6/01

ENCYCLOPEDIA OF
EUROPEAN SOCIAL HISTORY

EDITORIAL BOARD

ENCYCLOPEDIA OF
EUROPEAN SOCIAL HISTORY

FROM 1350 TO 2000

VOLUME 6

Peter N. Stearns

Editor in Chief

Charles Scribner's Sons

an imprint of the Gale Group

Detroit • New York • San Francisco • London • Boston • Woodbridge, CT

Library of Congress Cataloging-in-Publication Data
Encyclopedia of European social history from 1350 to 2000 / Peter N. Stearns, editor-in-chief.
     p.   cm.
    Includes bibliographical references and index.
    ISBN 0-684-80582-0 (set : alk. paper) — ISBN 0-684-80577-4 (vol. 1)—ISBN 0-684-80578-2 (vol. 2) — ISBN 0-684-80579-0 (vol. 3) — ISBN 0-684-80580-4 (vol. 4) — ISBN 0-684-80581-2 (vol. 5) — ISBN 0-684-80645-2 (vol. 6)
    1. Europe—Social conditions—Encyclopedias.   2. Europe—Social life and customs—Encyclopedias.   3. Social history—Encyclopedias.   I. Stearns, Peter N.
HN373 .E63 2000
306'.094'03—dc21

00-046376

CONTENTS OF THIS VOLUME

CONTENTS OF OTHER VOLUMES

ALPHABETICAL TABLE OF CONTENTS

COMMON ABBREVIATIONS USED IN THIS WORK

A.D.   *Anno Domini,* in the year of the Lord
AESC   *Annales: Économies, Sociétés, Civilisations*
ASSR   Autonomous Soviet Socialist Republic
b.   born
B.C.   before Christ
B.C.E.   before the common era (= B.C.)
c.   *circa,* about, approximately
C.E.   common era (= A.D.)
cf.   *confer,* compare
chap.   chapter
CP   Communist Party
d.   died
diss.   dissertation
ed.   editor (pl., eds.), edition
e.g.   *exempli gratia,* for example
et al.   *et alii,* and others
etc.   *et cetera,* and so forth
EU   European Union
f.   and following (pl., ff.)
fl.   *floruit,* flourished
GDP   gross domestic product
GDR   German Democratic Republic (East Germany)
GNP   gross national product
HRE   Holy Roman Empire, Holy Roman Emperor
ibid.   *ibididem,* in the same place (as the one immediately preceding)

i.e.   *id est,* that is
IMF   International Monetary Fund
MS.   manuscript (pl. MSS.)
n.   note
n.d.   no date
no.   number (pl., nos.)
n.p.   no place
n.s.   new series
N.S.   new style, according to the Gregorian calendar
OECD   Organization for Economic Cooperation and Development
O.S.   old style, according to the Julian calendar
p.   page (pl., pp.)
pt.   part
rev.   revised
S.   *san, sanctus, santo,* male saint
ser.   series
SP   Socialist Party
SS.   saints
SSR   Soviet Socialist Republic
Sta.   *sancta, santa,* female saint
supp.   supplement
USSR   Union of Soviet Socialist Republics
vol.   volume
WTO   World Trade Organization
?   uncertain, possibly, perhaps

ENCYCLOPEDIA OF
EUROPEAN SOCIAL HISTORY

BIOGRAPHIES

Texts of biographies are taken from sources published by the Gale Group and included in the Gale Biography Resource Center; sources are indicated by initials following the biography. The texts have been edited by the Scribner staff.

Sources: CA = *Contemporary Authors;* DAA = *International Dictionary of Architects and Architecture;* EOP = *Enyclopedia of Occultism and Parapsychology;* EWB = *Encyclopedia of World Biography;* HWL = *Historical World Leaders;* NWS = *Notable Women Scientists*

A

Adorno, Theodor   (1903–1969), German philosopher. Retaining his intellectual roots in Hegel and Marx, the German philosopher Theodor W. Adorno moved freely across diverse academic disciplines to probe into the nature of contemporary European culture and the predicament of modern man. He was a leading member of the influential intellectual movement known as the Frankfurt School.

Adorno was born in Frankfurt-am-Main, Germany, on September 11, 1903, as the only son of an upper middle class family. His father, Oskar Wiesengrund, was an assimilated Jewish merchant, and his mother, Maria Calvalli-Adorno, was a musically gifted person of Italian-Catholic descent. He adopted his mother's patronomic Adorno in the late 1930s.

Adorno became associated with the Institute for Social Research, which was established in 1923 as an affiliated body of the Frankfurt, but it was personal rather than formal because of his youth and student status. It was Max Horkheimer, eight years Adorno's senior, who introduced Adorno to other senior scholars there who were embarked on a variety of projects aimed at determining the social conditions of Europe. Although Marxist and progressive in outlook, the researchers at the Institute were concerned with intellectual work rather than direct political action. Together they constituted what came to be known as the Frankfurt School credited with the creation of the Critical Theory.

Adorno began teaching philosophy at his alma mater in 1931 but the seizure of political power by Hitler disrupted his academic career and eventually forced him into exile. He took refuge first at Oxford, England, between 1934 and 1937 and thereafter in the United States until his return to Germany in 1949 to resume teaching at the Frankfurt University. The sufferings of the Jews and the crimes of the Third Reich became two of the major concerns in his philosophical reflections to the end of his life.

During his stay in the United States between 1937 and 1949 Adorno was engaged in a number of projects which the members of the Institute for Social Research conducted individually or collectively. Although Adorno was disappointed by the quantitative analysis of cultural phenomena which he undertook at Princeton, he played a leading role in a large collaborative project which resulted in the publication of the influential book *Authoritarian Personality*.

Toward the end of the war Adorno and Horkheimer wrote *Dialectic of Enlightenment* published in Amsterdam in 1947. Defining enlightenment as demythologizing, the authors trace the process of taming of nature in Western civilization. The main thrust of the argument is that in the name of enlightenment a technological civilization which sets humans apart from nature has been developed and that such a civilization has become a cause of dehumanization and regimentation in modern society. They contend that the notion of reason is accepted in that civilization mainly in the sense of instrument for controlling nature, and subsequently people, rather than in the sense of enhancing human dignity and originality. In the new edition of the book published in 1969, shortly before Adorno's death, the authors declare that the enlightenment led to positivism and the identification of intelligence with what is hostile to spirit (Geistfeindschaft).

After World War II many members of the Frankfurt School remained in the United States or in Great Britain, but Horkheimer and Adorno returned to Germany. They were expected to provide intellectual leadership for postwar Germany. Horkheimer ac-

1

cepted the position of the Rector of the Frankfurt University and invited Adorno to join him. Adorno returned to Germany in 1949 although he spent a year in the United States in 1952.

Adorno lived up to what was expected of him by pouring out articles and books and by training a new generation of German scholars. His writings, voluminous as they were, however, did not contain many innovative ideas but rather restatement, in more elaborate forms and in a somewhat extravagant writing style, of the ideas which he had presented in his previous articles and books. But the true extent of his originality cannot be determined until the projected 23 volumes of his complete works are available.

In 1951 he published *Minima Moralia: Reflections from Damaged Life* consisting of articles which he wrote during the war. The most personal of his writings, the short essays in this book were written in an aphoristic style reminiscent of Arthur Schopenhauer and Friedrick Nietzsche. The purpose of the book is to examine how "objective forces" determine even the most intimate and immediate experience of an individual in contemporary society.

The *Negative Dialectics,* published in 1966, is a sustained polemic against the dream of philosophers from Aristotle to Hegel to construct philosophical systems enclosing coherently arranged propositions and proofs. One of the most terse statements in the book is "Bluntly put, closed systems are bound to fail." As this statement indicates, his aim in this book is to vindicate the vitality and intractability of reason.

Prisms, another major work published in 1967, contains essays on a wide range of topics from Thorstein Veblen to Franz Kafka. However, the main theme running throughout the book is the gradual decomposition of culture under the impact of instrumental reason. In this book and in *Aesthetic Theory,* his last major work unfinished at the time of his death in 1969 but edited and published posthumously, Adorno advances the thesis that the integrity of creative works lies in the autonomous acts of the artists who are at once submerged under and yet triumphant over social forces.

A persistent critic of positivism in philosophy and sociology and a bitter foe of commercialism and dehumanization promoted by the culture industry, Adorno championed individual dignity and creativity in an age increasingly menaced by what he regarded as mindless standardization and abject conformity. At a time when many academic philosophers were weary of dealing with large questions for fear of violating the canon of rigorous philosophical reasoning, Adorno boldly asserted that the function of philosophy is to make sense out of the totality of human experience.

Adorno, who was hailed as one of the ideological godfathers of the New Left Movement in the 1960s because of his indictment of both capitalism and communism, was criticized and humiliated by his former followers for his opposition to violent social activism. He was once forced out of his lecture room by female students at the Frankfurt University.

EWB

Alberti, Leon Battista (1414–1472), Italian writer, humanist, and architect. Through his theoretical writings on painting, sculpture, and architecture, Alberti raised them from the level of the mechanical arts to that of the liberal arts.

Alberti, as a scholar and philosopher who moved in humanist circles in Florence and the papal court in Rome, was involved in all the central concepts of the Renaissance. He was concerned with reforming his society and the arts in the image of ancient Roman culture. Throughout most of his writings the problem of man's relation to society is fundamental.

Alberti was born in Genoa on Feb. 14, 1404. He was the illegitimate son of Lorenzo Alberti, who belonged to one of the most prominent and oldest Florentine families but had been banished in 1401 from his native city. As a young boy, Leon Battista attended the famous school of the humanist Gasparino Barzizza in Padua, probably at the time Lorenzo Alberti was in Venice (1414). By 1421 Leon Battista was at the University of Bologna; while there he wrote a Latin comedy, *Philodoxeus* (ca. 1424). He received a degree in canon law prior to 1428, and it is probable that after earning his degree in Bologna he went to Rome. Sometime before 1431 Alberti was appointed prior of S. Martino in Gangalandi, Tuscany, which benefice he held until his death. In 1431 and early 1432 he accompanied Cardinal Albergati on a tour of northern Europe. On his return to Rome, Alberti became secretary to the patriarch of Grado and in October 1432 abbreviator at the papal court.

Soon after this Alberti wrote *Descriptio urbis Romae* as an index for an archeological map of Rome and in 3 months composed the first three books of *Della famiglia,* which is concerned with domestic life and the education of children. The fourth book of the treatise on the family, dealing with friendship, was written in Florence in 1437, and the entire work was revised in 1443. The sociological approach of this treatise remained central to his later writings.

The Treatises. In June 1434 Alberti accompanied the court of Pope Eugenius IV to Florence when it fled from the unrest in Rome. Florence, under the leadership of artists such as Donatello, Masaccio, and Filippo Brunelleschi, was then the art capital of Europe. Here Alberti composed his theoretical treatises on the visual arts. His treatise in Latin on painting, *De pictura*, was completed in 1435; the following year he prepared in Italian a briefer, more popular version, *Della pittura*. The Latin edition, dedicated to Gianfrancesco Gonzaga of Mantua, was written to persuade patrons that the art of painting was not merely a mechanical craft. The treatise explained for the first time in writing the mathematical foundations of one-point linear perspective as it was developed by the architect Brunelleschi, to whom the Italian version was dedicated; it also discussed antique themes and their appropriate expression. A Latin treatise on sculpture, *De sculptura*, may have originated at this time, although there is much uncertainty about its date.

As a member of the papal court, Alberti accompanied the Pope to Bologna in April 1436, and in January 1438 he was at Ferrara for the convocation of the council of the Latin and Greek churches. During this period Alberti wrote a work on law, *De iure* (1437), and another on the priest, *Pontifex* (1437). In 1442 Leonello d'Este, the ruler of Ferrara, recalled Alberti to advise him on a memorial equestrian statue of his father, Niccolo d'Este. Alberti's treatise on the horse, *De equo animante*, is related to this commission. His philosophical dialogue on peace of mind, *Della tranquillità dell'animo*, probably dates from the same period.

Alberti followed the papal court back to Rome in September 1443 and, probably at the instigation of Leonello d'Este, began to write the first five books of his important Latin treatise on architecture, *De re aedificatoria*. After Nicholas V was elected pope in 1447, Alberti finished the remaining five books, and the complete work was presented to the Pope in 1452 (first printed in 1485). The treatise not only relates architecture to the classical principles enunciated by the ancient Roman writer Vitruvius but, inspired by Alberti's previous concern for the family and society, studies architecture as a sociological phenomenon. For the remainder of his life, however, Alberti was more involved with the design and execution of architecture than with theoretical treatises.

Widespread Influence. Alberti's treatises on painting and architecture exerted a great influence on 16th- and 17th-century artistic thought. The teachings of the French 17th-century academies of painting and architecture represent a codification of artistic principles first formulated less rigidly by Alberti.

Of his architecture, the plan of S. Andrea, through its impact on Giacomo da Vignola's design for the Jesuit church, the Gesù, at Rome, was impor-

tant for two centuries of church architecture. In the same way, the facade of S. Maria Novella, with its great scrolls, became the model for classicizing church facades, as seen also in the Gesù. In both his architecture and architectural theory Alberti paved the way for the High Renaissance architecture of Rome, exemplified in Donato Bramante's work of the early 16th century.

EWB

Alembert, Jean Le Rond d' (1717–1783), French mathematician and philosophe. The chief contribution by the French mathematician and physicist Jean le Rond d'Alembert (1717–1783) is D'Alembert's principle, in mechanics. He was also a pioneer in the study of partial differential equations.

Jean le Rond d'Alembert was born on Nov. 16, 1717, and abandoned on the steps of the church of St-Jean-le-Rond in Paris. He was christened Jean Baptiste le Rond. The infant was given into the care of foster parents named Rousseau. Jean was the illegitimate son of Madame de Tencin, a famous salon hostess, and Chevalier Destouches, an artillery officer, who provided for his education. At the age of 12, Jean entered the Collège Mazarin and shortly afterward adopted the name d'Alembert. He became a barrister but was drawn irresistibly toward mathematics.

Two memoirs, one on the motion of solid bodies in a fluid and the other on integral calculus, secured d'Alembert's election in 1742 as a member of the Paris Academy of Sciences. A prize essay on the theory of winds in 1746 led to membership in the Berlin Academy of Sciences. D'Alembert wrote the introduction and a large number of the articles on mathematics and philosophy for Denis Diderot's *Encyclopédie*. He entered the Académie Française as secretary in 1755.

D'Alembert had a generous nature and performed many acts of charity. Two people especially claimed his affection; his foster mother, with whom he lived until he was 50, and the writer Julie de Lespinasse, whose friendship was terminated only by her death. D'Alembert died in Paris on Oct. 29, 1783.

D'Alembert's principle appeared in his *Traité de dynamique* (1743). It concerns the problem of the motion of a rigid body. Treating the body as a system of particles, d'Alembert resolved the impressed forces into a set of effective forces, which would produce the actual motion if the particles were not connected, and a second set. The principle states that, owing to the connections, this second set is in equilibrium. An outstanding result achieved by d'Alembert with the aid of his principle was the solution of the problem of the precession of the equinoxes, which he presented to the

Berlin Academy in 1749. Another form of d'Alembert's principle states that the effective forces and the impressed forces are equivalent. In this form the principle had been applied earlier to the problem of the compound pendulum, but these anticipations in no way approach the clarity and generality achieved by d'Alembert.

In his *Traité de l'équilibre et du mouvement des fluides* (1744), d'Alembert applied his principle to the problems of fluid motion, some of which had already been solved by Daniel Bernoulli. d'Alembert recognized that the principles of fluid motion were not well established, for although he regarded mechanics as purely rational, he supposed that the theory of fluid motion required an experimental basis. A good example of a theoretical result which did not seem to correspond with reality was that known as d'Alembert's paradox. Applying his principle, d'Alembert deduced that a fluid flowing past a solid obstacle exerted no resultant force on it. The paradox disappears when it is remembered that the inviscid fluid envisaged by d'Alembert was a pure fiction.

Applying calculus to the problem of vibrating strings in a memoir presented to the Berlin Academy in 1747, he showed that the condition that the ends of the string were fixed reduced the solution to a single arbitrary function. D'Alembert also deserves credit for the derivation of what are now known as the Cauchy-Riemann equations, satisfied by any holomorphic function of a complex variable.

Research on vibrating strings reflected only one aspect of d'Alembert's interest in music. He wrote a few of the musical articles for the *Encyclopédie.*

He favored the views of the composer Jean Philippe Rameau and expounded them in his popular *Élemens de musique théorique et pratique* (1752).

EWB

Alexander II (1818–1881), tsar of Russia (1855–1881). Alexander II is called the "tsar liberator" because he emancipated the serfs in 1861. His reign is famous in Russian history as the "era of great reforms."

Eldest son of Nicholas I, Alexander was born in Moscow on April 17, 1818. Vasili Zhukovski, the poet and courtier, was his principal tutor. Alexander spoke Russian, German, French, English, and Polish. He acquired a knowledge of military arts, finance, and diplomacy. From an early age he traveled extensively in Russia and abroad; in 1837, for example, he visited 30 Russian provinces, including Siberia, where no member of the royal family had ever been. Unlike his father, Alexander had experience in government before he acceded to the throne. He held various military commands and was a member of the state council

(from 1840) and of the committee of the ministers (from 1842); during Nicholas's absence Alexander acted as his deputy.

Alexander's political philosophy eludes precise definition. However, there is ample evidence to indicate that he was an admirer of Nicholas's autocracy and bureaucratic methods.

Emancipation of the Serfs. Before he became tsar, Alexander was not sympathetic to emancipation. He changed his mind because of Russia's technological and military backwardness in the Crimean War and because he believed that the liberation of the serfs was the only way to prevent a peasant uprising. Through a burdensome arrangement in which local commissions made studies and reported their findings to the government, an emancipation law was eventually formulated and proclaimed in 1861.

The new law stated that serfs were free to marry, acquire property, engage in trades, and bring suits in courts. Each estate proprietor had to prepare within a year an inventory determining the area of land actually in the possession of the peasants and defining the annual payment or services due from the liberated serfs. Each peasant household received its homestead and a certain amount of land (generally the same amount the family had cultivated for its own use in the past). The land usually became the property of the village commune, which had the power to redistribute it periodically among the households. The government bought the land from the owners, but the peasants had to redeem it by payments extending over 49 years. The proprietor kept only the portion of his estate that had been farmed for his own purposes.

The emancipation law of 1861, which liberated more than 40 million serfs, has been called the greatest single legislative act in history. It was a moral stimulus to peasant self-dignity. Yet there were many problems. The peasants had to accept the allotments, and generally they did not receive enough land and were overcharged for it. Since they became obligated for the payment of taxes and redemption reimbursements, their mobility was greatly limited. The commune replaced the proprietor as master over the peasants. The settlement, however, was on the whole liberal, despite some unsolved problems and the agrarian crises that emerged in part from its inadequacies.

Because the emancipation of the serfs ended the landlords' rights of justice and police on their estates, it was necessary to reform the entire local administrations. The statute of 1864 created provincial and district assemblies, which handled local finances, education, scientific agriculture, medical care, and maintenance of the roads. The elaborate electoral system dividing voters into categories by class provided substantial representation to the peasants in the assemblies. Peasant and proprietor were brought together in order to work out local problems.

During Alexander's reign other reforms were initiated. The cities were granted municipal assemblies with functions similar to those of the provincial assemblies. The Russian judicial system and legal procedures, which were riddled with inequities, were reformed. For the first time in Russian history, juries were permitted, cases were debated publicly and orally, all classes were made equal before the law, and the court system was completely overhauled. Censorship was relaxed, and the universities were freed from the restrictions imposed on them by Nicholas I. The army, too, was reformed by Gen. Dimitri Miliutin, military schools were reorganized along liberal lines, and conscription was borne equally by all social groups.

Despite all these reforms, Alexander II became the target of revolutionaries in 1866. Terrorist activity continued throughout the 1870s. The underlying reasons were the lack of far-reaching social and constitutional reforms; the bloody suppression of the peasant uprisings, especially the slaughter of Bezna; the Polish insurrection of 1863 and its bloody defeat; and the general ultrareactionary trend of official policies. Conservatives and nationalists were welcomed by the tsar, but the liberals were alienated. The radicals went underground and espoused the cause of political and social revolution. A member of a terrorist group murdered Alexander II on March 1, 1881.

EWB

Aretino, Pietro (1492–1556), Italian playwright and poet. Aretino rose from very humble origins in Arezzo to fame and eminence, simply by the calculated use of his pen. He operated mainly at the papal court in Rome until 1525; then, after a brief stay with the Duke of Mantua, he settled in Venice. He flattered and cajoled his chosen patrons, attacked their current adversaries, wrote outspoken letters to popes, kings and emperors, and earned from Ariosto the title of Scourge of Princes which has stuck with him ever since. His output ranged from Counter-Reformation devotional literature to outright pornography, everything being tackled, perplexingly, with equal apparent conviction and verbal skill.

His *Letters* tend to be seen as his crowning glory, but his comic drama is also of great significance. (He produced one tragedy, *Orazia*, printed in 1546.) He opened in 1525 with the absurd scurrilous *Cortigiana* (The Courtier's Play), combining two plots of elaborate practical jokes. The play was clearly written for a specific audience at a specific time, and its vigorous verbal by-play is larded with topical jokes. It was not printed in its first version before 1970, and the edition which appeared in 1534 is toned down in its aspects of vaudeville performance, and re-written to fit the topicalities and preoccupations of Aretino and his readers at that later date. Meanwhile *Il marescalco* (*The Stablemaster*) was written for the court of Mantua, probably in 1527, and published in 1533.

Both these early plays appear un-classical in structure, and owe little to Roman comedy in terms of plot. They seem to draw their inspiration more from the *beffa* tradition of practical joke in the medieval novella on the one hand; and from the harangues, dramatized dialogues, and sketches of street and court entertainment on the other. In fact a large part of both texts consists of one or two characters making speeches, to the audience or to each other: the content can be moralistic, satirical, sarcastic, celebratory, or just verbally fanciful, always supported by a level of language which is more dense and creative than that of most *commedia erudita*, though whether one would call it poetic is more debatable.

La Talanta and *Lo ipocrito* were both published in 1542, the former certainly being staged in Venice in the same year. The plays are named after a central character in each, Talanta being a rapacious prostitute, and the Hypocrite remaining named only by his principal characteristic. Both comedies have the surface function of detailing, in complex fictional plots, the dangers which prostitutes and religious hypocrites respectively pose to society and to individuals. But mixed in with these satirical aims, which continue to some extent the aggressive mockery of the first two plays, we find other elements sitting uneasily together for a modern reader, but foreshadowing quite separate developments in Italian theatre of the late 16th century. On the one hand, there are plots relating to marriages and family unity, traditional to classical comedy, but stretched by Aretino to such mannered lengths that one does not know whether they are to be taken at face value or as caricatures. The moral rhetoric is so stylized, the romantic misunderstandings and errors of identity so tortuous and implausible and yet a couple of decades later plots very similar to these were to become the norm. On the other hand, Aretino cannot renounce (or knows that his audience cannot renounce) more scurrilous low-life scenes involving backchat and practical jokes. What is more, in *Talanta* in particular, there are clear hints of the nascent *commedia dell'arte*, both in certain stereotyped characters and in the dialogue structure of some scenes, which may well have been played by professional buffoons alongside the gentlemen amateurs who took the more dignified roles.

Aretino's personal reputation was so bad by 1600 that his comedies were issued in a slightly re-written form, under altered titles and authorship. That they were reprinted at all at that period attests to their enduring influence. On the surface they are aimed firmly at a specific audience, and thus tend to date rapidly; their plots are fragmentary, and their structure over-leisurely; but their merciless satirical vein and their verbal creativity (the latter sadly rare in Italian, as opposed to English Renaissance comedy) seem to have made them hard to forget.

International Dictionary of Theatre,
volume 2: *Playwrights.* St. James Press, 1993.

Ariès, Philippe (1914–1984), French historian. Though an agronomic researcher by profession, Philippe Ariès avocationally studied the evolution of social attitudes, a hobby that brought him international renown. For his research on social attitudes, Aries developed a system of demographic study based on emotions and reactions to birth and death. His first major work, published in translation as *Centuries of Childhood: A Social History of Family Life,* explores attitudes toward children. The book, stated a *Newsweek* writer, "has never been surpassed," having held its appeal not only for historians and history buffs, but also for militant feminists in the United States. The latter are attracted to the book, *Newsweek* said, as "an ideological weapon against the idea of cohesive family." Ariès's own comment was, "each generation asks something new of history."

Ariès is best known, however, for his historical studies of death in the West, including *Western Attitudes Toward Death, The Hour of Our Death,* and the award-winning *Man Facing Death.* With the publication of *Western Attitudes Toward Death,* he "has enriched history with a supply of hypotheses that will reorient research," Robert Darnton pointed out, "even if many of them prove to be false."

Ariès's writings also include *History of French People* and his autobiography *Sunday Historian. Newsweek* described Philippe Ariès as "a maverick social historian whose pioneering studies of nonevents . . . have helped to create a new kind of history." He has explored "those elusive dimensions of social consciousness that once were considered static and too inaccessible for historical investigation." Ariès was completing a history of private life at the time of his death.

CA

Arkwright, Richard (1732–1792), English inventor and industrialist. Richard Arkwright developed several inventions which mechanized the making of yarn and thread for the textile industry. He also helped to create the factory system of manufacture.

Arkwright was born on Dec. 23, 1732, in Preston, Lancashire, England. Little is known of his early life except that he was from a large family of humble origin and obtained only the rudiments of an education. He was apprenticed to a barber in Preston, and when about 18 he set up on his own in Bolton, a textile town in Lancashire.

Sometime in the 1760s Arkwright began working on a mechanical device for spinning cotton thread, the spinning frame, which he patented in 1769. Problems still remained: the raw cotton had to be prepared for the invention by a hand process, and the invention had to be made practical and commercially successful. For this he needed funds and a mill where he could install the frame.

Probably for this reason in 1771 he moved to Nottingham, where a highly specialized kind of weaving, that of stockings, had already been fairly well mechanized. There Arkwright, whose inventions had reduced him to poverty, found a partner who supported his work and backed the construction of a mill run by waterpower (hence the later name of water frame).

Arkwright found that he could successfully use his thread for stockings and also as the warp, or longitudinal threads, in an ordinary loom onto which the weft, or cross threads, were woven. Heretofore, cotton thread had been used for the weft, but only linen threads had been strong enough for the warp. Now a textile made solely of cotton could be produced in England, and it eventually became one of the country's chief exports.

The production of thread was further improved in 1775 by Arkwright's patenting a practically continuous method which prepared the raw cotton for spinning. Apart from a completely mechanical loom, Arkwright had thus eliminated all the major obstacles to producing cotton cloth by machine.

Because thread production was now completely mechanized, all the hitherto separate operations could be coordinated and carried out under one roof, in a mill, or, as it was increasingly called, a factory. Arkwright paid as careful attention to the mill's operation as he did to his inventions. It was typical of his aggressive entrepreneurship that he was one of the first to apply the steam engine to his mills. While such a concentration of machines, driven by a prime mover, was not a new invention, Arkwright's rationalization of the factory system was nevertheless to become one of the most characteristic features of the industrial revolution.

Wealth and honors, including the bestowal of knighthood, came to him in the 1780s. He died in Nottingham on Aug. 3, 1792.

EWB

Arnold, Thomas (1795–1842), English educator. Thomas Arnold was a headmaster of Rugby School, and through his efforts it became the model for other English public schools and for boarding schools throughout the Western world.

Arnold was born in West Cowes, Isle of Wight, England, on June 13, 1795, the seventh child of William and Martha Arnold. His father was the postmaster and customs agent for the Isle of Wight. Arnold received his early education from his mother and an aunt. He attended the preparatory schools Warminster and Winchester from 1803 to 1811, prior to his admittance to Corpus Christi College of Oxford University. He graduated first class in classics in 1814. Through the influence of a friend he became a fellow of Oriel College, Oxford University, in 1814 a position he held until 1819. While there, he was ordained a deacon in the Church of England in 1818.

Arnold married Mary Penrose in 1820. He taught in several preparatory schools until 1827, when he became headmaster of Rugby School. He retained this post until his sudden death on June 12, 1842. Arnold also held a position in the senate of the University of London during 1836–1838 and was appointed a lecturer in history at Oxford in 1841.

Arnold was very much interested in Church reform. A radical in terms of religious thought of the day, he sought a simplified base on which to build a reunited Christian Church. He entered into a well-publicized dialogue with John Henry (later Cardinal) Newman over the nature of the Christian Church and what it ought to be. Arnold's religious ideas influenced the way in which he approached his job as headmaster of Rugby. He assumed the duties of the chaplain when the post became vacant, and he was noted for his sermons to the student body, later published. He emphasized the "Christian scholar" and "good character."

Social reform also interested Arnold. Although he maintained that the class structure of England was essentially natural and unchangeable, he actively sought to improve the lot of the lower and emerging middle classes. His convictions regarding the aristocracy centered on its responsibility and duty to do what was "right." In short, he wanted a useful aristocracy and a polished middle class. During the height of Parliament's debate over the reform bills of the early 1830s, Arnold published the *Englishman's Register,* a weekly journal supporting reform; it lasted only 3 months.

It is as headmaster of Rugby that Arnold is primarily remembered, however. The whole tone of the school was improved during his tenure. He is credited with broadening its curriculum, improving living conditions, raising the status of the masters, and inaugurating administrative reforms (for example, masters' conferences and student involvement in school affairs). What was once regarded as one of England's worst schools was, by the time of his death, famous for its successful graduates.

EWB

Atatürk, Ghazi Mustapha Kemal (1881–1938), was a Turkish nationalist and political leader who was instrumental in the fall of the Ottoman sultanate and in the creation of modern Turkey.

Mustapha Kemal devoted his life to freeing Turkey from foreign domination. Under his benevolent dictatorship as president of the republic, he instituted lasting reforms that earned him the name Atatürk (the father of the Turks).

Mustapha was born in Salonika (now Greece, but then part of Turkish Macedonia), the son of a lower-middle-class Turkish customs official. He received a military education, and a teacher dubbed him Kemal (perfection) because of the youth's demand for quality performance. Kemal graduated from the military academy in Monastir in 1899 and then attended the war and staff colleges in Istanbul.

Military Career. In 1905, on the day Kemal was commissioned a lieutenant at the General Staff Academy in Istanbul, he was arrested for political agitation. Banishment to Syria failed to dampen his revolutionary ardor. He organized some officers of the 5th Army Corps in Damascus into a secret society, Vatan (fatherland). Kemal established branches during a secret visit to Salonika, where the organization became Fatherland and Liberty, then the Ottoman Society of Liberty, and subsequently part of the Committee of Union and Progress. Despite this political activity and narrow escape from a second arrest, Kemal was not active in the 1908 coup or in the Young Turk movement which toppled Abdul Hamid.

In 1911 Kemal secretly went to Libya to organize Senussi resistance against the invading Italians. A major in the Second Balkan War, he served as chief of staff to the army on Gallipoli. When World War I broke out, Col. Mustapha Kemal was serving in Bulgaria as the Ottoman military attaché. During the war he commanded armies on every one of the several Ottoman fronts. He gained national recognition during the defense of Gallipoli. Promoted to pasha and given command of the 2d Army Corps, he led his troops and 3d Army forces in the Caucasus campaigns of 1916 and then was sent to the Hejaz. Correctly predicting the reverses to be expected in the Iraq campaign, he resigned but returned to service in 1918. Kemal was in command of the 7th Army withstanding the assault on Aleppo at war's end.

Reunification of Turkey. Peace was restored by the Mudros armistice of Oct. 30, 1918. The following May, 4 days after the Greeks landed troops in Turkey, Kemal was appointed inspector general of the 3d Army in Anatolia. From here he launched an anti-foreign movement that was to unify the Turkish elements in the empire against partition. At two conferences, at Erzerum on July 23 and at Sivas on September 11, he organized the Committee for the Defense of Eastern Asia Minor.

The Ferid Pasha government fell under this pressure, and new elections returned a Nationalist parliament. Its program, however, was sufficiently independent to prompt British occupation of the capital ostensibly to protect the Sultan. On March 20, 1920, the Ottoman parliament was dissolved. Some deputies fled to Ankara, where Kemal's committee convoked the first session of a new Grand National Assembly on April 23. It undertook both legislative and executive functions, with Kemal as president. Two governments were now functioning: the Sultan's in occupied Istanbul and Kemal's in Anatolia. This anomalous condition continued until the Allies forced the Sultan's assent to the Treaty of Sèvres on August 10, which established foreign control over large parts of the Turkish Empire. Thereupon the last vestige of the Sultan's power disappeared in Anatolia.

Opposition to foreign occupation was the keystone of Turkish nationalism, but dissension among the Allies was to be of major benefit to the Kemalists. Kemal's first success was peace with Russia in December. This border settlement was followed by a friendship treaty in March 1921. The Italians and the French, apparently anticipating an eventual Nationalist victory, were enticed into exchanging territorial claims for economic concessions. The result was that by mid-1921 only the Greeks and British occupied Turkish territory.

Greek troops moved through Anatolia in 1921 with considerable success to enforce the rule of the Sultan. As generalissimo of Turkish forces, Kemal had unlimited power during this campaign, and he was supplied by Russia, Italy, and France. The Greeks were stopped at Sakarya in September 1921 and driven out in a big campaign the following year. The Nationalists made Kemal a marshal and designated him Ghazi (victorious). The British concluded an armistice with the Turks at Mundanya on Oct. 11, 1922.

An international gathering at Lausanne in November 1920 set about revising the Treaty of Sèvres. The concurrent invitations issued the Nationalists and the Sultan's government precipitated the Grand National Assembly's dissolution of the sultanate of Mehmed VI on Nov. 1, 1922. On Oct. 29, 1923, Mustapha Kemal was elected president of the newly proclaimed Turkish Republic.

The interim period had been filled with the difficult task of negotiating the new treaty. The final document, signed July 24, 1923, established the compact, homogeneous entity known today as Turkey, freed of the onerous capitulations the Allies had expected to reimpose.

Turkish Republic. It had been Kemal's image as a national military hero which had assured the Nationalists a following in 1919. It was Kemal's determined leadership which assured the victory of 1923. It was to be Kemal's dictatorial guidance which subsequently defined the new Turkey.

Throughout the 1920s reform followed reform as the Turks undertook a shift from an Eastern to a Western orientation. President Kemal and his colleagues were Western-educated; the constitution of April 20, 1924, established in the republic a democratic state with elected representatives and all the typical popular guarantees. Yet Turkey remained a dictatorship throughout Kemal's time; he was a paternalistic ruler, convinced that he knew the nation's needs and how to satisfy them. Although democratic institutions were in existence, it was not the legislature which dominated but the Peoples' (in 1923 Republican Peoples') party, an outgrowth of the 1919 national group founded at Erzerum-Sivas. Kemal was party president. Policy was made in party caucus and then enacted as legislation by the Assembly. The party also selected and placed candidates, and there was no opposition slate. Kemal was reelected president of Turkey in 1927, 1931, and 1935 by the Assembly.

Kemal's Reforms. The haphazard reforms of the late 1920s were systematized by President Kemal in 1931 under six topics termed collectively "Kemalism": (1) republicanism, marked by the ending of the sultanate, the new republican constitution, and adoption of Western law codes in 1926; (2) secularism, eliminating the all-pervasive aspects of Islam from daily life, including polygamy, the Moslem calendar, and dervish religious orders; (3) populism, ending special privileges characterized formerly by religious exemptions, minority distinctions, and capitulations; the ancient Turkish peasant's democratic past was rediscovered and reemphasized, education fostered, the language purified, and the script romanized; (4) nationalism, concentrating on building Turkish pride through rewritten patriotic histories, emphasis on vernacular studies, and adoption of family names; (5) statism, introducing a form of state enterprise freed from outside manipulation and the foreign concessions of the past; it provided for the development of tariff-protected industries and increased government concern over agricultural output; (6) reformism, the continual revitalization of the movement to avoid its leadership's turning conservative and stagnating.

These Kemalist principles became the party platform in the 1935 elections and were added to the constitution in 1937. Kemal was an active president. Noted for his oratorical skill while in military school, he now utilized this asset to considerable advantage, moving readily about the country, eagerly explaining new laws. In one famous speech the President spoke over a period of 6 days.

Kemalist Turkey's foreign relations involved territorial settlements on Mosul and Alexandretta, an active role in the League of Nations after admission in 1932, and neighborly alliances in the Balkan Entente (1934) and the Saadabad Pact (1937). The most notable achievement was the Montreux Convention of 1936, by which Turkey regained control of the Straits.

Despite his posts as chief of state and party leader, Kemal was not a glory-grabber. He abhorred shallow ceremony and scorned pomp. In public life he was an incorruptible dynamo, but his riotous private life confounded many. Cirrhosis killed Atatürk on Nov. 10, 1938, his death accelerated by wild living and too much drinking.

EWB

B

Bacon, Francis (1561–1626), English philosopher, statesman, and author. Bacon was the chief figure of the English Renaissance. His advocacy of "active science" influenced the culture of the English-speaking world.

Francis Bacon was born in London on Jan. 22, 1561, the younger son of Sir Nicholas Bacon and his second wife, Lady Anne Bacon. Through the families of both parents he had important connections with the political and cultural life of Tudor England. His father was lord keeper of the great seal under Elizabeth I, and his maternal grandfather had been tutor to Edward VI.

Bacon entered Trinity College, Cambridge, in April 1573 and completed his studies there in December 1575. He began to study law at Gray's Inn, but his studies were interrupted for 2½ years while he served with Sir Amyas Paulet, the English ambassador to France. Upon his father's death Bacon returned to England, reentered Gray's Inn, and became a barrister in June 1592.

Bacon's literary work was accomplished, for the most part, during a life taken up with affairs of state. His public career began with his first election to Parliament in 1584. He early sought a position at court and Elizabeth I did make him Queen's counsel, but his ambitions for higher positions, supported by the Earl of Essex, were frustrated.

In 1592, on the anniversary of the Queen's coronation, Essex presented an entertainment composed by Bacon. In the speech in praise of knowledge he states his lifelong theme: "the sovereignty of man lieth hid in knowledge . . . now we govern nature in opinions, but are thrall to her in necessities; but if we would be led by her in invention, we should command her in action." Bacon tied himself closely to Essex and received many favors from him but later helped prosecute him for treason. While his part in the fate of Essex has been criticized as an ungrateful betrayal, it has also been defended as a duty painfully performed.

His Publications.   Bacon's first publication, in 1597, was a collection of 10 essays mainly devoted to aphorisms on political behavior. These were expanded and 29 new essays published with them in 1612. A still further enlarged edition, including 58 essays, appeared in 1625.

Bacon was knighted 4 months after the accession of James I in 1603, and in 1607 he was appointed solicitor general. In the meantime he had published *The Advancement of Learning* (1605), hoping to move James to support science. *De sapientia veterum* (*On the Wisdom of the Ancients*), an interpretation of ancient myths, was published in 1609. In the next dozen years Bacon's fortunes soared. In 1613 he was appointed attorney general; in 1616 to the Privy Council; in 1617 lord keeper; and in 1618 lord chancellor and Baron Verulam.

In 1620 *Novum organum* (*New Method*), was published as Part II of *The Great Instauration*. The entire project was never completed, and this part is not complete itself, but Bacon's reputation as a philosopher of science rests mainly upon it. The plan for the renewal of the sciences had six parts: a survey of existing knowledge, Bacon's inductive logic, an encyclopedia of all natural phenomena, examples of the New Method's application, Bacon's discoveries, and an exposition of the New Philosophy that would finally emerge.

Last Years.   In 1621, on his sixtieth birthday, Bacon was at the height of his career. He celebrated the occasion with a party at York House on the Strand, his birthplace. Among the guests was Ben Jonson. Five days later Bacon was created Viscount St. Albans. Disaster struck soon after. He was convicted by the High Court of Parliament for accepting bribes, sentenced to a fine and imprisonment, and banned from public office and Parliament. Here again, the degree of Bacon's guilt, which he admitted, and its moral evaluation have raised controversy.

The last 4 years of his life he devoted to writing *History of Henry VII, De augmentis scientiarum* (1623), *The New Atlantis* (1624), *Sylva sylvarum* (1627), and a number of other pieces.

He died on April 9, 1626, appropriately, however unfortunately, as the combined result of a scientific experiment and a political gesture. Leaving London, he decided to try the effect of cold in inhibiting putrefaction, and he stuffed with snow a hen he purchased from a woman along the way. He caught a chill and went to the nearby house of Lord Arundel, where the servants, in deference to his importance, made available the best bed. It, disastrously, was in a room that had not been adequately warmed or aired out, and Bacon contracted the bronchitis that brought about his death a week later.

Bacon's Philosophy.   Bacon developed a dislike for Aristotelian philosophy at Trinity College, and he also opposed Platonism. He felt that Aristotle's system was more suited to disputation than to discovery of new truth and that Plato's doctrine of innate knowledge turned the mind inward upon itself, "away from observation and away from things." Bacon's new method emphasized "the commerce of the mind with things." Science was to be experimental, to take note of how human activity produces changes in things and not merely to record what happens independently of what men do. This is part of what Bacon means by "active science." Still more fundamental is an ethical component. Science should be a practical instrument for human betterment. Bacon's attitude is best summed up in a passage from "Plan of the Work" in *The Great Instauration,* describing the sixth part, on "The New Philosophy or Active Science." "Man is the helper and interpreter of Nature. He can only act and understand insofar as by working upon her he has come to perceive her order. Beyond this he has neither knowledge nor power. For there is no strength that can break the causal chain. Accordingly these twin goals, human sci-ence and human power, come in the end to one. To be ignorant of causes is to be frustrated in action."

In the aphorism which concludes Book I of *Novum organum,* two rules of scientific procedure are emphasized: "to drop all preconceived notions and make a fresh start; and . . . to refrain for a while from trying to rise to the most general conclusions or even near to them." The fresh start requires the mind to overcome the influence of four "Idols," tendencies that inhibit the search for truth. The Idols of the Tribe are common to mankind generally. The Idols of the Cave are the tendencies of each man to see truth in relation to his own particular interests and disposition. The Idols of the Theater are the traditional philosophical systems. The Idols of the Market Place are errors that arise from language.

Science should start with what Bacon called Tables of Investigation. The Table of Presence lists instances in which the phenomenon being studied occurs. The Table of Absence in Proximity includes the important negative instances; these are the ones most like the positive instances. The Table of Comparison compares the degrees of the phenomenon.

Interpretation begins with a brief survey which will suggest the correct explanation of the phenomenon. Although this "anticipation" resembles a hypothesis, there is in Bacon's discussions no clear indication that he recognized the central scientific importance of devising and testing hypotheses. He goes on to consider "prerogative instances," those most likely to facilitate interpretation, of which he classifies 27 different types. By following the method outlined, scientific investigation is supposed to produce, almost mechanically, a gradually increasing generality of understanding, a "ladder of axioms" upon which the mind can climb up or down.

Bacon's program was too ambitious and in its particulars it has been of little influence. His approach did serve, however, to encourage detailed, concrete observation and experimentation and a system of scientific theory tied to them. His identification as the Moses of modern science or the Columbus of the mind is therefore not entirely inapt.

EWB

Baden-Powell, Robert   (1857–1941), British military officer, administrator, author and the founder of the Boy Scouts and the Girl Guides. Baden-Powell served with the British Army for thirty-four years beginning in 1876. Early in his career he displayed an aptitude for military scouting and in 1876 wrote a handbook entitled *Reconnaissance and Scouting.* Baden-Powell distinguished himself as a leader with his participation in the defense of Mafeking during the Boer

War. In 1900 he organized the South African Constabulary and acted as its inspector general until 1903, when he was named inspector general of cavalry.

Baden-Powell is said to have conceived of the idea of Boy Scouting in 1908 while on a camping trip with a group of English schoolboys. Later that year his book *Scouting for Boys: A Handbook for Instruction in Good Citizenship* elicited public enthusiasm for a scouting organization. At the urging of King Edward VII, Baden-Powell retired from the Army in 1910 to develop the Boy Scout and Girl Guide movements. A knight commander of the Royal Victorian Order and a conferee of the Grand Cross of St. Michael and St. George, Baden-Powell was named chief scout of the world at the first Boy Scout Jamboree, held in London in 1920. He was a prolific author whose books included *Sport in War* (1900), *An Old Wolf's Favourites: Animals I Have Known* (1921), and an autobiography titled *Lessons of a Lifetime* (1933). He also founded *The Scout* magazine.

CA

Bakhtin, Mikhail Mikhailovich (1895–1975), Russian philosopher and literary critic. Mikhail Bakhtin was the central figure of an intellectual circle that focused on the social nature of language, literature, and meaning in the years between World War I and World War II. Though his major works were not widely read until after the 1960s, his ideas were later adopted by many academic spheres and have contributed to new directions in philosophy, linguistics, and literary theory.

Although relatively unknown outside Soviet intellectual circles during his lifetime, the writings of Mikhail Mikhailovich Bakhtin have a had a significant influence in the fields of literary theory, linguistics, and philosophy. In works such as *Problems of Dostoevsky's Poetics* (1929, 1963), *Rabelais and His World* (1965), and *The Dialogic Imagination* (1975), Bakhtin outlined theories on the social nature of language, literature, and meaning. With the spread of his ideas in the Western academic world, Bakhtin has become one of the major figures of twentieth-century literary theory.

Bakhtin was born on November 16, 1895, in the city of Orel in the southern part of Russia. He was the third of five children in a family that had been part of the nobility since the Middle Ages, but no longer held land or title. His father was a state bank official, as his grandfather had been. Although the family relocated at various times throughout Bakhtin's childhood, he was provided with a thorough education. At home, he and his older brother, Nikolai, received lessons in Greek poetry from a German gov-

erness. After the family moved to Vilnius, Lithuania, when he was nine, he attended schools in the Russian-ruled city. At the age of 15, Bakhtin traveled with his family to Odessa in the Ukraine, where he graduated from the First Gymnasium and then studied philology (the study of literature and language) at the University of Odessa for a year.

Attracted by Philosophical Ideas. In his early adolescent years, Bakhtin began to develop an interest in radical philosophical ideas. He immersed himself in a wide range of books, including the works of German philosophers Friedrich Nietzsche and Georg Wilhelm Friedrich Hegel. He was encouraged in his pursuits and exposed to a developing spirit of revolutionary change by his brother and a circle of friends, with whom he would hold discussions and debates about new concepts. This early habit of questioning established ideas would become a lifelong practice for Bakhtin. Another important theme of his life first appeared during these years. At the age of 16, he was stricken with osteomyelitis, a disease that causes inflammation and destruction of bone tissue. This chronic condition and other bouts of poor health affected his work and activities for the rest of his life.

Bakhtin entered the University of St. Petersburg in Russia in 1914. There he studied philosophy and literature with a number of professors while sharing living quarters with his older brother. When the political turmoil of the Russian Revolution broke out in 1917, Nikolai joined the White Army, the military group supporting Russian royal rule against the Bolshevik revolutionary forces. With the defeat of the royal forces, Nikolai left for England. Bakhtin, however, stayed in school throughout this time and graduated in 1918.

Bakhtin Circle Established. Over the next ten years, Bakhtin began to develop the ideas that would lead to his major writings. Having moved with his family to the Belorussian town of Nevel in 1918, Bakhtin began meeting with a group of intellectuals that would become known as the "Bakhtin Circle." The members of the group discussed such topics as the effects of the Russian Revolution on the social and cultural lives of Soviet citizens and the role of social reality in the meaning of artistic works and language. Bakhtin published his first paper the following year in a local journal. The two-page article was titled, "Art and Responsibility." He would not publish again for another decade.

In 1920, he moved to the town of Vitebsk, where he held a number of jobs, including a teaching position at the Vitebsk Higher Institute of Education.

His intellectual work from this time included a number of unpublished writings, including the notebooks he kept. At Vitebsk, Bakhtin was joined by his friends from his circle in Nevel, including Lev Vasilyevich Pumpiansky and Valentin Nikolayevich Voloshinov. In addition, new people such as Ivan Ivanovich Sollertinsky and Pavel Nikolayevich Medvedev joined the group. In 1921, Bakhtin formed another important relationship. Suffering from his continued battle with osteomyelitis, his health declined even further when he contracted typhoid. A woman who nursed him through this period of illness, Elena Aleksandrova Okolovich, became his wife later in the same year.

From 1924 to 1929, Bakhtin lived in Leningrad (the name given to St. Petersburg after the Revolution). Prevented from working because of his poor health, his only income was a small medical pension. He did, however, continue to meet with the members of the Bakhtin Circle in their homes, where he would occasionally give lectures. Papers published by his associates during this time reflect many of Bakhtin's ideas; whether the critic was the sole author, co-author, or simply the philosophical inspiration for these writings is a matter of debate. Some of the works in question include the book *The Formal Method in Literary Scholarship,* published in 1928 by Medvedev and the 1929 work *Marxism and the Philosophy of Language* by Voloshinov. These works reflect the basic idea of the Bakhtin Circle that language is fundamentally a sociological force. Just as society, or popular culture, is continually changing and growing with the exchange of experiences and ideas, so does the meaning of language take on new dimensions with every act of reading, listening, or responding. In this way, Bakhtin and his colleagues established the concept of the "dialogic," or social nature of language, which was also extended to all artistic acts and utterances. These works by Medvedev and Voloshinov were couched in the language and themes of Marxism, making them acceptable for publication in the young communist state.

In 1929, Bakhtin and several members of his circle were arrested. The official reasons for Bakhtin's arrest included his religious practices: he had retained his Christian practices and beliefs even after all expressions of religion had been banned in the Soviet Union. He was sentenced, without a trial, to ten years of exile in the northern Soviet region of Siberia. With his health problems, such a severe sentence was a serious threat to Bakhtin's life. Several prominent political and cultural figures sympathized with the author's plight and lobbied for a reduced sentence. Due perhaps in large part to a favorable review of his Dostoevsky book by the Commissar of Enlightenment,

Bakhtin's sentence was eventually reduced to six years in Kazakhstan. In 1930 he received permission to travel to the city of Kustani and find work himself, rather than being assigned a job by the government. He secured a position as an accountant in a local government office; he also helped train workers in the area in clerical skills. Although his exile officially ended in 1934, Bakhtin opted to remain in Kustani for another two years.

He returned to Russia in 1936, settling in Saransk and taking a teaching job at the Mordovian Pedagogical Institute. In 1937, he moved to the town of Savelovo; being only a hundred kilometers outside Moscow, he was able to once again appear in intellectual and academic gatherings. But the coming years were filled with a number of frustrations and disappointments. His physical health suffered another blow in 1938 when his right leg was amputated. Professionally, he seemed assured of success when a number of his papers were accepted for publication. But with the start of World War II, these works were not printed.

Carnival Theory Applied to Literature.   This adversity seemed to spark a period of great productivity in Bakhtin. He gave lectures on the novel at Moscow's Gorky Institute and completed a dissertation on sixteenth-century French satirist Francois Rabelais for the institute in 1940. This work, which was expanded and published in 1965 as *Rabelais and His World,* stands alongside *Problems of Dostoevsky's Poetics* as one of Bakhtin's most important writings. In this work, Bakhtin examines the cultural and political hierarchies that existed in European society in the Middle Ages and the early Renaissance period. He postulated that popular culture embraced an earlier way of life that stressed communal living and working that directly clashed with the increasing power of central governments and noble classes. The tension between the "official" world of power, government, and religion and the unacknowledged world of popular culture was only free to be expressed, according to Bakhtin, in the environment of the carnival—a holiday atmosphere in which all things held sacred and mighty were free to be subjected to laughter and satire, a time when all boundaries were temporarily dissolved. Bakhtin finds this kind of carnivalesque subversion in the novels of Rabelais, whom he credits with heralding the modern era and a new philosophy of history.

Although he began working as a German instructor in the schools of Savelovo in 1941, Bakhtin continued to concentrate on his writing, turning out articles on the novel that were later collected in *The Dialogic Imagination,* published in 1975. Bakhtin worked in Savelovo from 1942 to 1945 as an instructor in Russian. He returned to the Mordovian Pedagogical Institute in Saransk in 1945, where he attained the rank of department chair. After submitting and defending his dissertation in the late 1940s, he was finally awarded a degree of candidate in 1951. When the institute became a university six years later, Bakhtin's scholarship and reputation as a teacher earned him the position of head of the department of Russian and foreign literatures.

Reputation Increased in Later Years. Despite these advancements, Bakhtin's ideas were little known outside his academic and intellectual circles of friends. Beginning in the mid-1950s, his work began to earn a limited amount of recognition elsewhere.

At this time of rising acclaim, Bakhtin continued to publish, but once again ill health limited his activities. He and his wife—who was also unwell—moved to Moscow in 1967 and then to Grevno in 1970 for medical care. After his wife's death in 1971 from a heart condition, Bakhtin settled in an apartment in Moscow. He spent his last years fighting both emphysema and his osteomyelitis, but he did not abandon his writing. He died in Moscow on March 7, 1975. After his death, more of his works were published and his influence gradually spread throughout the world, due in great part to the interest of Western academics. In this way, his own work took on a life of ongoing growth and interpretationthe kind of existence that Bakhtin had claimed for all acts of language. Long after the moment of writing and years after the death of the author, the works of Bakhtin have been the subject of numerous readings and responses that have added new dimensions to fields concerned with language and the nature of meaning, including linguistics, philosophy, and literary criticism.

EWB

Bakunin, Mikhail Aleksandrovich (1814–1876), Russian revolutionary agitator was the leading spirit of 19th-century anarchism. Mikhail Bakunin viewed revolution as the necessary means of destroying the political domination of individuals by the state.

Mikhail Bakunin was born on May 18, 1814, in Premukhino in the Tver Province to a retired diplomat and landowner. After finishing his studies at the artillery school, he received a commission as an officer in the Guards. It is said that his father was angry with him and asked that Mikhail be transferred to the regular army. Stranded in a desolate village of White Russia with his battery, Bakunin became depressed and unsociable. He neglected his duties and would lie for days wrapped in a sheepskin. The battery commander felt sorry for him; he had no alternative, however, but to remind Bakunin that he must either perform his duties or be discharged. Bakunin chose to take the latter course and asked to be relieved of his commission.

Bakunin went to Moscow in 1836, and from that date life began in earnest for him. He had studied nothing before, he had read nothing, and his knowledge of German was very poor. But he was blessed with a gift for dialectics and for constant, persistent thinking. He mastered German to study the philosophies of Immanuel Kant, Johann Fichte, and G. W. F. Hegel. In 1842, while living in Berlin, Bakunin published an impassioned essay declaring Hegelianism a revolutionary tool and ending with the dictum that was to become the motto of international anarchism: "The passion for destruction is also a creative passion." Bakunin participated in the Paris Revolution of 1848, made a fruitless attempt to organize a secret revolutionary international campaign for a Czech revolt, and participated in the Dresden rebellion of 1849. He was imprisoned in Russia until 1857 and then exiled to Siberia. In 1861 he escaped from Siberia to Japan, and on his way to Europe he stopped off in the United States. He declared his intention of becoming an American citizen. The poet Henry Wadsworth Longfellow portrayed the Russian in his diary as "a giant of a man with a most ardent, seething temperament."

Mission in Life. In 1862 Bakunin joined the revolutionary leaders Aleksandr Herzen and Nicholas Ogarev in London. Bakunin's intention was to devote all his energies to fighting for the freedom of the Russians and all the Slavs. He had not yet devised his anarchist doctrines, and he found himself advocating some of Herzen's views. Temperamentally the two men were so incompatible that they could not be comrades-in-arms, though they remained good friends. Bakunin's instincts were all against moderation, and conspiratorial intrigue was his goal. He embraced the cause of land and liberty and plunged into plotting with immense zest. He had plans for agitating in the army and among the peasantry, and he played with the idea of a vast revolutionary organization ringing Russia with a network of agents at strategic points on the border. Siberia was to be served by a branch located on the western coast of the United States.

Concept of Revolution. Bakunin reached the conclusion that revolution is necessary, regardless of the point of the critique of society from which it starts. He frequently attempted to give a philosophical foundation to revolution. The whole history of mankind appeared to him as "the revolutionary negation of the past. . . . Man has liberated himself (by breaking the divine commandment not to eat of the tree of knowledge); he has divided himself from animal and made himself man; he began his history and his human development with his act of disobedience and knowledge, that is, with rebellion and thought."

Bakunin held that there are principles which are the moving force of both the individual and the historical process. These are human animality, thought, and revolt. Social and private economy correspond to the first, science to the second, and freedom to the third. Man has an innate instinct for revolt. therefore, man's perpetual rebellion, which may lead to self-sacrifice and self-destruction, does not depend on either right or obligation but is immediately bestowed along with his humanity. Revolution can be looked upon as a theoretically perpetual situation or as an almost-infinite process. In theory, revolution may at some time cease and be replaced by a new order; in practice, it lasts so long that it must claim the attention of at least a whole generation. According to Bakunin, the goal of his generation was to destroy; the reconstruction would be done by others who would be better, fresher, and wiser. Bakunin never abandoned this view.

Exponent of Anarchism. The failure of the Polish insurrection in 1863 was a big disappointment to Bakunin, who henceforth became absorbed in a campaign of universal anarchy. Anarchism called for the replacement of the state with a loose confederation of autonomous units that would both end the injustices of private property and assure individual freedom. The millennium was to be achieved through an international rebellion set off by small groups of anarchist conspirators. Bakunin's anarchism, in theory, meant not disorder but lack of domination, a system without political power. Bakunin was also a militant atheist and thought religion was as great an enemy of freedom as the state was. At the end he appears to have lost his confidence in spontaneous popular uprising as the only sure method of destroying state governments.

Bakunin died in Bern, Switzerland, on July 1, 1876. His lifelong friend Herzen once remarked about Bakunin: "This man was born not under an ordinary star, but under a comet."

EWB

Barthes, Roland (1919–1980), French critic. Roland Barthes was a leading figure in semiology, a critical method that analyzes expression—from the artistic to the merely communicative—as a system of signs. His principal subject was, inevitably, language

itself, and his principal theme was the imprecision of language as a means of communicating a fixed idea. For Barthes, any literary work yields a multiplicity of interpretations, and even literary interpretations of a given work are open to varied readings. Therefore, a reduction of Barthes's own work is somewhat paradoxical: His basic premise is that there is no such thing as one basic premise.

The development of Barthes's critique of language was influenced by several schools of thought: first by Marxism and the work of Jean-Paul Sartre; second by structuralism; third by such post-structuralist thinkers as Jacques Derrida and Julia Kristeva; and fourth by aesthetic introspection. Of the first phase, Barthes's most significant work is *Le Degre zero de l'ecriture* (*Writing Degree Zero*), in which he considers both language and literature within historical contexts. Prior to the class upheavals of the mid-nineteenth century, Barthes claims, all literature adhered to basic premises of logic and continuity. In the alienating, chaotic twentieth century, however, literature fragmented into various dissimilar styles. For Barthes, the only response to this confusing state, in which a work's style becomes its content, is to promote a colorless, "objective" literature—what he called "writing degree zero"—as exemplified by such writers as Albert Camus and Alain Robbe-Grillet. With *Writing Degree Zero* Barthes showed himself to be a provocative critical theorist.

Another among Barthes's early works is the essay collection *Mythologies*. Included in this volume is "Myth Today, " in which Barthes explicates and elaborates his notion of myth as a form of expression within an historical context. He sees such phenomena as professional wrestling and the fashion industry as contemporary myths, and he finds these myths consistent with the increasing prevalence of bourgeois ideology, which, as a Marxist, he disdains as benefiting only the ruling class. But the political left, he laments, offers little alternative, wedded as it is to sociopolitical issues.

In *Mythologies* Barthes discusses a wide range of topics, and in subsequent books he continues to apply himself broadly. In *Elements de semiologie* (*Elements of Semiology*), first published in France in 1964, he moves into his second, structuralist, phase, outlining semiology as a method for perceiving virtually anything—even physical movements or noises—as systems. Beginning with an overview of the concepts of Swiss linguist Ferdinand de Saussure (1857–1913), whose groundbreaking work in the theoretical foundation of the study of language resulted in the consideration of language as a social phenomenon, Barthes expands them into such areas as food selection and clothing.

After entering into an explication of such semiological relationships as signifier- signified-signification, he then takes up the consideration of the dual "axes" of language—syntagmas (individual "utterances") and the entire language system taken as a whole—and illustrates their application.

In a related work, *Systeme de la mode* (*The Fashion System*), Barthes examines fashion magazines for their semiological content. He maintains that "discourse" through the language of clothing occurs on two levels—denotation and connotation—and that the significance of such discourse is valued independently of the wearer.

Among Barthes's other works devoted to the visual forms of language are *The Eiffel Tower and Other Mythologies,* first published in France in 1964, and his controversial *The Empire of Signs.* Written as a sequel to *Mythologies, The Eiffel Tower* comprises a series of twenty-nine essays devoted to the continued examination of the many layers of "language" structures that underlie modern culture and social interaction.

In the radical *S/Z* Barthes devotes himself to an exhaustive post-structuralist semiological analysis of Honore de Balzac's story "Sarrasine." Barthes further explores reading in *Le Plaisir du texte* (*The Pleasure of the Text*), a relatively accessible work that characterizes reading as a sensual, nearly hedonistic activity. Reading, Barthes charges, is a deliberate, contemplative means of obtaining pleasure and satisfaction, and as such it is far more than mere intellectual process.

When *The Pleasure of the Text* appeared in French in 1973 (and in English in 1975), Barthes was recognized as a leading figure in French critical thought. With other intellectuals, ranging from radical psychoanalyst Jacques Lacan to controversial socio-historical theorist Michel Foucault, Barthes enjoyed immense influence in both Europe and the United States. Throughout the remainder of the 1970s, with works such as *Roland Barthes par Roland Barthes* (*Roland Barthes by Roland Barthes*) and *Fragments d'un discours amoureux* (*A Lover's Discourse*), Barthes added to his stature as a provocative, engaging thinker. *A Lover's Discourse* proved a particularly intriguing work, for in it Barthes presents uncharacteristically poignant ruminations on love, its expression, and its articulations. Despite its subject, however, *A Lover's Discourse* is hardly an uplifting work. Barthes views love as an exhausting, enslaving emotion, one that often seems masochistic.

In 1980, only a few years after publishing *A Lover's Discourse,* Barthes was fatally struck by an automobile while crossing a Paris street; one month later he died from the massive chest injuries incurred during the accident. But with the *Barthes Reader* anthology—edited by Sontag—and several posthumous volumes, Barthes continues to hold high standing in academia as one of his country's most important contemporary thinkers.

Barthes died of chest injuries sustained in an automobile accident, March 25, 1980, in Paris.

CA

Beauvoir, Simone de (1908–1986), French writer. Simone Beauvoir first articulated what has since become the basis of the modern feminist movement. She was the author of novels, autobiographies, and nonfiction analysis dealing with women's position in a male-dominated world.

Simone Beauvoir set out to live her life as an example to her contemporaries and chronicled that life for those who followed. Fiercely independent, an ardent feminist before there was such a movement, her life was her legacy and her work was to memorialize that life.

"I was born at four o'clock in the morning on the ninth of January 1908, in a room fitted with white-enameled furniture and overlooking the Boulevard Raspail." Thus begins the first of four memoirs written by Beauvoir. It is through these autobiographies that Beauvoir's readers best know her, and it is in her book *The Second Sex*, an early feminist manifesto, that Beauvoir synthesized that life into the context of the historical condition of women.

The first child of a vaguely noble couple, Beauvoir was a willful girl, prone to temper tantrums. Her sister, Poupette, was born when Beauvoir was two and a half, and the two had a warm relationship. After World War I her father never fully recovered his financial security and the family moved to a more modest home; the daughters were told they had lost their dowries. Forced to choose a profession, Beauvoir entered the Sorbonne and began to take courses in philosophy to become a teacher. She also began keeping a journal—which became a lifetime habit—and writing some stories.

Link with Sartre. When Beauvoir was 21 she joined a group of philosophy students including Jean-Paul Sartre. Her relationship with Sartre intellectually, emotionally, and romantically was to continue throughout most of their lives. Sartre, the father of existentialism a school of thought that holds man is on his own, "condemned to be free," as Sartre says in *Being and Nothingness* was the single most important influence on Beauvoir's life.

In 1929 Sartre suggested that, rather than be married, the two sign a conjugal pact which could be renewed or cancelled after two years. When the pact

15

came due, Sartre was offered a job teaching philosophy in Le Havre and Beauvoir was offered a similar job in Marseilles. He suggested they get married, but they both rejected the idea for fear of forcing their free relationship into the confines of an outer-defined bond. It is indeed ironic that de Beauvoir, whose independence marked her life at every juncture, was perhaps best known as Sartre's lover.

The first installment of Beauvoir's autobiography, *Memoirs of a Dutiful Daughter*, is the story of the author's rejection of the bourgeois values of her parents' lives. The second volume, *The Prime of Life*, covers the years 1929 through 1944. Written in the postwar years, she separated the events taking place in Europe that led to the war from her own, isolated life. By 1939, however, the two strands were inseparable. Both Beauvoir and Sartre were teaching in Paris when the war broke out. Earlier she had written two novels that she never submitted for publication and one collection of short stories that was rejected for publication. She was, she said, too happy to write.

That happiness ended in the 1940s with the outbreak of World War II and the interruption of her relationship with Sartre. The introduction of another woman into Sartre's life, and then the anxiety and loneliness Beauvoir felt while Sartre was a prisoner for more than a year led to her first significant novel, *She Came to Stay*, published in 1943. *She Came to Stay* is a study of the effects of love and jealousy. In the next four years she published *The Blood of Others, Pyrrhus et Cinéas, Les Bouches Inutiles*, and *All Men Are Mortal*.

America Day By Day, a chronicle of Beauvoir's 1947 trip to the United States, and the third installment of her autobiography, *Force of Circumstances*, cover the period during which the author was formulating and writing *The Second Sex*, her feminist tract.

The Second Sex.   Written in 1949, *The Second Sex* is blunt and inelegant like her other writing. Its power comes from its content. Her themes and method of attack in *The Second Sex* are also the reoccurring issues of her work. The book rests on two theses: that man, who views himself as the essential being, has made woman into the inessential being, "the Other," and that femininity as a trait is an artificial posture. Both theses derive from Sartre's existentialism.

The Second Sex was perhaps the most important treatise on women's rights through the 1980s. When it first appeared, however, the reception was less than overwhelming. The lesson of her own life—that womanhood is not a condition one is born to but rather a posture one takes on—was fully realized here. Beauvoir's personal frustrations were placed in terms of the general, dependent condition of women. Historical, psychological, sociological, and philosophical, *The Second Sex* does not offer any concrete solutions except "that men and women rise above their natural differentiation and unequivocally affirm their brotherhood."

If *The Second Sex* bemoans the female condition, Beauvoir's portrayal of her own life revealed the possibilities available to the woman who can escape enslavement. Hers was a life of equality, yet Beauvoir remained a voice and a model for those women whose lives were not liberated.

The fourth installment of her autobiography, *All Said and Done*, was written when Beauvoir was 63. It portrays a person who has always been secure in an imperfect world. She writes: "Since I was 21, I have never been lonely. The opportunities granted to me at the beginning helped me not only to lead a happy life but to be happy in the life I led. I have been aware of my shortcomings and my limits, but I have made the best of them. When I was tormented by what was happening in the world, it was the world I wanted to change, not my place in it."

Beauvoir died of a circulatory ailment in a Parisian hospital April 14, 1986. Sartre had died six years earlier.

EWB

Behn, Aphra   (ca. 1640–1689), English poet, novelist, and playwright. Aphra Behn was the first of her gender to earn a living as a writer in the English language.

Aphra Behn was a successful author at a time when few writers, especially if they were women, could support themselves solely through their writing. For the flourishing London stage she penned numerous plays, and found success as a novelist and poet as well and through much of her work ran a decidedly feminist strain that challenged society's restrictions upon women of her day. For this she was scorned, and she endured criticism and even arrest at times. Another similarly free-thinking female novelist of a more recent era, Virginia Woolf, declared that "all women together ought to let flowers fall upon the tomb of Aphra Behn," according to Carol Howard's essay on Behn in the *Dictionary of Literary Biography*, ". . . for it was she who earned them the right to speak their minds."

A Childhood in Kent.   It is likely that Behn was the infant girl Eaffry Johnson, born in late 1640 according to baptismal records from the church of St. Michael's in Harbledown, a small village near Canterbury, England. This region of England, Kent, was a conservative, insular county during Behn's youth, but the English realm itself was anything but calm during her era; Behn's fortunes and alliances would be tied to the series of political crises that occurred during the seventeenth century, and her literary output drew from and even satirized the vying factions. First came a Civil War that pitted Puritans against King Charles I; the monarchy was abolished with the king's beheading in 1649. Until 1658 England was ruled by Puritan revolt leader Oliver Cromwell, and upon his death in 1658 the monarchy was restored; hence the term for the era in which Behn wrote, Restoration England.

Behn was likely the daughter of a barber and a wet-nurse, and through her mother's care for the children of local landed gentry, the Colepeppers, Behn probably had access to some educational opportunities. Literary scholars agree that Behn most likely left England as a young woman with her family in 1663 when her father was appointed to a military post in Surinam, on the northeast coast of South America. It was an arduous journey, and some evidence suggests that Behn's father did not survive the trip. In any event, Behn, her mother, and sister stayed on at the English settlement for a time until a return trip home was possible, and the experience provided the basis for her most famous literary work, *Oroonoko; or, The Royal Slave.*

Oroonoko in the Annals of English Literature. This novel, published only near the end of Behn's career in 1688, chronicles the tale of a cultivated, intelligent West African prince who speaks several European languages. Literary historians trace the development of realism in the novel back this 1688 volume. Realism is a literary style that uses real life as the basis for fiction, without idealizing it or imbuing it with a romantic bias, and it became prevalent in the nineteenth century. Behn's *Oroonoko* has also been termed groundbreaking for its depiction of the institution of slavery as cruel and inhumane, making it one of literary history's first abolitionist proclamations. Behn has been praised for her characterization of Oroonoko, a just and decent man who encounters some very cruel traits among his white enemies; critics point to him as European literature's first portrayal of the "noble savage."

Astrea the Spy. England's troubles with Holland played a decisive part in Behn's fortunes as a young woman. Following her return to England in 1664, she met and married a Dutch merchant by the name of Hans Behn. Though it has been hinted that her brief marriage may have been her own fiction—widows were more socially respectable than single

women during her era—other sources indicate the unfortunate Hans Behn died in an outbreak of the bubonic plague that swept through London in 1665. Later, many of Behn's works satirized Dutch merchants, the cultural icons of the era when Holland was growing rich from trade and giving birth to the first class of savvy capitalists. Behn may have been well-off herself for a time, and became a favorite at the Court of Charles II for her ebullient personality and witty repartee.

But then Behn's fortunes took a turn for the worse. It appears that she suddenly became destitute—perhaps after her husband died—and in 1666 was summoned into the service of the King as an agent in the war against Holland. She went to Antwerp to renew contact with a former lover, William Scot, who was a spy in the city; Scot was an Englishman who was involved in an expatriate group who once again wanted to abolish the monarchy. Behn's mission was to get him to switch sides, and to send reports on behalf of Charles II back to England in invisible ink using the code name "Astrea." During her work as an infiltrator Behn learned of plans to annihilate the English fleet in the Thames and, in June of 1667, Dutch naval forces did so. Yet her English spymasters left her virtually abandoned in a foreign enemy nation with no money—for a woman in the seventeenth century, this necessitated a very distressing and extreme crisis. She probably borrowed a sum, managed to return to England, and still was unremunerated by Charles II. Her numerous pleading letters, which still survive, were met with silence. She landed in debtor's prison in 1668, but at this point someone paid her debt and she was released.

Writing as a Profession. It was at this juncture that Behn resolved to support herself. She moved to London, and took up writing in earnest—not a revolutionary act at the time for a woman, but to expect to make a living at it certainly was. In Behn's day, a woman possessed no assets, could not enter into contracts herself, and was essentially powerless. Financial support came from a woman's father, and then her husband. Some well-born women escaped such strictures by becoming mistresses; others did so by entering a convent. The Restoration was a somewhat debauched period in English history, however, and its libertine ways were well-documented. Behn's ambitions coincided with the revival of the London stage; the Civil War had darkened the city's already-famed theaters in the 1640s and the London plague further shuttered them, but as England regained stability Charles II re-instituted the two main companies. Behn began writing for one of them, Duke's Company at

Dorset Garden, and her first play was produced in September of 1670. *The Forc'd Marriage; or, The Jealous Bridegroom* ran for six nights, a successful run, since playwrights usually went unpaid until the third evening's box-office take. The plot concerned a romantic comedy of errors, which was standard fare for the day.

Behn would pen a number of works for the stage over the next dozen years. Most were light-hearted tales of thwarted love and cavalier seduction.

Found Fodder in Restoration Foibles. One of her final plays, *The Roundheads; or, The Good Old Cause,* was produced in 1682 and achieved notoriety for the way in which Behn's pen ridiculed a faction of republican parliamentarians. But Behn's strong opinions landed her in trouble that same year when she was arrested for writing a polemic on the Duke of Monmouth, Charles II's illegitimate son and claimant to the throne. This also coincided with a merging of London's two main theaters and a subsequent decline of the medium. Behn then turned to writing novels. One of her best-known works was published in three volumes between 1684 and 1687, and was based on an actual scandal of the time. *Love-Letters Between a Nobleman and His Sister* was a thinly-disguised fictional treatment of the antics of one Lord Grey, who in 1682 eloped with his wife's sister; Grey was a Whig, or anti-monarchist, and would go on to play a real-life role in other political machinations between the throne and Parliament.

In the twilight years of her brief career, Behn earned a living from Latin and French translations, and also penned versions of *Aesop's Fables* and poetry some of which was quite racy. Yet she still struggled financially, and historians surmise that her lack of funds forced her to submit to substandard medical care when her health began to decline, which only worsened the situation. During the winter of 1683–1684, she was involved in a carriage accident, and also may have been plagued by arthritic joints; from some of her letters it can be inferred that she was also suffering from some sort of serious illness that may have been syphilis.

Behn died on April 16, 1689. She was buried in the cloisters at Westminster Abbey, and her admirers paid for a tombstone with an epitaph that read: "Here lies a proof that wit can never be/Defence enough against mortality," which she probably penned herself. Behn's literary reputation then sunk into obscurity for the next few centuries, and in England's Victorian era she was vilified. In 1871 a collection of her works, *Plays, Histories, and Novels of the Ingenious Mrs. Aphra Behn,* appeared in print, and the *Saturday Review,* a leading London periodical of the time, condemned it as a sordid assemblage. The reviewer noted that any person curious about the forgotten Behn and her infamous works will "find it all here, as rank and feculent as when first produced." It was not until well into the twentieth century that literary scholarship restored Behn's contribution to English letters.

EWB

Benjamin, Walter (1892–1940), German-born Jewish philosopher and critic. Walter Benjamin published widely on such topics as technology, language, literature, the arts, and society during the years between the world wars. When Benjamin committed suicide in 1940, he left behind a large body of mostly unfinished work that has been slowly published in his native Germany and translated into English and other European languages. Since the 1980s, this fragmented oeuvre has elicited much commentary and become the focus of steady scholarly activity, including several thousand studies. Some of his most noted works include *Illuminations, Essay, and Reflections, Reflections: Essays, Aphorisms, Autobiographical Writings,* and *The Correspondence of Walter Benjamin.*

The son of well-to-do Jewish parents, Benjamin was privately schooled, entering the University of Freiburg in 1912. Seven years later, he completed a doctorate at the University of Bern, for which he wrote a dissertation on German Romantic art and literature. Although he decried the bourgeoise existence he was a part of, he aspired to a university position. In order to procure one, he wrote a second study, this time on German tragic drama of the seventeenth century. This work was incomprehensible to the faculty at the University of Frankfurt, and his application was rejected. Without the sponsorship of a university, Benjamin was forced to become a freelance translator, journalist, and critic. He contributed to many influential journals of his day. He espoused Marxism, yet declined to become an "official" member of any political party. He admired the work of Bertolt Brecht, an avant-garde German dramatist whose plays reflected the communism of the time, and in 1927 Benjamin traveled to Moscow to view communism firsthand.

As a Jew, Benjamin saw the danger of Adolf Hitler's rise to power, and in 1933 he left Germany permanently. In Paris and in Denmark, Benjamin eked out a living by writing radio scripts and reviews and essays for various periodicals. In 1935 he accepted a stipend from the Institute for Social Research to write essays for their *Zeitschrift für Sozialforschung.* Benjamin and the editors of the review, Theodor Adorno and Max Horkheimer, often disputed the content of the essays and they required him to rework them endlessly. Despite the pleas of friends to relocate to Palestine, Benjamin settled in Paris in 1939, where he soon found himself in German-occupied territory. Benjamin and a group of refugees managed to escape from an increasingly hostile Paris and travel to Spain en route to the United States. When the group was not allowed to board a boat, and were instead turned over to the Gestapo, Benjamin took an overdose of morphine, feigned illness so no one would suspect what he had done, and refused medical attention, dying a short while later.

Benjamin is best known in the United States for his literary and cultural criticism, though his political, philosophical, and religious essays have been studied in greater detail by European commentators. Benjamin was first introduced to the American public in 1968 by Hannah Arendt in a long article in the *New Yorker*. In his literary and cultural analyses, Benjamin employed many different methodologies, including modernist, structuralist, and materialist approaches.

In approaching Benjamin, commentators have focused on his literary works. Among his essays are seminal works on Czech author Franz Kafka, French poet Charles Baudelaire, French novelist Marcel Proust, German playwright Bertolt Brecht, as well as on photography and the mechanical reproduction of artwork. Critics have debated heatedly the depth of Benjamin's conversion and commitment to communism. Several commentators purported that Benjamin chose Marxism as the "lesser of two evils," when compared with fascism.

For many years, Benjamin wrote letters that combined his latest philosophical and critical concerns with personal news, often of his struggles to earn a living. Among his correspondents were Gershom Scholem, a longtime friend and scholar who established the modern study of Jewish mysticism, Theodor Adorno, a Marxist and editor for whom Benjamin wrote important essays, Austrian theologian and philosopher Martin Buber, Christian theologian Florens Christian Rang, and dramatist Bertold Brecht. In the 1980s and 1990s several selections of Benjamin's translated letters were published; however, all were flawed by faulty translations or omissions due to stipulations made by the German publisher.

The slow publication and translation of Benjamin's works, some as many as fifty years after their original publication, have made it difficult for non-German-speaking scholars to appreciate the scope and significance of Benjamin's efforts. Even basing their judgments on an incomplete body of work, however, many commentators have declared Benjamin to be among the brightest intellectuals of his generation.

CA

Bentham, Jeremy (1748–1832), English philosopher, political theorist, and jurist. Jeremy Bentham expounded the ethical doctrine known as utilitarianism. Partly through his work many political, legal, and penal reforms were enacted by Parliament.

Jeremy Bentham, the son of a lawyer, was born on Feb. 15, 1748, in Houndsditch, near London. A precocious child, he learned Latin, Greek, and French before he was 10. The "philosopher," as he was known to his family, was an avid reader. After attending the famous Westminster school (1755–1760), he went to Queen's College, Oxford, and took his degree in 1763 at the age of 15. He studied at Lincoln's Inn, receiving a master of arts degree in 1766. The following year he was called to the bar.

Bentham cared little for his formal education, insisting that "mendacity and insincerity . . . are the only sure effects of an English university education," and he cared even less about succeeding as a practicing lawyer. He preferred to read and write papers on legal reform and to study physical science, especially chemistry. His father, who had amassed a considerable fortune in real estate speculations, died in 1792, and from that time on Bentham retired from public life and devoted himself to writing. In 1814 he purchased a mansion, and his home became a center of English intellectual life.

Bentham's Utilitarianism. In 1776 Bentham published *Fragment on Government*, which criticized the interpretations of English common law by Sir William Blackstone. Bentham attacked the notion that a social contract or compact had a legal basis. He continued to write on jurisprudence throughout his career: *Introductory View of the Rationale of Evidence* (1812), edited by James Mill, and the five-volume *Rationale of Juridical Evidence* (1827), edited by John Stuart Mill. In these criticisms of law, evidence, and even language (anticipating the "definition in use" theory of linguistic philosophy), Bentham was a consistent nominalist and instinctive utilitarian. Words and laws, men and institutions must be judged solely in terms of their actual usage and consequences.

Utilitarianism may be defined as the thesis that an act is right or good if it produces pleasure, and evil if it leads to pain. Although this doctrine is almost as old as philosophy itself, the principle of utility received its classic expression in Bentham's *Introduction to the Principles of Morals and Legislation* (1789). Bentham had a talent for simplification; he reduced all ethical considerations to an immediate source. "Nature has placed mankind under the governance of two sovereign masters, pain and pleasure." Utilitarianism aims to make morals and politics an exact science based on these objective criteria and to offer a quantitative method for evaluating both individual and institutional actions.

Men are often unhappy or are deprived of happiness by governments because they fail to perceive that the terms value, ought, good, and right are meaningless unless identical with utility, which is understood as pleasure or happiness. Bentham avoided the subjectivism of most hedonistic theories by acknowledging altruistic as well as egoistic pleasures and recognizing that pleasure often consists primarily in avoiding pain. He defined the community as "the sum of the interests of its members" and stated that utilitarianism aims at the "greatest happiness of the greatest number."

To determine the specific utility of actions, Bentham proposed a "felicific calculus" by which one can balance the pleasures and pains consequent upon one's acts. The value of an action will be greater or less in terms of the intensity and duration of pleasure and its certainty and possibility. One should also consider how an act will affect other people. In addition, the circumstances should be taken into account but not the motives, which do not matter.

Bentham's Personality. Bentham was a man of considerable irony and personal eccentricity. Given honorary citizenship by the new Republic of France in 1792, he scorned the French Revolution's "Declaration of the Rights of Man," commenting that all talk of rights was "nonsense" and talk of absolute rights was "nonsense on stilts." Although he spent 7 or 8 hours daily on his writing for more than 50 years, virtually all his published books are the product of editors. He habitually worked on several projects simultaneously without finishing them, and often there were several incomplete versions of the same topic. Bentham was fortunate in having editors of dedication and genius such as Étienne Dumont, James Mill, and John Stuart Mill. Bentham gave the editors total freedom; consequently some of the works bearing his name were thoroughly rewritten by others from conflicting versions or even scraps and notes.

Bentham's eccentricity took the form of obsession with certain ideas. Prison reform was a central concern of his for several years, and he solicited and received charters and money from the King for a model prison, the "Panopticon." Bentham attributed the failure of this project to royal envy and added to his thousands of written pages on the subject a treatise on the conflict between Jeremy Bentham and George III "by one of the disputants." Throughout his life Bentham conducted a lengthy, and largely unsolicited, correspondence with various heads of state suggesting methods of legal and constitutional reform. Late in life he became concerned with how the dead could be of use to the living; in the work *Auto Icon* he suggested that, with proper embalming, every man could become his own monument and that notables might be interspersed with trees in public parks. In his will, which contributed to establishing University College, London, he stipulated that his clothed skeleton and wax head be preserved. He died on June 6, 1832.

EWB

Bernstein, Eduard (1850–1932), German socialist. Eduard Bernstein was a leader of the revisionist, or evolutionary, wing of the German Social Democratic party.

Eduard Bernstein was born in Berlin on Jan. 6, 1850. As the family's financial resources were limited, his educational opportunities were restricted, and at 16 he became an apprentice in a bank. Within a few years he had risen to the position of bank clerk. In 1872 he joined the Social Democratic party (SPD) and became an active member of the party's Berlin organization. In 1878, shortly prior to the adoption of Chancellor Bismarck's antisocialist legislation, Bernstein traveled to Switzerland.

As a consequence of Bismarck's continued hostility toward the socialists, Bernstein remained in Switzerland and became the editor of the official SPD newspaper. After Bismarck brought pressure to bear in order to halt the smuggling of the newspaper into Germany, the Swiss government forced Bernstein to leave in 1880. He then went to London, where he met the German socialist Friedrich Engels, eventually becoming one of his close associates. Bernstein was also able to study the British labor movement and associate with the recently organized Fabian Society, an organization of socialists. Early Fabians such as George Bernard Shaw and Sidney and Beatrice Webb rejected revolutionary Marxism and advocated what they termed "the inevitability of gradualness." This idea was to form a central part of Bernstein's mature "revisionist" position.

During the 1890s Bernstein began to make his break with orthodox Marxism clear. His revisionist position emerged in a series of articles in an official party publication, *Die neue Zeit,* in 1898. The reaction to these articles by groups within the SPD caused him to write a defense, *Evolutionary Socialism* (1899). In this classic statement of the revisionist position, Bernstein used scientific analysis to attack the premises of revolutionary Marxism. He demonstrated through statistics that workers were not becoming more impoverished and that capitalism was not becoming less stable and thus its collapse was not imminent. He rejected revolutionary tactics as self-defeating and advocated achieving reforms through moderate and constitutional methods. He also urged that the SPD, a working-class party, should attempt to win over the middle classes. Revisionism was officially condemned by the SPD in 1903, and the polarization of the party's revolutionary and evolutionary wings existed until after World War II.

By his death in 1932 Bernstein had long since ceased to be regarded as a leader or major theorist of the SPD. But when the party was reorganized in West Germany after World War II, many of Bernstein's ideas were incorporated in its programs. The new party gave up its revolutionary theory, emphasized action and reform, and attempted to broaden its political base by cutting across ideological and class lines.

EWB

Binet, Alfred (1857–1911), French psychologist and the founder of French experimental psychology. Alfred Binet devised tests for measuring intelligence that have been widely used in schools.

Alfred Binet was born in Nice on July 11, 1857. He studied law and medicine in Paris and then obtained a doctorate in natural science. He became interested in hysteria and hypnosis and frequented Jean Martin Charcot's neurological clinic at the Sâlpétrière Hospital. During this time Binet wrote *La Psychologie du raisonnement* (1886; The Psychology of Reasoning), *Le Magnétisme animal* (1887; Animal Magnetism), and *On Double Consciousness* (1889).

In 1891 Binet joined the Laboratory of physiological Psychology of the École Pratique des Hautes Études; the following year he became assistant director and in 1895 director. He held this post for the rest of his life. In 1895 he founded the experimental journal *L'Année psychologique,* in which he published articles on emotion, memory, attention, and problem solvingarticles which contained a considerable number of methodological innovations.

Although trained in abnormal psychology, Binet never ceased to be interested in the psychology of intelligence and individual differences. After publishing *Les Altérations de la personnalité* (1892; The Alterations of the Personality) with C. Féré, Binet studied complex calculators, chess players, and literary creativity by the survey method. In 1900 he also became interested in suggestibility, a normal continuation of his work on hysteria.

Binet's major interest, however, was the development of intelligence, and in 1899 he established a laboratory at the École de la Rue de la Grange aux Belles. Here he devised a series of tests to study intellectual development in his daughters Armande and Marguerite. His wellknown work, *L'Étude expérimentale de l'intelligence* (1903; The Experimental Study of Intelligence), in which he showed that there could be imageless thought, was based on these studies with his daughters.

Two years later, in response to the request of the minister of public instruction to find a means for enabling learning disabled children to benefit from some kind of schooling, Binet, in collaboration with Théodore Simon, created "new methods for the diagnosis of retarded children's mental level," which were partly based on his earlier work. His scale for measuring intelligence was widely adopted. In 1908 the American psychologist Lewis M. Terman revised it (Stanford Revision). Binet himself improved his test in 1908 and 1911. He also continued to be interested in psychological applications to pedagogical problems: *Les Enfants anormaux* (1907; Abnormal Children), written with Simon; and *Less Idées modernes sur les enfants* (1909; Modern Ideas on Children). Binet died on Oct. 8, 1911.

EWB

Bismarck, Otto von (1815–1898), German statesman. Otto von Bismark was largely responsible for the creation of the German Empire in 1871. A leading diplomat of the late 19th century, he was known as the Iron Chancellor.

Otto von Bismarck, born at Schönhausen on April 1, 1815, to Ferdinand von Bismarck-Schönhausen and Wilhelmine Mencken, displayed a willful temperament from childhood. He studied at the University of Göttingen and by 1836 had qualified as a lawyer. But during the following decade he failed to make a career of this or anything else. Tall, slender, and bearded, the young squire was characterized by extravagance, laziness, excessive drinking, needlessly belligerent atheism, and rudeness. In 1847, however, Bismarck made a number of significant changes in his life. He became religious, entered politics as a substitute member of the upper house of the Prussian parliament, and married Johanna von Puttkamer.

In 1851 Frederick William IV appointed Bismarck as Prussian representative to the Frankfurt Diet of the German Confederation. An ingenious but cautious obstructionist of Austria's presidency, Bismarck described Frankfurt diplomacy as "mutually distasteful espionage." He performed well enough, however, to gain advancement to ambassadorial positions at Vienna in 1854, St. Petersburg in 1859, and Paris in 1862. He was astute in his judgment of international affairs and often acid in his comments on foreign leaders; he spoke of Napoleon III as "a sphinx without a riddle," of the Austrian Count Rechberg as "the little bottle of poison," and of the Russian Prince Gorchakov as "the fox in wooden shoes."

Minister-President of Prussia. In 1862 Frederick William's successor, William I, faced a crisis. He sought a larger standing army as a foundation for Prussian foreign policy; but he could not get parliamentary support for this plan, and he needed a strong minister-president who was willing to persist against opposition majorities. War Minister Roon persuaded the King to entrust the government to Bismarck. William attempted to condition the Sept. 22, 1862, appointment by a written agreement limiting the chief minister's part in foreign affairs, but Bismarck easily talked this restriction to shreds.

Bismarck's attempt to conciliate the budget committee foundered on his September 29 remark, "The great questions of the day will not be decided by speeches and resolutions of majorities that was the mistake of 1848 and 1849but by iron and blood." Bismarck complained that the words were misunderstood, but "blood and iron" became an unshakable popular label for his policies.

Bismarck soon turned to foreign affairs. He was determined to achieve Prussian annexation of the duchies of Schleswig and Holstein at the expense of Denmark. The history of Schleswig-Holstein during the preceding two decades had been stormy, and there were a number of conflicting claims of sovereignty over the territories. Bismarck let the Hohenzollerns, the Prussian ruling family, encourage the Duke of Augustenburg in his claim for Holstein, and the duke established a court at Kiel in Holstein in December 1863. Bismarck then, however, persuaded Austria's Count Rechberg to join in military intervention against the Hohenzollern protégé. This ability to take opposite sides at the same time in a political quarrel for motives ulterior to the issue itself was a Bismarckian quality not always appreciated by his contemporaries. Austro-Prussian forces occupied Holstein and invaded Schleswig in February 1864. The Danes resisted, largely because of a mistaken hope of English help, which Bismarck reportedly assessed with the comment, "If Lord Palmerston sends the British army to Germany, I shall have the police arrest them."

Denmark's 1864 defeat by Austro-Prussian forces led to the 1865 Austro-Prussian Gastein Convention, which exposed Rechberg's folly in committing Austrian troops to an adventure from which only Prussia could profit. Prussia occupied Schleswig, and Austria occupied Holstein, with Prussia to construct, own, and operate a naval base at Kiel and a Kiel-Brunsbüttel canal, both in Holstein. King William made Bismarck a count.

Austro-Prussian War. Bismarck gave Austria a number of opportunities to retreat from its Holstein predicament; when Austria turned to the German Confederation and France for anti-Prussian support, however, Bismarck allied Prussia to Italy. In 1866 Austria mobilized Confederation forces against Prussia, whose Frankfurt representative declared this to be an act of war dissolving the Confederation. The resulting Seven Weeks War led to the defeat of Austria at Königgrätz (July 3) by the Prussian general Moltke. Bismarck persuaded king William to accept the lenient Truce of Nikolsburg (July 26) and Treaty of Prague (August 23).

Prussia's victory enabled Bismarck to achieve Prussian annexation of Schleswig-Holstein, Hanover, Hesse-Cassel, and Frankfurt. The newly formed North German Confederation, headed by Prussia and excluding Austria, provided a popularly elected assembly; the Prussian king, however, held veto power on all political issues. The victory over Austria increased Bismarck's power, and he was able to obtain parliamentary approval of an indemnity budget for 4 years of unconstitutional government. Bismarck was also voted a large grant, with which he bought an estate in Farther Pomerania.

Franco-Prussian War. As payment for its neutrality during the Austro-Prussian War, France claimed Belgium. Bismarck held that the 1839 European treaty prevented this annexation, and instead he agreed to neutralize Luxembourg as a concession to the government of Napoleon III. The French were, however, antagonized by Bismarck's actions. In 1870 he heightened French hostility by supporting the claim of Leopold von Hohenzollern-Sigmaringen to the Spanish throne. The French government demanded Leopold's withdrawal, and Vincent Benedetti, the French ambassador to Prussia, requested formal assurance that no Hohenzollern would ever occupy the Spanish throne. William, who was staying at Bad Ems, declined the request and telegraphed Bismarck an account of the interview. Bismarck edited this "Ems Dispatch" and published an abrupt version that suggested that discussions were over and the guns loaded. His action precipitated the French declaration of war against Prussia on July 19, 1870.

Bismarck's treaties with the South German states brought them into the war against France, and his work at field headquarters transformed these wartime partnerships into a lasting federation. Within 6 weeks the German army had moved through Alsace-Lorraine and forced the surrender of Napoleon III and his army at Sedan (Sept. 2, 1870). But Paris defiantly proclaimed a republic and refused to capitulate. The annexation of occupied Alsace-Lorraine became Bismarck's territorial justification for continuing the war, and the siege of Paris ended in French surrender (Jan. 28, 1871). Alsace-Lorraine became a German imperial territory by the Treaty of Frankfurt (May 10, 1871). The Prussian victory led to the formation of the Reich, a unified German empire under Prussian leadership. William was proclaimed kaiser, or emperor, and Bismarck became chancellor of the empire. Bismarck was also elevated to the rank of prince and given a Friedrichsruh estate.

Chancellor of the Reich (1871–1890). Bismarck modernized German administration, law, and education in harmony with the economic and technological revolution which was transforming Germany into an industrial society. However, he developed no political system, party, or set of issues to support and succeed him. His *Kulturkampf,* or vehement opposition to the Catholic Church, was unsuccessful, and his anti-Socialist policies contributed to the wreckage of the Bismarckian parties in the 1890 election.

Among Bismarck's major diplomatic achievements of this period were the establishment of the Dreikaiserbund, or Three Emperors' League (Germany, Russia, Austria), of 1872–1878 and 1881–1887 and the negotiation of the 1879 Austro-German Duplice, the 1882 Austro-German-Italian Triplice, and the secret 1887 Russo-German Reinsurance Treaty. He served as chairman of the 1878 Congress of Berlin, and he also guided the German acquisition of overseas colonies.

The alliances that Bismarck established were not so much instruments of diplomacy as the visible evidence of his comprehensive effort to postpone a hostile coalition of the powers surrounding Germany. Restraining Russia, the strongest of these powers, required the greatest diplomatic effort. Bismarck's diplomacy is sometimes described as aimed at isolating France, but this is a misleadingly simplistic description of the complicated and deceptive methods he employed to lend substance to his statement, "We Germans fear God, but nothing else in the world."

Fall from Power. William I died March 9, 1888, but Bismarck remained as chancellor for Frederick III (who died June 15, 1888) and for 21 months of the reign of William II, last of the Hohenzollern monarchs. Court, press, and political parties discovered in the 29-year-old William an obvious successor to the power of the 73-year-old chancellor. William was intelligent and glib, with a singular capacity as a phrase maker, and his instability was as yet not widely recognized.

On March 15, 1890, William asked either for the right to consult ministers or for Bismarck's resignation; Bismarck's March 18 letter gave the Kaiser a choice between following Bismarck's Russian policy or accepting his resignation. Suppressing this letter, the Kaiser published an acceptance of Bismarck's retirement because of ill health and created him Duke of Lauenburg. Bismarck referred to this title as one he might use for traveling incognito.

Bismarck did not retire gracefully. Domestically he was happy at Friedrichsruh with Johanna, whom he outlived; and their children, Herbert, William, and Marie, frequently visited them there. Bismarck, however, used the press to harass his political successors, and he briefly stumped the country calling for more power to the parliament, of which he was an absent member from 1891 to 1893. Despite charades of reconciliation, he remained, to his death on July 30, 1898, thoroughly opposed to William II.

Historical estimates of Otto von Bismarck remain contradictory. The later political failure of the state he created has led some to argue that by his own standards Bismarck was himself a failure. He is, however, widely regarded as an extraordinarily astute statesman who understood that to wield power successfully a leader must assess not only its strength but also the circumstances of its application. In his analysis and management of these circumstances, Bismarck showed himself the master of realpolitik.

EWB

Blanc, Louis (1811–1882), French journalist, historian, and socialist politician. Louis Blanc greatly influenced the evolution of French socialism and modern social democracy.

Louis Blanc was born on Oct. 29, 1811, in Madrid, where his father was comptroller of finance for King Joseph, Napoleon's brother. Financially ruined by the fall of the French Empire, the Blanc family returned to Paris, and Louis managed to earn enough from his writings to study law.

In 1839 Blanc published his most famous essay, *L'Organisation du travail* ("The Organization of Labor"). He outlined his social thought, which was based on the principle, "From each according to his abilities, to each according to his needs." His theories were based on solid research and expressed in vivid language. He argued that unequal distribution of wealth, unjust wages, and unemployment all stemmed from competition. Unlike his predecessors, Blanc looked to the state to redress social injustice, but he believed that only a democratic republic could achieve an egalitarian commonwealth. Since every man has a "right to work," the state must provide employment and aid the aged and sick. It would accomplish these aims through establishing "social workshops"—producers' cooperatives, organized on a craft basis. The workers would manage these workshops, share in the profits, and repay the government loan. Eventually, the worker-owned factories, farms, and shops would replace those that were privately owned. Thus the whole process of production would become cooperative.

Though Marx criticized Blanc's ideas as utopian, French workers of the 1840s were intrigued by them. In 1846 there was a widespread demand for national workshops, and by 1848 "the organization of labor" had become a popular slogan. Articles in *La Réforme,* a radical newspaper, popularized Blanc's proposals among the workers, who adopted them as a practical reform program.

Blanc supported the cause of liberals throughout Europe. In 1841 in *Histoire de dix ans, 1830–1840 (History of Ten Years, 1830–1840)*, he denounced King Louis Philippe's foreign policy as pusillanimous. France, he thought, had missed a golden opportunity in 1830 to give Europe liberal institutions.

A member of the provisional government formed on Feb. 24, 1848 (after the fall of the July Monarchy), Blanc persuaded his colleagues to guarantee the right to work, to create national workshops, and to establish the Luxembourg Commission to study and propose social experiments. But the national workshops became a makeshift relief program, a mockery of Blanc's ideas, and the government rejected his proposal for a ministry of labor.

By the middle of May, the coalition of right- and left-wing republicans, which had overthrown the Orleanist regime, collapsed. Though Blanc had been elected to the conservative National Assembly, that body expelled him from the government in May. It also abolished the Luxembourg Commission and on June 21 closed the workshops. These actions provoked a workers' revolt, which General Cavaignac suppressed during the bloody June Days, and the ensuing reaction forced Blanc to seek asylum in England. While in exile he wrote a 12-volume history of the French Revolution to 1795 and a history of the Revolution of 1848. Blanc returned to France in 1871 and entered the Chamber of Deputies. There he led a futile fight for a radical constitution, opposing the one that was eventually adopted in 1875. In January 1879 he climaxed his long career by persuading the Assembly to grant amnesty to the Communards of 1871. Blanc died at Cannes on Dec. 6, 1882.

EWB

Bloch, Marc (1886–1944), French historian. Marc Bloch was the leading French medievalist of the 20th century. He inspired two generations of historians through his teaching and writing.

Marc Bloch was born at Lyons on July 6, 1886, the son of Gustave Bloch, a professor of ancient history. Marc studied in Paris at the École Normale and the Fondation Thiers, in Berlin, and in Leipzig. During World War I he served in the infantry, winning four citations and the Legion of Honor. When the French University at Strasbourg was revived in 1919, Bloch went there to organize the seminar on medieval history. He remained until 1936, when he was called to the Sorbonne to succeed Henri Hauser in the chair of economic history.

In 1920 Bloch presented his thesis *Kings and Serfs,* in which he tried to discover what freedom and servitude meant in the Middle Ages. It was a question he pondered throughout his career, continuing his investigations in major articles of 1921, 1928, and 1933 and in the pages of his *Feudal Society.* The thesis was symptomatic of Bloch's interests and sympathies. He saw the problem of liberty and servitude as one involving economic structures and systems of belief as well as legal norms and institutional practices. From then until his death he continued to affirm that history must concern itself with the whole man, that the economic or legal historian must be first of all a historian of civilization.

Bloch's interest in men and their beliefs inspired his second major work, *The Royal Touch* (1924), a study of the supernatural character attributed to kings in the Middle Ages, in particular the belief in their miraculous powers of healing. His interest in men and their works inspired a series of articles on the spread of labor-saving inventions in the Middle Ages, medieval monetary problems, rural land distribution, and many other topics. In all of these, as in a series of lectures, *The Original Characteristics of French Rural History* (1931), he insisted that the economic and technical questions he was discussing were also questions of "collective psychology."

In 1929 Bloch and Lucien Febvre founded the *Annales d'histoire économique et sociale* to provide a place for innovative historians to express their views. The two editors made themselves the champions of "history as one of the sciences of man" which the resources of sociology, psychology, economics, medicine, and all other disciplines that study man should be used to serve. Bloch also contributed to the *Revue de synthèse,* whose objective was to overcome the barriers between academic disciplines. His last historical work was *Feudal Society* (2 vols., 1939–1940), in which he described the legal institutions of feudalism in their broad cultural setting.

In 1939 Bloch was called back to the army. Avoiding capture in the defeat, he found refuge at Guéret, where he wrote a memoir of his war experiences, *The Strange Defeat* (1946). In this time of forced repose he also set down his reflections on his vocation, *The Historian's Craft*. The anti-Semitic laws soon forced him to leave the University of Paris for Clermont-Ferrand and then for Montpellier. When persecutions increased, he disappeared into the Resistance. In 1943 he reappeared briefly as "Blanchard," then as "Arpajon," "Chevreuse," and "Narbonne." Captured by the Germans in 1944, he was tortured and, on June 16, shot by a firing squad at Saint-Didier-de-Formans, near Lyons.

EWB

Bloomer, Amelia (1818–1894), American advocate of woman's rights in the early days of the feminist movement. Amelia Bloomer spent most of her life working for the cause. She was also a reformer of women's clothing and helped promote "bloomers."

Amelia Jenks was born into a family of modest means in Homer, N.Y., on May 27, 1818. Her formal education was negligible, consisting of only a few years in grammar school. At the age of 22 she married Dexter Bloomer, a lawyer and part owner of the *Seneca Falls County Courier*. A man of Quaker background and progressive social principles, he encouraged his wife to write articles on temperance and other social issues for his newspaper and for other periodicals.

In 1848, at the age of 30, Bloomer attended the first public Woman's Rights Convention at Seneca Falls, N.Y., but she took no part in the proceedings. A few months later she began to publish her own temperance newspaper, *The Lily*, which was immensely successful, gaining a circulation of 4,000 within a few years. At this time in her career Amelia Bloomer was a small, slight, dark-haired woman with good features and a pleasant expression. Timid and retiring by nature, she was a sternly serious person, seemingly lacking in any sense of humor.

Prodded by Elizabeth Cady Stanton, who also lived in Seneca Falls, Bloomer devoted increasing space in *The Lily* to questions concerning woman's rights, such as unequal educational opportunities, discriminatory marriage and property laws, and suffrage. In 1851 *The Lily* supported the reform in women's dress which came to bear Bloomer's name. Female fashion in the 1850s consisted of unhealthy, tightly laced corsets, layers of petticoats that could weigh well over 10 pounds, and floor-length dresses that dragged in the filth of the era's unpaved and unswept streets.

The bloomer costume dispensed with corsets in favor of loose bodices, substituted baggy ankle-length pantaloons for petticoats, and cut the gowns to above the knee. Such a costume had been worn at the utopian New Harmony colony in Indiana in the 1820s and as resort wear during the 1830s, and Mrs. Bloomer was by no means the originator of the revival in 1851. But her promotion of it attached her name to the sensation. Woman's-rights advocates, such as Elizabeth Cady Stanton and Susan B. Anthony, wore the reform dress for a year or so but abandoned it when they concluded that the ridicule it frequently elicited was preventing a fair hearing of their views. Mrs. Bloomer continued to wear the dress until the late 1850s, but, conservative by nature (she never shared the liberal religious views or abolitionist sentiments of her sisters in the movement), even she eventually opposed bloomers as inexpedient.

Bloomer moved to Council Bluffs, Iowa, in 1855, where she abandoned *The Lily* but continued to work actively in the woman's-suffrage movement of that state. She lectured and wrote widely, served as president of the state Woman Suffrage Association between 1871 and 1873, and corresponded with and arranged lectures for Lucy Stone, Susan B. Anthony, and Elizabeth Cady Stanton in Iowa. She retired increasingly into private life in the 1870s, troubled by poor health. She died at Council Bluffs on the last day of 1894.

Amelia Bloomer's work never matched the incessant and selfless activity of some of her contemporaries, but she contributed to the suffrage movement far more profoundly than the generally facetious use of her name would indicate.

EWB

Bodin, Jean (1529–1596), French political philosopher. Jean Bodin influenced European intellectual history through his formulation of economic theories and of principles of good government and through his advocacy of religious tolerance in an intolerant age.

Jean Bodin was born in Angers, the son of a tailor. He received his early education in Angers and Paris as a member of the religious order of Carmelites. After leaving the monastic life, he studied and later taught law at the University of Toulouse. In 1561 he began to practice law in Paris and at about the same time published two significant books. In *Methodus ad facilem historiarum cognitionem* (A Method for the Easy Learning of History), Bodin attempted to determine the principles of universal law through a study of history; in *Response aux paradoxes de M. Malestroit* (1568; Response to the Paradoxes of Monsieur Malestroit), he contended that the revolutionary rise in prices in the 16th century was caused by the great influx of gold and silver analysis which has earned him a distinguished position among early modern European economists.

Bodin won the favor of King Henry III of France and of his brother, the Duke of Alençon. In 1571 he became counselor to the duke and was appointed king's attorney at Laon in 1576. In the same year he served as a delegate of the Third Estate (commoners) at the Estates General of Blois. There Bodin antagonized the clergy and nobility by favoring negotiation instead of war with the French Protestants. He also opposed the King's demand to gain additional revenue by selling public lands and royal demesnes. Because of his stand, Bodin lost favor with the King, but he continued to serve the duke.

Bodin's most famous work, *Six livres de la république* (1576; Six Books of the Republic), reflects his distress over the chaos in France during the Wars of Religion. The principles Bodin proposes for a well-ordered state are based on the doctrine of sovereignty. He believed the state needed one supreme authority to make and enforce law, an authority whose power was limited only by natural and divine law and by the "fundamental laws" of the land. Although he conceded that there could be different types of government, he thought monarchy the most stable because its sovereignty was not divided.

In 1583 Bodin returned to Laon as procurator to the presidial court and spent the rest of his life there. Bodin's interest turned from politics to religion, and his writings reflect this change. In *La Demonomanie des sorciers* (1580; The Demonomania of Witches), he advocated the burning of witches. In the *Heptaplomeres* (1588)—a colloquy between a Jew, a Moslem, a Calvinist, a Lutheran, a Catholic, a theist, and an epicurean-his characters eventually decide that since one religion is as good as another, they should live together in charity. In 1596 Bodin died of plague in Laon.

EWB

Borromeo, St. Charles (1538–1584), Italian prelate. Charles Borromeo was a leading reformer in the Roman Catholic Church.

Charles Borromeo was born into a family of means in the town of Rocca d'Arona in northern Italy on Oct. 2, 1538. He was a bright and personable boy of 12 when he received tonsure, the official initiation into the ranks of the clergy. After studying with tutors, he enrolled at the University of Padua, where in 1559 he received the degree of doctor of laws. That same year his mother's brother was elected Pope Pius IV. Within a few months the new pope had called Charles, then 21, to Rome to help in administering the affairs of the Church.

Charles was given the rank of cardinal to go with his position as personal assistant to the Pope. Pius IV made his talented and dedicated nephew secretary of state and relied heavily on his energy in directing the third session of the Council of Trent (1562–1563), as well as in handling the practical, political affairs of the city of Rome. In 1563 Charles was ordained a priest and consecrated archbishop of Milan, but he continued to live in Rome and work with his uncle. When he was given responsibility in Rome for the Church reform commanded by the Council of Trent, he brought about proper religious instructions in the parishes, saw that the elaborate worship rituals were toned down in the interest of devotion, and built a new seminary for the proper training of the clergy.

From 1566 Charles directed the Church in Milan, since his services in Rome had come to an end with his uncle's death in 1565. Over the years he was a remarkably effective bishop. The diocese of Milan was split among five diplomatic fronts on which he had to operate simultaneously. His popularity with the people disturbed the Milanese senate, and his disciplinary directives antagonized several religious groups. At one point an assassin was hired to kill him but failed.

Almost all of the people of Milan respected Charles's courage and tireless concern. When the plague of 1576–1578 struck Milan, Charles spent much of his time nursing the sick. The catechetical centers he established were so effective that Protestantism made no headway in Milan. He died on Nov. 3, 1584, and was canonized in 1610.

EWB

Broca, Pierre Paul (1824–1880), French surgeon and anthropologist. Pierre Paul Broca was born near Bordeaux, France, in 1824. After studying mathematics and physical science at the local university, he entered medical school at the University of Paris in 1841. He received his M.D. in 1849. Though trained as a pathologist, anatomist, and surgeon, Broca's interests were not limited to the medical profession. His versatility and tireless dedication to science permitted him to make significant contributions to other fields, most notably to anthropology.

The application of his expertise in anatomy outside the field of medicine began in 1847 as a member of a commission charged with reporting on archaeological excavations of a cemetery. The project permitted Broca to combine his anatomical and mathematical skills with his interests in anthropology.

The discovery in 1856 of Neanderthal Man once again drew Broca into anthropology. Controversy surrounded the interpretation of Neanderthal. It was clearly a human skull, but more primitive and apelike than a modern skull and the soil stratum in which it was found indicated a very early date. Neanderthal's implications for evolutionary theory demanded thorough examination of the evidence to determine decisively whether it was simply a congenitally deformed *Homo sapiens* or a primitive human form. Both as an early supporter of Charles Darwin and as an expert in human anatomy, Broca supported the latter view. Broca's view eventually prevailed, though not until the discovery of the much more primitive Java Man (then known as *Pithecanthropus*, but later *Homo erectus*).

Broca is best known for his role in the discovery of specialized functions in different areas of the brain. In 1861, he was able to show, using post-mortem analysis of patients who had lost the ability to speak, that such loss was associated with damage to a specific area of the brain. The area, located toward the front of the brain's left hemisphere, became known as Broca's convolution. Aside from its importance to the understanding of human physiology, Broca's findings addressed questions concerning the evolution of language.

All animals living in groups communicate with one another. Non-human primates have the most complex communication system other than human language. They use a wide range of gestures, facial expressions, postures, and vocalizations, but are limited in the variety of expressions and are unable to generate new signals under changing circumstances. Humans alone possess the capacity for language rather than relying on a body language vocabulary. Language permits humans to generate an infinite number of messages and ultimately allows the transmission of information—the learned and shared patterns of behavior characteristic of human social groups, which anthropologists call culture—from generation to generation. The development of language spurred human evolution by permitting new ways of social interaction, organization, and thought.

Given the importance assigned to human speech in human evolution, scientists began to look for the physical preconditions of speech. The fact that apes have the minimal parts necessary for speech indicated that the shape and arrangement of the vocal apparatus was insufficient for the development of speech. The vocalizations produced by other animals are involuntary and incapable of conscious alteration. However, human speech requires codifying thought and transmitting it in patterned strings of sound. The area of the brain isolated by Broca sends the code to an-

other part of the brain that controls the muscles of the face, jaw, tongue, palate, and larynx, setting the speech apparatus in motion. This area and a companion area that controls the understanding of language, known as Wernicke's area, are detectable in early fossil skulls of the genus *Homo*. The brain of *Homo* was evolving toward the use of language, although the vocal chamber was still inadequate to articulate speech. Broca discovered one piece in the puzzle of human communication and speech, which permits the transmission of culture.

Equally important, Broca contributed to the development of physical anthropology, one of the four subfields of anthropology. Craniology, the scientific measurement of the skull, was a major focus of physical anthropology during this period. Mistakenly considering contemporary human groups as if they were living fossils, anthropologists became interested in the nature of human variability and attempted to explain the varying levels of technological development observed worldwide by looking for a correspondence between cultural level and physical characteristics. Broca furthered these studies by inventing at least twenty-seven instruments for making measurements of the human body, and by developing standardized techniques of measurement.

Broca's many contributions to anthropology helped to establish its firm scientific foundation at a time when the study of nature was considered a somewhat sinister science.

World of Scientific Discovery

Bruno, Giordano (1548–1600) Italian philosopher and poet. Giordano Bruno attempted to deal with the implications of the Copernican universe. Although he made no scientific discoveries, his ideas had much influence on later scientists and philosophers.

Giordano Bruno was born at Nola in southern Italy. His baptismal name was Filippo, but he took the name Giordano when he entered a Dominican monastery in Naples in 1565. During his stay in different monastic houses in southern Italy, he acquired a vast knowledge of philosophy, theology, and science. Because he developed unorthodox views on some Catholic teachings, Bruno was suspected of heresy and finally fled the monastic life in 1576. This experience reveals much about Bruno's personality. His love for knowledge and hatred of ignorance led him to become a rebel, unwilling to accept traditional authority. The price he paid for this independence was persecution and condemnation in many countries.

After making his way through northern Italy, Bruno sought refuge at Geneva in 1579. His criticism of a Genevan professor, however, forced his withdrawal from that city. The next two years were spent in Toulouse, where he was granted a master's degree and lectured on Aristotle. In 1581–1582 he stayed in Paris and published his first significant set of writings, in which he explained a new method for memory training and commented on the logical system of Raymond Lully.

In 1583 Bruno traveled to England, where he lived for 2 years. While there, he became friendly with some prominent Englishmen, publicly praised Queen Elizabeth I, and held a disputation at Oxford on the Copernican and Aristotelian conceptions of the universe. Most important, he published some of his best works in England during 1584–1585, namely, *La Cena de le Ceneri* (*The Ash Wednesday Supper*); *De l'infinito universo et mondi* (*On the Infinite Universe and Worlds*); and *De la causa, principio et uno* (*Concerning the Cause, Principle, and One*). In these works Bruno attempted to come to grips with the meaning of the new conception of the universe that Copernicus had developed. Bruno conceived of the universe as infinite, composed of a plurality of worlds. For him the universe has a unity that signifies a prevailing order-individual things are not isolated but are animated by a common life and a common cause. This cause is immanent, not transcendent, and the soul which gives life to the whole is God. It is God who "is not above, and not outside, but within and through, all things." It is not surprising that later examiners of Bruno's system described it as pantheistic. Bruno also published an Italian dialogue, *De gli eroici furori* (1585; *The Heroic Furies*), in which he presents the Renaissance conception of Platonic love.

Returning to France in 1585, Bruno was forced to leave that country in 1586 because of his attacks on Aristotelian philosophy. He then went to Germany, where he achieved some acclaim as a result of his lectures at the University of Wittenberg and published some works centered primarily on logic. After further travels he settled briefly in Frankfurt am Main, where he wrote a series of poems in Latin. In the three most important ones (all 1591), *De minimo* (*On the Minimum*), *De monade* (*On the Monad*), and *De immenso* (*On the Immense*), he examined what is infinitely small and infinitely great in the universe.

In 1592 Bruno went to Venice on the invitation of a Venetian nobleman who later betrayed him to the Catholic Inquisition. Bruno was arrested and imprisoned in Rome, where after a lengthy confinement and a trial for heresy he was burned at the stake on Feb. 17, 1600.

EWB

Braudel, Fernand (1902–1985), French sociologist. Fernand Braudel was the leading exponent of the so-called "*Annales*" school of history, which emphasizes total history over long historical periods and large geographical space.

Fernand Braudel was born August 24, 1902, in the small town of Luneville in eastern France. His father was an academic administrator. As a young *agrégé* in history, he went to Algeria in 1923 to teach in a lycée and to work on his *thèse d'état*, which was to be on Philip II of Spain and the Mediterranean. His thesis director, Lucien Febvre, made the fateful suggestion that Braudel invert the emphasisthe Mediterranean and Philip II. In 1935 he went to Brazil to teach in the university in São Paulo, Brazil, returning two and a half years later to France just before World War II, with an appointment in the IVe Section of the Ecole Pratique des Hautes Etudes (E.P.H.E.) in Paris. He spent the war in German prison camps in Mainz and Lübeck. During this time he wrote from memory his thesis, which has come to be considered the classic exemplary work of the *Annales* school of history. It was titled *The Mediterranean and the Mediterranean World in the Age of Philip II* (two volumes, 1949).

Elected in 1946 to the Collège de France, he joined his mentor, Febvre, as one of the founders in 1947 of the new VIe Section (economic and social sciences) of the E.P.H.E. He created the Centre de Recherches Historiques. On Febvre's death in 1956, he succeeded him as president of the VIe Section and editor of the journal *Annales E. S. C.* In 1963 he founded the Maison des Sciences de l'Homme, a structure housing national and international research groups, and became its administrator. From 1971 to 1984 he served as the president of the Scientific Commission of the annual Study Weeks sponsored by the Istituto Internazionale di Storia Economica 'Francesco Datini' in Prato, Italy. These were major meetings of economic historians of Europe (both east and west) specializing in the period between the 12th and the 18th centuries. In 1985 he was received in the Académie Française. He was awarded a long list of honorary degrees, memberships in national academies of science, and similar honors. He was widely read and influential in southern Europe (Spain, Portugal, Italy, Greece, and Turkey), Eastern Europe (Poland and Hungary), Germany and the Low Countries, Britain, Quebec, and, since the 1970s, the United States, where a research center named after him was established at the State University of New York, Binghamton.

What was the nature of his accomplishment that he achieved so many honors, so much prestige and influence? Obviously he was a great organizer of scientific activity, as the list of his successive activities attests. But more important than that, he symbolized, incarnated, and promulgated an approach to history which responded to and was of great help in interpreting the long-term structures and middle-run cyclical shifts of the real social world.

There are three central themes which one may associate with Braudel as the culminating figure of the so-called *Annales* school of history. The roots of the *Annales* school itself, often traced to the work of French historian Henri Berr at the turn of the 20th century, was the creation in a formal sense of the collaboration of Lucien Febvre and Marc Bloch at the University of Strasbourg in 1929, where they founded the journal *Annales d'histoire économique et social*. The very title of the journal indicates the initial concern, the enormous neglect of both economic and social history in the standard kind of political history that had prevailed in France, Germany, and Britain since the mid-19th century. The *Annales* school was determined to get at the long-term economic and social structures beneath the surface "events" which Braudel was later to describe as "dust." They turned toward the neglected arenas of rural life, demography, social ecology, everyday life, commerce, and mentalities and away from princes, generals, civil servants, and diplomats.

They were pushed by their subject matter to the work of sociologists, anthropologists, and economists for one fundamental reason. It was not only that the subject matter of *Annales* history was concerned with explaining, as opposed to merely describing, history. It was also that history was no longer seen as a mere collection of "facts." Facts "existed" only as responses to historical "problems." Intellectually, and therefore organizationally as well, the quest became the "totality" of human experience, and therefore the close collaboration of history and the social sciences.

Secondly, and this became Braudel's own great contribution, the *Annales* school saw time as a social—more than as a physical—phenomenon, whence the idea of a plurality of social times. The great trinity that Braudel constructed and used as the framework for his book on the Mediterranean was *structure, conjoncture, événement*: long-term, very slowly evolving structures; medium-term, fluctuating cyclical processes; and short-term, ephemeral, highly visible events. Braudel downplayed the time of events and rejected a fourth time, the universal very long-term, as mythical. History was consequently the story of the interweaving of the long-term structures and the cyclical movements (*conjonctures*).

Finally, 30 years after *The Mediterranean,* his second great work appeared in 1979, the three-volume *Civilization and Capitalism, 15th-18th Century*. In it he developed the theme of the three layers of eco-

nomic life, the bottom layer of everyday life, the middle layer of exchange (the arena of freedom), and the top layer of capitalist monopolies and constraints. This metaphor served to reorganize all of modern history into a constant struggle between the two bottom layers and the top layer of monopoly.

The contribution of Braudel was his sweep and therefore his relevance to the fundamental assessment of large-scale, long-term social change. His intellectual voice was stentorian, a firm line but one uncluttered by dogmatisms. His was a unifying influence, respectful of many strains but impatient of pomposity or foolishness. Above all, Braudel and the *Annales* school stood as a challenge to the narrow, the petty, the arrogance of power in the name of enduring realities, and the social change that is slow but inexorable.

EWB

Bunyan, John (1628–1688), English author and Baptist preacher. John Bunyan wrote *The Pilgrim's Progress* and some 60 other pious works. The sincere evangelical urgency of his religious thought and the vivid clarity of his prose have won wide admiration.

John Bunyan, born in Elstow near Bedford, was baptized on Nov. 30, 1628. His father, the brazier-tinker "Thomas Bonnion," derived from an old Bedfordshire family which had declined in fortune and status. Bunyan had a rudimentary education and at an early age became a tinker. From 1644 to 1647 he served with the parliamentary army during the Puritan Revolution, but he saw little or no fighting.

Religious Development. About 1649 Bunyan married a pious Anglican who introduced him to Arthur Dent's *The Plain Man's Pathway to Heaven*. Under their combined influence Bunyan became an attentive churchgoer and delighted in Anglican ceremonial and bell ringing. But he soon recognized that he was desperately bound by sin and that only Christ could provide redemption. He turned for guidance to John Gifford; once a roistering Cavalier, Gifford had been rescued from debauchery by the Gospel and was pastor of the Congregational Church in Bedford. "Mr. Gifford's doctrine," wrote Bunyan, "was much for my stability." Like Joan of Arc and St. Theresa, Bunyan heard voices, and like William Blake, he had visions. He saw Jesus looking "through the tiles on the roof" and felt Satan pluck his clothes to stop him from praying.

Bunyan was no fornicator, drunkard, or thief; but so urgent was his religion, so passionate his nature, that any sin, however small, was an enormous burden. With Gifford's guidance he made a spiritual pilgrimage and in 1653 was baptized in the Ouse River. Two years later, induced by his Baptist coreligionists, he started "the mighty work of preaching the Gospel." Soon his pen became as active as his tongue, and in 1658–1659 he published *Sighs from Hell* and other tracts.

Triumph in Adversity. The restoration of monarchy and Anglicanism in 1660 meant that Bunyan could no longer preach freely as he had under the Puritan Commonwealth. In January 1661 he was jailed for "pertinaciously abstaining" from Anglican services and for holding "unlawful meetings." Because he was unwilling to promise silence, his 3-month sentence stretched to 12 years with a few respites. After his wife's death he had remarried, and he worked while in prison to support his second wife and children. He also preached to his fellow sufferers and wrote a variety of religious works, including *Grace Abounding* published in 1666—one of the world's most poignant spiritual autobiographies. During this period he also wrote most of Part I of *The Pilgrim's Progress*, but he hesitated to release it because of its fictional structure.

After the Declaration of Indulgence (1672), Bunyan was freed and licensed as a preacher. He built a Nonconformist congregation of 3,000 or 4,000 souls in Bedfordshire; he ministered assiduously to his flock and helped to found about 30 other congregations. But in 1673 the edict of toleration was repealed. When Bunyan was imprisoned for about 6 months in 1675, he again worked on his masterpiece, and Part I of *The Pilgrim's Progress* was published in 1678. It won immediate popularity, and before Bunyan's death there were 13 editions, with some additions. Since then it has been continuously in print and has been translated into well over a hundred languages.

Bunyan's own experience and the language of the Bible were the sources of *The Pilgrim's Progress*. Unlike *Grace Abounding*, this work reveals his spiritual development through allegory. The countryside through which the hero, Christian, progresses is a blend of the English countryside, the world of the Bible, and the land of dreams. Despite his assertion that "manner and matter too was all my own," Bunyan owed a good deal to oral tradition and wide reading—folk tales, books of emblems and characters, sermons, homilies in dialogue form, and traditional allegories.

Bunyan's last decade was fertile. Like *The Pilgrim's Progress*, *The Life and Death of Mr. Badman* (1680) made a significant advance toward the English novel. *The Holy War* (1682) is a dramatic, allegorical account of siege warfare against the town of Mansoul. Although, like all his works, it is based on Calvinist

theology, Bunyan should not be considered a rigid determinist but should be viewed as a Christian humanist who assigned personal responsibility to his characters. Part II of *The Pilgrim's Progress* (1684) emphasizes human relationships and the sanctification of the world, especially through marriage and family life. Bunyan produced 14 more books before he died at the age of 60 on Aug. 31, 1688. He was buried in Bunhill Fields, where he lies near other great Nonconformists William Blake, George Fox, and Daniel Defoe.

Despite the Protestant evangelical cast of his mind, Bunyan transcended Puritanism and remains relevant in an age of ecumenism. Nor was he a pessimistic prophet: if his Pilgrim knew the Hill of Difficulty and the Slough of Despair, he also enjoyed the Delectable Mountains and reached the Celestial City.

EWB

Burckhardt, Jacob (1818–1897), Swiss historian. Jacob Burckhardt was a philosophical historian whose books dealt with cultural and artistic history and whose lectures examined the forces that had shaped European history.

Through the use of eyewitness accounts, diplomatic documents, and the contents of government archives, the teachers and contemporaries of Jacob Christoph Burckhardt sought to reconstruct political events "as they had really happened." Burckhardt, however, viewed history as the record of the achievement of the human spirit. Politics was only part of that record. The highest expression of any age was to be found in its poetry, art, literature, and philosophy. The historian's task was to seek the spirit these works expressed, so the reader might be "not smarter for the next time but wiser forever."

Burckhardt was born in Basel on May 25, 1818. His father, a pastor at the Basel Minster, was elected administrative head of the Reformed Church in the canton in 1838. The year before, Jacob had begun theological studies at the University of Basel. Within 18 months, however, he lost his orthodox religious beliefs and turned from theology to history. He studied in Berlin for 4 years, attending the lectures of Johann Droysen, August Boeckh, and Franz Kugler, and Leopold von Ranke's seminar. Burckhardt formed close friendships with a group of poets and students of revolutionary liberal political views.

In 1843 Burckhardt returned to Basel, where he took a post as political correspondent with the conservative *Basler Zeitung*, and lectured at the university on art history. He immersed himself in the political crisis then shaking Switzerland, a crisis brought on by the return of the Jesuits to the Catholic canton of

Lucerne. Then in 1846, disgusted by what he had seen, he left for Italy. His political views had turned to cultural and aristocratic conservatism. During the next 12 years he taught and wrote in Berlin, Basel, and Zurich, with lengthy trips to Italy in 1847, 1848, and again in 1853 to prepare the *Cicerone.*

"The Age of Constantine" and "Cicerone."

During the winter of 1847–1848 Burckhardt planned a series of cultural histories, beginning with the age of Pericles and ending with the age of Raphael. The first to appear was *The Age of Constantine the Great* (1852). The structure of this work was one that Burckhardt would use again in his later cultural histories and analyze in detail in his *Reflections on World History:* the "three great powers"—state, religion, and culture—and the ways in which they determine each other. The book is thus concerned as much with art and literature as with politics and religion.

Burckhardt's *Cicerone* (1854) was "a guide for the enjoyment of art in Italy." In form a traveler's guidebook, it was in reality a history of Italian art. In it Burckhardt first tried to solve the problem of systematic art history, tried, as he later put it, to get away from "the mess of art history as the history of artists," to go beyond biography to the analysis of historical and geographical styles.

"The Civilization of the Renaissance."

While still a student in Berlin, Burckhardt had come to the conclusion that the French Revolution had "pulled the historical ground from under the feet" of all European peoples. Just as in art the styles of every age now coexisted, "one beside the other," with no single tradition dominating, so with the state "the nineteenth century began with a clean slate." The individual now had free choice in politics, and nothing to fall back on but his own "inner truth." The application of this insight to the culture of Renaissance Italy resulted in Burckhardt's masterpiece, *The Civilization of the Renaissance in Italy* (1860).

In this work Burckhardt proposed that the conflict between popes and emperors had deprived 13th-century Italy of legitimate political rule, had left it with that "clean slate" he saw in his own times. This climate allowed political units to appear "whose existence was founded simply on their power to maintain it." But it also freed the individual of all traditional constraints, whether political, religious, or social. Expressed through artistic and literary forms revived from antiquity, this freed and self-conscious individualism, this "genius of the Italian people . . . achieved the conquest of the western world." In the Italian Re-

naissance, Burckhardt saw the major characteristics of the modern world, its evil as well as its good.

Later Years.

Burckhardt explained his thesis in his lectures of 1868–1869, "On the Study of History," in the course of a wideranging analysis of the "three powers" at the heart of his historical vision. Culture, in contrast to the constants, state and religion, "is the sum of those spiritual developments that appear spontaneously." Its form and its vehicle–language—are the product of societies and epochs, but its source is always the individual. To study culture is thus to study the individual giving expression to his place and his age as well as himself.

After publishing his notes on Italian architecture in 1867, Burckhardt prepared nothing more for the press but devoted himself until his retirement in 1893 to lecturing at the university. His series of cultural histories was never completed, but his lectures covered the entire sweep of European history from the ancient Greeks to the European crisis of 1870. In an age of ever-narrower nationalisms, Burckhardt reached back to the universal humanism of Goethe.

After 1870 Burckhardt became increasingly pessimistic about the future of European culture. Though he hoped for another Renaissance, he feared the arrival of the "fearful simplifiers," the demogogues who would lead the "masses" to tyranny and destroy the European culture he loved. "The world is moving toward the alternative of complete democracy or absolute, ruthless despotism," he wrote to a friend in 1882. The day would come when "the military state will turn industrialist." He withdrew to two sparsely furnished rooms above a bakery shop and devoted himself to his work on Italian art, which he never completed. He died on Aug. 8, 1897.

EWB

Burke, Edmund (1729–1797), British statesman and noted political theorist and philosophical writer. Edmund Burke was born in Ireland, spent most of his active life in English politics, and died the political oracle of conservative Europe.

Edmund Burke's view of society was hierarchical and authoritarian, yet one of his noblest characteristics was his repeated defense of those who were too weak to defend themselves. Outstanding in 18th-century British politics for intellect, oratory, and drive, he lacked the ability either to lead or to conciliate men and never exerted an influence commensurate with his capabilities. His career as a practical politician was a failure; his political theories found favor only with posterity.

Burke was born on Jan. 12, 1729, in Dublin of middle—class parents. His mother suffered from what Burke called "a cruel nervous disorder," and his relations with his authoritarian father, a Dublin attorney, were unhappy. After attending Trinity College, Dublin, Burke in 1750 crossed to England to study law at the Middle Temple. But he unconsciously resisted his father's plans for him and made little progress in the law. Indecision marked his life at this time: he described himself as "a runaway son" and his "manner of life" as "chequered with various designs." In 1755 he considered applying for a post in the Colonies but dropped the idea when his father objected.

In 1756 Burke published two philosophical treatises, *A Vindication of Natural Society* and *A Philosophical Enquiry into the Origin of Our Ideas of the Sublime and Beautiful.* In the *Vindication* Burke exposed the futility of demanding a reason for moral and social institutions and, with the foresight which was one of the most remarkable of his gifts, distinguished the coming attack of rationalistic criticism on the established order. The *Enquiry,* which he had begun when only 19, was considered by Samuel Johnson to be "an example of true criticism." These works were followed in 1757 by *An Account of the European Settlement in America,* to which Burke, although he denied authorship, clearly contributed a great deal. The early sheets of *The Abridgement of the History of England* were also printed in 1757, although the book itself was not published until after Burke's death. These works introduced Burke's name into London literary circles and seemed to open up a reputable career.

Family unity, which he had never known as a boy, became an article of Burke's adult philosophy. In 1757 he married the daughter of his physician and settled into family life with his father-in-law, his brother Richard, and his so-called cousin William. With them he found a domestic harmony he had never known in his father's home.

Early Political Career. Financial security, however, was elusive, and Burke was forced to take a minor secretarial post in the government establishment in Ireland. But contact with the depressed and persecuted Irish Catholics unsettled him, and early in 1765 he resigned his position. Necessity now led Burke into politics. In July 1765, when the Whig administration of Lord Rockingham was being formed, he was recommended to Rockingham, who took him on as his private secretary. In December, Burke entered Parliament as member for the Buckinghamshire constituency of Wendover.

Burke's subsequent political career was bound inextricably to the fortunes of the Rockingham group. Emotional and hysterical by nature, without a profession or a secure income, he found stability and independence through his attachment to the Whig aristocrats. When Rockingham lost the premiership in 1766, Burke, though offered employment under the new administration, followed him into opposition. "I believe in any body of men in England I should have been in the minority," he later said. "I have always been in the minority." Certainly the dominant characteristic of his political career was an overwhelming impulse to argue and oppose; to that was added enormous persistence, courage, concentration, and energy. Endowed with many of the qualities of leadership, he lacked the sensitivity to gauge and respect the feelings and opinions of others. Hence his political life was a series of negative crusades against the American war, Warren Hastings, and the French Revolution and his reputation as a statesman rests on his wisdom in opposition, not on his achievements in office.

Burke's theory of government was essentially conservative. He profoundly distrusted the people and believed in the divine right of the aristocracy to govern. "All direction of public humour and opinion must originate in a few," he wrote in 1775. "God and nature never meant [the people] to think or act without guidance or direction." Yet all Burke's writings, despite their rather narrow propaganda purpose, include valuable generalizations on human conduct.

Views on America and Ireland. Burke found difficulty in applying his political philosophy to practical issues. He was one of the first to realize the implications of Britain's problems with colonial America. He saw the British Empire as a family, with the parent exercising a benevolent authority over the children. Perhaps influenced by his own upbringing, he believed the British government to have been harsh and tyrannical when it should have been lenient. "When any community is subordinately connected with another," he wrote, "the great danger of the connexion is the extreme pride and self-complacency of the superior."

In 1774 Burke argued against retaining the tea duty on the Colonies in his celebrated *Speech on American Taxation,* and twice in 1775 he proposed conciliation with the Colonies. His conception of the British Empire as an "aggregate of many states under one common head" came as near as was possible in the 18th century to reconciling British authority with colonial autonomy. Yet at the same time he repeatedly declared his belief in the legislative supremacy of the British Parliament. Thus the American war split Burke in two. He could face neither American independence nor the prospect of a British victory. "I do not know," he wrote in August 1776, "how to wish success to those whose victory is to separate us from a large and noble part of our empire. Still less do I wish success to injustice, oppression, and absurdity . . . No good can come of any event in this war to any virtuous interest."

In Ireland, Burke's sympathies were with the persecuted Roman Catholics, who were "reduced to beasts of burden" and asked only for that elementary justice all subjects had a right to expect from their government. He preferred their cause to that of the Protestant Anglo-Irish, who were striving to throw off the authority of the British Parliament. With Irish nationalism and its constitutional grievances he had little sympathy. "I am sure the people ought to eat whether they have septennial Parliaments or not," he wrote in 1766. As on the American problem, Burke always counseled moderation in Ireland. "I believe," he said only 2 months before his death, "there are very few cases which will justify a revolt against the established government of a country, let its constitution be what it will."

Hastings Incident. On the formation of the short-lived Rockingham ministry in March 1782, Burke was appointed paymaster general. But now, when he seemed on the threshold of political achievement, everything seemed to go wrong for Burke. In particular, his conduct at this time showed signs of mental disturbance, a tendency aggravated by the death of Rockingham in July 1782. James Boswell told Samuel Johnson in 1783 that Burke had been represented as "actually mad"; to which Johnson replied, "If a man will appear extravagant as he does, and cry, can he wonder that he is represented as mad?" A series of intemperate speeches in the Commons branded Burke as politically unreliable, an impression confirmed by his conduct in the impeachment of Warren Hastings, the governor general of Bengal, in 1790.

Ever since Rockingham had taken office, the punishment of those accused of corruption in India had been uppermost in Burke's mind. His strong aggressive instincts, sharpened by public and private disappointments, needed an enemy against which they could concentrate. Always inclined to favor the unfortunate, he became convinced that Hastings was the principal source of misrule in India and that one striking example of retribution would deter other potential offenders. In Burke's disordered mind, Hastings appeared as a monster of iniquity; he listened uncritically to any complaint against him; and the vehemence with which he prosecuted the impeachment indicates the depth of his emotions. His violent language and intemperate charges alienated independent men and convinced his own party that he was a political liability.

Last Years. Disappointment and nostalgia colored Burke's later years. He was the first to appreciate the significance of the French Revolution and to apply it to English conditions. In February 1790 he warned the Commons: "In France a cruel, blind, and ferocious democracy had carried all before them; their conduct, marked with the most savage and unfeeling barbarity, had manifested no other system than a determination to destroy all order, subvert all arrangement, and reduce every rank and description of men to one common level."

Burke had England and his own disappointments in mind when he published *Reflections on the Revolution in France and on the Proceedings of Certain Societies in London* in 1790. "You seem in everything to have strayed out of the high road of nature," he wrote. "The property of France does not govern it"; and in the *Letters on a Regicide Peace* (1796) he defined Jacobinism as "the revolt of the enterprising talents of a country against its property." If England, following the French example, was not to be governed by property, what would become of Burke's most cherished principles? In part the *Reflections* is also Burke's apologia for his devotion to Rockingham. For Rockingham's cause Burke had sacrificed his material interests through 16 long years of profitless opposition, and when his party at last came to power he failed to obtain any lasting advantage for himself or his family. In the famous passage on Marie Antoinette in the *Reflections,* Burke, lamenting the passing of the "age of chivalry," perhaps unconsciously described his own relations with the Whig aristocrats: "Never, never more, shall we behold that generous loyalty to rank and sex, that proud submission, that dignified obedience, that subordination of the heart, which kept alive, even in servitude itself, the spirit of an exalted freedom."

For the last 5 years of his life Burke occupied a unique position. "He is," remarked a contemporary, "a sort of power in Europe, though totally without any of those means . . . which give or maintain power in other men." He corresponded with Louis XVIII and the French royalists and counseled Stanislaus of Poland to pursue a liberal policy. The Irish Catholics regarded him as their champion. As each succeeding act of revolution became more bloody, his foresight was praised more widely. He urged the necessity of war with France, and the declaration of hostilities further increased his prestige. On the last day of his life he spoke of his hatred for the revolutionary spirit in France and of his belief that the war was for the good of humanity. He died on July 9, 1797, and in accordance with his wishes was buried in the parish church of Beaconsfield in Buckinghamshire.

EWB

Byron, George Gordon, known as Lord Byron (1788–1824), English poet. Byron was one of the most important figures of the romantic movement. Because of his works, active life, and physical beauty he came to be considered the personification of the romantic poet-hero.

George Gordon Noel Byron was born on Jan. 22, 1788, into a family of fast-decaying nobility. His lame foot, the absence of any fatherly authority in the household after Captain "Mad Jack" Byron's death in 1791, the contempt of his aristocratic relatives for the impoverished widow and her son, his Calvinistic upbringing at the hands of a Scottish nurse, the fickleness and stupidity of his mother all conspired to hurt the pride and sensitiveness of the boy. This roused in him a need for self-assertion which he soon sought to gratify in three main directions: love, poetry, and action.

On the death of his grand-uncle in 1798, Byron inherited the title and estate. After 4 years at Harrow (1801–1805), he went to Trinity College, Cambridge, where he became conscious for the first time of the discrepancy between the lofty aspirations of idealism and the petty realities of experience. "I took my gradations in the vices with great promptitude," he later reminisced, "but they were not to my taste." His obstinate quest for some genuine passion among the frail women of this world accounts for the crowded catalog of his amours.

Early Works. In 1807 Byron's juvenilia were collected under the title *Hours of Idleness;* although the little book exhibited only the milder forms of romantic *Weltschmerz,* it was harshly criticized by the *Edinburgh Review.* The irate author counterattacked in *English Bards and Scotch Reviewers* (1809), the first manifestation of a gift for satire and a sarcastic wit which single him out among the major English romantics, and which he may have owed to his aristocratic outlook and his classical education.

In 1809 a 2-year trip to the Mediterranean countries provided material for the first two cantos of *Childe Harold's Pilgrimage.* Their publication in 1812 earned Byron instant glory, as they combined the more popular features of the late-18th-century romanticism: colorful descriptions of exotic nature, disillusioned meditations on the vanity of earthly things, a lyrical exaltation of freedom, and above all, the new hero, handsome and lonely, somberly mysterious, yet strongly impassioned for all his weariness with life.

Social Life. While his fame was spreading, Byron was busy shocking London high society. After his affairs with Lady Caroline Lamb and Lady Oxford, his incestuous and adulterous love for his half sister Augusta not only made him a reprobate, but also crystallized the sense of guilt and doom to which he had always been prone. From then on, the theme of incest was to figure prominently in his writings, starting with the epic tales that he published between 1812 and 1816: *The Giaour, The Bride of Abydos, The Corsair, Lara, The Siege of Corinth,* and *Parisina.* Incestuous love, criminal although genuine and irresistible, was a suitable metaphor for the tragic condition of man, who is cursed by God, rebuked by society, and hated by himself because of sins for which he is not responsible. The tales, therefore, add a new dimension of depth to the Byronic hero: in his total alienation he now actively assumes the tragic fatality which turns natural instinct into unforgivable sin, and he deliberately takes his rebellious stance as an outcast against all accepted notions of the right order of things.

While thus seeking relief in imaginative exploration of his own tortured mind, Byron had been half hoping to find peace and reconciliation in a more settled life. But his marriage to Anna Isabella Milbanke (Jan. 1, 1815) soon proved a complete failure, and she left him after a year. London society could have ignored the peculiarities of Byron's private life, but a satire against the Prince Regent, "Stanzas to a Lady Weeping," which he had appended to *The Corsair,* aroused hysterical abuse from the Tories, in whose hands his separation from his wife became an efficient weapon. On April 25, 1816, Byron had to leave his native country, never to return.

His Travels. In Switzerland, Byron spent several months in the company of the poet Shelley, resuming an agitated and unenthusiastic affair with the latter's sister-in-law, Clare Clairmont. Under Shelley's influence he read Wordsworth and imbibed the high-flown but uncongenial spirituality which permeates the third canto of *Childe Harold.* But *The Prisoner of Chillon* and Byron's first drama, *Manfred,* took the Byronic hero to a new level of inwardness: his greatness now lies in the steadfast refusal to bow to the hostile powers that oppress him, whether he discovers new selfhood in his very dereliction or seeks in self-destruction the fulfillment of his assertiveness.

In October 1816 Byron left for Italy and settled in Venice, where he spent many days and nights in unprecedented debauchery. His compositions of 1817, however, show signs of a new outlook. The fourth canto of *Childe Harold* does not reject the cosmic pessimism of *Manfred*, but the mood of shrill revolt is superseded by a tone of resigned acceptance, and sizable sections of the poem are devoted to the theme of political freedom and national independence. Equally significant of Byron's renewed ability to face the world in laughter rather than in anger is the witty, good-humored satire of *Beppo*, which should be considered a preparation for *Don Juan*, begun in September 1818.

Spontaneous maturation had thus paved the way for the healing influence of Teresa Guiccioli, Byron's last love, whom he met in April 1819. The poet had at last begun to come to terms with his desperate conception of life, to the extent of being able to debunk all shams and to parody all posturing, including his own, in *Don Juan*, the unfinished masterpiece on which he was to work till the end of his life. But this new balance also found serious utterance in *Cain*, the best of the plays that he wrote in 1821. It is a closely argued dramatic restatement of Byron's lasting creed that as the universe is swayed by a loveless God, the only greatness to which man can aspire lies in his foredoomed struggle for reason and justice. *Marino Faliero* illustrates the same pattern in the field of action, exalting the selflessness of the man who sacrifices his life in the service of popular freedom.

It is characteristic of Byron's integrity that he increasingly sought to translate his ideas into action, repeatedly voicing the more radical Whig viewpoint in the House of Lords in 1812–1813, running real risks to help the Italian Carbonari in 1820–1821, and collaborating with Leigh Hunt in launching the *Liberal* in 1822. His early poetry had contributed to sensitizing the European mind to the plight of Greece under the Turkish yoke. In 1824 Byron joined the Greek liberation fighters at Missolonghi, where he died of malarial fever on April 19.

EWB

C

Calvin, John (1509–1564), French Protestant reformer. John Calvin is best known for his doctrine of predestination and his theocratic view of the state.

John Calvin was born at Noyon in Picardy on July 10, 1509. He was the second son of Gérard Cauvin, who was secretary to the bishop of Noyon and fiscal procurator for the province. The family name was spelled several ways, but John showed preference while still a young man for "Calvin."

An ecclesiastical career was chosen for John, and at the age of 12, through his father's influence, he received a small benefice, a chaplaincy in the Cathedral of Noyon. Two years later, in August 1523, he went to Paris in the company of the noble Hangest family. He entered the Collège de la Marche at the University of Paris, where he soon became highly skilled in Latin. Subsequently he attended the Collège de Montaigu, where the humanist Erasmus had studied before him and where the Catholic reformer Ignatius of Loyola would study after him. Calvin remained in the profoundly ecclesiastical environment of this college until 1528. Then at the behest of his father he moved to Orléans to study law. He devoted himself assiduously to this field, drawing from it the clarity, logic, and precision that would later be the distinguishing marks of his theology.

In 1531, armed with his bachelor of laws degree, Calvin returned to Paris and took up the study of classical literature. At this time Martin Luther's ideas concerning salvation by faith alone were circulating in the city, and Calvin was affected by the new Protestant notions and by pleas for Church reform. He became a friend of Nicholas Cop, who, upon becoming rector of the university in 1533, made an inaugural speech which immediately branded him as a heretic. Calvin suffered the penalties of guilt by association and would certainly have been arrested had he not been warned to flee. In January 1534 he hastily left Paris and went to Angoulême, where he began work on his theological masterpiece, the *Institutes of the Christian Religion*.

Several turbulent months later, after a secret journey and two brief periods of arrest, Calvin was forced to flee from France when King Francis I instituted a general persecution of heretics. In December 1534 he found his way to Basel, where Cop had gone before him.

Calvin's Theology. Sometime during his last 3 years in France, Calvin experienced what he called his sudden conversion and mentally parted company with Rome. He proceeded to develop his theological position and in 1536 to expound it in the most severe, logical, and terrifying book of all Protestantism, the *Institutes of the Christian Religion*. Calvin followed this first Latin edition with an enlarged version in 1539 and a French translation in 1540, a book that has been called a masterpiece of French prose. The reformer continued to revise and develop the *Institutes* until his death.

Its theme is the majesty of God. There is an unbridgeable chasm between man and his maker. Man is thoroughly corrupt, so base that it is unthinkable that he could lift a finger to participate in his own salvation. God is glorious and magnificent beyond man's highest capacity to comprehend; He is both omnipotent and omniscient, and He has, merely by His knowing, foreordained all things that ever will come to pass. Man is helpless in the face of God's will. He is predestined either to eternal glory or eternal damnation, and he can do nothing, even if he is the best of saints in his fellow's eyes, to alter the intention of God. To suggest that he could would be to imply that the Creator did not fore-know precisely and thus diminish His majesty. To Calvin there could be no greater sacrilege. This doctrine of predestination did not originate with Calvin, but no one ever expressed it more clearly and uncompromisingly. He did not flinch from the terrible consequences of God's omniscience.

To those few whom God has chosen to save, He has granted the precious gift of faith, which is undeserved. All are unworthy of salvation, and most are damned because God's justice demands it. But God is infinitely merciful as well as just, and it is this mercy, freely given, that opens the door to heaven for the elect.

Calvin knew that this doctrine was terrifying, that it seemed to make God hateful and arbitrary, but he submitted that human reason is too feeble to scrutinize or judge the will of God. The Creator's decision on who shall be damned is immutable. No purgatory exists to cleanse man of his sins and prepare him for heaven. Yet Calvin counsels prayer, even though it will not change God's will, because prayer too is decreed and men must worship even though they may be among the damned. The prayer should be simple, and all elaborate ceremony should be rejected. The Catholic Mass is sacrilegious, because the priest claims that in it he changes the bread and wine into the body and blood of Christ. Calvin held that Christ is present whenever believers gather prayerfully, but in spirit only and not because of any act undertaken by priests, who have no special powers and are in no way different from other Christians. There are only two Sacraments: Baptism and the Lord's Supper. Like Luther, Calvin rejects all other "sacraments" as not based on Holy Scripture.

Calvin makes a distinction between the visible Church and the true Church. The former is composed of those who participate in the Sacraments and profess their faith in Christ; the latter, invisible and unknown to all save God, is the community of the electdead, living, and yet unborn. One must belong to the visible Church in order to be saved, but belonging to it is no guarantee of salvation. Church and state are both ordained by God. The task of the former is to teach and prescribe faith and morals, while the latter preserves order and enforces the laws set forth by the Church. There is no separation of Church and state. Both must work in harmony to preserve the word of God, and to this end the state is enjoined to use force if necessary to suppress false teachings, such as Catholicism, Anabaptism, or Lutheranism.

That these ideas, particularly with their cornerstone of predestination, soon conquered much of the Christian world is baffling at first examination. But Calvin's followers were encouraged by hope of election rather than enervated by fear of damnation. It seems to be an essential part of human nature to see oneself as just, and Calvin himself, while he firmly maintained that no one is certain of salvation, always acted with confidence and trust in his own election.

Geneva Reformer. While publication of the *Institutes* was in progress, Calvin made preparations to leave his homeland permanently. He returned briefly to France early in 1536 to settle personal business, then set out for Strasbourg. Because of the war between France and the Holy Roman Empire, he was forced to take a circuitous route which brought him to Geneva. He intended to continue on to Strasbourg but was persuaded to remain by Guillaume Farel, who had begun a Protestant movement in Geneva. Except for one brief interruption he spent the remaining years of his life in Geneva, spreading the word of God as he understood it and creating a theocratic state unique in the annals of Christendom.

In 1537 Calvin was elected to the preaching office by the city fathers, who had thrown off obedience to Rome along with their old political ruler, the Duke of Savoy. A council, now operating as the government, issued decrees in July 1537 against all manifestations of Catholicism as well as all forms of immorality. Rosaries and relics were banished along with adulterers. Gamblers were punished and so were people who wore improper, that is, luxurious, clothing. The austere hand of Calvin was behind these regulations.

The new rules were too severe for many citizens, and in February 1538 a combination of *Libertines* (freedom lovers) and suppressed Catholics captured a majority of the council. This body then banished Calvin and Farel; Calvin went to Strasbourg and Farel to Neuchâtel, where he remained for the rest of his life.

At Strasbourg, Calvin ministered to a small congregation of French Protestants and in 1540 married Idelette de Bure. She bore him one child, who died in infancy, and she herself died in 1549. While Calvin was establishing himself at Strasbourg, things were going badly for the new Protestantism in Geneva. Strong pressure was being exerted on the council from within and without the city to return to Catholicism. Fearing that they might be removed from office and disgusted with the trend toward flagrant immorality among the citizenry, the councilors revoked the ban on Calvin on May 1, 1541. A deputation was sent immediately to Strasbourg to persuade the reformer to return, and he did so reluctantly, on Sept. 13, 1541, after being promised total cooperation in restoring discipline.

Rule of God. The law of a Christian state, according to Calvin, is the Bible. The task of the clergy is to interpret and teach that law, while the task of the state is to enforce it. Under this principle, while the clergy, including Calvin, were not civil magistrates, they held enormous authority over the government and all aspects of civil as well as religious life.

Immediately on his return to Geneva, Calvin set about organizing the Reformed Church. On Jan. 2, 1542, the city council ratified the *Ordonnances ecclésiastiques,* the new regulations governing the Church, formulated by a committee led by Calvin. The *Ordonnances* divided the ministry into four categories: pastors, teachers, lay elders, and deacons. The pastors governed the Church and trained aspirants to the ministry. No one could preach henceforth in Geneva without permission of the pastors.

The conduct of all citizens was examined and regulated by a consistory of 5 pastors and 12 lay elders elected by the council. The consistory had the right to visit every family annually and search its home; to summon any citizen before it; to excommunicate, which meant virtually automatic banishment from the city by the council; to force attendance at weekly sermons; to prohibit gambling, drunkenness, dancing, profane songs, and immodest dress; and to forbid all forms of the theater. The colors of clothing, hair styles, and amounts of food permissible at the table were regulated. It was forbidden to name children after saints, and it was a criminal offense to speak ill of Calvin or the rest of the clergy. The press was severely censored, with writings judged to be immoral and books devoted to Catholicism or other false teaching forbidden. Punishment for first offenses was usually a fine and for repetition of minor crimes, banishment. Fornication was punishable by exile, and adultery, blasphemy, and idolatry by death. Education, which Calvin regarded as inseparable from religion, was very carefully regulated, and new schools were established. Charity was placed under municipal administration to eliminate begging. Thus the whole life of Geneva was placed under a rigid discipline and a single Church from which no deviation was permitted.

The consistory and the city council worked hand in hand in enforcing the laws, but the moving spirit of all was Calvin, who acted as a virtual dictator from 1541 until his death. Calvin did not look the part of a dictator. He was a small, thin, and fragile man with an unsmiling ruthless austerity in his face. He was pale under a black beard and a high forehead. A poet would perhaps see these physical details as signs of enormous, orderly intellect and of little human warmth or appetite, a being all mind and spirit with almost no body at all. There were some ugly moments in theocratic Geneva. During these years 58 people were executed and 76 banished in order to preserve morals and discipline. Like most men of his century, the reformer was convinced that believing wrongly about God was so heinous a crime that not even death could expiate it.

Last Years. The last years of Calvin's life were spent in elaborating Geneva's laws, writing controversial works against spiritual enemies, and laboring prodigiously on the theology of the *Institutes.* Geneva became a model of discipline, order and cleanliness, the admiration of all who visited there.

Men trained to the ministry by Calvin carried his doctrines to every corner of Europe. The reformer lived to see his followers growing in numbers in the Netherlands, Scotland, Germany, and even France, the homeland he had been forced to leave. The impetus he gave to austerity, frugality, and hard, uncomplaining work may have had some influence in forming a capitalist mentality devoted to the acquisition but not the enjoyment of wealth. In any case his teachings have been carried to the present day and live on in the churches which descended from him, modified from their early severity by time but still vigorous in some of the more puritan aspects of modern life.

On May 27, 1564, after a long illness Calvin died. He left an indelible mark on the Christian world.

EWB

Carlyle, Thomas (1795–1881), British essayist and historian and the leading social critic of early Victorian England. Disseminating German idealist thought in his country, with Calvinist zeal Thomas Carlyle preached against materialism and mechanism during the industrial revolution.

Thomas Carlyle was born at Ecclefechan in Dumfriesshire, Scotland, on Dec. 4, 1795. His father, a stonemason, was an intelligent man and a pious Calvinist. Carlyle was educated at Annan Grammar School and Edinburgh University, where he read voraciously and distinguished himself in mathematics. He abandoned his original intention to enter the ministry and turned instead first to schoolteaching and then to literary hackwork, dreaming all the while of greatness as a writer. A reading of Madame de Staël's *Germany* introduced him to German thought and literature, and in 1823–1824 he published a *Life of Schiller* in the *London Magazine* and in 1824 a translation of Goethe's *Wilhelm Meister's Apprenticeship* .

Meanwhile Carlyle had passed through a religious crisis similar to the one he was to describe in *Sartor Resartus* and had met Jane Baillie Welsh, a brilliant and charming girl, who recognized his genius and gave him encouragement and love. Through a tutorship in the Buller family Carlyle made his first trip to London, where he met Samuel Taylor Coleridge and other leading literary figures. He returned to Scotland, married Jane Welsh on Oct. 17, 1826, and settled first in Edinburgh and subsequently at Craigenputtock, an isolated farmhouse belonging to his wife's family. It was during this period that he wrote a series of essays for the *Edinburgh Review* and the *Foreign Review* which were later grouped as *Miscellaneous and Critical Essays*. Among these were essays on Burns, Goethe, and Richter and the important "Signs of the Times," his first essay on contemporary social problems.

"Sartor Resartus." It was at Craigenputtock that Carlyle wrote *Sartor Resartus,* his most characteristic work. Originally rejected by London editors, it was first published in *Fraser's Magazine* in 1833–1834 and did not attain book form in England until 1838, after Ralph Waldo Emerson had introduced it in America and after the success of Carlyle's *The French Revolution.* The first appearance of *Sartor Resartus* was greeted with "universal disapprobation," in part because of its wild, grotesque, and rambling mixture of serious and comic styles. This picturesque and knotted prose was to become Carlyle's hallmark.

Career in London. Carlyle came into his maturity with *Sartor* and longed to abandon short articles in favor of a substantial work. Accordingly, he turned to a study of the French Revolution, encouraged in the project by John Stuart Mill, who gave him his own notes and materials. As a help in his researches he moved to London, settling in Chelsea. The publication of *The French Revolution* in 1837 established Carlyle as one of the leading writers of the day. The book demonstrates his belief in the Divine Spirit's working in man's affairs. Carlyle rejected the "dry-as-dust" method of factual history writing in favor of immersing himself in his subject and capturing its spirit and movement hence the focus on the drama and scenic quality of events and on the mounting impact of detail. His ability to animate history is Carlyle's triumph, but his personal reading of the significance of a great event lays him open to charges of subjectivity and ignorance of the careful study of economic and political detail so admired by later schools of historical research.

Carlyle's great popularity led him to give several series of public lectures on German literature, the history of literature, modern European revolutions, and finally, and most significantly, on heroes and hero worship. These lectures were published in 1841 as *On Heroes, Hero-Worship, and the Heroic in Literature.* This work reflects his increasing hostility to modern egalitarian democracy and his stress upon the inequality of men's wisdom and the incorporation, as it were, of divine purpose. Carlyle's insistence upon the need for heroic leadership is the reason why he was attacked, often mistakenly, as an apostle of force or dictatorial rule.

Late Works. Carlyle's hero worship is responsible for the two largest projects of his later career. He first intended to rehabilitate Oliver Cromwell by means of a history of the Puritan Revolution but later narrowed his project to a collection of Cromwell's letters and speeches connected by narrative and commentary (1845). And from 1852 to 1865 he labored on a biography of Frederick the Great (1865) against the mounting uncongeniality and intractability of the subject. During these years Carlyle exerted a great influence on younger contemporaries such as Alfred Tennyson, Robert Browning, Charles Kingsley, John Ruskin, and James Froude. He published a number of criticisms of the economic and social conditions of industrial England, among them *Chartism* (1839), "Latter-Day" Pamphlets (1850), and *Shooting Niagara, and After?* (1867). His most significant social criticism, *Past and Present* (1843), contrasted the organic, hierarchical society of the medieval abbey of Bury St. Edmunds with the fragmented world of modern parliamentary democracy. It hoped for a recognition of moral leadership among the new "captains of industry."

In 1865 Carlyle was elected lord rector of Edinburgh University, but in his last years he was more than ever a lonely, isolated prophet of doom. He died on Feb. 5, 1881, and was buried in Ecclefechan Churchyard.

EWB

Castiglione, Baldassare (1478–1529), Italian author, courtier, and diplomat. Baldassare Castiglione is known primarily for his "Book of the Courtier." This work, which portrays the ideal courtier, was a chief vehicle in spreading Italian humanism into England and France.

Baldassare Castiglione was born on Dec. 6, 1478, in Casatico in the province of Mantua of an illustrious Lombard family. After receiving a classical education in Mantua and in Milan, he served at the court of the Milanese duke Lodovico Sforza from 1496 to 1499. Castiglione then entered the service of Francesco Gonzaga, Duke of Mantua. In 1503 he fought with Gonzaga's forces against the Spanish in Naples. On his way north he visited Rome and Urbino; both cities fascinated him. His request to transfer to the court of Guidobaldo da Montefeltro at Urbino was grudgingly granted in 1504 by Gonzaga.

At Urbino, Guidobaldo's wife, Elizabetta, presided over the noble company depicted in the *Libro del cortegiano* (*Book of the Courtier*). Castiglione's service there gave him an entree into the court of Pope Julius II, where he became a friend of the artist Raphael. He was sent as ambassador to Henry VII of England and in 1513 was made Count of Nuvolara by Guidobaldo's successor, Francesco Maria della Rovere. Castiglione married in 1516 but became a cleric in 1521 after the death of his wife. In 1524 he was sent by Pope Clement VII as ambassador to Charles V in Spain, an unfortunate mission in that Castiglione reported wrongly the Emperor's intentions in the period leading up to the sack of Rome in 1527. Castiglione died in Toledo, Spain, on Feb. 7, 1529.

"Book of the Courtier."   Published in 1528, though it was begun in 1507 and written mainly from 1513 to 1516, Castiglione's *Book of the Courtier* was a huge and immediate success. His idealized picture of society at the court of Urbino quickly became a book of etiquette for both the bourgeoisie and the aristocracy even beyond the confines of Italy. Translated into Spanish (1534), French (1537), English (1561), and German (1566), *The Courtier* saw some 40 editions in the 16th century alone and a hundred more by 1900. Through it, the broad values of Italian humanism the ideal of the fully developed, well-rounded man, itself the rebirth of a classical ideal were helped to spread throughout western Europe. Yet it must be admitted that in *The Courtier* the high qualities of *humanitas* culture and virtue are exalted not for themselves but as tools of self-advancement.

Dignified, melancholy, and idealistic (qualities that Raphael captured in his famous portrait), Castiglione tended not only to soften society's rough edges but also to avoid thorny practical and moral issues. For instance, he says of the Italians' recent poor reputation in arms, "It is better to pass in silence that which cannot be recalled without pain." As to the question of what a courtier should do when ordered by his prince to commit an immoral act such as mur-

der, he states, "There would be too much to say; it must all be left to your discretion." Nevertheless, there is much that is positive in *The Courtier;* there is a lofty concept of human personality and dignity and of man's creative possibilities.

Castiglione's classical learning is deftly blended into the polite conversation of the courtiers and their ladies. His arguments in favor of literature are derived from those of Cicero in *Pro Archia,* and his description of the ideal courtier is strongly influenced by Cicero's *Deoratore.* The courtier should be noble, witty, pleasant, agile, a horseman and a warrior (his principal profession), and devoted to his prince. He should know Greek, Latin, French, and Spanish, and he should be skilled, though not ostentatiously so, in literature, music, painting, and dancing. The courtier's behavior should be characterized by grace and nonchalance (*sprezzatura*), and he should carefully avoid any affectation. As in Machiavelli and Guicciardini, there is a certain moral relativism: seeming is frequently more important than being.

EWB

Catherine II   (1729–1796), Russian empress, known as Catherine the Great. Catherine II reigned from 1762 to 1796. She expanded the Russian Empire, improved administration, and vigorously pursued the policy of Westernization. Her reputation as an "enlightened despot," however, is not wholly supported by her deeds.

Born in the German city of Stettin on April 21, 1729, Catherine was the daughter of Prince Christian August of Anhalt-Zerbst and Princess Johanna Elizabeth of Holstein-Gottorp. Her education emphasized the subjects considered proper for one of her station: religion (Lutheranism), history, French, German, and music.

When Catherine was 15, she went to Russia at the invitation of Empress Elizabeth to meet and perhaps marry the heir to the throne, the Grand Duke Peter, an immature and disagreeable youth of 16. As the Empress had hoped, the two proved amenable to a marriage plan; but Catherine later wrote that she was more attracted to the "Crown of Russia," which Peter would eventually wear, than to "his person." When Catherine had met the important condition imposed upon her as a prospective royal consort, that she be converted to the Russian Orthodox faith, she and the young Grand Duke were married in 1745.

The marriage turned out to be an unhappy one in which there was little evidence of love or even affection. Peter was soon unfaithful to Catherine, and after a time she became unfaithful to him. Whether

Peter was the father of Paul and Anna, the two children recorded as their offspring, remains a moot question.

Although amorous interests were important in Catherine's personal life, they did not overshadow her intellectual and political interests. A sharp-witted and cultivated young woman, she read widely, particularly in French, at that time the first language of educated Europeans. She liked novels, plays, and verse but was particularly interested in the writings of the major figures of the French Enlightenment, such as Diderot, Voltaire, and Montesquieu.

Catherine was ambitious as well as intelligent. She always looked ahead to the time when Peter would succeed to the throne and she, as his empress, would be able to exercise great political influence. In anticipation of her future status she sought the reputation of being a true Russian. She worked diligently at mastering the Russian language and took care to demonstrate devotion to the Russian Orthodox faith and the Russian state. Thus she gave prominence to a significant difference between her attitude and that of her husband, who displayed open contempt for the country he was to rule. She assured herself of further advantage by the studied use of her charm and vivacity in cultivating the goodwill of important personages.

Ascent to Power. When Empress Elizabeth died on Dec. 25, 1761, Peter was proclaimed Emperor Peter III, and Catherine became empress. Friends warned that she might not enjoy her status for long since Peter was planning to divorce her, and she was advised to flee. She decided to ignore the warning, and the wisdom of her decision was soon demonstrated. Within a few months after coming to the throne, Peter had aroused so much hostility among government, military, and church leaders that a group of them began plotting a coup to remove him, place his 7-year-old son, Paul, on the throne, and name Catherine as regent until the boy should come of age. But they had underestimated Catherine's ambition she aimed at a more exalted role for herself. On June 28, 1762, with the aid of her lover Gregory Orlov, she rallied the troops of St. Petersburg to her support and declared herself Catherine II, the sovereign ruler of Russia (she later named Paul as her heir). She had Peter arrested and required him to sign an act of abdication. When he sought permission to leave the country, she refused it, intending to hold him prisoner for life. But his remaining days proved few; shortly after his arrest he was killed in a brawl with his captors.

Early Reign (1762–1764). Catherine had ambitious plans regarding both domestic and foreign affairs, but during the first years of her reign her attention was directed toward securing her position. She knew that a number of influential persons considered her a usurper and her son, Paul, the rightful ruler; she also realized that without the goodwill of the nobility and the military she could be overthrown by a coup as readily as she had been elevated by one. Her reaction to this situation was to take every opportunity for conciliating the nobility and the military and at the same time striking sharply at those who sought to replace her with Paul.

As for general policy, Catherine understood that Russia needed an extended period of peace during which to concentrate on domestic affairs and that peace required a cautious foreign policy. The able Count Nikita Panin, whom she placed in charge of foreign affairs, was well chosen to carry out such a policy.

Attempts at Reform (1764–1768). By 1764 Catherine felt sufficiently secure to begin work on reform. In her thinking about the problems of reform, she belonged to the group of 18th-century rulers known as "enlightened despots." Influenced by the ideas of the Enlightenment, these monarchs believed that a wise and benevolent ruler, acting according to the dictates of reason, could ensure the well-being of his or her subjects.

It was in the spirit of the Enlightenment that Catherine undertook her first major reform, that of Russia's legal system, which was based on the antiquated, inequitable, and inefficient Code of Laws, dating from 1649. For more than 2 years, inspired by the writings of Montesquieu and the Italian jurist Beccaria, she worked on the composition of the "Instruction," a document to guide those to whom she would entrust the work of reforming the legal system. This work was widely distributed in Europe and caused a sensation because it called for a legal system far in advance of the times. It proposed a system providing equal protection under law for all persons and emphasized prevention of criminal acts rather than harsh punishment for them.

In June 1767 the Empress created the Legislative Commission to revise the old laws in accordance with the "Instruction." For the time and place, the Commission was a remarkable body, consisting of delegates from almost all levels of society except the lowest, the serfs. Like many others, Catherine had great hopes about what the Commission might accomplish, but unfortunately, the delegates devoted most of their time to the exposition of their own grievances, rather than to their assigned task. Consequently, though their meetings continued for more than a year, they made no progress, and Catherine suspended the meetings at the end of 1768. The fact that she never reconvened the Commission has been interpreted by some historians as an indication that she had lost faith in the delegates; others feel, however, that she was more interested in having the reputation of being an "enlightened" ruler than in actually being one.

War and Revolt (1768–1774). Foreign affairs now began to demand Catherine's major attention. She had sent troops to help the Polish king Stanislas (a former lover) in suppressing a nationalist revolt aimed at reducing Russia's influence in Poland. In 1768 the Polish rebels appealed to Turkey for aid, and the Turkish sultan, grateful for an opportunity to weaken a traditional enemy, declared war on Russia. But his act was based on serious miscalculation, and his forces were soundly beaten by the Russians. This turn of events led Austria to threaten intervention on Turkey's behalf unless Catherine agreed not to take full advantage of her victory. Faced by this dangerous alternative, she agreed to show restraint in return for a portion of Polish territory. Thus in 1772 Austria and Russia annexed Polish territory in the First Partition of Poland. Two years later, after lengthy negotiations, Catherine concluded peace with Turkey, restricting herself to relatively modest but nonetheless important gains. Russia received as a territorial concession its first foothold on the Black Sea coast, and Russian merchant ships were allowed the right of sailing on the Black Sea and through the Dardanelles.

Even before the conclusion of peace with the Turks, Catherine had to concern herself with a revolt led by the Cossack Yemelyan Pugachev. It proved to be the most ominous internal threat she ever had to face. The rebel leader claimed that reports of Peter III's death were false and that he himself was the deposed emperor. He convinced many serfs, Cossacks, and members of other dissatisfied groups that when Catherine II was deposed and "Peter III" was returned to the throne their oppression would be ended. Soon tens of thousands were following him, and the uprising, which started in the south and spread up the Volga River, was within threatening range of Moscow. Pugachev's defeat required several major expeditions by the imperial forces, and a feeling of security returned to the government only after his capture late in 1774. The revolt was a major landmark in Catherine's reign. Deeply alarmed by it, she concluded, along with most of the aristocracy, that the best safeguard against rebellion would be the strengthening of the local administrative authority of the nobility rather than measures to ameliorate the condition of the lower classes.

Domestic Affairs (1775–1787). Much of Catherine's fame rests on what she accomplished during the dozen years following the Pugachev uprising, when she directed her time and talent to domestic affairs, particularly those concerned with the administrative operations of government. Her reorganization in 1775 of provincial administration, in such a way as to favor the nobility, stood the test of time; but her reorganization of municipal government 10 years later was less successful.

Catherine attached high importance to expanding the country's educational facilities. She gave serious consideration to various plans and in 1786 adopted one providing for a large-scale educational system. Unfortunately she was unable to carry out the entire plan; but she did add to the number of the country's elementary and secondary schools, and some of the remaining parts of her plan were carried out during succeeding reigns.

Another of Catherine's chief domestic concerns was the enhancement of Russia's economic strength. To this end she encouraged trade by ending various restrictions on commerce, and she promoted the development of underpopulated areas by attracting both Russians and foreigners to them as settlers.

The arts and sciences received much attention during Catherine's reign not only because she believed them to be important in themselves, but also because she saw them as a means by which Russia could attain a reputation as a center of civilization. Under her direction St. Petersburg was beautified and made one of the world's most dazzling capitals. With her encouragement, theater, music, and painting flourished; stimulated by her patronage, the Academy of Sciences reached new heights. Indeed, during her reign St. Petersburg became one of the major cultural centers of Europe.

Foreign Affairs (1787–1795). Catherine gradually came to believe that it would be possible to strip Turkey of both Constantinople and its European possessions if only Austria would join Russia in the undertaking. And, having gained Austria's lukewarm support, she began the deliberate pursuit of a policy so intolerably aggressive toward Turkey that in 1787 the Sultan finally declared war on Russia. As in past encounters, the Russian forces proved superior to the Turks, but they required 4 years to achieve victory. By the Treaty of Jassy (1792) Catherine won from Turkey a large area on the Black Sea coast and gained Turkish agreement to Russia's annexation of the Crimean Peninsula. But she was not able to carry out her original plan of annexing Constantinople and Turkey's European territory, since Austria had withdrawn its support of this action and other powers vigorously opposed it.

While the Russo-Turkish War was in progress, Polish nationalists again tried to strengthen the Polish state and end Russian influence within it. As before, their efforts were futile, leading only to unqualified disaster for their unfortunate country—the Second Partition of Poland (1793), in which Russia and Prussia annexed Polish territory; and the Third Partition (1795), in which Russia, Austria, and Prussia divided what remained of an independent Poland.

Problem of Succession. As she grew older, Catherine became greatly troubled because her heir, Paul, who had long been given to violent and unpredictable extremes of emotion, was becoming so unsettled and erratic that she doubted his fitness to rule. She considered disclaiming him as heir and naming his oldest son, Alexander, as her successor. But before she was able to alter her original arrangement, she died of a stroke on Nov. 6, 1796.

EWB

Cavendish, Margaret (1623–1673), of the first prolific female science writers. As the author of approximately 14 scientific or quasi-scientific books, Margaret Cavaendish helped to popularize some of the most important ideas of the scientific revolution, including the competing vitalistic and mechanistic natural philosophies and atomism. A flamboyant and eccentric woman, Cavendish was the most visible of the "scientific ladies" of the seventeenth century.

Margaret Lucas was born into a life of luxury near Colchester, England, in 1623, the youngest of eight children of Sir Thomas Lucas. She was educated informally at home. At the age of eighteen, she left her sheltered life to become Maid of Honor to Queen Henrietta Maria, wife of Charles I, accompanying the queen into exile in France following the defeat of the royalists in the civil war. There she fell in love with and married William Cavendish, the Duke of Newcastle, a 52 year-old widower, who had been commander of the royalist forces in the north of England. Joining other exiled royalists in Antwerp, the couple rented the mansion of the artist Rubens. Margaret Cavendish was first exposed to science in their informal salon society, "The Newcastle Circle," which included the philosophers Thomas Hobbes, René Descartes and Pierre Gassendi. She visited England in 1651—52 to try to collect revenues from the Newcastle estate to satisfy their foreign creditors. It was at this time that Cavendish first gained her reputation for extravagant dress and manners, as well as for her beauty and her bizarre poetry.

Publishes Original Natural Philosophy. Cavendish prided herself on her originality and boasted that her ideas were the products of her own imagination, not derived from the writings of others. Cavendish's first anthology, *Poems, and Fancies,* included the earliest version of her natural philosophy. Although English atomic theory in the seventeenth century attempted to explain all natural phenomena as matter in motion, in Cavendish's philosophy all atoms contained the same amount of matter but differed in size and shape; thus, earth atoms were square, water particles were round, atoms of air were long, and fire atoms were sharp. This led to her humoral theory of disease, wherein illness was due to fighting between atoms or an overabundance of one atomic shape. However in her second volume, *Philosophical Fancies,* published later in the same year, Cavendish already had disavowed her own atomic theory. By 1663, when she published *Philosophical and Physical Opinions,* she had decided that if atoms were "Animated Matter," then they would have "Free-will and Liberty" and thus would always be at war with one another and unable to cooperate in the creation of complex organisms and minerals. Nevertheless, Cavendish continued to view all matter as composed of one material, animate and intelligent, in contrast to the Cartesian view of a mechanistic universe.

Challenges Other Scientists. Cavendish and her husband returned to England with the restoration of the monarchy in 1660 and, for the first time, she began to study the works of other scientists. Finding herself in disagreement with most of them, she wrote *Philosophical Letters: or, Modest Reflections upon some Opinions in Natural Philosophy, maintained by several Famous and Learned Authors of this Age, Expressed by way of Letters* in 1664. Cavendish sent copies of this work, along with *Philosophical and Physical Opinions,* by special messenger to the most famous scientists and celebrities of the day. In 1666 and again in 1668, she published *Observations upon Experimental Philosophy,* a response to Robert Hooke's *Micrographia,* in which she attacked the use of recently-developed microscopes and telescopes as leading to false observations and interpretations of the natural world. Included in the same volume with *Observations* was *The Blazing World* was a semi-scientific utopian romance, in which Cavendish declared herself "Margaret the First."

Invited to the Royal Society. More than anything else, Cavendish yearned for the recognition of the scientific community. She presented the universities of Oxford and Cambridge with each of her publications and she ordered a Latin index to accompany the writings she presented to the University of Leyden, hoping thereby that her work would be utilized by European scholars.

After much debate among the membership of the Royal Society of London, Cavendish became the first woman invited to visit the prestigious institution, although the controversy had more to due with her notoriety than with her sex. On May 30, 1667, Cavendish arrived with a large retinue of attendants and watched as Robert Boyle and Robert Hooke weighed air, dissolved mutton in sulfuric acid and conducted various other experiments. It was a major advance for the scientific lady and a personal triumph for Cavendish.

Cavendish published the final revision of her *Philosophical and Physical Opinions*, entitled *Grounds of Natural Philosophy*, in 1668. Significantly more modest than her previous works, in this volume Cavendish presented her views somewhat tentatively and retracted some of her earlier, more extravagant claims. Cavendish acted as her own physician, and her self-inflicted prescriptions, purgings and bleedings resulted in the rapid deterioration of her health. She died in 1673 and was buried in Westminster Abbey.

Although her writings remained well outside the mainstream of seventeenth-century science, Cavendish's efforts were of major significance. She help to popularize many of the ideas of the scientific revolution and she was one of the first natural philosophers to argue that theology was outside the parameters of scientific inquiry. Furthermore, her work and her prominence as England's first recognized woman scientist argued strongly for the education of women and for their involvement in scientific pursuits. In addition to her scientific writings, Cavendish published a book of speeches, a volume of poetry, and a large number of plays. Several of the latter, particularly *The Female Academy*, included learned women and arguments in favor of female education. Her most enduring work, a biography of her husband, included as an appendix to her 24 page memoir, was first published in 1656 as a part of *Nature's Pictures*. This memoir is regarded as the first major secular autobiography written by a woman.

NWS

Cavour, Camillo Benso, conte di (1810–1861), Italian statesman. Cavour devoted himself to the liberation of northern Italy from Austrian domination. A brilliant and steadfast diplomat, he played a leading role in the unification of Italy.

Camillo Benso di Cavour was born on Aug. 1, 1810, at Turin. As a younger son in a noble family, he was trained to be an officer in the army. But moved by a restless dissatisfaction with Italian social and political conditions, he resigned his commission in 1831, when he was only 21 years old. He applied himself to the agricultural improvement of his family estate. Then, widening his sphere of activity, he founded the Piedmontese Agricultural Society and became one of the chief promoters of railroads and steamships in Italy. The liberal Cavour grew ever more distrustful of the reactionary politics in force throughout Europe, particularly their manifestation in the repressive rule of Austria over a large area of Italy.

The Journalist.   Cavour believed that liberalism and love of country could be combined to cause a revolt against Austrian dominion in the north and then to establish an Italian constitutional monarchy. To spread his views, in 1847 at Turin he established the newspaper *Il Risorgimento* (the resurgence, the name given to the Italian movement for unification and freedom).

In January 1848 revolution did break out, but in Sicily, against the ancient and decadent Bourbon regime, rather than in the north. Cavour, however, saw this as an opportunity to press in public speeches and in *Il Risorgimento* for a constitution for the Piedmont. Charles Albert, King of the Piedmont, yielded to this pressure and on February 8 granted a charter of liberties to his kingdom. Within 6 weeks of this memorable day Cavour's principal hope was realized when the Milanese rose against the Austrians. He then threw all his journalistic power into persuading the King to enter the war. Cavour, more than anyone else, was responsible for Piedmont's March 25 declaration of war on Austria.

Elections were held during the hostilities, and Cavour became a member of Parliament, beginning a career of public service that would end only with his death. On March 23, 1849, almost exactly a year after the war had begun, the Piedmontese were decisively defeated. King Charles Albert abdicated in favor of his son Victor Emmanuel II, who had no recourse but to make a loser's peace with Austria. Although the effort to throw off the foreign yoke had failed, Cavour did not slacken his efforts to achieve Italian independence.

Diplomatic Activity.   By 1851 Cavour was serving as minister of agriculture, industry, commerce, and finance. On November 4 he became prime minister. He brooded over the Austrian repression of Lombardy in retribution for the abortive revolt of that possession. He waited for a situation in which he could successfully oppose Austria, and his opportunity came with the Crimean War (1853–1856). This conflict allowed the Piedmontese statesman to use diplomacy on a broad international scale and thus force the Great Powers to take cognizance of Italy's plight. He decided to enter the war against Russia, and on Jan. 10, 1855, over serious objections within the Piedmontese government, a treaty with France and England was signed. A contingent of Piedmontese soldiers was sent to the Crimea, and the distinguished combat record of these troops enabled Cavour to assume a prominent position at the Congress of Paris after the war. Through his diplomatic skill at this meeting he succeeded in making the Italian question a chief topic of discussion and in making Austria appear in an unfavorable light.

Anticipating war with Austria, Cavour began strengthening the Piedmontese army and negotiating an alliance with the French emperor, Napoleon III. He agreed to cede Nice and Savoy to France in return for French help in ousting Austria from northern Italy. By 1859 the plans had been completed, and volunteers under the guidance of Cavour and Giuseppe Garibaldi were ready to spring into action throughout Italy. But Napoleon III then threw Cavour into despair by accepting a Russian proposal to convene a congress to settle the Italian question.

The Austrians, however, made the mistake of rejecting this plan and on April 23, 1859, sent an ultimatum to Piedmont. This had the effect of sealing the alliance between that state and France, and Cavour delightedly led the Piedmontese into war. When the French unexpectedly signed an armistice with Austria on July 8, Victor Emmanuel II, over the objections of Cavour, ended Piedmontese hostilities after only a partial victory. Lombardy was to be ceded to the Piedmont and Venetia to remain Austrian.

Unwilling to see such a good beginning go to waste, Cavour secretly encouraged revolutions against the petty tyrants of central Italy. He also remained in communication with Garibaldi. In May 1860, acting in the name of King Victor Emmanuel, whom Cavour had persuaded to cooperate, Garibaldi and his force of "Red Shirts" sailed to Sicily and in a few days demolished the tottering structure of the Bourbon government. When Garibaldi crossed to the mainland and took Naples, Cavour feared that the Red Shirts might complicate matters by attacking the Papal States. To avoid this action, he sent troops to annex the papal holdings. Cavour believed in a free Church but not in one whose territories cut Italy in half.

Cavour lived to see Victor Emmanuel II proclaimed king of a united Italy in 1861. But the statesman's strength was waning, and on June 6, 1861, he died. There were many problems in Italy still unsolved, but Cavour's brilliance had transformed his country from a collection of feudal principalities into a modern state.

EWB

Chamberlain, Houston Stewart

(1855–1927), English-born German writer. Houston Chamberlain formulated the most important theory of Teutonic superiority in pre-Hitlerian German thought.

Houston Stewart Chamberlain was born in Southsea, England, on Sept. 9, 1855. He was the son of an English captain, later admiral. Two of his uncles were generals, and a third was a field marshal. Educated in England and France, he suffered from poor health throughout his life. This prevented him from entering the British military service and led him to take cures in Germany, where he became an ardent admirer of the composer Richard Wagner. In 1882 Chamberlain met Wagner at the Bayreuth Festival, and he later became a close friend of Wagner's widow.

During the 1880s Chamberlain studied natural sciences in Geneva and Vienna. He wrote a dissertation on plant structure, which was accepted by the University of Vienna in 1889, but he never sought an academic position. In 1908 Wagner's daughter Eva became Chamberlain's second wife. Thereafter he lived at Bayreuth, the "home of his soul." He became a German citizen in 1916 and died on Jan. 9, 1927.

Literary Works. Chamberlain preferred to write in German, and his major works were composed in that language. His first published books were studies of Wagner: *The Wagnerian Drama* (1892) and the biography *Richard Wagner* (1896).

Chamberlain's most significant work is *The Foundations of the Nineteenth Century* (1899), which demonstrates his thesis that the history of a people or race is determined by its racial character and abilities. He conceives of race in terms of attitudes and abilities rather than physical characteristics. In general he views abilities and attributes of personality as inherited.

Unlike Joseph Arthur Gobineau, Chamberlain applies the term "Aryan" only to a language group and doubts the existence of an elite Aryan race. Instead he views the Teutons as the superior European race. For him the Teutons include most importantly the Germanic peoples, but also the Celts and certain Slavic groups. He holds that the Jews are fundamentally alien in spirit to the Teutons and believes that they should be allowed no role in German history.

Foundations, despite its scientific underpinnings, is essentially an eloquent, even poetic, vision of the German people. The modern reader may justly criticize this work as self-contradictory and sometimes nonsensical, but it had deep meaning for the Germans of Chamberlain's day. By 1942 *Foundations* had gone through 28 editions.

During World War I Chamberlain advocated the German cause, and his pro-German, anti-English writings were published in English as *The Ravings of a Renegade* (1916). Chamberlain met the young Hitler in 1923 and wrote several articles favorable to him.

EWB

Chamberlain, Joseph (1836–1914), English politician. Joseph Chamberlain influenced the fate of the Liberal party and then of the Conservative party. He has been described as one of Britain's first "professional" politicians.

Born in London on July 8, 1836, of a middle-class family, Joseph Chamberlain moved to Birmingham when he was 18 to join his uncle's engineering firm. He was so successful in business that he was able to retire with a large and assured income at the age of 38 and devote the rest of his life to politics. His first political position (1873–1876) was as the reforming Liberal lord mayor of Birmingham, where he promoted a "civic gospel." The city acquired new municipally owned services along with new buildings and roads, and it became a mecca for urban reformers. Chamberlain worked through a Liberal caucus, a more sophisticated form of party organization than existed anywhere else in Britain. When Chamberlain was elected to Parliament in 1876, his stated object was to do for the nation what he had already done for his local community.

Liberal Party. Chamberlain's liberalism was different in tone and in content from that of his party leaders, particularly William Gladstone. Chamberlain was a radical in sympathy, with a Unitarian religious background, and he systematically set out to attract support not only from religious dissenters but also from workingmen. His proposals for social reform, entailing increased government intervention and expenditure, were attacked by old-fashioned radicals as well as by Conservatives and moderate Liberals.

When the Liberals were returned to power in 1880, Chamberlain became president of the Board of Trade and a member of the Cabinet. However, he was never at ease personally or politically with Gladstone, his prime minister. After pressing for his unauthorized radical program in the 1885 election, Chamberlain broke with Gladstone in 1886 over the issue of home rule for Ireland. Because of Chamberlain's vigorous opposition to Gladstone's Home Rule Bill, the Liberal party split and was unable to regain office, except for one brief interlude, for 20 years.

The nature of the Liberal split was important. There had always been an internal division between Whigs and radicals, and it had seemed on more than one occasion that the party would divide into a right and a left wing. Instead, as a result of the home rule crisis, many Whigs and radicals found themselves in league against Gladstone, who represented the middle. After 1886 there was little hope for accommodation between Gladstone and Chamberlain, and Chamberlain became the effective leader of a third force, the Liberal Unionists, of which the Whig S. C. C. Hartington (later the Duke of Devonshire) was titular leader. Chamberlain's position throughout the rest of his political life was greatly strengthened by the fact that Birmingham remained loyal to him. Indeed, many of the policies which he advocated had their origins in the politics of the city.

Colonial Secretary. In 1895 Chamberlain became colonial secretary in a predominantly Conservative government led by Lord Salisbury. In his new position Chamberlain pursued forceful policies promoting imperial development. Although he was interested in the development of the tropics and in the transformation of the empire into a partnership of self-governing equals, his colonial secretaryship is associated mainly with the Boer War (1899–1902). His critics called this conflict "Chamberlain's war"; this description was a drastic oversimplification, despite Chamberlain's belief that British "existence as a great Power" was at stake. After the Peace of Vereeniging ended the war, he visited South Africa and supported measures of conciliation between South Africans of British and Boer descent. Throughout this period he was keenly interested in wider questions of foreign policy and argued for closer relations with Germany and the United States.

In May 1903 Chamberlain once again disturbed the pattern of British domestic politics by announcing his support of tariffs favoring imperial products and his abandonment of belief in free trade. His motives were mixed, but the effect of his conversion was to split the Conservatives as well as the Liberal Unionists. In September 1903 he resigned from the Cabinet and began a campaign to educate the British public. The leading Conservative free traders resigned with him, but his influence was perpetuated by the appointment of his son Austen as chancellor of the Exchequer. Chamberlain himself never held office again, and his protectionist campaign failed. The Liberals were returned to power in 1906, the year Chamberlain became 70. Immediately after the birthday celebrations in Birmingham, Chamberlain had a stroke, which prostrated him for the rest of his life. He died on July

2, 1914, a few weeks before the outbreak of World War I. It was left to his son Neville to lead Britain away from free trade in 1932.

Despite Chamberlain's switches of party alignment, his political career was more consistent than it seemed on the surface. He preferred deeds to talk and candor to equivocation. He looked for issues with extraparliamentary appeal and never lost his belief in active government.

EWB

Chaplin, Charles (1889–1977), film actor, director, and writer and one of the most original creators in the history of the cinema. Charlie Chaplin's remarkable portrayal of "the tramp"—a sympathetic comic character in ill-fitting clothes and a trademark mustache—won admiration from international audiences.

Charles Chaplin was born in a poor district of London on April 16, 1889. His mother, a talented singer, spent most of her life in and out of mental hospitals; his father was a fairly successful vaudevillian until he began drinking. After his parents separated, Charlie and his half brother, Sidney, spent most of their childhood in the Lambeth Workhouse. Barely able to read and write, Chaplin left school to tour with a group of clog dancers. Later he had the lead in a comedy act; by the age of 19 he had become one of the most popular music-hall performers in England.

Arrival in the United States. In 1910 Chaplin went to the United States to tour in *A Night in an English Music Hall* and was chosen by film maker Mack Sennett to appear in the silent Keystone comedy series. In these early movies (*Making a Living, Tillie's Punctured Romance*), Chaplin made the transition from a comedian of overdrawn theatrics to one of cinematic delicacy and choreographic precision. He created the role of the tramp, a masterful comic conception, notable, as George Bernard Shaw remarked, for its combination of "noble melancholy and impish humour."

Appearing in over 30 short films, Chaplin realized that the breakneck speed of Sennett's productions was hindering his personal talents. He left to work at the Essanay Studios. Outstanding during this period were *His New Job, The Tramp,* and *The Champion,* notable for their comic pathos and leisurely exploration of character. More realistic and satiric were his 1917 films for the Mutual Company: *One A.M., The Pilgrim, The Cure, Easy Street,* and *The Immigrant.* In 1918 Chaplin built his own studio and signed a $1,000,000 contract with National Films, producing such silent-screen classics as *A Dog's Life,*

comparing the life of a dog with that of a tramp, *Shoulder Arms,* a satire on World War I, and *The Kid,* a touching vignette of slum life.

In 1923 Chaplin, D. W. Griffith, Douglas Fairbanks, and Mary Pickford formed United Artists to produce feature-length movies of high quality. *A Woman of Paris* (1923), a psychological drama, was followed by two of Chaplin's funniest films, *The Gold Rush* (1925) and *The Circus* (1928). Chaplin directed *City Lights* (1931), a beautifully lyrical, Depression tale about the tramp's friendship with a drunken millionaire and a blind flower girl, considered by many critics his finest work. *Modern Times* (1936), a savagely hilarious farce on the cruelty, hypocrisy, and greed of modern industrialism, contains some of the funniest sight gags and comic sequences in film history, the most famous being the tramp's battle with an eating machine gone berserk. Chaplin's burlesque of Hitler (as the character Hynkel) in *The Great Dictator* (1940), although a devastating satire, loses impact in retrospect. The last film using the tramp, it contains an epilogue in which Chaplin pleads for love and freedom.

It was with these more complex productions of the 1930s and 1940s that Chaplin achieved true greatness as film director and satirist. *Monsieur Verdoux,* brilliantly directed by Chaplin in 1947 (and subsequently condemned by the American Legion of Decency), is one of the subtlest and most compelling moral statements ever put on the screen. Long before European film makers taught audiences to appreciate the role of the writer-director, Chaplin revealed the astonishing breadth of his talents by functioning as such in his productions.

The love showered upon Chaplin in the early years of his career was more than equaled by the vilification directed toward him during the 1940s and early 1950s. The American public was outraged by the outspoken quality of his political views, the turbulence of his personal life, and the sarcastic, often bitter, element expressed in his art. An avowed socialist and atheist, Chaplin expressed a hatred for right-wing dictatorship which made him politically suspect during the early days of the cold war. This hostility was compounded when he released his version of the Bluebeard theme, *Monsieur Verdoux.*

During the next 5 years Chaplin devoted himself to *Limelight* (1952), a strongly autobiographical work with a gentle lyricism and sad dignity, in sharp contrast to the mordant pessimism of *Monsieur Verdoux.* On vacation in Europe in 1952, Chaplin was notified by the U.S. attorney general that his reentry into the United States would be challenged. The charge was moral turpitude and political unreliability.

Chaplin, who had never become a United States citizen, sold all his American possessions and settled in Geneva, Switzerland, with his fourth wife, Oona O'Neill, daughter of the American playwright Eugene O'Neill, and their children.

In 1957 Chaplin visited England to direct *The King in New York* a satire on American institutions, which was never shown in the United States. *My Autobiography,* published in 1964, is a long, detailed account that descends from a vivid, Dickensian mode to endless self—apologies and name-dropping.

By the 1970s times had changed, and Chaplin was again recognized for his rich contribution to film making. He returned to the United States in 1972, where he was honored by major tributes in New York City and Hollywood, including receiving an honorary Academy Award. In 1975, he became Sir Charles Chaplin after being knighted by Queen Elizabeth II. Two years later, on December 25, 1977, Chaplin died in his sleep in Switzerland.

In all his work Chaplin consistently displayed emotional expressiveness, physical grace, and intellectual vision characteristic of the finest actors. The classical austerity and deceptive simplicity of his directorial style (emulated by Ingmar Bergman and others) has not been surpassed.

EWB

Charles I (1600–1649), King of England from 1625 to 1649. Charles I was to witness and take part in the English civil war, or Puritan Revolution, which ultimately cost him his life.

The second son of James VI of Scotland (later James I of England) and Anne of Denmark, Charles I was born in Dunfermline, Scotland, on Nov. 19, 1600. He did not become heir apparent to the English throne until the death of his elder brother, Henry, in 1612. Whether it was his early physical infirmities or the stress caused by the antipathy between his parents, the future king showed signs of personality disturbance in childhood. He did not speak as a young child and later always stuttered. He betrayed deep feelings of inadequacy both in his formal silences and in his overdependence on self-confident favorites. From very early life he lied. This was to be the King's ultimate weakness.

Charles received a good education with tutors. His first emergence into public affairs came with the loss of the crown of Bohemia by his brother-in-law, Frederick V, in 1618. That loss and the subsequent occupation of Frederick's inheritance in the Palatinate by Spanish troops deeply shocked Charles. He conceived that if he were to marry the Spanish Infanta, the King of Spain would restore the Palatinate to Fred-

erick. Charles went to Spain in 1623 with the 1st Duke of Buckingham, who abetted the scheme. In Madrid it took Charles 5 months to comprehend that the Spanish would never agree to marriage with a heretic, much less to the restoration of the Palatinate.

Early Reign. When Charles perceived the truth, he and Buckingham went to the opposite extreme and stampeded an unwilling King James and an eager Parliament into war with Spain. At the same time a marriage treaty with Louis XIII of France was arranged for the hand of Louis's sister, Henrietta Maria. Charles became king on March 27, 1625. His marriage occurred by proxy in Paris on May 1. The union was accompanied by an alliance between England and France against Spain. From the first, however, there were misunderstandings. The English believed that the French were not active enough in helping to expel the Spanish from the Palatinate. The French did not believe that Charles had lived up to the religious promises of the marriage contract to allow freedom to the English Catholics. It is not surprising under these circumstances that Charles found the gawky adolescent princess less than compatible. Relations with the Queen's brother deteriorated until Charles declared war on France as well as Spain in 1627.

These wars necessitated the frequent summonses of Parliament during the first years of Charles's reign. Differences over supplies, religion, and economic policy were frequent and led to the Petition of Right in 1628, in which the Commons condemned the King's policy of arbitrary taxation and imprisonment. But the chief cause of the King's difficulties with Parliament was the resentment of the English aristocracy over the continued ascendancy of the Duke of Buckingham. His ill-managed expedition against Cadiz, Spain, in 1625 and his disastrous attack in 1627 on the French forces besieging La Rochelle completely discredited the King's government in the eyes of the aristocracy.

Buckingham's assassination in 1628, although it was a bitter personal blow to the King, opened up a period of constructive rule, known as the period of personal government. An aftermath of constitutional disputes rocked Parliament in 1629, but many of the peers and their allies in the Commons such as Thomas Wentworth and Dudley Digges had thrown in their lot with the King. The earls of Arundel and Pembroke, Clifford, and Weston divided up administrative patronage. The wars against France and Spain were terminated, and so long as no new foreign crisis arose, royal finances were sufficient to conduct government without calling Parliament and reviving constitutional and religious opposition. After Buckingham's death, too, Charles fell in love with Henrietta Maria, and they were ever after a devoted couple.

Charles spent his time hunting and acquiring perhaps the greatest art collection in Europe. The quintessence of the King's royal policy during these years was the enforcement of order and a decorous service in the English Church by William Laud, Archbishop of Canterbury. The attempt to extend this religious order to Scotland in 1637, however, brought down the edifice of personal government. Parliament again had to be summoned in 1640, and to the residue of constitutional resentment from the earlier parliaments was joined the fear that the Earl of Strafford, the King's deputy in Ireland, would be an even more powerful and dangerous minister than the Duke of Buckingham had been. Until Strafford's execution for treason in 1641, the King faced a united aristocracy; and he was forced to relinquish most of his ministers, abolish the Star Chamber (councilors and judges who sat as a court) and High Commission, agree to triennial parliaments, and promise that no customs would be raised in the future without specific parliamentary grant.

Civil War. Following Strafford's death, the King's untrustworthiness still barred a stable settlement with the leaders of Parliament. His attempt to get evidence against them in Scotland during the autumn of 1641 coincided with the Irish rebellion. The parliamentary leaders could not trust him with an army. Their fears were confirmed when he entered the House of Commons on Jan. 4, 1642, in order to arrest five of their leading members for treason. Parliament then began on their own authority to make military provision to suppress the Irish and to defend themselves. Charles could not allow the heart of his prerogative to be thus torn from him, and so on August 14 the King raised his standard at Nottingham and called upon all his loyal subjects to defend his right. The civil war had begun.

Charles attracted a majority of the peers and many of the gentry to his side, and he commanded the military populace of Wales and the North. Under the generalship of his nephew Prince Rupert, the royal cavalry in particular bore down the parliamentary forces during 1642 and 1643. But Charles again fell victim to incompetent courtiers, as a whole the King's cause was ill-managed. By contrast the few but important peers who remained to command Parliament proved masters at gaining popular support, money, control of the navy, and a sufficient military response. On July 2, 1644, they won a surprise victory over Rupert at Marston Moor; in the following year they professionalized their military force as the New Model Army and decisively defeated Charles and Rupert at Naseby. In 1646 Charles surrendered to the Scots allies of Parliament.

During the succeeding years the King's main effort was to restore his royal authority. The means he chose were contradictory deals with various political groups, now the political Presbyterians in Parliament, now Oliver Cromwell and the Independent army generals, and at all times the Scots. Just as his letter commissioning an Irish army to land in England and requesting French troops during the civil war had discredited him after their discovery on the field of Naseby, so these incompatible negotiations from 1646 to 1648 destroyed his moral position in the eyes of many Englishmen. His negotiations with the Scots led to their intervention in the second civil war, of 1648, and this sealed Charles's fate in the minds of the army generals. On Dec. 6–7, 1648, the generals purged Parliament of all who were negotiating for the King's restoration to power and prepared to bring the "Man of Blood" to trial.

The Trial. There was in England no legal method to try a king. But Henry Ireton and the other officers devised a High Court of Justice, consisting of members of the purged Commons and other public officials, to try Charles Stuart for high treason. The King refused to recognize their jurisdiction and would not plead. During the trial he gave his finest defense of his kingship: "I do stand more for the liberty of my people, than any here that come to be my pretended judges." "I am sworn to keep the peace, by that duty I owe to God and my country, and I will do it to the last breath of my body; and therefore ye shall do well to satisfy first God, and then the country, by what authority you [try me]." By such words, when the court condemned him to death, he created the myth that he died for liberty under the law. On Jan. 30, 1649, he was led onto a scaffold, where he prayed with Bishop Juxon, and was beheaded. Thereby he also became the sanctified champion of the Anglican Church, despite his many promises to Catholics, Presbyterians, and Independents during the days of his adversity. After a decade under Puritan military dictatorship, the King executed that day became the foundation for restored monarchy, established church, free Parliament, and the conservative rule of law in England.

EWB

Chmielnicki, Bogdan (1595–1657), Cossack leader. Bogdan Chmielnicki led the Dnieper Cossacks in the Ukrainian war of liberation against Polish rule in 1648.

Bogdan Chmielnicki, or Khmelnitskii, was born in Pereyaslav in the Polish-controlled Ukraine. His father was a registered Cossack and proprietor of a small farm and flour mill at Czehrin near the Dnieper River. Bogdan was educated in the school of one of the Orthodox brotherhoods and also studied at the Jesuit school in Yaroslav.

When his father died, Chmielnicki assumed management of the small family estate. He ran into difficulty, however, when a Polish lord claimed ownership of the land. Chmielnicki was summoned before a tribunal and dispossessed of his small estate. He eventually fled to the south, where he joined the Zaporozhan Cossacks. Anxious for revenge, Chmielnicki raised an army from among the Cossacks, and he also gained wide support from the Crimean Tatars and the oppressed Russian peasantry of the Ukraine. In the spring of 1648, with a force of about 300,000 men, he defeated two Polish armies sent against him.

The rather limited character of Chmielnicki's ambitions enabled a peace treaty to be concluded with the Polish king in August 1649. Chmielnicki was recognized as hetman, or Cossack leader, and allowed to retain an armed force of 40,000 Cossacks, but no provision was made for the peasantry, thousands of whom had immigrated to the Donets Basin under Russian protection. War broke out again in 1650, and Chmielnicki, now deserted by the Crimean Tatars, was compelled to accept a peace which reduced the number of registered Cossacks to 20,000.

At this point Chmielnicki sent an urgent appeal to Alexis, the Russian tsar, for support. Although he had ignored earlier appeals, Alexis agreed to take Hetman Chmielnicki and his entire army, "with their towns and lands," under his protection. The final agreement was made at Pereyaslav in January 1654. Although there is some debate over its meaning, the agreement seems to have represented unconditional Ukrainian acceptance of Moscow's authority. It should be noted, however, that in later years the Ukrainians acquired good reason to complain of the Russian government, which eventually abrogated entirely the considerable autonomy granted to the Ukrainians after they had sworn allegiance to the Muscovite tsar.

Chmielnicki died on Aug. 6, 1657. His death opened the way for a succession of hetmans, who thought of Poland as a lesser danger than their Russian protectors. Their policy split the Ukraine; the left bank of the Dnieper tended to support Muscovy and carried on a civil war with the Polish sympathizers on the right bank. The Treaty of Andrusovo in 1667 confirmed this division.

EWB

Cobb, Richard (1917–), British historian. Richard Cobb has built a reputation for himself as one of the leading British historians of the French Revolution, but he has made his niche by writing his history from the viewpoint of the common person.

Fascinated by French culture since he was sent to France at the age of eighteen to study the language, Cobb has spent much time in his adopted second country, writing his first historical works in French. One of them, a two-volume work first published in the early 1960s, was translated in 1987 by Marianne Elliott as *The People's Armies*. The title refers to the volunteer forces used in 1793 during the French Revolution to enforce the will of the Republic's government among the general population. Their duties included taking grain from the peasants for the use of the military, harassing counterrevolutionaries, and robbing and vandalizing churches.

Cobb's 1969 effort, *A Second Identity*, combines previously published book reviews with an introductory explanation of how his love for France has etched itself deeply into his personality.

Cobb exhibits his preference for the history of the lower classes in one of his more unusual volumes, the 1978 *Death in Paris*. The book examines the records of the Basse-Geole de la Seine, the precursor of the Paris morgue, concerning sudden or violent deaths during the French Revolution between 1795 and 1801. Of the 404 cases listed for those years, almost all were poor and most were suicides, the majority of which drowned themselves in the river Seine. There were only nine murder victims. From the detailed records of personal effects found on the bodies—often suicides wore every piece of clothing they owned when they did away with themselves, even if it meant wearing several pairs of pants or many skirts in the heat of summer—Cobb pieces together what kind of lives these people might have led.

In 1980 Cobb produced two books, *Promenades: A Historian's Appreciation of Modern French Literature* and *The Streets of Paris*. Both are guided tours of a sort; in *Promenades* Cobb shows his readers around various French regions, including Burgundy, Lyons, Marseilles, and Paris, through the eyes of French authors such as Henri Beraud, Marcel Pagnol, and—Cobb's favorite—Raymond Queneau. *The Streets of Paris*, with photographs by Nicholas Breach, however, focuses on just one city, specifically the less prominent features of that city—a vanishing Paris.

French and Germans, Germans and French compares two periods when German soldiers occupied France: World War I and World War II. Cobb takes into account regional differences during the second occupation by examining Paris and northern France in the area of Lille near the Belgian border, both directly administered by Hitler's Third Reich, and the puppet government of Vichy in southern France.

Though usually interspersing incidents from his own life with history in his work, Cobb turned to more straightforward autobiography in his *Still Life: Sketches From a Tunbridge Wells Childhood.* Published in 1983, *Still Life* presents a picture of the neighborhood Cobb lived in as a child. In its pages the reader meets personages such as R. Septimus Gardiner, a taxidermist with a shop full of stuffed squirrels, fish, hummingbirds, and badgers; Dr. Footner, who made housecalls on Cobb's mother in a carriage; and the Limbury-Buses—the mother never went outdoors, the son never spoke, and the whole family followed precisely the same routine each day. Overall it is a quiet, unchangeable Tunbridge Wells that Cobb records, though he recounts his youthful fears about the flats his family lived in.

People and Places, which explores some of the various locales Cobb has lived in, and *A Classical Education,* in which Cobb recounts his teenage friendship with a youth who murdered his own mother, both saw publication in 1985. A collection of articles and reviews, *People and Places* ranges in its observations from Aberystwyth, Wales, where Cobb was a lecturer in history during the 1950s, to Oxford, and to Parisian department stores.

Cobb's third autobiographical venture appeared in 1988 as *Something to Hold Onto.* In the book Cobb conveys his childhood relationships with relatives. Recreating life with his grandparents—as well as with such characters as Daisy, whose room was piled with thousands of copies of the *Daily Mail,* and his Uncle Primus, whose only occupation was to wind the clocks, bang the gong for meals, and take two walks each day—Cobb focuses on life's rituals and routines, somehow important and enjoyable in their pure banality.

CA

Cohn-Bendit, Daniel (1946–), French radical. Daniel Cohn-Bendit only occupied center stage in French politics for a few weeks in 1968. Still, more than anyone else, Cohn-Bendit came to personify the new left that swept Western Europe and North America in the late 1960s and early 1970s.

In early 1968, Daniel Cohn-Bendit was a little known leader of a tiny student movement at the brand new Nanterre campus of the University of Paris. He was only 22, having been born in France of German Jewish parents in 1946. Because he held dual citizenship he had chosen to pursue his studies in sociology at the newly opened campus in one of the grimier industrial suburbs of Paris.

That campus represented everything that was troubling the overcrowded French university system. It had been built without planning for the social lives of the students. The educational system suffered from the same problems as the rest of the huge university centered at the Sorbonne.

Gradually the students' discontent with the university merged with more general opposition to the Gaullist regime, which seemed to run everything in a heavy-handed manner. In March 1968 those resentments began to surface. On March 22 a ceremony was held to open officially the Nanterre campus's swimming pool, which Cohn-Bendit and a small group of his fellow students disrupted. They were summoned to a disciplinary hearing which, given the centralization of the university, was to be held at the Sorbonne on May 3.

That hearing marked the beginning of the "events" of May and June 1968, the largest protest movement in the history of the new left. While the accused students were inside, a small group of supporters held a sympathy demonstration in the courtyard. To everyone's surprise, for the first time in centuries the police entered the courtyard to break up a demonstration. That fact, plus the brutality of the police action, rippled throughout Paris.

Students, whose anger had been building and repressed for months, reacted quickly. Throughout the next week demonstrations occurred in the streets of the Latin Quarter. As the police grew more violent, sympathy for the students and their seemingly modest demands grew. Finally, on the night of May 10–11, things truly got out of hand. The police became more violent, and the students and other demonstrators responded by erecting barricades. The police moved in with armored personnel carriers, tear gas, and billy clubs. Echoes of past revolutions could be heard throughout Paris.

In the meantime, Daniel Cohn-Bendit had emerged as the informal leader of the protests. No organization had called or could control what was happening. And, even though Danny the Red—as Cohn-Bendit was called—was by no means in charge, his role at Nanterre thrust him onto the front line.

After the "night of the barricades" support for the students spread, especially into the trade unions who had their own grievances with the government, the same enemy the students were attacking. They called for a sympathy protest the following Monday. The students marched behind the workers, and afterward Cohn-Bendit led them down a few blocks to begin occupying the Sorbonne.

Within hours the occupations spread as workers began taking over factories, newspapers, even the radio and television system. Within days the country was at a virtual standstill.

At first, Danny the Red seemed even more important, especially after a senior government official referred to him as "that German Jew," prompting thousands of people to march through Paris chanting "we are all German Jews." Then Cohn-Bendit was forced into the background. On May 24 he was expelled from France. De Gaulle seized that opportunity to deny him permission to reenter France, even though he did have joint French-German citizenship. He was not able to legally reenter the country for more than a decade.

Within another week President de Gaulle had reassumed control and dissolved the National Assembly. The Gaullists, not the left, won an overwhelming victory in the parliamentary elections held in June.

For many years, Danny the Red receded from the public eye. After his exile, he settled in Frankfurt, Germany, where he held a variety of jobs while remaining active in politics. In the 1970s he founded RK, a German group which encouraged common action between students and workers, and took part in various housing-related protests and reforms. For employment, he taught at an "anti-authoritarian kindergarten," and worked as a salesperson in the Karl-Marx Bookstore near the city's main university. In the 1980s, Cohn-Bendit founded a radical city magazine, *Pflasterstand,* whose name referred to a slogan of the 1968 revolts: "Underneath the surface structures of cement [*das Pflaster*] and steel lies the beach [*der Strand*]." He also worked as publicist for a number of books and publications, and wrote extensively on radical issues.

In 1984, Cohn-Bendit became a member of the Green Party, which changed its name to the Alliance Green Party in 1989. The Greens made common cause with the German Socialist Party (SPD) in the so-called "Red-Green Coalition," which elected Cohn-Bendit to the honorary position of Commissioner for Multicultural Affairs in July 1989.

In 1994, Cohn-Bendit reemerged onto the world, or at least the Continental, stage with his election to the European Parliament as a member of the Alliance Green Party. Sitting on the Committees for External Affairs, Security, and Defense, he opposed nationalism and promoted a globalist agenda. (Because of his Franco-German background, Cohn-Bendit has often humorously referred to himself as a "bastard," someone who is not tied to a specific national identity.) He also served on the Committee for Basic Freedoms and Internal Affairs, and on the "Delegation Maghreb," which is concerned with issues relating to the nations of the Maghreb region of north Africa: Algeria, Morocco, and Tunisia. He has also been an active figure behind the European Forum for Active Conflict Avoidance (FEPAC.)

Cohn-Bendit was chosen to lead the Green party in the European parliamentary general election in 1999. French workers at the Cogema nuclear reprocessing plant in La Hague, France, protested the choice as many believed the environmental activist would continue to prompt the closure of nuclear plants, thus threatening their jobs. But phasing out nuclear power isn't the only controversial effort Cohn-Bendit has made. Legalizing soft drugs and allowing residency permits for illegal immigrants who ask are other issues that continue to keep him in the midst of controversy.

When he was only 22, Daniel Cohn-Bendit left an indelible mark on the history of the 1960s. The movement he helped spawn led to many improvements in the lives of students and workers in the short run; even more importantly, the events set the agenda for French politics for many years, culminating in the 1981 election of President Francois Mitterrand's socialist government. But Cohn-Bendit himself remained modest about his achievements. In his brief autobiography on the World Wide Web in the 1990s, he made scant reference to his role in the 1968 events, and concentrated more on his current activities in the European Parliament. Summing up his interests, he said, "In any event I remain: a wanderer through the worlds, cultures, languages, occupations, generations, and classes, and last but not least: still an active soccernut, as player and fan."

EWB

Colbert, Jean Baptiste (1619–1683), French statesman. Jean Baptiste Colbert was one of the greatest ministers of Louis XIV and is generally regarded as the creator of the economic system of prerevolutionary France.

Jean Baptiste Colbert was born at Reims on Aug. 29, 1619, of a family of prosperous businessmen and officials. He entered the service of the French monarchy under Michel le Tellier, the father of the Marquis de Louvois. In 1651 he became the agent of Cardinal Mazarin, whom he served so well that the cardinal bequeathed him to King Louis XIV in 1661. Almost immediately Colbert became the most important minister in France. He was made intendant of finances in 1661 and in the next few years assumed responsibility for public buildings, commerce, and the administration of the royal household, the navy, and the merchant marine. His only serious rival was the war minister, Louvois. The two men intrigued against each other for royal favor, with Louvois, especially after 1679, gradually winning the upper hand. Colbert, however, remained immensely powerful until his death.

Colbert's most successful years were from 1661 to 1672. The neglect and corruption of the Mazarin period were replaced by a time of prosperity with expanding industry and mounting employment. The tax system was made slightly fairer and much more efficient, thereby greatly increasing Louis XIV's revenues.

In a mercantilist age Colbert was the supreme mercantilist. His program was to build up the economic strength of France by creating and protecting French industries, encouraging exports, and restricting imports (especially of luxury goods). By endless regulation and supervision, he tried to make French industry, particularly in luxury items, first in Europe; he was partially successful, for the French tradition of high quality in certain fields (for example, tapestry and porcelain) dates from his time.

Colbert organized royal trading companies to compete with the English and the Dutch for the trade of the Far East and the Americas. Although these companies were almost all failures, he was successful in building up one of the strongest European navies and a more than respectable merchant marine. At the same time he laid the foundations of the French overseas empire in Canada, the West Indies, and the Far East. The great expansion of French commerce and industry in the next century was largely due to his groundwork.

Colbert carried through a series of legal codifications of enormous importance, and the Code Napoleon was partly inspired by, and based on, his monumental work. He also made himself responsible for the artistic and cultural life of France. He encouraged, patronized, and regimented artists and writers, and the magnificent building program of Louis XIV was primarily his work.

Colbert was not an innovator. His ideas came from other men, particularly Cardinal Richelieu, and his interpretation of them was often mistaken. But for 22 years he controlled the economic fortunes of France, and he did so with an all-embracing scope and an incredible capacity for work. Some of his projects, however, were unsuccessful. He was unable to unify the diverse systems of weights and measures in France or to secure free trade within the country. His regulation of industry by constant inspection was largely ineffective, as his orders were often disregarded.

The major failure of Colbert stemmed from his determination to end Dutch domination of Far Eastern and European trade. Unable to damage the Dutch by a vindictive tariff war, he supported Louis XIV's unprovoked invasion of Holland in 1672 in the hope that the Dutch would be overrun in a few weeks. But the resultant war lasted until 1679, and the strain on the French economy undid many of the good results of Colbert's work.

Colbert died on Sept. 6, 1683, to the great relief of the general public, with whom he was (for the most part undeservedly) very unpopular. The immense concentration of responsibilities in one minister was never repeated under the monarchy.

EWB

Cole, George Douglas Howard (1889–1959), English historian, economist, and guild socialist. G. D. H. Cole's teaching, writing, and commitment to political activism affected three generations of Englishmen.

The son of a builder in West London, G. D. H. Cole went from St. Paul's School to Balliol College, Oxford. He coedited the *Oxford Reformer,* acted in social causes, and joined the Fabian Society. He attempted to reconcile syndicalism and socialism in *World of Labour* (1913), a plea for public ownership of major industries under the democratic control of unions modeled upon medieval guilds. With a first class in classical moderns and greats, he was awarded a fellowship at Magdalen College. Elected to the Fabian executive in 1915, he rebelled against the old guard to head the quasi-independent Fabian Research Bureau.

During the next decade Cole was away from Oxford writing, often with his wife and fellow Fabian rebel, Margaret Postgate Cole; directing tutorial classes at the University of London; and organizing professional trade unions. He returned to Oxford in 1925 as fellow of University College and university reader in economics and was to have compelling influence upon students such as Hugh Gaitskell. From 1944 until his retirement in 1957 Cole was at All Souls College as first Chichele professor of social and political theory.

Cole was for many years chairman of the Fabian weekly, the *New Statesman,* contributing to almost every issue during his lifetime. In 1931 he formed the Society for Socialist Information and Propaganda but broke with the society when it moved toward communism. That year he formed the New Fabian Research Bureau as a politically neutral agency for accumulating objective information. This group formed the basis for union in 1938 with the older, badly splintered Fabian Society. Collectivization was omitted from the new rules as a concession to Cole.

Cole's prodigious writings (over 130 works) may be divided into five broad and overlapping categories: guild socialism; history; biography; economic, political, and social analysis; and fiction. His strongest treatment of guild socialism, *Self-government in Industry* (1917), was an appeal for the pluralistic and romantic socialism which moved Cole all his life. In *Case for Industrial Partnership* (1957) he tried to adjust the earlier plea to new times.

Cole's historical and biographical work provided the evidence against which he tested his socialist faith and reliance upon the individual. This was especially true in his classic five-volume *History of Socialist Thought* (1953–1960).

Of Cole's perceptive biographies, the two best are *The Life of William Cobbett* (1924) and *The Life of Robert Owen* (1925). The analytical writings, intended to influence or explain, include *Principles of Economic Planning* (1935) and *An Intelligent Man's Guide to the Post-war World* (1947). For recreation he wrote, largely with his wife, more than 15 detective novels.

EWB

Columbus, Christopher (1451–1506), Italian navigator and the discoverer of America. Though Columbus had set out to find a westward route to Asia, his explorations proved to be as important as any alternate way to the riches of Cathay and India.

The archives of Genoa show that the famous discoverer was born Cristoforo Colombo (Spanish, Cristóbal Colón) there between August and October 1451. His father, Domenico Colombo, followed the weaver's craft, and his mother, Suzanna Fontanarossa, came of equally humble stock. Christopher was the eldest child, and two brothers make some appearance in history under their Hispanicized names, Bartolomé and Diego.

Columbus had a meager education and only later learned to read Latin and write Castilian. He evidently helped his father at work when he was a boy and went to sea early in a humble capacity. Since he aged early in appearance and contemporaries commonly took him for older than he really was, he was able to claim to have taken part in events before his time.

In 1475 Columbus made his first considerable voyage to the Aegean island of Chios, and in 1476 he sailed on a Genoese ship through the Strait of Gibraltar. Off Cape St. Vincent they were attacked by a French fleet, and the vessel in which Columbus sailed sank. He swam ashore and went to Lisbon, where his brother Bartolomé already lived. Columbus also visited Galway, in Ireland, and an English port, probably Bristol. If he ever sailed to Iceland, as he afterward claimed to have done, it must have been as a part of this voyage. He made his presumably last visit to Genoa in 1479 and there gave testimony in a lawsuit.

Court procedure required him to tell his age, which he gave as "past 27," furnishing reasonable evidence of 1451 as his birth year.

Columbus returned to Portugal, where he married Felipa Perestrelo e Monis, daughter of Bartolomeu Perestrelo, deceased proprietor of the island of Porto Santo. The couple lived first in Lisbon, where Perestrelo's widow showed documents her husband had written or collected regarding possible western lands in the Atlantic, and these probably started Columbus thinking of a voyage of investigation. Later they moved to Porto Santo, where his wife died soon after the birth of Diego, the discoverer's only legitimate child.

Formation of an Idea. After his wife's death, Columbus turned wholly to discovery plans and theories, among them the hope to discover a westward route to Asia. He learned of the legendary Irish St. Brendan and his marvelous adventures in the Atlantic and of the equally legendary island of Antilia. Seamen venturing west of Madeira and the Azores reported signs of land, and ancient authors, notably Seneca and Pliny, had theorized about the nearness of eastern Asia to western Europe, though it is not known just when Columbus read them. He acquired incunabular editions of Ptolemy, Marco Polo, and Pierre d'Ailly, but again it is uncertain how early he read them. He possibly first depended on what others said of their contents.

From Marco Polo, Columbus learned the names of Cathay (north China) and Cipango (Japan). The Venetian traveler had never visited Japan and erroneously placed it 1,500 miles east of China, thus bringing it closer to Europe. Furthermore, Columbus accepted two bad guesses by Ptolemy: his underestimate of the earth's circumference and his overestimate of Asia's eastward extension. With the earth's sphericity taken for granted, all Columbus's mistaken beliefs combined to make his idea seem feasible.

In 1474 the Florentine scientist Paolo dal Pozzo Toscanelli sent a letter and map to Fernao Martins of Lisbon, telling Martins that a western voyage in the Atlantic would be a shorter way of reaching the Orient than circumnavigation of Africa. Columbus obtained a copy of the letter and used it to clarify his own ideas.

In 1484 Columbus asked John II of Portugal for backing in the proposed voyage. Rejected, Columbus went to Spain with young Diego in 1485, and for nearly 7 years he sought the aid of Isabella of Castile and her husband, Ferdinand of Aragon. The sovereigns took no action but gave Columbus a small annuity that enabled him to live modestly. He found influential friends, including the powerful Duke of Medinaceli and Juan Pérez, prior of La Rábida monastery.

While waiting, the widowed Columbus had an affair with young Beatriz Enriquez de Harana of Cordova, who in 1488 bore his other son, Ferdinand, out of wedlock. He never married her, though he provided for her in his will and legitimatized the boy, as Castilian law permitted.

First Voyage. In 1492 Columbus resumed negotiations with the rulers. The discussions soon broke down, apparently because of the heavy demands by Columbus, who now prepared to abandon Spain and try Charles VIII of France. Father Pérez saved Columbus from this probably fruitless endeavor by an eloquent appeal to the Queen. Columbus was called back, and in April he and the rulers agreed to the Capitulations of Santa Fe, by which they guaranteed him more than half the future profits and promised his family the hereditary governorship of all lands annexed to Castile.

Financing proved difficult, but three ships were prepared in the harbor of Palos. The largest, the 100-ton *Santa Maria,* was a round-bottomed nao with both square and lateen sails; the caravel *Pinta* was square-rigged; and the small *Niña,* also a caravel, had lateen sails. Recruitment proved hard, and sailing might have been delayed had not the Pinzón brothers, mariners and leading citizens of Palos, come to Columbus's aid and persuaded seamen to enlist. The eldest brother, Martin Alonso, took command of the *Pinta,* and a younger brother, Vicente Yañez, commanded the *Niña.*

The fleet left Palos on Aug. 3, 1492, and, visiting the Canaries, followed the parallel of Gomera westward. Weather remained good during the entire crossing, "like April in Andalusia," as Columbus wrote in his diary, and contrary to popular tales, there was no serious threat of mutiny.

By mid-Atlantic, Columbus evidently concluded he had missed Antilia, so Cipango became his next goal. Landfall came at dawn of October 12, at the Bahama island of Guanahani, straightway renamed San Salvador by Columbus (probably modern San Salvador, or Watlings Island). Arawak natives flocked to the shore and made friends with the Spaniards as they landed. Believing himself in the East Indies, Columbus called them "Indians," a name ultimately applied to all New World aborigines.

The ships next passed among other Bahamas to Colba (Cuba), where the gold available proved disappointing. Turning eastward, Columbus crossed to Quisqueya, renamed Española (Hispaniola), where on Christmas Eve the *Santa Maria* ran aground near

Cap-Haitien. No lives were lost and most of the equipment was salvaged. As relations with the local Taino Arawaks seemed good and Columbus wished to return to Spain immediately, he built a settlement named Navidad for the *Santa Maria's* crew and left, promising to return in a few months.

Columbus recrossed the Atlantic by a more northerly route than on his outward passage and reached Europe safely. He had an interview with John II of Portugal, who, by a farfetched interpretation of an old treaty with Castile, claimed the new western islands for himself. Columbus then sailed to Palos and crossed Spain to the court at Barcelona, bearing the artifacts he had brought from Hispaniola and conducting several natives he had induced or forced to accompany him. Strong evidence also suggests that his crew brought syphilis, apparently never reported in Europe before and known to have been endemic in mild form among the Arawaks.

Regarding John II's territorial claims, Isabella and Ferdinand appealed to Pope Alexander VI, an Aragonese Spaniard, for confirmation of their rights, and in 1493 the Pope obliged, granting Castile complete rights west of a line from pole to pole in the Atlantic. But the Treaty of Tordesillas (1494) established a new line, from pole to pole, 370 leagues west of the Cape Verde Islands. Spain was entitled to claim and occupy all non-Christian lands west of the line, and Portugal all those to the east.

Second Voyage. Following an enthusiastic reception by Ferdinand and Isabella, "Admiral" Columbus prepared for a second voyage. He sailed from Cadiz with 17 ships and about 1,200 men in September 1493. Columbus entered the West Indies near Dominica, which he discovered and named. Passing westward and touching Marie Galante, Guadeloupe, and other Lesser Antilles, the fleet came to large Borinquén (modern Puerto Rico).

On reaching the Navidad settlement on Hispaniola, Columbus found the place destroyed. The Spaniards had made themselves so hated in their quest of gold and women that Chief Caonabo, more warlike than the others, had exterminated them. Another settlement, Isabela, proved an equally unfortunate location, and in 1495 or 1496 Bartolomé Columbus founded Santo Domingo on the south side of Hispaniola.

From Isabela the Admiral sent home most of the ships, though retaining the bulk of the men. He dispatched expeditions into the center of the island in search of gold and accompanied one in person. Meanwhile, he installed himself as governor of Hispaniola, intending it to be a trading post for commerce with the rich Oriental empires he expected soon to discover.

Columbus now decided to explore Cuba further by tracing the island's southern coast. With three ships, including his favorite *Niña,* he left Isabela in the spring of 1494 and followed the Cuban coast nearly to its western end. Indians told him of Jamaica not far to the south, and the Admiral turned that way, discovered the island, and had several fights with hostile natives. Returning to the Cuban shore, Columbus sailed to Bahía Cortés, where leaky ships and sailors' complaints forced him to put back.

Back in Hispaniola, Columbus found the Spanish settlers unruly and nearly impossible to govern. Complaints against Columbus reached the Castilian court in such numbers that he at last decided to go to Spain to clear his name. He left in the *Niña* in March 1496 and reached Cadiz in June. Bartolomé, with the rank of *adelantado,* remained to govern the colony in his absence.

Third Voyage. The Admiral's reception at court was visibly cooler, but Vasco da Gama's departure from Portugal for India in 1497 caused the Spanish rulers to dispatch Columbus again the following year. There were reports of a great continent south of the Admiral's previous discoveries, and Columbus left Sanlúcar de Barrameda with six ships late in May 1498.

The first land sighted had three hills in view, which suggested the Holy Trinity, and Columbus promptly named the island Trinidad. Since it lies by the Gulf of Paria and the Venezuelan mainland, the Admiral became the discoverer of South America on Aug. 1, 1498. The welcome discovery of pearls from oysters in the shallow waters of offshore islands caused the name "Pearl Coast" to be applied for a time to Venezuela, which Columbus even then recognized as a land of continental proportions because of the volume of water flowing from one of its rivers.

Rebellion and Arrest. The Admiral had left Hispaniolan affairs in bad condition 2 years earlier and now hastened to return there and relieve his hard-pressed brother. On arrival he succeeded in partially quieting by compromise a revolt headed by Francisco Roldán, an officeholder, and resumed his governorship. But so many letters of complaint had gone back to Castile regarding the Columbus brothers that the rulers sent out a royal commissioner, Francisco de Bobadilla, with full powers to act as he saw best.

Bobadilla was honest and meant well, but he had already formed a bad opinion of the Columbus family. He put the Admiral and the *adelantado* in

chains and sent them to Spain. Andrés Martin, commanding the ship in which they sailed, offered to remove the shackles, but the Admiral refused permission, as he meant to appear fettered before the sovereigns. On arrival in Cadiz in late November 1500, Columbus went to court to receive a kind welcome and assurance by the monarchs that the chains and imprisonment had not been by their orders.

In 1501 the Admiral began preparing for a fourth voyage. The fleet, consisting of four ships, left Cadiz on May 9, 1502, arriving in Santo Domingo on June 29. The Admiral next sailed to Guanaja Island off Honduras, then down the coast of Central America. When Columbus learned from the natives about another saltwater body, the Pacific, not far away, he felt certain that he was coasting the Malay Peninsula, of which he had learned through the writings of Ptolemy. A strait or open water should permit entry to the Indian Ocean. Although Columbus followed the coast nearly to the Gulf of Darien, he found no strait.

In April 1503 the ships left the mainland, but the hulls were thoroughly bored by teredos and had to be abandoned as unseaworthy in Jamaica. The Admiral and his crews were marooned in Jamaica for a year, during which time Diego Mendez and Bartolomeo Fieschi fetched a small caravel from Hispaniola. Columbus finally reached Sanlúcar de Barrameda, Spain, on Nov. 7, 1504.

Columbus had 18 months of life remaining, and they were unhappy. Though only 53 he was physically an aged man, a sufferer from arthritis and the effects of a bout of malaria. But financially his position was good, as he had brought considerable gold from America and had a claim to much more in Hispaniola. He died in Valladolid on May 20, 1506.

EWB

Comte, Auguste (1798–1857), French philosopher. Auguste Comte developed a system of positive philosophy. He held that science and history culminate in a new science of humanity, to which he gave the name "sociology."

Born in Montpellier, Auguste Comte abandoned the devout Catholicism and royalism of his family while in his teens. He entered the École Polytechnique in 1814 and proved himself a brilliant mathematician and scientist. Comte was expelled in 1816 for participating in a student rebellion. Remaining in Paris, he managed to do immense research in mathematics, science, economics, history, and philosophy.

At 19 Comte met Henri de Rouvroy, Comte de Saint-Simon, and as a "spiritually adopted son," he became secretary and collaborator to the older man until 1824. The relationship between Saint-Simon and Comte grew increasingly strained for both theoretical and personal reasons and finally degenerated into an acrimonious break over disputed authorship. Saint-Simon was an intuitive thinker interested in immediate, albeit utopian, social reform. Comte was a scientific thinker, in the sense of systematically reviewing all available data, with a conviction that only after science was reorganized in its totality could men hope to resolve their social problems.

In 1824 Comte began a common-law marriage with Caroline Massin when she was threatened with arrest because of prostitution, and he later referred to this disastrous 18-year union as "the only error of my life." During this period Comte supported himself as a tutor. In 1826 he proposed to offer a series of 72 lectures on his philosophy to a subscription list of distinguished intellectuals. After the third lecture Comte suffered a complete breakdown, replete with psychotic episodes. At his mother's insistence he was remarried in a religious ceremony and signed the contract "Brutus Napoleon Comte." Despite periodic hospitalization for mental illness during the following 15 years, Comte was able to discipline himself to produce his major work, the six-volume *Course of Positive Philosophy* (1830–1842).

Positivist Thought. Positivism as a term is usually understood as a particular way of thinking. For Comte, additionally, the methodology is a product of a systematic reclassification of the sciences and a general conception of the development of man in history: the law of the three stages. Comte, like the Marquis de Condorcet whom he acknowledged as a predecessor and G. W. F. Hegel whom he met in Paris, was convinced that no data can be adequately understood except in the historical context. Phenomena are intelligible only in terms of their origin, function, and significance in the relative course of human history.

But unlike Hegel, Comte held that there is no *Geist,* or spirit, above and beyond history which objectifies itself through the vagaries of time. Comte represents a radical relativism: "Everything is relative; there is the only absolute thing." Positivism absolutizes relativity as a principle which makes all previous ideas and systems a result of historical conditions. The only unity that the system of positivism affords in its pronounced antimetaphysical bias is the inherent order of human thought. Thus the law of the three stages, which he discovered as early as 1820, attempts to show that the history of the human mind and the development of the sciences follow a determinant pattern which parallels the growth of social and political institutions. According to Comte, the system of pos-

itivism is grounded on the natural and historical law that "by the very nature of the human mind, every branch of our knowledge is necessarily obliged to pass successively in its course through three different theoretical states: the theological or fictitious state; the metaphysical or abstract state; finally, the scientific or positive state."

These stages represent different and opposed types of human conception. The most primitive type is theological thinking, which rests on the "empathetic fallacy" of reading subjective experience into the operations of nature. The theological perspective develops dialectically through fetishism, polytheism, and monotheism as events are understood as animated by their own will, that of several deities, or the decree of one supreme being. Politically the theological state provides stability under kings imbued with divine rights and supported by military power. As civilization progresses, the metaphysical stage begins as a criticism of these conceptions in the name of a new order. Supernatural entities are gradually transformed into abstract forces just as political rights are codified into systems of law. In the final stage of positive science the search for absolute knowledge is abandoned in favor of a modest but precise inquiry into the relative laws of nature. The absolutist and feudal social orders are replaced gradually by increasing social progress achieved through the application of scientific knowledge.

From this survey of the development of humanity Comte was able to generalize a specific positive methodology. Like René Descartes, Comte acknowledged a unity of the sciences. It was, however, not that of a univocal method of thinking but the successive development of man's ability to deal with the complexities of experience. Each science possesses a specific mode of inquiry. Mathematics and astronomy were sciences that men developed early because of their simplicity, generality, and abstractness. But observation and the framing of hypotheses had to be expanded through the method of experimentation in order to deal with the physical sciences of physics, chemistry, and biology. A comparative method is required also to study the natural sciences, man, and social institutions. Thus even the history of science and methodology supports the law of the three stages by revealing a hierarchy of sciences and methodological direction from general to particular, and simple to complex. Sociology studies particular societies in a complex way since man is both the subject and the object of this discipline. One can consider social groups from the standpoint of "social statics," which comprises the elements of cohesion and order such as family and institutions, or from the perspective of "social dynamics," which analyzes the stage of continuous development that a given society has achieved.

Later Years. By 1842 Comte's marriage had dissolved, and he was supported by contributions from various intellectuals, including the English philosopher J. S. Mill. In 1844 he met Clothilde de Vaux, and they fell deeply in love. Although the affair was never consummated because Madame de Vaux died in the next year, this intense love influenced Comte in his later work toward a new religion of humanity. He proposed replacing priests with a new class of scientists and industrialists and offered a catechism based on the cult of reason and humanity, and a new calendar replete with positivist saints. While this line of thought was implicit in the aim of sociology to synthesize order and progress in the service of humanity, the farcical elements of Comte's mysticism has damaged his philosophical reputation. He died in obscurity in 1857.

EWB

Condorcet, Marquis de (1743–1794), French thinker. Marie Jean Antoine Nicolas Caritat, Marquis de Condorcet, expressed the spirit of the Enlightenment in reform proposals and writings on progress. He was the only philosophe to participate in the French Revolution.

Born in Ribemont in Picardy on Sept. 17, 1743, Condorcet was educated at the Jesuit college in Reims and later at the College of Navarre in Paris. He excelled in mathematics and in 1765 wrote the *Essay on Integral Calculus.* In 1769 he became a member of the Academy of Science, later becoming its perpetual secretary, and in 1782 was elected to the French Academy. He married Sophie de Grouchy in 1786, and their home became one of the famous salons of the period.

Prior to the French Revolution, Condorcet wrote biographies of A. R. J. Turgot and Voltaire and essays on the application of the theory of probabilities to popular voting, on the American Revolution and the Constitutional Convention, and on the abolition of the slave trade and slavery. In 1791 he was elected to the Legislative Assembly and later to the National Convention, where he continued to manifest his liberal and egalitarian sentiments.

In the report of the Committee on Public Education, Condorcet advocated universal primary school education and the establishment of a self-regulating educational system under the control of a National Society of Sciences and Arts to protect education from political pressures. However, the Legislative Assembly was hostile to all autonomous corporate structures and

ignored Condorcet's plan. His proposal for a new constitution, establishing universal male suffrage, proportional representation, and local self-government, was similarly set aside by the Jacobin-dominated National Convention, which considered it too moderate.

Condorcet's moderate democratic leanings and his vote against the death penalty for Louis XVI led to his being outlawed by the Jacobin government on July 8, 1793. He went into hiding in the home of a close friend, Madame Varnet, where he wrote the *Sketch of an Historical Picture of the Progress of the Human Mind,* his most famous and most optimistic work. This capsulized history of progress presented a set of intellectual and moral goals toward which men ought to work, and it was based on the utilitarian conviction that invention and progressive thought arise out of social need. According to Condorcet, the future progress of reason had become inevitable with the invention of the printing press and the advances in science and criticism. Rather than emphasizing the role of the solitary genius as the agent of progress, the *Sketch* stressed the dissemination of useful knowledge among the masses.

After 8 months of hiding, Condorcet fled Paris but was arrested on March 27, 1794, and imprisoned in Bourg-la-Reine. On March 29 he was found dead in his cell. His identity was unknown, and it is ironic that this critic of classical education was eventually identified by a copy of Horace's *Epistles* that he had been carrying at the time of his arrest.

EWB

Copernicus, Nicolaus (1473–1543), Polish astronomer. Copernicus was the founder of the heliocentric ordering of the planets.

Nicolaus Copernicus was born on Feb. 19, 1473, in Torun about 100 miles south of Danzig. He belonged to a family of merchants. His uncle, the bishop and ruler of Ermland, was the person to whom Copernicus owed his education, career, and security.

Copernicus studied at the University of Cracow from 1491 to 1494. While he did not attend any classes in astronomy, it was during his student years there that Copernicus began to collect books on astronomy and mathematics. Some of these contain marginal notes by him dating back to that period, but it remains conjectural whether Copernicus had already made at that time a systematic study of the heliocentric theory.

Copernicus returned to Torun in 1494, and in 1496, through the efforts of his uncle, he became a canon at Frauenburg, remaining in that office for the remainder of his life. Almost immediately Copernicus set out for Bologna to study canon law. In Bologna,

Copernicus came under the influence of Domenico Maria de Novara, an astronomer known for his admiration of Pythagorean lore. There Copernicus also recorded some planetary positions, and he did the same in Rome, where he spent the Jubilee Year of 1500.

In 1501 there followed a brief visit at home. His first official act as canon there was to apply for permission to spend 3 more years in Italy, which was granted him on his promise that he would study medicine. Copernicus settled in Padua, but later he moved to the University of Ferrara, where he obtained in 1503 the degree of doctor in canon law. Only then did he take up the study of medicine in Padua, prolonging his leave of absence until 1506.

Upon returning to Ermland, Copernicus stayed in his uncle's castle at Heilsberg as his personal physician and secretary. During that time he translated from Greek into Latin the 85 poems of Theophylactus Simacotta, the 7th-century Byzantine poet. The work, printed in Cracow in 1509, evidenced Copernicus's humanistic leanings. At this time Copernicus was also mulling over the problems of astronomy, and the heliocentric system in particular. The system is outlined in a short manuscript known as the *Commentariolus,* or small commentary, which he completed about 1512. Copies of it circulated among his friends eager to know the "Sketch of Hypotheses Made by Nicolaus Copernicus on the Heavenly Motions," as Copernicus referred to his work. In it, right at the outset, there was a list of seven axioms, all of which stated a feature specific to the heliocentric system. The third stated in particular: "All the spheres revolve about the sun as their midpoint, and therefore the sun is the center of the universe." The rest of the work was devoted to the elaboration of the proposition that in the new system only 34 circles were needed to explain the motion of planets.

The *Commentariolus* produced no reaction, either in print or in letters, but Copernicus's fame began to spread. Two years later he received an invitation to be present as an astronomer at the Lateran Council, which had as one of its aims the reform of the calendar; he did not attend. His secretiveness only seemed to further his reputation. In 1522 the secretary to the King of Poland asked Copernicus to pass an opinion on *De motu octavae spherae* (On the Motion of the Eighth Sphere), just published by Johann Werner, a mathematician of some repute. This time he granted the request in the form of a letter in which he took a rather low opinion of Werner's work. More important was the concluding remark of the letter, in which Copernicus stated that he intended to set forth elsewhere his own opinion about the motion of the

sphere of stars. He referred to the extensive study of which parts and drafts were already very likely extant at that time.

Copernicus could pursue his study only in his spare time. As a canon, he was involved in various affairs, including legal and medical, but especially administrative and financial matters. In fact, he composed a booklet in 1522 on the remedies of inflation, which then largely meant the preservation of the same amount of gold and silver in coins. For all his failure to publish anything in astronomy, to have his manuscript studies circulate, or to communicate with other astronomers, more and more was rumored about his theory, still on the basis of the *Commentariolus.*

Not all the comments were flattering. Luther denounced Copernicus as "the fool who will turn the whole science of astronomy upside down." In 1531 a satirical play was produced about him in Elbing, Prussia, by a local schoolmaster. In Rome things went better, for the time being at least. In 1533 John Widmanstad, a papal secretary, lectured on Copernicus's theory before Pope Clement VII and several cardinals. Widmanstad's hand was behind the letter which Cardinal Schönberg sent in 1536 from Rome to Copernicus, urging him to publish his thoughts, or at least to share them with him.

It was a futile request. Probably nobody knew exactly how far Copernicus had progressed with his work until Georg Joachim (Rheticus), a young scholar from Wittenberg, arrived in Frauenburg in the spring of 1539. When he returned to Wittenberg, he had already printed an account, known as the *Narratio prima,* of Copernicus's almost ready book. Rheticus was also instrumental in securing the printing of Copernicus's book in Nuremberg, although the final supervision remained in the care of Andrew Osiander, a Lutheran clergyman. He might have been the one who gave the work its title, *De revolutionibus orbium coelestium,* which is not found in the manuscript. But Osiander certainly had written the anonymous preface, in which Copernicus's ideas were claimed to be meant by their author as mere hypotheses, or convenient mathematical formalism, that had nothing to do with the physical reality.

The printed copy of his work, in six books, reached Copernicus only a few hours before his death on May 24, 1543. The physics of Copernicus was still Aristotelian and could not, of course, cope with the twofold motion attributed to the earth. But Copernicus could have done a better job as an observer. He added only 27 observations, an exceedingly meager amount, to the data he took over uncritically from Ptolemy and from more recent astronomical tables. The accuracy of predicting celestial phenomena on the basis of his system did not exceed the accuracy achieved by Ptolemy. Nor could Copernicus provide proof for the phases of Mercury and Venus that had to occur if his theory was true. The telescope was still more than half a century away. Again, Copernicus could only say that the stars were immensely far away to explain the absence of stellar parallax due to the orbital motion of the earth. Here, the observational evidence was not forthcoming for another 300 years. Also, while Ptolemy actually used only 40 epicycles, their total number in Copernicus's system was 84, hardly a convincing proof of its greater simplicity.

Still, the undeniable strength of Copernicus's work lay in its appeal to simplicity. The rotation of the earth made unnecessary the daily revolution of thousands of stars. The orbital motion of the earth fitted perfectly with its period of 365 days into the sequence set by the periods of other planets. Most importantly, the heliocentric ordering of planets eliminated the need to think of the retrograde motion of the planets as a physical reality. In the tenth chapter of the first book Copernicus made the straightforward statement: "In the center rests the sun. For who would place this lamp of a very beautiful temple in another or better place than this wherefrom it can illuminate everything at the same time."

The thousand copies of the first edition of the book did not sell out, and the work was reprinted only three times prior to the 20th century. No "great book" of Western intellectual history circulated less widely and was read by fewer people than Copernicus's *Revolutions*. Still, it not only instructed man about the revolution of the planets but also brought about a revolution in human thought by serving as the cornerstone of modern astronomy.

EWB

Cortés, Hernán (ca. 1485–1547), Spanish conquistadore. Hernán Cortés conquered the Aztec empire in Mexico and became the most famous of the Spanish conquistadores.

Hernán Cortés was born in Medellin. His parents were of the small landed gentry of the region. As a youth, he studied Latin for 2 years at the University of Salamanca, but lured by tales of new discoveries in America, he abandoned student life and in 1504 sailed for the New World.

Cortés settled initially on the island of Santo Domingo (Hispaniola) but in 1511 joined an expedition to Cuba, where he became a municipal official and an intimate friend of Diego Velázquez, the governor of the island. When Velázquez determined to dispatch an expedition to Mexico, he named Cortés for the command, but Velázquez soon came to suspect

Cortés of excessive ambition and determined to relieve him. Cortés, aware of this danger, managed to slip away with part of his followers before the governor could formally confront him. After meeting with other recruits, on Feb. 18, 1519, Cortés departed for Mexico with over 600 Spanish soldiers, sailors, and captains, some 200 Indian auxiliaries, and 16 horses.

Cortés's route took him first to Yucatán and thence up the Mexican coast to the vicinity of the modern city of Veracruz, where he founded a town, Villa Rica de Veracruz, which became the base for the conquest. There he arranged to have the municipal council which he had appointed name him captain general and principal judge, an act which gave him at least quasi-legal status. He also negotiated alliances with adjacent Indian tribes and gathered intelligence about the Aztecs.

In August 1519 Cortés struck inland for Tenochtitlán, an island city in Lake Texcoco and the capital of the Aztec confederation ruled by Montezuma II. The most consequential episode in the march was an alliance which Cortés negotiated with the Tlascala, an Indian nation hostile to the Aztecs. In early November the expedition reached the shores of Lake Texcoco. Montezuma, unsure of the intentions of the Spaniards and, indeed, of whether they were gods or men, had offered no overt resistance to their approach and now invited them into Tenochtitlán.

The Spaniards were treated as not entirely welcome guests, and Cortés responded by seizing Montezuma as hostage. At this time Cortés was faced with the arrival of an expedition sent by Governor Velázquez to chastise him. Cortés hastened to the coast to meet the newcomers and, after a surprise attack on them, induced them to join his forces. Upon returning to Tenochtitlán, however, he found the inhabitants in arms and his forces beleaguered in their quarters. Judging the situation to be hopeless, on the night of June 30, 1520, he led his forces from the city to refuge with his Tlascala allies.

In Tlascala, Cortés rebuilt his forces with newly arrived Spaniards and Indian auxiliaries. In May 1521 he began an attack on Tenochtitlán supported by a small navy which had been built in Tlascala, transported to Lake Texcoco, and reassembled. After 75 days of bitter street fighting, on August 13 the city fell to the Spaniards.

Success won legal status for Cortés. On Oct. 15, 1522, Emperor Charles V appointed him governor and captain general of New Spain, the name applied by the Spaniards to the conquered region. It also provided Cortés with an opportunity to display new dimensions of his abilities. He rebuilt Tenochtitlán as the Spanish city of Mexico and dispatched his lieutenants in all directions to subdue other Indian groups. Within a short time most of what is now central and southern Mexico was brought under Spanish rule. Cortés encouraged the introduction of European plants and animals. He vigorously supported the conversion of the native population to Christianity, and his government was marked by consideration for the physical welfare of the Indians.

The great conqueror's days of glory, however, were short. The Emperor was jealous of powerful and popular captains beyond his immediate control and soon began to withdraw or undermine the governmental powers conceded to Cortés. Royal officials were appointed to oversee the treasury of New Spain, royal judges arrived to dispense justice, and in 1526 he was deprived of the governorship. Cortés spent 2 years (1528–1530) in Spain defending himself against his enemies and attempting unsuccessfully to recover his administrative authority. He returned, retaining only the honorific military office of captain general but with the title of marquis of the valley of Oaxaca, which conferred on him a vast estate in southern Mexico.

Cortés remained in Mexico for the next 10 years, managing his estate and undertaking new expeditions which he hoped would recoup his power. His efforts were unsuccessful and in 1540 he returned to Spain, where he lived as a wealthy, honored, but disappointed man until his death in 1547. In compliance with his will, his remains were returned to Mexico, where they repose today in the church of the Hospital of Jesus in Mexico City, an institution which he himself had founded.

Cortés was unquestionably a man of immense abilities. As a conquistador, he displayed an exceptional combination of leadership, audacity, tenacity, diplomacy, and tactical skill. But he was more than a conqueror. He had a vision of a "New Spain" overseas and his statesmanship was instrumental in laying its foundations.

EWB

Cousin, Victor (1792–1867), French educator and philosopher. Victor Cousin helped to reorganize the French primary school system. He also established the study of philosophy as a major intellectual pursuit of the French secondary and higher schools.

Victor Cousin was born in Paris in the midst of the Revolution on Nov. 28, 1792, the son of a poor watchmaker. Like most boys of humble birth at that time, Cousin languished in the streets awaiting the appropriate age to enter an apprenticeship. When he was 11, a fateful event altered the course of his life: in a street fight between schoolboys Cousin came to

the rescue of the underdog, whose mother was looking on. A woman of means, she gratefully paid for Cousin's schooling at the Lycée Charlemagne, where he became one of the most brilliant students in the school's history. He continued his successful scholarly career first as a student at the prestigious École Normale, where he decided on a career in philosophy, and then as a teacher of philosophy and in several schools, and finally as a professor at the Sorbonne.

Development of Eclecticism. In 1817 and again in 1818 Cousin traveled to Germany to meet the leading lights of German letters, J. W. von Goethe, Friedrich Schleiermacher, Friedrich von Schelling, and, most important of all, G. W. F. Hegel. According to Cousin's "eclecticism," as he called his approach, the human mind can accept all carefully thought-out and moderate interpretations of the world. No system of thought is seen to be false, merely incomplete. By studying the history of philosophy, and Cousin directed his students to choose from each system what is true in it and in so doing to arrive at a complete philosophy. The introduction of the history of philosophy and as a major discipline in higher schools in France is a lasting accomplishment of Cousin. He organized the history of philosophy in two major works: *Cours de l'histoire de la philosophie* (Course of the History of Philosophy), written and revised between 1815 and 1841, portions of which have been translated into English; and the widely read *Du vrai, du beau, et du bien* (1836), which has been translated into English under the title *Lectures on the True, the Beautiful, and the Good,* and which came out in 31 editions over 90 years.

Political Pressures. During the repressive years of the Bourbon restoration (1820–1830), Cousin, considered too liberal, was fired from the Sorbonne. While traveling in Germany during that time, he was jailed for 6 months for being a liberal agitator, a charge that was wholly unfounded.

In the government of the July Monarchy (1830–1848) Cousin rose to the heights of power and success as an educator and statesman. As a member of the Council of State and later as a peer, he exercised the major influence over French schools and universities. Because of his knowledge of Germany, Cousin was sent to study the successful primary school systems of several German states, especially Prussia. His book *Report of the State of Public Instruction in Prussia* (1833), recommending reforms to the French, was read abroad and stirred many Americans, Horace Mann and Calvin Stowe among other, to visit Prussia to learn how the budding American common school could best be guided in its development. The Guizot Law of 1833, which was a constitution for the French primary school system, was written by Cousin and based on his *Report*.

The Revolution of 1848 left Cousin without a job. Yet his influence continued to be felt into the next two generations, since the leaders of the French nation were the graduates of the schools that for 18 years had felt the imprint of Cousin's dynamic style, thought, and personality. Cousin never married. His voluminous correspondence, which continued steadily until his death, attests to close friendships with many leaders in Europe and North America.

EWB

Cromwell, Oliver (1599–1658), English statesman and general. Oliver Cromwell won decisive battles in the English civil war. He then established himself and his army as the ruling force in England and later took the title Lord Protector of Great Britain and Ireland.

Oliver Cromwell was born on April 25, 1599, at Huntingdon. His father, Richard Cromwell, was a younger son of one of the richest men in the district, Sir Henry Cromwell of Hinchinbrook, known as the "Golden Knight." Cromwell's mother was the daughter of Sir William Steward, who managed the tithe revenues of Ely Cathedral. Little is known of Cromwell's childhood, except that his circumstances were modest and he was sent to the local school. His schoolmaster, Dr. Beard, was a devout Calvinist; most of Cromwell's intense religious convictions were derived from Beard, whom he venerated throughout his life.

In 1616 Cromwell entered Sidney Sussex College, Cambridge. He left the following year on the death of his father. For the next few years he lived in London, where in 1620 he married Elizabeth, the daughter of Sir James Bourchier, a wealthy leather merchant. Cromwell then returned to his small estate in Huntingdon, where he farmed his land and played a modest part in local affairs, acquiring a reputation as a champion of the poor and dispossessed. During these years Cromwell experienced periods of deep melancholy, suffused with religious doubt, but after much spiritual torment he became convinced that he was the instrument of God.

Political Situation in 1640. When Cromwell entered Parliament for Cambridge in 1640, England had been ruled personally by Charles I for 11 years. The King had pursued an authoritarian policy in religion and finance which had distressed many country gentlemen, including Cromwell. Furthermore, Charles had plunged into war with Scotland, which had risen in revolt when Archbishop William Laud had persuaded him to impose the English Prayer Book on the Scottish Church. The Scots rapidly defeated the King; destitute of money and at the mercy of the Scots, Charles I was forced to call Parliament.

The mood of Parliament was highly critical, and there was a closely knit body of Puritan country gentlemen and lawyers who were determined that the power of the King and the Anglican Church should be limited by Parliament. Several of Cromwell's relatives, particularly the influential John Hampden and Oliver St. John, belonged to this group, which was led by John Pym. Cromwell threw in his lot with these men. A middle-aged man without parliamentary experience, he spoke rarely, but when he did it was usually in support of extreme measures. Cromwell soon established his reputation as a firm upholder of the parliamentary cause; he was dedicated to the reform of the Church and of the court and was highly critical of the King.

Civil War. By 1642 the King and Parliament had become so antagonistic that armed conflict was inevitable. At the outbreak of war in August 1642, Cromwell headed a regiment whose prime duty was to defend East Anglia. He rapidly demonstrated not only his skill as a military leader by rapid raids into royalist territory combined with skillful retreat, but also his capacity to mold an effective army from his force of raw recruits.

Under the leadership of the Earl of Manchester, Cromwell's commander, regiments from other counties were brought together in a formidable body, known as the Eastern Association. In 1643 Cromwell's cavalry worsted the royalists in a number of sharp engagements—Grantham (May 13), Gainsborough (July 18), and Wincaby (October 13). These successes helped to create parliamentary supremacy in East Anglia and the Midlands. Cromwell's reputation as Parliament's most forceful general was made the next year, however, at the battle of Marston Moor (July 2, 1644), when his Ironsides routed the cavalry of Prince Rupert, the most successful royalist general. To Cromwell, whose religious convictions strengthened with every victory that he won, Marston Moor was God's work, and he wrote, "God made them stubble to our swords."

The victories in eastern England, however, were not matched by success elsewhere. After 2 years of war the King was still in the field, and there was a growing rift between Parliament and the army. Many disliked the price paid for alliance with the Scots (acceptance of the Presbyterian form of church government), and most longed for peace. Cromwell, however, yearned for victory. He bitterly attacked the Earl of Manchester, and after complex political maneuvering he emerged as the effective leader of the parliamentary armies. He proved his exceptional capacities as a general on June 14, 1645, when he smashed the royalists' army at Naseby in Northamptonshire. Within 12 months the royalist armies had capitulated.

In 5 years Cromwell had risen from obscurity to renown. A large man with a long, red face studded with warts, he nevertheless possessed considerable presence. His mood was usually somber, thoughtful, and deeply religious. His soldiers sang psalms as they went into battle, and every regiment had its preacher.

The next 3 years taxed Cromwell's skill and faith. His army became riddled with Levellers, whose radical doctrines called for a far more democratic social structure than Cromwell and his fellow generals would tolerate. Parliament and the Scots inclined not only to peace with the King but also to a rigid form of Presbyterianism, which Cromwell disliked. He claimed to believe in toleration, but excepted always Catholics and atheists.

In 1648 the royalists rose again, sided by the Scots, but in a lightning campaign Cromwell smashed both. The republicans were then determined to bring Charles I to trial, and Cromwell did nothing to stop them. At last agreeing that the King was "a man of blood" and should be executed, he signed Charles I's death warrant.

Further Campaigns. The execution of the King settled nothing. Legally, the House of Commons, purged to such an extent that it was called the Rump, ruled. But the army, Scotland, and Ireland were soon in rebellion. The Scottish Presbyterians proclaimed Charles II (Charles I's son) their lawful monarch, and the Irish Catholics did likewise. In England the radicals were a rampant minority, the royalists a stunned majority, but neither had any respect for the Rump.

Cromwell suppressed the Levellers by force and then set about subduing first Ireland and then Scotland. In the former Cromwell fought a tough, bloody campaign in which the butchery of thousands of soldiers at Drogheda (Sept. 11, 1649) and hundreds of civilians at Wexford (Oct. 11) caused his name to be execrated in Ireland for centuries.

On June 26, 1650, Cromwell finally became commander in chief of the parliamentary armies. He moved against the Scots and got into grievous difficulties. At Dunbar in August 1650 he was pressed between the hills and the sea and was surrounded by an army of 20,000 men. But the folly of the Scottish

commander, Leslie, enabled Cromwell to snatch a victory, he thought by divine help, on September 3. The next year Charles II and his Scottish army made a spirited dash into England, but Cromwell smashed them at Worcester on Sept. 3, 1651. At long last the war was over and Cromwell realized that God's humble instrument had been given, for better or worse, supreme power.

Cromwell's Rule: 1653–1658. For 5 years after the execution of the King, Parliament tried to formulate a new constitution. Its failure to do this so exasperated Cromwell that on April 20, 1653, he went with a handful of soldiers to the House of Commons, where he shouted at the members, "The Lord be done with you," and ordered them out.

Until his death Cromwell tried to create a firm new constitutional base for his power. His first attempt to establish a constitution by means of a nominated Parliament in 1653 ended in disaster, so the Council of Army Officers promulgated the Instrument of Government, by which Cromwell became Protector in December 1653. He was assisted by a Council of State on whose advice he acted, for Cromwell believed sincerely in the delegation and sharing of power. For 8 months Cromwell and his Council ruled most effectively, sweeping away ancient feudal jurisdictions in Scotland and Ireland and uniting those countries with England under one Parliament, which was itself reformed. When the Parliament met in 1654, however, it soon quarreled with Cromwell over the constitution. He once more took power into his own hands and dissolved Parliament on June 22, 1655.

Cromwell's government became more authoritarian. Local government was brought under major generals, soldiers whom he could trust. This infuriated the radical left as well as the traditionalists. Again attempting to give his authority a formal parliamentary base and also needing additional revenue, Cromwell reconvened Parliament. His successes abroad and his suppression of revolts at home had greatly increased his popularity; thus when Parliament met, he was pressed to accept the crown, but after much soul-searching he refused. He took instead the title Lord Protector under a new constitution—the Humble Petition and Advice (May 25, 1657). This constitution also reestablished the House of Lords and made Cromwell king in all but name. But Cromwell was no Napoleon; there were definite limits to his personal ambition. He did not train his son Richard to be his successor, nor did he try to establish his family as a ruling dynasty. And at the height of his power he retained his deep religious conviction that he was merely an instrument of God's purpose.

Cromwell pursued an effective foreign policy. His navy enjoyed substantial success, and the foundation of British power in the West Indies was laid by its capture of Jamaica (1655). He allied himself with France against Spain, and his army carried the day at the battles of the Dunes in 1658. These victories, combined with his dexterous handling of Scotland and brutal suppression of Ireland, made his personal ascendancy unassailable, in spite of failures in his domestic policy. But shortly after his death on Sept. 3, 1658, Cromwell's regime collapsed, and the restoration of the monarchy followed in 1660.

Critical Assessment. Cromwell's greatness will always be questioned. As a general, he was gifted yet lucky; as a statesman, he had some success but was unable to bring his plans to complete fruition. Although his religious conviction often appears to be a hypocritical cloak for personal ambition, his positive qualities are unmistakable. He believed in representative government (limited to men of property, however). He encouraged reform, and much of it was humane. He brought to the executive side of government a great degree of professionalism, particularly in the army and navy. Britain emerged from the Commonwealth stronger, more efficient, and more secure. Perhaps the most remarkable qualities of Cromwell were his sobriety and his self-control. Few men have enjoyed such supreme power and abused it less.

EWB

D

Danton, Georges Jacques (1759–1794), French statesman. Georges Jacques Danton was a leader during the French Revolution. Called the "orator of the streets," he was the most prominent early defender of popular liberties and the republican spirit.

Born in Arcis-sur-Aube in Champagne on Oct. 26, 1759, Georges Jacques Danton was the son of a lawyer and minor court official. He was educated by the Oratorians at Troyes and in 1785 earned a degree in law at the University of Reims. He was employed in the office of public prosecutor in Paris and in 1787 purchased the office of advocate to the King's Council.

Danton's massive stature, ready wit (which did much to overcome his physical ugliness), stentorious voice, and impromptu and fiery speeches made the public accept him as its champion of liberty. Danton was a pragmatist who believed that the Revolution could only succeed if it limited its program to the

possible, which meant upholding the rights of property, ending the war as quickly as possible by negotiation, and restoring order through a strong central government.

Danton had tendencies toward laziness and the dissolute life, which often blunted the force of his actions and made him appear capricious and unreliable to many of his contemporaries. There seems to be little doubt that he was implicated in financial corruption, but this appears more the result of thoughtlessness than a deliberate attempt to profit from the Revolution. At heart Danton appears to have been less a radical than an energetic and undisciplined individualist whose personality and the force of circumstances enabled him to become a great popular leader.

Danton's part in founding the Cordeliers Club, which became the advance guard of popular revolutionary activity, suggests that from the beginning of the Revolution he inclined toward the "people's cause." He was involved in the fall of the Bastille on July 14, 1789, and was the most outspoken critic of the commune and the Marquis de Lafayette. Following King Louis XVI's unsuccessful flight in June 1791, Danton was among those who called for the creation of a republic, and his speeches were considered responsible for the popular agitation that culminated in the massacre of the Champ de Mars.

In December 1791 Danton was elected first deputy prosecutor of the Paris Commune. Following the invasion of the Tuileries on June 20, 1792, he was elected president of the Théâtre Française Electoral District. He spoke out against the distinction between active and passive citizens and thus became one of the first to espouse the modern conception of the legal equality of all citizens. At the same time he began to play the primary role in the conspiracy that led to the overthrow of the monarchy on Aug. 10, 1792. He had become convinced, as had others, that as long as the monarchy continued to exist the Revolution would be endangered.

Danton was subsequently named minister of justice and became the predominant member of the Executive Committee. In this capacity he rallied the nation against the invading Prussians. It appears that he could have done little to prevent the September Massacres (1792), but his silent complicity in them deepened the split between himself and the Rolandists, which did much to force the trial of the King. Although Danton opposed this trial since it would make a negotiated peace impossible, he eventually voted in favor of execution of the King.

During this period Danton delivered his famous speech to the National Convention, which stated that to protect the Revolution it was necessary for France to secure its natural boundaries, although this might mean a perpetuation of the war. On April 6, 1793, he was elected to the newly established Committee of Public Safety and to the Revolutionary Tribunal; he was thus enabled to act as an emergency dictator. Although Danton believed that it was necessary to destroy internal dissent, his diplomatic policies continued to be moderate. He thus alienated the Commune, which began to look to Robespierre and more radical Jacobins for leadership. Setbacks in the Vandée and his attempted protection of the Girondists, even after their exclusion from the National Convention, resulted in Danton's not being reelected to the Committee on July 10, 1793. The leadership of the Revolution passed to Robespierre.

In October Danton retired to his home in Arcis; he returned to Paris the following month at the insistence of his friends, who feared Robespierre's terrorist policies. The increasingly radical demands of the Hébertists, however, were more frightening to Danton, and he lent his support to Robespierre. After the Hébertists had been suppressed, Robespierre moved against Danton, who had called for an end to the Terror. Danton and his followers were arrested and tried for antirevolutionary activity. On April 5, 1794, Danton went to the guillotine, which he had vowed to either pull down or die beneath.

EWB

Darwin, Charles Robert (1809–1882), English naturalist. Charles Darwin discovered that natural selection was the agent for the transmutation of organisms during evolution, as did Alfred Russel Wallace independently. Darwin presented his theory in *Origin of Species*.

The concept of evolution by descent dates at least from classical Greek philosophers. In the 18th century Carl Linnaeus postulated limited mutability of species by descent and hybridization. Charles Darwin's grandfather, Erasmus Darwin, and the Chevalier de Lamarck were the chief proponents of evolution about 1800. Such advocacy had little impact on the majority of naturalists, concerned to identify species, the stability of which was considered essential for their work. Natural theology regarded the perfection of adaptation between structure and mode of life in organisms as evidence for a beneficent, all-seeing, all-planning Creator. Organic structure, planned in advance for a preordained niche, was unchanged from the moment of creation. Variations in structure in these earthly imperfect versions of the Creator's idea were minor and impermanent.

In 1815 William Smith had demonstrated a sequence of fossil populations in time. Charles Lyell,

adopting James Hutton's uniformitarian view that present conditions and processes were clues to the past history of the earth, wrote his *Principles of Geology* (1830–1833), which Darwin on his *Beagle* circumnavigation found most apt for his own geological observations. Fossils in South America and apparent anomalies of animal distribution triggered the task for Darwin of assembling a vast range of material. A reading of Thomas Malthus's *Essay on the Principle of Population* in 1838 completed Darwin's conceptual scheme.

Critics, for whom the *Origin* is paramount among Darwin's considerable output, have accused him of vacillation and procrastination. But recent study of unpublished manuscripts and his entire works reveal a continuity of purpose and integrity of effort to establish the high probability of the genetic relationship through descent in all forms of life. Man is dethroned as the summit of creation and as the especial concern of the Creator. This revolution in thought has had an effect on every kind of human activity.

Darwin was born on Feb. 12, 1809, at Shrewsbury, the fifth child of Robert and Susannah Darwin. His mother, who was the daughter of the famous potter Josiah Wedgwood, died when Charles was 8, and he was reared by his sisters. At the age of 9 Charles entered Shrewsbury School. His record was not outstanding, but he did learn to use English with precision and to delight in Shakespeare and Milton.

In 1825 Darwin went to Edinburgh University to study medicine. He found anatomy and *materia medica* dull and surgery unendurable. In 1828 he entered Christ's College, Cambridge, with the idea of taking Anglican orders. He attended John Stevens Henslow's course in botany, started a collection of beetles that became famous, and read widely. William Paley's *Natural Theology* (1802) delighted Darwin by its clear logical presentation, and he later regarded this study as the most worthwhile benefit from Cambridge. He received his bachelor's degree in 1831.

Voyage of the *Beagle*. On Henslow's recommendation Darwin was offered the position of naturalist for the second voyage of H.M.S. *Beagle* to survey the coast of Patagonia and Tierra del Fuego and complete observations of longitude by circumnavigation with a formidable array of chronometers. The *Beagle* left on Dec. 27, 1831, and returned on Oct. 2, 1836. During the voyage Darwin spent 535 days at sea and roughly 1,200 on land. Enough identification of strata could be done on the spot, but sufficiently accurate identification of living organisms required systematists accessible only in London and Paris.

Darwin kept his field observations in notebooks with the specimens listed serially and their place and time of collection documented. Toward the end of the voyage, when sea passages were long, he copied his notes and arranged them to accord with systematics, concentrating on range and habits.

During the trip Darwin discovered the relevance of Lyell's uniformitarian views to the structure of St. Jago (Cape Verde Islands). He found that small locally living forms closely resembled large terrestrial fossil mammals embedded between marine shell layers and that the local sea was populated with living occupants of similar shells. He also observed the overlapping distribution on the continuous Patagonian plain of two closely related but distinct species of ostrich. An excursion along the Santa Cruz river revealed a section of strata across South America. He observed the differences between species of birds and animals on the Galápagos Islands.

Publications Resulting from Voyage. Darwin's *Journal of Researches* was published in 1839. With the help of a government grant toward the cost of the illustrations, the *Zoology of the Voyage of the Beagle* was published, in five quarto volumes, from 1839 to 1843. Specialist systematists wrote on fossil and living mammals, birds, fish, and reptiles. Darwin edited the work and contributed habits and ranges of the animals and geological notes on the fossils. Two themes run through his valuable and mostly neglected notes: distribution in space and time and observations of behavior as an aid to species diagnosis. He also published *The Structure and Distribution of Coral Reefs* (1842); he had studied the coral reefs in the Cocos Islands during the *Beagle* voyage.

Darwin abandoned the idea of fixity of species in 1837 while writing his *Journal.* A second edition, in 1845, had a stronger tinge of transmutation, but there was still no public avowal of the new faith. This delightful volume is his most popular and accessible work.

Darwin's Transmutation (Species) Notebooks (1837–1839) have been reconstructed. The notion of "selection owing to struggle" derived from his reading of Malthus in 1838. Earlier Darwin had read Pyrame de Candolle's works on plant geography, so his mind was receptive. The breadth of interest and profusion of hypotheses characteristic of Darwin, who could carry several topics in his mind at the same time, inform the whole. From this medley of facts allegedly assembled on Baconian principles all his later works derive.

It was not until Darwin's geological observations of South America were published in 1846 that

he started a paper on his "first Cirripede," a shell-boring aberrant barnacle, no bigger than a pin's head, he had found at Chonos Island in 1835. This was watched while living, then dissected, and drawn while the *Beagle* sheltered from a week of severe storms. The working out of the relationship to other barnacles forced him to study all barnacles, a task that occupied him until 1854 and resulted in two volumes on living forms and two on fossil forms.

Darwin married Emma Wedgwood, his first cousin, in 1839. They lived in London until 1842, when ill health drove him to Down House, where he passed the rest of his life in seclusion. Four of their sons became prominent scientists: George was an astronomer and mathematician, Francis a botanist, Leonard a eugenist, and Horace a civil engineer.

Development of Ideas on Evolution. In 1842 and 1844 Darwin wrote short accounts of his transmutation views. The 1844 sketch in corrected fair copy was a testament accompanied by a letter to his wife to secure publication should he die. Late in 1844 Robert Chambers's *Vestiges of Creation* appeared advocating universal development by descent. A great scandal ensued, and criticism of the amateur pretensions of the author was savage. Darwin decided to bide his time and become more proficient as a biologist.

In 1855 Darwin began to study the practices of poultry and pigeon fanciers and worldwide domesticated breeds, conducted experiments on plant and animal variation and its hereditary transmission, and worried about the problem of plant and animal transport across land and water barriers, for he was persuaded of the importance of isolation for speciation. The last step in his conceptual scheme had already occurred to him in 1852 while pondering Henri Milne-Edwards's concept of diversification into specialized organs for separation of physiological functions in higher organisms and the relevance of these considerations for classification when related to the facts of embryological development. Darwin's "principle of divergence" recognizes that the dominant species must make more effective use of the territory it invades than a competing species and accordingly it becomes adapted to more diversified environments.

In May 1856 Lyell heard of Darwin's transmutation hypothesis and urged him to write an account with full references. Darwin sent the chapter on distribution to Lyell and Sir Joseph Hooker, who were deeply impressed. Darwin continued his writing, and on June 14, 1858, when he was halfway through, he received an essay from Alfred Russel Wallace containing the theory of evolution by natural selection, the same theory Darwin was working on. Lyell and

Hooker arranged for a reading of a joint paper by Wallace and Darwin, and it was presented at a meeting of the Linnaean Society on July 1. The paper had little effect.

Origin of Species. On Nov. 24, 1859, Darwin published *On the Origin of Species by Means of Natural Selection, or the Preservation of Favoured Races in the Struggle for Life.* The analogy of natural selection was prone to misunderstanding by readers, since it carried for them an implied purpose on the part of a "deified" Nature. Herbert Spencer's phrase "survival of the fittest" was equally misleading because the essence of Darwin's theory is that, unlike natural theology, adaptation must not be too perfect and rigid. A mutable store of variation must be available to any viable population in nature.

The publication of Darwin's book secured worldwide attention for his hypothesis and aroused impassioned controversy. His main champion was T. H. Huxley. Darwin, remote in his retreat at Down House, took painstaking note of criticism and endeavored to answer points of detail in the five more editions of *Origin* produced during his lifetime. He avoided trouble and made several unfortunate concessions which weakened his presentation and made his views seem vague and hesitant. The first edition is easily the best.

Later Works. In *On the Various Contrivances by Which British and Foreign Orchids Are Fertilised by Insects* (1862) Darwin showed how the welfare of an organism may be hidden in apparently unimportant peculiarities. It became hard to say what is "useless" in nature. His *The Variation of Animals and Plants under Domestication* (1868; rev. ed. 1875) expanded on a topic he had introduced in *Origin.* A chapter in *Origin* on man as the most domesticated of animals grew into the book *The Descent of Man and Selection in Relation to Sex* (1871). *The Expression of the Emotions in Man and Animals* (1872) developed from material squeezed out of the *Descent.*

Plants became an increasing preoccupation, the more so since Darwin had his son Francis as collaborator and amanuensis. Papers Darwin had published in 1864 were collected into *The Movements and Habits of Climbing Plants* (1875), and these ideas were further generalized on uniformitarian lines and published as *The Power of Movement in Plants* (1880). All plants, not merely climbing ones, were shown to execute to some degree exploratory "circumnutation" movements. Studies on fertilization of plants by insects recorded as early as 1840 led to *The Effects of Cross and Self-Fertilisation in the Vegetable Kingdom* (1876) and *The Different Forms of Flowers on Plants of the Same Species*

(1877). *Insectivorous Plants* (1873) pursued the reactions of plants to stimuli. Darwin's last work returned to observations he had made in 1837: *The Formation of Vegetable Mould through the Action of Worms, with Observations on Their Habits* (1881). He died on April 19, 1882, and was buried in Westminster Abbey.

EWB

David, Jacques Louis (1748–1825), French painter. Jacques Louis David was the leader of the neoclassic movement. His style set the artistic standards for many of his contemporaries and determined the direction of numerous 19th-century painters.

Jacques Louis David early turned his back on the frivolous rococo manner, looking instead to antiquity for inspiration. Following the ideals of Nicolas Poussin, to whom the artist candidly admitted he owed everything, David sought to reduce classical principles to their barest, unencumbered essentials. In this endeavor he observed with avid interest the neoclassicism propounded by Johann Winckelmann and the illustrations of antiquity found in the paintings of Anton Raphael Mengs. An outspoken political firebrand, David espoused the cause of the French Revolution and under the Convention held sway as the virtual dictator of the arts; later when Napoleon came to power, he acted willingly as his artistic spokesman.

David was born in Paris on August 30, 1748. His well-to-do bourgeois family placed him in the studio of that arch-practitioner of the rococo manner, the eminent painter François Boucher, to whom David was apparently distantly related. Perhaps because of his own advanced years, Boucher encouraged David to study under Joseph Marie Vien, a painter who had been attracted by the new wave of interest in antiquity while studying in Rome. In 1771 David won second prize in the Prix de Rome competition, but it was not until 3 years later and after severe mental frustration that he won the first prize with his painting *Antiochus Dying for the Love of Stratonice.*

Early Works. David went to Rome in 1775 in the company of Vien, who had just been named the director of the French Academy there. David studied the ancient architectural monuments, marble reliefs, and freestanding statues. In addition, he strove for a clearer understanding of the classical principles underlying the styles of the Renaissance and baroque masters Raphael, the Carracci, Domenichino, and Guido Reni. The effects of David's Romanization were first witnessed in his *Belisarius Asking for Alms,* exhibited in Paris in 1781. When he returned to Paris in 1780, he was an artist already thoroughly imbued with the tenets of classicism. He was admitted to the

French Academy in 1783 with his painting *Andromache by the Body of Hector.*

The following year David returned to Rome in order to paint the *Oath of the Horatii,* a work which was immediately acclaimed a masterpiece both in Italy and in France at its showing at the Parisian Salon of 1785. The painting reflected a strong interest in archeological exactitude in the depiction of figures and settings. Its carefully calculated severity of composition and its emphasis on a sculptural hardness of precise drawing, which David saw as more important than color, contributed to the forceful moralistic tone of the subject: the oath being administered to the Horatii by their father, who demanded their sacrifice for the good of the state. In this single work, with its strong republican implications, those aspiring to do so could find a call to revolution, a revolution which was in fact only five years distant. The *Oath* was followed by other moralizing canvases such as the *Death of Socrates* (1787) and *Brutus and the Lictors Bringing Home to Brutus the Bodies of His Sons* (1789), both extolling the classical virtues.

French Revolution. With the Revolution in full swing, David for a time abandoned his classical approach and began to paint scenes describing contemporary events, among them the unfinished *Oath of the Tennis Court* (1791), glorifying the first challenge to royal authority by the parliamentarians of the period. He also concentrated on portraits of the martyred heroes of the fight for freedom, including the *Death of Marat* (1793), the *Death of Lepeletier de Saint-Fargeau* (1793) and the *Death of Joseph Bara* (1794), all executed with an unvarnished realism. The artist was deeply involved with the political scene; elected to the National Convention in 1792, he served as a deputy to that all-powerful body and was one of those who voted for the execution of King Louis XVI.

David had apparently long harbored great animosity toward the French Academy, perhaps because it had failed to fully recognize his talents when he had first submitted works for the Grand Prix competition. Though an honored member by the time of the Revolution, in 1793 he hastened its dissolution, forming a group called the Commune of the Arts; this group was almost immediately supplanted by the Popular and Republican Society of the Arts, from whose ranks the Institute ultimately would be formed.

A friend of Robespierre, David nearly accompanied him to the guillotine when the Jacobin fell from power in 1794. Imprisoned for seven months, first at Fresnes and then in the Luxembourg, the artist emerged a politically wiser man. It was while in prison that David executed one of his rare landscapes: the

Gardens of the Luxembourg (1794), a view from his prison window. By 1798 he was busy on what he proclaimed his masterpiece, the *Rape of the Sabine Women.* The subject matter, derived from the classical legend described by Livy in which the Sabine women intervened in the battle between their fathers and brothers and their Roman husbands, represented a calculated appeal by David to end the internecine conflict that had ripped France asunder; further, the vast canvas was planned as a sort of manifesto proclaiming the validity of the antique.

David and Napoleon. It was at this time that David met Napoleon Bonaparte, in whose person he recognized a worthy new hero whom he promptly proceeded to glorify. The Emperor in turn realized the rich potential of David as a propagandist born to champion his imperial regime, and it was probably with this in mind that he invited the artist to accompany him on his Egyptian campaign; that David declined to go was surely due only to the fact that he was then deeply absorbed in the creation of his avowed masterpiece, the *Sabine Women.* Named "first painter," David executed a number of portraits of the Emperor, the most notable of which is probably that entitled *Bonaparte Crossing the St. Bernard Pass* (1800), in which the subject was idealized in physical stature and romanticized as the effortless man of action. Among the major commissions granted David by the Emperor were the colossal scenes treating specific episodes of his reign. The best-known of these are the *Coronation of Napoleon and Josephine* (1805–1807), containing over 100 portraits, and the *Distribution of the Eagles* (1810).

Though David would have preferred to be remembered for his history painting, he was at his best as a portraitist. Certain of his portraits, such as *Madame Sériziat and Her Daughter* and *Monsieur Sériziat* (1795), are done with an incredible directness and thus retain a freshness and vivacity not often encountered in David's more serious works. His unfinished portrait *Madame Récamier* (1800), with the subject shown in long, loosely flowing robes, vaguely reminiscent of the antique, summarizes the studied elegance of the neoclassic age.

With Bonaparte's defeat at Waterloo and the subsequent restoration of the Bourbons, David tried to retreat into quiet seclusion, but his earlier political affiliation and, more particularly, his actions during the heat of the Revolution were not calculated to warm his relations with the new rulers. He was declared persona non grata and fled to Switzerland. A short time later he settled in Brussels, where he continued to paint until his death on December 29,

1825. His family's urgent request that his ashes be returned to France was denied. He was buried amidst great pomp and circumstance in the church of Ste-Gudule in Brussels.

David's Influence. There was scarcely a young painter of the following generation who was not influenced by David's style, a style which had within it such diverse aspects as classicism, realism, and romanticism. Among his foremost pupils, each of whom developed various different facets of his style, were Antoine Jean, Baron Gros; Pierre Narcisse Guérin; François Gérard; Girodet de Roucy-Trioson; and perhaps most important, J. A. D. Ingres.

EWB

Dee, John (1527–1608), mathematician and astrologer. John Dee is most remembered for his numerous experiments with crystal gazing. He was also a scholar, a fellow of Trinity College, Cambridge, England, and the author of 49 books on scientific subjects. His delving into the occult made him a person of strange reputation and career.

Born in London July 13, 1527, Dee is said to have descended from a noble old Welsh family, the Dees of Nant y Groes in Radnorshire. He claimed that one of his direct ancestors was Roderick the Great, Prince of Wales. Dee's father appears to have been a gentleman server at the court of Henry VIII and therefore affluent and able to give his son a good education. So at age 15, John Dee went to Cambridge University and after two years there took his bachelor of arts. Soon afterward he became intensely interested in astronomy and decided to leave England to study abroad. In 1547 he went to the Low Countries (modern Belgium, Luxembourg, and the Netherlands), where he consorted with numerous scholars. He returned to England with the first astronomer's staff of brass and also with two globes constructed by geographer Gerard Mercator (famed for his cartographic projection).

In 1548 he traveled to France, living for some time at Louvain. In 1550 he spent several months in Paris, lecturing on the principles of geometry. He was offered a permanent post at the Sorbonne, but declined, returning in 1551 to England, where on the recommendation of Edward VI he was granted the rectory of Upton-upon-Severn, Worcestershire.

Dee was now in a delightful and enviable position, having a comfortable home and assured income, and was able to devote himself exclusively to the studies he loved. But he had hardly begun to enjoy these benefits when, on the accession of Queen Mary in 1553, he was accused of trying to take the new

sovereign's life by means of magic and was imprisoned at Hampton Court.

He gained his liberty soon afterward, but he felt that many people looked at him with distrust because of his scientific predilections. In a preface he wrote for an English translation of Euclid, he complains bitterly of being regarded as "a companion of the hellhounds, a caller and a conjuror of wicked and damned spirits."

During the reign of Queen Elizabeth I his fortune began to improve again, and after making another long tour abroad (going on as far as St. Helena), he returned and took a house at Mortlake on the Thames.

While staying there he rapidly became famous for his intimate knowledge of astronomy. In 1572—on the advent of a new star—people flocked to hear Dee speak on the subject; when a mysterious comet appeared five years later, the scholar was again granted ample opportunity to display his learning. Queen Elizabeth herself was among those who came to ask him what this addition to the stellar bodies might portend.

First Crystal Visions. The most interesting circumstances in Dee's life are those dealing with his experiments in crystallomancy. Living in comparative solitude, practicing astrology for bread, but studying alchemy for pleasure, brooding over Talmudic mysteries and Rosicrucian theories, immersed in constant contemplation of wonders he longed to penetrate, and dazzled by visions of the elixir of life and the philosophers' stone, Dee soon reached such a condition of mystic exaltation that his visions seemed real, and he persuaded himself that he was the favored of the invisible world. In his *Diary* he recorded that he first saw spirits in his crystal globe on May 25, 1581.

One day in November 1582, while on his knees and fervently praying, Dee became aware of a sudden glory that filled the west window of his laboratory and in the midst of which shone the bright angel Uriel. It was impossible for Dee to speak. Uriel smiled benignly upon him, gave him a convex piece of crystal, and told him that when he wished to communicate with the beings of another world he had but to examine it intently, and they would immediately appear and reveal the mysteries of the future. Then the angel vanished.

Dee used the crystal but discovered that it was necessary to concentrate all his faculties upon it before the spirits would obey him. Also, he could never remember what the spirits said in their frequent conversations with him. He resolved to find a fellow worker, or a neophyte, who would converse with the spirits while he recorded the interesting dialogue. He found the assistant he sought in Edward Kelley, who unfortunately possessed the boldness and cunning for making a dupe of the amiable and credulous enthusiast.

Kelley was a native of Lancashire, born, according to Dee, in 1555. Nothing is known of his early years, but after having been convicted at Lancaster of coining, he was punished by having his ears cropped. He concealed the loss of his ears by a black skullcap. He later moved to Worcester and established himself as a druggist. Carnal, ambitious, and self-indulgent, he longed for wealth; and despairing of getting it through honest work, he began to seek the philosophers' stone and to employ what secrets he picked up in taking advantage of the ignorant and extravagant.

The Visions of Edward Kelley.   In his work with Kelley, Dee saw nothing. The visions seemed to exist solely in Kelley's fertile imagination. The entities who reportedly communicated through Kelley bore names such as Madini, Gabriel, Uriel, Nalvage, Il, Morvorgran, and Jubanladace. Some of them were said to be angels.

A record of the séances held in 1582–87 was published in Meric Casaubon's *A True and Faithful Relation of What Passed between Dr. Dee and Some Spirits; Tending, Had it Succeeded, to a General Alteration of Most States and Kingdoms in the World* (1659). The spirits offered occult instruction—how to make the elixir of life, how to search for the philosophers' stone, how to involve the spirits. They also gave information on the hierarchy of spiritual beings and disclosed the secrets of the primeval tongue that the angels and Adam spoke, which was corrupted into Hebrew after the Fall. This original speech bore an organic relation to the outer world. Each name expressed the properties of the thing spoken of, and the utterance of that name had a compelling power over that creature. Dee was supposed to write a book in this tongue under spirit influence. He was later relieved of the task, however. The prophecies that were given through the crystal mostly failed. The physical phenomena were few—occasional movements of objects, direct writing, and direct voice.

Dee and Kelley acquired a considerable reputation for the occult, which spread from Mortlake to continental Europe. Dee declared that he possessed the elixir of life, which he claimed to have found among the ruins of Glastonbury Abbey, so the curious were drawn to his house by a double attraction. Gold flowed into his coffers, but his experiments in the transmutation of metals absorbed a great portion of his money.

At that time the court of England was visited by a Polish nobleman named Albert Laski, Count Palatine of Siradz, who wanted to see the famous "Gloriana." Queen Elizabeth received him with the flattering welcome she always accorded to distinguished strangers and placed him in the charge of the earl of Leicester. Leicester promised to introduce him to the learned philosopher on their return to London, and so soothed his discontent.

A few days afterward Laski and the earl of Leicester were waiting in the antechamber at Whitehall for an audience with the queen when Dee arrived. Leicester embraced the opportunity and introduced him to Laski. The interview between two genial spirits was interesting and led to frequent visits from Laski to Dee's house at Mortlake. Kelley consulted the "great crystalline globe" and began to reveal hints and predictions that excited Laski's fancy. A careful perusal of Dee's *Diary* suggests that he was duped by Kelley and that he accepted all his revelations as the actual utterances of the spirits. It seems that Kelley not only knew something of the optical delusions then practiced by pretended necromancers, but also may have possessed considerable ventriloquial powers, which assisted him in deceptions.

It did not serve Kelley's purposes to bring matters too suddenly to an end, and hoping to show the value of his services, he renewed his complaints about the wickedness of dealing with spirit and his fear of the perilous enterprises they might enjoin. He threatened to abandon his task, which greatly disturbed Dee. Where indeed could he hope to meet with another scryer of such infinite ability?

Kelley then returned to Dee's crystal and his visions and soon persuaded Laski that he was destined by the spirits to achieve great victories over the Saracens and win enduring glory. To do he needed to return to Poland.

Adventures in Europe.   Laski returned to Poland, taking with him Dee and Kelley and their wives and families. The spirits continued to respond to their inquiries even while at sea. They landed at the Brill on July 30, 1583, and traversed Holland and Friesland to the wealthy town of Lubeck. There they lived sumptuously for a few weeks, and with new strength set out for Poland. On Christmas Day they arrived at Stettin, where they stayed until the middle of January 1584. They reached Lasco, Laski's estate, early in February.

Immediately work began for the transmutation of iron into gold, since boundless wealth was obviously needed for so grand an enterprise as the regeneration of Europe. Laski liberally supplied them with means, but the alchemists always failed on the very threshold of success.

It became apparent to the swindlers that Laski's fortune was nearly exhausted. At the same time, ironically, the angels Madini, Uriel, and their comrades in the crystal began to doubt whether Laski was, after all, the great regenerator intended to revolutionize Europe.

The whole party lived at Cracow from March 1584 until the end of July and made daily appeals to the spirits in reference to the Polish prince. They grew more and more discouraging in their replies, and Laski began to suspect that he had been duped. He proposed to furnish the alchemists with sufficient funds for a journey to Prague and letters of introduction to Emperor Rudolph. At that very moment the spirits revealed that Dee should bear a divine message to the emperor, and so Laski's proposal was gladly accepted.

At Prague the two alchemists were well received by the emperor. They found him willing to believe in the existence of the famous philosophers' stone. He was courteous to Dee, a man of European celebrity, but was very suspicious of Kelley. They stayed several months at Prague, living on the funds Laski had supplied and hoping to be drafted into the imperial service.

At last the papal nuncio complained about the tolerance afforded to heretical magicians, and the emperor was obliged to order them to leave within 24 hours. They complied, and so escaped prison or the stake, to which the nuncio had received orders from Rome to consign them in May 1586.

Dee's enthusiasm and credulity had made him utterly dependent on Kelley, but the trickster was nevertheless jealous of the superior respect that Dee enjoyed as a man of remarkable scholarship and considerable ability. Frequent quarrels broke out between them, aggravated by the passion Kelley had developed for the doctor's young and beautiful wife, which he was determined to gratify.

Soon afterward, Dee requested permission from Queen Elizabeth to return to England and left the castle of Trebona after finally separating from Kelley. The latter, who had been knighted at Prague, proceeded to the Bohemian capital, taking with him the elixir found at Glastonbury Abbey. He was immediately arrested by order of the emperor and imprisoned.

Kelley was later released and wandered throughout Germany, telling fortunes and propagating the cause of magic. He was again arrested as a heretic and sorcerer. In a desperate attempt to avoid imprisonment he tried to escape, but fell from the dungeon wall and broke two ribs and both his legs. He died of his injuries in February 1593.

Dee's Final Years. Dee set out from Trebona with a splendid train, the expenses of his journey defrayed by the generous Bohemian noble Count Rosenberg. In England he was well received by the queen and settled again at Mortlake, resuming his chemical studies and his pursuit of the philosophers' stone.

But nothing went well with the unfortunate enthusiast. He employed two scryers—a rogue named Bartholomew and a charlatan named Heckman—but neither could discover anything satisfactory in the "great crystalline globe." He grew poorer and poorer; he sank into indigence and wearied the queen with his importunity. At length he obtained a small appointment as chancellor of St. Paul's Cathedral, which in 1595 he exchanged for the wardenship of Manchester College. He served in this position until age and failing intellect compelled him to resign it about 1602 or 1603. He then retired to his old house at Mortlake, where he practiced as a fortune-teller, gaining little in return but an unenviable reputation as a wizard, "a conjuror, a caller, or invocator of devils."

Dee was an exceptionally interesting figure, and he must have been a man of rare intellectual activity. His calculations facilitated the adoption of the Gregorian calendar in England, and he foresaw the formation of the Historical Manuscripts Commission, addressing to the Crown a petition on the desirability of preserving the old, unpublished records of England's past, many of which were kept in the archives of monasteries. He was a voluminous writer on science, his works including *Monas Hieroglyphica* (1564), *De Trigono* (1565), *Testamentum Johannis Dee Philosophi Summi ad Johannem Guryun Transmissum* (1568) and *An Account of the Manner in which a Certayn Copper-smith in the Land of Moores, and a Certayn Moore Transmuted Copper to Gold* (1576).

It is usual to dismiss Kelley as a rogue and Dee as his dupe, but if the angelic visions were purely for money, they both could have done better for themselves. Dee seemed to be an honest man of unusual talents, devoting his life to science and the pursuit of mystical knowledge. The angelic language called Enochian, which Dee and Kelley used when invoking spirits in the crystal, is a construction of great intricacy, far beyond the capacity or the requirements of simple fraud. It combines magic, mathematics, astrology, and cryptography. An intriguing suggestion is that the angelic conversations were a system of codes to convey secrets, and that Dee and Kelley's visits in Europe were for purposes of espionage. In later times, Enochian rituals were revived by the magical Hermetic Order of the Golden Dawn and became a common element in ceremonial magic. Some Enochian rituals were adapted by Anton LaVey and the Church of Satan, which he founded.

Dee was miserably poor in his last years and was even obliged to sell his precious books in order to sustain himself. He was planning a journey to Germany when he died in December 1608; he was buried in the chancel of Mortlake Church.

EOP

Defoe, Daniel (1660–1731), English novelist, journalist, poet, and government agent. Daniel Defoe wrote more than 500 books, pamphlets, articles, and poems. Among the most productive authors of the Augustan Age, he was the first of the great 18th-century English novelists.

Daniel Defoe was the son of a dissenting London tallow chandler or butcher. He early thought of becoming a Presbyterian minister, and in the 1670s he attended the Reverend Charles Morton's famous academy near London. In 1684 he married Mary Tuffley, who brought him the handsome dowry of £3,700. They had seven children. Defoe participated briefly in the abortive Monmouth Rebellion of 1685 but escaped capture and punishment. From 1685 through 1692 he engaged in trade in London as a wholesale hosier, importer of wine and tobacco, and part owner and insurer of ships. In later life he also dealt in real estate and manufactured bricks.

Defoe evidently knew King William III; indeed, his bankruptcy in 1692 for the enormous sum of £17,000 was primarily because of losses suffered from underwriting marine insurance for the King. Although he settled with his creditors in 1693, he was plagued by the threat of bankruptcy throughout his life and faced imprisonment for debt and libel seven times.

Arrested in 1703 for having published *The Shortest Way with the Dissenters* in 1702, Defoe was tried and sentenced to stand in the pillory for 3 days in July. He languished in Newgate Prison, however, until Robert Walpole released him in November and offered him a post as a government agent. Defoe continued to serve the government as journalist, pamphleteer, and secret agent for the remainder of his life. The most long-lived of his 27 periodicals, the *Review* (1704–1713), was especially influential in promoting the union between England and Scotland in 1706–1707 and in supporting the controversial Peace of Utrecht (1713).

Defoe published hundreds of political and social tracts between 1704 and 1719. During the 1720s he contributed to such weekly journals as *Mist's* and *Applebee's,* wrote criminal biographies, and studied economics and geography as well as producing his major works of fiction. He died in a comatose lethargy in Ropemaker's Alley on April 24, 1731, while hiding from a creditor who had commenced proceedings against him.

Defoe's interests and activities reflect the major social, political, economic, and literary trends of his age. He supported the policies of William III and Mary after the Glorious Revolution of 1688–1689, and analyzed England's emergence as the major sea and mercantile power in the Western world. He pleaded for leniency for debtors and bankrupts and defended the rights of Protestant dissenters. Effectively utilizing newspapers and journals to make his points, he also experimented with the novel form, which was still in its infancy.

His Nonfiction. No brief account of Defoe's works can do more than hint at the range, variety, and scope of his hundreds of publications. His first major work, *An Essay upon Projects* (1697), which introduced many topics that would reappear in his later works, proposed ways of providing better roads, insurance, and education, and even planned a house for fools to be supported by "a Tax upon Learning, to be paid by the Authors of Books."

In 1701 Defoe published *The True-Born Englishman,* the most widely sold poem in English up to that time. He estimated that more than 80,000 copies of this defense of William III against the attacks of John Tutchin were sold. Although Defoe's prose satire against the tyranny of the Church of England, *The Shortest Way with the Dissenters* (1702), led to his arrest, the popularity of his *Hymn to the Pillory* (1703) indicated the favor that he had found with the London public. From 1704 to 1713 in his monumental *Review,* Defoe discussed almost every aspect of the political, economic, and social life of Augustan England.

Defoe's allegorical moon voyage, *The Consolidator: Or Memoirs of Sundry Transactions from the World in the Moon* (1705), reviews the political history of the previous century, defends his political activities, and describes the ingenious machine which lifts the narrator to Terra Luna: a chariot powered by 513 feathers, one for each member of the British Parliament. His *Appeal to Honour and Justice* (1715) is perhaps his most moving and personal account of his services to the English crown.

Robinson Crusoe. At the age of 59, after a full career as businessman, government servant, political pamphleteer, and journalist, Defoe embarked upon a career as novelist and within 6 years produced the half-dozen novels which have given him his greatest fame.

In April 1719 Defoe published his most enduring work, *The Life and Strange Surprizing Adventures of Robinson Crusoe.* The immediate success of the story of the shipwrecked Crusoe's solitary existence on a desert island for more than 20 years, of his encounter with the native Friday, and of his eventual rescue inspired Defoe to write *The Farther Adventures of Robinson Crusoe* later in 1719 and *Serious Reflections during the Life and Surprizing Adventures* in 1720. That year he published another travel novel, *The Life, Adventures, and Pyracies of the Famous Captain Singleton.*

The greatness of *Robinson Crusoe* lies not only in Defoe's marvelously realistic descriptive passages but in the fact that the novel recounts one of the great myths of Western civilizationman's ability to endure, survive, and conquer a hostile environment. As a fictional adaptation of the story of Alexander Selkirk, who had been stranded on an island near Chile early in the century, the novel shows Augustan England's interest in travel literature, religious allegory, and mercantilist economics.

Other Major Fiction. Defoe published comparatively little in 1721 because he was hard at work on the three major books that were to appear the following year. In January 1722 he published *The Fortunes and Misfortunes of the Famous Moll Flanders,* probably the most successful of his novels. Its irony, vivid details, and psychologically valid individual scenes more than compensate for its structural weaknesses. The elderly Moll writes of her early life, of her five husbands, of her life as a prostitute, and of her adventures as a thief.

A Journal of the Plague Year, issued in March 1722, presents a stunning picture of life in London during the Great Plague of 1665, and it was thought to be history rather than fiction for more than a hundred years. The third important novel to appear in 1722, *The History and Remarkable Life of the Truly Honourable Col. Jacque,* was published in December. In this study of a young man's rise to gentility, Defoe characteristically combined a brilliant command of detail and individual scene with an interesting but awkwardly plotted story.

Defoe published *The Fortunate Mistress; or, . . . Roxana* early in 1724. Though Roxana moves in a more fashionable world than did Moll Flanders, she shares with Moll native cunning and an instinct for self-preservation. Like *Moll Flanders, Roxana* juxtaposes moral homilies with titillating narrative passages. In 1724 Defoe also published *A Tour Thro' the Whole Island of Great Britain,* one of the most thorough and fascinating guide-books of the period.

The History of the Remarkable Life of John Sheppard (1724), one of Defoe's finest criminal biographies, was followed in 1725 by *The True and Genuine Account of the Life and Actions of the Late Jonathan Wild.* Defoe's intimate knowledge of London's underworld and of its prisons explains the vitality and accuracy of these hastily written criminal lives. These works also display his characteristically clear, strong, idiomatic English prose.

Although he continued to write until his death in 1731, only a few of Defoe's later works are worthy of note: *The Complete English Tradesman* (1725), *The Political History of the Devil* (1726), *A New Family Instructor* (1727), and *Augusta Triumphans* (1728), which was Defoe's plan to make "London the most flourishing City in the Universe."

EWB

Derrida, Jacques (1930–), French philosopher. Jacques Derrida, by developing a strategy of reading called "deconstruction," challenged assumptions about metaphysics and the character of language and written texts.

Jacques Derrida was born in El Biar, Algiers, in 1930. He went to France for his military service and stayed on to study at the Ecole Normale with the eminent Hegel scholar Jean Hyppolite. Derrida taught at the Sorbonne (1960–1964) and after 1965 he taught the history of philosophy at the Ecole Normale Superieure. He was also a visiting professor in the United States at Johns Hopkins University and at Yale. His scholarly contribution included work with GREPH (Groupe de recherches sur l'enseignement philosophique), an association concerned about the teaching of philosophy in France.

Derrida gained recognition for his first book, a translation with lengthy introduction of Husserl's *Origin of Geometry* (1962), which won him the Prix Cavailles. His analysis of Husserl's phenomenology became the starting point for the criticism of Western philosophy developed in his numerous other works. Derrida was suspicious of all systematic metaphysical thought and sought to illuminate the assumptions and riddles found in language.

Metaphysics of Presence. Derrida depicted Western thought, from Plato onward, as a "metaphysics of presence." By this he meant the desire to guarantee the certainty of thought claims by finding an ultimate foundation or source of meaning and truth. This quest was seen in the Western preoccupation with such concepts as substance, essence, origin, identity, truth, and, of course, "Being." Moreover, he explored the way metaphysics is linked to a specific view of language. The assumption, Derrida contended, is that the spoken word is free of the paradoxes and possibilities of multiple meanings characteristic of written texts. He called this assumed primacy of the spoken word over text "logocentrism," seeing it closely linked to the desire for certainty. His task was to undo metaphysics and its logocentrism. Yet Derrida was also clear that we cannot easily escape metaphysical thought, since to think outside it is to be determined by it, and so he did not affirm or oppose metaphysics, but sought to resist it.

Derrida developed a strategy of reading texts called "deconstruction." The term does not mean "destruction" but "analysis" in the etymological sense of "to undo." Deconstructive reading attempts to uncover and undo tensions within a text showing how basic ideas and concepts fail to ever express only one meaning. Derrida's point was that language always defers any single reference to the world because it is a system of signs that are intelligible only because of their differences. He called this dual character of language "difference" linking deferral and difference. Traditional metaphysics, as the quest for a unequivocal mystery of meaning, is deconstructed by exposing the "difference" internal to metaphysical discourse.

Nothing outside the Text. Derrida's famous phrase, stated in *Of Grammatology* (1976), that "there is nothing outside the text" sums up his approach. What texts refer to, what is "outside" them, is nothing but another text. "Textuality" means that reference is not to external reality, the assumption of much Western thought, but to other texts, to "intertextuality." Thus Derrida's criticism of logocentrism also entails an attack on the assumption that words refer to or represent the world. If texts do not refer to the world then it is impossible to secure through language a foundation for meaning and truth. This requires a revision of what we mean by philosophical thinking. It can no longer be seen as the search for foundations, but as the critical play with texts to resist any metaphysical drive of thought.

Derrida applied deconstructive reading to a variety of texts, literary and philosophical. In *Dissemination* (1972) he offered subtle and complex readings of Plato and Mallarme. In works such as *Margins of Philosophy* (1972) and *Writing and Difference* (1978) he wrote on topics ranging from metaphor to theater. He refused, in a way similar to Nietzsche, to accept simple distinctions between philosophical and literary uses of language. Interestingly, his challenge to philosophy and his affirmation of the ambiguity of texts meant that his own work called for deconstruction.

Derrida's deconstructive strategy has implications for the study of literature. His contention was that the search for meaning, ideas, the author's intention, or truth *in* a text are misguided. What must be explored is the meanings that words have because of linguistic relations in the text. This opens up an infinite play of meaning possible with any text. Put differently, there is no one meaning to a text, its meaning is always open and strictly undecideable. Deconstruction requires the close readings of texts that highlight linguistic relations, particularly etymological ones, and relations between a text and other texts found in our culture without seeking to determine "the" meaning of the work. In short, it requires taking seriously "difference" and intertextuality.

Not Without Detractors. Derrida's work provoked the reconsideration of traditional problems and texts and suggested a strategy for reading. However, he did not offer a positive position but debunked metaphysic strains of thought found throughout Western philosophy and literature. His work had significant impact on philosophical and literary circles, particularly in France and the United States. Derrida and his ideas were not always accepted. Critics argued his philosophy undermines the rational dialogue essential to academic pursuits. Indeed, in 1992 a proposal to give Derrida an honorary degree from Cambridge University met with opposition.

Derrida's 1996 book *Archive Fever: A Freudian Impression,* explored the relationship between technologies of inscription and psychic processes. Because of the complexity of his writing, the need to deconstruct his texts, and the limitless potential of deconstructive reading, the influence and importance of his work is still in question.

EWB

Descartes, René (1596–1650), French thinker. René Descartes is called the father of modern philosophy. He initiated the movement generally termed rationalism, and his *Discourse on Method* and *Meditations* defined the basic problems of philosophy for at least a century.

To appreciate the novelty of the thought of René Descartes, one must understand what modern philosophy, or rationalism, means in contrast to medieval, or scholastic, philosophy. The great European thinkers of the 9th to 14th century were not incapable of logical reasoning, but they differed in philosophic interests and aims from the rationalists. Just as the moderns, from Descartes on, usually identified philosophy with the natural and pure sciences, so the medievals made little distinction between philosophical and theological concerns.

The medieval doctors, like St. Thomas Aquinas, wanted to demonstrate that the revelations of faith and the dictates of reason were not incompatible. Their universe was that outlined by Aristotle in his *Physics,* a universe in which everything was ordered and classified according to the end that it served. During the Renaissance, however, men began exploring scientific alternatives to Aristotle's hierarchical universe. Further, new instruments, especially Galileo's telescope, added precision to scientific generalizations.

By the beginning of the 17th century the medieval tradition had lost its creative impetus. But the schoolmen, so called because they dominated the European universities, continued to adhere dogmatically to the traditional philosophy because of its association with Catholic theology. The rationalists, however, persistently refused professorships in order to preserve their intellectual integrity or to avoid persecution. They rejected the medieval practice of composing commentaries on standard works in favor of writing original, usually anonymous, treatises on topics suggested by their own scientific or speculative interests. Thus the contrast is between a moribund tradition of professorial disputes over trivialities and a new philosophy inspired by original, scientific research.

Descartes participated in this conflict between the scholastic and rationalist approaches. He spent a great part of his intellectual effort, even to the extent of suppressing some of his writings, attempting to convince ecclesiastical authorities of the compatibility of the new science with theology and of its superiority as a foundation for philosophy.

Early Life. Descartes was born on March 31, 1596, in La Haye, in the Touraine region, between the cities of Tours and Poitiers. His father, Joachim, a member of the minor nobility, served in the Parliament of Brittany. Jeanne Brochard Descartes, his mother, died in May 1597. Although his father remarried, Descartes and his older brother and sister were raised by their maternal grandmother and by a nurse for whom he retained a deep affection.

In 1606 Descartes entered La Flèche, a Jesuit college established by the king for the instruction of the young nobility. In the *Discourse* Descartes tells of the 8-year course of studies at La Flèche, which he considered "one of the most celebrated schools in Europe." According to his account, which is one of the best contemporary descriptions of 17th-century education, his studies left him feeling embarrassed at the extent of his own ignorance.

The young Descartes came to feel that languages, literature, and history relate only fables which incline man to imaginative exaggerations. Poetry and eloquence persuade man, but they do not tell the truth. Mathematics does grasp the truth, but the certainty and evidence of its reasoning seemed to Descartes to have only practical applications. Upon examination, the revelations of religion and morals seem as mysterious to the learned as to the ignorant. Philosophy had been studied by the best minds throughout the centuries, and yet "no single thing is to be found in it which is not subject to dispute." Descartes says that he came to suspect that even science, which depends upon philosophy for its principles, "could have built nothing solid on foundations so far from firm."

Travel and First Writings. The 18-year-old Descartes left college with a reputation for extreme brilliance. In the next years he rounded out the education befitting a young noble. He learned fencing, horsemanship, and dancing and took a law degree from Poitiers.

From 1618 to 1628 Descartes traveled extensively throughout Europe while attached to various military units. Although a devout Catholic, he served in the army of the Protestant prince Maurice of Nassau but later enlisted in the Catholic army of Maximilian I of Bavaria. Living on income from inherited properties, Descartes served without pay and seems to have seen little action; he was present, however, at the Battle of Prague, one of the major engagements of the Thirty Years' War. Descartes was reticent about this period of his life, saying only that he left the study of letters in order to travel in "the great book of the world."

This period of travel was not without intellectual effort. Descartes sought out eminent mathematicians, scientists, and philosophers wherever he traveled. The most significant of these friendships was with Isaac Beeckman, the Dutch mathematician, at whose suggestion Descartes began writing scientific treatises on mathematics and music. He perfected a means of describing geometrical figures in algebraic formulas, a process that served as the foundation for his invention of analytic geometry. He became increasingly impressed with the extent to which material reality could be understood mathematically.

During this period Descartes was profoundly influenced by three dreams which he had on Nov. 10, 1619, in Ulm, Germany. He interpreted their symbols as a divine sign that all science is one and that its mastery is universal wisdom. This notion of the unity of all science was a revolutionary concept which contradicted the Aristotelian notion that the sciences were distinguished by their different objects of study. Descartes did not deny the multiplicity of objects, but rather he emphasized that only one mind could know all these diverse things. He felt that if one could generalize man's correct method of knowing, then one would be able to know everything. Descartes devoted the majority of his effort and work to proving that he had, in fact, discovered this correct method of reasoning.

From 1626 to 1629 Descartes resided mainly in Paris. He acquired a wide and notable set of friends but soon felt that the pressures of social life kept him from his work. He then moved to Holland, where he lived, primarily near Amsterdam, for the next 20 years. Descartes cherished the solitude of his life in Holland, and he described himself to a friend as awakening happily after 10 hours of sleep with the memory of charming dreams. He said his life in Holland was peaceful because he was "the only man not engaged in merchandise." There Descartes studied and wrote. He carried on an enormous correspondence throughout Europe, and in Holland he acquired a small, but dedicated, set of friends and disciples. Although he never married, Descartes fathered a natural daughter who was baptized Francine. She died in 1640, when she was 5.

First Works. Descartes's research in mathematics and physics led him to see the need for a new methodology, or way of thinking. His first major work, *Rules for the Direction of the Mind*, was written by 1629. Although circulated widely in manuscript form, this incomplete treatise was not published until 1701. The work begins with the assumption that man's knowledge has been limited by the erroneous belief that science is determined by the various objects of experience. The first rule therefore states that all true judgment depends on reason alone for its validity. For example, the truths of mathematics are valid independently of observation and experiment. Thus the second rule argues that the standard for any true knowledge should be the certitude demanded of demonstrations in arithmetic and geometry. The third rule begins to specify what this standard of true knowledge entails. The mind should be directed not by tradition, authority, or the history of the problem, but only by what can clearly be observed and deduced.

There are only two mental operations that are permissible in the pure use of reason. The first is intuition, which Descartes defines as "the undoubting conception of an unclouded and attentive mind"; the second is deduction, which consists of "all necessary inference from other facts that are known with cer-

tainty. "The basic assumption underlying these definitions is that all first principles are known by way of self-evident intuitions and that the conclusions of this "seeing into" are derived by deduction. The clarity and distinctness of ideas are for Descartes the conceptual counterpart of human vision. (For example, man can know the geometry of a square just as distinctly as he can see a square table in front of him.)

Many philosophers recognized the ideal character of mathematical reasoning, but no one before Descartes had abstracted the conditions of such thinking and applied it generally to all knowledge. If all science is unified by man's reason and if the proper functioning of the mind is identified with mathematical thinking, then the problem of knowledge is reduced to a question of methodology. The end of knowledge is true judgment, but true judgment is equivalent to mathematical demonstrations that are based on intuition and deduction. Thus the method for finding truth in all matters is merely to restrict oneself to these two operations.

According to the fourth rule, "By method I mean certain and simple rules, such that if a man observe them accurately, he shall never assume what is false as true . . . but will always gradually increase his knowledge and so arrive at a true understanding of all that does not surpass his powers." The remaining sixteen rules are devoted to the elaboration of these principles or to showing their application to mathematical problems. In Descartes's later works he refines these methodological principles, and in the *Meditations* he attempts a metaphysical justification of this type of reasoning.

By 1634 Descartes had written his speculative physics in a work entitled *The World*. Unfortunately, only fragments survive because he suppressed the book when he heard that Galileo's *Dialogue on the Two Great Systems of the Universe* had been condemned by the Catholic Church because of its advocacy of Copernican rather than Ptolemaic astronomy. Descartes also espoused the Copernican theory that the earth is not the center of the universe but revolves about the sun. His fear of censure, however, led him to withdraw his work. In 1634 he also wrote the brief *Treatise on Man*, which attempted to explain human physiology on mechanistic principles.

***Discourse* and *Meditations*.** In 1637 Descartes finished *Discourse on Method*, which was published together with three minor works on geometry, dioptrics, and meteors. This work is significant for several reasons. It is written in French and directed to men of good sense rather than professional philosophers. It is autobiographical and begins with a personal account of his education as an example of the need for a new method of conducting inquiry.

The work contains Descartes's vision of a unity of science based on a common methodology, and it shows that this method can be applied to general philosophic questions. In brief, the method is a sophistication of the earlier *Rules for the Direction of the Mind.* In the *Discourse* Descartes presents four general rules for reducing any problem to its fundamentals by analysis and then constructing solutions by general synthesis.

Meditations on First Philosophy appeared in 1641–1642 together with six (later seven) sets of objections by distinguished thinkers including Thomas Hobbes, Antoine Arnauld, and Pierre Gassendi and the author's replies. The *Meditations* is Descartes's major work and is one of the seminal books in the history of philosophy. While his former works were concerned with elaborating a methodology, this work represents the systematic application of those rules to the principal problems of philosophy: the refutation of skepticism, the existence of the human soul, the nature of God, the metaphysical basis of truth, the extent of man's knowledge of the external world, and the relation between body and soul.

The first meditation is an exercise in methodological skepticism. Descartes states that doubt is a positive means of ascertaining whether there is any certain foundation for knowledge. All knowledge originates either from the senses or from the mind. Examples of color blindness, objects seen in perspective, and so on testify to the distortions inherent in vague sense perception. The recognition of these phenomena as distorted suggests a class of clear perceptions which are more difficult to doubt. But Descartes then points out that such images appear as clear to man in dreams as in an awakened state. Therefore all sensory experience is doubtful because sense data in itself does not indicate whether an object is seen or imagined, true or false.

What about the realm of pure ideas? Descartes simplifies the argument by asking whether it is possible to doubt the fundamental propositions of arithmetic and geometry. Man cannot doubt that two plus two equals four, but he may suspect that this statement has no reality apart from his mind. The standard of truth is the self-evidence of clear and distinct ideas, but the question remains of the correspondence of such ideas to reality. Descartes imagines the existence of an all-powerful "evil genius" who deceives man as to the content of his ideas, so that in reality two plus two equals five.

The second meditation resolves these skeptical issues in a deceptively simple manner by arguing that even if it is doubtful whether sense images or ideas have objects, it is absolutely true that man's mind exists. The famous formula "I think, therefore, I am" is true even if everything else is false. Descartes's solution is known as subjectivism, and it is a radical reversal of previous theories of knowledge. Whereas nature had been assumed to be the cause of man's images and ideas, Descartes states that man is a "thinking thing" whose subjective images and ideas are the sole evidence for the existence of a world.

The third meditation demonstrates that God is "no deceiver," and hence clear and distinct ideas must have objects that exactly and actually correspond to them. Descartes argues that the idea of God is an effect. But an effect gets its reality from its cause, and a cause can only produce what it possesses. Hence either Descartes is a perfect being or God exists as the cause of the idea of God.

The fourth meditation deals with the problem of human error; insofar as man restricts himself to clear and distinct ideas, he will never err. With this connection between ideas and objects Descartes can emerge from his doubts about knowledge. The external world can be known with absolute certainty insofar as it is reducible to clear and distinct ideas. Thus the fifth meditation shows the application of methodology to material reality in its quantifiable dimensions, that is, to the extent to which material reality can be "the object of pure mathematics."

The sixth, and final, meditation attempts to explain the relation between the human soul and the body. Since Descartes believed in mechanism, there could be no absolute connection between a free soul and a bodily machine. After considerable hesitation he expresses the relation between mind and matter as a "felt union." The body is the active faculty that produces the passive images and imaginings man finds in his mind. Actually Descartes's explanation is logically impossible in terms of the "subjective" separation of mind; similarly, the unresolved dualism of the "felt union" violates the principle of assenting only to clear and distinct ideas.

The remainder of Descartes's career was spent in defending his controversial positions. In 1644 he published the *Principles of Philosophy,* which breaks down the arguments of the *Meditations* into propositional form and presents extra arguments dealing with their scientific application. In 1649 Descartes accepted an invitation from Queen Christina of Sweden to become her teacher. There he wrote *The Passions of the Soul,* which is a defense of the mind-body dualism and a mechanistic explanation of the passions. But Descartes's health was undermined by the severity of the northern climate, and after a brief illness he died in Stockholm in 1650.

EWB

Dickens, Charles (1812–1870), English author. Charles Dickens was, and probably still is, the most widely read Victorian novelist. He is now appreciated more for his "dark" novels than for his humorous works.

Charles Dickens was born on Feb. 7, 1812, at Port-sea (later part of Portsmouth) on the southern coast of England. He was the son of a lower-middle-class but impecunious father whose improvidence he was later to satirize in the character of Micawber in *David Copperfield.* The family's financial difficulties caused them to move about until they settled in Camden Town, a poor neighborhood of London. At the age of 12 Charles was set to work in a warehouse that handled "blacking," or shoe polish; there he mingled with men and boys of the working class. For a period of months he was also forced to live apart from his family when they moved in with his father, who had been imprisoned in the Marshalsea debtors' prison. This experience of lonely hardship was the most significant formative event of his life; it colored his view of the world in profound and varied ways and is directly or indirectly described in a number of his novels, including *The Pickwick Papers, Oliver Twist,* and *Little Dorrit,* as well as *David Copperfield.*

These early events of Dicken's life left both psychological and sociological effects. The sociological effect of the blacking factory on Dickens was to give him a firsthand acquaintance with poverty and to make him the most vigorous and influential voice of the lower classes in his age. Despite the fact that many of England's legal and social abuses were in the process of being removed by the time Dickens published his exposés of them, it remains true that he was the most widely heard spokesman of the need to alleviate the miseries of the poor.

Dickens returned to school after an inheritance (as in the fairy-tale endings of some of his novels) relieved his father from debt, but he was forced to become an office boy at the age of 15. In the following year he became a free-lance reporter or stenographer at the law courts of London. By 1832 he had become a reporter for two London newspapers and, in the following year, began to contribute a series of impressions and sketches to other newspapers and magazines, signing some of them "Boz." These scenes of London life went far to establish his reputation and were published in 1836 as *Sketches by Boz,* his first book. On the strength of this success he married; his wife, Catherine Hogarth, was eventually to bear him 10 children.

Early Works. In 1836 Dickens also began to publish in monthly installments *The Posthumous Papers of the Pickwick Club.* This form of serial publication became a standard method of writing and producing fiction in the Victorian period and affected the literary methods of Dickens and other novelists. So great was Dickens's success with the procedure—summed up in the formula, "Make them laugh; make them cry; make them wait," that *Pickwick* became one of the most popular works of the time, continuing to be so after it was published in book form in 1837. The comic heroes of the novel, the antiquarian members of the Pickwick Club, scour the English countryside for local points of interest and are involved in a variety of humorous adventures which reveal the characteristics of English social life. At a later stage of the novel, the chairman of the club, Samuel Pickwick, is involved in a lawsuit which lands him in the Fleet debtors' prison. Here the lighthearted atmosphere of the novel changes, and the reader is given intimations of the gloom and sympathy with which Dickens was to imbue his later works.

During the years of *Pickwick*'s serialization, Dickens became editor of a new monthly, *Bentley's Miscellany.* When *Pickwick* was completed, he began publishing his new novel, *Oliver Twist,* in this magazine, a practice he continued in his later magazines, *Household Worlds* and *All the Year Round. Oliver* expresses Dickens's interest in the life of the slums to the fullest, as it traces the fortunes of an innocent orphan through the London streets. It seems remarkable today that this novel's fairly frank treatment of criminals like Bill Sikes, prostitutes like Nancy, and "fences" like Fagin could have been acceptable to the Victorian reading public. But so powerful was Dickens's portrayal of the "little boy lost" amid the lowlife of the East End that the limits of his audience's tolerance were gradually stretched.

Dickens was now embarked on the most consistently successful career of any 19th-century author after Sir Walter Scott. He could do no wrong as far as his faithful readership was concerned; yet his books for the next decade were not to achieve the standard of his early triumphs. These works include: *Nicholas Nickleby* (1838–1839), still cited for its exposé of brutality at an English boys' school, Dotheboys Hall; *The Old Curiosity Shop* (1840–1841), still remembered for reaching a high (or low) point of sentimentality in its portrayal of the sufferings of Little Nell; and *Barnaby Rudge* (1841), still read for its interest as a historical novel, set amid the anti-Catholic Gordon Riots of 1780.

In 1842 Dickens, who was as popular in America as he was in England, went on a 5-month lecture tour of the United States, speaking out strongly for the abolition of slavery and other reforms. On his return he wrote *American Notes,* sharply critical of the cultural backwardness and aggressive materialism of American life. He made further capital of these observations in his next novel, *Martin Chuzzlewit* (1843–1844), in which the hero retreats from the difficulties of making his way in England only to find that survival is even more trying on the American frontier. During the years in which *Chuzzlewit* appeared, Dickens also published two Christmas stories, *A Christmas Carol* and *The Chimes,* which became as much part of the season as plum pudding.

First Major Novels. After a year abroad in Italy, in response to which he wrote *Pictures from Italy* (1846), Dickens began to publish *Dombey and Son,* which continued till 1848. This novel established a new standard in the Dickensian novel and may be said to mark the turning point in his career. If Dickens had remained the author of *Pickwick, Oliver Twist,* and *The Old Curiosity Shop,* he might have deserved a lasting reputation only as an author of cheerful comedy and bathetic sentiment. But *Dombey,* while it includes these elements, is a realistic novel of human life in a society which had assumed more or less its modern form. As its full title indicates, *Dealings with the Firm of Dombey and Son* is a study of the influence of the values of a business society on the personal fortunes of the members of the Dombey family and those with whom they come in contact. It takes a somber view of England at mid-century, and its elegiac tone becomes characteristic of Dickens's novels for the rest of his life.

Dickens's next novel, *David Copperfield* (1849–1850), combined broad social perspective with a very strenuous effort to take stock of himself at the midpoint of his literary career. This autobiographical novel fictionalized elements of Dickens's childhood degradation, pursuit of a journalistic and literary vocation, and love life. Its achievement is to offer the first comprehensive record of the typical course of a young man's life in Victorian England. *Copperfield* is not Dickens's greatest novel, but it was his own favorite among his works, probably because of his personal engagement with the subject matter.

In 1850 Dickens began to "conduct" (his word for edit) a new periodical, *Household Words.* His editorials and articles for this magazine, running to two volumes, cover the entire span of English politics, so-

cial institutions, and family life and are an invaluable complement to the fictional treatment of these subjects in Dickens's novels. The weekly magazine was a great success and ran to 1859, when Dickens began to conduct a new weekly, *All the Year Round.* In both these periodicals he published some of his major novels.

"Dark" Novels. In 1851 Dickens was struck by the death of his father and one of his daughters within 2 weeks. Partly in response to these losses, he embarked on a series of works which have come to be called his "dark" novels and which rank among the greatest triumphs of the art of fiction. The first of these, *Bleak House* (1852–1853), has perhaps the most complicated plot of any English novel, but the narrative twists serve to create a sense of the interrelationship of all segments of English society. Indeed, it has been maintained that this network of interrelations is the true subject of the novel, designed to express Thomas Carlyle's view that "organic filaments" connect every member of society with every other member of whatever class. The novel provides, then, a chastening lesson to social snobbery and personal selfishness.

Dickens's next novel is even more didactic in its moral indictment of selfishness. *Hard Times* (1854) was written specifically to challenge the prevailing view of his society that practicality and facts were of greater importance and value than feelings and persons. In his indignation at callousness in business and public educational systems, Dickens laid part of the charge for the heartlessness of Englishmen at the door of the utilitarian philosophy then much in vogue. But the lasting applicability of the novel lies in its intensely focused picture of an English industrial town in the heyday of capitalist expansion and in its keen view of the limitations of both employers and reformers.

Little Dorrit (1855–1857) has some claim to be regarded as Dickens's greatest novel. In it he provides the same range of social observation that he had developed in previous major works. But the outstanding feature of this novel is the creation of two striking symbols of his views, which operate throughout the story as the focal points of all the characters' lives. The condition of England, as he saw it, Dickens sums up in the symbol of the prison: specifically the Marshalsea debtors' prison, in which the heroine's father is entombed, but generally the many forms of personal bondage and confinement that are exhibited in the course of the plot. For his counterweight, Dickens raises to symbolic stature his traditional figure of the child as innocent sufferer of the world's abuses. By making his heroine not a child but a childlike figure of Christian loving-kindness, Dickens poses the central burden of his workthe conflict between the world's harshness and human valuesin its most impressive artistic form.

The year 1857 saw the beginnings of a personal crisis for Dickens when he fell in love with an actress named Ellen Ternan. He separated from his wife in the following year, after many years of marital incompatibility. In this period Dickens also began to give much of his time and energies to public readings from his novels, which became even more popular than his lectures on topical questions.

Later Works. In 1859 Dickens published *A Tale of Two Cities,* a historical novel of the French Revolution, which is read today most often as a school text. It is, while below the standard of the long and comprehensive "dark" novels, a fine evocation of the historical period and a moving tale of a surprisingly modern hero's self-sacrifice. Besides publishing this novel in the newly founded *All the Year Round,* Dickens also published 17 articles, which appeared as a book in 1860 entitled *The Uncommercial Traveller.*

Dickens's next novel, *Great Expectations* (1860–1861), must rank as his most perfectly executed work of art. It tells the story of a young man's moral development in the course of his life from childhood in the provinces to gentleman's status in London. Not an autobiographical novel like *David Copperfield, Great Expectations* belongs to the type of fiction called, in German, *Bildungsroman* (the novel of a man's education or formation by experience) and is one of the finest examples of the type.

The next work in the Dickens canon had to wait for the (for him) unusual time of 3 years, but in 1864–1865 he produced *Our Mutual Friend,* which challenges *Little Dorrit* and *Bleak House* for consideration as his masterpiece. Here the vision of English society in all its classes and institutions is presented most thoroughly and devastatingly, while two symbols are developed which resemble those of *Little Dorrit* in credibility and interest. These symbols are the mounds of rubbish which rose to become features of the landscape in rapidly expanding London, and the river which flows through the city and provides a point of contact for all its members besides suggesting the course of human life from birth to death.

In the closing years of his life Dickens worsened his declining health by giving numerous readings from his works. He never fully recovered from a railroad accident in which he had been involved in 1865 and yet insisted on traveling throughout the British Isles and America to read before tumultuous audiences. He broke down in 1869 and gave only a final series of

readings in London in the following year. He also began *The Mystery of Edwin Drood* but died in 1870, leaving it unfinished. His burial in Westminster Abbey was an occasion of national mourning.

EWB

Diderot, Denis (1713–1784), French philosopher, playwright, and novelist. Denis Diderot is best known as the editor of the *Encyclopédie.*

On Oct. 15, 1713, Denis Diderot was born in Langres, Compagne, into a family of cutlers, whose bourgeois traditions went back to the late Middle Ages. As a child, Denis was considered a brilliant student by his Jesuit teachers, and it was decided that he should enter the clergy. In 1726 he enrolled in the Jesuit college of Louis-le-Grand and probably later attended the Jansenist Collège d'Harcourt. In 1732 he earned a master of arts degree in philosophy. He then abandoned the clergy as a career and decided to study law. His legal training, however, was short-lived. In 1734 Diderot decided to seek his fortune by writing. He broke with his family and for the next 10 years lived a rather bohemian existence. He earned his living by translating English works and tutoring the children of wealthy families and spent his leisure time studying. In 1743 he further alienated his father by marrying Anne Toinette Champion.

The *Encyclopédie.* On Jan. 21, 1746, André François le Breton and his partners were granted permission to publish a 10-volume encyclopedia. On the advice of the distinguished mathematician Jean d'Alembert and with the consent of Chancellor d'Aguesseau, Diderot was named general editor of the project.

For more than 26 years Diderot devoted the bulk of his energies and his genius to the writing, editing, and publishing of the *Encyclopédie.* For Diderot, the aim of the work was "to assemble the knowledge scattered over the face of the earth; to explain its general plan to the men with whom we live . . . so that we may not die without having deserved well of the human race." Such was the plan and the purpose of the *Encyclopédie,* and it was also the credo of the Enlightenment. But the project was more than just the compilation of all available knowledge; it was also a learning experience for all those regularly connected with it. It introduced Diderot to technology, the crafts, the fine arts, and many other areas of learning. It was an outlet for his curiosity, his scholarly interests, and his creativity.

In 1751 d'Alembert's *Preliminary Discourse* and the first volume were published. In January 1752 the second volume appeared, but the opposition of the Jesuits and other orthodox critics forced a temporary suspension. Publication was soon resumed and continued at the rate of one volume a year until 1759, when the Royal Council forbade further operations. Diderot and Le Breton, however, continued to write and publish the *Encyclopédie* secretly until 1765, when official sanction was resumed. In 1772 the completed work was published in 17 volumes of text and 11 volumes of plates under the title *Encyclopédie, ou Dictionnaire raisonné des sciences, des arts, et des métiers.*

Other Writings. Throughout the period of his association with the *Encyclopédie,* Diderot continued to devote himself to other writing. In 1746 he published *Philosophical Thoughts,* which was concerned with the question of the relationship between nature and religion. He viewed life as self-sufficient and held that virtue could be sustained without religious beliefs. In *Sceptics Walk* (1747) and *Letters on the Blind* (1749) Diderot slowly turned from theism to atheism. Religion became a central theme in his writings, and he aroused the hostility of public officials who considered him a leader of the radicals, "a clever fellow, but extremely dangerous."

In 1749 Diderot was imprisoned for 3 months because of his opinions in *Philosophical Thoughts.* Although he had stated, "If you impose silence on me about religion and government, I shall have nothing to talk about," after his release he reduced the controversial character of his published works. Therefore most of his materialistic and antireligious works and several of his novels were not published during his lifetime.

During his long literary career Diderot moved away from the mechanical approach to nature, which was characteristic of the Englightenment's use of the discoveries of Sir Isaac Newton. Such works as *D'Alembert's Dream, Conversation between d'Alembert and Diderot, Thoughts on the Interpretation of Nature, Elements of Physiology,* and *Essay on Seneca* vividly point to the evolution of his thought and to its modernity.

In his mature writings Diderot tends to see man as an integral part of an organic and vitalistic nature, governed by laws that are incomprehensible to him. Nature, according to Diderot, is a continually unfolding process, which reveals itself, rather than being revealed by man. Forms in nature develop from earlier forms in a continually evolving process, in which all elements, animate and inanimate, are related to one another. Man can know nature only through experience; thus rationalistic speculation is useless to him in understanding nature.

Diderot is one of the pre-19th-century leaders in the movement away from mathematics and physics, as a source of certain knowledge, to biological problems and historical insight. As one modern scholar has stated, Diderot's approach to nature and philosophy was that of mystical naturalism.

Later Years. Following the completion of the *Encyclopédie,* Diderot went into semiretirement; he wrote but infrequently published his works. His earnings as editor of the *Encyclopédie* guaranteed him a modest income, which he supplemented by writing literary criticism. In addition, he sold his library to Empress Catherine of Russia, who allowed him to keep it while he lived and paid him an annual salary as its librarian. On July 30, 1784, Diderot died in the home of his daughter, only 5 months after the death of his beloved mistress and intellectual companion, Sophie Voland.

The great paradox of Diderot's life is found in the tensions that existed between his basically bourgeois nature and his bohemian tendencies. This struggle was mirrored in his novel *Rameau's Nephew,* in which the staid Rameau and his bohemian nephew represent aspects of Diderot's personality. Fittingly, Diderot's last words, "The first step toward philosophy is incredulity," are an adequate measure of the man.

EWB

Disney, Walt (1901–1966), American filmmaker and entrepreneur. Walt Disney created a new kind of popular culture in feature-length animated cartoons and live-action "family" films.

Walter Elias Disney was born in Chicago, Illinois, on December 5, 1901, the fourth of five children born to a Canadian farmer father and a mother from Ohio. He was raised on a Midwestern farm in Marceline, Missouri, and in Kansas City, where he was able to acquire some rudimentary art instruction from correspondence courses and Saturday museum classes. He would later use many of the animals and characters that he knew from that Missouri farm in his cartoons.

He dropped out of high school at 17 to serve in World War I. After serving briefly overseas as an ambulance driver, Disney returned in 1919 to Kansas City for an apprenticeship as a commercial illustrator and later made primitive animated advertising cartoons. By 1922, he had set up his own shop in association with Ub Iwerks, whose drawing ability and technical inventiveness were prime factors in Disney's eventual success.

Initial failure sent Disney to Hollywood in 1923, where in partnership with his loyal elder brother Roy, he managed to resume cartoon production. His first success came with the creation of Mickey Mouse in *Steamboat Willie. Steamboat Willie* was the first fully synchronized sound cartoon and featured Disney as the voice of a character first called "Mortimer Mouse." Disney's wife, Lillian, suggested that Mickey sounded better and Disney agreed.

Living frugally, he reinvested profits to make better pictures. His insistence on technical perfection and his unsurpassed gifts as story editor quickly pushed his firm ahead. The invention of such cartoon characters as Mickey Mouse, Donald Duck, Minnie, and Goofy combined with the daring and innovative use of music, sound, and folk material (as in *The Three Little Pigs*) made the Disney shorts of the 1930s a phenomenon of worldwide success. This success led to the establishment of immensely profitable, Disney-controlled sidelines in advertising, publishing, and franchised goods, which helped shape popular taste for nearly 40 years.

Disney rapidly expanded his studio facilities to include a training school where a whole new generation of animators developed and made possible the production of the first feature-length cartoon, *Snow White* (1937). Other costly animated features followed, including *Pinocchio, Bambi,* and the celebrated musical experiment *Fantasia.* With *Seal Island* (1948), wildlife films became an additional source of income, and in 1950 his use of blocked funds in England to make pictures like *Treasure Island* led to what became the studio's major product, live-action films, which practically cornered the traditional "family" market. Eventually the Disney formula emphasized slick production techniques. It included, as in his biggest hit, *Mary Poppins,* occasional animation to project wholesome, exciting stories heavily laced with sentiment and, often, music.

In 1954, Disney successfully invaded television, and by the time of his death, the Disney studio's output amounted to 21 full-length animated films, 493 short subjects, 47 live-action films, seven True-Life Adventure features, 330 hours of Mickey Mouse Club television programs, 78 half-hour *Zorro* television adventures, and 280 other television shows.

On July 18, 1957, Disney opened Disneyland, a gigantic projection of his personal fantasies in Anaheim, California, which has proved the most successful amusement park in history with 6.7 million people visiting it by 1966. The idea for the park came to him after taking his children to other amusement parks and watching them have fun on amusement rides. He decided to build a park where the entire family could have fun together. In 1971, Disney World, in Orlando, Florida, opened. Since then, Disney theme parks have opened in Tokyo and Paris.

Disney had also dreamed of developing a city of the future, a dream realized in 1982 with the opening of EPCOT, which stands for Experimental Prototype Community of Tomorrow. EPCOT, which cost an initial $900 million, was conceived of as a real-life community of the future with the very latest in high technology. The two principle areas of EPCOT are Future World and World Showcase, both of which were designed to appeal to adults rather than children.

In addition to his theme parks, Disney created and endowed a new university, the California Institute of the Arts, known as Cal Arts. He thought of this as the ultimate in education for the arts, where people in many different disciplines could work together, dream and develop, and create the mixture of arts needed for the future. Disney once commented: "It's the principle thing I hope to leave when I move on to greener pastures. If I can help provide a place to develop the talent of the future, I think I will have accomplished something."

Disney's parks continue to grow with the creation of the Disney-MGM Studios, Animal Kingdom, and a extensive sports complex in Orlando. The Disney Corporation has also branched out into other types of films with the creation of Touchstone Films, into music with Hollywood Records, and even vacationing with its Disney Cruise Lines. In all, the Disney name now lends itself to a multi-billion dollar enterprise, with multiple undertakings all over the world.

In 1939, Disney received an honorary Academy Award and in 1954 he received four Academy Awards. In 1965, President Lyndon B. Johnson presented Disney with the Presidential Medal of Freedom and in the same year Disney was awarded the Freedom Foundation Award.

Happily married for 41 years, this moody, deliberately "ordinary" man was moving ahead with his plans for gigantic new outdoor recreational facilities when he died of circulatory problems on December 15, 1966, at St. Joseph's Hospital in Los Angeles, California. At the time of his death, his enterprises had garnered him respect, admiration, and a business empire worth over $100 million-a-year, but Disney was still remembered primarily as the man who had created Mickey Mouse over two decades before.

EWB

Douglas, Mary (1921–), British anthropologist and social thinker. Mary Tew Douglas was born in San Remo, Italy, to Phyllis Twomey and Gilbert Charles Tew, and was the eldest of two daughters. She was educated as a Catholic at the Sacred Heart Convent, Roehampton, in England, and she was keenly interested in religion all her life. As an anthropologist she kept on with her faith. At Oxford (where she did a B.A. degree in 1943) she fell under the influence of the famous social anthropologist E. E. Evans-Pritchard, who was also interested in comparative religion; he died a Catholic. Douglas wrote a biography of her mentor in 1980.

She interrupted her graduate study at Oxford to be a volunteer in World War II in the British Colonial Office working on penal reform. Afterwards she earned a bachelor of science degree in 1948 in anthropology and went to Africa, to the Belgian Congo (now Republic of Congo), to study the folkways of a tribe, the Lele of the Kasai, for her Ph.D. under Professor Evans-Pritchard (1951). Also in 1951, Mary Tew married the economist James A. T. Douglas. They had one daughter and two sons. She lived in London and was associated with University College, London, from that time onwards (lecturer in anthropology, 1951–1962; reader, 1963–1970; professor, 1971 until her retirement in 1978). She was the 1994 Bernal prize recipient.

Subsequently she went to the United States. Douglas was in New York City at the Russell Sage Foundation as director of research on human culture from 1977 to 1981; in Chicago at Northwestern University in Evanston, Illinois, as Avalon Foundation professor in anthropology and religion, 1981–1985; and at Princeton University as visiting professor of religion and anthropology beginning in 1985. She maintained her residence in London.

Doctoral Dissertation.   Her doctoral dissertation, published as *The Lele of the Kasai* in 1963, studied the Lele tribe "as they cooked, divided food, talked about illness, babies and proper care of the body" and examined how taboos operated within tribal society and the way in which polygamous male elders of the tribe manipulated raffia cloth debts in order to restrict the access of younger men to Lele women. This field investigation led Douglas on to other studies in what she called "social accountability" and "classification schemes" of human relations, applied equally to "primitive" societies (pre-industrial, pre-modern) and to modern industrial society. She wrote books on a variety of subjects including pollution, the consumer society, and religion.

The anthropology of Douglas was derived partly from the work of the French sociologist Emile Durkheim (1858–1917). Douglas rejected his determinism, but accepted what Durkheim realized: the *social* basis for human thought. She used the Durkheimian method of drawing on "primitive" cultures to illuminate problems in modern society. For Douglas, rituals dramatize moral order in the human universe. "Culture" is rooted in daily social relations: the most

mundane and concrete things of daily life. From childhood on, the drama of life is constructed: the self concept; the linguistic code, which the individual learns as a child; the individual as a moral actor; the collective nature of human existence. Comparative studies have to be made of such things as dirt and pollution, food and meals, the biological body, speech, jokes, and material possessions. The biological body is a perfect metaphor or symbol for the social body or the tribe or nation.

Douglas' view of "culture" was of it being created afresh each day. Hers was a world of ordinary symbols, rituals, and activities, all of which dramatized the "construction of social life." Everyday life was *itself* the focus of interest. Every mundane activity carried ritual and ceremonial significance. Symbolic order reflected social order as she looked at the ritual dramatization of social patterns.

Pollution and Taboo.   Douglas was perhaps noted for her writings on pollution and taboo. Dirt in "primitive" (as in modern) society is relative to location: dirty shoes are dirty on the table, not dirty on the floor; cooking utensils are dirty in the bedroom; earth is dirty on chairs. Pollution *behavior* is the reaction of our cherished classifications: dirt takes us straight to the field of symbolism, to symbols of purity. In *Purity and Danger: An Analysis of Concepts of Pollution and Taboo* (1966) she stated that modern notions express basically the same idea as "primitive" notions of pollution: "Our practices are solidly based on hygiene; theirs are symbolic; we kill germs; they ward off spirits."

It was *Purity and Danger: An Analysis of Concepts of Pollution and Taboo* and *Natural Symbols* (1970), the two early books, that had such an impact on the emerging sociology of scientific knowledge.

Four related themes were presented in that early work. First, she invited attention to culture, to knowledge of nature, and specifically to cosmological and taxonomic notions, as embedded within systems of accountability. Culture is maintained and it is modified as people use it: it is a tool in everyday social action. There is no fundamental "problem" of "the relationship between culture and social action" because culture is the means by which social action is accomplished, by which members say "good" and "bad" about each other's actions, and by which they recognize them as actions of a certain sort. Second, knowledge, including natural knowledge, is treated as constitutively social. As we bring up our children, and as we talk to each other, so we build, maintain, and modify the categories of perception, thought, and language: "The colonisation of each other's minds is the price we pay for thought." For Douglas, anything but a fully general social epistemology followed from a misunderstanding of the sort of thing knowledge was.

Third, beliefs and representations become knowledge—a collective good—by successfully making the transition from the indivudal to the communal, the private to the public. The achievement of credibility is a practical problem attached to all beliefs: no belief or representation shines by its own lights, carries its crediblity with it. "Credibility," she says, "depends so much on the consensus of a moral community that it is hardly an exaggeration to say that a given community lays on for itself the sum of the physical conditions which it experiences."

Finally in the years between *Purity and Danger* and *Natural Symbols,* she developed a set of techniques for the systematic comparative study of "cultural bias." "The Great Divide" between the "modern" and the "scientific," on the one hand, and the "primitive" and "magical," on the other, was rejected. "We " are forms of "them." There is a finite range of predicaments faced and principles available for the maintenance of order. A specific form of these predicaments and principles might be as well devised by Sepik River tribes, by the Big Men of Conservative Party Central Office, or by a community of high-energy phsycists. Cultural diversity has finite forms, and, because these forms do not map onto exisiting Great Divide theories, the comparative study of cultural bias has the capacity to join up the conversations of those who study the "primitive" and those who study the "modern": anthropologists and students of modern science.

But when Douglas attempted to write about the contemporary environmental protection movement of the 1960s and 1970s in *Risk and Culture,* written with Aaron Wildavsky (1982), she was less sure of the material. Half the book is an attack on the beliefs of the environmentalists. She portrayed the antinuclear and environmental movements as freakish, quasireligious cults. She did not uncover anything about the actual physical environment, or nuclear plants, or offshore oil-drilling, or industrial pollution of rivers and lakes. Douglas was best when she was talking about the Lele and pollution and food taboos.

The World of Goods. *The World of Goods: An Anthropological Theory of Consumption,* written with Baron Isherwood (1979), is partly an attempt to explore the social context of modern consumer society. Goods are social markers and a means of communicating. Individuals attain and keep power in society by acts of consumption, which ritually reaffirm their status. The Douglas argument is very generalized and takes us not much further than the old (and much

more informative) notion of Thorstein Veblen of "conspicuous consumption" in his book *The Theory of the Leisure Class* (1899). Modern culture is supposedly a *secular* world, in which science replaces religion and ritual. Douglas as a scholar delved into comparative religion. She disagreed with the idea that religion and science could not coexist. There would be no demise of religion in the world, whatever science discovers, because religion originates in human social relations. Modernity changes the shape of society; but there are still human social relations and religion will survive. Douglas was of the opinion that so long as there is collective life, there will be religion, ritual, myths, ceremonies, and rites.

Modernity has three allegedly negative effects on the survival of religion: Douglas dismissed all three. Science is supposed to reduce the explanatory power of religion; for Douglas, religion and science pose no tension with each other—their explanations apply to different kinds of problems. Modern life is undergoing bureaucratization, and this reduces the sense of the unknown and sacred; but Douglas thought that bureaucracy existed in the Vatican in the 15th century, and so did religion. And modern life has little direct experience of nature; but Mary Douglas felt that the discoveries of modern science itself created a new sense of awe and religion. Thus, religion does not disappear in modern society, it just reappears in new forms.

Looking back on her life as a young anthropologist in Africa in *Implicit Meanings: Essays in Anthropology* (1976), she commented: "The central task of anthropology was to explore the effects of the social dimensions on behaviour. The task was grand, but the methods were humble . . . We had to stay with a remote tribe, patiently let events unfold and let people reveal the categories of their thought." From a fundamental Durkheimian belief in the role of ritual and symbol in the construction of social life and social relations, Douglas explained the rituals of meals and food, cleaning and tidying, material possessions, speech, and numerous other concrete things of daily life in modern as well as "primitive" society.

EWB

Dreyfus, Alfred (1859–1935), French army officer. Alfred Dreyfus was unjustly convicted of treason. The effort, eventually successful, to clear his name divided French society and had important political repercussions.

Alfred Dreyfus was born at Mulhouse on Oct. 9, 1859, into a Jewish textile-manufacturing family. After the Franco-Prussian War his family left Alsace in order to remain French citizens. Choosing a military career, Dreyfus entered the École Polytechnique in 1878. After further study, during which he attained the rank of captain in 1889, he was assigned as a trainee to the general staff. Dreyfus was a competent and hardworking, though not brilliant or popular, young officer. His ordeal was to prove that he was a man of great courage but limited vision: his whole life was devoted to the army, and he never lost confidence that it would recognize and remedy the wrong done him.

Arrest and Conviction. The Dreyfus case began in September 1894, when French Army Intelligence found among some papers taken from the office of the German military attaché in Paris, a list (bordereau) of secret documents given to the Germans by someone in the French army. A hasty and inadequate investigation convinced the anti-Semitic Intelligence chief, Col. Sandherr, that Dreyfus was the traitor. Apart from a certain resemblance between his handwriting and that of the bordereau, no very convincing evidence against Dreyfus could be discovered. He was arrested, however, on October 15.

Dreyfus's court-martial was held behind closed doors during December 19–21. A unanimous court found him guilty and imposed the highest legal penalty: perpetual imprisonment, loss of rank, and degradation. He was sent to the infamous Devil's Island, where he was to spend almost 5 years under the most inhumane conditions. Still protesting his innocence, Dreyfus was unaware that he had been convicted with the aid of a secret dossier prepared by Army Intelligence. Communication of the dossier to the judges without the knowledge of the defense violated due process and was the first of many actions that would bring discredit on the army and ruin the careers of the officers involved.

Convinced of his innocence, the Dreyfus family, led by his brother Mathieu, sought new evidence which would persuade the army to reopen its investigation. Aside from a few individuals such as the brilliant young writer Bernard Lazare and the respected Alsatian life-senator Scheurer-Kestner, they found few supporters, and their efforts stirred the anti-Semitic press to raise the bogey of a "Jewish syndicate" trying to corrupt the army.

Fortune came to Dreyfus's aid for the first time in July 1895, when the new Intelligence chief, Lt. Col. Marie Georges Picquart, became convinced of Dreyfus's innocence and discovered a Maj. Walsin-Esterhazy to be the real author of the bordereau. Although Picquart was unable to convince his superiors to reexamine the verdict, he remained determined to help free Dreyfus.

Still unable to persuade the government to act, the supporters of Dreyfus—the Dreyfusards—now took their case to the public, charging Esterhazy with the crime for which Dreyfus was being punished. The anti-Semitic press counterattacked, and the Dreyfus case began to turn into the Dreyfus Affair, as public passions were raised against the few who dared to challenge the verdict of the court-martial. Supported by friends within the command, Esterhazy demanded a court-martial to prove his innocence; he received a triumphant acquittal in January 1898. The evidence against Esterhazy was little better than that which had convicted Dreyfus, but his acquittal dashed the hopes of the Dreyfusards, who had expected his conviction to prove Dreyfus innocent.

Retrial and Exoneration. The controversial novelist Émile Zola, however, found a way to reopen the case: he charged in an open letter to the President of the Republic entitled *J'accuse* that the military court had acquitted Esterhazy although they knew him to be guilty. Zola hoped to bring the facts of Dreyfus's case before a civil court, where it would be more difficult for the army to conceal what had happened; he was only partially successful, but increased public concern and violence in the streets forced the authorities to take further action.

The minister of war, Godefroy Cavaignac, aiming to quiet criticism, publicly revealed much of the evidence against Dreyfus. But the Dreyfusards, headed by socialist leader Jean Jaurès, charged that forgery was obvious. Cavaignac's further investigation led to the confession and suicide (Aug. 31, 1898) of an Intelligence officer, Lt. Col. Joseph Henry, who had been manufacturing evidence to strengthen the case against Dreyfus. This was the turning point of the Affair. The government brought the case before the highest appeals court, which declared (June 3, 1899) Dreyfus entitled to a new trial.

Dreyfus was brought back to France to face a new court-martial at Rennes in September 1899. It returned, by a vote of 5 to 2, the incredible verdict of guilty with extenuating circumstances and sentenced him to 10 years' imprisonment. The honor of the army had been made such an issue by the anti-Dreyfusards that no military court could ever find him innocent. No one believed in the honor of the army more than Dreyfus, and only with difficulty could he be persuaded to accept the pardon offered by President Émile Loubet.

Dreyfus continued to seek exoneration, and his record was finally cleared by the civil courts in July 1906. He was returned to service, promoted, and decorated, but he soon retired. Returning to active duty during World War I, he then spent his retirement in complete obscurity, and his death on July 11, 1935, passed almost unnoticed.

Political Consequences. Dreyfus understood little of the battle that raged in his name. The question of his innocence became a secondary matter beside the public issue of individual human rights versus the demands of state policy. Political issues also played a part in the Affair: to many conservatives the army and the Church seemed the last bulwarks of social stability; both would be undermined by the victory of the Dreyfusards. On the left many welcomed the opportunity to strike at the monarchist and clerical forces, which they saw as enemies of the Republic. Last but not least was the question of anti-Semitism. The Affair saw the first outpouring of modern political anti-Semitism, which proved a harbinger of the Nazi terror.

The immediate political consequence of the Affair was to bring the Radicals to power; they made the Church the scapegoat for the sins of the anti-Dreyfusards, taking a number of anticlerical measures culminating in the separation of Church and state in 1905. The passions exposed by the Affair were submerged in World War I but reappeared in the defeat of 1940 and under the Vichy regime.

EWB

Dubcek, Alexander (1921–1992), Czechoslovakian politician. Alexander Dubcek served briefly as head of his country's Communist party. His attempts to liberalize political life led to the occupation of Czechoslovakia by the Soviet army and his dismissal from office, only to be vindicated years later when the Communist regime fell.

Alexander Dubcek was born on Nov. 27, 1921, the son of a cabinetmaker who had just returned from the United States. His family lived in the U.S.S.R. from 1925 to 1938, and it was there that he received his education. During World War II he was an active member of the underground resistance to the Germans in Slovakia.

After the war Dubcek made his career as a functionary of the Communist party. He was elected to the Presidium of the Slovakian and then of the Czechoslovakian Communist party in 1962, and in the following year he became first secretary of the Slovakian party's Central Committee. Yet when he succeeded Antonin Novotny in January 1968 as first secretary of the Czechoslovakian Communist party, he was not well known in his own country and was hardly known at all outside it.

Pressure for the relaxation of the rigid dogma prevailing in political life had been mounting in Czechoslovakia for a considerable time and had been strengthened by economic discontent. Dubcek became the personification of this movement and promised to introduce "socialism with a human face." After coming to power, censorship was relaxed and plans were made for a new federal constitution, for new legislation to provide for a greater degree of civil liberty, and for a new electoral law to give greater freedom to non-Communist parties.

The Soviet government became increasingly alarmed by these developments and throughout the spring and summer of 1968 issued a series of warnings to Dubcek and his colleagues. Dubcek had attempted to steer a middle course between liberal and conservative extremes, and at a midsummer confrontation with the Soviet leaders he stood firm against their demands for a reversal of his policies.

It was thought that Dubcek had won his point on this occasion, but on August 20 armies of the U.S.S.R. and the other Warsaw Pact countries occupied Czechoslovakia. Some historians believe that the immediate cause of the Soviet invasion was the Action Program, initiated by Dubcek the previous year. Mass demonstrations of support for Dubcek kept him in power for the time being, but his liberal political program was abandoned.

Over the next 2 years Dubcek was gradually removed from power. In April 1969 he resigned as first secretary of the party, to be replaced by the orthodox Dr. Gustav Husak. That September he was dismissed from the Presidium, and in January 1970 from the Central Committee. In December 1969 he was sent to Turkey as ambassador. The final blow came on June 27, 1970, when he was expelled from the Communist party, and shortly afterward he was dismissed from his ambassadorial post. From there he was confined for almost twenty years to a forestry camp in Bratislava, with little contact with the outside world and constant and intense supervision by the secret police.

Meanwhile, the attitudes that Dubcek had set in motion continued under their own power. A small underground movement known as Charter 77, named after its inaugural declaration on January 1, 1977, grew to 2,000 members over the next twelve years. Influenced by the movement in neighboring Poland for greater openness and human rights, Charter 77 was created by a broad spectrum of leaders, including former Communists and religious activists. They were constantly hounded and persecuted by the Communist government, but did not relent. Police arrested ten of the group's leaders, including Vaclav Havel and Jiri Dienstbier, who became, respectively, President and Foreign Minister of the new Czechoslovak government in 1989. Charter 77 continued until 1995, when it became apparent it had fulfilled its function.

Dubcek highly approved of Russian prime minister Mikhail Gorbachev's progressive policy of *glasnost*, and eventually its successor of *perestroika*. While he noted there were some fundamental differences, he believed it came from the same ethic he had tried to promote in the Prague Spring. After Gorbachev visited Czechoslovakia in 1987, the secret police started leaving Dubcek alone.

On November 17, 1989, a student commemoration of a Nazi atrocity in 1939 was brutally assaulted by riot police with little provocation. The factionalized oppositions to the government became united to a single purpose by the event, and formed the Civic Forum, led by Havel. He obtained video of the riot, interviewed victims, and had thousands of copies distributed across the country that were surreptitiously played on available televisions. The people became inflamed, and larger and larger demonstrating crowds filled Wenceslas Square. This rapid yet peaceful movement came to be known as the Velvet Revolution. Just a week after the riot, Havel and Dubcek appeared together to the throng, who in one voice demanded the latter's restoration.

At first, Havel, the playwright, insisted on standing in the shadow of Dubcek; by the time of the federal elections in 1990, it had been decided that Dubcek would become chairman of the federal parliament. Dubcek then proposed Havel for the presidency, which was accepted unanimously.

In his last years, Dubcek aligned himself with the ideas of European Social Democracy and especially with German chancellor Willy Brandt. In 1992, Dubcek became leader of the Social Democratic party in Slovakia. By that time he was already sick, having worked virtually around the clock for over two years as chairman of the Czechoslovak assembly. A huge shock, one he did not get over, was the death of his wife, Anna, in September 1991. A year later, Dubcek was in a car accident, and barely escaped immediate death. Physicians diagnosed him with with a broken spine, as well as other serious illnesses. He passed away on November 1, 1992. Shortly thereafter, Czechoslovakia peacefully separated into the Czech Republic and Slovakia, an event known as the Velvet Divorce.

EWB

Duby, Georges (1919–), French scholar and author. Georges Durby has gained renown both as a medieval scholar and author. Duby's research led him to write several books on the middle ages. Notable among these was *Le Temps des cathedrales: L'Art et la societe, 980–1420.*

Translated in 1981 as *The Age of the Cathedrals: Art and Society, 980–1420*, the work had also served as the basis for the series of television films Duby produced for Antenne 2 in Paris in 1980. A comprehensive study of the early Gothic cathedrals of France, *The Age of the Cathedrals* discusses the various building plans of the churches and explains the social and religious milieu that gave rise to their construction.

Other works by Duby include *The Knight, the Lady and the Priest: The Making of Modern Marriage in Medieval France*, which traces the evolution of marriage and societal attitudes toward it through an examination of medieval romance literature, religious drama, and early church records, and *William Marshal: The Flower of Chivalry*, in which Duby examines a manuscript from the thirteenth century which contains a long poem by a French trouvere about the life of Guillaume Marechal, a knight-errant who rose to greatness and wealth in the service of kings before his death in 1219. Duby continued to write books on medieval subjects in coming years, and in 1986 he collaborated with several scholars to produce *Historie de la vie privee*. The work comprises an anticipated five volumes, the first three of which were directed by Duby and the late Philippe Aries.

CA

Durkheim, Émile (1858–1917), French philosopher and sociologist. Émile Durkheim was one of the founders of 20th-century sociology.

Émile Durkheim was born at Épinal, Lorraine, on April 15, 1858. Following a long family tradition, he began as a young man to prepare himself for the rabbinate. While still in secondary school, however, he discovered his vocation for teaching and left Épinal for Paris to prepare for the École Normale, which he entered in 1879. Although Durkheim found the literary nature of instruction there a great disappointment, he was lastingly inspired by two of his teachers: the classicist Numa Denis Fustel de Coulanges and the philosopher Émile Boutroux. From Fustel he learned the importance of religion in the formation of social institutions and discovered that the sacred could be studied rationally and objectively. From Boutroux he learned that atomism, the reduction of phenomena to their smallest constituent parts, was a fallacious methodological procedure and that each science must explain phenomena in terms of its own specific principles. These ideas eventually formed the philosophical foundations of Durkheim's sociological method.

From 1882 to 1885 Durkheim taught philosophy in several provincial lycées. A leave of absence in 1885–1886 allowed him to study under the psychologist Wilhelm Wundt in Germany. In 1887 he was named lecturer in education and sociology at the University of Bordeaux, a position raised to a professorship in 1896, the first professorship of sociology in France.

On his return from Germany, Durkheim had begun to prepare review articles for the *Revue philosophique* on current work in sociology. In 1896, realizing that the task was too much for a single person to do adequately, he founded the *Année sociologique*. His purpose, he announced, was to bring the social sciences together, to promote specialization within the field of sociology, and to make evident that sociology was a collective, not a personal, enterprise. In 1902 Durkheim was named to a professorship in sociology and education at the Sorbonne. There he remained for the rest of his career.

Achieving Consensus. *The Division of Labor*, Durkheim's doctoral thesis, appeared in 1893. The theme of the book was how individuals achieve the prerequisite of all social existence: consensus. Durkheim began by distinguishing two types of "solidarities," mechanical and organic. In the first, individuals differ little from each other; they harbor the same emotions, hold the same values, and believe the same religion. Society draws its coherence from this similarity. In the second, coherence is achieved by differentiation. Free individuals pursuing different functions are united by their complementary roles. For Durkheim these were both conceptual and historical distinctions. Primitive societies and European society in earlier periods were mechanical solidarities; modern European society was organic. In analyzing the nature of contractual relationships, however, Durkheim came to realize that organic solidarity could be maintained only if certain aspects of mechanical solidarity remained, only if the members of society held certain beliefs and sentiments in common. Without such collective beliefs, he argued, no contractual relationship based purely on self-interest could have any force.

Collective Beliefs. At the end of the 19th century, social theory was dominated by methodological individualism, the belief that all social phenomena should be reduced to individual psychological or biological phenomena in order to be explained. Durkheim therefore had to explain and justify his emphasis on collective beliefs, on "collective consciousness" and "collective representations." This he did theoretically in *The Rules of Sociological Method* (1895) and empirically in *Suicide* (1897). In the first, he argued that the social environment was a reality and therefore an object of study in its own right. "Sociological method," he wrote, "rests wholly on the basic principle that social facts must be studied as things; that is, as realities external to the individual." The central methodological problem was therefore the nature of these realities and their relationship to the individuals who compose society.

In *Suicide* Durkheim demonstrated his sociological method by applying it to a phenomenon that appeared quintessentially individual. How does society cause individuals to commit suicide? To answer this question, he analyzed statistical data on suicide rates, comparing them to religious beliefs, age, sex, marital status, and economic changes, and then sought to explain the systematic differences he had discovered. The suicide rate, he argued, depends upon the social context. More frequently than others, those who are ill-integrated into social groups and those whose individuality has disappeared in the social group will kill themselves. Likewise, when social values break down, when men find themselves without norms, in a state of "anomie" as Durkheim called it, suicide increases.

From what source do collective beliefs draw their force? In *The Elementary Forms of Religious Life* (1912) Durkheim argued that the binding character of the social bond, indeed the very categories of the human mind, are to be found in religion. Behind religion, however, is society itself, for religion is communal participation, and its authority is the authority of society intensified by being endowed with sacredness. It is the transcendent image of the collective consciousness.

During his lifetime Durkheim was severely criticized for claiming that social facts were irreducible, that they had a reality of their own. His ideas, however, are now accepted as the common foundations for empirical work in sociology. His concept of the collective consciousness, renamed "culture," has become part of the theoretical foundations of modern ethnography. His voice was one of the most powerful in breaking the hold of Enlightenment ideas of individualism on modern social sciences.

Durkheim died in Paris on Nov. 15, 1917.

EWB

E

Eichmann, Adolf (1906–1962), German Nazi leader. Adolf Eichmann was responsible for the persecution and murder of millions of Jews in the death camps in Europe during World War II.

On May 13, 1960, Adolf Eichmann was seized by Israeli agents in Argentina and smuggled back to

Jerusalem to stand trial for his role in the murder of one-third of Europe's Jewish people during World War II. The Eichmann trial of April through August 1961 gained world wide attention as the most important trial of Nazi criminality since the Nuremberg trial of 1945–1946. For the first time a Jewish court convened in judgment upon a former persecutor. Eichmann was that SS (Schutzstaffel) officer responsible for transporting Jews and other victims to the extermination camps. What motivated him? The trial testimony showed him to be the ultimate conformist in a criminal state. As he said to an interrogator, "If they told me that my own father was a traitor and I had to kill him, I'd have done it. At that time I obeyed my orders without thinking, I just did as I was told. That's where I found my how shall I say? my fulfillment. It made no difference what the orders were."

Karl Adolf Eichmann was born into a religious middle-class Protestant family in Solingen in western Germany near the Rhine river on March 19, 1906. His father, an accountant for an electrical company, moved his family to Linz, Austria, in 1914. Eichmann's mother died when he was ten. Unlike his three brothers and one sister he was a poor student. Because of his dark looks he was apparently chided as "the little Jew." In Linz Eichmann went to the same secondary school Hitler had attended some 15 years before.

The resentment in Germany and Austria after defeat in World War I twisted an already inflamed nationalism, fed a lie that Germany had been "stabbed in the back" by the Jews. In 1919, amidst this new wave of anti-Semitism, the 13-year-old Eichmann was named in a newspaper as a member of a gang of youths who had tormented a Jewish classmate. Eichmann kept a precise record of each gang member's turn in beating up the victim (who died 20 years later in a death camp).

In the 1920s Eichmann drifted. He studied electrical engineering without success until his father decided that he should become an apprentice in an electrical appliance company, but his father wasn't satisfied with his son's progress there either. In 1928 Eichmann became a traveling salesman for an oil company through the help of Jewish relatives of his stepmother. He enjoyed his independence and his sporty car and became a joiner. As a member of the youth section of the Austro-German Veterans' Organization, he marched through the streets of Linz challenging the social democrats and cheering German nationalism. In 1932 the fanatical young Ernst Kaltenbrunner recruited Eichmann for the Austrian Nazi party and the SS. The Nazis promised that Austria would become part of a powerful German nation-state, and

being a member of the SS gave Eichmann the chance to act superior after years of feeling inferior. Kaltenbrunner's father and Eichmann's father had been friends; their sons would make careers together in the SS. Kaltenbrunner became chief of the Security Service of the SS, second to Heinrich Himmler (and was hung as a war criminal in 1946).

When the Austrian government banned the Nazi Party in 1933, Eichmann, who did not have a job at the time, moved to Nazi Germany and joined the SS "Austrian Legion in exile." After a year he transferred to the Security Service where he found a niche for himself as an "expert" on Jewish affairs. He learned about Zionism and even briefly visited Palestine. When Austria was annexed by the Third Reich in 1938 Eichmann efficiently organized the expulsion of 45,000 Austrian Jews, first stripping them of their possessions. He became known in SS circles as the expert on forced emigration. When Germany invaded Poland, Hitler decided to exterminate the Polish Jews, and Eichmann's organizing ability turned towards mass murder. In the summer of 1941 he was among the first to be told of the "Final Solution," and on January 20, 1942, he was one of 15 who attended the Wannsee Conference where the formal pact was drawn between the political leadership and the bureaucracy to send European Jewry to the death camps. Jews were forced to wear the yellow star of David for easy identification; they were assembled for easy transport to their doom. Eichmann's principal concern was to maintain the killing capacity of the camps by maintaining a steady flow of victims. All the principles of civilization were turned on their head. First into the gas chambers were children, mothers, and the old. About 25 percent of each train load, the strongest men and women, were spared for slave labor. Very many died of starvation, sickness, and overwork. In 1944 Eichmann reported to Himmler that some four million Jews were killed in the camps and some two million more had been shot or killed by mobile units.

Eichmann was a bureaucratic mass murderer; he avoided the extermination sites and shielded himself from his acts through a bureaucratic language that deadened his conscience. Eichmann was limited, compartmentalized in mind and spirit. "Officialese is my only language," he said at his trial. Eichmann exemplified the terrifying discrepancy between the unparalleled and monstrous crime and the colorless official who carried out the evil. He viewed his victims as objects to be transported to their deaths as if they were nuts and bolts, and in 1944 he unsuccessfully sought to trade the lives of one million Jews for 10,000 trucks.

At the end of the war Eichmann was rounded up, but he managed to disguise his identity and escaped detection. ODESSA, the secret SS organization, arranged his flight to Argentina in 1952. Under the alias of Ricardo Klement, Eichmann created a new identity as the unassuming employee of the Mercedes-Benz car factory in Buenos Aires. His wife and two sons joined him.

On December 15, 1961, the Israeli court sentenced Eichmann to hang. His last words on June 1, 1962, were that he would not forget Austria, Germany, and Argentina. He was 56; his corpse was cremated, and his ashes scattered over the sea. Eichmann's inhuman acts in the name of Germany seemingly confirmed one 19th-century Austrian's fear that Europe was moving from humanity through nationality to beastiality.

EWB

Elias, Norbert (1897–1990), German sociologist. Born in Breslau (now Wroclaw, Poland), Norbert Elias was the only child of Hermannn and Sophie Elias. His father was a small clothes manufacturer, who devoted his life to his family and business. His Jewish family lived in a spacious apartment, with a cook and a nanny. Though Elias himself escaped Hitler's Germany in 1933, his parents remained, with disastrous consequences: his mother died at Auschwitz in 1941. His failure to convince his parents to escape, and his mother's horrible death, left him devastated.

After World War I, Elias studied medicine and philosophy at the University of Breslau. He earned his doctorate in philosophy in 1924, after opting out of medicine, under Richard Honigswald (1875–1947), one of the great neo-Kantian philosophers in early 20th century. In 1925 Elias moved to Heidelberg to study sociology under Karl Mannheim (1893–1947), earning his habilitation in 1933, which was published thirty years later as *The Court Society.* Escaping Germany in 1933, Elias sought employment as a professor first in Switzerland then in France, without much luck in either country. Finally, he moved to London in 1935.

Receiving financial help from a committee who assisted Jewish refugees from Germany, Elias found the reading room of the British Museum an ideal place for his research. It was during his early years in London when Elias began writing what eventually became his most famous book, *The Civilizing Process,* which was published in 1939 in German as *Uber den Prozess der Zivilisation.* Publishing a book written by a Jew in German during that time, however, was problematic. Nonetheless, it was well received by a few prominent German and Dutch sociologists. But it did

not reach its fame until many years later when it was translated to several languages, with the English version being published in 1978.

In *The Civilizing Process,* Elias argued that what Westerners today perceive as Western civilization, with emphasis on "civilized" personal manners, was a result of a long historical process, where the movement away from barbarity to civilization could be traced through examining books on manners. The internalization of this civility by the Western individual, Elias argued, demonstrated his basic theory that the individual was not a static, self-contained unit, but a process, effected by society at large, that begins with birth and ends with death.

In 1954, at age 57, Elias was finally offered a position at Leicester University in England. With his colleague Ilya Neustadt, Elias established the Department of Sociology at Leicester, which eventually became the largest and most respected in England. Elias retired in 1962 and spent the next two years in Ghana, teaching sociology to African students.

About 1968, when student protests were staged in many European universities, sociologists were looking for a different approach to sociology from the dominant American one, with its emphasis on statistics and empirical analysis. Elias's book, *The Civilizing Process,* offered that new approach, by its redefinition of the individual in relation to society. Overnight thousands of copies were pirated by students, who could not afford the hardback version. The international recognition of Elias catapulted him into the limelight and made him an intellectual celebrity, with television interviews and lectures to eager students at various universities.

Elias lived mostly in Holland after 1979. His theories found fertile ground among Dutch sociologists, such as Cas Wouters, who built upon Elias's theory about the civilization process to question whether the permissive society was a trend in de-civilization. In 1988 the Dutch government awarded Elias the insignia of the Commander of the Order of Orange-Nassau in the name of Queen Beatrix of Holland.

Recognizing his intellectual achievements and its debt to him for Hitler's crimes against him and his people, the German Federal Republic conferred on Elias many awards and pensions, crowned in 1986 by its highest decoration, the *Grosskreuz der Bundesdienstordens.*

Though Norbert Elias may not have answered all the questions that he had raised, his positive contribution to sociology is beyond question. Some very basic sociological assumptions had to be reassessed as a result of his new theories. The redefinition of the individual as a social process, which cannot be understood outside of its social context, has profound implications not only for the study of sociology, but also for history and politics. His research and resulting theories on sports, community relations, violence, and civilization help us understand our past and prepare for the future.

Mohammed Arkawi

Elizabeth I (1533–1603), queen of England and Ireland from 1558 to 1603. Elizabeth I preserved stability in a nation rent by political and religious dissension and maintained the authority of the Crown against the growing pressures of Parliament.

Born at Greenwich, on Sept. 7, 1533, Elizabeth I was the daughter of Henry VIII and his second wife, Anne Boleyn. Because of her father's continuing search for a male heir, Elizabeth's early life was precarious. In May 1536 her mother was beheaded to clear the way for Henry's third marriage, and on July 1 Parliament declared that Elizabeth and her older sister, Mary, the daughter of Henry's first queen, were illegitimate and that the succession should pass to the issue of his third wife, Jane Seymour. Jane did produce a male heir, Edward, but even though Elizabeth had been declared illegitimate, she was brought up in the royal household. She received an excellent education and was reputed to be remarkably precocious, notably in languages (of which she learned Latin, French, and Italian) and music.

Edward VI and Mary. During the short reign of her brother, Edward VI, Elizabeth survived precariously, especially in 1549 when the principal persons in her household were arrested and she was to all practical purposes a prisoner at Hatfield. In this period she experienced ill health but pursued her studies under her tutor, Roger Ascham.

In 1553, following the death of Edward VI, her sister Mary I came to the throne with the intention of leading the country back to Catholicism. The young Elizabeth found herself involved in the complicated intrigue that accompanied these changes. Without her knowledge the Protestant Sir Thomas Wyatt plotted to put her on the throne by overthrowing Mary. The rebellion failed, and though Elizabeth maintained her innocence, she was sent to the Tower. After 2 months she was released against the wishes of Mary's advisers and was removed to an old royal palace at Woodstock. In 1555 she was brought to Hampton Court, still in custody, but on October 18 was allowed to take up residence at Hatfield, where she resumed her studies with Ascham.

On Nov. 17, 1558, Mary died, and Elizabeth succeeded to the throne. Elizabeth's reign was to be looked back on as a golden age, when England began to assert itself internationally through the mastery of sea power. The condition of the country seemed far different, however, when she came to the throne. A contemporary noted: "The Queen poor. The realm exhausted. The nobility poor and decayed. Want of good captains and soldiers. The people out of order. Justice not executed." Both internationally and internally, the condition of the country was far from stable.

At the age of 25 Elizabeth was a rather tall and well-poised woman; what she lacked in feminine warmth, she made up for in the worldly wisdom she had gained from a difficult and unhappy youth. It is significant that one of her first actions as queen was to appoint Sir William Cecil (later Lord Burghley) as her chief secretary. Cecil was to remain her closest adviser; like Elizabeth, he was a political pragmatist, cautious and essentially conservative. They both appreciated England's limited position in the face of France and Spain, and both knew that the key to England's success lay in balancing the two great Continental powers off against each other, so that neither could bring its full force to bear against England.

The Succession. Since Elizabeth was unmarried, the question of the succession and the actions of other claimants to the throne bulked large. She toyed with a large number of suitors, including Philip II of Spain; Eric of Sweden; Adolphus, Duke of Holstein; and the Archduke Charles. From her first Parliament she received a petition concerning her marriage. Her answer was, in effect, her final one: "this shall be for me sufficient, that a marble stone shall declare that a Queen, having reigned such a time died a virgin." But it would be many years before the search for a suitable husband ended, and the Parliament reconciled itself to the fact that the Queen would not marry.

Elizabeth maintained what many thought were dangerously close relations with her favorite, Robert Dudley, whom she raised to the earldom of Leicester. She abandoned this flirtation when scandal arising from the mysterious death of Dudley's wife in 1560 made the connection politically disadvantageous. In the late 1570s and early 1580s she was courted in turn by the French Duke of Anjou and the Duke of Alençon. But by the mid-1580s it was clear she would not marry.

Many have praised Elizabeth for her skillful handling of the courtships. To be sure, her hand was perhaps her greatest diplomatic weapon, and any one of the proposed marriages, if carried out, would have had strong repercussions on English foreign relations.

By refusing to marry, Elizabeth could further her general policy of balancing the Continental powers. Against this must be set the realization that it was a very dangerous policy. Had Elizabeth succumbed to illness, as she nearly did early in her reign, or had any one of the many assassination plots against her succeeded, the country would have been plunged into the chaos of a disputed succession. That the accession of James I on her death was peaceful was due as much to the luck of her survival as it was to the wisdom of her policy.

Religious Settlement. England had experienced both a sharp swing to Protestantism under Edward VI and a Catholic reaction under Mary. The question of the nature of the Church needed to be settled immediately, and it was hammered out in Elizabeth's first Parliament in 1559. A retention of Catholicism was not politically feasible, as the events of Mary's reign showed, but the settlement achieved in 1559 represented something more of a Puritan victory than the Queen desired. The settlement enshrined in the Acts of Supremacy and Conformity may in the long run have worked out as a compromise, but in 1559 it indicated to Elizabeth that her control of Parliament was not complete.

Though the settlement achieved in 1559 remained essentially unchanged throughout Elizabeth's reign, the conflict over religion was not stilled. The Church of England, of which Elizabeth stood as supreme governor, was attacked by both Catholics and Puritans. Estimates of Catholic strength in Elizabethan England are difficult to make, but it is clear that a number of Englishmen remained at least residual Catholics. Because of the danger of a Catholic rising against the Crown on behalf of the rival claimant, Mary, Queen of Scots, who was in custody in England from 1568 until her execution in 1587, Parliament pressed the Queen repeatedly for harsher legislation to control the recusants. It is apparent that the Queen resisted, on the whole successfully, these pressures for political repression of the English Catholics. While the legislation against the Catholics did become progressively sterner, the Queen was able to mitigate the severity of its enforcement and retain the patriotic loyalty of many Englishmen who were Catholic in sympathy.

For their part the Puritans waged a long battle in the Church, in Parliament, and in the country at large to make the religious settlement more radical. Under the influence of leaders like Thomas Cartwright and John Field, and supported in Parliament by the brothers Paul and Peter Wentworth, the Puritans subjected the Elizabethan religious settlement to great stress.

The Queen found that she could control Parliament through the agency of her privy councilors and the force of her own personality. It was, however, some time before she could control the Church and the countryside as effectively. It was only with the promotion of John Whitgift to the archbishopric of Canterbury that she found her most effective clerical weapon against the Puritans. With apparent royal support but some criticism from Burghley, Whitgift was able to use the machinery of the Church courts to curb the Puritans. By the 1590s the Puritan movement was in some considerable disarray. Many of its prominent patrons were dead, and by the publication of the bitterly satirical *Marprelate Tracts,* some Puritan leaders brought the movement into general disfavor.

Foreign Relations. At Elizabeth's accession England was not strong enough, either in men or money, to oppose vigorously either of the Continental powers, France or Spain. England was, however, at war with France. Elizabeth quickly brought this conflict to a close on more favorable terms than might have been expected.

Throughout the early years of the reign, France appeared to be the chief foreign threat to England because of the French connections of Mary, Queen of Scots. By the Treaty of Edinburgh in 1560, Elizabeth was able to close off a good part of the French threat as posed through Scotland. The internal religious disorders of France also aided the English cause. Equally crucial was the fact that Philip II of Spain was not anxious to further the Catholic cause in England so long as its chief beneficiary would be Mary, Queen of Scots, and through her, his own French rivals.

In the 1580s Spain emerged as the chief threat to England. The years from 1570 to 1585 were ones of neither war nor peace, but Elizabeth found herself under increasing pressure from Protestant activists to take a firmer line against Catholic Spain. Increasingly she connived in privateering voyages against Spanish shipping; her decision in 1585 to intervene on behalf of the Netherlands in its revolt against Spain by sending an expeditionary force under the Earl of Leicester meant the temporary end of the Queen's policy of balance and peace.

The struggle against Spain culminated in the defeat of the Spanish Armada in 1588. The Queen showed a considerable ability to rally the people around herself. At Tilbury, where the English army massed in preparation for the threatened invasion, the Queen herself appeared to deliver one of her most stirring speeches: "I am come amongst you . . . resolved in the midst and heat of battle, to live and die amongst you all. . . . I know I have the body but of a weak and feeble woman, but I have the heart and stomach of a king and of a King of England too."

That the Armada was dispersed owed as much to luck and Spanish incapacity as it did to English skill. In some ways it marked the high point of Elizabeth's reign, for the years which followed have properly been called "the darker years." The Spanish threat did not immediately subside, and English counteroffensives proved ineffectual because of poor leadership and insufficient funds. Under the strain of war expenditure, the country suffered in the 1590s prolonged economic crisis. Moreover, the atmosphere of the court seemed to decline in the closing stages of the reign; evident corruption and sordid struggling for patronage became more common.

Difficulties in Ireland. The latter years of Elizabeth's reign were marked by increasing difficulties in Ireland. The English had never effectively controlled Ireland, and under Elizabeth the situation became acute. Given Ireland's position on England's flank and its potential use by the Spanish, it seemed essential for England to control the island. It was no easy task; four major rebellions (the rebellion of Shane O'Neill, 1559–1566; the Fitzmaurice confederacy, 1569–1572; the Desmond rebellion, 1579–1583; and Tyrone's rebellion, 1594–1603) tell the story of Ireland in this period. Fortunately, the Spaniards were slow to take advantage of Tyrone's rebellion. The 2d Earl of Essex was incapable of coping with this revolt and returned to England to lead a futile rebellion against the Queen (1601). But Lord Mountjoy, one of the few great Elizabethan land commanders, was able to break the back of the rising and bring peace in the same month in which the Queen died (March 1603).

Internal Decline. The latter years of Elizabeth also saw tensions emerge in domestic politics. The long-term dominance of the house of Cecil, perpetuated after Burghley's death by his son, Sir Robert Cecil, was strongly contested by others, like the Earl of Essex, who sought the Queen's patronage. The Parliament of 1601 saw Elizabeth involved in a considerable fight over the granting of monopolies. Elizabeth was able to head off the conflict by promising that she herself would institute reforms. Her famous "Golden Speech" delivered to this, her last Parliament, indicated that even in old age she had the power to win her people to her side: "Though God hath raised me high, yet this I count the glory of my crown, that I have reigned with your loves. . . . It is my desire to

live nor reign no longer than my life and reign shall be for your good. And though you have had, and may have, many princes more mighty and wise sitting in this seat, yet you never had, nor shall have, any that will be more careful and loving."

The words concealed the reality of the end of Elizabeth's reign. It is apparent, on retrospect, that severe tensions existed. The finances of the Crown, exhausted by war since the 1580s, were in sorry condition; the economic plight of the country was not much better. The Parliament was already sensing its power to contest issues with the monarchy, though they now held back, perhaps out of respect for their elderly queen. Religious tensions were hidden rather than removed. For all the greatness of her reign, the reign that witnessed the naval feats of Sir Francis Drake and Sir John Hawkins and the literary accomplishments of Sir Philip Sidney, Edmund Spenser, William Shakespeare, and Christopher Marlowe, it was a shaky inheritance that Elizabeth would pass on to her successor, the son of her rival claimant, Mary, Queen of Scots. On March 24, 1603, the Queen died; as one contemporary noted, she "departed this life, mildly like a lamb, easily like a ripe apple from the tree."

EWB

Engels, Friedrich (1820–1895), German revolutionist and social theorist. Friedrich Engels was the cofounder with Karl Marx of modern socialism.

Friedrich Engels was born on Nov. 28, 1820, in Barmen, Rhenish Prussia, a small industrial town in the Wupper valley. He was the oldest of the six children of Friedrich and Elisabeth Franziska Mauritia Engels. The senior Engels, a textile manufacturer, was a Christian Pietist and religious fanatic. After attending elementary school at Barmen, young Friedrich entered the gymnasium in nearby Elberfeld at the age of 14, but he left it 3 years later. Although he became one of the most learned men of his time, he had no further formal schooling.

Under pressure from his tyrannical father, Friedrich became a business apprentice in Barmen and Barmen, but he soon called it a "dog's life." He left business at the age of 20, in rebellion against both his joyless home and the "penny-pinching" world of commerce. Henceforth, Engels was a lifelong enemy of organized religion and of capitalism, although he was again forced into business for a number of years.

While doing his one-year compulsory military service (artillery) in Berlin, Engels came into contact with the radical Young Hegelians and embraced their ideas, particularly the materialist philosophy of Ludwig Feuerbach. After some free-lance journalism, part of it under the pseudonym of F. Oswald, in November 1842 Engels went to Manchester, England, to work in the office of Engels and Ermens, a spinning factory in which his father was a partner. In Manchester, the manufacturing center of the world's foremost capitalist country, Engels had the opportunity of observing capitalism's operations, and its distressing effects on the workers, at first hand. He also studied the leading economic writers, among them Adam Smith, David Ricardo, and Robert Owen in English, and Jean Baptiste Say, Charles Fourier, and Pierre Joseph Proudhon in French. He left Manchester in August 1844.

On his way back to Germany, Engels stopped in Paris, where he met Karl Marx for a second time. On this occasion a lifelong intellectual rapport was established between them. Finding they were of the same opinion about nearly everything, Marx and Engels decided to collaborate on their writing.

Engels spent the next 5 years in Germany, Belgium, and France, writing and participating in revolutionary activities. He fought in the 1849 revolutionary uprising in Baden and the Palatinate, seeing action in four military engagements. After the defeat of the revolution, he escaped to Switzerland. In October 1849, using the sea route via Genoa, he sailed to England, which became his permanent home.

In November 1850, unable to make a living as a writer in London and anxious to help support the penniless Marx, Engels reluctantly returned to his father's business in Manchester. In 1864, after his father's death, he became a partner in the firm, and by early 1869 he felt that he had enough capital to support himself and to provide Marx with a regular annuity of £350. On July 1, 1869, Engels sold his share of the business to his partner. He exulted in a letter to Marx: "Hurrah! Today I finished with sweet commerce, and I am a free man!" Marx's daughter, Eleanor, who saw Engels on that day, wrote: "I shall never forget the triumphant 'For the last time,' which he shouted as he drew on his top-boots in the morning to make his last journey to business. Some hours later, when we were standing at the door waiting for him, we saw him coming across the little field opposite his home. He was flourishing his walking stick in the air and singing, and laughing all over his face."

In September 1870 Engels moved to London, settling near the home of Marx, whom he saw daily. A generous friend and gay host, the fun-loving Engels spent the remaining 25 years of his life in London, enjoying good food, good wine, and good company. He also worked hard, doing the things he loved: writing, maintaining contact and a voluminous correspondence with radicals everywhere, and, after Marx's death in 1883, laboring over the latter's notes and manuscripts, bringing out volumes 2 and 3 of *Das Kapital* in 1885 and 1894, respectively. Engels died of cancer on Aug. 5, 1895. Following his instructions, his body was cremated and his ashes strewn over the ocean at Eastbourne, his favorite holiday resort.

Personality and Character. Engels was medium-height, slender, and athletic. His body was disciplined by swimming, fencing, and riding. He dressed and acted like an elegant English gentleman. In Manchester, where he maintained two homesone for appearances, as befitted a member of the local stock exchange, and another for his Irish mistresshe rode to hounds with the English gentry, whom he despised as capitalists but by whose antic behavior he was sardonically amused.

Engels had a brilliant mind and was quick, sharp, and unerring in his judgments. His versatility was astonishing. A successful businessman, he also had a grasp of virtually every branch of the natural sciences, biology, chemistry, botany, and physics. He was a widely respected specialist on military affairs. He mastered numerous languages, including all the Slavic ones, on which he planned to write a comparative grammar. He also knew Gothic, Old Nordic, and Old Saxon, studied Arabic, and in 3 weeks learned Persian, which he said was "mere child's play." His English, both spoken and written, was impeccable. It was said of him that he "stutters in 20 languages."

Engels apparently never married. He loved, and lived with successively, two Irish sisters, Mary (who died in 1863) and Lydia (Lizzy) Burns (1827–1878). After he moved to London, he referred to Lizzy as "my wife." The Burns sisters, ardent Irish patriots, stirred in Engels a deep sympathy for the Irish cause.

His Writings. Engels published hundreds of articles, a number of prefaces (mostly to Marx's works), and about half a dozen books during his lifetime. His first important book, written when he was 24 years old, was *The Condition of the Working Class in England in 1844,* based on observations made when he lived in Manchester. It was published in German in 1845 and in English in 1892. His next publication was the *Manifesto of the Communist Party* (*Communist Manifesto*), which he wrote in collaboration with Marx between December 1847 and January 1848, and which was published in London in German a month later. An anonymous English edition came out in London in 1850.

Engels also collaborated with Marx on *The Holy Family,* an attack on the Young Hegelian philosopher Bruno Bauer, which was published in Germany in 1845. Another collaboration with Marx, *The German*

Ideology, was written in 1845–1846, but it was not published in full until 1932.

In 1870 Engels published *The Peasant War in Germany,* which consisted of a number of articles he had written in 1850; an English translation appeared in 1956. In 1878 he published perhaps his most important book, *Herr Eugen Dühring's Revolution in Science,* known in an English translation as *Anti-Dühring* (1959). This work ranks, together with Marx's *Das Kapital,* as the most comprehensive study of socialist (Marxist) theory. In it, Engels wrote, he treated "every possible subject, from the concepts of time and space to bimetallism; from the eternity of matter and motion to the perishable nature of moral ideas; from Darwin's natural selection to the education of youth in a future society."

Engels's *Development of Socialism from Utopia to Science* was published in German in 1882 and in English, under the title *Socialism, Utopian and Scientific,* in 1892. In 1884 he brought out *The Origins of the Family, Private Property and the State,* an indispensable work for understanding Marxist political theory. His last work, published in 1888, was *Ludwig Feuerbach and the End of Classical German Philosophy.* Both of these last books are available in English. Two works by Engels were published posthumously: *Germany: Revolution and Counter-Revolution* (German, 1896; English, 1933) and *Dialectics of Nature,* begun in 1895 but never completed, of which an English translation appeared in 1964.

Engels's Ideas. In his articles and books Engels elaborated and developed, both historically and logically, basic ideas that go under the name of Marxism. His work was not an limitation of Marx but constituted a consistent philosophy at which both men had arrived independently and had shared in common. Engels refined the concept of dialectical materialism, which Marx had never fully worked out, to include not only matter but also form. He stressed that the materialist conception takes into consideration the whole cultural process, including tradition, religion, and ideology, which goes through constant historical evolution. Each stage of development, containing also what Engels called "thought material," builds upon the totality of previous developments. Thus every man is a product both of his own time and of the past. Similarly, he elaborated his view of the state, which he regarded as "nothing less than a machine for the oppression of one class by another," as evolving, through class struggles, into the "dictatorship of the proletariat."

EWB

Erasmus, Desiderius (1466–1536), Dutch scholar. Erasmus was the dominant figure of the early-16th-century humanist movement. The intellectual arbiter during the last years of Christian unity, he remains one of European culture's most controversial giants.

The evidence about the youth and adolescence of Erasmus is hard to evaluate. A major source of knowledge is autobiographical, a product of his middle age when international fame made him most sensitive about his illegitimate birth at Rotterdam, probably in October 1466, the second son of a priest, Roger Gerard, and a physician's daughter. School life, rather than a household environment, shaped Erasmus from his fifth year onward. He later disparaged the effort of his teachers and the guardians established after the parents' deaths about 1484; in fact, his father provided Erasmus a solid education with the Brethren of the Common Life from 1475 to 1484. From this religious community, which for a century had deflected education in the Low Countries from scholastic rigidity and had relieved its discipline of the strictest monastic severity, Erasmus obtained a firm grounding in classical Latin and an appreciation of a spirit of Christianity beyond its doctrinal basis.

From Steyn to Cambridge. His unpromising birth and his guardians' business sense gave the monastic cloister an obvious, if grim, place in Erasmus' future. He entered the Augustinian monastery at Steyn in 1487 and took monastic vows in 1488; he was ordained a priest in 1492. His reading in classical literature and Christian sources matured, but Erasmus found Steyn crude and rustic. Scholarship offered the first step out, when the bishop of Cambrai employed Erasmus as his secretary in 1493 and rewarded his work with a stipend for study at Paris in 1495.

Paris provided a diverse environment which Erasmus cultivated between recalls to the Low Countries in the late 1490s. He moved in literary circles, writing poetry and dedications and experimenting with styles of educational writing which bore fruit in the later publications *Adagia* and *Colloquia.* He sought students and patrons until, in 1499, his student Lord Mountjoy took him to England.

The visit was decisive to Erasmus. English humanists were studying Scripture and the early Church fathers and advocating reform of the Church and the educational process that served it. Friendships with John Colet, Sir Thomas More, and others restored Erasmus' interest in devotional studies and turned him to the Greek language as the key for his research. *Enchiridion militis Christiani* (*Handbook of the Militant Christian,* published 1503, though begun a decade before) outlined conduct which would foster

94

man's spiritual capacities and usher in the ethics and piety of what Erasmus' group called the "philosophy of Christ." It gave these scholars an international audience and steady patronage among educated laymen.

In 1506 Erasmus fulfilled a long-standing ambition by traveling to Italy. He watched Pope Julius II conquer Bologna that year; the sharpest edge of his wit can be discerned in a tract, *Julius exclusus* (published anonymously in 1517; he never admitted authorship), in which St. Peter bars Julius from heaven and scathingly damns his wars and treasure. Erasmus polished his Greek in Italy and formed, with Aldus Manutius's press in Venice, the first of the crucial links to publishing enterprises that secured his financial and professional independence.

Back in England by 1509, disillusioned with the Church's wars and its clergy's shortcomings, Erasmus wrote *Encomium moriae* (*The Praise of Folly*), a satiric exposition of the obstacles restricting the fulfillment of Christ's teaching. Though not formally released from monastic vows until 1517, Erasmus was now effectively freed of Steyn by his mounting reputation. He held a professorship at Cambridge (1511–1514) and settled into the vocation for which his study and travel had prepared him.

Major Publications. Erasmus' *Novum instrumentum,* a heavily annotated edition of the New Testament placing texts in Greek and revised Latin side by side, appeared in 1516 from the Basel press of Johannes Froben. As the first published Greek text and a basis for further clarification of the New Testament, it was a landmark for scholars and reformers. It attuned educated Europeans more closely to Erasmus' early works, which were now widely translated from the Latin of his originals, and paved the way for the literary and educational classics of the Christian humanist fellowship.

Erasmus had now returned to the Continent to the manuscripts and printing houses on which his massive efforts relied. Froben published his nine-volume edition of St. Jerome in 1516 and in the next two decades issued Erasmus' comprehensive editions of early Christian authors, including St. Cyprian (1520), St. Ambrose (1527), and St. Augustine (1529); he also circulated commentaries and treatises on divinity and revised editions of the literary works.

Another dimension to Erasmus' writing appeared in 1516, while he briefly served the future emperor Charles V as councilor. Following current humanist practice, he prepared a guide for educating princes to rule justly, *Institutio principis Christiani,* and in 1517 composed *Querela pacis* (*The Complaint of Peace*), condemning war as an instrument of tyranny and warning temporal rulers to fulfill their obligation to preserve Christian harmony. Erasmus thus demonstrated, before Luther's impact was clear, his sensitivity to Europe's impending fragmentation.

Erasmus and Reformation Europe. Erasmus' influence could not realize the vision of Christian renovation expressed in his New Testament dedication and preface, which urged Pope Leo X to make Rome the center of reform and to make Christ's words available to every plowboy in the field. Following Luther's lead, many intellectuals, impatient for action, rejected humanism's "halfway house" and used presses and pulpits to move Europe's masses as Erasmus never had. The Erasmians' style of persuasion was countered by simpler, vernacular tracts on theology, the Sacraments, and Church structure, sometimes linked with social and political issues. In 1516 Erasmus had foreseen a golden age, but by 1521, dismayed by the partisan tone and substance of the reformers' appeals, he was calling his own times the worst since Christianity began.

Erasmus' eventual response, after an important exchange with Luther in 1524–1525 about the role of human will in salvation to which he contributed *De libero arbitrio* (*On the Freedom of the Will*), was a gradual disengagement from the disputing theologians and their secular sponsors. He avoided Europe's major courts and capitals, and he left congenial intellectual homes in Catholic Louvain in 1521 and Protestant Basel in 1529, when denominational advocacy invaded their scholarship and governance. Printing presses continued to hold his audience: they were the lifelines of this complex man, rootless at birth, whose temperament, circumstances, and dislike of permanent commitments consistently separated him from friends and institutions eager to harness his talents.

He died on July 12, 1536. The embattled Catholic Church, which he never left, condemned some of Erasmus' work for its critical attitude and moderation against heretics, while much modern opinion based on Protestant, nationalist viewpoints has judged him harshly.

EWB

Evans-Pritchard, Sir Edward (1902–1973), English social anthropologist. Edward Evans-Pritchard did pioneer research in the social structure, history, and religion of African and Arab peoples.

Edward Evans-Pritchard was one of the foremost anthropologists of the mid-twentieth century. The son of an Anglican clergyman, Evans-Pritchard read history at Exeter College, Oxford, and received a doctorate in anthropology at the London School of

Economics. His first research was from 1926 to 1932 with the Azande of the southern Sudan and the Congo. He did further fieldwork in 1935–1936 and in 1938, mainly with the Nuer and other Nilotic peoples of the southern Sudan.

Acclaimed Scholar. Before World War II Evans-Pritchard served on the faculties of the London School of Economics, the Egyptian University in Cairo, and Cambridge University. During this period he produced his two most famous works: *Witchcraft: Oracles and Magic among the Azande* (1937) and *The Nuer* (1940). The first is a brilliant exposition of the internal logic of a preliterate philosophy, indicating how such ideas may reasonably persist in the face of what, to an outsider, may appear to be damning discrepancies and disproofs. The second volume examines the mode of political organization of the Nuer, a society lacking any formal government. It served as a model for much of the subsequent anthropological research in the social organization of African societies. In its analysis of the blood feud, conflict, and limits set by environment on a seminomadic society, it owes much to the earlier work of William Robertson Smith.

During World War II Evans-Pritchard served as an officer in military intelligence in East Africa, Ethiopia, Libya, and the Middle East, and he was able to do some anthropological fieldwork in these areas. He converted to Roman Catholicism in 1944, which may have influenced his subsequent attempts to reconcile the purported differences between social science and religious faith. In 1946 he was appointed to the chair of social anthropology at All Souls College at Oxford, which he held until his retirement in 1970. Twice he journeyed to the United States for scholarly pursuits: in 1950 he was a visiting professor at the University of Chicago, and seven years later he spent a year at Stanford University's Center for Advanced Study in the Behavioral Sciences.

Set a Standard for Anthropology Writing. An extraordinarily prolific writer, Evans-Pritchard produced works that touch upon nearly every facet of social anthropology. In general his writings exhibit a blend of rich ethnographic detail with subtle and suggestive theoretical insights. Among his better-known books are *The Sanusi of Cyrenaica* (1949), *Kinship and Marriage among the Nuer* (1951), *Social Anthropology* (1951), *Nuer Religion* (1956), and *Theories of Primitive Religion* (1965).

A year following his retirement, Evans-Pritchard was knighted for his contributions to science. He was father to five children with Ioma Nicholls, whom he married in 1939. Even after he retired from Oxford,

he continued to teach and to produce influential publications in his field, including *Man and Woman Among the Azande* (1971). He was one of the strongest proponents of the value of historical perspective in anthropology and of recording African oral literature. Evans-Pritchard died in Oxford on September 11, 1973.

EWB

F

Fénelon, François de Salignac de la Mothe (1651–1715), French prelate, theologian, and preacher. Born on Aug. 6, 1651, François Fénelon was educated by the Jesuits. He became a priest at the famous Seminary of St. Sulpice and spent 3 years preaching to Protestants. He became an ardent disciple and friend of Jacques Bossuet. Fénelon produced his *Treatise on the Existence of God* as well as his *Treatise on the Education of Young Girls* at this time. Both were highly successful.

In 1688 Fénelon met Madame Guyon, who claimed to have mystical experiences and to have the secret of loving God. She had been imprisoned by the archbishop of Paris in a convent because he feared that she was in error. Fénelon believed in her stoutly; he visited her infrequently but corresponded with her voluminously. He was suffering at this time from an intense aridity of mind in regard to God. Intellectually he could prove God's existence, but emotionally he felt little or nothing toward God. Guyon seemed to him to have discovered or received the secret of such "feeling" in her childlike surrender to God and the simplicity of her approach to divine things.

About this time there was a controversy in the French Church about a heresy called quietism, a teaching according to which progress in virtue and in the love of God was achieved by submitting to God's action and grace. Its opponents maintained that quietists made no positive effort at being virtuous, that they depended passively on God's grace, and even neglected basic rules of Christian virtue and behavior. Fénelon was involved in this unpleasant controversy through his association with Guyon. She used to visit, on Fénelon's suggestion, a school for girls run by Madame de Maintenon. The latter disliked Guyon and reported her to the authorities. Guyon also submitted her doctrine for approval to Bossuet on Fénelon's suggestion. Bossuet, although fundamentally ignorant of theology, attacked both Guyon and Fénelon in 1697.

Hate now replaced friendship for Fénelon in Bossuet's mind. He saw him as a rival in public speaking and as the nation's foremost theologian and religious counselor. He sought to have Fénelon discredited. The teaching of Fénelon and Guyon was condemned by Pope Innocent XII on the insistence of Louis XIV under Bossuet's constant prodding. Fénelon submitted and then set out to outline his teaching on Catholic mysticism on a scale never before attempted.

In February 1695 Fénelon was made archbishop of Cambrai and from then until his death he spent his time in writing, teaching, and preaching. He was appointed tutor to Louis XIV's eldest grandson, the Duc de Bourgogne. For the duke he composed his *Dialogues* and *Telemachus,* together with other minor works. His ideas on politics were based on the universal brotherhood of man, an unpopular idea in the 18th century. He proved himself a first-rate literary judge in his *Letter* to the French Academy in 1714. He spent his last years writing against Jansenism. In his writings he explained the love of God and the simplicity of heart required in man in order to be able to practice that love. Fénelon died on Jan. 7, 1715.

EWB

Ferry, Jules François Camille (1832–1893), French statesman. Jules Ferry was a major political leader during the first 2 decades of the Third Republic. He played a key role in expanding public education and in developing France's colonial empire.

Jules Ferry was born at Saint-Dié, Vosges Department, on April 5, 1832. On receiving his law degree in 1851, he was admitted to the Paris bar, but he first made his name in journalism as one of the most vigorous critics of the Second Empire. His successes led him into more active politics, and in 1869 he was elected to the legislature from Paris.

Entering the Government of National Defense after the fall of the Empire, Ferry became the top civil administrator for Paris and had to struggle with the difficult problems caused by the siege. His stringent but necessary measures earned him an unpopularity in the capital that lasted throughout his career.

Ferry became minister of public instruction in 1879 and initiated a number of reforms, the most controversial being those aimed at reducing the influence of the Church on education. The state recovered its monopoly in the awarding of degrees, but his proposal to prohibit teaching by members of religious orders (the famous Article 7) was defeated in the Senate. In 1880 he took administrative measures to dissolve unauthorized religious orders. More important was his introduction of legislation to make elementary education compulsory, free, and laic. In September 1880 he became premier and was able to further his program by decrees, but lack of funds and personnel prevented his ambitious plans from being implemented at once.

An ardent colonial expansionist when most republican politicians saw foreign questions only in terms of Alsace-Lorraine and the German menace, Ferry was charged with diverting attention and troops—away from the Continent. His first ministry ended in November 1881 as a result of criticism of the Tunisian expedition which led to the French protectorate.

Ferry returned to the Ministry of Public Instruction in January 1882. In February 1883 he was again premier and carried out a purge of antirepublican elements in the judiciary. Although his power and prestige seemed as great as ever, this time the opposition to his foreign policy proved fatal to Ferry's career. He supported French involvement in Indochina, but news of a minor defeat there, much exaggerated in the first report, compelled his resignation on March 30, 1885. He was an unsuccessful candidate for the presidency in 1887 and never again played a leading role in government. Shot by an Alsatian fanatic on Dec. 10, 1892, Ferry died in Paris on March 17, 1893.

EWB

Fichte, Johann Gottlieb (1762–1814), German philosopher of ethical idealism. Johann Gottlieb Fichte posited the spiritual activity of an "infinite ego" as the ground of self and world. He believed that human life must be guided by the practical maxims of philosophy.

Johann Gottlieb Fichte was born Rammenau on May 19, 1762, the son of a Saxon peasant. As a child, he impressed a visiting nobleman, Baron Miltitz, who adopted him and had him schooled at Pforta. In 1780 he became a student of theology at the University of Jena and later studied at Wittenberg and Leipzig. He soon assimilated three major ideas that became the foundations of his own philosophy: Spinoza's pantheism, Lessing's concept of striving, and Kant's concept of duty.

Fichte's patron died in 1788, leaving him destitute and jobless, but Fichte was able to obtain a position as tutor in Zurich, where he met Johanna Rahn, whom he would marry in 1794. Having unsuccessfully tried to make his mark in the world of letters, he finally succeeded in 1792, when he wrote his *Versuch einer Kritik aller Offenbarung* (*Critique of All Revelation*), an application of Kant's ethical principle of duty to religion. Since this work was published anonymously, it was believed to be Kant's; but Kant publicly praised Fichte as the author, earning him the attention of Goethe and the other great minds at the court of Weimar.

In 1794, through the influence of Goethe, Fichte was offered a professorship at Jena, where he proved an impassioned, dynamic teacher. He was a short, strongly built man with sharp, commanding features. His language had a cryptic ring; to Madame de Staël he once remarked, "Grasp my metaphysics, Madame; you will then understand my ethics."

Fichte displayed a strong moral concern for the lives of his students; he criticized the fraternities and gave public lectures on university life, which were published as *Einige Vorlesungen über die Bestimmung des Gelehrten* (1794; *The Vocation of the Scholar*). Despite all this extracurricular activity, Fichte developed his basic system, the *Wissenschaftslehre,* the doctrine of knowledge and metaphysics, in two works, *Über de Begriff der Wissenschaftslehre* and *Grundlage der gesamten Wissenschaftslehre* (both 1794). Since he was obsessively concerned with the clarity of his writings, these works were later revised and published in several different versions in his lifetime (the English translation was entitled *The Science of Knowledge*).

Fichte's metaphysics is called subjective idealism because it bases the reality of the self and the empirical world on the spiritual activity of an infinite ego. From the principle of the infinite ego, Fichte deduced the finite ego, or subject, and the non-ego, or object. This split, or "oppositing," between subject and object cannot be overcome through knowledge. Only through moral striving and the creation of a moral order can the self be reunited with the infinite ego. The *System der Sittenlehre nach den Principien der Wissenschaftslehre* (1798; *The Science of Ethics as Based on the Science of Knowledge*) expresses the necessity of moral striving in the formula, "If I ought I can." Even God is identified with the moral order in the essay "On the Ground of Our Belief in a Divine World Order" (1798). Fichte was wont to claim that in his own life "he created God every day."

Because of his radical political ideas and his intense moral earnestness, Fichte attracted the hostility of several groups: fraternity students, monarchists, and the clergy. The last group charged Fichte with atheism, since he had stated that "there can be no doubt that the notion of God as a separate substance is impossible and contradictory." He refused to compromise with his critics, even publicly attacking their idolatry of a personal God, and was forced to leave Jena in 1799.

These years of professional insecurity did not diminish Fichte's philosophical activity. He produced a popular account of his philosophy in *Die Bestimmung des Menschen* (1800; *The Vocation of Man*). In *Der geschlossene Handelsstaat* (1800; *The Closed Commercial State*) he argued for state socialism, and in

Grundzüge der Gegenwärtigun Zeitalters (1806; *Characteristics of the Present Age*) he presented his philosophy of history. Fichte's metaphysics became more theologically oriented in *Die Anweisung zum seligen Leben, order Religionslehre* (1806; *The Way towards the Blessed Life*). But his most memorable accomplishment during the time of the siege of Napoleon was his *Reden au die deutsche Nation* (*Addresses to the German Nation*), given in the winter of 1807–1808. These speeches rallied the German people on the cultural and educational "leadership of humanity."

In 1810, after teaching two terms at the universities of Erlangen and Königsberg, Fichte was appointed dean of the philosophy faculty and later rector of the University of Berlin. But Napoleon's siege of Berlin was to cut short his new teaching career. Johanna, his wife, nursing the wounded, fell ill with typhus and recovered; Fichte, however, succumbed to the disease and died on Jan. 27, 1814. His philosophy was quickly superseded by the philosophies of Schelling and Hegel.

EWB

Filmer, Sir Robert (c.1588–1653), English political theorist. Robert Filmer was influential in the development of English conservative thought. His treatises formed the basis for a royalist or Tory theory of kingship and government.

The eldest son of Sir Edward Filmer, Robert Filmer was born in the last decade of Elizabeth I's reign. After being educated at Trinity College, Cambridge, he retreated to his country estates in Kent, where he devoted himself to scholarly pursuits and to winning the hand of Anne, daughter of the bishop of Ely. At the beginning of Charles I's reign Filmer was knighted, but he appears to have played no major role either in local government or in Parliament.

As the conflict between Crown and Parliament deepened, Filmer took a strong royalist stand. When civil war erupted in 1641, Filmer's response was to write his *Patriarcha or the Natural Powers of Kings,* which, though not published, was circulated in manuscript form. His writings earned him the active hostility of Charles's parliamentary opponents. His house was looted by a parliamentary force in 1643, and the next year he was temporarily imprisoned in Leeds Castle.

With the end of the first civil war, Filmer regained his freedom and apparently played no part in the second internecine struggle, which broke out soon after. He did, however, return to his writing, and before the execution of Charles I he authored his most thoughtful treatise, *The Anarchy of Limited or Mixed Monarchy,* in which he argued for the establishment of a "pure" monarchy such as existed in France. Like his earlier work, this was not published at the time.

After the establishment of the Commonwealth, Filmer retreated into deeper obscurity. He continued to write, but as his ideas were anathema to England's new rulers, publication was impossible. After an appeal to the landed classes to restore traditional government in *The Free-holders' Grand Inquest,* he undertook an analysis of Aristotle's *Politics* which dealt with the question of "mixt" as opposed to "pure" forms of government, and Filmer argued, as did the French writer Jean Bodin, for the superiority of the latter type.

In 1652 Filmer wrote *Observations Concerning the Original of Governments,* in which he enunciated a theory of absolutism that not only opposed the more liberal ideas of John Milton and Hugo Grotius, but that also differed with the more (to him) congenial ideas of his other contemporary Thomas Hobbes. Filmer rejected any sort of "social compact" whether stemming from man's "natural goodness" as Milton would have had it or from his depravity as Hobbes averred, as the original basis for government. He also rejected extreme mechanism and thus alienated many contemporaries. Filmer was, however, a rationalist; before his death in 1653 he wrote two works which cast doubt on the validity of witchcraft, *An Advertisement to the Jurymen of England Touching Witches* and *The Difference between a Hebrew and an English Witch.*

After the Restoration a genuine wave of pro-monarchical sentiment existed, and Filmer's once unpopular ideas were gradually resurrected. In 1679 his treatises (except the *Patriarcha*) were published. The remaining work appeared in print the following year.

EWB

Foucault, Michel (1926–1984), French philosopher, critic, and historian. Michel Foucault was an original and creative thinker who made contributions to historiography and to understanding the forces that make history.

Michel Foucault was born on October 15, 1926, in Pottiers, France, the son of Paul (a doctor) and Anne (Malapert) Foucault. He studied at the Ecole Normale Superieure and at the University of Paris, Sorbonne, where he received his diploma in 1952. He served as director of the Institut Francais in Hamburg and held academic posts at the Universities of Clermont-Ferrand and Paris-Vincennes. In 1970 he became professor and chairman of the History of Systems of Thought at the College de France. A creative thinker, Foucault made substantial contributions to philosophy, history, literary criticism, and, specifically, to theoretical work in the human sciences. Often de-

picted as a "structuralist," a designation he disavowed, Foucault had something of a following among French intellectuals. He died from a neurological disorder on June 25, 1984, cutting short a brilliant career.

Foucault was known for tracing the development of Western civilization, particularly in its attitudes toward sexuality, madness, illness, and knowledge. His late works insisted that forms of discourse and institutional practices are implicated in the exercise of power. His works can be read as a new interpretation of power placing emphasis on what happens or is done and not on human agency, that is, he sought to explore the conditions that give rise to forms of discourse and knowledge. Foucault was particularly concerned with the rise of the modern stress on human self-consciousness and the image of the human as maker of history. He argued that the 20th century is marked by "the disappearance of man" because history is now seen as the product of objective forces and power relations limiting the need to make the human the focus of historical causation.

Throughout his studies Foucault developed and used what he called an "archaeological method." This approach to history tries to uncover strata of relations and traces of culture in order to reconstruct the civilization in question. Foucault assumed that there were characteristic mechanisms throughout historical events, and therefore he developed his analysis by drawing on seemingly random sources. This gives Foucault's work an eclecticism rarely seen in modern historiography. His concern, however, was to isolate the defining characteristics of a period. In the *Order of Things* (1971) he claimed that "in any given culture and at any given moment there is only one *episteme* (system of knowledge) that defines the conditions of the possibility of all knowledge." The archaeological method seeks to "dig up and display the archeological form or forms which would be common to all mental activity." These forms can then be traced throughout a culture and warrant the eclectic use of historical materials.

Foucault's archaeological method entails a reconception of historical study by seeking to isolate the forms that are common to all mental activity in a period. Rather than seeking historical origins, continuities, and explanations for a historical period, Foucault constantly sought the epistemological gap or space unique to a particular period. He then tried to uncover the structures that render understandable the continuities of history. His form of social analysis challenged other thinkers to look at institutions, ideas, and events in new ways.

Foucault claimed that his interest was "to create a history of the different modes by which, in our culture, human beings are made subjects." By this he

99

meant the way in which human beings are made the subjects of objectifying study and practices through knowledge, social norms, and sexuality. Thus he applied his archeological method to sexuality, insanity, history, and punishment. Just prior to his death, *Concern for the Self,* the third of his projected five-volume *History of Sexuality,* was published in France. The first two volumes, *The Will to Know* (published in English as *The History of Sexuality Volume I,* 1981) and *The Use of Pleasure* (1985), explored the relation between morality and sexuality. *Concern for the Self* addresses the oppression of women by men. In these studies, as in his *Discipline and Punish* (1977) about the rise of penal institutions, Foucault isolated the institutions that are images of the *episteme* of modernity. His conclusion was that modernity is marked not by liberalization and freedom, but by the repression of sexuality and the "totalitarianism of the norm" in mass culture.

Foucault's work continues to have significance for historical, literary, and philosophical study. In his later years Foucault wrote and spoke extensively on varying topics ranging from language to the relations of knowledge and power. In the span of a short career Foucault had considerable impact on the intellectual world. Yet given the complexity, subtly, and eclecticism of his style, the full impact of his work has yet to be realized.

EWB

Fox, George (1624–1691), English spiritual reformer. George Fox was the chief inspirer of the Society of Friends, or Quakers.

The son of a weaver, George Fox was born in July 1624 at Fenny Drayton, Leicestershire. He became a cobbler with little book learning beyond the Bible. When he was 19, a voice told him to "forsake all"; so he became a dropout, wandering about England in a solitary quest for religious truth. Gradually he clarified his beliefs, convinced that he derived them from direct experiences of God's light within him, "without the help of any man, book, or writing."

Holding that every man and woman could be similarly enlightened by Christ, Fox began "declaring truth" in public and developed into a dynamic, fanatically sincere speaker. He preached in barns, houses, and fields and in churches "after the priest had done"; but because his zeal sometimes led him to interrupt services, he was imprisoned as a disturber of public order. Inspired by the "Inner Voice," he became spiritual leader of some Nottinghamshire former Baptists but then went to the north of England, preaching, praying, and protesting at every opportunity. In 1652 he trudged about Yorkshire, a sturdy figure in leather breeches wearing a broad-brimmed hat over the ringlets of hair which fell to his shoulders.

Though Fox denounced creeds, forms, rites, external sacraments, and a "man-made" ministry, he became something of a negative formalist, refusing to doff his hat to anyone or to call months and days by their pagan names; and he used "thee" and "thou" instead of "you." Such flouting of conventions provoked intense opposition. Fox was repeatedly beaten by rowdies and persecuted by the pious, and the forces of law and order imprisoned him eight times for not conforming to the establishment. But his indomitable courage and his emphasis on the spirit rather than the letter of religion won him converts, even among his persecutors.

Paradoxically, this opponent of institutional religion showed a genius for organizing fellowships of Friends complete with unpaid officers, regular meetings, and funding arrangements. As a result, though his message was universal, individualistic, and spiritual, Fox founded what, by 1700, became the largest Nonconformist sect in England. In 1654 he organized a team of some 60 men and women as a mission to southern England. After converting many there, he extended his own preaching to Scotland (1657–1658), Wales (1657), Ireland (1669), the West Indies and America (1671–1673), the Netherlands (1677 and 1684), and Germany (1677). By 1660 he was issuing epistles to the Pope, the Turkish Sultan, and the Emperor of China. He was a strange mixture of fanaticism and common sense, selflessness and exhibitionism, liberalism and literalism.

In 1669 Fox married the outstanding female leader in the Quaker movement, Margaret, widow of his friend and patron Thomas Fell. But God's service took priority over their partnership, which was interrupted by his missions, his imprisonments in 1673–1675, and his supervision of the movement. He died in London on Jan. 13, 1691.

Fox composed hundreds of tracts for his times, defending principles of the Friends and exposing other men as sinners and ministers of the Great Whore of Babylon; but it is by his *Journal,* a record of his day-to-day activities and thoughts, that he is best remembered.

EWB

France, Anatole (1844–1924), French novelist and essayist. The works of Anatole France combine classical purity of style with penetrating flashes of irony. He is a major figure in the tradition of liberal humanism in French literature.

Jacques Anatole François Thibault, who was to take the literary name of Anatole France, was born in

Paris on April 16, 1844, the son of a self-educated bookseller. He attended the Collège Stanislas, a Catholic school, but was far from a brilliant pupil and emerged with a lasting dislike of the Church. Greater intellectual profit came to him from browsing among his father's books and from friendships with influential customers, which led to work for a publisher. France's first book was a study of the poet Alfred de Vigny and was followed by poetry and a verse drama, politely received but not particularly successful. At the same time he was pursuing a career in literary journalism, and in 1877 he married Valérie Guéin, the daughter of a well-to-do family, with whom he had a daughter, Suzanne, in 1881.

Early Career.

France's first great literary success came in 1881 with *Le Crime de Sylvestre Bonnard* (*The Crime of Sylvester Bonnard*). This story of an aging scholar betrays to the present-day reader an excessive sentimentality, but its optimistic theme and kindly irony were welcomed as a reaction against the brutal realism of the prevailing school of Émile Zola. The novel which followed, *Les Désirs de Jean Servien* (1882; *The Aspirations of Jean Servien*), was less well received. By the close of the 1880s France had established himself as a literary figure and had also begun a liaison with Madame Arman de Caillavet, who had a celebrated literary salon. Their relationship ended only with her death in 1910. France's marriage was dissolved in 1893.

In 1890 appeared *Thaïs*, set in Egypt in the early Christian era, treating the story of the courtesan Thaïs and the monk Paphnuce with tolerant irony and skepticism. It was followed in 1893 by *La Rôtisserie de la Reine Pédauque* (*At the Sign of the Reine Pédauque*), another tale with philosophical implications, this time set in the 18th century; and in 1894 by *Le Lys rouge* (*The Red Lily*), a more conventional novel of love in the wealthier classes, set largely in Italy. *Le Jardin d'Épicure* (1884; *The Garden of Epicurus*) consists of reprinted articles but contains the essence of France's attitude to the world at that point: a weary skepticism redeemed by an appreciation of the delicate pleasures of the mind.

Elected to the French Academy in 1896, France was at the height of a successful career. But his journalistic articles had begun to include social as well as literary criticism, and when the Dreyfus case came to a head in 1897, he felt obliged to take sides with the Jewish officer, whom he considered to have been wrongly condemned. For the rest of his life France was to abandon the political skepticism of his earlier years, while the irony in his books turned sharply critical of the contemporary world. This becomes increasingly evident in four books of *L'Histoire contemporaine* (1897–1901; *Contemporary History*), in which the figure of Monsieur Bergeret acts as the representative of France's own views on the Dreyfus case and other social problems, and in the story *Crainquebille* (1901), in which the case was transposed into a parable of the unjust prosecution of a harmless and innocent street peddler.

Later Works.

The book in which France's political irony reached its height was, however, *L'Île des Pingouins* (1908; *Penguin Island*), a penetrating glance at French history and life and perhaps the only satire in French literature which can be compared to Voltaire's *Candide*. The novel generally regarded as France's finest came out 4 years later: *Les Dieux ont soif* (*The Gods Are Athirst*). Set during the French Revolution, the book portrays the gradual development of a young artist, Évariste Gamelin, from his initial idealism and good nature to a point at which, through membership in a Revolutionary tribunal, his virtues have been transformed into a bloodthirsty and merciless fanaticism. France's own attitude is made clear through the character of Brotteaux, a formerly wealthy tax collector whose only possession is now his edition of Epicurus. Brotteaux, unjustly condemned by Gamelin's tribunal, meets the guillotine with stoic resolution. The novel ends with the overthrow of Robespierre and Gamelin's own execution.

France's last major work was *La Révolte des anges* (1914; *The Revolt of the Angels*), another satire, in which a group of angels attempt to free themselves from divine despotism. Less bitter than *L'Île des Pingouins* the book is also less successful. In France's later years he was increasingly involved politically with the extreme left and for a time became a supporter of the French Communist party. In 1921 he was awarded the Nobel Prize for literature; a year later his works were put on the papal Index. France, who had married again in 1920, died 6 months after his eightieth birthday, in 1924.

The many other books by France include collected articles on literary and social topics, volumes of autobiography, and a life of Joan of Arc. Regarded at the turn of the century as probably the most important French writer of his age, France lived too long for his reputation not to be viewed with impatience by a younger generation of writers who had little time for either his clarity of style or his polished irony. He himself had said, "People will reproach me for my audacity until they start reproaching me for my timidity." But if overvalued earlier, looked at in perspective, France's achievement as a novelist and satirist and his stand for the principles of justice and tolerance mark him as a major writer.

EWB

Franco, Francisco (1892–1975), Spanish general and dictator. Francisco Franco played a major role in the Spanish Civil War and became head of state of Spain in 1939.

Born at El Ferrol, a town in the northeastern Spanish province of Galicia, on December 4, 1892, Francisco Franco was the second of five children born to Maria del Pilar Bahamonde y Pardo de Andrade and Don Nicolas Franco, who had continued the Franco family tradition by serving in the Naval Administrative Corp. The young Franco was rather active; he swam, went hunting, and played football. At 12, he was admitted to the Naval Preparatory Academy whose graduates were destined for the Spanish navy. However, international events conspired to cut short his anticipated naval career. In 1898, much of the navy had been sunk by the United States in the Spanish-American War. Spain was slow to rebuild, therefore many ports which had relied on naval contracts were plunged into an economic recession. El Ferrol was hit hard, and entrance examinations for the navy were cancelled, but not before Franco passed for entrance to the Toledo Infrantry Academy in 1907. Franco inherited the nicknames "Franquito" or "Frankie Boy," since he would not participate in the same activities as his fellow students. He became the object of malicious bullying and initiations, and graduated in the middle of his class in 1910. Until 1912, Franco served as a second lieutenant. He was first posted to El Ferrol but in 1912 saw service in Spanish Morocco, where Spain had become involved in a stubborn colonial war. By 1915, at age 22, he had become the youngest captain in the Spanish army. In 1916, he was severely wounded while leading a charge. He was decorated, promoted to major and transferred to Oviedo, Spain. During the next three years, he romanced Carmen Polo y Martinez Valdes, and delayed his plans for the Spanish Foreign Legion for marriage until 1923. Franco became commander in 1922 and rose to the rank of brigadier general (at the age of 33) by war's end in 1926.

During the next few years, Franco commanded the prestigious General Military Academy in Saragossa. In 1928 a daughter, Carmen, his only child, was born. He maintained friendships with the dictator, Miguel Primo de Rivera, and King Alfonso XIII, but when both were overthrown and the Second Republic began a radical reconstruction of Spanish society, Franco surprisingly remained neutral and avoided military conspiracies.

Military governorships in Corunna and the Balearic Islands were followed by promotion to major general in reward for his neutrality, but with the advent of a more conservative Cabinet Franco commanded the Foreign Legion in the suppression of the Asturias revolt (October 1934). Now identified with the right, in 1935 he was made commander in chief of the army.

The Spanish Civil War. In February 1936 the leftist government of the Spanish republic exiled Franco to an obscure command in the Canary Islands. The following July he joined other right-wing officers in a revolt against the republic which is when the Spanish Civil War began. In October they made him commander in chief and head of state of their new Nationalist regime. During the three years of the ensuing civil war against the republic, Franco proved an unimaginative but careful and competent leader, whose forces advanced slowly but steadily to complete victory on April 1, 1939. On July 18 Franco pronounced in the Nationalists' favor and was flown to Tetuán, Spanish Morocco. Shortly afterward he led the army into Spain. The tide was already turning against the Republicans (or Loyalists), and Franco was able to move steadily northward toward Madrid, becoming, on September 29, generalissimo of the rebel forces and head of state.

Franco kept Spain out of World War II, but after the Axis defeat he was labeled the "last of the Fascist dictators" and ostracized by the United Nations. Strong connections with the Axis powers and the use of the fascist Falange ("Phalanx") organization as an official party soon identified Franco's Spain as a typical antidemocratic state of the 1930s, but El Caudillo (the leader) himself insisted his regime represented the monarchy and the Church. This attracted a wide coalition linked to Franco, who, with the death of General Sanjurjo in 1936 and General Mola the next year, remained the only Nationalist leader of importance. By the end of the Civil War in March 1939, he ruled a victorious movement which was nevertheless hopelessly divided among Carlists, Requetés, monarchists, Falangists, and the army. Foreign opposition to Franco decreased and in 1953 the signing of a military assistance pact with the United States marked the return of Spain to international society.

The need to avoid immediate Axis involvement in order to begin recovery temporarily maintained the tenuous coalition. Franco's statement, "War was my job; I was sure of that," showed his hesitant attitude toward the prospect of civilian statecraft. Yet he maneuvered with finesse through World War II, beginning with his famous rebuff of Hitler at Hendaye on October 23, 1940.

Except for sending the Blue Division to the Russian front, Franco resisted paying off his obligations to Germany and Italy. Instead he allied with Antonio Salazar, the Portuguese dictator, who counseled neutrality. Negotiations with the United States solidified this stand, and in October 1943 relations with the Axis powers were broken. But Allied antagonism was only somewhat mollified by this belated effort, and on December 13, 1946, the United Nations recommended diplomatic isolation of Spain.

Peacetime Government. Franco met this new threat by dismissing Serrano Suñer from office, removing the overtly fascist content from the Falange, and limiting all factional political activity. In 1946 the newly created United Nations declared that all countries should remove their ambassadors from Madrid. He also issued a constitution in 1947 which declared Spain to be a monarchy with himself as head of state possessing the power to name his successor. This successor might be either king or regent, thus leaving the future unresolved, a tactic which Franco capitalized on throughout most of the postwar period to prevent any group or individual from making strong claims upon his government. Cabinet ministers were chosen with an eye to national balance, and so slowly Spain moved away from sectarianism.

The economic and diplomatic situation remained difficult. In 1948 France closed its border with Spain, and exile groups, sometimes supported by the U.S.S.R., maintained extensive propaganda campaigns. Flying the banner of anticommunism during the emerging Cold War served him well. In 1950, the United States returned its ambassador and three years later the Americans were allowed four military bases in Spain. President Dwight D. Eisenhower personally greeted Franco in Madrid in 1959. Indeed, considering his Concordat with the pope in 1953, Franco can be said to "have arrived." Franco's regime became somewhat more liberal during the 1950s and 1960s. It depended for support not on the Falange, renamed the National Movement. Almost as if this signaled the end of isolation, tourist trade began picking up until within a few short years Spain had a substantial surplus in international payments. Spain enjoyed rapid economic growth in the 1960s and by the end of the century, its previously agrigcultural economy had been industrialized.

This upsurge permitted Franco to engage in a slow process of modernization that contained a few liberal elements. In May 1958 he issued the principles of the National movement, which contained a new series of fundamental freedoms still dominated, however, by an absolute prohibition on political opposition or criticism of the government. On several later occasions control of the press was temporarily relaxed, and in 1966 the Cortes, up to then a purely appointive body, was made partially elective.

In matters of economic planning, however, Franco demonstrated more consistent liberal intent. He led a belated industrial recovery that raised the standard of living and decreased social unrest. Many of his later Cabinet technocrats, however, were members of Opus Dei, a relatively unknown Catholic laymen's organization reputed to have enormous economic power. Franco's reliance upon this group became obvious in 1969, when the Falange lost its official status.

Franco's health declined during the 1960s. In 1969 he designated Prince Juan Carlos, grandson of Spain's former king, Alfonso XIII, as his official successor. In 1973 Franco relinquished his position as premier but continued to be head of state. Such was the character of Franco's regime that the choice was rumored to have been made by the army, still the most important institution in Spanish society. In July 1974, Franco suffered an attack of thrombophlebitis, an attack that signaled a host of successive afflictions over the following 16 months: partial kidney failure, bronchial pneumonia, coagulated blood in his pharynx, pulmonary edema, bacterial peritonitis, gastric hemorrhage, endotoxic shock and finally, cardiac arrest. At one point, Franco exclaimed, "My God, what a struggle it is to die." On November 20, 1975, when relatives asked doctors to remove his support systems, the 82-year-old Franco passed away. After Franco's death in Madrid, Juan Carlos became king.

EWB

Frederick II, known as Frederick the Great (1712–1786), king of Prussia from 1740 to 1786. Frederick II combined the qualities of a warrior king with those of an enlightened despot.

The eldest son of Frederick William I of Prussia and of Princess Sophie Dorothea of Hanover, Frederick II was born in Berlin on Jan. 24, 1712. His father was a hardworking, unimaginative soldier-king, with no outward pretensions and no time to waste on superfluous niceties. Even as an adolescent Frederick, with the tacit support of his mother, rebelled against this mold. He preferred French literature to German and the company of young fops to that of old soldiers.

In 1730 Frederick and a young friend, Lieutenant Katte, planned a romantic escape to England, but their plot was discovered. The would-be escapees were arrested and condemned to death for desertion, and

Katte was executed in Frederick's presence. The crown prince was spared upon the entreaties of Emperor Charles VI, although it is doubtful that his father ever intended to go through with the execution. Frederick, however, was imprisoned in the fortress of Küstrin in the most rigorous conditions until, after some 6 months, he voluntarily approached Frederick William with a request for pardon. For the next 2 years, although still nominally a prisoner, Frederick was employed in a subsidiary position of the local administration of Küstrin, thus learning the intricacies of the Prussian administrative system.

In 1732 Frederick was appointed commandant of an infantry regiment and, having decided to obey his father, he learned soldiering with all the thoroughness with which he had previously avoided it. In 1733, at his father's insistence, he married Elisabeth Christine of Braunschweig, but his aversion to women was so pronounced that the marriage was, over the many years it lasted, never consummated.

Between 1733 and 1740 Frederick, who had grown into a young man whose unimposing stature was balanced by piercing blue eyes, an aquiline nose, and a good chin, exceeded even the expectations of his father in his dedication to hard, dull routine. But he also found time to devote himself further to French literature, to begin a lifelong correspondence with a number of French *philosophes,* and to try writing himself. One product of this period was the *Anti-Machiavel* (1739), a work in which he argued that the Italian's ruthlessly practical maxims for princes were no longer compatible with the more advanced ethics of a new age. He was soon given the opportunity to test his own conduct against these views.

War of the Austrian Succession. On May 31, 1740, Frederick William died, and Frederick became king of Prussia as Frederick II. Before he had time to accustom himself to his new position, the death of Emperor Charles VI on October 20 created a political crisis and presented Frederick with a unique opportunity. Like all the other leading powers of Europe, Prussia had subscribed to the Pragmatic Sanction, guaranteeing the succession of Charles's daughter Maria Theresa and the integrity of her dominions. But it was an open secret that at least France and Bavaria intended to make demands upon Austria as soon as the Emperor was dead, and Frederick saw no reason to stand by while others enriched themselves at Austria's expense. He offered to assist Austria in the maintenance of its possessions in exchange for the cession of the rich province of Silesia to Prussia. When this outrageous piece of blackmail was indignantly rejected, in December Frederick marched his troops into Silesia, thus launching the War of the Austrian Succession (1740–1748).

In the first phase of this struggle the combined onslaught of Prussian, French, and Bavarian forces threatened to overwhelm Austria. Not wishing to bring about a situation more favorable to his potential rivals than to himself, Frederick withdrew from the war in 1742 with most of Silesia as his price. When Austria, relieved of the necessity of fighting the Prussians, threatened to crush its remaining enemies, Frederick reentered the war in 1744. The conflict was finally ended in 1748 with Silesia still firmly in Prussian hands.

Seven Years' War. Since the Austrians were antagonistic over the loss of Silesia, Frederick had reason to fear a renewal of the struggle. In the aftermath of the war both sides engaged in complicated diplomatic maneuvers. Austria, which had enjoyed a tentative alliance with Russia since 1746, tried to strengthen this while making overtures toward its old enemy France. Frederick in turn concluded the Treaty of Westminster (1755) with Great Britain, promising Prussian neutrality in the war that had just broken out between France and England. These maneuvers led directly to the Diplomatic Revolution, which in 1756 left Prussia facing an overwhelming Continental alliance of Austria, Russia, France, and Saxony. Rather than await inevitable death by constriction, Frederick attacked Austria, which he regarded as the weakest among the great powers facing him. Thus began the Seven Years' War (1756–1763).

In this conflict Frederick distinguished himself by continually keeping at bay much more powerful antagonists. He took advantage of the natural lack of cohesion of coalitions and fought his enemies, so far as possible, one at a time. The superior discipline of the Prussian army allowed Frederick to march it to the theater of war in small detachments, from various directions, uniting only shortly before a battle was to be fought. He also made the most of the oblique order of battle which he had inculcated in the Prussian army and which allowed him to concentrate his forces against emerging weak spots in his enemies' more ponderous formations.

In spite of these advantages, by 1762 Prussia was on the verge of bankruptcy, its army was in no condition to continue the war, and Russian troops had occupied Berlin. At this juncture Empress Elizabeth of Russia died; her successor, the mad Peter III, an admirer of Frederick, pulled Russia out of the war. Thus saved, Frederick was able to conclude the Peace of Hubertusberg (1763), which restored the prewar status quo.

The Seven Years' War taught Frederick that, while Prussia's recently acquired position as a great power had been successfully defended, any further adventures in foreign policy had to be avoided at all costs. Hereafter his policy was a strictly defensive one, bent primarily on preventing changes in the balance of power. This became evident when, in 1772, it appeared as if Austria and Russia were about to succeed in partitioning the Ottoman Empire. As there was no chance of securing reasonable compensation for Prussia, Frederick blustered and threatened until the principals agreed on a three-way partition of Poland. In 1778, when Joseph II of Austria attempted to acquire Bavaria, Frederick reluctantly went to war but engaged in no more than a half-hearted war of maneuver of which the Austrians at last tired; and in 1784, when Joseph tried to trade the Austrian Netherlands for Bavaria, Frederick organized the League of German Princes to preserve the status of Germany.

Domestic Policies. Frederick had inherited a well-run state from his father, a circumstance that allowed him to fight his major wars. But he worked as hard at internal administration as at military leadership. He very reluctantly delegated authority, took all important decisions himself, and ruled through ministers responsible only to him. His ruthless insistence on hard work and honesty resulted in a doubling of the revenues of the state in his reign and a tripling of the available reserve fund, this last in spite of the devastation associated with the Seven Years War.

Frederick continued the traditional Prussian policy of encouraging immigration of economically productive elements, particularly peasants, into the more backward and underpopulated areas of the state. In contrast, his policy toward the established peasantry tended to be restrictive. In spite of the spirit of the times, he refused to abolish serfdom where it existed, fearing that such a measure would weaken the landed nobility, which produced both officers for his army and officials for his civil service.

In economics Frederick was a strict mercantilist, fostering the rather backward domestic industry with high tariffs wherever he could. He did not, however, extend these notions to the building of a fleet, so that Prussia did not participate in the great expansion of European overseas trade of the second half of the 18th century.

Apart from purely pragmatic measures, Frederick's reign was not a time of considerable reform. The one exception is the area of judicial procedure, where the efforts of his minister of justice, Cocceji, resulted not merely in a more extensive codification of the law

but in the acceptance of the principle that the law is foremost the protector of the poor and the weak.

During his reign Frederick continued to concern himself with literature and music. He became, in a sense, the host of the most famous salon in Europe. Voltaire was only the best known of the *philosophes* to take advantage of his hospitality. The Prussian Academy of Sciences, which had long languished and which he renewed in 1744, provided much-needed subsidies for both major and minor luminaries of the French Enlightenment. At the same time Frederick had no use for those obstinate enough to persist in writing in "barbaric" German, and the young Goethe was not the only German author deprived of royal assistance for this reason.

But Frederick was not content to be merely a patron of literature. He found time to produce, besides *Anti-Machiavel*, the *Mirror of Princes* and a series of histories dealing with his own affairs that at his death filled 15 volumes.

An Assessment. Frederick was both lionized and vilified long after his death. In Germany his more nationally minded admirers produced a cult of Frederick the Great, the precursor of the all-German hero. In other countries he was blamed as the inventor of an implacable German militarism let loose upon the world. Both these views are gross distortions. Frederick was always a Prussian nationalist, never a German one. And while he was a soldier-king, his pervasive interests throughout his life were nonmilitary. The latter part of his reign was unquestionably pacific and in some cases even propitiatory in nature.

Frederick did not have a first-rate analytical mind, but Voltaire's denunciations of him after their famous quarrel do not sound much more convincing than his panegyrics when he still hoped to get some of the royal money. Frederick was parsimonious, perhaps to a fault, but his funds were in fact severely limited. His treatment of his queen, whom he refused even the right to reside near him, was perhaps unforgivable. Frederick II died at his beloved summer residence, Sans-Souci, near Potsdam on Aug. 17, 1786, and was followed on the throne by his nephew Frederick William II.

EWB

Freud, Sigmund (1856–1939), Austrian founder of psychoanalysis. The work of Sigmund Freud marked the beginning of a modern, dynamic psychology by providing the first systematic explanation of the inner mental forces determining human behavior.

Early in his career Sigmund Freud distinguished himself as a histologist, neuropathologist, and clinical neurologist, and in his later life he was acclaimed as a talented writer and essayist. However, his fame is based on his work in expanding man's knowledge of himself through clinical researches and corresponding development of theories to explain the new data. He laid the foundations for modern understanding of unconscious mental processes (processes excluded from awareness), neurosis (a type of mental disorder), the sexual life of infants, and the interpretation of dreams. Under his guidance, psychoanalysis became the dominant modern theory of human psychology and a major tool of research, as well as an important method of psychiatric treatment which currently has thousands of practitioners all over the world. The application of psychoanalytic thinking to the studies of history, anthropology, religion, art, sociology, and education has greatly changed these fields.

Sigmund Freud was born on May 6, 1856, in Freiberg, Moravia (now a part of the Czech Republic). Sigmund was the first child of his twice-widowed father's third marriage. His mother, Amalia Nathanson, was 19 years old when she married Jacob Freud, aged 39. Sigmund's two stepbrothers from his father's first marriage were approximately the same age as his mother, and his older stepbrother's son, Sigmund's nephew, was his earliest playmate. Thus the boy grew up in an unusual family structure, his mother halfway in age between himself and his father. Though seven younger children were born, Sigmund always remained his mother's favorite. When he was 4, the family moved to Vienna, the capital of the Austro-Hungarian monarchy and one of the great cultural, scientific, and medical centers of Europe. Freud lived in Vienna until a year before his death.

Youth in Vienna.

Because the Freuds were Jewish, Sigmund's early experience was that of an outsider in an overwhelmingly Catholic community. However, Emperor Francis Joseph had emancipated the Jews of Austria, giving them equal rights and permitting them to settle anywhere in the monarchy. Many Jewish families came to Vienna, where the standard of living was higher and educational and professional opportunities better than in the provinces. The Jewish people have always had a strong interest in cultural and intellectual pursuits; this, along with Austria's remaining barriers to social acceptance and progress in academic careers, was influential in Freud's early vocational interests. Had it been easier for him to gain academic success, it might have been more difficult for the young scientist to develop and, later, to defend his unpopular theories.

Although as he grew older Freud never practiced Judaism as a religion, his Jewish cultural background

and tradition were important influences on his thinking. He considered himself Jewish and maintained contact with Jewish organizations; one of his last works was a study of Moses and the Jewish people. However, at times Freud was unhappy that the psychoanalytic movement was so closely tied to Jewish intellectualism.

Freud went to the local elementary school and attended the humanistic high school (or gymnasium) from 1866 to 1873. He studied Greek and Latin, mathematics, history, and the natural sciences, and was a superior student. He passed his final examination with flying colors, qualifying to enter the University of Vienna at the age of 17. His family had recognized his special scholarly gifts from the beginning, and although they had only four bedrooms for eight people, Sigmund had his own room throughout his school days. He lived with his parents until he was 27, as was the custom at that time.

Prepsychoanalytic Work.

Freud first considered studying law but then enrolled in medical school. Vienna had become the world capital of medicine, and the young student was initially attracted to the laboratory and the scientific side of medicine rather than clinical practice. He spent 7 instead of the usual 5 years acquiring his doctorate, taking time to work in the zoological and anatomical laboratories of the famous Ernst Brucke. At 19 he conducted his first independent research project while on a field trip, and at 20 he published his first scientific paper.

Freud received his doctor of medicine degree at the age of 24. An episode at about this time reveals that he was not simply the "good boy" his academic career might suggest: he spent his twenty-fourth birthday in prison, having gone AWOL from his military training. For the next few years he pursued his laboratory work, but several factors shifted his interest from microscopic studies to living patients. Opportunities for advancement in academic medicine were rare at best, and his Jewish background was a decided disadvantage. More important, he fell in love and wanted to marry, but the stipends available to a young scientist could not support a wife and family. He had met Martha Bernays, the daughter of a well-known Hamburg family, when he was 26; they were engaged two months later. They were separated during most of the four years which preceded their marriage, and Freud's over 900 letters to his fiancée provide a good deal of information about his life and personality. They were married in 1887. Of their six children, a daughter, Anna, became one of her father's most famous followers.

Freud spent 3 years as a resident physician in the famous Allgemeine Krankenhaus, a general hospital that was the medical center of Vienna. He rotated through a number of clinical services and spent 5 months in the psychiatry department headed by Theodor Meynert. Psychiatry at this time was static and descriptive. A patient's signs and symptoms were carefully observed and recorded in the hope that they would lead to a correct diagnosis of the organic disease of the brain, which was assumed to be the basis of all psychopathology (mental disorder). The psychological meaning of behavior was not itself considered important; behavior was only a set of symptoms to be studied in order to understand the structures of the brain. Freud's later work revolutionized this attitude; yet like all scientific revolutions, this one grew from a thorough understanding and acknowledged expertise in the traditional methods. He later published widely respected papers on neurology and brain functioning, including works on cerebral palsy in children and aphasia (disturbances in understanding and using words).

Another of Freud's early medical interests brought him to the brink of international acclaim. During his residency he became interested in the effect of an alkaloid extract on the nervous system. He experimented on himself and others and found that small doses of the drug, cocaine, were effective against fatigue. He published a paper describing his findings and also participated in the discovery of cocaine's effect as a local anesthetic. However, he took a trip to visit his fiancée before he could publish the later findings, and during his absence a colleague reported the use of cocaine as an anesthetic for surgery on the eye. Freud's earlier findings were overshadowed, and later fell into disrepute when the addictive properties of cocaine became known.

During the last part of his residency Freud received a grant to pursue his neurological studies abroad. He spent 4 months at the Salpêtrière clinic in Paris, studying under the neurologist Jean Martin Charcot. Here Freud first became interested in hysteria and Charcot's demonstration of its psychological origins. Thus, in fact, Freud's development of a psychoanalytic approach to mental disorders was rooted in 19th-century neurology rather than in the psychiatry of the era.

Beginning of Psychoanalysis. Freud returned to Vienna, established himself in the private practice of neurology, and married. He soon devoted his efforts to the treatment of hysterical patients with the help of hypnosis, a technique he had studied under Charcot. Joseph Breuer, an older colleague who had become Freud's friend and mentor, told Freud about a hysterical patient whom he had treated successfully by hypnotizing her and then tracing her symptoms back to traumatic (emotionally stressful) events she had experienced at her father's deathbed. Breuer called his treatment "catharsis" and attributed its effectiveness to the release of "pent-up emotions." Freud's experiments with Breuer's technique were successful, demonstrating that hysterical symptoms could consistently be traced to highly emotional experiences which had been "repressed," that is, excluded from conscious memory. Together with Breuer he published *Studies on Hysteria* (1895), which included several theoretical chapters, a series of Freud's cases, and Breuer's initial case. At the age of 39 Freud first used the term "psychoanalysis," and his major lifework was well under way.

At about this time Freud began a unique undertaking, his own self-analysis, which he pursued primarily by analyzing his dreams. As he proceeded, his personality changed. He developed a greater inner security while his at times impulsive emotional responses decreased. A major scientific result was *The Interpretation of Dreams* (1901). In this book he demonstrated that the dreams of every man, just like the symptoms of a hysterical or an otherwise neurotic person, serve as a "royal road" to the understanding of unconscious mental processes, which have great importance in determining behavior. By the turn of the century Freud had increased his knowledge of the formation of neurotic symptoms to include conditions and reactions other than hysteria. He had also developed his therapeutic technique, dropping the use of hypnosis and shifting to the more effective and more widely applicable method of "free association."

Development of Psychoanalysis. Following his work on dreams Freud wrote a series of papers in which he explored the influence of unconscious mental processes on virtually every aspect of human behavior: slips of the tongue and simple errors of memory (*The Psychopathology of Everyday Life*, 1901); humor (*Jokes and Their Relation to the Unconscious*, 1905); artistic creativity (*Leonardo da Vinci and a Memory of His Childhood*, 1910); and cultural institutions (*Totem and Taboo*, 1912). He recognized that predominant among the unconscious forces which lead to neuroses are the sexual desires of early childhood that have been excluded from conscious awareness, yet have preserved their dynamic force within the personality. He described his highly controversial views concerning infantile sexuality in *Three Essays on the Theory of Sexuality* (1905), a work which initially met violent protest but was gradually accepted by practically all schools of psychology. During this period he also published a number of case histories and a series of articles dealing with psychoanalysis as a therapy.

After 1902 Freud gathered a small group of interested people on Wednesday evenings for presentation of psychoanalytic papers and discussion. This was the beginning of the psychoanalytic movement. Swiss psychiatrists Eugen Bleuler and Carl Jung formed a study group in Zurich in 1907, and the first International Psychoanalytic Congress was held in Salzburg in 1908. In 1909 Freud was invited to give five lectures at Clark University in Worcester, Mass. He considered this invitation the first official recognition to be extended to his new science.

The new science was not without its difficulties. Earlier, Freud and Breuer had differed concerning their findings with regard to the role of sexual wishes in neurosis. Breuer left psychoanalysis, and the two men parted scientific company, not without some personal animosity. Ironically, Breuer saved his reputation at the time, only to be remembered by later generations because of his brief collaboration with Freud. During his self-analysis Freud developed a strong personal attachment to a philosophically inclined German otolaryngological physician, Wilhelm Fliess. From their letters one observes a gradual cooling of the friendship as Freud's self-analysis progressed.

At the same time Freud faced a major scientific reversal. He first thought that his neurotic patients had actually experienced sexual seductions in childhood, but he then realized that his patients were usually describing childhood fantasies (wishes) rather than actual events. He retracted his earlier statement on infantile sexuality, yet demonstrated his scientific genius when he rejected neither the data nor the theory but reformulated both. He now saw that the universal sexual fantasies of children were scientifically far more important than an occasional actual seduction by an adult. Later, as psychoanalysis became better established, several of Freud's closest colleagues broke with him and established splinter groups of their own, some of which continue to this day. Of such workers in the field, Jung, Alfred Adler, Otto Rank, and Wilhelm Reich are the best known.

Later Years. In 1923 Freud developed a cancerous growth in his mouth that led to his death 16 years and 33 operations later. In spite of this, these were years of great scientific productivity. He published findings on the importance of aggressive as well as sexual drives (*Beyond the Pleasure Principle,* 1920); developed a new theoretical framework in order to organize his new data concerning the structure of the

mind (*The Ego and the Id,* 1923); revised his theory of anxiety to show it as the signal of danger emanating from unconscious fantasies, rather than the result of repressed sexual feelings (*Inhibitions, Symptoms and Anxiety,* 1926); and discussed religion, civilized society, and further questions of theory and technique.

In March 1938 Austria was occupied by German troops, and that month Freud and his family were put under house arrest. Through the combined efforts of Marie Bonaparte, Princess of Greece, British psychoanalyst Ernest Jones, and W. C. Bullitt, the American ambassador to France (who obtained assistance from President Franklin D. Roosevelt), the Freuds were permitted to leave Austria in June. Freud's keen mind and ironic sense of humor were evident when, forced to flee his home at the age of 82, suffering from cancer, and in mortal danger, he was asked to sign a document attesting that he had been treated well by the Nazi authorities; he added in his own handwriting, "I can most warmly recommend the Gestapo to anyone." Freud spent his last year in London, undergoing surgery. He died on Sept. 23, 1939. The influence of his discoveries on the science and culture of the 20th century is incalculable.

Personal Life. Freud's personal life has been a subject of interest to admirers and critics. When it seemed necessary to advance his science, he exposed himself mercilessly, and, particularly in the early years, his own mental functioning was the major subject matter of psychoanalysis. Still, he was an intensely private man, and he made several attempts to thwart future biographers by destroying personal papers. However, his scientific work, his friends, and his extensive correspondence allow historians to paint a vivid picture.

Freud was an imposing man, although physically small. He read extensively, loved to travel, and was an avid collector of archaeological curiosities. Though interested in painting, the musical charms of Vienna had little attraction for him. He collected mushrooms and was an expert on them. Devoted to his family, he always practiced in a consultation room attached to his home. He valued a small circle of close friends and enjoyed a weekly game of cards with them. He was intensely loyal to his friends and inspired loyalty in a circle of disciples that persists to this day.

EWB

Froebel, Friedrich Wilhelm August (1782–1852), German educator and psychologist. Friedrich Froebel was a pioneer of the kindergarten system and influenced the growth of the manual training movement in education.

Friedrich Froebel was born on April 21, 1782, in Oberweissbach, a small village in Thuringia. His father was a Lutheran minister. His mother died 9 months after his birth. In 1797 Froebel was apprenticed to a forester in Thuringia. Two years later, while visiting his brother, Froebel took some courses at the University of Jena.

In 1801 Froebel returned home to be with his ailing father. After his father's death the following year he became a clerk in the forestry department of the state of Bamburg. From 1804 to 1805 he served as a private secretary to several noblemen.

Teaching Career. The year 1805 marked a turning point in Froebel's life. He went to Frankfurt intending to become an architect but instead ended up teaching in a preparatory school. The effect of this teaching experience on Froebel was such that he decided to make education his life's work. In 1808 he went to Yverdon, Switzerland, where he tutored boys attending Johann Pestalozzi's institute. Feeling somewhat lacking in his own educational background, he left Yverdon in 1811 and studied at the universities of Göttingen and Berlin until 1816. During this period he briefly served in the army raised by the German states to oppose Napoleon.

In 1816 Froebel opened the Universal German Educational Institute at Keilham, a school based on his own educational theories. Its curriculum was comprehensive in nature, covering all aspects of the student's growth and developmentboth physical and mental. In 1818 he married Henrietta Hoffmeister.

In Froebel's major educational work, *The Education of Man* (1826), he explained the basic philosophy which guided his educational undertakingsthe unity of all things in God. This doctrine is evident in his work in the area of early-childhood education, to which he turned his attention in 1836. This culminated in the development of his famous kindergarten in 1840. That same year Froebel began to instruct teachers in the principles and methods of the kindergarten. His *Mutter- und Koselieder* (1843) is a song and picture book for children. He spent the remainder of his life elaborating, propagandizing, and defending the principles and practices embodied in the kindergarten.

In 1849, after spending approximately 5 years touring Germany and spreading the idea of the kindergarten, Froebel settled in Liebenstein. He spent the remainder of his life combating conservative forces critical of his educational theories. These forces managed in 1851 to get the Prussian government to ban the kindergarten on the grounds that it was an atheistic and socialistic threat to the state. This action was based not so much on what Froebel had done but rather on his followers' misrepresentation of his educational ideas. He did what he could to restore confidence in his kindergarten but died on June 21, 1852, some 8 years before the ban was lifted by the Prussian government.

The Kindergarten. This preschool experience for children grew out of Froebel's belief that man is essentially part of the total universe that is God. He felt that the only way for one to become one's real self, as God intended, was through the natural unfolding of the innate qualities that made up the whole person. This process should begin as soon as possible and under as natural conditions as possible. The program encouraged free activity, so that forces within the child could be released; creativeness, since man, being part of the creative God, should also create; social participation, since man must by nature act in society (a departure from Rousseau); and motor expression, which is related to activity and learning by doing.

Analysis of Educational Theories. The favorable aspects of his view of the kindergarten lie in Froebel's emphasis on the child, the view that education is growth, the recognition of the importance of activity in education, and the position that knowledge is not the end of education. Less favorable in terms of modern thought is the heavy emphasis he placed on object teaching. Froebel believed in an almost mystical way that an object could in some way create *symbolic* meaning for a child (for example, association with a ball teaches the meaning of unity). In later years the use of objects was to become a formalized and fixed part of the kindergarten curriculum. The "unfolding of innate qualities" in a mystical manner has also been criticized as being unscientific.

EWB

Fry, Elizabeth (1780–1845), British reformer and Quaker lay evangelist. Elizabeth Fry worked for prison reform, particularly to relieve the physical misery and moral degradation of women prisoners.

An evangelist who relied on prayer and Bible-reading to inculcate virtue, Elizabeth Fry epitomized the reformer inspired by religious motives. She also relied on her access to the politically powerful, an advantage she enjoyed as a member of a well-connected Quaker family and enhanced by the celebrity status that she quickly attained through her prison visits. Her work on behalf of women prisoners caught the popular fancy, and she enjoyed a prestige in her country and in other European countries that few women in a society ruled by men could match. On the other hand, England soon rejected her approach to prison reform.

People worried about the increase in crime that had started with the Industrial Revolution; it had increased even more after the end of the long wars with France brought extensive unemployment. A combination of the 18th-century Enlightenment critique of traditional institutions and a humanitarianism largely rooted in Evangelical (and Quaker) religion encouraged a fresh look at crime and punishment.

Fry inspired confidence as a devout, motherly woman of unquestionable sincerity. Her prison visits belonged to a tradition of well-off, benevolent women visiting the unfortunate, a kind of unpaid social work. Helping women prisoners appeared to be a respectable philanthropy for pious women with time, energy, and money to spare. Although the Society of Friends had an English membership of less than 20,000 during Fry's lifetime, Quaker women took a disproportionate role in charity and reform.

Elizabeth Fry was born into a happy, prosperous family, the Gurneys, at Norwich in eastern England, blighted only by the early death of her mother. Her father's relaxed Quakerism abandoned many of the restrictions identified with that religion, such as the requirement to wear only simple clothing and to avoid worldly society. She grew up enjoying fashionable parties and dances that earlier Quakers would have avoided. Some of her sisters would eventually withdraw from Quakerism to join the state Anglican Church, and her banker brothers would greatly add to the family riches.

Fry was in her teens in 1798 when an American member of the Society of Friends attacked the luxurious "gayness" of the local Quakers and awakened in Fry a sense of God that began her conversion to a strict Quakerism. This was not the common Evangelical conversion experience—a realization of guilt, followed by a sense of God's forgiveness—but instead a mystical communion with God. She never desired religious ceremonies or theology or a highly organized church. Her religion was a very personal one, founded on silent meditation, aided by the reading of the Bible, that sometimes led to informal but eloquent sermons. Virtually alone among religious denominations of the early 19th century, the small Society of Friends allowed women and men an equal right to speak at religious services because of the Quaker principle of direct inspiration.

Fry gradually adopted the strict Quaker policies on dress and Quaker peculiarities of speech (such as saying "thee" and "thou" instead of "you"). She became what contemporaries called a plain Friend. By 1799, she rejected singing as a distraction from true piety. (Her younger brother Joseph John Gurney followed her in reviving many of the old distinctive practices of the Quakers that separated them from other people; although as the leader of the Evangelical Quakers, he encouraged good relations with all Evangelical Protestants.)

After her father's death in 1809, Fry began to speak at Quaker meetings and was recognized officially as a full minister two years later. Her marriage in 1800 to a London Quaker, Joseph Fry, delayed her wider public career; she bore ten children between 1801 and 1816 (and an 11th in 1822).

Prison Ministry Begins. Although at the urging of an American Quaker she had visited Newgate Gaol (jail) in London during 1813, it was at the end of 1816 that Elizabeth Fry began her systematic work as a prison reformer. She visited many prisons in the British Isles during the following years, but she made her special mission the reform of the women imprisoned in Newgate. Approximately 300 women and children were crowded in a women's ward comprising 190 square yards. Hardened criminals guilty of serious crimes were mixed with those jailed for minor offenses. Children lived in the prison with their mothers, in rags, filth, and idleness. As the prison furnished no uniforms, many poverty-stricken women existed half-naked. Prison policy combined occasional brutality with a permissiveness that allowed inmates considerable freedom tolerating drinking and fighting and made no attempt at rehabilitation, such as training the women for jobs outside prison walls.

In 1817, Fry organized the Association for the Improvement of Female Prisoners in Newgate. Two members visited the prisoners every day to read the Scriptures aloud. When Fry read from the Bible (and preached) at Newgate, so many people wanted to attend that the London magistrates authorized her to issue tickets. Association members adopted a personal approach toward women prisoners and tried to gain their active cooperation through kindness and persuasion. Fry's association put the women prisoners to work, sewing and knitting, under the supervision of prisoner monitors. With a prisoner as the instructor, it also organized a school for the women (and their children) to teach them to read the Bible. One of Fry's rules for the Newgate women declared "that there be no begging, swearing, gaming, card-playing, quarrelling, or immoral conversation."

Fry's work was not confined to Newgate. In 1818, she made a tour of prisons in northern England and Scotland with her brother Joseph John Gurney, described in a book published under his name, *Notes on a Visit Made to Some of the Prisons in Scotland and the North of England in Company with Elizabeth Fry.* Middle-class ladies' committees sprang up to visit prisons all over the country. In 1821, they joined together as the British Ladies' Society for Promoting the Reformation of Female Prisoners.

Fry was an activist, not in most respects an original thinker. Ironically, most of her ideas resembled those of Jeremy Bentham, an earlier prison reformer who often is contrasted with Fry because he despised religion. Like Bentham, Fry favored classifying prisoners (in contrast to the prevalent mixing of all types), providing productive work for them, and establishing healthful living conditions. Her more distinctive opinions favored the employment of matrons to supervise women prisoners, rejected capital punishment (and flogging) in principle, minimized the role of unproductive hard labor such as working the treadmill, and repudiated bread-and-water diets. She tried, with modest success, to mitigate the sufferings of the women sentenced to transportation to Australia, a form of penal exile. Above all, she insisted that women criminals could be redeemed.

Her Influence Wanes.   For a few years, Fry had the ear of Cabinet ministers and parliamentary committees, but she soon lost her influence. Overestimating what she could do, she offended those whom she wanted to persuade. This was the case in 1818 when she lobbied the Home Secretary, Lord Sidmouth, to stop the execution of a Newgate prisoner.

By 1827, when she published the short book *Observations on the Visiting, Superintendence and Government of Female Prisoners,* based on her practical experience, her time of importance had already passed. She continued to argue for the importance of local ladies' committees; the influence of public-spirited women was needed to supplement and correct the laws and regulations established by men. For the prisoners themselves, she urged the women visitors to show a spirit of mercy: "Great pity is due from us even to the greatest transgressors among our fellow-creatures."

Fry lost prestige (and money for her prison charities) when her husband's businesses failed in 1828. As a bankrupt, he was excluded from the Society of Friends, and the Fry family became dependent on the financial generosity of the wealthy Gurneys.

By the mid-1820s, other prison reformers increasingly advocated policies contrary to Elizabeth Fry's. Many Quakers (including two of her brothers-in-law) were prominent in the Society for the Improvement of Prison Discipline and the Reformation of Juvenile Reformers (founded in 1818), but after a brief period when it supported her, the Society lob-

bied for a centralized professional prison administration and detailed bureaucratic rules that left no place for the visits of "meddlesome" ladies' committees. Fry's rivals campaigned for the harsh prison policies pioneered in the United States in Philadelphia, such as solitary confinement and exhausting hard labor. These principles became law when Parliament adopted the Prison Act of 1835.

Although lacking any practical influence, Fry remained a celebrity, particularly on the continent of Europe. Acclaimed in 1838 and 1841 when she visited France and the German states, she was also honored in 1842 by the king of Prussia who visited her Bible-reading at Newgate and lunched at her home.

Two years after Elizabeth Fry died in 1845, two of her daughters published a *Memoir of the Life of Elizabeth Fry with Extracts from her Journal and Letters,* an abridgment in two volumes of her 44 volumes of handwritten journals. The *Memoir* sought to make Fry a saint and left out whatever the daughters regarded as not fitting that image. Until 1980, Fry's biographers failed to read the original journals.

Fry was not the perfect woman that her daughters presented. She embodied many contradictions. She adhered to a strict Quakerism that required plain living and the rejection of worldly vanities; yet, as some fellow Quakers grumbled, her simple clothes were cut from expensive fabrics, and she rejoiced in her opportunities to mingle with politicians, aristocrats, and royalty. Nothing was more important for her than her religion, yet, to her great anguish, she failed to nurture a commitment to Quakerism among her children, nearly all of whom left the Society of Friends when they grew up.

Despite her limitations, Elizabeth Fry deserves to be remembered as a genuinely good woman, as her contemporaries acknowledged, and a much wiser one than the men who belittled her as a naive amateur realized. In the early 19th century, women reformers were loved more often than they were respected. Although far from perfect, Fry's philosophy of prison reform avoided numbing bureaucracy and dehumanizing brutality and encouraged the participation of members of the general public in the conduct of prison life.

EWB

G

Galileo Galilei   (1564–1642), Italian scientist. Galileo is renowned for his epoch-making contributions to astronomy, physics, and scientific philosophy.

Galileo was born in Pisa on Feb. 15, 1564, the first child of Vincenzio Galilei, a merchant and musician and an abrasive champion of advanced musical theories of the day. The family moved to Florence in 1574, and that year Galileo started his formal education in the nearby monastery of Vallombrosa. Seven years later he matriculated as a student of medicine at the University of Pisa.

In 1583, while Galileo was at home on vacation, he began to study mathematics and the physical sciences. His zeal astonished Ostilio Ricci, a family friend and professor at the Academy of Design. Ricci was a student of Nicolò Tartaglia, the famed algebraist and translator into Latin of several of Archimedes' works. Galileo's life-long admiration for Archimedes started, therefore, as his scientific studies got under way.

Galileo's new interest brought to an end his medical studies, but in Pisa at that time there was only one notable science teacher, Francisco Buonamico, and he was an Aristotelian. Galileo seems, however, to have been an eager disciple of his, as shown by Galileo's *Juvenilia,* dating from 1584, mostly paraphrases of Aristotelian physics and cosmology. Because of financial difficulties Galileo had to leave the University of Pisa in 1585 before he got his degree.

Early Work. Back in Florence, Galileo spent 3 years vainly searching for a suitable teaching position. He was more successful in furthering his grasp of mathematics and physics. He produced two treatises which, although circulated in manuscript form only, made his name well known. One was *La bilancetta* (The Little Balance), describing the hydrostatic principles of balancing; the other was a study on the center of gravity of various solids. These topics, obviously demanding a geometrical approach, were not the only evidence of his devotion to geometry and Archimedes. In a lecture given in 1588 before the Florentine Academy on the topography of Dante's *Inferno,* Galileo seized on details that readily lent themselves to a display of his prowess in geometry. He showed himself a perfect master both of the poet's text and of the incisiveness and sweep of geometrical lore.

Galileo's rising reputation as a mathematician and natural philosopher (physicist) gained him a teaching post at the University of Pisa in 1589. The 3 years he spent there are memorable for two things. First, he became exposed through reading a work of Giovanni Battista Benedetti to the "Parisian tradition" of physics, which originated during the 14th century with the speculations of Jean Buridan and Nicole Oresme at the University of Paris. This meant the breakaway point in Galileo's thought from Aristotelian

physics and the start of his preoccupation with a truly satisfactory formulation of the impetus theory. Second, right at the beginning of his academic career, he showed himself an eager participant in disputes and controversies. With biting sarcasm he lampooned the custom of wearing academic gowns. The most he was willing to condone was the use of ordinary clothes, but only after pointing out that the best thing was to go naked.

The death of Galileo's father in 1591 put on his shoulders the care of his mother, brothers, and sisters. He had to look for a better position, which he found in 1592 at the University of Padua, part of the Venetian Republic. The 18 years he spent there were, according to his own admission, the happiest of his life. He often visited Venice and made many influential friends, among them Giovanfrancesco Sagredo, whom he later immortalized in the *Dialogue* as the representative of judiciousness and good sense.

In 1604 Galileo publicly declared that he was a Copernican. In three public lectures given in Venice, before an overflow audience, he argued that the new star which appeared earlier that year was major evidence in support of the doctrine of Copernicus. (Actually the new star merely proved that there was something seriously wrong with the Aristotelian doctrine of the heavens.) More important was a letter Galileo wrote that year to Father Paolo Sarpi, in which he stated that "the distances covered in natural motion are proportional to the squares of the number of time intervals, and therefore, the distances covered in equal times are as the odd numbers beginning from one." By natural motion, Galileo meant the unimpeded fall of a body, and what he proposed was the law of free fall, later written as $s = 1/2(gt^2)$, where s is distance, t is time, and g is the acceleration due to gravity at sea level.

In 1606 came the publication of *The Operations of the Geometrical and Military Compass,* which reveals the experimentalist and craftsman in Galileo. In this booklet he went overboard in defending his originality against charges from rather insignificant sources. It was craftsmanship, not theorizing, which put the crowning touch on his stay in Padua. In mid-1609 he learned about the success of some Dutch spectacle makers in combining lenses into what later came to be called a telescope. He feverishly set to work, and on August 25 he presented to the Venetian Senate a telescope as his own invention. The success was tremendous. He obtained a lifelong contract at the University of Padua, but he also stirred up just resentment when it was learned that he was not the original inventor.

Astronomical Works. Galileo's success in making a workable and sufficiently powerful telescope with a magnifying power of about 40 was due to intuition rather than to rigorous reasoning in optics. It was also the intuitive stroke of a genius that made him turn the telescope toward the sky sometime in the fall of 1609, a feat which a dozen other people could very well have done during the previous 4 to 5 years. Science had few luckier moments. Within a few months he gathered astonishing evidence about mountains on the moon, about moons circling Jupiter, and about an incredibly large number of stars, especially in the belt of the Milky Way. On March 12, 1610, all these sensational items were printed in Venice under the title *Sidereus nuncius* (*The Starry Messenger*), a booklet which took the world of science by storm. The view of the heavens drastically changed, and so did Galileo's life.

Historians agree that Galileo's decision to secure for himself the position of court mathematician in Florence at the court of Cosimo II (the job also included the casting of horoscopes for his princely patron) reveals a heavy strain of selfishness in his character. He wanted nothing, not even a modest amount of teaching, to impede him in pursuing his ambition to become the founder of new physics and new astronomy. In 1610 he left behind in Padua his common-law wife, Marina Gamba, and his young son, Vincenzio, and placed his two daughters, aged 12 and 13, in the convent of S. Matteo in Arcetri. The older, Sister Maria Celeste as nun, was later a great comfort to her father.

Galileo's move to Florence turned out to be highly unwise, as events soon showed. In the beginning, however, everything was pure bliss. He made a triumphal visit to Rome in 1611. The next year saw the publication of his *Discourse on Bodies in Water*. There he disclosed his discovery of the phases of Venus (a most important proof of the truth of the Copernican theory), but the work was also the source of heated controversies. In 1613 Galileo published his observations of sunspots, which embroiled him for many years in bitter disputes with the German Jesuit Christopher Scheiner of the University of Ingolstadt, whose observations of sunspots had already been published in January 1612 under the pseudonym Apelles.

First Condemnation. But Galileo's real aim was to make a sweeping account of the Copernican universe and of the new physics it necessitated. A major obstacle was the generally shared, though officially never sanctioned, belief that the biblical revelation imposed geocentrism in general and the motionlessness of the earth in particular. To counter the scriptural difficulties, he waded deep into theology. With the help of some enlightened ecclesiastics, such as Monsignor Piero Dini and Father Benedetto Castelli, a Benedictine from Monte Cassino and his best scientific pupil, Galileo produced essays in the form of letters, which now rank among the best writings of biblical theology of those times. As the letters (the longest one was addressed to Grand Duchess Christina of Tuscany) circulated widely, a confrontation with the Church authorities became inevitable. The disciplinary instruction handed down in 1616 by Cardinal Robert Bellarmine forbade Galileo to "hold, teach and defend in any manner whatsoever, in words or in print" the Copernican doctrine of the motion of the earth.

Galileo knew, of course, both the force and the limits of what in substance was a disciplinary measure. It could be reversed, and he eagerly looked for any evidence indicating precisely that. He obeyed partly out of prudence, partly because he remained to the end a devout and loyal Catholic. Although his yearning for fame was powerful, there can be no doubt about the sincerity of his often-voiced claim that by his advocacy of Copernicanism he wanted to serve the long-range interest of the Church in a world of science. The first favorable sign came in 1620, when Cardinal Maffeo Barberini composed a poem in honor of Galileo. Three years later the cardinal became Pope Urban VIII. How encouraged Galileo must have felt can be seen from the fact that he dedicated to the new pope his freshly composed *Assayer,* one of the finest pieces of polemics ever produced in the philosophy of science.

The next year Galileo had six audiences with Urban VIII, who promised a pension for Galileo's son, Vincenzio, but gave Galileo no firm assurance about changing the injunction of 1616. But before departing for Florence, Galileo was informed that the Pope had remarked that "the Holy Church had never, and would never, condemn it [Copernicanism] as heretical but only as rash, though there was no danger that anyone would ever demonstrate it to be necessarily true." This was more than enough to give Galileo the necessary encouragement to go ahead with the great undertaking of his life.

The *Dialogue*. Galileo spent 6 years writing his *Dialogue concerning the Two Chief World Systems.* When the final manuscript copy was being made in March 1630, Father Castelli dispatched the news to Galileo that Urban VIII insisted in a private conversation with him that, had he been the pope in 1616, the censuring of Copernicanism would have never taken place. Galileo also learned about the benevolent attitude of the Pope's official theologian, Father Nicolò Riccardi, Master of the Sacred Palace. The book was published with ecclesiastical approbation on Feb. 21, 1632.

Second Condemnation. The *Dialogue* certainly proved that for all his rhetorical provisos Galileo held, taught, and defended the doctrine of Copernicus. It did not help Galileo either that he put into the mouth of the discredited Simplicius an argument which was a favorite with Urban VIII. Galileo was summoned to Rome to appear before the Inquisition. Legally speaking, his prosecutors were justified. Galileo did not speak the truth when he claimed before his judges that he did not hold Copernicanism since the precept was given to him in 1616 to abandon it. The justices had their point, but it was the letter of the law, not its spirit, that they vindicated. More importantly, they miscarried justice, aborted philosophical truth, and gravely compromised sound theology. In that misguided defense of orthodoxy the only sad solace for Galileo's supporters consisted in the fact that the highest authority of the Church did not become implicated, as the Catholic René Descartes, the Protestant Gottfried Wilhelm von Leibniz, and others were quick to point out during the coming decades.

The proceedings dragged on from the fall of 1632 to the summer of 1633. During that time Galileo was allowed to stay at the home of the Florentine ambassador in Rome and was detained by the Holy Office only from June 21, the day preceding his abjuration, until the end of the month. He was never subjected to physical coercion. However, he had to inflict the supreme torture upon himself by abjuring the doctrine that the earth moved. One hundred years later a writer with vivid imagination dramatized the event by claiming that following his abjuration Galileo muttered the words "Eppur si muove (And yet it does move)."

On his way back to Florence, Galileo enjoyed the hospitality of the archbishop of Siena for some 5 months and then received permission in December to live in his own villa at Arcetri. He was not supposed to have any visitors, but this injunction was not obeyed. Nor was ecclesiastical prohibition a serious obstacle to the printing of his works outside Italy. In 1634 Father Marin Mersenne published in French translation a manuscript of Galileo on mechanics composed during his Paduan period. In Holland the Elzeviers brought out his *Dialogue* in Latin in 1635 and shortly afterward his great theological letter to Grand Duchess Christina. But the most important event in this connection took place in 1638, when Galileo's *Two New Sciences* saw print in Leiden.

Two New Sciences. The first draft of the work went back to Galileo's professorship at Padua. But cosmology replaced pure physics as the center of his attention until 1633. His condemnation was in a sense a gain for physics. He had no sooner regained his composure in Siena than he was at work preparing for publication old, long-neglected manuscripts. The *Two New Sciences,* like the *Dialogue,* is in the dialogue form and the discussions are divided into Four Days.

Galileo found the justification for such a geometrical analysis of motion partly because it led to a striking correspondence with factual data. More importantly, he believed that the universe was structured along the patterns of geometry. In 1604 he could have had experimental verification of the law of free fall, which he derived on a purely theoretical basis, but it is not known that he sought at that time such an experimental proof. He was a Christian Platonist as far as scientific method was concerned. This is why he praised Copernicus repeatedly in the *Dialogue* for his belief in the voice of reason, although it contradicted sense experience. Such a faith rested on the conviction that the world was a product of a personal, rational Creator who disposed everything according to weight, measure, and number.

This biblically inspired faith was stated by Galileo most eloquently in the closing pages of the First Day of the *Dialogue.* There he described the human mind as the most excellent product of the Creator, precisely because it could recognize mathematical truths. This faith is possibly the most precious bequest of the great Florentine, who spent his last years partially blind. His disciple Vincenzio Viviani sensed this well as he described the last hours of Galileo: "On the night of Jan. 8, 1642, with philosophical and Christian firmness he rendered up his soul to its Creator, sending it, as he liked to believe, to enjoy and to watch from a closer vantage point those eternal and immutable marvels which he, by means of a fragile device, had brought closer to our mortal eyes with such eagerness and impatience."

EWB

Galton, Sir Francis (1822–1911), English scientist, biometrician, and explorer. Francis Galton founded the science of eugenics and introduced the theory of the anticyclone in meteorology.

Francis Galton was born on Feb. 16, 1822, at Birmingham, the son of Samuel Galton, a businessman, and Violetta Galton. After schooling in Boulogne and privately, he began to study medicine in 1838 but also read mathematics at Trinity College, Cambridge.

The death of Galton's father in 1844 left him with considerable independent means, and he abandoned further medical study to travel in Syria, Egypt, and South-West Africa. As a result, he published *Tropical South Africa* (1853) and *The Art of Travel* (1855). His travels brought him fame as an explorer, and in 1854 he was awarded the Gold Medal of the Geographical Society. He was elected fellow of the Royal Society in 1856.

Turning his attention to meteorology, Galton published *Meteorographica* (1863), in which he described weather mapping, pointing out for the first time the importance of an anticyclone, in which air circulates clockwise round a center of high barometric pressure in the Northern Hemisphere. Cyclones, on the other hand, are low-pressure centers from which air rushes upward and moves counterclockwise.

Meanwhile, Galton had developed an interest in heredity, and the publication of *The Origin of Species* (1859) by Charles Darwin won Galton's immediate support. Impressed by evidence that distinction of any kind is apt to run in families, Galton made detailed studies of families conspicuous for inherited ability over several generations. He then advocated the application of scientific breeding to human populations. These studies laid the foundation for the science of eugenics (a term he invented), or race improvement, and led to the publication of *Hereditary Genius* (1869) and *English Men of Science: Their Nature and Nurture* (1874).

Finding that advances in the study of heredity were being hampered by the lack of quantitative information, Galton started anthropometric research, devising instruments for the exact measurement of every quantifiable faculty of body or mind. In 1884 he finally set up and equipped a laboratory, the Biometric Laboratory at University College, London, where the public were tested. He measured such traits as keenness of sight and hearing, color sense, reaction time, strength of pull and of squeeze, and height and weight. The system of fingerprints in universal use today derived from this work.

Galton's application of exact quantitative methods gave results which, processed mathematically, developed a numerical factor he called correlation and defined thus: "Two variable organs are said to be co-related when the variation of the one is accompanied on the average by more or less variation of the other, and in the same direction. Co-relation must be the consequence of the variations of the two organs being partly due to common causes. If wholly due . . . the co-relation would be perfect." Co-relation specified the degree of relationship between any pair of individuals or any two attributes.

The developed presentation of Galton's views on heredity is *Natural Inheritance* (1889). A difficult work, with mathematics not beyond criticism, it sets out the "law of 1885," which attempts to quantify the influence of former generations in the hereditary makeup of the individual. Parents contribute each one-quarter, grandparents each one-sixteenth, and so on for earlier generations. Claims that Galton anticipated Mendel's ratios seem without foundation. For Galton, evolution ensured the survival of those members of the race with most physical and mental vigor, and he desired to see this come about in human society more speedily and with less pain to the individual through applying eugenics. Evolution was an unresting progression, the nature of the average individual being essentially unprogressive.

Galton used his considerable fortune to promote his scientific interests. He founded the journal *Biometrika* in 1901, and in 1903 the Eugenics Laboratory in the University of London. He died at Haslemere, Surrey, on Jan. 17, 1911, after several years of frail health. He bequeathed £45,000 to found a professorship in eugenics in the hope that his disciple and pupil Karl Pearson might become its first occupant. This hope was realized.

EWB

Gama, Vasco da (ca. 1460–1524), Portuguese navigator. Vasco da Gama was the first to travel by sea from Portugal to India. The term "Da Gama epoch" is used to describe the era of European commercial and imperial expansion launched by his navigational enterprise.

Little is known of the early life of Vasco da Gama; his father was governor of Sines, Portugal, where Vasco was born. He first comes to historical notice in 1492, when he seized French ships in Portuguese ports as reprisal for piratical raids. When he was commissioned for his famous voyage, he was a gentleman at the court of King Manuel I.

Manuel, against the advice of a majority of his counselors, had decided to follow up Bartolomeu Dias's triumphal voyage round the Cape of Good Hope (1487–1488) with a well-planned attempt to reach all the way to the Malabar Coast of India, the ports of which were the major entrepôts for the Western spice trade with southeastern Asia. This trade had fallen under the control of Moslem merchants; the Venetians were only the final distributors to Europe of these valuable commodities.

Manuel hoped to displace the Moslem (and thus the Venetian) middlemen and to establish Portuguese hegemony over the Oriental oceanic trades. He also hoped to join with Eastern Christian forces (symbolized to medieval Europeans by the legend of the powerful priest-king, Prester John) and thus carry on a worldwide crusade against Islam. Da Gama's voyage was to be the first complete step toward the realization of these ambitions.

Da Gama, supplied with letters of introduction to Prester John and to the ruler of the Malabar city of Calicut, set sail from the Tagus River in Lisbon on July 8, 1497. He commanded the flagship *St. Gabriel*, accompanied by the *St. Raphael* and *Berrio* (commanded, respectively, by his brother Paulo and Nicolas Coelho) and a large supply ship. After a landfall in the Cape Verde Islands, he stood well out to sea, rounding the Cape of Good Hope on November 22. Sailing past the port of Sofala, the expedition landed at Kilimane, the second in a string of East African coastal cities. These towns were under Moslem control and gained their wealth largely through trade in gold and ivory. Proceeding to Mozambique, where they were at first mistaken for Moslems, the Portuguese were kindly received by the sultan. A subsequent dispute, however, led da Gama to order a naval bombardment of the city.

Traveling northward to Mombasa, the Portuguese escaped a Moslem attempt to destroy the small fleet and hurriedly sailed for the nearby port of Malindi. Its sultan, learning of the bombardment to the south, decided to cooperate with da Gama and lent him the services of the famous Indian pilot Ibn Majid for the next leg of the journey. On May 20, 1498, the Portuguese anchored off Calicut, then the most important trading center in southern India, well prepared to tap the fabulous riches of India.

Their expectations, however, were soon to be deflated. The Portuguese at first thought the Hindu inhabitants of the city to be Christians, although a visit to a local temple where they were permitted to worship "Our Lady"—Devaki, mother of the god Krishna—made them question the purity of the faith as locally practiced. The zamorin, the ruler of Calicut, warmly welcomed the newcomers until his treasurers appraised the inexpensive items sent as gifts by King Manuel. In fact, the potentates of the East were at that time wealthier than the financially embarrassed Western kings, and the zamorin quite naturally had looked for a standard tribute in gold. The Portuguese merchandise did not sell well in the port, and the Moslem merchants who dominated the city's trade convinced the zamorin that he stood to gain nothing by concluding a commercial agreement with the intruders.

Amid rumors of plots against his life but with his ships stocked with samples of precious jewels and spices, da Gama sailed from Calicut at the end of August 1498. The trip back to Portugal proved far more difficult than the voyage out, and many men died of scurvy during the 3-month journey across the Arabian Sea. The *St. Raphael* was burned and its complement distributed among the other ships. The remaining vessels became separated in a storm off the West African coast, and Coelho was the first to reach home (July 10, 1499). The da Gamas had gone to the Azores, where Paulo died, and Vasco arrived in Lisbon on September 9.

Da Gama returned twice to India: in 1502, when he bombarded Calicut in revenge for an attack on a previous Portuguese expedition; and in 1524, when he was appointed viceroy. On Dec. 24, 1524, Vasco da Gama died in the southwestern Indian city of Cochin. He was richly rewarded for his services by his sovereign, being made Count of Vidiguerira and Admiral of the Indian Seas and receiving pensions and a lucrative slice of the Eastern trade.

Da Gama's first voyage deserves to be compared with Columbus's more celebrated "discovery" of the New World. Neither man actually "discovered" unoccupied territories; rather, both linked anciently settled and developed parts of the world with Europe. The Spaniards subsequently conquered the "Indians" of the West, living in settler societies off their labor and natural resources; the Portuguese founded a seaborne commercial empire from which they tried to drain middlemen's profits from a trade still on the whole unfavorably balanced against Europe.

EWB

Gaulle, Charles André Joseph Marie de (1890–1970), French general and statesman. Charles de Gaulle led the Free French forces during World War II. A talented writer and eloquent orator, he served as president of France from 1958 to 1969.

Charles de Gaulle was born on Nov. 23, 1890, in the northern industrial city of Lille. His father, Henri, was a teacher of philosophy and mathematics and a veteran of the Franco-Prussian War of 1870, in which the Prussians humiliatingly defeated what the French thought was the greatest army in the world. This loss colored the life of the elder de Gaulle, a patriot who vowed he would live to avenge the defeat and win back the provinces of Alsace and Lorraine. His attitude deeply influenced the lives of his sons, whom he raised to be the instruments of his revenge and of the restoration of France as the greatest European power.

From his earliest years Charles de Gaulle was immersed in French history by both his father and mother. For many centuries de Gaulle's forebears had played a role in French history, almost always as patriots defending France from invaders. In the 14th century a Chevalier de Gaulle defeated an invading English army in defense of the city of Vire, and Jean de Gaulle is cited in the Battle of Agincourt (1415).

Charles's great-great-grandfather, Jean Baptiste de Gaulle, was a king's counselor. His grandfather, Julien Philippe de Gaulle, wrote a popular history of Paris; Charles received this book on his tenth birthday and, as a young boy, read and reread it. He was also devoted to the literary works of his gifted grandmother, Julien Philippe's wife, Josephine Marie, whose name gave him two of his baptismal names. One of her greatest influences upon him was her impassioned, romantic history, *The Liberator of Ireland, or the Life of Daniel O'Connell*. It always remained for him an illustration of man's resistance to persecution, religious or political, and an inspiring example he emulated in his own life.

Perhaps the major influence on De Gaulle's formation came from his uncle, also named Charles de Gaulle, who wrote a book about the Celts which called for union of the Breton, Scots, Irish, and Welsh peoples. The young de Gaulle wrote in his copybook a sentence from his uncle's book, which proved to be a prophecy of his own life: "In a camp, surprised by enemy attack under cover of night, where each man is fighting alone, in dark confusion, no one asks for the grade or rank of the man who lifts up the standard and makes the first call to rally for resistance."

Military Career. De Gaulle's career as defender of France began in the summer of 1909, when he was admitted to the elite military academy of Saint-Cyr. Among his classmates was the future marshal of France Alphonse Juin, who later recalled de Gaulle's nicknames in school, "The Grand Constable," "The Fighting Cock," and "The Big Asparagus."

After graduation Second Lieutenant de Gaulle reported in October 1912 to Henri Philippe Pétain, who first became his idol and then his most hated enemy. (In World War I Pétain was the hero of Verdun, but during World War II he capitulated to Hitler and collaborated with the Germans while de Gaulle was leading the French forces of liberation.) De Gaulle led a frontline company as captain in World War I and was cited three times for valor. Severely wounded, he was left for dead on the battlefield of Verdun and then imprisoned by the Germans when he revived in a graveyard cart. After he had escaped and been recaptured several times, the Germans put him in a maximum security prison-fortress.

After the war de Gaulle went to general-staff school, where he hurt his career by constant criticism of his superiors. He denounced the static concept of trench warfare and wrote a series of essays calling for a strategy of movement with armored tanks and planes. The French hierarchy ignored his works, but the Germans read him and adapted his theories to develop their triumphant strategy of blitzkrieg, or lightning war, with which they defeated the French in 1940.

When France fell, de Gaulle, then an obscure brigadier general, refused to capitulate. He fled to London, convinced that the British would never surrender and that American power, once committed, would win the war. On June 18, 1940, on BBC radio, he insisted that France had only lost a battle, not the war, and called upon patriotic Frenchmen to resist the Germans. This inspiring broadcast won him worldwide acclaim.

Early Political Activity. When the Germans were driven back, de Gaulle had no rivals for leadership in France. Therefore in the fall of 1944 the French Parliament unanimously elected him premier. De Gaulle had fiercely opposed the German enemy, and now he vigorously defended France against the influence of his powerful allies Joseph Stalin, Winston Churchill, and Franklin Roosevelt. De Gaulle once stated that he never feared Adolf Hitler, who, he knew, was doomed to defeat, but did fear that his allies would dominate France and Europe in the postwar period.

By the fall of 1945, only a year after assuming power, de Gaulle was quarreling with all the political leaders of France. He saw himself as the unique savior of France, the only disinterested champion of French honor, grandeur, and independence. He despised all politicians as petty, corrupt, and self-interested muddlers, and, chafing under his autocratic rule, they banded against him. In January 1946, disgusted by politics, he resigned and retreated into a sulking silence to brood upon the future of France.

In 1947 de Gaulle reemerged as leader of the opposition. He headed what he termed "The Rally of the French People," which he insisted was not a political party but a national movement. The Rally became the largest single political force in France but never achieved majority status. Although de Gaulle continued to despise the political system, he refused to lead a coup d'etat, as some of his followers urged, and again retired in 1955.

Years as President. In May 1958 a combination of French colonials and militarists seized power in Algeria and threatened to invade France. The weakened Fourth Republic collapsed, and the victorious rebels called de Gaulle back to power as president of the Fifth Republic of France. From June 1958 to April 1969 he reigned as the dominant force in France. But he was not a dictator, as many have charged; he was elected first by Parliament and then in a direct election by the people.

As president, de Gaulle fought every plan to involve France deeply in alliances. He opposed the formation of a United States of Europe and British entry into the Common Market. He stopped paying part of France's dues to the United Nations, forced the NATO headquarters to leave France, and pulled French forces out of the Atlantic Alliance integrated armies. Denouncing Soviet oppression of Eastern Europe, he also warned of the Chinese threat to the world. He liberated France's colonies, supported the Vietnamese "liberation movement" against the United States, and called for a "free Quebec" in Canada.

De Gaulle had an early success in stimulating pride in Frenchmen and in increasing French gold reserves and strengthening the economy. By the end of his reign, however, France was almost friendless, and his economic gains had been all but wiped out by the student and workers protest movement in spring 1968.

De Gaulle ruled supreme for 11 years, but his firm hand began to choke and then to infuriate many citizens. In April 1969 the French voted against his program for reorganizing the Senate and the regions of France. He had threatened to resign if his plan was rejected and, true to his word, he promptly renounced all power. Thereafter de Gaulle remained silent on political issues. Georges Pompidou, one of his favorite lieutenants, was elected to succeed him as president. Charles de Gaulle died at Colombey-les-Deux-Églises on Nov. 9, 1970.

EWB

Garbo, Greta (1905–1990), Swedish-born American film star. Greta Garbo became one of Hollywood's legendary personalities.

Born Greta Louisa Gustafsson on September 18, 1905, in Stockholm, Sweden, Greta Garbo grew up in respectable poverty—inhibited, self-conscious, and oddly mature. She was one of three children and became a legendary actress and one of the most fascinating women of all time. Garbo was a woman of remarkable beauty, intelligence, and independent spirit. Despite her beauty, Garbo was somewhat reclusive and photophobic. She once told a gossip columnist in France, "I feel like a criminal who is hunted . . . when photographers come, they draw crowds. I am frightened beyond control. When so many people stare, I feel almost ashamed."

She was a stagestruck girl of 14 when her job as a clerk in a department store led to photographic modeling for her employer's catalog. This in turn brought parts in two short advertising films and, at 16, a bathing beauty role in E. A. Petschler's film *The Vagabond Baron.* In 1923 Garbo was one of only seven students admitted to Sweden's prestigious Royal Dramatic Theatre Academy. While attending the training school, she chose her stage name and worked to develop her voice. Her studies at the academy served as both the foundation for her acting career and a source of several lifelong friendships with other actors and artists.

Within a year, one of Sweden's foremost film directors, Mauritz Stiller, recognized Garbo's unique beauty and immense talent. Stiller selected Garbo to play the role of Countess Elizabeth Dohna in the Swedish film *The Atonement of Gosta Berling* (1924). The film was considered a silent screen masterpiece and was a huge success throughout Europe. Garbo was soon cast in the leading role of *Joyless Street,* the definitive masterpiece of German realistic cinema, directed by G. W. Pabst. The film received international acclaim for its depth of feeling and technical innovations. The film and Garbo's performance were a critical success, shattering box office records.

Driving her unmercifully, Stiller molded her into an actress and insisted on bringing her with him to the Metro-Goldwyn-Mayer (MGM) studio in Hollywood in the summer of 1925. Through Stiller, she won an assignment in her first American film *The Torrent* (1926). Garbo quickly became the reigning star of Hollywood, due to both the box office success of her films and her captivating performances. She starred in eleven silent films. Her dramatic presence on the screen redefined acting. Garbo's aura created a unique balance between femininity and independence, proving that these qualities were not mutually exclusive. While many of her silent film contemporaries failed in making the transition to sound films, Garbo found artistic expression and thrived in this breakthrough medium. Her voice added a wonderful new dimension to her characters. She then starred in *The Temptress* (1926) and *Flesh and the Devil* (1927), which not only made her famous but introduced her to John Gilbert, with whom she conducted (both on and off the screen) a flaming romance which lasted several years. On the day they were to be married, Garbo left Gilbert standing at the altar.

Garbo's first sound picture was *Anna Christie* (1930), based on a play by American dramatist Eugene O'Neill. The sound scene was a tour de force, the longest, continuous sound take of the time. Because of the film's extraordinary success, MGM created a German language version with Garbo and an entirely new cast. Garbo's ability to act successfully in two languages demonstrates her remarkable range and linguistic talent.

Garbo's career continued to flourish. She starred in 15 sound films including such classics as *Mata Hari* (1932), *As You Desire Me* (1932), and *Queen Christina* (1933), one of her first classic roles. Director Rouben Mamoulian used Garbo's mask-like visage as a canvas upon which the audience ascribed an array of intense emotions. This use of her face as an expressive conduit became Garbo's signature style, and she created magic with it in her starring roles in *Susan Lennox: Her Fall and Rise* (1931 with Clark Gable), *Grand Hotel* (1932), *Anna Karenina* (1935), *Camille* (1936), *Conquest* (1937), and *Ninotchka* (1939).

Garbo gradually withdrew into an isolated retirement in 1941 after the failure of *Two-Faced Woman*, a domestic comedy. Her retirement was also partly because of World War II. She was tempted by a number of very interesting acting possibilities, but, unfortunately, none of the projects came to fruition.

Her twenty years of brilliant film portrayals created a cinematic legend characterized by financial success. During the mid-1930's she was America's highest paid female. Garbo's retirement from films did not mark the end of a very busy, independent life. Without the pressures of filmmaking, Garbo had the opportunity to turn to other creative pursuits such as painting, poetry, creative design of clothing and furnishings, gardening, and a rigorous daily exercise routine. In 1950 Garbo was chosen the best actress of the half-century in a poll conducted by the theatrical newspaper *Variety*. She became a U.S. citizen in 1951, and in 1954 she received (in absentia) a special Academy Award for "her unforgettable screen performances." Garbo moved to New York City in 1953 and traveled extensively. She died at her home in New York on April 15, 1990.

EWB

Geertz, Clifford (1926–), American cultural anthropologist. Clifford Geertz did ethnographic field work in Indonesia and Morocco, wrote influential essays on central theoretical issues in the social sciences, and advocated a distinctive "interpretive" approach to anthropology.

Clifford Geertz was born in San Francisco on August 23, 1926. After serving in the U.S. Navy during World War II, he received a B.A. from Antioch College in 1950 and a Ph.D. from Harvard University in 1956. Having held a number of brief appointments early in his career, he took a position at the University of Chicago in 1960, where he was rapidly promoted

to associate and then full professor. In 1970 he joined the Institute for Advanced Study in Princeton, New Jersey, as professor of social science, a position of rare distinction which he still occupied in 1999. Over the years Geertz received a considerable number of honors and awards, including honorary degrees from several institutions. In 1958 and 1959 he was a fellow at the Center for Advanced Study in the Behavioral Sciences (Stanford) and in 1978–1979 he served as Eastman Professor at Oxford University. His books won major prizes, including the prestigious 1988 National Book Critics Circle Award for Criticism for *Works and Lives: The Anthropologist as Author.*

In 1952 Geertz first went to Indonesia with a team of investigators to study Modjokuto, a small town in east central Java, where he and his wife lived for more than a year. On the basis of his research there Geertz wrote his dissertation, later published in 1960 as *The Religion of Java*. A comprehensive analysis of Javanese religion in its social context, this book presents a picture of a highly religious culture composed of at least three main strands (related to different population groups). These include a traditional kind of animism, Islam (itself internally diverse), and a Hindu-influenced refined mysticism.

In later years Geertz returned to Java but also spent extensive periods in Tabanan, a small town in Bali. Initially treated with complete indifference by the Balinese, Geertz and his wife gained significant access to their community. He presented his interpretation of his time there in a classic essay on the Balinese cockfight. Both in the matching of the cocks and in the bets surrounding the fight, the Balinese dramatized their concern with maintaining a definite hierarchy of rivalries and groups in which everyone had his or her fixed place.

Geertz carried out field work in Sefrou, a town in north central Morocco, in the 1960s and early 1970s, enabling him to compare two "extremes" of Islamic civilization: homogeneous and morally severe in Moroco and blended with other traditions and less concerned with scriptural doctrine in Indonesia. In both countries he found traditional religion affected by the process of secularization; whereas people used to "be held" by taken-for-granted beliefs, in modern societies they increasingly have to "hold" their beliefs in a much more conscious (and anxious) fashion. Geertz published *Islam Observed* in 1968.

In his early work Geertz investigated why certain communities achieved greater economic growth and modernization than others. For example, he found that the "ego-focused" market peddlers of Modjokuto, who only looked out for their own and their families' gain, were in a less favorable position than the "group-focused" Tabanan aristocrats. The latter group could use their traditional prestige to mobilize communal resources for new investments, even though they had to temper their modern entrepreneurial drive with concern for the well-being of their community.

Geertz also authored a number of essays which elaborate on his theories, including *The Interpretation of Cultures* in 1973 and *Local Knowledge* in 1983.

In 1995, Geertz published *After the Fact: Two Countries, Four Decades, One Anthropologist*. In the book, he charted the transformation of cultural anthropology from a study of primitive people to a multidisciplinary investigation of a culture's symbolic systems and its interactions with the larger forces of history and modernization. Geertz used the greatest strength of anthropology (the ability to compare cultures). His periods of extended fieldwork in Indonesia and Morocco enabled him to view each through the lens of the other. He also used anecdotes in the book of non-western countries tackling the same social questions as Western countries: national identity, moral order, and competing values.

Throughout his career Geertz tried to make sense of the ways people live their lives by interpreting cultural symbols such as ceremonies, political gestures, and literary texts. Geertz was also interested in the role of thought (especially religious thought) in society. Analyzing this role properly, he argued, requires "thick description," a probing appraisal of the meanings people's actions have for them in their own circumstances—a method Geertz tried to demonstrate in his own work. Skeptical of attempts to develop abstract theories of human behavior but sensitive to issues of universal human concern, he emphasized that anthropologists should focus on the rich texture of the lives of real human beings. Yet he showed that in writing about others one necessarily transforms "their" world; the very style in which social scientists write conveys their distinctive interpretation. Geertz' own highly sophisticated, but dense and occasionally convoluted writing style exemplifies his influential "interpretive" approach to cultural anthropology.

EWB

Goebbels, Joseph Paul (1897–1945), German politician. Joseph Goebbels directed the extensive system of propaganda in Nazi Germany.

Joseph Goebbels was born on Oct. 29, 1897, in the Rhenish textile city of Rheydt, the son of a pious Catholic bookkeeper of modest means. With the support of stipends granted by Catholic organizations, the young Goebbels attended the university and earned a doctorate in literature in 1922.

After a number of unsuccessful attempts as writer, journalist, and speaker, Goebbels joined the National Socialist organization in northern Germany under Gregor Strasser in 1924 and edited various publications of this group from 1924 to 1926. In the late summer of 1925 Goebbels first met Hitler, was immediately enamored with the Führer, and broke with Strasser in November 1926 to go to Berlin as *Gauleiter* (district leader) upon Hitler's request. Here he founded and edited the party weekly, *Der Angriff* (The Attack). He took over the propaganda machine of the party in 1928 and became minister of popular enlightenment and propaganda with Hitler's rise to power in 1933.

From this position Goebbels built a machinery of thought control, which not only served as an effective support for the Nazi regime and later the war effort, but also actively limited and shaped all forms of artistic and intellectual expression to conform to the ideals of National Socialism and, most particularly, racist anti-Semitism. This involved the control of the press through censorship and removal of Jewish and non-Nazi editors and the establishment of government-sponsored radio stations, newspapers, and magazines. Jewish artists, musicians, writers, and even natural scientists, many of Germany's ablest men and women, were removed and often sent to concentration camps. Works by Jewish composers and writers were burned and outlawed. "Decadent" modern art was replaced by a Nazi standard of pseudoromantic, sentimental art. Education on all levels was similarly controlled.

Mass rallies, ever-present loudspeaker systems, and the mass production and distribution of "people's radios" ensured wide dissemination of Hitler's demagogic appeals to the nation. Goebbels, who had an unusually appealing speaking voice, increasingly became the Führer's channel of communication with the population. Most notorious was Goebbels's speech in August 1944 in the Sports Palace of Berlin, in which he fanatically called for total war. His fanaticism lasted to the end. In 1945 Goebbels called for the destruction of the German people since they had not been able to win victory. He stayed with Hitler even after Hermann Göring and Heinrich Himmler had sought contacts with the Allies. Goebbels killed himself and his entire family in Berlin on May 1, 1945, only hours after Hitler's suicide.

EWB

Goethe, Johann Wolfgang von (1749–1832), German poet, dramatist, novelist, and scientist. Goethe, who embraced many fields of human endeavor, ranks as the greatest of all German poets. Of all modern men of genius, Goethe is the most universal.

The many-sided activities of Johann Wolfgang von Goethe stand as a tribute to the greatness of his mind and his personality. Napoleon I's oft-quoted remark about Goethe, made after their meeting at Erfurt—"Voilà un homme!" (There's a man!) reflects later humanity's judgment of Goethe's genius. Not only, however, does Goethe rank with Homer, Dante Alighieri, and William Shakespeare as a supreme creator, but also in his life itself incredibly long, rich, and filled with a calm optimism Goethe perhaps created his greatest work, surpassing even his *Faust,* Germany's most national drama.

Goethe was born in Frankfurt am Main on Aug. 28, 1749. He was the eldest son of Johann Kaspar Goethe and Katharina Elisabeth Textor Goethe. Goethe's father, of Thuringian stock, had studied law at the University of Leipzig. He did not practice his profession, but in 1742 he acquired the title of *kaiserlicher Rat* (imperial councilor). In 1748 he married the daughter of Frankfurt's burgomaster. Of the children born to Goethe's parents only Johann and his sister Cornelia survived to maturity. She married Goethe's friend J. G. Schlosser in 1773. Goethe's lively and impulsive disposition and his remarkable imaginative powers probably came to him from his mother, and he likely inherited his reserved manner and his stability of character from his stern and often pedantic father.

Early Life.

Goethe has left a memorable picture of his childhood, spent in a large patrician house on the Grosse Hirschgraben in Frankfurt, in his autobiography *Dichtung und Wahrheit.* He and Cornelia were educated at home by private tutors. Books, pictures, and a marionette theater kindled the young Goethe's quick intellect and imagination.

During the Seven Years War the French occupied Frankfurt. A French theatrical troupe established itself, and Goethe, through his grandfather's influence, was allowed free access to its performances. He much improved his knowledge of French by attending the performances and by his contact with the actors. Meantime, his literary proclivities had begun to manifest themselves in religious poems, a novel, and a prose epic.

In October 1765 Goethe, then 16 years old, left Frankfurt for the University of Leipzig. He remained in Leipzig until 1768, pursuing his legal studies with zeal. During this period he also took lessons in drawing from A. F. Oeser, the director of the Leipzig Academy of Painting. Art always remained an abiding interest throughout Goethe's life.

During his Leipzig years Goethe began writing light Anacreontic verses. Much of his poetry of these years was inspired by his passionate love for Anna Katharina Schönkopf, the daughter of a wine merchant in whose tavern he dined. She was the "Annette" for whom the collection of lyrics discovered in 1895 was named.

The rupture of a blood vessel in one of his lungs put an end to Goethe's Leipzig years. From 1768 to the spring of 1770 Goethe lay ill, first in Leipzig and later at home.

It was a period of serious introspection. The Anacreontic playfulness of verse and the rococo manner of his Leipzig period were soon swept away as Goethe grew in stature as a human being and as a poet.

Study in Strasbourg.

Goethe's father was determined his son should continue his legal studies. Upon his recovery, therefore, Goethe was sent to Strasbourg, the capital of Alsace and a city that lay outside the German Empire. There his true Promethean self and his poetic genius were fully awakened. One of the most important events of Goethe's Strasbourg period was his meeting with Johann Gottfried von Herder. Herder taught Goethe the significance of Gothic architecture, as exemplified by the Strasbourg Minster, and he kindled Goethe's love of Homer, Pindar, Ossian, Shakespeare, and the *Volkslied.* Without neglecting his legal studies, Goethe also studied medicine.

Perhaps the most important occurrence of this period was Goethe's love for Friederike Brion, the daughter of the pastor of the nearby village of Sesenheim. Later Goethe immortalized Friederike as Gretchen in *Faust.* She also inspired the *Friederike Songs* and many beautiful lyrics. *Kleine Blumen, kleine Blätter* and *Wie herrlich leuchtet mir die Natur!* heralded a new era in German lyric poetry.

During this Strasbourg period Goethe also reshaped his Alsatian *Heidenröslein.* His lyrical response to the Gothic architecture of Strasbourg Minster appeared in his essay *Von deutscher Baukunst* (1772). Goethe also probably planned his first important drama, *Götz von Berlichingen,* while in Strasbourg. In August 1771 Goethe obtained a licentiate in law, though not a doctor's degree. He returned to Frankfurt in September and remained there until early 1772.

"Sturm und Drang" Period.

From spring to September 1772 Goethe spent 4 months in Wetzlar in order to gain experience in the legal profession at the supreme courts of the empire. However, Goethe found a more genial society in a local inn among the "Knights of the Round Table," calling himself "Götz von Berlichingen."

Goethe's passionate love for Charlotte Buff, who was the daughter of the Wetzlar *Amtmann* (bailiff) and was engaged to Johann Christian Kestner, the secretary of legation and a member of the Round Table, created a crisis. Out of its agony—Goethe's obsession with Charlotte led him almost to suicide—the poet created the world-famous novel *Die Leiden des jungen Werthers* (1774). A Rhine journey in the autumn of 1772 and intense preoccupation with his literary projects on his return to Frankfurt brought partial recovery to Goethe.

Goethe remained in Frankfurt until the autumn of 1775, and these were years of fantastic productivity. *Götz von Berlichingen* was finished in 1773. This play established the Shakespearean type of drama on the German stage and inaugurated the *Sturm und Drang* movement. Another play, *Clavigo,* soon followed. A tragedy, *Clavigo* marked considerable advancement in Goethe's art. *Die Leiden des jungen Werthers* appeared in 1774. This novel, written in the epistolary style, brought Goethe international fame and spread "Werther fever" throughout Europe and even into Asia. A sentimental story of love and suicide, *Werther* utilized the private and social experiences of its author's months in Wetzlar, molding them into one of the most powerful introspective novels of all time. Its psychological impact upon Goethe's contemporaries and its influence on German literature can scarcely be exaggerated.

Many unfinished fragments, some of them magnificent, also date from these years. Goethe worked on the dramas *Caesar* and *Mahomet* and the epic *Der ewige Jude.* A fragment of *Prometheus,* a tragedy, ranks among the poet's masterpieces. Perhaps the greatest work from these years was Goethe's first dramatization of the Faust legend.

During these years Goethe's poetic genius found its own unique self. The masterpieces of this great *Sturm und Drang* period include *Wanderers Sturmlied* (1771); *Mahomets Gesang* (1772–1773); *An Schwager Kronos* (1774); *Prometheus* (1774), a symbol of the self-confident genius; and *Ganymed* (1774), the embodiment of man's abandonment to the mysteries of the universe.

In 1775 Goethe fell in love with Lili Schönemann, the daughter of a Frankfurt banker. Goethe became formally betrothed to her, and Lili inspired many beautiful lyrics. However, the worldly society Lili thrived in was not congenial to the poet. A visit to Switzerland in the summer of 1775 helped Goethe realize that this marriage might be unwise, and the engagement lapsed that autumn. *Neue Liebe, Neues Leben* and *An Belinden* (both 1775) are poetic expressions of Goethe's happiest hours with Lili, while *Auf dem See,* written on June 15, 1775, reflects his mood after he broke the spell that his love for Lili had cast upon him. Goethe also conceived another drama during these Frankfurt years and actually wrote a great part of it. However, he did not publish *Egmont* until 1788. Graf Egmont, its protagonist, is endowed with a demonic power over the sympathies of both men and women, and he represents the lighter side of Goethe's visiona foil to Faust, and his more optimistic outlook.

Career in Weimar. On Oct. 12, 1775, the young prince of Weimar, Duke Karl August, arrived in Frankfurt and extended an invitation to Goethe to accompany him to Weimar. On November 7 Goethe arrived in the capital of the little Saxon duchy that was to remain his home for the rest of his life. The young duke soon enlisted Goethe's services in the government of his duchy, and before long Goethe had been entrusted with responsible state duties.

As minister of state, Goethe interested himself in agriculture, horticulture, and mining, all fields of economic importance to the duchy's welfare. Eventually his many state offices in Weimar and his social and political commitments became a burden and a hindrance to his creative writing. Perhaps Goethe's most irksome responsibility was the office of president of the Treasury after 1782.

Goethe made his first long stay at Weimar from November 1775 until the summer of 1786. In 1782 Emperor Joseph II conferred a knighthood on him. During these 12 years Goethe's attachment for Charlotte von Stein, the wife of a Weimar official and the mother of seven children, dominated his emotional life. A woman of refined taste and culture, Frau von Stein was 7 years Goethe's senior and was perhaps the most intellectual of the poet's many loves.

The literary output of the first Weimar period included a number of lyrics (*Wanderers Nachtlied, An den Mond,* and *Gesang der Geister über den Wassern*), ballads (*Der Erlkönig*), a short drama (*Die Geschwister*), a dramatic satire (*Der Triumph der Empfindsamkeit*), and several *Singspiele* (*Lila; Die Fischerin; Scherz; List und Rache;* and *Jery und Bätely*). Goethe also planned a religious epic (*Die Geheimnisse*) and a tragedy (*Elpenor*). In 1777 Goethe began to write a theatrical novel, *Wilhelm Meisters theatralische Sendung.* In 1779 the prose version of his drama *Iphigenie auf Tauris* was performed.

Under Frau von Stein's influence Goethe matured as an artist as well as a personality. His course toward artistic and human harmony and renunciation was mirrored in several poems written during this period: *Harzreise im Winter* (1777); *Ein Gleiches* (1780), *Ilmenau* (1783), and *Zueignung* (1784).

Italian Journey. In September 1786 Goethe set out from Karlsbad on his memorable and intensely longed-for journey to Italy. He traveled by way of Munich, the Brenner Pass, and Lago di Garda to Verona and Venice. He arrived in Rome on Oct. 29, 1786, and soon established friendships in the circle of German artists. In the spring of 1787 Goethe traveled to Naples and Sicily, returning to Rome in June 1787. He departed for Weimar on April 2, 1788.

It would be almost impossible to overstate the importance of Goethe's Italian journey. Goethe regarded it as the high point of his life, feeling it had helped him attain a deep understanding of his poetic genius and his mission as a poet. No longer in sympathy with *Sturm und Drang* even before his departure from Weimar, Goethe was initiated into neoclassicism by his vision of the antique in Italy. Goethe returned to Weimar not only with a new artistic vision but also with a freer attitude toward life. He recorded this journey in his *Italienische Reise* at the time of his trip, but he did not publish this volume until 1816–1817.

Return to Weimar. Goethe returned from Italy unsettled and restless. Shortly afterward, his ties with Frau von Stein having been weakened by his extended stay in Italy and by lighter pleasures he had known there, Goethe took the daughter of a town official into his house as his mistress. Christiane Vulpius, although she could offer no intellectual companionship, provided the comforts of a home. Gradually, she became indispensable as a helpmate, although she was ignored by Goethe's friends and unwelcome at court. Their son August was born in 1789, and Goethe married her in 1806, when the French invasion of Weimar endangered her position.

Goethe had finished *Egmont* in Italy. Additional literary fruits of his trip were the *Römische Elegien*, which reflected Italy's pagan influences, written in 1788–1789; the iambic version of *Iphigenie auf Tauris* (1787); and a Renaissance drama, *Torquato Tasso* (1790). Goethe also planned an epic *Nausikaa* and a drama *Iphigenie auf Delphos. Faust* was brought an additional step forward, part of it being published in 1790 as *Faust, Ein Fragment.*

Meanwhile, two new interests engrossed Goethe and renewed his Weimar ties. In 1791 he was appointed director of the ducal theater, a position he held for 22 years; and he became increasingly absorbed in scientific pursuits. From his scientific studies in anatomy, botany, optics, meteorology, and mineralogy, he

gradually reached a vision of the unity of the outward and inward worlds. Not only nature and art but also science were, in his view, governed by one organic force that rules all metamorphoses of appearances.

It is absolutely misleading, however, to suggest as some critics have that after his Italian journeys Goethe became a scientist and ceased to be a poet. In 1793 Goethe composed *Reineke Fuchs,* a profane "World Bible" in hexameters. He also took up his abandoned novel of the theater. His projected study of a young man's theatrical apprenticeship was transformed into an apprenticeship to life. *Wilhelm Meisters Lehrjahre,* varying between realism and poetic romanticism, became the archetypal *Bildungsroman.* Its influence on German literature was profound and enduring after its publication in 1795–1796.

Goethe's unique literary friendship with Friedrich von Schiller began in 1794. To it Goethe owed in great degree his renewed dedication to poetry. Goethe contributed to Schiller's new periodical *Die Horen,* composed *Xenien* with him in 1795–1796, received Schiller's encouragement to finish *Wilhelm Meisters Lehrjahre,* and undertook at his urging the studies that resulted in the epic *Hermann und Dorothea* and the fragment *Achilleis.* Schiller's urging also induced Goethe to return once more to *Faust* and to conclude the first part of it. *Xenien,* a collection of distichs, contains several masterpieces, and *Hermann und Dorothea* (1797) ranks as one of the poet's most perfect creations.

From Goethe's friendly rivalry with Schiller issued a number of ballad masterpieces: *Der Zauberlehrling, Der Gott und die Bajadere, Die Braut von Korinth, Alexis und Dora, Der neue Pausias,* and the cycle of four *Müller-Lieder.*

Goethe's classicism brought him into eventual conflict with the developing romantic movement. To present his theories, he published, in conjunction with Heinrich Meyer, from 1798 to 1800 an art review entitled *Die Propyläen.* Goethe also defended his ideals of classical beauty in 1805 in *Winckelmann und sein Jahrhundert.* But the triumphant publication of the first part of Faust in 1808 defeated Goethe's own classical ideals. It was received as a landmark of romantic art.

Last Years. The last period of Goethe's life began with Schiller's death in 1805. In 1806 he published his magnificent tribute to Schiller *Epilog zu Schillers Glocke.* In 1807 Bettina von Arnim became the latest (but not the last) of Goethe's loves, for the poet soon developed a more intense interest in Minna Herzlieb, the foster daughter of a Jena publisher.

The publication of the first part of *Faust* in 1808 was followed by the issuance the next year of a novel,

Die Wahlverwandtschaften, an intimate psychological study of four minds. The most classical and allegorical of Goethe's works, *Pandora,* was published in 1808. The scientific treatise *Zur Farbenlehre* appeared in 1810.

In 1811 Goethe published the first volume of his autobiography, *Aus meinem Leben, Dichtung und Wahrheit.* Volumes 2 and 3 followed in 1812 and 1814. The fourth, ending with Goethe's departure from Frankfurt in 1775 for Weimar, appeared in 1833, after his death. Additional materials for a continuation of *Dichtung und Wahrheit* into the Weimar years were collected in *Tag und Jahreshefte* (1830).

Increasingly aloof from national, political, and literary partisanship in his last period, Goethe became more and more an Olympian divinity to whose shrine at Weimar all Europe made pilgrimage. In 1819 Goethe published another masterpiece, this one a collection of lyrics inspired by his young friend Marianne von Willemer, who figures as Sulieka in the cycle. Suggested by his reading of the Persian poet Hafiz, the poems that constitute *Westöstlicher Diwan* struck another new note in German poetry with their introduction of Eastern elements.

Meanwhile, death was thinning the ranks of Goethe's acquaintances: Wieland, the last of Goethe's great literary contemporaries, died in 1813; Christiane in 1816; Charlotte von Stein in 1827; Duke Karl August in 1828; and Goethe's son August died of scarlet fever in Rome in 1830.

In 1822 still another passion for a beautiful young girl, Ulrike von Levetzow, inspired Goethe's *Trilogie der Leidenschaft: An Werther, Marienbader Elegie,* and *Aussöhnung.* The trilogy is a passionate and unique work of art written in 1823–1824, when Goethe was approaching the age of 75. Between 1821 and 1829 Goethe published the long-promised continuation of *Wilhelm Meisters Lehrjahre, Wilhelm Meisters Wanderjahre,* a loose series of episodes in novel form. His *Novelle* appeared in 1828.

However, the crowning achievement of Goethe's literary career was the completion of the second part of *Faust.* This work had accompanied Goethe since his early 20s and constitutes a full "confession" of his life. The second part, not published until after Goethe's death, exhibited the poet's ripe wisdom and his philosophy of life. In his *Faust* Goethe recast the old legend and made it into one of Western literature's greatest and noblest poetic creations. The salvation of Faust was Goethe's main departure from the original legend, and he handled it nobly in the impressively mystical closing scene of the second part.

Goethe died in Weimar on March 22, 1832. He was buried in the ducal crypt at Weimar beside Schiller.

EWB

Gorbachev, Mikhail Sergeevich (1931–), Russian politician. Mikhail Gorbachev was a member of the Communist Party who rose through a series of local and regional positions to national prominence. In March 1985 the Politburo of the Soviet Communist Party elected him general secretary of the party and leader of the U.S.S.R. He resigned in 1991.

Mikhail Gorbachev was born into a peasant family in the village of Privolnoe, near Stavropol, on March 2, 1931, and grew up in the countryside. As a teenager, he worked driving farm machinery at a local machine-tractor station. These stations served regional state and collective farms, but were also centers of police control in the countryside. Gorbachev's experience here undoubtedly educated him well about the serious problems of food production and political administration in the countryside, as well as the practices of the KGB (the Soviet secret police) control, knowledge which would serve him well in his future career.

In 1952 Gorbachev joined the Communist Party and began studies at the Moscow State University, where he graduated from the law division in 1955. Student acquaintances from these years describe him as bright, hard working, and careful to establish good contacts with people of importance. He also met and married fellow student Raisa Titorenko, in 1953.

With Stalin's death in 1953 the Soviet Union began a period of political and intellectual ferment. In 1956 Nikita Khrushchev denounced Stalin and paved the way for a major restructuring of the Soviet Union's political system and economic administration. For young party activists like Gorbachev this was a period of exciting innovations and challenges.

Gorbachev returned after his graduation to Stavropol as an organizer for the Komsomol (Young Communist League) and began a successful career as a party administrator and regional leader. In 1962 he was promoted to the post of party organizer for collective and state farms in the Stavropol region and soon took on major responsibilities for the Stavropol city committee as well. Leonid Brezhnev rewarded his ability by appointing him Stavropol first secretary in 1966, roughly equivalent to mayor.

Climbing the Party Ladder. Soon afterwards, as part of the party's new campaign to assure that its best career administrators were thoroughly trained in economic administration, Gorbachev completed an advanced program at the Stavropol Agricultural Institute and received a degree in agrarian economics. With this additional training he moved quickly to assume direction of the party in the entire Stavropol region, assuming in 1970 the important post of first secretary for the Stavropol Territorial Party Committee. This position, roughly equivalent to a governor in the United States, proved a stepping stone to Central Committee membership and national prominence.

Gorbachev was assisted in his rise to national power by close associations with Yuri Andropov, who was also from the Stavropol region, and Mikhail Suslov, the party's principal ideologist and a confidant of Leonid Brezhnev, who had once worked in the Stavropol area as well. Gorbachev also proved himself a shrewd and intelligent administrator, however, with an extensive knowledge of agricultural affairs, and it was largely on this basis that Brezhnev brought him to Moscow in 1978 as a party secretary responsible for agricultural administration. His performance in this capacity was not particularly distinguished. The Soviet Union suffered several poor harvests in the late 1970s and early 1980s, and its dependency on foreign grain imports increased. Yet Gorbachev gained a solid reputation, despite these problems, as an energetic and informed politician, with an activist style contrasting rather sharply with that of most aging Kremlin leaders.

The ascension of Yuri Andropov to power after the death of Leonid Brezhnev in January 1980 greatly strengthened the position of his protegé Gorbachev. Both men showed impatience with outmoded administrative practices and with the inefficiencies of the Soviet Union's economy. Andropov's death returned the U.S.S.R. briefly to a period of drift under the weak and ailing Konstantin Chernenko, but Gorbachev continued to impress his colleagues with his loyal and energetic party service. Beginning in October 1980 he was a member of the ruling Politburo.

A New Type of Russian Leader? As he took power in March 1985, Gorbachev brought a fresh new spirit to the Kremlin. Young, vigorous, married to an attractive and stylish woman with a Ph.D., he represented a new generation of Soviet leaders, educated and trained in the post-Stalin era and free from the direct experiences of Stalin's terror which so hardened and corrupted many of his elders. His first steps as head of the party were designed to improve economic productivity. He began an energetic campaign against inefficiency and waste and indicated his intention to "shake up" lazy and ineffective workers in every area of Soviet life, including the party. He also revealed an unusual affability. Britons found him and his wife Raisa "charming" when he visited England in December 1984, and he showed a ready wit, "blaming" the British Museum, where Karl Marx studied and wrote, for Communism's success. Shortly after taking power Gorbachev also moved to develop greater

rapport with ordinary citizens, taking to the streets on several occasions to discuss his views and making a number of well-publicized appearances at factories and other industrial institutions. In addition, he began strengthening his position within the party with a number of new appointments at the important regional level.

A charismatic personality, Gorbachev also had the youthfulness, training, intelligence, and political strength to become one of the Soviet Union's most popular leaders. Upon assuming power in 1985, he was faced with the need to make significant improvements in the Soviet Union's troubled economy—an extremely difficult task—and to establish better relations with the United States, which might allow some reduction in Soviet defense expenditures in favor of consumer goods. In November 1985 he met with President Reagan in Geneva to discuss national and international problems. Little progress was made but both leaders agreed to hold another "summit" meeting in the United States in 1986.

When new tensions developed between the two superpowers, the leaders agreed to hold a preliminary meeting at Reykjavik, Iceland, October 11–12, 1986. But the clearest signs of improving Soviet-American relations came in 1988. Gorbachev made a positive impression when he entered a crowd of spectators in New York City to shake hands with people. In May and June of the same year, President Reagan visited Moscow.

Within the Soviet Union, Gorbachev promoted spectacular political changes. His most important measure came in 1989 when he set up elections in which members of the Communist Party had to compete against opponents who were not Party members. Later that same year, he called for an end to the special status of the Communist party guaranteed by the Soviet Constitution and ended the Soviet military occupation of Afghanistan.

Two issues, however, caused growing difficulty for Gorbachev. First, there was the problem of nationalities, as the Soviet Union consisted of nearly 100 different ethnic groups. As the political dictatorship began to disappear, many of these groups began to engage in open warfare against each other. Such bloodshed came from longstanding local quarrels that had been suppressed under Moscow's earlier control. Even more serious, some ethnic groups, like the Lithuanians and the Ukrainians began to call for outright independence. Second, the country's economy was sinking deeper into crisis. Both industrial and agricultural production were declining, and the old system, in which the economy ran under centralized control of the government, no longer seemed to work.

Yet, Gorbachev was apparently more willing to make changes in government and international affairs than to focus on the problems associated with ethnic diversity and the economy. Perhaps influenced by more conservative rivals, he cracked down on the Lithuanians when they declared their independence in the summer of 1990. Also, he gradually tried to move toward a private system of farming and privately owned industry.

At the same time, a powerful rival began to emerge: once considered an ally, Boris Yeltsin became the country's leading advocate of radical economic reform. Although forced from the Politburo, the small group at the top of the Communist Party, in 1987, Yeltsin soon established his own political base. He formally left the Communist Party in 1990, something Gorbachev refused to do, and was elected president of the Russian Republic in June 1991. Gorbachev, on the other hand, had been made president of the Soviet Union without having to win a national election. Thus, Yeltsin could claim a greater degree of popular support.

Fall From Power. In August 1991, a group of Communist Party conservatives captured Gorbachev while he was on vacation in the Crimea and moved to seize power. Some of these men, like Prime Minister Valentin Pavlov, were individuals Gorbachev had put in power to balance the liberal and conservative political forces. But Yeltsin, not Gorbachev, led the successful resistance to the coup, which collapsed within a few days. When Gorbachev returned to Moscow, he was overshadowed by Yeltsin, and there were rumors that Gorbachev himself had been involved in the coup.

By the end of 1991, the Soviet Union had fallen apart. When most of its major components like the Ukraine and the Baltic states declared themselves as independent, real power began to rest with the leaders of those components, among them Yeltsin, hero of the attempted coup and president of the Russian Republic. Gorbachev formally resigned his remaining political office on Christmas Day 1991.

Private Citizen. As a private citizen, Gorbachev faded from public view, but continued to write and travel. On one occasion, his travels struck an important symbolic note. On May 6, 1992, he spoke at Westminster College in Fulton, Missouri. There, in 1946, Winston Churchill had given his classic speech coining the term "the Cold War." Gorbachev's appearance was a vivid reminder of the changes he had helped bring about during his seven years in power.

In the spring of 1995, Gorbachev began touring factories in Russia, spoke to university students, and denounced President Yeltsin. He stopped just short of formally announcing his candidacy for the presidency in 1996. He wrote an autobiography, which was released in 1995 in Germany and 1997 in the United States.

Like many historical figures, Gorbachev's role will be interpreted in varying ways. While a Russian factory worker stated in *Newsweek,* "He destroyed a great state . . . the collapse of the Soviet Union started with Gorbachev . . . ," some critics in the West saw the fall of Communism as "altogether a victory for common sense, reason, democracy and common human values."

EWB

Gouges, Olympe de (d. 1793), French writer.

Feminists such as Benoîte Groult assert that Olympe de Gouges' absence from the historical record was caused by a single factor: she was a woman. It appears, however, that in the case of Olympe de Gouges, there were additional reasons. She was legally low-born, denied any formal education, married at 16, a mother and widow at 17, and too proud and too independent to use either her late husband's name or to remarry. Her temperament, politics, and primarily her gender put off possible supporters and employers in the literary world, making it enormously difficult for her to find publishers. The works she did manage to get printed were largely ignored and are only now being collected and published.

Beyond the obstacles associated with meddling in the 18th-century world of male politics and of asserting that woman had rights and responsibilities equal to those of man, de Gouges had three strikes against her. First, like her contemporary Count Mirabeau, she supported King Louis XVI but, unlike Mirabeau, she lived long enough to meddle in his trial. Second, she supported the losing political party in 1792, the Girondins. Third, in 1793 she attacked the leader of the victorious Jacobin political party, Maximilien Robespierre. He targeted her and she—like so many Girondin leaders, like the king and the queen, and like Robespierre himself less than a year later—was guillotined, lost in a crowd. De Gouges's one monument, her *Déclaration of the Rights of Woman and the Female Citizen,* was covered up, neglected until recently.

The only source for de Gouges's early life is her autobiographical novel Mémoire de Mme Valmont, and what of the novel is factual remains a question for debate. The Jean-Jacques of the novel was Jean-Jacques Le Franc de Pomignan (d. 1784), a magistrate and writer of local fame. Was de Pomignan her biological father, and did De Gouges inherit her intellect and creativity from him? Or did the fiction of a noble birth leaven the rough baker's dough so that it rose beyond itself? De Pompignan was correct about legitimate birth. There are witnesses to a birth certificate showing Marie Gouze born to Pierre Gouze, a butcher at Montauban, and Olympe Mouisset, a trinket seller. De Gouges wrote nothing, however, about these two, and there is no record of any formal education. Of her marriage at 16 to Louis-Yves Aubry, a restauranteur and caterer at Montauban, she wrote little, later calling him an old man she never loved, who was neither rich nor well-born. He died soon after the birth of their son Pierre, leaving a small pension.

In widowhood at Montauban, de Gouges developed a friendship with Jacques Biétrix de Roziéres, a contractor in military transport, and he took her to Paris. Her biographers believe that she refused to marry de Roziéres because she viewed marriage as "the tomb of faith and love."

She Begins Extensive Writing. In Paris from 1767 or 1768, de Gouges developed the reputation of a *"femme galante"*—an attractive, free-spirited, unattached female with an active social and cultural life replete with many friends, many of them respectable. She may have learned to write during this period, but most of her works seem to have been dictated to secretaries/friends. (In fact, many well-known writers of the day employed assistants.) Even with their assistance, her lack of formal education is reflected in her works. "Si j'ecris mal," she once wrote, "je pense bien." ("I write bad, but I think good.") Her biographer Olivier Blanc has identified 135 writings of de Gouges plus seven articles in six different newspapers—four of which are antislavery pieces. Twenty-nine are novels and short stories, 45 are theater pieces, and 64 are political pamphlets, tracts, brochures, and placards.

De Gouges's first play is considered her best dramatic work. She called it, "the first effort of my feeble talent." "Zamour and Mirza, or the Happy Shipwreck" (happy because two slaves were liberated) was written in 1784 and submitted anonymously to the selection committee of the Comédie Française, which accepted it the following year. Performance of the play was long delayed. Powerful colonial interests feared that sympathetic portrayal of blacks might threaten the profitability of French colonies. De Gouges was threatened with a *lettre de cachet* (arrest order signed by the king) and actors refused to blacken their faces. In 1789, the play was retitled "Slavery of Negroes" and was performed by the Comédie Française. Uproar

ensued. The mayor of Paris condemned it as an incendiary piece which would cause revolt in the colonies. One critic reviewed the play in only one sentence: "We can only say that in order to write a good dramatic work, one must have hair on the chin." The production closed after three performances.

During the five years between the writing and the performance of this first play, de Gouges wrote many dramas, of which only a few texts survive.

Early in 1787, Finance Minister Calonne persuaded King Louis XVI to assemble a blue-ribbon panel called the assembly of Notables to consider Calonne's reform package to rescue finances. Calonne hoped that the assembly would endorse his reforms, thus influencing the law courts to enregister them. Enthralled by the constant news reports of the Assembly's proceedings, de Gouges turned her imagination to politics.

In 1788, de Gouges published *Letter to the People, or Project for a Patriotic Bank by a Female Citizen*. She called for a voluntary tax to fund a bank which "would be the envy of all the courts of Europe and shame the law courts" which had refused the king's tax edict. Also in 1788, De Gouges published *Reflections on Blacks*. She used this work to urge performances of her play *Zamour and Myrza* (which would be performed the following year), but also made this argument: everywhere in nature one sees variety—different kinds of trees, different kinds of flowers, different kinds of birds, fish, and so forth. Likewise one sees different kinds of human beings. Every kind of human is as precious as trees and other parts of nature are precious. Soon, the Revolution would abolish slavery. Whether or not her work influenced this progress, she was—as in the case of a national bank—in advance of such change.

She Presents Her Declaration of Women's Rights. In the summer of 1791, de Gouges authored her *Déclaration des droits de la femme et de la citoyenne* (Declaration of the Rights of Woman and the Female Citizen) patterned after the *Declaration of the Rights of Man* and *The Citizen* decreed as the first part of the Constitution by the National Assembly in August 1789. De Gouges sent a copy to the National Assembly then ending its term and a copy with a cover letter to Queen Marie Antoinette. No one has found evidence that the queen, or the National Assembly, or its successor the Legislative Assembly, ever admitted to having received it. The Legislative Assembly once voted *hommage* to de Gouges for "patriotic acts" (not mentioning the *Déclaration*) and, in its closing days, even received her. The preamble to the *Déclaration* began with characteristic directness and lack of diplomacy: "Man, are you capable of being just? It is a woman who asks you this question. Who has given you the authority to oppress my sex?" Unspeakably radical then, the *Déclaration* is still radical today (in it, De Gouges insisted on exact equality, including combat roles in the military).

In 1792 de Gouges enthusiastically endorsed the proclamation of the Republic, but attempted to defend King Louis whom the Jacobins insisted on trying for treason. Having overthrown the constitution, the Jacobins now demanded the king's death for violating that same constitution. De Gouges and the Girondins opposed the death sentence and few still argue that they were wrong to do so. The execution of King Louis XVI on January 21, 1793, was followed by the entrance of England into the War of the First Coalition and by a bloodbath in France. The Girondin leadership was arrested in the early summer of 1793 and guillotined in the fall.

Increasingly, de Gouges viewed Robespierre as a dictator violating liberty and the Republic. In a public letter, *"Response to the Justification by Maximilien Robespierre, addressed to Jerome Petion, President of the Convention,"* she asked, "Do you know how far you are from Cato?" Then, continuing the comparison of Mirabeau to the virtuous Roman senator who opposed Pompey, Crassus, and Caesar, she added, "As far as Marat from Mirabeau, as far as the mosquito from the eagle, and as far as the eagle from the sun." That did it, of course. It was de Gouges or Robespierre. De Gouges recognized this. Arrested July 20, 1793, De Gouges was accused before the Paris Tribunal on November 2. The next day she was guillotined. Eight months later, in the Revolutionary month of Thermidor (July), the majority of Robespierre's Jacobin party surprised and guillotined him. Once again, De Gouges had been ahead of events.

Historic World Leaders

Goya y Lucientes, Francisco de Paula José de

(1746–1828), Spanish painter and printmaker. Francisco Goya was Spain's greatest painter and printmaker during the late 18th and early 19th centuries, a wayward genius who prefigured in his art the romantic, impressionist, and expressionist movements.

Born in Fuendetodos near Saragossa on March 30, 1746, Francisco Goya died a voluntary expatriate in Bordeaux, France. Tradition has it that a priest discovered talent in the boy upon seeing him draw a hog on a wall. Oddly enough, a testament submitted for the process of beatification of Father José Pignatelli disclosed (not detected until 1962) that he taught Goya, who "instead of paying attention, kept his head down so that his teacher couldn't see him and occu-

pied himself in sketching. . . ." Pignatelli ordered him to the front of the class but recognized an artistic gift in the sketches. The priest called upon José Goya, the boy's father, and advised him to dedicate his son to painting. Perhaps owing to this same priest's influence, Goya at 12 years of age painted three works (destroyed 1936) for the church in Fuendetodos.

Two years later, Goya was apprenticed to José Luzán y Martínez, a mediocre, Neapolitan-trained painter who set his pupil to copying the best prints he possessed. After 4 years of this training, Goya left. He went to Madrid in 1763 to compete unsuccessfully for a scholarship to San Fernando Academy. The tests ended on Jan. 15, 1764, and nothing is known of the artist until 2 years later, when he entered another academic competition calling for a painting of the following subject: Empress Martha presents herself to King Alphonse the Wise in Burgos to petition a third of the ransom required by the sultan of Egypt for the rescue of her husband, Emperor Valduin; the Spanish king orders the full sum to be given her. The competitors were granted 6 months to execute this theme; Goya failed again. On July 22 he entered a competition to sketch another complicated historical scene and lost for the third time.

Early Works. Little is known of Goya's subsequent activities until April 1771, when he was in Rome. Two small paintings, both dated 1771 and one signed "Goya," have been discovered: *Sacrifice to Pan* and *Sacrifice to Vesta*. The monumental figures are classical but executed with sketchy brushstrokes and bathed in theatrical lighting. From Rome he sent to the Academy of Parma for an open competition another painting, *Hannibal in the Alps Contemplating the Italian Lands*, and signed himself as a pupil of Francisco Bayeu in his accompanying letter. Although he was not the winner, he did receive six of the votes and laudatory mention. Immediately after he had received this news, Goya departed for Saragossa.

The aforementioned works, and a handful more, are all that is known of Goya's art between 1766 and 1771. Sánchez Cantón (1964) pointed out that there are no concrete incidents to document the usual explanation, adduced from his known temperament, that he was otherwise occupied in womanizing, bullfighting, and brawling.

In Saragossa, Goya received important commissions, which he executed with success. On July 25, 1775, he married Josefa Bayeu, Francisco's sister. Bayeu, who was a director of the San Fernando Academy, used his influence to help his brother-in-law. Goya was commissioned to paint cartoons of contemporary customs and holiday activities for the Royal

Tapestry Factory of Santa Barbara. This work, well suited to his nature, lasted from 1774 to 1792. He completed 54 cartoons in a rococo style that mingled influences from Michel Ange Houasse, Louis Michel Van Loo, Giovanni Battista Tiepolo, and Anton Raphael Mengs.

Following an illness in 1778, Goya passed his convalescence executing his first series of engravings from 16 paintings by Diego Velázquez. Goya began to enjoy signs of recognition: he was praised by Mengs, named as a court painter by Charles III in 1779, and elected to membership in San Fernando Academy after he presented a small, classical painting, the *Crucified Christ,* in 1780. On the crest of this wave of approval, a quarrel with his important brother-in-law had serious consequences upon his career: in 1780 he was commissioned to paint a dome and its pendentives for the Cathedral of El Pilar in Saragossa. Bayeu suggested certain corrections in the domical composition, which Goya rejected. Then the council of the Cathedral took objection to certain nudities in his preparatory sketches for the pendentives and ordered him to submit his designs to Bayeu for correction and final approval. Goya accepted this condition, but afterward he declared he would "take it to court first." Later he wrote to a friend that, just to think about the incident, "I burn alive." This affair seems to have caused a hiatus (1780–1786) in his cartoons for the royal factory.

The Portraits.

The King commissioned Goya in 1780 to paint an altarpiece for the church of S. Francisco el Grande, Madrid; this work, the *Preaching of St. Bernardino,* was completed in 1784. No works by Goya are known for the year 1782 and only portraits for 1783, among which is one of the Count of Floridablanca, First Secretary of State. Other portraits of this period include those of the members of the family of the infante Don Luis (1783–1784) and the brilliant portrait of the Duke of Osuna (1785).

The artist was back in favor sometime before May 11, 1785, when he was appointed lieutenant director of painting (under Bayeu) in the Academy of San Fernando. The following year he was again working on the tapestry cartoons, and in June he was named painter to the king. Bayeu, clearly reconciled, sat for his portrait in 1786. Goya also executed many portraits of the royal family and members of the nobility, including the very appealing picture of the little Manuel Osorio de Zuñiga (1788).

Goya fell gravely ill in Seville at the end of 1792. He was left totally deaf and underwent a personality change from extrovert to introvert with an intense interest in evil spirits, a temporary avoidance of large canvases, and a preference for sketches in preparation for prints. He was back at work in Madrid by July 1793, and that year he produced a series of panels which he presented to the Academy of San Fernando. They include a scene in a madhouse, a bullfight, and an Inquisition scene.

Duchess of Alba.

Goya received a commission from the noble house of Alba in 1795. Since he moved in aristocratic circles, it is clear that he must have known the duchess for some time before this. At any rate, after the duke's death in July 1796, she retired to her villa in Sanlucar, and Goya was one of her guests. Upon his return to Madrid in 1797, he painted the duchess in black but with a wide colored belt (therefore not a mourning garment), wearing two rings, one imprinted "Alba" and the other "Goya." He signed the work "Goya, always."

Whatever their relationship was, it is clear that Goya had high hopes. It is also true that in the spring following the duke's death the duchess's servants were gossiping in correspondence about her possible remarriage. Nevertheless, Señora Goya was still living, and Goya could not be the unnamed swain. In any event, the duchess never did remarry. At best, Goya's painting was a brazen flaunting of illicit hopes; at worst, a vulgar display of kiss-and-tell.

Goya's first great series of etchings, *Los caprichos* (1796–1798), were based on drawings from his *Madrid Sketchbook.* They include scenes of witchcraft, popular traditions, bullfights, and society balls. In the *Caprichos* Goya mercilessly and vindictively lampooned the duchess. The duchess died in 1802, following a long illness. Goya painted the *Nude Maja* and the *Clothed Maja* later (usually dated between 1805 and 1807). The heads in both appear to float, neckless, above the shoulders.

Inquisition and the Peninsular War.

By the first years of the 19th century Goya was a wealthy man able to purchase an impressive home in 1803 and marry his son to an heiress in 1805. Simultaneously he was attracting the attention of the Holy Office of the Inquisition owing to the anticlerical satire in the *Caprichos* as well as his salacious subject matter. He donated all the *Caprichos* plates and the 240 unsold sets of the edition to the King under the pretext of seeking a pension for his son to travel; once the donation was accepted, the Holy Office perforce withdrew. The inquisitors did not forget, however; they investigated him again in 1814 concerning the nude and dressed *Majas.* Incomplete documentation leaves this incident obscure.

During the Napoleonic usurpation of the Spanish throne and the consequent War of Independence (1808–1813) Goya had an enigmatic record. With 3,000 other heads of families in Madrid on Dec. 10, 1808, he swore "love and fidelity" to the invader. In 1810 he attended the Academy to greet its new protector appointed by Joseph Bonaparte, but that same year he began work on his series of 80 etchings, *Los desastres de la guerra* (*The Disasters of War*), which, in many cases, is a specific condemnation of the Napoleonic war, although the expressionistic rendering makes the series a universal protest against the horrors of war. He finished the *Desastres* in 1814, the same year he painted the *Executions of May 3, 1808,* a grim depiction of a brutal massacre.

Goya applauded, understandably, the French suppression of the Inquisition and the secularization of religious orders. Yet in the joint will he made with his wife in 1811, he requested that he be buried in the Franciscan habit and have Masses offered and prayers said for his soul, and he made grants to holy places. His wife died in 1812, the year in which Goya painted the *Assumption of the Virgin* for the parish church of Chinchón, where his brother, Camilo, was the priest.

Goya executed two more series of etchings. *Los proverbios* (1813–1815; 1817–1818), or *Disparates,* as he himself called the series, are monstrous in mood and subject. The *Tauromachia* (1815–1816) is a series devoted to the art of bullfighting.

Last Years. In 1819 Goya purchased a villa, La Quinta del Sordo (Villa of the Deaf Man), at a time when his son and daughter-in-law were estranged from him, perhaps owing to another affair. His housekeeper was Leocadia Zorrilla de Weiss, a distant relative who was separated from her German husband, by whom she had had a son and daughter. Goya was so fond of the latter, Rosario, born in 1814, that some believe he was her father. Goya frescoed two rooms of the villa with his "black paintings." These profoundly moving works are a strange mixture of the horrendous (*Saturn Devouring His Son*), the diabolic (*Witches' Sabbath*), the salacious (*The Jesters*), the devout (*Pilgrimage of San Isidro*), and the ordinary (*Portrait of Leocadia Zorrilla,* previously called *Una manola*). These subjects and the others in the series make an ensemble that is as puzzling to interpret psychologically as it is emotionally overpowering.

In 1823 political events greatly affected Goya's life: Ferdinand VII, discontented with the constitution that had been forced upon him, left his palace in Madrid and went to Seville. Two months later the Duke of Angoulême with "one hundred thousand sons of St. Louis" invaded Spain to help Ferdinand VII. Goya, a liberal, immediately turned over the title to his villa to his grandson Mariano and took refuge in a friend's house. The following year Goya sought permission to spend 6 months enjoying the waters of Plombières "to mitigate the sickness and attacks that molested him in his advanced age." All this time Goya was receiving his royal salaries (and continued to do so up to his death) even though he had ceased to create works as First Court Painter or to teach in the Academy of San Fernando.

When the King granted his request, Goya immediately went to Bordeaux with Leocadia and her children. He went back to Spain in 1825 to ask to be retired and was granted permission to return to France "with all the salary." His paintings in Bordeaux, especially the *Milkmaid of Bordeaux,* indicate a release from his dark emotions. He died of a stroke on April 15, 1828, in Bordeaux.

EWB

Gramsci, Antonio (1891–1937), Italian Communist leader. Antonio Gramsci was a highly original Marxist who, working from Leninist principles, developed a new and controversial conception of hegemony in Marxist theory.

Antonio Gramsci was born in Ales in Sardinia on January 22, 1891. As the fourth son of Francesco Gramsci, a clerk in the registrar's office at Ghilarza, Gramsci was brought up in poverty and hardship, particularly during the five years his father was in prison for alleged embezzlement. As a child Antonio was constantly ill and withdrawn, and his anguish was compounded by physical deformity.

He was compelled to leave school at the age of 12 but following his father's release he was able to resume his education at Santa Lussurgia and Cagliari. On winning a scholarship to the University of Turin in 1911 he came into contact with future Communist leader and fellow Sardinian Palmiro Togliatti. During the elections of 1913the first to be held in Sardinia with universal male suffrage—Gramsci became convinced that Sardinia's acute problems of underdevelopment could only be solved in the context of socialist policies for Italy as a whole. (Gramsci retained a lively interest in his native Sardinia throughout his life and wrote a major essay on *The Southern Question* in 1926.)

Like many of his generation at the university in Turin, Gramsci was deeply influenced by the liberal idealism of Benedetto Croce. Gramsci's hostility to positivism made him a fierce critic of all fatalistic versions of Marxism. By 1915 he was writing regularly for the socialist *Il Grido del Populo* (The Cry of the

People) and *Avanti* (Forward), often on cultural questions in which he stressed the importance of educating the workers for revolution.

Following a four-day insurrection in August 1917 Gramsci became a leading figure in the Turin workers' movement. He welcomed the Russian Revolution (although in Crocean style he presented it as a "Revolution against *Das Kapital*") and in May 1919 he collaborated with Togliatti, Angelo Tasca, and Umberto Terracini to found *L'Ordine Nuovo* (The New Order) as an organ of "proletarian culture." The paper saw the factory committees in Turin as Soviets in embryo and the nuclei of a future socialist state. Thousands responded to the call to establish workers' councils in the Turin area, and during the "red years" of 1919 and 1920 there was a general strike and factories were occupied. *L'Ordine Nuovo*'s critique of the passivity and reformism of the Italian Socialist Party won the approval of Soviet leader Lenin, and although Gramsci would have preferred to continue working within the Socialist Party at a time of rising fascist reaction, a separate Communist Party of Italy was formed at Livorno in 1921.

Gramsci was on the Communist Party's central committee, but the newly formed party was dominated by Amadeo Bordiga, a powerful figure whose purist elitism brought him into increasing conflict with the Third Communist International (Comintern). Gramsci became his party's representative on the Comintern, and it was while recovering from acute depression in a clinic in Moscow that Gramsci met his future wife Julia in 1922. They had two children, Delio and a younger boy, Giuliano, whom Gramsci never actually saw. Despite some happy moments, particularly when the two were together in Rome in 1925 and 1926, the relationship between Gramsci and Julia was a fraught one. Julia was in poor mental health, and later with Gramsci's imprisonment all communication between them more or less ceased. It was with Julia's sister, Tatiana, who was devoted to Gramsci's well-being during the torturing years of incarceration, that he found real companionship.

In October 1922 Mussolini seized power. The head of the Communist Party was arrested, and Gramsci found himself party leader. He was elected parliamentary deputy in 1924 and by 1926, when the party held its third congress in Lyons, Gramsci had won wide membership support for a Leninist strategy of an alliance with the peasants under proletarian hegemony. In his one and only speech to the Chamber of Deputies Gramsci brilliantly analyzed the distinctive and lethal character of fascism and in 1926 he was arrested. Two years later he was brought to trial—"we must prevent this brain from functioning for twenty years," declared the prosecutor—and Gramsci spent the first five years of his sentence in the harsh penal prison at Turi. He was able to start work on his famous *Prison Notebooks* early in 1929, but by the middle of 1932 his health was beginning to deteriorate rapidly. Suffering from (among other ailments) Potts disease and arterio-sclerosis, he was eventually moved as a result of pressure from an international campaign for his release to a prison hospital in Formia, but by August 1935 he was too ill to work. Transferred to a clinic in Rome, he died on April 27, 1937, after a cerebral hemorrhage.

Tatiana had his 33 notebooks smuggled out of Italy and taken to Moscow via the diplomatic bag. These notebooks, despite the often rudimentary state of their drafts, are undeniably Gramsci's masterpiece. They contain sharply perceptive analyses of Italian history, Marxist philosophy, political strategy, literature, linguistics, and the theater. At their core stands Gramsci's over-riding preoccupation with the need to develop critical ideas rooted in the everyday life of the people so that the Communist cause acquires irresistible momentum. Opposed both to Bordiga's elitism and the sectarian policies of the Comintern between 1929 and 1934, Gramsci's stress on the moral and intellectual element in political movements offers a challenge not only to Marxists but to all seeking to change the world radically.

EWB

Grimm, Jakob Karl (1785–1863) and ***Wilhelm Karl*** (1786–1859), German scholars. The Grimm brothers were known for their Fairy Tales and for their work in comparative linguistics, which included the formulation of Grimm's law.

The romantic movement in Germany awakened the Germans' interest in the past of their own country, especially its cultural origins, early language, and folklore. Although some work in the rediscovery and edition of medieval German literature had already been undertaken in the 18th century, it was the first generation of romantic poets and theorists about the beginning of the next century, especially Ludwig Tieck, Novalis, and the Schlegel brothers, who first focused national attention on the origins of German culture and literature. While most of the poets viewed medieval literature chiefly as an inspiration for their own writings, others turned their attention to the methodical investigation of the past. The Grimm brothers were the most important of these romantic historians of early medieval language and folklore.

Jakob Grimm was born on Jan. 4, 1785, in Hanau. His brother, Wilhelm, was born on February 24 of the following year. As small children, they were inseparable and, aside from a brief period of living apart, they were to remain together for the rest of their lives. Their even-tempered dispositions assured cooperation on all the projects they undertook together. The main difference in their personalities seems to be that Jakob, the more robust of the two, had more taste for grueling research work, and it was he who worked out most of their grammatical and linguistic theories. Wilhelm was physically weaker but had a somewhat warmer temperament and more taste for music and literature. His literary talent was responsible for the pleasant style of their collection of fairy tales.

The brothers first attended school in Kassel, then began legal studies at the University of Marburg. While there, however, the inspiration of Friedrich von Savigny awakened in them an interest in past cultures. In 1808 Jakob was named court librarian to the King of Westphalia in Wilhelmshöhe, and in 1816 he became librarian in Kassel, where Wilhelm had been employed since 1814. They were to remain there until 1830, when they obtained positions at the University of Göttingen.

Grimm's Fairy Tales.

For some years the brothers had been in contact with the romantic poets Clemens Brentano and Achim von Arnim, who in Heidelberg were preparing a collection of German folk songs. Following their own interests in folklore and legends, the brothers brought out their first collection of tales, *Kinder—und Hausmärchen* (*Tales of Children and the Home*), in 1812. These tales were collected by recording stories told by peasants and villagers. Wilhelm put them into literary form and gave them a pleasant, childlike style. The brothers added many scholarly footnotes on the tales' sources and analogs.

In addition, the Grimms worked on editing remnants of other folklore and primitive literature. Between 1816 and 1818 they published two volumes of *Deutsche Sagen* (*German Legends*), and about the same time they published a volume of studies in early literary history, *Altdeutsche Wälder* (*Old German Forests*).

Linguistic Research.

In later years their interest in older literature led the Grimm brothers increasingly to a study of older languages and their relationship to modern German. Jakob, especially, began to specialize in the history and structure of the German language. The first edition of his *Deutsche Grammatik* (*German Grammar*) was published in 1819. Later editions show increasing development of a scientific method in linguistics.

The brothers, and especially Jakob, were also working to codify the relationship between similar words of related languages, such as English *apple* and German *Apfel*. Their formulation of the rules for such relationships became known as Grimm's law. It was later elaborated to account for all word relationships in the Indo-European group of languages. The Grimm brothers were not the first to take note of such similarities, but they can be credited with amassing the bulk of linguistic data and working out the details of the rules.

Later Years.

In 1830 the brothers moved to the University of Göttingen, where Jakob was named professor and head librarian and Wilhelm was appointed assistant librarian. As professor, Jakob held lectures on linguistics and cultural history. Wilhelm also attained the rank of professor in 1835. Both were dismissed in 1835 for political reasons: they had joined in signing a protest against the King's decision to abolish the Hanover constitution. They first moved back to Kassel but later obtained professorships at Berlin, where they were to remain until their deaths.

Their last years were spent in preparing the definitive dictionary of the German language, tracing the etymological derivation of every word. The first volume, published in 1854, has 1,824 pages and gets only as far as the word *Biermolke*. Four pages are devoted to the letter A alone, which is termed the most noble and primeval of all sounds. The Grimms' dictionary was carried on by generations of scholars after the brothers' deaths, and it was finished in 1960. Its completed form consists of 16 weighty volumes.

Wilhelm died in Berlin on Dec. 16, 1859. Jakob continued the work on the dictionary and related projects until his death in Berlin on Sept. 20, 1863.

EWB

Guizot, François Pierre Guillaume (1787–1874), French statesman and historian. François Guizot was a cold and clever politician whose refusal to grant electoral reforms precipitated the February Revolution of 1848. His scholarly publications, however, have been widely praised.

Though born at Nîmes on Oct. 4, 1787, François Guizot was educated in Geneva, where his mother had emigrated after his father's execution in 1794. Returning to Paris in 1805, Guizot studied law but soon forsook it for a literary career. The publication of a critical edition of Edward Gibbon's *Decline and Fall of the Roman Empire* established his reputation as a historian and secured his appointment (1812) to the chair of modern history in the University of Paris.

There he became a disciple of the moderate royalist philosopher Pierre Paul Royer-Collard.

Guizot took no active part in politics under the Empire, but during the first Bourbon restoration he held the post of secretary general of the Ministry of the Interior. After the Hundred Days he twice held office: secretary general of the Ministry of Justice (1815–1816) and director in the Ministry of the Interior (1819–1820). But the assassination of the Duke of Berry in February 1820 produced a reactionary backlash that swept Guizot and the moderates from office.

Out of office for most of the next decade, Guizot concentrated on historical research and writing. From his productive pen came the *History of the Origin of Representative Government* (2 vols., 1821–1822); *History of the English Revolution from Charles I to Charles II* (2 vols., 1826–1827); *General History of Civilization in Europe* (3 vols., 1828); and *Histoire de la civilisation en France* (4 vols., 1830). Guizot's histories have been justly praised for their excellent scholarship, lucid and succinct style, judicious analysis, and impartiality.

Returning to active politics in January 1830, Guizot entered the Chamber as a deputy for Lisieux and immediately joined the opposition to the Polignac ministry. Since 1815 Guizot had shared with Royer-Collard the leadership of the Doctrinaires, who considered the Charter of 1814 the epitome of political wisdom since it established a balance between the power of the Crown, the nobility, and the upper middle classes. As right-wing liberals, they supported the restoration monarchy so long as it governed according to the Charter, but when Charles X attempted to rule by decree, they turned from the Bourbon to the Orleanist dynasty. During the July Revolution of 1830, they helped to elevate Louis Philippe, Duke of Orléans, to the throne.

In August 1830 Guizot became minister of the interior. For the next 2 years he gradually became more conservative as a series of Paris disorders instilled in him a fear of anarchy. But his conservatism had deeper roots. A devout Calvinist, he identified the sanctified elect with the political elite, who, he believed, had a divine mission to govern the masses.

By October 1832, when he became minister of public instruction, Guizot had assumed leadership of the right-center. His one great legislative act was the law of June 28, 1833, the charter of France's elementary school system, which required every commune to maintain a public primary school. Always the champion of the academic community, he reestablished the Académie des Sciences Morales et Politiques, which Napoleon had suppressed, founded the Société de

l'Histoire de France, and published at state expense huge collections of medieval documents and diplomatic dispatches.

In February 1840 Guizot went to London as ambassador, but in October he became foreign minister and the dominant personality in the Soult ministry. The tenets of his foreign policy were nonintervention, friendship with Britain, and cooperation with Austria. In 1847 Guizot became premier. But overthrown by the February Revolution of 1848, he went into exile in England. After a year in London, devoted primarily to research in the British archives, he retired to his estate at Val Richer near Lisieux in Normandy.

Though Guizot survived the Orleanist monarchy by 26 years, he never reentered the political arena but focused his energy on academic activities and writing historical works. Between 1854 and his death on Sept. 12, 1874, he published the *Histoire de la république d'Angleterre et de Cromwell* (2 vols., 1854); *Histoire du protectorat de Cromwell et du rétablissement des Stuarts* (2 vols., 1856); *Mémoires pour servir à l'histoire de mon temps* (9 vols., 1858–1868); and the *Histoire parlementaire de la France* (5 vols., 1863), which included his speeches.

EWB

Gutenberg, Johann (ca. 1398–1468), German inventor and printer. Johann Gutenberg was the inventor of movable-type mechanical printing in Europe.

Johann Gutenberg was born Johann Gensfleisch zur Laden, in Mainz. He was the third child of Freile zum Gensfleisch and his second wife, Else Wirick zum Gutenberg, whose name Johann adopted. Nothing is known of Gutenberg's studies or apprenticeship except that he learned the trade of a goldsmith while living in Mainz. About 1428 his family was exiled as a result of a revolt of the craftsmen against the noble class ruling the town, and in 1430 Gutenberg established himself in Strasbourg, where he remained until 1444.

Gutenberg's experiments in printing began during his years in Strasbourg. He was already familiar with the techniques of xylography, the process used to make books and other printed matter in Europe since the 14th century, and in the Far East much earlier. Then came the transition from xylography to typography, infinitely more practical for text printing since, instead of reproduction by means of wood carving, a small separate block (type) was used for each sign or character. The idea of movable type may have occurred to many people independently; Gutenberg may have worked in this field about 1436.

Business of Printing. There is no record of Gutenberg's whereabouts after 1444, but he appears again in Mainz according to a document dated October 1448. By 1450 he is known to have had a printing plant, for which he borrowed 800 guilders from the rich financier Johann Fust to enable him to manufacture certain tools and equipment. In December 1452 Gutenberg had to pay off his debt. Being unable to do so, he and Fust concluded a new agreement, under which Gutenberg received another similar loan and the financier became a partner in the enterprise. At that time Gutenberg already printed with movable type, thus making the idea conceived in Strasbourg a reality in Mainz. A very valuable assistant to Gutenberg was his young employee and disciple Peter Schoeffer, who joined the firm in 1452. In spite of their successes, the relationship between Gutenberg and Fust took a bad turn, Fust sued Gutenberg for 2,000 guilders, and in 1455 the partnership was dissolved. Fust won the court action and thereby acquired Gutenberg's materials and tools and went into partnership with Schoeffer.

Provenance of printed works of this period is therefore difficult, especially since there are no printed works surviving with Gutenberg's name on them. From that period dates the monumental and extremely beautiful 42-Line Bible, also called the Gutenberg Bible and Mazarin Bible, a work in big folio which is the crowning of many years of collaboration by the Gutenberg-Fust-Schoeffer team. However, when the first finished copies were turned out in early 1456, Gutenberg, undoubtedly the main creator of the work, no longer belonged to the partnership. Fust continued printing successfully with Gutenberg's equipment and also with machinery improved by Schoeffer. In the meantime Gutenberg, not at all favored by fortune in his various undertakings, had to start all over again. It is believed that the fruit of his work in these years is the 36-Line Bible and the famous *Catholicon,* a kind of encyclopedia. Again, as Gutenberg never put his name on any of his works, all ascriptions are hypothetical.

Later Years. In 1462 Mainz was sacked by the troops of Adolph II. Fust's printing office was set on fire and Gutenberg suffered losses as well, the same as other craftsmen. In consequence of this disaster many typographers left Mainz, and through their dispersion they also scattered their until now so jealously protected know-how. Gutenberg remained in Mainz, but he was again reduced to poverty, and he requested the archiepiscopal court for a sinecure, which he obtained on Jan. 17, 1465, including salary and privileges "for services rendered . . . and to be rendered in the future." Gutenberg's post at the court allowed him some economic relief, but nevertheless he carried on with his

printing activities. The works from this final period in his life are unknown because of lack of identification.

Reportedly, Gutenberg became blind in the last months of his life, living partly in Mainz and partly in the neighboring village of Eltville. He died in St. Victor's parish in Mainz on Feb. 3, 1468, and was buried in the church of the Franciscan convent in that town. His physical appearance is unknown, though there are many imaginary depictions of his face and figure, including statues erected in Mainz and Strassburg. In 1900 the Gutenberg Museum was founded in Mainz with a library annexed to it to which all the objects and documents related to the invention of typography were entrusted.

EWB

H

Haeckel, Ernst Heinrich Philipp August (1834–1919), German biologist and natural philosopher. Ernst Haeckel was famous for his work in evolutionary theory, especially the construction of phylogenetic trees. In the late 19th and early 20th centuries he was as famous as Charles Darwin, whom he admired, though his views were closer to those of Jean Baptiste Lamarck.

Ernst Haeckel was born in Potsdam, Germany, on February 16, 1834, to Carl and Charlotte (Sethe) Haeckel. His father was the chief administrator for religious and educational affairs in Merseburg, while his mother was the daughter of a privy councillor in Berlin. Haeckel thus had the social advantage of growing up in an educated and cultured family. He was publicly educated at the *Domgymnasium* in Merseburg, graduating in 1852. He then, on the advice of his parents, studied medicine at Berlin, later at Würzburg and Vienna, before returning to Berlin to earn his medical degree in 1857.

In 1858 he passed the state medical examination, but he did not practice medicine. In fact, he had never been truly interested in being a physician, only pursuing that degree for his parents' sake. Yet he discovered, after initial reluctance, that medical school would provide him with the most solid foundation on which to build a scientific career. It was in this medical training that Haeckel met many of the most important biologists of his day. At Würzburg he studied under Albert von Kölliker and Franz Leydig, learning embryological and comparative anatomy as well as perfecting his skills in microscopical investigations— later to prove essential for his research in ontogeny and phylogeny.

It was also at Würzburg that Haeckel's philosophical views began to develop, confronted as he was by mechanistic and materialistic views of life developed by Rudolf Virchow and Carl Vogt and expressed by young scientists and physicians with whom he came into contact. In response to such strongly asserted materialism Haeckel's own Christian beliefs began to be transformed, and though he never relinquished the idea of god, his own god was eventually so radically changed that it seemed scarcely personal, perhaps nothing more than the principle of causality in the universe. Meanwhile, his medical education continued. At Berlin in 1854–1855 Haeckel studied under Johannes Müller, whom he greatly respected as the paradigm of the great scientist. Under Müller, he increased his understanding of comparative anatomy and he was introduced to marine zoology, one of Müller's specialties.

In 1858, after finishing his medical studies and final examination, Karl Gegenbaur offered him the chance of a future professorship in zoology at Jena if he would first undertake a zoological research expedition in the Mediterranean. This research occupied his time from 1859 to 1860 and resulted in the publication in 1862 of *The Radiolarians,* in which he announced his support of Darwinism. Haeckel determined to reinterpret all of morphology (study and comparison of animal forms) in terms of the theory of evolution, which meant the linking of animal species phylogenetically through "geneological" trees. He argued that all processes could be reduced to mechanical-materialistic causes, that evolution was driven by such causality, and that the true philosophy of nature should be Monism, a system stressing the unity of mind and matter, in contrast to all vitalistic or teleological dualism stressing the separation of mind and matter. He differed from Darwin in two fundamental waysHaeckel's was the more speculative mind, and he relied much more upon the Lamarckian principle of the inheritance of acquired characteristics than Darwin ever did.

Also in 1862, Haeckel married his cousin, Anna Sethe, who died in 1864, at which time he married Agnes Huschke, daughter of anatomist Emil Huschke. They had three children. In 1861, upon his return from his research expedition, Haeckel had been given the post of *Privatdozent* at the University of Jena. In 1862 he was named professor extraordinary in comparative anatomy and was made director of the Zoological Institute. And in 1865 a chair in zoology was established for him, which he held until 1909. During that more than 40 year period Haeckel continued his herculean labors on behalf of his science, going on four major scientific expeditions (Canary Islands, 1866–1867; Red Sea, 1873; Ceylon, 1881–1882; Java, 1900–1901) and further elaborating on his evolutionary schemes.

In 1901 he was the recipient of the Turin Bressa Prize for his outstanding work in biology. Throughout his life he received many honors and was elected to many scientific societies, among them the Imperial Academy of Sciences at Vienna (1872), the American Philosophical Society (1885), and the Royal Society of Edinburgh (1888). His most characteristic ideas and tendencies are evident in his early work of 1886, *General Morphology*all his subsequent efforts were reworkings of this book. He retired in 1909 and still lived in Jena when he died in 1919.

EWB

Hall, Marguerite Radclyffe (1886–1943), British writer. Radclyffe Hall, the name under which British literary figure Marguerite Radclyffe-Hall wrote, is perhaps best known for her 1928 novel, *The Well of Loneliness,* one of the first modern literary works whose plot concerned a same-sex relationship between women. Despite its laudatory critical reception, Hall's book was the subject of a ban under Britain's Obscene Libel Act, but scholars today consider it one of the premiere fictional portrayals of contemporary gay and lesbian life, a sensitive work that helped open doors of cultural acceptance for later writers.

Hall was born into a wealthy family in Hampshire, England, in 1886. Raised as a boy by her emotionally unstable parents, she was known as "John" to her friends and found security and support in her maternal grandmother, who encouraged the young girl's creative gifts. After receiving a large inheritance at the age of seventeen, Hall attended King's College in London and spent a year abroad in Germany. An accomplished amateur musician, she often wrote lyrics to accompany her compositions, and at the urging of her grandmother published some of this writing as a volume of verse entitled *'Twixt Earth and Stars* in 1906.

Around this time Hall became acquainted with Ladye Mabel Batten, a literary figure who became her companion and mentor for several years to follow. In these early years preceding World War I, Hall produced several other volumes of poetry, including *A Sheaf of Verses* and *Songs of Three Counties, and Other Poems,* works noteworthy for their frank expressions of passion between women. During this period Hall had become a Catholic, like Batten, and her new faith was to become an integral element in her later works of fiction. Batten encouraged Hall to branch out into fiction, and the writer's first foray into this genre came with the 1924 publication of *The Forge.* However, Batten had passed away in 1916, and the grieving Hall felt in part responsible, since the writer had developed a romantic interest in Batten's niece, Una Troubridge.

The Unlit Lamp, Hall's second novel, was also published in 1924 and is seen by scholars as a thematic precursor to *The Well of Loneliness.* Much more subtle in its addressing of same-sex romance, the work's possibly scandalous subject matter was so restrained that little was mentioned of it in reviews.

Hall's 1926 novel, *Adam's Breed,* is the story of a young man besieged by a collective guilt about the excess consumption of modern society, and is a reflection of her compassion for the plight of animals. By this time Hall and Troubridge, the wife of a naval officer, had become involved in a long-term relationship. Hall had originally wished to title *Adam's Breed* "Food," but her publisher feared that it would be mistaken for a cookbook.

Hall's landmark novel, *The Well of Loneliness,* appeared in print in 1928. The proclivities of its protagonist are explicit, and the passions depicted toward other female characters in the novel are also frank. Some details are autobiographical: the heroine's parents wished for a boy while the mother was expecting, and thus named the baby girl Stephen. Hall herself was raised as a boy and went by the nickname John for much of her life. As a young girl, Stephen develops a crush on one of the maids of the household, an incident which the scholar Dickson noted had also taken place in Hall's own youth. As a young girl, Stephen feels that she is not like other young girls, and finds herself more drawn to masculine pursuits; like Hall, the protagonist is an accomplished equestrienne.

After its publication in 1928, *The Well of Loneliness* was publicly condemned by a writer for the *Sunday Express* and a trial soon followed. Hall lost the case and the novel was banned in England; in a later case in a New York court the obscenity charges were dropped. Critical reaction to the novel was mixed, and was often tied in with a defense of it due to the controversy. Leonard Woolf, part of the influential British literary circle known as the Bloomsbury Group and husband to novelist Virginia, commented in *The Nation and The Athenaeum* that Hall's novel "is written with understanding and frankness, with sympathy and feeling," but charged that as a work of literary merit, it fell short.

Hall penned two other novels before ill health curtailed her writing in the years before her death. In 1932, she published *The Master of the House,* the story of a man whose life paralleled that of Jesus Christ. The critic Lawrence, writing in *The School of Femininity,* deemed it an appropriate companion to *The Well of Loneliness.* "While the heroine in the one book lives the life of a man within the body of a woman, the man in the other book lives the life of a Christ within the body of a mortal," Lawrence wrote. "Neither of them has any concern with normal experience. They should be kept together and read together. They are part of the same mysterious saga." Many elements of *The Master of the House* correspond to the life of Christ as presented in the Bible: Christophe is the son of a carpenter and his wife, Jouse and Marie; his cousin Jan, like John the Baptist, will remain a close confidant through adulthood. Hall set her updated version of the Biblical tale shortly before the outbreak of World War I, and the two men are sent to Palestine to defend it against the Turkish army. There Christophe is ambushed and his journey to death closely follows Christ's procession to the cross.

Hall's seventh and final novel, *The Sixth Beatitude,* appeared in 1936. It is the story of a poor woman, Hannah Bullen, whose somewhat unconventional life (she is unmarried, but mother to two) in a small English seaside town is marked by poverty and strife within her immediate family. The title of the work refers to the Roman Catholic notion of purity of mind and chastity of heart, and Hall attempts to portray the goodness of her protagonist despite the squalor of her surroundings.

Hall died of cancer in 1943. Although *The Well of Loneliness* is often cited as seminal to modern gay and lesbian fiction, the rest of her novels and poetry have often been overshadowed by the scandal that is associated with her best-known title—yet they also evince many of the same themes and convictions important to her.

CA

Hammond, John Lawrence Le Breton (1872–1952) and **Lucy Barbara** (1873–1961), English historians. The Hammonds were joint authors of a number of histories of the English working class.

Lawrence Hammond was born at Drighlington, Yorkshire, on July 18, 1872. His future wife, Lucy Barbara Bradby, was born in London in July 1873. Both were children of Anglican clergymen with working-class parishes, Lawrence's in the industrial north, Barbara's among the London docks. Both Lawrence and Barbara attended Oxford University, he at St. John's College, where he studied classics, and she at Lady Margaret Hall, where she was known as one of the most brilliant students of her time. They were married in 1901.

In 1897 Lawrence Hammond entered a career in journalism as a writer for the *Leeds Mercury* and the *Liverpool Post.* Two years later he became editor of the new liberal weekly, the *Spectator,* which had been launched to oppose British imperialism in South

Africa. In 1907 he left journalism to become secretary of the Civil Service Commission for six years. He returned to journalism after the war as correspondent for the *Manchester Guardian* and remained with this newspaper for the rest of his life.

After their marriage, the Hammonds began work on a series of social histories of the British labor class, extending from the later 18th to the mid-19th century. *The Village Labourer, 1760–1832* (1911) was the first to appear. In it they describe the changes that 18th-century parliamentary enclosures brought about in the villagers' way of life, the gradual isolation of the poor, and the laborers' revolts of the early 1830s. The book, wrote Gilbert Murray, had on its readers almost the effect of a revelation. Enclosures and the transformation of the laboring class had been looked upon as the necessary requisites for Britain's industrialization. Historians had emphasized the way these had contributed to Britain's progress in the 19th century. Here, however, the Hammonds assessed the cost of industrialization to its victims. They showed the suffering and degradation of the dispossessed amid the material success and the idealism of the early 19th century. Their next work, *The Town Labourer, 1760–1832,* appeared in 1917, and the last volume in the trilogy, *The Skilled Labourer, 1760–1832,* in 1919. They also wrote *Lord Shaftesbury* (1923), *The Rise of Modern Industry* (1925), *The Age of the Chartists* (1930), *The Bleak Age* (1934), and *C. P. Scott of the Manchester Guardian* (1934).

The Hammonds spent most of their later lives at Picott's End outside London. Here, wrote Arnold Toynbee, they lived in Desert-Father austerity, surrounded by dogs, cats, and a permanent congregation of birds, standing as expectantly as the birds in Giotto's picture of St. Francis.

Lawrence Hammond died on April 7, 1952. Barbara Hammond, grieving, went into a slow and irreversible decline. She died, after prolonged illness, on Nov. 14, 1961.

EWB

Hargreaves, James (d.1786), English inventor. Early in the eighteenth century John Kay (1704–1764) invented the flying shuttle, allowing weavers to produce material much faster than ever before. While this solved one problem, it created another: the spinning of yarn was still done by hand on the "Great Wheel," one thread at a time, and could not keep up with the demand brought on by Kay's new loom. To help increase the supply of yarn, the Royal Society of Arts offered cash prizes to anyone who invented a faster spinning machine. The first one to do so was James Hargreaves.

Hargreaves grew up in Lancashire, England, learning the trades of carpentry and weaving. He did not become an inventor until 1740, when he was employed by a local businessman to construct a better carding machine. A few years later, it is said, Hargreaves accidentally toppled the spinning wheel in his home. As it lay on its side, Hargreaves noticed the wheel and the spindle were still in motion, even though they had been tipped ninety degrees. It occurred to him that a mechanical spinner could be designed in which many spindles, set vertically and side-by-side, could spin a number of threads from just one horizontal wheel.

Hargreaves began constructing just such a machine in 1754; fourteen years and many prototypes later, the spinning jenny was complete. The spinning jenny was the first machine that accurately simulated the drafting motion of human fingers. This was vitally important to the success of the spinner, for it eliminated the need to draw cotton fibers out by hand. The jenny had one large wheel playing out cotton roving to eight different spindles, thus spinning eight threads at once.

Because the design was essentially the same as a spinning wheel (only eightfold) the yarn produced was still lumpy and uneven in places; however, it was sufficient for the weaving of many different fabrics, particularly when woven together with threads of linen. It was also ideal for the spinning of wool thread and yarn. Unlike many inventors who would follow him, Hargreaves did not plan to become wealthy from his invention—in fact, the first U jennies were used only in his home. Soon, however, the Hargreaves family suffered some financial setbacks, and he was forced to sell a few of his machines to mills.

His neighbors feared the new machine, thinking it would soon replace them all, and in 1768 they formed a mob that gutted the Hargreaves home and destroyed his jenny. Understandably upset, Hargreaves and his family moved to Nottingham. There he entered a partnership with Thomas James, and the two men opened their own cotton mill.

In 1769, Richard Arkwright successfully patented his water frame spinning machine (along with most of the machines associated with the spinning process, not all of which were of Arkwright's design). Inspired, Hargreaves enlisted legal aid to help him patent the jenny. By that time, many Lancashire mills had copied the jenny design illegally, an infringement for which Hargreaves sought restitution. His case was dismissed, however, when the court discovered that he had sold jennies in Lancashire a few years earlier.

By 1777 the water frame had almost completely replaced the jenny as England's most popular spinning machine: the yarn it produced was stronger and smoother, much more suited to the needs of the now-dominant hosiery industry. (Both the jenny and the water frame would ultimately be replaced by Samuel Crompton's spinning mule.) Hargreaves was never awarded the patent or the restitution he fought for; he died poor (compared, at least, to Arkwright) in 1778.

World of Invention

Haussmann, Baron Georges Eugène (1809–1891), French administrator. As French prefect of the Seine, Baron Haussmann carried out under Napoleon III a huge urban renewal program for the city of Paris.

During the administration of Baron Haussmann, 71 miles of new roads, 400 miles of pavement, and 320 miles of sewers were added to Paris; 100,000 trees were planted, and housing, bridges, and public buildings were constructed. Elected a member of the Académie des Beaux-Arts in 1867, the year of the International Exhibition in Paris, Haussmann stated, "My qualification? I was chosen as demolition artist" (*Memoires,* 3 vols., 1890–1893).

Admittedly Haussmann destroyed a considerable portion of the historic city, but the purpose was to tear down the worst slums and discourage riots, make the city more accessible, accommodate the new railroads, and beautify Paris. Long, straight boulevards for parades and for the circulation of traffic could also foil would-be rioters, since the mob could not defend boulevards as readily as barricaded slum alleyways.

Georges Eugène Haussmann was born in Paris. Exceedingly ambitious, he studied law solely with the aim of becoming an administrator within the prefectorial corps. He was appointed prefect of the Seine in 1853.

The instigator of the beautification of Paris was Napoleon III, who admired London, especially its squares. Such a program of beautification would in addition stimulate the banks and solve the problems of unemployment. Haussmann spent a total of 2,115,000,000 francs, the equivalent of $1.5 billion in today's currency.

Haussmann began by continuing the Rue de Rivoli as a great east-west link across Paris and by developing the areas of the Louvre and the Halles. He brought a competent engineer named Alphand from Bordeaux to continue the development of the Bois de Boulogne. Other acquaintances were introduced into the administration, notably in the construction of the famous sewers. The sewers, although underground, did not go unnoticed; Haussmann ensured that they became showplaces and even provided transportation for their viewing. One critic cynically considered the sewers "so fine that something really great should happen in them" (*Memoires*).

Three-quarters of the Île de la Cité was destroyed to create a central area for the Palais de Justice and police headquarters and barracks. The Boulevard de Sebastopol, beginning at the Gare de l'Est, was extended across the Île to provide a north-south route across Paris. The Gare du Nord was linked to the business district by the Rue La Fayette. Radial roads linked the core of the city to the suburbs. A green belt around the fortifications linking the Bois de Boulogne in the west to the Bois de Vincennes in the east did not materialize.

Haussmann was forced to retire in 1869, having succumbed to his critics, who accused him of "Haussmannnomania," heavy spending, and disrespect for the laws governing finance. One of his last acts for Napoleon III was the drafting of a proclamation for the siege of Paris in 1870.

EWB

Hébert, Jacques René (1757–1794), French journalist and revolutionist. Jacques René Hébert published the journal "Le Père Duchesne" and was a spokesman for the sans-culottes, the extreme republicans of revolutionary France.

Like other popular leaders of the French Revolution, Jacques René Hébert was a member of the bourgeoisie. He was born in Alençon, the son of a successful master jeweler who was a member of the municipal nobility. At the beginning of the French Revolution he was a destitute in Paris, but by 1790 he had established himself as a successful pamphleteer of political satires, appealing to popular antagonisms toward the nobility and the clergy. After the flight of the King, he attacked the Crown as the enemy of the Revolution.

In June 1792 Hébert founded the Revolutionary journal *Le Père Duchesne,* which became his vehicle for expounding his conception of proletarian interests and for venting his own frustrations. Its symbol was the caricature of a well-known braggarta sinister-looking man, a pistol in one hand and a hatchet in the other, standing over a kneeling priest, continually calling for the death of the enemies of the people. On Dec. 22, 1792, Hébert was elected assistant prosecutor of the Paris Commune.

During 1793 Hébert became the advocate of sans-culottism, which demanded all-out war against the enemies of the people. These enemies included the Church, counterrevolutionaries, profiteers, and political moderates. Although he has been associated with the dechristianization movement, Hébert claimed

138

he was not an atheist. He maintained that all good Jacobins ought to see Christ as the first Jacobin.

Hébertists were closely linked to the program of the Terror. Their fierce hatred of those classified as "enemies of the people" was influential in the Law of the Suspects, which made official their demands for justice. Their demands for price-fixing and enforced consumer protection led to the Laws of the Maximum of September and December 1793. Hébertists were also fanatical terrorists, and their influence was great in the police apparatus of the Committee of General Security. As such, they were deeply implicated not only in the Reign of Terror in Paris but also in the massacres of Lyons, Nantes, and the Vendée.

Hébert's base of power was the Commune and the influence it wielded on the Committee of Public Safety. The Committee's actions in December 1793 in suppressing the Commune did much to arouse the ire of Hébert and the sans-culottes. They began to attack the Committee, blaming it for the failure of price controls and for complicity with war profiteers. Finally, on March 4, 1794, Hébert—egged on by his supporters—called for an insurrection of the Commune. His call met with little success, but it served as a reason for his proscription as a counterrevolutionary. He was arrested on March 14, 1794, and was executed on March 24.

All historians have agreed that Hébert was an opportunist, but recently social historians have suggested that his opinions were widely held by the people. In particular, he seems to have been representative in his belief that by 1794 a conspiracy of sellers against consumers did exist.

EWB

Henry VIII (1491–1547), king of England from 1509 to 1547. As a consequence of the Pope's refusal to nullify his first marriage, Henry VIII withdrew from the Roman Church and created the Church of England.

The second son of Henry VII, Henry VIII was born on June 28, 1491, at Greenwich Palace. He was a precocious student; he learned Latin, Spanish, French, and Italian and studied mathematics, music, and theology. He became an accomplished musician and played the lute, organ, and harpsichord. He composed hymns, ballads, and two Masses. He also liked to hunt, wrestle, and joust and drew "the bow with greater strength than any man in England."

On his father's death on April 21, 1509, Henry succeeded to a peaceful kingdom. He married Catherine of Aragon, widow of his brother Arthur, on June 11, and 13 days later they were crowned at Westminster Abbey. He enthused to his father-in-law, Ferdi-

nand, that "the love he bears to Catherine is such, that if he were still free he would choose her in preference to all others."

Foreign Policy. In short order Henry set course on a pro-Spanish and anti-French policy. In 1511 he joined Spain, the papacy, and Venice in the Holy League, directed against France. He claimed the French crown and sent troops to aid the Spanish in 1512 and determined to invade France. The bulk of the preparatory work fell to Thomas Wolsey, the royal almoner, who became Henry's war minister. Despite the objections of councilors like Thomas Howard, the Earl of Surrey, Henry went ahead. He was rewarded by a smashing victory at Guinegate (Battle of the Spurs, Aug. 13, 1513) and the capture of Tournai and Théorouanne.

Peace was made in 1514 with the Scots, who had invaded England and been defeated at Flodden (Sept. 9, 1513), as well as with France. The marriage of Henry's sister Mary to Louis XII sealed the French treaty. This diplomatic revolution resulted from Henry's anger at the Hapsburg rejection of Mary, who was to have married Charles, the heir to both Ferdinand and Maximilian I, the Holy Roman emperor. Soon the new French king, Francis I, decisively defeated the Swiss at Marignano (Sept. 13–14, 1515). When Henry heard about Francis's victory, he burst into tears of rage. Increasingly, Wolsey handled state affairs; he became archbishop of York in 1514, chancellor and papal legate in 1515. Not even his genius, however, could win Henry the coveted crown of the Holy Roman Empire. With deep disappointment he saw it bestowed in 1519 on Charles, the Spanish king. During 1520 Henry met Emperor Charles V at Dover and Calais, and Francis at the Field of Cloth of Gold, near Calais, where Francis mortified Henry by throwing him in an impromptu wrestling match. In 1521 Henry joyfully received the papally bestowed title "Defender of the Faith" as a reward for writing the *Assertion of the Seven Sacraments,* a criticism of Lutheran doctrine. He tried to secure Wolsey's election as pope in 1523 but failed.

English Reformation. Catherine was 40 in 1525. Her seven pregnancies produced but one healthy child, Mary, born May 18, 1516. Despairing of having a legitimate male heir, Henry created Henry Fitzroy, his natural son by Elizabeth Blount, Duke of Richmond and Somerset. More and more, he conceived Catherine's misfortunes as a judgment from God. Did not Leviticus say that if a brother marry his brother's widow, it is an unclean thing and they shall be childless? Since Catherine was Arthur's widow, the matter was apparent.

The Reformation proceeded haphazardly from Henry's negotiations to nullify his marriage. Catherine would not retire to a nunnery, nor would Anne Boleyn consent to be Henry's mistress as had her sister Mary; she grimly demanded marriage. A court sitting in June 1529 under Wolsey and Cardinal Campeggio heard the case. Pope Clement VII instructed Campeggio to delay. When the Peace of Cambrai was declared between Spain and France in August 1529, leaving Charles V, Catherine's nephew, still powerful in Italy, Clement revoked the case to Rome. He dared not antagonize Charles, whose troops had sacked Rome in 1527 and briefly held him prisoner.

Henry removed Wolsey from office. Actually, Wolsey's diplomacy had been undermined by Henry's sending emissaries with different proposals to Clement. Catherine had a valid dispensation for her marriage to Henry from Pope Julius II; furthermore, she claimed that she came a virgin to Henry. She was a popular queen, deeply hurt by Henry's forsaking her bed in 1526. Henry's strategy matured when Thomas Cromwell became a privy councilor and his chief minister. Cromwell forced the clergy in convocation in 1531 to accept Henry's headship of the Church "as far as the law of Christ allows."

Anne's pregnancy in January 1533 brought matters to a head. In a fever of activity Henry married her on Jan. 25, 1533, secured papal approval to Thomas Cranmer's election as archbishop of Canterbury in March, had a court convened under Cranmer declare his marriage to Catherine invalid in May, and waited triumphantly for the birth of a son. His waiting was for naught. On Sept. 7, 1533, Elizabeth was born. Henry was so disappointed that he did not attend her christening. By the Act of Succession (1534) his issue by Anne was declared legitimate and his daughter Mary illegitimate. The Act of Supremacy (1534) required an oath affirming Henry's headship of the Church and, with other acts preventing appeals to Rome and cutting off the flow of annates and Peter's Pence, completed the break. Individuals unwilling to subscribe to the Acts of Succession and Supremacy suffered, the two most notable victims being John Fisher, Bishop of Rochester, and Thomas More (1535). Their executions led to the publication of the papal bull excommunicating Henry.

Although Henry allowed the publication of an English Bible (1538), the Henrician Reformation was basically conservative. Major liturgical and theological revisions came under his son, Edward VI. Henry's financial need, however, made him receptive to Cromwell's plan for monastic dissolutions via parliamentary acts in 1536 and 1539, in which the Crown became proprietor of the dissolved monasteries. The scale of monastic properties led to important social and economic consequences.

Later Marriages. Anne's haughty demeanor and moody temperament suited Henry ill, and her failure to produce a male heir rankled. She miscarried of a baby boy on Jan. 27, 1536, 6 days after fainting at the news that Henry had been knocked unconscious in a jousting accident in which the king fell under his mailed horse. It was a costly miscarriage, for Henry was already interested in Jane Seymour. He determined on a second divorce. He brought charges of treason against Anne for alleged adultery and incest; she was executed on May 19. The following day Henry betrothed himself to Jane and married her 10 days later. Jane brought a measure of comfort to Henry's personal life; she also produced a son and heir, Edward, on Oct. 12, 1537, but survived his birth a scant 12 days.

Henry was deeply grieved, and he did not remarry for 3 years. He was not in good health. Headaches plagued him intermittently; they may have originated from a jousting accident of 1524, in which Charles Brandon's lance splintered on striking Henry's open helmet. Moreover his ulcerated leg, which first afflicted him in 1528, occasionally troubled. Both legs were infected in 1537. In May 1538 he had a clot blockage in his lungs which made him speechless, but he recovered.

The course of diplomatic events, particularly the fear that Charles V might attempt an invasion of England, led Henry to seek an alliance with Continental Protestant powers; hence, his marriage to the Protestant princess Anne of Cleves on Jan. 12, 1540. His realization that Charles did not intend to attack, coupled with his distaste for Anne, led to Cromwell's dismissal and execution in June 1540 and to the annulment of his marriage to Anne on July 9, 1540.

Cromwell's fall was engineered by the conservative leaders of his Council, Thomas Howard, Duke of Norfolk, and Bishop Gardiner. They thrust forward the 19-year-old niece of Norfolk, Catherine Howard, and Henry found her pleasing. He married Catherine within 3 weeks of his annulment and entered into the Indian summer of his life. He bore his by now tremendous girth lightly and was completely captivated, but his happiness was short-lived. Catherine's indiscretions as queen consort combined with her sexual misdemeanors as a protégé of the old dowager Duchess of Norfolk ensured her ruin. Inquiry into her behavior in October 1541 led to house arrest and her execution on Feb. 13, 1542, by means of a bill of attainder.

Henry's disillusionment with Catherine plus preoccupation with the Scottish war, begun in 1542, and plans for renewal of hostilities with France delayed remarriage. The French war commenced in 1543 and dragged on for 3 years, achieving a solitary triumph before Boulogne (1545). Henry married the twice-widowed Catherine Parr on July 12, 1543. Though she bore him no children, she made him happy. Her religious views were somewhat more radical than those of Henry, who had revised the conservative Six Articles (1539) with his own hand. During his last years he attempted to stem the radical religious impulses unleashed by the formal break with Rome.

No minister during Henry's last 7 years approached the power of Wolsey or Cromwell. Henry bitterly reflected that Cromwell was the most faithful servant that he had ever had. He ruled by dividing his Council into conservative and radical factions. When Norfolk's faction became too powerful, he imprisoned him and executed his son the poet Henry Howard, Earl of Surrey. The King was unwell in late 1546 and early 1547, suffering from a fever brought on by his ulcerated leg. Before he died on Jan. 28, 1547, Henry reflected that "the mercy of Christ [is] able to pardon me all my sins, though they were greater than they be."

Assessment. Henry came to the throne with great gifts and high hopes. Ministers like Wolsey and Cromwell freed him from the burdensome chores of government and made policy, but only with Henry's approval. His relentless search for an heir led him into an accidental reformation of the Church not entirely to his liking. Ironically, had he waited until Catherine of Aragon died in 1536, he would have been free to pursue a solution to the succession problem without recourse to a reformation. His desire to cut a figure on the European battlefields led him into costly wars. To pay the piper, it was necessary to debase the coinage, thus increasing inflationary pressures already stimulated by the influx of Spanish silver, and to use the tremendous revenues from the sale of monastic properties. Had the properties been kept in the royal hand, the revenue could have made the Crown self-sufficient, perhaps so self-sufficient that it could have achieved an absolutism comparable to that of Louis XIV.

Though personally interested in education, Henry sponsored no far-reaching educational statutes. However, his avid interest in naval matters resulted in a larger navy and a modernization of naval administration. He brought Wales more fully into union with the English by the Statute of Wales (1536) and made Ireland a kingdom (1542). Through the Statute of Uses (1536) he attempted to close off his subjects' attempts to deny him his feudal dues, but this was resisted and modified in 1540. The great innovations came out of the Reformation Statutes, not the least of which was the Act in Restraint of Appeals, in which England was declared an empire, and the Act of Supremacy, in which Henry became supreme head of the Anglican Church. The politically inspired Henrician Reformation became a religiously inspired one under his son, Edward VI, and thus Henry's reign became the first step in the forging of the Anglican Church.

Henry ruled ruthlessly in a ruthless age; he cut down the enemies of the Crown, like the Duke of Buckingham in 1521 and the Earl of Surrey. He stamped out the Pilgrimage of Grace (1536–1537), which issued from economic discontent, and set up a council in the north to ensure that there would be no more disorder. Though he had political gifts of a high order, he was neither Machiavelli's prince in action nor Bismarck's man of blood and iron. He was a king who wished to be succeeded by a son, and for this cause he bravely and rashly risked the anger of his fellow sovereigns. That he did what he did is a testament to his will, personal gifts, and good fortune.

EWB

Henry IV (1553–1610), king of France from 1589 to 1610. The first Bourbon monarch, Henry IV, he faced internal discord caused by the Wars of Religion and the economic disasters of the late 16th century and external danger posed by the powerful Hapsburg monarchy of Spain.

Born at Pau in Béarn on Dec. 14, 1553, Henry IV was the son of Antoine, Duc de Bourbon, and Jeanne d'Albret, daughter of the king of Navarre. Henry's parents were sympathetic to the Huguenot (Calvinist) faith, and Henry was raised a Huguenot. Through his father, Henry was a descendant of King Louis IX of France and hence a prince of the blood royal, next in succession to the French throne should the children of Henry II and Catherine de Médicis have no issue.

Henry's early childhood was supervised by his grandfather, Henri d'Albret, the king of Navarre, and, after his grandfather's death in 1555, by his mother, now queen of Navarre. He was trained in physical as well as intellectual disciplines, and his later career showed the results of both aspects of his early life. His physical endurance and vigor were matched by a quick and tolerant mind, his skill as a soldier matched by his diplomatic and political astuteness in the course of his reign.

Historical Background. From 1559 to 1590 France was the scene of internal political and religious conflicts exacerbated by the constant threat of military intervention by Spain, the greatest military power in Europe. During this period France was ruled by the three children of Henry II and Catherine de Médicis in succession: Francis II (1559–1560), Charles IX (1560–1574), and Henry III (1574–1589). All three were weak-willed, and the first two had political minorities, thus making political power a prize to be controlled either by the queen mother, Catherine, or by one of the rival aristocratic factions, whose dynastic rivalry was further embittered by their religious differences.

The greatest of these rival clans were the ducal house of Lorraine, the family of Guise, and the house of Bourbon, led by Antoine of Navarre, Henry's father, and Antoine's brother, Louis, Prince of Condé. The Guise faction was the champion of orthodox Roman Catholicism, while the Bourbon faction spoke for French Protestantism. During the reign of Francis II the Guise faction acquired greater influence. Catherine's regency during the minority of Charles IX, however, favored playing off one faction against the other, and the French Wars of Religion began in 1562 and continued until 1598. The rival aristocratic houses used warfare or the threat of warfare to increase their own political power, calling for aid from their coreligionists outside France—Spain, the papacy, England, or the Protestant princes of Germany. Warfare, religious hatred, economic disorder, and the continual threat of outside intervention dominated the late 16th century in France.

The Reformation and its ensuing political complications thus struck France in a different way from that in which it had affected Germany and England. Exacerbating political rivalries, playing upon the instability and minority of French kings, and affording all dissident social elements the opportunity of evening old scores, the Reformation in France was not so much the arguing of theological points (as in Germany) or the vehicle of increasing royal authority (as in England), but the unleashing of political forces which the French monarchy was unable to contain. It was to be the task of Henry IV to create a monarchical state out of political and religious anarchy.

King of Navarre. Henry was brought into the center of political infighting before he was 20. Catherine de Médicis arranged for a marriage between Henry and her daughter, Margaret of France. Henry's mother, Jeanne, was in Paris to be persuaded that her son should marry the Catholic princess but died in 1572. Henry then became King Henry III of Navarre. He and Margaret were married in August 1572, a week before Catherine, fearful of Huguenot influence over Charles IX, ordered the execution of Huguenots in Paris and other French cities. Henry himself was spared, but he was kept a prisoner in various degrees of security from 1572 to 1576, when he escaped to his own kingdom.

Henry's appearance and personality in these years made him a favorite not only of his own subjects but even of many people at court who had every reason to wish him dead. Between his amorous adventures (which continued all his life) and his new role as king of Navarre and leader of French Huguenots, Henry's life moved out of Navarre exclusively and out of the choking world of the court into France itself. From 1576 to his conversion to Catholicism in 1594, Henry was the center of opposition both to Catholic persecution of Huguenots and to the powerful political League, which the Duke of Guise had created to control the crown of France under the semblance of defending it from Protestants.

King of France. In 1584 the Duke of Anjou, the youngest son of Catherine de Médicis, died, thus making Henry of Navarre the heir apparent to the reigning king, Henry III. The League immediately became more powerful, fearing a Protestant king. The League, allied with Philip II of Spain, exceeded in power even Henry III, who in despair arranged the assassination of the Duke of Guise and allied himself with Henry of Navarre.

When Henry III was assassinated in 1589, France faced the prospect of a Protestant king, kept from most of his kingdoms by a League of Catholics backed by the power of Spain. Henry had to fight his way to his own throne. But Henry IV refused to fight in the way his predecessors had done. Although he agreed to be instructed in the Catholic faith, he promised his coreligionists that he would end persecution on both sides, and from the death of Henry III to his own death, Henry IV had to create a political state over the skepticism of both Catholics and Protestants and in the presence of bitter memories of a kind that few states have been able to survive.

Between 1589 and 1594 Henry fought his way to the throne. He slowly wore down the Catholic front, declared war on Philip II of Spain in 1595, and guaranteed his earlier promises of religious toleration with the Edict of Nantes in 1598, the first successful attempt in modern European history to reconcile the presence of two religions within a single kingdom.

Henry's actions were dictated by political necessity as well as personal conviction. France was in dire economic straits and in the midst of a social crisis. He was aided by a strong civil service and by a minister of exceptional talents, Maximilien de Bethune, Duc de Sully, his director of finance. In 1599 Henry IV divorced his wife and in 1600 married Marie de Médicis, who in 1601 bore him a son, his successor Louis XIII.

In the course of his reign Henry turned his attention vigorously to those aspects of the kingdom which had virtually been ignored during the period of the civil wars: justice, finance, agriculture, the exploitation of foreign acquisitions in Canada, the calming of old religious and social hatreds, and the perennial task of the 16th-century French monarchy, the control of Spain and Hapsburg Austria through alliances with England and the United Provinces. In the case of Hapsburg power, Henry devised a general program for checking the ambitions of this great imperial house. Whether or not Henry was responsible for the famous "Grand Design" which Sully later attributed to him is doubtful, but his last act in the area of foreign affairs was to launch an invasion of the Spanish Netherlands.

As he left Paris for the new war, Henry IV was stabbed by the assassin Ravaillac on May 14, 1610. He died before he could be brought back to the Louvre. Henry's reign had witnessed the worst of the civil wars which had been fought in many parts of Europe in the name of religion. It had witnessed the immense threat of Spanish power as well as the fire of internal rebellion. It had begun the slow political, social, and economic reconstruction of France. Much of the success of the reign was directly the result of Henry's personality and political and military ability. In an age when monarchy is no longer considered a viable form of government, it is well to be aware of a point in European history when a victory for absolute monarchy meant social and political reform on a scale that no other form of government could provide—and meant, too, a victory for a monarch who was as personally appealing as any other figure in those 2 centuries his life touched.

EWB

Henry the Navigator (1394–1460), Portuguese prince. Henry launched the first great European voyages of exploration. He sought new lands and sources of revenue for his kingdom and dynasty and searched for eastern Christian allies against Islam.

Born at Oporto on March 4, 1394, Henry was the third son of John I of Portugal and Philippa of Lancaster. He grew to maturity at a time when John

I was bringing to a close a confused period of civil strife and war with Castile and securing Portugal's independence. The conflicts of this period had left the nobility decimated and impoverished and the monarchy's revenues greatly depreciated. Thus the ruling families began to look abroad for new worlds of wealth, land, and honors to conquer.

John and his sons became involved in a threefold movement of Portuguese expansion, comprising the campaign to conquer Moorish North Africa; the movement to explore and conquer the Atlantic island groups to the west and south; and the exploring, trading, and slaving expeditions down the West African coast. These ventures were united not by geographical curiosity but by Henry's overreaching desire to continue abroad the traditional Portuguese crusade against Moors and Berbers in the peninsula itself. He hoped also to catch Islam in a gigantic pincers movement by joining forces with the mythical "Indies" Christian kingdom of Prester John, the wealthy and powerful priest-king of medieval legend. The Prester's domains had been variously located in present-day India and in East Africa (Ethiopia).

North Africa and the Atlantic Islands. King John wished to satisfy the avarice and lust for battle of his warriors; Prince Henry and his brothers wanted to prove their manhood and strike a blow for the faith on the battlefield. A campaign launched in July 1415 during a civil war in North Africa left the port of Ceuta stripped of its navy. Henry was knighted and made Duke of Viseu. With the fall of Ceuta the Portuguese learned of the long-established gold trade with black Africa conducted by caravan across the Sahara. Gold hunger had been growing in late medieval Europe in response to the growth of commerce, but Portugal had lacked gold coinage since 1383. Prince Henry may thus have sought to tap the supply at its source by venturing down the West African coast.

Henry's first sponsored voyages of exploration were to the Atlantic islands of Madeira and Porto Santo (1418–1419); colonization followed. These islands, as well as the Azores and Canaries, had been known to the earlier Middle Ages; they were now rediscovered and exploited by the Portuguese (the Azores ca. 1439), except the Canaries, which fell under the control of Castile. The Cape Verde Islands, much farther to the south, were discovered and settled in 1455–1460. Colonization of these islands was important for the entire subsequent history of Iberian expansion: they provided bases for voyages to the New World and for the development of practices used later in American colonization. More immediately, they brought in returns on capital loans extended by Prince Henry to island settlers.

Meanwhile, the Portuguese involvement in North Africa was proving to be a costly and dangerous undertaking. During Henry's disastrous attempt in 1437 to conquer Tangier, the Moslems roundly defeated the Portuguese and took Prince Henry's younger brother, Fernando, as a hostage against the return of Ceuta. Over the objections of Henry and his eldest brother, Duarte (then king), the royal council refused to make the trade, and Fernando lived out the rest of his days in a dungeon at Fez.

African Voyages. The repeated probes made down the West African coast at Henry's behest constitute the most significant achievement of his career. Only the most important of these expeditions will be mentioned here.

After many unsuccessful attempts Gil Eannes in 1434 rounded Cape Bojador on the North African coast. This point was the southernmost limit of previous European exploration, and Eannes's feat in sailing beyond it—and returning—constitutes the most important navigational achievement of the early Portuguese maritime enterprise. Further voyages under Nuno Tristão led to the rounding of Cape Blanco (1442), the occupation of Arguin Island (1443), and the discovery of the mouths of the Senegal (1444) and Gambia (1446) rivers. Cape Verde was attained by Dinas Dias in 1444, and the islands of that name were first visited by Alvise da Cadamosto in 1555. The mouths of the Geba and Casamance rivers were discovered by Diogo Gomes in 1456, and in 1460 Pedro da Sintra reached Sierra Leone. A total of about 1,500 miles of African coast had been explored by these expeditions.

The economic and political consequences of African "discovery" were momentous. The Portuguese obtained an ever-increasing flow of gold through trade with inhabitants of the coastal regions and in 1457 resumed minting gold coins. With a coarse African red pepper (*malagueta*) the Portuguese made their first incursion into the Italian monopoly of the spice trade. However, the most important long-range economic development was the beginnings of the African slave trade, which became significant after 1442. The Portuguese obtained slaves through raids on coastal villages and trade with the inhabitants of Gambia and Upper Guinea. In this way the Portuguese, at the very beginning of Europe's overseas expansion, provided the "woeful solution" for the problem of colonial labor power.

Equally important for future patterns of colonization were developments in economic, religious, and political policy. At this time the papacy commenced to issue its long series of bulls defining the rights of the colonizing powers. The Portuguese crown was awarded an exclusive monopoly over both present and future exploration, commerce, and conquest all the way to South Africa and the "Indies," as well as a spiritual monopoly over these same regions.

Henry supported and defined the missions of his captains and patronized map makers and others who could make practical contributions to the progress of discovery. But he sponsored no "school" of pure science and mathematics, and his reputation as a patron of learning has been grossly inflated. Henry died at Vila do Infante near Sagres on Nov. 13, 1460.

EWB

Herder, Johann Gottfried von (1744–1803), German philosopher, theologian, and critic. Johann Gottfried von Herder is best known for his contribution to the philosophy of history.

Johann Gottfried von Herder was born into a religious middle-class family in East Prussia on Aug. 25, 1744, and was raised in the town of Mohrongen, where his father was the schoolmaster. A surgeon in the occupying Russian army offered to be young Herder's patron and finance his university education in the capital city of Königsberg. In 1762 Herder enrolled as a medical student only to discover that he was unable to attend dissections or operations without fainting. He transferred to theology, and during this period he met Immanuel Kant and Johann George Hamann. Despite their later disagreements, Herder wrote a moving description of Kant, then a young teacher, and Kant, equally impressed, remitted his usual lecture fees. In Hamann, Herder discovered a kindred spirit who wished to preserve the integrity of faith by exposing the limitations of "enlightened" rationalism. Their lifelong friendship and correspondence reinforced the interests of both philosophers in literature, language, translation, and esthetics.

Between 1764 and 1769 Herder lived in Riga, where he worked as a teacher and minister and wrote a number of reviews and essays. His first important works *Fragments concerning Recent German Literature* (1767) and *Critical Forests* (1769) display an early tendency to treat problems of esthetics and language historically.

In the following years Herder traveled throughout Europe and held a minor pastorate. In Paris he met the *encyclopédistes* Denis Diderot and Jean d'Alembert, and in Strasbourg he began his lifelong association with the poet J. W. von Goethe. Through Goethe's intervention, Herder eventually secured a permanent appointment as superintendent of the Lutheran clergy at Weimar in 1776. Herder worked conscientiously at his considerable administrative and clerical career in order to provide for his family of four children. Nonetheless, his prolific writings run to 33 volumes and include *Letters for the Advancement of Humanity, Christian Writings,* two works criticizing Kant (*Metakritik* and *Kalligone*), as well as collections of folk literature, translations, and poetry. He died in Weimar on Dec. 18, 1803.

His Thought. The speculative dimension of history is concerned with the search for philosophic intelligibility or meaning in the study of human events. Ancient historians saw the repetitive pattern of history, and in this *cyclical* perspective the justification for studying the past was to anticipate the future. Christianity introduced a linear conception of time and the notion of *Providence* by dating history from a specific event and envisioning a definite end. Beginning with the late 17th century, philosophers secularized Providence: God's story was replaced by a belief in human *progress* and man's future perfectibility. By and large, professional historians and philosophers have discarded such theories in favor of a position known as *historicism*. In this view there are no general patterns, and each historical epoch is unique in its individual character and culture.

Herder's work is the first to incorporate elements of historicism. In an early work, ironically entitled *Another Philosophy of History for the Education of Mankind* (1774), and his later four-volume *Idea for a Philosophy of History for Mankind* (1784–1791), he displays an ambivalence toward the goals of rationalism and the Enlightenment. In the *Idea* Herder's Protestant pessimism about the perfectibility of human nature is reinforced by physical-cultural relativism: on a star among stars, man, as a creature among creatures, plays out his unique destiny in proportion to the "force" or "power" resulting from the interaction between individual, institution, and environment. Like Kant, Herder was among the first to strike upon the ingenious solution, later favored by G. W. F. Hegel and Karl Marx, of locating progress in the species rather than in the individual. Thus humanity progresses, through God's mysterious ways, in spite of the individuals who compose it. History offers a synthesis of Providence, progress, and individuality since "whatever could be has been, according to the situation and wants of the place, the circumstances and occasions of the times, and the native or generated character of the people."

EWB

Herzen, Aleksandr Ivanovich (1812–1870), Russian author and political agitator. Aleksandr Her-

zen developed a socialist philosophy that was the ideological basis for much of the revolutionary activity in Russia.

Aleksandr Herzen, whose real surname was Yakovlev, was born on March 25, 1812, in Moscow. He was the illegitimate son of a wealthy Moscow aristocrat, Ivan Alexeevich Yakovlev, and a German woman of humble birth. Herzen was 13 when the Decembrist rising took place, and he was present at the thanksgiving service in the Kremlin after the hangings. The scene made a lasting impression on him. His foreign tutors exposed him to radical ideas, and in his early teens he dedicated himself to the fight for freedom. In 1829 Herzen entered the University of Moscow to study natural sciences and became the leader of a small group of like-minded students. The news of the fighting on the barricades in Paris in July 1830 and the November rebellion in Warsaw profoundly moved them.

Influence of Saint-Simon. During his university years Herzen and his friends discovered the writings of the Comte de Saint-Simon and Charles Fourier. Socialist teachings were just beginning to take root in Russia. What impressed Herzen most was Saint-Simon's vision of mankind totally regenerated by a new Christianity, a faith that exalted both the individual and the community. He was fascinated by Saint-Simon's doctrines that denounced the failings of the existing order and promised to stop the exploitation of man by man. He was somewhat repelled by Saint-Simon's emphasis on the role of government and was inclined to accept Fourier's plan for phalansteries that relied on private initiative and the free cooperation of the workers. The French Revolution, the Polish uprising, and the teachings of Saint-Simon made him feel that the time was ripe for change.

Arrest and Deportation. Herzen completed his studies in 1833, and his circle broke up the following year, when he and his lifelong friend Nikolai Ogarev were arrested. The charge against them was that they sang songs containing "vile and ill-intentioned expressions against the oath of allegiance to the monarch." The official investigators considered Herzen to be "a bold free thinker, very dangerous to society." Herzen and Ogarev were suspected of having founded a secret organization aiming to overthrow the existing order through the propagation of revolutionary ideas permeated with Saint-Simon's pernicious doctrine. The two friends were deported to the provinces, where Herzen remained until 1842.

Toward the end of his confinement and afterward Herzen studied the works of G. W. F. Hegel.

He perceived in the Hegelian dialectical conception of history a sanction for political and social change. If, as Hegal maintained, everything real is rational, Herzen then thought that rebellion against the order of things grown oppressive is also justified by reason. Herzen concluded that the "philosophy of Hegel is the algebra of revolution."

Protagonist of Westernism.

Moscow was the Slavophile center, and Herzen participated in the endless disputations that raged in the literary salons there. He found Slavophile theories extremely dangerous, seeing in them "fresh oil for anointing the Czar, new claims laid upon thought." By 1845 the relations between the Slavophiles and the Westerners were severed. Nevertheless, Herzen retained a certain predilection for some ideas of the Slavophiles. He shared the Slavophiles' partiality for everything Russian and their faith in the common people, and he was impressed by the Slavophile emphasis on the collectivist spirit of the Russian folk, as it was embodied in the *obshchina* (village commune).

Travel Abroad.

Herzen went abroad with his family in 1847 to escape the suffocating atmosphere of despotism of Nicholas I. He never returned to Russia. His first experience with life in western Europe was disheartening. Herzen discovered that France was dominated by the bourgeoisie, the segment of the population that had appropriated all the gains of the Revolution. He thought the bourgeoisie had all the vices of the nobleman and the plebeian and none of the virtues, and he rarely wavered in his dislike of the European middle class.

As Herzen's disillusionment with the West deepened, his country appeared to him in a different light. He came to believe that the Slavophiles were right: unlike effete Europe, Russia was full of vigor, self-confidence, and courage. Like most Slavs, Russians "belonged to geography, rather than to history." Above all, Russia possessed the village commune, "the life-giving principle of the Russian people." Herzen argued that the commune was in effect the seed of a socialist society because of its tradition of equality, collective ownership of land, and communal self-government. The Russian *muzhik* (peasant) was the man of destiny. Since the Russian *muzhik*'s whole existence was keyed to a collective way of life, Russia, or rather Slavdom, was in a position to assure the triumph of socialism. Taking advantage of Russian backwardness and European experience, Russia might indeed bypass capitalism and middle-class culture on its way to socialism.

In 1852 Herzen arrived in London. He was a bereaved and heartbroken man; one of his small sons and his mother had been drowned, and his wife had died in childbirth afterward. He desperately needed work in which he could submerge himself, and he used a portion of his considerable inheritance to set up the Free Russian Press in 1853.

The first pages produced were an appeal to the gentry to take the initiative in liberating the serfs. Otherwise, Herzen held that the serfs would be emancipated by the Tsar, strengthening his despotism, or else abolition would come as the result of the popular uprising. He went on to tell the landlords that Russia was on the eve of an overturn, which would be close to the heart of the people living out their lives within the commune. Herzen concluded, "Russia will have its rendezvous with revolution in socialism."

The "Bell."

On July 1, 1857, Herzen with Ogarev's help launched *Kolokol* (the *Bell*), first as a monthly, then as a biweekly. The *Bell* summoned the living to bury the past and work for the glorious future. It spoke for freedom and against oppression, for reason and against prejudice, for science and against fanaticism, for progressive peoples and against backward governments. Specifically, the *Bell* was dedicated to the "liberation of Russia."

Since Herzen had the privilege of freedom from censorship, his office at the *Bell* was flooded with communications from Russia, and there was a constant stream of Russian visitors. With their help and that of scores of correspondents scattered through Russia, the *Bell* conducted a most successful muckraking campaign. It cited particulars and named names. Minutes of secret sessions of the highest bodies appeared in its columns. The journal was read by all literate Russia. Fear of exposure in the *Bell* became a deterrent to administrative corruption, and there was talk in high government places of buying Herzen off, perhaps with an important post.

After the failure of the Polish rebellion of 1863 Herzen continued to berate the administration and to preach "Russian socialism," stemming from the *muzhik*'s way of life and reaching out for that "economic justice" which is a universal goal sanctioned by science. But the *Bell* was now reduced in readership and influence. Herzen antagonized the many who had drifted to the right, as well as the few who had moved to the left. In 1868 the *Bell* was silenced for good, and on Jan. 9, 1870, Aleksandr Herzen, a crusading journalist possessed of a powerful pen, died in Paris.

EWB

Herzl, Theodor (1860–1904), Hungarian-born Austrian Jewish author. Theodor Herzl founded the

World Zionist Organization and served as its first president.

Theodor Herzl, son of Jacob and Jeanette Herzl, was born on May 2, 1860, in Budapest, Hungary, where he attended elementary and secondary schools. In 1878 he was admitted as a law student to the University of Vienna, but after a year of legal studies he switched to journalism. He worked for the *Allgemeine Zeitung* of Vienna until 1892, when he took an assignment in Paris as correspondent for the Vienna *Neue Freie Presse*. In this capacity he reported on the Dreyfus Affair in 1894, and he was greatly troubled by the anti-Semitism he saw in France at the time. In 1896 Herzl started his political career with the publication of his pamphlet *The Jewish State: An Attempt at a Modern Solution of the Jewish Question*.

According to *The Jewish State*, persecution could not destroy the Jewish people but would accomplish the opposite: it would strengthen Jewish identification. In Herzl's view, effective assimilation of the Jews would be impossible because of the long history of prejudice and the competition between the non-Jewish and Jewish middle classes. Because of conditions in the Jewish Diaspora, some communities might disintegrate, but the people as a whole would always survive. Herzl believed that the Jews had little choice but to begin the concentration of the Jewish people in one land under its own sovereign authority. To achieve this purpose, he organized the First Zionist Congress, which met in Basel, Switzerland, in August 1897. This meeting marked the establishment of the World Zionist Organization, whose executives were to be the diplomatic and administrative representatives of the Zionist movement. Herzl became president of the organization, a post he held until his death.

The official goal of the World Zionist Organization was the establishment of "a secured homeland in Palestine for the Jewish people." Because Palestine was part of Turkey and because Germany enjoyed a special relationship with Turkey, in 1898 Herzl met with Kaiser William II in an unsuccessful effort to win his support. In May 1901 Herzl was received by the sultan of Turkey, Abdul-Hamid II. But this meeting too had no positive results, since Turkey was not willing to allow mass immigration without restrictions to Palestine.

In view of the deteriorating situation of eastern European Jewry, Herzl considered other territorial solutions for the Jewish problem. The British government suggested Uganda for the Jewish mass immigration, but this plan was rejected by the Fourth Zionist Congress in 1903, which again stated the ultimate goal of Zionism as the establishment of a Jewish national home in Palestine.

During the Uganda polemics Theodor Herzl showed signs of grave illness. On July 3, 1904, he died and was buried in Vienna. According to his wishes, his remains were transferred by the government of the independent state of Israel to Jerusalem in 1949 and buried on Mt. Herzl, the national cemetery of Israel.

EWB

Hill, Christopher (1910–), British historian. Christopher Hill is recognized in Great Britain as the foremost historian of the English Revolution (1640–1660), its origins and its aftermath. Hill's numerous books and essay collections examine the Revolution not only from the perspectives of those who engineered it, but also from the position of common citizens, radical religious fringe groups, the expanding mercantile class, and seminal writers such as John Milton and Gerrard Winstanley.

Although *New York Review of Books* correspondent J. P. Kenyon claims that Hill made "a spectacular leap to the very apex of the academic establishment," the more common view of Hill's career holds that the historian achieved prominence through his more than forty years of contributions to his field. John Brewer recalls that Hill was "an early member of what was to become the most important and influential group of historians in Britain after World War II," an association that "emanated not from an academic institution but a political party." Brewer refers to the Historians' Study Group of the British Communist Party, an organization that encouraged socialist and Marxist writing within the universities. When the Soviet Union invaded Hungary in 1956, Hill and many of his colleagues withdrew from the British Communist Party, expressing their dissatisfaction with Soviet policy. Hill did not abandon the task of writing socialist history, however. According to David Underdown, the scholar "has always emphasized that two distinct groups were central in transforming early modern English society: the 'industrious sort of people' or 'middling sort,' . . . and the radical intellectuals. . . . The period of Hill's greatest influence was probably during the late 1960s and early 1970s, when university students (and many of their elders) on both sides of the Atlantic found in his work inspiring echoes of their visions of a freer cultural and social order, and a sense of being sustained by a tradition of radical criticism stretching back over the centuries."

"The age of the Puritan Revolution must now be regarded as 'Hill's half-century,'" writes *New York Review of Books* contributor Lawrence Stone, "and for years to come students will be testing, confirming, modifying, or rejecting his hypotheses. It is given to few historians to achieve such intellectual dominance over their chosen field, for it requires sustained capacity for taking pains in the drudgery of research, a fertile and facile pen, and tremendous imaginative powers. Together, these are the marks of the great historian." Philip Rosenberg feels that with so many scholars "tending to treat their subjects as grist for their intellectual mills," Christopher Hill's "more humanistic approach is a valuable asset in no small part responsible for his preeminence among contemporary historians." Having retired as master of Balliol in 1978, Hill continues to write and lecture on aspects of the English Revolution and its ramifications for the history of modern Europe. According to Kenyon in the *Washington Post Book World*, Hill's "feel for the English language, the great breadth of his reading, and his patient and compassionate understanding of human eccentricity, make it possible for us to understand through him something of the feelings and emotions of these extraordinary men and women who peopled 'the Puritan Revolution.'"

CA

Himmler, Heinrich (1900–1945), German National Socialist politician. Heinrich Himmler commanded the SS, Hitler's elite troops, and was head of the Gestapo. He was perhaps the most powerful and ruthless man in Nazi Germany next to Hitler himself.

Born in Munich, Bavaria, on Oct. 7, 1900, Heinrich Himmler was the son of the former tutor of one of the Bavarian princes. In World War I he took his first opportunity to join the army (1917), but owing to his frail health he never reached the front. Yet he continued soldiering in veterans' bands after the war while a student at the university in Munich, and in November 1923 he marched in Hitler's ill-fated Beer Hall Putsch. After a brief flirt with the leftist Strasser faction of the Nazis, the young anti-Semitic fanatic joined Hitler in 1926 as deputy propaganda chief.

In January 1929 Himmler found his "calling" with his appointment as commander of the blackshirt SS (*Schutzstaffel*), then still a small, untrained bodyguard. With characteristic drive and pedantic precision he rapidly turned this organization into an elite army of 50,000, including its own espionage system (SD). After the Nazis came to power in 1933, Himmler took over and expanded the Gestapo (*Geheime Staatspolizei*, secret police). In 1934 he liquidated Ernst Roehm, chief of the SA (storm troopers), and thus gained autonomy for the SS, which took charge of all concentration camps.

From this power base, to which he added the position of chief of all German police forces in June 1936 and that of minister of the interior in August 1943, Himmler coordinated the entire Nazi machinery of political suppression and racial "purification." From 1937 on, the entire German population was screened for "Aryan" racial purity by Himmler's mammoth bureaucratic apparatus. After the invasion of eastern Europe it became Himmler's task to "Germanize" the occupied areas and to deport the native populations to concentration camps.

After the plot of July 1944 against Hitler, Himmler also became supreme commander of all home armies. In 1943 he made contacts with the Western Allies in an attempt to preserve his own position and to barter Jewish prisoners for his own safety, an action which caused his expulsion from the party shortly before Hitler's death. On May 21, 1945, Heinrich Himmler was captured while fleeing from the British at Bremervoerde. Two days later he took poison and died.

EWB

Hitler, Adolf (1889–1945)

The German dictator led the extreme nationalist and racist Nazi party and served as chancellor-president of Germany from 1933 to 1945. Probably the most effective and powerful demagogue of the 20th century, his leadership led to the extermination of approximately 6 million Jews.

Adolf Hitler and his National Socialist movement belong among the many irrationally nationalistic, racist, and fundamentally nihilist political mass movements that sprang from the ground of political, economic, and social desperation following World War I and the deeply upsetting economic dislocations of the interwar period. Taking their name from the first such movement to gain power—Mussolini's fascism in Italy (1922)-fascist-type movements reached the peak of their popular appeal and political power in the widespread panic and mass psychosis that spread to all levels of the traditional industrial and semi-industrial societies of Europe with the world depression of the 1930s. Always deeply chauvinistic, antiliberal and antirational, and violently anti-Semitic, these movements varied in form from the outright atheistic and industrialist German national socialism to the lesser-known mystical-religious and peasant-oriented movements of eastern Europe.

Early Life. Adolf Hitler was born on April 20, 1889, in the small Austrian town of Braunau on the Inn River along the Bavarian-German border, son of an Austrian customs official of moderate means.

His early youth in Linz on the Danube seems to have been under the repressive influence of an authoritarian and, after retirement in 1895, increasingly short-tempered and domineering father until the latter's death in 1903. After an initially fine performance in elementary school, Adolf soon became rebellious and began failing in the *Realschule* (college preparatory school). Following transfer to another school, he finally left formal education altogether in 1905 and, refusing to bow to the discipline of a regular job, began his long years of dilettante, aimless existence, reading, painting, wandering in the woods, and dreaming of becoming a famous artist. In 1907, when his mother died, he moved to Vienna in an attempt to enroll in the famed Academy of Fine Arts. His failure to gain admission that year and the next led him into a period of deep depression and seclusion from his friends. Wandering through the streets of Vienna, he lived on a modest orphan's pension and the money he could earn by painting and selling picture post-cards. It was during this time of his vagabond existence among the rootless, displaced elements of the old Hapsburg capital, that he first became fascinated by the immense potential of mass political manipulation. He was particularly impressed by the successes of the anti-Semitic, nationalist Christian-Socialist party of Vienna Mayor Karl Lueger and his efficient machine of propaganda and mass organization. Under Lueger's influence and that of former Catholic monk and race theorist Lanz von Liebenfels, Hitler first developed the fanatical anti-Semitism and racial mythology that were to remain central to his own "ideology" and that of the Nazi party.

In May 1913, apparently in an attempt to avoid induction into the Austrian military service after he had failed to register for conscription, Hitler slipped across the German border to Munich, only to be arrested and turned over to the Austrian police. He was able to persuade the authorities not to detain him for draft evasion and duly presented himself for the draft physical examination, which he failed to pass. He returned to Munich, and after the outbreak of World War I a year later, he volunteered for action in the German army. During the war he fought on Germany's Western front with distinction but gained no promotion beyond the rank of corporal. Injured twice, he won several awards for bravery, among them the highly respected Iron Cross First Class. Although isolated in his troop, he seems to have thoroughly enjoyed his success on the front and continued to look back fondly upon his war experience.

Early Nazi Years. The end of the war suddenly left Hitler without a place or goal and drove

him to join the many disillusioned veterans who continued to fight in the streets of Germany. In the spring of 1919 he found employment as a political officer in the army in Munich with the help of an adventurer-soldier by the name of Ernst Roehm, later head of Hitler's storm troopers (SA). In this capacity Hitler attended a meeting of the so-called German Workers' party, a nationalist, anti-Semitic, and socialist group, in September 1919. He quickly distinguished himself as this party's most popular and impressive speaker and propagandist, helped to increase its membership dramatically to some 6,000 by 1921, and in April that year became Führer (leader) of the now-renamed National Socialist German Workers' party (NSDAP), the official name of the Nazi party.

The worsening economic conditions of the two following years, which included a runaway inflation that wiped out the savings of great numbers of middle-income citizens, massive unemployment, and finally foreign occupation of the economically crucial Ruhr Valley, contributed to the continued rapid growth of the party. By the end of 1923 Hitler could count on a following of some 56,000 members and many more sympathizers and regarded himself as a significant force in Bavarian and German politics. Inspired by Mussolini's "March on Rome," he hoped to use the crisis conditions accompanying the end of the Ruhr occupation in the fall of 1923 to stage his own coup against the Berlin government. For this purpose he staged the well-known Nazi Beer Hall Putsch of Nov. 8–9, 1923, by which he hoped—in coalition with right-wingers around World War I general Erich Ludendorff—to force the conservative-nationalist Bavarian government of Gustav von Kahr to cooperate with him in a rightist "March on Berlin." The attempt failed, however. Hitler was tried for treason and given the rather mild sentence of a year's imprisonment in the old fort of Landsberg.

It was during this prison term that many of Hitler's basic ideas of political strategy and tactics matured. Here he outlined his major plans and beliefs in *Mein Kampf,* which he dictated to his loyal confidant Rudolf Hess. He planned the reorganization of his party, which had been outlawed and which, with the return of prosperity, had lost much of its appeal. After his release Hitler reconstituted the party around a group of loyal followers who were to remain the cadre of the Nazi movement and state. Progress was slow in the prosperous 1920s, however, and on the eve of the Depression, the NSDAP still was able to attract only some 2.5 percent of the electoral vote.

Rise to Power. With the outbreak of world depression, the fortunes of Hitler's movement rose rapidly. In the elections of September 1930 the Nazis polled almost 6.5 million votes and increased their parliamentary representation from 12 to 107. In the presidential elections of the spring of 1932, Hitler ran an impressive second to the popular World War I hero Field Marshal Paul von Hindenburg, and in July he outpolled all other parties with some 14 million votes and 230 seats in the Reichstag (parliament). Although the party lost 2 million of its voters in another election, in November 1932, President Hindenburg on Jan. 30, 1933, reluctantly called Hitler to the chancellorship to head a coalition government of Nazis, conservative German nationalists, and several prominent independents.

Consolidation of Power. The first 2 years in office were almost wholly dedicated to the consolidation of power. With several prominent Nazis in key positions (Hermann Göring, as minister of interior in Prussia, and Wilhelm Frick, as minister of interior of the central government, controlled the police forces) and his military ally Werner von Blomberg in the Defense Ministry, he quickly gained practical control. He persuaded the aging president and the Reichstag to invest him with emergency powers suspending the constitution in the so-called Enabling Act of Feb. 28, 1933. Under this act and with the help of a mysterious fire in the Reichstag building, he rapidly eliminated his political rivals and brought all levels of government and major political institutions under his control. By means of the Roehm purge of the summer of 1934 he assured himself of the loyalty of the army by the subordination of the Nazi storm troopers and the murder of its chief together with the liquidation of major rivals within the army. The death of President Hindenburg in August 1934 cleared the way for the abolition of the presidential title by plebiscite. Hitler became officially Führer of Germany and thereby head of state as well as commander in chief of the armed forces. Joseph Goebbels's extensive propaganda machine and Heinrich Himmler's police system simultaneously perfected totalitarian control of Germany, as demonstrated most impressively in the great Nazi mass rally of 1934 in Nuremberg, where millions marched in unison and saluted Hitler's theatrical appeals.

Preparation for War. Once internal control was assured, Hitler began mobilizing Germany's resources for military conquest and racial domination of the land masses of central and eastern Europe. He put Germany's 6 million unemployed to work on a vast rearmament and building program, coupled with a propaganda campaign to prepare the nation for war.

Germany's mythical enemy, world Jewry—which was associated with all internal and external obstacles in the way of total power—was systematically and ruthlessly attacked in anti-Semitic mass propaganda, with economic sanctions, and in the end by the "final solution" of physical destruction of Jewish men, women, and children in Himmler's concentration camps.

Foreign relations were similarly directed toward preparation for war: the improvement of Germany's military position, the acquisition of strong allies or the establishment of convenient neutrals, and the division of Germany's enemies. Playing on the weaknesses of the Versailles Peace Treaty and the general fear of war, this policy was initially most successful in the face of appeasement-minded governments in England and France. After an unsuccessful coup attempt in Austria in 1934, Hitler gained Mussolini's alliance and dependence as a result of Italy's Ethiopian war in 1935, illegally marched into the Rhineland in 1936 (demilitarized at Versailles), and successfully intervened in cooperation with Mussolini in the Spanish Civil War. Under the popular banner of national self-determination, he annexed Austria and the German-speaking Sudetenland of Czechoslovakia with the concurrence of the West in 1938 (Munich Agreement), only to occupy all of Czechoslovakia early in 1939. Finally, through threats and promises of territory, he was able to gain the benevolent neutrality of the Soviet Union for the coming war (Molotov-Ribbentrop Pact, August 1939). Alliances with Italy (Pact of Steel) and Japan followed.

The War. On Sept. 1, 1939, Hitler began World War II which he hoped would lead to his control of most of the Eurasian heartland with the lightning invasion of Poland, which he immediately followed with the liquidation of Jews and the Polish intelligentsia, the enslavement of the local "subhuman" population, and the beginnings of a German colonization. Following the declaration of war by France and England, he temporarily turned his military machine west, where the lightning, mobile attacks of the German forces quickly triumphed. In April 1940 Denmark surrendered, and Norway was taken by an amphibious operation. In May-June the rapidly advancing tank forces defeated France and the Low Countries.

The major goal of Hitler's conquest lay in the East, however, and already in the middle of 1940 German war production was preparing for an eastern campaign. The Air Battle of Britain, which Hitler had hoped would permit either German invasion or (this continued to be his dream) an alliance with "Germanic" England, was broken off, and Germany's naval operations collapsed for lack of reinforcements and matériel.

On June 22, 1941, the German army advanced on Russia in the so-called Operation Barbarossa, which Hitler regarded as Germany's final struggle for existence and "living space" (*Lebensraum*) and for the creation of the "new order" of German racial domination. After initial rapid advances, the German troops were stopped by the severe Russian winter, however, and failed to reach any of their three major goals: Leningrad, Moscow, and Stalingrad. The following year's advances were again slower than expected, and with the first major setback at Stalingrad (1943) the long retreat from Russia began. A year later, the Western Allies, too, started advancing on Germany.

German Defeat. With the waning fortunes of the German war effort, Hitler withdrew almost entirely from the public; his orders became increasingly erratic and pedantic; and recalling his earlier triumphs over the generals, he refused to listen to advice from his military counselors. He dreamed of miracle bombs and suspected treason everywhere. Under the slogan of "total victory or total ruin," the entire German nation from young boys to old men, often barely equipped or trained, was mobilized and sent to the front. After an unsuccessful assassination attempt by a group of former leading politicians and military men on July 20, 1944, the regime of terror further tightened.

In the last days of the Third Reich, with the Russian troops in the suburbs of Berlin, Hitler entered into a last stage of desperation in his underground bunker in Berlin. He ordered Germany destroyed since it was not worthy of him; he expelled his trusted lieutenants Himmler and Göring from the party; and made a last, theatrical appeal to the German nation. Adolf Hitler committed suicide on April 30, 1945, leaving the last bits of unconquered German territory to the administration of non-Nazi Adm. Karl Doenitz.

EWB

Hobbes, Thomas (1588–1679), English philosopher and political theorist. Thomas Hobbes was one of the central figures of British empiricism. His major work, "Leviathan," published in 1651, expressed his principle of materialism and his concept of a social contract forming the basis of society.

Born prematurely on April 5, 1588, when his mother heard of the impending invasion of the Spanish Armada, Thomas Hobbes later reported that "my mother gave birth to twins, myself and fear." His father was the vicar of Westport near Malmesbury in Gloucestershire. He abandoned his family to escape punishment for fighting with another clergyman "at the church door." Thereafter Thomas was raised and educated by an uncle. At local schools he became a proficient classicist, translating a Greek tragedy into Latin iambics by the time he was 14. From 1603 to 1608 he studied at Magdalen College, Oxford, where he was bored by the prevailing philosophy of Aristotelianism.

The 20-year-old future philosopher became a tutor to the Cavendish family. This virtually lifelong association with the successive earls of Devonshire provided him with an extensive private library, foreign travel, and introductions to influential people. Hobbes, however, was slow in developing his thought; his first work, a translation of Thucydides's *History of the Peloponnesian* Wars, did not appear until 1629. Thucydides held that knowledge of the past was useful for determining correct action, and Hobbes said that he offered the translation during a period of civil unrest as a reminder that the ancients believed democracy to be the least effective form of government.

According to his own estimate the crucial intellectual event of Hobbes's life occurred when he was 40. While waiting for a friend he wandered into a library and chanced to find a copy of Euclid's geometry. Opening the book, he read a random proposition and exclaimed, "By God that is impossible!" Fascinated by the interconnections between axioms, postulates, and premises, he adopted the ideal of demonstrating certainty by way of deductive reasoning. His interest in mathematics is reflected in his second work, *A Short Treatise on First Principles*, which presents a mechanical interpretation of sensation, as well as in his brief stint as mathematics tutor to Charles II. His generally royalist sympathy as expressed in *The Elements of Law* (1640) caused Hobbes to leave England during the "Long Parliament." This was the first of many trips back and forth between England and the Continent during periods of civil strife since he was, in his own words, "the first of all that fled." For the rest of his long life Hobbes traveled extensively and published prolifically. In France he met René Descartes and the anti-Cartesian Pierre Gassendi. In 1640 he wrote one of the sets of objections to Descartes's *Meditations*.

Although born into the Elizabethan Age, Hobbes out-lived all of the major 17th-century thinkers. He became a sort of English institution and continued writing, offering new translations of Homer in his 80s because he had "nothing else to do." When he was past 90, he became embroiled in controversies with the Royal Society. He invited friends to suggest appropriate epitaphs and favored one that read "this is the true philosopher's stone." He died on December 4, 1679, at the age of 91.

His Philosophy. The diverse intellectual currents of the 17th century, which are generically called modern classical philosophy, began with a unanimous repudiation of the authorities of the past, especially Aristotle and the scholastic tradition. Descartes, who founded the rationalist tradition, and his contemporary Sir Francis Bacon, who is considered the originator of modern empiricism, both sought new methodologies for achieving scientific knowledge and a systematic conception of reality. Hobbes knew both of these thinkers, and his system encompassed the advantages of both rationalism and empiricism. As a logician, he believed too strongly in the power of deductive reasoning from definitions to share Bacon's exclusive enthusiasm for inductive generalizations from experience. Yet Hobbes was a more consistent empiricist and nominalist, and his attacks on the misuse of language exceed even those of Bacon. And unlike Descartes, Hobbes viewed reason as summation of consequences rather than an innate, originative source of new knowledge.

Psychology, as the mechanics of knowing, rather than epistemology is the source of Hobbes's singularity. He was fascinated by the problem of sense perception, and he extended Galileo's mechanical physics into an explanation of human cognition. The origin of all thought is sensation which consists of mental images produced by the pressure of motion of external objects. Thus Hobbes anticipates later thought by distinguishing between the external object and the internal image. These sense images are extended by the power of memory and imagination. Understanding and reason, which distinguish men from other animals, consist entirely in the ability to use speech.

Speech is the power to transform images into words or names. Words serve as the marks of remembrance, signification, conception, or self-expression. For example, to speak of a cause-and-effect relation is merely to impose names and define their connection. When two names are so joined that the definition of one contains the other, then the proposition is true. The implications of Hobbes's analysis are quite modern. First, there is an implicit distinction between objects and their appearance to man's senses. Consequently knowledge is discourse about appearances. Universals are merely names understood as class concepts, and they have no real status, for everything which appears "is individual and singular." Since "true and false are attributes of speech and not of things," scientific and philosophic thinking consists in using names correctly. Reason is calculation or "reckoning the consequences of general laws agreed upon for either marking or signifying." The power of the mind is the capacity to reduce consequences to general laws or theorems either by deducing consequences from principles or by inductively reasoning from particular perceptions to general principles. The privilege of mind is subject to unfortunate abuse because, in Hobbes's pithy phrase, men turn from summarizing the consequences of things "into a reckoning of the consequences of appellations," that is, using faulty definitions, inventing terms which stand for nothing, and assuming that universals are real.

The material and mechanical model of nature offered Hobbes a consistent analogy. Man is a conditioned part of nature, and reason is neither an innate faculty nor the summation of random experience but is acquired through slow cultivation and industry. Science is the cumulative knowledge of syllogistic reasoning which gradually reveals the dependence of one fact upon another. Such knowledge is conditionally valid and enables the mind to move progressively from abstract and simple to more particular and complex sciences: geometry, mechanics, physics, morals (the nature of mind and desire), politics.

Political Thought. Hobbes explains the connection between nature, man, and society through the law of inertia. A moving object continues to move until impeded by another force, and "trains of imagination" or speculation are abated only by logical demonstrations. So also man's liberty or desire to do what he wants is checked only by an equal and opposite need for security. A society or commonwealth "is but an artificial man" invented by man, and to understand polity one should merely read himself as part of nature.

Such a reading is cold comfort because presocial life is characterized by Hobbes, in a famous quotation, as "solitary, poor, nasty, brutish and short." The equality of human desire is matched by an economy of natural satisfactions. Men are addicted to power because its acquisition is the only guarantee of living well. Such men live in "a state of perpetual war" driven by competition and desire for the same goods. The important consequence of this view is man's natural right and liberty to seek self-preservation by any means. In this state of nature there is no value above self-interest because where there is no common, coercive power there is no law and no justice. But there is a second and derivative law of nature that men may surrender or transfer their individual will to the state. This "social contract" binds the individual to treat others as he expects to be treated by them. Only a constituted civil power commands sufficient force to compel everyone to fulfill this original compact by which men exchange liberty for security.

In Hobbes's view the sovereign power of a commonwealth is absolute and not subject to the laws and obligations of citizens. Obedience remains as long as the sovereign fulfills the social compact by protecting the rights of the individual. Consequently rebellion is unjust, by definition, but should the cause of revolution prevail, a new absolute sovereignty is created.

EWB

Hobsbawm, Eric J. (1917–), British historian. Eric Hobsbawm has long been considered one of the leading European experts on the history of working classes.

Despite his reputation as a historian of revolution and the lower classes, one of Hobsbawm's most popular works is a study of jazz. *The Jazz Scene*, which was originally published in 1959 under a pseudonym (the author felt that a work on popular culture would hurt his professional reputation), is the work of "an abject jazz fan who sees his subject, good and bad, in the full economic, social, and political perspective of a historian," declares Roderick Nordell in the *Christian Science Monitor*.

Working-class issues and revolution are major themes throughout Hobsbawm's work. In *Politics for a Rational Left: Political Writing, 1977–1988,* the historian argues against the Conservatism of British politics during the 1980s. One of Hobsbawm's early works, *Captain Swing* (co-written with fellow historian George Rude), looks at nineteenth-century English working-class issues. It tells of a series of uprisings by agricultural laborers in rural England during the 1830s. The bands gathered together under the leadership of a mythical captain "Swing," whose name was signed to threatening letters addressed to local landowners. When the uprisings were suppressed, the convicted rebels were deported to Australia and Tasmania.

Hobsbawm looks at the question of revolution and its relationship to the development of the nation-state in *Nations and Nationalism since 1780: Programme, Myth, Reality.* The existence of a nation is something that developed only in the recent past, the historian concludes, and nationalism developed to its greatest extent (in one direction) in Nazi Germany during the 1930s and early 1940s.

So influential have Hobsbawm's writings been in the field of historical study, Tony Judt points out in the *New York Review of Books,* that "among historians in the English-speaking world there is a discernible 'Hobsbawm generation.' It consists of men and women who took up the study of the past at some point in the 'long nineteen-sixties,' between . . . 1959

and 1975, and whose interest in the recent past was irrevocably shaped by Eric Hobsbawm's writings, however much they now dissent from many of his conclusions." "But Hobsbawm's most enduring imprint on our historical consciousness," Judt continues, "has come through his great trilogy on the 'long nineteenth century,' from 1789 to 1914, the first volume of which, *The Age of Revolution, 1789–1848,* appeared in 1962." The interpretation put forth by Hobsbawm in this volume was that a single social class from northern Europe—the bourgeoisie—rose to power in a time of great social upheaval.

The Age of Revolution was followed by *The Age of Capital, 1848–1875,* a study that begins with another series of revolutions—the series of uprisings that shook Europe in 1878—and ends with an economic catastrophe: an economic depression that stretched across the world in 1875. Hobsbawm relates many events in world history during this time to the influence of capitalism: the collapse of black slavery in the United States, the urbanization of Western Europe, the massive emigration of agricultural and light industrial workers to the Americas, Australia, and New Zealand, and, David Brion Davis concludes, "the realization that no corner of the globe could escape the irresistible impact of Western capitalism and Western culture."

The Age of Empire, 1875–1914 continues Hobsbawm's examination of the expansion of capitalism into the twentieth century. Hobsbawm continues his examination of the twentieth century with *The Age of Extremes: A History of the World, 1914–1991,* which won the Lionel Gelber Prize in 1995.

EWB

Hugo, Victor (1802–1885), French author. Victor Hugo was the supreme poet of French romanticism. He is noted for the breadth of his creation, the versatility that made him as much at ease in the novel as in the short lyric, and the mystical grandeur of his vision.

Victor Hugo had a nomadic and anxious childhood. He was erratically schooled, a fact which accounts in part for the eclectic and unsystematic aspect of his poetic thought. At age 14 he wrote, "I want to be Chateaubriand or nothing." He had begun to write in every poetic genre—odes, satires, elegies, riddles, epics, madrigals, and to receive recognition while still in his adolescence, never having to face the long years of obscurity and struggle that are the lot of most poets.

In 1822 Hugo married his childhood sweetheart, Adèle Foucher, one and a half years after the death of his mother, who opposed the match. They later had four children, and their apartment, on the rue Cherche-midi in Paris, became the meeting place for the avant-garde of the romantic movement. In 1822 Hugo also published his first signed book, *Odes et poésies diverses.* In the preface to this book, which contains many poems celebrating his love for Adèle, the poet wrote, "Poetry is the most intimate of all things."

Hugo's work may be roughly divided into three periods. First in time is the intimate lyrical vein typical of the odes. Second is an involved or committed poetry speaking directly to political and social conditions. The epic novel *Les Misérables,* for example, fits into this group. (But this vein is also present in the very first volume, where a number of poems praise the throne and the altar; Hugo, who was to end as a staunch republican, began as a royalist.) In the last phase of his career Hugo rose to the heights of mysticism and poetic vision, as in *La Fin de Satan.*

Development of Romanticism. In 1824 some of Hugo's friends founded a review called *Muse française* which claimed as its contributors Alfred de Musset, Charles Nodier, and Hugo himself. All were young writers who were beginning to break with neoclassicism. After his visit to Alphonse de Lamartine and his discovery of German balladry, in 1826 Hugo published *Odes et ballades,* in which his rejection of neoclassicism became increasingly clear.

The years 1826 and 1827 were triumphant ones for the *Cénacle,* the name given to the young romantics who recognized Hugo as their chief and called him the "prince of poets." What Lamartine and the Vicomte de Chateaubriand had begun, Hugo was dedicated to complete. He ceased writing complimentary odes to King Charles X and began praising Napoleon I instead. With critics like Nodier and Charles Sainte-Beuve to advise him and with the support of geniuses such as the painter Eugène Delacroix and the poets Musset and Gerard de Nerval, Hugo formulated the doctrine of romanticism. This doctrine was expressed in the preface to his unproduced play, *Cromwell,* published in October 1827. Where classics and neoclassics had repudiated the Middle Ages as "barbaric," Hugo saw richness and beauty in this period, and he called for a new poetry inspired by medieval Christianity. He vindicated the ugly and grotesque as elements of the "new beauty." Poetry, he said, should do as nature does, "mixing in its creations yet without confusion shadow with light, the grotesque with the sublime, in other words, the body with the soul, the bestial with the spiritual." The vivifying sources of this new literature were to be the Bible, Homer, and Shakespeare.

Convinced that the new vision must prove itself in the theater, Hugo followed *Cromwell* with a number of other plays. On Feb. 25, 1830, the famous "battle of *Hernani*" took place, with Hugo's supporters outshouting the neoclassicists and antiromantics who had come to hiss the play. *Hernani* was performed 45 times (an unusual success for those days) and brought Hugo the friendship of such notable figures as Dumas *père* and George Sand.

But Hugo did not confine himself to the drama. In 1831 he published his magnificent novel *Notre Dame de Paris,* the work for which he is best known in the United States. He was originally inspired by Sir Walter Scott, on whom he hoped to improve by adding "sentiment" and "poetry" to the historical novel. In addition, he wished to convey the true spirit of the late Middle Ages through his evocation of the Cathedral of Notre Dame and his characters: Frollo the archdeacon, Quasimodo the hunchback, and Esmeralda the gypsy girl. Hugo wrote the novel nonstop during the fall and early winter of 1830 in order to meet his publisher's deadline. Although some readers were shocked that Frollo (who had taken holy orders) should fall in love with Esmeralda, the tale was an immense success. Théophile Gautier compared it to Homer's *Iliad.*

Also in 1831 Hugo published one of his most beautiful collections of poetry, *Les Feuilles d'automne.* Once again, Hugo wrote in the intimate vein: "Poetry speaks to man, to man as a whole. . . . Revolution changes all things, except the human heart." This volume expressed the sadness of things past as the poet approached his significant thirtieth birthday. The tone was personal and elegiac, sometimes sentimental.

It was not merely the passage of time that accounted for Hugo's melancholy. His wife, tired of bearing children and frustrated by the poet's immense egoism (*Ego Hugo* was his motto), turned for consolation to the poet's intimate friend, the waspish critic Sainte-Beuve. The sadness of this double betrayal is felt in *Feuilles d'automne.*

Tormented by his wife's coldness and his own inordinate sexual cravings, Hugo fell in love with the young actress and courtesan Juliette Drouet and took it upon himself to "redeem" her. He paid her debts and forced her to live in poverty, with her whole being focused entirely upon him. For the next 50 years Juliette followed the poet wherever he went. She lived in his shadow, unable to take a step without his permission, confined to a room here, a mere hovel there, but always near the magnificent houses where Hugo settled with his family. She lived henceforth solely for the poet and spent her time writing him letters, of which many thousands are extant.

With the advent of the July Monarchy, which ended the Bourbon succession and brought Louis Philippe of the house of Orléans to power, Hugo achieved wealth and recognition, and for 15 years he was the official poet of France. During this period a host of new works appeared in rapid sequence, including three plays: *Le Roi s'amuse* (1832), *Lucrézia Borgia* (1833), and the triumph, *Ruy Blas* (1838).

In 1835 came *Chants du crépuscule*, which included many love lyrics to Juliette, and in 1837 *Les Voix intérieures*, an offering to the memory of his father, who had been a Napoleonic general. *Les Rayons et les ombres* (1840) showed the same variety of inspiration, the same sonorous harmony, the same brilliance of contrasting images. His devotion to Juliette here found its deepest poetic expression in the beautiful poem entitled *Tristesse d'Olympio*, which directly rivals Lamartine's *Le Lac* and Alfred de *Vigny's Maison du berger*. Like these famous poets, Hugo evoked the past, searching for permanence of love; but unlike the pantheistic Lamartine or the skeptical Vigny, Hugo found permanence in memory.

Political Involvement.　Hugo published no more lyric poetry until 1853. He was now seized with a new ambition: he wished to become a statesman. At first a royalist, then a moderate, Hugo moved steadily toward liberalism. After the July Revolution he wrote in a more stirring vein than he ever had before: "I hate oppression with a profound hatred. . . . I curse those kings who ride in blood up to the bridle!" Hugo claimed that he had a "crystal soul" that reflected the same evolution as that the French people had gone through: from royalism to opposition to royalism, from the cult of Bonaparte to republicanism.

When Louis Philippe was deposed in the Revolution of 1848, Hugo at first found it hard to identify himself with the provisional government of Lamartine, for he still believed that a constitutional monarchy was the best form of government for France. Nevertheless, he allowed himself to be elected a deputy to the Assembly.

When Louis Napoleon, the nephew of the great man Hugo had always idolized, began to achieve notoriety, Hugo supported him. But his enthusiasm for the new president was short-lived. He wrote: "Upon the barricades I defended order. Before dictatorship I defended liberty." He made a stirring plea for freedom of the press and clemency to the rebel elements; at last, in 1849, he broke with Napoleon III with the words, "Because we have had a Great Napoleon must we now have a Little one?"

Louis Napoleon seized power by a coup d'etat on the night of Dec. 2, 1850, and proclaimed himself emperor. Hugo called for armed resistance and, witnessing the ensuing slaughter, Hugo believed the "Little Napoleon" to be a murderer. At great peril to her own life, Juliette saved the poet, found him shelter, and organized his escape to Brussels. From there he went to the British Channel islands of Jersey and Guernsey.

In November 1853 Hugo's fiercely anti-Napoleonic verse volume, *Les Châtiments,* was published in Belgium. Two different editionsone published under a false name with rows of dots in place of the individuals attacked, and the other, which was complete, with only "Geneva and New York" in place of the author's namewere culled from the 6,000 verses of the original manuscript. Though banned in France, the books were smuggled in (a favorite trick being to stuff them into hollow busts of the Emperor) and widely circulated.

His Mysticism.　During his exile Hugo gave vent to the mystical side of his personality. There were many séances in his home, first on Jersey, then in his splendid Hauteville House overlooking the coast of Guernsey. For Hugo, the supernatural was merely the natural. He had always felt premonitions, always heard premonitory sounds and messages during the night. Now, under the influence of a female voyante, he believed that he was communicating with spirits, among them Dante, Shakespeare, Racine, and even Jesus. But the "visit" that touched him most was that of his favorite daughter, Léopoldine, tragically drowned in the Seine with her young husband in 1843.

Indeed, Hugo's family was stricken with multiple tragedies. While exile refreshed and nourished his poetry, his wife and children languished. They longed for their friends and the familiar surroundings of Paris. His daughter, Adèle, retreated into a fantasy world, till at last she ran away in pursuit of an English officer who was already married. Hugo's wife left him to live in Brussels, where she died in 1868. Only Juliette remained loyal during the 17 years the poet spent in Hauteville House.

Hugo continued his experiments with the supernatural until stopped by the threatened insanity of his son, Charles. He never abandoned, however, the syncretic and magical religious views that he reached at this time. He believed that all matter was in progress toward a higher state of being, and that this progress was achieved through suffering, knowledge, and the love that emanates from God. Evil was not absolute but rather a necessary stage toward the Good. Through suffering and the experience of evil, man made progress toward higher states of being.

In 1856 Hugo published *Les Contemplations.* Many of these poems anticipate Hugo's next major work, the epic cycle *La Légende des siècles* (1859), conceived as part of an enormous uncompleted work whose mission was to "express humanity." Like his heroes Homer, Shakespeare, Dante, and his own contemporary Honoré de Balzac, Hugo dreamed of an all-inclusive cosmic poem. It would show the ascent of the universal soul toward the Good, and the emergence of Spirit from Matter.

In 1862 Hugo published *Les Misérables,* an immense novel, the work of many years. His guiding interest was similar to that of Charles Dickens, a social and humanitarian concern for the downtrodden. The book was meant to show the "threefold problem of the century": the degradation of proletarian man, the fall of woman through hunger, and the destruction of children. The sympathetic portrayal of the waif, Gavroche, and the escaped convict, Jean Valjean, won a vast readership for Hugo. The book was not merely an adventure story but a love story and a mystery as well. It crystallized Hugo's concern for social injustice and once again astounded the reading public with the scope of his literary powers.

When Victor Hugo died on May 22, 1885, it was as a venerable man, crowned with worldwide glory, still robust and emotionally ardent to the last.

EWB

Humboldt, Wilhelm von (1767–1835), German educator, statesman, political theorist, and philologist. Wilhelm von Humboldt reformed the Prussian school system and founded the University of Berlin. He was influential in developing the science of comparative philology.

Wilhelm von Humboldt was born in Potsdam on June 22, 1767. He studied law in Berlin and Göttingen. In his essay *Über das Studium des Klassischen Altertums* (1793) he summarized his program for educational reform, which was basically the program of German neohumanism. In Jena (1794–1797) he was a member of Friedrich von Schiller's circle. After traveling through Spain and France, during which Humboldt became interested in philology, he was appointed Prussian resident minister in Rome (1802–1808).

Humboldt was influenced by the educational principles of Johann Pestalozzi. As Prussian minister of education (1809–1810), he sent teachers to Switzerland to study Pestalozzi's methods, and he founded the University of Berlin (1809). Humboldt's ideas profoundly influenced European and American elementary education.

From 1810 to 1819 Humboldt served the government as minister in Vienna, London, and Berlin. He resigned from the ministry in protest against the reactionary policies of the government. His philological works on the Basque language (1821) and on Kavi, the ancient language of Java, published posthumously (1836–1840), were landmarks in their field. He died at Tegel on April 8, 1835.

Political Theory. In *The Sphere and Duties of Government* (published in part in 1792 and completely in 1851) Humboldt held that although the nation-state is a growing body, government is only one of the means aiding its welfare, a means whose sole aim should be to provide security for social development. As in biological evolution, all growth is good, as it brings forth an organism more complex, more diverse, and richer, and government—while a major agent in fostering this development—is not the only one. If it tries to do too much, it interferes with and retards the beneficial effects of other agencies.

Under the influence of romanticism Humboldt became almost mystical as he placed more stress on supra-individual and historically conditioned nationality and viewed individual nationality in turn as part of the universal spiritual and divine life which was the characteristic expression of humanity. In essays on the German (1813) and Prussian (1819) constitutions he advocated a liberalism which would preserve the unique character and traditions of individual states, provinces, and regions, with the constitution of any state adapted to the particular genius of its national character. He rejected both the artificial and atomistic liberalism of the French Revolution, which derived the state from the isolated and arbitrary wills of individuals, and the ultraconservative program to revive the old feudal estates. He advocated a liberalism grounded in tradition with regional self-governing bodies participating in governing a monarchical civil service state.

EWB

Hume, David (1711–1776), Scottish philosopher. David Hume developed a philosophy of "mitigated skepticism," which remains a viable alternative to the systems of rationalism, empiricism, and idealism.

If one was to judge a philosopher by a gauge of relevance—the quantity of issues and arguments raised by him that remain central to contemporary thought—David Hume would be rated among the most important figures in philosophy. Ironically, his philosophical writings went unnoticed during his lifetime, and the considerable fame he achieved derived from his work as an essayist and historian. Immanuel

Kant's acknowledgment that Hume roused him from his "dogmatic slumbers" stimulated interest in Hume's thought.

With respect to Hume's life there is no better source than the succinct autobiography, *My Own Life,* written 4 months before his death. He was born on April 26, 1711, on the family estate, Ninewells, near Edinburgh. According to Hume, the "ruling passion" of his life was literature, and thus his story contains "little more than the History of my writings." As a second son, he was not entitled to a large inheritance, and he failed in two family-sponsored careers in law and business because of his "unsurmountable aversion to everything but the pursuits of Philosophy and general learning." Until he was past 40, Hume was employed only twice. He spent a year in England as a tutor to a mentally ill nobleman, and from 1745 to 1747 Hume was an officer and aide-de-camp to Gen. James Sinclair and attended him on an expedition to the coast of France and military embassies in Vienna and Turin.

Major Works. During an earlier stay in France (1734–1737) Hume had written his major philosophic work, *A Treatise of Human Nature.* The first two volumes were published in 1739 and the third appeared in the following year. The critical reception of the work was singularly unfortunate. In Hume's own words, the *Treatise* "fell dead born from the press." Book I of the *Treatise* was recast as *An Enquiry concerning Human Understanding* and published in 1748. The third volume with minor revisions appeared in 1751 as *An Enquiry concerning the Principles of Morals.* The second volume of the *Treatise* was republished as Part 2 of *Four Dissertations* in 1757. Two sections of this work dealing with liberty and necessity had been incorporated in the first *Enquiry.* Hume's other important work, *Dialogues concerning Natural Religion,* was substantially complete by the mid-1750s, but because of its controversial nature it was published posthumously.

During his lifetime Hume's reputation derived from the publication of his *Political Discourses* (1751) and six-volume *History of England* (1754–1762). When he went to France in 1763 as secretary to the English ambassador, Hume discovered that he was a literary celebrity and a revered figure among the *philosophes.* He led a very happy and active social life even after his retirement to Edinburgh in 1769. He died there on Aug. 25, 1776. He specified in his will that the gravestone be marked only with his name and dates, "leaving it to Posterity to add the rest."

"Mitigated Skepticism." Skepticism is concerned with the truthfulness of human perceptions and ideas. On the level of perception, Hume was the first thinker to consistently point out the disastrous implications of the "representative theory of perception," which he had inherited from both his rationalist and empiricist predecessors. According to this view, when I say that I perceive something such as an elephant, what I actually mean is that I have in my mind a mental idea or image or impression. Such a datum is an internal, mental, subjective *representation* of something that I assume to be an external, physical, objective fact. But there are, at least, two difficulties inherent in ascribing any truth to such perceptions. If truth is understood as the conformity or adequacy between the image and the object, then it is impossible to establish that there is a true world of objects since the only evidence I have of an external world consists of internal images. Further, it is impossible to judge how faithfully mental impressions or ideas represent physical objects.

Hume is aware, however, that this sort of skepticism with regard to the senses does violence to common sense. He suggests that a position of complete skepticism is neither serious nor useful. Academic skepticism (the name derives from a late branch of Plato's school) states that one can never know the truth or falsity of any statement (except, of course, this one). It is, however, a self-refuting theory and is confounded by life itself because "we make inferences on the basis of our impressions whether they be true or false, real or imaginary." Total skepticism is unlivable since "nature is always too strong for principle." Hume therefore advances what he calls "mitigated skepticism." In addition to the exercise of caution in reasoning, this approach attempts to limit philosophical inquiries to topics that are adapted to the capacities of human intelligence. It thus excludes all metaphysical questions concerning the origin of either mind or object as being incapable of demonstration.

Theory of Knowledge. Even though an ultimate explanation of both the subject or object of knowledge is impossible, Hume provides a description of how man senses and understands. He emphasizes the utility of knowledge as opposed to its correctness and suggests that experience begins with feeling rather than thought. He uses the term "perception" in its traditional sense—that is, whatever can be present to the mind from the senses, passions, thought, or reflection. Nonetheless he distinguishes between impressions which are felt and ideas which are thought. In this he stresses the difference between feeling a toothache and thinking about such a pain, which had been obscured by both rationalists and empiricists. Both impressions and ideas are subdivided further into simple and complex; for example, the idea of heat is simple, while the idea of combustion is complex.

These simple divisions are the basis for Hume's "phenomenalism" (that is, knowledge consists of "appearances" in the mind). Hume distinguishes the various operations of the mind in a descriptive psychology, or "mental geography." Impressions are described as vivacious and lively, whereas ideas are less vivid and, in fact, derived from original impressions. This thesis leads to the conclusion that "we can never think of any thing which we have not seen without us or felt in our own minds." Hume often overestimates the importance of this discovery with the suggestion that the sole criterion for judging ideas is to remove every philosophical ambiguity by asking "from what impression is that supposed idea derived." If there is no corresponding impression, the idea may be dismissed as meaningless. This assumption that all ideas are reducible, in principle, to some impression is a primary commitment of Hume's empiricism. Hume did admit that there are complex ideas, such as the idea of a city, that are not traceable to any single impression. These complex ideas are produced by the freedom of the imagination to transform and relate ideas independently of impressions; such ideas are not susceptible to empirical verification. This represents the major paradox of Hume's philosophy—the imagination which produces every idea beyond sensible immediacy also denies the truth of ideas.

Theory of Ideas. Hume accepts the Cartesian doctrine of the distinct idea—conceivability subject only to the principle of contradiction—as both the unit of reasoning and the criterion of truth. But the doctrine of the distinct idea means that every noncontradictory idea expresses an a priori logical possibility. And the speculative freedom of the imagination to conceive opposites without contradiction makes it impossible to demonstrate any matter of fact or existence. This argument leads to a distinction between relations of ideas (demonstrations which are true a priori) and matters of fact (the opposite of which is distinctly conceivable). And this distinction excludes from the domain of rational determination every factual event, future contingent proposition, and causal relation. For Hume, since truth is posterior to fact, the ideas of reason only express what the mind thinks about reality.

Distinct ideas, or imaginative concepts, are pure antinomies apart from experience as every factual proposition is equally valid a priori. But Hume does acknowledge that such propositions are not equally meaningful either to thought or action. On the level of ideas, Hume offers a conceptual correlative to the

exemption of sensation as a form of cognition by his recognition that the meaning of ideas is more important than their truth. What separates meaningful propositions from mere concepts is the subjective impression of belief.

Belief, or the vivacity with which the mind conceives certain ideas and associations, results from the reciprocal relationship between experience and imagination. The cumulative experience of the past and present—for example, the relational factors of constancy, conjunction, and resemblance—gives a bias to the imagination. But it is man's imaginative anticipations of the future that give meaning to his experience. Neither the relational elements of experience nor the propensive function of the imagination, from the viewpoint of the criterion of truth, possesses the slightest rational justification. Hence the interplay between the criterion of truth and the logic of the imagination explains both Hume's skepticism and his conception of sensation and intellection.

Because of his skeptical attitude toward the truths of reason Hume attempted to ground his moral theory on the bedrock of feeling, "Reason is, and ought only to be, the slave of the passions." In this, Hume followed the "moral sense" school and, especially, the thought of Francis Hutcheson. The notion that virtue and vice are to be derived ultimately from impressions of approbation and blame or pleasure and pain shows that Hume anticipated Jeremy Bentham's utilitarianism, a debt which the latter acknowledged. Although Hume considered himself to be primarily a moralist, this doctrine is the least original part of his philosophical writings.

EWB

I

Ignatius of Loyola (1491–1556), Spanish soldier and ecclesiastic. Ignatius of Loyola was the founder of the Society of Jesus, or Jesuit order.

Ignatius was born in the castle of Loyola in the Basque province of Guipúzcoa. His real name was Iñigo de Oñaz y Loyola, but from 1537 on he also used the more widely known Ignatius, especially in official documents. From the age of about 15 to 26 he lived at the fortress town of Arévalo as a page of Juan Velázquez de Cuéllar, a treasurer general for Ferdinand the Catholic. After 1516 he participated in military expeditions for the Duke of Nájera. On May 20, 1521, he was wounded in the defense of Pamplona.

During convalescence at Loyola, Ignatius read from the *Life of Christ* by Ludolph of Saxony and from the short lives of saints by Jacobus de Voragine entitled *Legenda aurea.* This resulted in a conversion, whereby he resolved to live as a knight wholly devoted to Christ and to go to the Holy Land. He abandoned Loyola in 1522 and lived for 11 months in austerity and prayer at Manresa. Here he had religious experiences which rank him among the greatest mystics of Christianity, and he composed at least the core of his famous *Spiritual Exercises* (published in 1548).

Through the intensive experiences of Manresa and later, Ignatius gradually developed a world view centered on cooperation with Christ and the pope as His vicar in efforts to achieve God's plan in creating and redeeming men. His constant endeavor was to lead men to give greater praise to God through both prayer and apostolic service. Hence arose his phrase, reiterated so often that it became a motto, "For the greater glory of God."

Ignatius reached Jerusalem in 1523 but could not remain because of the enmity between Christians and Turks. He returned to Barcelona and began studies (1524–1526) toward the priesthood. He then studied at the universities of Alcalá (1526–1527), Salamanca (1527), and Paris (1528–1535), where he received the degree of master of arts in April 1534. On the following August 15 he and six companions vowed to live in poverty and chastity and to go to the Holy Land or, should this prove impossible, to put themselves at the apostolic service of the pope. When war prevented passage to Jerusalem in 1537, they accepted a suggestion of Pope Paul III to find their apostolate in Italy.

Ignatius was ordained a priest on June 24, 1537. In Rome in 1539 he and nine companions drew up a "First Sketch" of a new religious order devoted to apostolic service anywhere in the world by means of preaching and any other ministry. On Sept. 27, 1540, Paul III approved this new order and its title, the Society of Jesus. In April 1541 Ignatius was elected its general for a lifelong term.

Chiefly between 1547 and 1550 Ignatius composed his *Constitutions of the Society of Jesus,* a classic both of spiritual doctrine and of religious law. This work reveals Ignatius's genius as an organizer and administrator. To secure better cooperation in charity, he stressed obedience, but he placed many democratic procedures within the monarchical structure of his order.

From 1537 on Ignatius lived in Rome, engaging in various forms of priestly work. Twelve volumes of his correspondence have been preserved. He founded a chain of schools for the Christian education of youth. Between 1546 and 1556 he opened 33 colleges (3 of them universities) and approved 6 more. He was the first founder of a religious order to make the con-

ducting of schools for lay students a major work prescribed by the Constitutions.

At his death on July 31, 1556, the Society of Jesus had some 1,000 members distributed in 12 provinces. He was declared a saint by Pope Gregory XV on March 12, 1622.

EWB

Ivan IV (1530–1584), tsar of Russia, 1533–1584. Known as Ivan the Terrible, Ivan IV was the first Russian sovereign to be crowned tsar and to hold tsar as his official title in addition to the traditional title of grand duke of Moscow.

The reign of Ivan IV was the culmination of Russian historical developments that began with the rise of Moscow in the early 14th century. The results of these developments were the growth of a unified centralized state governed by an autocracy and the formation of a dominant class of serving gentry, the *pomeshchiki.*

Very little is actually known about Ivan. None of his papers, notes, or correspondence has survived. It is not possible to establish a precise chronology or to give a trustworthy factual account of Ivan's personal life. There are whole successions of years without a single reference to Ivan himself. All that is possible under these circumstances is to make surmises that are more or less in accord with the evidence of the scanty material that has survived.

One of the biggest stumbling blocks to contemporary students of Russian history in understanding Ivan is the epithet accorded him "the Terrible" or "the Dread." This epithet indicates sadistic and irrational traits in his character, and there is sufficient evidence to make Ivan's reign a study in abnormal psychology. It is said that as a boy he took delight in throwing young animals to their death from high rooftops. He also formed the habit of robbing and beating the people of his capital. There is also the terrible event in 1581, when Ivan, in a fit of anger, lashed out at his 27-year-old son, Ivan Ivanovich, and struck him dead with an iron-pointed staff.

It would, therefore, be foolish to argue that the personality of Ivan IV is irrelevant to an understanding of his reign. It has been shown, in fact, that there was a very real cause for the monstrous aspects of Ivan's personality. A contemporary study of Ivan's skeleton showed that he must have suffered horribly for many years from osteophytes, which virtually fused his spine.

Regency Period. Ivan was born on Aug. 25, 1530, in Moscow. His father was Basil III and his mother Helen Glinsky, a Russian of Lithuanian origin. Ivan was only 3 years old when his father died in 1533. His mother became regent, and the throne rapidly degenerated into a center of wild violence, intrigue, and denunciation as rival boyar families disputed the Glinksy regency. At times they brought their feuds into the Kremlin itself.

Evidence indicates that Ivan was a sensitive, intelligent boy with a remarkably quick and intuitive mind. He became quite aware of all the intrigues around him and of the precariousness of his own position. He was neglected and at times treated with scorn. Apparently, he was even short of food and clothes. This environment, therefore, nourished a hatred for the boyars that revealed itself in Ivan's later policies toward them.

Early Rule. In 1538 his mother died suddenly, and years of strife and misrule ensued. In 1547, however, Ivan decided, much to the astonishment of those around him, to be crowned, not as grand prince, but as tsar (God's anointed). In the same year Ivan married Anastasia Romanov. The marriage seems to have been a happy one, and when Anastasia died in 1560, deep grief overcame Ivan. Although he married four more times, he was never able to recapture the happiness he had enjoyed with Anastasia.

In 1547 Ivan also appointed the Selected Council, largely dominated by men of modest social standing. He allowed himself to be both directed and restrained by this Council, even agreeing to do nothing without its approval. The period following the Council's creation is generally considered the constructive period of Ivan's reign.

In 1550 Ivan called the first of two *zemskii sobors* (consultative assemblies) to meet during his reign. Although knowledge of the assemblies is fragmentary (some historians even deny that there was an assembly in 1550), they appear not to have been elected but appointed by Ivan himself and to have served in a purely advisory capacity. Approval was given, however, to several of Ivan's projected reforms. In 1552 a reform in local government was instituted. In those areas where the local population could guarantee a fixed amount of state dues to the treasury, officials elected from and by the local inhabitants were given the right to collect taxes in lieu of the old governors, who were abolished in such areas.

The Law Code of 1550 was another important reform of the early part of Ivan's reign. It was concerned primarily with discouraging the use of customary law in the courts, and it introduced the principle of statutory law.

Ivan, a devout churchman, called a church council in 1551. Among other matters, the council considered liturgical questions and passed reforms which tightened and perfected the organization of the Church. Ivan was also concerned with standardizing and organizing the responsibilities and duties of the service class. In 1556 he issued a decree which provided new regulations concerning the length, nature, and form of service which a member of the nobility was expected to render.

Foreign Policy. Among Ivan's military accomplishments was the destruction of the Tatar khanates of Kazan in 1552 and Astrakhan in 1556. Thus, of the three Tatar states in the region of Russia, only the Crimean Tatars remained unconquered by Muscovy. With the addition of Kazan and Astrakhan, Muscovy now extended to the Urals in the east and to the Caspian Sea in the south. Russia also began its expansion to the east beyond the Urals at this time and before Ivan's death had established itself in Siberia. Ivan's ambition to restore to Muscovy the western territories which had been annexed by Lithuania in the 16th century, however, was unrealized.

Another of Ivan's ambitions, contact with the West, was achieved. In 1553 an English sea captain, Richard Chancellor, landed on the Russian shore near the mouth of the Northern Dvina River and made his way to Moscow. Upon his return to England, Chancellor became one of the founders of the Muscovy Company, to which Ivan gave special trade privileges. Although traders of other nations, Dutch and French, began to appear, the English dominated the Russian trade with centers in many Russian towns.

Later Years. Despite governmental improvements at home and successes abroad, the constructive or early period of Ivan's rule was not to endure. He broke with his Selected Council, turned against many of his former advisers, and introduced a reign of terror against the boyars. The major turning point came in 1560, when Anastasia died quite suddenly. Convinced that his advisers, backed by the boyars, had caused her death, Ivan condemned them and turned against the nobility. In 1564 he abandoned Moscow. What his intentions were is not clear, although he threatened to abdicate and denounced the boyars for their greed and treachery. Confused and frightened, the people of Moscow begged the Tsar to return and rule over them. His eventual agreement to return was dependent upon two basic conditions: the creation of a territorial and political subdivision—the *oprichnina*—to be managed entirely at the discretion of the Tsar; and Ivan's right to punish traitors and wrongdoers, executing them when necessary and confiscating their possessions.

The area encompassed by the *oprichnina* was a large one, constituting about one-half of the existing Muscovite state. It also included most of the wealthy towns, trading routes, and cultivated areas and was, therefore, a stronghold of wealthy old boyar families. Ivan's establishment of his rule over the area necessarily involved, then, displacement (and destruction) of the major boyar families in Russia. This task fell to his special bodyguards, a select group known as the *oprichniki.*

In 1584 Ivan's health began to fail. As portents of death came to obsess him, he called on witches and soothsayers to aid him, but to no avail. The end came on March 18, 1584. In a final testament he willed his kingdom to Feodor, his oldest surviving son. Although the transition from Ivan to Feodor was relatively easy and quiet, Muscovy itself was, according to most observers, on the verge of anarchy.

EWB

J

James I (1566–1625), king of England from 1603 to 1625. As James VI, he was king of Scotland from 1567 to 1625.

The son of Mary Stuart, reigning queen of Scotland, and (presumably) her husband, Lord Darnley, James I was born in Edinburgh Castle on June 19, 1566. His mother's subsequent indiscretions forced her to renounce her title in her son's favor in 1567.

The infant king was placed in the trust of the Earl of Mar, a zealous Protestant, who was a firm believer in the value of education and discipline. The King's tutors, George Buchanan and Peter Young, were stern taskmasters, but James proved an apt pupil. By the age of 8 he was fluent in French, Latin, and reasonably conversant in English. But he received no instruction in the "courtly arts." James's sense of humor never outgrew the primitive, his language was coarse and vulgar, and his manner was most distinctly unregal.

In 1571 the regent, Lennox (James's paternal grandfather), was killed by the Marians, and he was then succeeded by the harsh Earl of Morton. In 1578 James was kidnapped by two of the Marians, Atholl and Argyle, only to be rescued within the month.

The two Catholic superpowers, France and Spain, both sought to influence developments in Scotland. From France came James's cousin, the corrupt Esmé Stuart, ostensibly to win James to the side of the house of Guise and the Catholic faith. The young king was completely smitten by this adventurer, and he gave him lands, income, and the title of Earl and then Duke of Lennox.

The new duke soon encompassed the downfall and execution of the regent, Morton. His influence over the King seemed paramount, and James's Protestant subjects vented their fears for the King's moral and religious state. In fact, the influence of Lennox and his equally corrupt accomplices seems to have been greatest in the field of politics: James completely turned from the basically democratic ideas espoused by his early tutors and began to think in terms of absolute monarchy.

In 1582 James was taken into custody at Ruthven Castle, and Lennox was driven from the country. Within a year the King had escaped from his new captors, but he succeeded merely in placing himself under the tutelage of Lennox's most aggressive companion, the Earl of Arran, who soon took over the actual running of the state.

Personal Rule. Egged on by Arran, James attacked the Presbyterian Church, and in 1584 he forced himself to be recognized as head of the Church. James's ambition to be king of England was matched by his need for English money; despite the attack on his favorite, Arran, the alliance with England was maintained. When his mother let herself be drawn into outright treason, James did little to prevent her execution in 1587.

James then turned his attention to dynastic (and romantic) matters, and he began his courtship of Anne of Denmark. The King, newly come of age, sailed after his bride, to the joy of his subjects. He married her in Norway, where severe weather had compelled her to remain. Six months later the royal couple returned to Scotland.

By 1592 the feuds between Lord Bothwell and the Catholic lords had reduced James to a virtual fugitive, pursued by one side and then the other. By 1593 Bothwell had made James his captive to the praise of the Presbyterians and Elizabeth, who both feared the influence of the Catholic Earl of Huntly. Bothwell, however, had overplayed his hand, James talked his way to freedom, and with the aid of the middle classes he proceeded against the man who had not merely held him a prisoner but had also sought his life through witchcraft and the black arts.

Bothwell, now desperate, allied himself with Huntly, Errol, and Angus. The result was the destruction of the Catholic earls as well as Bothwell. By the end of 1594 the position of the monarchy seemed exceptionally secure.

James's sense of security was heightened by another event of 1594the birth of a son and heir, Henry

Frederick. Entrusted to the care of the Dowager Countess of Mar, the young prince symbolized James's coming of age.

During the next 4 years James continued to consolidate his position. His finances were restored by the efforts of the "Octavians," and when the Catholic earls returned to Scotland they seemed a much chastened lot. Their return led to an excess of emotion on the part of the most zealous of the Presbyterians, and this in turn allowed the King to proceed against them and to further advance the episcopal form of ecclesiastical polity. His ideas on church-state relations, on the attitude of subjects toward their king, and on the nature of divine right appeared in print in 1598 in *The Trew Law of Free Monarchies*. Within 2 years James had further refined his ideas in his most important work, *Basilikon Doron* (written for the edification of the young Henry).

King of England.

James also accepted the advice offered by Robert Cecil, Elizabeth's most astute minister, to abandon his harebrained plots with Catholics and Protestants alike and to adopt a respectful and calm tone toward the aging queen. On Mar. 24, 1603, only 8 hours after Elizabeth's death, James was proclaimed king in London.

In a sense, the events of the first 2 years of James's reign in England serve to "set the stage" for the growing conflicts that marked the remainder of his 22 years on the throne. James had decisions to make in the areas of foreign policy, domestic religion, finance, and, in the broadest sense, in the field of governmental theory. In each of these areas, and in the matter of his northern kingdom and his royal favorites, he came into conflict with the English Parliament, especially with the House of Commons. James's great failure as an English king stemmed from his inability at first to perceive wherein the English assembly differed from the Scottish Parliament, and from his unwillingness to accept the differences when at last he became aware of them.

Especially in matters of secular domestic policies, James's first year on the English throne led to his asserting what he considered to be his "rightful" role in the government and in the constitution. Thus, in the first session of his first Parliament (1604), the King's speeches about his prerogative and the privileges that he had granted Parliament led that body to draft the "Apology of the Commons," in which the Commons equated their rights with those of all Englishmen. The Commons had suddenly assumed a new role. During James's first Parliament, which lasted until 1610, the opposition to him was sporadic and relatively uncoordinated. It tended to center on the

figure of James's heir, Henry, who was given his own household at the age of 9.

Affairs of Church and State.

The harsh treatment to which he had been subjected by some of his ministers of the Presbyterian Church as a youth, and the disruptive, highly anti-monarchical bias of the Church, led James to support an episcopal church— a church that moreover acknowledged him as its head. Indeed, James's instincts seemed to incline him toward a very highly ritualized form of worship, and he seemed at first disposed to move toward a more lenient position regarding Roman Catholicism. Whatever his real feelings on this issue might have been, the discovery of a Catholic conspiracy led by Guy Fawkes to blow up the royal family—and Parliament as well—robbed him of any initiative in dealing with the Catholics as a group. He was forced to bow to the harsh measures adopted by Parliament; his subsequent efforts to relieve the disabilities imposed on Catholics only made Parliament suspect his motives.

Suspicion clouded James's relations with Parliament over several other issues as well. His attempts to unite England and Scotland as one kingdom were thwarted; his meddling in the dealings of his common-law courts led him to quarrel with his own chief justice, Sir Edward Coke, and to espouse a more extreme view of his own prerogative; his arbitrary raising of customs duties further outraged the Commons; finally, his untoward fondness for a succession of worthless favorites (Scottish and English alike) annoyed Parliament, irked Prince Henry, and irritated Queen Anne.

Always impecunious, and without a trace of thrift, James maintained finances that were a source of embarrassment and of weakness. By 1610, amidst mutual recriminations and with the financial crisis unabated, James's first Parliament came to an end.

With Parliament in abeyance, government rested in the hands of James's favorite of the moment, Robert Carr, Earl of Somerset, and Carr's pro-Spanish in-laws, the Howards. Carr's implication in a scandalous murder trial, the death of Henry Howard, leader of the Spanish faction, and the emergence of a new favorite, George Villiers, seemed to undercut the Spanish party, but this eclipse was only temporary; the more the King seemed to incline toward Spain, the more he alienated his more substantial subjects. This mutual mistrust found expression in the "Addled Parliament" of 1614. For 2 months neither Commons nor King would concede a point to the other, and finally, despite his growing need for money, James dissolved his unruly legislature.

In his desperation, James now turned for help to Don Diego Sarmiento, the Spanish ambassador. His poverty really afforded him no choice, but his subjects saw this as further proof of duplicity. James began to consider a Spanish bride for Prince Charles, who had succeeded his late brother as Prince of Wales a most unpopular project, but one which endured for more than a decade. Sarmiento encouraged the King but demanded substantial concessions that would have been impossible for James to meet.

Thirty Years' War. The year 1616 saw the new favorite, Villiers (raised to the peerage as Baron, Viscount, Earl, Marquis, and finally, Duke of Buckingham), secure his position at court and become the focus of royal government. By 1618 he had destroyed the Howard family, and his power seemed to be complete. Buckingham's rise and his arrogance led to a quarrel with Prince Charles. James reconciled the two young men, and they soon became the best of friends.

By 1618, too, James's health was failing. He was badly crippled by gout and by attacks of kidney stones, and he clearly was no longer as alert mentally as he had been. It was precisely at this unfortunate moment that he was called upon to meet the greatest challenge of his reign: the outbreak of the Thirty Years' War.

James's potential reasons for action were immediate, urgent, personal, and obvious—the conflict revolved around his son-in-law, daughter, and grandchildren. On a broader level, the very existence of the reformed faith was in danger. Despite the virtually unanimous urging of his subjects, favorite, and son for an aggressive foreign policy, James vacillated, hesitated, and ultimately to his disgrace appeared to abandon his own family and to attempt an alliance with their enemies. That James sought to use Spanish friendship to aid his son-in-law's cause was neither apparent nor sensible to his subjects. When, in 1620, Spain invaded the Palatinate itself, even James was roused to anger.

Royal anger, to be effective, needed money, and money could only come from a Parliament. Reluctantly, against the advice of Buckingham (who had become pro-Spanish), James summoned Parliament in 1621. At first, despite James's habitual sermonizing to the Commons, things seemed to go well. Money was voted, and while the King refused to allow Parliament to discuss matters of foreign policy, he made no overt move to keep them from overhauling domestic affairs. By the end of the first session, Commons and King were closer together than they had been for years.

Spanish blandishments dissipated this goodwill, and when, during November and December 1620, the Commons refused to vote supplies blindly but insisted on presenting their views on foreign policy, the King was furious. He denied virtually all of Parliament's privileges, and when the Commons responded with a mild protestation, he dissolved Parliament.

Final Years and Death. The gulf between James and his subjects, indeed between the Crown and the nation, was now total. Morally as well as financially, James was bankrupt. He was also wholly dependent upon the goodwill of Spain, or so he thought.

As James grew senile, he lost control not only over his country but over his son and his favorite as well. Charles and Buckingham exposed themselves, their King, and their country to ridicule by their hasty and futile pursuit of the Spanish Infanta.

James's last Parliament was no more peaceful than his first had been. Again King and Commons clashed over prerogative and privilege, but now the Commons was joined by the Lords, and the King's harsh strictures were explained away by his own chief minister and his heir. In the end, the King, and not Parliament, gave way, and England's long flirtation with Spain was at an end.

James's end came soon after; always in poor health, he died on March 27, 1625. He left behind an empty treasury, a malcontented Parliament, and a son who would succeed him peaceably for a while.

EWB

Jaurès, Jean (1859–1914), French socialist. The greatest of the modern French Socialists, Jean Jaurès played a key role in the unification of the Socialist movement and in the struggle to prevent World War I.

On Sept. 3, 1859, Jean Jaurès was born at Castres, Tarn, into a lower-middle-class family. After studies there, he attended the lycée Louis-le-Grand in Paris. His intellect and articulateness won him first place in the 1878 entrance competition for the prestigious École Normale Supérieure, from which he graduated with a philosophy degree in 1881. While teaching at the lycée of Albi and then at the University of Toulouse, he became involved in politics.

In 1885 Jaurès was elected to the Chamber of Deputies from the Tarn as a moderate, unaffiliated republican. In the Chamber he worked for social welfare legislation and spoke vigorously against Gen. Boulanger. Defeated in 1889, he returned to teaching at Toulouse. His studies and his contact with the workers, especially the miners of Carmaux, whom he aided during the strike of 1892, led Jaurès to socialism.

Running on the platform of the Marxist French Workers' party, Jaurès was returned to the Chamber in January 1893, principally through the support of the Carmaux miners. Both within and without the Chamber he now emerged as one of the most effective spokesmen for the Socialist cause. His appeal was not limited to the working class; indeed, he was particularly effective with the petty bourgeoisie and the intelligentsia, who were impressed by his stand during the Dreyfus Affair, when he insisted that socialism stood for justice for every individual, regardless of class.

At the same time Jaurès was working to unify the Socialist movement, a role for which his eclectic formation, moralism, preference for synthesis over doctrinal purity, and conciliatory temperament well fitted him. The dogmatists, like Marxist leader Jules Guesde, distrusted him; but because he was the Socialists' most effective parliamentarian and most widely respected figure, they needed him. The first effort at federation (1899) broke down, largely over the entry of Socialist Alexandre Millerand into the ministry.

Jaurès defended ministerial participation under certain circumstances in a democratic regime, but this view was definitively rejected by the Second International (International Working Men's Association) in 1904. His decision to yield the point made possible the unification of French socialism in 1905, and his newspaper, *Humanité*, became the principal organ of the new party. Unification also forced him to abandon his leading role in the coalition which sustained the anticlerical ministry of J. L. E. Combes and to remain for the rest of his career an opposition leader.

The shadow of the coming war brought forth his greatest effort, to prevent France from causing conflict, to use the International to dissuade the powers, and to appeal to the common sense of mankind, but the forces for war were much stronger. His effort, mistakenly construed as unpatriotic, aroused bitter hatred that led to his assassination on July 31, 1914.

EWB

Jenner, Edward (1749–1823), English physician. Edward Jenner introduced vaccination against smallpox and thus laid the foundation of modern concepts of immunology.

Edward Jenner was born on May 17, 1749, in the village of Berkeley in Gloucestershire. At 8 his schooling began at Wooton-under-Edge and was continued in Cirencester. At 13 he was apprenticed to Daniel Ludlow, a surgeon, in Sodbury. In 1770 Jenner went to London to study with the renowned surgeon, anatomist, and naturalist John Hunter, returning to his native Berkeley in 1773.

Jenner had been interested in nature as a child, and this interest expanded under Hunter's guidance. For example, in 1771 the young physician arranged the zoological specimens gathered during Capt. James Cook's voyage of discovery to the Pacific. His thorough work led to his being recommended for the position of naturalist on the second Cook voyage, but he declined in favor of a medical career. Jenner aided in Hunter's zoological studies in many ways during his few years in London and then from Berkeley. Hunter's experimental methods, insistence on exact observation, and general encouragement are reflected in this work in natural history but are especially apparent in Jenner's introduction of vaccination.

In Eastern countries the practice of inoculation against smallpox with matter taken from a smallpox pustule was common. This practice was introduced into England in the early 18th century. Although such inoculation aided in the prevention of the dreaded and widespread disease, it was dangerous. There was a common story among farmers that if a person contracted a relatively mild and harmless disease of cattle called cowpox, immunity to smallpox would result. Jenner first heard this story while apprenticed to Ludlow, and when he went to London he discussed the possibilities of such immunity at length with Hunter. Hunter encouraged him to make further observations and experiments, and when Jenner returned to Berkeley he continued his observations for many years until he was fully convinced that cowpox did, in fact, confer immunity to smallpox. On May 14, 1796, he vaccinated a young boy with cowpox material taken from a pustule on the hand of a dairymaid who had contracted the disease from a cow. The boy suffered the usual mild symptoms of cowpox and quickly recovered. A few weeks later the boy was inoculated with smallpox matter and suffered no ill effects.

In June 1798 Jenner published *An Inquiry into the Causes and Effects of the Variolae Vaccinae, a Disease Discovered in Some of the Western Counties of England, Particularly in Gloucestershire, and Known by the Name of the Cowpox*. In 1799 *Further Observations on the Variolae Vaccinae or Cowpox* appeared and, in 1800, *A Continuation of Facts and Observations Relative to the Variolae Vaccinae, or Cowpox*. The reception of Jenner's ideas was a little slow, but official recognition came from the British government in 1800. For the rest of his life Jenner worked consistently for the establishment of vaccination. These years were marred only by the death in 1815 of his wife, Catherine Kingscote Jenner, whom he had married in 1788. Jenner died of a cerebral hemorrhage in Berkeley on Jan. 26, 1823.

EWB

Johnson, Samuel (1709–1784)

The writings of the English author and lexicographer express a profound reverence for the past modified by an energetic independence of mind. The mid-18th century in England is often called the Age of Johnson.

Samuel Johnson was born in Litchfield, Staffordshire, on September 18, 1709. His father was a bookseller—first successful, later a failure—and Johnson, whom Adam Smith described as the best-read man he had ever known, owed much of his education to the fact that he grew up in a bookstore. Though he lived to old age, from infancy Johnson was plagued by illness. He was afflicted with scrofula, smallpox, and partial deafness and blindness. One of his first memories was of being taken to London, where he was touched by Queen Anne, the touch of the sovereign then thought to be a cure for scrofula.

Johnson was educated at the Litchfield Grammar School, where he learned Latin and Greek under the threat of the rod. He later studied with a clergyman in a nearby village from whom he learned a lesson always central to his thinking that, if one is to master any subject, one must first discover its general principles, or, as Johnson put it, "but grasp the Trunk hard only, and you will shake all the Branches." In 1728–29 Johnson spent 14 months at Pembroke College, Oxford. He was poor, embarrassed by his poverty, and he could not complete the work for a degree. While at Oxford, Johnson became confirmed in his belief in Christianity and the Anglican Church, a belief to which he held throughout a life often troubled by religious doubts. His father died in 1731, and Johnson halfheartedly supported himself with academic odd jobs. In 1735 he married Mrs. Elizabeth Porter, a widow some 20 years older than he. Though Johnson's references to his "Tetty" were affectionate, the 17 years of their childless marriage were probably not very happy. Still casting about for a way to make a living, Johnson opened a boarding school. He had only three pupils, one of them being David Garrick—eventually to become the greatest actor of his day. In 1737 Johnson went to London to make a career as a man of letters.

Making His Name. Once in London, Johnson began to work for Edward Cave, the editor of the *Gentleman's Magazine*. Parliament did not then permit stenographic reports of its debates, and Cave published a column called "Debates in the Senate of Lil-

liput"—the name is taken, of course, from the first book of Jonathan Swift's *Gulliver's Travels*—for which Johnson, among others, wrote re-creations of actual parliamentary speeches. Years later, when someone quoted to him from a speech by William Pitt the Elder, Johnson remarked, "That speech I wrote in a garret in Exeter Street."

Johnson worked at a variety of other literary tasks. He published two "imitations" of the Roman satirist Juvenal, *London, a Poem* (1738) and *The Vanity of Human Wishes* (1749), transposing the language and situations of the classical originals into those of his own day. In 1744 Johnson published a biography of his friend Richard Savage. A neurotic liar and sponger and a failed writer, Savage had been one of Johnson's friends when they were both down and out, and to such early friends Johnson was always loyal. The *Life of Savage* is a sympathetic study of a complex and initially unsympathetic man. In 1749 Johnson completed his rather lifeless tragedy in blank verse *Irene;* it was produced by Garrick and earned Johnson £300.

In the early 1750s Johnson, writing usually at the rate of two essays a week, published two series of periodical essays *The Rambler* (1750–1752) and *The Adventurer* (1753–1754). The essays take various forms—allegories, sketches of representative human types, literary criticism, lay sermons. Johnson constantly lived in the presence of the literature of the past, and his essays refer to the classics as if they were the work of his contemporaries. He has a satirist's eye for discrepancies and contradictions in human life, yet he is always in search of the central and universal, for whatever is unchanging in man's experience. His prose is elaborate and richly orchestrated, and he seems to have tried to enlarge the language of moral philosophy by using scientific and technical terms.

Johnson's interest in specialized vocabularies can be easily explained. In 1746 he had, with the help of six assistants, begun work on a dictionary of the English language. The project was finally completed in 1755. Johnson had originally tried to interest Lord Chesterfield in becoming patron for this vast project, but he did little to help Johnson until help was no longer needed. Johnson wrote Chesterfield a public letter in which he declared the author's independence of noble patronage. Johnson's *Dictionary* is probably the most personal work of its kind that will ever be compiled; though Johnson received help from others, it was not the work of a committee. His own definition of *lexicographer* was a "writer of dictionaries; a harmless drudge," yet the work bears his personal stamp: it is notable for the precision of its definitions, for its appreciation of the paramount importance of metaphor in use of language, and for its examples, which draw on Johnson's reading in 200 years of English literature.

Johnson's *Rasselas, Prince of Abissinia* appeared in 1759, the year of the publication of Voltaire's *Candide,* a work which it somewhat resembles. Both are moral fables concerned with an innocent young man's search for the secret of happiness. The young Prince Rasselas, accompanied by his sister and the philosopher Imlac, leaves his home in the Happy Valley and interviews men of different kinds in the hope of discovering how life may best be lived. Disillusioned at last, Rasselas returns to his old home. Though Johnson was given to fits of idleness, he could at other times work with great facility; he wrote *Rasselas* in the evenings of one week to pay for the expenses of his mother's funeral. The work was immediately successful; six editions appeared during Johnson's lifetime and also a number of translations.

Years of Success and Fame. In 1762 Johnson, though he had been anti-Hanoverian in his politics, accepted a pension of £300 a year from George III. A year later he met James Boswell, the 22-year-old son of a Scottish judge. Boswell became Johnson's devoted companion; he observed him closely, made notes on his conversation, and eventually wrote the great biography of his hero. Boswell's Johnson is a formidable and yet endearing figure: bulky, personally untidy, given to many eccentricities and compulsions, in conversation often contentious and even pugnacious, a man of great kindness who delighted in society but was also the victim of frequent black moods and periods of religious disquiet. In 1773 Boswell persuaded Johnson, who pretended a stronger dislike of the Scots than he actually felt, to join him in a tour of Scotland, and there are records of the trip made by both men—Johnson's *A Journey to the Western Islands of Scotland* (1775) and Boswell's journal.

In 1764 Johnson and the painter Joshua Reynolds founded a club whose members eventually numbered some of the most eminent men of the time; they included the writer Oliver Goldsmith, Johnson's old pupil David Garrick, the economist Adam Smith, the historian Edward Gibbon, and the politicians Edmund Burke and Charles James Fox. In 1765 Johnson met Mr. and Mrs. Henry Thrale. He was a well-to-do brewer, and in the Thrales home Johnson found a refuge from the solitude which had oppressed him since his wife's death in 1752. In 1765 Johnson published an eight-volume edition of the works of Shakespeare; in his "Preface" Johnson praises Shakespeare for his fidelity to nature and defends him against the

charge that his failure to observe the three classical unities was a limitation on his achievement.

Last Years. Johnson's last great literary enterprise, a work in 10 volumes, was completed in his seventy-second year; it is the *Prefaces, Biographical and Critical, to the Works of the English Poets,* better known as the *Lives of the Poets.* It is a series of biographical and critical studies of 52 English poets, the earliest being Abraham Cowley; it is a magisterial revaluation of the course of English poetry from the early 17th century until his own time by a man whose taste had been formed by the poetry of John Dryden and Alexander Pope and who was thus in varying degrees out of sympathy with the metaphysicals and John Milton, as he was with the more "advanced" writers of his own time. Even when he deals with writers whom he does not much like, Johnson shows his genius for precise definition and for laying down fairly the terms of a critical argument.

Johnson's last years were saddened by the death of his old friend Dr. Robert Levett (to whom he addressed a beautiful short elegy), by the death of Thrale, and by a quarrel with Mrs. Thrale, who had remarried with what seemed to Johnson indecorous haste. In his last illness Johnson, always an amateur physician, made notes on the progress of his own disease. He died on December 13, 1784, in his house in London, and he was buried in Westminster Abbey.

EWB

Jones, Inigo (1573–1652), English architect and designer. Inigo Jones was the most talented native artist in England in the first half of the 17th century. He was responsible for introducing Italian Renaissance architecture into England.

Inigo Jones was born in London on July 15, 1573. Little is known of his early life and education, but between 1596/1597 and 1605 he traveled on the Continent and spent some years in Italy. In and around Venice and Vicenza he observed the buildings of Andrea Palladio, one of the major architects of the Late Renaissance, whose theories and designs had a profound effect on him.

During this period Jones may have worked for a time for King Christian of Denmark. In 1609 Jones traveled in France, and in 1613–1614 he toured the Continent, spending most of the time in Italy. During this Italian sojourn Jones undertook a professional study of Palladio's architecture and architectural theories.

In 1615 James I appointed Jones surveyor of the King's works, an important position, which was essentially that of chief architect to the Crown. He also held this position under Charles I until 1642, when the outbreak of the civil war disrupted court life.

Court Masques. During the reigns of both monarchs Jones designed and produced court masques, elaborate theatrical festivals which were common at courts on the Continent, especially in Italy. Ben Jonson often wrote scripts for the masques, and between 1605 and 1640 Jones worked on at least 25 of these productions. James I's queen, Anne of Denmark, was devoted to lavish entertainment and to the masques, and the tradition was continued in the reign of Charles I.

The masques, in which the sovereigns and courtiers participated, were dazzling spectacles organized around allegorical or mythological themes; they involved music, ballet, and spoken parts and required fantastic costumes, complex stage machinery, and brilliant stage settings. Hundreds of Jones's drawings for the costumes and stage designs are extant, none of which would have been possible without his knowledge of Italian art and draftsmanship. The masques allowed him to exercise an imaginative fantasy which rarely appears in the sobriety of his architectural designs.

His Architecture. Jones was the first professional architect in England in the modern sense of the term, and he turned English architecture from its essentially medieval Gothic and Tudor traditions into the mainstream of the Italian Renaissance manner. He designed many architectural projects, some of them vast in scale; but of the buildings actually executed from his designs only seven remain, most of them in an altered or restored state.

The earliest of Jones's surviving buildings is the Queen's House at Greenwich, a project he undertook for Queen Anne in 1616. The lower floor was completed at the time the Queen died in 1619. Work then stopped but was resumed in 1630 for Queen Henrietta Maria, Charles I's wife, and was completed in 1635. The building is marked by a symmetrical plan, simplicity of classical detail, harmonious proportions, and severe purity of line, all elements that reflected Italian Renaissance sources and constituted an architectural revelation to the English.

The building now most associated with Jones is the Banqueting House at Whitehall (1619–1622). Intended to serve as a setting for state functions, it is a sophisticated manipulation of Italian classical elements and owes much to Palladio. The main facade consists of seven bays and two stories gracefully unified in an elegant, rational pattern of classical columns and pilasters, lightly rusticated stone, discreetly carved ornamentation, and a delicate contrast of textures. The interior is one large double-cube room; its classical severity contrasts dramatically with the richly baroque ceiling containing paintings by Peter Paul Rubens that were installed in 1635.

The Queen's Chapel, Marlborough Gate, completed in 1627, has a coffered barrel vault derived from imperial Roman architecture; it was Jones's first design for a church and the first church structure in England in the classical style. In 1631 he became associated with a city planning project in the Covent Garden district of London and designed St. Paul's Church there. The church, which still exists in a restored condition, is in the form of an austere classical temple with a deep portico and severe Tuscan columns. Between 1634 and 1642 Jones was occupied with extensive restoration of the old St. Paul's Cathedral (now destroyed), which he fronted with a giant classical portico of 10 Corinthian columns. From about 1638 Jones was involved in preparing designs for a vast baroque palace projected by Charles I, but it was not realized.

In 1642 the conflict between Parliament and King erupted in open warfare which swept away the elegant Cavalier court of Charles I, and Jones's world disappeared with it. His last important work was undertaken in 1649, when he and John Webb, who had been his assistant for many years, provided designs for the Double- and Single-Cube Rooms at Wilton House. The architectural decoration of this splendidly proportioned suite of rooms is essentially French in character; the cream-colored walls are decorated with a rich variety of carved and gilded moldings and ornaments to create an effect both opulent and disciplined. Jones died in London on June 21, 1652, the same year that Wilton House was completed.

EWB

Joseph II (1741–1790), Holy Roman emperor from 1765 to 1790. He is one of the best examples of Europe's enlightened despots.

Born in Vienna on March 13, 1741, the first son of Maria Theresa, Archduchess of Austria, and Francis Stephen of Lorraine, Grand Duke of Tuscany, Joseph achieved his first triumph merely by being born a boy. A year earlier, as Joseph's grandfather Charles VI left no male heirs, Maria Theresa had succeeded to the hereditary dominions of the house of Hapsburg. Her succession, challenged by Frederick II of Prussia, had unleashed a general European war (War of the Austrian Succession), and the fact that Maria Theresa had previously given birth to three daughters had raised further questions about the succession.

The War of the Austrian Succession cost the house of Austria one of its richest provinces, Silesia, a loss confirmed in the Seven Years' War (1756–1763). Maria Theresa and her chief ministers were determined first to recover that province and later to compensate themselves somehow for its loss. Both of these aims required a general overhaul of the monarchy's inadequate armed forces, which in turn would require a general overhaul of the machinery of state in order to raise the necessary funds. Joseph was educated with these considerations in mind.

By the time he had reached the age of 20, with a high forehead, piercing blue eyes, a Roman nose, pouting lips, and a somewhat receding chin, Joseph had learned his lessons rather too well. In 1761 he submitted to his mother a memorandum proposing a general reform of the state that suggested a general centralization so pervasive that it not only would have done away with all of the remaining powers of the provincial estates but also would have overridden most of the national differences of the widespread dominions of the house of Austria. He was politely told to tend to his business. Meanwhile, he had married Isabella of Bourbon Parma in 1760; in 1762 she gave birth to a daughter, Maria Theresa; a year later Isabella died, a blow from which Joseph was never to recover. Although, for reasons of state, he entered into a second marriage, with Josepha of Bavaria, he treated her with disdain, and when she died in 1767, he refused to consider a third marriage. The death of his daughter in 1768 confirmed him in his growing misanthropy and finished the job of making him a compulsive worker.

Early Reign. In 1765 Joseph's father, who had with his wife's backing been elected Holy Roman emperor in 1742, died. Joseph was duly elected to succeed him in that dignity. His position was now an anomaly. His father, in spite of his high-sounding title, had been essentially a prince consort; Maria Theresa had given him no share in the administration of her dominions. Joseph was unwilling to play such a passive role. His mother now granted him the title of coregent, but it soon became clear that it too was an empty one. For the next 15 years Joseph would complain that he was unable to initiate what he regarded as necessary reforms.

The Empress did turn over to Joseph prime responsibility for the conduct of foreign affairs. In 1772, in the wake of a joint Prussian-Russian initiative, the kingdom of Poland was partitioned. Maria Theresa was reluctant to participate in what she regarded as a blatantly immoral action, but Joseph insisted and Austria received the southern Polish province of Galicia.

In 1778 Joseph attempted to take advantage of the fact that the ruling family of Bavaria, the house of Wittelsbach, had died out. Pressing some rather doubtful Hapsburg claims to the succession, he sent in Austrian troops. This action provided an opportunity for Frederick II of Prussia to pose as the defender of German liberties by declaring war on Austria. As neither side was anxious for a major war, operations soon degenerated into a desultory war of maneuver, contemptuously dubbed the "Potato War" by participants, who spent more time in digging up fields for food than in fighting. The Treaty of Teschen (1779) gave Austria insignificant territorial gains.

Enactment of Reforms. In 1780 Maria Theresa died, and Joseph, who now became sole ruler of all the Hapsburg dominions as well as emperor, was in the position of implementing the program of changes he had long desired. The reforms that Joseph now introduced had, with few exceptions, been under consideration in his mother's reign and were organically related to policies formulated under her. At any rate, the Josephinian reforms addressed themselves broadly to the inequities of the old regime.

In 1781 Joseph abolished serfdom, although the Austrian peasantry still was left with serious financial and work obligations. In the same year an edict of toleration lifted the Protestant and Greek Orthodox subjects of the monarchy to a condition of near equality. The next year the Jews of Austria also were granted a measure of toleration. The dominant position of the Catholic Church was further undermined by the creation of the Commission on Spiritual Affairs, which came perilously close to establishing secular control over the Church. At the same time Joseph ordered the dissolution of the majority of the monasteries in Austria. These events moved Pope Pius VI to take the unprecedented step of traveling to Vienna, but Joseph refused to give way on any question of substance, and Pius returned to Rome empty-handed.

In 1783 Joseph commuted the robot, the work obligation owed by the Austrian peasants to the noble owners of the land, to money payments, an action that led to untold difficulties. In order to assess the amount due by the peasants accurately, it was necessary to survey and register all land holdings. But, as the nobility had traditionally concealed a portion of its holdings in order to escape taxation, it now began to oppose Joseph in earnest and could do so more easily, for the Emperor had all but abolished censorship. In 1786 he did away with the restrictive craft guilds, a reform which was designed to create a distinct economic advantage but which added considerably to the number of Joseph's enemies. Finally, in 1789, Joseph abolished the robot entirely.

These reforms, striking as they did at the economic advantage enjoyed by the privileged orders, would have been difficult to enforce under ideal circumstances. As it was, Joseph's peculiar conduct of foreign policy in the 1780s did not contribute to the strength of his position. In 1784 he had tried to acquire Bavaria once more, this time in exchange for the Austrian Netherlands. Frederick II managed to block the scheme once more, this time by representing himself as the leader of the League of German Princes, dedicated to the maintenance of the status quo. Far worse, in 1787, as the result of an alliance recently concluded with Russia, Joseph involved Austria in a war with the Ottoman Empire. It was meant to be a joint venture with the Russians, but they were involved in a separate campaign against Sweden and left him to his own devices. The result was a military fiasco that brought on painful losses of territory and ruined Joseph's health. Concurrently his subjects in the Netherlands, resenting his attempts to enforce his ecclesiastical reforms there, rose in rebellion. Hungary, with the support of Prussian agents, was threatening secession. In 1790 Joseph was forced to repeal his reforms for Hungary. On Feb. 20, 1790, he died.

EWB

Jung, Carl Gustav (1875–1961), Swiss psychologist and psychiatrist. Carl Jung was a founder of modern depth psychology.

Carl Jung was born on July 26, 1875, in Kesswil, the son of a Protestant clergyman. When he was four, the family moved to Basel. As he grew older, his keen interest in biology, zoology, paleontology, philosophy, and the history of religion made the choice of a career quite difficult. However, he finally decided on medicine, which he studied at the University of Basel (1895–1900). He received his medical degree from the University of Zurich in 1902. Later he studied psychology in Paris.

In 1903 Jung married Emma Rauschenbach, his loyal companion and scientific collaborator until her death in 1955. The couple had five children. They lived in Küsnacht on the Lake of Zurich, where Jung died on June 6, 1961.

Jung began his professional career in 1900 as an assistant to Eugen Bleuler at the psychiatric clinic of the University of Zurich. During these years of his internship, Jung, with a few associates, worked out the so-called association experiment. This is a method of testing used to reveal affectively significant groups of ideas in the unconscious region of the psyche. They usually have a disturbing influence, promoting anxi-

eties and unadapted emotions which are not under the control of the person concerned. Jung coined the term "complexes" for their designation.

Association with Freud. When Jung read Sigmund Freud's *Interpretation of Dreams,* he found his own ideas and observations to be essentially confirmed and furthered. He sent his publication *Studies in Word Association* (1904) to Freud, and this was the beginning of their collaboration and friendship, which lasted from 1907 to 1913. Jung was eager to explore the secrets of the unconscious psyche expressed by dreaming, fantasies, myths, fairy tales, superstition, and occultism. But Freud had already worked out his theories about the underlying cause of every psychoneurosis and also his doctrine that all the expressions of the unconscious are hidden wish fulfillments. Jung felt more and more that these theories were scientific presumptions which did not do full justice to the rich expressions of unconscious psychic life. For him the unconscious not only is a disturbing factor causing psychic illnesses but also is fundamentally the seed of man's creativeness and the roots of human consciousness. With such ideas Jung came increasingly into conflict with Freud, who regarded Jung's ideas as unscientific. Jung accused Freud of dogmatism; Freud and his followers reproached Jung for mysticism.

Topology and Archetypes. His break with Freud caused Jung much distress. Thrown back upon himself, he began a deepened self-analysis in order to gain all the integrity and firmness for his own quest into the dark labyrinth of the unconscious psyche. During the years from 1913 to 1921 Jung published only three important papers: "Two Essays on Analytical Psychology" (1916, 1917) and "Psychological Types" (1921). The "Two Essays" provided the basic ideas from which his later work sprang. He described his research on psychological typology (extro- and introversion, thinking, feeling, sensation, and intuition as psychic functions) and expressed the idea that it is the "personal equation" which, often unconsciously but in accordance with one's own typology, influences the approach of an individual toward the outer and inner world. Especially in psychology, it is impossible for an observer to be completely objective, because his observation depends on subjective, personal presuppositions. This insight made Jung suspicious of any dogmatism.

Next to his typology, Jung's main contribution was his discovery that man's fantasy life, like the instincts, has a certain structure. There must be imperceptible energetic centers in the unconscious which regulate instinctual behavior and spontaneous imagination. Thus emerge the dominants of the collective unconscious, or the archetypes. Spontaneous dreams exist which show an astonishing resemblance to ancient mythological or fairy-tale motifs that are usually unknown to the dreamer. To Jung this meant that archetypal manifestations belong to man in all ages; they are the expression of man's basic psychic nature. Modern civilized man has built a rational superstructure and repressed his dependence on his archetypal nature—hence the feeling of self-estrangement, which is the cause of many neurotic sufferings.

In order to study archetypal patterns and processes, Jung visited so-called primitive tribes. He lived among the Pueblo Indians of New Mexico and Arizona in 1924–1925 and among the inhabitants of Mt. Elgon in Kenya during 1925–1926. He later visited Egypt and India. To Jung, the religious symbols and phenomenology of Buddhism and Hinduism and the teachings of Zen Buddhism and Confucianism all expressed differentiated experiences on the way to man's inner world, a world which was badly neglected by Western civilization. Jung also searched for traditions in Western culture which compensated for its one-sided extroverted development toward rationalism and technology. He found these traditions in Gnosticism, Christian mysticism, and, above all, alchemy. For Jung, the weird alchemical texts were astonishing symbolic expressions for the human experience of the processes in the unconscious. Some of his major works are deep and lucid psychological interpretations of alchemical writings, showing their living significance for understanding dreams and the hidden motifs of neurotic and mental disorders.

Process of Individuation. Of prime importance to Jung was the biography of the stages of inner development and of the maturation of the personality, which he termed the "process of individuation." He described a strong impulse from the unconscious to guide the individual toward its specific, most complete uniqueness. This achievement is a lifelong task of trial and error and of confronting and integrating contents of the unconscious. It consists in an ever-increasing self-knowledge and in "becoming what you are." But individuation also includes social responsibility, which is a great step on the way to self-realization.

Jung lived for his explorations, his writings, and his psychological practice, which he had to give up in 1944 due to a severe heart attack. His academic appointments during the course of his career included the professorship of medical psychology at the University of Basel and the titular professorship of philosophy from 1933 until 1942 on the faculty of phil-

osophical and political sciences of the Federal Institute of Technology in Zurich. In 1948 he founded the C. G. Jung Institute in Zurich. Honorary doctorates were conferred on him by many important universities all over the world.

EWB

K

Kant, Immanuel (1724–1804), German philosopher. The major works of Immanuel Kant offer an analysis of speculative and moral reason and the faculty of human judgment. He exerted an immense influence on the intellectual movements of the 19th and 20th centuries.

The fourth of nine children of Johann Georg and Anna Regina Kant, Immanuel Kant was born in the town of Königsberg on April 22, 1724. Johann Kant was a harness maker, and the large family lived in modest circumstances. The family belonged to a Protestant sect of Pietists, and a concern for religion touched every aspect of their lives. Although Kant became critical of formal religion, he continued to admire the "praiseworthy conduct" of Pietists. Kant's elementary education was taken at Saint George's Hospital School and then at the Collegium Fredericianum, a Pietist school, where he remained from 1732 until 1740.

In 1740 Kant entered the University of Königsberg. Under the influence of a young instructor, Martin Knutzen, Kant became interested in philosophy, mathematics, and the natural sciences. Through the use of Knutzen's private library, Kant grew familiar with the philosophy of Christian Wolff, who had systematized the rationalism of Leibniz. Kant accepted the rationalism of Leibniz and Wolff and the natural philosophy of Newton until a chance reading of David Hume aroused him from his "dogmatic slumbers."

The death of Kant's father in 1746 left him without income. He became a private tutor for 7 years in order to acquire the means and leisure to begin an academic career. During this period Kant published several papers dealing with scientific questions. The most important was the "General Natural History and Theory of the Heavens" in 1755. In this work Kant postulated the origin of the solar system as a result of the gravitational interaction of atoms. This theory anticipated Laplace's hypothesis (1796) by more than 40 years. In the same year Kant presented a Latin treatise, "On Fire", to qualify for the doctoral degree.

Kant spent the next 15 years (1755–1770) as a nonsalaried lecturer whose fees were derived entirely from the students who attended his lectures. In order to live he lectured between 26 and 28 hours a week on metaphysics, logic, mathematics, physics, and physical geography. Despite this enormous teaching burden, Kant continued to publish papers on various topics. He finally achieved a professorship at Königsberg in 1770.

Critique of Pure Reason. For the next decade Kant published almost nothing. But at the age of 57 he published the first edition of the *Critique of Pure Reason* (1781; 2d ed. 1787). This enormous work, one of the most important and difficult books in Western thought, attempts to resolve the contradictions inherent in perception and conception as explained by the rationalists and empiricists.

On the level of experience, Kant saw the inherent difficulties in the "representative theory of perception." Our percepts, or intuitions of things, are not themselves objects but rather images or representations. Since these perceptual images are the only evidence for an external, physical world, it can be asked how faithfully mental images represent physical objects. On the level of conception, mathematical, scientific, and metaphysical judgments make predictions about the connections and consequences of events. As these judgments tell us about the past, present, and future, they cannot be derived from our immediate experience. Some events, however, can be experienced as conforming to these universal and necessary laws; hence, these judgments are more than mere definitions. The aim of the critique is to explain how experience and reason interact in perception and understanding.

Philosophers had long recognized two kinds of judgment. The first is *analytic,* which is the product of the analysis or definition of concepts. All analytic propositions are reducible to statements of identity, that is, they define what a thing is. For example, a triangle is a three-sided figure universally (always) and necessarily (could not be otherwise) by definition. As such, all analytic judgments are true a priori, or independent of experience. The content and form of the second type of judgment is exactly the reverse. *Synthetic* propositions expand or amplify our knowledge, but these judgments are a posteriori, or derived from experience.

Kant's position is that of the first thinker to posit the problem of pure reason correctly by isolating a third order of judgment. Consider the following propositions: 10 times 2 is 20; every event has a cause; the universe is created. As universal and necessary, all three judgments are a priori but also, according to Kant, synthetic, in that they extend our knowledge of reality. Thus the fundamental propositions of mathe-

matics, science, and metaphysics are synthetic a priori, and the question that the *Critique of Pure Reason* poses is not an analysis of whether there is such knowledge but a methodology of *how* "understanding and reason can know apart from experience."

The solution to this problem is Kant's "Copernican Revolution." Until Copernicus hypothesized that the sun was the center of the universe and the earth in its rotation, science had assumed the earth was the center of the universe. Just so, argues Kant, philosophers have attempted and failed to prove that our perceptions and judgments are true because they correspond to objects. "We must therefore make trial whether we may not have more success . . . if we suppose that objects must conform to our knowledge." This radical proposal means that the mind constitutes the way the world appears and the way in which the world is thought about.

But, unlike later idealists, Kant does not say that the mind creates objects but only the conditions under which objects are perceived and understood. According to Kant, "we can know a priori of things only what we ourselves put into them." The attempt to preserve a realist orientation leads Kant to distinguish between the appearances of things (*phenomena*), as conditioned by the subjective forms of intuition, and the categories of the understanding and things-in-themselves (*noumena*). In brief, mathematics and science are true because they are derived from the ways in which the mind conditions its percepts and concepts, and metaphysics is an illusion because it claims to tell us about things as they really are. But since the mind constitutes the appearances and their intelligibility, we can never know noumenal reality (as it exists apart from mind) with any certainty. Although Kant considers the denial of metaphysics inconsequential because it has consisted only of "mock combats" in which no victory was ever gained, he is at some pains to establish that the restriction of pure reason to the limits of sensibility does not preclude a practical knowledge of morality and religion. In fact, the limitation of pure reason makes such faith more positive.

Later Works. In 1783 Kant restated the main outlines of his first critique in a brief, analytic form in the *Prolegomena to Any Future Metaphysics*. In 1785 he presented an early view of the practical aspects of reason in *Fundamental Principles of the Metaphysic of Morals*. In 1788 he published the *Critique of Practical Reason.*

While theoretical reason is concerned with cognition, practical reason is concerned with will, or self-determination. There is only one human reason, but after it decides what it can know, it must determine how it shall act. In the analytic of practical reason Kant attempts to isolate the a priori element in morality. The notion that happiness is the end of life is purely subjective, and every empirical morality is arbitrary.

Thus the freedom of the will, which is only a speculative possibility for pure reason, becomes the practical necessity of determining how one shall lead his life. And the fundamental, rational principle of a free morality is some universal and necessary law to which a man commits himself. This principle is called by Kant the "Categorical Imperative," which states that a man should obligate himself to act so that any one of his actions could be made into a universal law binding all mankind. The dignity of man consists in the freedom to overcome inclination and private interest in order to obligate oneself to the duty of performing the good for its own sake. In examining the consequences of man's freedom, Kant insists that practical reason postulates the immortality of the soul and the existence of God as the conditions for true freedom.

In 1790 Kant completed his third critique, which attempts to draw these conflicting tensions together. In pure reason the mind produces constitutive principles of *phenomena,* and in practical reason the mind produces regulative principles of noumenal reality. The *Critique of Judgment* attempts to connect the concepts of nature with the concepts of freedom. The reflective or teleological judgment of finality, which is derived from our esthetic feelings about the fittingness of things, mediates between our cognition and our will. This judgment neither constitutes nature like the understanding nor legislates action like practical reason, but it does enable us to think of the "purposiveness" of nature as a realm of ends that are in harmony with universal laws.

Although Kant continued writing until shortly before his death, the "critical works" are the source of his influence. Only a life of extraordinary self-discipline enabled him to accomplish his task. He was barely 5 feet tall and extremely thin, and his health was never robust. He attributed his longevity to an invariable routine. Rising at five, he drank tea and smoked his daily pipe and meditated for an hour. From six to seven he prepared his lectures and taught from seven to nine in his own home. He worked in his study until one. He invited friends for long dinners, which lasted often until four. After his one daily meal he walked between four and five so punctually that people were said to set their watches on his passing. He continued to write or read until he retired at ten. Toward the end of his life he became increasingly antisocial and bitter over the growing loss of his mem-

ory and capacity for work. Kant became totally blind and finally died on Feb. 12, 1804.

EWB

Kautsky, Karl Johann (1854–1938), German-Austrian socialist. Karl Kautsky was the major theoretician of German Social Democracy before World War I and one of the principal figures in the history of the international Socialist movement.

Born in Prague, Karl Kautsky was the son of a Czech painter and his actress wife. His studies at the University of Vienna were mainly scientific, however, rather than artistic. Although he considered himself a Socialist by 1875, it was his encounter with Wilhelm Liebkneckt and Eduard Bernstein about 1880 that brought him to Marxism, and in 1883 he became editor of *Die neue Zeit,* which soon became the leading Marxist theoretical journal in Germany and perhaps the world. In 1887 he published *The Economic Doctrines of Karl Marx,* which did much to popularize Marxist ideas.

Ideologically, Kautsky (along with August Bebel) represented the Socialist "center" which retained its belief in the inevitable—indeed imminent—collapse of capitalism, but which differed from the radical left in holding that socialism was possible only through political democracy. Unlike the Socialist right, however, Kautsky maintained that imperial Germany was too undemocratic for Socialists to participate in governmental coalitions and that therefore they must remain in the opposition. Kautsky was the author of much of the Erfurt program of 1891, strongly Marxist and revolutionary in tone, which was to remain the official program of the party throughout the imperial period, and he strongly resisted the revisionist tendencies associated with Bernstein that subsequently challenged many of the basic assumptions laid down at Erfurt.

Kautsky broke with the majority of the Social Democrats during World War I. Convinced of the war guilt of Germany and Austria, he joined the pacifist Independent Socialists (USPD), which cost him the editorship of *Die neue Zeit.* Though most of the Independent Socialists came from the radical wing of the prewar party, Kautsky did not share their enthusiasm for the Bolshevik revolution in Russia, and he became one of its most vocal Socialist opponents (especially in his *Dictatorship of the Proletariat,* 1918).

After the German revolution of 1918 Kautsky served briefly in the republican government in the Foreign Office and on the Socialization Commission. In 1919 he helped edit a collection of documents on the outbreak of the war, tending to show the guilt of the Kaiser. But in general Kautsky was without much influence in the post-war Social Democratic party or in the Weimar regime. He moved to Vienna, which he had to flee at the time of the Anschluss, just before his death in 1938.

EWB

Kepler, Johannes (1571–1630), German astronomer. Johannes Kepler was one of the chief founders of modern astronomy because of his discovery of three basic laws underlying the motion of planets.

Johannes Kepler was born on Dec. 27, 1571, in the Swabian town of Weil. His father, Heinrich Kepler, was a mercenary; although a Protestant, he enlisted in the troops of the Duke of Alba fighting the Reformed insurgents in the Low Countries. Kepler's grandmother brought him up; for years he was a sickly child. At 13 he was accepted at a theological seminary at Adelberg.

Kepler wanted to become a theologian, and following his graduation from the University of Tübingen, as bachelor of arts in 1591, he enrolled in its theological faculty. But he was also interested in French literature and astronomy. His poor health and proclivity to morbidness singled him out no less than did his precocious advocacy of the doctrine of Copernicus.

It seems that the University of Tübingen gladly presented Kepler for the post of the "mathematician of the province" when request for a candidate came from Graz. He arrived there in April 1594 and set himself to work on one of his duties, the composition of the almanac, in which the main events of the coming year were to be duly predicted. His first almanac was a signal success. The occurrence of two not too unlikely events, an invasion by the Turks and a severe winter, which he had predicted, established his reputation.

Far more important for astronomy was the idea that seized Kepler on July 9, 1595. It appeared to him that the respective radii of the orbits of the planets corresponded to the lengths determined by a specific sequence in which the five regular solids were placed within one another, with a sphere separating each solid from the other. The sphere (orbit) of Saturn enveloped a cube which in turn enveloped another sphere, the orbit of Jupiter. This circumscribed a tetrahedron, a sphere (the orbit of Mars), a dodecahedron, a sphere (the orbit of earth), an icosahedron, a sphere (the orbit of Venus), an octahedron, and the smallest sphere (the orbit of Mercury). The idea was the main theme of his *Mysterium cosmographicum* (1596).

The next year Kepler married Barbara Muehleck, already twice widowed, "under an ominous sky," according to Kepler's own horoscope. Of their five children only one boy and one girl reached adulthood. It was with reluctance that Kepler, a convinced Copernican, first sought the job of assistant to Tycho Brahe, the astrologer-mathematician of Rudolph II in Prague. He took his new position in 1600. On the death of Tycho the following year, Kepler was appointed his successor.

His Three Laws. Kepler's immediate duty was to prepare for publication Tycho's collection of astronomical studies, *Astronomiae instauratae progymnasmata* (1601–1602). Kepler fell heir to Tycho's immensely valuable records. Their outstanding feature lay in the precision by which Tycho surpassed all astronomers before him in observing the position of stars and planets. Kepler tried to utilize Tycho's data in support of his own layout of the circular planetary orbits. The facts, that is, Tycho's observations, forced him to make one of the most revolutionary assumptions in the history of astronomy. A difference of 8 minutes of arc between his theory and Tycho's data could be explained only if the orbit of Mars was not circular but elliptical. In a generalized form this meant that the orbits of all planets were elliptical (Kepler's first law). On this basis a proper meaning could be given to another statement of his which he had already made in the same context. It is known as Kepler's second law, according to which the line joining the planet to the sun sweeps over equal areas in equal times in its elliptical orbit.

Kepler published these laws in his lengthy discussion of the orbit of the planet Mars, the *Astronomia nova* (1609). The two laws were clearly spelled out also in the book's detailed table of contents. Thus they must have struck the eyes of any careful reader sensitive to an astronomical novelty of such major proportion. Still, Galileo failed to take cognizance of them in his printed works, although he could have used them to great advantage to buttress his advocacy of the Copernican system.

The relations between Galileo and Kepler were rather strange. Although Galileo remained distinctly unappreciative of Kepler's achievements, the latter wrote a booklet to celebrate Galileo's *Starry Messenger* immediately upon its publication in 1610. On the other hand, Kepler argued rather vainly in his *Conversation with the Starry Messenger* (1610) that in his *Astronomiae pars optica* (1604), or *Optics*, which he presented as a commentary to Witelo's 13th-century work, one could find all the principles needed to construct a telescope.

In 1611 came Rudolph's abdication, and Kepler immediately looked for a new job. He obtained in Linz the post of provincial mathematician. By the time he moved to Linz in 1612 with his two children, his wife and his favorite son, Friedrich, were dead. Kepler's 14 years in Linz were marked, as far as his personal life was concerned, with his marriage in 1613 to Suzanna Reuttinger and by his repeated efforts to save his aged mother from being tried as a witch.

As for Kepler the scientist, he published two important works while he was in Linz. One was the *Harmonice mundi* (1618), in which his third law was announced. According to it the squares of the sidereal periods of any two planets are to each other as the cubes of their mean distances from the sun. The law was, however, derived not from celestial mechanics (Newton's *Principia* was still 6 decades away) but from Kepler's conviction that nature had to be patterned along quantitative relationships since God created it according to "weight, measure and number." Shortly after his first book appeared, he wrote in a letter: "Since God established everything in the universe along quantitative norms, he endowed man with a mind to comprehend them. For just as the eye is fitted for the perception of colors, the ear for sounds, so is man's mind created not for anything but for the grasping of quantities." In the *Harmonice mundi* he wrote merely a variation on the same theme as he spoke of geometry which "supplied God with a model for the creation of the world. Geometry was implanted into human nature along with God's image and not through man's visual perception and experience." The second work was the *Epitome astronomiae Copernicanae,* published in parts between 1618 and 1621. It was the first astronomical treatise in which the doctrine of circles really or hypothetically carrying the various planets was completely abandoned in favor of a physical explanation of planetary motions. It consisted in "magnetic arms" emanating from the sun.

Kepler was already in Ulm, the first stopover of the wanderings of the last 3 years of his life, when his *Tabulae Rudolphinae* (1628) was published. It not only added the carefully determined position of 223 stars to the 777 contained in Tycho's *Astronomiae instauratae progymnasmata* but also provided planetary tables which became the standard for the next century. Kepler died on Nov. 15, 1630. He was a unique embodiment of the transition from the old to the new spirit of science.

EWB

Kerensky, Aleksandr Fedorovich (1881–1970), Russian revolutionary and politician. Aleksandr Kerensky was the central figure around whom the fate of representative government and socialism revolved in Russia during the Revolution of 1917.

Aleksandr Kerensky was born on April 22, 1881, in Simbirsk (now Ulyanovsk), the son of a teacher who also served as a middle-ranked provincial official. He entered St. Petersburg University (1899), where he studied jurisprudence, philology, and history. By 1904 he had completed his formal training and joined the St. Petersburg bar. He gained a reputation for public controversy and civil liberty; among other things, he worked with a legal-aid society and served as a defense lawyer in several celebrated political cases.

Kerensky's formal political career began when he stood successfully for election to the Fourth Duma (legislative assembly) in 1912. As a candidate of the Labor (Trudovik) party, he continued to champion civil rights. By 1914 he had been imprisoned twice for acts considered unfriendly or seditious by the government.

With the outbreak of World War I (1914), Kerensky was one of the few Duma members to speak against it, denouncing, in a public speech, the "devouring, fratricidal war." As Russian defeat followed defeat, support for the government dwindled and then disappeared, setting the stage for the Revolution of 1917 that swept Kerensky to power for a brief time.

During the revolutionary months of 1917, power in the major cities of Russia and at many points of military concentration was effectively divided between the provisional government, which derived its authority from the Duma, and the soviets—or representative councils—of workers' and soldiers' deputies. Among the members of the provisional government, Kerensky had a unique position because, for a time, he bridged the gap between these competing agencies of the revolution. Although a well-known member of the Duma, he was an articulate spokesman for the left and a member of the executive committee of the Petrograd soviet.

Kerensky was minister of justice in the first provisional government, organized by a liberal, Prince Lvov. This government's policy of honoring the war aims and obligations of the tsarist government proved sufficiently unpopular that the minister of foreign affairs (Pavel Miliukov) and the minister of war and navy (Aleksandr Guchkov) were forced to resign; Kerensky succeeded to the latter position. He fared little better in this position than had Guchkov, however. In spite of initial successes, a major offensive, which Kerensky inspired, resulted in fresh military disasters (June 1917). Thus, amidst military failure and broadly based, disruptive demonstrations, Lvov resigned as prime minister in July and Kerensky succeeded him.

Kerensky's own view was that in the succeeding weeks the Russian political situation was tending toward stability. Radical leftist agitators (including Lenin and Trotsky) had been imprisoned or forced to flee the country, and Kerensky himself enjoyed a certain amount of popularity. Moreover, the time was thought to be drawing closer when it would be possible to convene a constituent assembly that would formally establish a democratic regime. The stroke that destroyed these hopes came unexpectedly from the right in the form of the Kornilov uprising (September 9–14), which was an attempt to establish a conservatively backed military government. Kerensky managed to halt the attempted coup only by calling upon the radical left for support. Similarly, he was unable from this time forward to count on the military leadership for support against this same radical left. Soon after, Lenin and Trotsky, at large again, planned their own coup, the Bolshevik Revolution of November. When the blow fell, Kerensky was out of Petrograd searching for troops loyal enough to defend the government against the Bolsheviks. Failing in this, he returned to Petrograd and then Moscow, futilely attempting to organize opposition against the revolution.

In the spring of 1918 Kerensky finally fled Russia, and, for a short time thereafter, he strove to rally international opposition against the Bolshevik government. Failing this, he began to write and lecture in Europe on the affairs of his native land. In 1940 he moved to the United States, writing, lecturing, and teaching at Stanford University. He died on June 11, 1970, in New York City.

EWB

Keynes, John Maynard (1883–1946), English economist. John Maynard Keynes revolutionized economic theory and policy by linking employment and income to public and private expenditure. He is also known for his role in the creation of new international monetary institutions in World War II.

John Maynard Keynes was born on June 5, 1883, the son of John Neville Keynes, registrar of the University of Cambridge and eminent logician and economist. John Maynard's mother, a charming and talented woman, was onetime mayor of Cambridge. He was educated at Eton and King's College, Cambridge, and began a career in the civil service, where he was assigned to the India Office from 1906 to 1909. There he acquired an intimate knowledge of the government service and an interest in Indian currency and finance that was to bear fruit a few years later.

His Writings. In 1909 Keynes was elected fellow of King's College and returned to Cambridge. In 1911 he was chosen, in spite of his youth and inexperience, as editor of the *Economic Journal,* the publication of the Royal Economic Society and one of the leading professional journals. From that time until 1945 his duties were carried out with outstanding promptness and efficiency. In 1913 his first book, *Indian Currency and Finance,* was published shortly after he was appointed to the Royal Commission on Indian Currency and Finance. His book has been referred to as the best in the English language on the gold exchange standard.

With the outbreak of World War I Keynes entered the Treasury, first as an unofficial and unpaid assistant. Before the end of the war he held a position equivalent to an assistant secretary and was largely responsible for handling Interallied finances.

At the conclusion of the war Keynes went to the Paris Conference as principal representative of the Treasury and deputy for the chancellor of the Exchequer on the Supreme Economic Council. It soon became apparent to him that the economic terms of the treaty and particularly the reparations settlement were impossible of fulfillment. He resigned in June 1919 and set forth his case in *The Economic Consequences of the Peace* (1919). Although the book aroused tremendous controversy, subsequent events have demonstrated the substantial correctness of his position.

Having left the public service, Keynes returned to Cambridge as second bursar of King's College. In 1921 he assumed the first of a number of important company directorships. Also that year, he published *A Treatise on Probability* and, a year later, *A Revision of the Treaty,* a sequel to *The Economic Consequences.* In 1923 his *Tract on Monetary Reform* appeared. From 1924 until his death he was first bursar of King's College and through his expert management made King's what a contemporary has described as "indecently rich."

In 1925 Keynes married Lydia Lopokova, a Russian ballerina, who was as outstanding a person in her own way as he was in his. Although he had for many years been a collector of rare books and fine art, he now became an active patron of the theater, helping in later years (1932) as treasurer of the Camargo Society to bring about a union of the resources of the Camargo, the Vic-Wells, the Rambert Ballet, and others. In 1936 he founded and generously financed the Cambridge Arts Theatre.

Keynes's *Treatise on Money,* a two-volume work that generations of students have found full of brilliant insights but incomprehensible as a whole, was published in 1930. In it Keynes attempted with little success to break free of the shortcomings and limitations of the Cambridge version of the quantity theory of money. In retrospect, one can see the germ of many of the ideas that distinguish his later work, but as isolated flashes of insight lacking the proper framework and, as a result, not leading to any very useful or interesting conclusions.

Finally, in 1936, came Keynes's *General Theory of Employment, Interest and Money*, a book that not only revolutionized economic theory but also had a direct impact on the lives of a large proportion of the world's population. Here Keynes took issue with the classical theory which found in a competitive capitalist economy a set of mechanisms that automatically move the economy toward a state of full employment. (The term "classical" is used here to mean the mainstream of orthodox economic theory beginning with Adam Smith and running through the work of Ricardo, Mill, Marshall, and others.) These mechanisms functioned in the labor market and in the market for goods and services.

Return to Public Service. With the beginning of World War II, Keynes again entered the public service. In July 1940 he was asked to serve as adviser to the chancellor of the Exchequer, and he was soon after elected to the Court of the Bank of England and was raised to the peerage as Lord Tilton in 1942. Through his work, national income and expenditure accounts were developed and utilized in the preparation of wartime budgets. In addition to internal finance, he had special responsibility for intergovernmental finance, lend-lease, and mutual aid. This work required that he become a sort of special envoy to Washington and Ottawa in particular.

In the closing days of the war, Keynes played a major role in negotiating the United States loan to Great Britain and in the establishment of the International Monetary Fund and the Bank for Reconstruction and Development. Keynes died of a heart attack on Easter Sunday, April 21, 1946, shortly after having returned from the inaugural meetings of the International Monetary Fund and the World Bank in Savannah, Ga.

EWB

Khrushchev, Nikita Sergeevich (1894–1971), Soviet political leader. Nikita Khrushchev was a major force in world politics in the post-Stalin period.

Nikita Khrushchev was born in Kalinovka in southern Russia on April 17, 1894. At 15 he became an apprentice mechanic in Yuzovka, where his father was working as a miner. When his apprenticeship ended, he was employed as a machine repairman in coal mines and coke plants of the region.

In 1918 Khrushchev joined the Communist party, and he enrolled in the Red Army to fight in the civil war then in progress. After nearly 3 years of service, he returned to Yuzovka and was appointed assistant manager of a mine. Soon thereafter, he entered the Donets Industrial Institute, from which he graduated in 1925. He then took up his career as a full-time party official, beginning as secretary of a district party committee near Yuzovka.

Four years later Khrushchev attended the Industrial Academy in Moscow for training in industrial administration, leaving in 1931 to become secretary of a district party committee in Moscow. Within 4 years he became head of the party organization of Moscow and its environs, thus joining the highest ranks of party officialdom. In Moscow he used his industrial training as he helped to supervise the construction of the city's subway system.

When Stalin began purging the Communist party's leadership of those he mistrusted, Khrushchev was fortunate to be one of the trusted. In 1938, when most of the chief party leaders in the Ukraine were purged, he was made first secretary of the Ukrainian Communist party and at the same time was named to the Politburo, the ruling body of the Soviet Communist party. As first secretary, he was in fact, though not in name, the chief executive of the Ukraine. Except for a short interval in 1947, he retained his authority in that area until 1949.

During World War II, while still first secretary of the Ukrainian Communist party, Khrushchev served in the Red Army both in the Ukraine and in other southern parts of the former U.S.S.R., finally advancing to the rank of lieutenant general.

In 1949 Khrushchev was summoned to Moscow to serve in the party's Secretariat, directed by Stalin. Then, after Stalin's death in 1953, Khrushchev was among the eight men in whose hands power became concentrated. In the allocation of the various spheres of power, the party was recognized as his sphere; within a few months he became first secretary of the Central Committee of the Soviet Communist party that is, its chief official.

By installing his supporters in important party positions and making some shrewd political alliances, Khrushchev gained ascendancy over the seven who shared power with him; by 1955 he was clearly the foremost political figure in the Soviet Union. Even that prestigious status was enhanced 3 years later, when he became chairman of the Council of Ministers, succeeding Nikolai Bulganin. With that, he became the most powerful man in the country: as chairman of the Council of Ministers, he was head of the government; and, as first secretary of the Soviet Communist party's Central Committee, he was head of the party.

Instead of emulating Stalin by becoming a dictator, Khrushchev encouraged the policy of de-Stalinization, which the government had been following since 1953, for the purpose of ending the worst practices of the Stalin dictatorship. Although the Soviet Union under Khrushchev continued to be a one-party totalitarian state, its citizens enjoyed conditions more favorable than had been possible under Stalin. The standard of living rose, intellectual and artistic life became somewhat freer, and the authority of the political police was reduced. In addition, relations with the outside world were generally improved, and Soviet prestige rose.

Khrushchev's fortunes eventually began to take a downward turn, however. Some of his ambitious economic projects failed; his handling of foreign affairs resulted in a number of setbacks; and de-Stalinization produced discord in the Communist ranks of other countries. These developments caused concern among party leaders in the U.S.S.R., many of them already fearful that Khrushchev might be planning to extend his power. In October 1964, while Khrushchev was away from Moscow, they united in an effort whereby they managed to deprive him of his office and require his retirement. He died on Sept. 11, 1971, in Moscow.

EWB

Kipling, Joseph Rudyard (1865–1936), British poet and story writer. Rudyard Kipling was one of the first masters of the short story in English and the first to use Cockney dialect in serious poetry.

Rudyard Kipling's early stories and poems about life in colonial India made him a great favorite with English readers. His support of English imperialism at first contributed to this popularity but caused a reaction against him in the 20th century. Today he is best known for his *Jungle Books* and *Kim,* a story of India.

Kipling was born on December 30, 1865, in Bombay, India, where his father was professor of architectural sculpture in the School of Art. In 1871 he was sent to England for his education. In 1878 Rudyard entered the United Services College at "Westward Ho!," a boarding school in Devon. There young "Gigger" endured bullying and harsh discipline but also enjoyed the close friendships, practical jokes, and merry pranks he later recorded in *Stalky & Co.* (1899). Kipling's closest friend at Westward Ho!, George Beresford, described him as a short, but "cheery, capering, podgy, little fellow" with a thick pair of spectacles over "a broad smile." His eyes were brilliant blue, and over them his heavy black eyebrows moved up and down as he talked. Another close friend was the head-

master, "Crom" Price, who encouraged Kipling's literary ambitions by having him edit the school paper and praising the poems which he wrote for it. When Kipling sent some of these to India, his father had them privately printed as *Schoolboy Lyrics* (1881), Kipling's first published work.

In 1882 Kipling rejoined his parents in Lahore and became a subeditor for the *Civil and Military Gazette.* In 1887 he moved to the *Allahabad Pioneer,* a better paper which gave him greater liberty in his writing. The result was a flood of satiric verses, published as *Departmental Ditties* in 1886, and over 70 short stories published in 1888 in seven paperback volumes. In style, the stories showed the influence of Edgar Allan Poe, Bret Harte, and Guy de Maupassant; but the subjects were Kipling's own: Anglo-Indian society, which he readily criticized with an acid pen, and the life of the common British soldier and the Indian native, which he portrayed accurately and sympathetically.

Fame in England and America. In 1889 Kipling took a long voyage through China, Japan, and the United States. When he reached London, he found that his stories had preceded him and established him as a brilliant new author. He was readily accepted into the circle of leading writers, including William Ernest Henley, Thomas Hardy, George Saintsbury, and Andrew Lang. For Henley's *Scots Observer,* he wrote a number of stories and some of his best-remembered poems: "A Ballad of East and West," "Mandalay," and "The English Flag." He also introduced English readers to a "new genre" of serious poems in Cockney dialect: "Danny Deever," "Tommy," "Fuzzy-Wuzzy," and "Gunga Din." Kipling's first novel, *The Light That Failed* (1891), was unsuccessful. But when his stories were collected as *Life's Handicap* (1891) and poems as *Barrackroom Ballads* (1892), Kipling replaced Tennyson as the most popular English author.

In 1892 Kipling married Caroline Balestier. They settled on the Balestier estate near Brattleboro, Vt., and began four of the happiest years of Kipling's life, during which he wrote some of his best work—*Many Inventions* (1893), perhaps his best volume of short stories; *The Jungle Book* (1894) and *The Second Jungle Book* (1895), two books of animal fables which attract readers of all ages by illustrating the larger truths of life; *The Seven Seas* (1896), a new collection of poems in experimental rhythms; and *Captains Courageous* (1897), a novel-length sea story. These works not only assured Kipling's lasting fame as a serious writer but also made him a rich man.

His Imperialism. In 1897 the Kiplings settled in Rottingdean, a village on the British coast near Brighton. The outbreak of the Spanish-American War in 1898 and the Boer War in 1899 turned Kipling's attention to colonial affairs. He began to publish a number of solemn poems in standard English in the *London Times.* The most famous of these, "Recessional" (July 17, 1897), issued a warning to Englishmen to consider their accomplishments in the Diamond Jubilee year of Queen Victoria's reign with humility and awe rather than pride and arrogance. The equally well-known "White Man's Burden" (February 4, 1899) clearly expressed the attitudes toward empire implicit in the stories in *The Day's Work* (1898) and *A Fleet in Being* (1898). He referred to less highly developed peoples as "lesser breeds" and considered order, discipline, sacrifice, and humility to be the essential qualities of colonial rulers. These views have been denounced as racist, elitist, and jingoistic. But for Kipling, the term "white man" indicated citizens of the more highly developed nations, whose duty it was to spread law, literacy, and morality throughout the world.

During the Boer War, Kipling spent several months in South Africa, where he raised funds for soldiers' relief and worked on an army newspaper, the *Friend.* In 1901 Kipling published *Kim,* the last and most charming of his portrayals of Indian life. But anti-imperialist reaction following the end of the Boer War caused a decline in Kipling's popularity. When he published *The Five Nations,* a book of South African verse, in 1903, he was attacked in parodies, caricatures, and serious protests as the opponent of a growing spirit of peace and democratic equality. Kipling retired to "Bateman's," a house near Burwash, a secluded village in Essex.

Later Works. Kipling now turned from the wide empire as subject to England itself. In 1902 he published *Just So Stories for Little Children.* He also issued two books of stories of England's past, intended, like the *Jungle Books,* for young readers but suitable for adults as well: *Puck of Pook's Hill* (1906) and *Rewards and Fairies* (1910). But his most significant work was a number of volumes of short stories written in a new style: *Traffics and Discoveries* (1904), *Actions and Reactions* (1904), *A Diversity of Creatures* (1917), *Debits and Credits* (1926), and *Limits and Renewals* (1932). These later stories treat more complex, subtle, and somber subjects in a style more compressed, allusive, and elliptical. Consequently, these stories have never been as popular as his earlier work. But modern critics, in reevaluating Kipling, have found

a greater power and depth that make them his best work.

In 1907 Kipling became the first English writer to receive the Nobel Prize for literature. He died on January 18, 1936, and is buried in Westminster Abbey. His autobiography, *Something of Myself,* was published posthumously in 1937.

EWB

Knox, John (ca. 1505–1572), Scottish reformer. John Knox was one of the most celebrated followers of John Calvin and became the chief force in the introduction and establishment of the Presbyterian form of Calvinism in Scotland.

The Scotland of John Knox's time was used to reform movements. Long before Martin Luther's theses of 1517, men were executed for importing the doctrines of John Wyclif and John Hus. During Knox's adolescence he could not but be aware of the agitation for an evangelical Christianity abroad in the land.

The day and even the year of Knox's birth is disputed. The best estimate is probably 1505. His prosperous peasant father, William Knox, sought to prepare him for the priesthood. His autobiographical writings leave doubt over his early education. It is certain that Knox attended a university, either Glasgow or St. Andrews, but did not earn a degree. After ordination in 1532 he returned to Haddington, the region of his birth.

Conversion to Protestantism. Knox's conversion to Protestantism seemingly occurred between 1543 and 1546. In 1543 he was loyally serving the Catholic Church under the archbishop of St. Andrews. He styled himself "minister of the sacred altar." By 1546 he was vigorously defending the reformer George Wishart, who had introduced Swiss Protestantism into Scotland with his translation of the First Helvetic Confession in 1543 and impressed many before being executed for heresy in 1546.

The following year David Beaton, the cardinal responsible for Wishart's arrest, was murdered. Knox, hearing of the deed, eagerly joined the murderers in the castle of St. Andrews and, after protesting his unworthiness, became their preacher, thereby making his revolt from Rome complete and courting death. Curiously enough, his voluminous writings give no clue as to what transformed him in such a short time from a Catholic priest to a fiery, sword-bearing Protestant.

For fiery Knox was, denouncing the Catholic Church as a "synagogue of Satan" and the beast of the Apocalypse. While the castle trembled with spiritual thunder, the French laid siege, eventually capturing the occupants and making them galley slaves.

After 19 months Knox emerged in February 1549, his body intact, his spirit unbroken, and his Protestantism strengthened.

The release of Knox and his comrades may have been engineered by the new Protestant regency in England. In any case Knox took a paid position as preacher there. His popularity grew rapidly. In 1551 he was made chaplain to the king and in 1552 declined a bishopric. He worked to rid the religious services of all vestiges of Catholic ritual and to fix austerity of worship firmly in English Protestant doctrine. This made his life precarious when the fanatically Catholic Mary Tudor acceded to the throne in 1553. The following year Knox left England, wandered for a time, and unknowingly took the most important step of his career by moving to Geneva.

Calvin's Influence.

In the "Bible Commonwealth," Knox came to believe fully in Calvinism, in the right of the true church to impose strict rules of conduct and belief on the individual, and in the right of the people to rebel against a civil authority that attempts to enforce adherence to a false doctrine. He called Calvin's Geneva "the most perfect school of Christ that ever was on earth since the days of the apostles."

On a trip to Scotland in 1555, then under a regency in preparation for the reign of Mary Stuart, Knox organized Protestant congregations and preached quietly. After he left under pressure, in 1556, an ecclesiastical court burned him in effigy. Back in Geneva he worked effectively as pastor of an English congregation.

Calvinism suited his austerity, and Knox preached with certitude that those not of his and Calvin's church were damned for eternity and that no Christian love was due them. Since they were sons of Satan, one could take joy in hating them, reveling over the prospect of their damnation, and even cheating and deceiving them. Knox saw himself as the prophet of a biblical society in which virtuous priests would guide men, and statesmen would be bound by the precepts of the Bible.

Knox's Writings.

While he was at Geneva, Knox's pen was busy. His admonitions and letters to followers in England and Scotland are filled with burning condemnations of the Roman Church, a "harlot . . . polluted with all kinds of spiritual fornication," and of its priests, who were "pestilent papists" and "bloody wolves." His best-known work, *History of the Reformation of Religion within the Realm of Scotland,* is more polemic than history.

Preaching in the Reformed manner was forbidden in Scotland in 1559, and on May 2 Knox arrived in Edinburgh. Pursued as a criminal, he managed to remain free and become the architect of a new Scottish church. Under his guidance, Catholicism, the regency, and French influence were repudiated, and in 1560 a democratic form of church structure in which congregations elected their ministers and elders was adopted.

Under these conditions it is not surprising that Mary, Queen of Scots, a Catholic reared in France, found Scotland uncongenial soon after her arrival in 1561. Since Catholic worship was forbidden, Mary's private Masses had to be defended with the sword. In 1568 she was driven from Scotland in the midst of a scandal; Knox was in the forefront of her pursuers.

Death took the reformer on Nov. 24, 1572. Knox was a small man but of immense physical and moral strength. He was not without contradictions in his work and his life. Although an authoritarian, he did more to stimulate the growth of democracy than any man of his age. He left an independent Scotland under a severe but democratically elected church.

EWB

Kropotkin, Peter Alekseevich

(1842–1921), Russian scientist and anarchist. Peter Kropotkin combined biological and historical fact to derive a theory of "mutual aid" to support his belief in the superiority of an anarchist society.

Peter Kropotkin was born in Moscow on Dec. 12, 1842, to an ancient and noble Russian family. At 15 he entered the aristocratic Corps des Pages of St. Petersburg, and at 19 he became personal page to Czar Alexander II. A precocious and widely read youth, he rejected the opportunity for a fashionable military career in the Imperial Guards and volunteered to help implement the Alexandrian reforms in Siberia. Disappointed by the results after 5 years, he undertook geographical exploration in East Siberia, and his theory on the mountain structure of Siberia brought him fame and an offer of the position of secretary to the Imperial Geographical Society. However, Kropotkin was aware of the gulf between the educated elite and the impoverished masses, and he decided to enter the Russian revolutionary movement. He was arrested in 1874 but managed to escape from Russia in 1876.

Anarchist and Writer.

In Switzerland, Kropotkin developed his ideas on anarchism, which were later published as *Paroles d'un révolté* (1885). In 1881 Kropotkin was expelled from Switzerland and settled in France. But in 1883 the French government arrested Kropotkin for belonging to the First International. His observations on prison life were later published as *In Russian and French Prisons* (1887).

Released in 1886 after much political agitation on his behalf, Kropotkin moved to England, where he became very active in the international socialist movement. There he also began a series of articles against social Darwinism and its emphasis on the benefits of competition. Kropotkin tried to prove that sociability existed among animals, and that cooperation rather than struggle accounted for the evolution of man and human intelligence. The publication of *Mutual Aid* (1902), following his *Memoirs of a Revolutionist* (1899), brought Kropotkin worldwide fame. He elaborated on the economic and social implications of mutual aid for society in *Conquest of Bread* (1892) and *Fields, Factories and Workshops* (1901).

After the failure of the Russian Revolution of 1905, Kropotkin tried to find its significance for anarchists by studying the French Revolution. In *The Great French Revolution, 1789–1793* (1909) he interpreted the Revolution as a joining together of ideas from the upper class with action from the masses.

Although, as an anarchist, Kropotkin opposed war, the outbreak of World War I in 1914 brought him to the side of Russia. He saw in Germany the major support of reaction in Russia and Europe. After the collapse of the Russian autocracy in 1917, Kropotkin returned home to a warm welcome. Although he refused a Cabinet post in the provisional government, Kropotkin supported it against the Bolsheviks, whom he called "state socialists." After the Bolshevik coup d'etat in October 1917, Kropotkin found himself as strongly opposed to Western intervention as he was to the Bolsheviks, for he feared that intervention would only poison future Russian-European relations. In ill health, he moved from Moscow to Dmitrov and returned to his work on ethics, which he never completed. It was published posthumously from his notes as *Ethics, Origin and Development* (1922). Peter Kropotkin died of pneumonia on Feb. 8, 1921.

Kropotkin is a prototype of the non-Marxist Russian revolutionary thinker of the 19th century. In him were combined the major themes of the revolutionary socialists: populism, materialism, communalism, anarchism, and scientism. Kropotkin's distinctive contribution was to combine these themes into an original philosophy of anarchism based on mutual aid.

EWB

L

Lacan, Jacques (1901–1981), French psychoanalyst. After World War II Jacques Lacan became a cult hero, a formidable intellectual superstar whose "structural psychoanalysis," first in France and later at American elite universities, dominated much of intellectual life.

Jacques Lacan was born in Paris on April 13, 1901, the eldest child of Emilie and Alfred Lacan, a *representant de commerce* dealing in soap and oils. The family belonged to the prosperous middle bourgeoisie, and Lacan went to the Collège Stanislas, a well-known Jesuit establishment. Too thin to be accepted into military service, he went straight to the study of medicine and then to psychiatry. He took his clinical training at Sainte-Anne, the major psychiatric hospital in central Paris.

In 1931 he received his license as a forensic psychiatrist, and in 1932 was awarded his Doctorat d'état for his thesis, *De la psychose paranoiaque dans les rapports avec la personnalité*. While this thesis drew considerable acclaim outside psychoanalytic circles, particularly among the surrealist artists, it seems to have been ignored by psychoanalysts. But in 1934 he became a candidate for the Société Psychanalytique de Paris. During this period he is said to have befriended the surrealists André Breton and Georges Bataille. Because Lacan, like Freud, apparently destroyed most of the records of his past, and unlike Freud did not reveal much of it later on, it is difficult to distinguish between the many myths, anecdotes, and rumors that have surrounded him. There are, for instance, many contradictory tales about his romantic life with Sylvia Bataille in southern France during World War II and of his attachment to her daughter Laurance. He married Sylvia in 1953 and had another daughter, Judith, whose husband Jacques-Alain Miller served as Lacan's literary executor.

In 1934 Lacan developed the first version of his "mirror stage," which was to become the cornerstone of his theory when presented at the meetings of the International Psychoanalytic Association two years later in Marienbad. Due to World War II and the decimation of psychoanalysis on the Continent, Lacan's ideas lay dormant until 1949. Then he presented a more complex and complete variant of his "mirror stage" theory. Extrapolating from his work with patients, he maintained that the child's first perception of itself in the mirror, how it becomes aware of itself as a biological organism, sets the stage for its future psychic development. During this stage (from about six to eighteen months) the child realizes that its parents are not totally responsive to inarticulate demands, that it has to acquire language. And what happens during this process determines psychic development.

Lacan's Freudian peers did not appreciate his contributions. In fact, the so-called American ego psychologists, who held that infantile experiences are being resolved during the oedipal period, could not accept Lacan's "rereading of Freud." They mandated different types of interactions between analyst and patient, different assumptions about human growth and about the structure of the unconscious.

Lacan and his peers in the International Psychoanalytic Association eventually split up, in 1953, because they could not agree on how best to help patients reach and then overcome early unconscious trauma. Classical psychoanalysts were agreed that, optimally, this could happen only by means of regular sessions, four to five times a week, for at least 45 minutes, and over a period of around four years. Lacan was seeing his patients once or twice a week, for five to 25 minutes, and attacking his American and Parisian adversaries as authoritarian. However, a part of these attacks was incorporated in his theories when he played on, for instance, such terms as the *nom du père* and the *non du père* to accuse the "sons of Freud"— that is, the leaders in the psychoanalytic movement—of paternalism and of domination counterproductive to the relationship between psychoanalyst and analysand.

Lacanian psychoanalytic theory differentiated itself also by underpinning it with Ferdinand de Saussure's structural linguistics which in the 1960s was inspiring the other leading "structuralists," Michel Foucault, Roland Barthes, Louis Althusser, and Claude Lévi-Strauss. They all set out to uncover systematically the deep universal mental structures that manifest themselves in language. And they expected to find them by unveiling the relationships between *signs* (concepts) and *signifiers* (acoustic images); between language and words; and by studying their changing meanings. Lacan concentrated on "the language of the unconscious," not only in his work with patients but in the public seminars which certainly helped make him central to Parisian intellectual life, along with psychoanalysis, from the late 1960s until long after he died in 1981.

Lacan's analysis of literary texts as well used Saussurean means of "rereading." Whereas Freud and his followers (both literary figures and psychoanalysts) in a way were "diagnosing" artists and their works, Lacan's technique introduced a new dimension. His own imagination coupled to the linguistic method allowed him to make all sorts of jumps, in both metaphoric and metonymic directions. His famous seminar on *Poe's "Purloined Letter"* particularly intrigued American literary critics.

Lacan always deemed the psychoanalytic relationship central to everything he did. When he stated, for instance, that psychoanalysis is "structured like a language," he referred to the interaction between the analyst's and his patient's unconscious. His American followers, however, primarily were located in universities and, for the most part, ignored the therapeutic realm. Consequently, his Parisian adherents tended to be therapists working with patients who disregarded American textual analyses.

Urbane, brilliant, and provocative, Lacan continued to influence French intellectual life even while his ideas were questioned and debated.

EWB

Lamennais, Hugues Félicité Robert de   (1782–1854), French political writer. Félicité de Lamennais was a priest whose liberal political and religious ideas greatly agitated 19th-century France.

Félicité de Lamennais was born on June 19, 1782, into a well-to-do family in the town of Saint-Malo in Brittany. As a bright, sensitive young man, he was deeply impressed by the ideals as well as the horrors of the French Revolution. He gradually became convinced that social revolution must be accompanied by a firm religious faith. In 1816 he was ordained a Roman Catholic priest. Over the next 6 years Lamennais became widely known in Europe for his *Essay on Indifference in Matters of Religion,* in which he argued that a genuine improvement in man's social condition must be based on religious truth. Since the Roman Catholic Church possessed the fullest expression of religious truth, Europe's hope for a better future lay in accepting that Church's beliefs and structure.

Pope Leo XII invited Lamennais to Rome and offered to make him a cardinal. The passionate and dedicated young priest refused and returned to France, where, with a group of talented and equally dedicated disciples, including the Comte de Montalembert and Jean Baptiste Lacordaire, he started the journal *L'Avenir* (The Future) in 1830. The group pressed the Church's officials to renounce its connections with the government and take up instead the cause of the people. Lamennais wrote that the Church should support democratic and revolutionary movements wherever they appeared. Most of the French bishops, who owed their positions to an agreement the Pope had made with Napoleon, reacted strongly against Lamennais. His ideas were labeled subversive by the governments of both France and Austria, which joined with the bishops in pressuring the Pope to silence *L'Avenir.*

In 1832 Pope Gregory XVI issued an encyclical letter, *Mirari vos,* calling the ideas advocated in *L'Avenir* "absurd, and supremely dangerous for the Church." Lamennais, bitterly disappointed, submitted. But a year later, after the Pope had publicly supported the Russian Tsar in suppressing the Polish peasants, he left the Church. In 1834 he wrote a short, biting book, *Words of a Believer,* in which he denounced all authority, civil as well as ecclesiastical. In the next decade his thinking moved further and further to the left. He believed in the moral superiority of the working class and foresaw a time when governments would be overthrown and the workers would rule. During his last years he spent time in prison and was also elected to the Chamber of Deputies. After his death in Paris on Feb. 27, 1854, Lamennais was buried without funeral rites, mourned by thousands of intellectual and political sympathizers around the world.

EWB

Lamprecht, Karl (1856–1915), German historian. The highly original and combative Karl Lamprecht stirred up a violent controversy over the nature, methods, and purposes of history.

Karl Lamprecht was born in Jessen in Saxony on Feb. 25, 1856, the son of a liberal Lutheran pastor. He studied at the universities of Göttingen, Leipzig, and Munich, taking his doctorate at Munich in 1879. After a year of private tutoring, he qualified as lecturer at Bonn; he was promoted to assistant professor in 1885. Lamprecht's first major work, *German Economic Life in the Middle Ages* (3 vols.), came out in 1886. In 1890 he accepted a full professorship at Marburg but removed the following year to Leipzig, where he remained until his death on May 10, 1915.

In 1891 appeared the first volume (of the eventual 21 volumes) of what was to be Lamprecht's lifework, the *German History.* Controversy broke out immediately, reaching its climax with volume 6 in 1897. History, he explained in later articles and books, has

been a discipline that explores useless individual facts and concentrates too narrowly on politics. It should deal with the whole life of human society and, like the natural sciences, generalize and seek causal laws that will provide a few basic principles that will enable one to explain the whole human past.

Lamprecht thought that he had discovered such general principles in the sociopsychological realm. Once one has discovered the thought and behavior patterns of a people for a given period, one has the key by which to explain the whole society, its economic and social life, its art and thought, and its politics. Art, he thought, was particularly revealing about such thought and behavior patterns. Furthermore, such patterns of thinking and acting never completely disappear but live on into the next age, so that, as new ones come along, they tend to accumulate, leading to a progressive complexity and intensity of social life.

These theories of history hit the historical profession at a very sensitive time, when nature, methods, and purposes of history were being painfully examined. Men such as Wilhelm Dilthey and Max Weber were seeking to give history a rationale distinct from, but equally as reputable as, that of natural science. Others were seeking ways to treat history in all its aspects, even to find a universal history. What was lacking was a way to deal with these things within a single discipline. They were being treated as separate subjects, often collaboratively, and without any integrating principle. To this extent, Lamprecht found a sympathetic hearing. But his own solution the "psychogenetic" met with universal rejection as being too vague and not amenable to rigorous, disciplined study. The literature of controversy grew enormously after 1900, but the controversy quickly became tiresome, even for those engaged in it. Lamprecht's influence, therefore, was slight, not to say negative, but he was a symptom and child of his age.

In 1909 he founded, with private funds, the Institute for Cultural and Universal History at Leipzig in order to train scholars to carry on his work. It produced many admirers but few followers.

EWB

Las Casas, Bartolomé de (1474–1566), Spanish priest, social reformer, and historian. Bartolomé de Las Casas was the principal organizer and champion of the 16th-century movement in Spain and Spanish America in defense of the Indians.

Bartolomé de Las Casas, the son of a merchant, was born in Seville. Apparently he did not graduate from a university, although he studied Latin and the humanities in Seville. The facts of his life after 1502 are well known. In that year Las Casas sailed for Española in the expedition of Governor Nicolás de Ovando. In the West Indies he participated in Indian wars, acquired land and slaves, and felt no serious qualms about his actions, although he had been ordained a priest.

Not until his fortieth year did Las Casas experience a moral conversion, perhaps the awakening of a dormant sensitivity as a result of the horrors he saw about him. His early efforts at the Spanish court were largely directed at securing approval for the establishment of model colonies in which Spanish farmers would live and labor side by side with Indians in a peaceful coexistence that would gently lead the natives to Christianity and Christian civilization. The disastrous failure of one such project on the coast of Venezuela (1521) caused Las Casas to retire for 10 years to a monastery and to enter the Dominican order. He had greater success with an experiment in peaceful conversion of the Indians in the province of Tezulutlán—called by the Spaniards the Land of War—in Guatemala (1537–1540).

Las Casas appeared to have won a brilliant victory with the promulgation of the New Laws of 1542. These laws banned Indian slavery, prohibited Indian forced labor, and provided for gradual abolition of the *encomienda* system, which held the Indians living on agricultural lands in serfdom. Faced with revolt by the *encomenderos* in Peru and the threat of revolt elsewhere, however, the Crown made a partial retreat, repealing the provisions most objectionable to the colonists. It was against this background that Las Casas met Juan Ginés de Sepúlveda, defender of the *encomienda* and of Indian wars, in a famous debate at Valladolid in 1550. Sepúlveda, a disciple of Aristotle, invoked his theory that some men are slaves by nature in order to show that the Indians must be made to serve the Spaniards for their own good as well as for that of their masters. The highest point of Las Casas' argument was an eloquent affirmation of the equality of all races, the essential oneness of mankind.

To the end of a long life Las Casas fought passionately for justice for his beloved Indians. As part of his campaign in their defense, he wrote numerous tracts and books. The world generally knows him best for his flaming indictment of Spanish cruelty to the Indians, *Brief Account of the Destruction of the Indies* (1552), a work based largely on official reports to the Crown and soon translated into the major European languages. Historians regard most highly his *Historia de las Indias,* which is indispensable to every student of the first phase of the Spanish conquest. His *Apologética historia de las Indias* is an immense accumulation of ethnographic data designed to demonstrate that the Indians fully met the requirements laid down by Aristotle for the good life.

EWB

Lassalle, Ferdinand (1825–1864), German socialist leader. Ferdinand Lassalle is considered the founder of the German Social Democratic party and a major theoretician of "scientific" socialism.

Ferdinand Lassalle, whose real name was Lasal, was born in Breslau on April 11, 1825, the only son of a wealthy Jewish silk merchant. While still a boy, he rejected both Judaism and a career in the family business for what he felt was the freedom of secular thought and demanded an academic career.

Lassalle changed his last name purportedly to give it a French (that is revolutionary) sound, an action that has been described as characteristic and symptomatic of his posturing personality. Virtually all commentators, including those most sympathetic to

Lassalle and his program, agree that, while he was one of the most romantic and colorful figures in modern politics, he was also a rather foppish and quixotic person of colossal vanity and arrogance.

Lassalle studied at the universities of Breslau and Berlin where he became enthralled with the philosophy of G. W. F. Hegel and was convinced that the Hegelian "World Spirit" was realizing itself in the current age through himself.

As the prosecutor in a lengthy and much-publicized divorce suit (1846–1854), which Lassalle entered out of his hatred of aristocratic and male privilege, he became famous. During this period he acquainted himself with Karl Marx's writings and developed his own theory of socialism, which is sometimes described as "state socialism," although many of his followers deny that he was an adherent of that brand of socialism. Nevertheless, he denied in contrast to Marx that the bourgeoisie must be totally destroyed and also emphasized the positive role of nationalism. He thus generally advocated state action rather than revolution, that is, a take-over, not destruction of the bourgeois state by a workers' party, and favored a state system of workers' cooperatives.

At the conclusion of the lawsuit, Lassalle became the teacher and political leader of the emerging German labor movement. He advocated universal suffrage as the means by which the workers could force the bourgeois state to turn over to them the entire fruit of their labor and not just a percentage of it. Trade union activity, as he saw it, would be of little or no use in itself. The working class embodied the spirit of the people, whose higher will was manifest in the state. Labor could emancipate itself only through capturing the concentrated political power found in the machinery of the state.

Lassalle's chief significance, however, was in the realm of practical politics rather than in theory. He laid the groundwork for the modern German Social Democratic party. In 1862 he drew up the Program for the Workingman, a document similar to Marx and Engels's Communist Manifesto. The following year his General Association of German Workers was formed, the lineal ancestor of the Social Democratic party.

In 1864, however, before the party had grown beyond a few thousand members, Lassalle became involved in a dispute over a girl half his age, which led to a duel. He was killed before he managed to draw his pistol, on Aug. 28.

EWB

Lavisse, Ernest (1842–1922), French historian. Ernest Lavisse was active in educational reform and edited two multivolume histories of France.

Ernest Lavisse was born on Dec. 17, 1842, in the village of Nouvion-en-Thiérache. He retained a lifelong fondness for his native town and even as professor at the Sorbonne returned each year to address the school's graduating class. After secondary school in the nearby city of Laon, Lavisse continued his education at the Lycée Charlemagne in Paris and the École Normale Supérieure.

After a short student flirtation with republican politics, Lavisse returned to the Bonapartist sympathies he had learned from his family and in 1868 became secretary to Napoleon III's minister of education. Soon afterward he was named private tutor to the prince imperial, with whom he maintained a correspondence for many years after his teaching job was ended by the War of 1870.

Convinced by the defeat of 1870 that France had something to learn from Germany, Lavisse left for Berlin in 1873. There he remained for 3 years, studying with Georg Waitz and observing the structure of German education. When he was appointed lecturer at the École Normale in 1878, he entered the campaign to reform the French educational system, a campaign he pushed even more vigorously when named to the Sorbonne, first as assistant in 1883 and finally as professor of modern history in 1888. To the Sorbonne he introduced the Rankean method of seminar instruction in historical research. His untiring advocacy was largely responsible for the law of 1896 that united the various faculties of law, medicine, letters, and science into a single university. He also campaigned for changes in primary and secondary education. The history textbooks he wrote for the public schools went through many editions and, for almost two generations, made his name a household word even in the remotest corner of the French countryside.

Lavisse's historical writing was devoted largely to Germany, the most important being *The Youth of Frederick the Great* (1891) and *Frederick the Great before His Accession* (1893). His great work, however, was editing a *History of France from the Beginnings to the Revolution* (9 vols., 1900–1911), to which he attracted the greatest French historians of the day. His careful editing and his inspiration gave an unusual unity to a work composed by a number of strong-minded individuals. To the work he himself contributed a two-volume history of Louis XIV, painting brilliant portraits of the men and women of the reign but also depriving Louis of the heroic structure that Voltaire and Michelet had given him and fastening on the aging king the responsibility for the miseries of the end of his reign.

During World War I Lavisse was an active propagandist, writing numerous anti-German articles for the *Revue de Paris*. After the war he edited a second collection, *History of Contemporary France* (10 vols., 1920–1922), which he concluded with a remarkable statement of hope in the future of republican institutions. He died on Aug. 18, 1922.

EWB

Le Bon, Gustave (1841–1931), French social scientist and philosopher. Although Gustave Le Bon was originally trained as a physician, Le Bon's primary contribution was in sociology, where he developed major theories on crowd behavior.

The electric interests and abilities of Gustave Le Bon led to a full and productive life. Studies ranging from components of tobacco smoke, through physical anthropology, to atomic energy and structure describe the broad range of scholarly interests Le Bon maintained until his death. Because of this wide range, many have thought of Le Bon's work as shallow and dilettantish. No one in the course of a lifetime could possibly master all the disciplines observed in Le Bon's scholarly work. Nevertheless, men such as Sigmund Freud and Gordon Allport acknowledged the vital importance of Le Bon's work.

While Le Bon made contributions to theories of social evolution and political revolution, probably his most widely known work concerned the psychology of crowd behavior. He stated that crowds maintained a collective mind and that the group mind was not simply a summary of the individual persons. Instead, a new distillation of traits emerged, primarily unconscious in nature, which reflected racially inherited characteristics.

The consequence of these innate traits was a regression in the direction of more primitive, instinctual determinants of behavior, in contrast to more rational intellectual determinants. Le Bon also believed in the contagion of ideas in a crowd such that individual members, in a heightened state of suggestibility and with feelings of omnipotence, are subjugated to the will and emotion of the crowd mind. He also indicated that crowds are capable of engaging in positive social actions as well.

Le Bon's ideas about social evolution and political revolution were related again to racial stock. History, for Le Bon, is a consequence of racial temperament; to understand the history of a people, one must look to the soul of the people. Just as a people cannot choose its appearance, it cannot freely opt for its cultural institutions.

Le Bon's beliefs with respect to political behavior consistently revealed a basic mistrust of the masses. On the last day of his life he repeated the theme that where the common people continue to maintain, or gain, control of government, civilization is moved in the direction of barbarism. It was this view that earned Le Bon the occasional label of antidemocrat and elitist.

An interesting incident attributed to Le Bon concerns his return in 1884 from an anthropological expedition to India, where he was commissioned by France to study Buddhist monuments. Marie François Sadi Carnot, then the minister of public works, was given an opportunity to choose for himself an artifact from a group Le Bon had brought back. Carnot chose a statuette which Le Bon quickly indicated was not appropriate because it carried a curse. Le Bon told Carnot that the owner of the statuette would be killed upon reaching the highest office in France. The warning was disregarded, and on June 24, 1894, Carnot, the fourth president of the French Republic, was assassinated by an Italian anarchist at Lyons.

Le Bon was a physician, anthropologist in the field, and finally professor of psychology and allied sciences at the University of Paris. His best-known book is *La Psychologie des foules* (1895; translated as *The Crowd: A Study of the Popular Mind,* 1897). He died on Dec. 13, 1931, at Marne-la-Coquette near Paris.

EWB

Le Corbusier (1887–1965), Swiss architect, city planner, and painter. Le Corbusier practiced in France and was one of the most influential architects of the 20th century.

Le Corbusier, the pseudonym for Charles Édouard Jeanneret-Gris, was born on October 6, 1887, at La-Chaux-de-Fonds, where he attended the School of Fine Art until the age of 18 and was then apprenticed to an engraver. He studied architecture in Vienna with Josef Hoffmann (1908), in Paris with Auguste Perret (1908–1909), and in Berlin with Peter Behrens (1910–1911). In 1911 Le Corbusier traveled in the Balkans, Greece, Asia Minor, and Italy. The Acropolis in Athens and the sculpture of the 5th century B.C. by Phidias on the Parthenon made a great impression on him, as did Michelangelo's contributions to St. Peter's in Rome.

In 1904 Le Corbusier designed and built a small house at La-Chaux-de-Fonds, a building so picturesque that it would have fitted into the 18th-century hamlet at Versailles. Of the half-dozen villas that he built in his native town, one (1916) is as playful as any 16th-century mannerist structure by Sebastiano Serlio or Andrea Palladio. The dominating blank panel of the main facade of Le Corbusier's villa of 1916 relates to a similar motif that Palladio used on his own house in Vicenza, Italy, of 1572. Such a par-

allel between architects of the 16th and 20th centuries is relevant to an understanding of Le Corbusier. His system of geometric proportion, first used in the 1916 villa and expounded in two books, *Le Modulor I* (1950) and *Le Modulor II* (1955), follows in the tradition of Vitruvius, Leon Battista Alberti, and Palladio, and his concept of "modulor man" is an extension of Leonardo da Vinci's "Vitruvian man."

His Purism. The influence of Perret, Tony Garnier, and other architects became evident in Le Corbusier's 1915 Domino project for prefabricated houses, a solution to spatial construction consisting of columns, floor slabs, and stair-cases for vertical circulation. To reduce a building to such simple elements was cubistic, and it was perhaps a preview of things to come in Paris, where Le Corbusier settled in 1917. Architectural commissions were slow in coming, and he turned to painting. He and Amédée Ozenfant evolved a form of cubism known as purism, in which they attempted to restore to ordinary objects their basic architectonic simplicity. Le Corbusier's *Still Life* (1920) depicts a bottle and other everyday objects; the bottle is seen from the side, above, and below. By fragmenting the bottle in such a manner, the viewer has a greater understanding of the bottle than a photograph or a realistic painting would provide. From 1920 to 1925 Ozenfant and Le Corbusier published the magazine *L'Esprit nouveau,* which preached purist theories.

This painterly expression of Le Corbusier influenced his architecture. The clean-cut planes and their relationships to the volume of a space of the Domino house and the *Still Life* bottle were combined in the Pavillon de l'Esprit Nouveau at the 1925 Paris International Exposition of Decorative Arts. Even the interior of the Chapel of Notre-Dame-du-Haut at Ronchamp (1950–1955) is cubist, since, like the bottle, it expresses more than what the eye can actually see. The 6-inch slit between the top of the walls and the roof suggests a continuation of the billowing ceiling shape beyond the external walls, and the undulating shapes of the walls suggest spaces which exist but which are cut off from the viewer.

Machine for Living. Le Corbusier's most influential book, *Towards a New Architecture* (1923), is illustrated with his sketches of the Acropolis in Athens and other sites, the architecture of Michelangelo, the "industrial city" of Tony Garnier, American grain silos, ships, airplanes, and automobiles. Under the diagram of a "Delage Front-Wheel Brake" is the caption: "This precision, this cleanness in execution go further back than our reborn mechanical sense. Phidias felt in this way: the entablature of the Parthenon is a witness." The perfection to be found in Phidias's sculpture on the Parthenon and in the front-wheel brake design for a Delage car was demanded by Le Corbusier for 20th-century architecture. A house would be a "machine for living," not reducing man to the level of an automaton but uplifting him by as precise an environment in totality as the precision of an automobile brake. Ventilation, sound insulation, sun-traps in winter, and sun shields (*brises-soleil*) in summer were all a part of this precision and of Le Corbusier's ideals for a total environment.

Collaboration with Jeanneret.

From 1922 to 1940 Le Corbusier was in partnership with his cousin Pierre Jeanneret, and they collaborated on the project for the League of Nations Palace in Geneva (1927; not executed). The houses in the Weissenhof quarter of Stuttgart that they designed for the Deutsche Werkbund exposition (1927) were "perhaps the most imaginative structures at the Weissenhof" (Peter Blake, 1964). Le Corbusier's Centrosoyus (Palace of Light Industry) in Moscow (1929–1935) was one of the last major structures of post-World War I modern architecture in the Soviet Union.

Two notable villas designed by Le Corbusier are the Villa Monzie at Garches (1927), which derives its proportions, plan, and volumetric elements from Palladio's Villa Malcontenta of 1560, and the Villa Savoye at Poissy (1930), which incorporates the five tenets of his architecture: the *piloti* (freestanding structural column), the independence of the structural frame from the external skin, the free plan of the interior accommodation, the free elevation, and the roof garden.

City Planning.

The Swiss Hostel (1931–1933) and the Brazilian Pavilion (1956–1959) at University City in Paris and the Unité d'Habitation in Marseilles (1947–1952) were designed as though they were part of Le Corbusier's projected Radiant City, just as Frank Lloyd Wright's post-1932 projects were for Broadacre City. The Unité d'Habitation, which is an enormous housing block, has a wide variety of apartments, lead-encased for sound insulation, with east-west ventilation, sun-trap balconies which let in the winter sun but exclude the summer sun, and access streets at every third floor. *Pilotis* raise the building off the ground to maximize open space for pedestrian use, which, in the Radiant City of 3 million people, would amount to 85 percent of the total area.

In the Voisin Plan for Paris (1925) Le Corbusier developed his urbanistic concepts, and thereafter he projected a score of plans for cities on four continents.

Only one was realized, that for Chandigarh, the capital of the Punjab, India (begun 1953). Geometrically classical, Chandigarh is divided into different sectors: the Capital, consisting of the governor's palace (not built), the Parliament, the High Courts of Justice, and a ministries building; a commercial area; an industrial area; and a cultural center. Le Corbusier also designed the Open Hand monument, the democratic symbol of giving (that is, elected representatives are granted the privilege of giving good government in return).

Last Works and Influence.

Le Corbusier's last major buildings were the Chapel at Ronchamp, one of the most personal and expressive statements by the architect, and the Dominican monastery of Ste-Marie-de-la-Tourette at Eveux-sur-Arbresle (1957–1959). On August 27, 1965, Le Corbusier died of a heart attack at Cap-Martin.

The Ministry of Education and Health building in Rio de Janeiro, Brazil (1936–1945), by Lúcio Costa and Oscar Niemeyer, for which Le Corbusier was the consultant, gave impetus to a slowly emerging modern movement in South America. His Maison Jaoul at Neuilly (1952–1956) spawned a movement termed the "new brutalism" in England, a country which had already accepted Le Corbusier's philosophy in spirit and had developed upon it. Kunio Mayekawa and Junzo Sakakura, who worked for Le Corbusier in Paris, returned to Japan to glorify the master. Le Corbusier's buildings have been an inspiration in whatever country they have been constructed, including his Carpenter Visual Arts Center (1961–1963) at Harvard University, Cambridge, Mass. He was the principal founder of the International Congress of Modern Architecture (CIAM) in 1928, which propagated the objectives of the new architecture; it was disbanded in 1959. He was also a prolific writer, and his books have been extremely influential.

EWB

Lefebvre, Georges (1874–1959), French historian. Georges Lefebvre was one of the major 20th-century historians of the French Revolution.

Georges Lefebvre was born at Lille on Aug. 6, 1874. His father had little money to spend on his son's education. Young Lefebvre attended the local public school, followed the "special curriculum" in the local lycéewhich emphasized modern languages, mathematics, and economics instead of the classical languagesand graduated from the University of Lille. This education, he later wrote, "opened my mind to economic and social realities, and gave me the air of an independent, self-taught individual among my colleagues later on." He began research on his doctoral thesis in 1904, but as a provincial school-teacher, pre-occupied by supporting a family and his aged parents, he did not complete it until 1924, when he was 50 years old.

Lefebvre's doctoral thesis, "The Peasants of the Nord Department and the French Revolution," was a detailed statistical study of the effect of the Revolution on the countryside. It was based on a thorough analysis of thousands of tax rolls, notarial records, and the registers of rural municipalities, whose materials he used to trace the effects of the abolition of feudalism and ecclesiastical tithes, the consequences of property transfers, the movement of the bourgeoisie into the countryside, and the destruction of collective rights in the peasant villages. He argued that the Revolution completed the breakdown of peasant solidarity and transformed the village community. It created a class of peasant proprietors attached to the gains of the Revolution and to the principle of private property.

After his thesis appeared, Lefebvre was named professor at Clermont-Ferrand. In 1928 Marc Bloch succeeded in having him brought to Strasbourg, and in 1935 he was named to Paris. He reached retirement age in 1941 but was invited by his colleagues to remain until the Liberation.

Lefebvre was a man of the left and called himself a Marxist. He considered Jules Guesde and Jean Jaurès to have had the greatest influence on his intellectual life. He had seen Jaurès only twice, from a distance, but the latter's *Socialist History of the Revolution* determined the direction of Lefebvre's research. Lefebvre's Marxism, however, was thoroughly tempered: "Marx clarified the dominant influence of the mode of production, but it was never his intention to exclude other factors, especially man . . . It is man who makes history."

Lefebvre showed the breadth of his views when he turned from statistical social history to social psychology. In *The Great Fear of 1789* (1932) he sought the causes of this movement in the peasant mind: the fear of "brigands," poverty, and unemployment, to which 1789 added a political crisis and fear of an "aristocratic plot." He also wrote several general histories of the Revolution, integrating the social and economic history of the period with the political. The most famous are *Napoleon* (1935), *1789* (1939), and *The French Revolution* (1951). He died in Paris on Aug. 28, 1959.

EWB

Lenin, Vladimir Ilich (1870–1924), Russian statesman. Vladimir Lenin was the creator of the Bolshevik party, the Soviet state, and the Third International. He was a successful revolutionary leader and an important contributor to revolutionary socialist theory.

Few events have shaped contemporary history as profoundly as the Russian Revolution and the Communist revolutions that followed it. Each one of them was made in the name of V. I. Lenin, his doctrines, and his political practices. Contemporary thinking about world affairs has been greatly influenced by Lenin's impetus and contributions. From Woodrow Wilson's Fourteen Points to today's preoccupation with wars of national liberation, imperialism, and decolonization, many important issues of contemporary social science were first raised or disseminated by Lenin; even some of the terms he used have entered into everyone's vocabulary. The very opposition to Lenin often takes Leninist forms.

Formative Years. V. I. Lenin was born in Simbirsk (today Ulianovsk) on April 10 (Old Style), 1870. His real family name was Ulianov, and his father, Ilia Nikolaevich Ulianov, was a high official in the tsarist educational bureaucracy who had risen into the nobility. Vladimir received the conventional education given to the sons of the Russian upper class but turned into a radical dissenter. One impetus to his conversion doubtless was the execution by hanging of his older brother Alexander in 1887; Alexander and a few associates had conspired to assassinate the Emperor. Lenin graduated from secondary school with high honors, enrolled at Kazan University, but was expelled after participating in a demonstration. He retired to the family estate but was permitted to continue his studies in absentia. He obtained a law degree in 1891.

When, in 1893, he moved to St. Petersburg, Lenin was already a Marxist and a revolutionary by profession, joining like-minded intellectuals in study groups, writing polemical pamphlets and articles, and seeking to organize workers. The St. Petersburg Union for the Struggle for the Liberation of Labor, which Lenin helped create, was one of the important nuclei of the Russian Marxist movement. The most important work from this period is a lengthy pamphlet, "What Are the 'Friends of the People,' and How Do They Fight against Social-Democracy?" In it Lenin presents the essentials of his entire outlook.

In 1897 Lenin was arrested, spent some months in jail, and was finally sentenced to 3 years of exile in the Siberian village of Shushenskoe. He was joined there by a fellow Marxist, Nadezhda Konstantinovna Krupskaya, whom he married in 1898. In his Siberian exile he produced a major study of the Russian economy, *The Development of Capitalism in Russia*, in which he sought to demonstrate that, despite its backwardness, the economy of his country had definitely transformed itself into a capitalist one. If Lenin had produced nothing else than this learned though controversial work, he would today be known as one of the leading Russian economists of his period.

Emigration to Europe.   Not long after his release from Siberia in the summer of 1900, Lenin moved to Europe, where he spent most of the next 17 years, moving from one country to another at frequent intervals, periods of feverish activity alternating with those of total frustration. His first step was to join the editorial board of *Iskra* (*The Spark*), then the central newspaper of Russian Marxism, where he served together with the top leaders of the movement. After parting from *Iskra,* he edited a succession of papers of his own and contributed to other socialist journals. His journalistic activity was closely linked with organizational work, partly because the underground organizational network within Russia to some extent revolved around the distribution of clandestine literature.

Organizational activity, in turn, was linked with the selection and training of personnel. For some time Lenin conducted a training school for Russian revolutionaries at Longjumeau, a suburb of Paris. A perennial problem was that of financing the movement and its leaders' activities in their European exile. Lenin personally could usually depend on financial support from his mother; but her pension could not pay for his political activities. Much of the early history of Russian Marxism can be understood only in the light of these pressing money problems.

His Thought.   A Marxist movement had developed in Russia only during the last decade of the 19th century as a response to the rapid growth of industry, urban centers, and a proletariat. Its first intellectual spokesmen were people who had turned away from populism (*narodnichestvo*), which they regarded as a failure. Instead of relying on the peasantry, they placed their hopes on the workers as the revolutionary class. Rejecting the village socialism preached by the Narodniks, they opted for industrialization, modernization, and Westernization. Their immediate aim they declared to be a bourgeois revolution which would transform Russia into a democratic republic.

In accepting this revolutionary scenario, Lenin added the important proviso that hegemony in the coming bourgeois revolution should remain with the proletariat as the most consistently revolutionary of all classes.

At the same time, Lenin, more than most Marxists, made a clear distinction between the workers'

movement, on the one hand, and the theoretical contribution to be made by intellectuals, on the other. Of the two, he considered the theoretical contribution the more important, the workers' movement being a merely spontaneous reaction to capitalist exploitation, whereas theory was an expression of consciousness, meaning science and rationality. Throughout his life Lenin insisted that consciousness must maintain leadership over spontaneity for revolutionary Marxism to succeed. This implies that the intellectual leaders must prepare the proletariat for its political tasks and must guide it in its action. Leadership and hierarchy thus become key concepts in the Leninist vocabulary, and the role and structure of the party must conform to this conception. The party is seen as the institutionalization of true consciousness. It must turn into the general staff of the revolution, subjecting the working class and indeed all its own members to command and discipline.

Lenin expressed these ideas in his important book *What's To Be Done?* (1902), the title of the work expressing his indebtedness to Nikolai Chernyshevsky. When, in 1903, the leaders of Russian Marxism met for the first important party congress, formally the Second Congress, these ideas clashed head on with the conception of a looser, more democratic workers' party advanced by Lenin's old friend Luli Martov. This disagreement over the nature and organization of the party was complicated by numerous other conflicts of view, and from its first important congress Russian Marxism emerged split into two factions. The one led by Lenin called itself the majority faction (*bolsheviki*); the other got stuck with the name of minority faction (*mensheviki*). Lenin's reaction to the split was expressed in his pamphlet "One Step Forward Two Steps Back," published in 1904.

Mensheviks and Bolsheviks disagreed not only over organizational questions but also over most other political problems, including the entire conception of a Marxist program for Russia and the methods to be employed by the party. Bolshevism, in general, stresses the need for revolution and the futility of incremental reforms; it emphasizes the goals of Marxism rather than the process, with its timetable, by which Marx thought the new order was to be reached; in comparison to menshevism it is impatient, pragmatic, and tough-minded.

The Revolution of 1905 surprised all Russian revolutionary leaders, including the Bolsheviks. Lenin managed to return to Russia only in November, when the defeat of the revolution was a virtual certainty. But he was among the last to give up. For many more months he urged his followers to renew their revolutionary enthusiasm and activities and to prepare for an armed uprising. For some time afterward the technology of revolutionary warfare became the focus of his interest. His militancy was expressed in an anti-Menshevik pamphlet published in 1905, "Two Tactics of Social-Democracy in the Democratic Revolution."

The major impact of the aborted revolution and its aftermath was a decided change in Lenin's attitude toward the peasantry. Lenin came to recognize it as a class in its own right—not just as a rural proletariat—with its own interests, and as a valuable ally for the revolutionary proletariat. His pamphlet "The Agrarian Question in the Russian Revolution of 1905–7" presents these new views in systematic fashion.

Bolshevism as an Independent Faction.

In the 12 years between the Revolution of 1905 and that of 1917, bolshevism, which had begun as a faction within the Russian Social-Democratic Workers party, gradually emerged as an independent party that had cut its ties with all other Russian Marxists. The process entailed prolonged and bitter polemics against Mensheviks as well as against all those who worked for a reconciliation of the factions. It involved fights over funds, struggles for control of newspapers, the development of rival organizations, and meetings of rival congresses. Disputes concerned many questions about the goals and strategies of the movement, the role of national liberation movements within the Marxist party, and also philosophic controversies. Lenin's contribution to this last topic was published in 1909, *Materialism and Empirio-criticism.*

Since about 1905 the international socialist movement had begun also to discuss the possibility of a major war breaking out. In its congresses of 1907 and 1912, resolutions were passed which condemned such wars in advance and pledged the parties of the proletariat not to support them. Lenin had wanted to go further than that. He had urged active opposition to the war effort and a transformation of any war into a proletarian revolution. He called his policy "revolutionary defeatism." When World War I broke out, most socialist leaders in the countries involved supported the war effort. For Lenin, this was proof that he and they shared no aims or views. The break between the two schools of Marxism had become irreconcilable.

During the war Lenin lived in Switzerland. He attended several conferences of radical socialists opposed to the war or even agreeing with Lenin's revolutionary defeatism. He read extensively on the Marxist theory of state and wrote a first draft for a book on the subject, *The State and Revolution.* He also immersed himself in literature dealing with contemporary world politics and wrote a book which may, in

the long run, be his most important one, *Imperialism: The Highest Stage of Capitalism* (1916), in which Marxism is effectively made applicable to the 20th century. By the beginning of 1917 he had fits of despondency and wrote to a close friend that he despaired of ever witnessing another revolution. This was about a month before the fall of tsarism.

Lenin in 1917.

It took a good deal of negotiation and courage for Lenin and a group of like-minded Russian revolutionaries to travel from Switzerland back to Russia through enemy country (Germany). Much has been made of Lenin's negotiations with an enemy power and of the fact that some Bolshevik activities were supported financially by German intelligence agencies. There is no convincing evidence, however, which might show that acceptance of funds from objectionable sources made Lenin an agent of these sources in any way. And from his point of view the source of aid was immaterial; what counted was the use to which it was put.

The man who returned to Russia in the famed "sealed train" in the spring of 1917 was of medium height, quite bald, except for the back of his head, with a reddish beard. The features of his face were arresting slanted eyes that looked piercingly at others, and high cheekbones under a towering forehead. The rest of his appearance was deceptively ordinary: a man of resolute movements clad quite conservatively in a middle-class suit.

Versed in many languages, Lenin spoke Russian with a slight speech defect but was a powerful orator in small groups as well as before mass audiences. A tireless worker, he made others work tirelessly. Self-effacing, he sought to compel his collaborators to devote every ounce of their energy to the revolutionary task at hand. He was impatient with any extraneous activities, including small talk and abstract theoretical discussions. Indeed, he was suspicious of intellectuals and felt most at home in the company of simple folk. Having been brought up in the tradition of the Russian nobility, Lenin loved hunting, hiking, horseback riding, boating, mushrooming, and the outdoor life in general. He sought to steel himself by systematic physical exercise and generally forbade himself those hobbies which he considered time-wasting or corrupting: chess, music, and companionship. While his life-style was that of a dedicated professional revolutionary, his tastes in art, morals, and manners were rather conventional.

Once he had returned to Russia, Lenin worked feverishly and relentlessly to utilize the revolutionary situation that had been created by the fall of tsarism so as to convert it into a proletarian revolution which would bring his own party into power. These were the crucial 6 months of his life, but space does not permit a detailed account of his activities in the period. The result of his activities is well known: Opinions in Russia quickly became more and more polarized. Moderate forces found themselves less and less able to maintain even the pretense of control. In the end, the so-called provisional government, then headed by Kerensky, simply melted away, and power literally fell into the hands of the Bolsheviks. As a result of this so-called October Revolution, Lenin found himself not only the leader of his party but also the chairman of the Council of People's Commissars (equivalent to prime minister) of the newly proclaimed Russian Socialist Federative Soviet Republic.

Ruler of Russia. During the first years of Lenin's rule as dictator of Russia, the major task he faced was that of establishing his and his party's authority in the country. Most of his policies can be understood in this light, even though he alienated some elements in the population while satisfying others. Examples are the expropriation of landholdings for distribution to the peasants, the separate peace treaty with Germany, and the nationalization of banks and industrial establishments.

From 1918 to 1921 a fierce civil war raged which the Bolsheviks finally won against seemingly overwhelming odds. During the civil war Lenin tightened his party's dictatorship and eventually eliminated all rival parties from the political arena. A spirited defense of his dictatorship can be found in his "The Proletarian Revolution and the Renegade Kautsky" (1918), in which he answers criticism from some more moderate Marxists. Lenin had to create an entirely new political system with the help of inexperienced personnel; he was heading a totally exhausted economy and had to devise desperate means for mobilizing people for work. Simultaneously he created the Third (Communist) International and vigorously promoted the spread of the revolution to other countries; and meanwhile he had to cope with dissent among his own party comrades, some of whom criticized him from the left. The pamphlet "Left-wing Communism: An Infantile Disorder" is a response to this criticism.

When the civil war had been won and the regime established firmly, the economy was ruined, and much of the population was bitterly opposed to the regime. At this point Lenin reversed many of his policies and instituted a trenchant reform, called the New Economic Policy. It signified a temporary retreat from the goal of establishing communism at once and a resolve to make do with the social forces available: the

Communist party declared itself ready to coexist and cooperate with features of the past, such as free enterprise, capitalist institutions, and capitalist states across the borders. For the time being, the Soviet economy would be a mixture of capitalist and socialist features. The stress of the party's policies would be on economic reconstruction and on the education of a peasant population for life in the 20th century. In the long run, Lenin hoped that both these policies would make the blessings of socialism obvious to all, so that the country would gradually grow into socialism. The wariness, the caution, the fear of excessive haste and impatience which Lenin showed in the years 1921–1923 are expressed only inadequately in the last few articles he wrote, such as "On Cooperation," "How We Must Reorganize the Workers and Peasants Inspectorate," and "Better Less but Better."

In 1918 an assassin wounded Lenin; he recovered but may have suffered some lasting damage. On May 26, 1922, he suffered a serious stroke from which he recovered after some weeks, only to suffer a second stroke on December 16. He was so seriously incapacitated that he could participate in political matters only intermittently and feebly. An invalid, he lived in a country home at Gorki, near Moscow, where he died on Jan. 21, 1924. His body was preserved and is on view in the Lenin Mausoleum outside the walls of the Moscow Kremlin.

EWB

Leo XIII (1810–1903), pope from 1878–1903. Leo XIII is known for his social reforms and his recognition of the rights of the worker. During his reign the Roman Catholic Church achieved an international prestige it had not enjoyed since the Middle Ages.

Vincenzo Gioacchino Pecci, who became Pope Leo XIII, was born on March 2, 1810, in Carpineto, Italy. He was educated by the Jesuits at Viterbo and in Rome. After becoming a priest on Dec. 31, 1837, he was named apostolic delegate to Benevento. After a period as delegate to Perugia, he was appointed apostolic nuncio to Brussels in January 1843 and became an archbishop. Already at Perugia he had shown himself to be a social reformer. At Louvain he mediated in the bitter controversy between the Jesuits and the university. Reappointed to Perugia in 1846, he was made cardinal in 1853 by Pius IX. He spent the next 25 years restoring churches, promoting education of the clergy, and advocating social reform.

Political Revival. Leo became pope at a low ebb in the prestige of the papacy. The Pope had been a "prisoner" in the Vatican since 1870. Tension existed between the Vatican and most European governments. There were no strong Catholic political parties in Europe. The democracies and the Vatican traded no friendship. Within the Church there existed a polarization because of the authoritarian rule of Pius IX. Between the Italian state and the Vatican there were the utmost frigidity and ill feeling.

Elected pope at the age of 68, Leo was not expected to hold the post long or to make any great changes. His pontificate, however, lasted 25 years. One of his first undertakings was to offset the secularizing philosophies of governments imbued with anticlerical, antipapal, and anti-Church policies. It was the age of the *Kulturkampf* in Germany and of governmental anticlericalism in France, Belgium, and the Netherlands.

Leo's methods were in the main conciliatory and quite simple in intent. His strength lay in his obvious and proven enthusiasm for learning, for scientific achievement, and for a relatively open-minded discussion with all comers. As part of his program he set out to strengthen the Catholic political parties in Europe. His policies bore fruits within his lifetime, and their acceptance was aided mightily by the ever-growing threat of socialism and an early form of communism which had started with the Communist Manifesto of Friedrich Engels and Karl Marx in 1848. Thus Germany's chancellor Otto von Bismarck came to see the newly revived Catholic Center party as a bulwark against socialism. Extreme anticlerical legislation was repealed by his government by 1887. In 1881 the Prussian government had reappointed an envoy to the Vatican (the first since 1874). Similarly, in Belgium, Catholics gained political power and helped mitigate anticlericalism and secularizing policies. In France, Leo was less successful. His appeal was laced with too political a motivation, which divided Catholic supporters and created antagonism lasting well beyond Leo's death.

Italian Policy. For Italy, Leo adopted a policy marked by an intransigence which produced more or less the same bitter fruits as in France. Leo hoped Germany would force a solution of the "Roman question" and restore the papacy to a position of temporal power. But the Triple Alliance between Germany, Austria, and Italy dashed these aspirations. Leo could expect no help from France, where his policies had, rather, fomented antipapal feeling. When Mariano Rampolla became secretary of state for Italy in 1887, he sought the friendship of the democracies, the United States, and France particularly. Leo was much more in favor of a monarchical paternalism than of a democratic form of government; he feared the latter

as an open door to anticlerical and secular policies. In Italy, Leo allowed Catholics to participate in municipal politics, but he maintained the traditional ban on all Catholic participation in national politics almost to the end of his life. In his encyclical letter *Immortale Dei* (Nov. 1, 1885) Leo denounced democracy as irreconcilable with the authority of the Church, although he did allow that with proper conditions Catholics could work within such a democratic framework. In *Libertas praestantissimum* (June 20, 1888) he declared personal liberty and freedom to be a legitimate political goal, but he tied the success of such a goal to adherence to Roman Catholicism. Leo sought, in other words, to reconcile the liberalism of his day with traditional Roman Catholic teaching. Although he did not succeed, he laid the foundations for a later development in the mid-20th century. The policies of John XXIII, for instance, reflected Leo's thoughts but took some essential steps forward.

Diplomatic Relations. On the general plane of diplomatic relations, Leo was successful. He established cordial relations with Spain, Austria, Great Britain, Switzerland, Germany, the United States, and many South American countries. The tension between the Vatican and Russia was relaxed. His centralization policies included a new organization of pilgrimages to Rome, more frequent audiences for the visiting faithful as well as for non-Catholics, an expanding panache of papal ceremonial and glory, and the encouragement of cordial ties of collaboration and mutual respect between Catholic academic institutions and corresponding institutions in Europe and the Americas.

Social Reform. Leo is remembered more for his encyclical letter *Rerum novarum* (May 15, 1891) than for many other acts. The letter was part of his attempt to halt the drift of working people and industrial labor away from his Church. In part a rather dramatic departure from traditional policies of the Vatican and the Roman Catholic Church's outlook, the letter vindicated for workers and poor people the rights which never before had received such papal or ecclesiastical sanction.

The minimum standards Leo demanded for workers, such as a means of frugal sustenance and a minimum wage, now seem to be grossly underestimated. But in Leo's day, they represented violent if well-timed departures from the traditional norms. The letter's value lay much more in its accurate prediction of social reforms which, if implemented, might have averted such later developments as the Russian Revolution and the rise of Soviet bolshevism.

In *Rerum novarum* Leo also defended the rights of the family and the right to private property, themes which later became acute when communism spread throughout Europe and these rights were attacked and encroached upon by a dictatorial statism. His recommendations for effective legislation, his approval of labor unions and cooperative organizations, and his lauding of labor and its fruits as worthwhile and as dignified human elements helped shape the policies of many labor movements throughout the world. Concretely, *Rerum novarum* strongly influenced the formation of Catholic political parties and labor syndicates outside Italy and Spain, thus combating the spread of Marxism.

Leo also strengthened Rome's ties with Eastern-rite churches and carried the centralization policies of his predecessors to a considerable length. He relaxed the intransigence of his predecessor, Pius IX, by opening the Vatican archives and library to qualified historians of all faiths.

It would be a mistake, however, to assess Leo's pontificate as a radical or even a strong departure from that of his predecessors. He built on the strong centralization of Pius IX, who, although he failed in international politics, left Leo a strongly united Church and a store of spiritual resources. When Leo died on July 20, 1903, he enjoyed a vast personal prestige; his Church was enthusiastic for the papacy; but Leo, like his predecessor, had not been able to adapt Church structure and thought to the new realities of the emergent 20th century.

EWB

Leopold II (1835–1909), king of the Belgians from 1865–1909. Leopold II founded the Congo Free State.

Leopold was born in Brussels on April 9, 1835. He was the second child of the reigning Belgian monarch, Leopold I, and his second wife, Louise, the daughter of King Louis Philippe of France. His elder brother had died a few months after his birth in 1834, and thus Leopold was heir to the throne. When he was 9 years old, Leopold received the title of Duke of Brabant.

Leopold's public career began in 1855, when he became a member of the Belgian Senate. That same year Leopold began to urge Belgium's acquisition of colonies. In 1853 he married Marie Henriette, daughter of the Austrian archduke Joseph. Four children were born of this marriage; three were daughters, and the only son, Leopold, died when he was 9 years old.

In 1865 Leopold became king. His reign was marked by a number of major political developments. The Liberals governed Belgium from 1857 to 1880 and during their final year in power legislated the Frère-Orban Law of 1879. This law created free, secular, compulsory primary schools supported by the state and withdrew all state support from Roman Catholic primary schools. In 1880 the Catholic party obtained a parliamentary majority and 4 years later restored state support to Catholic schools. In 1885 various socialist and social democratic groups drew together and formed the Labor party. Increasing social unrest and the rise of the Labor party forced the adoption of universal male suffrage in 1893.

In 1876 Leopold organized, with the help of Henry Stanley, the International Association for the Exploration and Civilization of the Congo. The Congo Free State was established under Leopold II's personal rule at a European conference on African affairs held in Berlin in 1884–1885. Leopold then amassed a huge personal fortune by exploiting the Congo. His rule there, however, was subject to severe criticism, especially from British sources. Criticism from both Social Catholics and the Labor party at home forced Leopold to give the Congo to the Belgian nation. The Congo Free State was transformed into a Belgian colony under parliamentary control in 1908.

On Dec. 17, 1909, Leopold II died at Laeken, and the Belgian crown passed to Albert, the son of Leopold's brother, Philip, Count of Flanders.

EWB

Lévi-Strauss, Claude Gustave (1908–), French social anthropologist. Claude Lévi-Strauss became a leading scholar in the structural approach to social anthropology.

Claude Lévi-Strauss was born on November 28, 1908, in Brussels, Belgium, of a cultured Jewish family. He grew up in France, attended a lycée in Paris, and studied philosophy at the Sorbonne, University of Paris. After holding several provincial teaching posts, he became interested in anthropology and accepted an appointment as professor of sociology at São Paulo University, Brazil (1935–1939), which enabled him to do field research among Brazil's Indian tribes.

Lévi-Strauss returned to wartime France and served in the army (1939–1941). He taught in New York City at the New School for Social Research and at the École Libre des Hautes Études (1942–1945). He was also cultural attaché in the French embassy (1946–1947).

Back in France, Lévi-Strauss was associate director of the Musée de l'Homme, director of the École Pratique des Hautes Études, and editor of *Man: Review of French Anthropology*. From 1960 he was professor of social anthropology, professor of comparative religions of nonliterate people, and director of the Laboratory of Social Anthropology at the College of France.

Lévi-Strauss's fame began with his book *Tristes Tropiques* (*A World on the Wane,* 1961). It is partly biographical, partly a philosophical reflection on travel, and mainly a systematic account of four primitive South American Indian tribes. In this and his next influential book, *The Savage Mind* (1966), he expressed his belief that in their potential all men are intellectually equal. Instead of primitive man's being frozen in his culture, he wrote, "A primitive people is not a backward or retarded people; indeed it may possess a genius for invention or action that leaves the achievements of civilized peoples far behind."

Citing examples, Lévi-Strauss argued that primitive man's conceptual mental structures, though of a different order from those of advanced man, are just as rich, utilitarian, theoretical, complex, and scientific. There is no primitive mind or modern mind but "mind-as-such," in which is locked a structural way of thinking that brings order out of chaos and enables man to develop social systems to suit his needs. Man's mental structures and ways of achieving order are derived as much from primitive magic as from Western science, as much from primitive myth as from Western literature, and as much from primitive totemism as from Western morality and religion.

Lévi-Strauss's thesis, which excited world attention, is that if social scientists can understand man's mental structures, they can then build a study of man which is as scientific as the laws of gravity. If order exists anywhere, says Lévi-Strauss as a structuralist, then order exists everywhere, even in the brain.

Lévi-Strauss's search for the common denominator of human thought derives from structural linguistics, a 20th-century science which set out to uncover the possible relationships between the origins of human speech and the origins of culture. He goes beyond language in adding as concepts for social order such activities as music, art, ritual, myth, religion, literature, cooking, tatooing, intermarriage, the kinship system, and the barter of goods and services. He sees each as another related way by which a society maintains itself. Man's mental structures in bringing order out of chaos, no matter how divergent his patterns may seem in old and new cultures, may derive from a common mental code.

The work of Lévi-Strauss seeks to stimulate thinking and research on breaking the mystery of this code. His popularity rests on his belief that there are no superior cultures, that man acts according to a logical structure in his brain, and that once the code of this logical structure can be discovered, the human sciences can be as scientific as the natural sciences.

Lévi-Strauss was awarded the Wenner-Gren Foundation's Viking Fund Medal for 1966 and the Erasmus Prize in 1975. He has been awarded several honorary doctorate degrees from prestigious institutions such as Oxford, Yale, Harvard, and Columbia. He has also held several academic memberships including the National Academy of Sciences, the American Academy and Institute of Arts and Letters, the American Academy of Arts and Sciences, and the American Philosophical Society.

EWB

Lévy-Bruhl, Lucien (1857–1939), French philosopher, sociologist, and anthropologist. Lucien Lévy-Bruhl concerned himself primarily with the nonrational belief systems of primitive man.

Lucien Lévy-Bruhl was born in Paris on April 10, 1857. He attended the Lycée Charlemagne, pursuing studies in music, philosophy, and natural science, and graduated from the École Normale Supérieure in philosophy in 1879. He taught philosophy at Poitiers and Amiens before he attended the University of Paris to pursue his doctorate in 1884. He taught in Paris until his appointment to the Sorbonne in 1896 as titular professor of the history of modern philosophy. Lévy-Bruhl's scholarly work began with a history of modern French philosophy in 1889; a book on German philosophy (since Gottfried Wilhelm von Leibniz) appeared in 1890, one on Jacobean philosophy in 1894, and one on Comtean philosophy in 1900. *Ethics and Moral Science* (1902) marked the beginning of Lévy-Bruhl's anthropological interests. He recognized the impossibility of an absolute ethic because of the incommensurability of thought systems in different cultures, and he called for scientific study of the known range of moral systems, including the primitive. This book was probably influential in the appointment of Lévy-Bruhl to a chair in the history of modern philosophy at the Sorbonne in 1904.

Although Lévy-Bruhl remained more interested in primitive thought than in social institutions, his work moved from philosophy toward sociology under the influence of the Durkheimian sociologists. In 1925 he, along with Marcel Mauss and Paul Rivet, founded the Institute of Ethnology at the Sorbonne, dedicated to the memory of Émile Durkheim, who had died in 1917. Lévy-Bruhl, however, disagreed with some tenets of Durkheim's methodology, particularly the rationality of primitive man. He thus resigned from the institute and the Sorbonne in 1927 to devote himself to writing and travel.

Lévy-Bruhl wrote six books elaborating his concept of the nature of the primitive mind: *Mental Functions in Primitive Societies* (1910), *Primitive Mentality* (1922), *The Soul of the Primitive* (1928), *The Supernatural and the Nature of the Primitive Mind* (1931), *Primitive Mythology* (1935), and *The Mystic Experience and Primitive Symbolism* (1938). Never a fieldworker, he had access to more adequate descriptions of primitive cultures at the end of his life. He rejected some evolutionary implications of his earlier formulation of civilized and "primitive," or "prelogical," mentalities as polar and irreconcilable types. Later books dealt more fully with intermediate types. Posthumously published notebooks (1949) indicated his willingness to compromise even on the term "prelogical."

Lévy-Bruhl was aware of similarities between primitive and civilized thought but, in response to previous attributions of extreme rationality to primitive man, preferred to stress differences. Although postulation of a "primitive mentality" at first glance relegates primitive man to an inferior cultural status, Lévy-Bruhl was more concerned to demonstrate that primitive cultures must be studied in terms of their own categories. Though this view should encourage extensive fieldwork, his equation of all primitive thought patterns in practice minimized descriptive efforts.

After his retirement Lévy-Bruhl lectured at Harvard, Johns Hopkins, and the University of California. He died in Paris on March 13, 1939.

EWB

Livingstone, David (1813–1873), Scottish physician and explorer. David Livingstone was possibly the greatest of all African missionaries, explorers, and antislavery advocates.

Before Livingstone, Africa's interior was almost entirely unknown to the outside world. Vague notions prevailed about its geography, fauna, flora, and human life. Livingstone dispelled much of this ignorance and opened up Africa's interior to further exploration.

David Livingstone was born on March 19, 1813, in Blantyre, coming from Highlanders on his father's side and Lowlanders on his mother's. The Livingstones were poor, so at the age of 10 David worked in the textile mills 14 hours a day, studying at night and on weekends. After some hesitation he joined the Congregational Church of his father. In 1836 he entered the University of Glasgow to study medicine and theology, working during holidays to support himself. In 1840 he received his medical degree, was ordained, and was accepted by the London Missionary Society. He had been influenced by Robert Moffat and the first Niger expedition to apply for service in Africa.

After a 98-day voyage Livingstone arrived in Cape Town on March 15, 1841. He reached Moffat's station, Kuruman, at the time the outpost of European penetration in southern Africa, on July 31.

But Livingstone soon moved north to the Khatla people. It was here he permanently injured his left shoulder in an encounter with a lion. In 1845 he married Mary Moffat and settled farther north at Kolobeng. From here he set out with two friends, Oswell and Murray, to cross the Kalahari Desert, discovering Lake Ngami on Aug. 1, 1849. On another journey, in 1851, Livingstone and Oswell discovered the Zambezi River.

Crossing the Continent. In April 1852 at Cape Town, Livingstone saw his wife and four children off to England. Returning to Kolobeng, he found that some Boers had destroyed his station, the last settled home he ever had. In December he set out to walk to the west coast. He reached Linyanti, in Barotseland, where Chief Sekeletu of the Makololo gave him 27 men to go with him. They walked through hostile, unknown country, and after incredible hardship he reached Luanda on May 31, 1854.

The British consul there nursed him back to health, but Livingstone refused passage back to England. He had not found the hoped-for waterway, and he wanted to return the Makololo to their chief. Having been reequipped by the British and Portuguese in Luanda, he left on Sept. 19, 1854, but reached Linyanti only on Sept. 11, 1855. Sickness, rain, flooded rivers, and hostile tribes delayed him and forced him to spend all his equipment. He was given fresh supplies and men by Sekeletu. On November 15 he reached the spectacular falls on the Zambezi, which the Africans called the "Smoke which Thunders" but which Livingstone named Victoria Falls in honor of the queen of England. He finally reached Quelimane on the east coast on May 20, 1856. For the first time Africa had been crossed from coast to coast. He waited 6 months for a ship which returned him to England.

Livingstone was now a famous man. In 1855 the Royal Geographical Society had awarded him the Gold Medal; now at a special meeting they made him a fellow of the society. The London Missionary Society honored him; he was received by Queen Victoria; and the universities of Glasgow and Oxford conferred upon him honorary doctorates. In November 1857 his first book, the tremendously successful *Missionary Travels and Researches in South Africa,* was published.

Livingstone caught the imagination not only of England but the world. He opened the eyes of the world to the tremendous potentialities of Africa for human development, trade, and Christian missions; he also disclosed the horrors of the East African slave trade.

Zambezi Expeditions. With mutual regrets he severed his ties with the London Missionary Society, but the British government agreed to support an expedition to explore the Zambezi River led by Livingstone, who was made a British consul for the purpose. He sailed for Africa in March 1858.

The Zambezi expedition met with many difficulties. It was marred by friction among the Europeans, mainly caused by Livingstone's brother Charles. The steam launch *Ma Robert* proved unsuitable, and the Kebrabasa Rapids killed the dream of Zambezi as an inland waterway. The *Ma Robert* was taken into the Shire River but was blocked by the Murchison Falls.

The explorers learned of the existence of two lakes to the north, and on a second journey they discovered Lake Chilwa on April 16, 1859. On a third journey up the Shire they left the boat, walked 3 weeks overland, and discovered Lake Nyasa on Sept. 17, 1859. A new steamer, the *Pioneer,* arrived in 1861, by which they explored the Ruvuma River in an effort to bypass the Portuguese. Later they managed to get the *Pioneer* to Lake Nyasa, which they explored but did not circumnavigate.

In January 1862 a third boat, the *Lady Nyassa,* arrived together with Mrs. Livingstone, giving him fresh hope. But Mary Livingstone died from fever at the end of April. The *Lady Nyassa* never reached the lake, and finally the British government recalled the expedition. The Royal Navy took over the *Pioneer* at Quelimane, but Livingstone took the *Lady Nyassa* on a daring voyage to Bombay, India, where it was sold. In July 1864 Livingstone reached England.

In 1865 Livingstone published his second successful book, *Narrative of an Expedition to the Zambesi and Its Tributaries,* and the Royal Geographical Society equipped him for another expedition to explore the watersheds of Africa. He reached Zanzibar in January 1866 and began exploring the territory near Lakes Nyasa and Tanganyika. On Nov. 8, 1867, he discovered Lake Mweru and the source of the Lualaba River. On July 18, 1868, he found Lake Bangweulu. In March 1869 he reached Ujiji only to discover that there was no mail and that his supplies had been stolen. He was sick, depressed, and exhausted, but in September he set out again, witnessing at Nyangwe the horrors of the Arab slave trade. He returned to Ujiji in October 1871.

Search for Livingstone. Europe and America thought that the lonely man was lost, so the *London Daily Telegraph* and the *New York Herald* sent Henry Stanley to search for him. Stanley found Livingstone at Ujiji and stayed 4 months. Unable to persuade Livingstone to return to England, Stanley reequipped him and departed from him near Tabora on March 14, 1872. In August, Livingstone was on his way again. Near Bangweulu he got bogged down in swamps but finally reached Chitambo's village. On May 1, 1873, his servants found him in his tent kneeling in prayer at the bedside. He was dead. His men buried his heart but embalmed the body and carried it to the mission of the Holy Ghost fathers at Bagamoyo. It reached England, where it was identified by the lion wound in the left shoulder. On April 18, 1874, Livingstone was buried in great honor in London's Westminster Abbey.

Livingstone's Influence. No one made as many geographical discoveries in Africa as Livingstone, and his numerous scientific observations were quickly recognized. He was right in using quinine as an ingredient for the cure of malaria.

Regarding himself as a missionary to the end, Livingstone inspired many new enterprises such as the Makololo, Ndebele, and Tanganyika missions of his own society, the Universities' Mission to Central Africa, and the Livingstonia Mission of the Church of Scotland. His life caught the imagination of the Christian world.

Livingstone drew the world's attention to the great evil of the African slave traffic. He taught the world to see the African as "wronged" rather than depraved, and the world did not rest until slavery was outlawed. He saw the cure for it in Christianity and commerce and also inspired enterprises such as the African Lakes Company. But in his wake came also European settlement and the colonial scramble for Africa with all its ambiguities.

Although the Zambezi expedition proved that Livingstone was no ideal leader for white men, he nevertheless greatly influenced men who knew him, such as Stanley, John Kirk, and James Stewart. He made a lasting impression on the Africans he met, which was amply attested to by those who followed him. His peaceful intentions and moral courage were immediately recognized.

EWB

Lloyd George, David (1863–1945), English statesman. The 1st Earl Lloyd George of Dwyfor, David Lloyd George, was prime minister from 1916 to 1922. Although he was one of Britain's most successful wartime leaders, he contributed greatly to the decline of the Liberal party.

It has been said of David Lloyd George that he "was the first son of the people to reach supreme power." His life is representative of the transition in leadership from the landed aristocracy of the 19th century to the mass democracy of the 20th. But his career is almost unique in the manner in which he attained power and held it by his indifference to tradition and precedent, by his reliance on instinct rather than on reason, and by the force of his will and of his capacity despite personal unpopularity.

Lloyd George, as in later days he would have his surname, was born on Jan. 17, 1863, in Manchester, the son of William George, a schoolmaster of Welsh background, and of Elizabeth Lloyd. William George died in 1864, and Richard Lloyd, brother of the widow, took his sister and the three children into the family home at Llanystumdwy, Wales. From his uncle, a shoemaker by trade, a Baptist preacher, and an active Liberal in politics, young David absorbed much of the evangelical ethic and the radical ideal. He went to the village school. Barred from the Nonconformist ministry because it was unpaid, and excluded from teaching because that would have required joining the Church of England, he was articled, at age 16, to a firm of solicitors in Portmadoc. He soon began writing articles and making speeches on land reform, temperance, and religion. He often preached in the chapel. In 1884 he passed the Law Society examinations. He opened his office at Criccieth, helped organize the farmers' union, and was active in anti-tithe agitation. In 1888 he married Margaret Owen, the daughter of a well-to-do farmer; they had five children.

Early Political Career.   Lloyd George's activity in the politics of the new county council (created 1888) led to his election in 1890 as the member of Parliament for Caernarvon Borough, which he was to represent for the next 55 years. His maiden speech was on temperance, but his primary interest was in home rule for Wales. He led a revolt within the Liberal party against Lord Rosebery in 1894–1895 and successfully carried through its second reading a bill for the disestablishment of the Church of England in Wales. The Conservatives returned in 1895, and the bill could go no further. But his reputation was made by his bitter and uncompromising opposition to the Boer War as morally and politically unjustified. The Liberals were badly split, but in the reconstruction of the party after the war, the "center point of power," declared a Liberal journalist, was in Lloyd George and other young radicals.

In the strong Liberal Cabinet formed in 1905, Lloyd George became president of the Board of Trade.

He pushed through legislation on the merchant marine, patents, and copyrights. A chaos of private dock companies in London was replaced by a unified Port of London Authority. The Welsh agitator had become the responsible minister and brilliant administrator.

Chancellor of the Exchequer.   When Herbert Asquith became prime minister in 1908, Lloyd George was promoted to chancellor of the Exchequer. To pay for old-age pensions as well as for dreadnoughts, he presented in April 1909 a revolutionary "People's Budget" with an innovative tax on unearned increment in land values and a sharp rise in income tax and death duties. He lashed out, in his celebrated Limehouse speech, against landlords waxing rich on rising land values. When the Lords obstructed, spurred on by Arthur Balfour, the Conservative leader, he said that the House of Lords was not the watchdog of the Constitution; it was only "Mr. Balfour's poodle." The Lords' delay in accepting the budget precipitated the controversy with the Commons over the Lords' veto. At a secret conference of party leaders Lloyd George suggested a nonpartisan Cabinet, interesting in view of his later reliance on coalition.

Eventually the Lords' veto was limited, and Lloyd George proceeded with the National Insurance Act, providing protection against sickness, disability, and unemployment in certain trades. But in so doing he encountered charges of "demagoguery." His future was unclear. His popularity was undoubtedly increased by his Mansion House speech in 1911. Germany had sent a gunboat to Agadir in French-controlled Morocco, and Britain was committed to supporting the French interest. Lloyd George, the man of peace, startled the world by warning Germany that Britain would not harbor interference with its legitimate interests. In the next year came the Marconi scandal, involving Lloyd George and other ministers who had invested in the American Marconi Company just when its British associate was contracting with the government for development of radiotelegraph. Though a motion of censure was defeated, Lloyd George and the others remained suspect.

Prime Minister.   In August 1914 the Cabinet was divided on the war issues. Lloyd George at first wavered but with violation of Belgian neutrality aligned himself against Germany. His reputation soared in the newly created Ministry of Munitions, to which he was appointed in the coalition government organized by Asquith in May 1915. Lloyd George settled labor disputes, constructed factories, and soon replaced serious shortages with an output exceeding demand. When Lord Kitchener was lost at sea in June

1916, Lloyd George became minister of war. "The fight must be to the finishto a knockout blow," he declared. In such direction, however, Asquith's rather aimless leadership did not seem to be moving.

In December 1916 Asquith, faced by a revolt from Conservatives along with Lloyd George, resigned. Lloyd George succeeded. In the new War Cabinet of five, the "Welsh Wizard" was the only Liberal, but he "towered like a giant." His role is controversial, but he galvanized the war effort, and it is generally accepted that without him England could hardly have emerged from the conflict so successfully.

At the end of the war, despite the defection of Asquith and his Liberal following, Lloyd George, with strong Conservative support, decided to continue the coalition. He received overwhelming endorsement in the election of 1918. At the peace conference he mediated successfully between the idealism of U.S. president Woodrow Wilson and the punitive terms sought by French premier Georges Clemenceau. And he led in the formation of the Irish Free State in 1921, though losing Conservative support in the process.

But at home Lloyd George's oratory about constructing "a new society" came to naught; he did not have Conservative backing for reform, and his own efforts were equivocal. Conservative disenchantment reached the breaking point in the Turkish crisis of 1922—he was pro-Greek, the Conservatives pro-Turk. The Conservatives in the Commons voted, more than 2 to 1, to sever ties. Lloyd George was only 59, but his ministerial career was over. He never reestablished himself in the Liberal party, which, now divided between his supporters and those of Asquith, and suffering defection to Labor of its leadership and its rank and file, disintegrated beyond recovery. Lloyd George attempted a personal comeback in 1929, espousing massive programs of state action in the economy. His popular vote (25 percent) was respectable, but in the Commons the Liberals remained a poor third. He relinquished party leadership, and his power in the Commons was reduced to his family party of four.

Later Years. Lloyd George's influence in the 1930s was peripheral. Distrusted in many quarters, he was listened to but little heeded. He attacked the Hoare-Laval bargain over Abyssinia. But his misgivings over Versailles led to his respect for Hitler's Germany; in 1936 he visited the Führer at Berchtesgaden. As the crisis deepened, Lloyd George urged an unequivocal statement of Britain's intentions. In his last important intervention in the Commons, in May 1939, he called for the resignation of Neville Chamberlain, who did give way to Winston Churchill.

Lloyd George had urged serious consideration of the peace feelers Hitler had broadcast in October 1939, after his conquest of Poland. In July 1940, while preparing for an invasion of England, Hitler made further overtures of peace and toyed with the idea of restoring the Duke of Windsor to the throne and Lloyd George to 10 Downing Street.

Lloyd George's last years were largely spent in his home at Churt in Surrey. His wife died in 1941, and 2 years later he married Frances Louise Stevenson, his personal secretary for 30 years. In 1944 they left Churt to reside in Wales near his boyhood home. On Dec. 31, 1944, he was elevated to the peerage. He died on March 26, 1945.

EWB

Locke, John (1632–1704), English philosopher and political theorist. John Locke began the empiricist tradition and thus initiated the greatest age of British philosophy. He attempted to center philosophy on an analysis of the extent and capabilities of the human mind.

John Locke was born on Aug. 29, 1632, in Wrington, in Somerset, where his mother's family resided. She died during his infancy, and Locke was raised by his father, who was an attorney in the small town of Pensford near Bristol. John was tutored at home because of his always delicate health and the outbreak of civil war in 1642. When he was 14, he entered Westminster School, where he remained for 6 years. He then went to Christ Church, Oxford. In 1658 he was elected a senior student at his college. In this capacity he taught Greek and moral philosophy. Under conditions at the time he would have had to be ordained to retain his fellowship. Instead he changed to another faculty, medicine, and eventually received a license to practice. During the same period Locke made the acquaintance of Robert Boyle, the distinguished scientist and one of the founders of the Royal Society, and, under Boyle's direction, took up study of natural science. Finally, in 1668, Locke was made a fellow of the Royal Society.

In 1665 Locke traveled to the Continent as secretary to the English ambassador to the Brandenburg court. Upon his return to England he chanced to medically attend Lord Ashley, 1st Earl of Shaftesbury, and later lord chancellor of England. Their friendship and lifelong association drew Locke into political affairs. He attended Shaftesbury as physician and adviser, and in this latter capacity Locke drafted *The Fundamental Constitutions of Carolina* and served as secretary to the Board of Trade. In 1676 Locke went to France for his health. An inheritance from his father made him financially independent, and he remained in Montpellier for 3 years.

Locke rejoined Shaftesbury's service, and when the latter fled to Holland, the philosopher followed. He remained in exile from 1683 to 1689, and during these years he was deprived of his studentship by express order of Charles III. Most of his important writings were composed during this period. After the Glorious Revolution of 1689 Locke returned to England and later served with distinction as a commissioner of trade until 1700. He spent his retirement at Oates in Essex as the guest of the Mashams. Lady Masham was the daughter of Ralph Cudworth, the philosopher. Locke died there on Oct. 28, 1704.

Major Works. Locke, by virtue of his temperament and mode of existence, was a man of great circumspection. None of his major writings was published until he was nearly 60. In 1690 he brought out his major works: *Two Treatises* and the *Essay Concerning Human Understanding*. But the four books of the *Essay* were the culmination of 20 years of intellectual labor. He relates that, together with a few friends, probably in 1670, a discussion arose concerning the basis of morality and religion. The conclusion was that they were unable to resolve the question until an investigation had been made to see "what objects our understandings were or were not fitted to deal with." Thus the aim of this work is "to inquire into the origin, certainty, and extent of human knowledge, together with the grounds of belief, opinion, and assent."

The procedure employed is what he called the "historical, plain method," which consists of observations derived from external sensations and the internal processes of reflection or introspection. This psychological definition of experience as sensation and reflection shifted the focus of philosophy from an analysis of reality to an exploration of the mind. The new perspective was Locke's major contribution, and it dominated European thought for at least 2 centuries. But if knowledge consists entirely of experience, then the objects of cognition are ideas. The term "idea" was ambiguously defined by Locke as "whatsoever is the object of the understanding when a man thinks." This broad use means that sensations, memories, imaginings, and feelings as well as concepts are ideas insofar as they are mental. The danger of Locke's epistemology is the inherent skepticism contained in a technique which describes what is "in" the mind. For if everything is an idea, then it is difficult to distinguish between true and false, real and imaginary, impressed sensations and expressed concepts. Thus Locke, and the subsequent history of philosophy, had to wrestle with the dilemma that a psychological de-

scription of the origin of ideas seriously undermines the extent of their objective validity.

Nonetheless the intention of the *Essay* was positive in that Locke wished to establish the dependence of all human knowledge upon everyday experience or sensation. The alternative theory of innate ideas is vigorously attacked. Although it is not historically certain whether anyone seriously maintained such a doctrine, Locke's general criticism lends indirect support to an experiential view of knowledge. Innatism can be understood in a naive way to mean that there are ideas of which we are fully conscious at birth or which are universally acknowledged, so that the mind possesses a disposition to think in terms of certain ideas. The first position is refuted by observation of children, and the second by the fact that there are no acknowledged universal ideas to which everyone agrees. The sophisticated version falls into contradiction by maintaining that we are conscious of an unconscious disposition.

Theory of Knowledge. Having refuted the a priori, or nonexperiential, account of knowledge, Locke devotes the first two books of the *Essay* to developing a deceptively simple empirical theory of knowledge. Knowing originates in external and internal sources of sensation and reflection. The objects or ideas present to consciousness are divided into simple and complex.

In this view the actual extent of man's knowledge is less than his ideas because he does not know the real connections between simple ideas, or primary and secondary qualities. Also, an intuitive knowledge of existence is limited to the self, and the only demonstrable existence is that of God as an eternal, omnipotent being. With the exception of the self and God, all knowledge of existing things is dependent upon sensation, whose cognitive status is "a little bit better than probability." The poverty of real knowledge is compensated to some extent by human judgment, which presumes things to be true without actually perceiving the connections. And, according to Locke's commonsense attitude, the severe restrictions placed upon knowledge merely reflect that man's mental capacity is suitable for his nature and condition.

EWB

Lombroso, Cesare (1835–1909), Italian criminologist. Cesare Lombroso devised the now-outmoded theory that criminality is determined by physiological traits. Called the father of modern criminology, he concentrated attention on the study of the individual offender.

Born in Verona on Nov. 6, 1835, Cesare Lombroso studied medicine at the universities of Pavia,

Padua, Vienna, and Genoa. His interests in psychology and psychiatry merged with his study of the physiology and anatomy of the brain and ultimately led to his anthropometric analysis of criminals. While he was in charge of the insane at hospitals in Pavia, Pesaro, and Reggio Emilia (1863–1872), his interest in physiognomical characteristics of the mentally disturbed increased.

In 1876 Lombroso became professor of legal medicine and public hygiene at the University of Turin. That year he wrote his most important and influential work, *L'uomo delinquente,* which went through five editions in Italian and was published in various European languages but never in English. A deep and lasting friendship developed between Lombroso and his chief student, Enrico Ferri, who became Italy's leading criminologist.

Concept of Atavism. Lombroso's general theory suggested that criminals are distinguished from noncriminals by multiple physical anomalies. He postulated that criminals represented a reversion to a primitive or subhuman type of man characterized by physical features reminiscent of apes, lower primates, and early man and to some extent preserved, he said, in modern "savages." The behavior of these biological "throwbacks" will inevitably be contrary to the rules and expectations of modern civilized society.

Through years of postmortem examinations and anthropometric studies of criminals, the insane, and normal individuals, Lombroso became convinced that the "born criminal" (*reo nato,* a term given by Ferri) could be anatomically identified by such items as a sloping forehead, ears of unusual size, asymmetry of the face, prognathism, excessive length of arms, asymmetry of the cranium, and other "physical stigmata." Specific criminals, such as thieves, rapists, and murderers, could be distinguished by specific characteristics, he believed. Lombroso also maintained that criminals had less sensibility to pain and touch; more acute sight; a lack of moral sense, including an absence of remorse; more vanity, impulsiveness, vindictiveness, and cruelty; and other manifestations, such as a special criminal argot and the excessive use of tattooing.

Besides the "born criminal," Lombroso also described "criminaloids," or occasional criminals, criminals by passion, moral imbeciles, and criminal epileptics. He recognized the diminished role of organic factors in many habitual offenders and referred to the delicate balance between predisposing factors (organic, genetic) and precipitating factors (environment, opportunity, poverty).

Lombroso's research methods were clinical and descriptive, with precise details of skull dimension and other measurements. But he did not enjoy the benefits of rigorous statistical comparisons of criminals and noncriminals. Adequate control groups, which he lacked, might have altered his general conclusions. Although he gave some recognition in his later years to psychological and sociological factors in the etiology of crime, he remained convinced of, and identified with, criminal anthropometry. He died in Turin on Oct. 19, 1909.

Lombroso's theories were influential throughout Europe, especially in schools of medicine, but not in the United States, where sociological studies of crime and the criminal predominated. His notions of physical differentiation between criminals and noncriminals were seriously challenged by Charles Goring (*The English Convict,* 1913), who made elaborate comparisons and found insignificant statistical differences.

EWB

Louis XIV (1638–1715), king of France from 1643–1715. Louis XIV brought the French monarchy to its peak of absolute power and made France the dominant power in Europe. His reign is also associated with the greatest age of French culture and art.

After the chaos of the Wars of Religion, the French monarchy had been reestablished by Louis XIV's grandfather, Henry IV. Successive rulers and ministers (Henry himself, Louis XIII, Cardinal Richelieu, and Cardinal Mazarin) had done all in their power to make the king absolute ruler within France and to make France, instead of the Hapsburg coalition of Spain and the empire, the dominant power in Europe. By the time Louis assumed personal control, the groundwork for final success had been laid. It was Louis who brought the work to completion, enforcing his will over France and Europe to an unprecedented extent and establishing the administrative machinery that made France a modern state.

Louis was born at Saint-Germain on Sept. 5, 1638, the son of Louis XIII and his wife, Anne of Austria. His birth was greeted with immense national rejoicing, and he was hailed as *le Dieudonné,* "the God-given." On May 16, 1643, his father died, and Louis became king. As he was only 4, the country was governed by his mother as regent; this meant, in effect, by Cardinal Mazarin, with whom Anne was in love. The successive rebellions known as the Fronde failed to dislodge Mazarin, although they left the boy king with a lifelong horror of rebellion and a resentment of Paris, where the uprising had started. Mazarin remained in power for the rest of his life, and only when he died, on March 9, 1661, did Louis astonish the court by announcing that henceforward he would direct his government himself. He meant what he said. The government remained under Louis's personal control for the next 54 years.

His Character.   Unlike his father, Louis enjoyed excellent health almost all his life. His appetites for food, hunting, and sex were enormous, and he had a passion, unusual in those days, for fresh air and walking. Though not tall, he was extremely impressive in appearance due to his great dignity and royal presence, particularly as he grew older and left his youthful exuberance behind. While he frequently displayed gross and even brutal selfishness, he was courteous, considerate, and good-natured, and he showed great loyalty to his friends and his servants. His concept of his royal position was undoubtedly arrogant, but he was always conscious of his duty as king and sincerely believed that he was devoting himself to the well-being of his subjects. He detested inefficiency, corruption, and the abuse of privilege and stamped them out wherever he encountered them. However, his own passion for personal glory led him to drag France into a series of wars, ultimately at appalling cost to his people. On his deathbed he confessed to having loved war too much, but there are no signs that he really understood what his passion had cost his country.

Louis began with a team of excellent ministers inherited from Mazarin, but only now put to full and proper use. The most important were Michel Le Tellier, in charge of military affairs (assisted, and ultimately succeeded, by his son the Marquis de Louvois), and Jean Baptiste Colbert, whose immense sphere included the navy, the royal household, religion, cultural activities, colonies, and the whole direction of the economy. Nicolas Fouquet, who as superintendent of finances had been Mazarin's most important lieutenant, was regarded by Louis as dangerous. He was charged with peculation, found guilty, and imprisoned; Louis intervened to change his sentence from banishment to imprisonment for life. This uncharacteristic act of injustice reveals Louis's fear of another Fronde.

There was no first minister. Louis had resolved to allow no minister primacy after Mazarin, and in fact he preferred to keep his ministers divided into mutually hostile groups. He himself supported his ministers without reservation if he thought them right and never yielded to pressure to get rid of them; but he never allowed them to become presumptuous. Always suspicious of any subject who might grow too powerful, he would not allow any great nobles, even his own brother, onto the council.

Military Activities.   For the next 11 years Louis's primary commitment was the restoration of the French economy to health and vigor after the neglect of Mazarin's time. In 1672, however, exasperated at his failure to destroy the economic supremacy of the Dutch, he invaded their country, assisted by England whose king, Charles II, was on his payroll. Instead of the easy triumph he had expected, he found himself faced by dogged Dutch resistance, resolutely led by William of Orange and supported by a growing number of allies. The war lasted for 6 years and ended with Dutch economic ascendancy as strong as ever. France had acquired Franche-Comté from Spain and useful gains in the Spanish Netherlands, but at the cost of permanently abandoning the economic and fiscal progress made by Colbert down to 1672. For the rest of the reign the economic progress of France was first halted and then reversed.

Louis then pursued a policy of deliberate, though limited, aggression, bullying his neighbors and encroaching on their territory. This aroused increasing fear and resentment in Europe, and Louis was finally confronted by a coalition which plunged him into the War of the League of Augsburg. This war, which lasted from 1689 till 1697, left France in possession of Strasbourg, which Louis had seized in 1681, but exhausted and in no shape to meet the still greater war that was about to break out.

This was the War of the Spanish Succession. The last Spanish Hapsburg, Charles II, was certain to die without children and would leave a vast inheritance. To avoid conflict, the two claimants to the inheritance, Louis and the Emperor, had already reached an agreement to divide this inheritance between them. Just before his death, however, Charles offered to make Louis's grandson Philip his sole heir, with the stipulation that if Louis refused, the inheritance was to pass undivided to the Emperor's younger son. Louis considered that this offer made his previous agreement invalid and against the advice of his council accepted it. This inevitably meant war with Austria, but it was owing to Louis's greed and tactlessness that Britain and Holland were brought in as well. Once again France found itself facing an immense coalition, and this time it had only begun to recover from the last war.

This final war lasted from 1701 to 1714 and did France incalculable damage. Thanks to the courage and determination of Louis and his people, the fighting did not end in disaster. Philip retained the Spanish throne, and the only losses of territory France suffered were overseas. But the country had suffered years of appalling hardship; the population was sharply reduced by famine; industry and commerce were at a standstill; and the peasantry was crushed by an unprecedented load of taxation. The King's death the next year was greeted with a relief almost as great as the joy that had welcomed his birth.

Domestic Policy. Louis's religion was a rather unintelligent and bigoted Catholicism. At the same time he regarded himself as God's deputy in France and would allow no challenge to his authority, from the Pope or anyone else. As a result, he was involved in a series of unedifying quarrels with successive popes, which dragged on for years of futile stalemate and gave rise to the probably baseless suspicion that he might be contemplating a break with the Church on the lines of Henry VIII.

To reassure Catholic opinion as to his orthodoxy, Louis kept up a steady pressure against the Protestants in France. Finally, in 1685, he revoked the Edict of Nantes (by which Protestants had been granted toleration in 1598), forbade the practice of the Calvinist religion in France (he was less concerned about Lutherans), expelled all Calvinist pastors, and forbade lay Protestants, under savage penalties, to emigrate. There was great indignation abroad, even in Catholic circles, but in the intolerant atmosphere then prevailing in Catholic France, Louis's action was very popular.

At intervals throughout his reign Louis mounted a campaign against the Jansenists, a rigorist sect within the Catholic Church. He became so bitter toward them that he ended by reversing his antipapal policy in the hope of enlisting the Pope's support. This was forthcoming, and the Jansenists were condemned by the bull *Unigenitus* in 1713; but this interference outraged French national feeling, and the Jansenist cause gained considerably in popularity as a result.

Neither the government of France by a group of overlapping councils nor the administration of the provinces by intendants (royal agents equipped with full powers in every field) originated with Louis, but he took over these systems, making them more comprehensive and efficient, and extending the system of intendants for the first time to the whole of France. Government became much more efficient in his day, but much of this efficiency was lost after his death. It also became more bureaucratic, and this change was permanent. Increasingly, the affairs of provincial France came to be decided by the council, and local initiative was discouraged. Remembering the Fronde, Louis no doubt believed that anything was better than the semianarchy of the old days; but it can be argued that he carried the spirit of regimentation a good deal too far. Governmental overcentralization is a source of endless friction in France to this day. Louis neither initiated this centralization nor carried it to its final completion, but he certainly accelerated it.

The basic factor in the Fronde had been noble anarchy, and Louis was determined to keep the nobility in line. All through his reign he did his best to undercut the independent position of the nobles and turn them, particularly the richer and more powerful of them, into courtiers. In this he was largely successful. Versailles, which became the seat of government in 1682 (although the palace was still far from completion), became the magnet to which the nobility were attracted. No nobleman could hope for appointment to any important position without paying assiduous court at Versailles. The cult of monarchy, which Louis deliberately strengthened to the utmost of his ability, made them in any case flock to Versailles of their own free will; exclusion from the charmed circle of the court came to be regarded as social death. Louis has been criticized by some historians for turning the French nobility into gilded parasites, but it may be doubted, as the Fronde demonstrated, whether they were fit to play any more constructive role. Although he preferred to select his generals, his bishops, and (contrary to legend) his ministers from the nobility, Louis did not make the mistake of his successors and exclude the Third Estate from all the best positions. He made some of his appointments from the bourgeoisie.

Culture and Art. The reign of Louis XIV is often equated with the great age of French culture. In fact, this age began under Richelieu and was clearly over some years before Louis died. Nor did he do very much to help it. In the 1660s he indulged in some patronage of writers, but his benevolence was capriciously bestowed, frequently on second-rate men, and it dried up almost entirely when economic conditions worsened after 1672. Nevertheless, Jean Racine and Molière were substantially helped by Louis, and it was largely thanks to the king that Molière's plays were performed in spite of conservative opposition. The King's enthusiasm for building (Versailles, Marly, Trianon, and others), while costing the country more than it could afford, certainly furnished artists and architects with valuable commissions, and the King's love of musical spectacles offered a golden opportunity for composers. The flowering of painting, architecture, music, and landscape gardening in France at this time must be largely credited to Louis.

Personal Life. Louis was married to Maria Theresa, daughter of Philip IV of Spain, as part of the settlement by which Mazarin ended the Spanish war. He married her reluctantly (he was in love with Mazarin's own niece at the time) and made no pretense of being faithful to her; but he was fond of her after his fashion, and at her death observed, "This is the first sorrow she has ever caused me. " Overcharged with sexual energy practically all his life, he had a number of mistresses, whose jealousy of each other was a principal topic of court gossip. By the two best-known, Louise de La Vallière and Athénaïs de Montespan, he had a number of illegitimate children, of whom he was very fond; his fatherly attempts to secure for them, after his death, a position above their station caused a good deal of trouble. His attention was finally caught by Françoise Scarron, who had become the governess of these children; he made her Marquise de Maintenon and settled down in domestic respectability with her. In later life he became very puritanical, and Madame de Maintenon has sometimes been blamed for this, but it seems likely that the change was inherent in Louis's own nature.

Louis did not allow the pursuit of pleasure to interfere with his professional duties; all his life he worked indefatigably at the business of government. He also fancied himself, without justification, as a soldier and derived much pleasure from conducting lengthy sieges of towns that were bound to surrender in any case and giving his generals unsought and unwelcome advice as to how to conduct their campaigns.

The King's last years were darkened not only by the successive disasters of the war and the desperate condition of his people but by a series of personal tragedies. In quick succession his son, the two grandsons still with him, and one of his two infant great-grandsons died. With them died his grandson's wife, the young Duchess of Burgundy, whom Louis adored. Only his other great-grandson survived, to succeed him at the age of 5 as Louis XV. When Louis died, France had long been sick of him, and his funeral procession was insulted in the streets.

History can see him in a fairer perspective. He was not "Louis the Great," as he was sycophantically hailed in his lifetime; he was a man of average intelligence and human failings who committed many blunders and several crimes. Nevertheless, he did his duty as he saw it, with a quite exceptional conscientiousness and devotion. He saw himself as responsible to God for the well-being of his people, and though his interpretation of this responsibility was often strange, it was always sincere. More than any other man except Richelieu, he was the architect of the French national state. The greatness which France achieved in his lifetime was largely his doing.

EWB

Louis XVI (1754–1793), king of France from 1774–1792. Louis XVI failed to understand the revolutionary forces at work in France and thus contributed to the fall of the monarchy.

Louis XVI had the virtues of an admirable private individual but few of those required for a successful ruler, particularly during a turbulent period. He was a devoted father and husband, uncommon virtues for royalty in his day (in 1770 he married Marie Antoinette, daughter of Emperor Francis I and Maria Theresa). His chief vices were a tendency to overeat and a love of hunting. Although historians often cite with some condescension his skill as a locksmith, Louis was not entirely devoid of intellectual interests, particularly in the area of the sciences and geography. However, although sincerely interested in the well-being of his people, he was indecisive, was easily influenced, and lacked the strength to support reforming ministers against the hostility of the Queen, his family, the court, and the privileged classes whose position was threatened by change.

At the beginning of his reign Louis XVI restored the powers of the Parlement, for long the main obstacle to reform, thus reversing the actions of Louis XV, who had drastically curtailed its authority. However, at the same time he appointed as controller general (actually first minister) A. R. J. Turgot, a friend of the *philosophes* and advocate of reform. At first Louis supported the attempts of his minister to accomplish such reforms as abolition of the monopoly of the guilds, the royal *corvée* (required labor on roads and bridges), and the elimination of internal barriers to the circulation of grain. However, he was unable to resist the pressure of those opposed to reform and in 1776 reluctantly dismissed the minister, saying, "You and I, M. Turgot, are the only ones who really love the people."

Turgot was succeeded by the Genevan banker Jacques Necker, who acquired a reputation as a financial genius for his skill in negotiating loans; he financed French aid to the American colonies in their struggle against England without raising taxes. Necker's popularity became even greater when the King yielded to pressure from the court and privileged groups and also dismissed Necker.

After several brief ministries C. A. de Calonne was named controller general in 1783. In 1787, after attempting various expedients, Calonne, like several of his predecessors, concluded that the only solution for the growing deficit was to tax the privileged groups. Once more Louis XVI failed to support his minister, who had to resign. By 1788, however, as it became clear that France was on the verge of bankruptcy, pressure mounted on Louis XVI to convoke the Estates General, which had not met for 175 years, to deal with the fiscal crisis. In the summer of 1788 the King yielded to the popular outcry, and the following year (May 1789) the Estates General met at Versailles, opening the era of the French Revolution.

French Revolution. From the outset Louis XVI's actions and failure to act pushed the French people (as of May 1789 almost all accepted the institution of monarchy) along the path to revolution. Before the meeting of the Estates General he had agreed at the urging of Necker, who had been recalled to office, to allow the Third Estate representation equal to that of the other two Estates combined. The King was vague, however, on whether each Estate would meet and vote separately, in which case the privileged Estates could outvote the Third, or whether the vote would be by "head." On June 23 the King finally ordered the three Estates to meet separately, but when the Third Estate refused to obey, Louis XVI, characteristically, yielded. Before this the Estates General had adopted the title National Constituent Assembly, sign of its determination to give France a written constitution.

The response of the King, under the influence of reactionary court circles, was to summon troops to Versailles and to dismiss Necker, who had urged cooperation with the Third Estate. This was the immediate cause for the taking of the royal fortress, the Bastille, by the Parisian crowd (July 14).

Such acts as the refusal of the King to approve the Declaration of the Rights of Man and the decrees of Aug. 4–5, 1789, abolishing the remnants of the seigneurial regime, as well as a severe inflation, led to the Revolutionary days of Oct. 5–6, 1789, when a Parisian crowd forced the court to move from Versailles to Paris, where it could be controlled more easily. On June 20–21, 1791, Louis XVI sought to escape from Paris to eastern France, in the hope that with the aid of loyal troops he could return to Paris and reestablish his authority. However, at Varennes the royal party was recognized and forced to return to Paris, where the Revolutionaries had lost all confidence in the monarchy.

In September 1791 the National Assembly adjourned and was succeeded by the Legislative Assembly. By now Louis believed that the only hope for the monarchy was foreign intervention. He anticipated that the French armies, severely weakened by the desertion of royalist officers, would be quickly defeated and that the country would then turn to him to obtain more favorable terms. For reasons of their own some of the Revolutionaries, the Girondists, also wanted war. On April 20, 1792, France declared war on Austria, which was soon joined by Prussia.

From the outbreak of the war, events moved rapidly. Revolutionary France was incensed by the manifesto of the Prussian commander, the Duke of Brunswick, threatening dire punishment on Paris if the royal family were harmed. On Aug. 10, 1792, the crowd forced the Legislative Assembly to suspend the King, who, with the royal family, became prisoner of the Commune of Paris. The National Convention, which succeeded the Legislative Assembly, abolished the monarchy and decided to try "Citizen Capet," as Louis XVI was now called, for treason. He was found guilty, sentenced to death, and on Jan. 21, 1793, guillotined.

EWB

Lukács, Gyorgy (1885–1971), Hungarian literary critic and philosopher. Gyorgy Lukács was one of the foremost Marxist literary critics and theorists. His influence on criticism has been considerable in both Western and Eastern Europe.

Gyorgy Lukács was born April 13, 1885, in Budapest, into a wealthy, intellectual, Jewish banking family. He was a brilliant student and was given a cosmopolitan education in Hungary and Germany. Until 1917 he devoted himself to art and esthetics and was not interested in politics. Writing primarily in German, he achieved his first fame as a literary critic with *The Soul and the Forms* (Hungarian, 1910; German, 1911) and *The Theory of the Novel* (1916 as an article; 1920 as a book), a study of the spiritual aspects of the novel. During World War I he taught in a German university.

Because of the shock of the war and the impressions made on him by the Russian Revolution, Lukács completed a move from Neo-Kantianism through Hegelianism to Marxism and joined the Hungarian Communist party. Despite the party's often official displeasure with his intellectual work, he remained faithful to it. In 1919 he served as deputy commissar of culture in the revolutionary Béla Kun Communist government in Hungary. After the government was overthrown, he had to emigrate to Vienna and for about a decade participated actively in party affairs and disputes.

In 1923 he wrote *History and Class Consciousness*. This complex, theoretical, sociological work explored important but, until then, little-emphasized aspects of Marx's work: the strong connection with Hegel, the importance of the dialectic, and the concept of alienation. He also examined the nature of the working class's own self-consciousness. Lukács argued that genuine Marxism was not a body of rigid economic truths but a method of analysis which could enable the revolution to be created. His interpretation of Marxism influenced many European intellectuals but was attacked as dangerously revisionist by Soviet dogmatists, and his career in party politics was over by the late 1920s.

With the danger of fascism growing in Europe, Lukács emigrated to the Soviet Union in 1933. He worked as a literary editor and critic, emphasizing the relationship between a work of art and its sociohistorical period. Several times he publicly repudiated all his previous work and occasionally shifted his views to conform to the official party line and paid lip service to official Soviet socialist realism, but he later regarded this as a tactical necessity to survive physically in Stalin's Russia and still get his ideas heard. Despite occasional Marxist-Leninist dogmatisms, he wrote perceptive criticism and concentrated on realistic 19th-century literature. Whether through personal predilection or the exigencies of the Communist party line, he became cold to almost the entire modernist movement in literature.

Returning to Hungary in 1945, Lukács was active in cultural affairs and as a professor of esthetics and cultural philosophy, but he was again stigmatized for his heterodox views. Deeply affected by Nikita Khrushchev's revelations of Stalin's crimes, he spoke out publicly against Stalinist dogmatism in Hungary, and in 1956, joined the short-lived Imré Nagy government. After the Soviet invasion of Hungary, he was exiled to Romania, allowed to return in 1957, and forced to retire and go into seclusion. However, after 1965 he was again publicly honored in Hungary. Lukács died on June 4, 1971, in Budapest.

EWB

Lumière, Auguste (1862–1954) and ***Louis*** (1864–1948), French inventors. The Lumière brothers was responsible for a number of practical improvements in photography and motion pictures. Their work on color photography resulted in the Autochrome process, which remained the preferred method of creating color prints until the 1930s. They also applied their technological talents to the new idea of motion picture photography, creating the first projection system that allowed a film to be seen by more than one person at a time.

Auguste and Louis Lumière were pioneers in the improvement of photographic materials and processes in the late 1800s and early 1900s. Using their scientific abilities and business talents, they were responsible for developing existing ideas in still photography and motion pictures to produce higher quality products that were practical enough to be of commercial value. Their initial business success was manufacturing a "dry" photographic plate that provided a new level of convenience to photographers. The brothers later turned to less viable experiments with color pho-

tography, producing a more refined, but expensive, method known as the Autochrome process. The best-known of the Lumières' achievements, however, was the Cinematograph system of projected motion pictures. Their 1895 screening of a series of short films created with the Cinematograph at a Paris cafe is considered the first public cinema performance in history.

Auguste Marie Louis Lumière was born on October 19, 1862, in Besançon, France. His younger brother and future collaborator, Louis Jean Lumière, was born October 5, 1864, in the same town. The brothers also had two other siblings, a sister, Jeanne, and a brother, Èdouard, who was killed while serving as a pilot in World War I. The Lumière children were influenced by the artistic and technological interests of their father, Claude-Antoine (known as Antoine) Lumière, a painter and award-winning photographer. In 1860, Antoine had established his own studio in Besançon, where he met and married Jeanne-Josèphine Costille. He entered into a partnership with another photographer in Lyons in 1871, and over the coming years won medals in places such as Paris and Vienna for his photographs. His sons Auguste and Louis would also be avid photographers throughout their lives.

Produced New Photographic Plates. Antoine Lumière encouraged the scientific interests of his sons, and over the years the brothers developed their own specialities. Both had a firm grasp of organic chemistry, an asset that would become valuable in their later photographic work. But while Auguste had a preference for topics in biochemistry and medicine, Louis was more interested in the subject of physics. While attending Martinière Technical School, Louis distinguished himself as the top student in his class in 1880. It was during his school years that Louis began working on an improved photographic plate. Originally, "wet" photographic plates had been the only available medium for photography; these were very inconvenient, however, because they required treatment in a dark room immediately before and after the exposure of the plate. A new, more convenient, "dry" plate had been developed and marketed in the 1870s. Louis developed a better version of the dry plate that became known as the "blue label" plate.

The Lumière brothers and their father saw the potential for marketing such a product, and so, with financial backing from Antoine Lumière, the brothers began producing the plates in 1882. The following year, the venture opened a manufacturing facility in Lyons as the Antoine Lumière and Sons company. As the "blue label" plate became more popular among photographers, production increased from a few thousand a year to more than one million a year by 1886 and 15 million a year by 1894. The contributions of each brother to the success of the company and its products are difficult to isolate, because throughout their careers, the brothers both engaged in refining scientific techniques and they shared all credit on their works and patents. Although their interests varied as the focus of the company changed, a profound professional respect was always obvious between the two and certainly played a major role in their fruitful research and business partnership.

The Problem of Color Photography. The financial security the Lumière brothers enjoyed, from their booming sales of the dry plate, allowed them to carry out experiments in other aspects of photography. In the early 1890s, they turned to the problem of color photography. Since the advent of photography in the 1830s, numerous attempts had been made to create color photographs, with mixed success. The British scientist James Clerk Maxwell had devised a method in which a color reproduction could be created by using variously colored filters to photograph a subject; the resulting picture, however, could only be viewed by projecting the image—no prints were possible. This obstacle was overcome in the 1860s by the French researcher Louis Ducos du Hauron, who produced a color image by superimposing positive and negative shots taken through colored filters. While a print could be produced in this way, it was a complicated and time-consuming process that never gained much popularity. The Lumières set themselves to the task of creating a more practical application of color photography, but they eventually set the topic aside in favor of pursuing the exciting new field of motion pictures. Their early experiments in color photography, however, provided the groundwork for later innovations.

The interest in film technology had begun as a sort of hobby for the brothers, but soon they realized that work in this area could have great commercial value. Beginning in the summer of 1894, they began to look for a way to project motion pictures. The moving picture had been pioneered more than a decade earlier by the English photographer and bookseller Eadweard Muybridge. In an attempt to find a way to analyze the movement of a horse, around 1880 Muybridge had taken a series of photos of a horse in motion and placed the images on a glass disc that allowed him to project the images in quick succession. The result was a moving image, but one that was limited by the number of pictures that could fit on the disc. The idea was taken up later in the 1880s by French physiologist Étienne-Jules Marey and U.S. in-

ventor Thomas Edison. Edison led experiments that resulted in the 1889 creation of his kinetograph, a machine that used strips of photographic paper to take motion pictures. In 1893 Edison and his researchers produced the kinetoscope, a device also known as a "peep box," which allowed a single person to view the moving image. The Lumière brothers' goal was to improve on Edison's ideas by finding a way to project motion picture films for a larger audience.

Created First Projected Motion Pictures. Louis realized that the main obstacle to their goal of projection was finding a way to automatically create a continuous movement of the film containing the images. Part of the answer to the problem was found by Louis, who suddenly was inspired while lying awake one night. He realized that the same "presser foot" mechanism that drives a sewing machine could be adapted to move small sections, or frames, of film across the lens in quick succession, allowing a short period of time for each frame to be stationary to allow for exposure. Louis drew up the plans for a prototype camera, which was constructed by one of his technicians at the family factory. This machine, known as the Cinematograph, underwent a number of further developments that made it an extremely versatile tool. Not only could it create the negatives of an image on film, but it could also print a positive image as well as project the results at a speed of 12 frames per second.

Louis made the first use of his new camera in the summer of 1894, filming workers leaving the Lumière plant. He presented the film to the Société d'Encouragement pour l'Industrie Nationale on March 22, 1895. He and Auguste then made arrangements to bring a series of short films to a public audience. They rented a room at the Grand Café in Paris, and on December 28, 1895, held the first public show of projected moving pictures. The audience wasn't quite sure what to make of the new technology. Louis's creative use of the camera had led him to photograph an approaching train from a head-on perspective; some people in the audience were frightened at the image on the oncoming locomotive and in a panic tried to escape—others simply fainted. Despite their surprise, even shock, at the sight of moving pictures, audiences flocked to the Lumières' demonstrations and the Cinematograph was soon in high demand all around the world.

Autochrome Process Invented. Both Auguste and Louis created films for a while, but eventually they handed this work over to others so they could pursue other interests. Louis returned to research on color photography, developing the Auto-chrome process in 1904. His method, although still fairly expensive, provided a level of convenience similar to the dry plate. Autochrome achieved recognition as the best means of producing color images at that time and remained the favored means of color photography for the next 30 years. In later years, Louis would continue his interest in visual reproduction by developing a photographic method for measuring objects in 1920 and inventing relief cinematography techniques in 1935. Auguste spent the early 1900s investigating medical topics such as tuberculosis, cancer, and pharmacology. He joined the medical profession in 1914 as the director of a hospital radiology department. In 1928, Auguste published a medical book entitled *Life, Illness, and Death: Colloidal Phenomena.*

The Lumière brothers were each recognized for their numerous technological and scientific achievements: Auguste was named a member of the Legion of Honor, and Louis was elected to the French Academy of Sciences. At the age of 83, Louis Lumière died in Bandol, France, on June 6, 1948. His older brother lived to the age of 91 and died in his longtime home of Lyons, France, on April 10, 1954. For their work together in creating improvements in both photography and motion pictures, the Lumière brothers are recognized as symbols of an age of technological creativity and growth. They are also remembered for their lifelong aims of bringing such technology to a wider marketplace, a value seen most clearly in their contributions to the motion picture industry, which has become a popular form of entertainment in countries around the world.

EWB

Luther, Martin (1483–1546, German reformer. Martin Luther was the first and greatest figure in the 16th-century Reformation. A composer of commentaries on Scripture, theology, and ecclesiastical abuses, a hymnologist, and a preacher, from his own time to the present he has been a symbol of Protestantism.

Martin Luther was born at Eisleben in Saxony on Nov. 10, 1483, the son of Hans and Margaret Luther. Luther's parents were of peasant stock, but his father had worked hard to raise the family's status, first as a miner and later as the owner of several small mines, to become a small-scale entrepreneur. In 1490 Martin was sent to the Latin school at Mansfeld, in 1497 to Magdeburg, and in 1498 to Eisenach. His early education was typical of late-15th-century practice. To a young man in Martin's circumstances, only the law and the church offered likely avenues of success, and Hans Luther's anticlericalism probably influenced his decision that his son should become a lawyer

and increase the Luther family's prosperity, which Hans had begun. Martin was enrolled at the University of Erfurt in 1501. He received a bachelor of arts degree in 1502 and a master of arts in 1505. In the same year he enrolled in the faculty of law, giving every sign of being a dutiful and, likely, a very successful son.

Religious Conversion. Between 1503 and 1505, however, Martin experienced a religious crisis which would take him from the study of law forever. His own personal piety, fervently and sometimes grimly instilled by his parents and early teachers, and his awareness of a world in which the supernatural was perilously close to everyday life were sharpened by a series of events whose exact character has yet to be precisely determined. A dangerous accident in 1503, the death of a friend a little later, and Martin's own personal religious development had by 1505 started other concerns in him.

Then, on July 2, 1505, returning to Erfurt after visiting home, Martin was caught in a severe thunderstorm in which he was flung to the ground in terror, and he suddenly vowed to become a monk if he survived. This episode, as important in Christian history as the equally famous (and parallel) scene of St. Paul's conversion, changed the course of Luther's life. Two weeks later, against the opposition of his father and to the dismay of his friends, Martin Luther entered the Reformed Congregation of the Eremetical Order of St. Augustine at Erfurt. Luther himself saw this decision as sudden and based upon fear: "I had been called by heavenly terrors, for not freely or desirously did I become a monk, much less to gratify my belly, but walled around with the terror and agony of sudden death I vowed a constrained and necessary vow."

Luther's early life as a monk reflected his precipitate reasons for entering a monastery: "I was a good monk, and kept strictly to my order, so that I could say that if the monastic life could get a man to heaven, I should have entered." Monastic life at Erfurt was hard. Monks had long become (with the friars and many of the secular clergy) the targets of anticlerical feeling. Charged with having forsaken their true mission and having fallen into greed and ignorance, monastic orders made many attempts at reform in the 15th and 16th centuries. The congregation at Erfurt had been reformed in 1473. The year before Luther entered the Augustinian order at Erfurt, the vicar general Johann Staupitz (later Luther's friend) had revised further the constitution of the order.

Luther made his vows in 1506 and was ordained a priest in 1507. Reconciled with his father, he was then selected for advanced theological study at the University of Erfurt, with which his house had several connections.

Luther at Wittenberg. In 1508 Luther was sent to the newer University of Wittenberg to lecture in arts. Like a modern graduate student, he was also preparing for his doctorate of theology while he taught. He lectured on the standard medieval texts, for example, Peter Lombard's *Book of Sentences;* and he read for the first time the works of St. Augustine. In 1510 Luther was sent to Rome on business of the order and in 1512 received his doctorate in theology. Then came the second significant turn in Luther's career: he was appointed to succeed Staupitz as professor of theology at Wittenberg. Luther was to teach throughout the rest of his life. Whatever fame and notoriety his later writings and statements were to bring him, his work was teaching, which he fulfilled diligently until his death.

Wittenberg was a new university, founded in 1502–1503, strongly supported by the elector Frederick the Wise. By 1550, thanks to the efforts of Luther and his colleague Philip Melancthon, it was to become the most popular university in Germany. In 1512, however, it lacked the prestige of Erfurt and Leipzig and was insignificant in the eyes of the greatest of the old universities, that of Paris. It was not a good place for an ambitious academic, but Luther was not ambitious in this sense. His rapid rise was due to his native ability, his boundless energy, his dedication to the religious life, and his high conception of his calling as a teacher.

The intellectual climate which shaped Luther's thought is difficult to analyze precisely. The two competing philosophic systems of the late Middle Ages— scholasticism (derived from the Aristotelianism of St. Thomas Aquinas) and nominalism (derived from the skepticism of William of Ockham and his successors)—both appear to have influenced Luther, particularly in their insistence on rigorous formal logic as the basis of philosophic and theological inquiry. From Ockhamism, Luther probably derived his awareness of the infinite remoteness and majesty of God and of the limitation of the human intellect in its efforts to apprehend that majesty.

Luther's professional work forced him further to develop the religious sensibility which had drawn him to monasticism in 1505. In the monastery and later in the university Luther experienced other religious crises, all of which were based upon his acute awareness of the need for spiritual perfection and his equally strong conviction of his own human frailty, which caused him almost to despair before the overwhelming majesty and wrath of God. In 1509 Luther published his lectures on Peter Lombard; in 1513–1515 those on the Psalms; in 1515–1516 on St. Paul's Epistle to the Romans; and in 1516–1518 on the epistles to the Galatians and Hebrews. Like all other Christians, Luther read the Bible, and in these years his biblical studies became more and more important to him. Besides teaching and study, however, Luther had other duties. From 1514 he preached in the parish church; he was regent of the monastery school; and in 1515 he became the supervisor of 11 other monasteries.

Righteousness of God. Luther's crisis of conscience centered upon the question of his old monastic fears concerning the insufficiency of his personal efforts to placate a wrathful God. In his own person, these fears came to a head in 1519, when he began to interpret the passage in St. Paul's Epistle to the Romans which says that the justice of God is revealed in the Gospels.

Luther, the energetic monk and young theologian, felt himself to be "a sinner with an unquiet conscience." After an intense period of crisis, Luther discovered another interpretation of St. Paul's text: "I began to understand that Justice of God . . . to be understood passively as that whereby the merciful God justifies us by faith. . . . At this I felt myself to be born anew, and to enter through open gates into paradise itself." Only faith in God's mercy, according to Luther, can effect the saving righteousness of God in man. "Works," the term which Luther used to designate both formal, ecclesiastically authorized liturgy and the more general sense of "doing good," became infinitely less important to him than faith.

The doctrine of justification, taking shape in Luther's thought between 1515 and 1519, drew him into further theological speculation as well as into certain positions of practical ecclesiastical life. The most famous of these is the controversy over indulgences. In 1513 a great effort to dispense indulgences was proclaimed throughout Germany. In spite of the careful theological reservations surrounding them, indulgences appeared to the preachers who sold them and to the public who bought them as a means of escaping punishment in the afterlife for a sum of money. In 1517 Luther posted the 95 Theses for an academic debate on indulgences on the door of the castle church at Wittenberg. Both the place and the event were customary events in an academic year, and they might have gone unnoticed had not someone translated Luther's Latin theses into German and printed them, thus giving them widespread fame and calling them to the attention of both theologians and the public.

News of Dr. Luther's theses spread, and in 1518 Luther was called before Cardinal Cajetan, the papal legate at Augsburg, to renounce his theses. Refusing to do so, Luther returned to Wittenberg, where, in the next year, he agreed to a debate with the theologian Johann Eck. The debate, originally scheduled to be held between Eck and Luther's colleague Karlstadt, soon became a struggle between Eck and Luther in which Luther was driven by his opponent to taking even more radical theological positions, thus laying himself open to the charge of heresy. By 1521 Eck secured a papal bull (decree) condemning Luther, and Luther was summoned to the Imperial Diet at Worms in 1521 to answer the charges against him.

Diet of Worms.   Luther throughout his life always revealed a great common sense, and he always retained his humorous understanding of practical life. He reflected an awareness of both the material and spiritual worlds, and his flights of poetic theology went hand in hand with the occasional coarseness of his polemics. His wit and thought were spontaneous, his interest in people of all sorts genuine and intense, his power of inspiring affection in his students and colleagues never failing. He was always remarkably frank, and although he became first the center of the Reform movement and later one of many controversial figures in it, he retained a sense of self-criticism, attributing his impact to God.

Great personal attraction, absolute dedication to his theological principles, kindness and loyalty to his friends, and an acute understanding of his own human weakness—these were the characteristics of Luther when he came face to face with the power of the papacy and empire at Worms in 1521. He was led to a room in which his collected writings were piled on a table and ordered to repudiate them. He asked for time to consider and returned the next day and answered: "Unless I am proved wrong by the testimony of Scripture or by evident reason I am bound in conscience and held fast to the Word of God. Therefore I cannot and will not retract anything, for it is neither safe nor salutary to act against one's conscience. God help me. Amen." Luther left Worms and was taken, for his own safety, to the castle of Wartburg, where he spent some months in seclusion, beginning his great translation of the Bible into German and writing numerous tracts.

Return to Wittenberg.   In 1522 Luther returned to Wittenberg, where he succeeded in cooling the radical reforming efforts of his colleague Karlstadt and continued the incessant writing which would fill the rest of his life. In 1520 he had written three of his most famous tracts: *To The Christian Nobility of the German Nation,* which enunciates a social program of religious reform; *On the Babylonian Captivity of the Church,* on Sacraments, the Mass, and papal power; and *Of the Liberty of a Christian Man,* a treatise on faith and on the inner liberty which faith affords those who possess it.

The Lutheran Bible, which was "a vehicle of proletarian education" as well as a monument in the spiritual history of Europe, not only gave Luther's name and views wider currency but revealed the translator as a great master of German prose, an evaluation which Luther's other writings justify.

Besides these works, Luther had other matters at hand. His name was used now by many people, including many with whom he disagreed. The Reformation had touched society and its institutions as well as religion, and Luther was drawn into conflicts, such as the Peasants' Rebellion of 1524–1525 and the affairs of the German princes, which drew from him new ideas on the necessary social and political order of Christian Germany. Luther's violent antipeasant writings from this period have often been criticized. His fears of the dangerous role of extreme reformers like Karlstadt and Thomas Münzer, however, were greater than his hope for social reform through revolution. Luther came to rely heavily upon the princes to carry out his program of reform. In 1525 Luther married Katherine von Bora, a nun who had left her convent. From that date until his death, Luther's family life became not only a model of the Christian home but a source of psychological support to him.

Luther's theological writings continued to flow steadily. Often they were written in response to his critics or in the intense heat of debate with Protestant rivals. Among those great works not brought about by conflict should be numbered the *Great Catechism* and the *Small Catechism* of 1529 and his collection of sermons and hymns, many of the latter, like *Ein Feste Burg,* still sung today.

Debates with Theologians.   In 1524–1525 Luther entered into a discussion of free will with the great Erasmus. Luther's *On the Will in Bondage* (1525) remained his definitive statement on the question. In 1528 Luther turned to the question of Christ's presence in the Eucharist in his *Confession concerning the Lord's Supper,* which attracted the hostility of a number of reformers, notably Ulrich Zwingli. In 1529 Luther's ally Melancthon arranged a discussion between the two, and the Marburg Colloquy, as the debate is known, helped to close one of the early breaches in Protestant agreement.

In 1530, when Charles V was once again able to turn to the problems of the Reformation in Germany, Luther supervised, although he did not entirely agree with, the writing of Melancthon's Augsburg Confession, one of the foundations of later Protestant thought. From 1530 on Luther spent as much time arguing with other Reformation leaders on matters of theology as with his Catholic opponents.

Luther's disputes with other theologians were carried out with the same intensity he applied to his other work: he longed for Christian unity, but he could not accept the theological positions which many others had advanced. He was also fearful of the question of a general council in the Church. In 1539 he wrote his *On Councils and Churches* and witnessed in the following years the failure of German attempts to heal the wounds of Christianity. On the eve of his death he watched with great concern the calling of the Council of Trent, the Catholic response to the Reformation.

In the 1540s Luther was stricken with diseases a number of times, drawing great comfort from his family and from the lyrical, plain devotional exercises which he had written for children. In 1546 he was called from a sickbed to settle the disputes of two German noblemen. On the return trip he fell sick and died at Eisleben, the town of his birth, on Feb. 18, 1546.

EWB

Luxemburg, Rosa (1871–1919), Polish revolutionary and theorist. Rosa Luxemburg led the German workers' uprisings which followed World War I and is considered one of the pioneer activists and foremost martyrs of the international Communist movement.

Rosa Luxemburg was born in Zamo in Russian Poland and brought up in Warsaw. She was the daughter of a middle-class, Polish-speaking Jewish merchant. Dainty, almost tiny, she walked with a limp as the result of a childhood disease.

From her earliest years Rosa possessed "one of the most penetrating analytical minds of her age." In a period when the czarist government was increasing its religious and political oppression in Poland, especially of the Jews, she gained admission to the best girls' high school in Warsaw, usually reserved for Russians. There she joined a revolutionary cell and began a lifelong association with the socialist movement. When she was 18, her activities came to the attention of the Russian secret police, and she fled to Switzerland to avoid arrest.

Luxemburg continued her interests in socialist and revolutionary activities there. She earned a doctorate of laws at the University of Zurich in 1898.

Her thesis on industrial development in Poland later served as a basis for the program of the Social Democratic party of Poland. She decided to go to Germany and attach herself to the large, vital, and well-organized Social Democratic party (SPD). In Berlin she obtained German citizenship through a fictitious marriage and quickly became one of the most effective, respected, and even beloved leaders of the international socialist movement.

With Karl Kautsky, Luxemburg headed the revisionist wing of the SPD in opposition to its major theorist, Eduard Bernstein. She wrote articles in socialist newspapers increasingly critical of Bernstein's political and economic theories. Gradually, in a series of works published before the outbreak of World War I, she drifted apart from Kautsky and established herself as the acknowledged leader of the left, or revolutionary, wing of the SPD. She gave new life and theoretical form to the revolutionary goals of the party in a period when most factions were oriented toward parliamentary reform.

During World War I Luxemburg, now dubbed the "Red Rose" by police, was imprisoned for her revolutionary activities. Released for a short time in 1916, she helped to found the revolutionary Spartacus Union with Karl Liebknecht. When she again emerged from prison, in 1918, dissatisfied with the failure to effect a thoroughgoing socialist revolution in Germany, she helped to found the German Communist party (KPD) and its newspaper, the *Rote Fahne,* and drafted its program. She and Liebknecht urged revolution against the Ebert government, which came to power after the armistice, and were largely responsible for the wave of strikes, riots, and violence which swept across Germany from the end of 1918 until June 1919.

In January 1919 one of the most violent outbreaks occurred in Berlin. Luxemburg and Liebknecht, in spite of their doubts as to the timing, supported the Berlin workers in their call for revolution. The troops that were called in acted with extreme violence and brutality, crushing the revolt in a few days. On January 15 Liebknecht and Luxemburg were caught and murdered by the soldiers who held them prisoner.

EWB

M

Machiavelli, Niccolò (1469–1527), Italian author and statesman. Niccolò Machiavelli is best known for *The Prince,* in which he enunciated his political philosophy.

209

Niccolò Machiavelli was born in Florence of an aristocratic, though by no means wealthy, family. Little is known of the first half of his life, prior to his first appointment to public office. His writings prove him to have been a very assiduous sifter of the classics, especially the historical works of Livy and Tacitus; in all probability he knew the Greek classics only in translation.

In 1498 Machiavelli was named chancellor and secretary of the second (and less important) chancellery of the Florentine Republic. His duties consisted chiefly of executing the policy decisions of others, carrying on diplomatic correspondence, digesting and composing reports, and compiling minutes; he also undertook some 23 missions to foreign states. His embassies included four to the French king and two to the court of Rome. His most memorable mission is described in a report of 1503 entitled "Description of the Manner Employed by Duke Valentino [Cesare Borgia] in Slaying Vitellozzo Vitelli, Oliverotto da Fermo, Signor Pagolo and the Duke of Gravina, Orsini"; with surgical precision he details Borgia's series of political murders, implicitly as a lesson in the art of politics for Florence's indecisive and timorous gonfalonier, Pier Soderini.

In 1502 Machiavelli married Marietta Corsini, who bore him four sons and two daughters. To his grandson Giovanni Ricci we owe the preservation of many of his letters and minor works.

In 1510 Machiavelli, inspired by his reading of Roman history, was instrumental in organizing a citizen militia of the Florentine Republic. In August 1512 a Spanish army entered Tuscany and sacked Prato. The Florentines in terror deposed Soderini, whom Machiavelli characterized as "good, but weak," and allowed the Medici to return to power. On November 7 Machiavelli was dismissed; soon afterward he was arrested, imprisoned, and subjected to torture as a suspected conspirator against the Medici. Though innocent, he remained suspect for years to come; unable to secure an appointment from the reinstated Medici, he turned to writing.

In all likelihood Machiavelli interrupted the writing of his *Discourses on the First Ten Books of Titus Livius* to write the brief treatise on which his fame rests, *Il Principe* (1513; *The Prince*). Other works followed: *The Art of War* and *The Life of Castruccio Castracani* (1520); three extant plays, *Mandragola* (1518; The Mandrake), *Clizia*, and *Andria*; the *Istorie fiorentine* (1526; History of Florence); a short story, *Belfagor*; and several minor works in verse and prose.

In 1526 Machiavelli was commissioned by Pope Clement VII to inspect the fortifications of Florence. Later that year and the following year his friend and critic Francesco Guicciardini, Papal Commissary of War in Lombardy, employed him in two minor diplomatic missions. He died in Florence in June 1527, receiving the last rites of the Church that he had bitterly criticized.

The Prince. Machiavelli shared with Renaissance humanists a passion for classical antiquity. To their wish for a literary and spiritual revival of ancient values, guided by such authors as Plato, Cicero, and St. Augustine, he added a fierce desire for a political and moral renewal on the model of the Roman Republic as depicted by Livy and Tacitus. Though a republican at heart, he saw as the crying need of his day a strong political and military leader who could forge a unitary state in northern Italy to eliminate French and Spanish hegemony from Italian soil. At the moment that he wrote *The Prince* he envisioned such a possibility while the restored Medici ruled both Florence and the papacy. He had taken to heart Cesare Borgia's energetic creation of a new state in Romagna in the few brief years while Borgia's father, Alexander VI, occupied the papal throne. The final chapter of *The Prince* is a ringing plea to his Medici patrons to set Italy free from the "barbarians." It concludes with a quotation from Petrarch's patriotic poem *Italia mia*: "Virtue will take arms against fury, and the battle will be brief; for the ancient valor in Italian hearts is not yet dead." This exhortation fell on deaf ears in 1513 but was to play a role 3 centuries later in the Risorgimento.

Other Works. Certain passages in the *Discourses* (I, 11 and 12; II, 2) set forth Machiavelli's quarrel with the Church: by the bad example of the court of Rome, Italy has lost its devotion and religion; the Italian states are weak and divided because the Church, too feeble politically to dominate them, has nevertheless prevented any one state from uniting them. He suggests that the Church might have been destroyed by its own corruption had not St. Francis and St. Dominic restored it to its original principles by founding new orders. However, in an unusual if not unique departure from traditional anticlericalism, Machiavelli contrasts favorably the fiercely civil and militaristic pagan religion of ancient Rome with the humble and otherworldly Christian religion.

The *Mandragola*, the finest comedy of the Italian Renaissance, is not unrelated to Machiavelli's political writings in its comic indictment of contemporary Florentine society. In a well-knit intrigue the simpleton Nicia contributes to his own cuckolding. Nicia's beautiful and virtuous wife, Lucrezia (so named by the author with an eye to Roman history), is corrupted by those who should be her closest protectors: her mother, her husband, and her unscrupulous confessor, Fra Timoteo, all pawns in the skillful hands of the manipulator Ligurio.

Although not equaling Guicciardini as a historian, Machiavelli in his *History of Florence* nevertheless marks an advance over earlier histories in his attention to underlying causes rather than the mere succession of events as he tells the history of the Florentines from the death of Lorenzo de' Medici in 1492.

Machiavelli closely adhered to his maxim that a servant of government must be loyal and self-sacrificing. He nowhere suggests that the political morality of princes is a model for day-to-day dealings between ordinary citizens. His reputation as a sinister and perfidious counselor of fraud is largely undeserved; it began not long after his death. His works were banned in the first printed Index (1559). In Elizabethan England, Machiavelli was represented on the stage and in literature as diabolically evil. The primary source of this misrepresentation was the translation into English by Simon Patericke in 1577 of a work popularly called *Contre-Machiavel,* by the French Huguenot Gentillet, who distorted Machiavelli and blamed his teachings for the St. Bartholomew Night massacre of 1572. A poem by Gabriel Harvey the following year falsely attributed four principal crimes to Machiavelli: poison, murder, fraud, and violence. Christopher Marlowe's *The Jew of Malta* (1588) introduces "Machiavel" as the speaker of an atrocious prologue; Machiavellian villains followed in works by other playwrights.

Many of Machiavelli's authentic values are incorporated into 19th-century liberalism: the supremacy of civil over religious power; the conscription of citizen armies; the preference for republican rather than monarchical government; and the republican Roman ideals of honesty, work, and the people's collective responsibility for values that transcend those of the individual.

EWB

Malraux, André (1901–1976), French writer and politician. André Malraux was generally regarded as one of the most distinguished novelists of the 20th century. Malraux holds the distinction of having been France's first minister of culture, serving from 1959–69. In addition, his wartime activities and adventures were legendary and well-documented. Malraux was a Communist supporter until World War II, and principal themes in his writing were revolution and its philosophical implications. He was an existentialist, believing that man determines his own fate by the choices he makes.

The novels of André Malraux depart sharply from the traditional form, with their middle-class settings, careful plot development and concentration on psychological analysis. His heroes and protagonists are adventurers determined to "leave a scar on the map," and violent action, usually in a revolutionary setting, is mixed with punctuated dialogue and passages containing philosophical reflection.

Malraux was born in Paris on Nov. 3, 1901, the son of a wealthy banker, and was educated in Paris. He attended the Lycée Condorcet and the School of Oriental Languages and would eventually develop a serious interest in China. Malraux began to move on the fringes of the surrealist movement, publishing criticism and poems. He married Clara Goldschmidt in 1921, and in 1923 the couple set off for Indochina (a former French colony consisting of Cambodia, Laos, and Vietnam) to search for buried temples. After removing sculpture from the temples, Malraux and his wife were arrested by the French authorities and narrowly avoided prison.

It was during this period that Malraux, now hostile to the French colonial regime, came into contact with Vietnamese and Chinese Nationalists, many with Communist sympathies. He became a supporter of the international Communist movement, and during a stay in Saigon he organized a subversive newspaper.

Malraux's first novel, *Les Conquérants* (*The Conquerors*), was published in 1928. Set in Canton in 1925, it deals with the attempts of Chinese Nationalists and their Communist advisers to destroy imperialist influence and economic domination. The hero of the book provides a vigorously drawn portrait of the professional revolutionary. Malraux lamented the potential influences of Western culture, using China as an example, with *The Temptation of the West* (1926). In this work, the character of Ling says that many Chinese thought they could retain their cultural identities after being exposed to European influence and technology. Instead, that influence results in the "disintegrating soul" of China, a country newly "seduced" by music and movies.

Malraux's next novel, *La Voie Royale* (*The Royal Way,* 1930), was less successful; it had an autobiographical basis in the search for buried treasures, but treated the search as a kind of metaphysical adventure.

In 1933 appeared Malraux's most celebrated novel, *La Condition humaine* (*Man's Estate, Man's Fate*). Set in Shanghai, the novel describes the 1927 Communist uprising there, its initial success and ultimate failure. The novel continues to illustrate Malraux's favorite theme: that all men will attempt to escape, or to transcend, the human condition and that revolutionary action is one way of accomplishing this. In the end there is failure, but man attains dignity in making the attempt and by his very failure achieves tragic greatness.

Malraux's next novel, *Days of Wrath* (1936), a short account of a German Communist's imprisonment by the Nazis, was poorly received, considered more propaganda than art. But after Malraux assisted the Republican forces by organizing an air corps during the Spanish Civil War in 1936–1937, his inspiration was renewed. He then published *L'Espoir* (*Man's Hope*, 1938). In this book, the Republican forces gradually organize to meet the Fascist threat, and the novel ends at a point where the "hope" of the title might have been realized.

Following the Soviet Union's signing of a non-aggression pact with Germany, Malraux broke with the Communist cause. He was captured twice while fighting with the French army and underground resistance movement, but he escaped and would become a military leader. In 1943 he published his last novel, *Les Noyers de l'Altenburg* (*The Walnut Trees of Altenburg*).

The feel of this book is very different from that of Malraux's earlier novels. The narrator, captured by the Germans in 1940, reflects on his father's experiences before and during World War I—as an agent in central Asia, at a meeting of intellectuals in Germany, and while fighting on the Russian front. Malraux explores the fundamental problem of whether men are essentially the same in different epochs and different civilizations. Intellectually the answer seems to be negative, but emotionally it is positive, and human solidarity is maintained. Political action is seen as an illusion, and the traditional values of European humanism are affirmed.

Following the liberation of France in 1944, Malraux served in the reconstituted army as a colonel, and would later work to subvert the French Communist party. He was a supporter of General Charles de Gaulle. He and de Gaulle became friends and, as president of France, de Gaulle appointed Malraux to the position of minister of information—a job Malraux held from 1945–46. After leaving the post, he remained a de Gaulle intimate and one of the leading members of the Gaullist political movement. He contributed to *The Case for de Gaulle; a Dialogue between André Malraux and James Burnham.*

Beset by marital tensions, André and Clara Malraux divorced in January 1946. Two years later, Malraux married his sister-in-law.

In the years that followed, Malraux wrote mainly on the subject of art. One highly philosophical volume on this subject was *The Psychology of Art* (1950), in which Malraux writes of an "imaginary museum"—a "museum without walls"—in which objects of art are important for their own intrinsic value rather than for their collective underlying meanings.

In *Les Voix du silence* (*The Voices of Silence*, 1951), Malraux develops the idea that in the modern world, where religion is of little importance, art has taken its place as man's triumphant response to his ultimate destiny and his means of transcending death. Also on the subject of art, Malraux penned "Saturn: an Essay on (Francisco de) Goya" (1957, translated by C. W. Chilton). Malraux also wrote *Picasso's Mask* (1976).

In 1958, after de Gaulle's return to power, Malraux became minister of cultural affairs where he remained until de Gaulle's resignation in 1969. In 1967 he published the first volume of his *Antimémoires* (*Antimemoirs*). These were not memoirs of the usual type, failing to mention the accidental deaths of his two sons and the murder of his half-brother by the Nazis. Instead, they contained reflections on various aspects of his experiences and adventures.

Malraux paid two visits to the White House; in 1972, he conferred with President Richard Nixon prior to Nixon's visit to China. That same year he also suffered a near-fatal heart attack.

Malraux died in Paris on Nov. 23, 1976. Exactly 20 years later, his ashes were moved to the Pantheon necropolis in Paris. His namesake, the André Malraux Cultural Center, is in Chambéry (France).

EWB

Malthus, Thomas Robert (1766–1834), English economist. Thomas Malthus was of the classical school and was the first to direct attention to the danger of overpopulation in the modern world.

Thomas Malthus was born at the Rookery near Guilford, Surrey, a small estate owned by his father, Daniel Malthus. After being privately educated, Malthus entered Jesus College, Cambridge, where he was elected to a fellowship at the age of 27. He took religious orders at the age of 31 and held a curacy for a short period.

In 1798 Malthus published his *Essay on the Principle of Population*. This pamphlet was turned into a full-scale book in 1803 with the aid of demographic data drawn from a number of European countries.

In 1805 Malthus married, and shortly thereafter he was appointed professor of modern history and political economy at the East India Company's College at Haileybury, the first appointment of its kind in England. Much to the amusement of his critics, since he advocated controlling the birthrate, he fathered five children. He died at Haileybury on Dec.

23, 1834, the year that saw the passage of a new Poor Law inspired by his writings.

Debates concerning Malthusian Theory. Few thinkers in the history of social science have aroused as much controversy as Malthus. It is not difficult to find reasons for the furor: he consistently opposed all methods of reforming society which did not act directly to reduce the birthrate, and his own remedies for bringing that about were impractical; he reduced all human suffering to the single principle of the pressure of population on the food supply, and all popular proposals for political or economic reform were exposed as irrelevant and immaterial; and he drove home his theme in one harsh passage after another, suggesting that literally every other possible social order was even worse than the existing one. Those on the left hated him because he seemed to be defending the society they hoped to change, and those on the right disliked him for defending that society as merely a necessary evil.

Toward the end of the 19th century, the discussion died down as the rise in living standards and the decline in fertility, at least in Western countries, took the sting out of the fear of overpopulation. But after World War II the problem of the underdeveloped countries brought Malthus back in favor. Most of the emerging nations of Africa, Asia, and Latin America combine the high birthrates typical of agrarian economies with the low death rates typical of industrialized economies, and there is the danger of too many mouths to feed. It is not surprising, therefore, that Malthus's name crops up repeatedly in debates on population policy in underdeveloped countries. The arguments are very different from those employed in Malthus's own day, but the participants of the debate still line up as for or against the Malthusian theory of population.

From Malthus's writings, one receives the impression of an inflexible fanatic and possibly a misanthrope, but everyone who met Malthus found him kind and benevolent. In terms of the politics of that age, he was almost, but not quite, a "liberal," and his professions of concern over the conditions of the poor must be regarded as perfectly genuine. He had unpleasant truths to tell but he told them, as it were, "for their own good."

His Theory of Population. Malthus's theory of population is baldly stated in the first two chapters of the *Essay*. The argument begins with two postulates: "that food is necessary to the existence of man" and "that the passion between the sexes is necessary, and will remain nearly in its present state." The "prin-

ciple of population" followed from these with the force of deductive logic: "Assuming, then, my postulata as granted, I say, that the power of population is indefinitely greater than the power in the earth to produce subsistence for man. Population, when unchecked, increases in a geometrical ratio. Subsistence increases only in an arithmetical ratio. A slight acquaintance with numbers will show the immensity of the first power in comparison with the second. By that law of nature which makes food necessary to the life of man, the effects of these two unequal powers must be kept equal. This implies a strong and constantly operating check on population from the difficulty of subsistence."

In 1798 Malthus described all the checks, such as infanticide, abortion, wars, plagues, and death from disease or starvation, as resolvable into "misery and vice." In 1803 he added a third pigeonhole, moral restraint, defined as "that restraint from marriage which was not followed by irregular gratification." It should be noted that he did not include birth control achieved by artificial devices. In his view, man was naturally lazy and would not work to provide a livelihood for himself and his family except under the threat of starvation. Birth control, even if it could be adopted, would only remove the incentive to work and would, therefore, amount to more "misery and vice." Moral restraint was something else: it implied postponement of marriage and strict chastity until marriage. He doubted that moral restraint would ever become a common practice, and it is precisely this that gave his doctrine a pessimistic hue: there were remedies against the pressure of population, but they were unlikely to be adopted.

The Malthusian law of population has some resemblance to Newtonian mechanics in assuming tendencies which are never observed as such in the real world: the arithmetical ratio is simply a loose generalization about things as they are, whereas the geometrical ratio is a calculation of things as they might be but never are. The saving clause in the theory is the check of moral restraint, which permits the food supply to increase without a corresponding increase in population. But how shall we know that it is in operation, as distinct from the practice of birth control? By virtue of the fact that the food supply is outstripping the growth of numbers, Malthus would answer. In short, the Malthusian theory explains everything by explaining nothing. No wonder that Malthus's critics bitterly complained that the Malthusian theory could not be disproved, because it was always true on its own terms.

EWB

213

Mandeville, Bernard (ca. 1670–1733), English satirist and moral philosopher. Bernard Mandeville is famous as the author of *The Fable of the Bees.*

Bernard Mandeville was probably born in Rotterdam, Holland, the son of a prominent doctor. In 1685 he entered the University of Rotterdam and in 1689 went on to study medicine at the University of Leiden, where he received his medical degree in 1691. Afterward he went to England to "learn the language" and set up practice as a physician. However, he had very few patients and after a short time virtually gave up medicine to devote himself exclusively to his writings.

Mandeville's best-known work is *The Fable of the Bees, or Private Vices, Publick Benefits* (1714), originally published as a poem, "The Grumbling Hive, or Knaves Turned Honest" (1705). This was intended at first to be a political satire on the state of England in 1705, when the Tories accused the ministry of favoring the French war for their own personal gains. In the later version, however, enlarged to two volumes, Mandeville, in agreement with Thomas Hobbes, declares that men act essentially in terms of egoistical interests, in contrast to the easy optimism and idealism of Shaftesbury. The material concerns of individuals are the basic force behind all social progress, while what rulers and clergymen call virtues are simply fictions that those in power employ to maintain their control. Francis Hutcheson and Bishop Berkeley wrote treatises opposing Mandeville's views. Others, including Adam Smith, as some interpreters claim, were affected in a more positive way by Mandeville's ideas.

In some of his other works Mandeville shows an intelligent and open interest in controversial and, for the time, scandalous subjects, such as whoring and the execution of criminals. On some issues, however, Mandeville seems strangely callous. In "An Essay on Charity and Charity Schools" he objects to educating the poor because the acquisition of knowledge has the effect of increasing desires and thereby making it more difficult to meet the needs of the poor. Moreover, he seems to regard even wars as valuable to the economic development of a nation since by destroying houses and property laborers are provided an opportunity to replace the destroyed goods.

On the basis of his views Mandeville is usually placed in the moral-sense school. Some interpreters insist that he is the forerunner of the doctrine of utilitarianism.

EWB

Manet, Édouard (1832–1883), French painter. The art of Édouard Manet broke with 19th-century academic precepts and marks the beginning of modern painting.

Édouard Manet was born in Paris on January 23, 1832, to Auguste Édouard Manet, an official at the Ministry of Justice, and Eugénie Désirée Manet. The father, who had expected to study law, vigorously opposed his wish to become a painter. The career of naval officer was decided upon as a compromise, and at the age of 16 Édouard sailed to Rio de Janeiro on a training vessel. Upon his return he failed to pass the entrance examination of the naval academy. His father relented, and in 1850 Manet entered the studio of Thomas Couture, where, in spite of many disagreements with his teacher, he remained until 1856. During this period Manet traveled abroad and made numerous copies after the Old Masters in both foreign and French public collections.

Early Works. Manet's entry for the Salon of 1859, the *Absinthe Drinker,* a thematically romantic but conceptually already daring work, was rejected. At the Salon of 1861, his *Spanish Singer,* one of a number of works of Spanish character painted in this period, not only was admitted to the Salon but won an honorable mention and the acclaim of the poet Théophile Gautier. This was to be Manet's last success for many years.

In 1863 Manet married Suzanne Leenhoff, a Dutch pianist. That year he showed 14 paintings at the Martinet Gallery; one of them, *Music in the Tuileries,* remarkable for its freshness in the handling of a contemporary scene, was greeted with considerable hostility. Also in 1863 the Salon rejected Manet's large painting *Luncheon on the Grass,* and the artist elected to have it shown at the now famous Salon des Refusés, created by the Emperor under the pressure of the exceptionally large number of painters whose work had been turned away. Here, Manet's picture attracted the most attention and brought forth a kind of abusive criticism which was to set a pattern for years to come. Although this painting is a paraphrase of Giorgione's *Concert champetre,* the combination of clothed men and a nude woman in a modern context was found offensive.

In 1865 Manet's *Olympia* produced a still more violent reaction at the official Salon, and his reputation as a renegade became widespread. Upset by the criticism, Manet made a brief trip to Spain, where he admired many works by Diego Velázquez, to whom he referred as "the painter of painters."

Support of Baudelaire and Zola. Manet's close friend and supporter during the early years was Charles Baudelaire, who, in 1862, had written a quatrain to accompany one of Manet's Spanish subjects, *Lola de Valence,* and the public, largely as a result of the strange atmosphere of the *Olympia,* linked the two men readily. In 1866, after the Salon jury had rejected two of Manet's works, Émile Zola came to his defense with a series of articles filled with strongly expressed, uncompromising praise. In 1867 he published a book which contains the prediction, "Manet's place is destined to be in the Louvre." This book appears on Zola's desk in Manet's portrait of the writer (1868). In May of that year the Paris World's Fair opened its doors, and Manet, at his own expense, exhibited 50 of his works in a temporary structure, not far from Gustave Courbet's private exhibition. This was in keeping with Manet's view, expressed years later to his friend Antonin Proust, that his paintings must be seen together in order to be fully understood.

Although Manet insisted that a painter be "resolutely of his own time" and that he paint what he sees, he nevertheless produced two important religious works, the *Dead Christ with Angels* and *Christ Mocked by the Soldiers,* which were shown at the Salons of 1864 and 1865, respectively, and ridiculed. Only Zola could defend the former work on the grounds of its vigorous realism while playing down its alleged lack of piety. It is also true that although Manet despised the academic category of "history painting" he did paint the contemporary *Naval Battle between the Kearsarge and the Alabama* (1864) and the *Execution of Maximilian* (1867). The latter is based upon a careful gathering of the facts surrounding the incident and composed, largely, after Francisco Goya's *Executions of the Third of May,* resulting in a curious amalgam of the particular and the universal. Manet's use of older works of art in elaborating his own major compositions has long been, and continues to be, a problematic subject, since the old view that this procedure was needed to compensate for the artist's own inadequate imagination is rapidly being discarded.

Late Works. Although the impressionists were influenced by Manet during the 1860s, during the next decade it appears that it was he who learned from them. His palette became lighter; his stroke, without ever achieving the analytical intensity of Claude Monet's, was shorter and more rapid. Nevertheless, Manet never cultivated pleinairism seriously, and he remained essentially a figure and studio painter. Also, despite his sympathy for most of the impressionists with whom the public associated him, he never exhibited with them at their series of private exhibitions which began in 1874.

Manet had his first resounding success since the *Spanish Singer* at the Salon of 1873 with his *Bon Bock,*

which radiates a touch and joviality of expression reminiscent of Frans Hals, in contrast to Manet's usually austere figures. In spite of the popularity of this painting, his success was not to extend to the following season. About this time he met the poet Stéphane Mallarmé, with whom he remained on intimate terms for the remainder of his life. After Manet's rejection by the jury in 1876, Mallarmé took up his defense.

Toward the end of the 1870s, although Manet retained the bright palette and the touch of his impressionist works, he returned to the figure problems of the early years. The undeniable sense of mystery is found again in several bar scenes, notably the *Brasserie Reichshoffen,* in which the relationships of the figures recall those of the *Luncheon on the Grass.* Perhaps the apotheosis of his lifelong endeavors is to be found in his last major work, *A Bar at the Folies-Bergère.* Here, in the expression of the barmaid, is all the starkness of the great confrontations of the 1860s, but bathed in a profusion of colors. While we are drawn to the brilliantly painted accessories, it is the girl, placed at the center before a mirror, who dominates the composition and ultimately demands our attention. Although her reflected image, showing her to be in conversation with a man, is absorbed into the brilliant atmosphere of the setting, she remains enigmatic and aloof. Manet produced two aspects of the same personality, combined the fleeting with the eternal, and, by "misplacing" the reflected image, took a step toward abstraction as a solution to certain lifelong philosophical and technical problems.

In 1881 Manet was finally admitted to membership in the Legion of Honor, an award he had long coveted. By then he was seriously ill. Therapy at the sanatorium at Bellevue failed to improve his health, and walking became increasingly difficult for him. In his weakened condition he found it easier to handle pastels than oils, and he produced a great many flower pieces and portraits in that medium. In the spring of 1883 his left leg was amputated, but this did not prolong his life. He died peacefully in Paris on April 30.

Manet was short, unusually handsome, and witty. His biographers stress his kindness and unaffected generosity toward his friends. The paradoxical elements in his art are an extension of the man: although a revolutionary in art, he craved official honors; while fashionably dressed, he affected a Parisian slang at odds with his appearance and impeccable manners; and although he espoused the style of life of the conservative classes, his political sentiments were those of the republican liberal.

EWB

Marat, Jean Paul (1743–1793), French journalist and political leader. Jean Paul Marat was an influential advocate of extreme revolutionary views and measures.

Jean Paul Marat was born in Boudry, Neuchâtel, Switzerland, on May 24, 1743, the son of lower-middle-class parents. Of his early years very little is known. He acquired a medical education and for some years was a successful physician in both England and France. He also conducted scientific experiments in the fields of optics and electricity. But failure to achieve what he considered to be proper recognition for this work left him with a feeling of persecution.

Marat also published several books on philosophical and political themes, the most important of which was *The Chains of Slavery,* in which he voiced an uncompromising denunciation of royal despotism, a defense of the sovereignty of the people, and a sympathy for the poor and downtrodden which he never abandoned. The coming of the French Revolution in 1789 gave him his opportunity to pursue these themes, and before the year was out, he had begun to publish his journal, *Ami du peuple* (*Friend of the People*). In his opinion the moderate Revolution of 1789, although it had ended royal despotism, had left a new aristocracy of the rich in control, with the grievances of the poor still unsatisfied. Thus a radical revolutionary uprising was necessary, in his opinion, and he bluntly called time and again for popular executions and a temporary dictatorship to save the Revolution and bring about a regime of social justice.

Marat's radical views and the ferocity with which he voiced them won him great popularity among the lower classes in Paris and the provinces. But he was the object of particular fear and hatred to those who supported the moderate revolution that had produced the limited monarchy. The authorities frequently tried to silence him, but he avoided arrest by hiding with the aid of his supporters and published his journal at least intermittently.

When the moderate experiment with limited monarchy failed in the midst of disastrous military reverses, the King was deposed in August 1792, and less than a month later the September massacres, an outbreak of popular executions such as Marat had been urging, took place in Paris. These events inaugurated the radical phase of the French Revolution. The Paris voters elected Marat to the Convention, which was to serve France as a legislature for the next 3 years, and he sat and voted with the "Mountain," the left-wing Jacobin faction. But he was blamed by many for the September massacres, and his continued incitement to direct action and purges, plus his advocacy of an extensive program of social legislation, kept all but the most radical aloof from him. His extreme ideas and language were matched by his informality of dress and unkempt appearance, which was heightened by the evidence of a chronic skin disease.

Marat concentrated his invective during the early months of 1793 against the moderate Girondin party, and they responded in kind. They tried to silence him and persuaded the Convention to decree his arrest and trial. But he emerged from hiding and by a brilliant speech won a triumphant acquittal in April 1793. His Girondin opponents now came under attack from the Jacobin Mountain, and Marat reached the height of his influence as he led the attack in his journal. With the decisive aid of the Paris masses, the Convention was forced to unseat and then order the arrest of the Girondin leaders (June 2, 1793).

Marat's triumph led ironically to his own death. Charlotte Corday, an idealistic young girl of Girondin sympathies from the provinces, came to Paris to seek revenge and to rid her country of the monster Marat. By this time his health had so deteriorated that he was living and working in seclusion in his apartment under a regimen of medicinal baths. On July 13, 1793, she managed to gain admittance to his apartment, under the pretense of bringing information to aid him in his continued campaign against the Girondins, and stabbed him to death in his bath.

EWB

Maria Theresa (1717–1780) was Holy Roman empress from 1740 to 1780. Ruling in the most difficult period of Austrian history, she modernized her dominions and saved them from dissolution.

The eldest daughter of the emperor Charles VI, Maria Theresa was born in Vienna on May 13, 1717. Her education did not differ in the main from that given any imperial princess, being both clerical and superficial, even though by the time she was an adolescent it was becoming increasingly probable that Charles would produce no male heir and that one day Maria Theresa would succeed to all his dominions. Charles did not act upon the insistent advice of his most capable adviser, Prince Eugene of Savoy, and marry his daughter off to a prince powerful and influential enough himself to protect her dominions in time of need. Instead he chose to rely upon the fanciful diplomatic guarantees offered by the Pragmatic Sanction. Thus, in 1736 Maria Theresa was permitted to marry for love. Her choice was Duke Francis Stephen of Lorraine. So that France might not object to the prospect of an eventual incorporation of Lorraine into the empire, Francis Stephen was forced to exchange his beloved province for the rather less valuable Tuscany.

In spite of this, and even though the marriage in its first 3 years produced three daughters, Maria Theresa was boundlessly happy. Then suddenly, in October 1740, her father died. At the age of 23, without anything in the way of formal preparation, without the least acquaintance with affairs of state, Maria Theresa had supreme responsibility thrust upon her.

War of the Austrian Succession. Francis Stephen was designated coregent and put in charge of restoring the finances of the empire, a task to which he brought considerable ability but for which he was not to have the requisite time. The treasury was empty, the army had been badly neglected, and as Prince Eugene had warned, Austria's neighbors now engaged in a contest to establish which of them could repudiate most completely the obligations they had subscribed to in the Pragmatic Sanction. Bavaria advanced claims to a considerable portion of the Hapsburg lands and was supported in this venture by France. Spain demanded the empire's Italian territories. Frederick II of Prussia, himself very recently come to the throne of his country, now offered to support Maria Theresa against these importunities if Austria would pay for this service by turning over to Prussia the province of Silesia. When this cynical offer was indignantly rejected in Vienna, Frederick sent his troops into Silesia in December 1740. Bavaria and France soon joined in this attack, thus launching the 8-year War of the Austrian Succession.

At first it seemed as if the young Maria Theresa could quickly be overwhelmed. The elector Charles of Bavaria secured his election as Emperor Charles VII and with German and French troops captured Prague. If his army had achieved a juncture with the Prussians, the Austrians would no longer have been in a position to defend themselves. But Frederick II had not launched his attack on Silesia to introduce a French hegemony in central Europe. He now concluded an armistice with the Austrians, who were, in 1742, able to concentrate their forces against the French and Bavarians, whom they threw out of Bohemia. Frederick came back into the war in 1744, withdrew again the next year, in which, the Bavarian Charles VII having died, Francis Stephen was elected emperor. The war was ended at last in 1748, Austria being forced to acquiesce in the Prussian retention of Silesia and losing also the Italian districts of Parma, Piacenza, and Guastalla to France. The loss of Silesia was very painful indeed, as it was perhaps the richest of all the Hapsburg provinces.

Domestic Reform. Maria Theresa had learned her job under the most difficult conditions during the war. But she had soon found that, among the members of the high court aristocracy, the only class from which, traditionally, important servants of the Crown could be drawn, there was no dearth of able men willing to unite their fate with that of the house of Hapsburg. Although she had never, in the course of the war, found a really satisfactory general, she had recognized the talents of, and placed in responsible positions, a number of able administrators, men such as counts Sinzendorf, Sylva-Tarouca, and Kaunitz. Thus, at the end of the war, the basis for a reform of the governmental apparatus already existed.

The actual work of reform, with the explicit end of strengthening Austria so that one day in the not too distant future Silesia might be recovered, was turned over to a Silesian exile, Count Frederick William Haugwitz. The key to Haugwitz's reform program was centralization. Bohemia and Austria were placed under a combined ministry, and the Provincial Estates were, insofar as possible, deprived of their authority or at least circumvented. At the same time industry was encouraged as a producer of wealth that could most readily be tapped by the state. In the provinces to which it was applied, the system produced dramatic results: on the average, the military contributions of the districts in question rose by 150 percent. Unfortunately, the concerted opposition of the nobility in Hungary prevented it from being applied there. Moreover, Haugwitz's position was being continually undermined by his colleague Kaunitz, who himself wished to play the role of Austria's savior.

Foreign Policy. In 1753 Kaunitz was given the title of state chancellor with unrestricted powers in the realm of foreign policy. While serving as Austrian ambassador to France, he had convinced himself that Austria's defeat in the recent war had been due largely to an unfortunate choice of allies. In particular, he thought, the empire had been badly let down by England. He now set about forging a new alliance whose chief aim was to surround Prussia with an insurmountable coalition. Saxony, Sweden, and Russia became Austria's allies. In 1755 Kaunitz's diplomatic efforts were crowned with the conclusion of an alliance with Austria's old enemy France, a circumstance that led to the conclusion of an alliance between Prussia and England. This diplomatic revolution seemed to leave the Prussians at a hopeless disadvantage, but Frederick II was not the man to await his own funeral, and in 1756 he opened hostilities, thus launching what was to become the Seven Years War.

Maria Theresa, although no lover of warfare for its own sake, welcomed the war as the only practical means of at last recovering Silesia. It was not to be. In spite of a much more energetic conduct of the war on the part of Austria, Frederick was for the most part able to fight his enemies one at a time. And when, in 1762, his situation at last appeared desperate, the death of Empress Elisabeth brought about a Russian withdrawal from the war, which now could no longer be won by the allies. In 1763 peace was concluded, and Silesia remained firmly in Prussian hands.

In the course of this second war, Maria Theresa developed the habit of governing autocratically, excluding Francis Stephen from all participation in the affairs of state. In spite of this the marriage was a happy one. From the dynastic point of view, the birth of Archduke Joseph in 1741 had assured the male succession. His birth was followed by numerous others, the imperial couple producing 16 children in all. Then suddenly, in 1765, the Emperor died of a stroke. Maria Theresa was inconsolable. For a time she thought of withdrawing to a cloister and turning the government over to Joseph, who was then 24. It was only with great difficulty that her ministers, with Kaunitz in the lead, managed to dissuade her from this course. And when she did return to public life, it was as a different woman. For the rest of her days she wore only black; she never again appeared at the gay divertisements of what had been a very lighthearted court; and if she had all her life been a pious Catholic, her devotion to religion now came to border on both fanaticism and bigotry.

Later Reign. At his father's death Joseph had been appointed coregent. Unlike his father, the archduke meant in fact to share in the governance of the realm. But this Maria Theresa was unwilling to let him do. After many recriminations, a compromise was arrived at: Joseph was to take charge of army reform and to share with Kaunitz the responsibility of making foreign policy. This arrangement was unfortunate not only because it deprived Joseph of any real influence on the internal affairs of Austria, the sector in which his ideas were most promising, but also because he had no talent whatever either for diplomacy or for warfare.

The 15 years of the coregency were a time of continual struggle between mother and son, but it would be a mistake to construe them as an unrelenting struggle between the forces of progress, as represented by Joseph, and those of reaction, led by Maria Theresa. Although the archduke vigorously defended the principle of religious toleration, anathema to his mother, and once threatened to resign when she proposed to expel some Protestants from Bohemia, on the equally important question of peasant emancipation, Maria Theresa took a stand distinctly more favorable to the peasants than Joseph. In foreign affairs, she opposed Joseph's adventurous attempt to acquire Bavaria, which, as she had feared, led to war with Prussia in 1778; and when Joseph lost his nerve in the midst of the struggle, she took matters into her own hands and negotiated a by no means disadvantageous peace that resulted in the acquisition of the Innviertel.

These last events, incidentally, confirm that after the unsatisfactory conclusion of the Seven Years War the main Austrian objective was no longer a redress of balance against Prussia. If political and social reforms continued, it was in part because reform had become a way of life, in part because Maria Theresa recognized that a more centralized and effective government was an end worth pursuing for itself. Although it is true that throughout the coregency Joseph kept up a clamor for various changes, some of the major reforms of the period can nevertheless be attributed chiefly to the desires of the Empress. This is particularly true of the new penal code of 1768 and of the abolition of judicial torture in 1776. The penal code, although objected to as still unduly harsh, nevertheless had the virtue of standardizing both judicial proceedings and punishments. In spite of her devotion to the Catholic Church, Maria Theresa insisted on defending with great vigor the rights of the state vis-à-vis the Church.

In her reign, neither papal bulls nor the pastoral letters of bishops could circulate in her dominions without her prior permission, and in 1777 Maria Theresa joined a number of other European monarchs in banishing the Society of Jesus from her lands. In the course of 1780 Maria Theresa's health deteriorated rapidly. She died on November 29 of that year, probably of a heart condition.

EWB

Marie Antoinette (1755–1793), queen of France. Marie Antoinette was queen of France at the outbreak of the Revolution. Her activities and reputation contributed to the decline of the prestige of the French monarchy.

Marie Antoinette was the daughter of the Holy Roman emperor Francis I and the empress Maria Theresa. In 1770 she was married to the French Dauphin, who 4 years later ascended the throne as Louis XVI. The personalities of the two rulers were very different: while Louis XVI was phlegmatic and withdrawn, Marie Antoinette was gay, frivolous, and imprudent in her actions and choice of friends. She soon became unpopular in the court and the country, antagonizing many of the nobles, including the King's brothers and those Frenchmen who regretted the recently concluded alliance with Austria, long regarded as the traditional enemy; for the population as a whole she became the symbol for the extravagance of the court.

Although Marie Antoinette did not intervene in foreign affairs as frequently as has been asserted, she soon forgot her statement on first entering France, when she interrupted an official greeting in German, "Speak French, Monsieur. From now on I hear no language other than French." She sometimes sought, usually without great success, to obtain French support for Austrian objectives, for example, against Prussia and the Low Countries.

The Queen's influence on domestic policy before 1789 has also been exaggerated. Her interventions in politics were usually in order to obtain positions and subsidies for her friends. It is true, however, that she usually opposed the efforts of reforming ministers such as A. R. J. Turgot and became involved in court intrigues against them. Such activities, as well as her associates and personal life, particularly the "diamond necklace affair," when it appeared that the Queen had yielded herself to a wealthy cardinal for an expensive diamond necklace, increased her unpopularity and led to a stream of pamphlets and satires against her. The fact that after the birth of her children Marie Antoinette's way of life became more restrained did not alter the popular image of an immoral and extravagant woman.

In the summer of 1788, when Louis XVI yielded to pressure and convoked the Estates General to deal with the fiscal crisis, Marie Antoinette agreed, or appeared to agree, to the return of Jacques Necker as chief minister and to granting the Third Estate as many representatives as the other two combined. However, after the meeting of the Estates General in May 1789 and such events as the taking of the Bastille (July 14, 1789), Marie Antoinette supported the conservative court faction most insistent upon maintaining the Old Regime.

On Oct. 1, 1789, the Queen was received enthusiastically at a royalist banquet at Versailles during which the Revolution was denounced and its symbols insulted. A few days later (October 4–5) a Parisian crowd forced the court to move to Paris, where it could be controlled more readily. Marie Antoinette's role in the efforts of the monarchy to work with such moderates as the Comte de Mirabeau and later with the constitutional monarchist A. P. Barnave is unclear, but it appears that she lacked confidence in them. After the attempt of the royal couple to escape was thwarted at Varennes (June 21, 1791), the Queen, convinced that only foreign intervention could save the monarchy, sought the aid of her brother, the Holy Roman emperor Leopold II. Convinced that France, in its weakened condition, with many officers already émigrés, would be easily defeated, she favored the declaration of war on Austria in April 1792. On

Aug. 10, 1792, the Paris crowd stormed the Tuileries Palace and ended the monarchy (the following month the National Convention established the First French Republic).

On August 13 Marie Antoinette began a captivity that was to end only with her death. She was first imprisoned in the Temple with her family and, after Aug. 1, 1793, in the Conciergerie. After a number of unsuccessful attempts to obtain her escape failed, Marie Antoinette appeared before the Revolutionary Tribunal, charged with aiding the enemy and inciting civil war within France. The Tribunal found her guilty and condemned her to death. On Oct. 16, 1793, she went to the guillotine. As did Louis XVI, Marie Antoinette aroused sympathy by her dignity and courage in prison and before the executioner.

EWB

Mathiez, Albert (1874–1932), French historian. Albert Mathiez was one of the major 20th-century historians of the French Revolution.

Albert Mathiez was born to an innkeeper's family at La Bruyère in eastern France on Jan. 10, 1874. He graduated from the École Normale in 1897. After teaching for a short time in the provinces, he returned to Paris to prepare a doctoral thesis under the direction of Alphonse Aulard. The thesis, on Revolutionary religious cults (1904), marked him as a historian of independent mind. Mathiez argued that these cults were profoundly related to the Revolutionaries' views of the role of religion in society. Though the thesis derived much of its argument from the work of the sociologist Émile Durkheim, Mathiez later became dubious about the use of sociology in historical writing.

Three years after presenting his thesis Mathiez broke with Aulard, beginning a feud that continued for the rest of his life. Whether the feud was caused by personal pique, psychological conflict, or scholarly ambition, it took public form as a dispute over the characters and historical roles of Georges Jacques Danton and Maximilien de Robespierre. Danton, whom Aulard admired as a patriot, was to Mathiez a corrupt demagogue; Robespierre, a tyrant to Aulard, became for Mathiez the champion of social democracy. To prove his point Mathiez, in 1908, founded a new journal, the *Annales revolutionnaires,* and the Society for Robespierre Studies. In a series of articles and books—*Robespierre Studies* (2 vols., 1917–1918); *Danton and the Peace* (1919); and *The India Company* (1920)he exposed Danton's graft and his "defeatist" attempts to negotiate with the enemies of the Revolution. In *Danton* (1926) he covered his subject's entire career. At the same time he explored Robespierre's career and promoted an edition of his writings. In these articles and books Mathiez demonstrated his mastery of critical history, illuminating with his forceful imagination the new evidence he had found in the archives.

Strongly influenced by Jean Jaurès, Mathiez also wrote on the economic history of the Revolution. He had early come to see the Revolution as a class conflict, and the Russian Revolution confirmed his view that political events had to be related to economic and social movements.

Mathiez wrote one narrative of the Revolution (3 vols., 1922–1927). Writing for the general public, and confined to a short text by the publisher, Mathiez here showed his mastery of French style and his ability to convince his readers. He continued this narrative in a much more detailed manner in *The Thermidorian Reaction* (1929) and *The Directorate* (1934).

Mathiez's dispute with Aulard, his brusque manner toward those who were not his friends, his criticism of the government during World War I, and his defense of bolshevism left him few supporters in the Parisian academic world. Professor at Dijon (1919–1926), he was finally called to Paris in 1926 as a substitute and then as a lecturer. On Feb. 25, 1932, while delivering a lecture, he suffered a stroke and died.

EWB

Marx, Karl (1818–1883), German philosopher, radical economist, and revolutionary leader. Karl Marx founded modern "scientific" socialism. His basic ideas known as Marxism form the foundation of socialist and communist movements throughout the world.

Karl Marx spent most of his life in exile. He was exiled from his native Prussia in 1849 and went to Paris, from which he was expelled a few months later. He then settled in London, where he spent the rest of his life in dire poverty and relative obscurity. He was hardly known to the English public in his lifetime. His reputation as a radical thinker began to spread only after the emergence of the socialist parties in Europe, especially in Germany and France, in the 1870s and 1880s. From then on, Marx's theories continued to be hotly debated in the growing labor and socialist movements everywhere, including Tsarist Russia.

By the end of the 19th and beginning of the 20th century, socialist parties everywhere had by and large accepted a considerable measure of Marxism, even though with modifications. This was especially true of the idea of the class struggle and the establishment of a socialist society, in which economic exploitation and social inequality would be abolished. Marxism achieved its first great triumph in the Russian Revolution of 1917, when its successful leader, V. I. Lenin, a lifelong disciple of Marx, organized the So-

viet Union as a proletarian dictatorship based on Marx's philosophy, as Lenin interpreted it. Henceforth, Marx became a world figure and his theories a subject of universal attention and controversy.

Early Life. Marx was born in Trier, Rhenish Prussia, on May 5, 1818, the son of Heinrich Marx, a lawyer, and Henriette Presburg Marx, a Dutchwoman. Both Heinrich and Henriette were descendants of a long line of rabbis. Barred from the practice of law as a Jew, Heinrich Marx became converted to Lutheranism about 1817, and Karl was baptized in the same church in 1824, at the age of 6. Karl attended a Lutheran elementary school but later became an atheist and materialist, rejecting both the Christian and Jewish religions. It was he who coined the aphorism "Religion is the opium of the people," a cardinal principle in modern communism.

Karl attended the Friedrich Wilhelm Gymnasium in Trier for 5 years, graduating in 1835, at the age of 17. The gymnasium curriculum was the usual classical onehistory, mathematics, literature, and languages, particularly Greek and Latin. Karl became proficient in French and Latin, both of which he learned to read and write fluently. In later years he taught himself other languages, so that as a mature scholar he could also read Spanish, Italian, Dutch, Russian, and English. As his articles in the *New York Daily Tribune* show, he came to handle the English language masterfully (he loved Shakespeare, whose works he knew by heart), although he never lost his heavy Teutonic accent in speaking.

In October 1835 Marx matriculated in Bonn University, where he attended courses primarily in jurisprudence, as it was his father's ardent wish that he become a lawyer. Marx, however, was more interested in philosophy and literature than in law. He wanted to be a poet and dramatist, and in his student days he wrote a great deal of poetry—most of it preserved—which in his mature years he rightly recognized as imitative and mediocre. He spent a year at Bonn, studying little but roistering and drinking. He spent a day in jail for disturbing the peace and fought one duel, in which he was wounded in the right eye. He also piled up heavy debts.

Marx's dismayed father took him out of Bonn and had him enter the University of Berlin, then a hub of intellectual ferment. In Berlin a galaxy of brilliant thinkers was challenging existing institutions and ideas, including religion, philosophy, ethics, and politics. The spirit of the great philosopher G. W. F. Hegel was still palpable there. A group known as the Young Hegelians, which included teachers such as Bruno Bauer and bright, philosophically oriented students, met frequently to debate and interpret the subtle ideas of the master. Young Marx soon became a member of the Young Hegelian circle and was deeply influenced by its prevailing ideas.

Marx spent more than 4 years in Berlin, completing his studies there in March 1841. He had given up jurisprudence and devoted himself primarily to philosophy. On April 15, 1841, the University of Jena awarded "Carolo Henrico Marx" the degree of doctor of philosophy on the strength of his abstruse and learned dissertation, *Difference between Democritean and Epicurean Natural Philosophy*, which was based on Greek-language sources.

His Exile. Marx's hopes of teaching philosophy at Bonn University were frustrated by the reactionary policy of the Prussian government. He then turned to writing and journalism for his livelihood. In 1842 he became editor of the liberal Cologne newspaper *Rheinische Zeitung*, but it was suppressed by the Berlin government the following year. Marx then moved to Paris. There he first came in contact with the working class, gave up philosophy as a life goal, and undertook his serious study of economics.

In January 1845 Marx was expelled from France "at the instigation of the Prussian government," as he said. He moved to Brussels, where he lived until 1848 and where he founded the German Workers' party and was active in the Communist League. It was for the latter that he, with his friend and collaborator Friedrich Engels, published, in 1848, the famous Manifesto of the Communist Party (known as the Communist Manifesto). Expelled by the Belgian government for his radicalism, Marx moved back to Cologne, where he became editor of the *Neue Rheinische Zeitung* in June 1848. Less than a year later, in May 1849, the paper was suppressed by the Prussian government, and Marx himself was exiled. He returned to Paris, but in September the French government expelled him again. Hounded from the Continent, Marx finally settled in London, where he lived as a stateless exile (Britain denied him citizenship and Prussia refused to renaturalize him) for the rest of his life.

In London, Marx's sole means of support was journalism. He wrote for both German- and English-language publications. From August 1852 to March 1862 he was correspondent for the *New York Daily Tribune*, contributing a total of about 355 articles, many of which were used by that paper as leading (unsigned) editorials. Journalism, however, paid wretchedly (£2 per article); Marx was literally saved from starvation by the continuous financial support of Engels. In 1864 Marx helped to found in London the

International Workingmen's Association (known as the First International), for which he wrote the inaugural address. In 1872 he dissolved the International, to prevent it from falling into the hands of the anarchists under the leadership of Mikhail Bakunin. Thereafter, Marx's political activities were confined mainly to correspondence with radicals in Europe and America, offering advice and helping to shape the socialist and labor movements.

Marx was married to his childhood sweetheart, Jenny von Westphalen, who was known as the "most beautiful girl in Trier," on June 19, 1843. She was totally devoted to him. She died of cancer on Dec. 2, 1881, at the age of 67. For Marx it was a blow from which he never recovered.

Marx spent most of his working time in the British Museum, doing research both for his newspaper articles and his books. He was a most conscientious scholar, never satisfied with secondhand information but tracing facts and figures to their original sources. In preparation for *Das Kapital*, he read virtually every available work in economic and financial theory and practice in the major languages of Europe.

In the last two decades of his life Marx was tormented by a mounting succession of ailments that would have tried the patience of Job. He suffered from hereditary liver derangement (of which, he claimed, his father died); frequent outbreaks of carbuncles and furuncles on his neck, chest, back, and buttocks (often he could not sit); toothaches; eye inflammations; lung abscesses; hemorrhoids; pleurisy; and persistent headaches and coughs that made sleep impossible without drugs. In the final dozen or so years of his life, he could no longer do any sustained intellectual work. He died in his armchair in London on March 14, 1883, about two months before his sixty-fifth birthday. He lies buried in London's Highgate Cemetery, where the grave is marked by a bust of him.

His Works. Marx's writings fall into two general categories, the polemical-philosophical and the economic-political. The first reflected his Hegelian-idealistic period; the second, his revolutionary-political interests.

Marx wrote hundreds of articles, brochures, and reports but few books as such. He published only five books during his lifetime. Two of them were polemical, and three were political-economic. The first, *The Holy Family* (1845), written in collaboration with Engels, was a polemic against Marx's former teacher and Young Hegelian philosopher Bruno Bauer. The second was *Misère de la philosophie* (The Poverty of Philosophy), written by Marx himself in French and published in Paris and Brussels in 1847. As its subtitle indicates, this polemical work was "An Answer to the *Philosophy of Poverty* by M. Proudhon."

Marx's third book, *The Eighteenth Brumaire of Louis Bonaparte,* published serially in a German publication in New York City in 1852, is a brilliant historical-political analysis of the rise and intrigues of the Bonaparte who became Napoleon III. The remaining two books, both on economics, are the ones on which Marx's worldwide reputation rests: *Critique of Political Economy* and, more particularly, *Das Kapital* (Capital).

Critique was published in 1859, after about 14 years of intermittent research. Marx considered it merely a first installment, expecting to bring out additional volumes, but he scrapped his plan in favor of another approach. The result was *Das Kapital,* subtitled *Critique of Political Economy,* of which only the first volume appeared, in 1867, in Marx's lifetime. After his death, two other volumes were brought out by Engels on the basis of the materials Marx left behind. Volumes 2 (1885) and 3 (1894) can be properly regarded as works by Marx and Engels, rather than by Marx himself. Indeed, without Engels, as Marx admitted, the whole monumental enterprise might not have been produced at all. On the night of Aug. 16, 1867, when Marx completed correcting the proof sheets of volume 1, he wrote to Engels in Manchester: "I have YOU alone to thank that this has been made possible. Without your sacrifices for me I could never possibly have done the enormous work for the three volumes. I embrace you, full of thanks!"

A fourth volume of *Das Kapital* was brought together by Karl Kautsky after Engels's death. It was based on Marx's notes and materials from *Critique of Political Economy* and was published in three parts, under the title *Theories of Surplus Value,* between 1905 and 1910. A Russian edition, also in three parts, came out between 1954 and 1961, and an English translation in 1968.

Two of Marx's books were published posthumously. *The Class Struggles in France, 1848–1850,* written in 1871, appeared in 1895. It was, Engels wrote in his introduction, "Marx's first attempt, with the aid of his materialist conception, to explain a section of contemporary history from the given economic situation." The second posthumous work, *The German Ideology,* which Marx wrote in collaboration with Engels in 1845–1846, was not published in full until 1932. The book is an attack on the philosophers Ludwig Andreas Feuerbach and Max Stirner and on the so-called true socialists.

The rest of Marx's publications, mostly printed posthumously, consist of brochures. *Herr Vogt* (1860) is a furious polemic against a man named Karl Vogt,

whom Marx accused of being a police spy. *Wage-Labor and Capital* (1884) is a reprint of newspaper articles. *Critique of the Gotha Programme* (1891) consists of notes which Marx sent to the German Socialist party congress in 1875. *Wages, Price and Profit* (1898) is an address that Marx delivered at the General Council of the International in 1865.

His Ideas. Marx's world importance does not lie in his economic system, which, as critics point out, was not original but was derived from the classical economists Adam Smith and David Ricardo. *Das Kapital,* indeed, is not primarily a technical work on economics but one that uses economic materials to establish a moral-philosophical-sociological structure. Marx's universal appeal lies in his moral approach to social-economic problems, in his insights into the relationships between institutions and values, and in his conception of the salvation of mankind. Hence Marx is best understood if one studies, not his economics, but his theory of history and politics.

The central idea in Marx's thought is the materialistic conception of history. This involves two basic notions: that the economic system at any given time determines the prevailing ideas; and that history is an ongoing process regulated—predetermined—by the economic institutions which evolve in regular stages.

The first notion turned Hegel upside down. In Hegel's view, history is determined by the universal idea (God), which shapes worldly institutions. Marx formulated the reverse: that institutions shape ideas. This is known as the materialistic interpretation of history. Marx's second notion, that of historical evolution, is connected with his concept of dialectics. He saw in history a continuing dialectical process, each stage of development being the product of thesis, antithesis, and synthesis.

Thus thesis corresponds to the ancient, precapitalist period, when there were no classes or exploitation. Antithesis corresponds to the era of capitalism and labor exploitation. Synthesis is the final product— communism, under which capital would be owned in common and there would be no exploitation.

To Marx, capitalism is the last stage of historical development before communism. The proletariat, produced by capitalism, is the last historical class. The two are fated to be in conflict—the class struggle, which Marx proclaimed so eloquently in the Communist Manifesto—until the proletariat is inevitably victorious and establishes a transitional order, the proletarian dictatorship, a political system which Marx did not elaborate or explain. The proletarian dictatorship, in turn, evolves into communism, or the classless society, the final stage of historical development, when there are no classes, no exploitation, and no inequalities. The logical implication is that with the final establishment of communism, history comes to a sudden end. The dialectical process then presumably ceases, and there are no more historical evolutions or social struggles. This Marxist interpretation of history, with its final utopian-apocalyptic vision, has been criticized in the noncommunist world as historically inaccurate, scientifically untenable, and logically absurd.

Nevertheless, Marx's message of an earthly paradise has provided millions with hope and new meaning of life. From this point of view, one may agree with the Austrian economist Joseph A. Schumpeter that "Marxism is a religion" and Marx is its "prophet."

EWB

Maurras, Charles Marie Photius (1868–1952), French political writer and reactionary. Moving spirit and principal spokesman of Action Française, Charles Maurras was an antidemocrat, racist, monarchist, and worshiper of tradition and of the organic nation-state.

Charles Maurras was born in Martigues near Marseilles. He studied philosophy in Paris, where he was influenced by Auguste Comte, George Sorel, Henri Bergson, Maurice Barrès, and the racist journalist Édouard Drumont.

With Jean Moreas, in 1891 Maurras helped found the École Romane, and in 1892, with Frederico Amouretti, successfully took over the *Felibrige de Paris,* both movements dedicated to the purification of the French language and culture.

In both literature and politics Maurras sought to identify in history, especially in 17th-century classical traditions, all these concepts, ideals, institutions, and attributes of character which seemingly had succeeded. He considered his historical approach empirical and from this data sought to distill or induce a method for correcting evils and solving problems. He was committed to rescuing France from supposed literary and political degradation and corruption brought on by the Revolution, individualistic materialism, and predisposition toward relativism, eclecticism, and nihilism.

Believing the liberal individualism of the Revolution had opened the floodgates to degrading foreign forces—especially Jews—Maurras was clearly racist. Though nominally a man of letters, by 1899 his interests inclined toward politics, and he carried both his ideas and energies into the Ligue d'Action Française, which he and Barrès quickly appropriated and converted into the still-existing Action Française. Maurras's reverence for the past remained, and applying his literary methods to political analysis, he coined

in 1900 the term "integral nationalism"—"the exclusive pursuit of national policies, the absolute maintenance of national integrity, and the steady increase of national power"—a concept remarkably paralleling Barrès's "collective egotism." Then, combining the classical ideals of order, hierarchy, and discipline with attitudes of authoritarianism and the spirit of romantic patriotism, he sought to lay the foundations of an effective political movement.

Having conceived the principle, Maurras then developed his method—"organizing empiricism"—the use of historical experience as a model and guide for programs of action. Application of the method, in his hands, indicated that a return to monarchy alone could save France. This movement, too, was perhaps as much literary as political, despite Maurras's fanatic insistence upon the latter orientation. His insistence brought him imprisonment. In 1926 five of his works were put on the Index, and the Action Française was banned by the Church.

Though against collaboration, following the German invasion, Maurras strongly supported Marshal Pétain. His efforts were in vain. His anachronistic ideas could not effectively be written into Vichy legislation. In 1945, for his part in the Vichy regime, he was sentenced to life imprisonment and deprived of his civil rights by Liberation leaders. Simultaneously, he was condemned and dismissed from the French Academy, to which he had been elected in 1938. Because of illness, in 1952 he was released to a clinic in Tours, where he died a few months later. Throughout these years, except for reconciliation with the Church, he remained intransigent and wrote prodigiously, both literary works (reminiscences) and political polemics. Maurras provided footnotes for French rightists—so long as such remain. The Action Française still exists, is admired by some, and lists a few members in the French Academy.

EWB

Mazarin, Jules (1602–1661), French statesman. Jules Mazarin was the chosen successor of Richelieu. He governed France from 1643 until his death and laid the foundations for the monarchy of Louis XIV.

Jules Mazarin was born Giulio Mazarin on July 14, 1602, at Pescina, a village in the Abruzzi, Italy. He began his career as a soldier and diplomat in the service of the Pope. In this capacity he met Cardinal Richelieu in 1629 and decided to transfer his allegiance to him. He earned Richelieu's regard by acting in the French interest rather than the Pope's in certain treaty negotiations. He went to France as papal nuncio in 1636 and was naturalized as a French subject in 1639. In 1641 Richelieu persuaded the Pope to make Mazarin a cardinal, though he was not a priest.

Before Richelieu died in December 1642, he recommended Mazarin to Louis XIII as his successor, and the king accepted. Louis XIII died in May 1643, and the regent for the 5-year-old Louis XIV was his widow, Anne of Austria. The nobility welcomed the change. Anne was known to have been Richelieu's enemy, and Mazarin, though acknowledged as his nominee, was universally regarded as soft, ingratiating, and harmless. To everyone's utter astonishment, Anne confirmed Mazarin as first minister, and it soon became clear that she was in love with him. It is possible, though there is no proof, that later they were secretly married. They remained intimate friends and allies to the end of Mazarin's life.

Mazarin's task was to maintain the royal authority established by Richelieu and to win the war against France and Spain that he had started. Austria was humbled at the Peace of Westphalia in 1648; the war with Spain dragged on until 1659. The maintenance of royal authority was the most difficult task. Nobles who had reluctantly given way to Richelieu would not accept his successor, who was despised as a lowborn foreigner and thought to be weak-willed. The country was bitter at the taxes imposed by Richelieu to support the war, and its mounting resentment found dangerous expression in the Parliament of Paris, whose opposition was supported by all classes in the city.

To suppress the defiance that immediately arose in Paris, Mazarin had to call on the Prince de Condé, a cousin of the King and a very successful general. Finding himself indispensable, Condé became intolerably greedy and arrogant, and Mazarin finally had him and his friends arrested. The result was that the civil war that had already broken out became much worse, and several times it appeared as if Mazarin could not survive.

This war was called the Fronde, a name used to this day in France to denote irresponsible opposition. Paris, led by its Parliament, had rebelled in 1648. When this revolt was settled a year later, it was soon followed by the break with Condé. More humane than Richelieu, Mazarin imprisoned his enemies but did not put them to death, and as a result he could not make himself feared. The Fronde dragged on until 1653, but in the end, thanks to his own cleverness, the Queen's loyalty, and the mistakes of his enemies, Mazarin was completely victorious.

For the rest of his life Mazarin was the unchallenged master of France. His final triumph came with the Peace of the Pyrenees in November 1659. France had finally defeated Spain and was rewarded with ter-

ritorial acquisitions and the fateful marriage of Louis XIV to a Spanish princess. When Mazarin died on March 9, 1661, he had accomplished his task as he saw it. He had also accumulated a colossal fortune for himself.

In some ways Mazarin was a worthy successor to Richelieu. Behind a mask of affability, he was equally resolved to tolerate no opposition; his method of eliminating it was more devious and much less bloody but equally effective. As far as any man could have done, he fulfilled Richelieu's declared purpose of making "the king supreme in France, and France supreme in Europe." But, unlike Richelieu, he took no interest in the economic or cultural development of France. Once the Fronde was over, the country simply stagnated. The recovery that came in the 1660s was essentially the work of Jean Baptiste Colbert, whom Mazarin had picked out and recommended to the King.

EWB

Mérimée, Prosper (1803–1870), French author. Prosper Mérimée was a prose writer of the romantic period in France, important for his short stories, which mark the transition from romanticism toward the more objective works of the second half of the century.

Prosper Mérimée, a Parisian born and bred, grew up with the other French romantics. Although he shared some of their traits—a love of the exotic and the violent, for instance—his skeptical, pessimistic temperament kept him from their emotional excesses. He hid his emotional sensitivity beneath a cover of ironic objectivity. As restraint and ironic objectivity were among the principal goals of the later French realists, he stands as their precursor.

Mérimée's initial writings were entertaining frauds, published as alleged translations. A more important work under his own name, *Chronique du règne de Charles IX,* brought him to serious public attention in 1829. The *Chronique* is a historical novel, but it differs from the contemporary romantic ones in its impartial stance in recounting the Protestant and Catholic positions during the Wars of Religion in 16th-century France. True to form, Mérimée refused to provide an ending and mockingly invited his readers to invent one for themselves. Like his friend Stendhal, he feared being mocked himself and never allowed himself to appear to take any of his writings seriously, posing usually as an amateur who happened for the moment to be writing a story.

A very learned man, Mérimée was appointed inspector general of historical monuments in 1831. He performed major services by saving many ancient monuments from destruction, among others the church of St-Savin with its important 12th-century frescoes. He traveled widely through France, southern Europe, and the Near East, finding there the settings for many of his short stories (*nouvelles*).

Mateo Falcone (1829) and the longer *Colomba* (1841) and *Carmen* (1845) are the principal works for which Mérimée is now remembered, typical in their settings in Spain or Corsica, their portrayal of primitive passions, and their clear, concise style. Each story is a new experiment in form. The author's position remains distant, and Mérimée usually prefers the concrete to the abstract, giving a character life by a gesture or pose alone. *Carmen* is the source for Georges Bizet's opera (1875).

Mérimée ended his career as a writer in 1848, but he was a familiar figure at the court of the Second Empire, in part owing to his long prior acquaintance with the empress Eugénie. He was also among the first in France to appreciate Russian literature, translating Aleksandr Pushkin, Ivan Turgenev, and Nikolai Gogol.

EWB

Mesmer, Franz Anton (1734–1815), German physician. Franz Mesmer developed a healing technique called mesmerism that is the historical antecedent of hypnosis.

Franz Mesmer was born on May 23, 1734, in the village of Itznang, Switzerland. At age 15 he entered the Jesuit College at Dillingen in Bavaria, and from there he went in 1752 to the University of Ingolstadt, where he studied philosophy, theology, music, and mathematics. Eventually he decided on a medical career. In 1759 he entered the University of Vienna, receiving a medical degree in 1766.

Mesmer then settled in Vienna and began to develop his concept of an invisible fluid in the body that affected health. At first he used magnets to manipulate this fluid but gradually came to believe these were unnecessary, that, in fact, anything he touched became magnetized and that a health-giving fluid emanated from his own body. Mesmer believed a rapport with his patients was essential for cure and achieved it with diverse trappings. His treatment rooms were heavily draped, music was played, and Mesmer appeared in long, violet robes.

Mesmer's methods were frowned upon by the medical establishment in Vienna, so in 1778 he moved to Paris, hoping for a better reception for his ideas. In France he achieved overwhelming popularity, except among physicians. On the basis of medical opinion, repeated efforts were made by the French government to discredit Mesmer. At a time of political turmoil and revolution, such efforts were viewed as attempts to prevent the majority's enjoyment of health, and the popularity of mesmerism continued unabated. However, under continued pressure Mesmer retired to Switzerland at the beginning of the French Revolution, where he spent the remaining years of his life.

Critics focused attention of Mesmer's methods and insisted that cures existed only in the patient's mind. The 19th-century studies of Mesmer's work by James Braid and others in England demonstrated that the important aspect of Mesmer's treatment was the patient's reaction. Braid introduced the term "hypnotism" and insisted that hypnotic phenomena were essentially physiological and not associated with a fluid. Still later studies in France by A. A. Liebeault and Hippolyte Bernheim attributed hypnotic phenomena to psychological forces, particularly suggestion. While undergoing this scientific transformation in the 19th century, mesmerism, in other quarters, became more closely associated with occultism, spiritualism, and faith healing, providing in the last instance the basis for Christian Science.

EWB

Michelet, Jules (1798–1874), French historian. Jules Michelet wrote the *Histoire de France* and *Histoire de la Révolution française*, which established him as one of France's greatest 19th-century historians.

Jules Michelet was born on Aug. 21, 1798, in Paris. His father was a printer by trade, and his mother's family was from peasant stock. The family was poor, especially after Napoleon ordered the closing of his father's press. This family background prompted Michelet's initial sympathy with the French Revolution.

In 1822 Michelet began his long and devoted career as a teacher, becoming professor of history and philosophy at the École Normale Supérieure in 1827. In one of his earliest works, a translation of Giovanni Battista Vico's *Scienza nuova*, Michelet introduced such ideas as the importance of myth and language in historical understanding and the ability of man to forge his own history. His first volumes of French history treated the Middle Ages; already he revealed a passionate adherence to the role of the common people in history.

When Michelet joined the faculty at the Collège de France in 1838, his writing became more liberal and more oriented toward contemporary issues. Collaboration with a colleague, Edgar Quinet, on a book against the Jesuits raised the Church's suspicions. In addition, Michelet was waking up to the *esclavage* (slavery) of classes in an industrial society, a concern he expressed in his moving book *Le Peuple* (1846).

Thus Michelet and other writers of the period, encouraged by the revolutionary spirit growing since 1830, were attracted to the French Revolution. Michelet's seven-volume *Histoire de la Révolution française* illustrates his famous concept of history as a resurrection of the past in its spontaneous entirety. Although in this immense achievement the portraits of certain revolutionaries are masterfully drawn, Michelet is more sympathetic when narrating crowd scenes, for example, the fall of the Bastille.

The failure of the 1848 revolutions, Louis Napoleon's coup d'etat of 1851, and the proclamation of the Second Empire in 1852 profoundly disturbed Michelet. Although he was not exiled, he spent the following year in Italy.

Worn by arduous work and depressing historical events, Michelet discovered new life in his second marriage with 20-year-old Atanaïs Mialaret. Inspired by her love of nature, he wrote four poetical studies: *The Bird* (1856), *The Insect* (1857), *The Sea* (1861), and *The Mountain* (1867). These fecund later years saw two other outstanding books: one on the medieval witch (*La Sorcière,* 1862) and the other on world religions, including an attack on Christianity (*La Bible de l'humanité,* 1864). Michelet finally completed his history of France in 1867. Working continuously, he had written three volumes on 19th-century France up to the time of his death on Feb. 9, 1874, when he suffered a heart attack at Hyères.

EWB

Mill, John Stuart (1806–1873), English philosopher and economist. John Stuart Mill was the most influential British thinker of the 19th century. He is known for his writings on logic and scientific methodology and his voluminous essays on social and political life.

John Stuart Mill was born on May 20, 1806, in London to James and Harriet Burrow Mill, the eldest of their nine children. His father, originally trained as a minister, had emigrated from Scotland to take up a career as a freelance journalist. In 1808 James Mill began his lifelong association with Jeremy Bentham, the utilitarian philosopher and legalist. Mill shared the common belief of 19th-century psychologists that the mind is at birth a *tabula rasa* and that character and performance are the result of experienced associations. With this view, he attempted to make his son into a philosopher by exclusively supervising his education. John Stuart Mill never attended a school or university.

Early Years and Education. The success of this experiment is recorded in John Stuart Mill's *Autobiography* (written 1853–1856). He began the study of Greek at the age of 3 and took up Latin between his seventh and eighth years. From six to ten each morning the boy recited his lessons, and by the age of 12 he had mastered material that was the equivalent of a university degree in classics. He then took up the study of logic, mathematics, and political economy with the same rigor. In addition to his own studies, John also tutored his brothers and sisters for 3 hours daily. Throughout his early years, John was treated as a younger equal by his father's associates, who were among the preeminent intellectuals in England. They included George Grote, the historian; John Austin, the jurist; David Ricardo, the economist; and Bentham.

Only later did Mill realize that he never had a childhood. The only tempering experiences he recalled from his boyhood were walks, music, reading *Robinson Crusoe,* and a year he spent in France. Before going abroad John had never associated with anyone his own age. The year with Bentham's relatives in France gave young Mill a taste of normal family life and a mastery of another language, which made him well informed on French intellectual and political ideas.

When he was 16, Mill began a debating society of utilitarians to examine and promote the ideas of his father, Bentham, Ricardo, and Thomas Malthus. He also began to publish on various issues, and he had written nearly 50 articles and reviews before he was 20. His speaking, writing, and political activity contributed to the passage of the Parliamentary Reform Bill in 1830, which culminated the efforts of the first generation of utilitarians, especially Bentham and James Mill. But in 1823, at his father's insistence, Mill abandoned his interest in a political career and accepted a position at India House, where he remained for 35 years.

The external events of Mill's life were so prosaic that Thomas Carlyle once disparagingly described their written account as "the autobiography of a steam engine." Nonetheless in 1826 Mill underwent a mental crisis. He perceived that the realization of all the social reforms for which he had been trained and for which he had worked would bring him no personal satisfaction. He thought that his intellectual training had left him emotionally starved and feared that he lacked any capacity for feeling or caring deeply. Mill eventually overcame his melancholia by opening himself to the romantic reaction against rationalism on both an intellectual and personal level. He assimilated the ideas and poetry of English, French, and German thought. When he was 25 he met Harriet Taylor, and she became the dominant influence of his life. Although she was married, they maintained a close association for 20 years, eventually marrying in 1851, a few years after her husband's death. In his *Autobiography* Mill maintained that Harriet's intellectual ability was superior to his own and that she should be understood as the joint author of many of his major works.

"System of Logic."   The main purpose of Mill's philosophic works was to rehabilitate the British empirical tradition extending from John Locke. He argued for the constructive dimension of experience as an antidote to the negative and skeptical aspects emphasized by David Hume and also as an alternative to rationalistic dogmatism. His *System of Logic* (1843) was well received both as a university text and by the general public. Assuming that all propositions are of a subject-predicate form, Mill began with an analysis of words that constitute statements. He overcame much of the confusion of Locke's similar and earlier analysis by distinguishing between the connotation, or real meaning, of terms and the denotation, or attributive function. From this Mill described propositions as either "verbal" and analytic or "real" and synthetic. With these preliminaries in hand, Mill began a rather traditional attack on pure mathematics and deductive reasoning. A consistent empiricism demanded that all knowledge be derived from experience. Thus, no appeal to universal principles or a priori intuitions was allowable. In effect, Mill reduced pure to applied mathematics and deductive reasoning to "apparent" inferences or premises which, in reality, are generalizations from previous experience. The utility of syllogistic reasoning is found to be a training in logical consistency—that is, a correct method for deciding if a particular instance fits under a general rule—but not to be a source of discovering new knowledge.

By elimination, then, logic was understood by Mill as induction, or knowledge by inference. His famous canons of induction were an attempt to show that general knowledge is derived from the observation of particular instances. Causal laws are established by observations of agreement and difference, residues and concomitant variations of the relations between A as the cause of B. The law of causation is merely a generalization of the truths reached by these experimental methods. By the strict application of these methods man is justified in extending his inferences beyond his immediate experience to discover highly probable, though not demonstrable, empirical and scientific laws.

Mill's logic culminates with an analysis of the methodology of the social sciences since neither individual men nor patterns of social life are exceptions to the laws of general causality. However, the variety of conditioning factors and the lack of control and repeatability of experiments weaken the effectiveness of both the experimental method and deductive attempts, such as Bentham's hedonistic calculus, which attempted to derive conclusions from the single premise of man's self-interest. The proper method of the social sciences is a mixture: deductions from the inferential generalizations provided by psychology and sociology. In several works Mill attempted without great success to trace connections between the generalizations derived from associationist psychology and the social and historical law of three stages (theological, metaphysical, and positivist or scientific) established by Auguste Comte.

Mill's Reasonableness.   The mark of Mill's genius in metaphysics, ethics, and political theory rests in the tenacity of his attitude of consistent reasonableness. He denied the necessity and scientific validity of positing transcendent realities except as an object of belief or guide for conduct. He avoided the abstruse difficulties of the metaphysical status of the external world and the self by defining matter, as it is experienced, as "a permanent possibility of sensation," and the mind as the series of affective and cognitive activities that is aware of itself as a conscious unity of past and future through memory and imagination. His own mental crises led Mill to modify the calculative aspect of utilitarianism. In theory he maintained that men are determined by their expectation of the pleasure and pain produced by action. But his conception of the range of personal motives and institutional attempts to ensure the good are much broader than those suggested by Bentham. For example, Mill explained that he overcame a mechanical notion of determinism when he realized that men are capable of being the cause of their own conduct through motives of self-improvement. In a more important sense, he attempted to introduce a qualitative dimension to utility.

Mill suggested that there are higher pleasures and that men should be educated to these higher aspirations. For a democratic government based on consensus is only as good as the education and tolerance of its citizenry. This argument received its classic formulation in the justly famous essay, "On Liberty." Therein the classic formula of liberalism is stated: the state exists for man, and hence the only warrantable imposition upon personal liberty is "self-protection." In later life, Mill moved from a laissez-faire economic theory toward socialism as he realized that government must take a more active role in guaranteeing the interests of all of its citizens.

The great sadness of Mill's later years was the unexpected death of his wife in 1858. He took a house in Avignon, France, in order to be near her grave and divided his time between there and London. He won election to the House of Commons in 1865, although he refused to campaign. He died on May 8, 1873.

EWB

Mitterrand, François (1916–1996), French politician and statesman. François Mitterrand served in different governments under the Fourth Republic (1946–1958) and became a major opponent of Charles de Gaulle under the Fifth Republic beginning in 1958. In 1981 he was elected president of France and served for 14 years, longer than any other head of state in the five Republics since the Revolution of 1789.

François Maurice Adrien Marie Mitterrand was born into a middle-class Catholic family on October 26, 1916, in Jarnac, a small town in southwestern France near Cognac. During his childhood Mitterrand was influenced by his parents' concern for the plight of the poor. In 1934 he traveled to Paris where he entered the University of Paris and pursued degrees in political science and law. The rise of European fascism in the 1930s during his university years attracted Mitterand to attend demonstrations organized by the pro-fascists in 1935 and 1936. After obtaining his degree in law and letters and a diploma from the Ecole Libre des Science Politiques, Mitterrand began his mandatory military service in 1938.

Serving as a sergeant in the war, he was wounded and captured near Verdun in May of 1940 by the Germans. After three escape attempts, he fled his Nazi captors and returned to France. There he worked as a minor government official in Marshal Petain's Vichy government which collaborated with the Nazis. In 1943 he enlisted in the French Resistance movement when it became clear that the Nazis would lose the war. He used his position with the government for the Resistance while he headed the National Movement of War Prisoners and Deportees to forge the necessary papers needed in the resistance. Mitterand claimed that his government job had been a cover for his Resistance activities all along. He was awarded the Rosette de la Resistance for his efforts.

At the end of the war he became secretary general for war prisoners and deportees in the provisional government of Gen. Charles de Gaulle. In 1945 Mitterrand was one of the founders of the Democratic and Socialist Resistance Union, a moderate political party with a strong anti-Communist bent.

Legislative and Executive Positions. With the founding of the Fourth Republic, Mitterrand ac-

tively entered politics and gained valuable parliamentary experience, being elected a deputy to the National Assembly (1946–1958) and serving in 11 different governments. Under the Fourth Republic his ministerial appointments included minister of war veterans (1947–1948), minister for information (1948–1949), minister for overseas territories (1950–1951), minister of state (1952), minister for the Council of Europe (1953), minister of the interior (1954–1955), and minister of justice (1956–1957).

The founding of the Fifth Republic in 1958 by de Gaulle in the midst of the Algerian independence movement pushed Mitterrand into the opposition and, subsequently, his political thought and leanings gravitated toward the left. He opposed de Gaulle's founding of the Fifth Republic and charged that the general's "new republic" represented a permanent *coup d'etat.* During the first 23 years of the Fifth Republic, Mitterrand dedicated himself to opposing de Gaulle and his heirs. While no longer holding a ministerial post, he was elected to the Senate (1959–1962) and to the Chamber of Deputies (beginning in 1962). (He was also mayor of Château-Chinon beginning in 1959.) In time Mitterrand came to realize that to defeat de Gaulle the non-Communist left needed to be revitalized and an alliance established with the French Communist Party (PCF).

In the presidential election of 1965 Mitterrand opposed de Gaulle and ran as the candidate of the Federation of the Democratic and Socialist Left (FGDS), an alliance of non-Communist leftist parties. Realizing the advantages of electoral cooperation, the Communists backed Mitterrand in this election. Though he was defeated by de Gaulle, in the final round of the presidential contest Mitterrand obtained 44.8 percent of the vote.

Rise of the "Red Rose" Party. The popular appeal of the left, however, was set back by the momentous student-worker revolt of 1968 (the Events of May) and de Gaulle's manipulation of the crisis. Then, partially as a result of the disastrous outcome of the June 1968 legislative elections for the left, Mitterrand resigned as chairman of the FGDS and decided not to run in the 1969 presidential elections. From 1970 to 1971 he headed a political grouping known as the Convention of Republican Institutions. In 1971 he was chosen first secretary of a new Socialist Party (PS) founded in the aftermath of the 1968 revolt and created to replace the old bankrupt Socialist Party (SFIO). The PS, symbolized by a clenched first holding a red rose, eventually catapulted Mitterrand and his Socialist colleagues to power in 1981.

Shortly after assuming the leadership of the PS, Mitterrand and the Socialists agreed to support the Common Program (1972), an electoral alliance and program comprised of the Socialists, the Communists, and the left radicals (MRG). After signing the Common Program, the membership of Mitterrand's new party increased from 75,000 in 1972 to 200,000 in 1981. These numbers encouraged Mitterrand's hope of constructing a large non-Communist left in France. Several days after signing the Common Program, in fact, he declared at an international Socialist congress in Vienna that he wanted "to reconquer an important part of the communist electorate." This bold statement foreshadowed the competition that would develop between the PS and the PCF.

In addition to the competition with the PCF, Mitterrand also had to deal with rivalries developing within the PS itself, a catch-all party that cut across class lines and had three major tendencies or groupings: the radical tradition represented by Mitterrand, the revolutionary socialism of Jean-Pierre Chevènement, and the social democracy of Michel Rocard. After the founding of the PS, Mitterrand adroitly played one tendency against another to maintain his leadership of the party.

Third Try for Presidency Succeeds. After 1972 the rising popularity of Mitterrand's PS encouraged the Socialists but worried the PCF and the majority in power. In the 1973 legislative election the Socialists captured a respectable 18.9 percent of the vote, while the PCF garnered 21.4 percent. Then, in the 1974 presidential elections Mitterrand ran as the standard bearer of the left and almost defeated Valéry Giscard d'Estaing by winning 49.19 percent of the vote in the final round. In the cantonal elections of 1976 the PS became the first party of the French left by capturing 30.8 percent of the vote, while the PCF received only 17.3 percent. Fearing that the Socialists would make even further gains in the 1978 legislative elections at the expense of the PCF, the Communists sabotaged the Common Program on the eve of the elections. Consequently, instead of taking a majority of seats in the Chamber of Deputies as predicted earlier, the leftist parties suffered a setback due to their own disunity.

Between 1978 and 1981 the discord between the Socialists and Communists continued, revolving around both domestic and international issues (for example, the crisis in Poland and the Soviet invasion of Afghanistan). As a result of this breakdown of leftist unity, the PS and the PCF ran separate candidates in the 1981 presidential elections: the Socialists backed Mitterrand and the Communists supported Georges Marchais, head of the PCF. However, Marchais' poor showing in the first round of the elections convinced the PCF to back Mitterrand in the second round. Aided by Communist support and disunity now on the right, Mitterrand toppled Giscard by winning 51.75 percent of the vote. Mitterrand was aided, however, by a number of other factors: Giscard's so-called imperial image, the need for economic and social reform, and the twin problems of unemployment and inflation.

The April/May presidential elections were hailed as historic in France because they ended 23 years of right-wing government under the Fifth Republic. The elections also proved that *alternance,* or a change in government, was possible under the institutions of the Fifth Republic, a republic that Mitterrand had rejected earlier. The legislative elections held in June of 1981 constituted another historic dimension. In these elections Mitterrand's Socialist Party won an absolute majority of seats in the National Assembly. The year 1981 marked the first time since the French Revolution of 1789 that the left had captured the executive and the legislative branches of government.

An Administration of Reforms. In forming his new government Mitterrand took some noteworthy steps. He chose Pierre Mauroy, the Socialist mayor of Lille, as prime minister. To reward the Communists for their backing and to maintain leftist unity, Mitterrand included four Communist ministers in his government. He also created a Ministry for the Rights of Women and staffed his new ministry with Yvette Roudy, a long-time feminist activist.

Now in power, Mitterrand's government launched a series of reforms designed to change France. A nationalization program was carried out that extended state control over nine industrial groups, including electronics, chemical, steel, and arms industries. Social reforms were also made: the work week was reduced to 39 hours; workers received more rights at their workplace; the retirement age was reduced to 60; the vacation period was extended to five weeks of paid vacation instead of four; allocations for the elderly, for women who live alone, and for the handicapped were increased; the minimum wage was substantially increased; reimbursement for abortions was provided; a wealth tax was imposed; and approximately 100,000 jobs were created in the public sector.

The Mitterrand government also adopted a number of reforms to strengthen justice for its citizens and residents by abolishing the death penalty, striking down the old *ad hoc* state security court, amending laws against homosexuals, and trying to regularize the status of France's four million immigrant workers. In addition, the government launched a decentralization program designed to transfer some of the power and decision making from Paris to local regions. Year One of Mitterrand's Socialist experiment was a year of reforms, but an expensive one.

During the first year in power the Mitterrand government pursued a neo-Keynesian reflationary economic policy, believing that "pump priming" would help pull France out of the recession so troubling to the Western world. Yet this policy, coupled with the expensive reforms of the first year, only exacerbated the economic problems in France. Consequently, in June of 1982 Mitterrand was forced to announce that his government would pursue an austerity program. This program involved a second devaluation of the franc, a four-month-long wage and price freeze, an attempt to hold down the public debt, and a cap placed on state expenses. Such a change in economic policy meant that France was now focusing on reducing inflation instead of unemployment. The June 1982 austerity program was followed by even more rigorous austerity measures in March of 1983.

Trouble for the Socialist Government. While Mitterrand and his government enjoyed a "state of grace" during their first year, the austerity programs of 1982 and 1983, accompanied by rising unemployment, contributed to growing opposition in France and decline in the popularity of Mitterrand and his government. The Socialist government also sparked opposition with its educational policy, namely its attempt to gain more control over the 10,000 private, mainly religious, schools in France. Concerns over educational reform as well as a climate of general discontent led to a massive demonstration on June 24, 1984, by more than one million protesters at the Bastille in Paris, constituting the largest public demonstration in France since liberation.

Facing this mounting opposition, plus a setback in the European Parliament elections of June 17, 1984, Mitterrand began to move his government toward the center. The French president made a major television address on July 12, 1984, announcing that he would renegotiate the proposed reform for private schools and that he wished henceforth to consult the French on questions of public liberties through referendums. Then, only six days later the Mitterrand government announced several key resignations from the cabinet. Mitterrand picked Laurent Fabius, a young loyal *Mitterrandiste,* as his new prime minister. Shortly thereafter, Fabius announced that the government would continue the austerity program in an effort to redress the economic crisis and to modernize France. More austerity, coupled with declining popularity at

the polls, led the Communists to refuse to participate in Fabius's cabinet. Mitterrand hoped that these changes would help to defuse the opposition and also prepare the PS for the upcoming 1986 legislative elections and the 1988 presidential elections.

In foreign policy, where the French president exercises enormous power, Mitterrand was both pragmatic and Gaullist in his approach. Strongly anti-Soviet, Mitterrand supported the North Atlantic Treaty Organization (NATO) decision to begin the deployment of almost 600 new Pershing II and Cruise missiles in Western Europe in 1983. While Mitterrand tried to promote solidarity with members of the NATO alliance, especially West Germany, he closely guarded French autonomy on foreign policy matters. At the same time, Mitterrand supported the idea of a strong and more independent Europe. He, too, tried to encourage a North-South dialogue between the rich and the poor nations and attempted to develop and to strengthen French spheres of influence in the Third World.

The 1986 legislative elections were a blow to the Socialists. They lost their majority in the National Assembly to the rebuilt Gaullist Party, now called the Rally for the Republic (RPR). As a result Mitterrand had to give the office of prime minister to the RPR leader, Jacques Chirac. It was the Fifth Republic's first government divided between a Socialist president and a conservative legislature (called "co-habitation" in France).

Mitterand's most ambitious and visible projects were to order the construction of $6 billion of public buildings and in 1986 to a work with Great Britain to build the Channel Tunnel ("Chunnel") linking Europe's mainland with Great Britain. Scandal and accusations of corruption plagued the Mitterand presidency. His private presidential police force was accused of illegally tapping the phones of judges, journalists, senior officials, and even the prime minister. A 1994 biography *Une Jeunesse Francaise* (*Youth of a Frenchman*) brought his early career back to haunt him. In particular he was criticized for maintaining his friendship with Rene Bousquet, the Vichy police chief who deported thousands of French Jews to Germany's death camps.

Although he married Danielle Gouze, whom he had met while working for the Resistance, in 1944, Mitterrand was rumored to have several mistresses. The Mitterands had two sons. In 1994 it was revealed that Mitterand's mistress and their daughter had been living at state expense in an annex to the Elysee Palace.

In 1992 Mitterand discovered he had prostate cancer. After undergoing chemotherapy, he managed to complete his term in office, but decided not to seek a third term. He died on January 8, 1996 at age 79.

EWB

Montaigne, Michel Eyquem de (1533–1592),
French author. Michel Eyquem de Montaigne created a new literary genre, the essay, in which he used self-portrayal as a mirror of humanity in general.

Michel Eyquem de Montaigne was born on Feb. 23, 1533, at the family estate called Montaigne in Périgord near Bordeaux. His father, Pierre Eyquem, was a Bordeaux merchant and municipal official whose grandfather was the first nobleman of the line. His mother, Antoinette de Louppes (Lopez), was descended from a line of Spanish Jews, the Marranos, long converted to Catholicism. Michel, their third son, was privately tutored and spoke only Latin until the age of 6. From 1539 until 1546 he studied at the Collège de Guyenne, in Bordeaux, where the Scottish humanist George Buchanan was one of his teachers, as was the less-known French poet and scholar Marc Antoine Muret. Very little is known of Montaigne's life from age 13 to 24, but he may have spent some time in Paris, probably studied law in Toulouse, and certainly indulged in the pleasures of youth.

In 1557 Montaigne obtained the position of councilor in the Bordeaux Parlement, and it was there that he met his closest friend and strongest influence, Étienne de la Boétie. La Boétie and Montaigne shared many interests, especially in classical antiquity, but this friendship was ended by La Boétie's death from dysentery in August 1563. Montaigne was with him through the 9 days of his illness. The loss of his friend was a serious emotional blow that Montaigne later described in his essay "On Friendship." In 1571 Montaigne published his friend's collected works.

Two years after La Boétie's death, after a number of diversionary affairs, Montaigne married Françoise de la Chassaigne, daughter of a cocouncilor in the Bordeaux Parlement. She bore him six daughters, of whom only one survived to adulthood. The marriage was apparently amiable but sometimes cool—Montaigne believed that marriage was of a somewhat lower order than friendship.

In 1568 the elder Montaigne died, thus making Michel lord of Montaigne. Before his death, Pierre Eyquem had persuaded his son to translate into French the *Book of Creatures or Natural Theology* by the 15th-century Spanish theologian Raymond Sebond. The work was an apologia for the Christian religion based on proofs from the natural world. The translation was published early in 1569 and gave clear indication of Montaigne's ability both as translator and as author in his own right. From his work on this translation Montaigne later developed the longest of his many essays, "The Apology for Raymond Sebond." In this pivotal essay, Montaigne presented his skeptical philosophy of doubt, attacked human knowledge as presumptuous and arrogant, and suggested that self-knowledge could result only from awareness of ignorance.

In April 1570 Montaigne resigned from the Bordeaux Parlement, sold his position to a friend, and as lord of Montaigne formally retired to his country estate, his horses, and his beautiful and isolated third-floor library. He carefully recorded his retirement on his thirty-eighth birthday and soon began work on his *Essais*. Ten years later (1580) the first edition, containing books I and II, was published in Bordeaux.

Late in 1580 Montaigne began a 15-month trip through Germany, Switzerland, Austria, and Italy. He visited many mineral baths and watering spas in hopes of finding relief from a chronic kidney stone condition. His journal of these travels, though not intended for publication, was published in 1774. Toward the end of his trip Montaigne learned of his election in August 1580 to the mayoralty of Bordeaux, an office in which he then spent two 2-year terms. By all accounts he served the city with conscientious distinction during a troubled period, although public service was clearly not his aspiration at that time. He himself obliquely defended his regime in the essay "Of Husbanding Your Will."

At the end of his term of office Montaigne spent the best part of a year revising the first two books of the *Essais* and preparing book III for inclusion in the 1588 Paris edition, the fifth edition of the work. In 1586 both war and plague reached his district, and he fled with his household in search of peace and healthier air, receiving at best reluctant hospitality from his neighboring squires. When he returned 6 months later, he found the castle pillaged but still habitable.

Montaigne's last years were brightened by his friendship and correspondence with his so-called adoptive daughter, Marie de Gournay (1565–1645), an ardent young admirer who edited the expanded 1595 edition of his works (mainly from annotations made by Montaigne) and, in its preface, defended his memory to posterity. (It was from her edition that John Florio produced the 1603 English-language edition, which was a source for Shakespeare's *Tempest* and other playwrights' work.)

After 2 years of illness and decline Montaigne died peacefully in his bed while hearing Mass on Sept. 13, 1592. He died a loyal Catholic, but he was always tolerant of other religious views.

The "Essais." It is difficult if not impossible to summarize the ideas of Montaigne's *Essais*. He was not a systematic thinker and defied all attempts to be pinned down to any single point of view. He preferred to show the randomness of his own thought as representative of the self-contradiction to which all men are prone. His characteristic motto was "*Que sais-je?*" ("What do I know?") He was skeptical about the power of human reason, yet argued that each man must first know himself in order to live happily. The *Essais* constitute Montaigne's own attempt at self-knowledge and self-portrayal—in effect, they are autobiography. Since he argued that "each man bears the complete stamp of the human condition" ("*chaque homme porte la forme entière de l'humaine condition*"), these autobiographical exercises can also be seen as portraits of mankind in all its diversity. Although he constantly attacked man's presumption, arrogance, and pride, he nonetheless held the highest view of the dignity of man, in keeping with the dignity of nature.

As a skeptic, Montaigne opposed intolerance and fanaticism, believing truth never to be one-sided. He championed individual freedom but held that even repressive laws should be obeyed. He feared violence and anarchy and was suspicious of any radical proposals that might jeopardize the existing order in hopes of childish panaceas. Acceptance and detachment were for him the keys to happiness. In both the form and content of his *Essais,* Montaigne achieved a remarkable combination of inner tranquility and detachment, together with the independence and freedom of an unfettered mind.

EWB

More, Sir Thomas (1478–1535), English humanist and statesman.

The life of Thomas More exemplifies the political and spiritual upheaval of the Reformation. The author of *Utopia*, he was beheaded for opposing the religious policy of Henry VIII.

Thomas More was born in London on Feb. 6, 1478, to parents whose families were connected with the city's legal community. His education began at a prominent London school, St. Anthony's. In 1490 Thomas entered the household of Archbishop John Morton, Henry VII's closest adviser. Service to Morton brought experience of the world, then preferment in 1492 to Oxford, where More first encountered Greek studies. Two years later he returned to London, where legal and political careers were forged. By 1498 More had gained membership in Lincoln's Inn, an influential lawyers' fraternity.

Christian Humanism. A broader perspective then opened. The impact of humanism in England was greatly intensified about 1500, partly by Eras-

mus's first visit. His biblical interests spurred the work of Englishmen recently back from Italy; they had studied Greek intensively and thus were eager for fresh scrutiny of the Gospel texts and the writings of the early Church Fathers. John Colet's Oxford lectures on the Pauline epistles, and his move in 1504 to London as dean of St. Paul's Cathedral and founder of its famous humanist school, epitomized this reformist, educational activity among English churchmen. Lay patronage of the movement quickly made Cambridge, where Erasmus periodically taught, a focus of biblical scholarship and made London a favored meeting ground for Europe's men of letters.

England thus shed its cultural provincialism, and More, while pursuing his legal career and entering Parliament in 1504, was drawn to the Christian humanist circle. He spent his mid-20s in close touch with London's austere Carthusian monks and almost adopted their vocation. His thinking at this stage is represented by his interest in the Italian philosopher Giovanni Pico della Mirandola, who had also become increasingly pious when approaching the age of 30 a decade before; More's 1505 translation of Pico's first biography stressed that development.

But More then decided that he could fulfill a Christian vocation while remaining a layman. Both his subsequent family life and public career document the humanist persuasion that Christian service could be done, indeed should be pursued, in the world at large. He first married Jane Colt, who bore three sons and a daughter before dying in 1511, and then Alice Middleton. His household at Bucklersbury, London, until 1524 and then at Chelsea teemed with visitors, such as his great friend Erasmus, and formed a model educational community for the children and servants; More corresponded with his daughters in Latin. His legal career flourished and led to appointment as London's undersheriff in 1511. This meant additional work and revenue as civic counsel at Henry VIII's court and as negotiator with foreign merchants.

More's first official trip abroad, on embassy at Antwerp in 1515, gave him leisure time in which he began his greatest work, *Utopia.* Modeled on Plato's *Republic,* written in Latin, finished and published in 1516, it describes an imaginary land, purged of the ostentation, greed, and violence of the English and European scenes that More surveyed. Interpretations of *Utopia* vary greatly. The dialogue form of book I and *Utopia*'s continual irony suggest More's deliberate ambiguity about his intent. Whatever vision More really professed, *Utopia* persists and delights as the model for an important literary genre.

Service under Henry VIII. *Utopia*'s book I and More's history of Richard III, written during the same period, contain reflections about politics and the problems of counseling princes. They represent More's uncertainty about how to handle frequent invitations to serve Henry VIII, whose policies included many facets distasteful to the humanists. More had written in *Utopia:* "So it is in the deliberations of monarchs. If you cannot pluck up wrongheaded opinions by the root . . . yet you must not on that account desert the commonwealth. You must not abandon the ship in a storm because you cannot control the winds." He finally accepted Henry's fee late in 1517 and fashioned a solid career in diplomacy, legal service, and finance, crowned in 1529 by succession to Cardinal Wolsey as chancellor of England.

More's early doubts, however, proved justified. Under Wolsey's direction More as Speaker of the House of Commons in 1523 promoted a war levy so unpopular that its collection was discontinued. In European negotiations, Henry's belligerence and Wolsey's ambition frustrated More's desire to stop the wars of Christendom so that its faith and culture could be preserved.

By the time that Wolsey's inability to obtain the annulment of Henry's marriage to Catherine of Aragon had raised More to highest office and placed him in the increasingly distressing role of Henry's chief agent in the maneuvering that began to sever England from Rome, More was deeply engaged in writings against Lutherans, defending the fundamental tenets of the Church whose serious flaws he knew. More cannot justly be held responsible for the increased number of Protestants burned during his last months in office, but this was the gloomiest phase of his career. The polemics, in English after 1528, including the *Dialogue Concernynge Heresyes* (1529) and *Apologye* (1533), were his bulkiest works but not his best, for they were defensive in nature and required detailed rebuttal of specific charges, not the light and allusive touch of the humanist imagination. He continued writing until a year after his resignation from office, tendered May 16, 1532, and caused by illness and distress over England's course of separation from the Catholic Church.

Break with the King. More recognized the dangers that his Catholic apologetics entailed in the upside-down world of Henry's break with Rome and tried to avoid political controversy. But Henry pressed him for a public acknowledgment of the succession to the throne established in 1534. More refused the accompanying oath that repudiated papal jurisdiction in England, and the Christian unity thereby manifest, in favor of royal supremacy.

More's last dramatic year—from the first summons for interrogation on April 12, 1534, through imprisonment, trial for treason, defiance of his perjured accusers, and finally execution on July 6, 1535—should not be allowed to overshadow his entire life's experience. Its significance extends beyond the realm of English history. For many of Europe's most critical years, More worked to revitalize Christendom. He attacked those who most clearly threatened its unity; once convinced that Henry VIII was among their number, More withdrew his service and resisted to his death the effort to extract his allegiance. His life, like *Utopia,* offers fundamental insights about private virtues and their relationship to the politics of human community.

EWB

Mosley, Oswald (1896–1980), British politician and author. Oswald Mosley was a member of Parliament from 1918 to 1931, during which time he served alternately as a Conservative, Independent, and Labour representative. In the mid-1930s, though, Mosley became a follower of Hitler, Mussolini, and the fascists, and organized the British Union of Fascists. He lead his fellow fascist "blackshirts," armed with rubber hoses, pipes, and brass knuckles, on raids of London's Jewish areas. Hitler himself attended Mosley's wedding in 1936. When war with Germany erupted, Mosley was imprisoned by the British as a security risk. After the Allied victory, Mosley went into voluntary exile in France.

Lord Boothby wrote of Mosley: "I discerned in him . . . this kind of quality of leadership that I discerned in only two other men during all my period of political life. One is Lloyd George and the other is Churchill." Michael Foot equally admired Mosley: "[*My Life*] could cast a dazzling gleam across the whole century. . . . Within a few years of joining the Labour Party, he came near to diverting the whole course of British history. More surely than any other comparable figure of the time, Mosley had grasped the reality of Britain's economic plight. Vigour, intelligence, dramatic gesture and coruscating wit combined to give to this would-be Caesar a touch of Cicero as well. . . . What Mosley so valiantly stood for could have saved his country from the Hungry Thirties and the Second World War . . . the deep-laid middle-class love of mediocrity and safety-first which consigned political genius to the wilderness and the nation to the valley of the shadow of death."

CA

Mozart, Wolfgang Amadeus (1756–1791), Austrian composer. Mozart's mastery of the whole range of contemporary instrumental and vocal forms—including the symphony, concerto, chamber music, and especially the opera—was unrivaled in his own time and perhaps in any other.

Wolfgang Amadeus Mozart was born on Jan. 27, 1756, in Salzburg. His father, Leopold Mozart, a noted composer and pedagogue and the author of a famous treatise on violin playing, was then in the service of the archbishop of Salzburg. Together with his sister, Nannerl, Wolfgang received such intensive musical training that by the age of 6 he was a budding composer and an accomplished keyboard performer. In 1762 Leopold presented his son as performer at the imperial court in Vienna, and from 1763 to 1766 he escorted both children on a continuous musical tour across Europe, which included long stays in Paris and London as well as visits to many other cities, with appearances before the French and English royal families.

Mozart was the most celebrated child prodigy of this time as a keyboard performer and made a great impression, too, as composer and improviser. In London he won the admiration of so eminent a musician as Johann Christian Bach, and he was exposed from an early age to an unusual variety of musical styles and tastes across the Continent.

Salzburg and Italy, 1766–1773. From his tenth to his seventeenth year Mozart grew in stature as a composer to a degree of maturity equal to that of his most eminent older contemporaries; as he continued to expand his conquest of current musical styles, he outstripped them. He spent the years 1766–1769 at Salzburg writing instrumental works and music for school dramas in German and Latin, and in 1768 he produced his first real operas: the German *Singspiel* (that is, with spoken dialogue) *Bastien und Bastienne* and the opera buffa *La finta semplice*. Artless and naive as *La finta semplice* is when compared to his later Italian operas, it nevertheless shows a latent sense of character portrayal and fine accuracy of Italian text setting. Despite his reputation as a prodigy, Mozart found no suitable post open to him; and with his father once more as escort Mozart at age 14 (1769) set off for Italy to try to make his way as an opera composer, the field in which he openly declared his ambition to succeed and which offered higher financial rewards than other forms of composition at this time.

In Italy, Mozart was well received: at Milan he obtained a commission for an opera; at Rome he was made a member of an honorary knightly order by the Pope; and at Bologna the Accademia Filarmonica awarded him membership despite a rule normally requiring candidates to be 20 years old. During these years of travel in Italy and returns to Salzburg between

journeys, he produced his first large-scale settings of opera seria (that is, court opera on serious subjects): *Mitridate* (1770), *Ascanio in Alba* (1771), and *Lucio Silla* (1772), as well as his first String Quartets. At Salzburg in late 1771 he renewed his writing of Symphonies (Nos. 14–21).

In these operatic works Mozart displays a complete mastery of the varied styles of aria required for the great virtuoso singers of the day (especially large-scale da capo arias), this being the sole authentic requirement of this type of opera. The strong leaning of these works toward the singers' virtuosity rather than toward dramatic content made the opera seria a rapidly dying form by Mozart's time, but in *Lucio Silla* he nonetheless shows clear evidence of his power of dramatic expression within individual scenes.

Salzburg, 1773–1777. In this period Mozart remained primarily in Salzburg, employed as concertmaster of the archbishop's court musicians. In 1773 a new archbishop took office, Hieronymus Colloredo, who was a newcomer to Salzburg and its provincial ways. Unwilling to countenance the frequent absences of the Mozarts, he declined to promote Leopold to the post of chapel master that he had long coveted. The archbishop showed equally little understanding of young Mozart's special gifts. In turn Mozart abhorred Salzburg, but he could find no better post. In 1775 he went off to Munich, where he produced the opera buffa *La finta giardiniera* with great success but without tangible consequences. In this period at Salzburg he wrote nine Symphonies (Nos. 22–30), including the excellent No. 29 in A Major; a large number of divertimenti, including the *Haffner Serenade;* all of his six Concertos for violin, several other concertos, and church music for use at Salzburg.

Mannheim and Paris, 1777–1779. Despite his continued productivity, Mozart was wholly dissatisfied with provincial Austria, and in 1777 he set off for new destinations: Munich, Augsburg, and prolonged stays in Mannheim and Paris. Mannheim was the seat of a famous court orchestra, along with a fine opera house. He wrote a number of attractive works while there (including his three Flute Quartets and five of his Violin Sonatas), but he was not offered a post.

Paris was a vastly larger theater for Mozart's talents (his father urged him to go there, for "from Paris the fame of a man of great talent echoes through the whole world," he wrote his son). But after 9 difficult months in Paris, from March 1778 to January 1779, Mozart returned once more to Salzburg, having been unable to secure a foothold and depressed by the entire experience, which had included the death of his mother in the midst of his stay in Paris. Unable to get a commission for an opera (still his chief ambition), he wrote music to order in Paris, again mainly for wind instruments: the Sinfonia Concertante for four solo wind instruments and orchestra, the Concerto for flute and harp, other chamber music, and the ballet music *Les Petits riens*. In addition, he was compelled to give lessons to make money. In his poignant letters from Paris, Mozart described his life in detail, but he also told his father (letter of July 31, 1778), "You know that I am, so to speak, soaked in music, that I am immersed in it all day long, and that I love to plan works, study, and meditate." This was the way in which the real Mozart saw himself; it far better reflects the actualities of his life than the fictional image of the carefree spirit who dashed off his works without premeditation, an image that was largely invented in the 19th century.

Salzburg, 1779–1781. Returning to Salzburg once more, Mozart took up a post as court conductor and violinist. He chafed again at the constraints of local life and his menial role under the archbishop. In Salzburg, as he wrote in a letter, "one hears nothing, there is no theater, no opera." During these years he concentrated on instrumental music (Symphony Nos. 32–34), the Symphonie Concertante for violin and viola, several orchestral divertimenti, and (despite the lack of a theater) an unfinished German opera, later called *Zaide*.

In 1780 Mozart received a long-awaited commission from Munich for the opera seria *Idomeneo*, musically one of the greatest of his works despite its unwieldy libretto and one of the great turning points in his musical development as he moved from his peregrinations of the 1770s to his Vienna sojourn in the 1780s. *Idomeneo* is, effectively, the last and greatest work in the entire tradition of dynastic opera seria, an art form that was decaying at the same time that the great European courts, which had for decades spent their substance on it as entertainment, were themselves beginning to sense the winds of social and political revolution. Mozart's only other work in this genre, the opera seria *La clemenza di Tito* (1791), was a hurriedly written work composed on demand for a coronation at Prague, and it is significantly not cast in the traditional large dimensions of old-fashioned opera seria, with its long arias, but is cut to two acts like an opera buffa and has many features of the new operatic design Mozart evolved after *Idomeneo*.

Vienna, 1781–1791. Mozart's years in Vienna, from age 25 to his death at 35, encompass one of the most prodigious developments in so short a span in the history of music. While up to now he had demonstrated a complete and fertile grasp of the techniques of his time, his music had been largely within the range of the higher levels of the common language of the time. But in these 10 years Mozart's music grew rapidly beyond the comprehension of many of his contemporaries; it exhibited both ideas and methods of elaboration that few could follow, and to many the late Mozart seemed a difficult composer. Franz Joseph Haydn's constant praise of him came from his only true peer, and Haydn harped again and again on the problem of Mozart's obtaining a good and secure position, a problem no doubt compounded by the jealousy of Viennese rivals.

This decade also saw the composition of the last 17 of Mozart's Piano Concertos, almost all written for his own performance. They represent the high point in the literature of the classical concerto, and in the following generation only Ludwig van Beethoven was able to match them.

A considerable influence upon Mozart's music during this decade was his increasing acquaintance with the music of Johann Sebastian Bach and George Frederick Handel, which in Vienna of the 1780s was scarcely known or appreciated. Through the private intermediacy of an enthusiast for Bach and Handel, Baron Gottfried van Swieten, Mozart came to know Bach's *Well-tempered Clavier,* from which he made arrangements of several fugues for strings with new preludes of his own. He also made arrangements of works by Handel, including *Acis and Galatea*, the *Messiah,* and *Alexander's Feast.*

In a number of late works—especially the *Jupiter* Symphony, *Die Zauberflöte* (*The Magic Flute*), and the *Requiem*—one sees an overt use of contrapuntal procedures, which reflects Mozart's awakened interest in contrapuntal techniques at this period. But in a more subtle sense much of his late work, even where it does not make direct use of fugal textures, reveals a subtlety of contrapuntal organization that doubtless owed something to his deepened experience of the music of Bach and Handel.

Operas of the Vienna Years. Mozart's evolution as an opera composer between 1781 and his death is even more remarkable, perhaps, since the problems of opera were more far-ranging than those of the larger instrumental forms and provided less adequate models. In opera Mozart instinctively set about raising the perfunctory dramatic and musical conventions of his time to the status of genuine art forms. A reform of opera from triviality had been successfully achieved by Christoph Willibald Gluck, but Gluck cannot stand comparison with Mozart in pure musical invention. Although *Idomeneo* may indeed owe a good deal to Gluck, Mozart was immediately thereafter to turn away entirely from opera seria. Instead he sought German or Italian librettos that would provide stage material adequate to stimulate his powers of dramatic expression and dramatic timing through music.

The first important result was the German *Singspiel* entitled *Die Entführung aus dem Serail* (1782; Abduction from the Seraglio). Not only does it have an immense variety of expressive portrayals through its arias, but what is new in the work are its moments of authentic dramatic interaction between characters in ensembles. Following this bent, Mozart turned to Italian opera, and he was fortunate enough to find a librettist of genuine ability, a true literary craftsman, Lorenzo da Ponte. Working with da Ponte, Mozart produced his three greatest Italian operas: *Le nozze di Figaro* (1786; The Marriage of Figaro), *Don Giovanni* (1787, for Prague), and *Cosi fan tutte* (1790).

Figaro is based on a play by Pierre Caron de Beaumarchais, adapted skillfully by da Ponte to the requirements of opera. In *Figaro* the ensembles become even more important than the arias, and the considerable profusion of action in the plot is managed with a skill beyond even the best of Mozart's competitors. Not only is every character convincingly portrayed, but the work shows a blending of dramatic action and musical articulation that is probably unprecedented in opera, at least of these dimensions. In *Figaro* and other late Mozart operas the singers cannot help enacting the roles conceived by the composer, since the means of characterization and dramatic expression have been built into the arias and ensembles. This principle, grasped by only a few composers in the history of music, was evolved by Mozart in these years, and, like everything he touched, totally mastered as a technique. It is this that gives these works the quality of perfection that opera audiences have attributed to them, together with their absolute mastery of musical design.

In *Don Giovanni* elements of wit and pathos are blended with the representation of the supernatural onstage, a rare occurrence at this time. In *Cosi fan tutte* the very idea of "operatic" expression—including the exaggerated venting of sentiment—is itself made the subject of an ironic comedy on fidelity between two pairs of lovers, aided by two manipulators.

In his last opera, *The Magic Flute* (1791), Mozart turned back to German opera, and he produced a work combining many strands of popular theater but with means of musical expression ranging from quasi-folk song to Italianate coloratura. The plot, put together by the actor and impresario Emanuel Schi-

kaneder, is partly based on a fairy tale but is heavily impregnated with elements of Freemasonry and possibly with contemporary political overtones.

On concluding *The Magic Flute,* Mozart turned to work on what was to be his last project, the *Requiem.* This Mass had been commissioned by a benefactor said to have been unknown to Mozart, and he is supposed to have become obsessed with the belief that he was, in effect, writing it for himself. Ill and exhausted, he managed to finish the first two movements and sketches for several more, but the last three sections were entirely lacking when he died. It was completed by his pupil Franz Süssmayer after his death, which came on Dec. 5, 1791. He was given a third-class funeral.

EWB

Mussolini, Benito (1883–1945), Italian dictator. Benito Mussolini was head of the Italian government from 1922 to 1943. A Fascist dictator, he led Italy into three successive wars, the last of which overturned his regime.

Benito Mussolini was born at Dovia di Predappio in Forlì province on July 29, 1883. His father was a blacksmith and an ardent Socialist; his mother taught elementary school. His family belonged to the impoverished middle classes. Benito, with a sharp and lively intelligence, early demonstrated a powerful ego. Violent and undisciplined, he learned little at school. In 1901, at the age of 18, he took his *diploma di maestro* and then taught secondary school briefly. Voluntarily exiling himself to Switzerland (1902–1904), he formed a dilettante's culture notable only for its philistinism. Not surprisingly, Mussolini based it on Friedrich Nietzsche, Georges Sorel, and Max Stirner, on the advocates of force, will, and the superego. Culturally armed, Mussolini returned to Italy in 1904, rendered military service, and engaged in politics full time thereafter.

Early Career and Politics. Mussolini became a member of the Socialist party in 1900, and his politics, like his culture, were exquisitely bohemian. He crossed anarchism with syndicalism, matched Peter Kropotkin and Louis Blanqui with Karl Marx and Friedrich Engels. More Nietzschean than Marxist, Mussolini's socialism was *sui generis,* a concoction created entirely by himself. In Socialist circles, nonetheless, he first attracted attention, then applause, and soon widespread admiration. He "specialized" in attacking clericalism, militarism, and reformism. Mussolini urged revolution at any cost. In each attack he was extremist and violent. But he was also eloquent and forceful.

236

Mussolini occupied several provincial posts as editor and labor leader until he suddenly emerged in the 1912 Socialist Party Congress. Shattering all precedent, he became editor of the party's daily paper, *Avanti*, at a youthful 29. His editorial tenure during 1913–1914 abundantly confirmed his promise. He wrote a new journalism, pungent and polemical, hammered his readership, and injected a new excitement into Socialist ranks. On the Socialist platform, he spoke sharply and well, deft in phrase and savage in irony.

The young Mussolini proved a formidable opponent. In a party long inert, bureaucratic, and burdened with mediocrity, he capitalized on his youth, offered modernity with dynamism, and decried the need for revolution in a moment when revolutionary ferment was sweeping the country. An opportunist to his bones, Mussolini early mastered the direction of the winds and learned quickly to turn full sail into them.

From Socialist to Fascist. This much-envied talent led Mussolini to desert the Socialist party in 1914 and to cross over to the enemy camp, the Italian bourgeoisie. He rightly understood that World War I would bury the old Europe. Upheaval would follow its wake. He determined to prepare for "the unknown." In late 1914 he founded an independent newspaper, *Popolo d'Italia,* and backed it up with his own independent movement (Autonomous Fascists). He drew close to the new forces in Italian politics, the radicalized middle-class youth, and made himself their national spokesman.

Mussolini developed a new program, substituting nationalism for internationalism, militarism for antimilitarism, and the aggressive restoration of the bourgeois state instead of its revolutionary destruction. He had thus completely reversed himself. The Italian working classes called him "Judas" and "traitor." Drafted into the trenches in 1915, Mussolini was wounded during training exercises in 1917, but he managed to return to active politics that same year. His newspaper, which he now reinforced with a second political movement (Revolutionary Fascists), was his main card; his talents and his reputation guaranteed him a hand in the game.

After the end of the war, Mussolini's career, so promising at the outset, slumped badly. He organized his third movement (Constituent Fascists) in 1918, but it was stillborn. Mussolini ran for office in the 1919 parliamentary elections but was defeated. Nonetheless, he persisted.

Head of the Government. In March 1919 Mussolini founded another movement (Fighting Fascists), courted the militant Italian youth, and waited for events to favor him. The tide turned in 1921. The elections that year sent him victoriously to Parliament at the head of 35 Fascist deputies; the third assembly of his fledgling movement gave birth to a national party, the National Fascist party (PNF), with more than 250,000 followers and Mussolini as its uncontested leader, its *duce.*

The following year, in October 1922, Mussolini successfully "marched" on Rome. But, in fact, the back door to power had been opened by key ruling groups (industry and agriculture, military, monarchy, and Church), whose support Mussolini now enjoyed. These groups, economically desperate and politically threatened, accepted Mussolini's solution to their crisis: mobilize middle-class youth, repress the workers violently, and set up a tough central government to restore "law and order." Accordingly, with the youth as his "flying wedge," Mussolini attacked the workers, spilled their blood liberally over the Italian peninsula, and completed triumphantly the betrayal of his early socialism. Without scruple or remorse, Mussolini now showed the extent to which ambition, opportunism, and utter amorality constituted his very core. He was in fact eminently a product of a particular crisis, World War I, and a special social class, the petty bourgeoisie. Mussolini's capture of power was classic: he was the right national leader at the right historical moment.

Fascist State. Once in power, Mussolini attacked the problem of survival. With accomplished tact, he set general elections, violated their constitutional norms freely, and concluded them in 1924 with an absolute majority in Parliament. But the assassination immediately thereafter of the Socialist leader Giacomo Matteotti, a noted opponent, by Fascist hirelings suddenly reversed his fortunes, threw his regime into crisis, and nearly toppled him. Mussolini, however, recouped and with his pivotal speech of Jan. 3, 1925, took the offensive. He suppressed civil liberties, annihilated the opposition, and imposed open dictatorship. Between 1926 and 1929 Mussolini moved to consolidate his regime through the enactment of "the most Fascist laws" (*le leggi fascistissime*). He concluded the decade on a high note: his Concordat with the Vatican in 1929 settled the historic differences between the Italian state and the Roman Catholic Church. Awed by a generosity that multiplied his annual income fourfold, Pope Pius XI confirmed to the world that Mussolini had been sent "by Divine Providence."

As the 1930s opened, Mussolini, seated safely in power and enjoying wide support from the middle classes, undertook to shape his regime and fix its image. Italy, he announced, had commenced the epoch of the "Third Rome." The "Fascist Revolution," after the French original, would itself date civilized progress anew: 1922 became "Year I of the New Era"; 1932, Year X. The regime called itself the "Corporate State" and offered Italy a bewildering brood of institutions, all splendidly titled but sparsely endowed. For if the rhetoric impressed, the reality denied.

The strongest economic groups remained entrenched. They had put Mussolini into power, and they now reaped their fruits. While they accumulated unprecedented economic control and vast personal fortunes, while a class of nouveau riche attached itself to the regime and parasitically sucked the nation's blood, the living standard of the working majority fell to subsistence. The daily consumption of calories per capita placed Italy near the bottom among European nations; the average Italian worker's income amounted to one-half his French counterpart's, one-third his English, and one-fourth his American. As national leader, Mussolini offered neither solutions nor analyses for Italy's fundamental problems, preferring slogans to facts and propaganda to hard results. The face of the state he indeed refashioned; its substance he left intact. The "new order" was coating only.

Il Duce ruled from the top of this hollow pyramid. A consummate poseur, he approached government as a drama to be enacted, every scene an opportunity to display ample but superficial talents. Cynical and arrogant, he despised men in the same measure that he manipulated them. Without inspired or noble sentiments himself, he instinctively sought the defects in others, their weaknesses, and mastered the craft of corrupting them. He surrounded himself with ambitious opportunists and allowed full rein to their greed and to their other, unnameable vices while his secret agents compiled incriminating dossiers. Count Galeatto Ciano, his son-in-law and successor-designate, defined Mussolini's entourage as "that coterie of old prostitutes." Such was Mussolini's "new governing class."

Mussolini's Three Wars. In 1930 the worldwide economic depression arrived in Italy. The middle classes succumbed to discontent; the working people suffered aggravated misery. Mussolini initially reacted with a public works program but soon shifted to foreign adventure. The 1935 Ethiopian War, a classic diversionary exercise, was planned to direct attention away from internal discontent and to the myth of imperial grandeur. The "Italian Empire," Mussolini's creation, was announced in 1936. It pushed his star to new heights. But it also exacted its price. The man

of destiny lost his balance, and with it that elementary talent that measures real against acclaimed success. No ruler confuses the two and remains in power long. Mussolini thus began his precipitous slide.

The 1936 Spanish intervention, in which Mussolini aided Francisco Franco in the Civil War, followed hard on Ethiopia but returned none of its anticipated gains. Mussolini compounded this error with a headlong rush into Adolf Hitler's embrace. The Rome-Berlin Axis in 1936 and the Tripartite Pact in 1937 were succeeded by the ill-fated Steel Pact in 1939. Meanwhile, Mussolini's pro-Hitlerism struck internally. Having declared earlier that the racial problem did not exist for Italy, Mussolini in 1938 unleashed his own anti-Semitic blows against Italian Jewry. As the 1930s closed, Mussolini had nearly exhausted all toleration for himself and his regime within Italy.

World War II's surprise outbreak in 1939 left Mussolini standing on the margins of world politics, and he saw Hitler redrawing the map of Europe without him. Impelled by the prospect of easy victory, Mussolini determined "to make war at any cost." The cost was clear: modern industry, modern armies, and popular support. Mussolini unfortunately lacked all of these. Nonetheless, in 1940 he pushed a reluctant Italy into war on Hitler's side. He thus ignored the only meaningful lesson of World War I: the United States alone had decided that conflict, and consequently America, not Germany, was the key hegemonic power.

Disaster and Death. In 1940–1941 Mussolini's armies, badly supplied and impossibly led, strung their defeats from Europe across the Mediterranean to the African continent. These defeats constituted the full measure of Mussolini's bankruptcy. Italy lost its war in 1942; Mussolini collapsed 6 months later. Restored as Hitler's puppet in northern Italy in 1943, he drove Italy deeper into the tragedy of invasion, occupation, and civil war during 1944–1945. The end approached, but Mussolini struggled vainly to survive, unwilling to pay the price for folly. The debt was discharged by a partisan firing squad on April 28, 1945, at Dongo in Como province.

In the end Mussolini failed where he had believed himself most successful: he was not a *modern* statesman. His politics and culture had been formed before World War I, and they had remained rooted there. After that war, though land empire had become ossified and increasingly superfluous, Mussolini had embarked on territorial expansion in the grand manner. In a moment when the European nation-state had passed its apogee and entered decline (the economic depression had underscored it), Mussolini had pursued ultranationalism abroad and an iron state within. He had never grasped the lines of the new world already emerging. He had gone to war for more territory and greater influence when he needed new markets and more capital. Tied to a decaying world about to disappear forever, Mussolini was anachronistic, a man of the past, not the future. His Fascist slogan served as his own epitaph: *Non si torna indietro* (There is no turning back). A 19th-century statesman could not survive long in the 20th-century world, and history swept him brutally but rightly aside.

EWB

N

Nagy, Imre (1896–1958), Hungarian politician. Imre Nagy served as prime minister of Hungary between 1953 and 1955, then again in 1956 during the revolution. He was tried and executed in 1958.

Imre Nagy was born into a peasant family at Kaposvar on July 6, 1896. As a young man he was an engineering apprentice, then a worker in Budapest. He was sent to the Russian front during World War I. Taken prisoner, he joined the Red Army in 1917 and the Bolshevik Party in 1918. He returned to Hungary in the early 1920s and joined the then illegal Communist Party. He organized the peasants in a movement calling for agrarian reform. He was in charge of Communist Party work in the countryside, concentrating on agrarian questions. Politically very active, he was tried and sentenced several times by the Hungarian government.

In 1928 Nagy left the country and settled in Vienna. In March 1930 he joined the staff of the International Agronomy Institute in Moscow. He published several articles in the Hungarian emigre journal *Sarló es Kalapács* (Sickle and Hammer). In 1932, commissioned by the Comintern, he drafted the Communist program of action on agrarian problems. He never joined any of the emigre Hungarian Communist factions, which may be one of the reasons why he escaped the Stalinist purges of the 1930s.

In 1941 he became assistant editor, then editor-in-chief, of Radio Kossuth, which broadcast programs directed to Hungary. In 1944 Nagy drew up a plan for Hungarian agrarian reform. At the end of the year he returned to Hungary and was appointed minister for agriculture in the provisional government at Debrecen. In April 1945, following the World War II liberation of the country by the Red Army, the government moved to Budapest, where life began to resume its normal course. The agrarian reform implemented in Hungary was based on Nagy's plan and carried out under his direction. This made him very popular among the peasants.

In the elections held on November 4, 1945, the conservative Smallholders Party won 57.7 percent of the votes, the Social Democratic Party 17.4 percent, the Communist Party 17 percent, and the National Peasant Party 8 percent. These parties formed a coalition government. Imre Nagy became minister of the interior. On March 12, 1946, the Communist, Social Democrat, and National Peasant parties formed a "left block" inside the government coalition and organized demonstrations against the deputies from the right wing of the Smallholders Party. Under pressure, the Smallholders Party expelled 23 deputies. Later in March 1946 the Communist Party charged Imre Nagy with "lack of vigor" and relieved him of his post. It appointed Laszlo Rajk as his successor.

In order to force further nationalization, the Communist Party in February 1947 launched fresh attacks on the Smallholders Party. The secretary general of the party was arrested by the Soviet Control Commission and charged with anti-Soviet activities. He was tried and condemned to death, together with other party leaders.

In May the three largest banks were nationalized. New elections were held in August, in which 60 percent of the votes were won by the government coalition. Imre Nagy was elected president of the Parliament, a largely ceremonial office.

In March 1948, under pressure from the Communist Party, which was seeking a merger with the Social Democrats, the latter expelled some of its leading members who were opposed to such a union. Later that month businesses with more than 100 employees were nationalized. In June the Communist and Social Democratic parties decided to unite; for all practical purposes, the Social Democratic Party was absorbed by the Communists. A large-scale purge began in September, leading to the expulsion of some 100,000 members from the Communist Party: "former Social Democrats or unreliable elements."

Nagy had serious disputes with Matyas Rákosi, the Communist Party leader, from 1948. Nagy disagreed with the "personality cult" and the forced pace of collectivization, pointing out the dangers of this policy. In 1949 he was forced to withdraw from political life, having been removed from the politboro. He became director of the University of Agronomy and devoted himself to the study of agrarian questions.

A show trial of Rajk took place in September 1949; it was designed to justify the attacks on Yugoslavia. Rajk was sentenced to death. By December the nationalization of industry was completed. In the beginning of 1950 the first Five Year Plan took effect. It concentrated on the development of heavy industry and on intensified collectivization.

In 1951 Nagy was allowed to return to political life. He was again elected to the politboro and was made a member of the secretariat. In 1952 he was made minister for farm deliveries, and later, when Rákosi became president of the council, he was appointed as his second deputy.

In 1953, three months after Stalin's death, the new leaders of the Soviet Communist Party made a vigorous attack on the Hungarian party leaders and forced them to adopt a new line and to appoint Imre Nagy as prime minister. In his new post he introduced a series of measures. In addition to a reorganization of the economy, he announced measures of political liberalization. The peasants were allowed to withdraw from the cooperatives and were promised tax relief. Agricultural credit was eased. The deportations were ended. A new Patriotic People's Front was formed. In October 1954 Nagy announced intensified democratization. In December Rákosi attacked the line of policy adopted by Nagy. New instructions from Moscow strengthened Rákosi's position. In March 1955 the Central Committee condemned Imre Nagy's course, and in April he was expelled from the Central Committee and relieved of all his offices. At the end of 1955 he was expelled from the party.

After the 20th Congress of the Soviet Communist Party in 1956 it was important to rehabilitate Nagy's policy. In July Rákosi was removed; in October Nagy was readmitted to the party. On October 23 and 24 workers went on strike; there were demonstrations in the streets against occupying Soviet troops; and the demand was raised for the return to power of Nagy. Nagy delivered a radio address calling for an end to the fighting. On October 26 delegations from all over the country urged Nagy to take new measures to liberate the country. During the following days a new government was formed and discussions began concerning the complete withdrawal of the Soviet troops. But more Soviet troops entered the country. The Hungarian government denounced the Warsaw Pact and declared the country neutral. Soviet forces launched a general offensive against Hungary, crushing the uprising. Nagy took refuge at the Yugoslav embassy (some 200,000 Hungarians fled the country).

Nagy remained under the protection of the embassy until November 22, when he was duped into leaving it. On his way home he was captured. He was tried, sentenced to death, and executed in 1958.

EWB

Namier, Sir Lewis Bernstein (1888–1960), English historian. Lewis Namier was a major force in introducing stronger empirical methods and social analysis into the study of 18th-century politics.

Lewis Namier was born Ludvik Bernstein near Warsaw on June 22, 1888. He studied briefly at Lausanne and the London School of Economics before entering Balliol College, Oxford. The Oxford years, from 1908 to 1912, were crucial in his development. There he acquired a British self-identity, changing his name to Namier (derived from his family's older name, Niemirowski); there he also acquired a deep and permanent interest in British history of the 18th century.

Throughout his life Namier was strongly attracted to the world of power and policy making. At the start of World War I, he enlisted in the British army but was discharged in 1915 because of poor eyesight. As a civilian, he served in the Propaganda Department (1915–1917), the Department of Information (1917–1918), and the Political Intelligence Department of the Foreign Office (1918–1920). He attended the Versailles Peace Conference as a technical expert on eastern European affairs.

Namier started his serious work on the "imperial problem during the American Revolution" while a postgraduate student at Oxford in 1912 and continued these researches while in business in New York in 1913–1914. In 1920 he returned to academic life at Balliol College. Finding that this did not allow him sufficient time for research, he resigned to go into business during 1921–1923, hoping to save enough to support his serious studies. Without any regular income, living on grants, loans, and savings, he devoted the years 1924 through 1929 entirely to research and writing. From these fruitful years came his two great works on 18th-century politics.

During the 1920s Namier became active in the Zionist movement and in 1929 accepted the position of political secretary of the Jewish Agency for Palestine. Finding that he lacked the personal political skills necessary for such a delicate job, he resigned after 2 years. From 1931 until his retirement in 1953, Namier was professor of modern history at Manchester University. He was knighted in 1952 and received many academic honors during the 1950s. Sir Lewis died in London Aug. 19, 1960.

Historical Work: 18th Century. Namier's scholarly reputation is based primarily on his two related works on 18th-century politics. In *The Structure of Politics at the Accession of George III* (1929), he attempted a static analysis of political society and the political process as it existed from 1754 until 1762, during the ascendancy of the Duke of Newcastle. In this great work he broke forever the remnants of the

"Whig myth," deriving ultimately from Horace Walpole and Edmund Burke, which saw the politics of the first 2 decades of the reign of George III as adhering to the two-party model of the 19th century. He showed parliamentary politics to be based not upon coherent parties but, rather, on a congeries of familial-personal factions and interests, with a significant element supporting the government of the day regardless of its composition and another congenitally but unstably "independent." In most constituencies, family favor and personal dependency best explained voting patterns.

In *England in the Age of the American Revolution* (1930), Namier moved from static analysis to narrative history, in which he was less masterful. He intended to follow volume 1, which covered only 1760–1762, with other volumes but was deflected by teaching, other scholarly interests, and international events.

In his work on 18th-century parliaments, Namier collected data on hundreds of members of Parliament. He realized that the work of all scholars doing such work would be immensely aided by the compilation of a biographical dictionary of all members of the House of Commons, with collective analysis where possible. As early as 1928 he helped publicize the project for such a history of Parliament, and after World War II, when the reorganized project obtained government support, Namier joined the new editorial board and devoted the years after his retirement in 1953 to editing the volumes on the period 1754–1790. His *History of Parliament* (3 vols., 1964) is a tool of inestimable value for students of pre-Victorian politics.

Historical Work: 19th and 20th Centuries. Namier was deeply interested in European history, particularly central and east-central Europe, in the years since 1815. Starting with a propaganda piece, *Germany and Eastern Europe* (1915), he published a number of short interpretive essays (many republished in *Vanished Supremacies,* 1962) rich in insight and fresh interpretation. On a somewhat larger scale was his *1848: Revolution of the Intellectuals* (1946), which measured the formal liberal ideology of the central European revolutionaries against their class and national prejudices.

After 1940 Namier became involved in the problem of the diplomatic origins of World War II. Using government publications, early memoirs, and interviews with exiled officials in London, he published a series of articles, starting in 1943, on the diplomatic origins of the war. These were republished in 1948 as *Diplomatic Prelude 1938–1939.* He continued to publish articles and review essays in this area, subsequently republished in *Europe in Decay* (1950) and *In the Nazi Era* (1952). These were important for the rigorous scrutiny he gave to the dubious evidence and arguments advanced by some self or national apologists.

Though he did not produce a major work on the 19th century, Namier had considerable influence on A. J. P. Taylor and others working since 1945 on central European history. His work on the diplomatic origins of World War II has stood up well and is still the starting point for all students in the field. The influence of his 18th-century studies is likely to last, for it has given us a whole new way of approaching the historical study of political behavior.

EWB

Napoleon I (1769–1821), emperor of the French. Napoleon ranks as one of the greatest military conquerors in history. Through his conquests he remade the map of Europe, and through his valuable administrative and legal reforms he promoted the growth of liberalism.

Napoleon Bonaparte was born Napoleon Buonaparte (the spelling change was made after 1796) on Aug. 15, 1769, in the Corsican city of Ajaccio. He was the fourth of 11 children of Carlo Buonaparte and Letizia Romolino. His father derived from the lesser Corsican nobility. Following the annexation of Corsica by France in 1769, Carlo was granted the same rights and privileges as the French nobility. After an elementary education at a boys' school in Ajaccio, young Napoleon was sent in January 1779 with his older brother Joseph to the College of Autun in the duchy of Burgundy. In May of the same year he was transferred to the more fashionable College of Brienne, another military school, while his brother remained at Autun. Here Napoleon's small stature earned him the nickname of the "Little Corporal."

At Brienne, Napoleon received an excellent military and academic education, and in October 1784 he earned an appointment to the École Militaire of Paris. The royal military school of Paris was the finest in Europe in the years before the Revolution, and Napoleon entered the service of Louis XVI in 1785 with a formal education that had prepared him for his future role in French history. Napoleon joined an artillery unit at Valence, where he again received superior training.

First Military Assignments. Now a second lieutenant, Napoleon continued his education on his own, but he was distracted by Corsica. Until 1793 his thoughts, desires, and ambitions centered on the island of his birth. Following the death of his father, he received an extended leave (1786) to return to Corsica to settle his family's affairs. After rejoining his regiment at Auxonne, he again spent more than a year on his native island (1789–1790), during which time he was influential in introducing the changes brought about by the Revolution. Returning to France, Napoleon was transferred to Valence in June 1791. But by October he had returned to Corsica, where he remained for 7 months. He spent the critical summer of 1792 in Paris and then returned to Corsica for one last episode in October. On this visit he took part in the power struggle between the forces supporting Pasquale Paoli and those supported by the French Republic. After Paoli was victorious, Napoleon and the Bonaparte family were forced to flee to the mainland, and the young officer then turned his attention to a career in the French army.

The Revolution of 1789 did not have a major effect upon Bonaparte in its early years. He did not sympathize with the royalists. Nor did he take an active part in French politics, as his thoughts were still taken up with affairs in Corsica. Napoleon was in Paris when the monarchy was overthrown in August 1792, but no evidence indicates that he was a republican. Upon his return from Corsica in the spring of 1793, Capt. Bonaparte was given a command with the republican army that was attempting to regain control of southern France from the proroyalist forces. He took part in the siege of Avignon, and then while on his way to join the French Army of Italy Napoleon was offered command of the artillery besieging the port of Toulon.

National Acclaim. The siege of Toulon provided Napoleon with his first opportunity to display his ability as an artillery officer and brought him national recognition. France had gone to war with Prussia and Austria in 1792. England, having joined the struggle in 1793, had gained control of Toulon. After his distinguished part in dislodging the British, Napoleon was promoted to the rank of brigadier general. He also made the acquaintance of Augustin Robespierre, the younger brother of the powerful Maximilien, and though Napoleon was not politically a Jacobin, he derived benefits from his association with influential party members. The overthrow of the Jacobin regime on 9 Thermidor (July 1794) led to Napoleon's imprisonment in Fort Carré on August 9. When no evidence could be found linking him to the British, Napoleon was released after 10 days of confinement.

Throughout the winter of 1794–1795 Napoleon was employed in the defense of the Mediterranean coast. Then, in April 1795, he was ordered to

Paris, and in June he was assigned to the Army of the West. He refused this position, pleading poor health. This refusal almost brought an end to his military career, and he was assigned to the Bureau of Topography of the Committee of Public Safety. While serving in this capacity, he sought unsuccessfully to have himself transferred to Constantinople. Thus Napoleon was in Paris when the royalists attempted to overthrow the Directory on Oct. 5, 1795.

Gen. Paul Barras had been placed in command of the defense of Paris by the government, and he called upon Gen. Bonaparte to defend the Tuileries. Napoleon put down the uprising of 13 Vendémiaire by unhesitatingly turning his artillery on the attackers, dispersing the mob with what he called "a whiff of grapeshot." In gratitude he was appointed commander of the Army of the Interior and instructed to disarm Paris.

Marriage and Italian Campaign. In the winter of 1795 Napoleon met Josephine de Beauharnais, the former Mademoiselle Tascher de La Pagerie. Born on the island of Martinique, she had been married to Alexandre de Beauharnais at the age of 16 and had borne him two children, Eugène and Hortense, before separating from him. Alexandre, a nobleman from Orléans, was executed in the last days of the Terror in 1794, leaving Josephine free to marry Napoleon. Their civil ceremony took place on March 9, 1796. Within a few days Napoleon left his bride behind in Paris and took up his new command at the head of the Army of Italy.

On March 26 Napoleon reached his headquarters at Nice, and on March 31 he issued the first orders for the invasion of Italy. The campaign opened on April 12, and within several weeks he had forced Piedmont out of the war. In May, Napoleon marched across northern Italy, reaching Verona on June 3. The campaign was then bogged down by the Austrian defense of Mantua, which lasted 18 months. During this period Napoleon beat back Austrian attempts to relieve the fortified city at Castiglione, Arcole, and Rivoli. Finally, in the spring of 1797, Napoleon advanced on Vienna and forced the Austrians to sign the Treaty of Campoformio (Oct. 17, 1797). The treaty gave France the territory west of the Rhine and control of Italy.

After spending the summer and fall at the palace of Monbello, where he established with Josephine what in reality was the court of Italy, Napoleon returned to Paris the hero of the hour. He was the man who could make war and peace. Napoleon was given command of the Army of England after drawing up a plan to invade that island. However, after a brief visit to the English Channel he abandoned any hope of crossing that turbulent body of water with the available French fleet. Returning to Paris, he gave up his command.

Egyptian Campaign. Napoleon did not wish to remain idle in Paris; nor did the government wish to see a popular general in the capital without a command to occupy him. Thus, when an expedition to Egypt was proposed, probably by Charles Maurice de Talleyrand, both the general and his government gave it their support. Strategically, the expedition would extend French influence into the Mediterranean and threaten British control in India. Napoleon sailed from Toulon on May 19, 1798, with an army of 35,000 men. On June 11–12 he captured Malta, and on June 30 the task force reached Alexandria, Egypt. The city was taken, and Napoleon's army marched up the west branch of the Nile to Cairo. In sight of the city and of the Pyramids, the first major battle took place. With minimal losses the French drove the Mamluks back into the desert in the Battle of the Pyramids, and all of lower Egypt came under Napoleon's control.

Napoleon reorganized the government, the postal service, and the system for collecting taxes; introduced the first printing presses; created a health department; built new hospitals for the poor in Cairo; and founded the Institut d'Egypte. During the French occupation the Rosetta Stone was discovered, and the Nile was explored as far south as Aswan. But the military aspect of Napoleon's Egyptian venture was not so rewarding. On Aug. 1, 1798, Horatio Nelson destroyed the French fleet in Aboukir Bay, leaving the French army cut off from France. Then Napoleon's Syrian campaign ended in the unsuccessful siege of Acre (April 1799) and a return to the Nile. After throwing a Turkish army back into the sea at Aboukir (July 1799), Napoleon left the army under the command of Gen. Jean Baptiste Kléber and returned to France with a handful of officers.

The Consulate. Landing at Fréjus on Oct. 9, 1799, Napoleon went directly to Paris, where the political situation was ripe for a coup d'etat. France had become weary of the Directory, and in collaboration with Emmanuel Joseph Sieyès, Joseph Fouché, and Talleyrand, Napoleon overthrew the government on 18 Brumaire (Nov. 9–10, 1799). The Constitution of the Year VIII provided for the Consulate. Napoleon was named first consul and given virtually dictatorial powers. The trappings of the republic remained— there were two legislative bodies, the Tribunate and the Corps Legislatif—but real power rested in the hands of the first consul.

Napoleon began at once to solve the problems that faced France at the turn of the century. With mailed fist and velvet glove he ended the civil war in the Vendée. He then personally led an army over the Grand-Saint-Bernard Pass into Italy and defeated the Austrians, who had declared war on France while Napoleon was in Egypt, at the Battle of Marengo (June 14, 1800). This victory, which Napoleon always considered one of his greatest, again brought Italy under French control. After a truce that lasted into December, French armies forced Austria out of the war for the second time. The Treaty of Lunéville (Feb. 9, 1801) reconfirmed the Treaty of Campoformio. It was followed on March 25, 1802, by the Treaty of Amiens, which ended, or at least interrupted, the war with England. The Concordat that Napoleon signed with Pope Pius VII in 1801 restored harmony between Rome and Paris, and it ended the internal religious split that had originated in the Revolution. Napoleon also reformed France's legal system with the Code Napoleon.

The Empire. By 1802 Napoleon was the most popular dictator France had ever known, and he was given the position of first consul for life with the right to name his successor. The establishment of the Empire on May 18, 1804, thus changed little except the name of the government. The Constitution of the Year VIII was altered only to provide for an imperial government; its spirit was not changed. The Emperor of the French created a new nobility, set up a court, and changed the titles of government officials; but the average Frenchman noticed little difference.

The Treaty of Amiens proved to be no more than a truce, and in May 1803 the war with England was renewed. The Emperor planned to invade the island kingdom in the summer of 1805, but his naval operations went amiss. In September, Napoleon turned his back on the Channel and marched against Austria, who together with Russia had formed the Third Coalition. At Ulm (October 14) and Austerlitz (December 2) Napoleon inflicted disastrous defeats upon the Allies, forcing Alexander I of Russia to retreat behind the Neman and compelling Austria to make peace. At the Battle of Austerlitz, Napoleon reached the height of his military career. The Treaty of Pressburg (Dec. 27, 1805) deprived Austria of additional lands and further humiliated the once mighty Hapsburg state.

Victory throughout the Continent. The year 1806 was marked by war with Prussia over increased French influence in Germany. The overconfident Prussian army sang as it marched to total destruction at the battles of Jena and Auerstädt (Oct. 14, 1806), and Napoleon entered Berlin in triumph. Prussia was reduced to a second-rate power, and the fighting moved eastward into Poland as the Russians belatedly came to the aid of their defeated ally. Although at the Battle of Eylau (Feb. 8, 1807) the French were brought to a standstill, on June 14 at Friedland the Emperor drove the Russian army from the field. Alexander I made peace at Tilsit on June 25, 1807. This understanding between the two emperors divided Europe. Alexander was to have a free hand in the east to take Finland and Bessarabia, while Napoleon was free to reshape western and central Europe as he pleased. The most significant result was the creation of the grand duchy of Warsaw (1807). Sweden was defeated in 1808 with Russia's help. Napoleon was now master of the Continent. Only England remained in the field.

Problems with England and Spain. On Oct. 21, 1805, Adm. Horatio Nelson had destroyed the combined Franco-Spanish fleet off Cape Trafalgar, Spain. This loss made it virtually impossible for Napoleon to invade England. He, therefore, introduced the Continental system, or blockade, designed to exclude all British goods from Europe. In this manner he hoped to ruin the British economy and to force the "nation of shopkeepers" to make peace on French terms. His plan did not work, and it led Napoleon into conflicts with Spain, the papacy, and Russia, and it undoubtedly formed a major cause for the downfall of the Empire.

In Spain in 1808 French interference led to the removal of the Bourbon dynasty and to the placement of Joseph Bonaparte as king. But the Spanish people refused to accept this Napoleonic dictate and, with aid from Great Britain, kept 250,000 French troops occupied in the Peninsular War (1808–1814). The refusal of Pope Pius VII to cooperate with Napoleon and the blockade led to the Pope's imprisonment and a French takeover of the Papal States. In the case of Russia refusal proved even more serious. Alexander's refusal to close Russian ports to British ships led to Napoleon's Russian campaign of 1812, which was highlighted by the Battle of Borodino (September 7) and the occupation of Moscow (September 14–October 19). However, the ultimate result of this Russian campaign was the destruction of the Grand Army of 500,000 troops.

Fall from Glory. The Napoleonic system now began to break up rapidly. At its height three of the Emperor's brothers and his brother-in-law sat on European thrones. Napoleon had also secured an annulment of his marriage to Josephine and then married Marie Louise, the daughter of Emperor Francis II of Austria, in March 1810. Despite this union, Napoleon's father-in-law declared war on him in 1813. Napoleon's defeat at the Battle of the Nations at Leipzig (Oct. 16–18, 1813) forced him behind the Rhine, where he waged a brilliant, but futile, campaign during the first 3 months of 1814. Paris fell to the Allies on March 31, 1814, and the hopelessness of the military situation led the Emperor to abdicate at Fontainebleau (April 4, 1814) in favor of his son Napoleon II. However, the Allies refused to recogize the 3-year-old boy, and Louis XVIII was placed on the French throne.

Napoleon was exiled to the island of Elba, where he was sovereign ruler for 10 months. But as the alliance of the Great Powers broke down during the Congress of Vienna and the French people became dissatisfied with the restored royalists, Napoleon made plans to return to power. Sailing from Elba on Feb. 26, 1815, with 1,050 soldiers, Napoleon landed in southern France and marched unopposed to Paris, where he reinstated himself on March 21. Louis XVIII fled, and thus began Napoleon's new reign: the Hundred Days. The French did not wish to renew their struggle against Europe. Nevertheless, as the Allies closed ranks, Napoleon was forced to renew the war if he was to remain on the throne of France.

The Waterloo campaign (June 12–18) was short and decisive. After a victory over the Prussian army at Ligny, Napoleon was defeated by the combined British and Prussian armies under the Duke of Wellington and Gebhard von Blücher at Waterloo on June 18, 1815. He returned to Paris and abdicated for a second time, on June 22. Napoleon at first hoped to reach America; however, he surrendered to the commander of the British blockade at Rochefort on July 3, hoping to obtain asylum in England. Instead, he was sent into exile on the island of St. Helena. There he spent his remaining years, quarreling with the British governor, Sir Hudson Lowe, and dictating his memoirs. He died on St. Helena, after long suffering from cancer, on May 5, 1821.

EWB

Napoleon III (1808–1873), emperor of France from 1852 to 1870. Elected president of the Second French Republic in 1848, Napoleon III staged a coup d'etat in 1851 and reestablished the Empire.

Between 1848 and 1870 France underwent rapid economic growth as a result of the industrial revolution, and Napoleon III's government fostered this development. These years were also the period of the

Crimean War and the unifications of Italy and Germany, and France played a pivotal role in these affairs.

Napoleon was born in Paris on April 20, 1808, the youngest son of Louis Bonaparte, the king of Holland and brother of Napoleon, I, and of Hortense de Beauharnais, daughter of Josephine. His full name was Charles Louis Napoleon Bonaparte, but he was generally known as Louis Napoleon. After 1815 Louis Napoleon lived with his mother in exile in Augsburg, Bavaria, where he attended the Augsburg gymnasium, and at Arenburg Castle in Switzerland. In 1831 he and his brother joined rebels against papal rule in Romagna.

The Pretender. The death of his brother during this rebellion, followed by the death of Napoleon I's son, made Louis Napoleon the Bonaparte pretender. He took this position seriously, beginning his career as propagandist and pamphleteer in 1832 with *Rêveries politiques*. He also joined the Swiss militia, becoming an artillery captain in 1834 and publishing an artillery manual in 1836. Louis Napoleon attempted a military coup d'etat at Strasbourg on Oct. 30, 1836, but the ludicrous venture failed. Louis Philippe deported him to America, but Louis Napoleon returned to Arenburg to attend his mother, who died in October 1837.

France threatened invasion when the Swiss government refused to expel him, but Louis Napoleon withdrew voluntarily to England. There he produced his most famous pamphlet, *Des Idées napoléoniennes* (Napoleonic Ideas), effectively stating his political program, which combined the ideas of liberty and authority, social reform and order, and glory and peace. Louis Napoleon attempted a second coup d'etat on Aug. 6, 1840, at Boulogne-sur-Mer, but failed again. He was tried by the Chamber of Peers, condemned to perpetual imprisonment, and interned in the fortress of Ham (Somme). There he studied, and he wrote, among other things, *L'Extinction du paupérisme,* which increased his reputation as a social reformer. In 1846 he escaped to England.

Second Republic. Louis Napoleon hastened to Paris when he received news of the Revolution of 1848, but he withdrew on request of the provisional government. He declined to be a candidate in the April elections and resigned his seat when elected in four constituencies in June. In September 1848 he was again chosen by five districts and took his seat in the Assembly.

Louis Napoleon was not a particularly impressive figure. Nonetheless, the appeal of the Bonaparte name, strengthened by the spread of the Napoleonic legend, and a general demand for order following the workers' uprising of June 1848 won him overwhelming election as president of the Second French Republic on Dec. 10, 1848.

Louis Napoleon used a French expeditionary force to restore, and then to protect, papal supremacy in Rome, thus winning Roman Catholic support at home. In 1850 the legislature established residence requirements that disenfranchised nearly 3 million workers. The next year it rejected a constitutional amendment permitting re-election to the presidency. Louis Napoleon used these actions to justify his overthrow of the republic by a coup d'etat on Dec. 2, 1851. His action was endorsed by nearly 7,500,000 votes, with fewer than 650,000 negative votes. A year later more than 7,800,000 Frenchmen approved reestablishment of the Empire, which was inaugurated on Dec. 2, 1852.

Domestic Policies of the Emperor. Napoleon III governed by the principle of direct, or Caesarean, democracy, through which power was transferred directly from the people to an absolute ruler who was responsible to them and whose acts were confirmed by plebiscite. Although he established a senate and a legislative assembly chosen by universal suffrage, they had little power. Elections were carefully manipulated, and political activities and the press were closely controlled. The Emperor's ideal was to serve as representative of the whole nation, and hence he never organized a true Bonapartist party. In 1853 he married the Spanish beauty Eugénie de Montijo, and in 1856 she bore him an heir, thus providing for the succession.

In economic affairs Napoleon III considered himself a socialist, and he believed that government should control and increase national wealth. His ideals resembled those of the Saint-Simonians, emphasizing communications, public works, and credit. The imperial government built canals, promoted railroad development, and fostered the extension of banking and credit institutions. The Emperor inaugurated great public works programs in Paris and in leading provincial cities, sponsored trade expositions, and in 1860 introduced free trade, which was unpopular with industrial leaders but ultimately strengthened French industry.

Foreign Policy. In policy statements Napoleon III consistently asserted that the Empire stood for peace, but in practice Bonapartism demanded glory. Napoleon III believed in national self-determination, and he wished to assume leadership in redrawing European frontiers in accordance with his "principle of nationalities." Thus he hoped to restore France to the position of arbiter of Europe that it had enjoyed under Napoleon I. In practice, Napoleon III vacillated between his principles and promotion of France's self-interest, and he involved France in three European wars and several colonial expeditions.

The first European conflict, the Crimean War (1854–1856), brought little material gain, but Napoleon III defended France's protectorate of the holy places and joined the British to avenge Russia's defeat of Napoleon I. In the Congress of Paris, Napoleon III came close to his ideal of serving as arbiter of Europe. Among other things, he championed Romanian nationalism, gaining autonomy for Moldavia and Walachia and later aiding those provinces to achieve unification.

Napoleon III's second war was fought in 1859 for the Italian nationalist cause. Shortly after Felice Orsini's attempt to assassinate him in 1858, Napoleon III planned the liberation of Italy with Camillo di Cavour at Plombières. He envisaged the creation of a federation of four states under the presidency of the pope. Although French battles against Austria were successful, Napoleon III was unable to control the Italian nationalist movement, was threatened on the Rhine by Prussia, and lost support from proclerical elements in France, who saw Italian unification as a threat to the papacy. Napoleon III therefore made peace at Villafranca di Verona without freeing Venetia, thus disappointing the Italians and alienating French liberals. Although he had not fully honored his commitment, Napoleon III later received Nice and Savoy, and this brought an end to the British alliance that had been a cornerstone of his early diplomacy.

In 1862 Napoleon III became involved in an attempt to establish a friendly, pro-Catholic regime in Mexico under the Austrian prince Maximilian. Mexican resistance proved stronger than expected; the United States concluded its Civil War and exerted pressure; and Napoleon III withdrew his forces in 1866–1867. This fiasco provoked powerful criticism in France, which was intensified by the subsequent execution of Maximilian in Mexico. Meanwhile, the Emperor had also failed in his attempt to gain compensation for France in the Austro-Prussian War of 1866.

Liberal Empire. Growing opposition after 1859 encouraged Napoleon III to make concessions to liberalism. In 1860–1861 he gave the legislature additional freedom and authority, and in 1868 he granted freedom of press and assembly. The elections of 1869, fought with virulence, brought more than 3 million votes for opposition deputies. The results in-

duced Napoleon III to appoint the former Republican Émile Ollivier to form a responsible ministry. After further turbulence following a Bonaparte scandal, the Emperor resorted to plebiscite, and on May 8, 1870, more than 7,300,000 Frenchmen voted to accept all liberal reforms introduced by Napoleon III since 1860.

Franco-Prussian War. In 1870, when the Spanish invited Leopold of Hohenzollern-Sigmaringen to become their king, French protests induced Prussia's William I to have the candidacy withdrawn. The ambassador to Prussia was then instructed to demand a Prussian promise that no Hohenzollern would ever become king of Spain. William's refusal to consider this enabled Otto von Bismarck to provoke war by publishing William's dispatch from Ems in slightly altered form, making it appear that insults had been exchanged. France declared war on July 19, 1870, and Napoleon III took command of his troops although he was so ill from bladder stones, which had long troubled him, that he could scarcely ride his horse. The Emperor's troops were surrounded at Sedan, and Napoleon III surrendered with 80,000 men on Sept. 2, 1870. Two days later the Third Republic was proclaimed in Paris.

When the Germans released him in 1871, Napoleon III joined his wife and son at Chislehurst in England. He still hoped to regain the throne for his son, but he died on Jan. 9, 1873, following a series of bladder operations. His son was killed in South Africa in 1879 while serving in the British army.

EWB

Nerval, Gérard de (1808–1855), French poet. Gérard de Nerval was an early romantic. His prose and poetry mark him as a precursor of the many movements, from symbolism to surrealism, that shaped modern French literature.

Gérard de Nerval was born Gérard Labrunie on May 22, 1808, in Paris. Because of his parents' immediate departure for Silesia, where his mother died, Nerval was taken to the home of maternal relatives in the Valois. This region played a prominent part in many of his works. The fact that his early years were bereft of parental care probably contributed to his subsequent lack of mental equilibrium.

Upon his father's return from the Napoleonic Wars in 1814, Nerval returned to Paris. As a day pupil at the Lycée Charlemagne, he distinguished himself by his precocious literary gifts and made the acquaintance of a lifelong friend, the poet Théophile Gautier.

Nerval's translation in 1827 of J. W. von Goethe's *Faust* (*Part I*) earned him the praise of Goethe and opened influential Parisian literary circles to him.

His admiration for Victor Hugo converted him to the romantic movement. In the 1830s Nerval belonged to the *petit cénacle,* a group of minor artistic figures that gravitated around Gautier.

In 1834 Nerval received an inheritance from his maternal grandparents that enabled him to pursue exclusively the literary career of which his father disapproved. Nerval gave up his nominal study of medicine and made a brief trip to Italy, a tour that had a powerful and lasting effect on his imagination.

Meanwhile, Nerval fell in love with Jenny Colon, an actress, for whom he founded a theatrical review, *Le Monde dramatique.* It failed after 2 years. The brilliant and gay life that Nerval led during this brief period of prosperity was succeeded by a lifetime of financial difficulties and personal sadness. The poet lost both his small patrimony and Jenny Colon, who married another. During this period Nerval centered his main literary efforts on the theater, a genre basically uncongenial to his talents. In spite of an occasional success, such as *Piquillo* (1837), his efforts in the theater generally met with failure.

The years 1839–1841 were ones of growing eccentricities and depression for Nerval. His translation of *Faust* (*Part II*), which appeared in 1840, culminated in a mental breakdown that caused him to be hospitalized in 1841. His mental stability thus shattered, Nerval's life became more precarious and difficult because he depended upon his pen for his living. In order to mend his health, Nerval made a trip to the Orient in 1843. His health regained, he published articles dealing with his travels in serial form in various periodicals. During these years of remission from mental breakdown, he also published chronicles, essays, poems, and novellas in many magazines, all the time trying unsuccessfully to establish himself in the theater. He also traveled in foreign countries and in the Valois. Wandering had become a temperamental necessity, and it is an important theme in his major works.

In 1848 Nerval published his translation of Heinrich Heine's poetry. In 1851 *Le Voyage en Orient* appeared. Under the guise of a travelog, it concerned itself with the pilgrimage of a soul, being more revealing of the inner geography of Nerval than of Egypt, Lebanon, or Turkey.

Nerval's major works were all written in the last few years of his life under the threat of incurable insanity. A serious relapse in 1851 marked him irrevocably. In 1852 he published *Les Illuminés,* a series of biographical sketches of unorthodox and original figures. In 1853 *Les Petits châteaux de Bohême* appeared. It was a nostalgic recounting of his happy years. It also contained the *Odelettes,* early poems in the manner of Pierre de Ronsard. Nerval then published his best and most famous story, *Sylvie,* in the *Revue des deux mondes.* In this tale he explored the sources of memory and transfigured the Valois of his childhood. It was included in *Les Filles du feu* in 1854. That same year *Les Chimères,* a series of 12 hermetic sonnets, also appeared.

During this period Nerval was also writing an autobiographical work, *Les Nuits d'Octobre,* and *Aurélia,* his last and most occult work. In *Aurélia* Nerval described the experience of madness and his attempt to overcome it by means of the written word.

In January 1855, destitute and desperate, Nerval committed suicide by hanging himself in a Parisian alley.

EWB

Newton, Sir Isaac (1642–1727), English scientist and mathematician. Isaac Newton made major contributions in mathematics and theoretical and experimental physics and achieved a remarkable synthesis of the work of his predecessors on the laws of motion, especially the law of universal gravitation.

Isaac Newton was born on Christmas Day, 1642, at Woolsthorpe, a hamlet in southwestern Lincolnshire. In his early years Lincolnshire was a battleground of the civil wars, in which the challenging of authority in government and religion was dividing England's population. Also of significance for his early development were circumstances within his family. He was born after the death of his father, and in his third year his mother married the rector of a neighboring parish, leaving Isaac at Woolsthorpe in the care of his grandmother.

After a rudimentary education in local schools, he was sent at the age of 12 to the King's School in Grantham, where he lived in the home of an apothecary named Clark. It was from Clark's stepdaughter that Newton's biographer William Stukeley learned many years later of the boy's interest in her father's chemical library and laboratory and of the windmill run by a live mouse, the floating lanterns, sundials, and other mechanical contrivances Newton built to amuse her. Although she married someone else and he never married, she was the one person for whom Newton seems to have had a romantic attachment.

At birth Newton was heir to the modest estate which, when he came of age, he was expected to manage. But during a trial period midway in his course at King's School, it became apparent that farming was not his métier. In 1661, at the age of 19, he entered Trinity College, Cambridge. There the questioning of long-accepted beliefs was beginning to be apparent in new attitudes toward man's environment, expressed in the attention given to mathematics and science.

After receiving his bachelor's degree in 1665, apparently without special distinction, Newton stayed on for his master's; but an epidemic of the plague caused the university to close. Newton was back at Woolsthorpe for 18 months in 1666 and 1667. During this brief period he performed the basic experiments and apparently did the fundamental thinking for all his subsequent work on gravitation and optics and developed for his own use his system of calculus. The story that the idea of universal gravitation was suggested to him by the falling of an apple seems to be authentic: Stukeley reports that he heard it from Newton himself.

Returning to Cambridge in 1667, Newton quickly completed the requirements for his master's degree and then entered upon a period of elaboration of the work begun at Woolsthorpe. His mathematics professor, Isaac Barrow, was the first to recognize Newton's unusual ability, and when, in 1669, Barrow resigned to devote himself to theology, he recommended Newton as his successor. Newton became Lucasian professor of mathematics at 27 and stayed at Trinity in that capacity for 27 years.

Experiments in Optics.

Newton's main interest at the time of his appointment was optics, and for several years the lectures required of him by the professorship were devoted to this subject. In a letter of 1672 to the secretary of the Royal Society, he says that in 1666 he had bought a prism "to try therewith the celebrated phenomena of colours." He continues, "In order thereto having darkened the room and made a small hole in my window-shuts to let in a convenient quantity of the Suns light, I placed my prism at its entrance, that it might be thereby refracted to the opposite wall." He had been surprised to see the various colors appear on the wall in an oblong arrangement (the vertical being the greater dimension), "which according to the received laws of refraction should have been circular." Proceeding from this experiment through several stages to the "crucial" one, in which he had isolated a single ray and found it unchanging in color and refrangibility, he had drawn the revolutionary conclusion that "Light itself is a heterogeneous mixture of differently refrangible rays."

These experiments had grown out of Newton's interest in improving the effectiveness of telescopes, and his discoveries about the nature and composition of light had led him to believe that greater accuracy could not be achieved in instruments based on the refractive principle. He had turned, consequently, to suggestions for a reflecting telescope made by earlier investigators but never tested in an actual instrument. Being manually dexterous, he built several models in which the image was viewed in a concave mirror through an eyepiece in the side of the tube. In 1672 he sent one of these to the Royal Society.

Newton felt honored when the members were favorably impressed by the efficiency of his small reflecting telescope and when on the basis of it they elected him to their membership. But when this warm reception induced him to send the society a paper describing his experiments on light and his conclusions drawn from them, the results were almost disastrous for him and for posterity. The paper was published in the society's *Philosophical Transactions,* and the reactions of English and Continental scientists, led by Robert Hooke and Christiaan Huygens, ranged from skepticism to bitter opposition to conclusions which seemed to invalidate the prevalent wave theory of light.

At first Newton patiently answered objections with further explanations, but when these produced only more negative responses, he finally became irritated and vowed he would never publish again, even threatening to give up scientific investigation altogether. Several years later, and only through the tireless efforts of the astronomer Edmund Halley, Newton was persuaded to put together the results of his work on the laws of motion, which became the great *Principia.*

His Major Work.

Newton's *magnum opus, Philosophiae naturalis principia mathematica,* to give it its full title, was completed in 18 monthsa prodigious accomplishment. It was first published in Latin in 1687, when Newton was 45. Its appearance established him as the leading scientist of his time, not only in England but in the entire Western world.

In the *Principia* Newton demonstrated for the first time that celestial bodies follow the laws of dynamics and, formulating the law of universal gravitation, gave mathematical solutions to most of the problems concerning motion which had engaged the attention of earlier and contemporary scientists. Book 1 treats the motion of bodies in purely mathematical terms. Book 2 deals with motion in resistant mediums, that is, in physical reality. In Book 3, Newton describes a cosmos based on the laws he has established. He demonstrates the use of these laws in determining the density of the earth, the masses of the sun and of planets having satellites, and the trajectory of a comet; and he explains the variations in the moon's motion, the precession of the equinoxes, the variation in gravitational acceleration with latitude, and the motion of the tides. What seems to have been an early version of book 3, published posthumously as *The System of the World,* contains Newton's calculation, with illustrative diagram, of the manner in which, according to the law of centripetal force, a projectile could be made to go into orbit around the earth.

In the years after Newton's election to the Royal Society, the thinking of his colleagues and of scholars generally had been developing along lines similar to those which his had taken, and they were more receptive to his explanations of the behavior of bodies moving according to the laws of motion than they had been to his theories about the nature of light. Yet the *Principia* presented a stumbling block: its extremely condensed mathematical form made it difficult for even the most acute minds to follow. Those who did understand it saw that it needed simplification and interpretation. As a result, in the 40 years from 1687 to Newton's death the *Principia* was the basis of numerous books and articles. These included a few peevish attacks, but by far the greater number were explanations and elaborations of what had subtly evolved in the minds of his contemporaries from "Mr. Newton's theories" to the "Newtonian philosophy."

London Years. The publication of the *Principia* was the climax of Newton's professional life. It was followed by a period of depression and lack of interest in scientific matters. He became interested in university politics and was elected a representative of the university in Parliament. Later he asked friends in London to help him obtain a government appointment. The result was that in 1696, at the age of 54, he left Cambridge to become warden and then master of the Mint. The position was intended to be something of a sinecure, but he took it just as seriously as he had his scientific pursuits and made changes in the English monetary system that were effective for 150 years.

Newton's London life lasted as long as his Lucasian professorship. During that time he received many honors, including the first knighthood conferred for scientific achievement and election to life presidency of the Royal Society. In 1704, when Huygens and Hooke were no longer living, he published the *Opticks,* mainly a compilation of earlier research, and subsequently revised it three times; he supervised the two revisions of the *Principia;* he engaged in the regrettable controversy with G. W. von Leibniz over the invention of the calculus; he carried on a correspondence with scientists all over Great Britain and Europe; he continued his study and investigation in various fields; and, until his very last years, he conscientiously performed his duties at the Mint.

His "Opticks." In the interval between publication of the *Principia* in 1687 and the appearance of the *Opticks* in 1704, the trend was away from the use of Latin for all scholarly writing. The *Opticks* was written and originally published in English (a Latin translation appeared 2 years later) and was consequently accessible to a wide range of readers in England. The reputation which the *Principia* had established for its author of course prepared the way for acceptance of his second published work. Furthermore, its content and manner of presentation made the *Opticks* more approachable. It was essentially an account of experiments performed by Newton himself and his conclusions drawn from them, and it had greater appeal for the experimental temper of the educated public of the time than the more theoretical and mathematical *Principia.*

Of great interest for scientists generally were the queries with which Newton concluded the text of the *Opticks,* for example, "Do not Bodies act upon Light at a distance, and by their action bend its rays?" These queries (16 in the first edition, subsequently increased to 31) constitute a unique expression of Newton's philosophy; posing them as negative questions made it possible for him to suggest ideas which he could not support by experimental evidence or mathematical proof but which gave stimulus and direction to further research for many generations of scientists. "Of the Species and Magnitude of Curvilinear Figures," two treatises included with the original edition of the *Opticks,* was the first purely mathematical work Newton had published.

Mathematical Works. Newton's mathematical genius had been stimulated in his early years at Cambridge by his work under Barrow, which included a thorough grounding in Greek mathematics as well as in the recent work of René Descartes and of John Wallis. During his undergraduate years Newton had discovered what is known as the binomial theorem; invention of the calculus had followed; mathematical questions had been treated at length in correspondence with scientists in England and abroad; and his contributions to optics and celestial mechanics could be said to be his mathematical formulation of their principles.

But it was not until the controversy over the discovery of the calculus that Newton published mathematical work as such. The controversy, begun in 1699, when Fatio de Duillier made the first accusation of plagiarism against Leibniz, continued sporadically for nearly 20 years, not completely subsiding even with Leibniz's death in 1716.

The inclusion of the two tracts in the first edition of the *Opticks* was certainly related to the controversy, then in progress, and the appearance of other tracts in 1707 and 1711 under the editorship of younger colleagues suggests Newton's release of this material under pressure from his supporters. These tracts were for the most part revisions of the results of early research long since incorporated in Newton's working equipment. In the second edition of the *Principia,* of 1713, the four "Regulae Philosophandi" and the four-page "Scholium Generale" added to book 3 were apparently also designed to answer critics on the Continent who were expressing their partisanship for Leibniz by attacking any statement of Newton's that could not be confirmed by mathematical proof; the "Scholium" is of special interest in that it gives an insight into Newton's way of thought which the more austere style of the main text precludes.

Other Writings and Research. Two other areas to which Newton devoted much attention were chronology and theology. A shortened form of his *Chronology of Ancient Kingdoms* appeared without his consent in 1725, inducing him to prepare the longer work for publication; it did not actually appear until after his death. In it Newton attempted to correlate Egyptian, Greek, and Hebrew history and mythology and for the first time made use of astronomical references in ancient texts to establish dates of historical events. In his *Observations upon the Prophecies of Daniel and the Apocalypse of St. John,* also posthumously published, his aim was to show that the prophecies of the Old and New Testaments had so far been fulfilled.

Another of Newton's continuing interests was the area in which alchemy was evolving into chemistry. His laboratory assistant during his years at Cambridge wrote of his chemical experiments as being a major occupation of these years, and Newton's manuscripts reflect the importance he attached to this phase of his research. His Mint papers show that he made use of chemical knowledge in connection with the metallic composition of the coinage. Among the vast body of his manuscripts are notes indicating that his *Chronology* and *Prophecy* and also his alchemical work were parts of a larger design that would embrace cosmology, history, and theology in a single synthesis.

The mass of Newton's papers, manuscripts, and correspondence which survives reveals a person with qualities of mind, physique, and personality extraordinarily favorable for the making of a great scientist: tremendous powers of concentration, ability to stand long periods of intense mental exertion, and objectivity uncomplicated by frivolous interests. The many portraits of Newton (he was painted by nearly all the leading artists of his time) range from the fashionable, somewhat idealized, treatment to a more convincing realism. All present the natural dignity, the serious mien, and the large searching eyes mentioned by his contemporaries.

When Newton came to maturity, circumstances were auspiciously combined to make possible a major change in men's ways of thought and endeavor. The uniqueness of Newton's achievement could be said to lie in his exploitation of these unusual circumstances. He alone among his gifted contemporaries fully recognized the implications of recent scientific discoveries. With these as a point of departure, he developed a unified mathematical interpretation of the cosmos, in the expounding of which he demonstrated method and direction for future elaboration. In shifting the emphasis from quality to quantity, from pursuit of answers to the question "Why?" to focus upon "What?" and "How?" he effectively prepared the way for the age of technology. He died on March 20, 1727.

EWB

Nicholas I (1796–1855), Russian tsar, statesman, and autocrat. Nicholas I reigned from 1825 to 1855. During his reign Russian 19th-century autocracy reached its greatest power.

The third son of Tsar Paul I, Nicholas was tutored in political economy, government, constitutional law, jurisprudence, and public finance. He learned to speak Russian, French, German, and English, and he studied Greek and Latin. Nicholas showed great aptitude for the science of warfare, especially military engineering, and became an expert drillmaster. His education ended in the middle of 1813. In 1814 Nicholas joined the army, for which he retained a strong affection throughout his life. On July 1, 1817, he married Charlotte of Prussia, daughter of King Frederick William III. Nicholas took no part in the administration of public affairs during the reign of his brother Alexander I. He was put in charge of a brigade of the guards and was inspector general of army engineers.

Paul I's second son had renounced his right to the throne, and on Alexander's death in 1825 Nicholas became tsar. But the confusion over the succession led to the Decembrist Rebellion of 1825. This uprising was a shock to Nicholas, for it involved the army, especially the guards, whom the Tsar regarded as the backbone of the throne. Nicholas supervised the investigation of the conspiracy. He labeled the Decembrists "a handful of monsters." In spite of numerous secret committees and proposals, no significant reforms were enacted. The general attitude of Nicholas is pointed out by his remarks on the emancipation of serfs. "There is no doubt that serfdom, in its present form, is a flagrant evil which everyone realizes," Nicholas proclaimed in the state council on March 20, 1842, "yet to attempt to remedy it now would be, of course, an evil even more disastrous."

Nicholas's rigid conservatism, his fear of the masses, and his desire to preserve autocracy and to protect the interests of the nobility hindered reforms. Thus, his regime became a dictatorship.

Nicholas's conservative views determined Russian foreign policy, over which he exercised personal control. His opposition to the principle of national self-determination, which spread throughout Europe, caused him to come into conflict with every democratic and liberal movement in England and on the Continent. His aggressive and unpredictable foreign policy in Asia and the Near East annoyed the European powers and caused suspicion. His bloody suppression of the Polish insurrection of 1830–1831 and the destruction of Polish autonomy enhanced Nicholas's unpopularity.

Under Nicholas I the first railway between St. Petersburg and Tsarskoe Selo (Pushkin), 17 miles long, was opened to the public in 1837. By the end of his reign Russia had 650 miles of railways. Some progress was also made with river shipping.

It is a paradox that during the absolutism of Nicholas I the golden age of Russian literature occurred. Of the authors whose work does not extend beyond the chronological limits of Nicholas's rule, the most prominent were Aleksandr Pushkin, Mikhail Lermentov, Aleksei Koltsov, and Nikolai Gogol. In addition, intellectual movements emerged to debate the destiny and the contributions to civilization of Russia. The two best-known movements were the Westerners and the Slavophiles. The Westerners were primarily Russian humanitarians. They admired European science and wanted constitutional government, freedom of thought and of the press, and emancipation of the serfs.

Slavophilism of the 1840s was a romantic nationalism that praised Russian virtues as superior to those of the decadent West. The Orthodox Church, according to this movement, was the source of strength in the past and Russia's hope for the future. The Slavophiles criticized the Westernization of Peter the Great as an interruption in the harmonious course of Russian history.

Certainly, Nicholas's defeat in the Crimean War exposed the military and technological backwardness of Russia to the world. He was aware of the failure of his reign, and whatever illusions he might have cherished were dispelled by the Crimean War. He died in St. Petersburg on March 2, 1855.

EWB

Nicholas II (1868–1918), Tsar of Russia from 1894 to 1917. Nicholas II was a staunch defender of autocracy. A weak monarch, he was forced to abdicate, thus ending more than 300 years of Romanov rule in Russia.

The son of Alexander III, Nicholas was born on May 6, 1868. He studied under private tutors, was an accomplished linguist, and traveled extensively in Russia and abroad. In 1890–1891 he made a voyage around the world. Nicholas held customary commissions in the guards, rising, while heir apparent, to the rank of colonel. His participation in affairs of state prior to the death of his father was limited to attendance at meetings of the committee of ministers and of the state council.

His Personality. Throughout his life Nicholas kept with remarkable regularity a diary that throws much light on his character and interests. Hardly a day passed without a record of what Nicholas regarded as its most noteworthy events. These entries, comprising merely a few lines each, noted official visits; dwelt with affection on the doings of his wife and children; and listed his recreational activities. In his relations with courtiers and officials, Nicholas was considerate and kind, but his ministers could never be certain that the policies seemingly agreed upon would actually receive his assent or that a gracious audience would not be followed by a curt dismissal from office.

Nicholas became emperor on the death of his father on Oct. 20, 1894. Less than a month after his coronation, he married Princess Alix of Hesse-Darmstadt. It was a marriage of love, and he remained to the end an exemplary husband and devoted father. His son Alexis, born in 1904, suffered from hemophilia. Desperate efforts to save Alexis's life later led to the incredible episode of Rasputin, a monk who employed hypnotic power to stop Alexis's bleeding. In this manner Rasputin became a dominating influence at the royal court. The deeper cause of Rasputin's influence, as well as of many of Nicholas's difficulties, lay in the Tsar's refusal to concern himself with political questions and his staunch conviction that he must maintain the autocracy of his father.

Reaction and Oppression. Nicholas carried on his father's nationalism, his curtailment of the rights of minority nationalities, and his restrictions on nonorthodox religious groups. He limited Finnish autonomy, which had been honored by Russian monarchs since 1809. The Tsar's manifesto of February 1899 abolished the Finnish constitution and placed the function of making laws for Finland under the Russian imperial council.

Nicholas pursued a strongly anti-Semitic policy. Jews could enroll in higher schools only under quota limits and were excluded from law practice, zemstvos (local district and provincial assemblies), and city councils. Christian dissenters also were persecuted.

The industrial boom of the early 1890s led to Russia's first important strike movement between 1895 and 1897. In 1897 the government passed legislation curtailing the workday to 11½ hours, but it also ordered the capture and punishment of all strike leaders. University students had also begun to organize demonstrations and strikes. The students' confrontations with the officials of St. Petersburg University led to a general strike in Russian higher education. Nicholas unsuccessfully tried both leniency and harshness as methods of alleviating student disturbances.

The Socialist Revolutionary Battle Organization undertook a terrorist campaign with a series of political murders or attempted murders of provincial governors and other officials. The revolutionary movement was spreading widely. Nicholas and his government lacked a policy to deal effectively with the situation.

Imperialism in the Far East.   In form, Nicholas's foreign policy was similar to, and shaped after, that of the other eastern European monarchies: Germany and Austria-Hungary. Nor was it so different from the foreign policy of the western European democracies: France and Great Britain. The main effort of all the Great Powers was not so much to win control over new territories as to preserve the European status quo. However, mutual distrust and the suspicion of one power that another sought to change the status quo often provoked a crisis. In the last quarter of the 19th century, most of the European Great Powers were active in extending their influence and possessions into Africa and Asia. As a result, there was much concern as to whether "imperialist gains, losses, or transfers abroad might upset the balance of interests in Europe itself."

Nicholas's Russia began to challenge Japan in Manchuria and in Korea. An adventurer named Bezobrazov convinced Nicholas to finance a timber concession on the Yalu River on the northern border of Korea. When Tokyo concluded that Bezobrazov had won the support of the Tsar, the Japanese attacked the Russian fleet at Port Arthur in January 1904 without declaring war.

Russia suffered a series of defeats on land and sea in the war with Japan. The main factors for the Japanese victory over the Russians were the inade-

quate supply route of the Trans-Siberian Railway, the outnumbering of the Russian forces in the Far East by Japan, and Russian mismanagement in the field. A peace treaty, negotiated between Russia and Japan on Sept. 5, 1905, called for Russia's recognition of Japanese hegemony in Korea, annexation of southern Sakhalin by Japan, and Japan's lease of the Liaotung Peninsula and the South Manchurian Railway. The war had ended without forcing too excessive a price for peace.

Revolution of 1905.   In 1905 Father George Gapon, leader of a workers' group, led a procession of workers to Nicholas II in order to seek relief for their grievances. The procession was fired upon, and the incident—known as "Bloody Sunday"—may be considered the beginning of the Revolution of 1905. Millions of people participated in this mass movement. The primary goal of the rebellion was a "four-tail constituent assembly"—that is, universal, secret, equal, and direct suffrage to decide the country's future form of government. Other demands included civil liberties, especially freedom of speech, press, and assembly, and the enactment of an 8-hour workday.

When the general strike of October materialized, Minister of Finance Sergei Witte advised Nicholas to choose between a constitutional regime and a military dictatorship, but he added that he would participate only in the former. On Oct. 5, 1905, Nicholas promulgated the October Manifesto. It was drafted by Witte, who became Russia's first prime minister. The manifesto promised: "(1) To grant to the population the inviolable right of free citizenship, based on the principles of freedom of person, conscience, speech, assembly, and union. (2) Without postponing the intended elections for the State Duma and insofar as possible . . . to include in the participation of the work of the Duma those classes of the population that have been until now entirely deprived of the right to vote, and to extend in the future, by the newly created legislative way, the principles of the general right of election. (3) To establish as an unbreakable rule that without its confirmation by the State Duma, no law shall go into force and that the persons elected by the people shall have the opportunity for actual participation in supervising the legality of the acts of authorities appointed by it." Nicholas ended with an appeal to "all the true sons of Russia" to help reestablish law and order.

Fall of the Monarchy.   At the beginning of February 1917 Nicholas left the capital and went to supreme headquarters at Mogilev. On March 8 demonstrations were held to celebrate International

Women's Day, and these throngs merged with rioting crowds protesting the scarcity of bread in Petrograd. As the riots continued, Nicholas could do nothing but prorogue the Duma, which he did on March 11. The next day the Duma gathered in defiance of his order and chose a provisional committee, composed of members of the progressive bloc and two representatives of parties to the left of it. On March 15, 1917, Nicholas decided to abdicate in favor of his brother Michael. A delegation from the provisional committee, which by now had become the provisional government, waited on the Grand Duke Michael, who refused to be crowned tsar of Russia. The monarchy "thus perished without a murmur from either the dynasty or its supporters."

Nicholas abdicated his throne peacefully. On his train the next day he wrote in his diary: "I had a long and sound sleep. Woke up beyond Dvinsk. Sunshine and frost . . . I read much of Julius Caesar." Nicholas and the entire imperial family were forced to depart for Siberia in the summer of 1917. They were murdered by the Communists in July 1918. The Bolshevik zealots who carried out the killings then tried to erase all traces of the corpses.

After the collapse of the Soviet Union, the bodies were finally unearthed from a forest outside Yekaterinburg in 1991, and years of tests were conducted to confirm their identification. On July 17, 1998, Nicholas II, his wife, three of their daughters, and four faithful retainers received a formal burial ceremony in St. Petersburg, Russia.

EWB

O

Ortega y Gasset, José (1883–1955), Spanish philosopher and essayist. Jose Ortega y Gasset is best known for his analyses of history and modern culture, especially his penetrating examination of the uniquely modern phenomenon "mass man."

Ortega y Gasset was born in Madrid on May 9, 1883. He studied with the Jesuits at the Colegio de Jesuítas de Miraflores del Palo, near Málaga, and from 1898 to 1902 he studied at the University of Madrid, from which he received the degree of *licenciado en filosofía y letras*. From 1905 to 1907 he did postgraduate studies at the universities of Leipzig, Berlin, and Marburg in Germany. Deeply influenced by German philosophy, especially the thought of Hermann Cohen, Wilhelm Dilthey, Edmund Husserl, and Martin Heidegger, as well as by the French philosopher Henri Bergson, Ortega sought to overcome the traditional provincialism and isolation of philosophical study in his native Spain.

From 1910 to 1936 Ortega taught philosophy at the University of Madrid. Early in his career he gained a reputation through his numerous philosophical and cultural essays, not only in literary journals but also in newspapers, which were a peculiar and important medium of education and culture in pre-Civil War Spain. Ortega's most famous book, *The Revolt of the Masses* (1930), first appeared in the form of newspaper articles. Throughout his career he was generally active in the cultural and political life of his country, both in monarchist and in republican Spain. In 1923 Ortega founded the journal *Revista de Occidente,* which flourished until 1936.

After the outbreak of the Spanish Civil War in 1936, Ortega left Spain and lived abroad, dwelling in France, Holland, Argentina, and Portugal until the end of World War II. He returned to Spain in 1945, living there and in Portugal, with frequent trips and stays abroad, until his death. In 1948, together with Julián Marías, Ortega founded the Instituto de Humanidades, a cultural and scholarly institution, in Madrid. In 1949 Ortega lectured in the United States, followed by lectures in Germany and in Switzerland in 1950 and 1951. He received various honorary degrees, including a doctorate *honoris causa* from the University of Glasgow. Ortega died in Madrid on Oct. 18, 1955.

Ortega's numerous and varied writings, in addition to *The Revolt of the Masses,* include *The Modern Theme* (1923), *The Mission of the University* (1930), *On Love* (1940), *History as System* (1941), *Man and People* (1957), *Man and Crisis* (1958), and *What Is Philosophy?* (1958). Often mentioned, as is Miguel de Unamuno, with the existentialists, Ortega expounded a philosophy that has been called "ratiovitalism" or "vital reason," in which he sought to do justice to both the intellectual and passional dimensions of man as manifestations of the fundamental reality, "human life."

Ortega's philosophy is closest to that of Heidegger. He described human life as the "radical reality" to which everything else in the universe appears, in terms of which everything else has meaning, and which is therefore the central preoccupation of philosophy. Man is related to the world in terms of the "concerns" to which he attends. The individual human being is decisively free in his inner self, and his life and destiny are what he makes of them within the "given" of his heredity, environment, society, and culture. Thus man does not so much *have* a history; he *is* his history, since history is uniquely the manifestation of human freedom.

EWB

Orwell, George (1903–1950), British novelist and essayist. George Orwell is best known for his satirical novels *Animal Farm* and *Nineteen Eighty-four.*

George Orwell was born Eric Arthur Blair at Motihari, Bengal, India. His father, Richard Walmesley Blair, was a minor customs official in the opium department of the Indian Civil Service. When Orwell was four years old, his family returned to England, where they settled at Henley, a village near London. His father soon returned to India. When Orwell was eight years old, he was sent to a private preparatory school in Sussex. He later claimed that his experiences there determined his views on the English class system. From there he went by scholarship to two private secondary schools: Wellington for one term and Eton for four and a half years.

Orwell then joined the Indian Imperial Police, receiving his training in Burma, where he served from 1922 to 1927. While home on leave in England, Orwell made the important decision not to return to Burma. His resignation from the Indian Imperial Police became effective on Jan. 1, 1928. He had wanted to become a writer since his adolescence, and he had come to believe that the Imperial Police was in this respect an unsuitable profession. Later evidence also suggests that he had come to understand the imperialism which he was serving and had rejected it.

Establishment as a Writer. In the first 6 months after his decision, Orwell went on what he thought of as an expedition to the East End of London to become acquainted with the poor people of England. As a base, he rented a room in Notting Hill. In the spring he rented a room in a working-class district of Paris. It seems clear that his main objective was to establish himself as a writer, and the choice of Paris was characteristic of the period. Orwell wrote two novels, both lost, during his stay in Paris, and he published a few articles in French and English. After stints as a kitchen porter and dishwasher and a bout with pneumonia, he returned to England toward the end of 1929.

Orwell used his parents' home in Suffolk as a base, still attempting to establish himself as a writer. He earned his living by teaching and by writing occasional articles, while he completed several versions of his first book, *Down and Out in London and Paris.* This novel recorded his experiences in the East End and in Paris, and as he was earning his living as a teacher when it was scheduled for publication, he preferred to publish it under a pseudonym. From a list of four possible names submitted to his publisher, he chose "George Orwell." The Orwell is a Suffolk river.

First Novels. Orwell's *Down and Out* was issued in 1933. During the next three years he supported himself by teaching, reviewing, and clerking in a bookshop and began spending longer periods away from his parents' Suffolk home. In 1934 he published *Burmese Days.* The plot of this novel concerns personal intrigue among an isolated group of Europeans in an Eastern station. Two more novels followed: *A Clergyman's Daughter* (1935) and *Keep the Aspidistra Flying* (1936).

In the spring of 1936 Orwell moved to Wallington, Hertfordshire, and several months later married Eileen O'Shaughnessy, a teacher and journalist. His reputation up to this time, as writer and journalist, was based mainly on his accounts of poverty and hard times. His next book was a commission in this direction. The Left Book Club authorized him to write an inquiry into the life of the poor and unemployed. *The Road to Wigan Pier* (1937) was divided into two parts. The first was typical reporting, but the second part was an essay on class and socialism. It marked Orwell's birth as a political writer, an identity that lasted for the rest of his life.

Political Commitments and Essays. In July 1936 the Spanish Civil War broke out. By the end of that autumn, Orwell was readying himself to go to Spain to gather material for articles and perhaps to take part in the war. After his arrival in Barcelona, he joined the militia of the POUM (Partido Obrero de Unificacion Marxista) and served with them in action in January 1937. Transferring to the British Independent Labour party contingent serving with the POUM militia, Orwell was promoted first to corporal and then to lieutenant before being wounded in the middle of May. During his convalescence, the POUM was declared illegal, and he fled into France in June. His experiences in Spain had made him into a revolutionary socialist.

After his return to England, Orwell began writing *Homage to Catalonia* (1938), which completed his disengagement from the orthodox left. He then wished to return to India to write a book, but he became ill with tuberculosis. He entered a sanatorium where he remained until late in the summer of 1938. Orwell spent the following winter in Morocco, where he wrote *Coming Up for Air* (1939). After he returned to England, Orwell authored several of his best-known essays. These include the essays on Dickens and on boys' weeklies and "Inside the Whale."

After World War II began, Orwell believed that "now we are in this bloody war we have got to win it and I would like to lend a hand." The army, however, rejected him as physically unfit, but later he served for a period in the home guard and as a fire watcher. The Orwells moved to London in May 1940. In early 1941 he commenced writing "London Letters" for *Partisan Review,* and in August he joined the British Broadcasting Corporation (BBC) as a producer in the Indian section. He remained in this position until 1943.

First Masterpiece. The year 1943 was an important one in Orwell's life for several reasons. His mother died in March; he left the BBC to become literary editor of the *Tribune;* and he began book reviewing on a more regular basis. But the most important event occurred late that year, when he commenced the writing of *Animal Farm.* Orwell had completed this satire by February 1944, but several publishers rejected it on political grounds. It finally appeared in August 1945. This fantasy relates what happens to animals who free themselves and then are again enslaved through violence and fraud.

Toward the end of World War II, Orwell traveled to France, Germany, and Austria as a reporter. His wife died in March 1945. The next year he settled on Jura off the coast of Scotland, with his youngest sister as his housekeeper.

Crowning Achievement. By now, Orwell's health was steadily deteriorating. Renewed tuberculosis early in 1947 did not prevent the composition of the first draft of his masterpiece, *Nineteen Eighty-four.* The second draft was written in 1948 during several attacks of the disease. By the end of 1948 Orwell was seriously ill. *Nineteen Eighty-four* (1949) is an elaborate satire on modern politics, prophesying a world perpetually laid waste by warring dictators.

Orwell entered a London hospital in September 1949 and the next month married Sonia Brownell. He died in London on Jan. 21, 1950.

Orwell's singleness of purpose in pursuit of his material and the uncompromising honesty that defined him both as a man and as a writer made him critical of intellectuals whose political viewpoints struck him as dilettante. Thus, though a writer of the left, he wrote the most savage criticism of his generation against left-wing authors, and his strong stand against communism resulted from his experience of its methods gained as a fighter in the Spanish Civil War.

EWB

Owen, Robert (1771–1858), British socialist pioneer. The attempts of Robert Owen to reconstruct society widely influenced social experimentation and the cooperative movement.

Robert Owen was born in Newtown, Wales, on May 14, 1771, the son of a shopkeeper. Though he left school at the age of 9, he was precocious and learned business principles rapidly in London and Manchester. By 18 he was manager of one of Manchester's largest cotton mills. In 1799 he purchased the mills at New Lanark, Scotland; they became famous for fine work produced with high regard for the well-being of the approximately 2,000 employees, of whom several hundred were poor children.

A reader and thinker, Owen counted among his acquaintances Robert Fulton, Jeremy Bentham, and the poet Samuel Coleridge. Owen's reforms emphasized cleanliness, happiness, liberal schooling without recourse to punishment, and wages in hard times. As his fame spread, he considered implementing ideas that would increasingly negate competitive economics. His attack on religion at a London meeting in 1817 lost him some admirers. His pioneer papers of the time, including "Two Memorials on Behalf of the Working Classes" (1818) and "Report to the County of Lanark" (1821), held that environment determined human development.

Owen learned of the religious Rapp colony in America at New Harmony, Ind., and determined to prove his principles in action there. In 1825 he purchased New Harmony and drew some 900 individuals to the community for his experiment. Despite the work of talented individuals, New Harmony did not prosper. By 1828 Owen had lost the bulk of his fortune in New Harmony, and he left it.

Following an unsuccessful attempt to institute a comparable experiment in Mexico that year, Owen returned to England to write and lecture. He propagated ideas first developed in 1826 in *Book of the New Moral World.* A kind, selfless man, he failed to perceive that the industry and responsibility that had made New Lanark great were not present in New Harmony and in other experiments he sponsored. Nevertheless, his views created theoretical bases for developing socialist and cooperative thought.

In *The Crisis* (1832) Owen advocated exchanging commodities for labor rather than money to relieve unemployment. The Equitable Labour Exchange founded that year failed but led to the Chartist and Rochdale movements. Labor unrest further fed on Owenite tenets, and in 1833 the Grand National Consolidated Trades Union was formed. It rallied half a million workers and fostered such new tactics as the general strike but fell apart within a few months, owing to opposition by employers and the government.

Owen continued to write and propagandize. Such experiments as Harmony Hall, in Hampshire, England (1839–45), derived from his theories. But new revolutionary forces and leaders put him out of the main current. His conversion to spiritualism in 1854 and his *New Existence of Man upon the Earth* (1854–1855) seemed to him a broadening of reality, rather than a retreat. His *Autobiography* (1857–1858) is one of the great documents of early socialist experience. He died in Newtown, Wales, on Nov. 17, 1858.

EWB

Oxenstierna, Count Axel Gustafsson (1583–1654), Swedish statesman. Axel Oxenstierna was a major architect of his country's brief rise to greatness among the powers of 17th-century Europe.

Axel Oxenstierna was born at Uppsala on June 16, 1583. His was among the most influential families of the Swedish nobility. His social background, as well as a quick intelligence honed by education in German universities, enabled Oxenstierna to enter top government circles at an early age. He received his first appointment in 1605; by the decade's end he was the leader of the nobility in the Royal Council.

As in other states of eastern and central Europe, the relative weakness of the local bourgeoisie had enhanced the standing of the Swedish nobility. This enabled the aristocracy to wrest concessions from the monarchy, the better to be able to exploit the peasantry. Nevertheless, a dispute within the reigning Vasa dynasty during the 1590s had split the nobility along religious lines, thus shifting the balance of forces back in the King's favor.

King Sigismund Vasa III, a Catholic who had also been elected King of Poland, tried to bring Lutheran Sweden back into the Roman fold. The result was a coup (1598) which put his uncle into power as Charles IX and led to a purge of the aristocratic minority loyal to Sigismund. Such a purge could only strengthen the incoming King. However, Charles IX had to contend with Sweden's relatively weak power position with respect to other Baltic states, especially Denmark. Too weak to challenge Denmark's hold over the Baltic Sound (and thus over revenues from the wealthy Baltic commerce), he attacked Muscovy. He was in Moscow in 1610 and was planning to add the Tsar's domains to his own, when death cut short further expansion.

His youthful heir, Gustavus Adolphus (Gustavus II), now had to face the power of a reunited nobility under Oxenstierna's leadership. A first round of concessions was granted in the charter of 1611; in 1612 Oxenstierna was made the King's chancellor, and a noble monopoly of higher state offices was secured by the formal coronation oath of 1617. Yet, for all this, Sweden did not suffer the fate of Poland and other countries where the nobility ran unchecked. The chancellor and the king found it more convenient to collaborate than quarrel. The pressure to bolster Sweden's security by territorial expansion and to augment its wealth by exploiting its mineral resources and metallurgical industries (chiefly gun manufactures) made for sufficient cooperation among the country's leaders to thrust Sweden dramatically on the stage of European Great Power politics.

At home, succeeding years brought administrative measures similar to those applied by centralizing monarchies to the West. Central and local government, the Estates (Riksdag), and the judiciary were all affected. Oxenstierna played a key role in all decisions taken. Particularly significant was his reorganization of the nobility itself. By the Riddarhusordning of 1626 it was restructured according to criteria for membership in one of three newly formed aristocratic subclasses.

When Gustavus came to power, Sweden was at war with Denmark. Oxenstierna was instructed to conclude the 1613 Peace of Knäred with that country. This removed the Danish threat and gave some concessions to Sweden with respect to Baltic commerce. Gustavus now resumed the Swedish march to the east. By the time Oxenstierna negotiated the Treaty of Altmark with Poland (1629), his country was in effective command of eastern Baltic commerce. The impetus provided by this aggressive policy, coupled with the outbreak of the Thirty Years War in 1618, sufficed to draw Sweden into the broader conflict in Germany. Oxenstierna now added the duties of war leader to those of administrator and diplomat. In 1630, with financial support from Russia, France, and the Dutch, Gustavus marched into Germany; in 1631 he called Oxenstierna to his side; and when the King was slain at the battle of Lützen (November 1632), his chancellor assumed control of the Swedish war effort.

By that date, Sweden had become the strongest power inside Germany. After Gustavus's death, however, Sweden's position began to slip. Oxenstierna's armies were badly defeated at Nördlingen (1634), and his German allies made their separate Peace of Prague with the emperor in 1635. But the war went on, with France playing a role on the "Protestant" (anti-Hapsburg) side equal to Sweden's. Denmark took Austria's side in 1643 but was handily defeated by the Swedes. In the same year (1645) in which the two countries signed the Treaty of Brömsebro, Swedish armies marched all the way to Vienna. Oxenstierna now retired from the war with profit and honor. After 1648, strengthened by acquisitions from Denmark and the German princes, Sweden emerged as the greatest Baltic power.

Gustavus was succeeded by his daughter, Queen Christina, and Oxenstierna remained the dominant figure in the regime throughout her reign. He died in Stockholm on Aug. 28, 1654.

EWB

P

Palladio, Andrea (1508–1580), Italian architect. The buildings of Andrea Palladio were the most refined of the Renaissance period. Through them and his book on architectural theory he became the most influential architect in the history of Western art.

Roman architecture of the early 16th century had developed a mature classicism in the work of Donato Bramante and his followers. With the sack of Rome in 1527 young architects, such as Michele Sanmicheli and Jacopo Sansovino, brought the style to northern Italy. Andrea Palladio with further study of ancient Roman architecture, refined the classical mode to produce an elegant architecture befitting the opulent culture of the Veneto in the third quarter of the century. The aristocratic, mercantile society of Venice desired a splendid and sumptuous art to express pride in its accomplishments.

Andrea di Pietro dalla Gondola, called Andrea Palladio, was born in Padua on Nov. 30, 1508. In 1521 he was apprenticed for 6 years to a local stonecutter; 3 years later he broke the contract and moved to Vicenza, where he was immediately enrolled in the guild of masons and stonecutters. His first opportunity came about 1538 while he was working as a stone carver on the reconstruction of the Villa Cricoli, near Vicenza, owned by the local humanist Giangiorgio Trissino, who had a classical school for young Vicenzan nobility. Trissino recognized Andrea's ability and took him into his home and educated him. Trissino gave Andrea his humanist name Palladio as a reference to the wisdom of the Greek goddess Pallas Athene.

Early Architecture. Probably Palladio's first independent design was the Villa Godi (ca. 1538–1542) at Lonedo. Its simplified, stripped-down style reveals very little influence of ancient architecture, but its emphasis on clean-cut cubical masses foreshadows his mature style. The Casa Civena (1540–1546) in Vicenza, with its paired Corinthian pilasters above the ground-floor arcade, is more in the Roman High Renaissance manner, perhaps inspired by the publications of Sebastiano Serlio.

In 1541 Trissino took Palladio to Rome to study the ancient monuments. At this time Palladio began a magnificent series of drawings of ancient buildings.

The incomplete Palazzo Thiene (commissioned 1542, constructed ca. 1545–1550) in Vicenza is in the style of Giulio Romano, particularly in its heavy rustication of the ground floor and the massive stone blocks superimposed on the window frames of the main story. As Giulio Romano was in Vicenza in 1542, it is possible that he contributed to the design, since Palladio was still designated as a mason in the contract. The grandiose project, never completed, for the Villa Thiene (before 1550) at Quinto was influenced by Palladio's study of ancient Roman sanctuaries and baths. The only completed pavilion has a temple front facade, his first use of a temple front to decorate a villa, which became a hallmark of his style.

For many years the city of Vicenza had been considering how to refurbish its Gothic law court, the Palazzo della Ragione. In 1546 Palladio's project to surround the old building with loggias was approved, and he was commissioned to erect one bay in wood as a model. In 1547 and 1549 Palladio made further trips to Rome. In 1549 he began to construct two superimposed, arcaded loggias around the Palazzo della Ragione (completed 1617), known ever since as the Basilica Palladiana. Each bay of the loggias is composed of an arch flanked by lintels supported by columns. The motif of the arch flanked by lintels, although it was first used by Bramante and was popularized in Serlio's book, has been called in English the Palladian motif since Palladio used it on the Basilica.

Mature Style. Palladio created on the mainland around Venice a magnificent series of villas for the Venetian and Vicenzan nobility. The most renowned is the Villa Capra, or the Rotonda (1550–1551, with later revisions), near Vicenza. It is a simplified, cubelike mass capped by a dome over the central, round salon and has identical temple front porches on the four sides of the block. The absolute symmetry of the design was unusual in Palladian villas; the architect explained that it permitted equal views over the countryside around the hill on which the villa sits.

The city of Vicenza was almost completely rebuilt with edifices after Palladio's designs. The Palazzo Chiericati (now the Museo Civico) is a two-story structure facing on the square with a continuous Doric colonnade on the ground floor after the idea of an ancient Roman forum; the walled and fenestrated central section of the upper floor is flanked by Ionic colonnades. The facade of the Palazzo Iseppo Porto (ca. 1550–1552) is based on Bramante's Palazzo Caprini in Rome, but the plan is Palladio's version of an ancient Roman house with an entrance atrium and a large peristyle, or court, on the central axis behind the building block.

In 1554 Palladio made his last trip to Rome and in the same year published a fine guidebook to the antiquities of Rome, *Le antichità di Roma*. During the next year a group of Vicenzans, including Palladio, founded the Accademia Olimpica for the furthering of arts and sciences. In 1556 Daniele Barbaro, a Venetian humanist, published a commentary on the architectural treatise of the ancient Roman writer Vitruvius for which Palladio made the illustrations. At the same time Palladio designed for Barbaro and his brother at Maser (ca. 1555–1559) one of the loveliest of all villas. The Villa Barbaro (now Volpi) is set into a gentle hillside. The central, two-storied casino with a temple front of Ionic half-columns and pediment is flanked by single-story arcades connecting it to the service buildings, for the villa also served as a farm. In the 16th century the nobility of the Veneto attempted to improve the agricultural productivity of the land, and their villas served as residences during the periods when they supervised the farming.

Palladio's first architecture in the city of Venice was the commencement of the monastery of S. Giorgio Maggiore, whose refectory he completed (1560–1562). This was followed by the church of S. Giorgio Maggiore (1565–1610), which has a basilical plan with apsidal transept arms and a deep choir. The facade (designed 1565, executed 1607–1610), with its temple front on four giant half columns flanked by two half temple fronts on smaller pilasters, is Palladio's solution to the translation of a Christian church design into the classical mode. He applied a similar facade to the older church of S. Francesco della Vigna (ca. 1565). The Palazzo Valmarana (1565–1566) in Vicenza uses giant Corinthian pilasters, except at the ends, to emphasize the planar aspect of the facade adapted to its urban location.

Late Style.   Palladio's treatise on architecture, *I quattro libri dell' architettura* (1570), consists of four books. The first is devoted to technical questions and the classical orders, the second to domestic architecture, the third to civic architecture, and the fourth to ecclesiastical architecture. It is illustrated by ancient architecture and the works of Bramante and Palladio himself.

The truncated Loggia del Capitaniato (1571–1572) in Vicenza has giant half columns with an arcaded loggia below. In many of its details this design reveals an unclassical spirit. The short side, however, is modeled on an ancient triumphal arch and commemorates the victory of Lepanto in October 1571, which occurred while the loggia was being executed.

As the chief architect of Venice, Palladio designed the festival triumphal arch and the decorations to welcome the entry of King Henry III of France to Venice in July 1574.

To fulfill a vow of salvation from the disastrous plague of 1575–1576 the Venetian Senate commissioned Palladio to build the Church of the Redentore (1576–1592). Perhaps influenced by the Church of the Gesù in Rome, it is a wide basilica with side chapels and a trilobed crossing with deep choir. The facade, approached by monumental stairs, is a more unified version of his earlier church facades. For the Villa Barbaro at Maser he designed a separate chapel, the Tempietto (1579–1580), modeled on the ancient Roman Pantheon.

Palladio executed a theater, the Teatro Olimpico (1580), in Vicenza for the Accademia Olimpica. Based on the design of an ancient Roman theater, the auditorium is segmental in plan, facing a stage modeled on a Roman *scaenae frons*. The perspective stage scenery in wood and stucco was added by Vincenzo Scamozzi after Palladio's design. On Aug. 19, 1580, Palladio died in Vicenza:

His Influence.   Through his treatise Palladio exerted a dominant influence on architecture for over 2 centuries, particularly in northern Europe. There were two major periods of Palladianism in England. In the first half of the 17th century Inigo Jones converted English architecture to the Italianate Renaissance by introducing Palladio's style, seen best in the Banqueting Hall, Whitehall, London, and the Queen's House, Greenwich. The second wave of Palladianism was fostered in the early 18th century by the Earl of Burlington. Palladio's treatise was published in 1715 in an English translation by Giacomo Leoni. American architecture felt the impact in the late 18th and early 19th century, as seen in Thomas Jefferson's Monticello.

EWB

Pareto, Vilfredo   (1848–1923), Italian sociologist, political theorist, and economist. Vilfredo Pareto is chiefly known for his influential theory of ruling elites and for his equally influential theory that political behavior is essentially irrational.

Vilfredo Pareto was born in Paris on July 15, 1848. His father, an aristocratic Genoese, had gone into political exile in France about 1835 because he supported the Mazzinian republican movement. He returned to Piedmont in 1855, where he worked as a civil engineer for the government. Vilfredo followed his father's profession after graduating from the Polytechnic Institute at Turin in 1869. He worked as director of the Rome Railway Company until 1874, when he secured an appointment as managing director of an iron-producing company with offices in Florence.

In 1889 Pareto married a Russian girl, Dina Bakunin, resigned his post with the iron company for a consultancy, and for the next 3 years wrote and spoke against the protectionist policy of the Italian government domestically and its military policies abroad. His reputation as a rebellious activist led to an intimate acquaintance with the economist Maffeo Pantaleoni. This association led to Pareto's interest in pure economics, a field in which he quickly became proficient and well known. His reputation gained him an appointment in 1893 to the prestigious post of professor of political economy at Lausanne University.

In 1894 Pareto published his first noted work, *Cours d'économie politique,* which evoked a great deal of commentary from other economists. Two years later he inherited a small fortune from an uncle, a windfall which caused him to think of retiring to pursue research. At this point he began to develop the theories for which he is most famous, elitism and irrationalism in politics.

In his own earlier political career Pareto had been an ardent activist in behalf of democracy and free trade, as had been his father before him. The reasons for the marked change in his political outlook have been much disputed, ranging from the Neo-Freudian analytical account, to the interpretation which stresses certain developments in his own career, to the explanation which maintains that, quite simply, he changed because of the results of his own vast studies. By the time his next book, *The Manual of Political Economy,* was published in 1906, his ideas on elites and irrationalism were already well developed. The following year he resigned from his chair of political economy at Lausanne to devote all his energies to researching his theories.

Pareto retired to his villa at Celigny, where he lived a solitary existence except for his 18 Angora cats (the villa was named "Villa Angora") and his friend Jane Régis, a woman 30 years younger than he who had joined his household in 1901, when his wife left him. In 1907 he began writing his most famous and quite influential work, *The Treatise on Sociology;* he completed it in 1912 and published it in 1916. (The work was published in English translation as *The Mind and Society* in 1935 in a four-volume edition.) In 1923 he secured a divorce from his wife and married Jane Régis. Later the same year he died.

Pareto's theory of elitism is sometimes simplistically explained on the basis of his aristocratic heritage. However, as recent scholarship has shown, throughout his life and in his published works he often expressed extreme distaste with the titled Italian aristocracy, just as he was anti-socialist, anti-government-interventionist, anti-colonialist, anti-militarist, anti-racialist, and "anti-anti-Semitic." Attracted to fascism when it first came to power in Italy, he later opposed it. He is perhaps best described as an iconoclastic individualist.

The Mind and Society is at one and the same time a debunking of Marxism and of the bourgeois state. Pareto's method of investigation is inductive or positivistic, contemptuously rejecting natural law, metaphysics, and deductive reasoning. On the basis of very extensive historical and empirical studies, Pareto maintained that in reality and inevitably the true form of government in any state is never a monarchy, hereditary aristocracy, or democracy but that always all social organizations, including states, are governed by a ruling elite. This ruling elite, which has greater vitality and usefulness than other elites, dominates them until it in turn is overturned by a more powerful elite—Pareto's theory of "the circulation of elites." Political behavior itself, both of the masses and of the elites, is basically emotional and nonrational. The function of reason is to justify past behavior or to show the way to future goals, which are determined not by reason but by emotional wants.

EWB

Parnell, Charles Stewart (1846–1891), Irish nationalist leader. Charles Parnell made home rule for Ireland a major factor in Irish nationalism and British politics.

Charles Parnell's County Wicklow, Anglo-Irish, Protestant-gentry family had earned a patriotic reputation in Ireland by opposing the Act of Union with Britain and by supporting Catholic emancipation. His American mother was a passionate Anglophobe. Although Parnell was educated in England, used English speech patterns, and possessed the aloof manner associated with the English establishment, he inherited his family's devotion to Irish interests.

His Obstructionist Tactics. In 1875 Parnell entered the House of Commons, lending his Protestant-gentry respectability to home rule. Two years later he joined Joseph Biggar in systematic obstruction of British legislation. Described by Parnell as an active parliamentary policy, obstruction was a reaction to British indifference to Irish problems, to the cautious and conciliatory parliamentary tactics and leadership of Isaac Butt—father of home rule and chairman of the Irish party—and to the growing cynicism of Irish opinion toward nationalist politics.

Butt joined outraged British politicians and journalists in denouncing the "barbarian" tactics of Parnell and Biggar, claiming they had damaged home rule by alienating British opinion. Parnell insisted that the achievement of home rule depended on the determination of Irish nationalist members of Parliament to demonstrate that the union could be as unpleasant for the British as it was for the Irish.

Avoiding a direct challenge to Butt's control over the moribund Irish party or the impoverished Home Rule League, Parnell awaited the next general election. He used obstruction to attract notice and favor, courting Irish opinion at home and in the ghettos of Britain and the United States. In 1879 Parnell accepted the presidency of the National Land League, a New Departure instrument designed by Irish-Americans to bring republicans into contact with the Irish peasant masses. Financed by Irish-American dollars, the Land League demanded the end of landlordism, but it was prepared to accept agrarian reform along the way.

Leader of the Irish Party. The results of the general elections of 1880 gave Parnell the votes to command the Irish party. William Gladstone, the prime minister, responded to the near-revolutionary Land League agitation with a mixed coercion-conciliation policy. The 1881 Land Act gave Irish tenant farmers secure tenures at fair rents, freeing them from serfdom. But Parnell rejected the act as inadequate, and the government imprisoned him for encouraging agrarian disturbances. He was released in 1882 after promising to accept government improvements in the Land Act in exchange for Irish party support of future Liberal efforts to solve the Irish question. The truce was known as the Kilmainham Treaty.

After 1882 Parnell concentrated on building an effective Irish party to promote home rule. Instead of reviving the outlawed Land League, he used Irish-American money to pay the expenses of talented and sincere nationalists prepared to stand for Parliament. Parnell's genius, Irish-American dollars, and the Reform Bill of 1884 gave the Irish party more than 80 members in the House of Commons.

Irish-Liberal Alliance. With an effective party behind him, Parnell in 1885 played balance-of-power politics in the House of Commons, forcing both Liberals and Conservatives to bid for Irish votes. Gladstone made the highest offer: home rule. The Irish then turned the Conservatives out of office and installed the Liberals. In 1886 Gladstone introduced a home-rule bill which was defeated by defections in Liberal ranks. The Irish-Liberal alliance lasted for 30 years, limiting the freedom of the Irish party and pushing British anti-Irish, no-popery, imperialistic opinion in a conservative direction. Home rule became the most emotional issue in British politics.

At the beginning of December 1889, Parnell was the unchallenged master of Irish nationalism. He dominated Irish opinion, bringing extremist types into the mainstream of constitutional nationalism. He commanded Irish-American financial resources, and he had captured the Liberal party for home rule. But that month the tides of Parnell's fortune began to recede when Capt. William O'Shea submitted a petition suing his wife, Katherine, for divorce, naming Parnell as correspondent.

Downfall and Death. Irish nationalists assumed that Parnell would emerge from the courtroom an honorable man. Parnell, however, anxious to marry Katherine O'Shea who had been his mistress since 1880, decided not to contest William O'Shea's charges, and his image was tarnished by the captain's testimony. Although the Irish party reelected Parnell its chairman in November 1890—just after the divorce—British Nonconformists demanded that Gladstone separate the Liberals from a public sinner. Gladstone insisted that the Irish party drop Parnell as its leader. On Dec. 6, 1890, after days of bitter debate, a majority of home-rule members of Parliament decided that the fate of Irish freedom was more important than the position of one man. Parnell, a supreme egotist, refused to accept the realities of the Liberal alliance. He appealed to the Irish people in three by-election

contests. Opposed by the Catholic hierarchy and clergy, Parnell lost the by-elections and his health in the process. He died of rheumatic fever at Brighton on Oct. 6, 1891.

Parnell bequeathed a shattered parliamentary party, a bitter and divided nationalist opinion, and the myth of a martyred messiah. He became a symbol of resistance to British dictation, clericalism, and inhibiting Victorian and Irish Catholic moralities.

EWB

Pascal, Blaise (1623–1662), French scientist and philosopher. Blaise Pascal was a precocious and influential mathematical writer, a master of the French language, and a great religious philosopher.

Blaise Pascal was born at Clermont-Ferrand on June 19, 1623. He was the son of Étienne Pascal, king's counselor and later president of the Court of Aids at Clermont. Blaise's mother died in 1626, and he was left with his two sisters, Gilberte and Jacqueline. In 1631 the family moved to Paris.

Young Geometer. When Pascal was 12, he began attending meetings of a mathematical academy. His father taught him languages, especially Latin and Greek, but not mathematics. This ban on mathematics merely served to whet the boy's curiosity. He experimented with geometrical figures, inventing his own names for standard geometrical terms.

In 1640 the Pascal family moved to Rouen. There, still taught mainly by his father, Blaise worked with such intensity that his health deteriorated. Nevertheless, he had arrived at one of the most beautiful theorems in geometry. Sometimes called by him his "mystic hexagram," it is a theorem concerned with the collinearity of intersections of lines. It does not concern metrical properties of figures but is, in fact, at the very foundation of an important, and at the time almost entirely undeveloped, branch of mathematics—projective geometry. Pascal then set to work on a book, *Essay on Conics*, finished in 1640, in which the mystic hexagram was given central importance. It contained several hundred propositions on conic sections, bringing in the work of Apollonius and his successors, and was remarkable not only because of the writer's age (16) but also because of its treatment of tangency, among other things.

Jansenists and Port Royal. In 1646 Pascal's father had an accident and was confined to his house. He was visited by some neighbors who were Jansenists, a group formed by Cornelis Jansen, a Dutch-born professor of theology at Louvain. Their beliefs were contrary to the teachings of the Jesuits. The Pascals came under the influence of the Jansenists, with resultant fierce opposition to, and from, the Jesuits. Jacqueline wished to join the Jansenist convent at Port Royal. Étienne Pascal disliked the idea and took the family away to Paris, but after his death in 1651 Jacqueline joined Port Royal. Pascal still enjoyed a more worldly life, having a number of aristocratic friends and a little more money to spend from his patrimony. In 1654, however, he was completely converted to Jansenism, and he commenced an austere life at Port Royal.

Provincial Letters. In 1655 Antoine Arnauld, a prolific writer in defense of Jansen, was formally condemned by the Sorbonne for heretical teaching, and Pascal took up his defense in the first part of the famous *Provincial Letters.* Their framework is that of a correspondence between a Parisian and a friend in the provinces from Jan. 13, 1656, to March 24, 1657. They were circulated in the thousands through Paris under a pseudonym (Louis de Montalte), and the Jes-

uits tried to discover the author, whose wit, reason, eloquence, and humor made the order a laughingstock.

The *Pensées.* Knowledge of Pascal's personal life is slight after his entry to Port Royal. His sister Gilberte tells of his asceticism, of his dislike of seeing her caress her children, and of his apparent revulsion from talk of feminine beauty. He suffered increasingly after 1658 from head pains, and he died on Aug. 19, 1662.

At his death Pascal left an unfinished theological work, the *Pensées,* an apology for Christianity, in effect, which was published 8 years later by the Port Royal community in a thoroughly garbled and incoherent form. A reasonably authentic version first appeared in 1844. It deals with the great problems of Christian thought, faith versus reason, free will, and preknowledge. Pascal explains the contradictions and problems of the moral life in terms of the doctrine of the Fall and makes faith and revelation alone sufficient for their mutual justification.

The *Pensées,* unlike the *Provincial Letters,* were not worked over and over by their author, and in style they would not, perhaps, mark him out as a great literary figure. The *Letters,* however, give Pascal a place in literary history as the first of several great French writers practicing the polite irony to which the language lends itself. The *Pensées* could almost have been written by another man, for in them reason is ostensibly made to take second place to religion. But they are both, in their different ways, among the great books in the history of religious thought.

Later Mathematical and Scientific Work. Pascal's writings on hydrostatics, relating his experiments with the barometer to his theoretical ideas on the equilibrium of fluids, were not published until a year after his death. His *Treatise on the Equilibrium of Liquids* extends Simon Stevin's analysis of the hydrostatic paradox and enunciates what may be called the final law of hydrostatics: in a fluid at rest the pressure is transmitted equally in all directions (Pascal's principle). Pascal is important as having forged links between the theories of liquids and gases, and between the dynamics of rigid bodies and hydrodynamics.

Pascal's principal contribution to mathematics after his entry to Port Royal related to problems associated with the cycloida curve, with the area of which the best mathematicians of the day were occupied. He published many of his theorems without proof, as a challenge to other mathematicians. Solutions were found by John Wallis, Christopher Wren, Christian Huygens, and others. Pascal published his own solutions under the assumed name of Amos Dettonville (an anagram of Louis de Montalte), and contemporary mathematicians often referred to him by this name.

The mathematical theory of probability made its first great step forward when a correspondence between Pascal and Pierre de Fermat revealed that both had come to similar conclusions independently. Pascal planned a treatise on the subject, but again only a fragment survived, to be published after his death. He never wrote at great length on mathematics, but the many short pieces which survive are almost always concise and incisive.

EWB

Paul, St. Vincent de (1581–1660), French priest. Vincent de Paul organized works of charity, founded hospitals, and started two Roman Catholic religious orders.

Vincent de Paul was born into a peasant family on April 24, 1581, in the village of Pouy in southwestern France. He studied theology at the University of Toulouse, was ordained a priest at 19, and completed his theological studies 4 years later. Using his status as a priest to escape the dull village life of southern France, Vincent went to Paris in 1608. He wrote a curious letter to some friends at this time, telling in detail how he had been captured by Barbary pirates and taken as a slave to Tunisia. This story is not supported by any other evidence, and Vincent never referred to it later in his life.

In Paris, Vincent came under the influence of a wise spiritual guide who gradually caused him to see that helping others was more important than helping himself. For a few years he worked as a parish priest in Clichy near Paris. In 1613 he tutored the children of the general of the French galleys and in 1617 became chaplain to the galley slaves. He was concerned for all the peasants on the general's properties because of the terrible conditions in which they lived. By 1625 he had influenced a number of young men, some of them priests, to join him in forming a religious group to be called the Congregation of the Mission. Vincent and his friends worked with the poor people of the countryside near Paris, helping them obtain food and clothing and teaching them about Christ.

Vincent formed associations of wealthy lay people in Paris, persuading them to dedicate some of their time and money to helping the poor. He started several hospitals, including one in Marseilles for convicts sentenced to the galleys. Several times he was asked to act as a mediator in the wars of religion that were tearing France apart. With Louise de Marillac, a talented and sensitive friend, he started the first religious group of women dedicated entirely to works of charity

outside the cloister, a group called the Daughters of Charity.

Vincent was a man of action rather than of theory. The religious spirit he communicated was simple, practical, and straightforward. He looked to Christ as his leader and tried to translate the Gospel message into concrete results. He died on Sept. 27, 1660, and was canonized a saint in the Roman Catholic Church in 1737. The religious groups he founded continue to carry on his work.

EWB

Pavlov, Ivan Petrovich (1849–1936), Russian physiologist. Ivan Pavlov pioneered in the study of circulation, digestion, and conditioned reflexes. He believed that he clearly established the physiological nature of psychological phenomena.

Ivan Pavlov was born in Ryazan on Sept. 26, 1849, the son of a poor parish priest, from whom Pavlov acquired a lifelong love for physical labor and for learning. At the age of 9 or 10, Pavlov suffered from a fall which affected his general health and delayed his formal education. When he was 11, he entered the second grade of the church school at Ryazan. In 1864 he went to the Theological Seminary of Ryazan, studying religion, classical languages, and philosophy and developing an interest in science.

Making of a Physiologist. In 1870 Pavlov gained admission to the University of St. Petersburg, electing animal physiology as his major field and chemistry as his minor. There he studied inorganic chemistry under Dmitrii Mendeleev and organic chemistry under Aleksandr Butlerov, but the deepest impression was made by the lectures and the skilled experimental techniques of Ilya Tsion. It was in Tsion's laboratory that Pavlov was exposed to scientific investigations, resulting in his paper "On the Nerves Controlling the Pancreatic Gland."

After graduating, Pavlov entered the third course of the Medico-Chirurgical Academy (renamed in 1881 the Military Medical Academy), working as a laboratory assistant (1876–1878). In 1877 he published his first work, *Experimental Data Concerning the Accommodating Mechanism of the Blood Vessels,* dealing with the reflex regulation of the circulation of blood. Two years later he completed his course at the academy, and on the basis of a competitive examination he was awarded a scholarship for postgraduate study at the academy.

Pavlov spent the next decade in Sergei Botkins laboratory at the academy. In 1883 Pavlov completed his thesis, *The Centrifugal Nerves of the Heart,* and received the degree of doctor of medicine. The following year he was appointed lecturer in physiology at the academy, won the Wylie fellowship, and then spent the next 2 years in Germany. During the 1880s Pavlov perfected his experimental techniques which made possible his later important discoveries.

In 1881 Pavlov married Serafima Karchevskaia, a woman with profound spiritual feeling, a deep love for literature, and strong affection for her husband. In 1890 he was appointed to the vacant chair of pharmacology at the academy, and a year later he assumed the directorship of the department of physiology of the Institute of Experimental Medicine. Five years later he accepted the chair of physiology at the academy, which he held until 1925. For the next 45 years Pavlov pursued his studies on the digestive glands and conditioned reflexes.

Scientific Contributions. During the first phase of his scientific activity (1874–1888), Pavlov developed operative-surgical techniques that enabled him to perform experiments on unanesthetized animals without inflicting much pain. He studied the circulatory system, particularly the oscillation of blood pressure under various controlled conditions and the regulation of cardiac activity. He noted that the blood pressure of his dogs hardly varied despite the feeding of dry food or excessive amounts of meat broth. In his examination of cardiac activity he was able to observe the special nerve fibers that controlled the rhythm and the strength of the heartbeat. His theory was that the heart is regulated by four specific nerve fibers; it is now generally accepted that the vagus and sympathetic nerves produce the effects on the heart that Pavlov noticed.

In the course of his second phase of scientific work (1888–1902), Pavlov concentrated on the nerves directing the digestive glands and the functions of the alimentary canal under normal conditions. He discovered the secretory nerves of the pancreas in 1888 and the following year the nerves controlling the secretory activity of the gastric glands. Pavlov and his pupils also produced a considerable amount of accurate data on the workings of the gastrointestinal tract, which served as a basis for Pavlov's *Lectures on the Work of the Principal Digestive Glands* (published in Russia in 1897). For this work Pavlov received in 1904 the Nobel Prize in physiology or medicine.

The final phase of Pavlov's scientific career (1902–1936) was primarily concerned with ascertaining the functions of the cerebral cortex by means of conditioned reflexes. Prior to 1900, Pavlov observed that his dogs would secrete saliva and gastric juices before the meat was actually given to them. The sight, odor, or even the footsteps of the attendant were suf-

ficient to trigger the flow of saliva. Pavlov realized that the dogs were responding to activity associated with their feeding, and in 1901 he termed such a response a "conditioned reflex," which was acquired, or learned, as opposed to the unconditioned, or inherited, reflex. He faced a dilemma: could he embark on the study of conditioned reflexes by applying physiological methods to what was generally viewed as psychic phenomena? He opted to follow Ivan Sechenov, who considered that, in theory, psychic phenomena are essentially reflexes and therefore subject to physiological analysis.

The important lectures, papers, and speeches of Pavlov dealing with conditioned reflexes and the cerebral cortex are presented in *Twenty Years of Objective Study of the Higher Nervous Activity (Behavior) of Animals: Conditioned Reflexes* (1923) and *Lectures on the Work of the Cerebral Hemispheres* (1927). He not only concerned himself with the formation of conditioned responses but noted that they were subject to various kinds of manipulation. He discovered that conditioned responses can be extinguished—at least temporarily—if not reinforced; that one conditioned stimulus can replace another and yet produce identical conditioned responses; and that there are several orders of conditioning. In time Pavlov developed a purely physiological theory of cortical excitation and inhibition which considered, among other things, the process of sleep identical with internal inhibition. However magnificent his experiments were in revealing the responses of animals to conditioning stimuli, he encountered difficulty in experimentally proving his assertion that conditioned responses are due to temporary neuronal connections in the cortex.

In 1918 Pavlov had an opportunity to study several cases of mental illness and thought that a physiological approach to psychiatric phenomena might prove useful. He noted that he could induce "experimental neuroses" in animals by overstraining the excitatory process or the inhibitory process, or by quickly alternating excitation and inhibition. Pavlov then drew an analogy between the functional disorders in animals with those observed in humans. In examining the catatonic manifestations of schizophrenia, he characterized this psychopathological state as actually being "chronic hypnosis"—chiefly as a consequence of weak cortical cells—which functions as a protective mechanism, preserving the nerve cells from further weakening or destruction.

In Pavlov's last scientific article, "The Conditioned Reflex" (1934), written for the *Great Medical Encyclopedia,* he discussed his theory of the two signaling systems which differentiated the animal nervous system from that of man. The first signaling system, possessed both by humans and animals, receives stimulations and impressions of the external world through sense organs. The second signaling system in man deals with the signals of the first system, involving words, thoughts, abstractions, and generalizations. Conditioned reflexes play a significant role in both signal systems. Pavlov declared that "the conditioned reflex has become the central phenomenon in physiology"; he saw in the conditioned reflex the principal mechanism of adaptation to the environment by the living organism.

Philosophy and Outlook. Pavlov's endeavor to give the conditioned reflex widest application in animal and human behavior tended to color his philosophical view of psychology. Although he did not go so far as to deny psychology the right to exist, in his own work and in his demands upon his collaborators he insisted that the language of physiology be employed exclusively to describe psychic activity. Ultimately he envisioned a time when psychology would be completely subsumed into physiology. Respecting the Cartesian duality of mind and matter, Pavlov saw no need for it inasmuch as he believed all mental processes can be explained physiologically.

Politically, most of his life Pavlov was opposed to the extremist positions of the right and left. He did not welcome the Russian February Revolution of 1917 with any enthusiasm. As for the Bolshevik program for creating a Communist society, Pavlov publically stated, "If that which the Bolsheviks are doing with Russia is an experiment, for such an experiment I should regret giving even a frog." Despite his early hostility to the Communist regime, in 1921 a decree of the Soviet of People's Commissars, signed by Lenin himself, assured Pavlov of continuing support for his scientific work and special privileges. Undoubtedly, Soviet authorities viewed Pavlov's approach to psychology as confirmation of Marxist materialism as well as a method of restructuring society. By 1935 Pavlov became reconciled to the Soviet Communist system, declaring that the "government, too, is an experimenter but in an immeasurably higher category."

Pavlov became seriously ill in 1935 but recovered sufficiently to participate at the Fifteenth International Physiological Congress, and later he attended the Neurological Congress at London. On Feb. 27, 1936, he died.

EWB

Penn, William (1644–1718), English religious reformer and colonist. William Penn founded Pennsylvania and played a leading role in the history of New Jersey and Delaware.

The heritage of William Penn was his part in the growth of the Society of Friends (Quakers) and role in the settlement of North America. Penn's influence with the British royal family and his pamphlets on behalf of religious toleration were important factors in the consolidation of the Quaker movement. He gave witness in America to the liberal faith and social conscience he had propounded in England in a career committed to religious and political values that have become inseparable from the American way of life.

William Penn was born in London on Oct. 14, 1644, the son of Adm. William Penn and Margaret Jasper. Adm. Penn served in the parliamentary navy during the Puritan Revolution. Although rewarded by Cromwell and given estates in Ireland, he fell into disfavor and took part in the restoration of Charles II. An intimate of the Duke of York, Adm. Penn was knighted by Charles II. With so influential a father, there seemed little doubt that William's prospects were attractive.

Early Manhood. Nothing better demonstrates how young Penn represented his period than his early religious enthusiasm. At the age of 13 he was profoundly moved by the Quaker Thomas Loe. Afterward, at Oxford, he came under Puritan influences. When he refused to conform to Anglican practices, the university expelled him in 1662.

At his father's request Penn attended the Inns of Court, gaining knowledge of the law. A portrait of this time shows him dressed in armor, with handsome, strong features, and the air of confidence of a fledgling aristocrat.

Quaker Advocate. Appearances, in Penn's case, were deceiving. While supervising his father's Irish estates, Penn was drawn into the Quaker fold. His conversion was inspired by the simple piety of the Quakers and the need to provide relief for victims of persecution. At the age of 22, much to his father's distress, Penn became a Quaker advocate. His marriage in 1672 to Gulielma Maria Springett, of a well-known Quaker family, completed his religious commitment.

Penn's prominence and political connections were important resources for the persecuted Quakers. A major theme of his voluminous writings was the inhumanity and futility of persecution. One remarkable achievement during this period was Penn's handling of the "Bushell Case." Penn managed to persuade a jury not to subject a Quaker to imprisonment only for his faith. When the magistrate demanded that the jury change its verdict, Penn maintained successfully that a jury must not be coerced by the bench.

This landmark case established the freedom of English juries.

Colonial Proprietor. Religious persecution and colonization went hand in hand as the Quakers looked to America for a haven. Various problems invited Penn's association with the Quaker interests in New Jersey. Apart from his influence in England, Penn was active in mediating quarrels among the trustees. Doubtless, too, Penn contributed to the "Concessions and Agreements" (1677) offered to settlers, although he was not its principal author. This document gave the settlers virtual control over this colony through an elected assembly. It also offered a forthright guarantee of personal liberties, especially religious toleration and trial by jury, which the Quakers could not obtain in England.

The manifest liabilities of New Jersey formed a prelude to the founding of Pennsylvania. Of major importance, however, was Penn's Quaker faith and unyielding devotion to religious and political freedom; this underlaid his conception of Pennsylvania as a "Holy Experiment." In addition, Penn thought the colony could become a profitable enterprise to be inherited by his family.

Penn's proprietary charter contained many elements of previous grants. Penn and his heirs were given control over the land and extensive powers of government. The document reflected the period in which it was written: in keeping with new imperial regulations, Penn was made personally responsible for the enforcement of the Navigation Acts and had to keep an agent in London; he was required to send laws to England for royal approval.

In several ways Pennsylvania was the most successful English colony. Penn's initial treaties with the Indians, signed in 1683 and 1684, were based on an acceptance of Indian equality and resulted in an unprecedented era of peace. Penn also wrote promotional tracts for Pennsylvania and arranged circulation of these materials abroad. The response was one of the largest and most varied ethnic migrations in the history of colonization. Moreover, Pennsylvania's economic beginnings were usually successful. A fertile country, the commercial advantages of Philadelphia, and substantial investments by Quaker merchants produced rapid economic growth.

Despite this success Pennsylvania was not without problems. An immediate concern was its borders, especially those with Maryland. Because of anomalies in Penn's charter, an area along the southern border, including Philadelphia, was claimed by Lord Baltimore. This problem was only partly ameliorated when Penn secured control over what later became Dela-

ware from the Duke of York. Just as troublesome were political controversies within the colony. Although Penn's liberal spirit was evident in the political life of Pennsylvania, and he believed that the people should be offered self-government and that the rights of every citizen should be guaranteed, he did not think the colonists should have full power. In order to provide a balance in government, and partly to protect his own rights, he sought a key role in running the colony. What Penn envisaged in his famous "Frame of Government" (1682) was a system in which he would offer leadership and the elected assembly would follow his pattern.

Almost from the start there were challenges to Penn's conception. Controversies developed among the respective branches of government, with the representatives trying to restrict the authority of the proprietor and the council. Disputes centered on taxation, land policy, Penn's appointments, and defense. "For the love of God, me, and the poor country," Penn wrote to the colonists, "be not so governmentish, so noisy, and open in your dissafection." Other difficulties included Penn's identification with James II, which brought him imprisonment and a temporary loss of the proprietorship in 1692–1694. No less burdensome was his indebtedness. Penn's liabilities in the founding of Pennsylvania led to his imprisonment for debt, a humiliating blow.

Final Years. After the Glorious Revolution in England, Penn and his family went to live in Pennsylvania. Arriving in 1699, he reestablished friendly contacts with the Indians and worked hard to heal a religious schism among the Quakers. He also labored to suppress piracy and tried to secure expenditures for colonial self-defense, demanded by the Crown but resisted by pacifist Quakers.

Penn's major achievement was the new charter of 1701. Under its terms the council was eliminated, and Pennsylvania became the only colony governed by a unicameral legislature of elected representatives. This system, which lasted until 1776, permitted the Delaware settlers to have their own legislature. Penn was obliged to return to England late in 1701 to fight a proposal in Parliament which would have abrogated all proprietary grants. He never saw Pennsylvania again.

Penn's last years were filled with disappointment. His heir, William, Jr., was a special tribulation because of his dissolute lifestyle. After the death of his first wife in 1694, Penn married Hannah Callowhill in 1696. Perplexed by debts, colonial disaffection, and the general antipathy of the King's ministers toward private colonies, Penn almost completed the sale of

Pennsylvania to the Crown in 1712 before he suffered his first disabling stroke. He died at Ruscombe, Berkshire, on July 30, 1718.

EWB

Pepys, Samuel (1633–1703), English diarist and public official. Samuel Pepys kept a diary that provides a graphic account of English social life and conditions during the early period of the Restoration.

Samuel Pepys was born on Feb. 23, 1633, in London. His father was a tailor. Pepys was sent to school first at Huntingdon and later to St. Paul's in London. In June 1650 he entered Trinity College, Cambridge, but he transferred to Magdalene College the following October and graduated in 1653.

In 1655 Pepys married Elizabeth St. Michel, the young daughter of a Huguenot exile. The couple was apparently supported at first by Pepys's cousin Sir Edward Montagu, later the Earl of Sandwich, whose service Pepys entered. In 1660 Pepys accompanied Montagu as secretary on the voyage that returned Charles II to England. That same year Pepys was appointed clerk of the acts at the Navy Office. This appointment was significant because Pepys was to serve the navy in some capacity for the greater part of his life, working to improve its efficiency and to ensure its integrity.

In 1662 Pepys was appointed one of the commissioners for Tangier, which was then occupied by the English; 3 years later he was named treasurer. When the Dutch War broke out in 1665, he was appointed surveyor general of the Victualing Office in addition to his regular duties for the navy, and he remained at his post throughout the Great Plague of 1665 although most inhabitants left London. Pepys saved the Navy Office from the Great Fire of 1666 by having the buildings around it destroyed. When the Dutch War ended in 1668, the Duke of York entrusted Pepys with the task of acquitting the navy of mismanagement.

Pepys's appearance before Parliament evidently whetted his own aspirations for a seat. He was elected to Parliament in 1673 and again in 1679. In 1673 the King transferred Pepys from the Navy Office to the secretaryship of the Admiralty. At the time of the Popish Plot in 1678, Whig opponents of the Duke of York accused Pepys of giving naval secrets to the French. Pepys resigned his office and was imprisoned in the Tower in 1679, but the charges against him were unfounded, and Pepys was vindicated and freed in 1680.

Pepys's wife had died in 1669. His principal companions since then had been such men of taste and knowledge as John Evelyn, Christopher Wren, and John Dryden. In 1684 Pepys was elected president of the Royal Society. That same year he was also restored to the secretaryship of the Admiralty, retaining the post until the Glorious Revolution of 1688.

After Pepys retired from public life in 1689, he led a relatively quiet life. He published his *Memoirs . . . of the Royal Navy* in 1690. He corresponded with friends and acted as consultant to the navy. He died on May 26, 1703.

Pepys is remembered today for the diary he kept for 9½ years in the 1660s. In his diary, written in cipher, Pepys recorded both the significant and trivial events of his public and private worlds. Together with his impressions of his own domestic situation, he recorded his thoughts about Charles II, the Great Plague of 1665, the Great Fire of 1666, the Restoration theater, the King's mistresses, the Dutch War, and the Duke of York. Failing eyesight caused him to discontinue the diary while still a young man, but its intimate record of his daily life and of the early Restoration remains both interesting and historically valuable.

Pepys's diary was not transcribed and published until 1825. The first virtually complete edition was issued between 1893 and 1899, edited by H. B. Wheatley.

EWB

Perrault, Charles (1628–1703), Children's story writer. Though the stories of *Cinderella, Little Red Riding Hood, Puss in Boots,* and *Sleeping Beauty* are among the best known and most popular works of literature in the world, few people recognize the name of Charles Perrault, the man who is generally believed to be their author. Because his collection of stories, *Histories; or, Tales of Times Past,* was published under the name of Perrault's son, Pierre d'Armancour, there has always been some debate even about the authorship. Glenn S. Burne noted in *Writers for Children* that, according to the best evidence, "the stories were the work of Perrault in probable collaboration with the talented teenage boy, with whom he had a close relationship." Burne went on to say that Perrault published these tales near the end of his career, when his interests were elsewhere, and he probably had no idea that they would become so important.

Born on January 12, 1628, in Paris, France, Perrault was the youngest son of an eminent Parisian lawyer. Both his parents took an active part in educating their children and, when Perrault was sent to a private school at the age of eight, he was one of the top students in his class. Several years later his brilliance led him to argue with a teacher and leave school to study independently with a friend named Beaurain. In his autobiography, *Memoires de Charles Perrault,* Perrault described how the two boys got together mornings and afternoons for three or four years, reading in the course of that time most of the Bible and the classic authors. Perrault first tried his hand at writing when he, his older brother Claude (a medical student who became both a physician and an architect), and Beaurain adapted the sixth book of the *Aeneid* into comic verse, a popular literary practice of the time. Later the brothers collaborated on the first volume of *Les Murs de troie* ("The Walls of Troy").

In 1651 Perrault took the bar exam and was admitted to the practice of law. He soon became disillusioned with it, however, and left in 1654 to serve as a clerk to Claude, who had bought the post of Receiver General of Finances for the city of Paris—buying positions in the government and army was a common practice at the time. During this period Perrault was also continuing his studies and writing poetry, some of which was published and translated into Italian. In the mid-1660s he was appointed by Jean Baptiste Colbert, then Minister of Finance under King Louis XIV, to an advisory council that supervised the making of monuments, medals, and other works glorifying the king. Perrault became secretary to the council, which later became the French Academy, created "for the advancement and perfection of all sciences." When Colbert was appointed Superintendent of the Royal Buildings, he made Perrault his chief clerk. In this capacity Perrault had the pleasure of helping get his brother Claude's design chosen for the forefront of the Louvre Museum. In 1671 Perrault was formally admitted to the French Academy; in 1672 he became its chancellor and, in 1681, its director.

Perrault married Marie Guichon in 1672, and the couple had three sons and a daughter. Several years after his wife's death in 1678, Perrault decided to devote all of his time to writing and educating his children. As he stated in his autobiography, "With this in mind I went to live in the St. Jacques district [of Paris], which being near to the schools, gave me the great facility to send my children there, having always thought that it was best for children to come home to sleep in their father's house when it was possible rather than sending them to board in the school. . . . I gave them a tutor and I myself took great care to watch over their studies." Burne pointed out in *Writers for Children* that his wife's death may have been a factor in Perrault's writing the fairy tales, "since he maintained that such literature was an effective means of instilling values."

Though it is the fairy tales that are generally remembered, Perrault gained prominence as a literary figure with his poem "Le Siecle de Louis XIV," which he read to the Academy. In this poem he praised the superiority of modern letters as opposed to the classics, thus raising an argument that lasted for many years and brought his name into prominence.

Perrault died on May 16, 1703, at the age of seventy-five. Many critics believe that his now-familiar stories were half-forgotten folk tales that the author merely set down in a simple, readable form. In *Contes* Perrault said of them, "These sorts of tales have the gift of pleasing . . . great minds as well as lesser folk, the old as well as young folk; these idle fancies amuse and lull reason, although contrary to the same reason, and can charm reason better than all imaginable probability."

Major Authors and Illustrators
for Children and Young Adults

Pestalozzi, Johann Heinrich (1746–1827), Swiss educator. Johann Pestalozzi envisioned a science of education based on the psychology of child development. He laid the foundation of the modern primary school.

Johann Pestalozzi was born in Zurich on Jan. 12, 1746. His father died shortly afterward, and Pestalozzi was raised in poverty. This early experience with the life of degradation of the poor developed in him an acute sense of justice and a determination to help the underprivileged. He chose to enter the ministry, but his studies in theology at the University of Zurich were without distinction. He tried law and politics, but his humanitarianism was mistaken for radicalism and he became very unpopular even with those he sought most to help. In 1769 he settled on his farm, "Neuhof," at Birr, Switzerland, where he planned to fight poverty by developing improved methods of agriculture.

At Neuhof, Pestalozzi realized that schoolteaching was his true vocation and that as a schoolmaster he could fulfill his desire to improve society by helping the individual to help himself. In 1775 he turned his farm into an orphanage and began to test his ideas on child rearing. In 1780 he wrote *The Hours of a Hermit,* a series of generally sad maxims reflecting his view of man's somber plight in the world and the failure of his own attempts at reform at Neuhof. He first experienced success with *Leonard and Gertrude* (1783), which was widely acclaimed and read as a novel and not, as it was intended to be, as an exposition of his pedagogical ideas.

His newfound fame brought Pestalozzi to Stanz, where he took over an orphanage in 1798, and then to Burgdorf, where he ran a boarding school for boys from 1800 to 1804. In 1801 he published *How Gertrude Teaches Her Children,* a sequel to his earlier novel and an expansion of his educational thought. But it was at Yverdun, where he was the director for the next

20 years of a boarding school for boys of many nationalities, that Pestalozzian principles of education were applied and observed by world leaders.

According to Pestalozzi, "the full and fruitful development" of the child according to his own nature is the goal of education. The school and teachers provide only the environment and guidance, respectively, most appropriate to free expression that allows the natural powers of the child to develop. Instruction should be adapted to each individual according to his particular changing, unfolding nature. Rather than from books, the child should learn by observing objects of the real world. Sense perceptions are of supreme importance in the development of the child's mind. Pestalozzi described such a detailed methodology both for child development and for the study of the child that a definite system of teacher training evolved also.

Honors flowed in; Yverdun became a showplace. These were two causes of the ultimate collapse of the school. Pestalozzi's fame brought out some of his more disagreeable characteristics, and the original atmosphere of fellowship disappeared in the influx of visitors to the school. The school closed amid disputes and lawsuits; Pestalozzi died an embittered man on Feb. 17, 1827, in Brugg. But his ideas were used in establishing national school systems during the 19th century, and his influence among educators continues to be great to this day.

EWB

Pétain, Henri Philippe (1856–1951), French general and statesman. Philippe Pétain a military hero in World War I, headed the collaborationist Vichy regime during World War II. Officially considered a traitor, he is admired by many of his countrymen as a supreme patriot.

Philippe Pétain was born to peasant parents on April 24, 1856, at Cauchy-à-la-Tour. After a private boarding-school education, he entered Saint-Cyr in 1876 and graduated 2 years later. An advocate of defensive rather than offensive strategies, he became an instructor at the École de Guerre in 1888. Nearly 60 years old and without active-duty experience in 1914, Petain had had a far from brilliant career. World War I changed that radically.

Hero of Verdun. Promoted to brigadier general on Aug. 31, 1914, Pétain distinguished himself at the Battle of the Marne (1914) and in June 1915 was named a full general and given command of the 11th Army. When the Germans decided in 1916 to end the war with a massive concentrated attack on the French line at Verdun, Pétain was ordered to stop the offensive at all costs. Promising that "they shall not pass," he held Verdun but at the enormous cost of 350,000 men. Subsequently a great popular hero, he became chief of the general staff in April 1917, and a month later he succeeded Gen. Robert Nivelle as commander in chief.

Pétain assumed his command over a French army near disintegration. Years of indecisive war had sapped morale, and mutinies were endemic. Combining harsh disciplinary measures with humane redress of grievances, he very quickly reestablished order. Without these reforms the French army would not have withstood the final German offensives of 1918.

Between the World Wars. Named marshal of France on Nov. 21, 1918, Pétain emerged from the war second only to Ferdinand Foch in prestige. It was only natural that Pétain was regarded as a high military authority, but the consequences later proved catastrophic. Vice president of the Supreme War Council after 1920 and inspector general of the army after 1922, Pétain used his influence to orient French military planning along defensive lines. He favored the construction of heavily armed fortifications along the Franco-German frontier. Against the protests of such young rebels as Charles De Gaulle, who urged a strategy of mobile mechanized warfare, Pétain's influence was decisive, and the Maginot Line was constructed on the Franco-German border. French government and military leaders were determined to prepare France for any future war.

Retiring from the army in 1931, Pétain entered politics in 1934 as minister of war in the short-lived authoritarian government of Gaston Doumergue. Increasingly contemptuous of parliamentary politics and such Socialist experiments as the Popular Front, and a known partisan of dictatorial regimes, Pétain provided a figure in the late 1930s around which right-wing opponents of the Third Republic could rally.

Vichy Regime. Ambassador to Spain at the outbreak of World War II, Pétain was recalled and appointed vice-premier in May 1940 by Premier Paul Reynaud in an attempt to bolster his foundering government. With the fall of France imminent, Reynaud resigned on June 16, 1940, and President Albert Lebrun asked the 84-year-old Pétain to form a new government whose first task would be to negotiate an armistice with the Germans. No one seemed to care that the rapid collapse of the French army in 1940 had been largely due to the outdated principles on which Pétain had organized it and to its lack of mechanized equipment, whose supply he had opposed.

On June 22 Pétain concluded an armistice with the Nazis that divided France into two zones: the north and the Atlantic coastline under German military occupation, and the rest of France under the direct administration of Pétain's government. Militarily, France retained control of its fleet, but its army was drastically reduced to 100,000 men.

Meeting in national assembly at Vichy on July 10, 1940, a rump parliament voted full constituent powers to Pétain. The next day he was named chief of state, and with Pierre Laval he then began the task of constructing a hierarchical and authoritarian regime under the formula of his so-called National Revolution. Little more than empty rhetoric ("Work-Family-Fatherland") and the cult of Pétain, his Vichy regime was a scarcely disguised client state of Nazi Germany.

Of necessity, Pétain's central principle in foreign policy was collaboration with the Third Reich. Above all, he wanted to keep France out of the war and to keep Germany as faithful to the armistice terms as possible. Opposed, however, to the all-out collaboration urged by Laval, Pétain replaced him with Adm. Jean Darlan in 1941. Under pressure from Berlin, Laval returned to office in April 1942.

The crisis of the Vichy regime occurred in November 1942 following the Allied landings in North Africa and the German occupation of Vichy France. Urged to flee, Pétain refused, believing that it was his duty to share the fate of his countrymen. He still refused even after ultracollaborationists were imposed upon him by the Germans, and thus he implicated himself in their treason. Arrested by the retreating Nazis on Aug. 20, 1944, and sent to Germany, Pétain voluntarily returned to France in April 1945. Immediately arrested and brought to trial by the provisional government of his onetime protégé Charles De Gaulle, Pétain was convicted of treason, militarily degraded, and sentenced to death. His sentence was commuted to life imprisonment by De Gaulle, and Pétain died 6 years later, on July 23, 1951, on the Île d'Yeu.

Estimates of Pétain's Career.   Pétain remains an acutely controversial figure in recent French history. He is the object of an as yet unsuccessful effort at rehabilitation, his right-wing admirers depicting him as the "crucified savior of France" and claiming that his self-sacrifice after 1940 "will one day count more for his glory than the victory of Verdun." Not only did Pétain save France from the fate of Poland, they insist, but by playing a double game he tricked Adolf Hitler into staying out of North Africa, which made possible the eventual Allied victory in 1945. Preposterous as these claims are, the impression they give of Pétain is only slightly more misleading than that given by official Resistance historiography, which unfailingly portrays him as an arch-villain and as a criminal traitor to France.

EWB

Peter I   (1672–1725), tsar of Russia (1682–1725). Peter the Great's reign was marked by a program of extensive reform known as Westernization and by the establishment of Russia as a major European power.

Contemporaries abroad tended to admire Peter I for his reforms and to fear him because of his country's growing power, but his reforms were generally unpopular with his subjects, not only because they entailed higher taxes and harder work for almost everyone but also because they disturbed ancient religious and cultural traditions. After his death, Russians soon came to realize that Peter had been the country's greatest ruler and that his reign had indeed been a high point in their history. That evaluation is still generally accepted by historians.

Peter was born in Moscow on May 30, 1672, the only son of Tsar Alexis and his second wife, Natalia Naryshkin. The 13 children of Alexis' previous marriage included 3 who became prominent during Peter's youth: able and ambitious Sophia, half-blind and half-witted Ivan, and amiable Feodor, who succeeded Alexis in 1676.

Peter's formal education, entrusted to private tutors, began when he was 7 but was interrupted 3 years later, when Tsar Feodor died without having named an heir. Sophia and a small group of supporters favored the frail Ivan, her 15-year-old brother, to succeed Feodor. Another group favored the robust and intelligent Peter and at once proclaimed him tsar, planning that his mother serve as regent. That arrangement was quickly upset, however, when Sophia received the help of the Moscow troops and compelled the installation of Ivan as "First Tsar," Peter as "Second Tsar," and herself as regent.

Formative Years.   During the next 7 years little was required of Peter except that he take part in formal ceremonies. Fascinated by military activities, he spent much time at games involving arms practice and battle maneuvers, at first with young friends and later with two regiments of soldiers that he was permitted to recruit and train. His curiosity and abundant energy led him also to the study and practice of the skills involved in navigation and such crafts as carpentry, stonecutting, and printing. In the course of these pursuits, he came into contact with a number of foreign residents and gained from them knowledge of the world outside Russia.

Disturbed by the trend of his development, Peter's mother mistakenly decided that she could change it by arranging for his marriage; at her direction, he was married to Eudoxia Lopukhin in January 1689. Still, he showed no inclination to forgo his first interests or his unconventional activities.

Political opposition to Sophia's regency came to a head during Peter's 17th year, and, impressed by the assurance of strong support if he would assert himself, Peter declared her office vacant and sent her away to a convent. That done, he returned to his habitual pursuits and continued to neglect personal responsibilities, even after Eudoxia had borne him a son, Alexis, in 1690. By that time he was a striking figure, impressive as a potential ruler but with scant interest in the duties involved.

It was not until 1695, when he had his first taste of actual fighting, against the Turkish forces at Azov, that Peter began to give serious thought to the problems he faced as czar. The death of "First Tsar" Ivan during the following year finally brought him close to the full import of his position.

First Steps.   Having been impressed at Azov by his country's lack of adequate fighting ships, Peter began with characteristic zeal to plan for an efficient navy. He sent groups of young men to western European countries to study navigation and shipbuilding; then, in 1697, he himself followed—an unprecedented step for a Russian tsar—to acquire firsthand information and to hire shipwrights for service in Russia. He visited Holland, England, Germany, and Austria. In those countries he was impressed not only by their technological superiority over Russia but also by what seemed to him a superior style of life. When he returned to Russia in 1698, he was ready to make many changes.

One of Peter's first acts was to order that men shave off their beards, and when he met stubborn resistance, he modified his order only to the extent of imposing a tax on those who chose to keep their beards. He also shattered tradition by requiring that the old Russian calendar (which reckoned time from the creation of the world) be abandoned in favor of the Julian calendar used in the West. At the same time, he was dealing with two other matters, a revolt among the Moscow troops and the annoying presence of his unwanted wife, Eudoxia; he speedily quelled the revolt with savage executions and terminated his marriage by forcing Eudoxia into a convent.

Great Northern War.   The handling of some of his problems, Peter soon learned, required more than his usual imperious tactics. During his European tour, he had obtained assurances of Western cooperation in forcing Sweden to cede the territory that Russia needed as an outlet to the Baltic Sea. He began the undertaking by a declaration of war on Sweden in 1700.

Peter led his forces in their first major encounter with the Swedes at Narva in November 1700 and was severely defeated by inferior numbers. Resorting to the means he had used with the navy—remodeling by Western patterns—he began at once to whip into shape a better organized, equipped, and trained army. In 1703 he led it to a redeeming victory and took from Sweden the mouth of the Neva River. He designated the site for a city to be named St. Petersburg and to become the imperial capital. A year later he captured Narva.

Taking advantage of a few years of respite while the Swedes were engaged with other enemies, Peter worked purposefully to strengthen Russian arms and to keep under control the domestic discontent that was breaking into open revolt in many areas, particularly along the Don and the Volga rivers. He was obliged to return to the war in mid-1709, however, to meet a Swedish invasion led by Charles XII. The opposing forces met at Poltava, where the Russians won a decisive victory. The battle did not end the war, but it marked a turning point and vindicated Peter's belief in his methods. Moreover, it had a profound psychological effect on the western European states, who now saw Russia as a formidable power.

Twelve years of indecisive hostilities followed the Poltava victory. In 1711 Peter had to divert some of his troops to the south, where the Turks, encouraged by Sweden, had attacked Russia. After a year of unsuccessful fighting, he had to cede the port of Azov, Russia's only point of access to the Black Sea. Meanwhile, intermittent fighting kept the main war going, and it was not until 1718 that Sweden reluctantly agreed to a consideration of peace terms. By the resulting Treaty of Nystad, signed in September 1721, Sweden ceded Ingria, Estonia, Livonia, and a portion of Karelia, thus giving Russia a firm foothold on the Gulf of Finland and the Baltic Sea. Since Peter had already established Russian influence in Courland, his country was now a major Baltic power, having been provided with "a window to Europe" by the new acquisitions. In recognition of what he had achieved, the Russian Senate, a body created by Peter, conferred upon him the titles of "the Great" and "Emperor."

Personal Problems.   After he freed himself of Eudoxia, Peter became attracted to Catherine Skavrenska, a Lithuanian girl of humble origin, and married her secretly, delaying until 1712 the public recognition of her as his consort. When Catherine bore a son, the Tsar had him christened Peter Petrovich and anticipated his succession to the throne. Alexis, the son by his first marriage, had become a lazy, weak-willed, and hostile young man who resisted being molded to his father's standards. In the belief that Alexis was actually plotting against the throne, Peter ordered that he be taken to prison; and there, after being questioned under torture, Alexis died. Yet the Tsar's problem was not solved: in 1719 Peter Petrovich died, leaving him no son as successor. Alexis had left a son, Peter Alekseyevich; but the Czar chose to bypass him and to decree, in 1722, that thereafter each ruler of Russia was free to name his heir. It is probable that Peter intended to name his wife, Catherine, as his heir, but he continued to postpone the formality.

Domestic Reforms. Although Peter carried out many reforms in his early years as tsar, his major work as a reformer was done in the last decade of his reign. His goal was to create a powerful and prosperous state, efficiently and honestly administered, to which every subject could contribute. To achieve that goal, he refashioned many existing institutions and initiated new policies, generally guided by what he had learned of western Europe. He reorganized the country's entire administrative structure and promulgated the Table of Ranks, classifying civil service, military, and naval positions and providing for advancement on the basis of merit from lower to higher positions. He encouraged industry and commerce, spurred the development of science, and laid the foundations of the Academy of Sciences, which was established soon after his death. He instituted Russia's secular schools, eliminated the obsolete characters from the Russian alphabet, and established the country's first newspaper.

Even the Church felt the force of Peter's great energy. Although a religious man, he had no respect for the privileges accorded to the Church, was critical of many of its policies, and resented its resistance to his reforms. When Patriarch Adrian, head of the Russian Orthodox Church, died in 1700, Peter did not permit the vacancy to be filled. Finally, in 1721, he abolished the post of patriarch, substituting for it the Holy Synod, a board of prelates who were to direct the affairs of the Church under the supervision of a layman appointed by the tsar.

Apparently, Peter found his greatest satisfaction in the development of St. Petersburg. He intended that this modern city become the center of the new Russia as Moscow had been the center of the old. He declared it to be the country's new capital and gradually transferred to it the central administrative offices. Built in Western style rather than the traditional Russian, it provided a visible symbol of his reforms.

Last Years. After the war with Sweden, Peter began to think seriously of his country's interests in Asia. At his direction, Russian forces conquered Kamchatka on the Pacific, and a Russian expedition explored the area now known as the Bering Strait. With prospects of more immediate value, he successfully pursued a war against Persia to strengthen Russia's position on the Caspian.

The treaty ending the war with Persia had yet to be ratified in 1724, when Peter's health began to fail rapidly. Characteristically, he continued to drive himself to the very limit of his strength, still postponing the designation of an heir. He died on Jan. 28, 1725, in the city that he had founded.

EWB

Petrarch (1304–1374), Italian poet. Francesco Petrarca is best known for the lyric poetry of his *Canzoniere* and is considered one of the greatest love poets of world literature. A scholar of classical antiquity, he was the founder of humanism.

Petrarch has been called the first modern man. He observed the external world and analyzed his own interior life with a new awareness of values. Painfully conscious of human transience, he felt it his mission to bridge the ages and to save the classical authors from the ravages of time for posterity. He also longed for fame and for permanence in the future. Petrarch attained a vast direct knowledge of classical texts, subjecting them to critical evaluation and prizing them as an expression of the living human spirit. His attitude provided the first great stimulus to the cultural movement that culminated in the Renaissance.

Petrarch's life was marked by restlessness, yet one of its constant motives was his devotion to cherished friends. Equally constant was an unresolved interior conflict between the attractions of earthly life, particularly love and glory, and his aspirations toward higher religious goals.

Early Years and Education. Petrarch was born on July 20, 1304, in Arezzo, where his family was living in political exile. His parents were the Florentine notary Ser Petracco and Eletta Canigiani. His childhood was spent at Incisa and Pisa until 1312, when his family moved to Avignon, then the papal residence. A housing shortage there obliged Petrarch, his younger brother Gherardo, and their mother to settle in nearby Carpentras, where he began to study grammar and rhetoric. Beginning in 1316, Petrarch pursued legal studies at the University of Montpellier.

But already he preferred classical poets to the study of law. During one surprise visit Petrarch's father discovered some hidden books and began to burn them; however, moved by his son's pleading, he spared Cicero's *Rhetoric* and a copy of Virgil from the fire. About this time Petrarch's mother died.

In 1320 Petrarch and Gherardo went to Bologna to attend the law schools. They remained in Bologna—with two interruptions caused by student riots—until their father's death in 1326. Free to pursue his own interests, Petrarch then abandoned law and participated in the fashionable social life of Avignon.

Laura and the *Canzoniere*. On April 6, 1327, in the church of St. Clare, Petrarch saw and fell in love with the young woman whom he called Laura. She did not return his love. The true identity of Laura is not known; there is, however, no doubt regarding her reality or the intensity of the poet's passion, which endured after her death as a melancholy longing. Petrarch composed and revised the love lyrics inspired by Laura until his very last years. The *Canzoniere,* or *Rerum vulgarum fragmenta,* contains 366 poems (mostly sonnets, with a few canzoni and compositions in other meters) and is divided into two sections: the first is devoted to Laura in life (1–263) and the second to Laura in death (264–366). Petrarch became a model for Italian poets. The influence of his art and introspective sensibility was felt for more than 3 centuries in all European literatures.

When the income of Petrarch's family was depleted, he took the four Minor Orders required for an ecclesiastical career, and in the fall of 1330 he entered the service of Cardinal Giovanni Colonna. In 1333, motivated by intellectual curiosity, Petrarch traveled to Paris, Flanders (where he discovered two of Cicero's unknown orations), and Germany. Upon returning to Avignon, he met the Augustinian scholar Dionigi di Borgo San Sepolcro, who directed him toward a greater awareness of the importance of Christian patristic literature. Until the end of his life, Petrarch carried with him a tiny copy of St. Augustine's *Confessions,* a gift from Dionigi. In 1336 Petrarch climbed Mt. Ventoux in Provence; on the summit, opening the *Confessions* at random, he read that men admire mountains and rivers and seas and stars, yet neglect themselves. He described this experience in spiritual terms in a letter that he wrote to Dionigi (*Familiares* IV, 1).

Major Works in Latin. Petrarch's reputation as a man of letters and the canonries to which he was appointed at various times assured him the ease and freedom necessary for his studies and writing. He par-

ticipated during this period in the polemic concerning the papal residence, expressing in two *Epistolae metricae* his conviction that the papacy must return to Rome. Early in 1337 Petrarch visited Rome for the first time. The ancient ruins of the city deepened his admiration for the classical age. In the summer he returned to Avignon, where his son, Giovanni, had been born, and then went to live at Vaucluse (Fontaine-de-Vaucluse) near the source of the Sorgue River. There he led a life of solitude and simplicity, and he also conceived his major Latin works. In 1338 Petrarch began his *De viris illustribus,* and about that time he also started his Latin epic on Scipio Africanus, the *Africa.* In Vaucluse, Petrarch probably also worked on his *Triumphus Cupidinis,* a poetic "procession," written in Italian, in which Cupid leads his captive lovers. In 1340 Petrarch received invitations simultaneously from Paris and Rome to be crowned as poet. He chose Rome. His coronation on April 8, 1341, was a personal victory and a triumph for art and knowledge as well.

Middle Years. On returning from Rome, Petrarch stopped at Parma. There, on the wooded plateau of Selvapiana, he continued his *Africa* with renewed inspiration. In April 1343, shortly after Petrarch had returned to Avignon, Gherardo became a Carthusian monk. That same year Petrarch's daughter, Francesca, was born. Gherardo's decision to become a monk deeply moved Petrarch, leading him to reexamine his own spiritual state. Though his Christian faith was unquestionably sincere, he felt incapable of his brother's renunciation. His inner conflict inspired the *Secretum* a dialogue in three books between St. Augustine and Petrarch. In it Petrarch expressed his awareness of his failure to realize his religious ideal and his inability to renounce the temporal values that motivated his life. That year Petrarch also began a treatise on the cardinal virtues, *Rerum memorandarum libri.*

In the fall of 1343 Petrarch went to Naples on a diplomatic mission for Cardinal Colonna. He recorded his travel impressions in several letters (*Familiares* V, 3, 6). Upon his return he stopped at Parma, hoping to settle at Selvapiana. But a siege of Parma by Milanese and Mantuan troops forced him to flee to Verona in February 1345. There, in the cathedral library, he discovered the first 16 books of Cicero's letters to Atticus and his letters to Quintus and Brutus. Petrarch personally transcribed them, and these letters of Cicero stimulated Petrarch to plan a formal collection of his own letters.

From 1345 to 1347 Petrarch lived at Vaucluse and undertook his *De vita solitaria* and the *Bucolicum carmen* the latter a collection of 12 Latin eclogues. Early in 1347 a visit to Gherardo's monastery inspired Petrarch to write his *De otio religioso*. In May of that year an event occurred in Rome that aroused his greatest enthusiasm. Cola di Rienzi, who shared Petrarch's fervent desire for the rebirth of Rome, gained control of the Roman government through a successful revolution. Petrarch encouraged Cola with his pen, exhorting him to persevere in his task of restoring Rome to its universal political and cultural missions. Petrarch then started out for Rome. But Cola's dictatorial acts soon brought down upon himself the hostility of the Pope and the antagonism of the Roman nobles. News of Cola's downfall, before the year was over, prompted Petrarch to write his famous letter of reproach (*Familiares* VII, 7), which tells of his bitter disillusionment.

The Black Death and Milanese Period. Rather than proceed to Rome, Petrarch remained in Parma, where in May 1348 news of Laura's death reached him. The Black Death deprived Petrarch of several of his close friends that year, among them Cardinal Colonna. His grief is reflected in the poems he then wrote to Laura and in his letters of this period, one of the most desolate letters being addressed to himself (*Ad se ipsum*). Three eclogues and the *Triumphus mortis* (following the *Triumph of Love* and the *Triumph of Chastity*) were also inspired by the pestilence.

Because of the losses Petrarch had suffered, a period of his life seemed to have ended. In 1350 he began to make the formal collection of his Latin prose letters called *Familiares*. Since 1350 was a Year of Jubilee, Petrarch also made a pilgrimage to Rome. On his way he stopped in Florence, where he made new friends, among whom was Giovanni Boccaccio. After a brief stay in Rome, Petrarch returned northward and arrived in Parma in January 1351. In the meantime, Pope Clement VI was soliciting Petrarch's return to Avignon, and Florence sent Boccaccio with a letter of invitation promising Petrarch a professorship at the university and the restitution of his father's property. Petrarch chose Provence, where he hoped to complete some of his major works. He arrived in Vaucluse in June 1351, accompanied by his son. In Avignon that August he refused a papal secretaryship and a bishopric offered to him. Petrarch was impatient to leave the papal "Babylon" and wrote a series of violent letters against the Curia (*Epistolae sine nomine*).

In the spring of 1352, Petrarch returned to Vaucluse, resolved to leave Provence. The following spring, after visiting Gherardo, he crossed the Alps and greeted Italy (*Epistolae metricae* III, 24). For 8 years he stayed in Milan under the patronage of Gio-

vanni Visconti and later Galeazzo II Visconti, enjoying seclusion and freedom for study while using his pen to urge peace among Italian cities and states. He worked on the *Canzoniere*, took up old works (*De viris illustribus*), and began the treatise *De remediis utriusque fortunae*. Petrarch was also entrusted with diplomatic missions that brought him into direct relationship with heads of state, including the emperor Charles IV.

Padua, Venice, and Arquà. In June 1361 Petrarch went to Padua because the plague (which took the life of his son and the lives of several friends) had broken out in Milan. In Padua he terminated the *Familiares* and initiated a new collection, *Seniles*. In the fall of 1362 Petrarch settled in Venice, where he had been given a house in exchange for the bequest of his library to the city. From Venice he made numerous trips until his definitive return to Padua in 1368. During this period a controversy with several Averroists gave rise to an *Invective* on his own ignorance.

Petrarch's Paduan patron, Francesco da Carrara, gave him some land at Arquà in the Euganean Hills near Padua. There Petrarch built a house to which he retired in 1370. He received friends, studied, and wrote, and there his daughter, Francesca, now married, joined him with her family. Despite poor health, Petrarch attempted a trip to Rome in 1370, but he had to turn back at Ferrara. Except for a few brief absences, Petrarch spent his last years at Arquà, working on the *Seniles* and on the *Canzoniere*, for the latter of which he wrote a concluding canzone to the Virgin Mary. The *Posteritati*, a biographical letter intended to terminate the *Seniles*, remained incomplete at Petrarch's death. He revised his four *Triumphs* (of Love, Chastity, Death, and Fame), adding two more (of Time and of Eternity). Petrarch died on the night of July 18/19, 1374, and he was ceremonially buried beside the church of Arquà.

EWB

Philip II (1527–1598), king of Spain from 1556 to 1598. During Philip II's reign the Spanish Empire was severely challenged and its economic, social, and political institutions strained almost to the breaking point.

The son of Emperor Charles V, Philip II inherited the larger portion of his father's dominions: Spain, the Low Countries (basically the Netherlands and Belgium of today), Franche-Comté, Sicily and southern Italy, the duchy of Milan, and Spain's colonies in the New World, including Mexico and much of South America. But the inheritance inevitably included the host of problems which his father had left unsolved or which were incapable of being solved. The other part of Charles's dominions, the Holy Roman Empire, was bequeathed to his brother Ferdinand, Philip's uncle.

Philip was born in Valladolid on May 21, 1527, at the outset of the religious and political wars that divided Europe and drained the resources of every major European country. France, the principal opponent of Emperor Charles's ambition, was likewise the chief rival of Philip's Spain. When he acceded to the throne in 1556, the two countries were still at war; peace was concluded at Cateau-Cambrésis in 1559, largely because both states were financially exhausted.

The need to find money and enforce order in his territories led to Philip's clash with his Dutch subjects, a clash that produced the first war for national independence in modern European history and eventually drew Philip into the ill-fated Armada expedition. Spain's resources, including its commercial and military lifeline to northern and southern Italy, were meanwhile threatened in the Mediterranean by the Turkish fleet and the incursions of pirates, largely operating out of North African ports.

On the one side combating rebellious Protestant subjects and on the other confronting the advance of Islam, Philip II has often been depicted as the secular arm of the Catholic Church, a religious zealot who sought to erase heresy and infidelity through military conquest. This, however, is a simplification and is misleading. He was indeed a devout Catholic and vitally concerned with the suppression of "heresy" in all the territory over which he ruled. But his policies and choices must also be viewed in the light of what he considered to be Spanish national interests.

Early Life. Philip's first marriage (1543) was to his cousin Maria of Portugal, who lived but 2 years, leaving a son, Don Carlos. To consolidate his empire and afford protection for his holdings in the Low Countries, Charles then married Philip to Mary Tudor of England, the Catholic queen of a basically Protestant country. Philip's stay in England was not a happy one, and Mary died in 1558 to be succeeded by her half sister, Elizabeth. His ties with England broken, Philip returned to Spain via Flanders in 1559. In that year the peace treaty with France was signed. The temporary harmony between the two powers was symbolized by Philip's marriage with Elizabeth of Valois, the daughter of the king of France, who proved to be his favorite wife.

Philip had succeeded his father as king of Spain in 1556. Unlike Charles V, Philip was to be a "national" monarch instead of a ruler who traveled from one kingdom to another. Though he was to travel

widely throughout the Iberian Peninsula, he would never leave it again.

Personally, Philip was fair, spoke softly, and had an icy self-mastery; in the words of one of his ministers, he had a smile that cut like a sword. He immersed himself in an ocean of paperwork, studying dispatches and documents and adding marginal comments on them while scores of other documents and dispatches piled up on tables and in anterooms.

With the problems of communication in Philip's far-flung empire, once a decision was made it could not be undone. As king, he preferred to reserve all final decisions to himself; he mistrusted powerful and independent personalities and rarely reposed much confidence in aides. This personal stamp of authority during Philip's reign was in sharp contrast to the era of minister-favorites in 17th-century Spain. His private life included a delight in art, in the cultivation of flowers, in religious reading (his reign coincided with the great age of Spanish mysticism), and above all in the conception and building of the Escorial, the royal palace outside Madrid whose completion was perhaps the greatest joy of his life.

A combination palace, monastery, and mausoleum, the Escorial was Philip's preferred place for working. In a complex that included a place for his own tomb, naturally the thought of his successor concerned Philip greatly. His son Don Carlos was abnormal, mentally and physically, and on no account fit to become a responsible ruler. Philip was aware that contacts had been made between his son and political enemies. He had Don Carlos arrested, and what followed is one of the great historical enigmas: Don Carlos died on July 25, 1568, under mysterious circumstances that have never been explained satisfactorily. Did Philip have his son executed or did he die of natural causes? There is no persuasive proof on one side or the other. This incident was one of the most publicized in Philip's reign and one which naturally served to blacken his reputation. In any event, his fourth marriage, to Anne of Austria, produced five children, one of whom survived to succeed as Philip III.

Relations with Rome. During the Council of Trent (1545–1563) there was usually strong doctrinal accord between the papacy and Spanish bishops. The major difference lay in varying interpretations of the rights of Spanish bishops and their king vis-à-vis the Holy See. The King had almost total control over the Spanish Catholic Church, and although Spanish arms could advance Catholic interests, if Philip's Spain were to become supreme in Europe the Pope risked being reduced to a chaplain. One momentous occasion when they worked together came in the joint venture of Spain, the Vatican, and Venice against the Turkish navy. At Lepanto, in 1571, the Catholic forces devastated the enemy fleet. It was the most signal victory of Philip's career. Although the Turks soon rebounded, Philip was never again to ally himself so strongly with Rome. The relations between Spain and the Vatican illustrate how senseless it is to speak of the "monolithic nature" of Catholicism in this era.

Dutch Revolt. In an attempt to shore up his depleted treasury and instill more centralization into his dominions, Philip disregarded the prerogatives and local traditions in the Low Countries, the most prosperous of the territories under his rule. In the 1560s he sought to exact more taxes, to impose more bishops, and to reshuffle the administration, thus provoking an increasingly militant opposition.

Protestant attacks upon Catholic churches, coupled with increasing resistance from the predominantly Catholic population, were followed by a severe response from Spain. A Spanish army moved against the rebels, executed several of their leaders, and opened the way to a broader war which lasted throughout Philip's reign. It was truly a war for national independence, with brutality and heroism on both sides and a growing identification of Protestantism (especially Calvinism) with opposition to Spain's political, religious, and economic policies. The rebels, entrenched in the north, declared themselves independent under the name of the United Provinces. The southern part (roughly the area comprising Belgium) remained under Spanish control.

Since the Dutch were subsidized by the English, and since Spanish supply ships could not safely move through the English Channel, Philip concluded that a conquest of England was necessary for the pacification of the Netherlands. But at the same time that the Dutch were in revolt, there were repeated clashes between the French royal armies and French Calvinists. The ups and downs of the warfare in France and in the Netherlands were viewed as barometers of the fortunes of European Protestantism versus Catholicism. After Philip's death, a truce with the Dutch was arranged in 1609. Though war was to break out again, the independence of the United Provinces was recognized in 1648.

The Armada. The need to cut off English subsidies and control the English Channel so as to throttle the Dutch revolt led Philip to undertake the Armada, the most famous event of his reign. The plan was for a huge fleet to rendezvous with Spanish troops in the Netherlands and then proceed to the military conquest of England, serving Philip's military and political ends and immeasurably injuring the Protestant cause. The skill of the English navy and adverse weather conditions led to a total fiasco. Though most of his ships eventually returned home to port and though Philip still dreamed of a future campaign, the expense of the expedition and the psychological shock of failure resulted in the "invincible" Armada's becoming the symbol of Philip's failure to achieve a Spanish predominance in Europe.

French Relations. As Philip sought to put down the rebellion in the Netherlands, he fomented dissension in France. French Protestants were sometimes subsidized by Spanish agents to ensure confusion in the enemy camp. Philip tried (unsuccessfully) to install his own candidate on the French throne, and Spanish troops became embroiled in the French wars. The struggle with France drew Spanish strength away from the Netherlands and so eased the pressure on the Dutch rebels. Peace was reached at the Treaty of Vervins in 1598, several months before Philip's death.

Domestic Affairs. The complexity and extent of these foreign ventures had, of course, a tremendous impact on the economy and life of Spain. There was a constant need for money and in a country where only careers in the Church and the army carried prestige and where commerce and manual labor in general were frowned upon, the already-staggering economy was crippled by a series of disasters. The costly adventures abroad were punctuated by abrasive relations between Philip and his Spanish domains over taxation and jurisdiction; a diminishing flow of silver from the American mines; a decreasing market for Spanish goods; a severe inflation; several declarations of government bankruptcy; and an agricultural crisis that sent thousands into the cities and left vast areas uncultivated. All these, together with plagues and the defeat of the Armada, were crushing blows—economically, socially, and psychologically.

Any one of these myriad problems and crises would have taxed the ingenuity of a government. Taken together and exacerbated by the strain of incessant warfare, they shook Spain to its roots. The union of Portugal to Spain in 1580 may have given Philip satisfaction but hardly lightened his burdens. He worked methodically, even fatalistically, puzzled by the workings of a God who would permit such calamities to occur. Spain had already entered into a period of sharp decline at his death on Sept. 13, 1598, at El Escorial.

EWB

275

Philip IV (1605–1665), king of Spain from 1621 to 1665. During Philip IV's reign Spain was engaged in foreign wars and torn by internal revolt.

Born on April 8, 1605, Philip IV succeeded his father, Philip III, in 1621. He was more intelligent than his father but like him allowed his government to be run by minister-favorites. Philip's principal minister, Gaspar de Guzmán, Count of Olivares, dominated his councils and was the effective ruler of Spain for more than 20 years. In 1627 the ruinous expenses of Spain's involvement in the Thirty Years War forced the government to declare itself bankrupt; the war effort continued, however, and the Mantuan campaign (1628–1631) led to an open conflict with France, which became intensified in 1635.

Spanish troops at first came close to Paris, but the situation rapidly deteriorated. Olivares's desperate attempts to raise funds for the prosecution of the war provoked dissent and rebellion, and in 1640 Catalonia went into open revolt, murdered the king's agent there, and welcomed French aid in its struggle against the government of Castile. Soon afterward, Portugal rebelled and declared itself independent from Spain. Olivares's counterpart in France, Cardinal Richelieu, supplied money to both Catalonia and Portugal as French troops occupied Catalonia.

In January 1643, after visiting the war front in Aragon, Philip dismissed Olivares and declared that he would rule without a favorite. However, he soon employed one in the person of Don Luis de Haro, a nephew of Olivares. On May 19, 1643, the Spanish infantry was vanquished by the French at Rocroi. Since the beginning of the 16th century, the Spanish infantry had been regarded as the best in Europe; its defeat symbolized the downfall of Spain as a military power.

A dreary succession of setbacks marked the second half of Philip's reign. Another bankruptcy was declared in 1647, and in the same year unsuccessful revolts against Spanish rule erupted in Sicily and Naples. These events convinced Richelieu and his successor, Cardinal Mazarin, that, by pursuing an all-out war against Spain, France could gain considerable land and power in the European theater. Thus the war between the two countries continued after the Peace of Westphalia (by which Spain officially recognized the independence of the United Provinces) had concluded the Thirty Years War in 1648. Although civil war in France (the Fronde) gave the Spanish some slight respite, it could not stave off the inevitable. For although Catalonia was won back in 1652, bankruptcy was again declared in 1653.

The union of Cromwell's England with France in the war against Spain proved to be the coup de grace. Spain lost both Dunkerque and Jamaica to the English. In the Peace of the Pyrenees, concluded with France in 1659, Spain gave up Artois and territories in the Spanish Netherlands, together with Rosellón and part of Cerdaña. As part of the "peace package," a marriage was arranged between Philip IV's daughter, Maria Theresa, and the young Louis XIV. The waiver of the Infanta's inheritance rights to Spanish territory was contingent on the payment of a dowry of 500,000 escudos, which the French as well as the Spanish knew could never be paid. After Philip's death this clause was used as a pretext for the seizure of still more Spanish territory in the Low Countries during the War of Devolution.

Philip IV died on Sept. 17, 1665, just before Portugal's independence was recognized. In the course of his reign he had married twice. His first wife, Elizabeth of Bourbon, died in 1644; their only child died 2 years later. His second wife, Maria Anna of Austria, gave birth to one son who survived, the hapless Charles II, who was destined to be the last Hapsburg monarch of Spain.

EWB

Pico della Mirandola, Giovanni (1463–1494), Italian philosopher and humanist. Giovanni Pico della Mirandola was a brilliant exemplar of the Renaissance ideal of man.

The youngest son of a princely Lombard house, Giovanni Pico della Mirandola received a Church benefice when he was 10 years old. However, Pico quickly surpassed the routine expectation of a career in Church or state. At the University of Padua from 1480 to 1482, when the city and its university enjoyed the liberal patronage of Venice, welcomed Eastern scholars, and offered one of Europe's richest civic cultures, he studied Aristotelianism and Hebrew and Arabic religion, philosophy, and science. By 1487 his travels and education, broadened to include Florence and Paris, had steeped Pico in a unique variety of languages and traditions. Committed to no exclusive source of wisdom and disappointed by the philosophic weakness of the Italian humanists' study of classical culture, he sought a core of truth common to this vast knowledge.

The young man's first and most famous venture was a challenge to Europe's scholars for public disputation at Rome in 1487. Pico prepared to defend 900 *conclusiones*—402 drawn from other philosophers (most heavily from scholastic, Platonic, and Arabic thinkers) and 498 his own. However, a papal commission, suspicious of such diversity, condemned 13 of Pico's theses. The assembly was canceled, and he fled to Paris, suffering brief imprisonment before settling in Florence late in 1487. His writings for the disputation were banned until 1493.

At Florence, Pico joined Lorenzo de' Medici's Platonic Academy in its effort to formulate a doctrine of the soul that would reconcile Platonic and Christian beliefs. Pico's ambition, which many critics attribute to youthful confusion, can be measured by his plan to harmonize Plato and Aristotle and to link their philosophies with revelations proclaimed by the major religions. Preparatory treatises included the *Heptaplus* of 1489, a commentary on Genesis stressing its correspondence with sacred Jewish texts, and the work *De ente et uno* of 1492, on the nature of God and creation.

Pico gradually renounced Medicean splendor, embraced the piety of the reforming friar Girolamo Savonarola, and began writing in defense of the Church. Pico's philanthropy kept pace with his purchase of manuscripts, as he built one of Europe's great private scholarly collections. He died of fever on Nov. 17, 1494, as French soldiers occupied Florence.

Described as being "of feature and shape seemly and beauteous," Pico combined physique, intellect, and spirituality in a way that captivated both the lovers of *virtù* and Christian reformers. In his *De hominis dignitate,* written to introduce his abortive Roman congress, Pico had God endow Adam with "what abode, what form, and what functions thou thyself shalt desire . . . so that with freedom of choice and with honor, thou mayest fashion thyself." This early tract asserted the philosophy that Pico's later and more complex works stressed: the active intellect can discern right from wrong, truth from illusion, and is free to guide the soul, indeed to bind all men, to union with a common creator. Pico's late work *Disputationes in astrologiam,* an unfinished attack on astrology, rejected occult thought which subordinated human will to deterministic forces.

EWB

Pisan, Christine de   (ca. 1364–ca. 1430), French author. Christine de Pisan wrote lyric poetry and also prose and verse works on a great variety of philosophical, social, and historical subjects.

Thomas de Pisan, father of Christine de Pisan, was an astrologer and medical doctor in the service of the republic of Venice when he accepted a similar appointment at the court of Charles V of France. Born in Venice, Christine was taken to Paris in 1368, where she was brought up in courtly surroundings and enjoyed a comfortable and studious childhood and adolescence. At 15 she married Étienne de Castel. In 1380 Charles V died, thereby dissolving the royal appointment of her father, who died 5 years later. Chris-

tine's husband, secretary of Charles VI, died in 1390, leaving her a widow at 25, with three children, considerable debts, and impatient creditors. Two years later Charles VI became insane, leaving the nation open prey.

Impoverished by multiple blows of adversity, Christine determined to earn her living by writing, composing her first ballades in 1393. Her works were successful, and richly illuminated copies of some of them were presented to noted patrons of letters. Thirty major titles followed until she retired to the convent at Poissy, where her only daughter had been a religious for 22 years. She wrote no more except one religious work and a eulogy on Joan of Arc after the victory at Orléans.

In verse, Christine's first work appears to be her *Hundred Ballades,* followed by 26 virelays, 2 lays, 69 rondeaux, 70 framed poems, 66 more ballades, and 2 complaints. In her *Epistle to the God of Love* (1399) she begins her battle for feminism, reproaching Ovid and Jean de Meun for their misogyny; a second attack appears in her *Tale of the Rose* (1402). Of her 15 other long poems the best is the *Changes of Fortune* (1403), in the 23,636 lines of which she traces changing "fortune" from the time of the Jews down to her own time.

In prose, after her allegorical *Epistle from Othea* (1400), Christine vigorously continues her feminism in the *City of Ladies* and the *Book of the Three Virtues* (both 1405). Other works in prose include the *Deeds and Good Morals of Wise King Charles V* (1404), a book on arms and knighthood (1410), and the *Book of Peace* (1414), which holds up Charles V as a model for the Dauphin. Her *Hours of Contemplation on the Passion,* containing lessons on patience and humility, was written during her last retreat.

EWB

Pius V   (1504–1572), was pope from 1566 to 1572. An austere man, Pius V put the decrees of the Council of Trent into effect and thus occupies a central position in the Catholic Reformation.

Antonio Ghislieri, who became Pius V, was born on Jan. 17, 1504, at Bosco Marengo near Alessandria in northern Italy. He was from a poor family. At 14 years of age Ghislieri entered the Order of Preachers and took the name Michele. He received his higher education as a friar at Bologna. In 1528 he was ordained at Genoa.

For more than 20 years Ghislieri gained a wide breadth of experience as professor of theology, superior in his order, and member of the Inquisition in Pavia, Como, and Bergamo. His dedication to the work of the Inquisition brought him to the attention of officials in Rome, including Giampietro Carafa, the future Pope Paul IV. In 1551 Pope Julius III appointed Ghislieri commissary general of the Roman Inquisition. Under Paul IV, Ghislieri was given greater responsibilities: in 1556 the bishopric of Sutri and Nepi, in 1557 the cardinalate, and in 1558 the post of grand inquisitor of the Roman Church. Pope Pius IV assigned him to the see of Mondovi in 1560. On Jan. 7, 1566, Ghislieri was elected pope and took the name Pius V.

Pius V had a twofold preoccupation: the preservation of the purity of the faith and the advancement of Church reform. He used the Inquisition, although more moderately than Paul IV; severely punished bishops who remained absent from their sees; examined the spiritual tenor of religious orders; implemented the decrees of the Council of Trent; and simplified to the point of austerity the style of life of the papal household. In 1566 Pius V issued the Roman Catechism.

Pius V influenced the liturgical life of the Church in a monumental way. In 1568 he issued the *Breviarium Romanum* and in 1570 the *Missale Romanum,* thereby removing the multiplicity of forms in the breviary and in the Mass and creating, with minor exceptions, a liturgical uniformity throughout the Church. In 1567 he made the greatest theologian of his order, St. Thomas Aquinas, a Doctor of the Church.

In his foreign policies Pius V experienced both failure and success. Misjudging the situation in England, he seriously blundered in 1570, when he announced that English Catholics no longer owed allegiance to Queen Elizabeth. His action worsened the situation of England's persecuted Catholics. Against the Turks he was successful. He built up the Holy League and on Oct. 7, 1571, a fleet of Spanish, Venetian, and papal ships defeated the Turkish fleet at Lepanto in the Gulf of Corinth. Pius V died on May 1, 1572. He was canonized in 1712 by the Church.

EWB

Pius IX (1792–1878), was pope from 1846 to 1878. Pius IX began his reign devoted to liberal ideals but, embittered by the anticlericalism of Italian liberals and by the assault on papal territories by the new kingdom of Italy, became an important foe of progress and change.

Pius IX was born Giovanni Maria Mastai-Ferretti on May 13, 1792, at Senigallia, Italy. He became archbishop of Spoleto in 1827 and bishop of Imola in 1832. He was already recognized as a liberal when he was created a cardinal in 1840. On the death of Gregory XVI a conclave divided between progressive and conservative prelates chose, on June 16, 1846,

Mastai-Ferretti as pope in preference to the reactionary Luigi Lambruschini.

The new pope began his pontificate—the longest in history—by initiating badly needed reforms. Improvements in financial administration and in the treatment of criminals in the Papal States were followed by an easing of the censorship. The political innovations of 1847 decreed that only the secretary of state had to be a priest and that the council of advisers to the pope and his ministers would be elected officials. A municipal government was established for Rome, part of which was made up of elected representatives. While presiding over these specific liberal changes in his own territories, Pius IX lent encouragement to Italian nationalism.

But that he was always a reformer and never a revolutionary Pius IX quickly proved after the revolutions of 1848. His enforced departure from Rome to Gaeta and the establishment of a Roman Republic cooled his ardor for Italian nationalism. Devoted first and always to the welfare of the Church, he had been willing to support the introduction into it of democratic elements, but he would never agree to the loss of the Pope's temporal power.

When the movement for Italian unity broke out into war in 1859, Pius IV attempted to remain neutral, but he could not keep the papal territories from being dismembered. His refusal to yield any part of these dominions in negotiations with the victorious Piedmontese caused him to lose them all. On Sept. 18, 1860, the Papal States were overrun, and only the presence of French troops protected Rome. The liberal kingdom of Italy was established, and to his dying breath Pius IX remained its bitterest enemy.

As long as the French garrisoned Rome, Pius IX was able to hold his capital, and from it he fired all the spiritual weapons in his arsenal. The famous *Syllabus of Errors* of 1864, a list of erroneous modernistic statements, specifically repudiated the notion that the Pope would ever ally himself with progress or modern civilization. The Vatican Council on July 18, 1870, made the ancient doctrine of papal infallibility into a dogma of the Church. Pius IX had made it his unremitting task to reimpose on the faithful the Ultramontane authority of the medieval Church.

The French withdrew their troops from Rome in 1870 upon the outbreak of the Franco-Prussian War. Italian soldiers took the city on September 20 of that year, and in October a plebiscite was held in which an overwhelming majority voted to make Rome a part of the Italian kingdom. Pius IX spent the rest of his life in the Vatican. He refused to negotiate with the new kingdom, whose Parliament unilaterally declared that the Pope still retained his sovereignty and absolute control over the Vatican. He could conduct diplomatic relations with other states and was compensated for the loss of his territories. These arrangements did not placate him, and he died unreconciled on Feb. 7, 1878.

EWB

Pius XII (1876–1958), was Pope from 1939 to 1958. Pius XII guided the Roman Catholic Church through the difficult years of World War II and the postwar period, when much of the eastern Catholic Church was heavily persecuted by Soviet communism.

Pius XII was born Eugenio Maria Giuseppe Pacelli in Rome on March 2, 1876. Because of poor health he was allowed to study for the priesthood at his home. Ordained a priest in 1899, he took up work in the Vatican Secretariat of State in 1901, working there until 1917. In that year he became archbishop of Sardis and was sent to Munich as apostolic nuncio to Bavaria. In 1918 he became nuncio in Berlin to the new Weimar Republic. During his German years Pacelli acquired a love of the German people and a knowledge of German affairs. He was a close observer and on a few occasions an eyewitness of Bolshevik riots in Germany, which developed a strong fear in him that Soviet Marxism was the prime enemy of Christendom. This fear, together with his love of Germany, influenced his judgments during World War II. Pius XI recalled Pacelli to Rome in 1929 and named him a cardinal. In 1930 he became secretary of state, remaining at this post until his election as pope on March 2, 1939.

Pius XII's main determination, upon the outbreak of World War II in September 1939, was to preserve cordial relations with all belligerents. He had concluded from his years in Germany that the Vatican should engage in the role of international peacemaker. He therefore refused, in spite of Anglo-American pressures, clearly to declare against the Axis Powers or publicly to describe the German invasion of Soviet Russia as a crusade against communism, as the Axis Powers wished him to do. His attempted neutrality in word and action led Pius XII into an extreme form of abstention from all effective moral protest in the war. He consequently did not intervene to denounce or to halt the Nazi campaign against the Jews or the genocidal acts of the Hitler regime.

This lack of action brought much public criticism of Pius after the war. The Pope, it was argued, had a moral obligation to speak out specifically against all and every kind of injustice. In his defense, it has been alleged—accurately—that any such denunciation might have brought the full wrath of Hitler upon the Church in all the occupied countries as well as in Germany. Privately, Pius organized shelters and other places of refuge for Jews. He also organized the highly effective Work of St. Raphael, which aided in locating and resettling war refugees. The Vatican itself and many Vatican buildings were used, with Pius's tacit approval, for sheltering war refugees, downed pilots, and Allied military personnel.

Toward the end of the war, when Communist partisans appeared in northern Italy, Pius XII communicated his fears to President Franklin Roosevelt of the United States, and in postwar Italy Pius organized Catholic Action groups, which played a great part in bringing the Christian Democrats to power in 1948, thus keeping Italy within the western orbit. Pius continued to battle against Italian communism to the end of his life, issuing a formal excommunication decree against all Catholics who joined the Communist party. At the end of Pius XII's reign, the status of the Church was high on the international scene; his popularity had waned among the intellectuals of the Church; and Pius had placed the Vatican in intransigent positions regarding both non-Catholics and non-Christians.

Role in the Church. Within the Roman Church, Pius XII exercised an authoritarian influence on all developments. In spite of his dogmatic intransigence regarding the ecumenical movement and his refusal to meet with leaders of Eastern Orthodox churches, many of Pius's provisions and reforms laid the ground for the more radical reforms achieved by the Second Vatican Council (called by his successor, John XXIII) and for the participation of Roman Catholics in the ecumenical movement. Pius introduced evening Mass, relaxed the laws on fasting, encouraged the indigenous hierarchies of Africa and Asia, permitted the use of the vernacular in certain Church ceremonies, and reformed the ancient liturgy of the Easter celebration. In doctrine and in theology, Pius was extremely conservative and fomented in the Roman government of the Church a repressive and reactionary spirit. The various offices and ministries of the Vatican, under his rule, exercised great control over the teachings and writings of Roman Catholic scholars and thinkers. This state of affairs provoked the counterreactions characteristic of John XXIII's reign and facilitated the work of the Second Vatican Ecumenical Council.

Pius ruled autocratically, imposed his views, and expected exact obedience from all. But not all of his directives concerning the teaching of the Church on dogmatic matters were repressive in their final effect. His *Divino afflante Spiritu* (1943) gave fresh life to Roman Catholic biblical studies by admitting that the

Bible as a book had been influenced in its literary forms by the cultures in which its various parts had been composed. His *Humani generis* (1950), although repressive in many ways, did not completely block all scientific inquiry into the natural truths underlying the facts of religion and religious territory.

Pius XII was the first pope to make use of the radio on an extensive scale. Indeed, he took every suitable occasion to address both Catholics and non-Catholics on a variety of subjects. During his pontificate the prestige of the Church rose enormously, and his presence in Rome attracted more pilgrims and visitors from varying faiths and countries than ever before in the history of the Vatican. Pius XII died at Castel Gandolfo, the summer residence of the popes, on Oct. 9, 1958.

EWB

Pizarro, Francisco (ca. 1474–1541), Spanish conquistador. Atahualpa, Pizarro was the obscure adventurer and ruffian who discovered and overthrew the Inca empire of Peru. Assassin of the Inca Atahualpa, Pizarro was assassinated in turn by his own countrymen.

Francisco Pizarro was born at Trujillo in Estremadura. The illegitimate son of a poor *hidalgo* (small landholder of the petty nobility), he never learned to read and may have earned his keep herding his father's swine. This allegation is often cited by Pizarro's detractors in terms of a comparison with Herná Cortés the better-born conqueror of Mexico. But the destruction wreaked by Cortés upon Aztec civilization was no less far-reaching than Pizarro's impact upon the society of Peru.

Pizarro left Spain for the New World in the wake of the early discoveries. He joined Alonso de Ojeda on the latter's disastrous expedition to Colombia and subsequently accompanied Vasco Núñez de Balboa on his march to the South Sea (Pacific Ocean). It was Pizarro who later arrested the condemned Balboa on orders from the great explorer's rival, Pedrarias de Ávila. He then settled down as an *encomendero* (lord of Indian serfs) in Panama.

Yet Pizarro remained a conquistador without a conquest. Emboldened by tales of fabulous kingdoms to the south, he went into partnership with another adventurer, Diego de Almagro, and a priest, Luque. This combination financed and led several voyages of reconnaissance. Pizarro then journeyed to Spain, where the Emperor commissioned him to undertake the southern conquest and to establish a province of New Castile. So empowered, he returned to the New World, accompanied by his half brothers Gonzalo, Hernando, and Juan Pizarro, his cousin Pedro Pizarro,

and Martin de Alcántara. At the end of 1530 Pizarro set sail with 180 men for Peru.

Conquest of Peru. Pizarro arrived at a time most favorable for his designs. Atahualpa, brother of the Inca Huáscar, had usurped the throne and moved the seat of government from the traditional Andean stronghold of Cuzco to Cajamarca in the north. It was on the northern coast, at Tumbes, that Pizarro's forces landed; and after consolidating his position, the conqueror marched on the new capital in 1532. Tricked into capture under cover of false negotiations, Atahualpa sought to buy his freedom with his gold. The loot delivered, the monarch was slain. Meanwhile, reinforced by troops under Almagro, the Spanish had captured and sacked Cuzco itself. In 1535 Pizarro founded his own capital of Lima near the coast, thus originating the troublesome later-day distinction between the Indian society of the mountains and the Hispanicized civilization of the seaboard.

The Spanish conquest has shed some of its glamour in the light of modern research. Peruvians under Manco Capac, successor to the deposed Huáscar, held out against the Spanish for 40 years more; Indian revolts recurred for another 200. The question persists: why was this great civilization mortally wounded, if not instantly overthrown, by the Estremaduran adventurer? The immediate answer lies in the outbreak of civil war within the Peruvian ruling class, a division which gave Pizarro his opportunity. Atahualpa's rivals rejoiced in his downfall, just as enemies of the Aztecs had at first welcomed and abetted the invasion of Cortés. Yet the explanation for the Spanish success must be sought deeper in the structure of society, where it can be grasped in the relation between the social divisions within these native American empires and the level of technology.

Like the leaders of the splendid civilizations of the ancient Near East, the priestly and military ruling classes of the Incas and Aztecs employed the surplus appropriated from producers to subsidize irrigation and flood-control projects, to build large cities and road networks, and to underwrite the production of craftsmen-artists. But unlike the agrarian producers of those earlier civilizations, the peasants lacked suitable draft animals, wheeled vehicles, and plows. Under these conditions the productivity of labor was extremely low, and it required a stern labor discipline, upheld by a powerful religiopolitical orthodoxy, to extract a level of surplus product sufficient to the requirements of the ruling classes. Divided among themselves, such rulers were further weakened by the hostility of subject peoples and the passivity of agrarian producers. Faced with a determined neo-feudal enemy skilled in the art of conquest from the center outward, they were less able to mobilize resistance, and to sustain it, than the primitive peoples of the north, the far south, and the east. In the final analysis, writes a historian of European expansion, J. H. Parry, these civilizations' "combination of wealth and technical weakness was their undoing."

His Death. Cortés had been able to overcome immediate challenges from Spanish competitors; Pizarro was not so fortunate. Tensions between original invaders and latecomers divided the conquistadors into two parties, respectively led by Pizarro and his sometime associate Almagro. The situation was only briefly eased by an Almagro expedition to Chile. Upon his return he seized Cuzco and confronted the Pizarros in the Las Salinas War. Captured by Hernando Pizarro in 1538, Almagro was executed; but his shade haunted Francisco until his own murder in Lima (June 26, 1541) by members of the defeated faction. Civil war persisted until 1548, when the Spanish government finally asserted its authority over the new colony. Of the band of marauding brothers, only Hernando survived the Pizarro "victory" over the Incan empire.

EWB

Plumb, J. H. (1911–), British historian. Though an historian by profession, J. H. Plumb nevertheless holds the rather unusual notion that history, or as he prefers to call it, The Past, deserves to be put to rest once and for all. In his book on the subject, *The Death of the Past*, Plumb argues that not only has technological innovation diminished the past's ability to provide guidance to modern industrial societies, but, more significantly, that people have always tended to rewrite the past to suit their own ends—be it a priest who seeks to confirm a particular religious belief, a king who needs to justify his rule, or a mere "commoner" who wants to add a few illustrious members to an otherwise undistinguished family tree. This "created ideology with a purpose," as the author defines conventional history, is what has made freedom and economic prosperity such rare commodities, for those in power have always manipulated the past at the expense of the "little guy."

Of course, Plumb does not advocate doing away with history and historians altogether. According to William Appleman Williams of the *Nation*, Plumb believes the modern historian should attempt to "defuse" the power of the past "by removing the ideology of the historian and thereby transform what has been an instrument of social control into a tool of human improvement." In order to "cleanse the story of man-

kind," as Plumb himself states, the historian must "try and understand what happened, purely in its own terms. . . . [He must] see things as they really were, and from this study. . . . attempt to formulate processes of social change which are acceptable on historical grounds and none other." But the ideal historian has to do more than just uncover and explain historical events; Williams reports that Plumb also expects him to make "positive statements about human life" while developing "principles about social living" with the ultimate goal of demonstrating that "the condition of mankind has improved" throughout history.

Few observers criticize the spirit behind such a cause, but most doubt that what Plumb proposes is possible. Though a *Times Literary Supplement* critic, for example, calls *The Death of the Past* a "stimulating, courageous, and frequently learned book" which "deserves to be pondered by all who teach or value history," William H. McNeill, himself a historian, comments in the *Saturday Review* that the distinction Plumb makes between "history" (what *really* happened) and "The Past" (what the chroniclers *say* happened) "strikes me as completely false. What Professor Plumb hails as a new genus, history, is merely the onset of a climate of opinion in which he feels at home. Older uses of the past he analyzes, often wittily and well, as self-serving, erroneous, naive. . . . [But Plumb's] view of man's past . . . seems quite as self-serving. . . . To claim that modern historians have a unique talisman that allows us to know things as they really were—apart, apparently, from the questions we ask and the conceptions we bring to the past—obscures rather than clarifies the real, indisputable advances that have occurred and are occurring in our understanding of mankind's history.

This little book . . . is briskly written, and abounds in arresting turns of phrase. But Plumb's brilliant style cannot really salvage a faulty idea."

The *New Statesman* reviewer agrees, remarking that "there is not much one can do with [such] a confession of faith except sign it, and with a good deal of mental reservation I should be prepared to sign this one. . . . [But] I have the impression that Plumb is skating on pretty thin ice." The *Nation's* Williams also sees "much truth in [Plumb's] analysis" but ultimately decides that following his advice "is to start down a path that will change the historian into a kind of superheated lay minister. At best, and by Plumb's own formulation, the historian becomes an advocate who offers one general answer to the questions he has raised. Plumb is trying to keep the crown on Clio's head even as he tells us that the old regime has collapsed."

Melvin Maddocks of the *Christian Science Monitor*, responding to Plumb's question, "Can man face the future with hope and with resolution without a sense of the past?," concludes that this "is not the final question. The final question must go beyond the morale problem to ask: Can man even function without a sense of the past? . . . Are not the very standards by which historians think bound to be a conscious and subconscious heritage of the past? . . . The Futurist is born with a love of the vacuum. He longs for a brave, new, empty world. What he hates most is the sight of footprints in the sand. But the question-to-end-all-questions he may have to ask himself is: Would I want to live in the kind of world where footprints were not at least a possibility?"

CA

Pobedonostsev, Konstantin Petrovich (1827–1907), Russian statesman and jurist.

As director general of the Holy Synod, Konstantin Pobedonostsev became a champion of tsarist autocracy, orthodoxy, and Russian nationalism.

Konstantin Pobedonostsev was born on May 21, 1827, in Moscow. His father, Peter V. Pobedonostsev, a professor at the University of Moscow, educated Konstantin at home until he enrolled at the St. Petersburg School of Jurisprudence in 1841. From his father, he learned to read Old Church Slavonic, French, Latin, and German. He also studied the Bible, the writings of the Russian Orthodox Church Fathers, Greek and Roman classics, Russian history, and Russian literature. He graduated from the School of Jurisprudence with a wide knowledge of Western judicial institutions, laws, and literatures.

Pobedonostsev first won acclaim as a historian of Russian judicial institutions and as a specialist in Russian civil law. In 1846 Pobedonostsev was assigned to the eighth department of the Senate in Moscow. In 1853 he became secretary of the seventh department. In 1859 he was named lecturer in Russian civil law at Moscow University

In 1861 Pobedonostsev was appointed tutor in Russian history and law to the heir to the throne, the future Alexander III, and was named executive secretary of the Senate. He moved to St. Petersburg into a life of great influence in the central governmental bureaucracy and the court. He employed his tutorial position to mold the views of the imperial heir. Pobedonostsev emphasized the ties between Russian Orthodoxy and Russian national history. By the late 1870s his influence on Alexander had become overwhelming.

In 1872 Pobedonostsev became a member of the State Council, a body that advised the Tsar concerning projected laws. Most of the significant legis-lation and decrees of the 19th century received their final review and drafting in this Council. Pobedonostsev's main responsibility as a Council member was civil and ecclesiastical matters. His work in the Council contributed to his appointment in 1880 as director general of the Holy Synod of the Russian Orthodox Church. For the remainder of his life he was a member of both the Council and the Senate. His service in the highest organs of the tsarist government naturally gave him power in shaping Russia's domestic policies.

Pobedonostsev's reputation in Russian history rests largely upon his accomplishments as director general of the Holy Synod. For 25 years his influence on the religious and political life of Russia was enormous as a result of his official positions and his relations with the czars, their wives, the imperial family, and the court.

In 1881 Pobedonostsev advised Alexander III concerning the selection of his ministers, most of whom were named upon his recommendation. The Tsar consented to Pobedonostsev's policy of the Russification of minority groups, particularly Jews and dissenters. As director general, Pobedonostsev attempted to restrict the number and the rights of other religious groups in Russia. Under his influence Alexander III opposed any limitation of his autocratic powers, tightened censorship, tried to suppress all opposition opinion, and persecuted religious nonconformists.

Pobedonostsev also tutored the future Nicholas II and was one of his most influential advisers until the Revolution of 1905. In his writing Pobedonostsev strongly attacked Western rationalism and liberalism. He died in St. Petersburg on March 23, 1907.

EWB

Pope, Alexander (1688–1744), English poet and satirist.

Alexander Pope was the greatest poet and verse satirist of the Augustan period. No other poet in the history of English literature has handled the heroic couplet with comparable flexibility and brilliance.

Alexander Pope inherited from John Dryden the verse from that he chose to perfect. He polished his work with meticulous care and, like all great poets, used language with genuine inventiveness. His qualities of imagination are seen in the originality with which he handled traditional forms, in his satiric vision of the contemporary world, and in his inspired use of classical models.

Pope was born on May 21, 1688, in London, where his Roman Catholic father was a linen merchant. After the Glorious Revolution of 1688 his family moved out of London and settled about 1700 at Binfield in Windsor Forest. Pope had little formal schooling, largely educating himself through extensive reading. Sir William Trumbull, a retired statesman of literary interests who lived nearby, did much to encourage the young poet. So did the dramatist and poet William Wycherley and the poet-critic William Walsh, with whom Pope became acquainted when he was about 17 and whose advice to aim at "correctness" contributed to the flawless texture and concentrated brilliance of Pope's verse.

A sweet-tempered child with a fresh, plump face, Pope contracted a tubercular infection in his later childhood and never grew taller than 4 feet 6 inches. He suffered curvature of the spine (necessitating the wearing of a stiff canvas brace) and constant headaches. His features, however, were striking, and the young Joshua Reynolds noticed in his "sharp, keen countenance . . . something grand, like Cicero's." His physical appearance, frequently ridiculed by his enemies, undoubtedly gave an edge to Pope's satire; but he was always warmhearted and generous in his affection for his many friends.

Early Poems. Precocious as a poet, Pope attracted the notice of the eminent bookseller Jacob Tonson, who solicited the publication of his *Pastorals* (1709). By this time Pope was already at work on his more ambitious *Essay on Criticism* (1711), an illuminating synthesis of critical precepts designed to expose the evils and to effect a regeneration of the contemporary literary scene.

The *Rape of the Lock* (1712, two cantos) immediately made Pope famous as a poet. The cutting off of a lock of Miss Arabella Fermor's hair by Robert, Lord Petre, had caused an estrangement between these prominent Catholic families; and Pope's friend John Caryll had suggested that he write a poem "to make a jest of it, and laugh them together again." In the poem Fermor is represented as Belinda and Lord Petre as the Baron. Adopting a mock-heroic style in the manner of Nicholas Boileau's *Le Lutrin,* Pope showed how disproportionate it was to treat the event overseriously, at the same time glancing good-humoredly at vanity and at the rococo-like glitter of the *beau monde.* Rejecting Joseph Addison's advice not to enlarge his design, Pope published an extended version (1714, five cantos) containing the "machinery" of the sylphs (adopted from the Rosicrucian system) and various other epic motifs and allusions. These not only heightened the brilliance of the poem's world but also helped to place its significance and that of the "rape" in proper perspective.

Several other poems published by 1717, the date of the first collected edition of Pope's works, deserve a brief mention. "Windsor Forest" (1713), written in the tradition of Sir John Denham's "Cooper's Hill," celebrated the peace confirmed by the Treaty of Utrecht. A rich tapestry of historical and poetic allusions, it showed the Stuarts, and especially Queen Anne, in a quasi-mythical light. In 1717 appeared the sophisticated yet moving "Elegy to the Memory of an Unfortunate Lady" and "Eloisa to Abelard," an example in the Ovidian manner of the currently popular form of heroic epistle. The representation of the cloistered Eloisa's conflicting emotions toward her former lover (the scholar Peter Abelard), the denouement, and the concluding epilogue make this poem, in effect, a drama in miniature.

Translations of Homer. Pope also engaged in poetic imitations and translations. His *Messiah* (1712), published by Sir Richard Steele in the *Spectator,* was an imitation of Virgil's fourth Eclogue, based on passages from Isaiah; and his early "translations" of Chaucer included the *Temple of Fame* (1715). In later life Pope published reworkings of several of John Donne's satires. But Pope's versions of Homer were his greatest achievement as a translator.

From an early age a frequenter of Will's Coffeehouse, Pope was for a time friendly with men of both political parties. He wrote the prologue for Joseph Addison's Cato (1713), and the Whigs naturally hoped to secure his talents for their party. But growing opposition between him and Addison's followers (who met at Button's) made inevitable Pope's adherence to his other and more congenial group of literary friends— Jonathan Swift, Dr. John Arbuthnot, John Gay, and Thomas Parnell. Together they combined to form the Scriblerus Club, which aimed at a burlesque treatment of all forms of pedantry and which indirectly contributed to the creation of such works as *Gulliver's Travels* and the *Dunciad.* In 1715 Addison tried to forestall the success of Pope's translation of the *Iliad* by encouraging Thomas Tickell to publish a rival version, and this caused Pope a great deal of anxiety until the superiority of his own translation was acclaimed.

Pope undertook the translation because he needed money—the result of a sharp drop in the interest from his father's French annuities. The translation occupied him until 1720, and it was a great financial success, making Pope independent of the customary forms of literary patronage. Parnell and William Broome were among those who assisted with the notes, but the translation was entirely Pope's own. It has been highly praised by subsequent critics.

From the time his *Iliad* began to appear, Pope became the victim of numerous pamphlet attacks on his person, politics, and religion, many of them instigated by the infamous publisher Edmund Curll. In 1716 an increased land tax on Roman Catholics forced the Popes to sell their place at Binfield and to settle near the Earl of Burlington's villa at Chiswick. The next year Pope's father died, and in 1719 the poet's increased wealth enabled him to move with his mother to a semirural villa at Twickenham. There he improved house and gardens, making a special feature of the grotto, which connected house and gardens beneath the intervening road. At Twickenham, Lady Mary Wortley Montagu soon became Pope's neighbor. Several years earlier she had rivaled Martha Blount as an object of Pope's affection, but later a good deal of enmity existed between her and Pope, and she joined Lord (John) Hervey in attacking him.

During the 1720s Pope was engaged on a version of the *Odyssey* (1725–1726). Broome and Elijah Fenton were his collaborators, completing half of the translation between them. It was Pope's name, however, that sold the work, and he naturally received the lion's share of the profits (Pope earned about £9,000 from his translations of Homer). It was this translation that led to Pope's association with the young Joseph Spence, who wrote a judicious and engaging criticism of it and who later recorded his valuable *Anecdotes* of Pope.

Editorial Work. Pope also undertook several editorial projects. Parnell's *Poems* (1721) was followed by an edition of the late Duke of Buckingham's *Works* (1723), subsequently suppressed on account of its Jacobite tendencies. The trial of his friend Francis Atterbury, Bishop of Rochester, for complicity in a Jacobite plot also caused Pope a good deal of concern. Then, in 1725, Pope's edition of William Shakespeare appeared. Pope's emendations and explanatory notes were notoriously capricious, and his edition was attacked by Lewis Theobald in *Shakespeare Restored* (1726), a work that revealed a superior knowledge of editorial technique and that gained for its author the unenviable distinction of becoming the original hero of the *Dunciad*.

The *Dunciad*. In 1726–1727 Swift was in England and a guest of Pope. Together they published three volumes of *Miscellanies* in 1727–1728, in the last of which the *Peri Bathous; or the Art of Sinking in Poetry* was included. Renewed contact with Swift must have given a great impetus to Pope's poem on "Dulness," which appeared as the three-book *Dunciad* (1728). Theobald was the prime dunce, and the next year the poem was enlarged by a ponderous apparatus (including "Notes Variorum") intended as a burlesque on the learned lumber of commentators and textual critics.

Clearly Pope used the *Dunciad* as personal satire to pay off many old scores. But it was also prompted by his distaste for that whole process by which worthless writers gained undue literary prominence. "Martinus Scriblerus" summarized the action of the poem as "the removal of the imperial seat of Dulness from the city to the polite world," and this parody of Virgil's epic was accompanied by further mock-heroic elementsthe intervention of the goddess, the epic games of the second book, and the visit to the underworld and the vision of future "glories," with the former city-poet Elkanah Settle acting the part of the sybil. Indeed, despite its devastating satire, the *Dunciad* was essentially a phantasmagoric treatment of the forces of anticulture by a great comic genius.

In 1742 Pope published a fourth book to the *Dunciad* separately, and his last published work was the four-book *Dunciad* (1743), which incorporated the new material and enthroned the brazen laureate Colley Cibber as prime dunce in place of Theobald. This revenge on Cibber, who had recently exposed a ridiculous escapade of the poet's youth, provided the poem with a more considerable hero. It also gained in artistic completeness, since the action of the fourth book depicted the fulfillment of Settle's prophecy.

Epistles and *An Essay on Man*. "The Epistle to Burlington" (1731), reminiscent of the *Dunciad* in its vivaciously satiric portrait of "Timon," was designed as part of a "system of ethics in the Horatian way" of which *An Essay on Man* (1733–1734) was to constitute the first book. Though this plan was never realized, the poem illustrates, along with its companion, "Epistle to Bathurst" (1733), antithetical vices in the use of riches. These two epistles were subsequently placed after those "To Cobham" (1734) and "To a Lady" (1735), which were thus intended to provide the projected *magnum opus* with an introductory section on the characters of men and women. "To Cobham" fits easily into this scheme, but "To a Lady" is rather a deliciously witty portrait gallery in Pope's best satiric manner.

"To Burlington" also compliments a nobleman friend of long standing who influenced Pope's appreciation of architecture as did Allen Bathurst his appreciation of landscape gardening. To these pursuits Pope devoted much of his time, being disposed to regard a cultivated esthetic taste as inseparable from a refined moral sense.

Pope's friendship with the former statesman Henry St. John Bolingbroke, who on his return from exile had settled a few miles from Twickenham, stimulated his interest in philosophy and led to the composition of *An Essay on Man*. Some ideas were doubtless suggested by Bolingbroke; certainly the argument advanced in Epistle 4—that terrestrial happiness is adequate to justify the ways of God to man—was consonant with his thinking. But Pope's sources were predominately commonplaces with a long history in Western thought, the most central being the doctrine of plenitude (expressed through the metaphors of a "chain" or "scale" of being) and the assertion that the discordant whole is bound harmoniously together. Even Pope's doctrine of the "ruling passion" was not original, though he gave it its most extended treatment. In essence, however, the *Essay* is not philosophy but a poet's apprehension of unity despite diversity, of an order embracing the whole multifarious creation.

The Correspondence.

In 1733 Pope's mother died. The same year he engaged in a cat-and-mouse game with Curll to have his letters published in the guise of a pirated edition. Appearing in 1735, this edition allowed him to publish an authoritative edition in 1737. Such maneuvers are not easy to justify. Nor is the careful rewriting and fabrication, designed to reflect the author in the best possible light. But at least Pope's letters suggest the extent of his many friendships and something of the hospitality he enjoyed whenever he indulged his love of traveling.

Imitations of Horace.

The 1730s were also the years of the *Imitations of Horace* (1733–1738), pungent and endearing by turns. How congenial to Pope were the conversational framework and Horatian independence of tone is evident from the fact that they read not like "imitations" but have the freshness of originals. Indeed, the best of them—the "Epistle to Arbuthnot" (1735) and the "Dialogues" (1738)— have no precise source. The "Epistle," with its famous portrait of Addison ("Atticus") and searing indictment of Hervey ("Sporus"), was both the satirist's *apologia pro vita sua* and his vindication of personally oriented satire. The two "Dialogues" continued this theme, introducing an additional element of political satire.

As Pope grew older, he came to rely more and more on the faithful Martha Blount, and to her he left most of his possessions. He described his life as a "long disease," and asthma increased his sufferings in his later years. At times during the last month of his life he became delirious. He died on May 30, 1744, and was buried in Twickenham Church.

EWB

Popper, Karl (1902–1994), Austrian philosopher. Karl Popper offered an original analysis of scientific research that he also applied to research in history and philosophy.

Karl Popper was born in Vienna on July 28, 1902, the son of a barrister. He studied mathematics, physics, and philosophy at the University of Vienna. Though not a member of the Vienna Circle, he was in sympathy with some, if not all, of its aims. His first book, *The Logic of Scientific Discovery* (1935), was published in a series sponsored by the Circle. In 1937 Popper accepted a post in New Zealand as senior lecturer in philosophy at Canterbury University College in Christchurch.

At the end of World War II, Popper was invited to the London School of Economics as a reader, and in 1949 he was made professor of logic and scientific method. Popper then made numerous visits to the United States as visiting professor and guest lecturer. In 1950 he gave the William James Lectures at Harvard University. In 1965 Popper was knighted by Queen Elizabeth II.

Foundations of Popper's Theory.

Popper's first book laid the foundations for all the rest of his work. It offered an analysis of the procedure to be used in scientific work and a criterion for the meaning of the statements produced in such work. According to Popper, the researcher should begin by proposing hypotheses. The collection of data is guided by a theoretical preconception concerning what is relevant or important. The examination of causal connections between phenomena is also guided by leading hypotheses. Such a hypothesis is scientific only if one can derive from it particular observation statements that, if falsified by the facts, would refute the hypothesis. A statement is meaningful, therefore, if and only if there is a way it can be falsified. Hence the researcher should strive to refute rather than to confirm his hypotheses. Refutation is real advancement because it clears the field of a likely hypothesis.

Understanding History and Society.

Popper later applied his analysis of knowledge to theories of society and history. In *The Open Society and Its Enemies* (1945) he attacked Plato, G. W. F. Hegel, and Karl Marx as offering untenable totalitarian theories that are easily falsifiable. *The Open Society* is often considered one of Popper's most influential books of this century. It also was responsible for the prevalent use of the term "open society." Critics argue that Popper succeeded in this book and in its sequel, *The Poverty of Historicism* (1957), in formulating a deterministic theory about general laws of historical development and then refuting it. A lively controversy ensued on the issue of which philosophers, if any, held the doc-

285

trine Popper refuted. Popper found himself embroiled in a decade of polemics, particularly with partisans of Plato. Popper was thus credited with a convincing logical refutation but one misdirected in its targets.

Popper's later works *Objective Knowledge* (1972) and *The Self and Its Brain* (1977) combined his scientific theory with a theory of evolution. In the 1980s, Popper continued to lecture, focusing mainly on questions of evolution and the role of consciousness. Karl Popper died of complications from cancer, pneumonia, and kidney failure on September 17, 1994 at the age of 92.

EWB

Power, Eileen (1889–1940), British educator and historian. Noted for her academic work in the area of medieval history in the years after World War I, Eileen Power's informative books on women's history were considered pioneering in their day. While not the first woman to undertake the study of medieval social and economic history, she became the most widely known because of her ability to engage not only an academic audience but the general reader as well. Power believed that the broad study of history was crucial to reducing and eliminating nationalism and provincialism. To that end she contributed to popular magazines, gave radio talks on historical topics, and wrote books on history for young readers.

Like many of her colleagues, Power was attracted to the Middle Ages because of its contrasts with the industrial age; unlike others she did not harbor any illusions about what life was like during this period. Her style of historical writing was unique in that she used individuals to represent historic "types" as a means of making the distant past easier for the average reader to relate to. This technique can be seen in her *Medieval People*, published in 1924. Ignoring high-profile individuals, the work presents the era through the lives of six "average" individuals, including a peasant, a prioress, and two men engaged in the wool trade. In engaging sketches Power includes a great deal of background information gleaned from various documents of the period.

At her untimely death in 1940, Power would leave, among other works, an unfinished world history for young people. Several of her lectures would be edited by her husband, Michael M. Postan, in 1975 and published as *Medieval Women*.

CA

Primo de Rivera y Orbaneja, Miguel (1870–1930), Spanish general. Miguel Primo de Rivera ruled Spain as a dictator from 1923 to 1930.

Miguel Primo de Rivera was born in Cadiz on Jan. 8, 1870, of a middle-class family that later became landowners in the Andalusian town of Jerez. He entered the General Military Academy in Toledo in 1884 and first saw service in Africa in 1893, where he won the Cross of San Fernando. Two years later he went to Cuba as an aide to Gen. Martinez de Campos. When his uncle, Gen. Fernando Primo de Rivera, was named captain general of the Philippines in 1897, Miguel went to Manila as an aide. A major in 1898, he was prevented by the collapse of Spanish military power from becoming a lieutenant general until 1919, the interim being filled with campaigns in Morocco, a stormy military governorship of Cadiz (1915), and service as an observer at the western front during World War I.

Public notice did not come Primo's way until 1922, when, as captain general of Barcelona, he attempted to reestablish law and order at just the moment that antiwar sentiment and social unrest were pointing toward revolution. Almost by chance Primo was selected as the chief figure in the military coup d'etat that on Sept. 12, 1923, overthrew parliamentary government (possibly with the aid of King Alfonso XIII) and imposed a military dictatorship. Overnight Primo became the most important political figure in Spain.

Primo has been described as a "glorified café politician" who, though he had made no preparation for rule, nevertheless aspired to political greatness. Order was restored by suspending constitutional guarantees, dissolving the Parliament, and imposing martial law. A new party, the Patriotic Union, became Primo's political vehicle and the only legal party in the country. Aside from the King's support of it, however, it had been put together so fast that it never developed great strength. Only because Primo was able to concentrate resources and to rally the army and defeat Abd el-Krim and the Moroccans did the new regime gain some respite from political dissension. The ending of the Moroccan War in December 1925 became Primo's one solid triumph.

Internal problems, surprisingly, continued to mount. Liberals rejected Primo's local government reforms and anticentralism, and radicals, despite the addition of a Socialist, Largo Cabellero, to his Cabinet, did not feel that the regime was moving fast enough in making social reforms. University students and intellectuals, fearing that Primo was another Benito Mussolini, led the opposition from 1925 on, and one of Spain's most distinguished intellectuals, Miguel de Unamuno, went into exile. Primo in fact was far from being a Fascist like Mussolini; if anything he had a paternalistic view of the state that unfortunately was out of step with the growing ideological sensitivities of the Spaniards.

By 1928, as the revolt of the cadets at the Academy of Segovia showed, even the army was dissatisfied with Primo, mainly because law and order were breaking down. The next 2 years witnessed one act of rebellion after the other, but King Alfonso XIII delayed replacing Primo because the monarchy had used the regime to hide its involvement in a series of disastrous political and military setbacks just prior to the dictatorship. Finally, however, Primo had no other recourse than to resign on Jan. 28, 1930, when he left for exile in Paris. He died in Paris on March 16, 1930.

Primo's son, José Antonio, frequently defended his father during the next few years of growing political bitterness, and many aspects of his father's paternalism could be found in José Antonio Primo de Rivera's much more overtly fascist philosophy. José Antonio founded the Falange party and became the martyr of the nationalist movement.

EWB

Proust, Marcel (1871–1922), French novelist. Marcel Proust ranks as one of the greatest literary figures of the 20th century. He abandoned plot and traditional dramatic action for the vision of the first-person narrator confronting his world.

Marcel Proust was born to wealthy bourgeois parents on July 10, 1871, in Auteuil, a suburb of Paris. The first son of Dr. Adrien Proust and Jeanne Weil, the daughter of a wealthy Jewish financier, he was hypersensitive, nervous, and frail. When he was 9 years old, his first attack of asthma, a disease that greatly influenced his life, nearly suffocated him. In 1882 Proust enrolled in the Lycée Condorcet. Only during his last two years of study there did he distinguish himself as a student, attracting the interest of his philosophy professor, Marie-Alphonse Daru. After a year of military service, Proust studied law and then philosophy.

In the meantime, Proust was creating a name for himself in high society as a brilliant conversationalist with an ear for speech patterns that enabled him to mimic others with devastating ease and accuracy. His verve, dark features, pale complexion, and elegant taste fascinated the hosts of the smart Parisian set that he eagerly courted. Although he soon earned the reputation of a snob and social climber, Proust's intimate friends saw him as generous, extremely intelligent, capable of serious thinking, and as an excellent intellectual companion. But he irritated through his eagerness to please, his intensity of emotion, and his indecisiveness. Proust was not indecisive, however, about his commitment to writing.

Early Works. In 1892 and 1893 Proust contributed a number of critical notes and sketches and two short stories to the ephemeral journal *Le Banquet* and to *La Revue blanche.* He published his first work in 1896, a collection of short stories, short verse portraits of artists and musicians, and incidental pieces written during the preceding six years. *Les Plaisirs et les jours* (*Pleasures and Days*) received cursory notice in the press despite its preface by Anatole France. The book did little to dispel the prevalent notion of Proust as an effete dandy. His interest in analysis of rare and exquisite feelings, his preoccupation with high society, and his refined style were all too familiar to allow his readers to see a talented and serious writer groping for eternal truths and a personal style.

In 1895, even before he published *Les Plaisirs et les jours,* Proust had made a first attempt at a major work. Unable to handle his material satisfactorily, unsure of himself, and unclear about the manner of achieving the goals he had set, Proust abandoned the work in 1899. It appeared, under the title of *Jean Santeuil,* only in 1952; from thousands of notebook pages, Bernard de Fallois had culled and organized the novel according to a sketchy plan he found among them. As a consequence the novel is uneven; many passages announce, duplicate, or are variations of passages in Proust's masterpiece, and others are incoherent or apparently irrelevant. Some, however, are beautifully lyric or analytic. *Jean Santeuil* is Proust's first attempt to come to grips with material that later yielded so much in *À la recherche du temps perdu. Jean Santeuil* is the biography of an imaginary character who struggles with himself, his family, and his environment in order to discover, justify, and affirm his artistic vocation. Through episodes and sketches Proust traced Jean Santeuil's progress toward maturity, touching upon many of the themes he later developed more fully: the impact of nature upon the sensibility; the silent work of the imagination in involuntary memory; memory bridging gaps in time; the effects of events such as the Alfred Dreyfus case upon society; the snobbery of social intercourse; the self-oriented nature of love; and the liberating power of art.

After abandoning *Jean Santeuil,* Proust returned to his studies. Although he read widely in other literatures, he was limited to translations. During 1899 he became interested in the works of John Ruskin, and after Ruskin's death (Jan. 20, 1900), Proust published an obituary of the English critic in *La Chronique des arts et de la curiosité* (Jan. 27, 1900) that established him as a Ruskin scholar. Proust's *Pélerinages ruskiniens en France* appeared in *Le Figaro* in February and was followed by several more articles on Ruskin in *Le Mercure de France* and in *La Gazette des beaux-arts.* With the help of an English-speaking friend, Marie Nordlinger, and his mother, Proust translated Ruskin's *The Bible of Amiens* (1904) and *Sesame and Lilies* (1906). Grappling with Ruskin's ideas on art and its relationship to ethics helped him clarify his own esthetic ideas and move beyond the impasse of *Jean Santeuil.*

In 1903 Proust's father died. His own health, deteriorating since 1899, suffered an even greater shock following the death of his mother in September 1905. These setbacks forced Proust into the sanatorium of Dr. Paul Sollier (in December 1905), where he entertained hopes of curing his asthma. Undoubtedly preferring his illness to any cure, Proust left, "fantastically ill," in less than 2 months. After more than 2 years of seclusion, he emerged once again into society and into print with a series of articles and pastiches published in *Le Figaro* during 1907 and 1908. From 1905 to 1908 Proust had been mysteriously working on a novel; he abandoned it, too, in favor of a new one he had begun to plan when he realized the necessity of still another dress rehearsal. He wrote pastiches of Honoré de Balzac, Gustave Flaubert, Edmond de Goncourt, Charles Sainte-Beuve, and others (February-March 1908), and this activity led Proust inadvertently to problems of literary criticism and to a clearer formulation of a literary work as an art object. By November 1908 Proust was planning his *Contre Sainte-Beuve* (published in 1954; *On Art and Literature*), a rebuttal of Sainte-Beuve, the recognized master of historical literary criticism. The true writer expresses a self, Proust felt, that is completely hidden beneath the one manifested "in our habits, in society, in our vices. If we want to try to understand that self, it is only by trying to re-create it deep in ourselves, that we can succeed." By reacting to Sainte-Beuve, Proust formulated, in terms applicable to the artist as well as to the reader, the notion that lies at the heart of *À la recherche du temps perdu,* Proust finished *Contre Sainte-Beuve* during the summer of 1909 and began almost immediately to compose his great novel.

Remembrance of Things Past.
Although Proust had, by 1909, accumulated and reworked most of the material that was to become *À la recherche du temps perdu* (*Remembrance of Things Past*), he still had not fully grasped the focal point that would enable him to structure and to orchestrate his vast material. In January 1909 he had a series of experiences that bore belated fruit during the early summer of that year. The sudden conjunction of flavors in a cup of tea and toast evoked in him sensations that recalled his youth in his grandfather's garden at Auteuil. Although he had had similar experiences in the past and

had considered them important, he had not realized that not only were these experiences a key element in an artist's work but also they could serve as the organizing principle of his novel. They revealed the hidden self that Proust had spoken of in *Contre Sainte-Beuve,* a present self identical to the one in various moments of past time. This process of artistic resurrection and the gradual discovery of its effectiveness, he realized, was the focal point his novel required. *À la recherche du temps perdu,* like Balzac's *La Comédie humaine,* depicts the many facets of a whole society in a specific period of history. Political events, such as the Dreyfus case; social transformations, such as the rise of the bourgeoisie and the decline of the nobility; artistic events; evaluations in music, art, and literature; and different social milieus from the working class to bohemian circles—all found their place in Proust's panorama of French life during the decades around the turn of the century. But Proust was primarily concerned with portraying not reality but its perception by his narrator, Marcel, and its capacity to provoke and reveal Marcel's permanent self, normally hidden by habit and social intercourse. From the very first words of his predominantly first-person narrative, Marcel traces his evolution through a multiplicity of recalled experiences to the final realization that these experiences, processed and stored in his memory, reflect his inner life more truly than does his outer life, that their resuscitation in their immediacy destroys spans of elapsed time, that their telling answers his long search for an artistic vocation, and that they form, in fact, the substance of his novel. A key event in the resolution of the novel is the narrator's discovery of the powers of involuntary memory.

Proust began his novel in July 1909, and he worked furiously on it until death interrupted his corrections, revisions, and additions. In 1913, after several rejections, he found in Grasset a publisher who would produce, at the author's expense, the first of three projected volumes (*Du Côté de chez Swann, Le Côté de Guermantes,* and *Le Temps retrouvé; Swann's Way, The Guermantes Way,* and *Time Regained*). After the appearance of the first volume, André Gide, who had earlier rejected Proust's manuscript on behalf of Gallimard, changed his mind and in 1916 obtained the rights to publish the subsequent volumes. Meanwhile, World War I interrupted publication but not Proust's continued expansion of his work. *À l'ombre des jeunes filles en fleur* (*Within a Budding Grove*), originally only a chapter title, appeared late in 1918 as the second volume and won the Goncourt Prize the following year. As volumes appeared, Proust continually expanded his material, inserting long sections as close to publication as the galley stage. *Le Côté de*

Guermantes appeared in 1920; *Sodome et Gomorrhe* (*Cities of the Plain*), Part 1, appeared in 1921 and the two volumes of Part 2 in 1922. Feeling his end approaching, Proust finished drafting his novel and began revising and correcting proofs, expanding the text as he went along with what he called "supernourishment." Proust had completed revisions of *La Prisonnière* (*The Captive*) and had begun reworking *Albertine disparue* (*The Sweet Cheat Gone*) when, on Nov. 18, 1922, he died of bronchitis and pneumonia contracted after a series of violent asthma attacks. The final volumes of his novel appeared owing to the interest of his brother, Robert, and to the editorial supervision of Jacques Rivière: *La Prisonnière*, two volumes, 1923; *Albertine disparue*, two volumes, 1925; and *Le Temps retrouvé*, two volumes, 1927.

EWB

Pugachev, Emelyan Ivanovich (1742–1775), Russian Cossack soldier. Emelyan Pugachev led the peasant rebellion in Russia in 1773–1775.

Emelyan Pugachev, a Don Cossack, was born in the village of Zimoveiskaya. The main course of his life was influenced initially by the fact that, as a Don Cossack, he was subject, when of age, to duty in the Russian army. In 1770, during a Russo-Turkish conflict in which he was serving, he was given a temporary leave and, at its expiration, refused to return to his regiment. Arrested, he managed to escape, thus beginning his life as a strong-willed fugitive.

In the course of his subsequent wanderings Pugachev was struck by the bitter unrest he found among the lower classes in Russia. What he saw convinced him that the time was ripe for revolt, and being a rebel by nature and having a bent toward leadership, he took upon himself the task of directing a revolt. As a basis for appeal, he decided to assume the character of Tsar Peter III, having observed that many credulous people distrusted the official report that Peter had died in 1762.

With about 80 Cossacks committed to his scheme, in September 1773 Pugachev proclaimed himself Peter III and called on the oppressed to follow him in an uprising against Catherine II (the Great). He began his campaign along the Yaik (now called the Ural) River, gathering followers among disgruntled Cossacks, fugitive serfs, released convicts, religious dissenters, Bashkirs, and Tatars. Although the force he assembled was neither well trained nor well disciplined, it was large enough to defeat local military units sent against it. To widen his campaign, Pugachev undertook the capture of Orenburg (Chkalov), the major center of government strength on the Yaik River, setting up headquarters and laying siege to the

city. Meanwhile, news of the revolt prompted bloody uprisings against landlords and government officials along the Volga River and in the region east of it. Thousands left their homes to join the rebel army, and they increased its numbers to about 25,000.

Late in 1773 Catherine II, judging the revolt dangerous enough to warrant her action, sent a large force to suppress it. Pugachev was compelled to end the siege of Orenburg, but he eluded capture by the government forces. Again he marshaled a sizable following and, in July 1774, was able to resume the offensive and capture the city of Kazan. At the same time, serf uprisings took place near Nizhni Novgorod (Gorki) only 275 miles east of Moscow.

Catherine, now deeply alarmed by the nearness of the revolt, sent new contingents against Pugachev. They succeeded in destroying most of his army, near Tsaritsyn (now Volgograd), but he once again evaded efforts to capture him. Still determined, Pugachev made his way to the Yaik Cossack region, hoping that Yaik and Don Cossacks would provide him with a new army. Instead of being given support, however, he was betrayed. A group of Cossacks opposed to his aims seized him and handed him over to the authorities.

Taken in chains to Moscow, Pugachev was tried and sentenced to death. On Jan. 10, 1775, he was beheaded and quartered before a large Moscow crowd.

EWB

Pushkin, Aleksandr Sergeevich (1799–1837), Russian poet and prose writer. Aleksandr Pushkin ranks as the country's greatest poet. He not only brought Russian poetry to its highest excellence but also had a decisive influence on Russian literature in the 19th and 20th centuries.

Aleksandr Pushkin is Russia's national poet. He established the norms of classical Russian versification, and he laid the groundwork for much of the development of Russian prose in the 19th century. His work is distinguished by brilliance of language, compactness, terseness, and objectivity. His poetry is supremely untranslatable, and consequently Pushkin has had less influence on world literature than on Russian literature. He may be described as a romantic in subject matter and a classicist in style and form.

Pushkin was born on May 26, 1799, the son of a family of the middle nobility. On his father's side he was a descendant of one of the oldest lines of Russian nobility, and on his mother's side he was related to an Abyssinian, Abram Petrovich Hannibal, who had been kidnaped in Africa, brought to Constantinople, and sent as a gift to Peter I (the Great). Pushkin was brought up in an atmosphere that was predominantly French, and at a very early age he became acquainted with the classic works of 17th- and 18th-century French literature. Several of the important figures of Russian literatureincluding Nikolai Karamzin and Vasily Zhukovskywere visitors to the Pushkin home during Aleksandr's childhood.

Between 1811 and 1817 Pushkin attended a special school established at Tsarskoye Selo (later renamed Pushkin) by Tsar Alexander I for privileged children of the nobility. Pushkin was an indifferent student in most subjects, but he performed brilliantly in French and Russian literature.

Early Works, 1814–1820. After finishing school, Pushkin led the reckless and dissipated life of a typical nobleman. He wrote about 130 poems between 1814 and 1817, while still at school, and these and most of his works written between 1817 and 1820 were not published because of the boldness of his thoughts on political and erotic matters. In 1820 Pushkin completed his first narrative poem, *Russlan and Ludmilla.* It is a romance composed of fantastic adventures but told with 18th-century humor and irony. Before *Russlan and Ludmilla* was published in June 1820, Pushkin was exiled to the south of Russia because of the boldness of the political sentiments he had expressed in his poems. His "Ode to Liberty" contained, for example, a reference to the assassination of Paul I, the father of Tsar Alexander I. Pushkin left St. Petersburg on May 6 and he did not return to the capital for more than 6 years.

South of Russia, 1820–1824. Pushkin spent the years 1820–1823 in various places in the Caucasus and in the Crimea, and he was at first charmed by the picturesque settings and relieved to be free of the intoxications and artificialities of the life of the capital. Subsequently, however, he felt bored by the life in small towns and took up again a life of gambling, drinking, and consorting with loose women. He was always short of money, for his salary in the civil service was small and his family refused to support him. He began to earn money with his poetic works, but these sums were seldom sufficient to permit him to compete comfortably with his affluent friends. In 1823 he was transferred to Odessa, where he found the life of a large city more to his liking.

The poet's life in Odessa in 1823–1824 was marked by three strong amorous attachments. First, he fell in love with Carolina Sobansky, a beauty who was 6 years older than he. He broke with her in October 1823 and then fell violently in love with the wife of a Dalmatian merchant, Amalia Riznich. She had many admirers and gave Pushkin ample cause for jealousy. Amalia, however, inspired some of Pushkin's best poems, such as "Night" and "Beneath the Blue Sky of Her Native Land," and he remembered her to the end of his life. His third love was for the wife of the governor general, the Countess Eliza Vorontsov. She was a charming and beautiful woman. Vorontsov learned of the affair, and having no special liking for Pushkin he resolved to have him transferred from Odessa. He was aided in this endeavor by an unfortunate letter that Pushkin had written to a friend in which he had questioned the immortality of the soul. The letter was intercepted, and because of it Pushkin was expelled from the service on July 18, 1824, by the Tsar and ordered to the family estate of Mikhailovskoye near Pskov.

Pushkin's poetic work during the 4 years that he spent in the south was rich in output and characterized by Lord Byron's influence, which can be seen in "The Caucasian Captive" (1820–1821), "The Fountain of Bakhchisarai" (1822), and "The Gypsies" (1824). These poems are mellifluous in verse and exotic in setting, but they already show the elements of Pushkin's classic style: measure, balance, terseness, and restraint.

Mikhailovskoye, 1824–1826. On Aug. 9, 1824, Pushkin arrived at Mikhailovskoye. His relations with his parents were not good. The father felt angry at his son's rebelliousness and on one occasion spread a story that his son had attempted to beat him. The family left the estate about mid-November, and Pushkin found himself alone with the family nurse, Arina Rodionovna, at Mikhailovskoye. He lived fairly much as a recluse during the next two years, occasionally visiting a neighboring town and infrequently entertaining old Petersburg friends. During this period he fell in love with a Madame Kern, who was married to an old general and who encouraged the attention of many men. Also at this time the nurse told Pushkin many folk tales, and it is generally believed that she imbued him with the feeling for folk life that manifested itself in many of his poems.

Pushkin's two years at Mikhailovskoye were extremely rich in poetic output. He completed "The Gypsies," wrote the first three chapters of *Eugene Onegin,* and composed the tragedy *Boris Godunov.* In addition he composed many important lyrics and a humorous tale in verse entitled *Count Nulin. Boris Godunov* is a chronicle play. Pushkin took the subject from Karamzin's history, and it relates the claims of the impostor Demetrius to the throne of the elected monarch Boris Godunov.

Maturity, 1826–1831. After the end of his exile at Mikhailovskoye, Pushkin was received by the new czar, Nicholas I, who charmed Pushkin by his reasonableness and kindness. The Tsar placed Pushkin under a privileged tyranny by promising him that his works would be censored by the Tsar himself. The practical consequences of this arrangement were that Pushkin was placed under an honorable promise to publish nothing that was injurious to the government; in time this "privileged" censorship became increasingly onerous.

Pushkin continued his dissipated life after 1826 but with less gusto. Although he was still in his 20s, he began to feel the weight of his years, and he longed to settle down. On April 6, 1830, he proposed to Nathalie Goncharova for the second time and was accepted. She came from a noble family that had fallen on hard times financially. The Goncharovs were dissatisfied with Pushkin's standing with the government and were unimpressed by his reputation as a poet. Pushkin had to ask for economic favors for the Goncharovs from the government, and he persuaded his father to settle an estate on him.

Pushkin's output in the years 1826–1829 was not so great as in the years 1824–1826, but it was still impressive. He continued to work on *Eugene Onegin,* wrote a number of excellent lyrics, worked on but did not finish a prose novel entitled *The Nigger of Peter the Great,* and wrote *Poltava,* a narrative poem on Peter the Great's struggle with Charles XII which celebrates the Russian victory over the Swedes. This poem shows the continuing development of Pushkin's style toward objectivity and austerity.

In the fall of 1830 Pushkin left the capital to visit a small estate by the name of Boldino, which his father had left him, with the intention of spending a few weeks there. However, he was blocked from returning to the capital by measures taken by the authorities because of a cholera epidemic, and he was forced to return to Boldino. During that autumn at Boldino, Pushkin wrote some of his greatest lyrics; *The Tales of Belkin;* a comic poem in octaves, "The Little House in Kolomna"; and four small tragedies; and he virtually finished *Eugene Onegin.*

Eugene Onegin was begun in 1824 and finished in August 1831. This novel in verse is without doubt Pushkin's most famous work. It shows the influence in theme of Byron's *Don Juan* and in style of Laurence Sterne's novels. It is a "novel" about contemporary life, constructed in order to permit digressions and a variety of incidents and tones. The heart of the tale concerns the life of Eugene Onegin, a bored nobleman who rejects the advances of a young girl, Tatiana. He meets her later, greatly changed and now sophisticated, falls in love with her. He is in turn rejected by her because, although she loves him, she is married.

Pushkin's four little tragedies are models of spare, objective, and compact drama. The plays are short and vary in length from 240 to 550 lines. *The Feast during the Plague* is a translation of a scene from John Wilson's *The City of the Plague; The Stone Guest* is a variation of the Don Juan theme; *Mozart and Salieri* treats the tradition of Antonio Salieri's envy of Wolfgang Amadeus Mozart's effortless art and the injustice of Nature in dispensing her gifts; and *The Covetous Knight* has as its theme avariciousness and contains the famous monologue of the baron on his treasures.

The Tales of Belkin consists of five short stories: "The Shot," "The Snowstorm," "The Stationmaster," "The Undertaker," and "The Peasant Gentlewoman." The stories are models of swift, unadorned narration.

Marriage, Duel, and Death, 1831–1837.
After 1830 Pushkin wrote less and less poetry. "The Bronze Horseman" (1833) is considered by many to be his greatest poem. The setting is the great flood of 1824, which inundated much of St. Petersburg. The theme of the poem is the irreconcilable demands of the state and the individual.

The Golden Cockerel (1833) is a volume of Russian folktales. Pushkin's masterpiece in narrative is the short story "The Queen of Spades" (1834), about a gloomy engineer who is ruthless in his efforts to discover the secret of three winning cards. Mention should also be made of his *The History of the Pugachev Rebellion* (1834) and *The Captain's Daughter* (1837), a short novel about the Pugachev rebellion.

Pushkin married Nathalie Goncharova on Jan. 19, 1831. She bore him three children, but the couple was not happy together. She was beautiful and a favorite at court, but she was also somewhat uneducated and not free of vulgarity. She encouraged the attentions of Baron George d'Anthes, an exiled Alsatian Frenchman and a protégé of the minister of the Netherlands at St. Petersburg. Pushkin provoked D'Anthes to a duel on Jan. 26, 1837, and the duel took place the next day. Pushkin was wounded and died on January 29. There was great popular mourning at his death.

Many of Pushkin's works provided the basis for operas by Russian composers. They include *Ruslan and Ludmilla* by Mikhail Glinka, *Eugene Onegin* and *The Queen of Spades* by Peter Ilyich Tchaikovsky, *Boris Godunov* by Modest Mussorgsky, *The Stone Guest* by Aleksandr Dargomijsky, and *The Golden Cockerel* by Nicolai Rimsky-Korsakov.

EWB

R

Ranke, Leopold von (1795–1886), German historian. Leopold von Ranke was one of the most prolific and universal modern historians of his time. He imparted his expertise and methodology through the introduction of the seminar as an informal but intensive teaching device.

Leopold von Ranke was born on Dec. 21, 1795, in the rural Thuringian town of Wiehe, which then belonged to electoral Saxony. Although Ranke was born into the era of the French Revolution, his bourgeois, small-town, generally well-ordered, and peaceful background and upbringing did not provide much contact with the violent events of the times. After receiving his early education at local schools in Donndorf and Pforta, he attended the University of Leipzig (1814–1818), where he continued his studies in ancient philology and theology.

In the fall of 1818 Ranke accepted a teaching position at the gymnasium (high school) in Frankfurt an der Oder. His teaching assignments in world history and ancient literature, for which he disdained the use of handbooks and readily available prepared texts, as well as the contemporary events of the period, led him to turn to original sources and to a concern for the empirical understanding of history in its totality.

Making use of materials from the Westermannsche Library in Frankfurt and from the Royal Library in Berlin, Ranke produced his first work, *Geschichten der romanischen und germanischen Völker* (1824; *Histories of the Romanic and Germanic Peoples*), which earned him a professorial appointment at the University of Berlin in 1825, where he was to remain for the rest of his life except for extended research trips abroad.

Although this first work was still lacking in style, organization, and mastery of its overflowing detail, it had particular significance because it contained a technical appendix in which Ranke established his program of critical scholarship—"to show what actually happened" by analyzing the sources used, by determining their originality and likely veracity, and by evaluating in the same light the writings of previous historians "who appear to be the most celebrated" and who have been considered "the foundation of all the later works on the beginning of modern history." His scathing criticism of such historians led him to accept only contemporary documents, such as letters from ambassadors and others immediately involved in the course of historical events, as admissible primary evidence.

With Ranke's move to Berlin, the manuscripts of Venetian ministerial reports of the Reformation period became available to him and served as the basis for his second work, *Fürsten und Völker von Süd-Europa* (1827; *Princes and Peoples of Southern Europe*), which was republished in his complete works as *Die Osmanen und die spanische Monarchie im 16. und 17. Jahrhundert* (vols. 35 and 36; *The Ottomans and the Spanish Monarchy in the Sixteenth and Seventeenth Centuries*).

Travels and Research. The limited collection in Berlin whetted Ranke's appetite to investigate other European libraries and archives, especially those of Italy. Armed with a travel stipend from the Prussian government, he proceeded at first to Vienna, where a large part of the Venetian archives had been housed after the Austrian occupation of Venetia. A letter of introduction brought acquaintance with Friedrich von Gentz, who, through intercession with Prince Metternich, not only opened the Viennese archives to Ranke but also brought him into immediate contact with the day-to-day politics of the Hapsburg court. During his stay in Vienna he wrote *Die serbische Revolution* (1829), republished in an expanded version as *Serbien und die Türkei im 19. Jahrhundert* (1879; *Serbia and Turkey in the 19th Century*).

In 1828 Ranke traveled to Italy, where he spent 3 successful years of study visiting various public and private libraries and archives, although the Vatican Library remained closed to him. During this period he wrote a treatise, *Venice in the Sixteenth Century* (published 1878), and collected material for what is generally considered his masterpiece, *Die römischen Päpste, ihre Kirche und ihr Staat im 16. und 17. Jahrhundert* (1834–1836; *The Roman Popes, Their Church and State in the 16th and 17th Centuries*).

Returning from Italy in 1831, Ranke soon became involved in the publication of a journal designed to combat French liberal influence, which had alarmed the Prussian government in the aftermath of the revolutionary events of 1830. Although the *Historisch-Politische Zeitschrift*, with Ranke as editor and chief contributor, contained some of the best political thought published in Germany during this time, it lacked the polemical quality and anticipated success of a political fighting journal and was discontinued in 1836. In the same year Ranke was appointed full professor and devoted the rest of his life to the task of teaching and scholarly work. A Protestant counterpart to his *History of the Popes* was published as *Deutsche Geschichte im Zeitalter der Reformation* (1839–1847; *German History during the Era of the Reformation*), which was largely based on the reports of the Imperial Diet in Frankfurt.

Last Works. With the following works Ranke rounded out his historical treatment of the major powers: *Neun Bücher preussischer Geschichte* (1847–1848; *Nine Books of Prussian History*); *Französische Geschichte, vornehmlich im 16. and 17. Jahrhundert* (1852–1861; *French History, Primarily in the 16th and 17th Centuries*); and *Englische Geschichte, vornehmlich im 16. und 17. Jahrhundert* (1859–1868; *English History, Primarily in the 16th and 17th Centuries*). Other works, dealing mainly with German and Prussian history during the 18th century, followed in the 1870s.

During the last years of his life Ranke, now in his 80s and because of failing sight requiring the services of readers and secretaries, embarked upon the composition of his *Weltgeschichte* (1883–1888; *World History*), published in nine volumes. The last two were published posthumously from manuscripts of his lectures. He died in Berlin on May 23, 1886.

The complete work of Ranke is difficult to assess. Not many of his works achieved the artistic high point of *The Roman Popes* or its appeal for the general reader. Yet there is hardly a chapter in his total enormous production which could be considered without value. His harmonious nature shunned emotion and violent passion, and he can be faulted less for what he wrote than for what he left unwritten. His approach to history emphasized the politics of the courts and of great men but neglected the common people and events of everyday life; he limited his investigation to the political history of the states in their universal setting. Ranke combined, as few others, the qualities of the trailblazing scholar and the devoted, conscientious, and innovative teacher.

EWB

Reed, John Silas   (1887–1920), American revolutionist, poet, and journalist. John Reed became a symbol in many American minds of the Communist revolution in Russia.

John Reed was born in the mansion of his maternal grandparents outside Portland, Ore., on Oct. 22, 1887. His father sold agricultural implements and insurance. Reed was a frail youngster and suffered with a kidney ailment. He attended Portland public schools and graduated from Harvard in 1910. Although he felt like an outsider, Reed had been active at the university.

Reed went to work for *American Magazine,* of muckraking fame, and *The Masses,* a radical publication. Journalists Ida Tarbell and Lincoln Steffens awakened his liberal feelings, but he soon bypassed them as a radical. In 1914 *Metropolitan Magazine* sent Reed to Mexico, where he boldly walked within the lines of Pancho Villa's army. Villa reportedly made Reed a staff officer and called the journalist "brigadier general." Reed next gave sympathetic coverage to

striking coal miners in Colorado. He went to Europe for *Metropolitan Magazine* when World War I broke out in 1914. He covered the battle fronts in Germany, Russia, Serbia, Romania, and Bulgaria.

Reed and his wife, Louise Bryant, were in Russia during the October Revolution. In reporting the Bolshevik effort to gain control, Reed won V. I. Lenin's friendship. Here Reed gathered materials for his most noted work, *Ten Days That Shook the World* (1919). It is generally recognized that the book lacks factual accuracy, but Bertram Wolfe (1960) contends that "as literature Reed's book is the finest piece of eyewitness reporting the revolution produced."

In 1918 Reed was named Russian consul general at New York, a status never recognized by the United States. In 1919, after he had been expelled from the National Socialist Convention, he formed the Communist Labor party in the United States. He was arrested several times for incendiary speeches and finally, after printing articles in the *Voice of Labor,* was indicted for sedition. He fled to the Soviet Union on a forged passport. The thing usually unreported about Reed among the Muscovites was his unrelenting contention that decisions should be made democratically and his opposition to a monolithic society under dictatorial control. Twice he tried to return to the United States but was unsuccessful. Stricken by typhus, he died on Oct. 19, 1920, in Moscow. He was given a state funeral and buried in the Kremlin.

EWB

Renan, Ernest   (1823–1892), French author, philologist, archaeologist. Ernest Renan was the founder of comparative religion, and influenced European thought in the second half of the 19th century through his numerous writings.

Ernest Renan grew up in the mystical, Catholic French province of Brittany, where Celtic myths combined with his mother's deeply experienced Catholicism led this sensitive child to believe he was destined for the priesthood. He was educated at the ecclesiastical college at Tréguier, graduating in 1838, and then went to Paris, where he carried on the usual theological studies at St-Nicolas-du-Chardonnet and at St-Sulpice. In his *Recollections of Childhood and Youth* (1883) he recounted the spiritual crisis he went through as his growing interest in scientific studies of the Bible eventually made orthodoxy unacceptable; he was soon won over to the new "religion of science," a conversion fostered by his friendship with the chemist P. E. M. Berthelot.

Renan abandoned the seminary and earned his doctorate in philosophy. At this time (1848) he wrote *The Future of Science* but did not publish it until

1890. In this work he affirmed a faith in the wonders to be brought forth by a science not yet realized, but which he was sure would come.

Archaeological expeditions to the Near East and further studies in Semitics led Renan to a concept of religious studies which would later be known as comparative religion. His was an anthropomorphic view, first publicized in his *Life of Jesus* (1863), in which he portrayed Christ as a historical phenomenon with historical roots and needing a rational, nonmystical explanation. With his characteristic suppleness of intellect, this deeply pious agnostic wrote a profoundly irreligious work which lost him his professorship in the dominantly Catholic atmosphere of the Second Empire in France.

The *Life of Jesus* was the opening volume of Renan's *History of the Origins of Christianity* (1863–1883), his most influential work. His fundamental thesis was that all religions are true and good, for all embody man's noblest aspirations: he invited each man to phrase these truths in his own way. For many, a reading of this work made religion for the first time living truth; for others, it made religious conviction impossible.

The defeat of France in the Franco-Prussian War of 1870–1871 was for Renan, as for many Frenchmen, a deeply disillusioning experience. If Germany, which he revered, could do this to France, which he loved, where did goodness, beauty, or truth lie? He became profoundly skeptical, but with painful honesty he refused to deny what seemed to lie before him, averring instead that "the truth is perhaps sad." He remained sympathetic to Christianity, perhaps expressing it most movingly in his *Prayer on the Acropolis of Athens* (1876), in which he reaffirmed his abiding faith in the Greek life of the mind but confessed that his was inevitably a larger world, with sorrows unknown to the goddess Athena; hence he could never be a true son of Greece, any more than any other modern.

EWB

Rhodes, Cecil John (1853–1902), English imperialist, financier, and mining magnate. Cecil Rhodes founded and controlled the British South Africa Company, which acquired Rhodesia and Zambia as British territories. He founded the Rhodes scholarships.

Cecil Rhodes was born on July 5, 1853, at Bishop's Stortford, Hertfordshire, one of nine sons of the parish vicar. After attending the local grammar school, his health broke down, and at 16 he was sent to South Africa. Arriving in October 1870, he grew cotton in Natal with his brother Herbert but in 1871 left for the newly developed diamond field at Kimberley.

In the 1870s Rhodes laid the foundation for his later massive fortune by speculating in diamond claims, beginning pumping techniques, and in 1880 forming the De Beers Mining Company. During this time he attended Oxford off and on, starting in 1873, and finally acquired the degree of bachelor of arts in 1881. His extraordinary imperialist ideas were revealed early, after his serious heart attack in 1877, when he made his first will, disposing of his as yet unearned fortune to found a secret society that would extend British rule over the whole world and colonize most parts of it with British settlers, leading to the "ultimate recovery of the United States of America" by the British Empire!

From 1880 to 1895 Rhodes's star rose steadily. Basic to this rise was his successful struggle to take control of the rival diamond interests of Barnie Barnato, with whom he amalgamated in 1888 to form De Beers Consolidated Mines, a company whose trust deed gave extraordinary powers to acquire lands and rule them and extend the British Empire. With his brother Frank he also formed Goldfields of South Africa, with substantial mines in the Transvaal. At the same time Rhodes built a career in politics; elected to the Cape Parliament in 1880, he succeeded in focusing alarm at Transvaal and German expansion so as to secure British control of Bechuanaland by 1885. In 1888 Rhodes agents secured mining concessions from Lobengula, King of the Ndebele, which by highly stretched interpretations gave Rhodes a claim to what became Rhodesia. In 1889 Rhodes persuaded the British government to grant a charter to form the British South Africa Company, which in 1890 put white settlers into Lobengula's territories and founded Salisbury and other towns. This provoked Ndebele hostility, but they were crushed in the war of 1893.

By this time Rhodes controlled the politics of Cape Colony; in July 1890 he became premier of the Cape with the support of the English-speaking white and non-white voters and the Afrikaners of the "Bond" (among whom 25,000 shares in the British South Africa Company had been distributed). His policy was to aim for the creation of a South African federation under the British flag, and he conciliated the Afrikaners by restricting the Africans' franchise with educational and property qualifications (1892) and setting up a new system of "native administration" (1894).

Later Career. At the end of 1895 Rhodes's fortunes took a disastrous turn. In poor health and anxious to hurry his dream of South African federa-

294

tion, he organized a conspiracy against the Boer government of the Transvaal. Through his mining company, arms and ammunition were smuggled into Johannesburg to be used for a revolution by "out-landers," mainly British. A strip of land on the borders of the Transvaal was ceded to the chartered company by Joseph Chamberlain, British colonial secretary; and Leander Jameson, administrator of Rhodesia, was stationed there with company troops. The Johannesburg conspirators did not rebel; Jameson, however, rode in on Dec. 27, 1895, and was ignominiously captured. As a result, Rhodes had to resign his premiership in January 1896. Thereafter he concentrated on developing Rhodesia and especially in extending the railway, which he dreamed would one day reach Cairo.

When the Anglo-Boer War broke out in October 1899, Rhodes hurried to Kimberley, which the Boers surrounded a few days later. It was not relieved until Feb. 16, 1900, during which time Rhodes had been active in organizing defense and sanitation. His health was worsened by the siege, and after traveling in Europe he returned to the Cape in February 1902, where he died at Muizenberg on March 26.

Rhodes left £6 million, most of which went to Oxford University to establish the Rhodes scholarships to provide places at Oxford for students from the United States, the British colonies, and Germany. Land was also left to provide eventually for a university in Rhodesia.

EWB

Richardson, Samuel (1689–1761), English novelist. Samuel Richardson brought dramatic intensity and psychological insight to the epistolary novel.

Fiction, including the novel told in letters, had become popular in England before Samuel Richardson's time, but he was the first English novelist to have the leisure to perfect the form in which he chose to work. Daniel Defoe's travel adventures and pseudo-biographies contain gripping individual episodes and an astonishing realism, but they lack, finally, the structural unity and cohesiveness characteristic of Richardson's lengthy novels. Unlike his great contemporary Henry Fielding, who satirized every echelon of English society in such panoramic novels as *Tom Jones,* Richardson chose to focus his attention on the limited problems of marriage and of the heart, matters to be treated with seriousness. In so doing, however, he also provided his readers with an unparalleled study of the social and economic forces that were bringing the rising, wealthy English merchant class into conflict with the landed aristocracy.

Born in Derbyshire, Richardson was one of nine children of a joiner, or carpenter. He became an ap-prentice printer to John Wilde and learned his trade well from that hard master for 7 years. After serving as "Overseer and Corrector" in a printing house, he set up shop for himself in Salisbury Court, Fleet Street, in 1720, where he married, lived for many years, and carried on his business. Within 20 years he had built up one of the largest and most lucrative printing businesses in London. Although he published a wide variety of books, including his own novels, he depended upon the official printing that he did for the House of Commons for an important source of income.

Richardson claimed to have written indexes, prefaces, and dedications early in his career, but his first known work, published in 1733, was *The Apprentice's Vade Mecum; or, Young Man's Pocket Companion,* a conduct book addressed to apprentices. *A Seasonable Examination . . .* (1735) was a pamphlet supporting a parliamentary bill to regulate the London theaters.

Pamela. In 1739, while at work on a book of model letters for social occasions proposed to him as a publishing venture by two booksellers, Richardson decided to put together a series of letters that would narrate the tribulations of a young servant girl in a country house. His first epistolary novel, *Pamela, or Virtue Rewarded,* was published in two volumes in November 1740 and became an instantaneous and enormous success. When its popularity led to the publication of a spurious sequel, Richardson countered by publishing a less interesting and, indeed, less popular continuation of his work in December 1741.

Richardson claimed in a letter to the Reverend Johannes Stinstra in 1753 that the idea for the story of Pamela had been suggested to him 15 years before, a claim he repeated to Aaron Hill. Regardless of the source for the story, however, Richardson's audience accepted and praised his simple tale of a pretty 15-year-old servant girl, the victim of the extraordinarily clumsy attempts at seduction by her young master, Squire B(later named Squire Booby in the novels of Henry Fielding), who sincerely, shrewdly, and successfully holds out for marriage.

Richardson's use of the epistolary form, which made it possible for him to have Pamela writing at the moment, enabled him to give a minutely particular account of his heroine's thoughts, actions, fears, and emotions. Pamela's letters give the reader a continuous and cumulative impression of living through the experience and create a new kind of sympathy with the character whose experiences are being shared. But Richardson's decision to have the entire story told through Pamela's letters to her parents also raised technical problems that he was not to overcome until his second novel. Because she alone must report compliments about her charms, testify to her virtue, and relate her successful attempts to repulse Squire B's advances, she often seems coy and self-centered rather than innocent.

Richardson's continuation of *Pamela*, which describes her attempts to succeed in "high life" after her marriage to Squire B, is a less interesting story, more pretentiously told and far less moving.

He followed his triumph with *Pamela* in 1741 by publishing the delayed *Letters Written to and for Particular Friends, Directing the Requisite Style and Forms . . . in Writing Familiar Letters,* a collection of little interest to the modern reader.

Clarissa. By the summer of 1742 Richardson had evidently begun work on what was to become his masterpiece. *Clarissa Harlowe* was published in seven volumes in 1747–1748. Although he had finished the first version of the novel by 1744, he continued to revise it, to solicit the opinions of his friends (and disregard most of their advice), and to worry about its excessive length. The massive work, which runs to more than a million words and stands as one of the longest novels in the English language, contains 547 letters, most written by the heroine, Clarissa Harlowe, her friend, Anna Howe, the dashing villain, Lovelace, and his confidant, John Belford. Letters of enormous length and incredible intensity follow Clarissa's struggle with her family to avoid marriage to the odious Mr. Soames, her desperate flight from her unbending and despicable family into the arms of Lovelace, her drugged rape, her attempts to escape from Lovelace by soliciting the aid of her unforgiving family, and her dramatic death. Before the final volumes of the novel were published, many of Richardson's readers had pleaded with him to give the novel a happy ending by allowing Clarissa to live. Richardson, however, had set out to show that in losing her innocence a girl might be ennobled rather than degraded, but that no matter how much of a paragon of virtue and decorum she might be in this world, she would find true reward for her virtue only in the next. The novel shows clearly the influence of the Christian epic, the English stage, and the funereal literature popular in the period. With specific debts to Nicholas Rowe's *Fair Penitent* and John Milton's *Paradise Lost,* it explores the problem of humanity desperately, if futilely, seeking freedom in a society where duty and responsibility are constant limitations upon that search. Although its great length has earned for it the title of "one of the greatest of the unread novels," it maintains a commanding place in the corpus of major English fiction because of its exploration of property marriages in the shifting social milieu of mid-18th-century England, its dramatic and cumulative power, and its clear tie to such other great Western mythical stories as Romeo and Juliet and Tristan and Isolde.

Sir Charles Grandison. Richardson toiled for 5 years to depict the perfect Christian gentleman, especially in order to answer criticisms that he had allowed Lovelace to become too attractive a figure in *Clarissa.* His third and final novel, *Sir Charles Grandison,* was published in 1753–1754. Richardson's contemporaries, who had found Lovelace a fascinating and dramatic villain, thought Sir Charles chilly and priggish. Richardson's story of the earnest Christian gentleman who must choose between the English maiden, Harriet Byron, and the more attractive and more interesting Clementina della Porretta pleases few readers. Because Sir Charles is too faultless and too moral, he does not win the reader's sympathies.

After this Richardson wrote no more novels. He died in London on July 4, 1761.

EWB

Richelieu, Armand Jean du Plessis de (1585–1642), French statesman and cardinal. Richelieu devoted himself to securing French leadership in Europe and royal domination of the existing social order in France.

The policies and personal conduct of Richelieu were distinguished by self-restraint, flexibility in response to changing opportunities, and alertness to remote consequences. His long-range intentions could be achieved only at the expense of Spain abroad and of the King's family and the great noblemen at home.

In the early 17th century a precarious balance existed between reasons of state and religious sectarianism as principles for international action. A similar balance existed in France between the rights of the King and the particular rights of provinces, localities, classes, and persons. Each balance was tipped toward the first alternative during Richelieu's career. The alignments of European states shifted and their relative power changed. The French political system began to define anew the relation of each social group to the monarchy and thus to other social groups. These historical developments eventually went far beyond Richelieu's plans, but he played a significant part in them.

Armand du Plessis was born on Sept. 9, 1585, in Paris, fourth of the five children of François du Plessis, the lord of Richelieu, and Suzanne de La Porte. His father was provost of the King's central administrative establishment and grand provost of

France under Henry III and conducted the investigation of the King's murderer in 1589; he remained in the same post serving Henry IV but in 1590 died of a fever. His mother, the self-effacing daughter of a learned, vain lawyer prominent in the Paris bourgeoisie, was placed in severe financial difficulties by early widowhood. She moved to the old stone manor house of Richelieu, a few miles east of Loudun in Poitou, to reside with her mother-in-law, a proud noblewoman originally of the Rochechouart family. About 4 years later, Armand returned to Paris to study grammar and philosophy at the Collège de Navarre, from which he went on to a military academy.

The Du Plessis family's plans appeared to be settled. The eldest son, Henri, was seeking to become established in the entourage of the new queen, Maria de' Medici. The second son, Alphonse, was destined to be bishop of Luçon; the mother received the income of the benefice. But Alphonse declined the nomination and became a Carthusian monk. Armand was designated instead, and in 1603 he began serious study of theology. Younger than the canonical age to become a bishop, he went to Rome for a papal dispensation in 1607 and was consecrated there. He returned to Paris, obtained his degree in theology, and lingered to multiply his acquaintances among clergymen and among the associates of his brother Henri.

Career as Bishop. At the end of 1608 Richelieu arrived in Luçon, then little more than a village amid the marshes, a short distance from the Atlantic and north of La Rochelle. He found it "the most ignoble, mud-covered, unpleasant bishopric in France." He was an assiduous bishop, controlling his canons, carefully choosing parish priests, encouraging the preaching missions of the Capucin monks led by Father Joseph of Paris (François Le Clerc du Tremblay), and, while residing at his priory of Coussay between Loudun and Poitiers, cooperating with other active churchmen.

Richelieu's first important political opportunity came with the convocation of the Estates General in 1614. The clergy of Poitou elected him a deputy. At Maria de Medici's suggestion he was chosen to speak for the clergy as a whole at the last session of the Estates (Feb. 23, 1615). He then went back to Poitou but a year later returned to Paris, served her in negotiations with the Prince of Condé, and was appointed secretary of state for foreign affairs and war. He held the post for only 5 months because Louis XIII seized power in April 1617 and dismissed his mother's councilors. Further steps against them followed, and in 1618 the bishop of Luçon was ordered into exile in the papal city of Avignon.

From Poitou, in 1617, Richelieu had joined in a pamphlet controversy between the King's Jesuit confessor and four Protestant ministers. In *Les Principaux points de la foi de l'église Catholique,* he employed moderate terms and rejected force as a means of conversion. He answered the Protestant ministers on several issues and told them, "You give to the people a power much greater than the one you deny to the pope, which is greatly disadvantageous to kings." In Avignon, in 1618, he finished a catechism he had been preparing in his diocese, *L'Instruction du Chrétien,* a calm, simple explanation of dogma and commandments which makes clear the sovereignty of God by comparing it to the sovereignty of the King.

Among Louis XIII's advisers, Father Joseph and others believed that Richelieu would be a moderating influence on the King's mother. Accordingly the King recalled him from Avignon in March 1619 and ordered him to resume serving her. Thereafter Richelieu's biography merges increasingly with the history of the monarchy. Representing the queen mother that spring, he negotiated an agreement with the King's commissioners that she would reside in Anjou. She designated his brother Henri de Richelieu as governor of the provincial capital; but 7 weeks later Henri was killed in a duel at Angoulême. This event, the personal sorrow of Armand de Richelieu's life, deprived him of a valued political ally.

The queen mother aspired to sit in the King's council. She also wanted the King to obtain Richelieu's nomination as a cardinal; for him this would mean undisputed political eminence, a voice in important decisions of state, and greater security than a bishop could expect. She hoped in the end to control royal policy through the influence Richelieu would exercise as a member of the King's council. These motives played an important part in the threat of an armed uprising in the summer of 1620 and in the tangle of duplicity and argument that ensued, with Richelieu in the role of mediator between the queen mother and her opponents. The resistance of the King and his ministers gradually crumbled. The queen mother was invited into the council at the beginning of 1622; in the following September, the Pope appointed Richelieu a cardinal; finally, the King called Richelieu to his council in April 1624 and designated him chief councilor 3½ months later.

Position as Minister. Richelieu remained the King's principal minister until his death, and he was made a duke in 1631. He was never the only royal adviser, but he gradually built up in the council a group of men, his "creatures," loyal to him as well as to the King. He was never free from potential rivals.

He relied on his family, which he extended by carefully arranging marriages of his nieces and cousins into great families. Thus he used intensively the kind of patron-client relation that had assisted his early career. He made clear that the King was his patron, and he made sure that Louis XIII knew that Richelieu was the King's creature.

From the first, Richelieu encountered a strong current of "devout" Catholic opinion that regarded Protestants everywhere as the enemy or as possible converts and insisted on reforms within France. The queen mother, Maria, the queen consort, Anne, and the keeper of the seals, Michel Marillac, shared that opinion. Richelieu partly satisfied it for a time, negotiating the marriage of the King's sister Henriette to Charles I of England, conducting the siege of the Huguenot city of La Rochelle, and cooperating with Marillac on a program of proposed reforms. But he firmly advised Louis XIII to intervene in northern Italy, against the Spanish king and the Emperor, in order to maintain a foothold on the route between Madrid and Vienna. Over this question the queen mother finally broke with Richelieu in 1630. The King eliminated her clientele and influence from his court.

Opposition to Richelieu and his policies arose also from ambitious, dissatisfied noblemen. This led to plots sanctioned by the King's brother Gaston (1626, 1632, 1636, and 1642), Queen Anne (1633), and a second cousin of the King, the Comte de Soissons (1636 and 1641). These all failed. Three scions of great families were beheaded (the Comte de Chalais in 1626, the Duc de Montmorency in 1632, and the Marquis de Cinq-Mars in 1642).

Foreign Policy. Richelieu gave first priority to foreign policy. He concluded, probably very early, that war against Spain in the long run would be unavoidable. He strove to delay it by encouraging German resistance to the Hapsburg emperor in Vienna, thereby diverting into central Europe the resources and attention of the Hapsburg king in Madrid. In his German policy, he relied heavily on Father Joseph. He subsidized the Dutch Republic and the Swedish warrior king Gustavus Adolphus (Gustavus II) and in 1634 was prepared to aid the Bohemian general A. E. W. von Wallenstein against the Emperor.

From 1635 until his death Richelieu was preoccupied by an overt war against Spain and by the diplomacy it entailed. The fighting occurred principally on the northern and eastern frontiers of France, secondarily on the Mediterranean coast and in the Pyrenees. It was complicated by armed revolts of the populace, especially in western provinces. Richelieu negotiated often with emissaries of Spain but insisted on French control of Lorraine and French garrisons in northern Italy. The negotiations broke down. The war was still going on when Richelieu died on Dec. 4, 1642.

EWB

Riefenstahl, Leni (1902–), German film director. Leni Riefenstahl achieved fame and notoriety for her propaganda film *Triumph of the Will* and her two part rendition of the 1936 Olympic Games, *Olympia,* both made for Adolf Hitler's Third Reich.

Leni Riefenstahl was one of the most controversial figures in the world of film. A talented and ambitious dancer, actress, and director, she had already made a name for herself in her native Germany and abroad when Adolf Hitler came to power in 1933. She admired him, as he did her, and with his friendship and support became the "movie-queen of Nazi Germany," a position she much enjoyed but could not live down after the fall of the Third Reich. In spite of her energetic attempts to continue as a filmmaker and her protestations that she had done nothing but be an unpolitical artist, she never managed to complete another film. Eventually she turned to still photography, producing two books on the African tribe of the Nuba (*The Last of the Nuba,* 1974, and *The People of Kau,* 1976) and one of underwater pictures (*Coral Gardens,* 1978), for which she learned to scuba dive at the age of 73. These photographs continued her life-long fascination with the beauty and strength of the human body, especially the male, and her early interest in natural life away from modern civilization.

Early Career as Dancer and Actress. Helene Berta Amalie Riefenstahl was born in Berlin on August 22, 1902. Her father, Alfred Riefenstahl, owned a plumbing firm and died in World War II, as did her only brother, Heinz. Early on she decided to become a dancer and received thorough training, both in traditional Russian ballet and in modern dance with Mary Wigman. By 1920 Riefenstahl was a successful dancer touring such cities as Munich, Frankfurt, Prague, Zurich, and Dresden.

She became interested in cinema when she saw one of the then popular mountain films of Arnold Fanck. With characteristic decisiveness and energy she set out to meet Fanck and entice him to offer her the role of a dancer in his *Der heilige Berg* (*The Holy Mountain,* 1926). It was well-received and Riefenstahl made up her mind to stay with the relatively new medium of motion pictures. Over the next seven years she made five more films with Fanck: *Der grosse Sprung* (*The Great Leap,* 1927), *Die weisse Hölle vom Piz Palü* (*The White Hell of Piz Palü,* 1929), *Stürme über dem Mont Blanc* (*Storms over Mont Blanc,* 1930), *Der weisse Rausch* (*The White Frenzy,* 1931), and *S. O. S. Eisberg* (*S. O. S. Iceberg,* 1933). She also tried acting in another type of film with a different director, but *Das Schicksal derer von Habsburg* (*The Fate of the Hapsburgs,* 1929) turned out to be an unsatisfactory venture. In Fanck's films Riefenstahl was often the only woman in a crew of rugged men who were devoted to getting the beauty and the dangers of the still untouched high mountains (and for *S. O. S. Eisberg,* of the Arctic) onto their action-filled adventure films. Not only did she learn to climb and ski well, she also absorbed all she could about camera work, directing, and editing.

The Blue Light. Eventually Riefenstahl conceived of a different kind of mountain film, more romantic and mystical, in which a woman, played by herself, would be the central character and which she herself would direct. *Das blaue Licht* (*The Blue Light,* 1932) was based on a mountain legend and was shot in remote parts of the Tessin and the Dolomites. It demanded—and received—a great deal of dedication from those involved, many of whom were former associates of Fanck's who continued to work with her on other films. She also obtained the help of the well-known avant-garde author and film theoretician Bela Balazs, a Marxist and Jew, who collaborated on the script and as assistant director. *The Blue Light* won acclaim abroad, where it received the silver medal at the 1932 Biennale in Venice, and at home, where it also attracted the attention of Hitler.

Films for the Third Reich. When Adolf Hitler came to power he asked Riefenstahl to film that year's Nazi party rally in Nuremberg. *Sieg des Glaubens* (*Victory of Faith,* 1933) has been lost; presumably it was destroyed because it showed party members who were soon afterward liquidated by Hitler. With his power consolidated he wanted Riefenstahl to do the 1934 rally as well, a task she claims to have accepted only after a second "invitation" and the promise of total artistic freedom.

Triumph des Willens (*Triumph of the Will,* 1935) is considered by many to be *the* propaganda film of all times, even if its director later maintained that all she had made was a documentary. Carefully edited from over 60 hours of film by herself, with concern for rhythm and variety rather than chronological accuracy, it emphasizes the solidarity of the Nazi party, the unity of the German people, and the greatness of their leader who, through composition, cutting, and special camera angles, is given mythical dimensions. Filming Albert Speer's architechtural spectacle where the Nazi icons, swastika, and eagle are displayed prominently and, together with flags, lights, flames, and music, made a powerful appeal to the irrational, emotional side of the viewer, particularly the German of the time. Not surprisingly, the film was awarded the German Film Prize for 1935. But it was also given the International Grand Prix at the 1937 Paris World Exhibition, albeit over the protest of French workers.

Riefenstahl's next film, the short *Tag der Freiheit: Unsere Wehrmacht* (*Day of Freedom: Our Armed Forces,* 1935) was in a way a sequel, shot to placate the German Armed Forces, who were not at all pleased about having received little attention in *Triumph of the Will.*

Another major assignment from Hitler followed: to shoot the 1936 Olympic Games held in Germany. *Olympia,* Part 1: *Fest der Völker* (*Festival of Nations*) and Part 2: *Fest der Schönheit* (*Festival of Beauty*) premiered in 1938, again to great German and also international acclaim. Elaborate and meticulous preparation, technical inventiveness, and 18 months of laborious editing helped Riefenstahl elevate sports photography—until then a matter for newsreels only—to a level of art seldom achieved. From the naked dancers in the opening sequence and the emphasis upon the African American athlete Jesse Owens to the striking diving and steeplechase scenes, the film celebrated the beauty of the human form in motion in feats of strength and endurance.

Immediately after completing *The Blue Light* Riefenstahl had made plans to film *Tiefland* (*Lowlands*), a project that was to be interrupted by illness, Hitler's assignments, and the war. When it was finished in 1954 all fire had gone out of this tale of innocence and corruption, high mountains and lowlands, based on the opera by the Czech Eugene d'Albert. Many of Riefenstahl's other projects, most notably her plan to do a film on Penthisilea, the Amazon queen, were never completed at all. This was due partly to the fact that she was a woman in a man's profession but mostly to the war and the choices she made under the Nazis and for them. Ultimately, all her work, in spite of the great talent and dedication it so clearly demonstrates, is tainted by the readiness and skill with which she put her art at the service of the Third Reich, no matter whether it was from conviction, political naivete, ambition, or, most likely, a combination of all three.

In 1993, when she was 91 years old, German director Ray Mueller made a film biography (*The Wonderful, Horrible Life of Leni Riefenstahl*). The release of the film coincided with the English translation of her autobiography *Leni Riefenstahl: A Biography.* In both the film and the book, Riefenstahl claims her innocence and mistreatment, never realizing the effect that her films had on promoting the Nazi cause. Ray Muller was quoted in (*Time Magazine*) as declaring "she is still a 30's diva, after all and not accustomed to being crossed. By the second day, I was asking prickly questions and she was having choleric fits." In his review of the film, *New York Times* film critic Vincent Canby concluded "Ms. Riefenstahl doesn't come across as an especially likable character which is to her credit and Mr. Muller's. She is beyond likability. She is too complex, too particular and too arrogant to be seen as either sympathetic or unsympathetic. There's the suspicion that she had always had arrogance and that it, backed up by her singular talent, is what helped to shape her wonderful and horrible life."

EWB

Robespierre, Maximilien François Marie Isidore de (1758–1794), French Revolutionary leader. Maximilien de Robespierre was the spokesman for the policies of the dictatorial government that ruled France during the crisis brought on by civil and foreign war.

Maximilien de Robespierre was an early proponent of political democracy. His advanced ideas concerning the application of the revolutionary principle of equality won for him the fervent support of the lower middle and working classes (the *sans-culottes*) and a firm place later in the 19th century in the pantheon of European radical and revolutionary heroes. These ideas and the repressive methods used to implement and defend them, which came to be called the Reign of Terror, and his role as spokesman for this radical and violent phase of the French Revolution also won for him the opprobrium of conservative opponents of the Revolution ever since.

Career before the Revolution. Robespierre was born on May 6, 1758, in the French provincial city of Arras. He was educated first in that city and then at the Collège Louis-le-Grand in Paris. Upon completing his studies with distinction, he took up his father's profession of law in Arras and soon had a successful practice. But he had developed a sense of social justice, and as the Revolution of 1789 loomed, he assumed a public role as an advocate of political change, contributing to the pamphlet and *cahier* literature of the day, and being elected at the age of 30 a member of the Third Estate delegation from Arras to the Estates General, where he quickly associated himself with the Patriot party.

Role in Early Revolution. During the first period of the Revolution (1789–1791), in which the Estates General became the National (or Constituent) Assembly, Robespierre spoke frequently in that body. But his extremely democratic ideas, his emphasis on civil liberty and equality, his uncompromising rigidity in applying these ideas to the issues of the moment, and his hostility to all authority won him little support in this moderate legislature. He favored giving the vote to all men, not just property owners, and he opposed slavery in the colonies. On both of these issues he lost, being ahead of his time.

Robespierre found more receptive listeners at the Paris Jacobin Club, where throughout his career he had a devoted following that admired him not only for his radical political views but perhaps even more for his simple Spartan life and high sense of personal morality, which won for him the appellation of "the Incorruptible." His appearance was unprepossessing, and his old-fashioned, prerevolutionary style of dress seemed out of place. He lacked the warmth of personality usually associated with a popular political figure. Yet his carefully written and traditionally formal speeches, because of his utter sincerity and deep personal conviction, won him a wide following.

When his term as a legislator ended in September 1791, Robespierre remained in Paris, playing an influential role in the Jacobin Club and shortly founding a weekly political journal. During this period (1791–1792) he was an unremitting critic of the King and the moderates who hoped to make the experiment in limited, constitutional monarchy a success. Robespierre, profoundly and rightly suspicious of the King's intentions, spoke and wrote in opposition to the course of events, until August 1792, when events turned in his favor with the overthrow of the monarchy and the establishment of the First French Republic.

Period in Power. A Convention was quickly elected to perform the task of drafting a constitution, this time for a democratic republic, and to govern the country in the meantime. Robespierre was elected a member for Paris. As a spokesman for the Mountain, the radical Jacobin faction in the Convention, he played a prominent role in the successive controversies that developed. He was an uncompromising antagonist of the deposed king, who was finally placed on trial, convicted, and executed in January 1793.

The moderate Girondin faction had incurred the enmity of Robespierre and the leaders of the Mountain in the process, and for this and other reasons, both personal and political, there followed months of bitter controversy, climaxed by the victory of the Robespierrist faction, aided by the intervention of the Parisian *sans-culottes,* with the expulsion from the Convention and arrest of the Girondins (June 2,

1793) and the execution shortly thereafter of their leaders.

The dual crises of foreign war, in which most of Europe was now fighting against the Revolutionary government in France, and civil war, which threatened to overthrow that government, had led to the creation of the crisis machinery of government, the Reign of Terror. The central authority in this government was the Committee of Public Safety. For the crucial months from mid-1793 to mid-1794 Robespierre was one of the dominant members of and the spokesman for this dictatorial body. Under their energetic leadership the crisis was successfully surmounted, and by the spring of 1794 the threat of civil war had been ended and the French army was winning decisive victories.

Political controversy had continued, however, as Robespierre, having prevailed against the moderate Girondins, now faced new opposition on both the left and the right. The Hébertists, a radical faction that controlled the Paris city government and was particularly responsive to the grievances of the *sans-culottes* concerning wartime shortages and inflation, actively campaigned for rigorous economic controls, which Robespierre opposed. Nor could he support their vigorous anti-Christian campaign and atheistic Religion of Reason. Robespierre and his colleagues on the committee saw them as a threat, and in March 1794 the Hébertist leaders and their allies were tried and executed.

Two weeks later came the turn of the Indulgents, or Dantonists, the moderate Jacobins who, now that the military crisis was ended, felt that the Terror should be relaxed. Georges Jacques Danton, a leading Jacobin and once a close associate of Robespierre, was the most prominent of this group. Robespierre was inflexible, and Danton and those accused with him were convicted and guillotined.

Robespierre and his associates, who included his brother Augustin and his young disciple Louis de Saint-Just, were now in complete control of the national government and seemingly of public opinion. He thus could impose his own ideas concerning the ultimate aims of the Revolution. For him the proper government for France was not simply one based on sovereignty of the people with a democratic franchise, which had been achieved. The final goal was a government based on ethical principles, a Republic of Virtue. He and those of his associates who were truly virtuous would impose such a government, using the machinery of the Terror, which had been streamlined, at Robespierre's insistence, for the purpose. Coupled with this was to be an officially established religion of the Supreme Being, which Robespierre inaugurated in person.

Downfall and Execution. Opposition arose from a variety of sources. There were disaffected Jacobins who had no interest in such a program and had good reason to fear the imposition of such high ethical principles. More and more of the public, now that the military crisis was past, wanted a relaxation, not a heightening, of the Terror. The crisis came in late July 1794. Robespierre spoke in the Convention in vague but threatening terms of the need for another purge in pursuit of his utopian goals. His opponents responded by taking the offensive against him, and on July 27 (9 Thermidor by the Revolutionary calendar) they succeeded in voting his arrest. He and his colleagues were quickly released, however, and they gathered at the city hall to plan a rising of the Parisian *sans-culottes* against the Convention, such as had prevailed on previous occasions. But the opposition leaders rallied their forces and late that night captured Robespierre and his supporters. In the process Robespierre's jaw was fractured by a bullet, probably from his own hand. Having been declared outlaws, they were guillotined the next day. With this event began the period of the Thermidorian Reaction, during which the Terror was ended and France returned to a more moderate government.

EWB

Rousseau, Jean Jacques (1712–1778), Swiss-born philosopher, author, political theorist, and composer. Jean Jacques Rousseau ranks as one of the greatest figures of the French Enlightenment.

Both Jean Jacques Rousseau the man and his writings constitute a problem for anyone who wants to grasp his thought and to understand his life. He claimed that his work presented a coherent outlook; yet many critics have found only contradictions and passionate outbursts of rhetoric.

For Rousseau's biographers the man himself has been as puzzling as his work—a severe moralist who lived a dangerously "relaxed" life, a misanthrope who loved humanity, a cosmopolitan who prided himself on being a "citizen of Geneva," a writer for the stage who condemned the theater, and a man who became famous by writing essays that denounced culture. In addition to these anomalies, his biographers have had to consider his confessed sexual "peculiarities"—his lifelong habit of masturbation, his exhibitionism, his youthful pleasure in being beaten, his 33-year liaison with a virtual illiterate, and his numerous affairs—and, characteristic of his later years, his persecution suspicions that reached neurotic intensity.

Three major periods characterize Rousseau's life. The first (1712–1750) culminated in the succès de scandale of his *Discours sur les sciences et les arts*. The second (1750–1762) saw the publication of his closely related major works: *La Nouvelle Héloïse* (1761), *L'Émile* (1762), and *Du contrat social* (1762). The last period (1762–1778) found Rousseau an outcast, hounded from country to country, his books condemned and burned, and a personnage, respected and with influential friends. The *Confessions, Dialogues, and Les Rêveries du promeneur solitaire* date from this period.

Youth, 1712–1750.

Rousseau was the second child of a strange marriage. His mother, Suzanne Bernard, had at the age of 33 married Isaac Rousseau, a man less wellborn than she. Isaac, exhausted perhaps by his frequent quarrels over money with his mother-in-law, left his wife in 1705 for Constantinople. He returned to Suzanne in September 1711. Jean Jacques was born on June 28, 1712, at Geneva, Switzerland. Nine days later his mother died.

At the age of 3, Jean Jacques was reading and weeping over French novels with his father. From Isaac's sister the boy acquired his passion for music. His father fled Geneva to avoid imprisonment when Jean Jacques was 10. By the time he was 13, his formal education had ended. Apprenticed to a notary public, he was soon dismissed as fit only for watchmaking. Apprenticed again, this time to an engraver, Rousseau spent 3 wretched years in hateful servitude, which he abandoned when he found himself unexpectedly locked out of the city by its closed gates. He faced the world with no visible assets and no obvious talents.

Rousseau found himself on Palm Sunday, 1728, in Annecy at the house of Louise Eleonore, Baronne de Warens. She sent him to a hospice for catechumens in Turin, where among "the biggest sluts and the most disgusting trollops who ever defiled the fold of the Lord," he embraced the Roman Catholic faith. His return to Madame de Warens in 1729 initiated a strange alliance between a 29-year-old woman of the world and a sensitive 17-year-old youth.

Rousseau lived under her roof off and on for 13 years and was dominated by her influence. He became her *Petit;* she was his *Maman.* Charming and clever, a born speculator, Madame de Warens was a woman who lived by her wits. She supported him; she found him jobs, most of which he regarded as uncongenial. A friend, after examining the lad, informed her that he might aspire to become a village curé but nothing more. Still Rousseau read, studied, and reflected. He pursued music and gave lessons. For a time he was a not too successful tutor.

First Publications and Operas.

In 1733, disturbed by the advances made to Rousseau by the mother of one of his music pupils, Madame de Warens offered herself to him. Rousseau became her lover: "I felt as if I had been guilty of incest." The sojourn with Madame de Warens was over by 1742. Though she had taken other lovers and he had enjoyed other escapades, Rousseau was still devoted to her. He thought that the scheme of musical notation he had developed would make his fortune in Paris and thus enable him to save her from financial ruin. But his journey to Paris took Rousseau out of her life. He saw her only once again, in 1754. Reduced to begging and the charity of her neighbors, Madame de Warens died destitute in 1762.

Rousseau's scheme for musical notation, published in 1743 as *Dissertation sur la musique moderne,* brought him neither fame nor fortune—only a letter of commendation from the Académie des Sciences. But his interest in music spurred him to write two operas *Les Muses galantes* (1742) and *Le Devin du village* (1752)—and permitted him to write articles on music for Denis Diderot's *Encyclopédie; the Lettre sur la musique française,* which embroiled him in a quarrel with the Paris Opéra (1753); and the *Dictionnaire de musique,* published in 1767.

From September 1743 until August 1744 Rousseau served as secretary to the French ambassador to Venice. He experienced at firsthand the stupidity of officialdom and began to see how institutions lend their authority to injustice and oppression in the name of peace and order. Rousseau spent the remaining years before his success with his first *Discours* in Paris, where he lived from hand to mouth the life of a struggling intellectual.

In March 1745 Rousseau began a liaison with Thérèse Le Vasseur. She was 24 years old, a maid at Rousseau's lodgings. She remained with him for the rest of his life—as mistress, housekeeper, mother of his children, and finally, in 1768, as his wife. He portrayed her as devoted and unselfish, although many of his friends saw her as a malevolent gossip and troublemaker who exercised a baleful influence on his suspicions and dislikes. Not an educated woman—Rousseau himself cataloged her malapropisms—she nonetheless possessed the uncommon quality of being able to offer stability to a man of volatile intensity. They had five children—though some biographers have questioned whether any of them were Rousseau's. Apparently he regarded them as his own even though he abandoned them to the foundling hospital. Rousseau had no means to educate them, and he reasoned that they would be better raised as workmen and peasants by the state.

By 1749 Diderot had become a sympathetic friend, and Rousseau regarded him as a kindred spirit. The publication of Diderot's *Lettre sur les aveugles* had resulted in his imprisonment at Vincennes. While walking to Vincennes to visit Diderot, Rousseau read an announcement of a prize being offered by the Dijon Academy for the best essay on the question: has progress of the arts and sciences contributed more to the corruption or to the purification of morals?

Years of Fruition, 1750–1762. Rousseau won the prize of the Dijon Academy with his *Discours sur les sciences et les arts* and became "l'homme du jour." His famous rhetorical "attack" on civilization called forth 68 articles defending the arts and sciences. Though he himself regarded this essay as "the weakest in argument and the poorest in harmony and proportion" of all his works, he nonetheless believed that it sounded one of his essential themes; the arts and sciences, instead of liberating men and increasing their happiness, have for the most part shackled men further. "Necessity erected thrones; the arts and sciences consolidated them," he wrote.

The *Discours sur l'origine de l'inégalité des hommes,* written in response to the essay competition proposed by the Dijon Academy in 1753 (but which did not win the prize), elaborated this theme still further. The social order of civilized society, wrote Rousseau, introduced inequality and unhappiness. This social order rests upon private property. The man who first enclosed a tract of land and called it his own was the true founder of civilized society. "Don't listen to that imposture; you are lost if you forget that the fruits of the earth belong to everyone and the earth to no one," he wrote. Man's greatest ills, said Rousseau, are not natural but made by man himself; the remedy lies also within man's power. Heretofore, man has used his wit and art not to alter his wretchedness but only to intensify it.

Three Major Works. Rousseau's novel *La Nouvelle Héloïse* (1761) attempted to portray in fiction the sufferings and tragedy that foolish education and arbitrary social conventions work among sensitive creatures. Rousseau's two other major treatises, *L'Émile ou de l'éducation* (1762) and *Du contrat social* (1762) undertook the more difficult task of constructing an education and a social order that would enable men to be natural and free; that is, that would enable men to recognize no bondage except the bondage of natural necessity. To be free in this sense, said Rousseau, was to be happy.

Rousseau brought these three works to completion in somewhat trying circumstances. After having returned to the Protestant fold in 1755 and having regained his citizenship of Geneva that same year, Rousseau accepted the rather insistent offer of Madame Louise d'Épinay to install Thérèse and himself in the Hermitage, a small cottage on the d'Épinay estate at Montmorency. While Rousseau was working on his novel there, its heroine materialized in the person of Sophie, Comtesse d'Houdetot; and he fell passionately in love with her. He was 44 years old; Sophie was 27, married to a dullard, the mistress of the talented and dashing Marquis Saint-Lambert, and the sister-in-law of Rousseau's hostess. Rousseau was swept off his feet. Their relationship apparently was never consummated; Sophie pitied Rousseau and loved Saint-Lambert. But Madame d'Épinay and her paramour, Melchior Grimm, meddled in the affair; Diderot was drawn into the business. Rousseau felt that his reputation had been blackened, and a bitter estrangement resulted. Madame d'Épinay insulted Rousseau until he left the Hermitage in December 1757. However, he remained in Montmorency until 1762, when the condemnation of *L'Émile* forced him to flee from France.

La Nouvelle Héloïse appeared in Paris in January 1761. Originally entitled *Lettres de deux amants, habitants d'une petite ville au pied des Alpes,* the work was structurally a novel in letters, after the fashion of the English author Samuel Richardson. The originality of the novel won it hostile reviews, but its romantic eroticism made it immensely popular with the public. It remained a best seller until the French Revolution.

The notoriety of *La Nouvelle Héloïse* was nothing compared to the storm produced by *L'Émile* and *Du contrat social.* Even today the ideas promulgated in these works are revolutionary. Their expression, especially in *L'Émile,* in a style both readable and alluring made them dangerous. *L'Émile* was condemned by the Paris Parlement and denounced by the archbishop of Paris. Both of the books were burned by the authorities in Geneva.

L'Émile* and *Du contrat social. *L'Émile ou de l'éducation* remains one of the world's greatest speculative treatises on education. However, Rousseau wrote to a correspondent who tried to follow *L'Émile* literally, "so much the worse for you!" The work was intended as illustrative of an educational program rather than prescriptive of every practical detail of a proper education. Its overarching spirit is best sensed in opposition to John Locke's essay on education. Locke taught that man should be educated to the station for which he is intended. There should be one education for a prince, another for a physician, and still another for a farmer. Rousseau advocated one education for all. Man should be educated to be a man, not to be a doctor, lawyer, or priest. Nor is a child merely a little man; he is, rather, a developing creature, with passions and powers that vary according to his stage of development. What must be avoided at all costs is the master-slave mode of instruction, with the pupil as either master or slave, for the medium of instruction is far more influential than any doctrine taught through that medium. Hence, an education resting merely on a play of wills—as when the child learns only to please the instructor or when the teacher "teaches" by threatening the pupil with a future misfortune—produces creatures fit to be only masters or slaves, not free men. Only free men can realize a "natural social order," wherein men can live happily.

A few of the striking doctrines set forth in *L'Émile* are: the importance of training the body before the mind, learning first through "things" and later through words, teaching first only that for which a child feels a need so as to impress upon him that thought is a tool whereby he can effectively manage things, motivating a child by catering to his ruling passion of greed, refraining from moral instruction until the awakening of the sexual urge, and raising the child outside the doctrines of any church until late adolescence and then instructing him in the religion of conscience. Although Rousseau's principles have never been fully put into practice, his influence on educational reformers has been tremendous.

L'Émile's companion master work, *Du contrat social,* attempted to spell out the social relation that a properly educated man—a free man—bears to other free men. This treatise is a difficult and subtle work of a penetrating intellect fired by a great passion for humanity. The liberating fervor of the work, however, is easily caught in the key notions of popular sovereignty and general will. Government is not to be confused with sovereignty of the people or with the social order that is created by the social contract. The government is an intermediary set up between the people as law followers and the people as law creators, the sovereignty. Furthermore, the government is an instrument created by the citizens through their collective action expressed in the general will. The purpose of this instrument is to serve the people by seeing to it that laws expressive of the general will of the citizens are in fact executed. In short, the government is the servant of the people, not their master. And further, the sovereignty of the people—the general will of the people—is to be found not merely in the will of the majority or in the will of all but rather in the will as enlightened by right judgment.

As with *L'Émile, Du contrat social* is a work best understood as elaborating the principles of the social order rather than schematizing the mechanism for those general principles. Rousseau's political writings more concerned with immediate application include his *Considérations sur le gouvernement de la Pologne* (1772) and his incomplete *Projet de constitution pour la Corse,* published posthumously in 1862.

Other writings from Rousseau's middle period include the *Encyclopédie* article *Économie politique* (1755); *Lettre sur la Providence* (1756), a reply to Voltaire's poem on the Lisbon earthquake; *Lettre à d'Alembert sur les spectacles* (1758); *Essai sur l'origine des langues* (1761); and four autobiographical *Lettres à Malesherbes* (1762).

Exile and Apologetics, 1762–1778. Forced to flee from France, Rousseau sought refuge at Yverdon in the territory of Bern. Expelled by the Bernese authorities, he found asylum in Môtiers, a village in the Prussian principality of Neuchâtel. Here in 1763 he renounced his Genevan citizenship. The publication of his *Lettres écrites de la montagne* (1764), in which he defended *L'Émile* and criticized "established" reformed churches, aroused the wrath of the Neuchâtel clergy. His house was stoned, and Rousseau fled to the isle of St. Pierre in the Lake of Biel, but he was again expelled by the Bernese. Finally, through the good offices of the British philosopher David Hume, he settled at Wotton, Derbyshire, England, in 1766. Hume managed to obtain from George III a yearly pension for Rousseau. But Rousseau, falsely believing Hume to be in league with his Parisian and Genevan enemies, not only refused the pension but also openly broke with the philosopher. Henceforth, Rousseau's sense of persecution became ever more intense, even at times hysterical.

Rousseau returned to France in June 1767 under the protection of the Prince de Conti. Wandering from place to place, he at last settled in 1770 in Paris. There he made a living, as he often had in the past, by copying music. By December 1770 the *Confessions,* upon which he had been working since 1766, was completed, and he gave readings from this work at various private homes. Madame d'Épinay, fearing an unflattering picture of herself and her friends, intervened; the readings were forbidden by the police. Disturbed by the reaction to his readings and determined to justify himself before the world, Rousseau wrote *Dialogues ou Rousseau, Juge de Jean-Jacques* (1772–1776). Fearful lest the manuscript fall into the hands of his enemies, he attempted to place it on the high altar of Notre Dame. Thwarted in this attempt, he left a copy with the philosopher Étienne Condillac and, not wholly trusting him, with an English acquaintance, Brooke Boothby. Finally, in 1778 Rousseau entrusted copies of both the *Confessions* and the *Dialogues* to his friend Paul Moultou. His last work, *Les Rêveries du promeneur solitaire*, begun in 1776 and unfinished at his death, records how Rousseau, an outcast from society, recaptured "serenity, tranquility, peace, even happiness."

In May 1778 Rousseau accepted Marquis de Giradin's hospitality at Ermenonville near Paris. There, with Thérèse at his bedside, he died on July 2, 1778, probably from uremia. From birth he had suffered from a bladder deformation. From 1748 onward his condition had grown worse. His adoption of the Armenian mode of dress was due to the embarrassment caused by this affliction, and it is not unlikely that much of his suspicious irritability can be traced to the same malady. Rousseau was buried on the île des Peupliers at Ermenonville. In October 1794 his remains were transferred to the Panthéon in Paris. Thérèse, surviving him by 22 years, died in 1801 at the age of 80.

EWB

S

Sade, Donatien Alphonse François, comte de (1740–1814), French writer of psychological and philosophical works. The Marquis de Sade has been traditionally viewed as the greatest incarnation of evil that ever lived. However, new interpretations of his life and writings have begun to appear. It is now generally agreed that despite his reputation, his works, which were ignored for over a century, must be considered as of the first rank. Sade has been termed the "most absolute writer who has ever lived."

Born on June 2, 1740, to Marie Elénore de Maille de Carman, lady-in-waiting to and relative of the Princess de Condé, and Jean Baptiste Joseph François, Comte de Sade, who traced his ancestry to the chaste Laura of Petrarch's poems, the Marquis de Sade may be the most typical and the most unusual representative of the other side of the Enlightenment, the side at which the *philosophes* railed.

Very little is known of Sade's life. He graduated from the Collège Louis-le-Grand, was commissioned as a coronet in the French army, and later sold his commission. He was forced to marry the eldest daughter of a leading magisterial family, Renée Pélagie de Montreuil, who bore him three children. Because of his libertinage, which included the seduction of and elopement with his wife's sister, Anne Prospère, he incurred the unending enmity of his mother-in-law, who eventually had him imprisoned in 1781. Sade had tasted imprisonment before for libertinage and

indebtedness, and he spent half of his adult life in prisons and asylums. Only three public scandals can be proved against him, and none of these seems to merit the punishment meted out to him, reinforcing his claim that he was an unjust victim of his reputation and others' hatreds.

During the Revolution, Sade was released from prison, served as secretary and president of the Piques section of Paris, and represented it at least once before the National Convention, where he addressed a pamphlet calling for the abolition of capital punishment and the enfranchisement of women. His attitudes and actions gained the hatred of Maximilien de Robespierre, who had him imprisoned (1793). He was saved only by the death of the "Incorruptible." Released in 1794, Sade was arrested in 1801 for being the supposed author of a scandalous pamphlet against Napoleon. He spent the rest of his life at Charenton insane asylum, where he died on Dec. 8, 1814. His best-known books include *Justine; ou, Les Malheurs de la vertu* (1791) and its sequel, *Histoire de Juliette; ou, Les Prospérités du vice* (1797).

Thus the life of the Marquis de Sade. Who was he? Why did he acquire the unique reputation he possesses? There are no simple answers regarding the life of any man. For Sade, there is possibly no answer at all. Works on his life have justly sought answers in his literary works, and because of this most commentators tend to psychoanalyze him. Although many of these works have offered brilliant insights into the character of the man, none of them is definitive and most treat him out of context, as though his life and aberrations were apart from life. Most Sadean scholars tend to agree that his hostility to religion, to the established social and political order, and to the despotism of existing law was similar in many ways to that of the *philosophes*. Some writers believe that he carried the beliefs of the *philosophes* to the rational conclusions, which in the end negated the conclusions and opened for succeeding generations a moral abyss. Others focus on what is termed a philosophy of destruction found in Sade's writings. Sade's atheism is viewed as the first element in a dialectic which destroys divinity through sacrilege and blasphemy and raises to preeminence an indifferent and unfolding nature which destroys to create and creates to destroy. Nature itself is then destroyed by being constantly outraged because it takes on the same sovereign character as God. What emerges is the "Unique One," the man who rises above nature and arrogates to himself the creative and destructive capacities of nature in an extreme form, becoming solitary, alone, unique in the conscious awareness that he is the creative force and all others are but the material through which his energy is expressed.

EWB

Saint-Just, Louis Antoine Léon de (1767–1794), radical political leader during the French Revolution and member of the ruling Jacobin group in Paris during the Reign of Terror.

Louis de Saint-Just was born on Aug. 25, 1767, in Decize, the son of an army officer. After a period of schooling, he ran away from home to Paris, taking with him part of the family silver. He studied law for a time and also published a burlesque epic which was a mixture of the crudely erotic and of sharp criticism of the government and society of his day.

When the Revolution broke out in 1789, the youthful Saint-Just gave it his enthusiastic support, and he published in 1791 *The Spirit of the Revolution and of the Constitution of France.* He was too young to be elected to the Legislative Assembly that year, but in September 1792 he was elected a member of the Convention, whose task it was, now that the King had been deposed, to draft a new constitution and to govern France in the meantime. Saint-Just, handsome, proud, and self-possessed, spoke with the zeal of a dedicated revolutionist. He ruthlessly and brilliantly urged the trial and execution of the King; he participated actively in drafting the Constitution of 1793; and in the feverish atmosphere of foreign and civil war, he became the spokesman for the Jacobins in demanding the death of their moderate opponents, the Girondins.

In June 1793 Saint-Just became a member of the Committee of Public Safety, the executive body that ruled France in dictatorial fashion, using the so-called Reign of Terror as a means of repressing opposition. In October he was sent as a representative to the Army of the Rhine in Strasbourg, where the war was going badly and factionalism and opposition to the government in Paris were at their height. He was twice sent on similar missions to the Army of the North.

Back in Paris, Saint-Just defended the Terror in speeches and proposed a redistribution of the property of the disloyal rich, a plan that was never implemented. As spokesman for the Robespierrist faction, he denounced the extremist Hébertists; he also denounced Georges Jacques Danton and the Indulgents; and each time the objects of his scorn were sent to the guillotine.

Although a determined terrorist, Saint-Just was also an idealist. His unpublished *Fragments concerning Republican Institutions* reveals his Rousseauistic and Spartan utopianism. He and Robespierre were determined to fashion a new France, a "Republic of Virtue," and for that goal the continuation of the Terror was essential. But a moderate trend had begun, prompted in part by the military victory of Fleurus,

to which Saint-Just had contributed during his last mission to the army. For this and other reasons, a fatal split took place.

Saint-Just prepared a report denouncing his and Robespierre's opponents, to be delivered to the Convention on July 27, 1794. But he was interrupted by the opposition, and he, Robespierre, and their colleagues were arrested. Released by their supporters, they gathered at the city hall, hoping to prevail over their enemies with the aid of the Parisian populace. But shortly after midnight they were captured and executed. Saint-Just's youthful beauty and his terrible virtue have earned him the sobriquet of "archangel of the Revolution."

EWB

Saint-Simon, Claude Henri de Rouvroy, comte de (1760–1825), French social philosopher and reformer. Saint-Simon was one of the founders of modern industrial socialism and evolutionary sociology.

The Comte de Saint-Simon was born in Paris to the poorer side of a prominent noble family. From childhood on he was filled with great ambitions that took him on many different paths. First commissioned into the army at 17, he served 4 years, during which he fought with some distinction in the American Revolution.

On his return to Europe, Saint-Simon tried a series of bold commercial ventures but had limited success before the French Revolution. During the Terror of 1793–1794 he was imprisoned for a year and barely escaped execution. This experience left him deeply opposed to revolutionary violence. After his release, for a short time he obtained a sizable fortune by speculating in confiscated properties, which he spent on a lavish Paris salon that attracted many intellectual and government leaders. But his funds were soon exhausted, and he lived his remaining years in constant financial difficulties.

In 1802 Saint-Simon turned to a new career as writer and reformer. In numerous essays and brochures written during the chaotic years of Napoleon's rule and the Bourbon restoration that followed, he developed a broad-ranging program for the reorganization of Europe. Although many of its ideas were commonplace, his program is distinctive for its blending of Enlightenment ideals, the more practical materialism of the rising bourgeoisie, and the emphasis on spiritual unity of restorationists.

All three strands are joined in Saint-Simon's evolutionary view of history as a determined progression from one stable form of civilization to another, which gave his program a distinctive rationale. Each higher form was thought to be based on more advanced "spiritual" as well as "temporal" (that is, political-economic) principles, reflecting a more general process of cultural enlightenment. But each in turn also is destined to become obsolete as further cultural progress occurs.

Saint-Simon argued that all of Europe had been in a transitional crisis since the 15th century, when the established medieval order (based on feudalism and Catholicism) began to give way to a new system founded on industry and science. He wrote as the new system's advocate, urging influential leaders to hasten its inception as the only way to restore stability. In this he was one of the first ameliorators to argue for reform as an evolutionary necessity.

Saint-Simon's earlier writings, during Napoleon's reign (*Introduction aux travaux scientifiques du XIX siècle,* 1807–1808; and *Mémoire sur la science de l'homme,* 1813), stress the spiritual side of the transitional crisis. He argued that disorder was rampant because theistic Roman Catholicism, the spiritual basis of medieval society, was being undermined by the rise of science and secular philosophies. Although the trend was inevitable, Saint-Simon was highly critical of many scientists and intellectuals for their "negativism" in breaking down an established creed without providing a replacement. Instead, he called for the creation of an integrative social science, grounded in biology, to help establish a new "positive" credo for secular man in the emerging social order. This "positivistic" notion was developed by his one-time disciple Auguste Comte.

After Napoleon's downfall Saint-Simon shifted his attention from the ideology of the new system to its temporal structure and policies in a series of periodicals: *L'Industrie* (1816–1818); *La Politique* (1819); *L'Organisateur* (1819–1820); and *Du Système industriel* (1821–1822). These contain his main socialist writings, but his doctrines often are closer to venture capitalism and technocracy than to Marxism or primitive communalism. Saint-Simon's future society is above all one of productive achievement in which poverty and war are eliminated through large-scale "industrialization" (a word he coined) under planned scientific guidance. It is an open-class society in which caste privileges are abolished, work is provided for all, and rewards are based on merit. Government also changes from a haphazard system of class domination and national rivalries to a planned welfare state run by scientific managers in the public interest.

Saint-Simon's final work, *Le Nouveau Christianisme* (1825), inspired a Christian socialist movement called the Saint-Simonians, who were devoted to a secular gospel of economic progress and human brotherhood. After his death, his ideas were reworked by followers into the famous *Doctrine de Saint-Simon* (1829). This was the first systematic exposition of industrial socialism, and it had great influence on the Social Democratic movement, Catholic reforms, and Marxism.

EWB

Salazar, António de Oliveira (1889–1970), Portuguese statesman. The government of António de Oliveira Salazar once was considered to be the very model of a modern authoritarian political system.

António de Oliveira Salazar was born on April 28, 1889, in Vimieiro near Santa Comba Dão in the province of Beira Alta. His parents, owners of several small estates, as well as innkeepers, were António de Oliveira and María de Resgate Salazar, who, despite financial problems, saw to it that Salazar was well educated. He entered the seminary of Viseu in 1900, but after 8 years of religious training he decided to teach. In 1910 he began to study economics at the University of Coimbra, spending 4 years there as a student and another 7 as an economics professor. He obtained a chair of political economy in 1918. A knowledge of economics was valuable in underdeveloped Portugal, and soon Salazar was well known by the government for his monetary skills.

The emergence of Salazar as a national figure came at a difficult moment in Portuguese history. After more than a century of economic difficulties tied to imperial decline, political life had degenerated badly. The double assassination of Carlos I and the crown prince in February 1908 and the overthrow of Manuel II in October 1910 had led to creation of a republic which in the 16 years of its existence went from crisis to crisis. The University of Coimbra furnished many republican leaders in the first phase of the period, but spread of a deeper radicalism engendered a conservative reaction led by António Sardinha. He sought an "organic monarchy" that would be traditionalist and antiparliamentary, but chaos prevented any success.

Economic Policies. In the stalemate after 1918 Salazar's star rose. His economic thought was strongly influenced by Catholic corporatism and Leo XIII's *Rerum novarum.* He favored joint labor-management industrial commissions, compulsory arbitration, and Catholic trade unions. In January 1921 Salazar was one of three Catholic deputies elected to the Parliament, but turmoil was still so great that he attended only a few sessions before returning to the university. However, in May 1926, when a military dictatorship overthrew the republic, Salazar was offered the Ministry of Economic Affairs. He refused the position until 1928, when he received great powers which made him the most important figure in the government.

Salazar's reforms brought some national stability by prohibiting the import of foreign goods, cutting the state budget, and developing a new tax system. Soon he turned to a revision of the structure of government itself. "In an administrative system in which lack of sincerity and clarity were evident," he said, "the first requirement is a policy of truth. In a social order in which rights were competitive and unaccompanied by equivalent duties, the crying need is for a policy of sacrifice. And in a nation divided against itself by groups and clashing interests which threatened its unity, the main need is a national policy."

Ruler of Portugal. The national policy emerged during 1929 in the wake of Portugal's newfound stability, when Salazar's reforms stood the test of the Depression. The military leaders of the dictatorship no longer had as much prestige or interest in ruling, and Salazar informally became the strongest man in the regime. He immediately began to write a new constitution which was approved by plebiscite on March 19, 1933. It created a corporative state divided by levels into *sindicatos* (government unions by industry), *gremios* (guilds of employers), and *ordens* (white-collar organizations). Each of these handled welfare arrangements, employment of their members, and vocational training and negotiated national wage agreements. Each was also guided by special government secretariats that dictated policy. A fourth level was made up by the armed forces, although here there was more autonomy in honor of the role played by the services in establishing the new regime. All four levels elected representatives who then chose deputies for the national Parliament, giving the franchise to the corporative institutions rather than to the national electorate, a variation of the indirect franchise. Salazar's motto was "control by stability," which was facilitated further by the provision that only his National Union party had official status. The president of the party became president of the republic with enormous executive powers, not the least being control of the newly established secret police, the PIDE.

Much of this structure had been modeled on Mussolini's Italy, and Salazar remained diplomatically close to Mussolini in the 1930s. He intrigued several times against the Spanish Republic, and when the Civil War broke out in Spain, he recognized Franco's Nationalists in December 1937. Portugal supplied funds and arms to the Burgos government until the end of the war, and on March 17, 1939, a pact of friendship and nonaggression was signed between the two countries which pledged eternal opposition to communism and created an "Iberian bloc" linking them together against outside attack. For Portugal it was the first time since 1640 that it had cooperated directly with Spain, but even so Salazar was restrained by long-standing treaties with Great Britain, which kept him from closer cooperation with either Franco or Mussolini. Portugal, as a result, remained correctly neutral during World War II until 1943, when Salazar granted the Allies bases in Portuguese territory. His anticommunism brought Portugal into NATO in 1949 and won him backing to join the United Nations at the same time.

Postwar Period. The postwar period, despite these successes, was troubled, first because of domestic economic difficulties and then because of colonial unrest in Angola and Mozambique. Government mismanagement of both problems led to renewal of opposition to Salazar's dictatorship in 1956. Two years later, an opposition candidate, Humberto Delgado, polled a quarter million votes for the presidency, which Salazar had occupied since 1951. The PIDE became more active, but the opposition continued to grow until 1965, when Delgado was assassinated in Spain. By that time draconian measures in the colonies diminished the drive for independence to the point where there was less unrest in metropolitan Portugal, although vestiges of opposition continued to manifest themselves spasmodically until September 1968, when Salazar was incapacitated by a massive brain hemorrhage. His 36-year rule thus came to an end on September 27, when Marcelo Caetano of the National Union replaced him in the premiership. Salazar died on July 27, 1970, in Lisbon.

EWB

Sand, George (1804–1876), French novelist. The most successful woman writer of her century, George Sand's novels present a large fresco of romantic sentiment and 19th-century life, especially in its more pastoral aspects.

George Sand was born Amandine Aurore Lucille Dupin in Paris on July 1, 1804. On her father's side she was related to a line of kings and to the Maréchal de Saxe; her mother was the daughter of a professional bird fancier. Aurore's father, Maurice Dupin, was a soldier of the Empire. He died when Aurore was still a child.

At the age of 14, tired of being the "apple of discord" between her mother and grandmother, Aurore went to the convent of the Dames Augustines Anglaises in Paris. Though she did her best to disrupt the convent's peaceful life, she felt drawn to quiet contemplation and direct communication with God.

To save Aurore from mysticism, her grandmother called her to her home in Nohant. Here Aurore studied nature, practiced medicine on the peasants, read from the philosophers of all ages, and developed a passion for the works of François René Chateaubriand. Her eccentric tutor encouraged her to wear men's clothing while horseback riding, and she galloped through the countryside in trousers and loose shirt, free, wild, and in love with nature.

Marriage and Lovers. When her grandmother died, Aurore became mistress of the estate at Nohant. At 19 she married Casimir Dudevant, the son of a baron and a servant girl. He was good-hearted but coarse and sensual, and he offended her lofty and mystical ideal of love. Aurore soon began to seek her idealized love object elsewhere. For a time she maintained a platonic relationship with Aurélien de Sèze, but eventually this affair languished. She had begun to realize that it was impossible to sustain love without physical passion.

At the age of 27 Aurore moved to Paris in search of independence and love, leaving husband and children behind. She began writing articles to earn her living and met a coterie of writers. Henri de Latouche and Charles Sainte-Beuve became her mentors.

Aurore fell in love with Jules Sandeau, a charming young writer. They collaborated on articles and signed them collectively "J. Sand." When she published her first novel, *Indiana* (1832), she took as her pen name "George Sand."

George Sand made a home for Sandeau and for her daughter, Solange, but eventually she wearied of his jealousy and idle disposition. He, in turn, realized that he could never overcome her essential frigidity. She felt as though she had failed in marriage as well as in adultery. Several novels of disillusioned love were the fruit of this period of her life. Then she met the young poet Alfred de Musset, and they became lovers.

George Sand legally separated from her husband; she gained custody over Solange, while her husband kept the other child, Maurice. She now came to enjoy great renown in Paris both as a writer and as a bold and brilliant woman. She had many admirers and chose new lovers from among them. Her lovers included the Polish composer Frédéric Chopin and the doctor who attended Musset in Venice. Perhaps it was her inability to be aroused to physical passion that drove her from one lover to another. She compensated for this deficiency by the spiritual intensity of her love.

Political Views. George Sand was a democrat; she felt close to the people by birth, and she often praised the humble virtues of the urban and country poor in her novels. She was a Christian of sorts and advocated a socially conscious religion. Like Jean Jacques Rosseau, she believed that inherently good man was corrupted by civilization and faulty institutions.

Despite her own feminist leanings, George Sand never advocated political equality for women. It was in love that she demanded equality, in the free choice of the love object; the inequality of men and women before the law seemed to her a scandal.

Last Years. As she grew older, George Sand spent more and more time at her beloved Nohant and gave herself up to the intoxications of pastoral life, the entertainment of friends, the staging of puppet shows, and most of all to her grandchildren. Though she had lost none of her vital energy and enthusiasm, she grew less concerned with politics. Her quest for the absolute in love had led her through years of stormy affairs to the attainment of a tolerant and universal love of God, of nature, of children. She died in Nohant on June 9, 1876.

Early Novels. Every night from midnight until dawn, George Sand covered her daily quota of 20 pages with her large, tranquil writing, never crossing out a line. All her novels are love stories in which her romantic idealism unfolds in a realistic setting. The characters are people she knew, although their sentiments are idealized.

The early works by George Sand are novels of passion, written to alleviate the pain of her first love affairs. *Indiana* (1832) has as its central theme woman's search for the absolute in love. *Valentine* (1832) depicts an aristocratic woman, unhappily married, who finds that a farmer's son loves her. *Lélia* (1854) is a lyrical but searching confession of the author's own physical coldness. Lélia is a beautiful woman loved by a young poet, but she can show him only maternal affection.

Socialist Novels. During the 1840s George Sand wrote a number of novels in which she exposed her socialist doctrine joined with a humanitarian religion. *Le Compagnon du tour de France* (1840), *Consuelo* (1842–1843), and *Le Péché de Monsieur Antoine* (1847) are typical novels of this period. Her socialism was of an optimistic, idealistic nature. She sympathized in these novels with the plight of the worker and the farmer. She also wrote a number of novels devoted to country life, most produced during her retreat to Nohant at the time of the 1848 uprising. *La Mare au diable* (1846), *La Petite Fadette* (1849), and *Les Maîtres sonneurs* (1852) are typical novels of this genre. They celebrate the humble virtues of a simple life and offer idealized portraits of the peasants of Berry.

George Sand's last works show a tendency to moralize; in these novels the characters become incarnated theories rather than human beings.

EWB

Sartre, Jean-Paul (1905–1980), French philosopher and man of letters. Jean-Paul Sartre ranks as the most versatile writer and as the dominant influence in three decades of French intellectual life.

Jean-Paul Sartre was born in Paris on June 21, 1905. His father, a naval officer, died while on a tour of duty in Indochina before Sartre was two years old. His mother belonged to the Alsatian Schweitzer family and was a first cousin to Albert Schweitzer. The young widow returned to her parents' house, where she and her son were treated as "the children." In the first volume of his autobiography, *The Words* (1964), Sartre describes his unnatural childhood as a spoiled and precocious boy. Lacking any companions his own age, the child found "friends" exclusively in books. Reading and writing thus became his twin passions. "It was in books that I encountered the universe."

Sartre entered the École Normale Supérieure in 1924 and after one failure received first place in the *agrégation* of philosophy in 1929. The novelist Simone de Beauvoir finished second that year, and the two formed an intimate bond that endured thereafter. After completing compulsory military service, Sartre took a teaching job at a lycée in Le Havre. There he wrote his first novel, *Nausea* (1938), which some critics have called the century's most influential French novel.

From 1933 to 1935 Sartre was a research student at the Institut Français in Berlin and in Freiburg. He discovered the works of Edmund Husserl and Martin Heidegger and began to philosophize in the phenomenological vein. A series of works on the modalities of consciousness poured from Sartre's pen: two works on imagination, one on self-consciousness, and one on emotions. He also produced a first-rate volume of short stories, *The Wall* (1939).

Sartre returned to Paris to teach in a lycée and to continue his writing, but World War II intervened. Called up by the army, he served briefly on the Eastern front and was taken prisoner. After nine months he secured his release and returned to teaching in Paris, where he became active in the Resistance. During this period he wrote his first major work in philosophy, *Being and Nothingness: An Essay in Phenomenological Ontology* (1943).

After the war Sartre abandoned teaching, determined to support himself by writing. He was also determined that his writing and thinking should be *engagé*. Intellectuals, he thought, must take a public stand on every great question of their day. He thus became fundamentally a moralist, both in his philosophical and literary works.

Sartre had turned to playwriting and eventually produced a series of theatrical successes which are essentially dramatizations of ideas, although they contain some finely drawn characters and lively plots. The first two, *The Flies* and *No Exit*, were produced in occupied Paris. They were followed by *Dirty Hands* (1948), usually called his best play; *The Devil and the Good Lord* (1957), a blasphemous, anti-Christian tirade; and *The Prisoners of Altona* (1960), which combined convincing character portrayal with telling social criticism. Sartre also wrote a number of comedies: *The Respectful Prostitute* (1946), *Kean* (1954), and *Nekrassov* (1956), which the critic Henry Peyre claimed "reveals him as the best comic talent of our times."

During this same period Sartre also wrote a three-volume novel, *The Roads to Freedom* (1945–1949); a treatise on committed literature; lengthy studies of Charles Baudelaire and Jean Genet; and a prodigious number of reviews and criticisms. He also edited *Les Temps modernes*.

Though never a member of the Communist party, Sartre usually sympathized with the political views of the far left. Whatever the political issue, he was quick to publish his opinions, often combining them with public acts of protest.

In 1960 Sartre returned to philosophy, publishing the first volume of his *Critique of Dialectical Reason*. It represented essentially a modification of his existentialism by Marxist ideas. The drift of Sartre's earlier work was toward a sense of the futility of life. In *Being and Nothingness* he declared man to be "a useless passion," condemned to exercise a meaningless freedom. But after World War II his new interest in social and political questions and his rapprochement with Marxist thought led him to more optimistic and activist views.

Sartre has always been a controversial yet respected individual. In 1964, Sartre was awarded but refused to accept the Nobel Prize in literature. Sartre suffered from detrimental health throughout the 1970s. He died of a lung ailment in 1980.

EWB

Schmoller, Gustav Friedrich von (1838–1917), German economist. Gustav Friedrich von Schmoller broadened the study of economics by insisting that it be studied dynamically in the context of history and sociology.

Gustav von Schmoller was born on June 24, 1838, in Württemberg-Baden. He was from a family of civil servants and continued in that tradition. His studies in civic administration at the University of Tübingen included public finance, statistics, economics, administration, history, and sociology. He served as professor of civic administration at the universities of Halle (1864–1872), Strasbourg (1872–1882), and Berlin (1882–1913). He was also a member of academies in Berlin, Munich, St. Petersburg, Copenhagen, Vienna, and Rome.

In the early 1860s Schmoller defended the commercial treaty between France and the German Customs Union, negotiated with Prussian leadership. This defense curtailed his career in Württemberg but gained favor for him with Prussian authorities, and he was appointed official historian of Brandenburg and Prussia in 1887. He became a member of the Prussian state council in 1884 and representative of the University of Berlin in the Prussian upper house in 1889. He died at Bad Harzburg on June 27, 1917.

Schmoller was the founder and leader of the Association of German Academic Economists. He was also editor of several publications series, one of which was later known as *Schmoller's Yearbook* (from 1881). One of the first great organizers of research in the social sciences, he dominated for several decades the development of economics and of related social sciences. During this time hardly a chair of economics in German universities was filled without his approval.

In political activities Schmoller was a royalist, favored strong government, and had high regard for the Prussian civil service. He was a conservative social reformer who wanted to improve working-class conditions by means of better education, government regulations, cooperatives, and other reforms.

Schmoller's contribution to economics was to reject its study in a narrow analytical view and to place it in the context of the other social sciences. Opposing a theoretical approach, he preferred to include in economics relevant aspects of history, statistics, sociology, social psychology, social anthropology, geography, and even ethics and philosophy. He was eclectic in assembling these aspects into a panorama of the social sciences. He was challenged as superficial by theoretical economist Carl Menger of Vienna in an 1883 pamphlet, by historian Georg von Below in 1904, and by others. Modern critics view Schmoller's long dominance of German social scientists as unfortunate because its effect was to retard development of economic theory in Germany. Outside Germany his influence in economics was small, although he did influence American institutional economics.

EWB

Schopenhauer, Arthur (1788–1860), German philosopher. Schopenhauer's pessimistic philosophy, widely known in the late 19th century in Europe and the United States, held that ultimate reality was nothing but senseless striving or will, having no divine origin and no historical end.

Arthur Schopenhauer was born in Danzig on Feb. 22, 1788. His father, a successful Dutch businessman, had a taste for urbane living, travel, and bourgeois culture, while his mother aspired to the more exotic culture of writers and nonconformists. When Schopenhauer was 5, Danzig, formerly a free mercantile city, was annexed by Poland. As a consequence, his family moved to Hamburg, Germany, in search of a more congenial setting for his father's business. In 1797 Schopenhauer was sent to stay with a family in France, returning to Hamburg after 2 years to enter a private school. Later he became interested in literature, earning the disapproval of his father, who nonetheless gave him the choice of pursuing serious literary studies or traveling with the family for 2 years. Schopenhauer chose to travel.

His voyages over, Schopenhauer took a job as a clerk in a Hamburg merchant's office. That year, 1805, his father died, apparently a suicide. The mercantile world held only drudgery for young Schopenhauer, whose ambitions and desires were both unfocused and frustrated. Feeling constrained by a promise to his father, Schopenhauer remained at work until 1807, when he joyfully resigned in order to study Greek and Latin in a school at Gotha. Having enraged an unsympathetic instructor, he transferred to a school in Weimar, where his mother had already established herself as mistress of a literary salon frequented by Goethe and other notables. But Schopenhauer had earlier quarreled with his mother, whom he thought too free with her ideas and her favors. He therefore resided with his mentor, the philologist Franz Passow, who paid his tuition. Schopenhauer's studies went well, and in 1809, on acquiring a handsome legacy, he enrolled at the University of Göttingen. He studied mostly the sciences and medicine but eventually turned to philosophy.

Philosophical Studies. Schopenhauer's new passion for philosophy led him to the University of Berlin, where he hoped to cull the wisdom of Johann Gottlieb Fichte, then the foremost philosopher in Germany. He was disappointed in Fichte but remained at the university until 1813, when Prussia mobilized to expel the French after Napoleon's defeat. Seeing the dangers of staying in Berlin and having no heart for nationalistic fervor, Schopenhauer sought refuge in Rudolstadt. There he completed his doctoral dissertation, which he submitted successfully to the University of Jena. He published the dissertation at his own expense and then returned to Weimar. He met Goethe, who seemed sympathetic to his thinking. One fruit of their conversations was Schopenhauer's brief study *Über das Sehn und die Farben* (1816; *On Vision and Colors*).

The World as Will and Idea. Schopenhauer's unhappy relations with his mother finally terminated in open hostility, and he moved to Dresden. By this time the central and simple idea of his philosophy had taken hold in his mind. The principal source of this idea was his own experience and moods, but the expression of it owed much to the philosophies of Plato and Immanuel Kant and the mystical literature of India. He foresaw that his reflections would eventually lift him above the absurd stresses and conflicts of his life, and he thought that ultimately his writings would usher in a new era not only in philosophy but also in human history. Whereas former philosophies had been parceled into schools and special problems, his own, as he envisaged it, would be a single, simple fabric. The simplest expression of this potent idea is probably the very title of the book he wrote at Dresden, *Die Welt als Wille und Vorstellung* (*The World as Will and Idea*). The world is necessarily present to a subject that perceives it; thus the world is "idea" or "representation." Yet the world is not created or constructed by the subject or the mind; its own nature is will, or blind striving. "My body and my will are one," and in the final analysis one person's will is indistinguishable from every other form of willing.

The book was printed by a reluctant publisher in 1818 and failed to gain a public. Nevertheless, with two books to his credit, Schopenhauer was given a lectureship in philosophy at the University of Berlin. At that time G. W. F. Hegel was the center of attention, and Schopenhauer decided to compete with him by lecturing at the same hour. But he addressed an empty room, and shortly his academic career was over.

Other Writings. In 1831 cholera was epidemic in Berlin, and Schopenhauer fled to Frankfurt, where he stayed for the rest of his life. In 1836 he published a study of contemporary science, *Über den Willen in der Natur* (*On the Will in Nature*), showing that his philosophy was consistent with the sciences. In 1839 he won a prize from the Norwegian Scientific Society for an essay on freedom of the will. To this

essay he added another, publishing them in 1841 as *Die Beiden Grundprobleme der Ethik* (*The Two Fundamental Problems of Ethics*). During these years he revised and augmented the text of *The World as Will and Idea*, which was republished in 1844 with 50 new chapters. In 1847 he republished his dissertation, *Über die vierfache Wurzel des Satzes vom zureichenden Grunde* (*On the Fourfold Root of the Principle of Sufficient Reason*). By now he was attracting some notice, but the fame he had predicted for himself was still only a dream.

Schopenhauer's style of life in his Frankfurt years has always both fascinated and puzzled his admirers. Though he wrote about the ultimate value of negating the will, he displayed unusual willfulness; though he extolled tranquility, he was always energetic; though he wrote savage diatribes against women, he could not forgo female company.

Parerga und Paralipomena. At last, in 1851, Schopenhauer published the book that brought him fame and followers. Titled *Parerga und Paralipomena*, it was a collection of highly polished, insightful essays and aphorisms. Its style was probably the chief reason for the book's immediate success. Yet the ideas were important too, particularly the notion that will was primary over intellect. The pessimism that follows from such a notion was already in vogue, and Schopenhauer became its voice. Another reason for his fame was surely his appeal to the inner experience of moods and feelings, in contrast to the more traditional appeals to history, reason, authority, and objective evidence. His philosophy takes its source in "the selfsame unchangeable being which is before us." Life is all suffering, he said, but it can be reflected upon, and then it will be seen to be "nothing." Schopenhauer died on Sept. 21, 1860. By then he had countless followers, and he was idolized as a kind of savior.

EWB

Shakespeare, William (1564–1616), English playwright, poet, and actor. William Shakespeare is generally acknowledged to be the greatest of English writers and one of the most extraordinary creators in human history.

The most crucial fact about William Shakespeare's career is that he was a popular dramatist. Born six years after Queen Elizabeth I had ascended the throne, contemporary with the high period of the English Renaissance, Shakespeare had the good luck to find in the theater of London a medium just coming into its own and an audience, drawn from a wide range of social classes, eager to reward talents of the sort he possessed. His entire life was committed to the public theater, and he seems to have written nondramatic poetry only when enforced closings of the theater made writing plays impractical. It is equally remarkable that his days in the theater were almost exactly contemporary with the theater's other outstanding achievements the work, for example, of Christopher Marlowe, Ben Jonson, and John Webster.

Shakespeare was born on or just before April 23, 1564, in the small but then important Warwickshire town of Stratford. His mother, born Mary Arden, was the daughter of a landowner from a neighboring village. His father, John, son of a farmer, was a glove maker and trader in farm produce; he had achieved a position of some eminence in the prosperous market town by the time of his son's birth, holding a number of responsible positions in Stratford's government and serving as mayor in 1569. By 1576, however, John Shakespeare had begun to encounter the financial difficulties which were to plague him until his death in 1601.

Though no personal documents survive from Shakespeare's school years, his literary work shows the mark of the excellent if grueling education offered at the Stratford grammar school (some reminiscences of Stratford school days may have lent amusing touches to scenes in *The Merry Wives of Windsor*). Like other Elizabethan schoolboys, Shakespeare studied Latin grammar during the early years, then progressed to the study of logic, rhetoric, composition, oration, versification, and the monuments of Roman literature. The work was conducted in Latin and relied heavily on rote memorization and the master's rod. A plausible tradition holds that William had to discontinue his education when about 13 in order to help his father. At 18 he married Ann Hathaway, a Stratford girl. They had three children (Susanna, 1583–1649; Hamnet, 1585–1596; and his twin, Judith, 1585–1662) and who was to survive him by 7 years. Shakespeare remained actively involved in Stratford affairs throughout his life, even when living in London, and retired there at the end of his career.

The years between 1585 and 1592, having left no evidence as to Shakespeare's activities, have been the focus of considerable speculation; among other things, conjecture would have him a traveling actor or a country schoolmaster. The earliest surviving notice of his career in London is a jealous attack on the "upstart crow" by Robert Greene, a playwright, professional man of letters, and profligate whose career was at an end in 1592 though he was only 6 years older than Shakespeare. Greene's outcry testifies, both in its passion and in the work it implies Shakespeare had been doing for some time, that the young poet had already established himself in the capital. So does

the quality of Shakespeare's first plays: it is hard to believe that even Shakespeare could have shown such mastery without several years of apprenticeship.

Early Career. Shakespeare's first extant play is probably *The Comedy of Errors* (1590; like most dates for the plays, this is conjectural and may be a year or two off), a brilliant and intricate farce involving two sets of identical twins and based on two already-complicated comedies by the Roman Plautus. Though less fully achieved, his next comedy, *The Two Gentlemen of Verona* (1591), is more prophetic of Shakespeare's later comedy, for its plot depends on such devices as a faithful girl who educates her fickle lover, romantic woods, a girl dressed as a boy, sudden reformations, music, and happy marriages at the end. The last of the first comedies, *Love's Labour's Lost* (1593), is romantic again, dealing with the attempt of three young men to withdraw from the world and women for 3 years to study in their king's "little Academe," and their quick surrender to a group of young ladies who come to lodge nearby. If the first of the comedies is most notable for its plotting and the second for its romantic elements, the third is distinguished by its dazzling language and its gallery of comic types. Already Shakespeare had learned to fuse conventional characters with convincing representations of the human life he knew.

Though little read and performed now, Shakespeare's first plays in the popular "chronicle," or history, genre are equally ambitious and impressive. Dealing with the tumultuous events of English history between the death of Henry V in 1422 and the accession of Henry VII in 1485 (which began the period of Tudor stability maintained by Shakespeare's own queen), the three "parts" of *Henry VI* (1592) and *Richard III* (1594) are no tentative experiments in the form: rather they constitute a gigantic tetralogy, in which each part is a superb play individually and an integral part of an epic sequence. Nothing so ambitious had ever been attempted in England in a form hitherto marked by slapdash formlessness.

Shakespeare's first tragedy, *Titus Andronicus* (1593), reveals similar ambition. Though its chamber of horrors, including mutilations and ingenious murders, strikes the modern reader as belonging to a theatrical tradition no longer viable, the play is in fact a brilliant and successful attempt to outdo the efforts of Shakespeare's predecessors in the lurid tradition of the revenge play.

When the theaters were closed because of plague during much of 1593–1594, Shakespeare looked to nondramatic poetry for his support and wrote two narrative masterpieces, the seriocomic *Venus and Adonis* and the tragic *Rape of Lucrece,* for a wealthy patron, the Earl of Southampton. Both poems carry the sophisticated techniques of Elizabethan narrative verse to their highest point, drawing on the resources of Renaissance mythological and symbolic traditions.

Shakespeare's most famous poems, probably composed in this period but not published until 1609, and then not by the author, are the 154 sonnets, the supreme English examples of the form. Writing at the end of a brief, frenzied vogue for sequences of sonnets, Shakespeare found in the conventional 14-line lyric with its fixed rhyme scheme a vehicle for inexhaustible technical innovations—for Shakespeare even more than for other poets, the restrictive nature of the sonnet generates a paradoxical freedom of invention that is the life of the form—and for the expression of emotions and ideas ranging from the frivolous to the tragic. Though often suggestive of autobiographical revelation, the sonnets cannot be proved to be any the less fictions than the plays. The identity of their dedicatee, "Mr. W. H.," remains a mystery, as does the question of whether there were real-life counterparts to the famous "dark lady" and the unfaithful friend who are the subject of a number of the poems. But the chief value of these poems is intrinsic: the sonnets alone would have established Shakespeare's preeminence among English poets.

Lord Chamberlain's Men.   By 1594 Shakespeare was fully engaged in his career. In that year he became principal writer for the successful Lord Chamberlain's Men, one of the two leading companies of actors; a regular actor in the company; and a "sharer," or partner, in the group of artist-managers who ran the entire operation and were in 1599 to have the Globe Theater built on the south bank of the Thames. The company performed regularly in unroofed but elaborate theaters. Required by law to be set outside the city limits, these theaters were the pride of London, among the first places shown to visiting foreigners, and seated up to 3,000 people. The actors played on a huge platform stage equipped with additional playing levels and surrounded on three sides by the audience; the absence of scenery made possible a flow of scenes comparable to that of the movies, and music, costumes, and ingenious stage machinery created successful illusions under the afternoon sun.

For this company Shakespeare produced a steady outpouring of plays. The comedies include *The Taming of the Shrew* (1594), fascinating in light of the first comedies since it combines with an Italian-style plot, in which all the action occurs in one day, a more characteristically English and Shakespearean plot, the taming of Kate, in which much more time passes; *A*

Midsummer Night's Dream (1595), in which "rude mechanicals," artisans without imagination, become entangled with fairies and magic potions in the moonlit woods to which young lovers have fled from a tyrannical adult society; *The Merchant of Venice* (1596), which contributed Shylock and Portia to the English literary tradition; *Much Ado about Nothing* (1598), with a melodramatic main plot whose heroine is maligned and almost driven to death by a conniving villain and a comic subplot whose Beatrice and Benedick remain the archetypical sparring lovers; *The Merry Wives of Windsor* (1599), held by tradition to have been written in response to the Queen's request that Shakespeare write another play about Falstaff (who had appeared in *Henry IV*), this time in love; and in 1600 the pastoral *As You Like It,* a mature return to the woods and conventions of *The Two Gentlemen of Verona* and *A Midsummer Night's Dream,* and *Twelfth Night,* perhaps the most perfect of the comedies, a romance of identical twins separated at sea, young love, and the antics of Malvolio and Sir Toby Belch.

Shakespeare's only tragedies of the period are among his most familiar plays: *Romeo and Juliet* (1596), *Julius Caesar* (1599), and *Hamlet* (1601). Different from one another as they are, these three plays share some notable features: the setting of intense personal tragedy in a large world vividly populated by what seems like the whole range of humanity; a refusal, shared by most of Shakespeare's contemporaries in the theater, to separate comic situations and techniques from tragic; the constant presence of politics; and—a personal rather than a conventional phenomenon—a tragic structure in which what is best in the protagonist is what does him in when he finds himself in conflict with the world.

Continuing his interest in the chronicle, Shakespeare wrote *King John* (1596), despite its one strong character a relatively weak play; and the second and greater tetralogy, ranging from *Richard II* (1595), in which the forceful Bolingbroke, with an ambiguous justice on his side, deposes the weak but poetic king, through the two parts of *Henry IV* (1597), in which the wonderfully amoral, fat knight Falstaff accompanies Prince Hal, Bolingbroke's son, to *Henry V* (1599), in which Hal, become king, leads a newly unified England, its civil wars temporarily at an end but sadly deprived of Falstaff and the dissident lowlife who provided so much joy in the earlier plays, to triumph over France. More impressively than the first tetralogy, the second turns history into art. Spanning the poles of comedy and tragedy, alive with a magnificent variety of unforgettable characters, linked to one another as one great play while each is a complete and independent success in its own right, the four plays pose disturbing and unanswerable questions about politics, making one ponder the frequent difference between the man capable of ruling and the man worthy of doing so, the meaning of legitimacy in office, the value of order and stability as against the value of revolutionary change, and the relation of private to public life. The plays are exuberant works of art, but they are not optimistic about man as a political animal, and their unblinkered recognition of the dynamics of history has made them increasingly popular and relevant in our own tormented era.

Three plays of the end of Elizabeth's reign are often grouped as Shakespeare's "problem plays," though no definition of that term is able successfully to differentiate them as an exclusive group. *All's Well That Ends Well* (1602) is a romantic comedy with qualities that seem bitter to many critics; like other plays of the period, by Shakespeare and by his contemporaries, it presents sexual relations between men and women in a harsh light. *Troilus and Cressida* (1602), hardest of the plays to classify generically, is a brilliant, sardonic, and disillusioned piece on the Trojan War, unusually philosophical in its language and reminiscent in some ways of *Hamlet*. The tragicomic *Measure for Measure* (1604) focuses more on sexual problems than any other play in the canon; Angelo, the puritanical and repressed man of ice who succumbs to violent sexual urges the moment he is put in temporary authority over Vienna during the duke's absence, and Isabella, the victim of his lust, are two of the most interesting characters in Shakespeare, and the bawdy city in which the action occurs suggests a London on which a new mood of modern urban hopelessness is settling.

King's Men. Promptly upon his accession in 1603, King James I, more ardently attracted to theatrical art than his predecessor, bestowed his patronage upon the Lord Chamberlain's Men, so that the flag of the King's Men now flew over the Globe. During his last decade in the theater Shakespeare was to write fewer but perhaps even finer plays. Almost all the greatest tragedies belong to this period. Though they share the qualities of the earlier tragedies, taken as a group they manifest new tendencies. The heroes are dominated by passions that make their moral status increasingly ambiguous, their freedom increasingly circumscribed; similarly the society, even the cosmos, against which they strive suggests less than ever that all can ever be right in the world. As before, what destroys the hero is what is best about him, yet the best in Macbeth or Othello cannot so simply be commended as Romeo's impetuous ardor or Brutus's political idealism (fatuous though it is). The late tragedies are each in its own way dramas of alienation, and

their focus, like that of the histories, continues to be felt as intensely relevant to the concerns of modern men.

Othello (1604) is concerned, like other plays of the period, with sexual impurity, with the difference that that impurity is the fantasy of the protagonist about his faithful wife. Iago, the villain who drives Othello to doubt and murder, is the culmination of two distinct traditions, the "Machiavellian" conniver who uses deceit in order to subvert the order of the polity, and the Vice, a schizophrenically tragicomic devil figure from the morality plays going out of fashion as Shakespeare grew up. *King Lear* (1605), to many Shakespeare's masterpiece, is an agonizing tragic version of a comic play (itself based on mythical early English history), in which an aged king who foolishly deprives his only loving daughter of her heritage in order to leave all to her hypocritical and vicious sisters is hounded to death by a malevolent alliance which at times seems to include nature itself. Transformed from its fairy-tale-like origins, the play involves its characters and audience alike in metaphysical questions that are felt rather than thought.

Macbeth (1606), similarly based on English chronicle material, concentrates on the problems of evil and freedom, convincingly mingles the supernatural with a representation of history, and makes a paradoxically sympathetic hero of a murderer who sins against family and statea man in some respects worse than the villain of *Hamlet*.

Dramatizing stories from Plutarch's *Parallel Lives*, *Antony and Cleopatra* and *Coriolanus* (both written in 1607–1608) embody Shakespeare's bitterest images of political life, the former by setting against the call to Roman duty the temptation to liberating sexual passion, the latter by pitting a protagonist who cannot live with hypocrisy against a society built on it. Both of these tragedies present ancient history with a vividness that makes it seem contemporary, though the sensuousness of *Antony and Cleopatra*, the richness of its detail, the ebullience of its language, and the seductive character of its heroine have made it far more popular than the harsh and austere *Coriolanus*. One more tragedy, *Timon of Athens*, similarly based on Plutarch, was written during this period, though its date is obscure. Despite its abundant brilliance, few find it a fully satisfactory play, and some critics have speculated that what we have may be an incomplete draft. The handful of tragedies that Shakespeare wrote between 1604 and 1608 comprises an astonishing series of worlds different from one another, created of language that exceeds anything Shakespeare had done before, some of the most complex and vivid characters in all the plays, and a variety of new structural techniques.

A final group of plays takes a turn in a new direction. Commonly called the "romances," *Pericles* (1607), *Cymbeline* (1609), *The Winter's Tale* (1611), and *The Tempest* (1611) share their conventions with the tragicomedy that had been growing popular since the early years of the century. Particularly they resemble in some respects plays written by Beaumont and Fletcher for the private theatrical company whose operation the King's Men took over in 1608. While such work in the hands of others, however, tended to reflect the socially and intellectually narrow interests of an elite audience, Shakespeare turned the fashionable mode into a new kind of personal art form. Though less searing than the great tragedies, these plays have a unique power to move and are in the realm of the highest art. *Pericles* and *Cymbeline* seem somewhat tentative and experimental, though both are superb plays. *The Winter's Tale*, however, is one of Shakespeare's best plays. Like a rewriting of *Othello* in its first acts, it turns miraculously into pastoral comedy in its last. *The Tempest* is the most popular and perhaps the finest of the group. Prospero, shipwrecked on an island and dominating it with magic which he renounces at the end, may well be intended as an image of Shakespeare himself; in any event, the play is like a retrospective glance over the plays of the two previous decades.

After the composition of *The Tempest*, which many regard as an explicit farewell to art, Shakespeare retired to Stratford, returning to London to compose *Henry VIII* and *The Two Noble Kinsmen* in 1613; neither of these plays seems to have fired his imagination. In 1616, at the age of 52, he was dead. His reputation grew quickly, and his work has continued to seem to each generation like its own most precious discovery. His value to his own age is suggested by the fact that two fellow actors performed the virtually unprecedented act in 1623 of gathering his plays together and publishing them in the Folio edition. Without their efforts, since Shakespeare was apparently not interested in publication, many of the plays would not have survived.

EWB

Shaw, George Bernard (1856–1950), British playwright, critic, and pamphleteer. George Bernard Shaw produced more than 52 plays and playlets, three volumes of music and drama criticism, and one major volume of socialist commentary.

George Bernard Shaw's theater extended to his personal life. He considered himself a cultural miracle, and a partisan conflict among his readers and play-goers provoked a massive body of literature for and against him and his work. Much recent criticism concludes that he ranks as the greatest English dramatist since William Shakespeare.

Shaw was born in Dublin, Ireland, on July 16, 1856. At an early age he was tutored in classics by an uncle, and when he was 10 years old, he entered the Wesleyan Connexional School in Dublin. There his academic performance was largely a failure. Shaw later described his own education: "I cannot learn anything that does not interest me. My memory is not indiscriminate, it rejects and selects; and its selections are not academic." Part of his nonacademic training was handled by his mother, a music teacher and a mezzo-soprano; Shaw studied music and art at the same time. He became a Dublin office boy in 1871 at a monthly salary equivalent to $4.50. Success in business threatened him: "I made good," he wrote, "in spite of myself and found, to my dismay, that Business, instead of expelling me as the worthless imposter I was, was fastening upon me with no intention of letting me go. . . . In March, 1876, I broke loose." Resigning a cashier's position, Shaw joined his mother and two sisters in London, where they conducted a music school. Shaw had started writing, at the age of 16, criticism and reviews for Irish newspapers and magazines; in 4 years only one piece was accepted. Shaw lived in London for the 9 years after 1876 supported by his parents and continued to write criticism. He also entertained in London society as a singer.

Shaw as a Novelist. Between 1876 and 1885 Shaw wrote five novels. *Immaturity*, the first, remained unpublished, and the other four, after a series of rejections from London publishers, appeared in radical periodicals. *To-Day* published *An Unsocial Socialist* in 1884; it was designed as part of a massive projected work that would cover the entire social reform movement in England. *Cashel Byron's Profession* (1882) also appeared in *To-Day*; juvenile, nonsensical, at times hilarious, it was produced in 1901 as the drama *The Admirable Bashville; or, Constancy Unrewarded*. *The Irrational Knot*, a portrayal of modern marriage that Shaw asserted anticipated Henrik Ibsen's *A Doll's House*, appeared in another radical periodical, *Our Corner*, as did *Love among the Artists* (1887–1888).

Political Activities and Writings. At the age of 23 Shaw had joined a socialist discussion group, of which Sydney Webb was a member, and he joined the Fabian Society in 1884. *Fabian Essays* (1887), edited by Shaw, emphasized the importance of economics and class structure; for him, economics was "the basis of society." In 1882 Shaw's conversion to socialism began when he heard Henry George, the American author of *Progress and Poverty*, address a London meeting. George's message "changed the whole current of my life." His reading of Karl Marx's *Das Kapital* in the same year "made a man of me." For 27 years Shaw served on the Fabian Society's executive committee. In his role as an active polemicist he later published *Common Sense about the War* on Nov. 14, 1914, a criticism of the British government and its policies. *The Intelligent Woman's Guide to Capitalism and Socialism* (1928) supplied a complete summary of his political position. It remains a major volume of socialist commentary. For 6 years Shaw held office on a municipal level in a London suburb.

Shaw's other careers continued. Between 1888 and 1894 he wrote for newspapers and periodicals as a highly successful music critic. At the end of this period, he began writing on a regular basis for Frank Harris's *Saturday Review;* as a critic, he introduced Ibsen and the "new" drama to the British public. Shaw's *Quintessence of Ibsenism* appeared in 1890, *The Sanity of Art* in 1895, and *The Perfect Wagnerite* in 1898. All of them indicate the formation of his esthetics. He married Charlotte Payne-Townshend, an Irish heiress and fellow socialist, in 1898. She died in 1943.

The Plays. Shaw wrote drama between 1892 and 1947, when he completed *Buoyant Billions* at the age of 91. *Widowers' Houses,* his first play, was produced in 1892 at London's Royalty Theater. He identified this and the other early plays as "unpleasant." *Widowers' Houses* was about slum landlordship. Preoccupied by the "new" woman, Shaw wrote *The Philanderers* in 1893. Also written in the same year but not produced until 1902 because of British censorship, *Mrs. Warren's Profession* revealed, he wrote, "the economic basis of modern commercial prostitution." Shaw's first stage successes, *Arms and the Man* and *Candida,* both of them "pleasant" plays, were produced in 1894. *You Never Can Tell,* first produced in 1896 and not often revived, is Shaw's most underrated comedy. The Vedrenne-Barker productions at the Royal Court Theater in London of Shaw, Shakespeare, and Euripides between 1904 and 1907 established Shaw's permanent reputation; 11 of his plays received 701 performances.

Shaw began as a dramatist writing against the mechanical habits of domestic comedy and against the Victorian romanticizing of Shakespeare and drama in general. He wrote that "melodramatic stage illusion is not an illusion of real life, but an illusion of the embodiment of our romantic imaginings."

Shaw's miraculous period began with *Man and Superman* (1901–1903). It was miraculous even for him; in a late play, *Too True to Be Good* (1932), one of the characters speaks for him: "My gift is divine: it is not limited by my petty personal convictions. Lucidity is one of the most precious of gifts: the gift of the teacher: the gift of explanation. I can explain anything to anybody; and I love doing it."

Major Barbara (1905) is a drama of ideas, largely about poverty and capitalism; like most of Shaw's drama, *Major Barbara* poses questions and finally contains messages or arguments. *Androcles and the Lion* (1911) discusses religion. *John Bull's Other Island* (1904), which is the least known of his major plays, concerns political relations between England and Ireland. *Heartbreak House* analyzes the domestic effects of World War I; written between 1913 and 1916, it was first produced in 1920. Most of the plays after *Arms and the Man* carry long prefaces that are often not directly related to the drama itself. Shaw systematically explored such topics as marriage, parenthood, education, and poverty in the prefaces.

Shaw's popular success was coupled with a growing critical success. *Heartbreak House, Back to Methuselah* (1921; he called it his "metabiological pentateuch"), *Androcles and the Lion,* and *Saint Joan* (1923) are considered his best plays. They were all written between the ages of 57 and 67.

Shaw Explaining Shaw. The plays of Shaw express, as did his life, a complex range of impulses, ambitions, and beliefs. Reflecting on his life and his work, he explained at 70: "If I am to be entirely communicative on this subject, I must add that the mere rawness which soon rubs off was complicated by a deeper strangeness which has made me all my life a sojourner on this planet rather than a native of it. Whether it be that I was born mad or a little too sane, my kingdom was not of this world: I was at home only in the realm of my imagination, and at ease only with the mighty dead. Therefore I had to become an actor, and create for myself a fantastic personality fit and apt for dealing with men, and adaptable to the various parts I had to play as an author, journalist, orator, politician, committee man, man of the world, and so forth. In all this I succeeded later on only too well."

Shaw was awarded the 1925 Nobel Prize for literature. At the patriarchal age of 94, he died in his home at Ayot St. Lawrence, England, on November 2, 1950.

EWB

Sieyès, Emmanuel Joseph (1748–1836), French statesman and political writer. Emmanuel Joseph Sieyès, known as the Abbé Sieyès, upheld the interests of the Third Estate. His effort to consolidate a moderate republican government established Napoleon Bonaparte as the head of state.

Born at Fréjus on May 3, 1748, Emmanuel Joseph Sieyès got his primary education from the Jesuits in his hometown and continued into advanced study in theology. Appointment as a canon in the cathedral chapter of Tréguier (1775) brought him the appellation of Abbé (used in France not only for abbots but also for churchmen without a parish), and by the eve of the French Revolution he had been promoted to vicar general of the bishop of Chartres. But his interests in these years of intensive political debate turned from theology and Church administration to public affairs, and when the government called for proposals on ways to hold the elections to the Estates General, one of his three pamphlets on the issue was of critical importance in rallying the Third Estate as a force independent of, and even hostile to, clergy and nobility. This was the famous *Qu'est-ce que le tiers état?* (1789; *What Is the Third Estate?*), which proclaimed in phrases of ringing clarity that the commoners had been nothing and should be all, as the essential component of the French nation.

Sieyès was elected a deputy of the Third Estate and not of the First Estate, the clergy, and he played a key role in the events of the first months of the Revolution. He proposed the name National Assembly for the combined single chamber established unilaterally by the Third Estate, with some support from liberal clergy and nobles, on June 17; drew up the "Tennis Court Oath," by which the deputies pledged themselves to the defense of the National Assembly as the embodiment of the sovereignty of the people, on June 20; and took the initiative in the decision of the Constituent Assembly (as the National Assembly was called in its self-assumed task of writing a constitution) to continue its work despite the King's order to disband on June 23. He was also active in the formulation of the Declaration of the Rights of Man.

Further events showed Sieyès to be a moderate within the Revolutionary movement. He favored the widest personal rights of citizens as against arbitrary government power, limitation of the right to vote to property holders (because the votes of the poor, he argued, would be easily bought by the rich), and extreme economic individualism, without restriction upon the right of persons to amass wealth. He was not elected to the Legislative Assembly but was chosen a deputy to the Convention. As the Revolution swung into its radical phase, he chose the path of caution and avoided a prominent role during the Reign of Terror. Asked afterward what he had done during that perilous period, he answered tersely, "J'ai vécu" (I stayed alive). To do so, he had voted for the death penalty against Louis XVI; but after Maximilien de Robespierre's fall, he resumed political activity.

As a member of the Thermidorean Committee of Public Safety and then of the Council of Five Hundred, Sieyès favored an annexationist foreign policy and internal consolidation. After serving as ambassador to Berlin in 1798–1799, he returned to Paris to become a member of the Directory, the executive branch of government. When it became clear that the Directory was supported by only a minority in the nation, with both radical republicans and royalists in active opposition, he and a fellow Director sought the support of the army in the person of Gen. Bonaparte in the coup d'etat of 18 Brumaire (Nov. 9, 1799). However, in the new government of three consuls conceived by Sieyès, it was Napoleon Bonaparte who took the post of first consul for himself, and Sieyès was sent into innocuous but prestigious posts, especially after Bonaparte became Emperor Napoleon. He was named to the Senate and became its president, was named a count of the empire, and was elected to the French Academy.

However, when the Bourbon monarchy was finally restored in 1815, Sieyès was banned as a regicide and fled to Brussels, where he lived as an exile until the Revolution of 1830. Returning home, he died in Paris on June 20, 1836, remembered in history chiefly for his inflammatory pamphlet of 1789 and his dupe's part in the overthrow of the Directory.

EWB

Simmel, Georg (1858–1918), German sociologist and philosopher. Georg Simmel wrote important studies of urban sociology, social conflict theory, and small-group relationships.

Georg Simmel was born on March 1, 1858, in Berlin, the youngest of seven children. His father was a prosperous Jewish businessman who became a Roman Catholic. His mother, also of Jewish forebears, was a Lutheran. Georg was baptized a Lutheran but later withdrew from that Church, although he always retained a philosophical interest in religion.

His father died when Georg was very young. A family friend and music publisher became his guardian and left him an inheritance when he died which enabled Simmel to pursue a scholarly career for many years without a salaried position. He studied history and philosophy at the University of Berlin, earning a doctoral degree in 1881. He was a lecturer at the University of Berlin from 1885 to 1900 and professor extraordinary until 1914. He then accepted his only salaried professorship at the provincial University of Strasbourg. There he died on Sept. 26, 1918.

Simmel's wide interests in philosophy, sociology, art, and religion contrasted sharply with those of his more narrowly disciplined colleagues. Eschewing pure philosophy, he preferred to apply it functionally as the philosophy of culture, of money, of the sexes, of religion, and of art. Similarly in sociology, the field of his lasting renown, he favored isolating multiple factors. In 1910 he helped found the German Sociological Association. His sociological writings were on alienation and on urban stresses and strains; his philosophical writings foreshadowed modern existentialism.

Although a popular and even brilliant lecturer, academic advancement eluded Simmel. The reasons for this include prewar Germany's latent anti-Semitism, the unorthodox variety of subjects he pursued rather than following a more acceptable narrow discipline, and perhaps jealousy at his sparkling originality. Ortega y Gasset compared him to a philosophical squirrel, gracefully acrobatic in leaping from one branch of knowledge to another. Unable or unwilling to develop consistent sociological or philosophical systems, Simmel founded no school and left few disciples. "I know that I shall die without intellectual heirs," he wrote in his diary. "My legacy will be, as it were in cash, distributed to many heirs, each transforming his part into use conformed to *his* nature. . . ." This diffusion occurred, and his ideas have since pervaded sociological thought. His insightful writings still stimulate while more systematic contemporaries are less read.

EWB

Smith, Adam (1723–1790), Scottish economist and moral philosopher. Adam Smith believed that in a laissez-faire economy the impulse of self-interest would work toward the public welfare.

Adam Smith was born on June 5, 1723, at Kirkcaldy. His father had died two months before his birth, and a strong and lifelong attachment developed between him and his mother. As an infant, Smith was kidnaped, but he was soon rescued. At the age of 14 he enrolled in the University of Glasgow, where he remained for three years. The lectures of Francis Hutcheson exerted a strong influence on him. In 1740 he transferred to Balliol College, Oxford, where he remained for almost seven years, receiving the bachelor of arts degree in 1744. Returning then to Kirkcaldy, he devoted himself to his studies and gave a series of lectures on English literature. In 1748 he moved to Edinburgh, where he became a friend of David Hume, whose skepticism he did not share.

Theory of Moral Sentiments. In 1751 Smith became professor of logic at the University of Glasgow and the following year professor of moral philosophy. Eight years later he published his *Theory of Moral Sentiments*. Smith's central notion in this work is that moral principles have social feeling or sympathy as their basis. Sympathy is a common or analogous feeling that an individual may have with the affections or feelings of another person. The source of this fellow feeling is not so much one's observation of the expressed emotion of another person as one's thought of the situation that the other person confronts. Sympathy usually requires knowledge of the cause of the emotion to be shared. If one approves of another's passions as suitable to their objects, he thereby sympathizes with that person.

Sympathy is the basis for one's judging of the appropriateness and merit of the feelings and actions issuing from these feelings. If the affections of the person involved in a situation are analogous to the emotions of the spectator, then those affections are appropriate. The merit of a feeling or an action flowing from a feeling is its worthiness of reward. If a feeling or an action is worthy of reward, it has moral merit. One's awareness of merit derives from one's sympathy with the gratitude of the person benefited by the action. One's sense of merit, then, is a derivative of the feeling of gratitude which is manifested in the situation by the person who has been helped.

Smith warns that each person must exercise impartiality of judgment in relation to his own feelings and behavior. Well aware of the human tendency to overlook one's own moral failings and the self-deceit in which individuals often engage, Smith argues that each person must scrutinize his own feelings and behavior with the same strictness he employs when considering those of others. Such an impartial appraisal is possible because a person's conscience enables him to compare his own feelings with those of others. Conscience and sympathy, then, working together provide moral guidance for man so that the individual can control his own feelings and have a sensibility for the affections of others.

The Wealth of Nations. In 1764 Smith resigned his professorship to take up duties as a traveling tutor for the young Duke of Buccleuch and his brother. Carrying out this responsibility, he spent 2 years on the Continent. In Toulouse he began writing his best-known work, *An Inquiry into the Nature and Causes of the Wealth of Nations*. While in Paris he met Denis Diderot, Claude Adrien Helvétius, Baron Paul d'Holbach, François Quesnay, A. R. J. Turgot, and Jacques Necker. These thinkers doubtless had some influence on him. His life abroad came to an abrupt end when one of his charges was killed.

Smith then settled in Kirkcaldy with his mother. He continued to work on *The Wealth of Nations,* which was finally published in 1776. His mother died at the age of 90, and Smith was grief-stricken. In 1778 he was made customs commissioner, and in 1784 he became a fellow of the Royal Society of Edinburgh. Smith apparently spent some time in London, where he became a friend of Benjamin Franklin. On his deathbed he demanded that most of his manuscript writings be destroyed. He died on July 17, 1790.

The Wealth of Nations, easily the best known of Smith's writings, is a mixture of descriptions, historical accounts, and recommendations. The wealth of a nation, Smith insists, is to be gauged by the number and variety of consumable goods it can command. Free trade is essential for the maximum development of wealth for any nation because through such trade a variety of goods becomes possible.

Smith assumes that if each person pursues his own interest the general welfare of all will be fostered. He objects to governmental control, although he acknowledges that some restrictions are required. The capitalist invariably produces and sells consumable goods in order to meet the greatest needs of the people. In so fulfilling his own interest, the capitalist automatically promotes the general welfare. In the economic sphere, says Smith, the individual acts in terms of his own interest rather than in terms of sympathy. Thus, Smith made no attempt to bring into harmony his economic and moral theories.

EWB

Spencer, Herbert (1820–1903), English philosopher, scientist, engineer, and political economist. In Herbert Spencer's day his works were important in popularizing the concept of evolution and played an important part in the development of economics, political science, biology, and philosophy.

Herbert Spencer was born in Derby on April 27, 1820. His childhood, described in *An Autobiography* (1904), reflected the attitudes of a family which was known on both sides to include religious nonconformists, social critics, and rebels. His father, a teacher, had been a Wesleyan, but he separated himself from organized religion as he did from political and social authority. Spencer's father and an uncle saw that he received a highly individualized education that emphasized the family traditions of dissent and independence of thought. He was particularly instructed in the study of nature and the fundamentals of science, neglecting such traditional subjects as history.

Spencer initially followed up the scientific interests encouraged by his father and studied engineering. For a few years, until 1841, he practiced the profession of civil engineer as an employee of the London and Birmingham Railway. His interest in evolution is said to have arisen from the examination of fossils that came from the rail-road cuts.

Spencer left the railroad to take up a literary career and to follow up some of his scientific interests. He began by contributing to *The Non-Conformist,* writing a series of letters called *The Proper Sphere of Government.* This was his first major work and contained his basic concepts of individualism and laissez-faire, which were to be later developed more fully in his *Social Statics* (1850) and other works. Especially stressed were the right of the individual and the ideal of noninterference on the part of the state. He also foreshadowed some of his later ideas on evolution and spoke of society as an individual organism.

A System of Evolution. The concept of organic evolution was elaborated fully for the first time in his famous essay "The Developmental Hypothesis," published in the *Leader* in 1852. In a series of articles and writings Spencer gradually refined his concept of organic and inorganic evolution and popularized the term itself. Particularly in "Progress: Its Law and Cause," an essay published in 1857, he extended the idea of evolutionary progress to human society as well as to the animal and physical worlds. All nature moves from the simple to the complex. This fundamental law is seen in the evolution of human society as it is seen in the geological transformation of the earth and in the origin and development of plant and animal species.

Natural selection, as described by Charles Darwin in the *Origin of Species,* published in 1859, completed Spencer's evolutionary system by providing the mechanism by which organic evolution occurred. Spencer enthusiastically elaborated on Darwin's process of natural selection, applying it to human society, and made his own contribution in the notion of "survival of the fittest." From the beginning Spencer applied his harsh dictum to human society, races, and the state, judging them in the process: "If they are sufficiently complete to live, they do live, and it is well they should live. If they are not sufficiently complete to live, they die, and it is best they should die."

Spencer systematically tried to establish the basis of a scientific study of education, psychology, sociology, and ethics from an evolutionary point of view. Although many of his specific ideas are no longer fashionable, Spencer went a long way in helping to establish the separate existence of sociology as a social science. His idea of evolutionary progress, from the simple to the complex, provided a conceptual framework that was productive and that justifies granting to him the title father of comparative sociology. His views concerning a science of sociology are elaborated in two major works, *Descriptive Sociology* (published in 17 volumes, 1873–1934) and *The Study of Sociology* (1873).

Spencer was particularly influential in the United States until the turn of the century. According to William Graham Sumner, who used *The Study of Sociology* as a text in the first sociology course offered in an American university, it was Spencer's work which established sociology as a separate, legitimate field in its own right. Spencer's demand that historians present the "natural history of society," in order to furnish data for a comparative sociology, is also credited with inspiring James Harvey Robinson and the others involved in the writing of the New History in the United States.

Economic Theories. Social philosophy in the latter part of the 19th century in the United States was dominated by Spencer. His ideas of laissez-faire and the survival of the fittest by natural selection fitted very well into an age of rapid expansion and ruthless business competition. Spencer provided businessmen with the reassuring notion that what they were doing was not just ruthless self-interest but was a natural law operating in nature and human society. Not only was competition in harmony with nature, but it was also in the interest of the general welfare and progress. Social Darwinism, or Spencerism, became a total view of life which justified opposition to social reform on the basis that reform interfered with the operation of the natural law of survival of the fittest.

Spencer visited the United States in 1882 and was much impressed by what he observed on a triumphal tour. He prophetically saw in the industrial might of the United States the seeds of world power. He admired the American industrialists and became a close friend of the great industrialist and steel baron Andrew Carnegie.

By the 1880s and 1890s Spencer had become a universally recognized philosopher and scientist. His books were published widely, and his ideas commanded a great deal of respect and attention. His *Principles of Biology* was a standard text at Oxford. At Harvard, William James used his *Principles of Psychology* as a textbook.

Although some of Spencer's more extreme formulations of laissez-faire were abandoned fairly rapidly, even in the United States, he will continue to exert an influence as long as competition, the profit motive, and individualism are held up as positive social values. His indirect influence on psychology, sociology, and history is too strong to be denied, even

when his philosophical system as a whole has been discarded. He is a giant in the intellectual history of the 19th century.

Spencer spent his last years continuing his work and avoiding the honors and positions that were offered to him by a long list of colleges and universities. He died at Brighton on Dec. 8, 1903.

EWB

Stalin, Joseph (1879–1953), Soviet statesman. Joseph Stalin was the supreme ruler of the Soviet Union and the leader of world communism for almost 30 years.

Under Joseph Stalin the Soviet Union greatly enlarged its territory, won a war of unprecedented destructiveness, and transformed itself from a relatively backward country into the second most important industrial nation in the world. For these achievements the Soviet people and the international Communist movement paid a price that many of Stalin's critics consider excessive. The price included the loss of millions of lives; massive material and spiritual deprivation; political repression; an untold waste of resources; and the erection of an inflexible authoritarian system of rule thought by some historians to be one of the most offensive in recent history and one that many Communists consider a hindrance to further progress in the Soviet Union itself.

Formative Years. Stalin was born Iosif Vissarionovich Dzhugashvili on Dec. 21, 1879, in Gori, Georgia. He was the only surviving son of Vissarion Dzhugashvili, a cobbler who first practiced his craft in a village shop but later in a shoe factory in the city. Stalin's father died in 1891. His mother, Ekaterina, a pious and illiterate peasant woman, sent her teenage son to the theological seminary in Tpilisi (Tiflis), where Stalin prepared for the ministry. Shortly before his graduation, however, he was expelled in 1899 for spreading subversive views.

Stalin then joined the underground revolutionary Marxist movement in Tpilisi. In 1901 he was elected a member of the Tpilisi committee of the Russian Social Democratic Workers party. The following year he was arrested, imprisoned, and subsequently banished to Siberia. Stalin escaped from Siberia in 1904 and rejoined the Marxist underground in Tpilisi. When the Russian Marxist movement split into two factions, Stalin identified himself with the Bolsheviks.

During the time of the 1904–1905 revolution, Stalin made a name as the organizer of daring bank robberies and raids on money transports, an activity that V. I. Lenin considered important in view of the party's need for funds, although many other Marxists considered this type of highway robbery unworthy of a revolutionary socialist.

Stalin participated in congresses of the Russian Social Democratic Workers party at Tampere, London, and Stockholm in 1905 and 1906, meeting Lenin for the first time at these congresses. In 1912 Stalin spent some time with Lenin and his wife in Crakow and then went to Vienna to study the Marxist literature concerning the nationality problem. This study trip resulted in a book, *Marxism and the National Question.* In the same year Lenin co-opted Stalin into the Central Committee of the Bolshevik party.

Stalin's trips abroad during these years were short episodes in his life. He spent the major portion of the years from 1905 to 1912 in organizational work for the movement, mainly in the city of Baku. The secret police arrested him several times, and several times he escaped. Eventually, after his return from Vienna, the police caught him again, and he was exiled to the faraway village of Turukhansk beyond the Arctic Circle. He remained here until the fall of tsarism. He adopted the name Stalin ("man of steel") about 1913.

First Years of Soviet Rule.   After the fall of tsarism, Stalin made his way at once to Petrograd, where until the arrival of Lenin from Switzerland he was the senior Bolshevik and the editor of *Pravda,* the party organ. After Lenin's return, Stalin remained in the high councils of the party, but he played a relatively inconspicuous role in the preparations for the October Revolution, which placed the Bolsheviks in power. In the first Cabinet of the Soviet government, he held the post of people's commissar for nationalities.

During the years of the civil war (1918–1921), Stalin distinguished himself primarily as military commissar during the battle of Tsaritsyn (Stalingrad), in the Polish campaign, and on several other fronts. In 1919 he received another important government assignment by being appointed commissar of the Workers and Peasants Inspectorate. Within the party, he rose to the highest ranks, becoming a member of both the Political Bureau and the Organizational Bureau. When the party Secretariat was organized, he became one of its leading members and was appointed its secretary general in 1922. Lenin obviously valued Stalin for his organizational talents, for his ability to knock heads together and to cut through bureaucratic red tape. He appreciated Stalin's capabilities as a machine politician, as a troubleshooter, and as a hatchet man.

The strength of Stalin's position in the government and in the party was anchored probably by his secretary generalship, which gave him control over party personnel administration over admissions, training, assignments, promotions, and disciplinary matters. Thus, although he was relatively unknown to outsiders and even within the party, Stalin doubtless ranked as the most powerful man in Soviet Russia after Lenin.

During Lenin's last illness and after his death in 1924, Stalin served as a member of the three-man committee that conducted the affairs of the party and the country. The other members of this "troika" arrangement were Grigori Zinoviev and Lev Kamenev. The best-known activity of this committee during the years 1923–1925 was its successful attempt to discredit Leon Trotsky and to make it impossible for him to assume party leadership after Lenin's death. After the committee succeeded in this task, Stalin turned against his two associates, who after some hesitation made common cause with Trotsky. The conflict between these two groups can be viewed either as a power struggle or as a clash of personalities, but it also concerned political issues—a dispute between the left wing and the right wing of bolshevism. The former feared a conservative perversion of the revolution, and the latter were confident that socialism could be reached even in an isolated and relatively backward country. In this dispute Stalin represented, for the time being, the right wing of the party. He and his theoretical spokesman, Nikolai Bukharin, warned against revolutionary adventurism and argued in favor of continuing the more cautious and patient policies that Lenin had inaugurated with the NEP (New Economic Policy).

In 1927 Stalin succeeded in defeating the entire left opposition and in eliminating its leaders from the party. He then adopted much of its domestic program by initiating a 5-year plan of industrial development and by executing it with a degree of recklessness and haste that antagonized many of his former supporters, who then formed a right opposition. This opposition, too, was defeated quickly, and by the early 1930s Stalin had gained dictatorial control over the party, the state, and the entire Communist International.

Stalin's Personality.   Although always depicted as a towering figure, Stalin, in fact, was of short stature. He possessed the typical features of Transcaucasians: black hair, black eyes, a short skull, and a large nose. His personality was highly controversial, and it remains shrouded in mystery. Stalin was crude and cruel and, in some important ways, a primitive man. His cunning, distrust, and vindictiveness seem to have reached paranoid proportions. In political life he tended to be cautious and slow-moving. His style of speaking and writing was also ponderous and graceless. Some of his speeches and occasional writings read like a catechism. He was at times, however, a clever orator and a formidable antagonist in debate. Stalin seems to have possessed boundless energy and a phenomenal capacity for absorbing detailed knowledge.

About Stalin's private life, little is known beyond the fact that he seems always to have been a lonely man. His first wife, a Georgian girl named Ekaterina Svanidze, died of tuberculosis. His second wife, Nadezhda Alleluyeva, committed suicide in 1932, presumably in despair over Stalin's dictatorial rule of the party. The only child from his first marriage, Jacob, fell into German hands during World War II and was killed. The two children from his second marriage outlived their father, but they were not always on good terms with him. The son, Vasili, an officer in the Soviet air force, drank himself to death in 1962. The daughter, Svetlana, fled to the United States in the 1960s.

Stalin's Achievements.

In successive 5-year plans, the Soviet Union under Stalin industrialized and urbanized with great speed. Although the military needs of the country drained away precious resources and World War II brought total destruction to some of the richest areas of the Soviet Union and death to many millions of citizens, the nation by the end of Stalin's life had become the second most important industrial country in the world.

The price the Soviet Union paid for this great achievement remains staggering. It included the destruction of all remnants of free enterprise in both town and country and the physical destruction of hundreds of thousands of Russian peasants. The transformation of Soviet agriculture in the early 1930s into collectives tremendously damaged the country's food production. Living standards were drastically lowered at first, and more than a million people died of starvation. Meanwhile, Stalin jailed and executed vast numbers of party members, especially the old revolutionaries and the leading figures in all areas of endeavor.

In the process of securing his rule and of mobilizing the country for the industrialization effort, Stalin erected a new kind of political system characterized by unprecedented severity in police control, bureaucratic centralization, and personal dictatorship. Historians consider his regime one of history's most notorious examples of totalitarianism.

Stalin also changed the ideology of communism and of the Soviet Union in a subtle but drastic fashion. While retaining the rhetoric of Marxism-Leninism, and indeed transforming it into an inflexible dogma, Stalin also changed it from a revolutionary system of ideas into a conservative and authoritarian theory of state, preaching obedience and discipline as well as veneration of the Russian past. In world affairs the Stalinist system became isolationist. While paying lip service to the revolutionary goals of Karl Marx and Lenin, Stalin sought to promote good relations with the capitalist countries and urged Communist parties to ally themselves with moderate and middle-of-the-road parties in a popular front against the radical right.

From the middle of the 1930s onward, Stalin personally managed the vast political and economic system he had established. Formally, he took charge of it only in May 1941, when he assumed the office of chairman of the Council of Ministers. After Nazi Germany invaded the Soviet Union, Stalin also assumed formal command over the entire military establishment.

Stalin's conduct of Russian military strategy in the war remains as controversial as most of his activities. Some evidence indicates that he committed serious blunders, but other evidence allows him credit for brilliant achievements. The fact remains that under Stalin the Soviet Union won the war, emerged as one of the major powers in the world, and managed to bargain for a distribution of the spoils of war that enlarged its area of domination significantly, partly by annexation and partly by the transformation of all the lands east of the Oder and Neisse rivers into client states.

Judgments of Stalin.

Stalin died of a cerebrovascular accident on March 5, 1953. His body was entombed next to Lenin's in the mausoleum in Red Square, Moscow. After his death Stalin became a controversial figure in the Communist world, where appreciation for his great achievements was offset to a varying degree by harsh criticism of his methods. At the Twentieth All-Union Party Congress in 1956, Premier Nikita Khrushchev and other Soviet leaders attacked the cult of Stalin, accusing him of tyranny, terror, falsification of history, and self-glorification.

EWB

Stanley, Sir Henry Morton

(1841–1904), British explorer and journalist. Henry Stanley opened Central Africa to exploitation by Western nations.

Henry Stanley was originally named John Rowland. He was born near Denbigh Castle, Wales, to John Rowland, a farmer, and an unmarried woman. The boy lived with his maternal grandfather until he was about 6, when his grandfather died. The youngster was sent to a workhouse, where he remained until the age of 15, when he ran away.

323

Young Rowland lived on a hand-to-mouth basis with various relatives until he was 18, when he signed on as a cabin boy and shipped to New Orleans. There a cotton broker, Henry Morton Stanley, adopted him and gave him his name. Stanley's adopted father died without providing for him. The young man volunteered as a Confederate soldier and was captured at Shiloh. He was released from prison by changing sides and finished the war in the Union Navy.

After the war Stanley became a newspaper correspondent. He covered Indian campaigns in the American West. In 1868 he went to Abyssinia to cover a British expedition. In 1869 the publisher of the *New York Herald* commissioned Stanley to find Dr. David Livingstone, a Scottish missionary explorer, lost somewhere in Central Africa. Stanley found Livingstone at Ujiji in 1871 after an 8-month search. They did some exploring together, and when Livingstone died in 1873, Stanley stepped into his shoes.

In 1874 Stanley began a 3-year journey to measure the lakes of Central Africa. From 1879 to 1884 he opened the Congo River Basin and laid the groundwork for the Congo Free State after setting up 21 trading posts along the river. Between 1887 and 1890 he led a mission to rescue Emin Pasha, the governor of Equatoria. Stanley settled the question of the source of the Nile and opened a vast territory which accelerated the desire of European countries to control African soil.

On July 12, 1890, Stanley married Dorothy Tennant. In 1895 he became a member of Parliament, and 4 years later he was knighted, receiving the Grand Cross of the Bath. He died on May 10, 1904, in London.

EWB

Stead, William Thomas (1849–1912), British journalist. William Stead was a prolific early practitioner of expose journalism in England. As an editor and writer for such periodicals as the *Pall Mall Gazette* and his *Review of Reviews,* he uncovered social ills and agitated for reform. While his writings are generally criticized for their sensationalism, Stead had a profound effect on turn-of-the-century English politics and journalism.

Stead was born into a large family at Embleton Manse, Northumberland, England. His father, a Congregational minister, educated Stead and his siblings at home, instilling in them a love of literature and a reverence for the Bible. Stead also received two years of formal schooling at Silcoates, a school for clergymen's sons near Wakefield in West Yorkshire. At the age of twenty-one, after briefly working as a clerk to the Russian vice consul in Newcastle, Stead became

the editor of the Darlington *Northern Echo;* he held this position from 1871 to 1880. In that period he succeeded in making the paper a powerful provincial voice of radical political views and Nonconformist religious sentiment.

In 1880 Stead was invited to London to work as assistant editor to John Morley on the *Pall Mall Gazette.* During his nine-year stay with the *Gazette,* Stead launched sensational, successful press campaigns to forge a strong Royal Navy, to repeal the Contagious Diseases Act, to raise the age of consent for girls from thirteen to sixteen years, and to ruin the political careers of Sir Charles W. Dilke and Charles Stewart Parnell, both of whom Stead considered immoral. Stead was also an outspoken proponent of home rule for Ireland, British Imperialism, and women's rights.

Under Stead's editorship the *Pall Mall Gazette* became one of the most powerful dailies in Great Britain. Throughout his career at the *Gazette,* Stead popularized the techniques of what Matthew Arnold would later term "the new journalism," making generous use of illustrations, headlines, and the personal interview, all of which were relatively new to British journalism at that time. In 1889 Stead left the *Gazette* to found his *Review of Reviews,* a monthly that featured summaries of news, essays, and stories drawn from various foreign and domestic periodicals and books. Stead used the *Review,* as he had the *Gazette,* as a personal pulpit from which he preached his numerous social and religious causes.

Stead's most notorious expose was *The Maiden Tribute of Modern Babylon,* published serially in the *Pall Mall Gazette* in 1885 and compiled into pamphlet form later that year. In a four-day series of articles, Stead detailed in explicit terms the widespread and profitable activities of the vice underworld in London, focusing especially on child prostitution and white slavery. The series culminated with Stead's account of the purchase of a girl for five pounds, intended to demonstrate the ease with which children could be obtained by procurers.

The enormous public outcry against the articles intensified when it became apparent that this account was, as George Bernard Shaw later called it, a "put-up job" perpetrated by Stead himself. Enlisting the help of members of the Salvation Army, including the services of a converted procuress, Stead purchased thirteen-year-old Eliza Armstrong from her mother for five pounds, had Armstrong certified a virgin by a midwife, and installed the girl in a bordello. Before any harm could be done to the girl, she was removed from the house and sent to live with Salvationists in Paris. Stead and his cohorts were convicted on kidnapping charges; all received light sentences except

Stead, who was made to serve three months in Cold-bath Prison and Holloway Gaol.

Although his reputation and credibility were somewhat tarnished by the *Maiden Tribute* scandal, Stead continued to be a prominent critic of vice. Journeying to Chicago in 1894, he made a thorough investigation of the city's underworld, publishing a five hundred-page account of his findings titled *If Christ Came to Chicago: A Plea for the Union of All Who Love in the Service of All Who Suffer*. In 1895 Stead began publishing his "Masterpiece Library," a series of volumes aimed at making important literary works accessible to the working class and, especially, children. About one hundred pages each and profusely illustrated, the "Penny Poets," "Penny Novels," and "Books for the Bairns" series presented condensations or retellings of classics and biblical stories. The series sold over fourteen million copies during its more than thirty-year publication run.

In his efforts as a publisher of inexpensive pamphlet editions of his exposes and of the classics, Stead is regarded as a herald of the present era of cheap, accessible paperback books that place a diversity of reading matter within the reach of all classes of people. In later years Stead protested vociferously against the Boer War in South Africa; he also devoted himself increasingly to his interest in spiritualism, editing *Borderland,* a journal devoted to occultism, and publishing *Letter from Julia,* a volume of epistles that he claimed were transmitted to him by a deceased woman named Julia Ames. Stead died in the sinking of the *Titanic* in 1912.

In Stead's time the general public reacted to his journalism with distaste for his methods but appreciation for his sincerity and, usually, the realization that his exposes were truthful despite their often sensational tone. His detractors attacked his lack of regard for Victorian standards of propriety, or, questioned the truthfulness of his work. Although they often deplored his opinions and way of presenting information, Stead's associates agreed that he was a rigorous truth-seeker who thoroughly researched and believed in everything he published. Present-day critics praise Stead for his revitalizing role in British journalism, asserting that his work represented the advent of an aggressive new generation of correspondents who would not only report about political and social issues but would also raise those issues, effectively claiming an active role in revealing corruption and engendering change. Such works as *If Christ Came to Chicago* are recognized as models of journalistic research, requiring months of probing information sources as various as tax rolls, crime-ridden locales, the testimony of relief workers, and the statements of prostitutes and street people. While his writings and the political issues he covered have been largely forgotten, Stead's influence continues to be felt by any reader who buys an inexpensive paperback book or picks up an illustrated, headline-punctuated newspaper.

CA

Stolypin, Piotr Arkadevich (1862–1911), Russian statesman and reformer. Piotr Stolypin is known for his victory over anarchist forces, for his attempt to transform the Russian autocratic monarchy into a constitutional one, and for his land reform.

Piotr Stolypin was born in Baden. A country squire and landlord in Kovno, he was named marshal of the nobility of that province from 1887 to 1902. In 1903 he was appointed governor of the adjoining province of Grodno and a year later was transferred in the same capacity to Saratov on the Volga. There he ruthlessly put down the peasants, and his determination and personal courage led to his appointment as minister of the interior in 1906. Later that year he became prime minister.

Stolypin was the most competent and clear-sighted official to serve Tsar Nicholas II. His policy was twofoldto bring law and order to society and to institute reform. An enemy of revolution and a conservative, Stolypin tried to break up the revolutionary groups and also to undermine their popular support through social and political reforms. As a monarchist and a constitutionalist, he wished to work harmoniously with the elected Duma in the passage of reform legislation.

An intelligent and well-educated man, Stolypin pondered for some time the poor condition of the Russian villages and concluded that the low level of rural economy was due to the fact that the land did not belong to the peasants. He realized also that Russia could not become a strong power until the majority of the Russian population the peasants became interested in the preservation of individual property. The Revolution of 1905 with its agrarian excesses only strengthened Stolypin's conviction on this point. He came to believe finally that the primary need of Russia was the creation of a class of well-to-do landowners.

Under Stolypin's agrarian reform law peasants made remarkable progress in obtaining private land ownership. Stolypin spared no money in order to consolidate and to increase the peasantry. He encouraged the practice of granting the peasants small credits; he maintained an army of land experts, land surveyors, and agronomists; and he spent large sums of money on public education.

Stolypin's creative efforts in the work of the state were not always within the limits of the constitutional order at which he aimed. The introduction of local assemblies in the western province aroused the entire Russian people against him. The left wing and the center were indignant at such a flagrant violation of the constitution, and the right wing was indignant at his treatment of its leaders in the State Council. Stolypin was killed in Kiev on Sept. 18, 1911. His assassin was a double agent whose motives remain cloudy to this day.

EWB

Stopes, Marie (1880–1958), English scientist and writer.

Best known for her work as a pioneer in popularizing the use of birth control in the United Kingdom, Marie Stopes was also a prolific writer. While attracting the condemnation of the Catholic Church for her staunch advocacy of contraception and her establishment of Great Britain's first birth control clinic, Stopes's work as a social reformer would also pave the way for an increasing public acceptance of books on the subject of human sexuality.

Marie Stopes was a British scientist and writer who became an active proponent of sexual education and birth control in the early twentieth century. In books such as *Married Love* (1918), Stopes became one of the first people to publicly discuss romantic and sexual happiness in marriage. She also provided information on contraception through her clinics, lectures, and books, including *Wise Parenthood* (1918). While much of Stopes's information and advice was criticized by medical professionals and officials of the Roman Catholic church, her books enjoyed wide sales, demonstrating the public's need for the kind of well-explained practical advice that she offered.

Marie Charlotte Stopes was born in Edinburgh, Scotland, on October 15, 1880. Her parents were both well-educated with successful careers: her father, Henry Stopes, was an architect, and her mother, Charlotte Carmichael Stopes, was a Shakespeare expert who had been the first female graduate of a Scottish university. The family moved to London after Stopes's birth, and there she was educated at home by her mother until the age of 12. She was then sent to Edinburgh to begin classes at St. George's School. After a short period there, she moved to North London Collegiate, where she distinguished herself as a top student. Stopes attended University College, where she focused first on chemistry and later switched to an honors botany program. In 1902, she received her bachelor of science degree with honors in botany and geology.

Continuing to prepare herself for a scientific career, Stopes went to the Botanical Institute of Munich University in Germany. There, she conducted her doctoral research on the reproduction processes of cycads, a type of tropical plant. She was awarded a doctoral degree with highest honors in 1904. Returning to England, she earned a doctor of science degree from London University, becoming the youngest person in Britain to do so. The same year, she overcame another boundary by becoming the first woman to join the science faculty of Manchester University. Stopes had a very successful scientific career; she conducted well-respected research on the history of angiosperms and she also studied the composition of coal. Her work earned her a grant from the British Royal Society, an organization of leading scientists, which allowed her to travel to Japan to conduct research in 1907 and 1908. This award was another first for a woman.

Returning to her post at Manchester for a time, Stopes published the first of her scientific works, *Ancient Plants,* published in 1910. In 1913, she accepted a position at University College and for the next seven years she lectured in paleobotany and wrote other books in her fields of specialty. These included *The Constitution of Coal,* published in 1918, and *The Four Visible Ingredients in Banded Bituminous Coal: Studies in the Composition of Coal,* published in 1919.

In 1911, Stopes married Reginald Ruggles Gates, a Canadian botanist; she did not take his surname, however, and would retain her maiden name throughout her life. The marriage was not successful, primarily due to Stopes's discovery that her new husband was impotent. She filed for an annulment, which was granted in 1916. The experience apparently left a strong impression on Stopes, who increasingly turned her energies from her scientific research and teaching to writing on the topics of love, marriage, and sex. After completing her first book in this area, *Married Love,* she found that publishers were unwilling to handle a book that engaged in such unabashed discussions of sexual relationships. In order to get her work published, Stopes sought financial backing elsewhere. During this time, she met the wealthy pilot Humphrey Verdon Roe, who shared her interests in promoting birth control. Roe agreed to lend her the money to publish the book, which was finally printed in 1918. Stopes and Roe were married that year in a civil ceremony at a registry office in May and a religious ceremony on June 19. In July of 1919, Stopes delivered a stillborn son, a tragedy for which she held her doctors responsible. This event may have played a role in her strong distrust of doctors for the rest of her life. Roe and Stopes were successful in having a child in 1924, when their son Harry Stopes-Roe was born.

Married Love was a great success. Her marriage manual did not present many new ideas, but was unique in presenting instruction and advice with uncomplicated language that was accessible to a wide audience. Her main contribution was promoting the idea that people should expect and strive for happiness in their personal and sexual relationships, a fairly radical idea for the time. The book drew a substantial amount of letters from readers, most of whom desired information on birth control. Stopes willingly obliged her readers by compiling her ideas on the topic in the book *Wise Parenthood* in 1918. In the book, she suggested that a cervical cap be used for contraception; she felt that this was the best method to use and never supported any other methods despite the criticism she received from medical doctors on the subject. *Wise Parenthood* continued Stopes's practice of providing often unavailable information on reproduction by using detailed drawings of human anatomy to educate readers about the physical facts of sexuality.

Other books on sex, marriage, and birth control by Stopes followed throughout the 1920s and early 1930s, including *A Letter to Working Mothers* (1919), *Radiant Motherhood* (1920), and *Enduring Passion* (1928). In addition, in 1921 she and her husband founded the first birth control clinic in London, the Mother's Clinic. The early 1920s brought a number of attacks on Stopes's work. Doctors criticized her promotion of the cervical cap, arguing that it was one of the most harmful methods of birth control for women. A Roman Catholic doctor, Halliday Sutherland, wrote a treatise accusing Stopes of using poor women for birth control experiments; she vehemently denied the charges and countered by suing Sutherland for libel. The highly publicized trials that followed ultimately resulted in Sutherland being cleared of the charges, but brought Stopes an incredible amount of attention, resulting in her popularity as a public speaker. She also published a formal rebuttal to the Church's attacks on her work in the 1933 book, *Roman Catholic Methods of Birth Control.*

Stopes's later years were marked by a growing sense of frustration and isolation. She and Roe were separated in 1938, at which time she moved into a home in Norbury Park in England. After she expressed disapproval over her son's marriage, she also lost touch with him for a long time. She reportedly became disillusioned with her humanitarian causes and retreated into literary pursuits, producing a number of poorly received collections of love poetry such as *Love Songs for Young Lovers* (1939), *We Burn* (1950), and *Joy and Verity* (1952). The battles that she did take on were obscure and unsuccessful, notably her fight to obtain a state pension for the poet Lord Alfred Douglas. She held the belief that physical health could be maintained with a regimen of cold baths and drinking a daily glass of sea water; because of this and her distrust of doctors, she did not immediately seek medical attention when signs of illness appeared. She was finally diagnosed with advanced breast cancer, but refused standard treatment. Instead she underwent some holistic therapy in Switzerland before returning to Norbury Park and dying on October 2, 1958.

A flamboyant and often arrogant figure who considered herself the best authority on the topics of love, marriage, sex, and birth control, Stopes was criticized during her lifetime for advancing ideas that were in some cases outdated and not proper for all people. But much of the opposition she encountered also stemmed from the fact that she dared to address topics that were still considered improper for public discussion at that time. Fighting this mentality, which she felt led to ignorance and unhappiness in sexual matters, Stopes provided information that was eagerly sought by the public. Her success in changing attitudes about romantic relationships and parenthood was apparent in the popularity of her books and the enormous public response that they generated.

EWB

T

Taine, Hippolyte Adolphe (1828–1893), French critic and historian. Hippolyte Taine was one of the most prominent intellectual figures of his period in France. His emphasis on scientific methods in criticism formed the basis of contemporary critical techniques.

Hippolyte Taine was born in Vouziers in the Ardennes on April 21, 1828, into a family of civil servants. His childhood was spent in an enlightened cultural atmosphere in which earnest intellectual pursuits mingled with an early exposure to the arts and to nature. By the age of 14, when he moved to Paris with his widowed mother, he had developed an intense intellectuality matched only by his profound love of nature.

Taine's passion for knowledge and especially for philosophy made him highly receptive to the multitude of intellectual and scientific trends of his time. By the time he had completed his university studies at the École Normale Supérieure, he had investigated almost every philosophical and scientific concept known. Upon leaving the university he was prepared to formulate his own critical apparatus in order to investigate bodies of knowledge.

Taine's most productive years coincided with the reign of Napoleon III. The Second Empire, beneath its social glitter and economic growth, was highly oppressive to liberal intellectuals. Taine abandoned all hopes of a professorial career at the university. He withdrew from public life and devoted his energies to research in a large variety of fields. All of his studies centered on the problem of the human condition and were underlain by his naive but honest belief in the explicability of human nature by means of scientific inquiry.

The culmination of this belief found its expression in Taine's central work, *De l'intelligence* (1870). It summed up all his previous interests in psychology and philosophy and fused the converging lines of his critical thought. His works preceding *De l'intelligence* encompass a great variety of interests and touch on almost every phase of intellectual and artistic production. His dissertation on the fables of Jean de La Fontaine, completed in 1853 and published in its final form in 1860 (*La Fontaine et ses fables*), was a presentation of Taine's concept of esthetics. It expressed in essence his doctrine of scientific determinism by attributing "racial" distinctions to climatic and geographical differences. His work on the French philosophers of the 19th century (*Les Philosophes français du XIX siècle*, 1857) was a critical evaluation of the major philosophical concepts of the century, and his essays on a wide variety of subjects represented a further elaboration of his critical system. These volumes included *Essais de critique et d'histoire* (1858), *Nouveaux essais* (1865), and *Derniers essais* (1894).

Taine formulated his critical system most clearly in the introduction to the five volumes of one of his major works, *Histoire de la littérature anglaise* (1863). He stated that every reality, psychological, esthetic, or historical, can be reduced to a distinctly definable formula by discovering in each reality a single operative principle. This basic principle is governed by a system of laws that he reduced to his famous triad of race, environment, and time ("la race, le milieu, le moment"). Taine applied this critical system in all of his works, including his analyses of the development of the arts of Greece, Italy, and the Netherlands, presented in a series of lectures spanning more than 20 years at the École des Beaux-Arts and published in two volumes, *Philosophie de l'art* (1865–1869).

The Franco-Prussian War of 1870 profoundly disturbed Taine. From then until his death, he applied himself to an analysis of French history in an attempt to uncover the causes of France's defeat and the Commune of 1871 (*Les Origines de la France contemporaine*, 1875–1893). He died in Paris on March 9, 1893.

EWB

Talleyrand, Charles Maurice de, duc de Talleyrand-Périgord

Talleyrand, Charles Maurice de, duc de Talleyrand-Périgord (1754–1838), French statesman. Talleyrand remains the classic case of a successful turncoat in politics. For half a century he served every French regime except that of the Revolutionary "Terror."

Charles Maurice de Talleyrand was a masterful diplomat of the old school as ambassador and foreign minister. Admired and often distrusted, sometimes even feared by those he served, he was not easily replaced as a negotiator of infinite wiles. Talleyrand has been an extraordinarily difficult figure for historians to understand and appraise. His moral corruption is beyond question: he was an unabashed liar and deceiver; he not only took but sought bribes from those with whom he was negotiating; and he lived with a niece as his mistress for decades. He repeatedly shifted political allegiance without visible compunction and possessed no political principle on which he would stand firm to the last; and he was also at least technically guilty of treason, engaging in secret negotiations with the public enemies of his country while in its service.

Yet closer scrutiny of what Talleyrand did shows an apparent steady purpose beneath the crust of arrogant contempt for the ordinary standards of mankind's judgment, expressed in the comment attributed to him on the kidnaping and execution of the Duc d'Enghien at Napoleon's command: "It was worse than a crime, it was a mistake." Talleyrand had his own vision of the interests of France, which lay in making the transition from the Old Regime to the new as painless as possible, at the same time preserving the territorial interests of the French nation. His fidelity to whichever persons happened to be at the head of the French state lasted at best only as long as their power, but this matchless cynic seems to have possessed genuine devotion for France as a country, and his apparent treasons can be seen as the products of a higher loyalty. Yet this picture of him may be false, for Talleyrand destroyed many of the records by which the truth regarding his career could have been more closely reached. It is easier to decide his guilt than to specify what he was guilty of, easier to affirm his deeper innocence than to prove it. The problem lies both in the man himself and in the eye of the beholder.

Education and Priesthood. Talleyrand was born in Paris on Feb. 13, 1754, into one of the most ancient and distinguished families of the French nobility. As the eldest son of Charles Daniel, Comte de Talleyrand, a lieutenant general in the French army, he was destined to follow his father's career until a childhood accident caused a permanent injury. His father compelled him to accept a career in the Church over Talleyrand's protests, for he had no vocation as a priest. But he took Holy Orders in 1775 after studies at the Collège d'Harcourt, a secondary school, and at the seminary in Reims. His rapid promotions came to him as an ecclesiastical administrator with powerful backing, not as a shepherd of souls. His first important post was as general agent for the assembly of the French clergy in 1780, negotiating with the government for the "voluntary" payments made by churchmen in lieu of the taxes from which they were exempt. Then, in 1788, he was appointed bishop of Autun and was consecrated the next year, as the French Revolution was about to begin.

Elected to the Estates General as a deputy of the clergy, Talleyrand quickly showed that he wished the First Estate to cooperate in the transformation of the Old Regime into a new order, even at the expense of its own privileges. Passing over into open opposition to the court, he was influential in persuading his fellow ecclesiastics to join the Third Estate in the newly proclaimed National Assembly on June 19, 1789. He proposed on October 10 that the vast properties of the Church be put at the disposal of the state in exchange for salaries to be paid by the state, and in line with this policy he accepted the Civil Constitution of the Clergy and was one of the consecrators of the new bishops established under its provisions. For these violations of Church discipline, Pope Pius VI excommunicated Talleyrand in 1791. His report on public education in September 1791 won wide praise for its principles but was never applied.

Diplomatic Missions and Exile. In 1792 Talleyrand repeatedly went to England as an unofficial envoy with the mission of keeping that country neutral in the war beginning with Austria and Prussia, but the French invasion of the Austrian Netherlands (Belgium) as well as the rise of revolutionary extremism, culminating in the execution of Louis XVI, brought England into the war in 1793. Talleyrand, condemned as an émigré by the Revolutionary authorities at home, was expelled by England in 1794, and he went to the United States for 2 years. There he visited many parts of the country and probably engaged in land speculation.

In 1796, after the formation of the Directory, Talleyrand returned to France. He was named to the Institute and became foreign minister in July 1797. He took part in the coup d'etat of 18 Fructidor (Sept. 4, 1797), which confirmed the republican regime against royalist conspiracies, and he pocketed a fortune in bribes from those who wanted his favor (al-though the American negotiators in the "XYZ affair" not only rebuffed his demands for money but made them public on their return home). He was forced to resign the Foreign Ministry in July 1799, when his republicanism fell under suspicion. His destiny then became intertwined with that of Gen. Napoleon Bonaparte, whose expedition to Egypt Talleyrand had sponsored and whom he helped to come to power in the coup d'etat of 18 Brumaire (Nov. 9, 1799).

Napoleon's Foreign Minister. Talleyrand served as foreign minister for Napoleon under the Consulate and the Empire until August 1807 and was rewarded in 1804 with the post of grand chamberlain and in 1806 with the title of Prince de Benevento (French, Bénévent). However, his relations with the Emperor became clouded as Napoleon's obsessive aggressiveness became clear to him. Talleyrand wanted to end the exhausting wars against the recurring European coalitions by making peace with England and Russia, the principal foes, on terms that preserved for France its major territorial gains. Remaining in the Emperor's service, he began a perilous game of intrigues designed to thwart his master's ambitions. In 1808 at Erfurt he encouraged Tsar Alexander I to resist Napoleon's demands and was dismissed in 1809 by the suspicious Napoleon but allowed to reside at his country estate. However, after the invasion of Russia in 1812, Talleyrand began a secret correspondence with Louis XVIII and, as head of a provisional government established on April 1, 1814, was a principal figure in the King's first restoration.

Congress of Vienna. Again named foreign minister, Talleyrand skillfully maneuvered to win the full support of the Allies for the Bourbons, obtained relatively favorable terms for France in the first Peace of Paris, then played upon the dissensions of the victors to gain a place for France among the negotiators at the Congress of Vienna, and finally turned the victors against each other to France's advantage. This brilliant feat of diplomacy was partly dimmed by the wrath of the Allies when France welcomed Napoleon back in the Hundred Days, but the final peace terms that emerged from the Vienna negotiations brought France back to its prerevolutionary frontiers.

Upon the second restoration of Louis XVIII, Talleyrand served as prime minister and foreign minister from July until September, but the ultraroyalists who dominated the new government were less forgiving than the king, least of all of an apostate bishop, and Talleyrand lost his office. However, he received the title of Duc de Dino in 1815, in place of the princely title of Benevento, which had been extinguished with Napoleon's departure, and in 1817 he became Duc de Talleyrand-Périgord. During the remainder of the reign of Louis XVIII, Talleyrand was a member of the Chamber of Peers, where he often voted against the government.

Final Diplomatic Achievements. After the Revolution of 1830, in which he was a minor participant but encouraged Louis Philippe to take the crown, Talleyrand was sent to London as ambassador. He negotiated an agreement with England, upon recognition of the new independent Belgian state, that was favorable to French interests. The signing of the Quadruple Alliance of 1834 (with England, Spain, and Portugal), which assured Anglo-French collaboration in support of the constitutional government in Spain against the Carlist rebels, was Talleyrand's final achievement as a diplomat. He died in Paris on May 17, 1838, soon after becoming reconciled with the Roman Catholic Church.

EWB

Tawney, Richard Henry (1880–1962), British economic historian and social philosopher. Richard Tawney was an influential Fabian socialist and an adviser to governments.

Richard Tawney was born in Calcutta, India, on Nov. 30, 1880, the son of a distinguished civil servant and Sanskrit scholar. Educated at Rugby and Balliol College, Oxford, he graduated in classics in 1903 and then lived and worked at Toynbee Hall settlement in London. From 1906 to 1908 he lectured in economics at Glasgow University and then was a pioneer teacher for the Oxford University Tutorial Classes Committee until the outbreak of war in 1914. He was wounded at the Battle of the Somme in 1916.

Tawney was an ardent supporter of the Workers' Educational Association, serving as a member of its executive (1905) and president (1928–1944). His adult teaching, especially at Rochdale, is now legendary. His first seminal work of scholarship was *The Agrarian Problem in the Sixteenth Century* (1912), dedicated to his tutorial classes, in which he traced the impact of commercialism on English agriculture and society.

In 1918 Tawney became a fellow of Balliol. The following year he was appointed reader in economic history at the London School of Economics; he was professor of economic history there from 1931 to 1949. He was a founder member and later president of the Economic History Society and, for 7 years, joint editor of its *Review*. His editions of economic documents became standard sources for students, as did his two studies of economic morality and practice

in Tudor and Stuart England: his edition of Thomas Wilson's *Discourse upon Usury* (1925) and his classic *Religion and the Rise of Capitalism* (1926). Like his other major works, including *The Rise of the Gentry* (1954), *Religion and the Rise of Capitalism* was substantially criticized by later scholars, and its conclusions were later modified. Nevertheless, its power and seminal influence were universally recognized, so much so that the 17th century is often described as "Tawney's century." In 1958 he published his long-awaited study *Lionel Cranfield: Business and Politics under James I,* which was generally acclaimed by scholars.

Throughout Tawney's life, scholarship and action were interconnected. His 1914 monograph on wage rates in the chain-making industry led to his presidency of the Chain-Making Trade Board (1919–1922). In 1919 he was a leading figure on the Sankey Coal Commission, and subsequently he served as adviser on educational matters to the Labour party, member of the Consultative Committee of the Board of Education and the Cotton Trade Conciliation Board, and Labour attaché at the British embassy in Washington during World War II. His ideas exerted a profound influence on the philosophy of the British left. His expanded Fabian Society pamphlet *The Acquisitive Society* (1922) and his essay "Equality" (1931) contained severe moral condemnations of the capitalist economic and social system.

Tawney possessed a rare combination of qualities: humility, personal asceticism bordering on eccentricity, exceptional literary skills, deep scholarship, and a rare capacity to inspire his fellowmen with ideals of humanity and social justice. He died in London on Jan. 16, 1962.

EWB

Teresa of Avila (1515–1582), Catholic nun and reformer.

The Protestant Reformation of the early and mid-16th century provoked a crisis for those Christians who remained loyal to the Catholic Church. Aware that it was in many ways corrupt and that spiritual life had become diluted by secular concerns, Catholic reformers tried to recover the integrity of primitive Christianity without violating Catholic tradition and the religious authorities. The effort at an internal Catholic reformation was particularly intense in Spain, where Saint Ignatius Loyola, Saint John of the Cross, and an influential group of Christian humanists created new religious orders and a new form of spirituality. None of these Catholic reformers was more successful than Saint Teresa of Avila, creator of the Discalced Carmelites and an influential spiritual writer.

Spain in the 16th century was an aristocratic society obsessed by the idea of blood purity (*limpieza de sangre*) which in our eyes seems no better than a form of fanatical racism. Recently reunited by the "Catholic Kings"—Ferdinand and Isabella—after a long era of fragmentation and partial Muslim occupation, Spain had a large population of Moors and Jews who had converted to Christianity under threat of expulsion or death. The Spanish Inquisition, doubting the sincerity of some of these conversions, launched periodic investigations of *conversos;* among them, in 1485, was Juan Sanchez, a rich textile trader of Jewish descent and Teresa's grandfather. After a hearing where he confessed to "many grave crimes and offences against our Holy Catholic Faith," he was publicly humiliated in the Inquisition's *auto de fe,* a procession of backsliders bearing extinguished candles in the streets of Toledo (to show that the light of salvation had gone out in their souls). Despite his confession, his "crimes" cannot have been very grave or he would have been put to death.

Surviving the ordeal and working to expunge its memory by dynastic alliances with older Catholic families, Juan Sanchez moved to the nearby city of Avila in Castile; there, his son Alonso, a taxgatherer and financier, lived an ostentatious life, fathering Teresa de Ahumada by his second wife. Teresa grew up in the protected environment of an honor-conscious society and faced the prospect of either marriage or taking the veil; no other alternatives presented themselves to high-born women of her age. As a child, she enjoyed romantic fiction, of the kind which Cervantes later lampooned in *Don Quixote,* and she seems to have had a brief flirtation with a young man connected with her family. They responded by placing her in a nunnery, where—after an early shock at this comparatively spartan life—she came to believe that she had a lifetime's vocation.

The convent of the Incarnation in Avila was centrally placed in the city and, although the nuns were supposed to be cloistered, there was in fact a good deal of contact between the nuns and the other citizens of the town. The Carmelite nuns had for two centuries deviated from the austere ideals of their founders, and within the convent, social distinctions from the outside were still observed. Wealthier nuns, such as Teresa herself, had to bring a "dowry" to the convent, just as they would have had to take one to a husband; by this means, and by promises of payment from novices' parents, the convent was sure of a steady income. The more privileged and high-born nuns had private rooms rather than sleeping in the dormitory shared by poor nuns; they had their own servants (even slaves in a few cases); and they continued to enjoy the honorific name "Doña" inside the convent just as they had outside.

A custom had also developed that if a woman in one of the major families in Avila needed a female companion in times of bereavement or stress she could summon one from the convent to spend time with her; on several occasions, Teresa was thus called away from the Incarnation for periods of months at a time. Thus, she spent two years with Doña Guiomar de Ulloa, an influential widow who became one of Teresa's principal benefactors in her later experiments in reforming the Carmelite order. In the same way, she would return to her family in times of sickness. During one such sickness, when she was in her early 20s, Teresa was so near death that her family had dropped wax onto her eyes, a local custom with the dead, before she surprised them by reviving. The episodic nature of convent life, along with the free access of outsiders to the residents, made the Carmelite existence a relatively relaxed affair in Teresa's youth.

Teresa Experiences Revelations, Visions. Without ever complaining about the convent life, she began to draw attention to herself by an exceptional form of spirituality. Sometimes while praying, she would receive messages from Christ, usually in the form of sudden convictions sown in her mind as she meditated. As her life continued, they became more intense and insistent, giving her at times the radiant assurance that she was in direct contact with God. Fearing nevertheless that she might somehow be under the influence of the devil, like some recently denounced spiritual charlatans, she treated her own revelations guardedly and consulted a succession of confessors about how to proceed. Most of them, similarly afraid of a demonic visitation, and responding to the defensive Spanish religious mood of the times which regarded any novelty as a possible sign of "Lutheranism," discouraged her. But then a meeting at Doña Guiomar de Ulloa's house with Peter of Alcantara, a reformer who believed in reviving the early Christian life of heroic austerity, led her to recover confidence. Peter of Alcantara assured her that her visions came from God and that she should heed them.

Her religious development continued through her 20s and 30s and became progressively more intense; at times, she would enter a trancelike state, which local people sought to oversee out of fascination. Particularly embarrassing to her were episodes of involuntary levitation during prayer, which had induced weightlessness, widely reported and seemingly well authenticated at the time.

Whatever our judgment of Teresa's reports of divine visitation it is certain that she was a woman of courage, integrity, and resolve. In response to one confessor's request, she wrote her life history, which now constitutes our best source of information about her experiences; written in a form influenced by Saint Augustine's *Confessions*, which she had read and admired, it speaks of her as a dreadful sinner and attributes all her merits to God.

She Works to Reform Convent.   As she advanced into middle age at the Incarnation convent, her sense of dissatisfaction with life there, coupled with the promoting of her visions, led her to attempt a reform of the convent; in this project several of her relatives, also young nuns, were eager to cooperate. Hoping to revive the old simplicity of Carmelite life, she arranged to acquire a house in another part of Avila and to live there with a handful of like-minded disciples. It seemed to her that the only way she as a woman could help to prevent the spread of heresy throughout Europe was to pray more fervently and to live a more devout life, and in its way she saw her reform as a missionary activity, even though it did not require leaving home ground.

The experiment faced many obstacles. First, Teresa wanted to live without the financial security which was enjoyed by the other monastic houses of Avila, but to trust entirely to alms, like Jesus. She would accept "dowries" if they were offered but would not make them a condition of admission; a novice's character alone would be decisive. She would make no distinction between the rich and poor, noble and plebeian, within the house; all titles would be dropped and the nuns would call one another "sister." It may be that as the descendant of *conversos,* even rich ones, she remained sensitive to the disadvantages of those without the coveted degrees of blood purity. In her book *The Way of Perfection,* Teresa explained that this dramatic contrast with the outside world was a way of reminding the sisters that "it is the Lord who provides for all in common" and that they were freed from trying to please their relatives outside the walls.

The city authorities, the local bishop, and many noble families protested against the plan, on the grounds that it would disrupt a convenient way of life (in which convent and city interacted to the convenience of the city) and that it would deny their daughters the honors and dignity they had previously preserved as nuns. Besides, with the way things stood, the twice-yearly payments the families made to a convent guaranteed its continued association with, even dependence on, *them,* a dependence which was now threatened. They also feared that a convent without

regular means of support could easily become a burden on the finances of the city. As the gilt was already peeling off the facade of Spain's "golden age," in the form of bad harvests, inflation, and urban discontent, these were grave matters.

Teresa had sufficient supporters among the clergy and lay nobility, however, that she was able to persist, and she was steadied by a vision of Peter of Alcantara, recently deceased, who urged her not to falter. On the day that her convent opened, it was surrounded by a chanting mob of angry townsmen who tried to break down the door. Teresa's diplomatic gifts, and her capacity to win over once-intractable opponents, ultimately secured for her the right of the Convent of St. Joseph to exist in Avila and a law suit against it was resolved. The small but well-educated and influential religious reform party in Avila was pleased to see this example of discipline and religious humility in the heart of the city as a form of living sermon to the other residents. For Teresa, the simple life of this new convent was much superior to the luxuries of the old; most of her supporters, many of them cousins, agreed, but a few were unable to endure it and returned to the Incarnation with her consent. Sleeping on straw mattresses, without servants, wearing harsh sackcloth robes, the sisters at St. Joseph were soon afflicted by a plague of lice in their clothes and hair, but after intercessory prayers by Teresa she reported that the lice departed once and for all.

She called her reformed sisterhood the "Discalced Carmelites." *Discalced* means that they did not wear shoes but went barefoot, again in tribute to Jesus' simplicity and suffering.

When St. Joseph's was established, Teresa, again prompted by divine visitation, moved to establish another convent, at the market town of Medina del Campo. This and her other houses were usually in market centers (including Toledo, Segovia, and Seville) because urban centers alone seemed likely to be able to provide the money in occasional benefactions which her new rule specified. Later, when rural houses were established, some kind of regular financing became imperative or they would have foundered quickly. The cities also possessed large converso populations, and the merchants and professionals who sympathized with the new spirituality of Catholic reform, rather than the older legalistic form of faith, looked more favorably on Teresa's reforms.

Teresa Establishes More Convents.   Despite recurrent illnesses, Teresa lived into her late 60s, the last year being the most active, as she moved from place to place in Spain establishing new convents of the Discalced Carmelites—a total of 17 in her last 20 years. Inspired by her example, Carmelite friars as well as nuns began to organize reforms, the most distinguished of whom was Friar (ultimately Saint) John of the Cross, who for a time was Teresa's confessor. He was many years her junior and admired her greatly but could still rebuke her when necessary. "When you make your confession, Mother," he told her on one occasion, "you have a way of finding the prettiest excuses." Around him gathered many stories of supernatural events and stern dealings with demonic interventions; one of the nuns of St. Joseph's was "lifted bodily from her feet and left suspended upside down in the air until ordered back to her stall by St. John of the Cross" while another was "glued so firmly to the ground that no one could make her budge until she was released by a mere glance from the friar."

As the Discalced Carmelites established themselves, however, the older "Calced" branch became increasingly suspicious and resentful; they used their influence with the authorities to prevent new houses—even when guaranteed an income by wealthy enthusiasts—from being established, so that some of Teresa's long and difficult journeys across Spain were made in vain. They also arranged for the imprisonment of John of the Cross in Toledo where he was flogged and ordered to abandon the Reformers; although he steadfastly refused.

John of the Cross's sufferings ended after eight months when he managed to escape, but he was so sick that Teresa thought he would die in any case.

A papal nuncio to whom Teresa appealed that the Calced and Discalced Carmelites might be officially divided into two separate congregations (the only way she could see to end the conflict) was not at first disposed to listen sympathetically. His attack in turn, however, aroused Teresa's growing body of friends and supporters within Spain who sent reassuring messages to Rome about her good qualities (and those of John of the Cross). Finally, in June 1580, she managed to get a brief from the Pope officially dividing the Carmelites into two distinct provinces and settling most of the points of conflict between the branches.

Teresa traveled extensively right up to the end of her life and endured a long coach ride during her final illness. Neither did death bring an end to her peregrinations. The nuns who attended her in her final illness reported that her sickroom was filled with a delicious aroma, and those who laid her to rest discovered that her body was immune to decay, another sign, in their view, of her exceptional sanctity. Far from decomposing, her body emitted a sweet aroma ("the odor of sanctity") not only at first but for years thereafter as it was repeatedly dug up and examined. Not only was it inspected; the body was also moved

from place to place as rival convents and cities vied to get their hands on what was now a holy relic. And with each exhumation parts of the miraculously preserved body were hacked off to be used as relics: first a finger, next an arm, later the heart (which was said to bear signs of the angels piercing spear) until by the next century the incorruptible body was scarcely more than a fragment. Forty years after her death, in 1622, Teresa of Jesus was named a saint while the order she had founded continued to endure, though it had been forced early to accept permanent endowments as the only viable way of surviving the economic austerities of a Spain which was now entering a long period of decline and senescence.

HWL

Thiers, Louis Adolphe (1797–1877), French journalist, historian, and statesman. Adolphe Thiers was the most gifted of the literary statesmen who were an important feature of 19th-century French political life.

Born at Marseilles on April 16, 1797, Adolphe Thiers attended the local lycée and studied law at Aix. Though admitted to the bar, he forsook the legal profession to become a journalist. Moving to Paris in 1821, Thiers became a contributor to the *Constitutionnel,* a Liberal paper, and began the *History of the French Revolution* (10 vols., 1823–1827; trans., 5 vols., 1895), a sympathetic account which established his reputation as a man of letters. The work suffered from diffuseness, casuistry, bias against those with whom he disagreed, and omission of inconvenient facts, all of which evoked the protest from many participants in the described events that he had treated them and their cause unjustly.

Brilliant but arrogant, energetic but antagonistic, Thiers embarked upon a successful but controversial political career under the July Monarchy. With the financial backing of Jacques Lafitte, in 1830 Thiers joined F. A. M. Mignet and N. A. Carrel in founding the National and launching an editorial campaign to replace the Bourbon with an Orleanist dynasty. A member of the haute bourgeoisie, he played a prominent role in the July Revolution and in the ascendancy of the Duc d'Orléans to the throne. Elected deputy for Aix, he soon became the leader of the Left Center, which wanted to broaden the suffrage to include the lower bourgeoisie and thought that the King should reign but not rule.

After the fall of the Lafitte ministry (March 1831), Thiers became less liberal, and, following the suppression of the Republican insurrection of June 1832, he became minister of the interior in the Soult government. During the next 4 years Thiers advanced from one portfolio to another until he became premier (February–September 1836). The brevity of his ministry is explained by the opposition of François Guizot, leader of the Right Center, and the hostility of Louis Philippe, who resented his ambition and arrogance. In March 1840 Thiers again became premier but held the post only 6 months before his rash support of Egypt during the second Mohammed Ali crisis brought France to the brink of war with Britain and caused the King to dismiss him (Oct. 29, 1840). He continued to sit in the Chamber but seldom spoke until 1846, when he began a campaign of opposition against the Guizot ministry. When it fell on Feb. 23, 1848, the King again turned to Thiers, but this action came too late. The next day, Thiers, loyal to the end, advised Louis Philippe to leave the capital and besiege it until it could be assaulted. The King, however, rejected the plan and repaired instead to England.

Under the Second Republic, Thiers posed as a conservative republican. The "red scare" created by the June Days so intimidated him that he supported L. E. Cavaignac's bloody suppression of the workers. He backed Louis Napoleon for president, however, in the belief that, if Louis Napoleon was elected, his presumed ineptitude would pave the way for the restoration of the Orleanist dynasty. Elected to the Legislative Assembly in 1849, Thiers, Voltairean skeptic though he was, even voted for the Falloux Law (1850) because he saw the Church as an ally against the socialists. Arrested at the time of the coup of 1851, the former premier went into English exile, but within a year the Prince President granted him amnesty.

Returning to Paris in 1852, Thiers spent the next decade completing the *History of the Consulate and the Empire* (trans., 20 vols., 1845–1862), a work begun in 1840. So pro-Napoleon as to be panegyrical, it suffered, too, from the same faults which marred his first history and provoked the same criticism.

In 1863 Thiers resumed his political career as a deputy for Paris. A severe critic of Napoleon III's foreign policy, he blamed it for France's loss of prestige. After 1866 he repeatedly warned the Emperor of the Prussian menace, but few of his countrymen took his Philippics seriously. The consequences of unpreparedness were, of course, the defeat of France and the fall of Napoleon III.

On Sept. 4, 1870, the Third Republic replaced the Second Empire and opened the way for Thiers's third and greatest ascendancy. Elected provisional executive by the Assembly on Feb. 16, 1871, he at once negotiated with Bismarck the Treaty of Frankfurt (May 10) and soon thereafter (May 21–28) crushed the Paris Commune. On August 30 a grateful France elected him president, and for the next 2 years he gave the infant republic the stability and direction that it so desperately needed. A strong executive and a skillful parliamentary leader, Thiers earned the sobriquet "Adolphe I." But on May 24, 1873, a monarchist majority, which regarded him a turncoat, forced him to resign. The "grand old man" continued to sit in the Assembly until his death on Sept. 3, 1877.

EWB

Thomas, Keith (1933–), author and intellectual. The typical Englishman of the period 1500–1800 saw himself as the center of the universe, with the various animals and plants placed on earth to serve his own purposes. With *Man and the Natural World: A History of the Modern Sensibility*, author Keith Thomas examines the evolving relationship between civilized man and his wild environment in a book "alive with the color and charm of nature itself," according to Michael Kitch in a *Washington Post Book World* article.

As Thomas describes life during this technologically and socially active segment of English history, humans often had whimsical or complicated classifications regarding the animals in their lives:" Hanoverian cows were given names—Gentle, Lovely, Mother-like or Welcome Home—but pigs and sheep were not," writes London *Times* critic Michael Ratcliff. "Seventeenth-century dogs were allowed in church, even at the communion rail, but were hanged like felons if they had killed or been otherwise 'wicked'; cats and cocks were fair game for torture, but no creature was eaten which had been a worker or given pleasure as a pet, and horsemeat never took on." The author, says Ratcliff, "is an historian of infinite curiosity and vast reading, and [*Man and the Natural World*] covers an extraordinary range of subjects, among them gardening, folklore, forestry, cruelty, refinement, fashion, class, battery pig farmers in the sixteenth century, ornamental dogs at the Stuart court, the shift from country to town and the rise of a sentimental nostalgia for the land. In the process he surprises, informs and entertains on every page, and detects a tragic paradox within an inexhaustible comedy of English manners and life."

"There is a lot to trace," acknowledges Noel Perrin. Writing about *Man and the Natural World* in the *New York Times Book Review*, Perrin recounts: "At the beginning of the period, nearly all Englishmen took for granted that the sole function of other life-forms was to serve man. Flies served to remind us of the shortness of life. Lobsters were not only good to eat (a 16th-century gentleman remarked), they provided the diner with valuable exercise as he cracked their claws—and their wonderful armor made a good subject for military contemplation. Those plants that gave us neither food nor medicine often gave us messages from God. So did birds.'" Paradoxically, Thomas suggests that we turned our conscience to nature only when its conquest was nearly complete," states Kitch." The environmental ethic, he explains, arose with prosperity, but prosperity wrenched from nature itself. His explanation leads him to a dilemma. For man has come to look upon himself as a predator, if a remorseful one, saddled with reconciling the ascendancy over nature that civilization requires with the sensitivity to nature that civilization fosters."

While Perrin cites some faults with Thomas's work—the author, he says, "has a tendency to treat all his quotations equally, as if levels of seriousness in speech did not exist and context did not matter"—the reviewer also feels that the book "has two great charms. One is the almost incredible wealth of supporting detail. . . .[The other is the author's] gift for apt quotation. One hears a thousand or more voices in this book, most of them lively." As an example Perrin refers to "the voice of an indignant nobleman, Lord Sheffield, who said of his children's tutor, 'He would maintain to my face that both hawks and hounds, which I did then and do now moderately delight in, were not ordained by God for man's recreation, but for adorning the world.' The tutor failed to gain tenure. The book is full of these delights."

Concludes Kitch: "[The author] puts history to its highest purpose and achieves it in a style at once pleasing and perceptive. *Man and the Natural World*, like a favored guidebook, is both a reliable guide and a congenial companion."

CA

Thompson, E. P. (1924–1993), English historian. Edward Palmer Thompson was born in Boar's Hill in Oxford, England. His American mother, Theodosia Jessup Thompson, the daughter of Henry Jessup, who founded the American Mission in Lebanon, was a Methodist missionary in India. His British father, Edward John Thompson, whose parents were also Methodist missionaries in India, taught Bengali at Oxford, in addition to writing poetry, upon returning to England from India in 1923. Poets and Indian independence agitators, like Nehru, who gave young Edward few lessons in the game of cricket, gravitated to the Thompsons' home in Boar's Hill.

Like his father before him, Thompson attended the Methodist Kingswood private school near Bath. Too young to join the British Army in 1941, he enrolled for courses in literature and history at Cambridge University, joining the British Communist Party in the same year. A year after he joined the army in 1942, he was in charge of a tank company as a lieu-

tenant in the British Six Armoured Division, fighting first in North Africa then in Italy. Back in Cambridge, he met Dorothy Towers in 1946. They were married two years later in 1948, after working in Yugoslavia together with a group of young communists to build a 150-mile railroad from Slavonia to Bosnia. They moved to Halifax, Yorkshire, where Thompson taught English to adult education classes in the department of Extra-Mural Studies at Leeds University, during which time he wrote *The Making of the English Working Class,* the book that made him famous.

The book was published in 1963, during a time when the cold war was at its hottest, Stalin's barbarity had been exposed by Khrushchev in 1956, capitalism was showing impressive growth, contrary to what the communists had predicted, and the English working class was exhibiting alarming apathy. By writing the book, Thompson wanted to rescue the working class from historical oblivion. Rather than being a passive outcome of historical economic change, Thompson argued, the English working class had essentially created itself by 1832. Be that as it may, what is important about Thompson's book is that it forced a sharp turn to the left in the historical research and writing about the working class. It was no longer possible to dismiss the development of the working class simply as a result of changing economic conditions. The response to *The Making of the English Working Class* was immediate and forceful. Some questioned the theoretical purity of Thompson's method in interpreting social history within the Marxist model, and feminists pointed to his implicit gendered approach. The book, however impure theoretically and methodologically it was or not, had nonetheless introduced a new approach to writing social history.

In 1965 Thompson moved to Warwick to head Warwick University's Center of Social Studies. Six years later, in 1971, after his wife had secured a history professorship at Birmingham University, Thompson ended his teaching career to devote himself to the research and writing of history.

When the United States decided to position new nuclear missiles in England in 1979, Thompson joined Ken Coates in creating the European Nuclear Disarmament (END) organization. Thompson called for the de-nuclearization and neutralization of both East and West Europe. Hundreds of thousands would eventually listen to Thompson speak in antinuclear rallies. He believed that global nuclear holocaust was the only possible outcome if the cold war was allowed to continue. Though Thompson may have been justly accused of being naive, he nonetheless believed that ordinary people, in both East and West, could change the course of history and end the cold war in Europe by their demonstrations.

Through his historical research, his political activism and his teaching, Thompson has indeed rescued the working class from historical oblivion, as he had intended. He clearly demonstrated how individual working men and women, through their daily struggle, had been active agents in the creation of their own working class. Thompson's approach to history from below created doubts about the adequacy of the deterministic historical model, where the individual human agency in shaping history is completely lacking. After his resignation from the British Communist Party in 1956 and his rejection of Louis Althusser's structural-functionalism in his book, *The Poverty of Theory*, Thompson was determined to expose the terrible consequences of historical determinism by demonstrating how Althusser's structural-functionalism could be used to justify Stalin's atrocities.

Mohammed Arkawi

Tocqueville, Alexis Charles Henri Maurice Clérel de

(1805–1859), French statesman and writer. Alexis de Tocqueville was the author of *Democracy in America*, the first classic commentary on American government written by a foreigner.

Alexis de Tocqueville was born in Paris on July 29, 1805, of an aristocratic Norman family. He studied law in Paris (1823–1826) and then was appointed an assistant magistrate at Versailles (1827).

The July 1830 Revolution which, with middle-class support, put Louis Philippe on the throne, required a loyalty oath of Tocqueville as a civil servant. He was suspect because his aristocratic family opposed the new order and was demoted to a minor judgeship without pay. Tocqueville and another magistrate, Gustave de Beaumont, asked to study prison reform in America, then an interest of the French government. Granted permission but not funds (their families paid their expenses), Tocqueville and Beaumont spent from May 1831 to February 1832 in the United States. Their travel and interviews resulted in *On the Penitentiary System in the United States and Its Application in France* (1832). Then followed Tocqueville's famous *Democracy in America* (vol. 1, 1835; vol. 2, 1840), an immediate best seller. By 1850 it had run through 13 editions.

Tocqueville was elected to the Chamber of Deputies in 1839. He opposed King Louis Philippe but after the Revolution of 1848 again served as a deputy. Tocqueville was foreign minister for a few months in 1849 and retired from public affairs at the end of 1851. During his last years he wrote *The Old Regime and the French Revolution* (1856). He died in Cannes on April 16, 1859.

Democracy in America. Despite his aristocratic upbringing, Tocqueville believed that the spread of democracy was inevitable. By analyzing American democracy, he thought to help France avoid America's faults and emulate its successes. Chief among his many insights was to see equality of social conditions as the heart of American democracy. He noted that although the majority could produce tyranny its wide property distribution and inherent conservatism made for stability. American literature, then still under European influence, he felt would become independent in idiom and deal with plain people rather than the upper classes. The American zeal for change he connected with a restless search for the ideal. Noting the permissiveness of democracy toward religion, he anticipated denominational growth. Discerning natural hostility to the military, he foresaw an adverse effect of prolonged war on American society. He anticipated that democracy would emancipate women and alter the relationship of parents to children. He saw danger in the dominance of American politics by lawyers.

Though his work has been criticized for some biases, errors, omissions, and pessimism, Tocqueville's perceptive insights have been continually quoted. He ranks as a keen observer of American democracy and as a major prophet of modern societies' trends.

EWB

Tolstoy, Leo

(1828–1910), Russian novelist and moral philosopher. Leo Tolstoy ranks as one of the world's great writers, and his *War and Peace* has been called the greatest novel ever written.

Leo Tolstoy was one of the great rebels of all time, a man who during a long and stormy life was at odds with Church, government, literary tradition, and his own family. Yet he was a conservative, obsessed by the idea of God in an age of scientific positivism. He brought the art of the realistic novel to its highest development. Tolstoy's brooding concern for death made him one of the precursors of existentialism. Yet the bustling spirit that animates his novels conveys—perhaps—more of life than life itself.

Tolstoy's father, Count Nikolay Ilyich Tolstoy, came of a noble family dating back to the 14th century and prominent from the time of Peter I. Both Tolstoy's father and grandfather had a passion for gambling and had exhausted the family wealth. Nikolay recouped his fortunes, however, by marrying Maria Volkonsky, bearer of a great name and heiress to a fortune that included 800 serfs and the estate of Yasnaya Polyana in Tula Province, where Leo (Lev Nikolayevich) was born on Aug. 28, 1828, the youngest of four sons. His mother died when he was 2 years old, whereupon his father's distant cousin Tatyana Ergolsky took charge of the children. In 1837 Tolstoy's father died, and an aunt, Alexandra Osten-Saken, became legal guardian of the children. Her religious fervor was an important early influence on Tolstoy. When she died in 1840, the children were sent to Kazan to another sister of their father, Pelageya Yushkov.

Tolstoy was educated at home by German and French tutors. He was not a particularly apt pupil, but he was good at games. In 1843 he entered Kazan University; planning on a diplomatic career, he entered the faculty of Oriental languages. Finding these studies too demanding, he switched 2 years later to the notoriously easygoing law faculty. The university, however, had too many second-rate foreigners on its faculty, and Tolstoy left in 1847 without taking his degree.

Tolstoy returned to Yasnaya Polyana, determined to become a model farmer and a "father" to his serfs. His philanthropy failed because of his naiveté in dealing with the peasants and because he spent too much time carousing in Tula and Moscow. During this time he first began making those amazingly honest and self-lacerating diary entries, a practice he maintained until his death. These entries provided much material for his fiction, and in a very real sense his whole oeuvre is one long autobiography. In 1848 Tolstoy attempted to take the law examination, this time in St. Petersburg, but after passing the first two parts he again became disenchanted, returning to the concerts and gambling halls of Moscow when not hunting and drinking at Yasnaya Polyana.

Army Life and Early Literary Career. Nikolay, Tolstoy's eldest brother, visited him at this time in Yasnaya Polyana while on furlough from military service in the Caucasus. Leo greatly loved his brother, and when he asked him to join him in the south, Tolstoy agreed. After a meandering journey, he reached the mountains of the Caucasus, where he sought to join the army as a Junker, or gentleman-volunteer. In the autumn he passed the necessary exams and was assigned to the 4th Battery of the 20th Artillery Brigade, serving on the Terek River against the rebellious mountaineers, Moslem irregulars who had declared a holy war against the encroaching Russians.

Tolstoy's border duty on a lonely Cossack outpost became a kind of pagan idyll, hunting, drinking, sleeping, chasing the girls, and occasionally fighting. During the long lulls he first began to write. In 1852 he sent the autobiographical sketch *Childhood* to the leading journal of the day, the *Contemporary*. Nikolai Nekrasov, its editor, was ecstatic, and when it was published (under Tolstoy's initials), so was all of Russia. Tolstoy now began *The Cossacks* (finished in 1862), a thinly veiled account of his life in the outpost.

From November 1854 to August 1855 Tolstoy served in the battered fortress at Sevastopol. He had requested transfer to this area, where one of the bloodiest battles of the Crimean War was in process. As he directed fire from the 4th Bastion, the hottest area in the conflict for a long while, Tolstoy managed to write *Youth*, the second part of his autobiographical trilogy. He also wrote the three *Sevastopol Tales* at this time, revealing the distinctive Tolstoyan vision of war as a place of unparalleled confusion, banality, and heroism, a special space where men, viewed from the author's dispassionate, God-like point of view, were at their best and worst. Some of these stories were published while the battle they described still raged. The first story was the talk of Russia, attracting (for almost the last time in Tolstoy's career) the favorable attention of the Tsar.

School for Peasant Children. In 1856 Tolstoy left the service (as a lieutenant) to look after his affairs in Yasnaya Polyana; he also worked on *The Snowstorm* and *Two Hussars*. In the following year he made his first trip abroad. He did not like Western Europe, as his stories of this period, *Lucerne* and *Albert*, show. He was becoming increasingly interested in education, however, and he talked with experts in this field wherever he went. In the summer he returned to Yasnaya Polyana and set up a school for peasant children, where he began his pedagogic experiments. In 1860–1861 Tolstoy went abroad again, seeking to learn more about education; he also gambled heavily. During this trip he witnessed the death of his brother Nikolay in the south of France. More than all the grisly scenes of battle he had witnessed, this event brought home to Tolstoy the fact of death, the specter of which fascinated and terrified him throughout his long career.

After the freeing of the serfs in 1861, Tolstoy became a mediator (*posrednik*), an official who arbitrated land disputes between serfs and their former masters. In April he had a petty quarrel with Turgenev, actually challenging him to a duel. Turgenev declined, but the two men were on bad terms for years.

Tolstoy's school at Yasnaya Polyana went forward, using pioneering techniques that were later adopted by progressive educationists. In 1862 Tolstoy started a journal to propagate his pedagogical ideas, *Yasnaya Polyana*. He also took the first of his koumiss cures, traveling to Samara, living in the open, and drinking fermented mare's milk. These cures eventually became an almost annual event.

Golden Years. Since 1861 Tolstoy had been trying to write a historical novel about the Decembrist uprising of 1825. But the more he worked, the farther back in time he went. The first portion of *War and Peace* was published in 1865 (in the *Russian Messenger*) as "The Year 1805." In 1868 three more chapters appeared; and in 1869 he completed the novel. Tolstoy had been somewhat neglected by critics in the preceding few years because he had not participated in the bitter literary politics of the time. But his new novel created a fantastic outpouring of popular and critical reaction.

Tolstoy's next 10 years were equally crowded. He published the *Primer* and the first four *Readers* (1872–1875), his attempts to appeal to an audience that would include children and the newly literate peasantry. From 1873 to 1877 he worked on the second of his masterworks, *Anna Karenina,* which also created a sensation upon its publication.

Spiritual Crisis. The ethical quest that had begun when Tolstoy was a child and that had tormented him throughout his younger years now drove him to abandon all else in order to seek an ultimate meaning in life. At first he turned to the Russian Orthodox Church, visiting the Optina-Pustyn monastery in 1877. But he found no answer. He began reading the Gospels, and he found the key to his own moral system in Matthew: "Resist not evil." In 1879–1880 Tolstoy wrote his *Confession* (published 1884) and his *Critique of Dogmatic Theology.* From this point on his life was dominated by a burning desire to achieve social justice and a rationally acceptable ethic.

Tolstoy was a public figure now, and in 1881 he asked Alexander III, in vain, to spare the lives of those who had assassinated the Tsar's father. He visited Optina again, this time disguised as a peasant, but his trip failed to bring him peace. In September the family moved to Moscow in order to further the education of the older sons. The following year Tolstoy participated in the census, visiting the worst slums of Moscow, where he was freshly appalled.

Tolstoy had not gone out of his way to propagate his new convictions, but in 1883 he met V. G. Chertkov, a wealthy guards officer who soon became the moving force behind an attempt to start a movement in Tolstoy's name. In the next few years a new publication was founded (the *Mediator*) in order to spread Tolstoy's word in tract and fiction, as well as to make good reading available to the poor. In 6 years almost 20 million copies were distributed. Tolstoy had

long been under surveillance by the secret police, and in 1884 copies of *What I Believe* were seized from the printer. He now took up cobbling and read deeply in Chinese philosophy. He abstained from cigarettes, meat, white bread, and hunting. His image as a white-bearded patriarch in a peasant's blouse dates from this period.

Tolstoy's relations with his family were becoming increasingly strained. The more of a saint he became in the eyes of the world, the more of a devil he seemed to his wife. He wanted to give his wealth away, but she would not hear of it. An unhappy compromise was reached in 1884, when Tolstoy assigned to his wife the copyright to all his works before 1881.

In 1886 Tolstoy worked on what is possibly his most powerful story, *The Death of Ivan Ilyich,* and his drama of peasant life, *The Power of Darkness* (which could not be produced until 1895). In 1888, when he was 60 years old, his thirteenth child was born. In the same year he finished his sweeping indictment of carnal love, *The Kreutzer Sonata.*

Last Years and Death. In 1892 Tolstoy's estate, valued at the equivalent of $1.5 million, was divided among his wife and his nine living children. Tolstoy was now perhaps the most famous man in the world; people came from all over the globe to Yasnaya Polyana. His activity was unabated. In 1891 and in 1893 he organized famine relief in Ryazan Province. He also worked on some of his finest stories: *The Devil* (1890, published posthumously) and *Father Sergius* (1890). In order to raise money for transporting a dissenting religious sect (the Doukhobors) to Canada, Tolstoy published the third, and least successful, of his three long novels, *Resurrection* (1899). From 1896 to 1904 he worked on the story that was his personal favorite, *Hadji Murad,* the tale of a Caucasian mountaineer.

Tolstoy's final years were filled with worldwide acclaim and great unhappiness, as he was caught in the strife between his convictions, his followers, and his family. The Holy Synod excommunicated him in 1901. Unable to endure the quarrels at home he set out on his last pilgrimage in October 1910, accompanied by his youngest daughter, Alexandra, and his physician. The trip proved too much, and he died in the home of the stationmaster of the small depot at Astapovo on Nov. 9, 1910. He was buried at Yasnaya Polyana.

EWB

Toulouse-Lautrec, Henri de (1864–1901), French painter. Henri de Toulouse-Lautrec depicted Montmartre's night life of cafés, bars, and brothels, the world which he inhabited at the height of his career.

Henri de Toulouse-Lautrec, a direct descendant of the counts of Toulouse, was born on Nov. 24, 1864, at Albi. His eccentric father lived in provincial luxury, hunting with falcons and collecting exotic weapons. Henri began to draw at an early age. He suffered a fall in 1878 and broke one femur; in 1879 he fell again and broke the other one. His legs did not heal properly; his torso developed normally, but his legs were permanently deformed.

Encouraged by his first teachers, the animal painters René Princeteau and John Lewis Brown, Toulouse-Lautrec decided in 1882 to devote himself to painting, and that year he left for Paris. Enrolling at the École des Beaux-Arts, he entered the studio of Fernand Cormon. In 1884 Toulouse-Lautrec settled in Montmartre, where he stayed from then on, except for short visits to Spain, where he admired the works of El Greco and Diego Velázquez; Belgium; and England, where he visited Oscar Wilde and James McNeill Whistler. At one point Toulouse-Lautrec lived near Edgar Degas, whom he valued above all other contemporary artists and by whom he was influenced. From 1887 his studio was on the Rue Caulaincourt next to the Goupil printshop, where he could see examples of the Japanese prints of which he was so fond.

Toulouse-Lautrec habitually stayed out most of the night, frequenting the many entertainment spots about Montmartre, especially the Moulin Rouge cabaret, and he drank a great deal. His loose living caught up with him: he suffered a breakdown in 1899, and his mother had him committed to an asylum at Neuilly. He recovered and set to work again. He died on Sept. 9, 1901, at the family estate at Malromé.

Parisian Demimonde. Toulouse-Lautrec moved freely among the dancers, prostitutes, artists, and intellectuals of Montmartre. From 1890 on, his tall, lean cousin, Dr. Tapié de Celeyran, accompanied him, and the two, depicted in *At the Moulin Rouge* (1892), made a colorful pair. Despite his deformity, Toulouse-Lautrec was an extrovert who readily made friends and inspired trust. He came to be regarded as one of the people of Montmartre, for he was an outsider like them, fiercely independent, but with great ability and intellect.

Among the painter's favorite subjects were the cabaret dancers Yvette Guilbert, Jane Avril, and La Goulue and her partner, the contortionist Valentin le Désossé. Toulouse-Lautrec depicted his subjects in a style bordering on but rising above caricature through the seriousness of his intention. He took subjects who habitually employed disguise and charade as a way of life and stripped away all that was inessential to reveal each as an individual and yet as a prisoner of his destiny.

The two most direct influences on Toulouse-Lautrec's art were the Japanese print, as seen in his oblique viewpoints and flattened forms, and Degas, from whom he derived the tilted perspective, cutting of figures, and use of a railing to separate the spectator from the painted scene, as in *At the Moulin Rouge*. But the authentic feel of a world of depravity and the strident, artificial colors used to create it were Toulouse-Lautrec's own.

Unusual types performing in a grand, contrived spectacle attracted Toulouse-Lautrec. In his painting *In the Circus Fernando: The Ringmaster* (1888) the nearly grotesque, strangely cruel figure of the ringmaster is the pivot around which the horse and bareback rider must revolve. In 1892–1894 Toulouse-Lautrec did a series of interiors of houses of prostitution, where he actually lived for a while, becoming the confidant and companion of the girls. As with his paintings of cabarets, he caught the feel of the brothels and made no attempt to glamorize them. In the *Salon in the Rue des Moulins* (1894) the prostitutes are shown as ugly and bored beneath their makeup; the madame sits demurely in their midst. He neither sensationalized nor drew a moral lesson but presented a certain facet of the periphery of society for what it was—no more and no less.

Color Lithography and the Poster. Toulouse-Lautrec broadened the range of lithography by treating the tone more freely. His stroke became more summary and the planes more unified. Sometimes the ink was speckled on the surface to bring about a great textural richness. In his posters he combined flat images (again the influence of the Japanese print) with type. He realized that if the posters were to be successful their message had to make an immediate and forceful impact on the passerby, and he designed them with that in mind.

Toulouse-Lautrec's posters of the 1890s establish him as the father of the modern large-scale poster. His best posters were those advertising the appearance of various performers at the Montmartre cabarets, such as the singer May Belfort, the female clown Cha-U-Kao, and Loïe Fuller of the Folies-Bergère.

In a poster of 1893 the dancer Jane Avril, colored partially in bright red and yellow, is pictured kicking her leg. Below her, in gray tones so as not to detract attention, is the diagonally placed hand of the violinist playing his instrument. There is some indication of floorboards but no furniture or other figures.

The legend reads simply "Jane Avril" in white letters and "Jardin de Paris" in black letters.

EWB

Treitschke, Heinrich von (1834–1896), German historian, politician, and political publicist. Heinrich von Treitschke was the most famous and influential member of the Prussian school of history in 19th-century Germany. He advocated a powerful German state under Prussian leadership.

Heinrich von Treitschke was born on Sept. 15, 1834, in Dresden. His father, who rose to general officer's rank in the service of the Saxon monarchy, was of German-Czech descent, had been ennobled in 1821, and maintained his aristocratic conservatism and loyalty to the Saxon royal family throughout his life. Young Heinrich showed early intellectual promise in his schooling, which, however, was interrupted at the age of 8 by a severe case of measles complicated by glandular fever which led to increasing loss of hearing. Thus a career of public service as a soldier or statesman-politician became impossible, and Heinrich decided on a life of scholarship.

His Education. Attending Dresden's Holy Cross Gymnasium (high school) from 1846 to 1851, Treitschke was exposed not only to the traditional classical education but also to liberal ideas critical of the semiabsolutism of the times. The study of German literature under Julius Klee and personal observations of the political events of the revolutionary years 1848–1849 molded Treitschke's tendency toward strong political conviction into an attitude of enthusiastic support for a constitutional, united Germany under Prussian leadership.

From 1851 to 1854 Treitschke studied at the universities of Bonn, Leipzig, Tübingen, and Freiburg, attending classes under F. C. Dahlmann, the political economist Wilhelm Roscher, and the eminent Tübingen philosopher Friedrich Theodor Vischer.

After a brief interlude in Dresden, Treitschke studied at Göttingen and Leipzig. He succeeded in publishing two volumes of poems, *Patriotic Songs* (1856) and *Studies* (1857). In 1858 he finished his habilitation thesis, *Die Gesellschaftswissenschaft* (1859; *The Science of Society*), which earned him an appointment as lecturer at the University of Leipzig in 1859.

The political atmosphere in Leipzig did not prove congenial, and in 1863 Treitschke accepted a professorial appointment at Freiburg. Here he wrote his famous essay *Bundesstaat und Einheitsstaat* (1863–1864; *Federation and Centralization*). In 1866, when Baden joined Austria in war against Prussia, Treitschke resigned his position at Freiburg and demanded in a pamphlet, *The Future of the North German Middle States,* the annexation of Hanover, Hesse, and Saxony by Prussia.

Political Activities. Although Treitschke was estranged from his father, his fame as a political publicist had now reached national eminence. Positions at Kiel (1866) and Heidelberg (1867–1874) followed before he finally settled in Berlin. His strong Prussian sentiments had earned him appointment as editor of the *Preussische Jahrbücher* (Prussian Annals) in 1866 and election to the German Reichstag (House of Deputies) in 1871. Although originally affiliated with the National Liberal party, he left that party in 1879 to support Bismarck's new commercial policy and held his seat until 1884 as an independent member with conservative leanings.

The period from 1859 to 1871 is important for Treitschke's development. More and more he abandoned his original liberal constitutional attitude and became an ever more ardent advocate of the power state, of war as the noblest activity of man, and of a German expansionist, cultural mission under Prussian leadership which would establish Germany as an equal among the world powers. Although he counted among his close friends a number of Jews, he participated in the anti-Semitic movement of the late 1870s, proclaiming that Jewry could play an important role only if its individual members were to merge themselves with the nationality of their state.

History of Germany. Treitschke had planned to write a history of Germany since 1861; but not until he had settled in Berlin, where the Prussian archives were close at hand, did the work progress. The first volume of his *Deutsche Geschichte im 19. Jahrhundert* (*German History in the 19th Century*) was published in 1879, starting with the Napoleonic period. The fifth volume, published in 1894, brought the narrative only to the beginning of 1848. Although this, the greatest of his works, also suffered from the shortcomings of Treitschke's emotional patriotic nature and was limited to the almost exclusive use of the Prussian archives, it nevertheless constitutes a major contribution to historical writing. Its literary style and power of expression have been likened to Friedrich von Schiller's diction and Johann Gottlieb Fichte's rhetoric. In spite of his tendency to oversimplify complicated events, Treitschke exhibited a grasp of detail and power to synthesize that produced a general cultural historical setting uncommon among the works of historians of his time.

Other important historical and political essays were published in four volumes as *Historische und Pol-*

itische Aufsätze (1896; *Historical and Political Essays*); and his lectures on politics were collected and published in two volumes as *Vorlesungen über Politik* (1898; *Politics*).

Treitschke died on April 28, 1896, in Berlin. His influence during his lifetime was threefold: as teacher, political propagandist, and historian. A generation of students and of the general public was affected by his political lectures and nationalistic journalism, and even abroad he was often regarded as an official mouthpiece of German policy.

Although after his death Treitschke's influence among German historians, who generally preferred to follow the more balanced methodological example of the Ranke school of historical writing, became largely dormant, it was revived in coarsened form by Nazi ideologists, who utilized his unbridled nationalism as a point of departure for their thought and actions.

EWB

Trevelyan, George Macaulay (1876–1962), English historian. George Trevelyan is known for his defense and illustration of history as a literary art.

George Macaulay Trevelyan was born at Welcombe near Stratford-on-Avon on Feb. 16, 1876, the son of Sir George Otto Trevelyan. His maternal granduncle was the historian Thomas Babington Macaulay. Young Trevelyan went to Trinity College, Cambridge, where Bertrand Russell, G. E. Moore, and Ralph Vaughan Williams were among his friends. In 1898, his imagination caught by what he saw as the first stirring of national consciousness and individual freedom among the 14th century Lollards, he wrote *England in the Age of Wycliffe* as a dissertation for a Trinity fellowship. An immediate success, it remains one of the best books on the subject.

Awarded the fellowship, Trevelyan set out upon an academic career. Cambridge, however, was then dominated by a highly critical mode of historical writing, soon to be epitomized by J. B. Bury in the phrase, "History is a science, nothing more, nothing less." The ethos was not congenial for a writer of Trevelyan's literary and humanistic bent. In 1903 he left Cambridge for London, not to return until his appointment as regius professor in 1927.

Trevelyan's next work, *England under the Stuarts* (1904), showed a deeper historical understanding and more secure craftsmanship, particularly in its portrayal of King Charles I and the Cavaliers. The year of its publication, Trevelyan married Janet Penrose Ward. As a wedding gift, he received a copy of Giuseppe Garibaldi's *Memoirs,* which awakened memories of stories he had heard from his father (who had tried to join Garibaldi in 1867) and of his own walks in the

Umbrian hills. The result was *Garibaldi's Defence of the Roman Republic,* written in the heat of inspiration in 1906. It was a perfect match of event and author, giving full play to Trevelyan's poetic imagination. Its success was immediate, and he felt impelled to complete the story with *Garibaldi and the Thousand* (1909) and *Garibaldi and the Making of Italy* (1911).

Trevelyan's *History of England* (1926) quickly became one of the best-selling textbooks of its age. From its pages a generation of Englishmen learned the history of their country. In 1928, having succeeded Bury as regius professor, he began work on his three-volume *England under Queen Anne* (1931–1934), his major contribution to historical scholarship. He had long dreamed of telling the story, he later wrote, attracted by its "dramatic unity"; it was "like a five-act drama, leading up to the climax of the trumpets proclaiming King George." His last major work, *English Social History* (1944), written just before World War II, was his greatest commercial success.

In 1930 Trevelyan received the Order of Merit. He died at Cambridge on July 21, 1962.

EWB

Troeltsch, Ernst (1865–1923), German theologian, historian, and sociologist. Ernst Troeltsch, through his utilization of the objective methods of modern scholarship, contributed to the sociology of religion and the problems of historicism.

Ernst Troeltsch was born in Augsburg. After studying theology at the universities of Erlange, Göttingen, and Berlin from 1883 to 1888, he became a lecturer at Göttingen in 1891, an associate professor at Bonn in 1892, and a professor at Heidelberg in 1894; he remained at Heidelberg for 21 years. For a short time he was a Lutheran curate in Munich. In 1901 he married, and a son, Ernst Eberhard, was born in 1913. In 1915 he came to feel that theology was too confining and transferred to philosophy at the University of Berlin.

A conservative in politics, Troeltsch long served in the Baden upper house. From 1919 to 1921 he was a member of the Prussian Landtag and concurrently secretary of state for public worship. He was moved deeply by the war. Like Max Weber and others, he hailed the "great and wonderful" fervor of the Germans and saw their cause rooted in idealistic values as opposed to the materialism of the Allies. Soon, however, together with Weber and Friedrich Meinecke, he left the conservative majority, opposed annexationist war aims, and advocated increased democratization. After the war he defended the Weimar Republic, decried the "frightful demagoguery" of the right, and advocated a genuine conservatism in articles which bore the pseudonym of *Spektator* and appeared until 4 months before his death.

In *The Social Teaching of the Christian Churches* (1912) Troeltsch studied the relation between religion and the other elements of society and culture. He found that Christianity was not reducible to displaced social protest, as Karl Kautsky and the Marxists had suggested, but rather was a real and autonomous religious movement with its own immanent implications for development and its own independent effect upon history. Although the forms of belief and organization developed by the Church were historically conditioned, they also represented the unfolding of the implications of Christianity's inner meaning; and once the Church was established, it also in turn affected and influenced other aspects of society and culture.

Troeltsch carried out his study in four contexts—family, economic life, politics, and intellectual life—and found Christianity exhibiting two contrary but complementary tendencies—accommodation and protest. These two tendencies gave rise to two organizational types: the Church, which qualifiedly accepted the world in order to sanctify it, and the sect, which rejected the world and the whole idea of adjustment to it. Troeltsch stated that the Christian ideal could not be "realized within this world apart from compromise" and that consequently Christian history was "the story of a constantly renewed search for this compromise, and a fresh opposition to this spirit of compromise."

In an earlier work Troeltsch had examined the relationship between Protestantism and modern capitalism. He agreed with Weber that Calvinism had an important early influence upon the development of capitalism, but he saw the Protestant impact upon economic developments as chiefly "indirect and unconsciously produced" and religion as more affected than affecting with respect to modern developments. Despite the Christian derivation of modern civilization, Troeltsch came to see the future of Christianity as "unpredictable" and its survival demanding "very bold and far-reaching changes."

Historicism was a profound challenge to Troeltsch. If all beliefs and values are products of individual tendencies specific to particular conditions, is there then nothing suprahistorical resulting from man's search for truth and creation of value? He studied this problem in his *Historismus und seine Probleme* (1922), examining the "relation of individual historical facts to standards of value within the entire domain of history in connection with the development of political, social, ethical, esthetic, and scientific ideas." Earlier he had spoken of "polymorphous truth,"

which though beyond history is apprehended differently in different civilizations and epochs, and he had also sought for an extra-historical basis in morality. Now he concluded that "even the validity of science and logic seemed to exhibit, under different skies and on different soil, strong individual differences present even in their deepest and inner rudiments."

Troeltsch was concerned with historicism not simply as a scholar but as a deeply religious man as well. Although he failed to solve the problems intellectually, he concluded: "Skepticism and relativism are only an apparent necessary consequence of modern intellectual conditions and of historicism. They may be overcome by way of ethics"; and, "If there is any solution at all to these riddles and problems, with their conflicts and contradictions, that solution certainly is not to be found within their own sphere, but beyond it, in that unknown land, of which there are so many indications in the historic struggle of the spirit upward, but which itself is never revealed to our eyes."

EWB

Trotsky, Leon (1879–1940), Russian revolutionist. Leon Trotsky was a principal leader in the founding of the Soviet Union. He played an important role in the October Revolution, which brought the Bolsheviks to power; and he organized the Red Army during the ensuing civil war.

Leon Trotsky was born Lev Davidovich Bronstein near Elisavetgrad (later Kirovograd). He derived from an almost completely Russified Jewish family who lived in the province of Kherson, in the small town of Yanovka. His father, David Leontievich Bronstein, had by dint of hard labor grown fairly prosperous as a farmer, but his uncultured middle-class family lived an extremely simple life. At the age of 7 the boy was sent to a Jewish private religious school in the nearby town of Gromokla. Since he knew no Yiddish, his stay was brief and unhappy but nonetheless valuable, for he learned to read and write Russian.

Shortly after his return home, a cousin, Moisey Filippovich Shpenster, arrived at the Bronstein household to recuperate from an illness. He played the role of tutor to Lyova (Lev's nickname) and when it came time for him to return to Odessa, Lyova returned with him.

In Odessa, Lyova attended a preparatory class for an entire year. At St. Paul's Realschule he quickly overcame his early deficiencies and rose to the head of his class. Seven years in Odessa expanded the already existing differences between father and son. For some reason David Bronstein decided to have his son finish his last academic year in the nearby seaport of

Nikolaev instead of in Odessa. Here Lyova had his first contacts with the Russian revolutionary movement.

Revolutionary Activities and First Exile. A relatively large concentration of old exiles of the group called Narodnaia Volia (The People's Will) lived in this small town. Lyova became acquainted with this circle through Franz Shvigovsky, a gardener who played a prominent role in a small discussion club. One member of this Narodnik group, Alexandra Sokolovskaya, considered herself a Marxist and was almost immediately opposed by the 17-year-old Lyova. He knew almost nothing of Marxist doctrine, but his ability as an orator and his intellectual prowess soon made him the focal point of the group. The more involved he became, the more his schoolwork declined, although he graduated in 1897 with first-class honors.

As news of strikes began to grow, Lyova found himself becoming more and more inclined toward Marxism. This period saw the formation of the South Russian Workers' Union. The clandestine activities of its members were for the most part harmless, but police spies successfully infiltrated the group. After an extended period of interrogation, Bronstein was exiled to Siberia for 4 years by administrative verdict. While awaiting deportation, he first heard of V. I. Lenin and his book *The Development of Capitalism in Russia*. Before leaving, Bronstein married Alexandra Sokolovskaya.

During his stay in Verkholensk, Bronstein began forming his ideas on national coordination and on centralized party leadership. In a little-known essay he composed his thoughts on the subject, and the result was an organizational scheme that practically paralleled that of the Bolsheviks, of whom he later was so critical. He also turned to literary criticism, but the young revolutionary grew restless. Urged on by his wife, he escaped after 4½ years of prison and exile.

Exile and Formulation of Theory. The name on Bronstein's false passport was Trotsky, a name that remained with him. He joined Lenin in London in October and began writing for *Iskra*. Trotsky shared his quarters with V. I. Zasulich and J. Martov and drew closer to these two than to Lenin. Only Georgi Plekhanov showed any dislike for Trotsky. The split among the *Iskra* editors was already taking shape, and Trotsky became the special focus of Plekhanov's scorn.

In July 1903 at Brussels the Second Congress of the Russian Social Democratic Workers' Party produced, instead of one party, two. Trotsky emerged as Lenin's most implacable opponent on the question of

the organization of the party. Despite his early writings favoring a high degree of centralization, Trotsky sided with Martov and the Mensheviks in favoring a broader-based party. Plekhanov had sided with Lenin, but their relationship was a fragile one. When Plekhanov invited the Iskra board to return, Lenin broke with the editorial staff completely. Trotsky returned, but Plekhanov's dislike of him only grew. Thus began Trotsky's estrangement from the Menshevik wing of the party. No rapprochement, however, with Lenin was forthcoming.

Suspended between both factions, Trotsky came under the influence of A. L. Helfand, whose pen name was Parvus. Under this influence Trotsky adopted a theory of "permanent revolution" that called for a telescoping of the bourgeois revolution into a socialist one that would carry far beyond Russia's borders. An important basis for this concept was the recognition by Helfand, Trotsky, and Lenin that Russia, far from having been a feudal country, was an Asiatic despotism, with the consequence that Russia's cities, unlike those of the West, had not produced an advanced entrepreneurial bourgeois elite. This made it unlikely, in Trotsky's view, that a sophisticated capitalist development would occur in Russia, and thus it was unprofitable to rely on such development as a basis for revolution. Trotsky argued that the revolution should result in the immediate establishment of the dictatorship of the proletariat (meaning power for its vanguard, the Communist elite). The question of whether such a "permanent" or telescoped revolution could be attempted without a great risk of reestablishing the old bureaucratic despotism under Communist leadership preoccupied the Fourth (or Unity) Party Congress in Stockholm in 1906. Lenin offered certain relative guarantees against this Asiatic restoration (no police, no standing army, no bureaucracy, to avoid turning the proletarian dictatorship into a bureaucratic despotism) and an absolute guarantee of a socialist revolution in the West to follow the establishment of Communist power in Russia.

The first news of "Bloody Sunday," the outbreak of the 1905 Revolution, found Trotsky in Geneva. After a brief respite at Parvus's home, Trotsky went to Kiev in February. With the end of those hectic days at the beginning of the year, revolutionary turmoil abated, and Trotsky, under the assumed name of Peter Petrovich, moved in and out of the clandestine circles of St. Petersburg.

October 1905 Revolution and Second Exile. In the middle of October 1905 a general strike broke out in St. Petersburg, and Trotsky hurriedly returned to the capital from Finland. On the first day of his return he appeared at the Soviet, which had assembled at the Technological Institute. He was elected to the Executive Committee of the Soviet of St. Petersburg as the chief representative of the Menshevik wing and played the dominant role in the brief life of this new type of institution. For his part in the Revolution of 1905 Trotsky was exiled to Siberia in 1907 for life with the loss of all his civil rights. On the trip to Siberia, he decided to escape. His second exile lasted 10 years, until the February Revolution of 1917.

At the London Congress in April 1907, Trotsky maintained his position of aloofness and implored both sides to coalesce in the name of unity. For the next 7 years he lived with his second wife in Vienna, where he made the acquaintance of Rosa Luxemburg, Karl Kautsky, Rudolph Hilferding, Eduard Bernstein, Otto Bauer, Max Adler, and Karl Renner. It did not take long for Trotsky to become aware of the differences between "his" Marxism and theirs. He became the editor of a Viennese paper called *Pravda*. In August 1912 he organized in Vienna a conference of all Social Democrats, hoping that this would lead to a reconciliation, but Lenin's refusal to attend was a severe disappointment. An August bloc consisting of Mensheviks, Bolshevik dissenters, the Jewish Bund, and Trotsky's followers was formed.

With the outbreak of World War I Trotsky left Vienna for Zurich in order to avoid internment. The question of the war and the Zimmerwald Conference seemed to draw Lenin and Trotsky closer together, and, conversely, Trotsky and the August bloc seemed to become less and less amicable. Parvus's stand on the war also conflicted with Trotsky's internationalism, and their friendship was ended on Trotsky's initiative.

Return to Russia. In September 1916 Trotsky was deported from France, where he had resided during the previous 2 years. On January 13, 1917, he landed in New York. By mid-March the first news of the Revolution began to arrive. He took a negative view of the new government almost immediately. Certainly his stand was firmer on this issue than Stalin's. Trotsky's differences with Lenin were indeed growing less severe. With his family, Trotsky attempted to return to Russia, but he was removed from his ship at Halifax by British authorities, who forced him to remain in Canada for an entire month. Not until May 4 did he finally arrive in Petrograd.

Trotsky assumed the leadership of the Interborough Organization, a temporary body composed of many prominent personalities opposed to the "war, Prince Lvov, and the social patriots." At the Bolshevik party's Sixth Congress in July-August, Trotsky led the entire group into Lenin's fold even though at this time he was in prison as the result of the abortive July coup. With the growth of Bolshevik strength in Soviet representation, the Petrograd Soviet elected Trotsky as its chairman on September 23. He had also been raised to Central Committee status during his prison term.

Trotsky and Lenin prodded the Bolsheviks on to revolution over the objections of such men as Lev Kamenev, Trotsky's brother-in-law, and Grigori Zinoviev, and Trotsky alone forged the "machinery of insurrection." He scurried from meeting to meeting agitating whoever would listen. By his own estimate no more than 25,000 or 30,000 (the actual number was probably less) took part in the final coup, a testament to his organizational ability.

People's Commissar. In the Soviet government founded by Lenin after the coup, Trotsky was given the position of people's commissar for foreign affairs. He also led the Soviet delegation at the Brest-Litovsk Peace Conference. While he negotiated, Karl Radek distributed pamphlets among German soldiers designed to provoke unrest in the enemy camp.

The German demands were so extensive that the Bolshevik party split over the question of war or peace. Lenin was almost alone in wanting to accept the terms dictated by the Germans. Profound disagreement had existed between Lenin and Trotsky on the question of Brest-Litovsk, but Lenin convinced Trotsky once again to approach the Germans for terms. This time the terms were even more unfavorable, but again Lenin persuaded Trotsky to side with the peace faction. Trotsky cast the deciding vote in favor of signing the highly unfavorable Treaty of Brest-Litovsk.

Although Trotsky had resigned as commissar of foreign affairs he was immediately appointed to the post of commissar for war. In that capacity he rebuilt the Red Army and directed the campaigns on four fronts during the civil war. Despite wholesale opposition throughout the Bolshevik party, he persisted in the use of former tsarist officers, buttressed by a system of political commissars and terror. From a force of fewer than 10,000 reliable armed soldiers in October 1917, he had built an army numbering more than 5 million 2½ years later. He alone proved capable of imposing centralization upon a highly fragmented force.

Toward the end of the civil war in 1920, Trotsky proposed that the machinery for military mobilization be employed for the organization of civilian labor. Civilian labor was to be subjected to military discipline, and the army was to be reorganized on the basis of productive units. Lenin wholeheartedly supported

Trotsky's suggestions. Trotsky's strong-arm methods in shaping the army and in forcing industrial production created a large number of bitter enemies who were soon to be heard from.

Opposition to Stalin. From Lenin's death in 1924 until Trotsky's exile in 1928, Trotsky fought a long, hard, and losing battle against Stalin, who cultivated the many enemies that Trotsky had made as a revolutionary. Despite the fact that Lenin in his last testament seemed to favor Trotsky over Stalin and even had proposed removing Stalin from power, Trotsky proved no match for Stalin. The plethora of positions that Stalin had attained, some important and some not so important but all with patronage, strengthened his position and undermined the power of his opposition. In the final analysis, Trotsky had only his personal brilliance and the army as bases for power, the latter without its crucial political control apparatus. Stalin not only controlled a variety of organizations, but he skillfully appealed to the class interest of the new bureaucratic elite and decisively asserted his claim to Lenin's mantle at the funeral of the dead founder and in the *Foundations of Leninism,* published in early 1924. Trotsky did not bother to attend Lenin's funeral.

Exile and Assassination. Trotsky allied himself with the so-called left opposition of Kamenev and Zinoviev; but Stalin successfully opposed him by breaking up the alliance, aided by Nikolai Bukharin and the right wing of the party. After his defeat Trotsky was expelled from the party, and in 1928 he was exiled to Alma-Ata in Central Asia. Forced to flee the Soviet Union, he went first to Turkey, then to France and Norway, and finally to Mexico. Throughout his sojourn he continued to attack Stalin, returning to his early critical themes of bureaucratic centralism and one-man dictatorship. Implacable as he was in his criticism, Trotsky did not draw on the most powerful polemical weapon available to him: that the cause of socialism had been lost in an "Asiatic restoration," through the consolidation of a new bureaucratic despotism under Stalin. That would have meant the rejection of Soviet communism and the party. Trotsky, unable to do so, could attack only Stalin and his policies.

On August 20, 1940, Trotsky was mortally wounded in Mexico City by an ice ax wielded by Ramon Mercador, a Soviet assassin talked into this crime, according to one account, by his mother, who held the Order of Lenin for masterminding assassinations for the Soviet secret police.

EWB

Turgot, Anne Robert Jacques, Baron de l'Aulne

(1721–1781), French economist. A. R. J. Turgot was controller general under Louis XVI. His efforts to reform the Old Regime were thwarted by the failure of the King to support him against the opposition of the privileged classes.

Originally A. R. J. Turgot planned to enter the Church but experienced doubts concerning his religious calling and turned to a public career. After holding a number of legal positions he purchased, as was the practice, the office of master of requests, a post that often led to appointment as intendant, the chief administrator of a district. However, Turgot's interests extended beyond the law and administration. He was a friend of the *philosophes* and frequented the intellectual salons of Paris; in 1760 he visited Voltaire, then in exile. He also contributed articles to the *Encyclopédie,* wrote an essay on toleration, and planned an ambitious history of the progress of man which he never completed.

Turgot was, however, particularly interested in economics and knew Adam Smith, the great English economist, and François Quesnay, founder of the Physiocratic school. He shared their distrust of government intervention in the economy and their belief in free trade but disagreed with the Physiocratic view that only agriculture was productive, while commerce and industry were unproductive.

In 1761 the King named Turgot intendant of the *généralité* (district) of Limoges, a poor and backward region. During the 13 years that he spent at Limoges, Turgot attempted, despite local opposition and halfhearted support from the central government, a widespread reform of his district. Historians disagree on how successful he was. He brought tax lists up to date and sought to introduce a more equitable method of collecting taxes. He abolished the *corvée* (forced labor on the roads by peasants) and substituted for it a tax. Consistent with his belief in free trade, he resisted pressure to repeal legislation permitting the free circulation of grain within France during a period of shortages and suppressed riots against the movement of grain. At the same time he opened workshops to provide work for the unemployed which he financed in part by funds that he forced landowners to contribute. He encouraged improvement of agriculture by such means as an agricultural society. While at Limoges, Turgot also continued to study economics and in 1766 published his most important theoretical work on the subject, *Reflections on the Formation and Distribution of Wealth,* a book whose ideas anticipated Adam Smith's classic study in 1776.

In July 1774 Turgot was named secretary of the navy and the following month controller general of finances (actually prime minister). Although he saw the need for fundamental reforms of the government and society, Turgot also recognized that he must advance cautiously; basic reforms would not only be costly but certain to arouse the opposition of the privileged classes. His first efforts, therefore, emphasized modest reforms and reducing government expenditures by such measures as eliminating useless positions and aid for courtiers. However, even such minor reforms aroused the opposition of the privileged and of financiers whose interests had also been adversely affected. Churchmen, moreover, were suspicious of this friend of the *philosophes* who "did not attend Mass" and was suspected of favoring tolerance for Protestants.

In January 1776 Turgot presented to the King his famous Six Edicts, which went beyond his previous minor reforms and economies. The two most contested edicts were one ending the monopoly of the guilds and another abolishing the *corvée* Turgot implied that a tax would be levied upon the "landowners for whom public roads are useful." The Six Edicts now became the target of all the opponents of Turgot; the clergy, the nobles, the queen, Marie Antoinette, all clamored and conspired for his dismissal. They even forged a correspondence in which Turgot made offensive remarks about Louis XVI. The latter, who had at first supported his minister, of whom he had said, "Only Monsieur Turgot and I really love the people," was unable to resist the pressures upon him and in May 1776 requested Turgot's resignation. The dismissal of Turgot marked the failure of the last attempt to reform the monarchy from within. Turgot, who warned Louis XVI that Charles I of England had lost his head because of his weakness, spent his last years engaged in scholarly and literary work but still sought to influence the King.

EWB

V

Vasari, Giorgio (1511–1574), Italian painter, architect, and writer. Giorgio Vasari was the author of *The Lives of the Most Celebrated Painters, Sculptors, and Architects*. His book is the foundation of modern art historiography and the prototype for all biographies of artists.

Giorgio Vasari was born on July 30, 1511, in Arezzo. According to his own account, he was apprenticed as a boy to Andrea del Sarto in Florence. He apparently suffered at the hands of Andrea's wife, to judge from the waspish references to her in his life of Andrea. Vasari's career is well documented, the fullest source of information being the autobiography added to the 1568 edition of his *Lives*.

Vasari had an extremely active career, but much of his time was spent as an impresario devising decorations for courtly festivals and similar ephemera. He fulsomely praised the Medici family for forwarding his career from childhood, and much of his work was done for Cosimo I, Grand Duke of Tuscany. Vasari was a prolific painter in the mannerist style and was also active as an architect, his talents in the latter profession being superior to those he displayed as a painter. He supervised the building of Pope Julius III's Villa Giulia near Rome, but his masterpiece is the reconstruction of the Uffizi picture gallery in Florence (from 1560), originally the offices of the grand-ducal administration.

The *Lives*. Vasari's *Lives* was published in Florence in 1550; it was revised and enlarged in 1568. He venerated Michelangelo to the point of idolatry. In the latter years of Michelangelo's life Vasari came to know him quite well, and for this reason the two versions of his biography of Michelangelo are of the greatest importance as a contemporary assessment.

The tradition of such biographies goes back to antiquity; technical treatises on the arts were also written in classical times, Pliny the Elder and Vitruvius having produced two celebrated examples. As early as the time of Lorenzo Ghiberti there had been an attempt to imitate classical prototypes by writing on earlier and contemporary artists, and Ghiberti, in his *Commentaries* (ca. 1447–1455), also wrote the earliest autobiography by a modern artist.

During the late 15th and early 16th centuries similar treatises were projected and written, and Vasari knew and used some of these earlier works. What distinguishes the first edition of his *Lives* is the fact that it is far fuller (and better written) than any of its predecessors or potential rivals. As Vasari says himself, he wrote as an artist for other artists, with knowledge of technical matters.

The book opens with long introductions on the history and technique of painting, sculpture, and architecture, as practiced in Italy since the Dark Ages, and then proceeds to a chronological series of lives of the great revivers of painting (Giotto), sculpture (the Pisani), and architecture (Arnolfo di Cambio), reaching a climax in the life of Michelangelo, the master of all three arts, who was then 75 years old. Briefly, the plan of the book was to show how Italian—and specifically Tuscan—artists had revived the glories of classical art late in the 13th century, reaching a crescendo in Michelangelo. Vasari is extremely partisan in that Venetians such as Giorgione and Titian are not given the prominence they deserve; and he also shows an uneasy awareness that if Michelangelo had reached perfection only decline could follow.

Vasari took great care to gather material on his numerous journeys, and, more than any of his predecessors, he looked at works of art. On the other hand, his reverence for factual truth was less than would be required of a modern historian, and he was unable to resist an amusing anecdote. This gives his book a liveliness and directness which has ensured its continued popularity independent of its historical importance.

In 1568 Vasari produced a second edition, much larger than the original and containing a great many alterations, particularly in the earlier lives. It also has many new biographies of living (or recently dead) artists, so it is an essential source for Vasari's contemporaries. He gives more space to non-Florentine artists and even mentions one or two non-Italians.

The most important changes are in the life of Michelangelo, who had died in 1564. Part of the revision of Vasari's earlier life was occasioned by the publication, in 1553, of the *Life of Michelangelo,* written by Ascanio Condivi, a pupil of Michelangelo, and probably partly dictated by the master. The versions by Vasari and Condivi give us, therefore, a unique contemporary picture of the life and works of the greatest Italian artist of the age.

It is almost impossible to imagine the history of Italian art without Vasari, so fundamental is his *Lives.* It is the first real and autonomous history of art both because of its monumental scope and because of the integration of the individual biographies into a whole.

EWB

Victoria (1819–1901), queen of Great Britain and Ireland from 1837 to 1901 and empress of India from 1876 to 1901. Victoria presided over the expansion of England into an empire of 4 million square miles and 124 million people.

A woman who gave her name to an age, Victoria was a richly contradictory character. Intensely virtuous, at the age of 11 upon learning she was next in succession to the British crown, she reacted by promising "I will be good," a promise which she faithfully kept. With innate good manners and a great love of truth, she was also immensely selfish, keeping aged ministers and ladies-in-waiting out in all weathers and up to all hours, and ruining the life and character of her eldest son (later Edward VII) by refusing to allow him any responsibility. Her prudery was famous, yet her letters reveal her completely unafraid to face unpleasant facts, even about her nearest and dearest. Tremendously personal and partisan in her handling of

her ministers, she never succeeded in understanding the English party system; she considered that her own view of what would best benefit her country gave her the right to oppose any policy and person, and she frankly preferred coalitions, while accepting that the Crown must be above party. Living all her adult life subject to the guidance of wise men, she remained both innocent and devious, arbitrary and simple, courageous and timid, "unconstitutional in action while constitutional by temperament." In fact she was so completely an expression of the dominant views and characteristics of her time that she truly embodied and interpreted her people throughout her reign. As queen, she saw slavery abolished in the colonies, the Reform Bill passed, the Poor Law reformed, the Corn Laws repealed; she saw her country undertake successful wars in the Crimea, Egypt, the Sudan, and South Africa, acquire the Suez Canal, and establish constitutions in Australia and Canada.

Alexandrina Victoria was born in Kensington Palace, London, on May 24, 1819. She was the only child of Edward, Duke of Kent (1767–1820; fourth son of George III), by Mary Louis Victoria (1786–1861; fourth daughter of Francis Frederick Anthony, reigning Duke of Saxe-Coburg-Gotha, and widow of Edward, Prince of Leiningen). Victoria was baptized on June 24, 1819, Alexander I of Russia being one of her sponsors, and her uncle, the prince regent (later George IV), the other. She grew up under her mother's care and that of Louisa Lehzen, her German governess, and spoke only German until she was 3. From 1832 Victoria's mother took her on extended tours through England. On May 24, 1837, she came of age, and on June 20, on the death of her uncle William IV, she succeeded to the throne, receiving the news of her accession in a cotton dressing gown at 6 A.M. Her chief advisers at first were the prime minister, Lord Melbourne, a Whig (Liberal), and Baron Stockmar, a German sent to London by her uncle King Leopold of the Belgians as adviser to his 18-year-old niece.

First Years of Reign. Victoria's hand was kissed on her accession by members of her council, which included the Duke of Wellington, Sir Robert Peel, Lord John Russell, and Lord Palmerston, with all of whom she was to be closely associated. She opened her first Parliament on November 20, 1837, and read her own speech; Parliament voted her an annuity of £385,000, plus the revenues of the duchies of Lancaster and Cornwall, another £126,000. Victoria proceeded to pay her father's debts. On June 28, 1838, her coronation took place. Next year her initial popularity waned, resulting from her dependence on Lord Melbourne and from her unjust treatment of

Lady Flora Hastings, one of her ladies-in-waiting. When Lord Melbourne resigned, Victoria sent for the opposition leader, Sir Robert Peel; but when she refused to change her ladies, as was then the custom on a change of government, Peel refused to take office and Victoria recalled Melbourne.

In October her two first cousins, Ernest and Albert Edward (1819–1861) of Saxe-Coburg-Gotha, came to London. Albert had written in his diary at 11, "I intend to train myself to be a good and useful man." Victoria fell in love with him instantly and proposed to him; they were married on February 10, 1840. It was an ideally happy marriage and restored the prestige of the Crown, which had sadly deteriorated during the reigns of Victoria's three inept predecessors. Prince Albert was granted £30,000 annual income by Parliament, was named regent in the event of the Queen's death in childbirth, and in 1857 was made Prince Consort by Victoria. Albert described his functions to the Duke of Wellington in April 1850 as: "the husband of the Queen, the tutor of the Royal children, the private secretary of the sovereign and her permanent Minister."

In June 1842 Victoria made her first railway journey from Slough, the station nearest Windsor Castle, to Paddington, and in that same year she first went to Scotland, traveling by sea. In 1843 Victoria and Albert visited King Louis Philippe. She was the first English monarch to land in France since Henry VIII visited Francis I in 1520. King Louis Philippe's return visit was the first voluntary visit to England of any French ruler. In 1845 Victoria, with Albert, made the first of many trips to Germany, staying at Albert's birthplace, Rosenau.

Her Ministers. In 1834, after Lord John Russell had failed to form a ministry (principally owing to Victoria's opposition to Palmerston as foreign minister), Lord John "handed back the poisoned chalice," as Disraeli put it, to Peel. But Peel's ministry fell on a measure for Irish coercion, and by 1847 the Irish famine, in which 1½ million people died and 1 million emigrated, postponed Victoria's planned visit there, which did not take place until 1849, when she landed at Cove, changing its name to Queenstown. In 1846 Victoria tangled with Palmerston over the marriage of the Spanish queen Isabella, and in 1850 she informed him that he "(1) should inform her of the course of action he proposes, and (2) should not arbitrarily modify or alter a measure once it had received her sanction." Lord Palmerston "affected pained surprise" at these injunctions but did not alter his ways. In 1851 the Whig government was outvoted and Lord John resigned, but as Lord Derby, the Con-

servative (Tory) leader refused to form a government, Victoria again sent for Lord John Russell. She was at this time so happy and blessed in her homelife that she wrote, "Politics (provided my Country is safe) must take only 2nd place." In 1844 she had Osborne Palace built for her on the Isle of Wight and in 1848 Balmoral Castle in Scotland; thereafter until the end of her life she spent part of each spring and fall in these residences. In 1851 she and Prince Albert were much occupied with the Great Exhibition, held in London, the first of its kind.

In 1851 Victoria was furious with Palmerston for informing Walewski, the French ambassador to London, that he approved of the coup by which Prince Louis Napoleon made himself Emperor Napoleon III. Victoria was largely instrumental in compelling Lord John Russell to demand Palmerston's resignation. In 1852 the Whigs finally fell, and Lord Derby led a Tory Government. But in July the Tories were beaten in the general election, and in December Lord Derby resigned. At Victoria's request, Lord Aberdeen made a coalition government, with Palmerston relegated to the Home Office. In 1853 Victoria and Albert suffered unpopularity for their apparent pro-Russian stand but regained public approval after the British declared war on Russia February 28, 1854. In January 1855 the government was defeated on their conduct of the war, and Palmerston formed an administration. On March 30, 1856, Victoria admitted that she admired Palmerston's winning of the war. In 1856 Victoria and Albert visited Napoleon III in Paris, and in 1857 the Indian Mutiny against British rule, as represented by the East India Company, led to Victoria's writing that there now existed in England "a universal feeling that India [should] belong to *me*." In 1858 the East India Company was abolished. That same year Victoria's eldest child, Victoria, married Prince (later Emperor) Frederick of Prussia. In March 1861 Victoria's mother died, and her eldest son, Albert Edward, while in camp in the Curragh in Ireland, had an affair with an actress called Nelly Clifden, distressing Victoria and Albert, who were planning his marriage to Princess Alexandra of Denmark. Prince Albert, already ill, went in icy weather to Cambridge to remonstrate with his son; Albert was suffering from typhoid and died on December 14, 1861, aged 42.

The widowed Victoria held her erring son as partly the cause of his father's death and never forgave him. She retired into complete seclusion and wore mourning until her death.

In 1862 Victoria's daughter Alice married Prince Louis of Hesse, and a year later her eldest son, now created Prince of Wales, whom his family called "Bertie," married Princess Alexandra of Denmark. Victoria supported Prussia during its war with Denmark over Schleswig-Holstein, whereas her daughter-in-law, her ministers, and her people openly upheld Denmark. She approved Russia's brutal suppression of Poland's national uprising in 1863. In 1865 in the Seven Weeks War between Prussia and Austria, which ended in Prussia's victory at Sadowa, Victoria was again pro-Prussian. In 1867 Victoria entertained the Khedive of Egypt and the Sultan of Turkey. In 1868 Benjamin Disraeli became prime minister but was defeated by William Gladstone over the disestablishment of the Irish Church. Disraeli offered to resign, but Victoria kept him in office for six months after his defeat. Victoria, though she thought him "odd" and his wife odder, much appreciated Disraeli because he treated her as a woman. Gladstone, she complained, treated her as though she were a public department. In the Franco-Prussian War of 1870, Victoria was still pro-Prussian, though she welcomed the exiled French empress Eugénie and allowed her and the Emperor to live at Chislehurst. In 1873 Gladstone resigned, and in 1874, to Victoria's delight, Disraeli became prime minister. He called the plump, tiny queen "The Fäery" and admitted he loved her—"perhaps the only person left to me in this world that I do love." That same year Victoria's son Prince Alfred married Marie, daughter of the Russian tsar, who insisted she be called Imperial, not Royal, Highness. This encouraged Victoria to make "preliminary enquiries" about officially assuming the title Empress of India, which she did on May 1, 1876. In 1875 Disraeli, with the help of the Rothschilds, bought the majority of the Suez Canal shares from the bankrupt Khedive of Egypt, to Victoria's delight. That same year Gladstone roused the country with stories of "Bulgarian atrocities": 12,000 Bulgarian Christians had been murdered by Turkish irregulars. In 1877 Russia declared war on Turkey; Victoria and Disraeli were pro-Turk, sending a private warning to the Tsar that, were he to advance, Britain would fight. Disraeli complained that Victoria "writes every day and telegraphs every hour." In 1878 at the Congress of Berlin, Disraeli obtained, as he told Victoria, "peace with honour."

In 1879 Victoria visited Italy and Germany. In the fall Gladstone's Midlothian campaign led to the government's defeat in April 1880. In 1882 a third attempt was made on Victoria's life. Africa gave trouble, the Zulu killed Empress Eugénie's son, and the Sudanese killed General Gordon in Khartoum before Lord Wolseley, sent at Victoria's urging to relieve him, arrived. In 1885 Victoria went to Aix-les-Bains; she thought Gladstone a humbug, and "he talks so very much." In June he resigned, but Lord Salisbury, who became prime minister, lost the ensuing general elec-

tion. Gladstone, pledged to Irish home rule, came in again, to Victoria's unconcealed annoyance. When he was defeated on this issue, Lord Salisbury returned to power.

Last Years. In 1887 Victoria's golden jubilee was celebrated, and in 1888 she actually approved of Gladstone when he persuaded Parliament to vote £37,000 annually for the Prince of Wales' children. In 1889 the German Kaiser, Victoria's grandson, visited England; in 1892 Gladstone again became prime minister. His Home Rule Bill was passed in the House of Commons but thrown out by the House of Lords. Gladstone resigned, to be succeeded by Lord Rosebery. In 1897 Victoria's diamond jubilee was magnificently celebrated, the apotheosis of her reign and of her empire. In 1897 the repression of the Sudan culminated in Lord Kitchener's victory at Omdurman on September 2. Victoria was joyful; "Surely Gordon is avenged," she wrote. In 1899 the Boer War broke out, and in 1900 Victoria went to Ireland, where most of the soldiers who fought on the British side were recruited. In August she signed the Australian Commonwealth Bill and in October lost a grandson in the war. On January 22, 1901, she died in the arms of the Kaiser. Her last word was "Bertie." She was the mother of four boys and five girls, all of whom had issue. In her lifetime she had 40 grand-children and 37 great-grandchildren. During her reign the British crown ceased to be powerful but remained influential.

EWB

Virchow, Rudolf Ludwig Carl (1821–1902), German medical scientist, anthropologist, and politician. Rudolf Virchow was the founder of the school of "cellular pathology," which forms the basis of modern pathology.

Rudolf Virchow was born on Oct. 13, 1821, in Schivelbein, the only child of a farmer and city treasurer. In 1839 Virchow entered the Friedrich Wilhelms Institute in Berlin to undertake medical studies in preparation for a career as an army doctor. He came under the strong influence of Johannes Müller, who encouraged many German doctors to use experimental laboratory methods in their medical studies. Virchow received his medical degree in 1843, having already shown a keen interest in pathology.

In 1845, while still working as an intern, Virchow published his first scientific paper. By this year he had committed himself to a research methodology based on a mechanistic understanding of vital phenomena. Medical research, according to Virchow, needed to use clinical observation, experiments on animals, and microscopic examination of human tissues in order to understand how ordinary chemical and physical laws could explain the normal and abnormal phenomena associated with life. He accepted the cell theory as one basic element in this mechanistic understanding of life. In committing himself to this view, he joined a group of radical young medical scientists who were then challenging the dominant vitalism of an older generation.

In 1846 Virchow began to teach courses in pathological anatomy. In 1847 he was appointed to his first academic position with the rank of *privatdozent*. In the same year he and a colleague, Benno Reinhardt, published the first volume of a medical journal, the *Archives for Pathological Anatomy and Physiology and Clinical Medicine*. Virchow continued to edit this journal until his death in 1902.

Virchow's radical political views were clearly shown in 1848, the year of revolution in Germany. Early in the year Virchow presented a report on a typhus epidemic in Upper Silesia in which he recommended that the best way to avoid a repetition of the epidemic would be to introduce democratic forms of government. When the revolution broke out in Berlin, Virchow joined the revolutionaries fighting on the barricades. He threw himself wholeheartedly into the revolution, much to the displeasure of his father. He participated in a number of democratic clubs and helped edit a weekly paper, *Die medizinische Reform,* which promoted revolutionary ideas in relation to the medical profession.

Virchow's political views led to his suspension by the reestablished conservative government in 1849. The suspension was quickly revoked because of the hostile reaction of the medical fraternity. Later the same year Virchow was appointed professor at the University of Würzburg. Shortly after, he married Rose Mayer, the daughter of a leading German gynecologist.

The chair at Würzburg was the first one in Germany to be devoted to pathological anatomy. During Virchow's 7 years there, the medical school became recognized as one of the best in Europe, largely due to his teaching. He developed his concept of "cellular pathology," basing his interpretation of pathological processes on the recently formulated cell theory of Matthias Schleiden and Theodor Schwann. In the same period he became joint editor of an annual publication reviewing the year's progress in medical science. This publication later became known as Virchow's *Jahresbericht,* and he continued to edit it until his death. He also started work in 1854 on his *Handbook of Special Pathology and Therapeutics,* which became the model for later German "handbooks" in various sciences. Although Virchow's main interest at Würzburg was pathology, he also continued to work

in the field of public health and began researches in physical anthropology.

In 1856 Virchow accepted a chair at the University of Berlin on condition that a new building be constructed for a pathological institute. He remained in this position for the rest of his life. From 1859 Virchow renewed his activities in politics. In that year he was elected as a member of the city council, on which he served until his death. On the council he mainly interested himself in matters of public health. In 1861 Virchow was one of the foundation members of the Deutsche Fortschrittpartei and was elected in the same year to the Prussian Diet. He vigorously opposed Bismarck's preparations for war and his "blood and iron" policy of unifying Germany.

In the late 1860s and 1870s Virchow concentrated his attention on anthropology and international medical relations. He was active in numerous international medical congresses during this period and kept a continuing interest in the control and prevention of epidemics.

In 1873 Virchow was elected to the Prussian Academy of Science. All his contributions to this body were in the field of anthropology, mostly concerning physical anthropology and archaeology. In his new field as in others he took up the task of editing a leading journal, the *Zeitschrift fuer Ethnologie.* Virchow's later years continued to be active, especially in relation to his editorial duties. He died on Sept. 5, 1902.

EWB

Voltaire (1694–1778), French poet, dramatist, historian, and philosopher. Voltaire was an outspoken and aggressive enemy of every injustice but especially of religious intolerance. His works are an outstanding embodiment of the principles of the French Enlightenment.

François Marie Arouet rechristened himself Arouet de Voltaire, probably in 1718. A stay in the Bastille had given him time to reflect on his doubts concerning his parentage, on his need for a noble name to befit his growing reputation, and on the coincidence that *Arouet* sounded like both a *rouer* (for beating) and *roué* (a debauchee). In prison Voltaire had access to a book on anagrams, which may have influenced his name choice thus: *arouet, uotare, voltaire* (a winged armchair).

Youth and Early Success, 1694–1728. Voltaire was born, perhaps on Nov. 21, 1694, in Paris. He was ostensibly the youngest of the three surviving children of François Arouet and Marie Marguerite Daumand, although Voltaire claimed to be the "bastard of Rochebrune," a minor poet and songwriter. Voltaire's mother died when he was seven years old, and he was then drawn to his sister. She bore a daughter who later became Voltaire's mistress.

A clever child, Voltaire was educated by the Jesuits at the Collège Louis-le-Grand from 1704 to 1711. He displayed an astonishing talent for poetry, cultivated a love of the theater, and nourished a keen ambition.

When Voltaire was drawn into the circle of the 72-year-old poet the Abbé de Chaulieu, "one of the most complete hedonists of all times," his father packed him off to Caen. Hoping to squelch his son's literary aspirations and to turn his mind to the law, Arouet placed the youth as secretary to the French ambassador at The Hague. Voltaire fell in with a jilted French refugee, Catherine Olympe Dunoyer, pretty but barely literate. Their elopement was thwarted. Under the threat of a *lettre de cachet* obtained by his father, Voltaire returned to Paris in 1713 and was articled to a lawyer. He continued to write, and he renewed his pleasure-loving acquaintances. In 1717 Voltaire was at first exiled and then imprisoned in the Bastille for verses offensive to powerful personages.

As early as 1711, Voltaire, eager to test himself against Sophocles and Pierre Corneille, had written a first draft of *Oedipe*. On Nov. 18, 1718, the revised play opened in Paris to a sensational success. The *Henriade,* begun in the Bastille and published in 1722, was Voltaire's attempt to rival Virgil and to give France an epic poem. This work sounded in ringing phrases Voltaire's condemnation of fanaticism and advanced his reputation as the standard-bearer of French literature. However, his growing literary, financial, and social successes only partially reconciled him to his father, who died in 1722.

In 1726 an altercation with the Chevalier de Rohan, an effete but influential aristocrat, darkened Voltaire's outlook and intensified his sense of injustice. Rohan had mocked Voltaire's bourgeois origin and his change of name and in response to Voltaire's witty retort had hired ruffians to beat the poet, as Voltaire's friend and host, the Duc de Sully, looked on approvingly. When Voltaire demanded satisfaction through a duel, he was thrown into the Bastille through Rohan's influence and was released only on condition that he leave the country.

England willingly embraced Voltaire as a victim of France's injustice and infamy. During his stay there (1726–1728) he was feted; Alexander Pope, William Congreve, Horace Walpole, and Henry St. John, Viscount Bolingbroke, praised him; and his works earned Voltaire £1,000. Voltaire learned English by attending the theater daily, script in hand. He also imbibed English thought, especially that of John Locke and Sir Isaac Newton, and he saw the relationship between free government and creative speculation. More importantly, England suggested the relationship of wealth to freedom. The only protection, even for a brilliant poet, was wealth. Henceforth, Voltaire cultivated his Arouet business cunning.

At Cirey and at Court, 1729–1753. Voltaire returned to France in 1729. A tangible product of his English stay was the *Lettres anglaises* (1734), which have been called "the first bomb dropped on the Old Regime." Their explosive potential included such remarks as, "It has taken centuries to do justice to humanity, to feel it was horrible that the many should sow and the few should reap." Written in the style of letters to a friend in France, the 24 "letters" were a witty and seductive call for political, religious, and philosophic freedom; for the betterment of earthly life; for employing the method of Sir Francis Bacon, Locke, and Newton; and generally for exploiting the intellect toward social progress. After their publication in France in 1734, copies were seized from Voltaire's bookseller, and Voltaire was threatened with arrest. He fled to Lorraine and was not permitted to return to Paris until 1735. The work, with an additional letter on Pascal, was circulated as *Lettres philosophiques.*

Prior to 1753 Voltaire did not have a home; but for 15 years following 1733 he had a refuge at Cirey, in a château owned by his "divine Émilie," Madame du Châtelet. While still living with her patient husband and son, Émilie made generous room for Voltaire. They were lovers; and they worked together intensely on physics and metaphysics. The lovers quarreled in English about trivia and studied the Old and New Testaments. These biblical labors were important as preparation for the antireligious works that Voltaire published in the 1750s and 1760s. At Cirey, Voltaire also wrote his *Éléments de la philosophie de Newton.*

But joining Émilie in studies in physics did not keep him from drama, poetry, metaphysics, history, and polemics. Similarly, Émilie's affection was not alone enough for Voltaire. From 1739 he required travel and new excitements. Thanks to Émilie's influence, Voltaire was by 1743 less unwelcome at Versailles than in 1733, but still there was great resentment toward the "lowborn intruder" who "noticed things a good courtier must overlook." Honored by a respectful correspondence with Frederick II of Prussia, Voltaire was then sent on diplomatic missions to Frederick. But Voltaire's new diversion was his incipient affair with his widowed niece, Madame Denis. This affair continued its erotic and stormy course to the last years of his life. Émilie too found solace in other lovers. The idyll of Cirey ended with her death in 1749.

Voltaire then accepted Frederick's repeated invitation to live at court. He arrived at Potsdam with Madame Denis in July 1750. First flattered by Frederick's hospitality, Voltaire then gradually became anxious, quarrelsome, and finally disenchanted. He left, angry, in March 1753, having written in December 1752: "I am going to write for my instruction a little dictionary used by Kings. 'My friend' means 'my slave.'" Frederick was embarrassed by Voltaire's vocal lawsuit with a moneylender and angered by his attempts to ridicule P. L. M. de Maupertuis, the imported head of the Berlin Academy. Voltaire's polemic against Maupertuis, the *Diatribe du docteur Akakia*, angered Frederick. Voltaire's angry response was to return the pension and other honorary trinkets bestowed by the King. Frederick retaliated by delaying permission for Voltaire's return to France, by putting him under a week's house arrest at the German border, and by confiscating his money.

Sage of Ferney, 1753–1778. After leaving Prussia, Voltaire visited Strasbourg, Colmar, and Lorraine, for Paris was again forbidden him. Then he went to Geneva. Even Geneva, however, could not tolerate all of Voltaire's activities of theater, pen, and press. Therefore, he left his property "Les Delices" and bought an estate at Ferney, where he lived out his days as a kingly patriarch. His own and Madame Denis's great extravagances were supported by the tremendous and growing fortune he amassed through shrewd money handling. A borrower even as a schoolboy, Voltaire became a shrewd lender as he grew older. Generous loans to persons in high places paid off well in favors and influence. At Ferney, he mixed in local politics, cultivated his lands, became through his intelligent benevolence beloved of the townspeople, and in general practiced a self-appointed and satisfying kingship. He became known as the "innkeeper of Europe" and entertained widely and well in his rather small but elegant household.

Voltaire's literary productivity did not slacken, although his concerns shifted as the years passed at Ferney. He was best known as a poet until in 1751 *Le Siècle de Louis XIV* marked him also as a historian. Other historical works include *Histoire de Charles XII; Histoire de la Russie sous Pierre le Grand;* and the universal history, *Essai sur l'histoire générale et sur les moeurs et l'esprit des nations,* published in 1756 but begun at Cirey. An extremely popular dramatist until 1760, when he began to be eclipsed by competition from the plays of Shakespeare that he had introduced to France, Voltaire wrote in addition to the early *Oedipe La Mort de César, Ériphyle, Zaïre, Alzire, Mérope, Mahomet, L'Enfant prodigue, Nanine* (a parody of Samuel Richardson's *Pamela*), *L'Orphelin de la Chine, Sémiramis,* and *Tancrède.*

The philosophic *conte* was a Voltaire invention. In addition to his famous *Candide* (1759), others of his stories in this genre include *Micromégas, Vision de Babouc, Memnon, Zadig,* and *Jeannot et Colin*. In addition to the *Lettres Philosophiques* and the work on Newton, others of Voltaire's works considered philosophic are *Philosophie de l'histoire, Le Philosophe ignorant, Tout en Dieu, Dictionnaire philosophique portatif,* and *Traité de la métaphysique.* Voltaire's poetry includes in addition to the *Henriade* the philosophic poems *L'Homme, La Loi naturelle,* and *Le Désastre de Lisbonne,* as well as the famous *La Pucelle,* a delightfully naughty poem about Joan of Arc.

Always the champion of liberty, Voltaire in his later years became actively involved in securing justice for victims of persecution. He became the "conscience of Europe." His activity in the Calas affair was typical. An unsuccessful and despondent young man had hanged himself in his Protestant father's home in Roman Catholic Toulouse. For 200 years Toulouse had celebrated the massacre of 4,000 of its Huguenot inhabitants. When the rumor spread that the deceased had been about to renounce Protestantism, the family was seized and tried for murder. The father was broken on the rack while protesting his innocence. A son was exiled, the daughters were confined in a convent, and the mother was left destitute. Investigation assured Voltaire of their innocence, and from 1762 to 1765 he worked unceasingly in their behalf. He employed "his friends, his purse, his pen, his credit" to move public opinion to the support of the Calas family.

Voltaire's ingenuity and zeal against injustice were not exhausted by the Calas affair. Similar was his activity in behalf of the Sirven family (1771) and of the victims of the Abbeville judges (1774). Nor was Voltaire's influence exhausted by his death in Paris on May 30, 1778, where he had gone in search of Madame Denis and the glory of being crowned with laurel at a performance of his drama *Irène.*

Assessment of Voltaire. Voltaire was more than a thinker and activist. Style was nearly always nearly all to him in his abode, in his dress, and particularly in his writings. As poet and man of letters, he was demanding, innovative, and fastidious within regulated patterns of expression. Even as thinker and activist, he believed that form was all or at least the best part. As he remarked, "Never will twenty folio volumes bring about a revolution. Little books are the ones to fear, the pocket-size, portable ones that sell for thirty sous. If the Gospels had cost 1200 sesterces, the Christian religion could never have been established."

Voltaire's literary focus moved from that of poet to pamphleteer, and his moral sense had as striking a development. In youth a shameless libertine and in middle years a man notorious throughout the literary world, with more discreet but still eccentric attachments, in his later years Voltaire was renowned, whatever his personal habits, as a public defender and as a champion of human liberty. "Time, which alone makes their reputations of men," he observed," in the end makes their faults respectable." In his last days in Paris, he is said to have taken especially to heart a woman's remark: "Do you not know that he is the preserver of the Calas?"

Voltaire's life nearly spanned the 18th century; his writings fill 70 volumes; and his influence is not yet exhausted. He once wrote: "They wanted to bury me. But I outwitted them."

EWB

W

Wagner, Richard (1813–1883), German operatic composer. Richard Wagner was the most important seminal figure in 19th-century music. He was also a crucial figure in 19th-century cultural history for both his criticism and polemical writing.

Richard Wagner was born on May 22, 1813, in Leipzig into an unassuming family. His father died shortly after Richard's birth, and within the year his mother married Ludwig Geyer. There is still some controversy as to whether or not Geyer, an itinerant actor, was Wagner's real father. Wagner's musical training was largely left to chance until he was 18, when he studied with Theodor Weinlig in Leipzig for a year. He began his career in 1833 as choral director in Würzburg and composed his early works in imitation of German romantic compositions. Beethoven was his major idol at this time.

Wagner wrote his first opera, *Die Feen* (The Fairies), in 1833, but it was not produced until after the composer's death. He was music director of the theater in Magdeburg from 1834 to 1836, where his next work, *Das Liebesverbot* (Forbidden Love), loosely based on Shakespeare's *Measure for Measure* was performed in 1836. That year he married Minna Planner, a singer-actress active in provincial theatrical life.

In 1837 Wagner became the first music director of the theater in Riga, where he remained until 1839. He then set out for Paris, where he hoped to make his fortune. While in Paris, he developed an intense hatred for French musical culture that lasted the remainder of his life, regardless of how often he attempted to have a Parisian success. It was at this time that Wagner, in financial desperation, sold the scenario for *Der fliegende Holländer* (The Flying Dutchman) to the Paris Opéra for use by another composer. Wagner later set to music another version of this tale.

Disillusioned by his lack of success, Wagner returned to Germany, settling in Dresden in 1842, where he was in charge of the music for the court chapel. *Rienzi*, a grand opera in imitation of the French style, enjoyed a modest success; the Overture is still popular. In 1845 *Tannhäuser* was premiered in Dresden; this proved the first undoubted success of Wagner's career. In November of the same year he finished the poem for *Lohengrin* and began composition early in 1846. While at work on *Lohengrin* he also made plans for his tetralogy, *Der Ring des Nibelungen* (The Ring of the Nibelungen), being captivated by Norse sagas. In 1845 he prepared the scenario for the first drama of the tetralogy to be written, *Siegfried's Tod* (Siegfried's Death), which later became *Die Götterdämmerung* (The Twilight of the Gods).

Years of Exile. Wagner had to flee Dresden in 1849 in the aftermath of the Revolution of 1848. He settled in Switzerland, first in Zurich and then near Lucerne. He remained in Switzerland for the most part for the next 15 years without steady employment, banished from Germany and forbidden access to German theatrical life. During this time he worked on the *Ring*, which dominated his creative life over the next 2 decades.

The first production of *Lohengrin* took place in Weimar under Franz Liszt's direction in 1850 (Wagner was not to see *Lohengrin* until 1861). By this time Wagner was moderately notorious as a polemicist, and his most fundamental work of theory, *Opera and Drama*, dates from 1850–1851. In it he discusses the significance of legend for the theater and how to write singable poetry, and he presents his ideas with regard to the realization of the "total work of art" (Gesamtkunstwerk), which would effectively change the course of theatrical life in Germany if not the world.

The year 1850 also saw publication of one of Wagner's most scurrilous tracts, *The Jew in Music*, in which he viciously attacked the very existence of the Jewish composer and musician, particularly in German society. Anti-Semitism remained a hallmark of Wagner's philosophy the rest of his life.

Between 1850 and 1865 Wagner fashioned most of the material to which he owes his reputation. He purposefully turned aside from actual composition to plan an epic cycle of such grandeur and proportion as had never been created before. In 1851 he wrote the poem for *Der junge Siegfried* (Young Siegfried), the work now known as *Siegfried,* to prepare the way for *Götterdämmerung.* He realized he would need not only this drama to clarify his other work but two additional dramas as well, and he sketched the remaining poems for the *Ring* by the end of 1851. He completed *Das Rheingold* (The Rhinegold) in 1852 after he had revised the poem for *Die Walküre* (The Valkyrie).

In 1853 Wagner formally commenced composition on the *Rheingold;* he completed the scoring the following year and then began serious work on the *Walküre,* which was finished in 1856. At this time he was toying with the notion of writing the drama *Tristan und Isolde.* In 1857 he finished the composition of Act II of *Siegfried* and gave himself over entirely to *Tristan.* This work was completed in 1859, but it was mounted in Munich only in 1865.

Last Years. In 1860 Wagner received permission to reenter Germany except for Saxony. He was granted full amnesty in 1862. That year he began the music for *Die Meistersinger von Nürnberg* (The Mastersingers of Nuremburg), which he had first thought of in 1845. He resumed composition on *Siegfried* in 1865 and began sketching what would eventually become *Parsifal,* also a vague possibility since the mid-1840s. He began *Parsifal* at the urging of the Bavarian monarch, Ludwig II, then Wagner's patron. The *Meistersinger* was completed in 1867; the first performance took place in Munich the following year. Only then did he pick up the threads of the *Ring* and resume work on Act III of *Siegfried,* which was finished in September 1869, a month that also saw the first performance of the *Rheingold.* He wrote the music for *Götterdämmerung* from 1869 to 1874.

The first entire *Ring* cycle (*Rheingold, Walküre, Siegfried,* and *Götterdämmerung*) was given at the Festspielhaus, the shrine Wagner built for himself at Bayreuth, in 1876, over 30 years after the idea for it had first come to mind. He finished *Parsifal,* his final drama, in 1882. Wagner died on Feb. 13, 1883, in Venice and was buried at Bayreuth.

Philosophy of the *Ring.* The *Ring* is central to Wagner's career. Here he wished to present new ideas of morality and human activity that would completely alter the course of history. He envisioned a world made entirely free from subservience to supernatural bondage, which he believed had adversely affected Western civilization from ancient Greece to the present. Wagner also held that at the source of all human activity was fear, which must be purged so that man can live the perfect life. In the *Ring* he attempted

to set forth the standards for superior humans, those beings who would dominate individuals less fortunate; in turn, such lesser mortals would recognize their own inferior status and yield to the radiance offered by the perfect hero. The implications inherent in a quest for moral and racial purity are vital to Wagner's intentions in the *Ring.*

It is interesting to note that Wagner believed it was only by submitting completely to the sensuous experience that man could be liberated from the restraints imposed by rationality. However valuable the intellect might be, the rational life was regarded as a hindrance to achieving the fullest development of human awareness. Only when perfect man and perfect woman came together could a transcendental heroic image be created. Siegfried and Brünnhilde together are invincible after each has submitted to the other; apart they are imperfect.

There is no charity or idealism present in the Wagnerian myth world. The perfect ones exult only in each other. All men must recognize the superiority of certain creatures and then bow to their will. Man may quest for his destiny, but he must submit to the will of the superior one if the two come into conflict. In the *Ring* Wagner wanted to turn his back upon the civility inherent in the Hellenic-Judeo-Christian world. He preferred a realm dominated by the strength and savagery exemplified in the Norse sagas. The implications for the future of Germany were immense.

Philosophy of Other Operas. In *Tristan* Wagner rejected the affirmative way he developed in the *Ring.* Instead, he explored the dark side of love in order to plunge to the depths of negative experience. Tristan and Isolde, liberated and not doomed by a love potion they drink, willingly destroy a kingdom in order to love and to live; the sensual power of love is seen here as a destructive force, and the musical style of devious chromaticism and overwhelming orchestral pulsation is perfect for the messages of the drama.

Wagner's egomania, never tolerable to anyone save those who could blind themselves totally to his flaws, came to the fore in the *Meistersinger.* The tale of the young hero-singer who conquers the old order and forces a new, sensually more exciting style upon the tradition-bound Nuremburg society is the tale of the *Ring* in a slightly different guise. (Wagner openly claimed *Tristan* to be the *Ring* in microcosm.) It is obvious in the *Meistersinger* that Wagner identifies himself with the messianic figure of a young German poet and singer who wins the prize and is finally accepted as the leader of a new society.

In *Parsifal* Wagner identified himself even more intensely with the hero as the savior, the world's redeemer. The mysteries celebrated in *Parsifal* are those prepared for the glory of Wagner himself and not for any god.

Musical Language.

The scope of Wagner's vision is as breathtaking as his ideas and metaphysics are repugnant. Without the music his dramas would still be milestones in the history of Western thought. With the music, however, Wagner's importance is greatly magnified. He conceived a musical language that would most effectively present his philosophies. He intended to batter down the resistant forces of reason by means of the music. Ideally, there would be an unending melody in which the voice and text are but part of the fabric, united with a magnificent orchestral web which becomes the action at a distinctly musical pace. The verbal language, often very obscure and tortured in syntax, is acceptable only through the music.

For Wagner, music was in no sense additive, tacked onto the dramas after completion, anymore than it was an exercise in formal rhetoric, mere "art for art's sake." Music could bind all life, art, reality, and illusion together into one symbiotic union that would then work its own unique magic upon an audience. It is no accident that Wagner's musical language is intended to dethrone reason and to ask for unquestioning acceptance of the composer's beliefs. In Wagner's reading of Schopenhauer, the musical ideal in his dramas would be not a reflection of the world but would be that very world itself.

Personal Characteristics.

Such a summary of Wagner's creative life hardly hints at the extraordinary complications of his personal life which, in turn, affected his dramas. Wagner was that rare individuala truly charismatic figure who overcame all adversities. During the years in Switzerland he managed to live for the most part on charity by means of the most amazing conniving and manipulation of people conceivable. The Wesendonck family in particular contributed to his well-being, and Mathilde Wesendonck, one of Wagner's many mistresses, was credited with partially inspiring *Tristan*.

Wagner's life after leaving Saxony was a constant series of intrigues, harangues, and struggles to overcome the indifference of the world, to find the ideal woman worthy of his love, and to be the worthy recipient of the benefits offered by the perfect patron. Cosima Liszt von Bülow was the answer to his quest for the ideal female, subservient and fanatically devoted to his well-being. Although Wagner and Minna had lived apart for some time, Wagner did not marry Cosima until 1870, almost a decade after Minna's death. Over 30 years her husband's junior, Cosima was to be the dominating, guiding spirit in the Wagnerian shrine at Bayreuth until her death in 1930.

The perfect patron proved to be Ludwig II, who literally rescued Wagner from debtors' prison and brought the composer to Munich with a near carte blanche for life and creativity. Once salvaged, however, Wagner was so offensive to all save the blindly adoring young monarch that he was forced to flee within two years. Ludwig, despite eventually disillusionment, remained a loyal supporter of Wagner. It was his generosity that made possible the first festival performances of the *Ring* in Bayreuth in 1876.

Never one of amenable disposition, Wagner held convictions of his own superiority that developed monomaniacal proportions as he grew older. He was intolerant of any questioning, of any failure to accept him and his creation. His household revolved completely in his orbit, and his demands upon wives, mistresses, friends, musicians, and benefactors were legion. Those who ran afoul of him were pilloried unmercifully, often unscrupulously, such as Eduard Hanslick, the distinguished Viennese music critic who became the model for Beckmesser in the *Meistersinger*.

When the young philosopher Friedrich Nietzsche first met Wagner, he thought he had found his way into the presence of a god, so radiant and powerful did Wagner seem to him. Later Nietzsche realized that the composer was something less than the perfection of the superman incarnate he had imagined him to be and turned away in disgust. Wagner never forgave Nietzsche for his desertion.

Place in History.

In retrospect, Wagner's accomplishments outweigh both his personal behavior and his legacy for the 20th century. He has even managed to survive the predictable rejection by later generations of composers. Wagner created such an effective, unique musical language, especially in *Tristan* and *Parsifal*, that the beginnings of modern music are often dated from these scores.

Wagner demonstrated that music was not restricted to being pure formalism and abstract theoretical exploration but was a living, vibrant force capable of changing men's lives. He also proved that the music theater is a proper forum for ideas as opposed to being an arena for only escape and entertainment. And he demonstrated that a composer could rightfully take his place among the great revolutionary thinkers of Western civilization, questioning and attacking what seemed intolerable in traditional modes of behavior, experience, learning, and creation. Together with Karl Marx and Charles Darwin, Wagner must be given his rightful due as one of the greatest forces in 19th-century cultural history.

EWB

Webb, Beatrice Potter (1858–1943), English social reformer. Beatrice Potter Webb was a leading Fabian socialist and a partner with her husband, Sidney Webb, in their projects for social and educational reform and in their research into the history of political and economic institutions.

Beatrice Potter was born on Jan. 2, 1858, at Standish House near Gloucester. Her father, Richard Potter, was a man with large railroad interests and many contacts among politicians and intellectuals. She was educated at home by governesses and also by extensive travel, wide reading, and direct contact with many of the leading figures of politics, science, and industry. Herbert Spencer in particular gave her the attention and encouragement that she thought denied to her by her family.

Potter's involvement with social problems began in 1883, when she became a rent collector in London. This work, in turn, led to her participation in Charles Booth's survey published as *Life and Labour of the People in London*. In 1887 the results of her inquiries into dock life in the East End of London were published in *Nineteenth Century*, soon followed by other articles and studies of sweated labor.

Increased confidence and deeper study culminated in Potter's *The Co-operative Movement in Great Britain* (1891). It was in connection with this that she met Sidney Webb. They were married in 1892, and their life together became one of single-minded dedication to research and social reform. Together they produced a veritable torrent of books, pamphlets, essays, and memoranda amounting to over a hundred items.

Until 1906 Potter's role in the partnership was primarily that of researcher, writer, and hostess for gatherings of Cabinet ministers and members of Parliament who came to hear the Webb opinion on social legislation. At the end of 1905 Beatrice was appointed a member of the Royal Commission on the Poor Laws, which sat from 1906 to 1909. The minority report, drafted by the Webbs, played an important role in the dismantling of the old Poor Law and in its replacement by the new systems of social insurance.

In the period after 1910 the Webbs abandoned their nonpartisan stance and became an important force in building the Labour party. Another cornerstone of their earlier philosophy was abandoned with the publication of their *Soviet Communism: A New Society?* (1935). They, who had always held that social change cannot come about by the violent destruction of existing institutions, endorsed the Russian Revolution in spite of its totalitarianism. Beatrice Webb died at Liphook, Hampshire, on April 30, 1943. In 1947, shortly after Sidney's death, their ashes were buried in Westminster Abbey.

EWB

Webb, Sidney James, Baron Passfield (1859–1947), English social reformer and a leading Fabian Socialist. Sidney Webb a historian of social and economic institutions, founder of the London School of Economics and Political Science, and a Cabinet minister.

Sidney Webb was born in London on July 13, 1859. He was educated in Switzerland, Germany, the Birkbeck Institute, the City of London College, and through his own intensive reading. After a brief period of employment in the office of a firm of colonial brokers, he entered the civil service in 1878. In 1885 he was called to the bar and in the following year received his bachelor of laws degree from London University.

In 1885 Webb joined the Fabian Society and soon became a dominating influence on that organization. In 1891 he resigned from the civil service to run successfully for the London County Council. During most of the next 2 decades he was chairman of the Technical Education Committee of the council and brought about a thoroughgoing reform and centralization of the educational system in London. In 1895 he became the founder of the London School of Economics and Political Science.

In 1892 Webb married Beatrice Potter. From that time on, their work merged so thoroughly that it is impossible to distinguish their individual contributions. Among the earliest and most notable of their works are *The History of Trade Unionism* (1894) and *Industrial Democracy* (1897). Later there were nine massive volumes of the history of *English Local Government*, the first of which appeared in 1906 and the last in 1929.

By 1910 the Webbs decided that the Fabian policy of working through the existing political parties without partisan involvement had outlived its usefulness, and the Fabian Society threw its weight behind the Labour party. From 1915 to 1925 Sidney was a member of the party executive. In 1920 he was elected to Parliament, and in 1924 he was appointed president of the Board of Trade. Although he retired from office in 1928, he was called out of retirement in 1929 to serve (as Baron Passfield) as secretary of state for the colonies.

After the fall of the Labour government in 1932, the Webbs toured the Soviet Union and extolled it in their *Soviet Communism: A New Society?*

(1935). Beatrice died in 1943, and Sidney on Oct. 13, 1947.

EWB

Weber, Max (1864–1920), German social scientist. Max Weber was a founder of modern sociological thought. His historical and comparative studies of the great civilizations are a landmark in the history of sociology.

The work of Max Weber reflects a continued interest in charting the varying paths taken by universal cultural history as reflected in the development of the great world civilizations. In this sense, he wished to attempt a historical and analytical study of the themes sounded so strongly in G. W. F. Hegel's philosophy of history, especially the theme, which Weber took as his own, of the "specific and peculiar rationalism of Western culture." Along with this emphasis on universal cultural history, Weber's detailed training as a legal and economic historian led him to reject the overly simplistic formulas of economic base and corresponding cultural superstructure that were so often used to account for cultural development and were a strong part of the intellectual environment of Weber's early years as student and professor. His historical and comparative erudition and analytical awareness required that he go beyond both the Hegelian and Marxian versions of historical development toward a deep historical and comparative study of sociocultural processes in West and East.

Weber was born on April 21, 1864, in Erfaut, Thuringia, the son of a lawyer active in political life. An attack of meningitis at the age of 4 and his mother's consequent overprotectiveness helped contribute to Weber's sedentary yet intellectually precocious youth. He read widely in the classics and was bored with the unchallenging secondary education of his time, which he completed in 1882. He then attended Heidelberg University, where he studied law, along with history, economics, and philosophy.

After three terms at Heidelberg, Weber served a year in the military, which he found to be largely an "incredible waste of time" with its continued attempts to regiment the human intellect. Resuming his studies at the universities of Berlin and Göttingen in 1884, he passed his bar examination in 1886 and would later practice law for a time. He completed his doctoral thesis in 1889 with an essay on the history of the medieval trading companies, which embodied his interests in both legal and economic history. His second major work, a customary "habilitation" thesis that would qualify him to teach at the university level, appeared in 1891 and involved a study of the economic,

cultural, and legal foundations of ancient agrarian history.

In 1893 Weber married Marianne Schnitger. The following year he received an appointment as professor of economics at Freiburg University; in 1896 he accepted a professorship at Heidelberg. Shortly after his father's death in 1897, Weber began to suffer from a psychic disturbance that incapacitated him almost completely until 1902. By the next year he was well enough to join Werner Sombart in editing the *Archiv für Sozialwissenschaft and Sozialpolitik* (Archives for Social Science and Social Policy), the most prominent German social science journal of the period.

Protestantism and Capitalism.   Having assumed his full work load again, Weber began to write perhaps his most renowned essays, published in the *Archiv* in 1904–1905 under the title *The Protestant Ethic and the Spirit of Capitalism.* In them he attempted to link the rise of a new sort of distinctly modern capitalism to the religious ethics of Protestantism, especially the Calvinist variety, with its emphasis on work in a calling directed toward the rational ascetic mastery of this world.

Weber argued that, when the asceticism of the medieval Catholic monastery, oriented toward salvation in a world beyond this one through self-denial exercised by a religious few, was brought into the conduct of everyday affairs, it contributed greatly to the systematic rationalization and functional organization of every sphere of existence, especially economic life. He viewed the Reformation as a crucial period in western European history, one that was to see a fundamental reorientation of basic cultural frameworks of spiritual direction and human outlook and destined to have a great impact on economic life as well as other aspects of modern culture. Within the context of his larger questions, Weber tended to view Protestant rationalism as one further step in the series of stages of increasing rationalization of every area of modern society.

In 1904 Weber was invited to attend the St. Louis Exhibition in Missouri and to deliver a popular sociological lecture. While in America, he had substantial opportunity to encounter what he saw as added evidence for his special thesis in *The Protestant Ethic and the Spirit of Capitalism,* as well as for his more general philosophic and historical concerns. In the United States the religious foundations of modern economic life had seen perhaps their greatest fruition in the enormous "towers of capital," as Weber called them, of the eastern industrial centers of the country. However, he also recognized that the contemporary American economic life had been stripped of its original ethical and religious impulse. Intense economic competition assumed the character almost of sport, and no obvious possibilities appeared for the resuscitation of new spiritual values from what appeared to be the extensive mechanization of social and economic existence.

Employing a method that isolated the similarities and differences between features of sociocultural development in different societies, Weber attempted to weigh the relative importance of economic, religious, juridical, and other factors in contributing to the different historical outcomes seen in any comparative study of world societies. This larger theme formed one of his central intellectual interests throughout the remainder of his life, and it resulted in the publication of *The Religion of China* (1915), *The Religion of India* (1916–1917), and *Ancient Judaism* (1917–1919). Although he also planned comparable works on early Christianity, medieval Catholicism, and Islamic civilization, he died before they could be completed.

Later Work. After the essays of 1904–1905, Weber took on an even heavier burden of activities than before his illness. His break with the Verein für Sozialpolitik (Union for Social Policy), a long-standing German political and social scientific organization, over the question of the relation of social scientific research to social policy led to the establishment in 1910, with the collaboration of other great social scientists of his day, of the new Deutsche Soziologische Gesellschaft (German Sociological Society).

Weber and his collaborators argued that social science could not be simply subordinated to political values and policies. Rather, there was a logical distinction between the realms of fact and value, one which required a firmly grounded distinction between the analyses of the social scientist and the policies of any political order. Social science must develop "objective" frames of reference, ones "neutral" to any particular political policies and ethical values. This ever-renewed tension between particular ethical stances and "objectivity" in the sciences remained a central part of Weber's concerns in his political activities during and after World War I as well as in his academic writings and lectures.

Economy and Society. In 1909 Weber took over the editorship of a projected multivolume encyclopedic work on the social sciences entitled *Outline of Social Economics.* It was to contain volumes authored by prominent social scientists of the time. Although he was originally to contribute the volume *Economy and Society* to this effort, difficulties in obtaining completed manuscripts from some participants led Weber to expand his contribution into what became a prodigious attempt at the construction of a systematic sociology in world historical and comparative depth, one which was to occupy a large portion of his time and energies during the remainder of his life. He published his first contributions in 1911–1913, other still unfinished sections being published after his death.

Economy and Society differed in tone and emphasis from Weber's comparative studies of the cultural foundations of Chinese, Indian, and Western civilizations. This massive work was an attempt at a more systematic sociology, not directed toward any single comparative, historical problem but rather toward an organization of the major areas of sociological inquiry into a single whole. Weber never believed it possible to write a truly systematic sociology that would have separate analytical sections on each area of interest and that would form a general system of theory. Containing large sections on sociological analysis, the economy and social norms, economy and law, domination, and legitimacy, and still unsurpassed sections on religion, the city, and political rulership, *Economy and Society* remains today perhaps the only systematic sociology in world historical and comparative depth.

Last Years. Despite time spent in the medical service during World War I, Weber's efforts were largely devoted from 1910 to 1919 to the completion of his studies on China, India, and ancient Judaism and to his work on *Economy and Society.* Many younger as well as more established scholars formed part of Weber's wide intellectual circle during these years. Always desirous of championing the cause of scholars whose work was judged unfairly because of religious, political, or other external criteria, Weber on numerous occasions attempted to aid these young scholars—despite sometimes substantial intellectual differences with them—by securing for them the academic appointments they deserved. Often these attempts were unsuccessful and led Weber into bitter conflicts with many established scholars and political figures over the relation of science to values and the application of extrascientific criteria to the evaluation of a writer's work.

In 1918 Weber resumed his teaching duties. One result was a series of lectures in 1919–1920, "Universal Economic History," which was published posthumously from students' notes as *General Economic History*. Along with this lecture series, Weber delivered two addresses in 1918, "Science as a Vocation" and "Politics as a Vocation," in which he voiced ethical themes that had occupied him in his scholarly work and in his numerous discussions of social policy. In these two addresses he contrasted the ethic of unalterable ultimate ends so characteristic of uncompromising religious and political prophets with the ethic of consequences so necessary in political life, in which possible outcomes of actions and policies are agonizingly weighed and the least undesirable course determined in light of a plurality of given goals. Variants of this distinction pervaded much of Weber's own view of political and religious life and formed a central aspect of his ethical philosophy.

Thus, Weber sounded ethical themes that have become a central part of the "existentialist" philosophical orientation of our time. Understanding the dilemma of modern men caught between the older religious systems of the past and the cynical power politics of the present, he gave no simple solutions and was willing neither to wait for new prophets nor to abdicate all ethical responsibility for the conduct of life because of its seeming ultimate "meaninglessness."

Weber died in Munich on June 14, 1920. His work forms a major part of the historical foundation of sociology.

EWB

Wedgwood, Josiah (1730–1795), English potter. Josiah Wedgwood established the Wedgwood pottery factory. His work is most associated with the neoclassic style.

Josiah Wedgwood was born in August 1730 at Burslem, Staffordshire, into a family which had been engaged in the manufacture of pottery since the 17th century. His father owned a factory called the Churchyard Pottery, and Josiah began working in this family enterprise as an apprentice in 1744. He left the factory in the early 1750s and until 1759 was engaged with various partners in the manufacture of standard types of earthenware, including salt-glaze and stoneware products and objects in the popular agate and tortoiseshell glazes. During these years he experimented with improving glazes in color, and he achieved a particularly refined green glaze.

In Staffordshire at Ivy House in Burslem. The Ivy House pottery was so successful that in 1764 he moved his factory to larger quarters nearby; the new factory was first known as the Brick House Works and later as the Bell House. During this period Wedgwood created his first creamware, a pale-colored earthenware frequently decorated with painted or enameled designs. Wedgwood's creamware won the approval of Queen Charlotte and after about 1765 became known as "Queen's ware."

During the first half of the 18th century the prevailing taste was for the rococo, a decorative style which used sensuous and delicate colors, lavish ornament, and a complex interplay of curved lines and masses. From about the middle of the century, however, the exuberant gaiety of the rococo began gradually to be replaced by neoclassicism and a return to the comparative severity of the art of antiquity. In the early 1760s Wedgwood met Thomas Bentley, a cultivated man devoted to neoclassicism, and in 1769 they opened a factory near Burslem which was called Etruria and dedicated to the creation of ornamental pottery designed in the neoclassic manner. The factory at Bell House was retained for the production of functional tableware until the 1770s, when it was absorbed into Etruria.

The two products of the Etruria factory which became most fashionable were the basaltes and the jasperware objects. The basaltes were decorative and functional pieces made of a hard black stoneware, often with low-relief decoration, in designs based upon antiquity. The jasperware became the most famous of the Wedgwood products and is still the pottery most associated with the Wedgwood name. Jasperware, which Wedgwood perfected about 1775, is a fine stoneware with a solid body color in blue, soft green, lavender, pink, black, or other colors and generally decorated with delicate low-relief designs in white adapted from Greek vase paintings, Roman relief sculpture, and other antique sources. Jasperware was produced in a great variety of functional and decorative objects ranging from teapots to cameos and including vases, bowls, candlesticks, and portrait reliefs.

Bentley died in 1780, and Wedgwood continued the work at Etruria, producing some of the factory's finest jasper in the late 18th century. He employed many artists to provide designs for his products and to adapt designs from classical antiquity. The most notable of these modelers was John Flaxman, a famous sculptor who supplied designs for the Etruria factory from 1775 to 1800. From 1787 Flaxman was in Rome for several years studying antique sculpture and sending Wedgwood elegant interpretations of ancient art.

Wedgwood died at Etruria on Jan. 3, 1795. His tombstone states that he "converted a rude and inconsiderable Manufactory into an elegant Art and an important part of National Commerce." The factory remains in the family and since 1810 has been known as Josiah Wedgwood and Sons. The modern factory is primarily concerned with the production of dinnerware and functional objects but continues to manufacture the jasper and basaltes that Josiah made so popular.

EWB

Wesley, John (1703–1791), English evangelical clergyman, preacher, and writer. John Wesley was the founder of Methodism. One of England's greatest spiritual leaders, he played a major role in the revival of religion in 18th-century English life.

The 18th century found the Church of England out of touch with both the religious and social problems of the day. Its leadership was constituted largely by political appointees, its clergy were riddled with ignorance, and churchmen of genuine concern were rare. The influence of rationalism and deism even among dedicated clergymen caused the Anglican Church to be unaware of the spiritual needs of the masses. John Wesley's great achievement was to recognize the necessity of bringing religion to this wide and neglected audience.

Wesley was born in Epworth, Lincolnshire, on June 17, 1703. He was the fifteenth of the 19 children of Samuel Wesley, an Anglican minister who took his pastoral duties seriously and instilled this idea in his son. John's mother, a woman of great spiritual intensity, molded her children through a code of strict and uncompromising Christian morality, instilling in John a firm conception of religious piety, concern, and duty.

In 1714 Wesley entered Charterhouse School, and in 1720 he became a student at Christ Church, Oxford. Receiving his bachelor of arts degree in 1724, he was ordained a deacon in the Church of England in 1725 and was elected a fellow of Lincoln College, Oxford, in 1726. He became curate to his father in the following year and was ordained a priest in 1728. Returning to Oxford in 1729, Wesley, in addition to the duties of his fellowship at Lincoln, became active in a religious club to which his younger brother Charles belonged. The Holy Club, nicknamed "Methodists" by its critics, met frequently for discussion and study. Its members engaged in prayer, attended church services, visited prisoners, and gave donations to the needy. The Holy Club was one of Wesley's formative influences, and he soon became its acknowledged leader.

Ministry in Georgia. Buoyed by his years at Oxford and desirous of putting the principles of the Holy Club to work elsewhere, Wesley in 1735 accepted the invitation of James Oglethorpe to become a minister in the recently founded colony of Georgia. Accompanied by his brother Charles, Wesley spent two disappointing years in the New World. Despite his zeal to bring them the Gospel, he was rebuffed by the colonists and received unenthusiastically by the Indians. Moreover, he became involved in an unsuccessful love affair, the aftermath of which brought him the unwanted publicity of a court case. In 1737 Wesley returned to England.

Wesley's stay in Georgia was, however, not without benefit. Both on his trip over and during his two-year stay, he was deeply influenced by Moravian missionaries, whose sense of spiritual confidence and commitment to practical piety impressed him.

Conversion and Preaching. In England, Wesley continued to keep in close touch with the Moravians. At one of their meetings in Aldersgate Street, London, on May 24, 1738, he experienced conversion while listening to a reading of Martin Luther's preface to the Epistle to the Romans. "I felt I did trust in Christ, Christ alone, for salvation," Wesley wrote, "and an assurance was given me that He had taken away *my* sins, even *mine,* and saved *me* from the law of sin and death."

Through this personal commitment Wesley, though he later broke with the Moravians, became imbued with the desire to take this message to the rest of England. Finding the bishops unsympathetic or indifferent and most clergymen hostile to the point of closing their churches to him, Wesley, following the example of such preachers as George Whitefield, began an itinerant ministry that lasted more than 50 years. Forced to preach outside the churches, he became adept at open-air preaching and, as a result, began to reach many, especially in the cities, about whom the Church of England had shown little concern.

A small man (he was 5 feet 6 inches in height and weighed about 120 pounds), Wesley always had to perch on a chair or platform when he preached. He averaged 15 sermons a week, and as his *Journal* indicates, he preached more than 40,000 sermons in his career, traveling the length and breadth of England—altogether more than 250,000 miles—many times during an age when roads were often only muddy ruts. A contemporary described him as "the last word . . . in neatness and dress" and "his eye was 'the brightest and most piercing that can be conceived.' "

Preaching was not easy; crowds were often hostile, and once a bull was let loose in an audience he was addressing. Wesley, however, quickly learned the art of speaking and, despite opposition, his sermons began to have a marked effect. Many were converted immediately, frequently exhibiting physical signs, such as fits or trances.

Organization of Methodism. From the beginning Wesley viewed his movement as one within the Church of England and not in opposition to it. As he gained converts around England, however, these men and women grouped themselves together in societies that Wesley envisioned as playing the same role in Anglicanism as the monastic orders do in the Roman Catholic Church. He took a continual and rather authoritarian part in the life of these societies, visiting them periodically, settling disputes, and expelling the recalcitrant. Yearly conferences of the whole movement presented him with the opportunity to establish policy. Under his leadership each society was broken down into a "class," which dealt with matters of finance, and a "band," which set standards of personal morality. In addition, Wesley wrote numerous theological works and edited 35 volumes of Christian literature for the edification of the societies. A tireless and consummate organizer, he kept his movement prospering despite a variety of defections.

Yet the continual opposition of the Anglican bishops, coupled with their refusal to ordain Methodist clergy, forced Wesley to move closer to actual separation toward the end of his life. In 1784 he took out a deed of declaration, which secured the legal standing of the Methodist Society after his death. In the same year he reluctantly ordained two men to serve as "superintendents" for Methodists in North America. He continued the practice to provide clergymen for England but very sparingly and with great hesitation. Wesley always maintained that he personally adhered to the Church of England.

Methodism had a significant impact on English society. It brought religion to masses of people who, through the shifts of population brought about by the industrial revolution, were not being reached by the Anglican Church. In addition, it had a beneficial effect on many within both the Church of England and dissenting congregations. By emphasizing morality, self-discipline, and thrift to the deprived classes, Wesley has been credited by some historians as being a major force in keeping England free of revolution and widespread social unrest during his day. He himself was politically conservative, a critic of democracy, and a foe of both the American and French revolutions.

Throughout his life Wesley's closest confidant was his brother and coworker Charles, the composer of a number of well-known hymns. Wesley, always extraordinarily healthy, remained active to the end, preaching his final sermon at an open-air meeting just 4 months before his death on March 2, 1791, in London.

EWB

Wilberforce, William

Wilberforce, William (1759–1833), English statesman and humanitarian. William Wilberforce was a prominent antislavery leader. His agitation helped smooth the way for the Act of Abolition of 1833.

William Wilberforce was born to affluence at Hull on Aug. 24, 1759. He attended Hull Grammar School and St. John's College, Cambridge. He was elected to Parliament from Hull in 1780 and from Yorkshire in 1784. In 1812 he moved his constituency to Bramber, Sussex. He retired from the House of Commons in 1825.

Wilberforce was a friend and lifelong supporter of William Pitt the Younger, the great British prime minister and war leader. Like his leader, Wilberforce moved toward a more conservative position following the French Revolution and Britain's involvement in the French Revolutionary Wars and Napoleonic Wars. His antislavery ideas arose not out of a background of secular liberalism but out of his religious beliefs. England in the late 18th century experienced a powerful religious revival, and in 1785 Wilberforce was converted to Evangelical Christianity.

In 1787 Wilberforce was approached by the antislavery advocate Thomas Clarkson, who was already in touch with the abolitionist lawyer Granville Sharp. The three formed the nucleus of a group ridiculed as the "Clapham sect" (after the location of the house where they held their meetings). They were joined by such slavery opponents as John Newton, Hannah More, Henry Thornton, Zachary Macaulay, E. J. Eliot, and James Stephen. Clarkson organized a propaganda campaign throughout the country, while Wilberforce represented the group's interests in the House of Commons. Wilberforce created two formal organizations in 1787: the Committee for the Abolition of the Slave Trade and the Society for the Reformation of Manners.

The Claphams won a growing number of converts to their cause, but they were unable to make any legal headway against the West Indies slave traders and planters. Pitt personally supported the petitions presented to the House by Wilberforce; yet the slave trade was regarded as essential to economic health, and the West Indies interests were an important component of Pitt's Whig coalition. The 1790s witnessed some reform of the worst practices of the slavers and a resolution supporting the gradual abolition of the slave trade.

However, Wilberforce held firm in his views. His persistence was finally rewarded in 1807, when, following Pitt's death, a temporary Radical government coalition led by Charles James Fox united liberals and Evangelicals behind passage of an act prohibiting the slave trade. This act represented the culmination of Wilberforce's active participation in the movement.

In 1823 younger followers of Wilberforce founded the Antislavery Society, of which Wilberforce became a vice president. Once again a prolonged period of agitation produced results. Wilberforce, however, had been dead for a month when the Emancipation Act became law in August 1833.

EWB

Wilde, Oscar Fingall O'Flahertie Wills (1854–1900), British author. Oscar Wilde was part of the "art for art's sake" movement in English literature at the end of the 19th century. He is best known for his brilliant, witty comedies.

Oscar Wilde was born in Dublin, Ireland, on Oct. 16, 1854. His father, Sir William Wilde, was a well-known surgeon; his mother, Jane Francisca Elgee Wilde, wrote popular poetry and prose under the pseudonym Speranza. For three years Wilde was educated in the classics at Trinity College, Dublin, where he began to attract public attention through the eccentricity of his writing and his style of life.

At the age of 23 Wilde entered Magdalen College, Oxford. In 1878 he was awarded the Newdigate Prize for his poem "Ravenna." He attracted a group of followers, and they initiated a personal cult, self-consciously effete and artificial. "The first duty in life," Wilde wrote in *Phrases and Philosophies for the Use of the Young* (1894), "is to be as artificial as possible." After leaving Oxford he expanded his cult. His iconoclasm contradicted the Victorian era's easy pieties, but the contradiction was one of his purposes. Another of his aims was the glorification of youth.

Wilde published his well-received *Poems* in 1881. The next six years were active ones. He spent an entire year lecturing in the United States and then returned to lecture in England. He applied unsuccessfully for a position as a school inspector. In 1884 he married, and his wife bore him children in 1885 and in 1886. He began to publish extensively in the following year. His writing activity became as intense and as erratic as his life had been for the previous six years. From 1887 to 1889 Wilde edited the magazine *Woman's World*. His first popular success as a prose writer was *The Happy Prince and Other Tales* (1888). *The House of Pomegranates* (1892) was another collection of his fairy tales.

Wilde became a practicing homosexual in 1886. He believed that his subversion of the Victorian moral code was the impulse for his writing. He considered himself a criminal who challenged society by creating scandal. Before his conviction for homosexuality in 1895, the scandal was essentially private. Wilde believed in the criminal mentality. "Lord Arthur Savile's Crime," from *Lord Arthur Savile's Crime and Other Stories* (1891), treated murder and its successful concealment comically. The original version of *The Pic-*

ture of Dorian Gray in *Lippincott's Magazine* emphasized the murder of the painter Basil Hallward by Dorian as the turning point in Dorian's disintegration; the criminal tendency became the criminal act.

Dorian Gray was published in book form in 1891. The novel celebrated youth: Dorian, in a gesture typical of Wilde, is parentless. He does not age, and he is a criminal. Like all of Wilde's work, the novel was a popular success. His only book of formal criticism, *Intentions* (1891), restated many of the esthetic views that *Dorian Gray* had emphasized, and it points toward his later plays and stories. *Intentions* emphasized the importance of criticism in an age that Wilde believed was uncritical. For him, criticism was an independent branch of literature, and its function was vital.

His Dramas. Between 1892 and 1895 Wilde was an active dramatist, writing what he identified as "trivial comedies for serious people." His plays were popular because their dialogue was baffling, clever, and often epigrammatic, relying on puns and elaborate word games for its effect. *Lady Windermere's Fan* was produced in 1892, *A Woman of No Importance* in 1893, and *An Ideal Husband* and *The Importance of Being Earnest* in 1895.

On March 2, 1895, Wilde initiated a suit for criminal libel against the Marquess of Queensberry, who had objected to Wilde's friendship with his son, Lord Alfred Douglas. When his suit failed in April, counit charges followed. After a spectacular court action, Wilde was convicted of homosexual misconduct and sentenced to 2 years in prison at hard labor.

Prison transformed Wilde's experience as radically as had his 1886 introduction to homosexuality. In a sense he had prepared himself for prison and its transformation of his art. *De Profundis* is a moving letter to a friend and apologia that Wilde wrote in prison; it was first published as a whole in 1905. His theme was that he was not unlike other men and was a scapegoat. *The Ballad of Reading Gaol* (1898) was written after his release. In this poem a man has murdered his mistress and is about to be executed, but Wilde considered him only as criminal as the rest of humanity. He wrote: "For each man kills the thing he loves,/ Yet each man does not die."

After his release from prison Wilde lived in France. He attempted to write a play in his pretrial style, but this effort failed. He died in Paris on Nov. 30, 1900.

EWB

William II (1859–1941), last of the Hohenzollern rulers. William II was emperor of Germany and king

of Prussia from 1888 until his forced abdication in 1918.

In the crucial years before World War I, William II was the most powerful and most controversial figure in Europe. His domineering personality and the comparatively vague political structure of the post-Bismarck state combined to make his reign over the most advanced country in Europe both authoritarian and archaic.

William was born on Jan. 27, 1859. He was the son of Frederick III and Princess Victoria of England. William's views of his prerogatives were strongly influenced by his Prussian military education, amidst the subservience and flattery of his fellow cadets. After completing his studies at the University of Bonn, William entered the army and in 1881 married Princess Augusta Victoria of Schleswig-Holstein.

William was an intelligent, dashing, impulsive young man who loved military display and believed in the divine nature of kingship; his strong personality overcame the serious handicap (for a horseman) of a withered left arm. His father found William immature, but Chancellor Otto von Bismarck considered him a more acceptable successor to his grandfather (and to Frederick the Great) than his liberal father. Conservative circles in Germany breathed a sigh of relief when the death of William I in 1888 was quickly followed by that of Frederick III. William II ascended the throne that year.

Differences between the young kaiser and the aging Bismarck soon were public knowledge. Serious questions of policy separated them, such as whether to renew the anti-Socialist legislation on the books since 1878, and in foreign affairs, whether to keep the alliance with Russia as well as with Austria, as Bismarck insisted. But basically the split was a personal one, the question being which man was to rule Germany. William forced Bismarck to resign in 1890, and thereafter he steered his own course.

It seemed to mark the beginning of a new era. William was the representative of a new generation that had grown up since German unification, and he was at home in the world of technology and of neoromantic German nationalism. Indeed, William gave the impression of dynamism. He was always in the public eye and caught, for a time, the imagination of his country. But he cared little for the day-to-day problems of government, and his "policies" were often shallow, short-lived, and contradictory. Thus the "Labor Emperor" of the early years of the reign soon became the implacable enemy of the Social Democratic working-class movement. In foreign policy his inconsistencies were even more glaring. England and Russia, in particular, were alternately wooed and rebuffed;

both ultimately ended up as foes. Sometimes the Kaiser's sounder instincts were overridden by his advisers, as in the Morocco crisis of 1905, which William, who was essentially peaceful in intent, had not wished to provoke. But mainly his mistakes were his own.

Foreign opinion concerning the Kaiser was much more hostile than German opinion, and his often bellicose and pompous utterances did much to tarnish Germany's image abroad. Nevertheless, World War I and postwar depictions of him as the incarnation of all that was evil in Germany were grossly unfair. So little was he the martial leader of a militaristic nation that his authority in fact faded during World War I, and the military assumed increasing control. Belatedly, William tried to rally a war-weary nation with promises of democratic reforms, but at the end of the war the German Republic was proclaimed without serious opposition. William abdicated in November 1918.

After his abdication William lived in quiet retirement in Doorn, Holland, not actively involved with the movement for a restoration of the monarchy. He died in Doorn on June 4, 1941.

EWB

Wolff, Baron Christian von (1679–1754), German philosopher. Christian von Wolff systematized the doctrines of Leibniz. He is best known for his broad concept of philosophy.

Christian von Wolff was born in Breslau, Silesia, on Jan. 24, 1679. His father, a tanner, vowed that his son would enter the Lutheran ministry. At the University of Jena, Wolff studied theology but found that he was more interested in mathematics, physics, and philosophy. He took a master of arts degree at the University of Leipzig, where he taught from 1703 to 1706. He wrote a paper on universal practical philosophy, which he submitted to Gottfried Wilhelm von Leibniz, and on the strength of Leibniz's recommendation Wolff was appointed professor of mathematics at Halle in 1706. He remained there until 1723, when Frederick William I expelled him from Prussia for anti-Pietist teachings.

Wolff then taught at the University of Marburg, where he continued to publish various sections of his unified and deductive system of all branches of human knowledge. His productivity can be gauged by the fact that the collected edition of his major works fills 26 volumes. With the accession of Fredrick II (the Great) in 1740, Wolff was recalled in triumph to Halle. He was honored as professor, vice-chancellor, and finally chancellor of the university (1743). He died at Halle on April 9, 1754.

Wolff was well acquainted with the major developments of modern science and philosophy. He met and corresponded with Leibniz, and, like his mentor, Wolff knew ancient philosophy as well as the Roman Catholic and Protestant traditions of scholasticism. His aim was to systematically organize all knowledge in terms of logical deductions from first principles.

The metaphysics of this endeavor was Leibnizian in origin: the principles of identity and sufficient reason. Wolff believed that every idea or concept expresses a possibility. That some possibilities are actualized is a matter of historical fact. Thus the role of sensation and experience in general is historical. The transition from historical knowledge to philosophical knowledge is the difference between "the bare knowledge, the fact" and the reason for this fact. Philosophy is "the science of all possible things." Insofar as things are definite they have quantitive relations, and mathematics is the clearest expression of the demonstrable scientific connections between objects. Therefore the purview of all knowledge is encompassed in the disciplines of history, philosophy, and mathematics. With this plan, which Wolff presented in *Preliminary Discourse on Philosophy in General* (1728), he was able to offer a complete division of the sciences.

EWB

Wollstonecraft, Mary (1759–1797), British author.

Mary Wollstonecraft was the second of seven children and the eldest daughter of Edward John Wollstonecraft and Elizabeth Dixon Wollstonecraft. Edward came from a prosperous family of weavers in Spitalfields, London, and Elizabeth came from a well-placed family in Ballyshannon, Ireland.

Wollstonecraft was faced in 1782 with the need to support herself and her sisters, Eliza and Everina. With the help of Fanny Blood, the four women opened a boarding school for private pupils. They rented a large house in Newington Green, north of London, and were able to attract enough pupils to make the venture self-supporting. Additionally, Wollstonecraft joined a group of dissenting intellectuals who lived near the Green. Within this group there were discussions of politics, religion, and education led by its founder, Dr. Richard Price. Some of its members included Samuel Rodgers, James Sowerby, the Reverend John Hewlett, and Mrs. James Burgh; the group was often visited by Joseph Priestley. Here Wollstonecraft was to encounter an alternative to the dominant ideology of her childhood and to find support for her developing intellectual curiosity.

Within the Price circle, Wollstonecraft was exposed to the ideas and values that descended from the English empirical tradition in philosophy and English religious dissent. Wollstonecraft would subscribe to the essential elements of that philosophy all her life: experience is the basis of all knowledge; environment shapes character; men and women are innately good and potentially perfectible; and truth is something knowable, both through self-examination and through education in the widening social contexts of family, community, polite society, and ultimately humanity in general.

But her membership in this cohesive group and the educational community she was creating with her sisters was not to last. The school closed in 1786.

The spring of that year was an important period for Wollstonecraft; she spent March and April writing her first book, *Thoughts on the Education of Daughters* (1787), a collection of essays on education for parents, detailing a need for moral, social, and intellectual improvement of their daughters. The book follows existing patterns for such manuals by focusing on Lockean rationalism and Christian morality.

In midsummer of 1786 Wollstonecraft accepted a position as governess to the eldest daughters of Viscount Kingsborough. In the summer of 1787 she wrote her first novel, *Mary, A Fiction* (1788), and by the end of that summer she had received Joseph Johnson's assurance of a position as a reviewer and translator for his new journal, the *Analytical Review*.

From October 1787 to January 1789 Wollstonecraft spent most of her time reviewing fiction and educational works in the *Analytical Review*; translating works from French, Dutch, and German (which she was teaching herself); writing a children's book; and compiling an anthology of educational and inspirational writing for women. These were the months to which Wollstonecraft later referred as of hard labor and relative obscurity; they were her apprenticeship as a reviewer, translator, and political thinker.

In 1788 Wollstonecraft was living alone in London and earning enough from her writing to bring her sisters to the city for holidays, and then to send Everina to Paris to improve her French. During this period Wollstonecraft was also having to prove herself in the home of her publisher, for she was one of the youngest and one of the few women members of the Johnson circle. This group of writers, professionals, painters, and pamphleteers met at Johnson's home for debate, discussion, and dinner.

During 1788 Johnson also asked Wollstonecraft to begin two projects: one was a translation from the German of Joachim Heinrich Campe's *New Robinson Crusoe* (1779–1780), which was abandoned when another translation was published in that year; the second was a more interesting but time-consuming project, the anthology *The Female Reader*. The book was an imitation of one of the most popular elocution manuals of the day, *Enfield's Speaker*. William Enfield, head of Warrington Dissent in Academy, had written a book for his male students that would provide elocutionary models for teaching public speaking and writing. On the title page *The Female Reader* is attributed to a popular writer of conduct books; however, it was Wollstonecraft who wrote the preface and four short entries, and who arranged the other selections from published sources.

In November 1789 Wollstonecraft's old friend from Newington Green Dr. Richard Price delivered the annual address to the Society for Commemorating the Glorious Revolution of 1688 at the Dissenting Meeting House on the Old Jewry. Edmund Burke, a Whig statesman and writer, responded to Price's enthusiasm with a commendation of the man and the events to which he was paying homage. His famous pamphlet *Reflections on the Revolution in France* glorifies hereditary monarchy, aristocracy, and property, and condemns the individualism of French liberalism and dissenting religion. Burke offers a vision of collective English traditions in which eternal immutable laws can be found within the principles of religion and the hierarchy of a paternally controlled family.

Thirty days after the publication of Burke's pamphlet, Wollstonecraft's *A Vindication of the Rights of Men* (1790) appeared. It was written as a letter and was the first reply by an English radical writer to the challenge offered by Burke. Her authorship of the pamphlet was not known until the second edition, which appeared within a month. The pamphlet was well received, praised by reviewers for its eager warmth and positiveness. Suddenly Wollstonecraft was the center of attention, both within the Johnson circle and for the British press, who found her bold indignation infectious and her tone representative of a general consternation at Burke's hyperbolic rhetoric and political complacency.

When Johnson published Wollstonecraft's revision of the first edition of *A Vindication of the Rights of Men* on 14 December 1790, political expectations in Britain and France had shifted but so had those of the author. She wrote the second edition in the first person instead of the third, added examples from her family experience, and ended the work with an attack on what she saw as hypocritical liberals who agitated for equality but who had been subservient to British authority. Wollstonecraft sent a copy of the second edition to Price, and he acknowledged his pleasure in such an advocate. During this same period the three volumes of her translation from German of Christian Gotthilf Salzmann's *Elements of Morality, for the Use of Children* appeared, as did the second edition of *Original Stories*, with the Blake illustrations. Johnson now promoted her to editorial assistant of the *Analytical Review*, which meant she could choose the reviews she wanted to write as well as make assignments to other writers. After years of obscurity, struggles with indebtedness, and personal defeat, the opportunities of a new world of success and acclaim greeted Wollstonecraft. The multitude of possibilities unleashed in France seemed to be mirrored in her own career and in her personal life. She had established her own voice after years of writing anonymously or in forms dictated by others, and she could now openly declare her independence to her sisters, despite their still being a financial burden upon her.

Such freedom from family also had implications for her personal life. She could openly discuss her relationship with a painter and member of the Johnson circle, Henri Fuseli. From 1778 to 1790, Wollstonecraft and Fuseli had been seeing each other at least once a week and often daily. Although he was married, she saw no reason for that to be an impediment to unite herself to his mind. She consistently referred to their relationship as the meeting of two geniuses. Fuseli was the center of her new life, and, as William Godwin states, she made light of any difficulties such a relationship might create for either of them. During this period she also abandoned her shabby rooms for more spacious lodgings in Store Street on Bedford Square, only a few blocks from Fuseli's home, and she gave up her old ascetic habit of wearing black dresses. In 1791 she sat for a portrait commissioned by William Roscoe. Indeed, 1791 and 1792 were to be important years in Wollstonecraft's career.

In 1791 she had written to her good friend William Roscoe—a Liverpool businessman with radical political leanings—that she was beginning a new book. *A Vindication of the Rights of Woman* was intended as a two-volume work, with the second volume to focus on the legal and political situations of women. The second volume was never published; however, volume one sold well and was widely read and reviewed.

The book, like *A Vindication of the Rights of Men*, responded to a particular set of social and political events and personalities within Britain and in revolutionary France. In France, Charles-Maurice de Talleyrand-Périgord had just presented his Report on Public Instruction to the National Assembly in September 1791. It made no provision for woman's education. In fact, girls were to be educated with boys only until the age of eight and thereafter were to remain home in domestic employment. The immediate aim of Wollstonecraft's essay was to point out how little the French revolutionaries were doing to change the subordinate status of women, both in their attempts at political and education reform. Also, Wollstonecraft set out to attack Rousseau's *Emile*, (1762), a book she had previously admired. She now saw his educational schema as an attempt to degrade one half of the human species, and render women pleasing at the expense of every other virtue. Rhetorically, Wollstonecraft uses the essay to critique these two public figures in the same way she critiqued Burke; they become representative of a particular political and ideological position that degrades women.

A Vindication of the Rights of Woman also responded to the changing education of and literature for women in the later decades of the eighteenth century. Throughout the 1780s Wollstonecraft had the opportunity to read the major women novelists of the period, and her critiques for the *Analytical Review* had forced her to read most of the publications devoted to woman's education. She also wanted *A Vindication of the Rights of Woman* to add to the growing public debate over the role of education for women. This debate had reached the pages of the *Analytical Review* in a long and enthusiastic reaction Wollstonecraft had written to Catherine Macaulay's *Letters on Education, with Observations on Religious and Metaphysical Subjects* (1783).

With the completion of *A Vindication of the Rights of Woman*, Wollstonecraft returned to writing for the *Analytical Review* and concentrated her energies on her relationship with Fuseli. In November 1792 she proposed to Henry and Sophia Fuseli a social, but not sexual, menage a trois. She wrote to Sophia that being above deceit, I find that I cannot live without the satisfaction of seeing and conversing with him daily. Her overtures were rejected. She then decided to leave London, to travel to France, and to abandon her plans for a second volume of *A Vindication of the Rights of Woman*. She had tried to travel to France earlier in the year with Joseph Johnson and the Fuselis; however, they turned back because of the turmoil of revolutionary events. She now decided to go on her own and on 8 December 1792 left for Dover.

Sometime during February or early March of 1793 Mary Wollstonecraft met Gilbert Imlay, an American explorer, writer, and entrepreneur. Imlay was a former army officer in the American Revolutionary army who had written *A Topographical Description of the Western Territory of North America* (1792). He was in Paris on commercial business. Both shared liberal political views and met through connections within the expatriate community in Paris. By

all accounts she was immediately drawn to him; in fact Godwin states that she gave loose to all the sensibilities of her nature. They quickly became lovers, for by May 1793, when the Girondins fell, Wollstonecraft was registered as Imlay's wife at the American embassy. By this time it was becoming unsafe for British citizens to remain in Paris, and in June they moved to the suburban village of Neuilly. Imlay's business plans kept him traveling, and in Wollstonecraft's letters to him during this period one is given a full record of her emotional need for stability and her hopes for happiness. The letters are at once tender, demanding, and lavish in their unabashed sentimentality.

Wollstonecraft had very good reason to distrust Imlay, for as the months at Neuilly passed and her pregnancy confined her to the cottage, she found him spending more and more time traveling. In January 1794 Wollstonecraft pursued Imlay to Le Havre, and she finished her book on the French Revolution there. Her letters to him from this period give a clear indication of her complex feelings: her desire for affection, her confidence in their relationship as a form of sanity in a world gone mad, and her intense fear of abandonment and a growing sense that he embodied all the tensions to be found in her past disappointments with family and friends. On 14 May 1794 Wollstonecraft gave birth to a daughter, Fanny, named after Fanny Blood. Soon after Fanny's birth Imlay moved to Paris, and Wollstonecraft followed, but she was to spend the winter in Paris alone as Imlay had gone to London. She tried to make him return to Paris, and when this failed, she tried to join him in London in April 1795. She found him living with another woman, and in May of that year she attempted suicide, probably by taking laudanum.

Imlay responded, but not by agreeing to live with her. Instead, he suggested a distraction and a chance to reflect on her situation by undertaking a voyage to Scandinavia on his behalf. The shipping business he had embarked on when they were living in Le Havre had run into difficulties, and Imlay suggested Wollstonecraft go as his agent to sort out the problems with his business partner, Elias Backman, who was living in Goteborg, Sweden. Wollstonecraft, Fanny, and a French maid, Marguerite, sailed from Hull to Goteborg in late June and, after traveling along the southern Swedish and Norwegian coasts, crossed to Denmark. They returned to London via Hamburg in early October 1795, at a time when the rest of Europe was at war with France, and most travel was considered dangerous.

Wollstonecraft's mission was to try to recover a ship and its valuable cargo, both belonging to Imlay. This ship was packed with silver and had been appro-

priated and sold by its Norwegian captain, Peder El-
lefsen, of Risor. The ship and its cargo represented the
greater part of Imlay's assets, and to lose it would have
meant ruin. The irony of Wollstonecraft's journey
would not have been lost on her, for her assignment
was to discover the fate of the ship, the attitudes of
all parties concerned, and to try to come to a financial
settlement that would save Imlay's faltering fortunes
and, she thought, their relationship. The delicate negotiations were difficult and finally unsuccessful, but
all this is not mentioned in Wollstonecraft's account
of the journey, published in *Letters Written During a
Short Residence in Sweden, Norway, and Denmark*
(1796).

On 4 October 1795 Wollstonecraft returned to
London to attempt another reconciliation with Imlay,
only to find him living with a young actress. The next
day she attempted suicide by walking in the rain until
her clothing was sodden and then leaping into the
Thames River from Putney Bridge. Two fishermen
close by pulled her out and revived her; her friends
the Christies then took her to their home to recuperate. For the next few weeks she continued to write to
Imlay, but by the spring of 1796 she was able to see
that her relationship with him was self-destructive. She
may also have come to understand how, in her relationship with Imlay, she was her mother's daughter.

Wollstonecraft again had to find some way to
support herself, her daughter, and her French maid,
Marguerite. She resumed writing for the *Analytical
Review* and moved her family to rooms in Pentonville,
a suburb in north London. On 8 January 1796 she
renewed her acquaintance with William Godwin at a
tea party given by her new friend Mary Hays. Their
relationship developed slowly over the next months,
but by July, as Godwin writes, friendship was melting
into love. Wollstonecraft took new rooms near Godwin's in Somers Town, and by the middle of August
they had become lovers. Their letters from this period
provide a portrait of Wollstonecraft full of fears and
doubts about the choice she had made, while Godwin
provides an unquestioning loyalty. The letters show
that Wollstonecraft had found a friend who respected
her and whom she could respect, providing her with
the support and encouragement that she had sought
for so long in others. When she found that she was
pregnant, Godwin and Wollstonecraft married at St.
Pancras Church on 29 March 1797. Godwin agreed
to the ceremony despite his own stated opposition to
marriage. During the late spring and early summer
months of 1797, Wollstonecraft's letters are marked
by a calm self-confidence and a pleasure in their widening circle of friends.

At this time she served as Johnson's editorial
assistant on the *Analytical Review* and was writing a
novel. It was a fictional presentation of the material
in the promised second volume of *A Vindication of
the Rights of Woman*, in which the injustices of the
British legal system and the tyranny of marriage were
to be demonstrated. The novel was to be called *Maria;
or, The Wrongs of Woman*. Wollstonecraft began work
on it in the spring of 1796, but the novel was only
about one-third completed at the time of her death
in 1797. Godwin published it in *Posthumous Works of
the Author of A Vindication of the Rights of Woman*
(1798), adding his own preface, notes, and appendix.

During the summer of 1797 Wollstonecraft was
planning for the birth of her second child with a sense
of expectation and confidence. During her previous
pregnancy she had written *Origin and Progress of the
French Revolution*; now she sought to complete two
projects: *Maria* and a book, in the form of letters or
lessons, on pregnancy and the Management of Infants. She and Godwin were expecting a boy and had
selected his name, William. At 5 A.M. on Wednesday,
30 August, Wollstonecraft felt the first twinges of labor. At 11:30 A.M. she gave birth to a girl, Mary, the
future author of *Frankenstein* (1817). Eleven days after
the birth, Wollstonecraft died of septicemia.

Concise Dictionary of British Literary Biography, Vol. 3 (adapted)

Woolf, Virginia Stephen (1882–1941), English
novelist, critic, and essayist. Virginia Woolf ranks as one
of England's most distinguished writers of the period
between World War I and World War II. Her novels
can perhaps best be described as impressionistic.

Dissatisfied with the novel based on familiar,
factual, and external details, Virginia Woolf followed
experimental clues to a more internal, subjective, and
in a sense more personal rendering of experience than
had been provided by Henry James, Marcel Proust,
and James Joyce. In the works of these masters the
reality of time and experience had formed the stream
of consciousness, a concept that probably originated
with William James. Virginia Woolf lived in and responded to a world in which certitudes were collaps-
ing under the stresses of changing knowledge, the civilized savagery of war, and new manners and morals.
She drew on her personal, sensitive, poetic awareness
without rejecting altogether the heritage of literary
culture she derived from her family.

Early Years and Marriage. Virginia Stephen
was born in London on Jan. 25, 1882. She was the
daughter of Sir Leslie Stephen, a famous scholar and
agnostic philosopher who, among many literary oc-

cupations, was at one time editor of *Cornhill Magazine* and the *Dictionary of National Biography.* James Russell Lowell, the American poet, was her godfather. Virginia's mother died when the child was 12 or 13 years old, and she was educated at home in her father's library, where she also met his famous friends.

In 1912, eight years after her father's death, Virginia married Leonard Woolf, a brilliant young writer and critic from Cambridge whose interests in literature as well as in economics and the labor movement were well suited to hers. In 1917, for amusement, they originated the Hogarth Press by setting and handprinting on an old press *Two Stories* by "L. and V. Woolf." The volume was a success, and over the years they published many important books, including *Prelude* by Katherine Mansfield, then an unknown writer; *Poems* by T. S. Eliot; and *Kew Gardens* by Virginia Woolf. The policy of the Hogarth Press was to publish the best and most original work that came to its attention, and the Woolfs as publishers favored young and obscure writers. Virginia's older sister Vanessa, who married the critic Clive Bell, participated in this venture by designing dust jackets for the books issued by the Hogarth Press.

Quite early in her career Virginia Woolf's home in Tavistock Square, Bloomsbury, became a literary and art center, attracting such diverse intellectuals as E. M. Forster, Lytton Strachey, Arthur Waley, Victoria Sackville-West, John Maynard Keynes, and Roger Fry. These artists, critics, and writers became known as the Bloomsbury group. Roger Fry's theory of art may have influenced Virginia's technique as a novelist. Broadly speaking, the Bloomsbury group drew from the philosophic interests of its members (who had been educated at Cambridge) the values of love and beauty as preeminent in life.

As Critic and Essayist. Virginia Woolf began writing essays for the *Times Literary Supplement* when she was young, and over the years these and other essays were collected in a two-volume series called *The Common Reader* (1925, 1933). These studies range with affection and understanding through all of English literature. Students of fiction have drawn upon these criticisms as a means of understanding Virginia Woolf's own direction as a novelist. One passage frequently studied occurs in "Modern Fiction" in the *First Series:* "Life is not a series of . . . big lamps symmetrically arranged; but a luminous halo, a semitransparent envelope surrounding us from the beginning of consciousness to the end. Is it not the task of the novelist to convey this varying, this unknown and uncircumscribed spirit, whatever aberration or complex-

ity it may display, with as little mixture of the alien and external as possible?"

Another essay frequently studied is "Mr. Bennett and Mrs. Brown," written in 1924, in which Virginia Woolf describes the manner in which the older-generation novelist Arnold Bennett would have portrayed Mrs. Brown, a lady casually met in a railway carriage, by giving her a house and furniture and a position in the world. She then contrasts this method with another: one that exhibits a new interest in the subjective Mrs. Brown, the mysteries of her person, her consciousness, and the consciousness of the observer responding to her.

Achievement as Novelist. Two of Virginia Woolf's novels in particular, *Mrs. Dalloway* (1925) and *To the Lighthouse* (1927), follow successfully the latter approach. The first novels covers a day in the life of Mrs. Dalloway in postwar London; it achieves its vision of reality through the reception by Mrs. Dalloway's mind of what Virginia Woolf called those 'myriad impressionstrivial, fantastic, evanescent, or engraved with the sharpness of steel." *To the Lighthouse* is, in a sense, a family portrait and history rendered in subjective depth through selected points in time. Part I deals with the time between six o'clock in the evening and dinner. Primarily through the consciousness of Mrs. Ramsay, it presents the clash of the male and female sensibilities in the family; Mrs. Ramsay functions as a means of equipoise and reconciliation. Part II: Time Passes, is a moving evocation of loss during the interval between Mrs. Ramsay's death and the family's revisit to the house. Part III moves toward completion of this intricate and subjective portrait through the adding of a last detail to a painting by an artist guest, Lily Briscoe, and through the final completion of a plan, rejected by the father in Part I, for him and the children to sail out to the lighthouse. The novel is impressionistic, subjectively perceptive, and poignant.

Last Years and Other Books. Virginia Woolf was the author of about 15 books, the last, *A Writer's Diary,* posthumously published in 1953. Her death by drowning in Lewes, Sussex, on March 28, 1941, has often been regarded as a suicide brought on by the unbearable strains of life during World War II. The true explanation seems to be that she had felt symptoms of a recurrence of a mental breakdown and feared that it would be permanent.

Mrs. Dalloway, To the Lighthouse, and *Jacob's Room* (1922) constitute Virginia Woolf's major achievement. *The Voyage Out* (1915) first brought her critical attention. *Night and Day* (1919) is traditional in method. The short stories of *Monday or Tuesday* (1921) brought critical praise. In *The Waves* (1931) she masterfully employed the stream-of-consciousness technique. Other experimental novels include *Orlando* (1928), *The Years* (1937), and *Between the Acts* (1941). Virginia Woolf's championship of woman's rights is reflected in the essays in *A Room of One's Own* (1929) and in *Three Guineas* (1938).

EWB

Wundt, Wilhelm Max (1832–1920), German psychologist and philosopher. Wilhelm Wundt was the founder of experimental psychology. He edited the first journal of experimental psychology and established the first laboratory of experimental psychology.

Wilhelm Wundt was born on Aug. 16, 1832, in Baden, in a suburb of Mannheim called Neckarau. As a child, he was tutored by Friedrich Müller. Wundt attended the gymnasium at Bruschel and at Heidelberg, the University of Tübingen for a year, then Heidelberg for more than 3 years, receiving a medical degree in 1856. He remained at Heidelberg as a lecturer in physiology from 1857 to 1864, then was appointed assistant professor in physiology. The great physiologist, physicist, and physiological psychologist Hermann von Helmholtz came there in 1858, and Wundt for a while was his assistant.

During the period from 1857 to 1874 Wundt evolved from a physiologist to a psychologist. In these years he also wrote *Grundzüge der physiologischen psychologie* (*Principles of Physiological Psychology*). The two-volume work, published in 1873–1874, stressed the relations between psychology and physiology, and it showed how the methods of natural science could be used in psychology. Six revised editions of this work were published, the last completed in 1911.

As a psychologist, Wundt used the method of investigating conscious processes in their own context by "experiment" and introspection. This technique has been referred to as content psychology, reflecting Wundt's belief that psychology should concern itself with the immediate content of experience unmodified by abstraction or reflection.

In 1874 Wundt left Heidelberg for the chair of inductive philosophy at Zurich, staying there only a year. He accepted the chair of philosophy at the University of Leipzig, and in 1879 he founded the first psychological laboratory in the world. To Leipzig, men came from all over the world to study in Wundt's laboratory. In 1879 G. Stanley Hall, Wundt's first American student, arrived, followed by many other Americans. From this first laboratory for experimental psychology a steady stream of psychologists returned to their own countries to teach and to continue their researches. Some founded psychological laboratories of their own.

In 1881 Wundt founded *Philosophische Studien* as a vehicle for the new experimental psychology, especially as a publication organ for the products of his psychological laboratory. The contents of *Philosophische Studien* (changed to *Psychologische Studien* in 1903) reveal that the experiments fell mainly into four categories: sensation and perception; reaction time; time perception and association; and attention, memory, feeling, and association. Optical phenomena led with 46 articles; audition was second in importance. Sight and hearing, which Helmholtz had already carefully studied, were the main themes of Wundt's laboratory. Some of the contributions to the *Studien* were by Wundt himself. Helmholtz is reported to have said of some of Wundt's experiments that they were *schlampig* (sloppy). Comparing Wundt to Helmholtz, who was a careful experimentalist and productive researcher, one must conclude that Wundt's most important contributions were as a systematizer, organizer, and encyclopedist. William James considered Wundt "only a rather ordinary man who has worked up certain things uncommonly well."

Wundt's *Grundriss der Psychologie* (1896; *Outline of Psychology*) was a less detailed treatment than his *Principles,* but it contained the new theory of feeling. A popular presentation of his system of psychology was *Einführung in die Psychologie* (1911; *Introduction to Psychology*). His monumental *Völkerpsychologie* (1912; *Folk Psychology*), a natural history of man, attempted to understand man's higher thought processes by studying language, art, mythology, religion, custom, and law. Besides his psychological works he wrote three philosophical texts: *Logic* (1880–1883), *Ethics* (1886), and *System of Philosophy* (1889). Wundt died near Leipzig on Aug. 31, 1920.

EWB

Z

Zetkin, Clara (1857–1933), German political activist. Clara Zetkin was a prominent member of socialist and communist organizations in Europe in the nineteenth and twentieth centuries. As a longtime supporter of the German Social Democratic Party, she argued that equality of women could only be accomplished through a class revolution that overthrew the capitalist system. She later was a founder of the German Communist Party and became a respected political ally of Vladimir Lenin in the Soviet Union.

Clara Zetkin was a distinguished member of Socialist and Communist organizations in Europe in the late 1800s and early 1900s. Throughout her political career, she focused on the liberation of women in society through Marxist reforms of the capitalist system. For many years she promoted her radical thought as the editor of *Die Gleichheit*, the women's journal of the German Social Democratic Party. In her later years, Zetkin served as both a representative of the German Communist Party in the Reichstag legislative body and as an associate of Vladimir Ilich Lenin in the Soviet Union.

Zetkin was born Clara Eissner on July 5, 1857, in Wiederau, near Leipzig, Germany. She was the oldest of the three children of Gottfried Eissner, a schoolteacher and church organist, and Josephine Vitale Eissner, Gottfried's second wife, who was the widow of a local doctor. Josephine Eissner was active in women's education societies and a believer in equal rights and economic power for women. Her work was inspired by feminist organizations, including the German Women's Association and the Federation of German Women's Associations, led by women's rights activists such as Auguste Schmidt and Luise Otto. When Eissner was 15, her father retired and the family moved to Leipzig, where she was enrolled at Schmidt and Otto's Van Steyber Institute in 1875. She studied there until 1878, and her activities during these years included reading socialist newspapers and books and attending meetings of the Leipzig Women's Education Society and the National Association of German Women. These areas of feminist and socialist thought became the focus of her lifelong political activities.

Joined German Social Democrats. In 1878, Zetkin befriended some students from Russia, who introduced her to the political ideals of the German Social Democratic Party, or SPD. One of her new associates was Ossip Zetkin, a native of Odessa, Russia. Ossip Zetkin acted as a political mentor, teaching her about the writings of Karl Marx and Friedrich Engels and the ideas of scientific socialism. At his suggestion, she began to attend meetings of the Leipzig Workers' Education Society and reject her bourgeois lifestyle, which ultimately led to a split with her family and her feminist mentor, Auguste Schmidt. In 1879, Zetkin traveled to Russia to observe the activities of Marxist groups there.

These experiences gave Zetkin a strong sympathy for the proletariat struggle and she decided to devote her life to the Marxist reform of society. Due to a German law forbidding women to join political parties, she could not become an official member of the SPD, but she spent all her energies supporting its cause. After the passage of the 1878 Anti-Socialist Law in Germany, Ossip Zetkin was forced to leave the country, and Zetkin decided to leave as well. She first traveled to Linz, Austria, where she worked as a tutor of factory workers. She joined a group of SPD members in Zurich in 1882 to write propaganda to sneak into Germany. In November of that year, she was reunited with Ossip Zetkin in Paris. The two lived together and eventually had two sons, Maxim and Konstantine, but were never officially married because Zetkin did not want to give up her German citizenship. She did, however, adopt his surname, and remained Ossip's companion until the end of his life.

Linked Women's Rights to Social Revolution. In Paris, Zetkin began to concentrate on combining her interests in socialism and feminism in an attempt to accomplish equality for working women in the proletariat movement. Her return to feminist issues also led her to reestablish ties with her family, who came to her assistance after Zetkin contracted tuberculosis due to her impoverished conditions in Paris. Her family took her into their home at Leipzig while she recovered, and it was in Leipzig that she gave her first public speech on the liberation of women and all workers through a class revolution. She believed that once class equality was established in a Marxist society, the economic and social oppression of women would naturally come to an end. Because of this line of thought, for many years she fought against special provisions and laws to protect women in the workplace; her thought was that becoming satisfied with such measures would detract from the focus on a total restructuring of the class system. After her convalescence, Zetkin returned to Paris to nurse Ossip, who was suffering from spinal tuberculosis. He never recovered and died in January of 1889.

Zetkin overcame her grief at her partner's death by immersing herself in her political work. Her preoccupation with the socialist cause was so great, in fact, that rearing her two sons constituted her only personal considerations for many years. She would later be married to the painter Georg Friedrich Zundel, a man 18 years her junior. The marriage, which began in 1899, began to disintegrate during World War I and ended in divorce in 1927, primarily due to Zetkin's overwhelming commitment to her work. She became one of the leading women in the socialist movement and in July of 1889 served as one of the eight women delegates who attended the Second International Congress in Paris. She was there as a representative of the working class women of Berlin, Germany, and in a speech before the Congress, she clearly outlined the ideas in support of women's equality that she had been developing. Her speech, later published as *Working Women and the Contemporary Women*

Question, reiterated her belief that she and her comrades should not focus on winning specific rights for women, such as education or economic equality, but should instead concentrate on ending the capitalist system that oppressed women and all workers. In a move that foreshadowed her growing differences with her fellow socialists, the Congress did not support her extremism, voting in favor of equal pay for equal work by women and voicing opposition to hazardous labor by women. This stance did not undermine Zetkin's role in the party, however. She was selected during the Congress to help lead recruiting and education efforts for the SPD in Berlin; she and six other women returned to Germany to found the Berlin Agitation Committee.

Edited Socialist Journal for Women. With the expiration of the Anti-Socialist Law in 1890, SPD members were allowed to return to Germany. Zetkin received another assignment from the party at this time, editing an SPD journal for women. The first issue of *Die Gleichheit* appeared in January of 1892, and under Zetkin's guidance, the journal set an agenda reflecting her beliefs in spreading socialist and Marxist thought among women and fighting the kind of feminist legal reforms supported by bourgeois women's groups. Still forbidden by law from direct membership in the SPD, Zetkin became active in a less direct method of advocating socialism and recruiting women trade unionism. She helped to link unions in Germany with international organizations and organized strike funds in addition to giving hundreds of speeches. Her involvement with working people helped to moderate some of her views. At an 1896 SPD conference, she gave her support to measures protecting working mothers and advocating women's right to vote.

In general though, Zetkin refused to compromise her rigid adherence to Marxist ideology. After 1900, other members of the SPD were increasingly drawn to a revisionist interpretation of Marx's thought that proposed working within the legal system to accomplish reform. Revisionists saw Zetkin as too theoretical in her journal, and she was instructed to modify *Die Gleichheit* to reach a more general audience, including housewives and children. But although many complained about Zetkin, she was well established in the party and was in no danger of being removed. In 1895 she had become the first woman in the SPD governing body and in 1906 she was named to the central committee on education.

In 1908, women in Germany were given the right to join political parties. Zetkin felt that bringing women into the SPD would result in them being voiceless in an organization run by men, so she worked to form a separate women's group within the party. To this end, she participated in the first International Women's Conferences in 1907 and 1910 and became secretary of the International Women's Bureau, a group which adopted *Die Gleichheit* as its official publication. But her work in this area did not erase the tensions between her and the revisionists. World War I brought the conflict to the forefront. Zetkin, along with other radicals in the party, such as Rosa Luxemburg, wanted the SPD to condemn the imperialist stance of Germany and its military activities. When the party voted to support the government, Zetkin opposed the move in a series of writings in *Die Gleichheit,* resulting in her removal from the post of editor in 1917. Zetkin left the party to join antiwar socialists in the Independent Social-Democratic Party. Later she and three other radical socialists formed the Gruppe Internationale, also known as the Sparticus League, which became the German Communist Party, or KPD, in November of 1918.

Active in Communist Party. Although her political affiliation had changed, Zetkin's goals remained the same. At the 1919 Third International Congress, she gave a speech emphasizing the importance of having educated women as an active force in the international Communist struggle. In 1920 she was elected the international secretary for Communist women, a post in which she continued to argue that women's issues could only be addressed through reforms for all workers. In the years after World War I, her active role in Communist politics took her to the Soviet Union frequently. There she was an important ally of Soviet Communist leader Vladimir Lenin. She also held a post in the German Reichstag as a member of the KPD. As its oldest member, she was given the honor of convening the legislative body in 1932, and she used to occasion to speak out against Nazi leader Adolf Hitler and his Fascist policies.

Zetkin suffered from poor health in her later years, and she died outside of Moscow in the Soviet Union on June 20, 1933. She was honored with an elaborate funeral and buried in the Kremlin wall. The services were attended by leading Communists from across Europe, including Joseph Stalin and Nadezhda Krupskaya, the widow of Lenin. The presence of such luminaries demonstrated the importance of the life and work of Zetkin to supporters of Communism throughout the world.

EWB

Zola, Émile (1840–1902), French novelist. Émile Zola was the foremost proponent of the doctrine of naturalism in literature. He illustrated this doctrine chiefly in a series of 20 novels published between 1871 and 1893 under the general title *Les Rougon-Macquart*.

Shortly after his birth in Paris on April 2, 1840, Émile Zola was taken to the south of France by his father, a gifted engineer of Venetian extraction, who had formed a company to supply Aix-en-Provence with a source of fresh water. He died before the project had been completed, leaving his widow to struggle with an increasingly difficult financial situation. Despite this, Émile's boyhood and schooling at Aix were, on the whole, a happy period of his life. He retained a lasting affection for the sunbaked countryside of this part of France. One of his closest friends at school and his companion on many a summer's ramble was Paul Cézanne, the future painter.

Early Years in Paris. In 1858 Zola and his mother moved to Paris, where he completed his rather sketchy education. He never succeeded in passing his *baccalauréat* examinations. For a few years after leaving school, he led a life of poverty verging on destitution. Finally, in 1862, he was given a job in the publishing firm of Hachette, which he kept for 4 years. Here he learned much about the business and promotional sides of publishing and met several distinguished writers, among them the philosopher and literary historian Hippolyte Taine, whose ideas strongly influenced the development of Zola's thought. It was one of Taine's sayings ("Vice and virtue are chemical products like vitriol and sugar") that Zola took as the epigraph of his early novel *Thérèse Raquin* (1867). The formula was well suited to the uncompromising materialism that imbues this macabre story of adultery, murder, and suicide.

Les Rougon-Macquart. About 1868–1869, when Zola was working as a freelance journalist, he conceived the idea of writing a series of interlinked novels tracing the lives of various members of a single family whose fortunes were to counterpoint the rise and fall of the Second Empire (1852–1870). He proposed in particular to demonstrate how the forces of heredity might influence the character and development of each individual descendant of a common ancestress. The scheme enabled him to apportion to each novel the analysis of a particular section of society, ranging from the upper stratum of high finance and ministerial authority down to the suffering masses starving in the slums or toiling in the mines. *Les Rougon-Macquart* was originally planned in ten volumes; but the design was so obviously promising that Zola eventually extended it to twice that number. The volumes were designed as social documents rather

than as pure works of fiction, but his powerfully emotive imagination and primitive symbolism conferred on the best of them, nonetheless, many of the qualities of expressionistic prose poetry.

The first six volumes were largely ignored by the critics, although they included some powerful pieces of social satire. For example, *La Curée* (1872) dealt with real estate speculation; *Le Ventre de Paris* (1873) attacked the pusillanimous conservatism of the small-shopkeeper class; and *Son Excellence Eugène Rougon* (1876) was an exposure of political jobbery. Only with the seventh, *L'Assommoir* (1877), did Zola finally produce a best seller that made him one of the most talked of writers in France and one of the most bitterly assailed. The plot of this novel is almost nonexistent. He contented himself with tracing the life story of a simpleminded, good-hearted laundress who lived in a working-class district in the north of Paris. By dint of hard work she achieves at first a modest prosperity, until her husband's increasing fecklessness and addiction to drink drag her down to utter destitution. For the title of his novel Zola used a contemporary slang word for a liquor store. The problem of alcoholism among the poor looms large in the book, as do the related problems of overcrowded housing conditions, prostitution, and the risk of starvation during the periods of prolonged unemployment. Though in no sense a work of propaganda, *L'Assommoir* succeeded in drawing attention to the wretched conditions in which the urban proletariat had been living throughout the 19th century.

Succeeding volumes of the *Rougon-Macquart* cycle included many others that were universally read, even though savagely condemned by conservative critics. *Nana* (1880) dealt with the lives of the demimondaines and their wealthy, dissipated clients. The heroine's career was modeled on the careers of a number of successful courtesans of the heyday of the Second Empire. *Germinal* (1885), doubtless Zola's masterpiece, narrated the preliminaries, outbreak, and aftermath of a coal miners' strike in northeast France; it was the first novel in which the possibility of a social revolution launched by the proletariat against the middle classes was seriously mooted. In his descriptions of the dangerous daily labor in the pits and of the rioting of the exasperated strikers, Zola achieved effects of agony and terror of a kind never before realized in literature. *La Terre* (1887) represents his attempt to do for the farm laborer what he had done for the miner in *Germinal.* The picture of rural life he offered was anything but idyllic, rape and murder being shown as the inevitable concomitants of the narrowness of the peasant's horizons and his atavistic land hunger. Finally, *La Débâcle* (1892) gave an epic dignity to the story of France's calamitous defeat at the hands of the Prussians in 1870.

Naturalism in Theory and Practice. The immense sales of his works enabled Zola, by 1878, to purchase a property outside Paris, at Médan, a hamlet where he lived quietly for most of the year, occasionally entertaining the younger writers who made up the vanguard of the short-lived naturalist school. Five of them collaborated with him in the production of a volume of short stories issued in 1880 under the title *Soirées de Médan.* Of these five, the two most talented, Guy de Maupassant and Joris Karl Huysmans, forswore their allegiance shortly afterward. Zola did, however, have important disciples outside France: Giovanni Verga in Italy, Eça de Queiros in Portugal, George Moore in England, and Frank Norris and Stephen Crane in the United States.

Zola set out his fundamental theoretical beliefs in *Le Roman expérimental* (1880), but even he adhered very loosely to them in practice. Naturalism embraced many of the tenets of the older realist movement, such as an interest in average types rather than above-average individuals, the cultivation of a pessimistic and disillusioned outlook, a studious avoidance of surprising incident, and a strict obedience to consequential logic in plot development. The special innovation of naturalism lay in its attempt to fuse science with literature. This meant, in practice, that human behavior had to be interpreted along strictly materialistic or physiological lines ("the soul being absent," as Zola put it) and that the individual was to be shown as totally at the mercy of twin external forces, heredity and environment. The emphasis placed on environment accounts for the immense pains that Zola took to document the setting he proposed to use in any particular novel.

Last Years. Zola's private life was not free of strains. He married in 1870, but this union was childless. Then, in 1888, he set up a second home with a young seamstress, who bore him two children. This unexpected blossoming of domestic happiness probably accounts for the sunnier tone of the books he wrote after the completion of *Les Rougon-Macquart.* They included a trilogy, *Lourdes, Rome,* and *Paris* (1894–1898), dealing with the conflict between science and religion, and a tetralogy of utopian novels, *Les Quatre Évangiles,* of which only the first three were completed.

Zola's dramatic intervention on behalf of Alfred Dreyfus carried his name even further than had his literary work. Dreyfus, a Jewish officer in the French army, had been wrongfully condemned for espionage in 1894, and with much courage and recklessness of consequences Zola challenged the findings of the court-martial in an open letter to the President of the Republic (*J'accuse,* Jan. 13, 1898). Since his statement charged certain high-ranking army officers with falsification of evidence, Zola was put on trial. He lost his case, spent a year in hiding in England, and returned to France on June 5, 1899. His sudden death in Paris on Sept. 29, 1902, from carbon monoxide poisoning may not have been accidental as the inquest found. There is reason to believe that he was the victim of an assassination plot engineered by a few of the more fanatical of his political enemies.

EWB

Zwingli, Huldreich (1484–1531), Swiss Protestant reformer. Huldreich Zwingli paved the way for the Swiss Reformation. His influence on the church-state relations of the cantons that became Protestant was profound and durable.

An exact contemporary of Martin Luther, Huldreich Zwingli experienced and contributed to the profound changes in religious and intellectual life that, arising in the early 1500s, permanently affected Western civilization. He was born on Jan. 1, 1484, in the village of Wildhaus, one of ten children. His experience with ecclesiastical traditions came early, through an uncle who was a priest. Huldreich was destined by his parents for the priesthood.

Early Years and Education. Zwingli's education was markedly humanistic. In 1494 he was sent to school at Basel and in 1498 to Bern, where a famous classicist, Heinrich Wölflin, fired a love in him for ancient writers, including the pagans, that he never lost. In 1500 Zwingli entered the University of Vienna to study philosophy, and there too the ideals of humanism were nurtured and deepened in him, for at that time the university boasted the presence of Conradus Celtes, one of the leading scholars of the humanistic tradition. Zwingli also acquired a deep appreciation and understanding of music and learned to play several instruments.

At the age of 18 Zwingli was again in Basel, where he studied theology. In 1506 he received his master's degree and was ordained a priest by the bishop of Constance. After celebrating his first Mass at Wildhaus, he was elected parish priest of Glarus a few miles away. He spent ten years in Glarus, a decade that in several important respects formed the most decisive period of his life. He developed his character as a reformer, his knowledge and love of Greek, his admiration for the great humanist Erasmus, and his bitterness at the corruption in the Church. Zwingli became so enamored of Homer, Pindar, Democritus, and Julius Caesar that he refused to believe that they and other great pagans were unredeemed because they had not known Christ.

By 1516, when Zwingli moved to Einsiedeln in the canton of Schwyz, he was already arriving at doctrinal opinions divergent from those of Rome. He not only attacked such abuses as the sale of indulgences and the proliferation of false relics but also began to speak openly of a religion based only on the Bible. Independently of Luther, Zwingli concluded that the papacy was unfounded in Scriptures and that Church tradition did not have equal weight with the Bible as a source of Christian truth.

Reformation in Zurich.

Zwingli's preaching was so impressive that he was asked to become the vicar, or people's priest, of the Grossmünster in Zurich. This city bristled with intellectual activity, and on Dec. 10, 1518, he eagerly accepted the offer. At Zurich, under his leadership, the Swiss Reformation began. He preached against the excessive veneration of saints, the celibacy of the priesthood, and fasting. When his parishioners were accused of eating meat during Lent, he defended them before the city council and wrote a forceful tract on the subject. His stand against the celibacy of the clergy brought down the wrath of the bishop of Constance upon him. In 1523 Zwingli admirably defended his position on this topic with 67 theses presented in a public disputation. The city council not only found itself in accord with him but also voted to sever the canton from the bishop's jurisdiction. Thus Zurich adopted the Reformation.

During the 1520s Zwingli wrote much; not all of his writings were theological. Unlike Luther and John Calvin, the Swiss reformer possessed a profound patriotic element, a quality that caused him to inveigh heavily against the pernicious practice of hiring out soldiers to fight as mercenaries in the wars of other nations. In 1521 he convinced Zurich to abolish this policy.

Zwingli's Theology.

The doctrinal matter that set Zwingli apart from Luther on the one hand and Roman Catholicism on the other was that of the Eucharist. Zwingli denied the real presence of Christ in the Host and insisted that the Eucharist was not the repetition of Christ's sacrifice but only a respectful remembrance.

Since Jesus was God as well as man one performance of the act of redemption was enough. Moreover, the Scriptures contain all Christian truth and what cannot be found therein must be ruthlessly cast from the true Church. Thus the concept of purgatory, the hierarchy, the veneration of relics and images, the primacy of the pope, and canon law must all be cast aside. Zwingli expressed these views in the 67 theses of 1523 and in the tract *De vera et falsa religione* of 1525. In general, his theology was absorbed in and superseded by that of Calvin.

Zwingli's disagreement with Luther was fundamental, and after the two reformers met at Marburg in 1529 and had a profitless discussion, it became clear that no unification of their movements could result. Zwingli was also unsuccessful in winning over all of Switzerland to his cause. Uri, Schwyz, Unterwalden, Lucerne, and Zug—the conservative forest cantons—remained faithful to Roman Catholicism and formed a league to fight Protestant movements.

Tensions grew, and civil war threatened in 1529 and then broke out in 1531. Zwingli counseled the war and entered the fray as chaplain at the side of the citizens of Zurich and their allies. He was slain at the battle of Kappel on Oct. 11, 1531. His body was abused by the victorious Catholics, who quartered it and burned it on a heap of manure.

EWB

DIRECTORY OF CONTRIBUTORS

John Agnew is Professor of Geography at the University of California, Los Angeles. He is the author of *Place and Politics* and coeditor of *The Power of Place* and *Human Geography: An Essential Anthology.* He gave the Hettner Lectures at the University of Heidelberg in June 2000 on "Reinventing Geopolitics." PRINCIPLES OF REGIONALISM

Kathleen Alaimo is Associate Professor of History at Saint Xavier University, Chicago. She is coeditor of and a contributor to *Children as Equals: Exploring the Rights of the Child* (forthcoming) and is a member of the editorial board of *History of Education Quarterly.* JUVENILE DELINQUENCY AND HOOLIGANISM

James C. Albisetti is Professor of History at the University of Kentucky. He is the author of *Secondary School Reform in Imperial Germany* (1983), *Schooling German Girls and Women* (1989), "Portia ante Portas: Women and Legal Profession in Europe, ca. 1870–1925" (*Journal of Social History,* 2000), and other essays. PROFESSIONALS AND PROFESSIONALIZATION

Karl Appuhn is a junior fellow at the Columbia University Society of Fellows in the Humanities. He is the author of "Inventing Nature: Forests, Forestry, and State Power in Renaissance Venice" (*The Journal of Modern History*). MICROHISTORY

Amanda Carson Banks is Director of Development and Adjunct Associate Professor in the College of Arts and Letters at California State University, Sacramento. She is the author of *Birth Chairs, Midwives, and Medicine* (1999). CHILDBIRTH, MIDWIVES, WETNURSING

Andrew Barnes teaches European and African History at Arizona State University. He is author of *The Social Dimension of Piety* (1994) and coeditor of *Social History and Issues in Human Consciousness: Some Interdisciplinary Connections* (1989). He has written numerous articles on the historical evolution of Chris-

tian churches in Europe and Africa. CHURCH AND SOCIETY

Jay R. Berkovitz is Professor of Judaic and Near Eastern Studies at the University of Massachusetts at Amherst, where he directs the Center for Jewish Studies. He is the author of *The Shaping of Jewish Identity in Nineteenth-Century France* (1989) and *Rites and Passages: The Making of Jewish Culture in Modern France* (forthcoming). JUDAISM

Jeremy Black is Professor of History at the University of Exeter. He is the author of over thirty-five books, including *Maps and History: Constructing Images of the Past* (1997), *Maps and Politics* (1997), *War and the World: Military Power and the Fate of Continents, 1450–2000* (1998), and *A New History of England* (2000). WAR AND CONQUEST

Constance B. Bouchard is Professor of Medieval History at the University of Akron. She has been a Guggenheim Fellow. Her books include *Sword, Miter, and Cloister: Nobility and the Church in Burgundy, 980–1198* (1987) and *Strong of Body, Brave and Noble: Chivalry and Society in Medieval France* (1998). THE MEDIEVAL HERITAGE

Thomas E. Brennan is Professor of History at the United States Naval Academy. He is author of *Public Drinking and Popular Culture in Eighteenth-Century Paris* (1988) and *Burgundy to Champagne: The Wine Trade in Early Modern France* (1997), which won the Pinkney Prize for best monograph in French history. DRINKING AND DRUGS

Kristine Bruland is Professor of Economic History at the University of Oslo. Her work on history and technology includes *British Technology and European Industrialization: The Norwegian Textile Industry in the Mid-Nineteenth Century* (1989). She is the coeditor, with Maxine Berg, of *Technological Revolutions in Europe: Historical Perspectives* (1998). TECHNOLOGY

Gayle K. Brunelle is Professor of History at California State University, Fullerton. She is the author of *The New World Merchants of Rouen, 1559–1630* (1991) and "Contractual Kin: Women Servants and Their Mistresses in Early Modern Nantes" (*Journal of Early Modern History,* 1998). THE WORLD ECONOMY AND COLONIAL EXPANSION

Maria Bucur is an Assistant Professor and the John V. Hill Chair in East European History at Indiana University. She is the author of "Between the Mother of the Wounded and the Virgin of Jiu: Romanian Women and the Gender of Heroism during the Great War" (*Journal of Women's Studies,* 2000) and coeditor of *Staging the Past: The Politics of Commemoration in Habsburg Central Europe, 1848 to the Present* (forthcoming). She is the recipient of various fellowships, most recently a faculty Fulbright-Hays research grant in 1999. THE BALKANS

Peter Burke is Professor of Cultural History, University of Cambridge, and Fellow of Emmanuel College. He is the author of *Popular Culture in Early Modern Europe* (1978), *The Italian Renaissance: Culture and Society in Italy* (1987), *The Fabrication of Louis XIV* (1992), and *The Art of Conversation* (1993). THE ANNALES PARADIGM; LANGUAGE; POPULAR CULTURE

Nupur Chaudhuri is a history professor at Texas Southern University. She is the coeditor of *Western Women and Imperialism: Complicity and Resistance* (1992), *Nation, Empire, Colony: Historicism, Gender, and Race* (1998), and *Voices of Women Historians: Personal, Professional, and Political* (1999). She is author of several articles on British women in nineteenth-century India. IMPERIALISM AND GENDER

Palle Ove Christiansen is senior lecturer at the Department of History at the University of Copenhagen. He is the author of *A Manorial World: Lord, Peasants, and Cultural Distinctions on a Danish Estate, 1750–1980* (1996) and several books in Danish. At present he writes on cultural history. PEASANT AND FARMING VILLAGES

Anna Clark is Associate Professor of History at the University of Minnesota. She is the author of *Women's Silence, Men's Violence: Sexual Assault in England, 1770–1845* (1987) and *The Struggle for the Breeches: Gender and the Making of the British Working Class* (1995). GENDER AND POPULAR PROTEST

Linda L. Clark is Professor of History at Millersville University. She is the author of *Social Darwinism in*

France (1983), *Schooling the Daughters of Marianne: Textbooks and the Socialization of Girls in Modern French Primary Schools* (1984), and *The Rise of Professional Women in France: Gender and Public Administration since 1830* (forthcoming). She also wrote the introduction to and edited "France since 1789" in *The American Historical Association's Guide to Historical Literature* (1995). GENDER AND EDUCATION

Constance Classen is Distinguished Scholar at Lonergan College, Concordia University, Montreal. Her books include *World of Sense: Exploring the Senses in History and across Cultures* (1993) and *The Color of Angels: Cosmology, Gender, and the Aesthetice Imagination* (1998). She is the coauthor of *Aroma: The Cultural History of Smell.* THE SENSES

Alexander Cowan is Senior Lecturer in History at the University of Northumbria at Newcastle, England. He is the author of *Urban Europe 1500–1700* (1998) and has edited a book of essays, *Mediterranean Urban Culture 1400–1700* (1998). He is currently working on a monograph on women and social distinction in early modern Venice. SUBURBS AND NEW TOWNS; URBANIZATION

Thomas Cragin is Assistant Professor of European History at Widener University. JOURNALISM

Gary S. Cross is Professor of European History at the Pennsylvania State University. He is the author of *Time and Money: The Making of Consumer Culture* (1993) and *An All-Consuming Century* (2000). CONSUMERISM; TOYS AND GAMES; WORK TIME

David M. Crowe is a Professor of History at Elon College. He is President of the Association for the Study of Nationalities and a member of the Education Committee of the United States Holocaust Memorial Museum. He is the author of *The Baltic States and the Great Powers: Foreign Relations, 1938–1940* (1993) and *A History of the Gypsies of Eastern Europe and Russia* (1994), and coeditor of *The Gypsies of Eastern Europe* (1991). ROMA: THE GYPSIES

Rineke van Daalen is senior researcher at the Amsterdam School for Social Research, University of Amsterdam. She is the author of a thesis on public complaints and government intervention, based on letters to the municipal authorities of Amsterdam between 1865 and 1920. She is working on a project concerning children in European welfare states. THE EMOTIONS; DOMESTIC INTERIORS

Charles R. Day is Professor of History at Simon Fraser University in Vancouver, British Columbia. He is author of *Education for the Modern World: The Écoles d'Arts et Métiers and the Rise of French Industrial Engineering* (1987) and *Schools and Work: Technical and Vocational Education in France since the Third Republic* (2001). HIGHER EDUCATION

Alexander De Grand is Professor of History at North Carolina State University. He is the author of *Bottai e la cultura fascista, Italian Fascism: Its Origins and Development* (1982), and *Fascist Italy and Nazi Germany: The Fascist Style of Rule* (1995). FASCISM AND NAZISM

Jonathan Dewald is Professor of History at the State University of New York at Buffalo. He is the author of *The Formation of a Provincial Nobility: The Magistrates of the Parlement of Rouen, 1499–1610* (1980), *Pont-St-Pierre 1398–1789: Lordship, Community, and Capitalism in Early Modern France* (1987), *Aristocratic Experience and the Origins of Modern Culture: France, 1570–1715* (1993), and *The European Nobility, 1400–1800* (forthcoming). THE ARISTOCRACY AND GENTRY; THE EARLY MODERN PERIOD

Brian Dolan is Wellcome Research Lecturer at the University of East Anglia. He is the author of *Exploring European Frontiers: British Travellers in the Age of Enlightenment* (2000). His next book, *Ladies of the Grand Tour,* will be published in 2001. THE ENLIGHTENMENT

Andrew Donson is Visiting Assistant Professor at the University of Nevada–Reno. His dissertation is "War Pedagogy and Youth Culture: Nationalism and Authority in Germany in the First World War" (University of Michigan, 2000). YOUTH AND ADOLESCENCE

Brendan Dooley is Research Coordinator for the Medici Archive Project in Florence, Italy. He has recently taught at Harvard University and is the author of *Science, Politics, and Society in Eighteenth-Century Italy: The* Giornale de' letterati d'Italia *and Its World* (1991) and *The Social History of Skepticism: Experience and Doubt in Early Modern Culture* (1999). STUDENT MOVEMENTS

Robert S. Duplessis is Isaac H. Clothier Professor of History and International Relations at Swarthmore College. He has been a Fulbright Fellow (1985–1986), a National Endowment for the Humanities Fellow (1996–1997), a Guggenheim Fellow (2000–2001). He is author of *Lille and the Dutch Revolt*

(1991), *Transitions to Capitalism in Early Modern Europe* (1997), and numerous essays on European textile production and on the the history of consumption in the early modern Atlantic basin. CAPITALISM AND COMMERCIALIZATION

Geoff Eley is Professor of History at the University of Michigan. He is the author of *Reshaping the German Right* (1990) and *Remembering the Future: The History of the Left in Europe, 1850–2000.* GENERATIONS OF SOCIAL HISTORY

Steven A. Epstein is Professor of History at the University of Colorado at Boulder. He is the author of numerous works on medieval and modern social history, including *Speaking of Slavery: Color, Ethnicity, and Human Bondage in Italy.* PREINDUSTRIAL MANUFACTURING

Joanne M. Ferraro is Professor of History at San Diego State University. She is the author of *Family and Public Life in Brescia, 1580–1650: The Foundations of Power in the Venetian State* (1993) and *The Marriage Wars in Late Renaissance Venice* (forthcoming). COURTSHIP, MARRIAGE, AND DIVORCE

Caroline Ford is Associate Professor of History at the University of British Columbia in Vancouver, Canada. She is author of *Creating the Nation in Provincial France: Religion and Political Identity in Brittany* (1993) and recently completed a book-length manuscript entitled *Divided Houses: Religion and Gender in 19th-Century France.* NATIONALISM

Christopher E. Forth teaches European intellectual and cultural history at the Australian National University. He is the author of *Zarathustra in Paris: The Nietzsche Vogue in France, 1891–1918* (forthcoming) and is completing a study entitled *Conquering Virility: The Dreyfus Affair and the Crisis of French Manhood.* He is the coeditor (with Ivan Crozier) of *Body Parts: Critical Explorations in Corporeality* (forthcoming). CULTURAL HISTORY AND NEW CULTURAL HISTORY

Gregory L. Freeze is the Victor and Gwendolyn Beinfield Professor of History at Brandeis University. He is the author of *The Russian Levites* (1977) and *The Parish Clergy in Nineteenth-Century Russia* (1983). EASTERN ORTHODOXY

Christopher R. Friedrichs is Professor of History at the University of British Columbia. He is the author of *Urban Society in an Age of War: Nördlingen, 1580–1720* (1979), *The Early Modern City, 1450–1750*

(1995), and *Urban Politics in Early Modern Europe* (2000). THE CITY: THE EARLY MODERN PERIOD; URBAN INSTITUTIONS AND POLITICS: THE EARLY MODERN PERIOD

Cathy A. Frierson is Professor of History at the University of New Hampshire. She is the author of *Peasant Icons: Representations of Rural People in Late Nineteenth Century Russia* (1993) and *All Russia is Burning! A Cultural History of Fire and Arson in Rural Russia* (forthcoming). She is the editor and translator of *Aleksandr Nikolaevich Engelgardt's Letters from the Country, 1872–1887* (1993). PEASANTS AND RURAL LABORERS

Dick Geary is Professor of Modern History at the University of Nottingham and the author of several books on the European labor movement, as well as on Karl Kautsky (1987) and Hitler and Nazism (2d ed., 2000). He is currently completing a study of unemployment in the Weimar Republic. WORKING CLASSES

Marco Giugni is Researcher in the Department of Political Science at the University of Geneva, Switzerland. He is author and coauthor of numerous books and articles on social movements, including *Entre stratégie et opportunité: Les nouveaux mouvements sociaux en Suisse* (1995), *New Social Movements in Western Europe: A Comparative Analysis* (with Hanspeter Kriesi, Ruud Koopbant, and Jan Willem Duyvendak; 1995), and *Histoires de mobilisation politique en Suisse: De la contestation à l'intégration* (with Florence Passy; 1997). His current research interests include political claim making in the fields of immigration, unemployment, and social exclusion. MODERN PROTEST POLITICS

Paul F. Grendler is Professor of History Emeritus at the University of Toronto and was president of the Renaissance Society of America from 1992 to 1994. He is the author of *Schooling in Renaissance Italy: Literacy and Learning, 1300–1600* (1989), *The Universities of the Italian Renaissance* (forthcoming), and other books. He has received many fellowships, honors, and prizes. SCHOOLS AND SCHOOLING

Gay L. Gullickson is Professor of History at the University of Maryland, College Park. She is the author of *Spinners and Weavers of Auffay: Rural Industry and the Sexual Division of Labor in a French Village, 1750–1850* (1986) and *Unruly Women of Paris: Images of the Commune* (1996). PROTOINDUSTRIALIZATION

Allen Guttmann is Professor of English and American Studies at Amherst College. He is the author of

From Ritual to Record: The Nature of Modern Sports (1978) and eight other books on the history of sports. His most recent titles are *Games and Empires: Modern Sports and Cultural Imperialism* (1994) and *The Erotic in Sports* (1996). SPORTS

W. Scott Haine is adjunct assistant professor at Holy Names College, Oakland, California. He is author of *The World of the Parisian Café: Sociability among the French Working Class, 1789–1914* (1996) and *The History of France* (2000). He is currently working on three volumes on the history of the café during the twentieth century. STREET LIFE AND CITY SPACE

Michael R. Haines is Banfi Vinters Distinguished Professor of Economics at Colgate University and Research Associate at the National Bureau of Economic Research. He is the author of *Fertility and Occupation: Population Patterns in Industrialization* (1979), *Fatal Years: Child Mortality in Late Nineteenth-Century America* (with Samuel H. Preston; 1991), and *A Population History of North America* (edited with Richard Steckel; 2000), as well as numerous articles on historical demography. He was president of the Social Science History Association. THE POPULATION OF EUROPE: THE DEMOGRAPHIC TRANSITION AND AFTER

Lesley A. Hall is Senior Assistant Archivist in the Contemporary Medical Archives Centre, Wellcome Library for the History and Understanding of Medicine, London, and Honorary Lecturer in History of Medicine, University College London. She has published *Hidden Anxieties: Male Sexuality, 1900–1950* (1991), *The Facts of Life: The Creation of Sexual Knowledge in Britain, 1650–1950* (1995; with Roy Porter), and *Sex, Gender, and Social Change in Britain since 1880* (2000), as well as numerous articles on the history of gender and sexuality. MASTURBATION

Michael P. Hanagan teaches history at the New School for Social Research in New York City. He is the author of *The Logic of Solidarity* (1979) and *Nascent Proletarians: Class Formation in Post-Revolutionary France* (1989). He has coedited a number of books, including *Challenging Authority: The Historical Study of Contentious Politics* (1998) and *Extending Citizenship, Reconfiguring States* (1999). He is currently collaborating on a world history textbook and a comparative study of the welfare state. CLIOMETRICS AND QUANTIFICATION; LABOR HISTORY: STRIKES AND UNIONS; URBAN CROWDS

Julie Hardwick is Associate Professor of History at Texas Christian University. She is the author of *The*

Practice of Patriarchy: Gender and the Politics of Household Authority in Early Modern France (1998). INHERITANCE

Stephen L. Harp is Associate Professor of History at the University of Akron. He is the author of *Learning to be Loyal: Primary Schooling as Nation Building in Alsace and Lorraine, 1850–1940* (1998) and *Marketing Michelin: Advertising and National Culture in Twentieth-Century France* (forthcoming). TRAVEL AND TOURISM

Donna Harsch is Associate Professor of History at Carnegie Mellon University. She is the author of *German Social Democracy and the Rise of Nazism, 1928–1933* (1993) and "Society, the State, and Abortion in East Germany, 1950–1972," (*American Historical Review*). SINCE WORLD WAR II

Richard Hellie is Professor of Russian History and Director of the Center for Eastern European and Russian/Eurasian Studies at the University of Chicago. He is the author of *Enserfment and Military Change in Muscovy* (1971), *Slavery in Russia 1450–1725* (1982), and *The Economy and Material Culture of Russia 1600–1725* (19990). He is the translator of *The Russian Law Code* (Ulozhenie) *of 1649* (1988). SLAVES

John Henry is a Senior Lecturer in the Science Studies Unit at the University of Edinburgh, Scotland. He is the author of *The Scientific Revolutions and the Origins of Modern Science* (1997) and numerous articles in the history of science and medicine from the Renaissance to the nineteenth century. SCIENCE AND THE SCIENTIFIC REVOLUTION

Colin Heywood is Senior Lecturer in Economic and Social History at the University of Nottingham, England. He is the the author of *Childhood in Nineteenth-Century France* (1988) and *The Development of the French Economy* (1992). CHILD LABOR; CHILD REARING AND CHILDHOOD

Michael C. Hickey is Associate Professor of History at Bloomsburg University of Pennsylvania. He is author of more than a dozen articles on modern Russian and Russian-Jewish history. THE JEWS AND ANTI-SEMITISM

Bridget Hill most recently worked for the Open University; she is now retired. She is the author of *Women, Work, and Sexual Politics in Eighteenth-Century England* (1989), *The Republican Virago: The Life and Times of Catherine Macaulay, Historian* (1992), and

Servants: English Domestics in the Eighteenth Century (1996). She is in the process of completing a book on spinsters in England, 1660–1850. SERVANTS

Mack P. Holt is Associate Professor of History at George Mason University. He is the author of *The Duke of Anjou and the Politique Struggle during the Wars of Religion* (1986) and *The French Wars of Religion, 1562–1629* (1995). He has held fellowships from the National Endowment for the Humanities, the Andrew W. Mellon Foundation, and the John Simon Guggenheim Memorial Foundation. FESTIVALS

Young-Sun Hong is Associate Professor of History at the State University of New York, Stony Brook. She is the author of *Welfare, Modernity, and the Weimar State, 1919–1933* (1998) and book review editor of *Social History.* Her current project is on race, health, and citizenship in East and West Germany from 1945 to 1975. SOCIAL WELFARE AND INSURANCE

R. A. Houston is Professor of Early Modern History in the University of St Andrews, Scotland. He is the author of *Scottish Literacy and the Scottish Identity: Literacy and Society in Scotland and England, 1600–1850* (1985), *Literacy in Early Modern Europe: Culture and Education, 1500–1800* (1989), and *Madness and Society in Eighteenth-Century Scotland* (2000). He is the coauthor of *Autism in History: The Case of Hugh Blair of Borgue* (2000). LITERACY

Ronnie Po-Chia Hsia is Professor of History at New York University. He is the author of *Society and Religion in Münster 1535–1618* (1984), *The Myth of Ritual Murder: Jews and Magic in Reformation Germany* (1988), *Social Discipline in the Reformation; Central Europe 1550–1750* (1989), *Trent 1475: Stories of a Ritual Murder Trial* (1992), and *The World of Catholic Renewal 1540–1770* (1998). THE PROTESTANT REFORMATION AND THE CATHOLIC REFORMATION

Tamara L. Hunt is Associate Professor of History at Loyola Marymount University. She is the author of *Defining John Bull: Political Caricature and British National Identity, 1760–1820* (2000). Her fellowships include a Chandis Securities Company Fellowship at the Henry E. Huntington Library (1992) and a National Endowment for the Humanities Fellowship for College Teachers (1997–1998). MEMORY AND THE INVENTION OF TRADITIONS; HOLIDAYS AND PUBLIC RITUALS

Hartmut Kaelble is Professor of Social History at Humboldt University, Berlin. He is author of *Social Mobility in the 19th and 20th Centuries: Europe and*

America in Comparative Perspective (1985) and *A Social History of Western Europe, 1880–1980* (1989). COMPARATIVE EUROPEAN SOCIAL HISTORY; SOCIAL MOBILITY

Gisela Kaplan is Professor at the University of New England, Armindale, New South Wales, Australia, and teaches in social science. She has authored ten books, including *Hannah Arendt: Thinking, Judging, Freedom* (1989) and *Contemporary Western European Feminism* (1992), and over one hundred papers and chapters in books. She contributed to *Challenging Racism and Sexism* (edited by Ethel Tobach and Betty Rosoff, 1994), which won the Gustavus Myer award for the most outstanding publication on human rights in 1996. NEW SOCIAL MOVEMENTS; RACISM

Craig Keating is an instructor in the Department of History at the University of British Columbia and a research associate at the Institute for Governance Studies at Simon Fraser University, Vancouver. He has written on the work of Michel Foucault and Georges Canguilhem. He is currently writing a history of the cultural construction of old age in France. HOUSING

Kathleen J. Kete is Associate Professor of History at Trinity College, Hartford, Connecticut. She is the author of *The Beast in the Boudoir: Petkeeping in Nineteenth-Century Paris* (1994). ANIMALS AND PETS

Kenneth Kiple is Distinguished University Professor at Bowling Green State University. He is the author or editor of a number of books, including *The Cambridge World History of Human Disease* (1993) and *The Cambridge World History of Food* (2000). HEALTH AND DISEASE

Sherri Klassen is Instructor at Trent University, Peterborough, Ontario, and Visiting Scholar at the Institute for Human Development, Life Course and Aging in the University of Toronto. She is the author of *Aging Gracefully in the Eighteenth Century: A Study of Elderly Women in Old Regime Toulouse.* THE LIFE CYCLE; WIDOWS AND WIDOWERS

John Komlos is Professor of Economics at the University of Munich. He is the author of *The Habsburg Monarchy as a Customs Union: Economic Development in Austria-Hungary in the Nineteenth Century* (1983) and *Nutrition and Economic Development in the Eighteenth-Century Habsburg Monarchy: An Anthropometric History* (1989). ANTHROPOMETRY

Josef Konvitz is Head of Division, Territorial Development Policies and Prospects, Organization for Economic Cooperation and Development, Paris. Until 1992, he was professor of history at Michigan State University. He is the author of *Cities and the Sea* (1978), *The Urban Millennium* (1985), and numerous articles on urban history. The article "The City: The Modern Period" presents his own views and not those of the OECD. THE CITY: THE MODERN PERIOD

Rob Kroes is Chair of American Studies at the University of Amsterdam. He is the author of *If You've Seen One, You've Seen the Mall: Europeans and American Mass Culture* (1996) and of *Us and Them: Questions of Citizenship in a Globalizing World* (2000). AMERICA, AMERICANIZATION, AND ANTI-AMERICANISM

Hartmut Lehmann is Director at the Max-Planck-Institut for History in Göttingen, Germany. He is author of *Das Zeitalter des Absolutismus* (1980), *Martin Luther in the American Imagination* (1988), and *Protestantische Weltsichten* (1998). SECULARIZATION

James R. Lehning is Professor of History at the University of Utah. He is the author of *The Peasants of Marlhes: Family Organization and Economic Development in 19th-Century France* (1980) and *Peasant and French: Cultural Contact in Rural France in the 19th Century* (1995). AGRICULTURE

Beverly Lemire is Professor of History, University of New Brunswick. She is the author of *Fashion's Favourite: The Cotton Trade and the Consumer in Britain, 1660–1800* (1991) and *Dress, Culture, and Commerce: The English Clothing Trade before the Factory, 1660–1800* (1997). She holds a Killam Research Fellowship in 1999–2001. CLOTHING AND FASHION

David Levine is Professor of Educaton, Ontario Institute for Studies in Education of the University of Toronto. He is the author of *Family Formations in an Age of Nascent Capitalism* (1977), *Reproducing Families: The Political Economy of English Population History* (1987), and *At the Dawn of Modernity: Biology, Culture, and Material Life in Europe after the Year 1000* (2000). He is the coauthor of *The Making of an Industrial Society: Whickham, 1560–1765* (1977) and *Poverty and Piety in an English Village: Terling, 1525–1700* (1979). He edited *Proletarianization and Family History* (1984) and *The Quiet Revolution: European History in the Age of Fertility Decline* (1992). THE EUROPEAN MARRIAGE PATTERN; HISTORY OF THE FAMILY; THE POPULATION OF EUROPE: EARLY MODERN DEMOGRAPHIC PATTERNS

Brian Lewis is Assistant Professor of History at McGill University, Montreal. He is the author of *The Middlemost and the Milltowns: Bourgeois Culture and Politics in Early Industrial England* (forthcoming). BRITAIN

Mary Lindemann is Professor of History at Carnegie Mellon University. She is the author of *Patriots and Paupers: Hamburg, 1712–1830* (1990), *Health and Healing in Eighteenth-Century Germany* (1996), and *Medicine and Society in Early Modern Europe* (1999). THE SOURCES OF SOCIAL HISTORY

Keith P. Luria is Associate Professor of History at North Carolina State University. He is the author of *Territories of Grace: Cultural Change in the Seventeenth-Century Diocese of Grenoble* (1991). BELIEF AND POPULAR RELIGION; CATHOLICISM

Theresa M. McBride is Professor and Chair of the Department of History at the College of the Holy Cross. She is the author of *The Domestic Revolution: The Modernisation of Household Service in England and France, 1820–1920* (1977) and numerous articles and chapters in historical journals and other collections. She is a member of the board of editors of *The Journal of Social History* and a past member of the board of editors of the Society for French Historical Studies. URBAN INSTITUTIONS AND POLITICS: THE MODERN PERIOD

John Martin, a Professor of History, teaches medieval and early modern history at Trinity University, San Antonio, Texas. He is the author of *Venice's Hidden Enemies: Italian Heretics in a Renaissance City* (1993) and coeditor of *Venice Reconsidered: The History and Civilization of an Italian City-State* (2000). THE RENAISSANCE

Jason Martinek is a doctoral candidate in labor history at Carnegie Mellon University. His research examines the role of reading in European and American social movements in the nineteenth and twentieth centuries. READING

Stephen Maughan is Associate Professor of History at Albertson College of Idaho. He writes on British foreign missions and imperialism, most recently publishing "Civic Culture, Women's Foreign Missions, and the British Imperial Imagination, 1860–1914" in *Paradoxes of Civil Society: New Perspectives on Modern German and British History* (edited by Frank Trentmann; 2000). He is completing a book on Anglican foreign missions and imperial culture in Victorian and Edwardian Britain. EXPLORERS, MISSIONARIES, TRADERS

Laura E. Nym Mayhall is Assistant Professor of History at the Catholic University of America. She is coeditor of *Women's Suffrage in the British Empire: Citizenship, Nation, and Race* (2000). FEMINISMS

Mary Jo Maynes is Professor of German History at the University of Minnesota. She is the author of *Schooling for the People, Comparative Local Studies of Schooling History in France and Germany, 1750–1850* (1985) and *Schooling in Western Europe: A Social History* (1985). Her most recent monograph is *Taking the Hard Road: Lifecourse in French and German Workers' Autobiographies of the Industrial Era* (1995). She is one of the editors of the Encyclopedia. CENTRAL EUROPE

David W. Miller is Professor of History at Carnegie Mellon University. He is the author of *Church, State, and Nation in Ireland, 1898–1921* (1973) and *Queen's Rebels: Ulster Loyalism in Historical Perspective* (1978). IRELAND

Montserrat Miller is Associate Professor of History at Marshall University. She is working on a book on the social history of provisioning entitled *Neighborhood Nexus: Women, Food Markets, and Consumerism in Twentieth-Century Barcelona.* THE IBERIAN PENINSULA; SHOPS AND STORES

Arthur Mitzman is Professor Emeritus of Modern History at the University of Amsterdam, the Netherlands. Educated at Columbia University and Brandeis University in the history of ideas, he is the author of *The Iron Cage: An Historical Interpretation of Max Weber* (1970), *Sociology and Estrangement: Three Sociologists of Imperial Germany* (1973), *Michelet Historian: Rebirth and Romanticism in Nineteenth-Century France* (1990), and *Michelet ou la subversion du passé* (1998). HIGH CULTURE

Leslie Page Moch is Professor of History at Michigan State University. She is the author of *Moving Europeans: Migration in Western Europe since 1650* (1992) and coeditor of *European Migrants: Global and Local Perspectives* (with Dirk Hoerder; 1996) and *Challenging Authority: The Historical Study of Contentious Politics* (With Michael Hanagan and Wayne te Brake; 1998). MIGRATION

Scott Hughes Myerly is a historian, author, and consultant. His monograph *British Military Spectacle from Waterloo through the Crimean War* (1996) was a finalist in the Longmans/History Today Book of the Year Competition (1997). His fellowships include the Beatrice, Benjamin and Richard Bader Fellowship in the Visual Arts of the Theatre at Harvard University (1979) and a Fletcher Jones Fellowship in Theatre History at the Henry E. Huntington Library (1996). HOLIDAYS AND PUBLIC RITUALS; MEMORY AND THE INVENTION OF TRADITIONS

Michael Neiberg is Associate Professor of History at the United States Air Force Academy. He is the author of *Making Citizen-Soldiers: ROTC and the Ideology of American Military Service* (2000). THE MILITARY; MILITARY SERVICE

Emil Niederhauser is full member of the Hungarian Academy of Sciences and Professor Emeritus at the University of Budapest. His many books in Hungarian include: *History of Bulgaria; Serf Emancipation in Eastern Europe; Russian Culture in the Nineteenth Century; The Inflamed Peninsula; National Revival Movements in Eastern Europe; The Habsburgs;* and *History of Historical Writing in Eastern Europe.* His English and German books are *The Rise of Nationality in Eastern Europe; Die Habsburger;* and *1848: Sturm im Habsburgerreich.* EAST CENTRAL EUROPE

Kathryn Norberg is Associate Professor in the Department of History, University of California, Los Angeles. She is the author of *Rich and Poor in Grenoble, 1600–1814* (1984) and coeditor of *From the Royal to the Republican Body: Incorporating the Political in Seventeenth- and Eighteenth-Century France* (1998). She is currently coediting *SIGNS: A Journal of Women and Culture.* PROSTITUTION

Robert A. Nye is the Thomas Hart and Mary Jones Horning Professor of the Humanities and Professor of History at Oregon State University. He is the author of *Masculinity and Male Codes of Honor in Modern France* (1998) and *Sexuality* (1999). HONOR AND SHAME

Patrick K. O'Brien, FBA, is Centennial Professor of Economic History at the London School of Economics and Convener of the Programme in Global History at the Institute of Historical Research, University of London. He is the author of four books and editor of twelve, and has written about one hundred articles in academic journals. THE INDUSTRIAL REVOLUTIONS

Kenneth Orosz teaches European and African History at the University of Maine at Farmington. He is the author of several articles on colonial archives and

education policy in colonial Cameroon. His research interests also include missionaries, the role of women in the colonies, and the impact of imperialism on culture. EMIGRATION AND COLONIES

Bryan D. Palmer is Professor of History at Queen's University, Kingston, Ontario. He is the author of *E. P. Thompson: Objections and Oppositions* (1994) and *Cultures of Darkness: Night Travels in the Histories of Transgression* (2000), among other works. He currently edits the Canadian journal of labor studies *Labour/Le Travail.* MARXISM AND RADICAL HISTORY

Panikos Panayi is Professor of European History at De Montfort University, Leicester, England. He has published widely in the history of immigrants and other ethnic minorities in Europe. His most important publications in this area include *Outsiders: A History of European Minorities* (1999), *An Ethnic History of Europe since 1945: Nations, States, and Minorities* (2000), and *Ethnic Minorities in Nineteenth and Twentieth Century Germany: Jews, Gypsies, Poles, Turks, and Others* (2000). IMMIGRANTS

Nicholas Papayanis is Professor of History at the City University of New York. He is the author of *Alphonse Merrheim: The Emergence of Reformism in Revolutionary Syndicalism, 1871–1925* (1985), *The Coachmen of Nineteenth-Century Paris: Service Workers and Class Consciousness* (1993), and *Horse-Drawn Cabs and Omnibuses in Paris: The Idea of Circulation and the Business of Public Transit* (1996). THE URBAN INFRASTRUCTURE

David Parker is Senior Lecturer in Modern History at the University of Leeds, England. He is the author of numerous articles and books on the social and intellectual foundations of French absolutism, including *Class and State in Ancien Régime France: The Road to Modernity?* (1996). ABSOLUTISM

Andrew Pettegree is Professor of Modern History at the University of St. Andrews and Director of the St. Andrews Reformation Studies Institute. He is the author of several books on the English and European Reformations, including *Emden and the Dutch Revolt: Exile and the Development of Reformed Protestantism* (1992) and *Marian Protestantism* (1996). His most recent published project is a one-volume multiauthor survey of the Reformation, *The Reformation World* (2000). PROTESTANTISM

Roderick G. Phillips is Professor of History at Carleton University, Ottawa, Ontario, and editor of *The*

Journal of Family History. He has held fellowships in many countries and is the author of numerous books, including *Putting Asunder: A History of Divorce in Western Society* (1988), *Untying the Knot: A Short History of Divorce* (1991), *State, Society, and Nation in Twentieth-Century Europe* (1996), and *A Short History of Wine* (2000). Sex, Law, and the State

Andrejs Plakans is Professor of History at Iowa State University. He is the author of *Kinship in the Past: An Anthropology of European Family Life (1500–1900)* (1984) and *The Latvians: A Short History* (1995). He is coeditor, with Tamara K. Hareven, of *Family History at the Crossroads: Linking Familial and Historical Change* (1987). Kinship

Jeremy D. Popkin is Professor of History at the University of Kentucky. He has written extensively on the history of the French press and is the author of *A History of Modern France* (1993) and *A Short History of the French Revolution* (1993). France

Dorothy Porter is Professor of History at Birkbeck College, University of London. She is the author of *The History of Health and the Modern State: National Contexts Compared* (1994) and *Health, Civilisation, and the State: A History of Public Health from Antiquity to Modernity* (1999). She is the editor of *Social Medicine and Medical Sociology in the Twentieth Century* (1997). Public Health

Norman Pounds is Distinguished Professor Emeritus at Indiana University and an Honorary Fellow of Fitzwilliam College, Cambridge University. He is the author of *An Economic History of Medieval Europe* (1974), *Hearth and Home* (1989), *The Culture of the English People: Iron Age to the Industrial Revolution* (1994), and *A History of the English Parish* (2000). Standards of Living

Brian Pullan is Emeritus Professor of Modern History at the University of Manchester, England. His books include *Rich and Poor in Renaissance Venice* (1973), *The Jews of Europe and the Inquisition of Venice* (1983), and *Poverty and Charity: Europe, Italy, Venice* (1994). Charity and Poor Relief: The Early Modern Period

Panu Pulma is a senior research fellow of the Academy of Finland. His books deal with the relationship between central power and local communities in eighteenth-century Sweden/Finland, with the history of child care and child welfare, and with twentieth-century urban history. His current research deals with the

social policies of the Nordic capital cities (Oslo, Stockholm, and Helsinki) after World War II. The Nordic Countries

Matthew Ramsey is Associate Professor of History at Vanderbilt University. He is the author of *Professional and Popular Medicine in France, 1770–1830: The Social World of Medical Practice* (1988). Medical Practitioners and Medicine

David L. Ransel is Professor of History at Indiana University. He is author of *The Politics of Catherinian Russia: The Panin Party* (1975), *Mothers of Misery: Child Abandonment in Russia* (1988), and *Village Mothers: Three Generations of Change in Russia and Tataria* (2000). He was editor of *Slavic Review* from 1980 to 1985 and editor of *The American Historical Review* from 1985 to 1995. Orphans and Foundlings

Charles Rearick is Professor of History at the University of Massachusetts, Amherst. He is the author of *Beyond the Enlightenment: Historians and Folklore in Nineteenth-Century France* (1974), *Pleasures of the Belle Epoque: Entertainment and Festivity in Turn-of-the-Century France* (1985), and *The French in Love and War: Popular Culture in the Era of the World Wars* (1997). Consumer Leisure

Daniel P. Resnick is Professor of History at Carnegie Mellon University. He is the editor of *Literacy in Historical Perspectives* and the author of articles and essays on literacy development in Europe and America. Reading

Lucy Riall is Senior Lecturer in History at Birkbeck College, University of London. She is the author of *The Italian Risorgimento: State, Society, and National Unification* (1994) and *Sicily and the Unification of Italy: Liberal Policy and Local Power, 1859–1866* (1998). Italy

Michael D. Richards is the Hattie Mae Samford Professor of History at Sweet Briar College. He is the author of *Twentieth-Century Europe: A Brief History* (1998) and *Term Paper Resource Guide to Twentieth-Century World History* (2000). Revolutions

John M. Riddle is an Alumni Distinguished Professor of History at North Carolina State University. He is the author of *Contraception and Abortion from the Ancient World to the Renaissance* (1992) and *Eve's Herbs: A History of Contraception and Abortion in the West* (1997). Birth, Contraception, and Abortion

Priscilla R. Roosevelt is a fellow of the Institute of European, Russian, and Eurasian Studies at George Washington University and president of American Friends of the Russian Country Estate, Inc., a nonprofit foundation. She is the author of *Apostle of Russian Liberalism: Timofei Granovsky* (1985) and *Life on the Russian Country Estate: A Social and Cultural History* (1995). ESTATES AND COUNTRY HOUSES

Ellen Ross is Professor of History and Women's Studies at Ramapo College of New Jersey, where she is the coordinator of the Women's Studies Program. She is the author of many articles on women and poverty in late nineteenth- and early twentieth-century London and *Love and Toil: Motherhood in Working-Class London 1870–1918* (1993). Her current work is on philanthropic donors and recipients in Britain from 1860 to 1940. MOTHERHOOD

Don K. Rowney is Professor of History at Bowling Green State University. He is the author of *Transition to Technocracy: The Structural Origins of the Soviet Administrative State* (1989) and coauthor of *Russian Officialdom: The Bureaucratization of Russian Society from the Seventeenth to the Twentieth Century* (1979). BUREAUCRACY

John G. Rule is Professor of History at the University of Southhampton, England. He is the author of *The Labouring Classes in Early Industrial England, 1750–1850* (1986), a two-volume survey of the economic and social history of Hanoverian England, *The Vital Century: England's Developing Economy, 1714–1815* (1992), and *Albion's People: English Society, 1714–1815* (1992). MORAL ECONOMY AND LUDDISM

Paul Sant Cassia is Professor of Social Anthropology at the University of Durham, England. He is the coauthor of *The Making of the Modern Greek Family* (1991) and is working on a book dealing with memory and disappeared persons in Cyprus. He was the Founding Editor of *The Journal of Mediterranean Studies* and is currently editor of *History and Anthropology*. BANDITRY

Abby M. Schrader is Assistant Professor of History at Franklin and Marshall College and author of *Languages of the Lash: Corporal Punishment and the Construction of Identity in Imperial Russia.* PUNISHMENT

Alfred Erich Senn is Professor Emeritus of History at the University of Wisconsin–Madison. He is the author of *The Emergence of Modern Lithuania* (1959), *Lithuania Awakening* (1990), *Gorbachev's Failure in*

Lithuania (1995), and *Power, Politics, and the Olympic Games* (1999). THE BALTIC NATIONS

Scott J. Seregny is Professor of History at Indiana University at Indianapolis. He is the author of *Russian Teachers and Peasant Revolution: The Politics of Education in 1905* (1989). Recent publications include "Zemstvos, Peasants, and Citizenship: The Russian Adult Education Movement and World War I" (*Slavic Review,* 2000). TEACHERS

Peter Shapely is currently a lecturer at the University of Wales, Bangor. His recent publicatons include *Charity and Power in Victorian Manchester* (forthcoming), "Status and Parlimentary Candidates in Manchester" (*International Review of Social History,* 1999), "Charity, Status, and Social Leadership" (*Journal of Social History,* 1998), and "Urban Charity, Class Reflections, and Social Cohesion" (*Urban History,* forthcoming) WORK AND THE WORK ETHIC

Haia Shpayer-Makov is Senior Lecturer of History at the University of Haifa. She is the author of *The Making of a Policeman: A Social History of a Labor Force in Metropolitan London, 1829–1914* (forthcoming) and has published articles on anarchism and the Metropolitan Police of London. POLICE

Adrian Shubert is Professor of History at York University, Toronto. His books include *A Social Hiistory of Modern Spain* (1990) and *Death and Money in the Afternoon* (1999). THE LIBERAL STATE

Lisa Z. Sigel is Assistant Professor of History at Millsaps College and Visiting Lecturer at DePaul University. She is author of *Governing Pleasures: A History of British Pornography, 1815–1914* (forthcoming). THE BODY AND ITS REPRESENTATIONS; PORNOGRAPHY; SEXUAL BEHAVIOR AND SEXUAL MORALITY

Bonnie G. Smith teaches history at Rutgers University. She is the author of *The Gender of History: Men, Women, and Historical Practice* (1998), *Global Feminisms since 1945* (2000), and *Imperialism* (2000). She is the coauthor of *The Making of the West* (2000). THE DEVELOPMENT OF GENDER HISTORY; GENDER THEORY; WOMEN AND FEMININITY

Ginnie Smith holds a Ph.D. from the London School of Economics and Political Science. She is the author of articles on seventeenth-century cosmetics, eighteenth-century regimen, and nineteenth-century "Physical Puritanism." She is working on a book pro-

384

visionally entitled *Cleanliness, c. 300,000 B.C. to A.D. 2000.* CLEANLINESS

Timothy B. Smith is Associate Professor of History at Queen's University, Kingston, Ontario. He has published in the field of the history of French social policy. MARGINAL PEOPLE; THE NINETEENTH CENTURY; CHARITY AND POOR RELIEF: THE MODERN PERIOD

George Snow is Professor of History at Shippensburg University in Pennsylvania. He is author of a number of articles on alcoholism and temperance in imperial and Soviet Russia, including "Drinking and Drunkenness in Russia and the Soviet Union: A Review Essay" (*Social History of Alcohol Review*, 1988), "Alcohol and Alcoholism in Russia and the Soviet Union" (*Social History of Alcohol Review*, 1992), and "Alcoholism in the Russian Military: The Public Sphere and the Temperance Discourse, 1883–1917" (*Jahrbücher für Geschichte Osteuropas,* 1997). ALCOHOL AND TEMPERANCE

Anne-Marie Sohn is Professor of Contemporary History at the University of Rouen, France. She is a specialist in women's history and the history of private life. She is the author of *Chrysalides: Femmes dans la vie privée (XIX–XX siècles)* (1996), *Du premier baiser à l'alcôve: Les Français et la sexualité au quotidien (1850–1950)* (1996), and *Une histoire sans les femmes est-elle possible?* (1998). ILLEGITIMACY AND CONCUBINAGE

Pieter Spierenburg is Professor of Preindustrial History at Erasmus University, Rotterdam, the Netherlands. He is author of a number of works, including *The Spectacle of Suffering* (1984), and the editor of *Men and Violence: Gender, Honor, and Rituals in Modern Europe and America* (1998). CRIME

Peter N. Stearns is Provost at George Mason University and editor of *The Journal of Social History.* He has published widely in social history and in world history, focusing on aspects of human experience such as old age and emotion. He is the editor in chief of the Encyclopedia. ARTISANS; MEN AND MASCULINITY; MIDDLE-CLASS WORK; MODERNIZATION; PERIODIZATION IN SOCIAL HISTORY

Laura Tabili is Associate Professor of Modern European History at the University of Arizona. She is the author of *"We Ask for Justice": Workers and Racial Difference in Late Imperial Britain* (1994). IMPERIALISM AND DOMESTIC SOCIETY

Charles Tilly is Joseph L. Buttenwieser Professor of Social Science at Columbia University and a student of social change in Europe and North America. COLLECTIVE ACTION; DEMOCRACY; SOCIAL CLASS

Louise A. Tilly is Professor Emerita of History and Sociology at the New School University and Department Associate, History Department, Northwestern University. She is the author of *Politics and Class in Milan* (1992); coauthor of *Women, Work, and Family* (1978); and coeditor of *Women, Politics, and Change* (1990), *The European Experience of Declining Fertility* (1992), and *European Integration in Social Perspective* (1997). She is currently editing and coauthoring a textbook in world history. INTERDISCIPLINARY CONTACTS AND INFLUENCES

Elizabeth Townsend earned her doctorate in modern European intellectual and cultural history from the University of California, Los Angeles, in 1998. She is completing a law degree with an emphasis on copyright law at the University of Arizona. Her book in progress, *Reconstructing the First World War Generation: A Comparative Biography,* examines the definitional elements of generation, with particular emphasis on the role of gender. She is also working on issues relating to the cultural materials used by scholars and copyright law. GENERATIONS AND GENERATIONAL CONFLICT

David G. Troyansky is Associate Professor of History at Texas Tech University. He is the author of *Old Age in the Old Regime: Image and Experience in Eighteenth-Century France* (1989) and principal editor of *The French Revolution in Culture and Society* (1991). DEATH; THE ELDERLY

Randolph Trumbach is Professor of History at Baruch College and the Graduate Center, City University of New York. He is the author of *The Rise of the Egalitarian Family* (1978) and *Sex and the Gender Revolution* (volume 1; 1998). HOMOSEXUALITY AND LESBIANISM

Liana Vardi is Associate Professor of History at the State University of New York at Buffalo. She is the author of *The Land and the Loom: Peasants and Profit in Northern France 1680–1800* (1993) and of "Farmers, Gleaners, and Officials in Early Modern France," and "Imagining the Harvest in Early Modern Europe,", both of which appeared in *The North American Historical Review.* LAND TENURE; SERFDOM: WESTERN EUROPE

Steven Béla Várdy is McAnulty Distinguished Professor of European History at Duquesne University. He is the author of over a dozen books and several hundred articles and essays. His books include *Modern Hungarian Historiography* (1976), *The Hungarian Americans* (1985), *Clio's Art in Hungary and Hungarian America* (1985), *Baron Joseph Eötvös, 1813–1871: A Literary Biography* (1987), *The Austro-Hungarian Mind at Home and Abroad* (1989), *Historical Dictionary of Hungary* (1997), and *Magyarok az Újvilágban* [Hungarians in the World]. EAST CENTRAL EUROPE

Alexander Varias teaches European cultural history at Villanova University and Chestnut Hill College. He is the author of *Paris and the Anarchists* (1996) and of numerous articles on art and cinema. He is the coauthor (with Lorraine Coons) of a forthcoming book on the cultural history of twentieth-century French and British ocean liners. He holds a Ph.D. in European history from New York University. ARTISTS

Keith Vernon is a senior lecturer in social history at the University of Central Lancashire, England. He has written on several aspects of the history of science and education and currently researching the history of British universities from 1850 to 1939. STUDENTS

Lynne Viola is Professor of History at the University of Toronto. She is the author of *The Best Sons of the Fatherland: Workers in the Vanguard of Soviet Collectivization* (1987) and *Peasant Rebels under Stalin: Collectivization and the Culture of Peasant Resistance* (1996). COLLECTIVIZATION

Rex Wade is Professor at George Mason University. He is the author of *The Russian Search for Peace, February–October 1917* (1969), *Red Guards and Workers' Militias in the Russian Revolution* (1984), *The Russian Revolution, 1917* (2000), and numerous articles. He is the compiler and editor of *Documents of Soviet History* (volumes 1–3; 1991) and coeditor of *State and Society in Provinical Russia: Saratov, 1590–1917* (1989). RUSSIA AND THE EAST SLAVS

Rosemary Wakeman is Visiting Associate Professor at Fordham University. She is the author of *Modernizing the Provincial City: Toulouse, 1945–1975* (1997). THE URBAN INFRASTRUCTURE

John K. Walton is Professor of Social History at the University of Central Lancashire, Preston, U.K. His books include *The English Seaside Resort: A Social History, 1750–1914* (1983) and *The British Seaside: Hol-*

idays and Resorts in the Twentieth Century. POLICING LEISURE; VACATIONS

Whitney Walton is Associate Professor of History at Purdue University. She is the author of *France at the Crysal Palace: Bourgeois Taste and Artisan Manufacture in the Nineteenth Century* (1992) and *Eve's Proud Descendants: Four Women Writers and Republican Politics in Nineteenth-Century France.* MATERIAL CULTURE

William Weber is Professor of History at California State University, Long Beach. He is the author of *Music and the Middle Class* (1975) and *The Rise of Musical Classics in Eighteenth-Century England* (1992). MUSIC AND DANCE

Eric D. Weitz is Associate Professor of History at the University of Minnesota. He is the author of *Creating German Communism, 1890–1990: From Popular Protests to Socialist State* (1997) and is currently writing a comparative history of genocides, *For Race and Nation: Genocides in the Twentieth Century* (forthcoming). He has been the recipient of grants and fellowships from the German Academic Exchange Service, the American Council of Learned Societies and the Social Science Research Council, and the National Council for Soviet and East European Research, among others. CENTRAL EUROPE; COMMUNISM; SOCIALISM

Robert Whaples is Associate Professor of Economics at Wake Forest University. He is Associate Director and Book Review Editor for EH.NET (www.eh.net) and winner of the Hughes Prize (for teaching) and Nevins Prize (for dissertation research) from the Economic History Association. His research focuses primarily on the history of American labor markets. He has coedited *Historical Perspectives on the American Economy* (1995) and *Public Choice Interpretations of American Economic History* (2000). ANTHROPOMETRY

Merry E. Wiesner-Hanks is Professor and Chair of the Department of History at the University of Wisconsin–Milwaukee. She is the author of *Women and Gender in Early Modern Europe* (2d ed., 2000), *Christianity and Sexuality in the Early Modern World* (2000), and many other books and articles. She is one of the editors of *The Sixteenth Century Journal* and *Becoming Visible: Women in European History* (3d ed., 1997). GENDER AND WORK; PATRIARCHY

Jay Winter is Reader in Modern History, University of Cambridge, and Fellow of Pembroke College. He is author of *Sites of Memory, Sites of Mourning: The*

386

Great War in European Cultural History (1995). THE WORLD WARS AND THE DEPRESSION

Thomas C. Wolfe is Assistant Professor of History and Anthropology at the University of Minnesota, Twin Cities. He is currently at work on a study of the role of journalism and communications in the governance of late Soviet society. COMMUNICATIONS, THE MEDIA, AND PROPAGANDA

Isser Woloch is Moore Collegiate Professor of History at Columbia University. His most recent books include *The New Regime: Transformations of the French Civic Order, 1789–1820s* (1994) and *Napoleon and His Collaborators: The Making of a Dictatorship* (2000). THE FRENCH REVOLUTION AND THE EMPIRE

Cas Wouters is a Researcher at the Faculty of Social Sciences at Utrecht University, the Netherlands. He has published many articles and books on twentieth-century changes, mainly in the West, in manners or codes of behavior and emotion management. The focus of his research has been on the norms regulating interactions between men and women, between people of various social status, and between the generations, including the codes of conduct dealing with dying and mourning. MANNERS

David Wright is Hannah Chair in the History of Medicine at McMaster University, Hamilton, Ontario. He has published widely on the history of mental health and disability, including (with Peter Bartlett) *Outside the Walls of the Asylum: The History of Care in the Community, 1750–2000* (1999) and (with Anne Digby) *From Idiocy to Mental Deficiency: Historical Perspectives on People with Learning Disabilities* (1996). DEVELOPMENTAL AND PHYSICAL DISABILITIES: THE "BLIND," "DEAF AND DUMB," AND "IDIOT"

387

INDEX

Page numbers in boldface refer to the main entry on the subject.
Page numbers in italics refer to figures, illustrations, maps, tables, and sidebars.

A

A. U., **1**:516, 519
Abbott, Berenice, **2**:264
Abel, Wilhelm, **2**:*24,* 27
    Agricultural Fluctuations in Europe,
        2:*30 Fig. 1, 30 Fig. 2*
Abelard, Peter, **5**:353
Abelin, J. P., **1**:*339*
Abolition of Feudalism, The (Markoff),
        1:77–79
Aborigines of Australia, **1**:*467*
Abortion, **2**:185–186; **4**:30, 162
    in Britain, **1**:267
    campaigns against, **4**:252
    criminalization of, **2**:189
    as inheritance strategy, **5**:105
    in interwar years, **1**:224
    and the women's movement, **3**:294–
        295, *295;* **4**:52
About, Edmond, **3**:380
Abrams, Philip, **1**:13
Abrantes, Laure d', **4**:3
Absinthe, **3**:489, *490;* **5**:96, 99
Absolutely Fabulous, **5**:137
Absolutism, **2**:439–448
    definition, **2**:439
    in Denmark, **1**:359
    as history period, **1**:125
    legitimation of, **2**:445–446
    and ritual, **5**:191
    social foundations of, **2**:442–443
Abstract Expressionism, **3**:93
Académie de l'espée, L' (Thibault),
        5:168
Academies, **2**:317
    Académie Française, **5**:68, 72
    Accademia della Crusca, **5**:68, 72
    and civil society, **2**:493
    and development of languages, **5**:72
    and scientific revolution, **2**:85
Academy of the Lynxes, **2**:84
Accampo, Elinor, **1**:211
Accent (in language), **5**:68–69
Accommodations of servants, **3**:142–
    143
Accouchement sans Douleur (Lamaze
    method), **4**:434
Accoucheur, **4**:432, *432*
Achenbaum, W. A., **4**:239
Acid rain, **2**:128

Ackerman, James S., **2**:414
    Villa, The, **2**:*413*
Ackroyd's Loom-Shed at Halifax (Worsted
        Goods), **2**:*58*
Acquired immune deficiency syndrome.
    See AIDS
Acta sanctorum (Bolland), **1**:*159*
Acton, Lord, **1**:3
Acts of Mercy, The (della Robbia), **3**:*448*
Adages (Erasmus), **5**:410
Adam, Robert, **2**:415
Adam, Victor, **2**:*280*
Adams, Bruce F., **3**:424
Adams, Henry, **1**:525
Adas, Michael, **1**:205
Addison, Joseph, **1**:35; **2**:318
Adelswäärd-Fersen, Jacques d', **4**:252
Adler, Jules, **3**:*490*
Administration. *See also* Bureaucracy;
    Venality of office
    in absolutist states, **2**:440
    and control of the army, **3**:99
    language used in chanceries, **5**:71
    nobles in, **3**:34
    theory of, **2**:540
Administrative Behavior: A Study of
        Decision-Making (Simon), **2**:540
Adolescence (Hall), **4**:197
Adorno, Theodor, **1**:86; **5**:25, 77;
    6:1–2
    Dialectic of Enlightenment, **1**:189
    on vision, **4**:358
Adult education
    classes sponsored by teachers, **5**:370
    literacy class in Soviet Union, **4**:*79*
Adultery
    and divorce, **4**:157
    in England, **4**:303
    as grounds for divorce, **4**:303
    as justification for separation, **4**:303
    laws and, **4**:250
    severely punished for women, **4**:31
    sexual double standard, **4**:250
Advertising
    of consumer entertainment, **5**:206–
        207
    to expand readership of newspapers,
        5:426
    Pears' Soap, **1**:*511*
    printing and, **5**:386

"Aesthetic" dress, **5**:493
Afghans, **1**:535
Africa
    Christian converts in, **1**:485
    emigration and settlement in,
        1:497–500
    Italian emigrants in, **1**:331
    European interaction in early
        modern period, **1**:462–464,
        468–469
    exploration of, **1**:482
    German colonies in, **1**:347
    and gunboat diplomacy, **1**:462
    men viewed as effeminate by the
        British, **1**:519
    missions to
        competition between European
            churches, **5**:270–271
        European Protestant, **1**:484
    plantation agriculture in, **1**:471
    political economy distorted by trade
        with Europeans, **1**:463
    scramble for, **1**:471
    South Africa
        importation of indentured ser-
            vants from India, **1**:498
    trade networks
        Europe inserting itself in, **1**:461
African International Association, **1**:471
Africans. *See also* Blacks
    in Britain before World War II,
        1:533
    as immigrants
        in postwar period, **2**:140
        as slaves, **1**:533
    in Italy, **1**:331
Afro-Caribbeans in Britain, **1**:533
Age
    ages of life, **4**:220, *221*
    and childhood, **4**:176
    awareness of, **2**:197–198
        age pyramid, **2**:*198 Fig. 1*
    demographic aging, **4**:220
        French age pyramids, **4**:*222*
            Fig. 1
    life expectancy at birth in
        Europe, **4**:*223 Tab. 2*
    percentage of English population
        over age sixty, **4**:*223 Tab. 1*
    and juvenile delinquency, **3**:384

Banditry, 3:175, 181, 344–345, **373–382**
  bandits as folk heroes, 3:181, *345;* 5:9
  control of, in early modern Europe, 1:171
  in Italy, 1:328, 333
  juvenile delinquency and, 3:385
  myth of banditry, 3:375–376
    function of, 3:379
  surviving a bandit attack, 3:*5*
Bandits (Hobsbawm), 1:11; 3:344, 373–374, 375, 378, 380
Bang, J. L., 5:402
Banishment, 3:418
Banking and finance
  euro as new currency, 1:245
  and fairs in the Middle Ages, 2:427
  industry's links with, 2:56
  widows in, 4:211
Bank of England, 1:174
Banks, Amanda Carson, *as contributor,* 4:427–437
Banks, Joseph, 1:186
Bannister, Roger, 5:*174*
Banquet after the Hunt (Cane), 1:*325*
Banquet of the Officers of the St. George Militia Company, A (Hals), 2:*303*
Banquet Years, The (Shattuck), 3:90
Baptism as ritual of life-stage transition, 2:199
Baptists, 5:310
  in Britain, 1:259, 264
  and missions, 1:483
Barasch, Moshe, 4:368
Bar at the Folies-Bergère, A (Manet), 3:88
Baravalle, Lea, 4:520
Barbados, 1:481
Barbaro, Francesco, 1:147
Barber, Francis, 1:506
Barber-surgeons, 3:59; 4:415
Barbier, Charles, 3:509
Barcelona, 1:312
  exchange in, 2:427
  Exposición Mundial (1888), 2:432
  and its suburbs, 2:*333*
  markets in, 2:433–434
Bardet, Jean-Pierre, 2:219
Bardi, Giovanni, 5:168
Bari, Barbara, *as contributor,* 4:479–493
Barlach, Ernst, 3:92
Barlow, Edward, 4:516
Barnabites (Clerics Regular of St. Paul), 5:335
Barnard, Chester, 2:540
Barnes, Andrew E., *as contributor,* 5:263–273
Barnes, John, 5:181
Barometer, 2:86
Baronio, Cesare, 5:118
Baroque, 3:81
Barraclough, Geoffrey, 1:11

Barrie, J. M., 5:526
Barthes, Roland, 1:8, 88; **6:14–15**
Bartholomew Fair (Jonson), 5:159
Bartholomew's Fair, 4:331–332
Bartlett, Peter, *as contributor,* 3:429–443
Bartlett, Thomas, 1:273
Bartok, Béla, 1:453
Bartov, Omer, 2:548
Barzun, Jacques, 1:551
Basalla, George, 2:14
Basel, Switzerland
  divorce in, 4:158
  evil carnival, 5:56
  prostitution in, 3:351
Basin, Thomas, 2:121
Basketball, 5:181
Basque Country, 1:307
  anti-liberal movement in, 2:456
  regional nationalism, 1:314, 316; 2:504
Bassi, Laura, 1:187
Bastille Day, 1:287; 2:318; 3:234; 5:47–49, 193–194
  bicentennial, 5:*50*
  under the Third Republic, 5:*49*
Bataille, Georges, 4:297
Batavian Republic, 3:238
Baten, Jörg, 4:400
  Ernährung und wirtschaftliche Entwicklung in Bayern, 1730–1880, 4:*403 Fig. 4*
Bateson, Mary, 4:4
Bath, England
  Pump Room, 5:*222*
  as spa resort, 5:221, 231
Bathing, 4:336
  communal, 4:*349*
  domestic arrangements of bathing, 4:348
  modern bathroom, 4:*352*
  open-air, 4:*350*
  public, 4:345, 348
  during Renaissance, 4:348
  thermal baths, 4:*346*
Bathing at Ramsgate (Birch after West), 5:*234*
Battle between Carnival and Lent, The (Brueghel), 5:42, 56, *57*
Battle of Kappel wars, 5:305
Battle of Valle Giulia, The: Oral History and the Art of Dialogue (Portelli), 1:*20*
Battleship Building and Party Politics in Germany 1894–1901 (Kehr), 1:6
Baudelaire, Charles, 3:88; 4:362; 5:24
  as flaneur, 2:320
  mixture of low and high culture, 5:20
Bauer, Otto, 2:503
  Nationalities Question and Social Democracy, The, 1:50
Bauhaus school of architecture, 3:92; 5:467, 478
  and city design, 2:321

Baulant, Micheline, 2:43
Bavarian Republic, 3:244
Bax, Ernest Belfort, 1:153
  Peasants War in Germany, 1525–1526, The, 1:49
Baxandall, Michael, 4:368
Bayard, Émile, 3:*489*
Bayerland, Ortlof von, 4:428
Bayle, Antoine-Laurent, 3:431
Bayley, David, 3:401
Baylor, Michael G., 2:*32*
Bazelgette, Joseph, 2:284, *285*
Beach, Sylvia, 3:295
Beaches. See also seaside resorts and vacations
  bathing in Brighton, 5:*235*
  bathing machine, 5:*234*
  Odessa, 5:*242*
  regulations of, 5:232
Be a Man!: Males in Modern Society (Stearns), 1:102
Beans, 1:477
Beard, Charles, 1:84
Bearman, Peter S., 1:75
Beast in the Boudoir, The (Kete), 5:515, 516
Beatles, 5:148
  Beatles Fans at Buckingham Palace, 4:*373*
Beaudoin, Steven M., *as contributor,* 2:477–487
Beaumarchais, Pierre Augustin, 2:373; 5:144
Beauvais et le Beauvaisis de 1600 à 1730: Contribution de l'histoire sociale de la France du XVIIe siècle (Goubert), 1:8
Beauvoir, Simone de, 1:97; 3:23; 4:5, *51;* **6:15–16**
  Amérique au jour le jour, L', 3:22
  Deuxième sexe, Le, 1:55, 95; 4:51
Beaux Gestes: A Guide to French Body Talk (Wylie and Stafford), 4:368
Bebel, August, 3:109, 128, 270
  Frau und der Sozialismus, Die, 4:50; 5:412
Beccaria, Cesare, 1:184
Beckford, William, 4:320
Bederman, Gail, 1:102
Bedroom behavior, etiquette about, 4:374
Beds, 5:441
Beer, 3:483; 5:89, 96, 502
  aristocracy and, 3:32
  commercialization of beer making in Renaissance, 5:91
  considered less harmful than distilled alcohol, 3:485
  distinguished from spirits, 5:97
  gardens and prostitution, 3:358
Beethoven, Ludwig van, 3:86
Beffes, 5:132

collectivization, 2:410
communist party loyal to Soviet
Union, 2:529
expulsion of Turks, 1:*431*
1989 revolution, 3:247
socialism in, 3:272
women in medical profession, 4:79
Bulgars, 1:421
Bull-baiting, 5:507, 509
policing of, 5:160
Bulletin of the Labour History Society,
1:12
Bullfight, 5:171–172
Bullinger, Heinrich, 5:305
Bull running, 5:507
policing of, 5:160
Bulwer, John, 4:367
Bunsen, R. W., 5:356
Bunyan, John, 5:*307;* 6:29–30
Pilgrim's Progress, 2:195; 5:3, 413
Burckhardt, Jacob, 1:3; 3:79; 4:366;
6:30–31
*Civilization of the Renaissance in
Italy, The,* 1:84, 143; 5:15
and tradition, 5:116
*Burdens of History: British Feminists,
Indian Women, and Imperial
Culture, 1865–1915* (Burton),
1:18
Bureaucracy, 2:533–543. *See also*
Administration
hereditary officeholding, 2:444
housing of, 2:536
as new class in east central Europe,
1:388
nobles in, 1:175
of Russian Orthodox Church,
5:316
in seventeenth century, 1:174
*Bureaucracy, Aristocracy, and Autocracy:
The Prussian Experience, 1660–
1815* (Rosenberg), 1:5
Bure de Boo, Anders, 1:*358*
Burgkmair, Hans, 5:*132*
Burgos, Javier de, 2:451
Burguière, André, 4:384
Burial, 2:230
at night, 2:227, 228
Burial at Ornans (Courbet), 2:*220;*
3:87
Burial of the Count of Orgaz, The (El
Greco), 5:*288*
Burke, Edmund, 5:424, 427; 6:31–34
Burke, Peter, 1:12, 83; 2:171; 4:369;
5:281
as contributor, 1:41–48; 5:3–13,
67–76
on humor restrictions, 5:132
Burnett, John, 1:509
Burney, Charles, 5:145
Burns, Robert, 1:257
Burstyn, Joan, 4:7
Burt, Cyril, 4:178
Burton, Antionette, 1:18
Burton, Richard, 1:482; 4:295

Burton, Robert
Anatomy of Melancholy, The, 5:170
laughter as remedy of melancholy, 5:133
as source about humor, 5:135
owner of collection of jest books,
5:135
Bush, Michael, 2:366
on medieval serfdom, 2:370
Bushnell, John, 2:550
Business
Americanization of practices, 1:529
cycles and strikes, 3:256–257, 257
of the Enlightenment, 1:186
immigrants in, 1:538
opportunities of the seventeenth
century, 1:174
records as sources of social history,
1:34
Business and Politics under James I
(Tawney), 1:4
Butler, Eleanor, 4:31
Butler, Josephine, 3:357, 457
Butler, Judith, 1:98
Butler, Samuel, 5:*307*
Butlin Holiday Camps, 5:85–86
Buttinger, John, 1:55
Buxton, Thomas Fowell, 5:513
Buytewech, Willem Pietersz, 2:416
Bynum, Caroline, 1:37
Bynum, W. F., 4:357
Byrd, William, 5:145
Byron, George Gordon (Lord Byron),
3:*49;* 5:20; 6:34–35
epitaph to his dog, 5:516
and Grand Tour, 5:231
Byzantine Empire, and the Balkans,
1:421

C

Cabarets, 5:146, 210
Cabet, Étienne, 1:289; 3:123, 268, 269
Cabinets of curiosities, 1:186; 2:83, *84;*
5:31
consumerism and, 5:77
Cabral, Pedro Álvarez, 1:462
Cabs, 2:279
Cacao, 1:505
Cadastres as source of social history,
1:33
Cadbury family, 4:457
Cade, John, 3:346, *432,* 435
Cádiz, 1:312
Cafés. *See also* coffeehouses
in Italy, 1:326
in villages, 2:41
working class café, 2:318–319, 321
Caffè, Il (journal), 1:184
Cage, John, 5:148
Cahiers de doléances, 3:234
analysis by Markoff, 1:76
machine-readable sample of, 1:78
roots of women's movement, 3:316
and soil erosion, 2:124

Cahusac, Louis, 5:149
Caillois, Roger, 5:521
Caius, Johannus, 5:515
Calasanz, José, 5:337
Calendar
and New Year, 5:45
revolutionary, 5:47
Calhoun, Craig, 3:213
Callaway, Helen, 4:11
Callot, Jacques, 1:*451;* 4:*366;* 5:168
Calvin, John, 5:305; 6:35–37
on Catholicism as form of magic,
5:29
Institutes of the Christian Religion,
5:305
on marriage being a civil contract,
4:136–137
and religious instructions, 5:408
and sexuality, 4:302
strong critic of popular culture,
5:59
university student, 5:354
Calvinism
adultery as capital offense, 4:303
in east central Europe, 1:*391*
in Low Countries, 1:300–301
and reform of morals, 5:59
and ritual of death, 2:227–228
"Calvinist Communion Service"
(Picart), 5:*305*
Cambridge Group for the History of
Population and Social Structure,
1:13, 21, 77; 2:39
database built by, 1:37
and family reconstitution, 1:62
and kinship, 4:101, 103
Laslett and, 4:86
Cambridge Modern History, 1:3
Cambridge University, 3:69; 5:353,
354, 356
during the Middle Ages, 1:137
protests against women at, 4:*77*
Cameron, Charles, 2:415
Campaign for Nuclear Disarmament,
3:298
Campan, Jeanne, 4:72
Campbell, Colen, 2:415
Campbell, Colin, 5:78
Camporesi, Piero, 4:357
Canada
conditions for emigrants, 1:*495*
French imperial ventures in,
1:174
French peasants shipped to Quebec,
1:493
Italian immigrants in, 1:331
monopolistic church in French
Canada, 1:481
Canaletto (Giovanni Antonio Canal),
5:*5*
Canaries, sugar plantations in, 1:463
Candide (Voltaire), 1:*190*
Candolle, Alphonse de, 2:*89*
Cane, Carlo, 1:*325*
Canetti, Elias, 3:217

Havinden, M. A., 2:346
Hawkins John, 5:145
Hay, Douglas, 1:15
    "Poaching and the Game Laws on
        Cannock Chase," 5:511–512
    on punishment, 3:424
    "State and the Market in 1800,
        The: Lord Kenyon and Mr.
        Waddington," 3:207
    "War, Dearth, and Theft in the
        Eighteenth Century," 3:338
Haydn, Franz Joseph, 1:*190*
Hayek, Friedrich von, 2:538
Hayes, Carlton, 2:504
    *Historical Evolution of Modern
        Nationalism, The,* 2:503
Hayn, Hugo, 4:296
Hazard, Paul, 1:176
Hazing, 4:148
Hazlett, John
    *My Generation: Collective Autobiog-
        raphy and Identity Politics,*
        4:235
Health. *See also* Disease
    and disease, 2:205–217
    influence of child labor on, 4:519
    modernization of, 2:5
    and poverty, 3:525
    standard of living and, 5:452–453
Health, H., 5:*161*
Health care
    gender hierarchies in, 4:59
    in Germany
        in nineteenth century, 1:215
    for military veterans, 2:548
    state programs, 4:420–421
Health insurance
    in Germany, 1:346
    in Scandinavia, 1:365
Health resorts, 5:*225*
*Heart of the Race, The: Black Women's
    Lives in Britain* (Bryan et al.),
    4:11
Hebdige, Dick, 5:7
Heber, Reginald, 1:519
Hébert, Jacques-René, 3:236; 5:425;
    6:138–139
Hebra Kadishah, 5:*278*
He Cast a Look and Was Hurt (Min-
    kowski), 5:*284*
Hechter, Michael, 1:244
Heemskerck, Egbert, 5:*490*
Hegel, Georg Wilhelm Friedrich, 1:85;
    3:268; 4:457
    and civil society, 2:489
Heideken, Pehr Gustaf von, 3:*140*
Heidelberg, University of, 5:353
Heidenheimer, Arnold J., 3:*475 Tab. 1*
    *Development of Welfare States in
        Europe and America, The,*
        1:115
Heimat, 1:*252 map;* 5:122
Heinsohn, Gunnar, 2:185
Hélias, Pierre-Jakez, 4:182, 184
Heller, Clément, 1:44

Hellerstein, Erna Olafson, 4:6
Hellie, Richard, *as contributor,* 3:165–
    174
Helmholtz, Hermann Ludwig Ferdi-
    nand von, 3:511
Helsinki, 1:364
Helsinki Watch, 1:456
Hemingway, Ernest, 4:*239*
Hempel, Carl Gustav, 1:71
Henderson, W. O., 4:484
Hendrick, Harry
    on childhood, 4:522
    Male Youth Problem, The, 4:197
Henry VII (England)
    use of printing press to communi-
        cate news, 5:419
Henry VIII (England), **6:139–141**
    and Church of England, 1:259
    cockfights and, 5:169
    integration of Wales into the
        English system of govern-
        ment, 1:257
    and printing, 5:381, 421
    and tournaments, 5:167
Henry II (France)
    killed in tournament, 5:167
Henry IV (France), **6:141–143**
    etiquette at court of, 4:*372*
Henry the Navigator, 1:462; **6:143–
    144**
Henry, John, *as contributor,* 2:77–94
Henry, Louis, 1:73; 2:151
    and family reconstitution, 1:33, 62,
        77
    historical demography, 1:44
Herbalists, 3:59; 4:414, 428
Herbart, J. F., 4:442
Herder, Johann Gottfried von, 1:85,
    373; 5:3, 176; **6:144–145**
    and invention of tradition, 5:121
    and nationalism, 2:501
Heretics, persecution of
    including witches, 1:161; 3:362,
        364
    in Italy, 1:328
    in Spain, 1:310
Herlihy, David, 2:28, 29, *198 Fig. 1;*
    4:88, 89
    and history from the bottom up,
        1:31
    Toscans et leurs familles, Les, 4:*208
    Fig. 1*
Hermeneutics, 5:116
Hermes Trismegistus, 2:81; 5:30
Hermetic Order of the Golden Dawn,
    5:35
Herodotus, 1:244
Heroes of Their Own Lives (Gordon),
    1:92
Herrigel, Gary, 1:244
    Industrial Constructions, 2:538
    subnational regions in, 1:247
Hertwig, Oskar, 2:189
Herz, Henri, 5:146
Herzegovina, 3:305

Herzen, Aleksandr, 3:304; **6:145–146**
Herzl, Theodor, 1:441; **6:146–147**
Herzog, Dagmar, 1:*19,* 342
    *Intimacy and Exclusion: Religious
        Politics in Pre-Revolutionary
        Baden,* 1:101
Hesse, 5:302
Hetherington, Henry, 5:427
Hettling, Manfred, *as contributor,*
    2:489–498
Hewitt, Charles, 5:*90*
Hewitt, Nancy, 1:66
Hexter, J. H., 3:*40*
Heywood, Colin, *as contributor,* 4:175–
    191, 513–524
Hickey, Michael C., *as contributor,*
    1:433–447
Hidden from History (Rowbotham),
    1:15
Hide and Seek (Tissot), 5:*445*
High culture, 2:247; **5:15–28**
    in cities, 2:251
    defined, 5:15, 16
    distancing itself from low culture,
        4:391
    secular, 5:17–20
Higher education, 5:353–364. *See also*
    Universities; specific schools and
    universities
    in Britain, 5:359
        civic universities, 5:356
        for women, 4:76, 77, 79
    in France, 5:355, 359–360
        grandes écoles, 2:540
        school of mines, 3:61
        for women, 4:77, 79
        women in, 4:80
    in Germany, 5:359
        medical education, 4:*421*
        university reform, 5:356
        women in, 4:78
    in Italy, 4:77
    mass, 5:358
    medical education, 3:60
        women and, 3:63, 70
    and 1968 student protests, 3:*320–
        321*
    technical institutes, 3:69
    tourism studies, 5:219
    university lecture hall, 5:*361*
    women, 1:304
        for women, 4:*76*
Hiking, 4:336; 5:225
    on Grand Tour, 5:231
    societies, 5:83
    youth organizations, 4:198
Hildegard of Bingen, 3:81; 4:274
Hilferding, Rudolf, 1:50
Hill, Bridget, *as contributor,* 3:139–
    147
Hill, Christopher, 1:7, 10, 11, 55;
    2:*89;* 5:410; **6:147–148**
    English Revolution, 1640, 3:*40*
    Lenin and the Russian Revolution,
        1:52

Professionalization project, 3:57–58
Professionals and professionalization,
  3:57–65
  comparative history of, 1:115
  Jews as, 1:440
  of soccer teams, 5:174
  women in France, 1:291
Progressivism charity and, 3:469
Proletariat. *See also* Working classes
  as new class in east central Europe,
    1:388
  rural proletariat in Scandinavia,
    1:361, 362
Propaganda
  communications and media, 2:101–
    112
  definition of, 2:107
  deriving from print, 2:107
  of fascism and Nazism, 2:510
  of Soviet Union, 2:525
Propaganda (Bernays), 2:108
Property
  accounts as source of social history,
    1:32
  and civil society, 2:489, 490
  crimes, 3:336–340
    extension of the range of, 3:346
    informal handling of in early
      modern time, 3:339–340
    no longer linked to periods of
      depression, 3:347
  deeds as source of social history,
    1:31
  feminism and law, 4:49
  ownership as basis of the bourgeois
    political order, 1:209
  rights
    in nineteenth century, 1:209
    of women during the Middle
      Ages, 1:135
  transmission
    between generations, 4:224
    importance of timing, 4:125
*Property, Production, and Family in
  Neckarhausen, 1700–1870*
  (Sabean), 1:21, *22*, 67
Prophetic Sons and Daughters (Valenze),
  1:101
Proportional representation, 2:472
Propriétaire des choses, 2:*370*
Prosopography, 1:62
  late twentieth century, 1:66
  and research on kinship, 4:101
  sources for, 1:33
Prost, Antoine, 1:221
Prostitution, 3:351–360; 4:60, *247*.
  See also Brothels
  asylums for, 3:459
  court cases as source for study of,
    1:33
  domestic servants and, 3:145
  in early modern cities, 2:254
  as economic necessity, 3:175
  intermingling with mollies, 4:318
  in Italy, 1:326

  juvenile delinquency and, 3:384,
    390
  as life strategy, 4:6
  male, 4:314
  *Miroir des plus belles courtisanes de ce
    temps* (Crispin de Passe),
    3:*352*
  in nineteenth century, 4:337
  policing of, 5:160
  in postwar period, 4:254
  and public drinking places, 5:92
  *Reception Room in the Brothel on the
    Rue des Moulins* (Toulouse-
    Lautrec), 3:*356*
  red light districts during Middle
    Ages, 3:351
  regulation of, 3:518
  social history of, 1:100
  as social problem, 4:49
  as topic of amateur history, 4:4
  *Transport of Prostitutes to the Salpê-
    trière Prison* (Jeaurat), 3:*354*
  as vector of sexual disease, 4:251
*Prostitution and Victorian Society:
  Women, Class, and the State*
  (Walkowitz), 1:18, 100
Prostitution in Paris (Parent-
  Duchâtelet), 3:355
Protein energy malnutrition (PEM),
  2:212
Protest. *See* Collective action; Popular
  protest
Protestant churches
  approach to poverty, 3:449–450
  national churches similar to
    Catholic national churches,
    5:266
  and prototype of social worker,
    5:270
Protestant countries
  church lands for sale, 3:33
  and divorce, 4:157–158
  supervision of religious matters,
    1:339
  and temperance, 5:97
Protestant Dissenters, 1:263
*Protestant Ethic and the Spirit of Capi-
  talism, The* (Weber), 1:4; 2:534;
  3:43
Protestantism, 5:301–312
  in Central Europe, 1:337
  clergy, 1:160
  cultural world of, 5:*307*
  and death, 2:227–228
  development of Protestant identity
    in Ireland, 1:280
  differences with Catholic societies,
    1:159–160
  in Germany, 1:345
  and good witches, 3:367
  and linear life-course model, 2:200
  and literacy, 5:396
  in Low Countries, 1:300
  and marriage, 2:*174;* 4:146, 157
  in Old Regime France, 1:286

  social impact of, 5:*304*
  strengthening of patriarchy at the
    household and state level,
    4:19–20
  and unwed mothers, 3:500
  worship, 5:*268*
Protestant Reformation, 1:153–163,
  338
  broadsides and pamphlets, 5:421
  and Carnival, 5:43
  and cities, 2:257
  contrasted with Catholic Reforma-
    tion, 1:*155*
  early optimism of, 5:*302*
  and east central Europe, 1:384
  and education, 5:333
  and England, 1:259
  and family
    increased importance, 4:38
    and state regulation, 4:136–137
  and humanism, 5:58
  and image of the elderly, 4:219
  importance of printing for, 5:381
  key role of cities, 2:250
  and legislation against adultery,
    4:302–303
  and literacy, 4:70–71
    in Sweden, 5:333
  and marriage, 4:247
  and patriarchy, 4:38
  socialist interpretation of, 1:153
  and social restrictions of girls, 3:388
  and work, 4:495–496
Protoindustrialization, 1:149; 2:39–49,
  40. See also Putting-out system
  in Britain, 4:480
  in Central Europe, 1:340
  defined, 2:39–41
  eastern European serfs in, 2:385
  and formation of working-class
    identity, 3:125
  and gender, 4:57
  in Ireland, 1:277
  and periodization, 1:128
  symbiotic relationship with factory
    work, 2:53; 4:479
  Tilly and Scott on, 4:94
  women and, 4:27
  worker displaced by mechanization,
    4:481
Protonationalism, popular, 2:501–502
Proudhon, Pierre-Joseph, 4:22
Proust, Marcel, 5:15, 23; 6:287–289
  and passage of time, 2:199
Prout, Alan, 4:175
Provence, 2:219
Proxemics, 4:368
Prussia
  as absolutist state, 2:440
    cantonal system of maintenance
      of army, 2:441
  agriculture
    growth after 1850, 2:350
    land reforms, 2:348, 399
  child labor laws, 4:522

ISBN 0-684-80645-2

90000